Lecture Notes in Computer Science 11443

Commenced Publication in 1973
Founding and Former Series Editors:
Gerhard Goos, Juris Hartmanis, and Jan van Leeuwen

Editorial Board Members

David Hutchison
Lancaster University, Lancaster, UK
Takeo Kanade
Carnegie Mellon University, Pittsburgh, PA, USA
Josef Kittler
University of Surrey, Guildford, UK
Jon M. Kleinberg
Cornell University, Ithaca, NY, USA
Friedemann Mattern
ETH Zurich, Zurich, Switzerland
John C. Mitchell
Stanford University, Stanford, CA, USA
Moni Naor
Weizmann Institute of Science, Rehovot, Israel
C. Pandu Rangan
Indian Institute of Technology Madras, Chennai, India
Bernhard Steffen
TU Dortmund University, Dortmund, Germany
Demetri Terzopoulos
University of California, Los Angeles, CA, USA
Doug Tygar
University of California, Berkeley, CA, USA

Dongdai Lin · Kazue Sako (Eds.)

Public-Key Cryptography – PKC 2019

22nd IACR International Conference on Practice and Theory of Public-Key Cryptography Beijing, China, April 14–17, 2019 Proceedings, Part II

Springer

Editors
Dongdai Lin
SKLOIS, Institute of Information
Engineering
Chinese Academy of Sciences
Beijing, China

Kazue Sako
Security Research Laboratories
NEC Corporation
Kawasaki, Japan

ISSN 0302-9743 ISSN 1611-3349 (electronic)
Lecture Notes in Computer Science
ISBN 978-3-030-17258-9 ISBN 978-3-030-17259-6 (eBook)
https://doi.org/10.1007/978-3-030-17259-6

Library of Congress Control Number: 2019936577

LNCS Sublibrary: SL4 – Security and Cryptology

This Springer imprint is published by the registered company Springer Nature Switzerland AG
The registered company address is: Gewerbestrasse 11, 6330 Cham, Switzerland

Preface

The 22nd IACR International Conference on Practice and Theory of Public-Key Cryptography (PKC 2019) was held April 14–17, 2019, in Beijing, China. The conference is sponsored by the International Association for Cryptologic Research (IACR) and focuses on all technical aspects of public-key cryptography. These proceedings consist of two volumes including 42 papers that were selected by the Program Committee from 173 submissions. Each submission was assigned to at least three reviewers while submissions co-authored by Program Committee members received at least five reviews. During the discussion phase, the Program Committee used quite intensively a recent feature of the review system, which allows Program Committee members to anonymously ask questions to the authors. The reviewing and selection process was a challenging task and we are deeply grateful to the Program Committee members and external reviewers for their hard and thorough work. Many thanks also to Shai Halevi for his assistance with the Web submission and review software. We thank the authors for promptly responding to the questions raised by the committee, which helped us understand the content of their submissions.

The conference program also included an invited talk by Tatsuaki Okamoto (NTT). We would like to thank the invited speaker as well as all the other speakers and the authors of all submissions for their contributions to the program and conference. Finally, we would like to thank Xiaoyun Wang, the general chair, and all the members of local Organizing Committee for organizing a great conference and all the conference attendees for making this conference a truly intellectually stimulating event through their active participation.

April 2019

Dongdai Lin
Kazue Sako

PKC 2019

22nd IACR International Conference on Practice and Theory of Public-Key Cryptography

Beijing, China
April 14–17, 2019

Sponsored and Organized by

International Association for Cryptologic Research
State Key Laboratory of Information Security
State Key Laboratory of Cryptology
TopSec Technologies Inc.
Institute of Information Engineering, Chinese Academy of Sciences
Chinese Association for Cryptologic Research

General Chair

Xiaoyun Wang	Tsinghua University, China

Program Co-chairs

Dongdai Lin	SKLOIS, Institute of Information Engineering, Chinese Academy of Sciences, China
Kazue Sako	Security Research Laboratories, NEC Corporation, Japan

Steering Committee

Michel Abdalla	Ecole Normale Supérieure, France
Yvo Desmedt	University of Texas at Dallas, USA
Goichiro Hanaoka	National Institute of Advanced Industrial Science and Technology, Japan
Aggelos Kiayias	University of Edinburgh, UK
Dongdai Lin	Chinese Academy of Sciences, China
David Naccache	Ecole Normale Supérieure, France
Tatsuaki Okamoto	NTT Labs, Japan
David Pointcheval	Ecole Normale Supérieure, France
Kazue Sako	NEC Security Research Laboratories, Japan
Moti Yung	Google and Columbia University, USA
Yuliang Zheng	University of Alabama at Birmingham, USA

Program Committee

Erdem Alkim	Ondokuz Mayis University, Turkey
Diego F. Aranha	Aarhus University, Denmark and University of Campinas, Brazil
Chris Brzuska	Alto University, Finland
Dario Catalano	University of Catania, Italy
Nishanth Chandran	Microsoft, India
Sanjit Chatterjee	Indian Institute of Sciences, India
Jie Chen	East China Normal University, China
Jung Hee Cheon	Seoul National University, Korea
Craig Costello	Microsoft Research, USA
Yi Deng	Chinese Academy of Sciences, China
Leo Ducas	CWI Amsterdam, The Netherlands
Nico Döttling	Cispa Helmholtz Center (i.G.), Germany
Dario Fiore	IMDEA Software Institute, Spain
Pierre-Alain Fouque	Rennes University, France
Feng Hao	University of Warwick, UK
Tibor Jager	Paderborn University, Germany
Marc Joye	OneSpan, Belgium
Tancrède Lepoint	SRI International, USA
Benoît Libert	CNRS and ENS de Lyon, France
Helger Lipmaa	University of Tartu, Estonia
Feng-Hao Liu	Florida Atlantic University, USA
Takahiro Matsuda	AIST, Japan
Pratyay Mukherjee	Visa Research, USA
Satoshi Obana	Hosei University, Japan
Miyako Okubo	NICT, Japan
Arpita Patra	Indian Institute of Science, India
Ludovic Perret	Sorbonne University, France
Thomas Peters	UC Louvain, Belgium
Benny Pinkas	Bar-Ilan University, Israel
Bertram Poettering	Royal Holloway, University of London, UK
Antigoni Polychroniadou	Cornell Tech, USA
Alessandra Scafuro	NC State University, USA
Jae Hong Seo	Hanyang University, South Korea
Qiang Tang	New Jersey Institute of Technology, USA
Huaxiong Wang	Nanyang Technological University, Singapore
Yu Yu	Shanghai Jiaotong University, China

Organizing Committee

Xiaofeng Chen	Xidian University, China
Yu Chen	SKLOIS, Institute of Information Engineering, CAS, China
Shuqin Fan	State Key Laboratory of Cryptology, China

Xinyi Huang	Fujian Normal University, China
Ming Li	SKLOIS, Institute of Information Engineering, CAS, China
Zhe Liu	Nanjing University of Aeronautics and Astronautics, China
Chunming Tang	Guangzhou University, China
Anyu Wang	SKLOIS, Institute of Information Engineering, CAS, China
Jian Weng	Jinan University, China
Baofeng Wu	SKLOIS, Institute of Information Engineering, CAS, China
Fangguo Zhang	Sun Yat-sen University, China
Yunlei Zhao	Fudan University, China

Additional Reviewers

Benjamin Dowling
Behzad Abdolmaleki
Masayuki Abe
Martin R. Albrecht
Pedro G. M. R. Alves
Gilad Asharov
Nuttapong Attrapadung
Karim Baghery
Shi Bai
Marshall Ball
Manuel Barbosa
Hridam Basu
Carsten Baum
Pascal Bemmann
Fabrice Benhamouda
Pauline Bert
Francesco Berti
Ward Beullens
Sauvik Bhattacharya
Olivier Blazy
Katharina Boudgoust
Florian Bourse
Xavier Bultel
Olive Chakraborty
Biniy Chen
Long Chen
Rongmao Chen
Yu Chen
Wonhee Cho
Ashish Choudhury
Peter Chvojka
Sadro Coretti
Geoffroy Couteau
Edouard Cuvelier
Prem Laxman Das
Bernardo David
Amit Deo
Apoorvaa Deshpande
Julien Devigne
Ning Ding
Lucas Enloe
Jieun Eom
Naomi Ephraim
Xiong Fan
Antonio Faonio
Luca De Feo
Daniele Friolo
Georg Fuchsbauer
Ben Fuller
Tommaso Gagliardoni
Steven Galbraith
Tatiana Galibus
Chaya Ganesh
Romain Gay
Peter Gazi
Kai Gellert
Nicholas Genise
Satrajit Ghosh

Irene Giacomelli
Junqing Gong
Alonso Gonzalez
Jens Groth
Fabrice Ben Hammouda
Kyoohyung Han
Abida Haque
Javier Herranz
Clemens Heuberger
Minki Hhan
Hyunsook Hong
Seungwan Hong
Jingwei Hu
Qiong Huang
Xinyi Huang
Huisu Jang
Christian Janson
Jinhyuck Jeong
Yun-Seong Ji
Shaoquan Jiang
Zhang Jiang
Charanjit Jutla
R. Kabaleeshwaran
Saqib A. Kakvi
Koray Karabina
Shuichi Katsumata
Yutaka Kawai
Hamidreza Khoshakhlagh
Dongwoo Kim
Duhyeong Kim
Jaeyun Kim
Jiseung Kim
Minkyu Kim
Fuyuki Kitagawa
Susumu Kiyoshima
Kamil Kluczniak
François Koeune
Yashvanth Kondi
Toomas Krips
Shravan Kumar
Rafael Kurek
Fabien Laguillaumie
Junzuo Lai
Qiqi Lai
Hyung Tae Lee
Joohee Lee
Kiwoo Lee
Jiangtao Li
Jie Li
Changlu Lin
Fuchun Lin
Qipeng Liu
Shengli Liu
Zhe Liu
Zhen Liu
Patrick Longa
Steve Lu
Yuan Lu
Lin Lyu
Shunli Ma
Varun Madathil
Monosij Maitra
Giulio Malavolta
Mark Manulis
Chloe Martindale
Daniel Masny
Peihan Miao
Rafael Misoczki
Payman Mohassel
Fabrice Mouhartem
Yi Mu
Sayantan Mukherjee
Pierrick Méaux
Michael Naehrig
Kartik Nayak
Khoa Nguyen
David Niehues
Ryo Nishimaki
Luca Nizzardo
Ariel Nof
Koji Nuida
Sai Lakshmi Bhavana Obbattu
Cristina Onete
Emmanuella Orsini
Jiaxin Pan
Tapas Pandit
Lorenz Panny
Jong Hwan Park
Alain Passelègue
Sikhar Patranabis
Alice Pellet–Mary
Geovandro Pereira

Olivier Pereira
Rachel Player
S. Puria
Erick Purwanto
Baodong Qin
Chen Qian
Mario Di Raimondo
Somindu C. Ramanna
Divya Ravi
Joost Renes
Amanda Cristina Davi Resende
Melissa Rossi
Arnab Roy
Paul Rösler
Mohamed Sabt
Yusuke Sakai
Jonas Schneider
Peter Scholl
Jacob Schuldt
Sven Schäge
Adam Sealfon
Sruthi Sekar
Minhye Seo
Akash Shah
Kazumasa Shinagawa
Adam Shull
Janno Siim
Luisa Siniscalchi
Benjamin Smith
Azam Soleimanian
Yongha Son
Katerina Sotiraki
Shifeng Sun
Willy Susilo
Koutarou Suzuki
Benjamin Hong Meng Tan
Radu Titiu
Junichi Tomida
Rotem Tsabary
Daniel Tschudi
Anselme Tueno
Dominque Unruh
Muthuramakrishnan Venkitasubramaniam
Daniele Venturi
Sameer Wagh
Michael Walter
Hailong Wang
Liping Wang
Luping Wang
Yu-chen Wang
Yuyu Wang
Zhedong Wang
Weiqiang Wen
Joanne Woodage
Shota Yamada
Takashi Yamakawa
Avishay Yanay
Guomin Yang
Kang Yang
Rupeng Yang
Xu Yanhong
Donggeon Yhee
Jingyue Yu
Yang Yu
Zuoxia Yu
Aaram Yun
Michal Zajac
Ming Zeng
Cong Zhang
Jiang Zhang
Juanyang Zhang
Kai Zhang
Liang Feng Zhang
Mingwu Zhang
Rui Zhang
Xiaojun Zhang
Qian Zhao
Yunlei Zhao
Linfeng Zhou
Giorgos Zirdelis

Contents – Part II

Re-encryption Schemes

Fundamental Primitives (II)

Post Quantum Cryptography

Contents – Part I

Cryptographic Protocols

Digital Signatures

Zero-Knowledge

Public Key Encryptions

Collusion Resistant Broadcast and Trace from Positional Witness Encryption

Rishab Goyal, Satyanarayana Vusirikala(✉), and Brent Waters

University of Texas at Austin, Austin, USA
{rgoyal,satya,bwaters}@cs.utexas.edu

Abstract. An emerging trend is for researchers to identify cryptography primitives for which feasibility was first established under obfuscation and then move the realization to a different setting. In this work we explore a new such avenue—to move obfuscation-based cryptography to the assumption of (positional) witness encryption. Our goal is to develop techniques and tools, which we will dub "witness encryption friendly" primitives and use these to develop a methodology for building advanced cryptography from positional witness encryption.

We take a bottom up approach and pursue our general agenda by attacking the specific problem of building collusion-resistant broadcast systems with tracing from positional witness encryption. We achieve a system where the size of ciphertexts, public key and private key are polynomial in the security parameter λ and independent of the number of users N in the broadcast system. Currently, systems with such parameters are only known from indistinguishability obfuscation.

1 Introduction

Over the past five years the introduction of candidate indistinguishability obfuscation schemes [27] has produced a dramatic shift in the community's view of which cryptographic primitives are plausibly achievable. Starting with [56] there have been several works [9,10,16,19,26,30,43,45,56] that leverage the power of indistinguishability obfuscation [6,7] to give new solutions for problems ranging from deniable encryption to showing the hardness of finding Nash equilibrium.

An emerging trend is for researchers to identify cryptography primitives for which feasibility was first established under obfuscation and then move the realization to a different setting. For example, several works [2,9,39,40,46,59] proposed solutions under the Learning with Errors [54] (LWE) assumption of primitives (or impossibility results) that to that point were known only under indistinguishability obfuscation. The motivation for this movement is that LWE is considered a standard assumption with connections to certain problems on lattices, while current indistinguishability obfuscation constructions are based on much newer multilinear map candidates. In a different line of researchers [31,47]

B. Waters—Supported by NSF CNS-1228599 and CNS-1414082, DARPA SafeWare, Microsoft Faculty Fellowship, and Packard Foundation Fellowship.

D. Lin and K. Sako (Eds.): PKC 2019, LNCS 11443, pp. 3–33, 2019.
https://doi.org/10.1007/978-3-030-17259-6_1

have shown how to base applications such as realizing trapdoor permutations and the hardness of Nash equilibrium from functional encryption. While sub exponentially hard functional encryption is known to imply indistinguishability obfuscation [4,5,11], this direction is motivated by building these primitives with only a polynomial loss in the reductions coupled with prospect of functional encryption schemes realized from the polynomial hardness of standard assumptions.

In this work we explore a new such avenue—to move obfuscation-based cryptography to the assumption of (positional) witness encryption [29,33]. Recall that in a witness encryption scheme, say for SAT, an encryption algorithm takes in a message m along with a boolean formula ϕ that operates an n bit input w producing a ciphertext ct. A decryptor can recover the message m from ct if it knows a w such that $\phi(w) = 1$. If no such w exists, then the message is computationally hidden. In addition to serving as its own application, witness encryption is known to give rise to primitives such as identity-based encryption [12,58] and attribute-based encryption [55].

A natural question is why push for moving cryptography from indistinguishability obfuscation to positional witness encryption when current constructions for both rely on multilinear maps [22,23,25,32]. The justification (like in [31,47]) relies on some projection to the future. Since witness encryption is a less powerful primitive than indistinguishability obfuscation, it is believed that the community will likely arrive at a standard assumption solution earlier. This conjecture is supported by some heuristic evidence:

- The work of [33] showing provably secure positional witness encryption from simple multilinear map assumptions came earlier than and was simpler than the later work [34] which gave a similar result for obfuscation.
- Recently, it was shown [18] that attribute-based encryption gives rise to a non-trivial form of witness encryption. This might lead to further advances in witness encryption which would not necessarily translate to general obfuscation.
- Recently, the concept of lockable obfuscation [39,59] was proposed and shown to be realizable under the LWE assumption. Like witness encryption this is a general class of obfuscation, but is more restricted than indistinguishability obfuscation.
- Very recently, Chen et al. [20] gave a new candidate for witness encryption (albeit not positional witness encryption) inspired by [32] multilinear encodings. An important feature of their candidate is that it directly encodes read-once branching program representations of the associated CNF formulae, thereby avoiding attacks such as input-mixing and more. Since read-once branching programs are much less expressive than general branching programs, this also points towards reaching the goal of witness encryption before obfuscation.

In addition, we expect future solutions to witness encryption to be practically more efficient than full blown indistinguishability obfuscation.

Our goal is to develop techniques and tools, which we will dub "witness encryption friendly" primitives[1], and use these to develop a methodology for building advanced cryptography from positional witness encryption. While we don't expect to move all or even "most" of obfuscation-based cryptography to positional witness encryption, we believe that a long term effort could yield a number of applications which are comparable to those achieved from the aforementioned efforts on building from functional encryption [31,47] or lockable obfuscation [39,59].

We will take a bottom-up approach and pursue our general agenda by attacking specific problems that are not known from witness encryption. To that end in this work we study building collusion-resistant broadcast systems with tracing from positional witness encryption. Our goal is to achieve where the size of ciphertexts, public key and private key are polynomial in the security parameter λ and independent of the number of users N in the broadcast system.[2] Below we provide an overview of prior work, present our new results, toolkit of "witness encryption friendly" primitives, and the techniques that allow us to achieve the above goals.

1.1 Overview

Broadcast Encryption with Tracing. Broadcast Encryption was introduced by Fiat and Naor [24]. A broadcast encryption scheme, like a standard public key encryption scheme, consists of three algorithms—setup, encryption and decryption. The setup algorithm outputs a public key and N secret keys, where N represents the number of users given as an input. Using the encryption algorithm, a sender can encrypt a message such that the corresponding ciphertext can only be decrypted by the "qualified" users $S \subseteq [N]$.[3] Here the set S is given as input to the encryption algorithm. The decryption algorithm is self-explanatory. For security it is required that no set of colluding users can decrypt a ciphertext if none of them are *qualified.*

Suppose that a set of users S_1 collude to create a decoding box D which is capable of decrypting ciphertexts intended for some (possibly different) set of users S_2 with some non-negligible probability. A broadcast system which provides tracing capabilities allows extraction of a non-empty set T (from the box D) such that $T \subseteq S_1$, i.e. contains at least one colluding user but none outside of it. Such broadcast systems are referred to as Trace and Revoke systems in the folklore [50,51]. However, we chose to refer to it as Broadcast and Trace system as it is more appropriate. They have an additional tracing algorithm which given only the oracle access to the box D can perform this traitor extraction.

Broadcast and Trace via Augmented Broadcast Encryption (AugBE). Boneh and Waters (BW) [14] built the first fully collusion resistant Broadcast and Trace

[1] This is intended to mirror the term "iO friendly" used elsewhere in the literature.

[2] Following prior broadcast encryption literature we will not count a description S of the recipients of a ciphertext toward the ciphertext overhead.

[3] Here *qualified* could alternatively be interpreted as "non-revoked".

scheme with sub-linear (in N) ciphertext size. They also provided a framework for building Broadcast and Trace schemes by introducing an intermediate primitive called augmented broadcast encryption (AugBE). We follow the same approach in this work and therefore we elaborate on it now.

An AugBE scheme, as the name suggests, is a broadcast encryption scheme with an augmented encryption functionality. Similar to a standard broadcast encryption scheme it consists of setup, encryption and decryption algorithms. In an AugBE system, the encryption algorithm also receives a "cutoff" index $i \in [N+1]$, in addition to a set $S \subseteq [N]$, as an input. This cutoff index affects the decryptability of the ciphertext in such a way that the resultant ciphertext can only be decrypted by the users $S' = S \setminus [i-1]$, i.e. users whose indices are as large as i and belong to the set S are now labelled as *qualified.* BW defined two security properties for an AugBE system—index hiding and message hiding security. The first security property (index hiding) states that an encryption of m under set S to index i is indistinguishable from an encryption of m under set S to index $i+1$, if either $i \notin S$ (even when the adversary has all the secret keys), or the adversary does not have the ith key. The second property (message hiding) states that an encryption of m_0 under set S to index $N+1$ is indistinguishable from an encryption of m_1 under set S to index $N+1$, even when the adversary is given all N secret keys.

BW argued that if an AugBE scheme satisfies these two properties, then that is sufficient for constructing a Broadcast and Trace (BT) scheme. In their transformation, the BT setup and decryption algorithm are identical to their AugBE counterparts. For encryption, a sender runs the AugBE encryption algorithm with the cutoff index value set to be 1. The tracing algorithm runs AugBE encryption varying the value of cutoff index. Given a decoder box D and target set S, the tracing algorithm encrypts random messages under set S to every index $i = 1$ to $N+1$, and estimates (for each index i) the probability D decrypts correctly. Suppose the probability decoder D is successful, i.e. decrypts standard (index 1) ciphertexts correctly, is at least ϵ. By message hiding property, we know that D can not have non-negligible success probability when run on ciphertexts encrypting to index $N+1$. This implies that there must exist an index $i^* \in [N]$ such that the decoder's success probability in decrypting index i^* ciphertexts is at least $\approx \epsilon/N$ more than in decrypting index i^*+1 ciphertexts. Every cutoff index i where there is a gap in the estimated success probabilities for index i and $i+1$, the tracing algorithm adds that user i to the set of traitors. The main idea here is that if an index $i \notin S$ or the adversary does not have the key for user i, then by index hiding security it should not be able to distinguish between index i and $i+1$ ciphertexts.

Although the above transformation seems to work (at least intuitively), we would like to point out that the proof provided in [14] was inaccurate. Very briefly, the problem lies in the fact that there is a "semantic gap" between the definitions of BT and AugBE schemes. The issue is that in a BT system an adversary outputs a box which performs some decoding/decryption operations, whereas in an AugBE system the adversary plays a distinguishing game. At first, it seems like one could use the decoder box to decrypt the ciphertext and use its output for distinguishing. The problem is that decoder might work incorrectly sometime and it would affect the success probability of the reduction algorithm. Similar issues were observed by Goyal, Koppula and Waters [41] in the context of (non-broadcast) traitor tracing. They resolved the issue by upgrading the security requirements from the underlying intermediate primitives to match the decoder-based security notions required for traitor tracing. In this work we fix the proof of security for the BW transformation showing that it does lead to a secure BT scheme.[4] More details are provided later in Sect. 3.

Our Results and Prior Work. Our main result are new collusion-resistant Broadcast and Trace schemes from positional witness encryption where the size of ciphertexts, public key and private key are polynomial in the security parameter λ and independent of the number of users N[5]. Currently, systems with such parameters are only known from indistinguishability obfuscation [52]. If we drop the tracing requirement, that is consider only broadcast encryption, there are constructions based on multilinear maps [15] and iO [16]. If we drop the revocation requirement, that is consider only traitor tracing, schemes with such parameters are known based on iO [16]. In bilinear groups we can achieve short ciphertexts [13,35], but with longer keys if we drop the tracing requirement. Additionally, we have solutions [14] with ciphertexts that grow proportionally to $\sqrt{N}$ if we keep it. Very recently, Goyal, Koppula and Waters [41] gave a polylog traitor tracing scheme from the LWE assumption. However, their system does not have the capability to broadcast to arbitrary sets.

We further develop a toolkit of certain simpler primitives such that these could be used in conjunction with positional witness encryption in similar vein to how we have *iO friendly* primitives to support applications of iO. Our BT scheme is secure assuming the existence of positional witness encryption and these simpler primitives. We provide numerous instantiations of these primitives from a wide variety of standard assumptions such as LWE, RSA and decision linear over bilinear groups. Now we describe our techniques and main ideas to build a Broadcast and Trace system.

Building Augmented Broadcast Encryption from Positional Witness Encryption. The main building block used in our construction is a positional witness encryption (PWE) scheme. In a PWE scheme, the encryption algorithm also takes as input a *cutoff* index $i \in \{0, \ldots, 2^n\}$ where n is the bit length of witnesses on which the corresponding boolean formula (witness relation) ϕ operates. A decryptor can recover the message m from ct if it knows a w such that $\phi(w) = 1$ and $w \geq i$.[6] For security it has two properties—message hiding and index hiding. First, message hiding states that a message encrypted for index 2^n (i.e., the last

---

[4] Here we only consider BT schemes with public traceability.

[5] Here we assume that number of users N is at most $\mathsf{poly}(\lambda)$.

[6] Here comparisons between bit-strings is performed by interpreting each bit-string as non-negative integer.

index) is hidden irrespective of the boolean formula used. Second, index hiding states that an encryption of m under formula ϕ for index i is indistinguishable from an encryption of m under ϕ to index $i+1$, if $\phi(i) = 0$.

We now provide an outline of our AugBE construction. Let us start with a simple idea. Suppose during setup, the algorithm samples a key pair for a standard signature scheme. Next, the secret key for i^{th} user consists of a signature σ_i on message i and the public key simply corresponds to the verification key vk. To encrypt a message m under set S and index i, the encryptor runs the PWE encryption algorithm on message m for index $i \,||\, 0^\ell$ and formula $\phi_{\mathsf{vk},S}$, where $\phi_{\mathsf{vk},S}(j, \sigma) = 1$ iff '$j \in S$' and 'σ is a valid signature on j under vk'. Here ℓ denotes the length of the signatures. For decryption a user simply runs the PWE decryption with its index and signature as the witness. Correctness of this scheme follows directly. However, this scheme is clearly not compact since the set S is embedded in the formula $\phi_{\mathsf{vk},S}$ and since the size of PWE ciphertexts could arbitrarily (but polynomially) depend on the size of the formula, thus the overall AugBE scheme could be highly inefficient. In a few words the problem is that we are implementing a trivial set membership check which breaks compactness.

To get around this problem we will use an alternate set membership check. Our idea is to embed only a succinct commitment to the set S in the formula ϕ such that there exists proofs of membership in S that grow at most logarithmically with the number of users N. Clearly such a primitive would resolve the inefficiency problem. One possible execution of this idea is via a Merkle hash tree.[7] Let $\mathbb{I}_S$ represent the N-bit indicator string corresponding to set S, i.e. i^{th} bit of $\mathbb{I}_S$ is 1 iff $i \in S$. We modify the encryption procedure as follows—first compute a hash h of string $\mathbb{I}_S$; next run the PWE encryption algorithm on message m for index $i \,||\, 0^\ell \,||\, 0^k$ and formula $\phi_{\mathsf{vk},h,N}$, where $\phi_{\mathsf{vk},h,N}(j, \sigma, \pi) = 1$ iff '$j \leq N$', 'π is a valid proof membership for index j w.r.t. hash h' and 'σ is a valid signature on j under vk'. Here proof π simply corresponds to the pre-images in the hash tree along the path from the root h to the leaf node containing the jth bit, and k denotes the length of proof π. The decryption is then performed analogously where the decryptor computes the membership proof by hashing $\mathbb{I}_S$ and using the appropriate leaf-to-root path as a proof. This seems to resolve the succinctness problem as the size of the ciphertext is independent of the number of users. Also, at least intuitively, it seems that the scheme should satisfy both index hiding and message hiding security properties. The intuition is that since $\phi_{\mathsf{vk},h,N}$ is not satisfied by any witness larger than $(N+1) \,||\, 0^\ell \,||\, 0^k$, by using security of PWE we can argue message hiding security for the above scheme.[8] For arguing

[7] The idea of using Merkle hash tree for efficiently committing to large sets has also been previously used in works such as [3,60].

[8] The proof will involve an exponential number of hybrids. This is because for applying message hiding security property of PWE the index used must be $2^{\lambda+\ell+k}$ (i.e., the last index), therefore we need to use index hiding security to go from index $(N+1) \,||\, 0^\ell \,||\, 0^k$ to $2^{\lambda+\ell+k}$ which takes an exponential number of hybrid steps. Here the exact ordering of witness components, i.e. i, σ, π, is very important for the proof to go through. We can only use the security of PWE scheme if index i is leading term and corresponds to the most significant bits.

index hiding security we would hope to use the fact that if $i \notin S$, or if the adversary does not receive the key for i^{th} user, then the adversary does not know of any witnesses of the form $i \,||\, \{0,1\}^{\ell} \,||\, \{0,1\}^{k}$ and thus we could use PWE index hiding security. In the first case (i.e., $i \notin S$) hardness of computing witnesses should follow from collision resistance of the hash function, and in the second scenario it should follow from unforgeability of the signature scheme. However, there is a problem here. Although we could argue that witnesses are hard-to-compute while proving index hiding for AugBE, this won't be sufficient overall as for applying PWE index hiding security as it is necessary that there does *not* exist *any* witness of the form $i \,||\, \{0,1\}^{\ell} \,||\, \{0,1\}^{k}$. Thus, unless the underlying PWE scheme provides some strong notion of extractable security, it is not clear how to prove security of the above construction.[9]

To this end, we develop a toolkit of certain simpler primitives, which aid us in proving our construction to be secure. Our motivation here is that using such primitives, we could somehow indistinguishably switch between instances/formulae which have hard-to-compute witnesses to instances/formulae which do not have any witnesses (in some particular pre-specified range). Thus this would enable applicability of the index hiding security property of PWE scheme in the corresponding proof. Below we elaborate on two such primitives—all-but-one signatures and somewhere perfectly binding hash functions (a primitive similar to somewhere statistically binding hash functions described in [44,53]).[10]

A Toolkit for Witness Encryption. The first primitive we consider is a special type of signature scheme called all-but-one (ABO) signatures. These are just like standard signatures, except the setup algorithm has a special "punctured" mode in which it takes a message m^* as an additional input and outputs a pair of signing and verification key $(\mathsf{sk}, \mathsf{vk})$ such that there does not exist any signature that gets verified for message m^*. In other words, the verification algorithm on inputs vk and m^* rejects *every* signature σ. Now instead of unforgeability-type security, we only require that an adversary should not be able to distinguish verification keys that are output by *punctured* setup with message m^* from those output by normal setup, even when given access to the signing oracle.[11] We note that the notion of ABO signatures is motivated by constrained signatures [16] and splittable signatures [45], but is much weaker than both of those. In this work, we also provide new constructions of ABO signatures from a wide variety

[9] Although the notion of witness encryption with extractable security has been well studied [28,36], extractability in the case of positional witness encryption is rather non-trivial to define due to the fact that PWE already requires index hiding to hold for all indices.

[10] We would like to point out that our techniques of relaxing extractably-secure assumptions to more standard indistinguishability-based assumptions are in part inspired by analogous results in the regime of moving from differing-inputs obfuscation (diO) to indistinguishability obfuscation (iO) [21,44,52].

[11] The adversary is not allowed to query the oracle on message m^* to allow trivial distinguishing attacks.

of standard assumptions. Next we discuss the second primitive we use, and later we will circle back to the new ABO signature constructions we provide.

The next primitive we employ is a somewhere perfectly binding (SPB) hash function [44,53]. An SPB hash consists of four algorithms—setup, hash, open and verify. The setup algorithm is used to sample a hash key hk, and has two modes (akin to ABO signatures)—normal and "binding". In the *binding* mode it takes an index i as an additional input, and it ensures that the corresponding hash function H_{hk} is perfectly binding for the ith message position (i.e., the hash value completely determines the ith bit of the pre-image). Additionally, SPB hashes have a local opening property which states that for any message m, any index $i \leq |m|$ and hash $h = H_{\mathsf{hk}}(m)$, one could create a *short* proof π proving that the message's i^{th} bit is $m[i]$ and it hashes to h.[12] Such proofs could be verified by running the verification algorithm which also take as input the hash key, hash value and a position. For security it is required that an adversary should not be able to distinguish between hash keys that are output by *binding* setup and those output by normal setup.

Next we show that if we use ABO signatures and SPB hash functions in the previously described AugBE construction then we can prove its security using positional witness encryption.

Completing AugBE Construction. As discussed earlier, ABO signature scheme and an SPB hash function enable us to indistinguishably turn instances with hard-to-compute witnesses into instances which have no witnesses (in a particular range). Therefore, by simply using an ABO signature scheme and an SPB hash function in our AugBE construction, we can also prove index hiding property of our construction. The construction is identical to the one described before, except that checking membership of index j will now be done by SPB verification algorithm as follows—'π proves that there exists a string x such that $x[j] = 1$ and $H_{\mathsf{hk}}(x) = h$'. The proof of AugBE message hiding stays the same as $\phi_{\mathsf{vk},\mathsf{hk},h,N}$ is not satisfied by any witness larger than $(N+1) \,||\, 0^\ell \,||\, 0^k$. The AugBE index hiding proof is divided in two parts. Let i be the challenge index, S the challenge set and $S_\mathcal{A}$ the set of keys in adversary's possession. We know that either $i \notin S$ or $i \notin S_\mathcal{A}$. Consider the following cases.

- $i \notin S_\mathcal{A}$: The idea here is that since the adversary does not have key for user i, thus we could instead generate the $(\mathsf{sk}, \mathsf{vk})$ key pair by running *punctured* setup for message i. From adversary's perspective this can not be distinguished with non-negligible probability by ABO security. And now, since the verification key vk no longer accepts any signature σ for message i, we get $\phi_{\mathsf{vk},\mathsf{hk},h,N}(w) = 0$ for all $i \,||\, 0^\ell \,||\, 0^k \leq w < (i+1) \,||\, 0^\ell \,||\, 0^k$. As a result, we could use PWE index hiding security to switch from index i AugBE ciphertexts to index $i+1$ ciphertexts. Finally, we could *un-puncture* the key vk to complete the proof.

[12] Technically one could visualize the proof π as only proving that the ith bit of pre-image is $m[i]$. The fact that it also proves that the message hashes to $H_{\mathsf{hk}}(m)$ is just due to the structure of the proof.

– $i \notin S$: The proof is very similar to the one described above. The only modification will be that instead of puncturing the verification key at index i, we *bind* the hash key for position i. The intuition is that since the ith bit of string $\mathbb{I}_S$ is zero (as $i \notin S$), thus if the hash key hk was (perfectly) binding at position i then there will not exist any proof π that proves that there exists a string x such that $H_{\mathsf{hk}}(\mathbb{I}_S) = H_{\mathsf{hk}}(x)$ the ith bit of x is 1. Thus, as before $\phi_{\mathsf{vk},\mathsf{hk},h,N}(w) = 0$ for all indices in that range and we can apply PWE index hiding security.

At a high level, the proposed paradigm is to first use the developed toolkit to turn formulae with *hard-to-compute* satisfying inputs into formulae with only *range-restricted* satisfying inputs, then use PWE security to cut through the range of *inactive* inputs, and finally switch back to original formulae using our toolkit. We believe that such a methodology will find more applications especially in bringing more primitives based on obfuscation to the assumption of (positional) witness encryption. Finally, we talk about the new ABO signature constructions that we provide.

ABO Signatures from Standard Assumptions. In this work we give two new pathways to build ABO signatures. First, we show that an ABO signature scheme can be generically built from any verifiable random function (VRF) [49] and a perfectly-binding (non-interactive) commitment scheme. Second, we show that any identity-based encryption (IBE) scheme [12,58], that is anonymous [8] as well as allows efficient key verifiability, also leads to an ABO signature scheme. VRFs can be based on a wide variety of assumptions such as decision-linear over bilinear maps as well as RSA-like assumptions [42,49] and perfectly-binding (non-interactive) commitment schemes can be based on assumptions such as DDH, LWE and LPN [37] and perfectly injective OWFs. IBE schemes with such verifiability and anonymity properties can be based on simple assumptions over bilinear maps as well as LWE [1,17,39,48,57,59]. Thus this leads to new constructions of ABO signatures. We also point out that ABO signatures can be built from constrained signatures [16] and splittable signatures [45] which have been constructed under iO and OWFs. Constrained signatures have also been constructed from non-interactive witness indistinguishable proofs and perfectly binding commitments [16].

We now briefly highlight the main ideas to build these from VRFs. A VRF is like a pseudorandom function (PRF) in which the secret key holder can also prove correctness and uniqueness of PRF evaluation. Concretely, using the secret key sk, it could efficiently evaluate the function $F_{\mathsf{sk}}(\cdot)$ on any input x as well as generate a proof π of the statement $y = F_{\mathsf{sk}}(x)$. An ABO signing key will simply correspond to the VRF secret key sk, and the ABO verification key will contain the VRF verification key vk as well as a commitment COM. Here COM commits to 0 during standard setup, whereas during punctured setup (with message x^*) COM commits to 1 where the random coins used are $F_{\mathsf{sk}}(x^*)$. A signature σ for any message x will simply correspond to its function evaluation $y = F_{\mathsf{sk}}(x)$ as well as corresponding proof π. While verifying a message-signature pair $x, (y, \pi)$

w.r.t. key (vk, COM), the verifier checks two things—(1) π proves that y is a correct evaluation on input x, and (2) COM does not match the commitment of bit 1 obtained using y as randomness. Clearly this scheme satisfies the ABO scheme correctness condition if the underlying commitment scheme is perfectly binding as in case of normal setup, condition (2) will never be satisfied. Both our ABO constructions are provided later in Sect. 5.

Lastly, one might think that the full power of ABO signatures is not needed to build the above Broadcast and Trace system. Instead a restricted version where the message space is fixed to be $\{1, 2, \ldots, N\}$ might suffice. It turns out that such a restricted ABO signature scheme can be directly constructed from any SPB Hash function and length doubling pseudo-random generator (PRG). The idea is to sample an SPB hash key hk, random λ bit strings s_i for each message $i \in [N]$ during setup. The verification key consists of the hash key hk and a hash value h, where h is computed as the SPB hash on the set $\{t_i = \mathsf{PRG}(s_i)\}_i$. The signature on message i consists of (s_i, π_i) where π_i is the SPB hash opening of hash h on index i. The verification procedure first checks correctness of the hash proof π_i, and then also checks that $\mathsf{PRG}(s_i)$ is i^{th} block value. For punctured setup at index i^*, the algorithm changes the following—(1) it samples SPB hash hk to be binding at index i^*, (2) it samples t_{i^*} uniformly at random from $\{0, 1\}^{2\lambda}$. With all-but-negligible probability, t_{i^*} will lie outside the range space of PRG, therefore no valid signature for i^* would exist under punctured setup.

However, such an ABO scheme can only be used to build a Broadcast and Trace system in which the numbers of users is a-priori (and polynomially) bounded. A more desirable setting would be where the number of users that can be supported is exponential (i.e., unbounded), while allowing the encryptor to choose any polynomial sized (a-priori unbounded) subset of users to broadcast to. Such a Broadcast and Trace system would still require the full power of ABO signatures, thus we stick to the more general setting.

2 Preliminaries

Notations. For a probability distribution D, we denote by $x \leftarrow D$ that x is sampled according to D. If S is a set, $y \leftarrow S$ denotes that y is sampled from S according to the uniform distribution on S. The set of contiguous integers $\{1, \ldots, k\}$ for some $k \geq 1$ is denoted by $[k]$. The set of contiguous integers $\{m, \ldots, n\}$ for some $m, n \in \mathbb{Z}$ is denoted by $[m, n]$. We sometimes slightly abuse notation and refer to bit strings in $\{0, 1\}^\ell$ by integers, where the left most bit of $x \in \{0, 1\}^\ell$ is considered as the most significant bit. For any set S, we denote the size of the set of $|S|$. We denote security parameter by λ in the rest of the paper. For any bit string t, we denote that $\mathsf{int}(t)$ as the integer representation of string t.

We define positional witness encryption in this section and defer the definitions of rest of the primitives to the full version of the paper due to space constraints.

2.1 Positional Witness Encryption

In this section, we formally define Positional Witness Encryption (PWE) [33] and list its correctness and security properties. The encryption system is defined for an NP language L and a message space $\{\mathcal{M}_\lambda\}_\lambda$. Let $R(\cdot,\cdot)$ be the witness relation corresponding to L i.e., for any string $x \in \{0,1\}^*$, $x \in L$ iff $\exists w \in \{0,1\}^{n(|x|)}$ s.t. $R(x,w) = 1$, where $n(|x|)$ is the witness length of instance x. For simplicity of notation, we hereby denote $n = n(|x|)$. A party can encrypt a message m with an instance x and index ind. Another party can decrypt the ciphertext using a witness w to the instance x such that $R(x,w) = 1$ and $w \geq \mathsf{ind}$. Given a string $w \in \{0,1\}^n$, we sometimes slightly abuse notation and also refer to w as an integer. Formally, the encryption system contains two procedures defined as follows.

- $\mathsf{Encrypt}(1^\lambda, x, m, \mathsf{ind}) \to \mathsf{ct}$. The encryption algorithm takes as input a security parameter 1^λ, an instance $x \in \{0,1\}^*$, a message m, an index $\mathsf{ind} \in [0, 2^n]$ and outputs a ciphertext ct.
- $\mathsf{Decrypt}(w, \mathsf{ct}) \to m$. The decryption algorithm takes as input a witness $w \in [0, 2^n - 1]$, a ciphertext ct and outputs either a message m or $\perp$.

Correctness. We say that a PWE scheme is correct if for every $\lambda \in \mathbb{N}$, any instance $x \in \{0,1\}^*$, any message $m \in \mathcal{M}_\lambda$, any witness $w \in [0, 2^n - 1]$, any position index $\mathsf{ind} \in [0, 2^n]$ such that $R(x,w) = 1$ and $w \geq \mathsf{ind}$, and $\mathsf{ct} \leftarrow \mathsf{Encrypt}(1^\lambda, x, m, \mathsf{ind})$, we have

$$\Pr\left[\mathsf{Decrypt}(w, \mathsf{ct}) = m\right] = 1$$

Security. A positional witness encryption scheme should satisfy 2 security properties: *message indistinguishability* and *position indistinguishability* defined as follows.

Definition 1 (Message Indistinguishability). *A PWE scheme for a language L is message indistinguishability secure if for any stateful PPT adversary $\mathcal{A}$, there exists a negligible function negl$(\cdot)$ such that for every $\lambda \in \mathbb{N}$, we have*

$$\Pr\left[\mathcal{A}(\mathsf{ct}) = b \;:\; \begin{array}{c} (x, m_0, m_1) \leftarrow \mathcal{A}(1^\lambda); \\ b \leftarrow \{0,1\}; \mathsf{ct} \leftarrow \mathsf{Encrypt}(1^\lambda, x, m_b, 2^n) \end{array}\right] \leq \frac{1}{2} + \mathit{negl}(\lambda).$$

Note that the above property needs to be satisfied even for instances $x \in L$.

Definition 2 (Position Indistinguishability). *A PWE scheme for a language L with witness relation $R(\cdot,\cdot)$ is position indistinguishability secure if for every stateful PPT adversary $\mathcal{A}$, there exists a negligible function negl$(\cdot)$ such that for every $\lambda \in \mathbb{N}$, we have*

$$\Pr\left[\mathcal{A}(\mathsf{ct}) = b \;:\; \begin{array}{c} (x, m, \mathsf{ind}) \leftarrow \mathcal{A}(1^\lambda); \\ b \leftarrow \{0,1\}; \mathsf{ct} \leftarrow \mathsf{Encrypt}(1^\lambda, x, m, \mathsf{ind} + b) \end{array}\right] \leq \frac{1}{2} + \mathit{negl}(\lambda).$$

where the adversary $\mathcal{A}$ is restricted to produce a challenge (x, m, ind) such that $R(x, \mathsf{ind}) = 0$.

3 Revisiting Broadcast and Trace System

3.1 Broadcast and Trace System

In this section, we formally define Broadcast and Trace system and describe its security properties. The security definition is motivated by a recent work by Goyal et al. [38] which points out problems with previously proposed notions of traitor tracing and proposes an indistinguishability based security definition for the primitive.

- $\mathsf{Setup}(1^\lambda, 1^N) \to (\mathsf{pk}, \{\mathsf{sk}_1, \mathsf{sk}_2, \dots, \mathsf{sk}_N\})$. The setup algorithm takes as input a security parameter λ and number of users N. It outputs a public key pk, and secret keys for N users $\{\mathsf{sk}_1, \mathsf{sk}_2, \dots, \mathsf{sk}_N\}$.
- $\mathsf{Encrypt}(\mathsf{pk}, S, m) \to \mathsf{ct}$. The encryption algorithm takes as input public key pk, a set $S \subseteq [N]$ of users, a message m and outputs a ciphertext ct.
- $\mathsf{Decrypt}(i, \mathsf{sk}_i, \mathsf{pk}, S, \mathsf{ct}) \to m/\perp$. The decryption algorithm takes as input an index $i \in [N]$, secret key of ith user, public key pk, a set of users $S \subseteq [N]$, a ciphertext ct and outputs either a message m or $\perp$.
- $\mathsf{Trace}^D(\mathsf{pk}, S_D, m_0, m_1, 1^{1/\epsilon}) \to S^*$. The tracing algorithm takes as input a public key pk, a set of users S_D, two messages m_0, m_1 and parameter $\epsilon < 1$. The algorithm has a black-box access to the decoder D and outputs a set of indices $S^* \subseteq [N]$.

Correctness. The Broadcast and Trace system is said to be correct if for every $\lambda \in \mathbb{N}$, any number of users $N \in \mathbb{N}$, every subset of users $S \subseteq [N]$, every message $m \in \mathcal{M}_\lambda$, every user $i \in S$, $(\mathsf{pk}, \{\mathsf{sk}_1, \mathsf{sk}_2, \dots, \mathsf{sk}_N\}) \leftarrow \mathsf{Setup}(1^\lambda, 1^N)$ and $\mathsf{ct} \leftarrow \mathsf{Encrypt}(\mathsf{pk}, S, m)$, we have

$$\mathsf{Decrypt}(i, \mathsf{sk}_i, \mathsf{pk}, S, \mathsf{ct}) = m.$$

Security. Intuitively, the system is said to be secure if it is IND-CPA secure and if no poly-time adversary can produce a decoder that can fool the tracing algorithm. We formally define both of these properties below.

Definition 3 (IND-CPA security). *We say that a Broadcast and Trace scheme is* IND-CPA *secure if for every stateful PPT adversary $\mathcal{A}$, there exists a negligible function negl$(\cdot)$ such that for all $\lambda \in \mathbb{N}$, the following holds*

$$\Pr\left[\mathcal{A}^{O(\cdot)}(\mathsf{ct}) = b : \begin{array}{c} 1^N \leftarrow \mathcal{A}(1^\lambda); (\mathsf{pk}, (\mathsf{sk}_1, \dots, \mathsf{sk}_N)) \leftarrow \mathsf{Setup}(1^\lambda, 1^N); \\ (S', m_0, m_1) \leftarrow \mathcal{A}^{O(\cdot)}(\mathsf{pk}); b \leftarrow \{0,1\}; \\ \mathsf{ct} \leftarrow \mathsf{Encrypt}(\mathsf{pk}, S', m_b) \end{array}\right] \leq \frac{1}{2} + negl(\lambda).$$

Here, $O(\cdot)$ is an oracle that has $\{\mathsf{sk}_i\}_{i\in[N]}$ hardwired, takes as input an index $i \in [n]$ and outputs sk_i. Let the set of indices queried by the adversary to the oracle be $S \subseteq [N]$. Then the adversary is restricted to output the challenge set S' such that $S' \subseteq [N] \setminus S$.

Experiment $\mathsf{Expt\text{-}BT}_{\mathcal{A},\epsilon}(\lambda)$

- $1^N \leftarrow \mathcal{A}(1^\lambda)$.
- $(\mathsf{pk}, (\mathsf{sk}_1, \ldots, \mathsf{sk}_N)) \leftarrow \mathsf{Setup}(1^\lambda, 1^N)$.
- $(D, S_D, m_0, m_1) \leftarrow \mathcal{A}^{O(\cdot)}(\mathsf{pk})$.
- $S^* \leftarrow \mathsf{Trace}^D(\mathsf{pk}, S_D, m_0, m_1, 1^{1/\epsilon(\lambda)})$.

Here, $O(\cdot)$ is an oracle that has $\{\mathsf{sk}_i\}_{i\in[N]}$ hardwired, takes as input an index $i \in [N]$ and outputs sk_i. Let S be the set of indices queried by $\mathcal{A}$.

Fig. 1. Experiment Expt-BT

Definition 4 (IND-secure Traitor Tracing). *Let* (Setup, Encrypt, Decrypt, Trace) *be a Broadcast and Trace scheme. For any non-negligible function* $\epsilon(\cdot)$ *and stateful PPT adversary* $\mathcal{A}$*, consider the experiment* $\mathsf{Expt\text{-}BT}_{\mathcal{A},\epsilon}(\lambda)$ *defined as follows.*

In order to define the security of tracing mechanism, we define the following events and probabilities as a function of security parameter λ.

- $\mathsf{Good\text{-}Dec}_{\mathcal{A},\epsilon}$: $\Pr[D(\mathsf{ct}) = b : b \leftarrow \{0,1\}, \mathsf{ct} \leftarrow \mathsf{Encrypt}(\mathsf{pk}, S_D, m_b)] \geq 1/2 + \epsilon(\lambda)$
  $\mathsf{Pr\text{-}Good\text{-}Dec}_{\mathcal{A},\epsilon}(\lambda) = \Pr[\mathsf{Good\text{-}Dec}_{\mathcal{A},\epsilon}]$
- $\mathsf{Correct\text{-}Tr}_{\mathcal{A},\epsilon}$: $|S^*| > 0, S^* \subseteq S \cap S_D$
  $\mathsf{Pr\text{-}Correct\text{-}Tr}_{\mathcal{A},\epsilon}(\lambda) = \Pr[\mathsf{Correct\text{-}Tr}_{\mathcal{A},\epsilon}]$
- $\mathsf{False\text{-}Tr}_{\mathcal{A},\epsilon}$: $S^* \not\subseteq S \cap S_D$
  $\mathsf{Pr\text{-}False\text{-}Tr}_{\mathcal{A},\epsilon}(\lambda) = \Pr[\mathsf{False\text{-}Tr}_{\mathcal{A},\epsilon}]$

The Broadcast and Trace scheme is said to have Ind-secure tracing mechanism if for every stateful PPT adversary $\mathcal{A}$*, polynomial* $q(\cdot)$ *and non-negligible function* $\epsilon(\cdot)$*, there exists negligible functions* $negl_1(\cdot)$ *and* $negl_2(\cdot)$ *such that for all* $\lambda \in \mathbb{N}$ *satisfying* $\epsilon(\lambda) > 1/q(\lambda)$, $\mathsf{Pr\text{-}Correct\text{-}Tr}_{\mathcal{A},\epsilon}(\lambda) \geq \mathsf{Pr\text{-}Good\text{-}Dec}_{\mathcal{A},\epsilon}(\lambda) - negl_1(\lambda)$ *and* $\mathsf{Pr\text{-}False\text{-}Tr}_{\mathcal{A},\epsilon}(\lambda) \leq negl_2(\lambda)$ *(Fig. 1).*

3.2 Augmented Broadcast Encryption

In this section, we define Augmented Broadcast Encryption (AugBE) and its security properties.

- $\mathsf{Setup}(1^\lambda, 1^N) \rightarrow (\mathsf{pk}, \{\mathsf{sk}_1, \ldots, \mathsf{sk}_N\})$. The setup algorithm takes as input security parameter λ and number of users N. It outputs a public key pk and secret keys $\{\mathsf{sk}_1, \ldots, \mathsf{sk}_N\}$, where sk_i is the secret key for user i.
- $\mathsf{Encrypt}(\mathsf{pk}, S, m, \mathsf{ind}) \rightarrow \mathsf{ct}$. The encryption algorithm takes as input public key pk, a set of users $S \subseteq [N]$, a message m, and an index $\mathsf{ind} \in [N+1]$. It outputs a ciphertext ct.
- $\mathsf{Decrypt}(i, \mathsf{sk}_i, \mathsf{pk}, S, \mathsf{ct}) \rightarrow m/\perp$. The decryption algorithm takes as input an index i, secret key for i^{th} user sk_i, public key pk, a set of users $S \subseteq [N]$, a ciphertext ct and outputs a message m or $\perp$.

Correctness. An AugBE scheme is said to be correct if for every security parameter $\lambda \in \mathbb{N}$, any number of users $N \in \mathbb{N}$, any message $m \in \mathcal{M}_\lambda$, any subset of users $S \subseteq [N]$, any index $\mathsf{ind} \in [N]$, any $i \in S \cap \{\mathsf{ind}, \mathsf{ind}+1, \ldots, N\}$, $(\mathsf{pk}, \{\mathsf{sk}_1, \mathsf{sk}_2, \ldots, \mathsf{sk}_N\}) \leftarrow \mathsf{Setup}(1^\lambda, 1^N)$ and $\mathsf{ct} \leftarrow \mathsf{Encrypt}(\mathsf{pk}, S, m, \mathsf{ind})$, we have

$$\mathsf{Decrypt}(i, \mathsf{sk}_i, \mathsf{pk}, S, \mathsf{ct}) = m.$$

Security. We need AugBE to satisfy 2 security properties. The first is *message hiding* property which states that no PPT adversary can distinguish between encryptions of m_0 and m_1 encrypted using the last index $N+1$. The second is *index hiding* property which states that ciphertexts encrypted to index ind do not reveal any non-trivial information about the index. We formally define the security properties below.

Definition 5 (Message Hiding). *We say that an AugBE scheme satisfies message hiding property if for every stateful PPT adversary $\mathcal{A}$, there exists a negligible function negl$(\cdot)$ such that for every $\lambda \in \mathbb{N}$, the following holds*

$$\Pr\left[\mathcal{A}^{O(\cdot)}(\mathsf{ct}) = b \ : \begin{array}{c} 1^N \leftarrow \mathcal{A}(1^\lambda); \\ (\mathsf{msk}, \mathsf{pk}, \{\mathsf{sk}_i\}_{i\in[N]}) \leftarrow \mathsf{Setup}(1^\lambda, 1^N); \\ (S', m_0, m_1) \leftarrow \mathcal{A}^{O(\cdot)}(\mathsf{pk}); b \leftarrow \{0,1\}; \\ \mathsf{ct} \leftarrow \mathsf{Encrypt}(\mathsf{pk}, S', m_b, N+1) \end{array}\right] \leq \frac{1}{2} + negl(\lambda).$$

Here, $O(\cdot)$ is an oracle that has $\{\mathsf{sk}_i\}_{i\in[N]}$ hardwired, takes as input an index $i \in [N]$ and outputs sk_i.

Definition 6 (Index Hiding). *We say that an AugBE scheme satisfies index hiding property if for every stateful PPT adversary $\mathcal{A}$, there exists a negligible function negl$(\cdot)$ such that for every $\lambda \in \mathbb{N}$, the following holds,*

$$\Pr\left[\mathcal{A}^{O(\cdot)}(\mathsf{ct}) = b \ : \begin{array}{c} (1^N, \mathsf{ind}) \leftarrow \mathcal{A}(1^\lambda); \\ (\mathsf{msk}, \mathsf{pk}, \{\mathsf{sk}_i\}_{i\in[N]}) \leftarrow \mathsf{Setup}(1^\lambda, 1^N); \\ (S', m) \leftarrow \mathcal{A}^{O(\cdot)}(\mathsf{pk}); b \leftarrow \{0,1\}; \\ \mathsf{ct} \leftarrow \mathsf{Encrypt}(\mathsf{pk}, S', m, \mathsf{ind}+b) \end{array}\right] \leq \frac{1}{2} + negl(\lambda).$$

Here, $O(\cdot)$ is an oracle that has $\{\mathsf{sk}_i\}_{i\in[N]}$ hardwired, takes as input an index $i \in [N]$ and outputs sk_i. Let the set of keys queried by the adversary be S. We restrict the adversary to satisfy $\mathsf{ind} \notin S' \vee \mathsf{ind} \notin S$.

3.3 Broadcast and Trace from AugBE

We construct a Broadcast and Trace system assuming we have an AugBE scheme. The construction is same as [14], but we would like to point out their security proof is inaccurate. The problem lies in the fact that there is a "semantic gap" between their definitions of BT and AugBE schemes. The issue is that in a BT system an adversary outputs a box which performs some decoding/decryption operations, whereas in an AugBE system the adversary plays a distinguishing game. We modify their security proof as per indistinguishability based definition of Broadcast and Trace. Due to space constraints, we present the construction in the full version of the paper.

4 Construction of Augmented Broadcast Encryption

In this section, we construct an augmented broadcast encryption (AugBE) scheme from positional witness encryption (PWE), somewhere perfectly binding hash (SPB hash) function and all-but-one (ABO) signatures. We also prove that the construction satisfies the message hiding and index hiding properties.

Let $\mathcal{ABO} = (\mathsf{Setup}_{\mathsf{ABO}}, \mathsf{Setup\text{-}Punc}_{\mathsf{ABO}}, \mathsf{Sign}_{\mathsf{ABO}}, \mathsf{Verify}_{\mathsf{ABO}})$ be an ABO signature scheme with message space $\{0,1\}^{\lambda}$, signature space $\{0,1\}^{k(\lambda)}$, secret key space $\{\mathcal{S}_\lambda\}_\lambda$ and verification key space $\{\mathcal{V}_\lambda\}_\lambda$. Let $\mathcal{SPB} = (\mathsf{Setup}_{\mathsf{SPB}}, \mathsf{Setup\text{-}Bind}_{\mathsf{SPB}}, \mathsf{Hash}_{\mathsf{SPB}}, \mathsf{Open}_{\mathsf{SPB}}, \mathsf{Verify}_{\mathsf{SPB}})$ be an SPB hash function with hash key space $\{\mathcal{K}_\lambda\}_\lambda$, hash space $\{\mathcal{H}_\lambda\}_\lambda$ and hash opening space $\{0,1\}^{\ell(\lambda)}$. For simplicity of notation, we hereby use $\ell = \ell(\lambda)$ and $k = k(\lambda)$. Let $\mathcal{PWE} = (\mathsf{Encrypt}_{\mathsf{PWE}}, \mathsf{Decrypt}_{\mathsf{PWE}})$ be a PWE scheme with message space $\{\mathcal{M}_\lambda\}_\lambda$ with respect to the following language $\mathcal{L}$. The language $\mathcal{L}$ contains instances of the form $(1^\lambda, N, h, \mathsf{hk}, \mathsf{vk}) \in 1^\lambda \times \{0,1\}^\lambda \times \mathcal{H}_\lambda \times \mathcal{K}_\lambda \times \mathcal{V}_\lambda$, where $\lambda \in \mathbb{N}$, with the following witness relation $\mathcal{R}$:

$$(1^\lambda, N, h, \mathsf{hk}, \mathsf{vk}) \in \mathcal{L} \iff \begin{array}{c} \exists (i, \sigma, \pi) \in \{0,1\}^\lambda \times \{0,1\}^k \times \{0,1\}^\ell \text{ s.t.} \\ 1 \le i \le N \wedge \mathsf{Verify}_{\mathsf{ABO}}(\mathsf{vk}, i, \sigma) = 1 \wedge \\ \mathsf{Verify}_{\mathsf{SPB}}(\mathsf{hk}, h, i, 1, \pi) = 1. \end{array}$$

Note that the above witness relation $\mathcal{R}$ is well defined as $\mathsf{Verify}_{\mathsf{ABO}}$ and $\mathsf{Verify}_{\mathsf{SPB}}$ are deterministic algorithms. We construct an AugBE scheme $\mathcal{AUGBE} = (\mathsf{Setup}, \mathsf{Encrypt}, \mathsf{Decrypt})$ with message space $\{\mathcal{M}_\lambda\}_\lambda$. We sometimes slightly abuse notation and denote the values in $\{0,1\}^z$ (for $z \in \mathbb{N}$) by integers. For any set $S \subseteq [N]$, let $\mathbb{I}_S$ be a bit vector of length N, where the ith element $\mathbb{I}_S(i)$ is defined as

$$\mathbb{I}_S(i) = \begin{cases} 1 & \text{if } i \in S, \\ 0 & \text{otherwise} \end{cases}.$$

- $\mathsf{Setup}(1^\lambda, 1^N)$: Sample $(\mathsf{vk}, \mathsf{sk}) \leftarrow \mathsf{Setup}_{\mathsf{ABO}}(1^\lambda)$ and $\mathsf{hk} \leftarrow \mathsf{Setup}_{\mathsf{SPB}}(1^\lambda, N)$. Compute signatures $\{\sigma_i \leftarrow \mathsf{Sign}_{\mathsf{ABO}}(\mathsf{sk}, i) : 1 \le i \le N\}$. Output $\mathsf{pk} = (1^\lambda, N, \mathsf{vk}, \mathsf{hk})$, and secret keys $\{\mathsf{sk}_i = \sigma_i : 1 \le i \le N\}$.
- $\mathsf{Encrypt}(\mathsf{pk}, S, m, \mathsf{ind})$: Let $\mathsf{pk} = (1^\lambda, N, \mathsf{vk}, \mathsf{hk})$. Compute SPB hash on $\mathbb{I}_S$ i.e., compute the hash $h = \mathsf{Hash}_{\mathsf{SPB}}\ (\mathsf{hk}, \mathbb{I}_S)$. Then encrypt the message m with PWE scheme using the instance $\mathsf{inst} = (1^\lambda, N, h, \mathsf{hk}, \mathsf{vk})$ and index $\mathsf{ind}||0^{k+\ell}$, i.e., computes $\mathsf{ct} \leftarrow \mathsf{Encrypt}_{\mathsf{PWE}}\ (\mathsf{inst}, m, \mathsf{ind}||0^{k+\ell})$.
- $\mathsf{Decrypt}(i, \mathsf{sk}_i, \mathsf{pk}, S, \mathsf{ct})$: Let $\mathsf{pk} = (1^\lambda, N, \mathsf{vk}, \mathsf{hk})$. Compute hash $h = \mathsf{Hash}_{\mathsf{SPB}}$ $(\mathsf{hk}, \mathbb{I}_S)$ and proof $\pi_i \leftarrow \mathsf{Open}_{\mathsf{SPB}}(\mathsf{hk}, \mathbb{I}_S, i)$. Then decrypt the ciphertext using the witness $w = i||\mathsf{sk}_i||\pi_i$ i.e., output message $m \leftarrow \mathsf{Decrypt}_{\mathsf{PWE}}(w = i||\mathsf{sk}_i||\pi_i, \mathsf{ct})$.

Note that the correctness properties of $\mathcal{SPB}$ hash and $\mathcal{ABO}$ signature schemes imply that $w = i||\mathsf{sk}_i||\pi_i$ is a valid witness to the instance $\mathsf{inst} = (1^\lambda, N, h, \mathsf{hk}, \mathsf{vk})$ (i.e., $R(x, w) = 1$). This along with the correctness of $\mathcal{PWE}$ scheme imply the correctness of the above scheme. In the following subsections, we prove that the above AugBE construction satisfies message hiding and index hiding properties. Formally, we prove the following theorem.

Theorem 1. *If $\mathcal{PWE}$ is a sub-exponentially secure PWE scheme as per Definitions 1 and 2, $\mathcal{ABO}$ is a secure ABO signature scheme and $\mathcal{SPB}$ is a secure SPB hash function, then $\mathcal{AUGBE}$ is a secure AugBE scheme as per Definitions 5 and 6.*

4.1 Message Hiding

In this subsection, we prove the message hiding property of the above scheme assuming sub-exponential security of $\mathcal{PWE}$ scheme. For any instance $(1^\lambda, N, h, \mathsf{hk}, \mathsf{vk})$, let $r(\lambda)$ be the length of witnesses accepted by the witness relation $\mathcal{R}$, i.e., $r(\lambda) = \lambda + k(\lambda) + \ell(\lambda)$. For simplicity of notation, we ignore the parameters and simply denote it by r. We first describe the following games that help us in proving the property.

$\mathsf{Game}\ N + 1||0^{k+\ell}$. This game is same as the AugBE message hiding game.

1. *Setup Phase.* The adversary $\mathcal{A}$ sends the number of users 1^N to the challenger. The challenger samples the keys $(\mathsf{vk}, \mathsf{sk}) \leftarrow \mathsf{Setup}_{\mathsf{ABO}}(1^\lambda)$, hash key $\mathsf{hk} \leftarrow \mathsf{Setup}_{\mathsf{SPB}}(1^\lambda, N)$ and signatures $\{\sigma_i \leftarrow \mathsf{Sign}_{\mathsf{ABO}}(\mathsf{sk}, i) : 1 \leq i \leq N\}$. It then sends the public key $\mathsf{pk} = (1^\lambda, N, \mathsf{vk}, \mathsf{hk})$ to $\mathcal{A}$.
2. *Pre-Challenge Query Phase.* The adversary then adaptively queries for secret keys. For each query j, the challenger responds with the secret key $\mathsf{sk}_j = \sigma_j$.
3. *Challenge Phase.* The adversary then sends a pair of messages m_0, m_1 and a set $S \subseteq [N]$ to the challenger. The challenger samples a bit $b \leftarrow \{0,1\}$ and computes hash $h = \mathsf{Hash}_{\mathsf{SPB}}(\mathsf{hk}, \mathbb{I}_S)$. It then samples ciphertext $\mathsf{ct} \leftarrow \mathsf{Encrypt}_{\mathsf{PWE}}\ (x = (1^\lambda, N, h, \mathsf{hk}, \mathsf{vk}), m_b, \mathsf{int}(N + 1||0^{k+\ell}))$ and responds with ct.
4. *Post-Challenge Query Phase.* This is identical to Pre-Challenge Query Phase.
5. *Output Phase.* The adversary sends a bit b' to the challenger. The adversary wins if $b' = b$.

$\mathsf{Game}\ y$ $(N + 1||0^{k+\ell} < y \leq 2^r)$. This game is similar to $\mathsf{Game}\ N + 1||0^{k+\ell}$, except that the challenger encrypts the challenge message using index y instead of index $\mathsf{int}(N + 1||0^{k+\ell})$.

3. *Challenge Phase.* The adversary then sends a pair of messages m_0, m_1 and a set $S \subseteq [N]$ to the challenger. The challenger samples a bit $b \leftarrow \{0,1\}$ and computes hash $h = \mathsf{Hash}_{\mathsf{SPB}}(\mathsf{hk}, \mathbb{I}_S)$. It then samples ciphertext $\mathsf{ct} \leftarrow \mathsf{Encrypt}_{\mathsf{PWE}}\ (x = (1^\lambda, N, h, \mathsf{hk}, \mathsf{vk}), m_b, y)$ and responds with ct.

For any stateful PPT adversary $\mathcal{A}$, we define the advantage of the adversary in Game x as $\mathsf{Adv}_x^{\mathcal{A}}(\lambda) = \Pr[\mathcal{A} \text{ wins}] - 1/2$. We prove that the advantage of any PPT adversary $\mathcal{A}$ in Game $N+1||0^{k+\ell}$ is negligible in security parameter. For any stateful PPT adversary $\mathcal{B}$ and $\lambda \in \mathbb{N}$, let $\mathsf{AdvPosInd}^{\mathcal{B}}(\lambda)$ denote the advantage of $\mathcal{B}$ in position indistinguishability game and $\mathsf{AdvMsgInd}^{\mathcal{B}}(\lambda)$ denote the advantage of $\mathcal{B}$ in message indistinguishability game of $\mathcal{PWE}$ scheme. For any $\lambda \in \mathbb{N}$, let $\mathsf{AdvPosInd}(\lambda) = \sup_{\text{PPT } \mathcal{B}} \mathsf{AdvPosInd}^{\mathcal{B}}(\lambda)$ and $\mathsf{AdvMsgInd}(\lambda) = \sup_{\text{PPT } \mathcal{B}} \mathsf{AdvMsgInd}^{\mathcal{B}}(\lambda)$. We now establish using the following lemma that the difference of the adversary's advantage between each adjacent game is at most $2 \cdot \mathsf{AdvPosInd}(\lambda)$. Finally we show that if any adversary wins in the last game, then it wins message indistinguishability game against PWE challenger as well.

Claim 1. *For every y s.t. $N+1||0^{k+\ell} \le y \le 2^r - 1$, every PPT adversary $\mathcal{A}$ and $\lambda \in \mathbb{N}$, we have* $\mathsf{Adv}_y^{\mathcal{A}}(\lambda) - \mathsf{Adv}_{y+1}^{\mathcal{A}}(\lambda) \le 2 \cdot \mathsf{AdvPosInd}(\lambda)$.

Proof. Consider any y s.t. $N+1||0^{k+\ell} \le y \le 2^r - 1$, any PPT adversary $\mathcal{A}$ and $\lambda \in \mathbb{N}$. We build a PPT algorithm $\mathcal{B}$ which uses $\mathcal{A}$ and has advantage $(\mathsf{Adv}_y^{\mathcal{A}}(\lambda) - \mathsf{Adv}_{y+1}^{\mathcal{A}}(\lambda))/2$ in the position indistinguishability game of the $\mathcal{PWE}$ scheme. The reduction algorithm $\mathcal{B}$ proceeds as follows.

$\mathcal{A}$ first sends the number of users 1^N to $\mathcal{B}$. $\mathcal{B}$ then samples $(\mathsf{sk}, \mathsf{vk}) \leftarrow \mathsf{Setup}_{\mathsf{ABO}}(1^\lambda)$, $\mathsf{hk} \leftarrow \mathsf{Setup}_{\mathsf{SPB}}(1^\lambda, N)$, signatures $\{\sigma_j \leftarrow \mathsf{Sign}_{\mathsf{ABO}}(\mathsf{sk}, j) : 1 \le j \le N\}$ and sends the public key $\mathsf{pk} = (1^\lambda, N, \mathsf{vk}, \mathsf{hk})$ to $\mathcal{A}$. $\mathcal{A}$ then adaptively queries for secret keys. For each query j, $\mathcal{B}$ responds with the secret key $\mathsf{sk}_j = \sigma_j$. After query phase, $\mathcal{A}$ sends a challenge set S and a pair of messages m_0, m_1 to $\mathcal{B}$. $\mathcal{B}$ samples a bit $b \leftarrow \{0,1\}$ and computes hash $h = \mathsf{Hash}_{\mathsf{SPB}}(\mathsf{hk}, \mathbb{I}_S)$. It then sends the challenge instance $\mathsf{inst} = (1^\lambda, N, h, \mathsf{hk}, \mathsf{vk})$, challenge message m_b and challenge index y to the challenger $\mathcal{C}$ of position indistinguishability game. The challenger samples a bit $\beta \leftarrow \{0,1\}$ and responds with a ciphertext $\mathsf{ct} \leftarrow \mathsf{Encrypt}_{\mathsf{PWE}}(\mathsf{inst}, m_b, y+\beta)$ to $\mathcal{B}$, which forwards it to $\mathcal{A}$. $\mathcal{A}$ further adaptively queries for secret keys. For each query j, $\mathcal{B}$ responds with the secret key $\mathsf{sk}_j = \sigma_j$. Finally, $\mathcal{A}$ sends a bit b' to $\mathcal{B}$. If $b' = b$, then $\mathcal{B}$ outputs 0 indicating its guess that the challenger encrypted m_b using index y. If $b' \ne b$, then $\mathcal{B}$ outputs 1 indicating its guess that the challenger encrypted m_b using index $y+1$.

We know that the index y cannot be a witness for the instance $(1^\lambda, N, h, \mathsf{hk}, \mathsf{vk})$ as $y \ge N+1||0^{k+\ell}$ (i.e., $y[1:\lambda] \ge N+1$). Therefore, the reduction algorithm $\mathcal{B}$ acts as a valid adversary in the position indistinguishability game. If $\beta = 0$, $\mathcal{B}$ simulates the view of Game y to $\mathcal{A}$ and $\Pr[b' = b] = 1/2 + \mathsf{Adv}_y^{\mathcal{A}}(\lambda)$. Otherwise, it simulates the view of Game $y+1$ to $\mathcal{A}$ and $\Pr[b' = b] = 1/2 + \mathsf{Adv}_{y+1}^{\mathcal{A}}(\lambda)$. Therefore, the advantage of $\mathcal{B}$ in position indistinguishability game is given by $\mathsf{AdvPosInd}^{\mathcal{B}}(\lambda) = 1/2 \cdot \Pr[b' = b | \beta = 0] + 1/2 \cdot \Pr[b' \ne b | \beta = 1] - 1/2 = 1/2 \cdot (\mathsf{Adv}_y^{\mathcal{A}}(\lambda) - \mathsf{Adv}_{y+1}^{\mathcal{A}}(\lambda))$. Therefore, $\mathsf{Adv}_y^{\mathcal{A}}(\lambda) - \mathsf{Adv}_{y+1}^{\mathcal{A}}(\lambda) \le 2 \cdot \mathsf{AdvPosInd}(\lambda)$.

Claim 2. *For every stateful PPT adversary $\mathcal{A}$ and every $\lambda \in \mathbb{N}$, we have* $\mathsf{Adv}_{2^r}^{\mathcal{A}}(\lambda) \le \mathsf{AdvMsgInd}(\lambda)$.

Proof. Consider any PPT adversary $\mathcal{A}$ and any $\lambda \in \mathbb{N}$. We build a PPT algorithm $\mathcal{B}$ which uses $\mathcal{A}$ and has advantage $\mathsf{Adv}^{\mathcal{A}}_{2^r}(\lambda)$ in message indistinguishability game of the $\mathcal{PWE}$ scheme. The reduction algorithm $\mathcal{B}$ proceeds as follows.

$\mathcal{A}$ first sends the number of users 1^N to $\mathcal{B}$. $\mathcal{B}$ then samples $(\mathsf{sk}, \mathsf{vk}) \leftarrow \mathsf{Setup}_{\mathsf{ABO}}(1^\lambda)$, hash key $\mathsf{hk} \leftarrow \mathsf{Setup}_{\mathsf{SPB}}(1^\lambda, N)$ and signatures $\{\sigma_j \leftarrow \mathsf{Sign}_{\mathsf{ABO}}(\mathsf{sk}, j) : 1 \leq j \leq N\}$. It then sends the public key $\mathsf{pk} = (1^\lambda, N, \mathsf{vk}, \mathsf{hk})$ to $\mathcal{A}$. $\mathcal{A}$ then adaptively queries for secret keys. For each query j, $\mathcal{B}$ responds with the secret key $\mathsf{sk}_j = \sigma_j$. After query phase, $\mathcal{A}$ sends a challenge set S and messages m_0, m_1 to $\mathcal{B}$. $\mathcal{B}$ computes hash $h = \mathsf{Hash}_{\mathsf{SPB}}(\mathsf{hk}, \mathbb{I}_S)$. It then sends challenge instance $\mathsf{inst} = (1^\lambda, N, h, \mathsf{hk}, \mathsf{vk})$ and challenge messages m_0, m_1 to message indistinguishability game challenger $\mathcal{C}$. The challenger samples a bit $b \leftarrow \{0,1\}$ and responds with ciphertext $\mathsf{ct} \leftarrow \mathsf{Encrypt}_{\mathsf{PWE}}(\mathsf{inst}, m_b, 2^r)$ to $\mathcal{B}$, which forwards ct to $\mathcal{A}$. $\mathcal{A}$ further adaptively queries for secret keys. For each query j, $\mathcal{B}$ responds with the secret key $\mathsf{sk}_j = \sigma_j$. Finally, $\mathcal{A}$ sends a bit b' to $\mathcal{B}$, which outputs b' as its guess in message indistinguishability game.

Clearly, $\mathcal{B}$ is a valid adversary of the message indistinguishability game, and also simulates the view of Game 2^r to $\mathcal{A}$. Note that advantage of $\mathcal{B}$ in message indistinguishability game is given by $\mathsf{AdvMsgInd}^{\mathcal{B}}(\lambda) = \mathsf{Adv}^{\mathcal{A}}_{2^r}(\lambda)$, and therefore $\mathsf{Adv}^{\mathcal{A}}_{2^r}(\lambda) \leq \mathsf{AdvMsgInd}(\lambda)$.

Note that by combining Claims 1 and 2, the advantage of any PPT adversary $\mathcal{A}$ in AugBE message hiding game is $\mathsf{Adv}^{\mathcal{A}}_{N+1||0^{k+\ell}}(\lambda) = \sum_{y=N+1||0^{k+\ell}}^{2^r-1}(\mathsf{Adv}^{\mathcal{A}}_{y}(\lambda) - \mathsf{Adv}^{\mathcal{A}}_{y+1}(\lambda)) + \mathsf{Adv}^{\mathcal{A}}_{2^r}(\lambda) \leq 2 \cdot (2^\lambda - N) \cdot 2^{k+\ell} \cdot \mathsf{AdvPosInd}(\lambda) + \mathsf{AdvMsgInd}(\lambda)$. Using complexity leveraging, we demand that $\mathsf{AdvPosInd}(\lambda) \leq 2^{-(\lambda+k+\ell+1)} \cdot \mathrm{negl}(\lambda)$ for some negligible function $\mathrm{negl}(\cdot)$. At the instantiation level, the security parameter will be increased to match this condition.

4.2 Index Hiding

In this section, we prove the index hiding property of the above scheme. We first describe the following 2 games that help us in describing the lemma formally.

Game 0. This game corresponds to AugBE index hiding game where the challenger always uses bit $b = 0$.

1. *Setup Phase.* The adversary $\mathcal{A}$ sends the number of users 1^N and index i s.t. $1 \leq i \leq N$ to the challenger. The challenger samples $(\mathsf{vk}, \mathsf{sk}) \leftarrow \mathsf{Setup}_{\mathsf{ABO}}(1^\lambda)$, hash key $\mathsf{hk} \leftarrow \mathsf{Setup}_{\mathsf{SPB}}(1^\lambda, N)$ and signatures $\{\sigma_j \leftarrow \mathsf{Sign}_{\mathsf{ABO}}(\mathsf{sk}, j) : 1 \leq j \leq N\}$ of the AugBE scheme. It then sends the public key $\mathsf{pk} = (1^\lambda, N, \mathsf{vk}, \mathsf{hk})$ to $\mathcal{A}$.
2. *Pre-Challenge Query Phase.* The adversary then adaptively queries for secret keys. For each query j, the challenger responds with the secret key $\mathsf{sk}_j = \sigma_j$.
3. *Challenge Phase.* The adversary then sends a message m and a set $S \subseteq [N]$ to the challenger. The challenger computes hash $h = \mathsf{Hash}_{\mathsf{SPB}}(\mathsf{hk}, \mathbb{I}_S)$ and responds with ciphertext $\mathsf{ct} \leftarrow \mathsf{Encrypt}_{\mathsf{PWE}}(x = (1^\lambda, N, h, \mathsf{hk}, \mathsf{vk}), m, \mathsf{int}(i||0^{k+\ell}))$.

4. *Post-Challenge Query Phase.* This is identical to Pre-Challenge Query Phase.
5. *Output Phase.* The adversary sends a bit b' to the challenger.

Let the set of all secret keys queried by the adversary be S^*. The adversary is restricted to query such that $i \notin S \vee i \notin S^*$.

Game 3. This game is similar to the first game, except that the challenger always uses bit $b = 1$.

3. *Challenge Phase.* The adversary then sends a message m and a set $S \subseteq [N]$ to the challenger. The challenger computes hash $h = \mathsf{Hash}_{\mathsf{SPB}}(\mathsf{hk}, \mathbb{I}_S)$ and responds with ciphertext $\mathsf{ct} \leftarrow \mathsf{Encrypt}_{\mathsf{PWE}}(x = (1^\lambda, N, h, \mathsf{hk}, \mathsf{vk}), m, \mathsf{int}(i + 1||0^{k+\ell}))$.

For any stateful PPT adversary $\mathcal{A}$, let the probability that $\mathcal{A}$ outputs 1 in Game y be $p_y^{\mathcal{A}}(\lambda)$. We denote the advantage of a PPT adversary $\mathcal{A}$ in distinguishing between any two games Game x and Game y by $\mathsf{Adv}_{x,y}^{\mathcal{A}}(\lambda) = |p_x^{\mathcal{A}}(\lambda) - p_y^{\mathcal{A}}(\lambda)|$.

Lemma 1. *If $\mathcal{ABO}$ is a secure ABO signature scheme, $\mathcal{SPB}$ is a secure SPB hash function, and $\mathcal{PWE}$ is a sub-exponentially secure PWE scheme as per Definition 2, for every stateful PPT Adversary $\mathcal{A}$, there exists a negligible function negl($\cdot$) such that for every security parameter λ, $\mathsf{Adv}_{0,3}^{\mathcal{A}}(\lambda) \leq negl(\lambda)$.*

Proof. We first classify the adversaries into the following 2 types.

- Type 1 adversary: Restricted to generate set of key queries S^* and challenge set S s.t. $i \notin S$.
- Type 2 adversary: Restricted to generate set of key queries S^* and challenge set S s.t. $i \in S \wedge i \notin S^*$.

We now prove Lemmas 2 and 3 which together imply Lemma 1.

Lemma 2. *If $\mathcal{SPB}$ is secure, and $\mathcal{PWE}$ is a sub-exponentially secure as per Definition 2, for every stateful* Type 1 *PPT Adversary $\mathcal{A}$, there exists a negligible function negl($\cdot$) such that for every security parameter λ, $\mathsf{Adv}_{0,3}^{\mathcal{A}}(\lambda) \leq negl(\lambda)$.*

Proof. We prove the lemma using the following sequence of hybrids.

Game 1.t (for $0 \leq t < 2^{k+\ell}$): Here t is a bit string of length $k + \ell$. This game is similar to Game 0 except that challenger samples SPB hash key using Setup-Bind and encrypts the challenge message using index $\mathsf{int}(i||0^{k+\ell}) + t$.

1. *Setup Phase.* The adversary $\mathcal{A}$ sends the number of users 1^N to the challenger. The challenger samples $(\mathsf{vk}, \mathsf{sk}) \leftarrow \mathsf{Setup}_{\mathsf{ABO}}(1^\lambda)$, $\mathsf{hk} \leftarrow \mathsf{Setup\text{-}Bind}_{\mathsf{SPB}}$ $(1^\lambda, N, i)$ and signatures $\{\sigma_j \leftarrow \mathsf{Sign}_{\mathsf{ABO}}(\mathsf{sk}, j) : 1 \leq j \leq N\}$. It then sends the public key $\mathsf{pk} = (1^\lambda, N, \mathsf{vk}, \mathsf{hk})$ to $\mathcal{A}$.
3. *Challenge Phase.* The adversary sends a message m and a set $S \subseteq [N]$ to the challenger. The challenger computes hash $h = \mathsf{Hash}_{\mathsf{SPB}}(\mathsf{hk}, \mathbb{I}_S)$ and responds with ciphertext $\mathsf{ct} \leftarrow \mathsf{Encrypt}_{\mathsf{PWE}}((1^\lambda, N, h, \mathsf{hk}, \mathsf{vk}), m, \mathsf{int}(i||0^{k+\ell}) + t)$.

$\mathsf{Game}\ 1.2^{k+\ell}$: This game is similar to $\mathsf{Game}\ 1.2^{k+\ell}-1$ except that challenger encrypts the challenge message using index $\mathsf{int}(i+1||0^{k+\ell})$.

1. *Setup Phase.* The adversary $\mathcal{A}$ sends the number of users 1^N to the challenger. The challenger samples $(\mathsf{vk},\mathsf{sk}) \leftarrow \mathsf{Setup}_{\mathsf{ABO}}(1^\lambda)$, hash key $\mathsf{hk} \leftarrow \mathsf{Setup\text{-}Bind}_{\mathsf{SPB}}(1^\lambda, N, i)$ and signatures $\{\sigma_j \leftarrow \mathsf{Sign}_{\mathsf{ABO}}(\mathsf{sk}, j) : 1 \le j \le N\}$ of the AugBE scheme. It then sends the public key $\mathsf{pk} = (\mathsf{vk},\mathsf{hk})$ to $\mathcal{A}$.
3. *Challenge Phase.* The adversary sends a message m and a set $S \subseteq [N]$ to the challenger, which computes hash $h = \mathsf{Hash}_{\mathsf{SPB}}(\mathsf{hk}, \mathbb{I}_S)$ and responds with ciphertext $\mathsf{ct} \leftarrow \mathsf{Encrypt}_{\mathsf{PWE}}((1^\lambda, N, h, \mathsf{hk}, \mathsf{vk}), m, \mathsf{int}(i+1||0^{k+\ell}))$.

For any PPT adversary $\mathcal{B}$ and $\lambda \in \mathbb{N}$, let $\mathsf{AdvSpbInd}^{\mathcal{B}}(\lambda)$ denote the advantage of $\mathcal{B}$ in index hiding game of $\mathcal{SPB}$ scheme and $\mathsf{AdvPosInd}^{\mathcal{B}}(\lambda)$ denote the advantage of $\mathcal{B}$ in position indistinguishability game of $\mathcal{PWE}$ scheme. For any $\lambda \in \mathbb{N}$, let $\mathsf{AdvPosInd}(\lambda) = \sup_{\mathrm{PPT}\ \mathcal{B}} \mathsf{AdvPosInd}^{\mathcal{B}}(\lambda)$ and $\mathsf{AdvSpbInd}(\lambda) = \sup_{\mathrm{PPT}\ \mathcal{B}} \mathsf{AdvSpbInd}^{\mathcal{B}}(\lambda)$. We prove Lemma 2 using the following sequence of claims.

Claim 3. *For every* Type 1 *PPT adversary* $\mathcal{A}$ *and any* $\lambda \in \mathbb{N}$, *we have* $\mathsf{Adv}^{\mathcal{A}}_{0,1.0}(\lambda) \le 2 \cdot \mathsf{AdvSpbInd}(\lambda)$.

Proof. Consider any Type 1 PPT adversary $\mathcal{A}$ and any $\lambda \in \mathbb{N}$. We build a PPT algorithm $\mathcal{B}$ which uses $\mathcal{A}$ and has advantage $\mathsf{Adv}^{\mathcal{A}}_{0,1.0}(\lambda)/2$ in index hiding game of the $\mathcal{SPB}$ scheme. The reduction algorithm $\mathcal{B}$ proceeds as follows.

$\mathcal{A}$ first sends the number of users 1^N and an index i s.t. $1 \le i \le N$ to $\mathcal{B}$. $\mathcal{B}$ then sends (N, i) to index hiding game challenger $\mathcal{C}$. The challenger samples a bit $b \leftarrow \{0,1\}$. If $b = 0$, it responds with $\mathsf{hk} \leftarrow \mathsf{Setup}_{\mathsf{SPB}}(1^\lambda, N)$. Otherwise, it responds with $\mathsf{hk} \leftarrow \mathsf{Setup\text{-}Bind}_{\mathsf{SPB}}(1^\lambda, N, i)$. $\mathcal{B}$ samples $(\mathsf{sk},\mathsf{vk}) \leftarrow \mathsf{Setup}_{\mathsf{ABO}}(1^\lambda)$, signatures $\{\sigma_j \leftarrow \mathsf{Sign}_{\mathsf{ABO}}(\mathsf{sk}, j) : 1 \le j \le N\}$ and sends the public key $\mathsf{pk} = (1^\lambda, N, \mathsf{vk}, \mathsf{hk})$ to $\mathcal{A}$. $\mathcal{A}$ then adaptively queries for secret keys. For each query j, $\mathcal{B}$ responds with secret key $\mathsf{sk}_j = \sigma_j$. After query phase, $\mathcal{A}$ sends a challenge set S and a message m to $\mathcal{B}$. $\mathcal{B}$ aborts if $i \in S$. Otherwise, it computes hash $h = \mathsf{Hash}_{\mathsf{SPB}}(\mathsf{hk}, \mathbb{I}_S)$ and responds with ciphertext $\mathsf{ct} \leftarrow \mathsf{Encrypt}_{\mathsf{PWE}}((1^\lambda, N, h, \mathsf{hk}, \mathsf{vk}), m, \mathsf{int}(i||0^{k+\ell}))$. $\mathcal{A}$ further adaptively queries for secret keys. For each query j, $\mathcal{B}$ responds with secret key $\mathsf{sk}_j = \sigma_j$. Finally, $\mathcal{A}$ sends a bit b' to $\mathcal{B}$, which outputs b' as its guess in the index hiding game.

As $\mathcal{A}$ is a Type 1 adversary, note that $i \notin S$ and $\mathcal{B}$ does not abort. Note that if $b = 0$, $\mathcal{B}$ simulates the view of $\mathsf{Game}\ 0$ to $\mathcal{A}$ and $\Pr[b' = 1] = p^{\mathcal{A}}_0(\lambda)$. Otherwise, it simulates the view of $\mathsf{Game}\ 1.0$ to $\mathcal{A}$ and $\Pr[b' = 1] = p^{\mathcal{A}}_{1.0}(\lambda)$. This implies, the advantage of $\mathcal{B}$ in the index hiding game is given by $\mathsf{AdvSpbInd}^{\mathcal{B}}(\lambda) = |1/2 \cdot \Pr[b' = 0 | b = 0] + 1/2 \cdot \Pr[b' = 1 | b = 1] - 1/2| = \mathsf{Adv}^{\mathcal{A}}_{0,1.0}(\lambda)/2$. Therefore, $\mathsf{Adv}^{\mathcal{A}}_{0,1.0}(\lambda) \le 2 \cdot \mathsf{AdvSpbInd}(\lambda)$.

Claim 4. *Assuming* $\mathcal{SPB}$ *is somewhere perfectly binding w.r.t. opening, for any* $0 \le t \le 2^{k+\ell}-1$, *any stateful* Type 1 *PPT Adversary* $\mathcal{A}$ *and any* $\lambda \in \mathbb{N}$, *we have* $\mathsf{Adv}^{\mathcal{A}}_{1.t,1.t+1}(\lambda) \le 2 \cdot \mathsf{AdvPosInd}(\lambda)$.

Proof. Consider any t s.t. $0 \leq t \leq 2^{k+\ell} - 1$, any Type 1 PPT adversary $\mathcal{A}$ and any $\lambda \in \mathbb{N}$. Assuming $\mathcal{SPB}$ is somewhere perfectly binding w.r.t. opening, we build a PPT algorithm $\mathcal{B}$ which uses $\mathcal{A}$ and has advantage $\mathsf{Adv}^{\mathcal{A}}_{1.t,1.t+1}(\lambda)/2$ in position indistinguishability game of the $\mathcal{PWE}$ scheme. The reduction algorithm $\mathcal{B}$ proceeds as follows.

$\mathcal{A}$ first sends the number of users 1^N and an index i s.t. $1 \leq i \leq N$ to $\mathcal{B}$. $\mathcal{B}$ then samples $(\mathsf{sk}, \mathsf{vk}) \leftarrow \mathsf{Setup}_{\mathsf{ABO}}(1^\lambda)$, hash key $\mathsf{hk} \leftarrow \mathsf{Setup\text{-}Bind}_{\mathsf{SPB}}(1^\lambda, N, i)$ and signatures $\{\sigma_j \leftarrow \mathsf{Sign}_{\mathsf{ABO}}(\mathsf{sk}, j) : 1 \leq j \leq N\}$. It then sends the public key $\mathsf{pk} = (1^\lambda, N, \mathsf{vk}, \mathsf{hk})$ to $\mathcal{A}$. $\mathcal{A}$ then adaptively queries for secret keys. For each query j, $\mathcal{B}$ responds with secret key $\mathsf{sk}_j = \sigma_j$. After query phase, $\mathcal{A}$ sends a challenge set S and a message m to $\mathcal{B}$. $\mathcal{B}$ aborts if $i \in S$. Otherwise, it computes hash $h = \mathsf{Hash}_{\mathsf{SPB}}(\mathsf{hk}, \mathbb{I}_S)$, and sends the challenge instance $\mathsf{inst} = (1^\lambda, N, h, \mathsf{hk}, \mathsf{vk})$, challenge message m and challenge index $\mathsf{int}(i||0^{k+\ell}) + t$ to the position indistinguishability game challenger $\mathcal{C}$. The challenger samples a bit $\beta \leftarrow \{0,1\}$ and responds with a ciphertext $\mathsf{ct} \leftarrow \mathsf{Encrypt}_{\mathsf{PWE}}(\mathsf{inst}, m, \mathsf{int}(i||0^{k+\ell}) + t + \beta)$[13] to $\mathcal{B}$. $\mathcal{B}$ forwards the ciphertext to $\mathcal{A}$. $\mathcal{A}$ further adaptively queries for secret keys. For each query j, $\mathcal{B}$ responds with secret key $\mathsf{sk}_j = \sigma_j$. Finally, $\mathcal{A}$ sends a bit b' to $\mathcal{B}$, which outputs b' as its guess in the position indistinguishability game.

As $\mathcal{A}$ is a Type 1 adversary, note that $\mathbb{I}_S(i) = 0$ and $\mathcal{B}$ does not abort. We know that, $\Pr[\mathsf{hk}$ is binding w.r.t. opening at index $i] = 1$. This implies that there does not exist a proof π such that $\mathsf{Verify}_{\mathsf{SPB}}(\mathsf{hk}, h, i, 1, \pi) = 1$ and $\mathsf{int}(i||0^{k+\ell}) + t$ cannot be a witness of the instance $(1^\lambda, N, h, \mathsf{hk}, \mathsf{vk})$. Therefore, $\mathcal{B}$ acts as a valid adversary of the position indistinguishability game. If $\beta = 0$, $\mathcal{B}$ simulates the view of $\mathsf{Game}\ 1.t$ to $\mathcal{A}$ and $\Pr[b' = 1] = p^{\mathcal{A}}_{1.t}(\lambda)$. Otherwise, it simulates the view of $\mathsf{Game}\ 1.t+1$ to $\mathcal{A}$ and $\Pr[b' = 1] = p^{\mathcal{A}}_{1.t+1}(\lambda)$. This implies, the advantage of $\mathcal{B}$ in the position indistinguishability game is given by $\mathsf{AdvPosInd}^{\mathcal{B}}(\lambda) = |1/2 \cdot \Pr[b' = 0|\beta = 0] + 1/2 \cdot \Pr[b' = 1|\beta = 1] - 1/2| = \mathsf{Adv}^{\mathcal{A}}_{1.t,1.t+1}(\lambda)/2$. Therefore, $\mathsf{Adv}^{\mathcal{A}}_{1.t,1.t+1}(\lambda) \leq 2 \cdot \mathsf{AdvPosInd}(\lambda)$.

Claim 5. *For every* Type 1 *PPT adversary* $\mathcal{A}$ *and any* $\lambda \in \mathbb{N}$, *we have* $\mathsf{Adv}^{\mathcal{A}}_{1.2^{k+\ell},3}(\lambda) \leq 2 \cdot \mathsf{AdvSpbInd}(\lambda)$.

Proof. Consider any Type 1 PPT adversary $\mathcal{A}$ and any $\lambda \in \mathbb{N}$. We build a PPT algorithm $\mathcal{B}$ which uses $\mathcal{A}$ and has advantage $\mathsf{Adv}^{\mathcal{A}}_{1.2^{k+\ell},3}(\lambda)/2$ in the index hiding game of the $\mathcal{SPB}$ scheme. We ignore the description of algorithm $\mathcal{B}$ as it proceeds similar to proof of Claim 3.

Note that by triangle inequality and combining Claims 3, 4, and 5, the advantage of any Type 1 PPT adversary $\mathcal{A}$ in AugBE index hiding game is $\mathsf{Adv}^{\mathcal{A}}_{0,3}(\lambda) \leq \mathsf{Adv}^{\mathcal{A}}_{0,1.0} + \sum_{t=0}^{2^{k+\ell}-1} \mathsf{Adv}^{\mathcal{A}}_{1.t,1.t+1} + \mathsf{Adv}^{\mathcal{A}}_{1.2^{k+\ell},3} \leq 4 \cdot \mathsf{AdvSpbInd}(\lambda) + 2 \cdot 2^{k+\ell} \cdot \mathsf{AdvPosInd}(\lambda)$. Using complexity leveraging, we demand that $\mathsf{AdvPosInd}(\lambda) \leq 2^{-(k+\ell+1)} \cdot \mathrm{negl}(\lambda)$ for some negligible function $\mathrm{negl}(\cdot)$. At the instantiation level, the security parameter will be increased to match these conditions.

[13] Note that index $\mathsf{int}(i||0^{k+\ell}) + 2^{k+\ell}$ is same as $\mathsf{int}(i+1||0^{k+\ell})$.

Lemma 3. *If $\mathcal{ABO}$ is a secure ABO signature scheme and $\mathcal{PWE}$ is a sub-exponentially secure as per Definition 2, for every stateful* Type 2 *PPT Adversary $\mathcal{A}$, there exists a negligible function negl($\cdot$) such that for every security parameter λ, $\mathsf{Adv}^{\mathcal{A}}_{0,3}(\lambda) \leq negl(\lambda)$.*

Proof. We prove the lemma using the following sequence of hybrids.

Game 2.t (for $0 \leq t < 2^{k+\ell}$): Here t is a bit string of length $k + \ell$. This game is similar to Game 0 except, the challenger samples ABO signature verification key using Setup-Punc algorithm and encrypts challenge message using index $\mathsf{int}(i||0^{k+\ell}) + t$.

1. *Setup Phase.* The adversary $\mathcal{A}$ sends the number of users 1^N to the challenger. The challenger samples $(\mathsf{vk}, \mathsf{sk}) \leftarrow \mathsf{Setup\text{-}Punc}_{\mathsf{ABO}}(1^\lambda, i)$, $\mathsf{hk} \leftarrow \mathsf{Setup}_{\mathsf{SPB}}$ $(1^\lambda, N, i)$ and signatures $\{\sigma_j \leftarrow \mathsf{Sign}_{\mathsf{ABO}}(\mathsf{sk}, j) : 1 \leq j \leq N\}$. It then sends the public key $\mathsf{pk} = (1^\lambda, N, \mathsf{vk}, \mathsf{hk})$ to $\mathcal{A}$.
3. *Challenge Phase.* The adversary sends a message m and a set $S \subseteq [N]$ to the challenger. The challenger computes hash $h = \mathsf{Hash}_{\mathsf{SPB}}(\mathsf{hk}, \mathbb{I}_S)$ and responds with ciphertext $\mathsf{ct} \leftarrow \mathsf{Encrypt}_{\mathsf{PWE}}((1^\lambda, N, h, \mathsf{hk}, \mathsf{vk}), m, \mathsf{int}(i||0^{k+\ell}) + t)$.

Game $2.2^{k+\ell}$: This game is similar to Game $2.2^{k+\ell} - 1$ except that the challenger encrypts the challenge message using index $\mathsf{int}(i + 1||0^{k+\ell})$.

1. *Setup Phase.* The adversary $\mathcal{A}$ sends the number of users 1^N to the challenger. The challenger samples $(\mathsf{vk}, \mathsf{sk}) \leftarrow \mathsf{Setup\text{-}Punc}_{\mathsf{ABO}}(1^\lambda, i)$, hash key $\mathsf{hk} \leftarrow \mathsf{Setup}_{\mathsf{SPB}}(1^\lambda, N, i)$ and signatures $\{\sigma_j \leftarrow \mathsf{Sign}_{\mathsf{ABO}}(\mathsf{sk}, j) : 1 \leq j \leq N\}$ of the AugBE scheme. It then sends the public key $\mathsf{pk} = (\mathsf{vk}, \mathsf{hk})$ to $\mathcal{A}$.
3. *Challenge Phase.* The adversary sends a message m and a set $S \subseteq [N]$ to the challenger, which computes hash $h = \mathsf{Hash}_{\mathsf{SPB}}(\mathsf{hk}, \mathbb{I}_S)$ and responds with ciphertext $\mathsf{ct} \leftarrow \mathsf{Encrypt}_{\mathsf{PWE}}((1^\lambda, N, h, \mathsf{hk}, \mathsf{vk}), m, \mathsf{int}(i + 1||0^{k+\ell}))$.

For any PPT adversary $\mathcal{B}$ and $\lambda \in \mathbb{N}$, let $\mathsf{AdvAboInd}^{\mathcal{B}}(\lambda)$ denote the advantage of $\mathcal{B}$ in VK indistinguishability game of $\mathcal{ABO}$ scheme and $\mathsf{AdvPosInd}^{\mathcal{B}}(\lambda)$ denote the advantage of $\mathcal{B}$ in position indistinguishability game of $\mathcal{PWE}$ scheme. For any $\lambda \in \mathbb{N}$, let $\mathsf{AdvPosInd}(\lambda) = \sup_{\mathrm{PPT}\ \mathcal{B}} \mathsf{AdvPosInd}^{\mathcal{B}}(\lambda)$ and $\mathsf{AdvAboInd}(\lambda) = \sup_{\mathrm{PPT}\ \mathcal{B}} \mathsf{AdvAboInd}^{\mathcal{B}}(\lambda)$. We prove Lemma 3 using the following sequence of claims.

Claim 6. *For every* Type 2 *PPT adversary $\mathcal{A}$ and any $\lambda \in \mathbb{N}$, we have* $\mathsf{Adv}^{\mathcal{A}}_{0,2.0}(\lambda) \leq 2 \cdot \mathsf{AdvAboInd}(\lambda)$.

Proof. Consider any Type 2 PPT adversary $\mathcal{A}$ and any $\lambda \in \mathbb{N}$. We build a PPT algorithm $\mathcal{B}$ which uses $\mathcal{A}$ and has advantage $\mathsf{Adv}^{\mathcal{A}}_{0,2.0}(\lambda)$ in VK indistinguishability game of the $\mathcal{ABO}$ scheme. The reduction algorithm $\mathcal{B}$ proceeds as follows.

$\mathcal{A}$ first sends the number of users 1^N and an index i s.t. $1 \leq i \leq N$ to $\mathcal{B}$. $\mathcal{B}$ sends challenge message i to VK indistinguishability game challenger $\mathcal{C}$. The challenger samples a bit $b \leftarrow \{0, 1\}$. If $b = 0$, it samples $(\mathsf{sk}, \mathsf{vk}) \leftarrow \mathsf{Setup}_{\mathsf{ABO}}(1^\lambda)$. Otherwise, it samples $(\mathsf{sk}, \mathsf{vk}) \leftarrow \mathsf{Setup\text{-}Punc}_{\mathsf{ABO}}(1^\lambda, i)$. It then sends vk to $\mathcal{B}$. $\mathcal{B}$

samples $\mathsf{hk} \leftarrow \mathsf{Setup}_{\mathsf{SPB}}(1^\lambda, N)$ and sends the public key $\mathsf{pk} = (1^\lambda, N, \mathsf{vk}, \mathsf{hk})$ to $\mathcal{A}$. $\mathcal{A}$ then adaptively queries for secret keys. For each query j, $\mathcal{B}$ aborts if $j = i$. Otherwise, it forwards the query to $\mathcal{C}$, which responds with $\sigma \leftarrow \mathsf{Sign}_{\mathsf{ABO}}(\mathsf{sk}, j)$. $\mathcal{B}$ forwards the reply to $\mathcal{A}$. After query phase, $\mathcal{A}$ sends a challenge set S and a message m to $\mathcal{B}$. $\mathcal{B}$ computes hash $h = \mathsf{Hash}_{\mathsf{SPB}}(\mathsf{hk}, \mathbb{I}_S)$ and responds with ciphertext $\mathsf{ct} \leftarrow \mathsf{Encrypt}_{\mathsf{PWE}}$ $(x = (1^\lambda, N, h, \mathsf{hk}, \mathsf{vk}),\ m, \mathsf{int}(i||0^{k+\ell}))$. $\mathcal{A}$ then adaptively queries for secret keys. For each query j, $\mathcal{B}$ aborts if $j = i$. Otherwise, it forwards the query to $\mathcal{C}$, which responds with $\sigma \leftarrow \mathsf{Sign}_{\mathsf{ABO}}(\mathsf{sk}, j)$. $\mathcal{B}$ forwards the reply to $\mathcal{A}$. Finally, $\mathcal{A}$ sends a bit b' to $\mathcal{B}$, which outputs b' as its guess in the VK indistinguishability game.

As $\mathcal{A}$ is a Type 2 adversary, it does not query for secret key sk_i and therefore, $\mathcal{B}$ does not abort and acts as a valid adversary of the VK indistinguishability game. If $b = 0$, then $\mathcal{B}$ simulates the view of Game 0 to $\mathcal{A}$ and $\Pr[b' = 1] = p_0^{\mathcal{A}}(\lambda)$. Otherwise, it simulates the view of Game 2.0 to $\mathcal{A}$ and $\Pr[b' = 1] = p_{2.0}^{\mathcal{A}}(\lambda)$. This implies, the advantage of $\mathcal{B}$ in the index hiding game is given by $\mathsf{AdvSpbInd}^{\mathcal{B}}(\lambda) = |1/2 \cdot \Pr[b' = 0|b = 0] + 1/2 \cdot \Pr[b' = 1|b = 1] - 1/2| = \mathsf{Adv}_{0,2.0}^{\mathcal{A}}(\lambda)/2$. Therefore, $\mathsf{Adv}_{0,2.0}^{\mathcal{A}}(\lambda) \leq 2 \cdot \mathsf{AdvAboInd}(\lambda)$.

Claim 7. *For every t s.t. $0 \leq t \leq 2^{k+\ell} - 1$, every* Type 2 *PPT adversary $\mathcal{A}$ and any $\lambda \in \mathbb{N}$, we have* $\mathsf{Adv}_{2.t,2.t+1}^{\mathcal{A}}(\lambda) \leq 2 \cdot \mathsf{AdvPosInd}(\lambda)$.

Proof. Consider any t s.t. $0 \leq t \leq 2^{k+\ell} - 1$, a Type 2 PPT adversary $\mathcal{A}$ and any $\lambda \in \mathbb{N}$. We build a PPT algorithm $\mathcal{B}$ which uses $\mathcal{A}$ and has advantage $\mathsf{Adv}_{2.t,2.t+1}^{\mathcal{A}}(\lambda)$ in position indistinguishability game of the $\mathcal{PWE}$ scheme. The reduction algorithm $\mathcal{B}$ proceeds as follows.

$\mathcal{A}$ first sends the number of users 1^N and an index i s.t. $1 \leq i \leq N$ to $\mathcal{B}$. $\mathcal{B}$ then samples $(\mathsf{sk}, \mathsf{vk}) \leftarrow \mathsf{Setup\text{-}Punc}_{\mathsf{ABO}}(1^\lambda, i)$, hash key $\mathsf{hk} \leftarrow \mathsf{Setup}_{\mathsf{SPB}}(1^\lambda, N)$ and signatures $\{\sigma_j \leftarrow \mathsf{Sign}_{\mathsf{ABO}}(\mathsf{sk}, j) : 1 \leq j \leq N, j \neq i\}$. It then sends the public key $\mathsf{pk} = (1^\lambda, N, \mathsf{vk}, \mathsf{hk})$ to $\mathcal{A}$. $\mathcal{A}$ then adaptively queries for secret keys. For each query j, $\mathcal{B}$ aborts if $j = i$. Otherwise, it responds with the secret key $\mathsf{sk}_j = \sigma_j$. After query phase, $\mathcal{A}$ sends a challenge set S and a message m to $\mathcal{B}$. $\mathcal{B}$ computes hash $h = \mathsf{Hash}_{\mathsf{SPB}}(\mathsf{hk}, \mathbb{I}_S)$ and sends the challenge instance $\mathsf{inst} = (1^\lambda, N, h, \mathsf{hk}, \mathsf{vk})$, challenge message m and challenge index $\mathsf{int}(i||0^{k+\ell}) + t$ to the position indistinguishability game challenger $\mathcal{C}$. The challenger samples a bit $\beta \leftarrow \{0, 1\}$ and responds with a ciphertext $\mathsf{ct} \leftarrow \mathsf{Encrypt}_{\mathsf{PWE}}(\mathsf{inst}, m, \mathsf{int}(i||0^{k+\ell}) + t + \beta)$[14] to $\mathcal{B}$. $\mathcal{B}$ forwards the ciphertext to $\mathcal{A}$. $\mathcal{A}$ further adaptively queries for secret keys. For each query j, $\mathcal{B}$ aborts if $j = i$. Otherwise, it responds with the secret key $\mathsf{sk}_j = \sigma_j$. Finally, $\mathcal{A}$ sends a bit b' to $\mathcal{B}$, which outputs b' as its guess in the position indistinguishability game.

As $\mathcal{A}$ is a Type 2 adversary, it does not make key query on i and therefore, $\mathcal{B}$ does not abort. As vk is punctured at i, $\nexists \sigma$ s.t. $\mathsf{Verify}_{\mathsf{ABO}}(\mathsf{vk}, i, \sigma) = 1$. This implies $\mathsf{int}(i||0^{k+\ell}) + t$ cannot be a witness of the instance $(1^\lambda, N, h, \mathsf{hk}, \mathsf{vk})$ and therefore, $\mathcal{B}$ acts as a valid adversary of the position indistinguishability game. If $\beta = 0$, $\mathcal{B}$ simulates the view of Game $2.t$ to $\mathcal{A}$ and $\Pr[b' = 1] = p_{2.t}^{\mathcal{A}}(\lambda)$.

[14] Note that index $\mathsf{int}(i||0^{k+\ell}) + 2^{k+\ell}$ is same as $\mathsf{int}(i + 1||0^{k+\ell})$.

Otherwise, it simulates the view of Game $2.t+1$ to $\mathcal{A}$ and $\Pr[b'=1] = p^{\mathcal{A}}_{2.t+1}(\lambda)$. This implies, the advantage of $\mathcal{B}$ in the position indistinguishability game is given by $\mathsf{AdvPosInd}^{\mathcal{B}}(\lambda) = |1/2 \cdot \Pr[b'=0|\beta=0] + 1/2 \cdot \Pr[b'=1|\beta=1] - 1/2| = \mathsf{Adv}^{\mathcal{A}}_{2.t,2.t+1}(\lambda)/2$. Therefore, $\mathsf{Adv}^{\mathcal{A}}_{2.t,2.t+1}(\lambda) \leq 2 \cdot \mathsf{AdvPosInd}(\lambda)$.

Claim 8. *For every* Type 2 *PPT adversary* $\mathcal{A}$ *and any* $\lambda \in \mathbb{N}$, *we have* $\mathsf{Adv}^{\mathcal{A}}_{2.2^{k+\ell},3}(\lambda) \leq 2 \cdot \mathsf{AdvAboInd}(\lambda)$.

Proof. Consider any Type 2 PPT adversary $\mathcal{A}$ and any $\lambda \in \mathbb{N}$. We build a PPT algorithm $\mathcal{B}$ which uses $\mathcal{A}$ and has advantage $\mathsf{Adv}^{\mathcal{A}}_{2.2^{k+\ell},3}(\lambda)$ in VK indistinguishability game of the $\mathcal{ABO}$ scheme. We ignore the description of algorithm $\mathcal{B}$ as it proceeds similar to proof of Claim 6.

Note that by combining triangle inequality and Claims 6, 7, and 8, the advantage of any Type 2 PPT adversary $\mathcal{A}$ in AugBE index hiding game is $\mathsf{Adv}^{\mathcal{A}}_{0,3}(\lambda) \leq \mathsf{Adv}^{\mathcal{A}}_{0,2.0} + \sum_{t=0}^{2^{k+\ell}-1} \mathsf{Adv}^{\mathcal{A}}_{2.t,2.t+1} + \mathsf{Adv}^{\mathcal{A}}_{2.2^{k+\ell},3} \leq 4 \cdot \mathsf{AdvAboInd}(\lambda) + 2 \cdot 2^{k+\ell} \cdot \mathsf{AdvPosInd}(\lambda)$. Using complexity leveraging, we demand that $\mathsf{AdvPosInd}(\lambda) \leq 2^{-(k+\ell+1)} \cdot \mathrm{negl}(\lambda)$ for some negligible function $\mathrm{negl}(\cdot)$. At the instantiation level, the security parameter will be increased to match this condition.

Note that Lemma 1 follows by combining Lemmas 2 and 3 as any adversary $\mathcal{A}$ of AugBE index hiding game is of either Type 1 or Type 2.

5 All-But-One Signatures from Standard Assumptions

In this section, we present two new constructions for all-but-one (ABO) signatures from standard assumptions. The first construction is based on verifiable random functions (VRF) and perfectly-binding (non-interactive) commitment schemes. The second construction is based on verifiable and anonymous identity-based encryption (VAIBE). The first ABO scheme satisfies perfect correctness, where as the second scheme satisfies correctness with all but negligible probability. We would like to point that using the second ABO signature scheme to instantiate the AugBE construction described in Sect. 4 results in AugBE scheme without perfect correctness. We finally note that VRFs can be based on simple assumptions over bilinear maps as well as RSA-like assumptions [42,49], and perfectly binding commitments can be constructed from any injective OWF as well as based on assumptions such as DDH, LWE and LPN [37], and VAIBE can be based on simple assumptions over bilinear maps as well as LWE [1,17,48,57].[15] Therefore, this leads to constructions of ABO signatures from a wide variety of standard assumptions listed above.

[15] We would like to point out that most existing IBE constructions based on LWE are already verifiable and they can be made anonymous by using the transformation from [39,59].

5.1 All-But-One Signatures from VRFs

Let $\mathcal{VRF} = (\mathsf{Setup}_{\mathsf{VRF}}, \mathsf{Eval}_{\mathsf{VRF}}, \mathsf{Verify}_{\mathsf{VRF}})$ be a verifiable random function (VRF) with input space $\{0,1\}^{i(\lambda)}$, output space $\{0,1\}^{o(\lambda)}$ and proof space $\{0,1\}^{p(\lambda)}$. Let $\mathcal{COM} = (\mathsf{Setup}_{\mathsf{COM}}, \mathsf{Commit}, \mathsf{Verify}_{\mathsf{COM}})$ be a perfectly binding computationally hiding commitment scheme with randomness space $\{0,1\}^{o(\lambda)}$ and commitment space $\{0,1\}^{k(\lambda)}$. We construct an ABO signature scheme $\mathcal{ABO} = (\mathsf{Setup}, \mathsf{Setup\text{-}Punc}, \mathsf{Sign}, \mathsf{Verify})$ on message space $\{0,1\}^{i(\lambda)}$ and signature space $\{0,1\}^{o(\lambda)+p(\lambda)}$ as follows. For the simplicity of notation, we hereby denote $i = i(\lambda)$, $o = o(\lambda)$, $p = p(\lambda)$ and $k = k(\lambda)$.

- $\mathsf{Setup}(1^\lambda)$. Sample $(\mathsf{sk}_{\mathsf{VRF}}, \mathsf{vk}_{\mathsf{VRF}}) \leftarrow \mathsf{Setup}_{\mathsf{VRF}}(1^\lambda)$ and $\mathsf{pp} \leftarrow \mathsf{Setup}_{\mathsf{COM}}(1^\lambda)$. Sample $y^* \leftarrow \{0,1\}^o$ and $\mathsf{cm} \leftarrow \mathsf{Commit}(\mathsf{pp}, 0; y^*)$. Output $\mathsf{sk} = \mathsf{sk}_{\mathsf{VRF}}$ and $\mathsf{vk} = (\mathsf{pp}, \mathsf{vk}_{\mathsf{VRF}}, \mathsf{cm})$.
- $\mathsf{Setup\text{-}Punc}(1^\lambda, m^*)$. Sample $(\mathsf{sk}_{\mathsf{VRF}}, \mathsf{vk}_{\mathsf{VRF}}) \leftarrow \mathsf{Setup}_{\mathsf{VRF}}(1^\lambda)$ and $\mathsf{pp} \leftarrow \mathsf{Setup}_{\mathsf{COM}}(1^\lambda)$. Sample $(y^*, \pi) \leftarrow \mathsf{Eval}_{\mathsf{VRF}}(\mathsf{sk}_{\mathsf{VRF}}, m^*)$ and $\mathsf{cm} \leftarrow \mathsf{Commit}(\mathsf{pp}, 1; y^*)$. Output $\mathsf{sk} = \mathsf{sk}_{\mathsf{VRF}}$ and $\mathsf{vk} = (\mathsf{pp}, \mathsf{vk}_{\mathsf{VRF}}, \mathsf{cm})$.
- $\mathsf{Sign}(\mathsf{sk}, m)$. Sample $(y, \pi) \leftarrow \mathsf{Eval}_{\mathsf{VRF}}(\mathsf{sk}, m)$. Output $\sigma = (y, \pi)$.
- $\mathsf{Verify}(\mathsf{vk}, m, \sigma)$. Let $\sigma = (y, \pi)$ and $\mathsf{vk} = (\mathsf{pp}, \mathsf{vk}_{\mathsf{VRF}}, \mathsf{cm})$. Output 1 iff $\mathsf{Verify}_{\mathsf{VRF}}(\mathsf{vk}_{\mathsf{VRF}}, m, y, \pi) = 1 \wedge \mathsf{Verify}_{\mathsf{COM}}(\mathsf{pp}, 1, \mathsf{cm}, y) = 0$.

Due to space constraints, we prove that the $\mathcal{ABO}$ signature scheme satisfies the required correctness properties in the full version of the paper.

We prove that the above scheme satisfies VK indistinguishability property using a sequence of hybrids. The first hybrid is same as the VK indistinguishability game, except that the challenger always uses punctured setup to generate verification key. The second hybrid is same as the first hybrid, except that the challenger samples y^* randomly during the setup phase. These two hybrids are indistinguishable to the adversary as the $\mathcal{VRF}$ scheme has pseudorandomness property and as the adversary is not allowed to query for signature on message m^*. The third hybrid is same as the VK indistinguishability game, except that the challenger always uses normal setup to generate verification key. The second and third hybrids are indistinguishable to the adversary as he cannot distinguish between commitment of 0 and commitment of 1 (computational hiding property of the $\mathcal{COM}$ scheme). Due to space constraints, we prove that the above scheme satisfies VK indistinguishability in the full version of the paper.

5.2 All-But-One Signatures from VAIBE

In this section, we construct all-but-one (ABO) signatures from verifiable and anonymous identity based encryption system (VAIBE). Let $\mathcal{VAIBE} = (\mathsf{Setup}_{\mathsf{VAIBE}}, \mathsf{KeyGen}, \mathsf{Encrypt}, \mathsf{Decrypt}, \mathsf{Verify}_{\mathsf{VAIBE}})$ be any VAIBE scheme for message space $\{0,1\}^{m(\lambda)}$, ciphertext space $\{0,1\}^{c(\lambda)}$, secret key space $\{0,1\}^{k(\lambda)}$, identity space $\{0,1\}^{i(\lambda)}$ and proof space $\{0,1\}^{r(\lambda)}$. We construct an ABO signature scheme $\mathcal{ABO} = (\mathsf{Setup}, \mathsf{Setup\text{-}Punc}, \mathsf{Sign}, \mathsf{Verify})$ for message space $\{0,1\}^{i(\lambda)} \backslash \{0^{i(\lambda)}\}$ and signature space $\{0,1\}^{k(\lambda)+r(\lambda)}$ i.e., for every $\lambda \in \mathbb{N}$, identity $0^{i(\lambda)}$ is not supported by the signature scheme. Let $\mathcal{I}_\lambda = \{0,1\}^{i(\lambda)} \setminus \{0^{i(\lambda)}\}$. For simplicity of notation, we hereby denote $m = m(\lambda), c = c(\lambda), k = k(\lambda), i = i(\lambda)$ and $p = p(\lambda)$. Also, we hereby refer to messages in $\mathcal{ABO}$ scheme by identities in $\mathcal{VAIBE}$ scheme. Formally, the construction proceeds as follows.

- $\mathsf{Setup}(1^\lambda)$. Sample VAIBE keys $(\mathsf{mpk}_{\mathsf{VAIBE}}, \mathsf{msk}_{\mathsf{VAIBE}}) \leftarrow \mathsf{Setup}_{\mathsf{VAIBE}}(1^\lambda)$. Sample a random message $x \leftarrow \{0,1\}^m$ and compute ciphertext $t \leftarrow \mathsf{Encrypt}(\mathsf{mpk}_{\mathsf{VAIBE}}, 0^i, x)$. Output secret key $\mathsf{sk} = \mathsf{msk}_{\mathsf{VAIBE}}$ and verification key $\mathsf{vk} = (x, \mathsf{mpk}_{\mathsf{VAIBE}}, t)$.
- $\mathsf{Setup\text{-}Punc}(1^\lambda, \mathsf{id}^*)$. Sample VAIBE keys $(\mathsf{mpk}_{\mathsf{VAIBE}}, \mathsf{msk}_{\mathsf{VAIBE}}) \leftarrow \mathsf{Setup}_{\mathsf{VAIBE}}(1^\lambda)$. Choose a random message $x \leftarrow \{0,1\}^m$. Encrypt the message x using identity id^* i.e., compute ciphertext $t \leftarrow \mathsf{Encrypt}(\mathsf{mpk}_{\mathsf{VAIBE}}, \mathsf{id}^*, x)$. Output secret key $\mathsf{sk} = \mathsf{msk}_{\mathsf{VAIBE}}$ and verification key $\mathsf{vk} = (x, \mathsf{mpk}_{\mathsf{VAIBE}}, t)$.
- $\mathsf{Sign}(\mathsf{sk}, \mathsf{id})$. Sample $(\mathsf{sk}_{\mathsf{id}}, \pi) \leftarrow \mathsf{KeyGen}(\mathsf{sk}, \mathsf{id})$. Output signature $\sigma = (\mathsf{sk}_{\mathsf{id}}, \pi)$.
- $\mathsf{Verify}(\mathsf{vk}, \mathsf{id}, \sigma)$. Let $\sigma = (\mathsf{sk}', \pi)$ and $\mathsf{vk} = (x, \mathsf{mpk}, t)$. Output 1 iff $\mathsf{Verify}_{\mathsf{VAIBE}}(\mathsf{mpk}, \mathsf{id}, \mathsf{sk}', \pi) = 1 \wedge x \neq \mathsf{Decrypt}(\mathsf{sk}', t)$.

We note that the $\mathcal{ABO}$ scheme does not achieve perfect correctness[16]. We now prove that the $\mathcal{ABO}$ scheme satisfies the required correctness properties with all but negligible probability.

Correctness of Setup

Claim 9. *There exists a negligible function negl(·) such that for all $\lambda \in \mathbb{N}$ and any identity* $\mathsf{id} \in \mathcal{I}_\lambda$, *we have*

$$\Pr\left[\mathsf{Verify}(\mathsf{vk}, \mathsf{id}, \sigma) = 0 \ : \ \begin{array}{c} (\mathsf{mpk}, \mathsf{msk}) \leftarrow \mathsf{Setup}_{\mathsf{VAIBE}}(1^\lambda), x_0 \leftarrow \{0,1\}^m, \\ t \leftarrow \mathsf{Encrypt}(\mathsf{mpk}, 0^i, x_0), \mathsf{vk} \leftarrow (x_0, \mathsf{mpk}, t), \\ \sigma = (\mathsf{sk}_{\mathsf{id}}, \pi) \leftarrow \mathsf{KeyGen}(\mathsf{msk}, \mathsf{id}) \end{array}\right] \leq \frac{1}{2^m} + negl(\lambda).$$

Proof. Suppose there exists a non-negligible function $\delta(\cdot)$ such that, for every $\lambda \in \mathbb{N}$, there exists an identity $\mathsf{id}'_\lambda \in \mathcal{I}_\lambda$ such that,

$$\Pr\left[\mathsf{Verify}(\mathsf{vk}, \mathsf{id}'_\lambda, \sigma) = 0 \ : \ \begin{array}{c} (\mathsf{mpk}, \mathsf{msk}) \leftarrow \mathsf{Setup}_{\mathsf{VAIBE}}(1^\lambda), x_0 \leftarrow \{0,1\}^m, \\ t \leftarrow \mathsf{Encrypt}(\mathsf{mpk}, 0^i, x_0), \mathsf{vk} \leftarrow (x_0, \mathsf{mpk}, t), \\ \sigma = (\mathsf{sk}_{\mathsf{id}'_\lambda}, \pi) \leftarrow \mathsf{KeyGen}(\mathsf{msk}, \mathsf{id}'_\lambda) \end{array}\right] > \frac{1}{2^m} + \delta(\lambda).$$

By the correctness of $\mathcal{VAIBE}$ scheme, we know that $\mathsf{Verify}_{\mathsf{VAIBE}}(\mathsf{mpk}, \mathsf{id}'_\lambda, \mathsf{sk}_{\mathsf{id}'_\lambda}, \pi) = 1$. This implies,

$$\Pr\left[\mathsf{Decrypt}(\mathsf{sk}_{\mathsf{id}'_\lambda}, t) = x_0 \ : \ \begin{array}{c} (\mathsf{mpk}, \mathsf{msk}) \leftarrow \mathsf{Setup}_{\mathsf{VAIBE}}(1^\lambda), \\ x_0 \leftarrow \{0,1\}^m, t \leftarrow \mathsf{Encrypt}(\mathsf{mpk}, 0^i, x_0), \\ \sigma = (\mathsf{sk}_{\mathsf{id}'_\lambda}, \pi) \leftarrow \mathsf{KeyGen}(\mathsf{msk}, \mathsf{id}'_\lambda) \end{array}\right] > \frac{1}{2^m} + \delta(\lambda). \quad (1)$$

[16] Using this ABO scheme in our AugBE construction results in an AugBE scheme without perfect correctness.

For any fixed $x_0 \in \{0,1\}^m$, let

$$p_{x_0} = \Pr\left[\mathsf{Decrypt}(\mathsf{sk}_{\mathsf{id}'_\lambda}, t) = x_0 \;:\; \begin{array}{r}(\mathsf{mpk}, \mathsf{msk}) \leftarrow \mathsf{Setup}_{\mathsf{VAIBE}}(1^\lambda),\\ x_1 \leftarrow \{0,1\}^m, t \leftarrow \mathsf{Encrypt}(\mathsf{mpk}, 0^i, x_1),\\ (\mathsf{sk}_{\mathsf{id}'_\lambda}, \pi) \leftarrow \mathsf{KeyGen}(\mathsf{msk}, \mathsf{id}'_\lambda)\end{array}\right].$$

We know that $\sum_{x_0} p_{x_0} = 1$. This implies,

$$\Pr\left[\mathsf{Decrypt}(\mathsf{sk}_{\mathsf{id}'_\lambda}, t) = x_0 \;:\; \begin{array}{c}(\mathsf{mpk}, \mathsf{msk}) \leftarrow \mathsf{Setup}_{\mathsf{VAIBE}}(1^\lambda), x_1 \leftarrow \{0,1\}^m,\\ x_0 \leftarrow \{0,1\}^m, t \leftarrow \mathsf{Encrypt}(\mathsf{mpk}, 0^i, x_1),\\ (\mathsf{sk}_{\mathsf{id}'_\lambda}, \pi) \leftarrow \mathsf{KeyGen}(\mathsf{msk}, \mathsf{id}'_\lambda)\end{array}\right] = \frac{1}{2^m}. \quad (2)$$

We build a non-uniform PPT adversary $\mathcal{A}$ that breaks IND-CPA security of $\mathcal{VAIBE}$ scheme. The algorithm proceeds as follows. Assume the adversary is given id'_λ as a non-uniform advice. $\mathcal{A}$ first samples two random messages $x_0 \leftarrow \{0,1\}^m, x_1 \leftarrow \{0,1\}^m$ and sends challenge messages (x_0, x_1) and challenge identity 0^i to VAIBE IND-CPA challenger $\mathcal{C}$. $\mathcal{C}$ samples VAIBE keys $(\mathsf{mpk}, \mathsf{msk}) \leftarrow \mathsf{Setup}_{\mathsf{VAIBE}}(1^\lambda)$, a bit $b \leftarrow \{0,1\}$, and computes ciphertext $t \leftarrow \mathsf{Encrypt}(\mathsf{mpk}, 0^i, x_b)$. $\mathcal{C}$ sends public key mpk and challenge response t to $\mathcal{A}$. The adversary then makes a key query on index id'_λ to the challenger, which responds with $(\mathsf{sk}_{\mathsf{id}'_\lambda}, \pi) \leftarrow \mathsf{KeyGen}(\mathsf{msk}, \mathsf{id}'_\lambda)$. $\mathcal{A}$ outputs 1 if $\mathsf{Decrypt}(\mathsf{sk}_{\mathsf{id}'_\lambda}, t) = x_0$ and outputs 0 otherwise.

By Eq. 1, if $b = 0$, $\mathcal{A}$ outputs 1 with probability greater than $\frac{1}{2^m} + \delta(\lambda)$. By Eq. 2, if $b = 1$, $\mathcal{A}$ outputs 1 with probability $\frac{1}{2^m}$. This implies that the advantage of $\mathcal{A}$ in the IND-CPA game is at least $1/2 \cdot \delta(\lambda)$.

Correctness of Punctured Setup

Claim 10. *For all* $\lambda \in \mathbb{N}$, *any identity* $\mathsf{id}^* \in \mathcal{I}_\lambda$, *any keys* $(\mathsf{sk}, \mathsf{vk}) \leftarrow \mathsf{Setup\text{-}Punc}(1^\lambda, \mathsf{id}^*)$, *any* $\sigma \leftarrow \{0,1\}^{k+r}$, *we have* $\mathsf{Verify}(\mathsf{vk}, \mathsf{id}^*, \sigma) = 0$.

Proof. Let $\mathsf{vk} = (x, \mathsf{mpk}, t)$ and $\sigma = (\mathsf{sk}', \pi)$. From the soundness of verifiability property of $\mathcal{VAIBE}$ scheme, we know that if $\mathsf{Verify}_{\mathsf{VAIBE}}(\mathsf{mpk}, \mathsf{id}^*, \mathsf{sk}', \pi) = 1$, then $\mathsf{Decrypt}(\mathsf{sk}', t) = x$. Therefore, $\mathsf{Verify}(\mathsf{vk}, \mathsf{id}^*, \sigma) = 0$.

The VK indistinguishability property of the above scheme follows from the IND-ANON security of the $\mathcal{VAIBE}$ scheme. Intuitively, if an adversary can distinguish between verification key generated by the normal setup and the punctured setup, then he can also distinguish between VAIBE ciphertext encrypted using identity 0^i and VAIBE ciphertext encrypted using identity id^*, which contradicts the IND-ANON security property of the $\mathcal{VAIBE}$ scheme. Due to space constraints, we defer the full proof to the full version of the paper.

Acknowledgement. We thank the anonymous reviewers of PKC 2019 for helpful feedback, especially for pointing out the connection between SPB hashes and (a weakening of) ABO signatures.

References

1. Agrawal, S., Boneh, D., Boyen, X.: Efficient lattice (H)IBE in the standard model. In: Gilbert, H. (ed.) EUROCRYPT 2010. LNCS, vol. 6110, pp. 553–572. Springer, Heidelberg (2010). https://doi.org/10.1007/978-3-642-13190-5_28
2. Alamati, N., Peikert, C.: Three's compromised too: circular insecurity for any cycle length from (Ring-)LWE. In: Robshaw, M., Katz, J. (eds.) CRYPTO 2016. LNCS, vol. 9815, pp. 659–680. Springer, Heidelberg (2016). https://doi.org/10.1007/978-3-662-53008-5_23
3. Ananth, P., Boneh, D., Garg, S., Sahai, A., Zhandry, M.: Differing-inputs obfuscation and applications. Cryptology ePrint Archive, Report 2013/689 (2013)
4. Ananth, P., Jain, A.: Indistinguishability obfuscation from compact functional encryption. In: Gennaro, R., Robshaw, M. (eds.) CRYPTO 2015. LNCS, vol. 9215, pp. 308–326. Springer, Heidelberg (2015). https://doi.org/10.1007/978-3-662-47989-6_15
5. Ananth, P., Jain, A., Sahai, A.: Achieving compactness generically: indistinguishability obfuscation from non-compact functional encryption. IACR Cryptology ePrint Archive (2015)
6. Barak, B., et al.: On the (im)possibility of obfuscating programs. In: Kilian, J. (ed.) CRYPTO 2001. LNCS, vol. 2139, pp. 1–18. Springer, Heidelberg (2001). https://doi.org/10.1007/3-540-44647-8_1
7. Barak, B., et al.: On the (im)possibility of obfuscating programs. J. ACM **59**(2), 6 (2012)
8. Bellare, M., Boldyreva, A., Desai, A., Pointcheval, D.: Key-privacy in public-key encryption. In: Boyd, C. (ed.) ASIACRYPT 2001. LNCS, vol. 2248, pp. 566–582. Springer, Heidelberg (2001). https://doi.org/10.1007/3-540-45682-1_33
9. Bitansky, N., Paneth, O.: ZAPs and non-interactive witness indistinguishability from indistinguishability obfuscation. In: Dodis, Y., Nielsen, J.B. (eds.) TCC 2015. LNCS, vol. 9015, pp. 401–427. Springer, Heidelberg (2015). https://doi.org/10.1007/978-3-662-46497-7_16
10. Bitansky, N., Paneth, O., Wichs, D.: Perfect structure on the edge of chaos. In: Kushilevitz, E., Malkin, T. (eds.) TCC 2016. LNCS, vol. 9562, pp. 474–502. Springer, Heidelberg (2016). https://doi.org/10.1007/978-3-662-49096-9_20
11. Bitansky, N., Vaikuntanathan, V.: Indistinguishability obfuscation from functional encryption. In: IEEE 56th Annual Symposium on Foundations of Computer Science, FOCS 2015, pp. 171–190 (2015)
12. Boneh, D., Franklin, M.: Identity-based encryption from the Weil pairing. In: Kilian, J. (ed.) CRYPTO 2001. LNCS, vol. 2139, pp. 213–229. Springer, Heidelberg (2001). https://doi.org/10.1007/3-540-44647-8_13
13. Boneh, D., Gentry, C., Waters, B.: Collusion resistant broadcast encryption with short ciphertexts and private keys. In: Shoup, V. (ed.) CRYPTO 2005. LNCS, vol. 3621, pp. 258–275. Springer, Heidelberg (2005). https://doi.org/10.1007/11535218_16
14. Boneh, D., Waters, B.: A fully collusion resistant broadcast, trace, and revoke system. In: Proceedings of the 13th ACM Conference on Computer and Communications Security, CCS 2006, pp. 211–220 (2006)
15. Boneh, D., Waters, B., Zhandry, M.: Low overhead broadcast encryption from multilinear maps. In: Garay, J.A., Gennaro, R. (eds.) CRYPTO 2014. LNCS, vol. 8616, pp. 206–223. Springer, Heidelberg (2014). https://doi.org/10.1007/978-3-662-44371-2_12

16. Boneh, D., Zhandry, M.: Multiparty key exchange, efficient traitor tracing, and more from indistinguishability obfuscation. In: Garay, J.A., Gennaro, R. (eds.) CRYPTO 2014. LNCS, vol. 8616, pp. 480–499. Springer, Heidelberg (2014). https://doi.org/10.1007/978-3-662-44371-2_27
17. Boyen, X., Waters, B.: Anonymous hierarchical identity-based encryption (without random oracles). In: Dwork, C. (ed.) CRYPTO 2006. LNCS, vol. 4117, pp. 290–307. Springer, Heidelberg (2006). https://doi.org/10.1007/11818175_17
18. Brakerski, Z., Jain, A., Komargodski, I., Passelegue, A., Wichs, D.: Non-trivial witness encryption and null-IO from standard assumptions. Cryptology ePrint Archive, Report 2017/874 (2017). https://eprint.iacr.org/2017/874
19. Canetti, R., Lin, H., Tessaro, S., Vaikuntanathan, V.: Obfuscation of probabilistic circuits and applications. In: Dodis, Y., Nielsen, J.B. (eds.) TCC 2015. LNCS, vol. 9015, pp. 468–497. Springer, Heidelberg (2015). https://doi.org/10.1007/978-3-662-46497-7_19
20. Chen, Y., Vaikuntanathan, V., Wee, H.: GGH15 beyond permutation branching programs: proofs, attacks, and candidates. In: Shacham, H., Boldyreva, A. (eds.) CRYPTO 2018. LNCS, vol. 10992, pp. 577–607. Springer, Cham (2018). https://doi.org/10.1007/978-3-319-96881-0_20
21. Cho, C., Döttling, N., Garg, S., Gupta, D., Miao, P., Polychroniadou, A.: Laconic oblivious transfer and its applications. In: Katz, J., Shacham, H. (eds.) CRYPTO 2017. LNCS, vol. 10402, pp. 33–65. Springer, Cham (2017). https://doi.org/10.1007/978-3-319-63715-0_2
22. Coron, J.-S., Lepoint, T., Tibouchi, M.: Practical multilinear maps over the integers. In: Canetti, R., Garay, J.A. (eds.) CRYPTO 2013. LNCS, vol. 8042, pp. 476–493. Springer, Heidelberg (2013). https://doi.org/10.1007/978-3-642-40041-4_26
23. Coron, J.-S., Lepoint, T., Tibouchi, M.: New multilinear maps over the integers. In: Gennaro, R., Robshaw, M. (eds.) CRYPTO 2015. LNCS, vol. 9215, pp. 267–286. Springer, Heidelberg (2015). https://doi.org/10.1007/978-3-662-47989-6_13
24. Fiat, A., Naor, M.: Broadcast encryption. In: Stinson, D.R. (ed.) CRYPTO 1993. LNCS, vol. 773, pp. 480–491. Springer, Heidelberg (1994). https://doi.org/10.1007/3-540-48329-2_40
25. Garg, S., Gentry, C., Halevi, S.: Candidate multilinear maps from ideal lattices. In: Johansson, T., Nguyen, P.Q. (eds.) EUROCRYPT 2013. LNCS, vol. 7881, pp. 1–17. Springer, Heidelberg (2013). https://doi.org/10.1007/978-3-642-38348-9_1
26. Garg, S., Gentry, C., Halevi, S., Raykova, M.: Two-round secure MPC from indistinguishability obfuscation. In: Lindell, Y. (ed.) TCC 2014. LNCS, vol. 8349, pp. 74–94. Springer, Heidelberg (2014). https://doi.org/10.1007/978-3-642-54242-8_4
27. Garg, S., Gentry, C., Halevi, S., Raykova, M., Sahai, A., Waters, B.: Candidate indistinguishability obfuscation and functional encryption for all circuits. In: FOCS (2013)
28. Garg, S., Gentry, C., Halevi, S., Wichs, D.: On the implausibility of differing-inputs obfuscation and extractable witness encryption with auxiliary input. In: Garay, J.A., Gennaro, R. (eds.) CRYPTO 2014. LNCS, vol. 8616, pp. 518–535. Springer, Heidelberg (2014). https://doi.org/10.1007/978-3-662-44371-2_29
29. Garg, S., Gentry, C., Sahai, A., Waters, B.: Witness encryption and its applications. In: STOC (2013)
30. Garg, S., Pandey, O., Srinivasan, A.: Revisiting the cryptographic hardness of finding a nash equilibrium. In: Robshaw, M., Katz, J. (eds.) CRYPTO 2016. LNCS, vol. 9815, pp. 579–604. Springer, Heidelberg (2016). https://doi.org/10.1007/978-3-662-53008-5_20

31. Garg, S., Pandey, O., Srinivasan, A., Zhandry, M.: Breaking the sub-exponential barrier in obfustopia. In: Coron, J.-S., Nielsen, J.B. (eds.) EUROCRYPT 2017. LNCS, vol. 10212, pp. 156–181. Springer, Cham (2017). https://doi.org/10.1007/978-3-319-56617-7_6
32. Gentry, C., Gorbunov, S., Halevi, S.: Graph-induced multilinear maps from lattices. In: Dodis, Y., Nielsen, J.B. (eds.) TCC 2015. LNCS, vol. 9015, pp. 498–527. Springer, Heidelberg (2015). https://doi.org/10.1007/978-3-662-46497-7_20
33. Gentry, C., Lewko, A., Waters, B.: Witness encryption from instance independent assumptions. In: Garay, J.A., Gennaro, R. (eds.) CRYPTO 2014. LNCS, vol. 8616, pp. 426–443. Springer, Heidelberg (2014). https://doi.org/10.1007/978-3-662-44371-2_24
34. Gentry, C., Lewko, A.B., Sahai, A., Waters, B.: Indistinguishability obfuscation from the multilinear subgroup elimination assumption. In: IEEE 56th Annual Symposium on Foundations of Computer Science, FOCS 2015, pp. 151–170 (2015)
35. Gentry, C., Waters, B.: Adaptive security in broadcast encryption systems (with short ciphertexts). In: Joux, A. (ed.) EUROCRYPT 2009. LNCS, vol. 5479, pp. 171–188. Springer, Heidelberg (2009). https://doi.org/10.1007/978-3-642-01001-9_10
36. Goldwasser, S., Kalai, Y.T., Popa, R.A., Vaikuntanathan, V., Zeldovich, N.: How to run turing machines on encrypted data. In: Canetti, R., Garay, J.A. (eds.) CRYPTO 2013. LNCS, vol. 8043, pp. 536–553. Springer, Heidelberg (2013). https://doi.org/10.1007/978-3-642-40084-1_30
37. Goyal, R., Hohenberger, S., Koppula, V., Waters, B.: A generic approach to constructing and proving verifiable random functions. In: Kalai, Y., Reyzin, L. (eds.) TCC 2017. LNCS, vol. 10678, pp. 537–566. Springer, Cham (2017). https://doi.org/10.1007/978-3-319-70503-3_18
38. Goyal, R., Koppula, V., Russell, A., Waters, B.: Risky traitor tracing and new differential privacy negative results. Cryptology ePrint Archive, Report 2017/1117 (2017). https://eprint.iacr.org/2017/1117
39. Goyal, R., Koppula, V., Waters, B.: Lockable obfuscation. In: 58th IEEE Annual Symposium on Foundations of Computer Science, FOCS 2017, pp. 612–621 (2017)
40. Goyal, R., Koppula, V., Waters, B.: Separating semantic and circular security for symmetric-key bit encryption from the learning with errors assumption. In: Coron, J.-S., Nielsen, J.B. (eds.) EUROCRYPT 2017. LNCS, vol. 10211, pp. 528–557. Springer, Cham (2017). https://doi.org/10.1007/978-3-319-56614-6_18
41. Goyal, R., Koppula, V., Waters, B.: Collusion resistant traitor tracing from learning with errors. In: STOC (2018)
42. Hofheinz, D., Jager, T.: Verifiable random functions from standard assumptions. In: Kushilevitz, E., Malkin, T. (eds.) TCC 2016. LNCS, vol. 9562, pp. 336–362. Springer, Heidelberg (2016). https://doi.org/10.1007/978-3-662-49096-9_14
43. Hofheinz, D., Jager, T., Khurana, D., Sahai, A., Waters, B., Zhandry, M.: How to generate and use universal samplers. In: Cheon, J.H., Takagi, T. (eds.) ASIACRYPT 2016. LNCS, vol. 10032, pp. 715–744. Springer, Heidelberg (2016). https://doi.org/10.1007/978-3-662-53890-6_24
44. Hubácek, P., Wichs, D.: On the communication complexity of secure function evaluation with long output. In: Proceedings of the 2015 Conference on Innovations in Theoretical Computer Science, ITCS 2015, pp. 163–172 (2015)
45. Koppula, V., Lewko, A.B., Waters, B.: Indistinguishability obfuscation for turing machines with unbounded memory. In: Proceedings of the Forty-Seventh Annual ACM on Symposium on Theory of Computing, STOC 2015, pp. 419–428 (2015)

46. Koppula, V., Waters, B.: Circular security separations for arbitrary length cycles from LWE. In: Robshaw, M., Katz, J. (eds.) CRYPTO 2016. LNCS, vol. 9815, pp. 681–700. Springer, Heidelberg (2016). https://doi.org/10.1007/978-3-662-53008-5_24
47. Liu, Q., Zhandry, M.: Decomposable obfuscation: a framework for building applications of obfuscation from polynomial hardness. In: Kalai, Y., Reyzin, L. (eds.) TCC 2017. LNCS, vol. 10677, pp. 138–169. Springer, Cham (2017). https://doi.org/10.1007/978-3-319-70500-2_6
48. Luo, S., Shen, Q., Jin, Y., Chen, Y., Chen, Z., Qing, S.: A variant of Boyen-Waters anonymous IBE scheme. In: Qing, S., Susilo, W., Wang, G., Liu, D. (eds.) ICICS 2011. LNCS, vol. 7043, pp. 42–56. Springer, Heidelberg (2011). https://doi.org/10.1007/978-3-642-25243-3_4
49. Micali, S., Rabin, M., Vadhan, S.: Verifiable random functions. In: Proceedings 40th IEEE Symposium on Foundations of Computer Science, FOCS, pp. 120–130. IEEE (1999)
50. Naor, D., Naor, M., Lotspiech, J.: Revocation and tracing schemes for stateless receivers. In: Kilian, J. (ed.) CRYPTO 2001. LNCS, vol. 2139, pp. 41–62. Springer, Heidelberg (2001). https://doi.org/10.1007/3-540-44647-8_3
51. Naor, M., Pinkas, B.: Efficient trace and revoke schemes. In: Frankel, Y. (ed.) FC 2000. LNCS, vol. 1962, pp. 1–20. Springer, Heidelberg (2001). https://doi.org/10.1007/3-540-45472-1_1
52. Nishimaki, R., Wichs, D., Zhandry, M.: Anonymous traitor tracing: how to embed arbitrary information in a key. In: Fischlin, M., Coron, J.-S. (eds.) EUROCRYPT 2016. LNCS, vol. 9666, pp. 388–419. Springer, Heidelberg (2016). https://doi.org/10.1007/978-3-662-49896-5_14
53. Okamoto, T., Pietrzak, K., Waters, B., Wichs, D.: New realizations of somewhere statistically binding hashing and positional accumulators. In: Iwata, T., Cheon, J.H. (eds.) ASIACRYPT 2015. LNCS, vol. 9452, pp. 121–145. Springer, Heidelberg (2015). https://doi.org/10.1007/978-3-662-48797-6_6
54. Regev, O.: On lattices, learning with errors, random linear codes, and cryptography. In: Proceedings of the 37th Annual ACM Symposium on Theory of Computing, pp. 84–93 (2005)
55. Sahai, A., Waters, B.: Fuzzy identity-based encryption. In: Cramer, R. (ed.) EUROCRYPT 2005. LNCS, vol. 3494, pp. 457–473. Springer, Heidelberg (2005). https://doi.org/10.1007/11426639_27
56. Sahai, A., Waters, B.: How to use indistinguishability obfuscation: deniable encryption, and more. In: Symposium on Theory of Computing, STOC 2014, New York, NY, USA, 31 May–03 June 2014, pp. 475–484 (2014)
57. Seo, J.H., Kobayashi, T., Ohkubo, M., Suzuki, K.: Anonymous hierarchical identity-based encryption with constant size ciphertexts. In: Jarecki, S., Tsudik, G. (eds.) PKC 2009. LNCS, vol. 5443, pp. 215–234. Springer, Heidelberg (2009). https://doi.org/10.1007/978-3-642-00468-1_13
58. Shamir, A.: Identity-based cryptosystems and signature schemes. In: Blakley, G.R., Chaum, D. (eds.) CRYPTO 1984. LNCS, vol. 196, pp. 47–53. Springer, Heidelberg (1985). https://doi.org/10.1007/3-540-39568-7_5
59. Wichs, D., Zirdelis, G.: Obfuscating compute-and-compare programs under LWE. In: 58th IEEE Annual Symposium on Foundations of Computer Science, FOCS 2017, pp. 600–611 (2017)
60. Zhandry, M.: How to avoid obfuscation using witness PRFs. In: Kushilevitz, E., Malkin, T. (eds.) TCC 2016. LNCS, vol. 9563, pp. 421–448. Springer, Heidelberg (2016). https://doi.org/10.1007/978-3-662-49099-0_16

Break-glass Encryption

Alessandra Scafuro(✉)

NCSU, Raleigh, USA
ascafur@ncsu.edu

Abstract. "Break-glass" is a term used in IT healthcare systems to denote an emergency access to private information without having the credentials to do so.

In this paper we introduce the concept of *break-glass encryption* for cloud storage, where the security of the ciphertexts – stored on a cloud – can be violated *exactly once*, for emergency circumstances, in a way that is *detectable* and without relying on a trusted party.

Detectability is the crucial property here: if a cloud breaks glass without permission from the legitimate user, the latter should detect it and have a proof of such violation. However, if the break-glass procedure is invoked by the *legitimate* user, then semantic security must still hold and the cloud will learn nothing. Distinguishing that a break-glass is requested by the legitimate party is also challenging in absence of secrets.

In this paper, we provide a formalization of break-glass encryption and a secure instantiation using hardware tokens. Our construction aims to be a feasibility result and is admittedly impractical. Whether hardware tokens are necessary to achieve this security notion and whether more practical solutions can be devised are interesting open questions.

1 Introduction

The purpose of an encryption scheme [GM84] is to protect data against any observer that is not the intended recipient of the data. Encryption has been historically used to protect messages in transmission over untrusted channels. Recently however, encryption is progressively being used in the context of cloud storage to protect the confidentiality of the data uploaded by the users to the cloud. In a cloud storage setting, the cloud is trusted to guarantee availability of the uploaded data at any time, but it is not necessarily trusted (or held accountable) for not leaking clients' data to third parties. Thus, the cloud can be seen as an untrusted but reliable channel that the client uses to communicate data to herself in the future.

The Need to Break. But what happens if the user loses the key? Or more generally, what if the user loses the ability to access to the secret key (e.g. because she lost her laptop, or simply because she is not alive anymore) but there is a need

A. Scafuro—Supported by NSF grant #1012798.

D. Lin and K. Sako (Eds.): PKC 2019, LNCS 11443, pp. 34–62, 2019.
https://doi.org/10.1007/978-3-030-17259-6_2

to retrieve the documents that she uploaded to the cloud? For this emergency condition, one would like to have a way to break the encryption *without knowing any cryptographic secret* associated to the user.

Break-glass Encryption. We introduce the concept of *break-glass*[1] encryption. This is an encryption scheme that guarantees semantic security – just like any traditional encryption scheme – but it additionally provides a new command called Break that allows one designated party (the cloud) to help an alleged user to break her ciphertexts. Each ciphertext can be broken *at most one time* in a way that is *detectable. Detectability is the crucial property.* If the cloud breaks the ciphertexts without having received any request from the user, then the user should be able to detect and publicly prove this violation. A bit more specifically, we consider a setting where a user uploads and updates a (potentially large) number of ciphertexts and we want two properties: (1) a *legitimate* break-glass procedure preserves semantic security, that is, an honest user should be able to use the cloud to break her ciphertexts in such a way that the cloud does *not* learn anything about the plaintexts; (2) an *illegitimate* break-glass procedure is detectable, that is, if the cloud breaks user's ciphertexts without any permission, this violation is detectable and can be proven to a third party. In other words, a legitimate break-glass procedure preserves the semantic security of the ciphertext, while an illegitimate break-glass procedure leaks data but provides a proof of the violation.

What Constitutes a Legitimate Break-glass Request? A peculiar aspect of a break-glass encryption is that the break-glass procedure should be requested *without knowing any secret.* This is indeed crucial since a user wants to break-glass exactly because he does not remember his secrets.

However, if no secret are required to request to break-glass, how do we distinguish a legitimate request – coming from the owner of the data – from an illegitimate one – coming from anyone else? What makes a request illegitimate?

This is a challenge unique for our setting. For any break-glass encryption, one has to first design a permission mechanism for creating legitimate permissions without any secret and identifying and/or denying illegitimate requests. To devise such a permission mechanism we leverage the following observation. If a user did *not* request a break-glass procedure, this means that she probably still possesses her secrets, and therefore she can use them to delegitimize the request.

More concretely, the high-level idea behind the permission mechanism is the following. Any user $\mathcal{U}$ has associated a (public) alert address (e.g., an email address, a Bitcoin account), which we call alert-info. When the cloud receives a break-glass request from a party on behalf of user $\mathcal{U}$, will first send an "alert" to user $\mathcal{U}$, by forwarding the break-glass request to the address alert-info. The

[1] The name break-glass encryption is inspired by the break-glass procedures used in access control of various systems (healthcare, computer systems, etc.). In a break-glass procedure the system administrator breaks into the account of a certain user without the legitimate credentials in order to retrieve his data.

cloud will then wait a certain interval of time $T_{\mathsf{WaitPermission}}$, this time could depend on the application and the permission mechanism. If the users knows the secret associated to alert-info, then she will be able to stop or endorse the permission by using her secrets. If not, the user will simply do nothing. After waiting $T_{\mathsf{WaitPermission}}$ steps, if no denying answer is received from $\mathcal{U}$, the silence is accepted as a proof that the user did indeed lose the key and a "silence" permission that $\mathcal{U}$ wishes to break the glass. Crucially, it is important that a cloud is not able to fabricate a "silence" permission; thus the silence response must be publicly verifiable. This is necessary for protecting the user against a malicious cloud that pretends that no answer was received; but also to protect the cloud in case a malicious user remains silent but then *later* accuses the cloud by fabricating a proof delegitimizing the request.

We abstract the properties of such verifiable permission mechanism in an ideal functionality $\mathcal{G}_{\mathsf{perm}}$ (see Fig. 2) and we discuss possible implementations using a blockchain or an email provider (see Sect. 4.3).

Detectability: Why Simple Solutions Do Not Work. At first sight, the break-glass property might seem trivial to achieve; after all we are adding a method to reveal something and not to conceal. Unfortunately, this is not the case, and the main reason is that for each breaking attempt we need to ensure detectability. To show this, we now discuss some trivial solutions that do not work.

A straightforward solution could be to upload the ciphertexts in one cloud, and give the secret key to another party, e.g., a friend, another cloud, a group of colleagues, etc. This approach fails in achieving detectability: if the cloud colludes with the party holding the key then ciphertexts can be decrypted at any time and without leaving any trace. Similarly, the approach of selecting a group of people that collectively holds the secret key suffers of the same problem: if the group comes together and decides to decrypt, there is no way for the user to ever notice. Furthermore, in this type of approach, it does not seem possible to guarantee semantic security in presence of legitimate break-glass procedure.

Another relatively straightforward approach is to use a one-time hardware token. Namely, the user prepares a token which has the secret key hardwired, and when queried, it will output the key and then stop responding. The user will then send to the cloud two things: the ciphertexts and the token, with the understanding that the token should be used only in case of emergency. To break the glass, the cloud simply queries the token and get the key. The user could detect if the break-glass procedure has been illegitimately performed by periodically pinging her token. This approach however does not achieve semantic security in presence of legitimate break-glass procedure. Indeed, since the cloud learns the key, will be able to decrypt everything even when following a legitimate request, and also trace the ciphertexts updates over time. Finally, this solution does not allow for any granularity in case of illegitimate break-glass procedure. Indeed, since the key is revealed, all ciphertexts are automatically broken. Instead, we would like a more fine-grained mechanism that tells the user exactly which ciphertexts have been compromised, or that it allows the user to setup a leaking threshold (e.g., not more then 50% of the data should be ever decrypted).

When to Use Break-glass Encryption? Break-glass security is reminiscent of covert security [AL07], and it is meaningful in scenarios where the loss of reputation is a strong deterrence against cheating. In particular, our definition is stronger than covert security in that we explicitly require that, for any illegitimate breaking attempt, the client will get a proof that can be used to publicly accuse the cloud. Thus, we target the scenario of cloud storage, where the cloud is a functional and mostly credible company (e.g., Dropbox, iCloud Apple, Google drive). In this scenario the stake for reputation is very high, therefore it is very reasonable to assume that the benefit from breaking the security of a single client, are less appealing than losing the reputation and thus all the other clients. Clearly, break-glass encryption is not suitable for scenarios where the cloud storage is an unknown server, that has not accountability or credibility. In this case indeed, there is no reputation to maintain, thus not deterrence against cheating.

What Break-glass Encryption is Not. Break-glass encryption is different from a "trapdoored" encryption scheme, where one can put a trapdoor that allows a designed party (who knows the trapdoor) to decrypt. The crucial difference is that a trapdoor allows to decrypt undetectably, while we want to make sure that each break is detectable and it can be performed at most one-time.

1.1 Our Contribution and Our Techniques

In this paper we provide two main contributions:

- **Definition of break-glass encryption.** We introduce the new concept of *break-glass encryption*. This is an encryption scheme for the **cloud storage setting**, that allows a honest user to break her own ciphertexts when necessary, while preserving semantic security. We formally define break-glass encryption via an ideal functionality $\mathcal{F}_{\mathsf{break}}$. In this context, we also introduce a new ideal functionality, $\mathcal{G}_{\mathsf{perm}}$, for generating verifiable permissions for a user $\mathcal{U}$.
- **Construction of a break-glass encryption.** As a feasibility result, we show that break-glass encryption can be constructed using (stateful) hardware token [Kat07] in the ($\mathcal{G}_{\mathsf{perm}}, \mathcal{G}_{\mathsf{clock}}$)-hybrid model, where $\mathcal{G}_{\mathsf{clock}}$ is the global clock functionality. We also suggest implementations of $\mathcal{G}_{\mathsf{perm}}$ using blockchain or email systems.

In the remaining part of this section we provide more details about the technical aspects of each contribution.

Definition of Break-glass Encryption. We consider a setting where there is a cloud $\mathcal{C}$ and a user $\mathcal{U}$, and the cloud is used for memory outsourcing. The user can perform the following actions (1) upload/download ciphertexts; (2) update a ciphertext; (3) break-glass of one (or many) ciphertexts. Our ideal functionality $\mathcal{F}_{\mathsf{break}}$ should satisfy the following properties. If the cloud honestly performs a legitimate break-glass procedure on behalf of a user, then semantic security should still hold, namely, the cloud does not learn anything about the decryption. If the cloud performs an illegitimate break-glass command, then this action must be detectable by the user the very next time the user attempts to read *any* ciphertext, and the violation should be publicly verifiable.

Defining Permission Without Secret: $\mathcal{G}_{\mathsf{perm}}$ *Functionality.* We introduce the $\mathcal{G}_{\mathsf{perm}}$ functionality. This a functionality used by cloud $\mathcal{C}$ and user $\mathcal{U}$ to obtain and verify valid permissions from $\mathcal{U}$. In $\mathcal{G}_{\mathsf{perm}}$ each user $\mathcal{U}_i$ is associated to a public information $\mathsf{alert\text{-}info}_i$. We stress that this information is public and a user can retrieve it even if she loses all her secrets. This functionality provides the following interface: Register, Create Permission, and Verify Permission. Register is used by $\mathcal{U}$ to register the public information $\mathsf{alert\text{-}info}$. Create Permission is used by the cloud to obtain a permission π_{perm}, which is either a publicly verifiable endorsement of the request or a publicly verifiable silence proof from $\mathcal{G}_{\mathsf{perm}}$. This step uses timing information and invoke ideal functionality $\mathcal{G}_{\mathsf{clock}}$. This is the global clock functionality, previously used in [BMTZ17] in the context of defining the public ledger functionality and analysing the security of the bitcoin protocol. VerifyPermission is used by any party who wishes to check that $(\mathsf{alert\text{-}info}, \pi_{\mathsf{perm}})$ is a valid permission granted by $\mathcal{U}$. We discuss realization of $\mathcal{G}_{\mathsf{perm}}$ based on blockchain or email in Sect. 4.3.

Defining Break-glass: $\mathcal{F}_{\mathsf{break}}$ *Functionality.* We capture the security properties of detectability, accountability and semantic security in presence of legitimate break-glass procedure in an ideal functionality $\mathcal{F}_{\mathsf{break}}$ (Fig. 1). $\mathcal{F}_{\mathsf{break}}$ interacts with two parties, a cloud $\mathcal{C}$ and a user $\mathcal{U}$. $\mathcal{F}_{\mathsf{break}}$ takes in input messages $m_1, \ldots, m_l$ from $\mathcal{U}$, who can then update and retrieve her messages many times (by invoking commands Update/Retrieve). $\mathcal{F}_{\mathsf{break}}$ provides a Break command that can be invoked by $\mathcal{C}$ only. It takes in input an index i (denoting the ciphertext that the party wishes to decrypt), a proof of permission $(\mathsf{alert\text{-}info}, \pi_{\mathsf{perm}})$ or a proof of cheating (π_{cheat}). $\mathcal{F}_{\mathsf{break}}$ verifies the permission $(\mathsf{alert\text{-}info}, \pi_{\mathsf{perm}})$ using $\mathcal{G}_{\mathsf{perm}}$, and then proceeds by sending m_i to the user $\mathcal{U}$ only. If the request is illegitimate, $\mathcal{F}_{\mathsf{break}}$ checks that π_{cheat} is a proof of cheating. If the check passes, $\mathcal{F}_{\mathsf{break}}$ sends m_i to the cloud, and records the cheating attempt.

For every operation requested by the user, $\mathcal{F}_{\mathsf{break}}$ proceeds only after receiving an ack from $\mathcal{C}$. This captures the real world fact that a cloud can always refuse to answer (note that this is true in any cloud system). In such case, our functionality give no explicit guarantees, since the user will just receive the message $(\mathsf{refuse}, \bot)$. In practice however, refusing the answer is a proof of misbehaviour and can be turned into a legal proof via court.

Construction. Our construction relies on hardware tokens. The token is the point of trust of the user. It is initialized with the secret key k used to encrypt the data, a signing key $\mathsf{ssk}_{\mathcal{T}}$, and the verification key of the cloud $\mathsf{vpk}_{\mathcal{C}}$. The token is sent to the cloud $\mathcal{C}$ at the very beginning, and it stays with the cloud throughout the execution. We consider the case where the user can encrypt arbitrarily long files, but the size of the token is constant, that is, it must be independent on the number of blocks encrypted. This size constraint rules out any solution where we just keep all the ciphertexts inside the token or have the token record all the ciphertexts for which the cloud invoked the Break command.

The token performs a computation only when the inputs are authenticated wrt the cloud's public key. Authenticated inputs serve two purposes: first, it provides a proof in case a cloud operated the token illegitimately; second, it protects the cloud from false accusations about the operation of the token. Finally, the outputs of the token is also authenticated, in order to avoid that the cloud sends wrong information to the user.

Warm Up Solution Without Granularity. As warm up, we describe a solution that does not provide any granularity. Namely, a user cannot detect which ciphertexts have been violated and when. The first solution works as follows. The user sends her ciphertexts $C = (c_1, \ldots, c_n)$, encrypted under a secret key k to the cloud. Then she initializes a token $\mathcal{T}$ with the secret key k, the verification key of the cloud $\mathsf{vpk}_{\mathcal{C}}$ and the signature key $\mathsf{ssk}_{\mathcal{T}}$ used to authenticate $\mathcal{T}$'s outputs. The token $\mathcal{T}$ performs a very simple functionality: on input a permission perm and a fresh public key pk, it outputs the encryption of the secret key k and stops. Note that the token only checks that the input perm, pk is correctly signed by $\mathcal{C}$; but does not check if the permission (if any) given in input is valid. This check will be done later by the parties only in case of dispute. This solution is simple, but it leaves little control on the illegitimate queries. Indeed, with one such query, the cloud can immediately decrypt 100% of the ciphertexts. We would like a more fine-grained approach that allows the user to identify precisely which ciphertexts have been broken and potentially to setup a threshold on the total number of ciphertexts that can be broken.

A Fine-Grained Solution: Breaking Ciphertexts Selectively. To break the ciphertexts selectively, the token should not output the key. Instead, we need the token to decrypt selectively. The idea is to give in input to the token also a ciphertext c_i, so that the token will answer with m_i, i.e., the decryption of c_i, rather than the key. More precisely, the token will output an encryption of m_i under the public key pk, where pk is the public key chosen by the person who is requesting to break ciphertext c_i. Moreover, to make sure that c_i is marked as broken, the token will output a new version, $c_i' = \mathsf{Enc}(m_i||broken||\mathsf{perm})$ that must replace c_i, where perm is the permission used to invoke the break procedure (perm might be empty). Next time the user will download the i-th ciphertext, she will obtain c_i' and if she still has the key k, she will detect that c_i' was illegitimately broken; similarly, next time the cloud inputs c_i' to the token, the token will refuse to decrypt.

This solution is too naive. A malicious cloud can simply ignore the new marked ciphertext c_i' and send the old unbroken c_i to the user. Namely, the cloud can always replay old ciphertexts, defeating the checks of the token/user. To overcome this problem, we propose a mechanism that makes valid ciphertext evolve over time, or in other words, *age*. We do so by simply adding bookkeeping information; namely, each encryption now will also contain a time t_i when it was last updated, the time T_0 when the first break occurred (if any). This means that by downloading *any* of the ciphertexts the user can determine if a break-glass has happened. Each ciphertext c_i needs to be refreshed every I timestamps (where I is a parameter that can vary with application). Since updating ciphertexts requires the use of the secret key, the cloud $\mathcal{C}$ will use the token to re-encrypt each ciphertext upon each interval I. Updating a ciphertex simply means to re-encrypt the message m_i concatenated with the *current* time, and the time of the first break-glass T_0 (if any). Now, when a user downloads the i-th ciphertext c_i, and tries to decrypt it, she expects to obtain the most updated time (within a window of I steps). If not, she will discard the ciphertext as stale, and consider this as a cheating attempt from the cloud.

Therefore, in this fine grained approach, the token performs two operations for the cloud: re-encryption and break. When the cloud inputs the command 're-encrypt', then the token expects in input a ciphertext c_i that needs to be re-encrypted with the current time. The token will accept to re-encrypt only if the time registered in c_i are at most I steps behind the current time.

Finally, there is a subtle issue that requires a careful tradeoff between the size of interval I and the size of the memory of the token. Consider the following attack. The cloud queries the token to re-encrypt c_i at time t obtaining c_i^t. The cloud then queries the token to break c_i^t, at time $t+1$ and obtains m_i as well as the new encryption c_i^{t+1} which is marked as broken. Then, the cloud completely discard c_i^{t+1} and instead queries the token to re-encrypt c_i^t at time $t+2$. If $t+I < t+2$ then the token accepts to re-encrypt c_i^t with the new time $t+2$, and output the new ciphertext c_i^{t+2} which is not marked as broken (however note that c_i^{t+2} will still have the field $T_0 \neq 0$ signaling that a break-glass took place). Thus, the cloud obtains a clean unmarked version of c_i which is updated to time $t+2$, even if c_i was broken at time $t+1$ and the user will not detect that this specific ciphertext was broken (however $\mathcal{U}$ will still know that a ciphertext was broken). This problem arises because we allow a interval I between re-encryptions and can be solved by simply remembering the indexes of the ciphertexts broken within a window of I steps. The size of this list depends on the size of I (and $logn$ where n is the number of ciphertexts).

How to Get Rid of Clocks in the Token. In the outlined solution, the token uses a clock to check the current time and identify stale ciphertexts. However, requiring a clock (even only loosely synchronized) in the token is a strong assumption (the token cannot simply connect to a public server to check the time). We remove this assumption by having the cloud $\mathcal{C}$ provide the current time as input to the token. Time is simply a monotonic function, and time is "correct" if it moves forward. Thus, instead of requiring the token to keep its own clock, the token could receive the time as input, store the last time it was queried, and accept a new "current" time only if it goes in the forward direction. Checking whether the time provided by $\mathcal{C}$ is actually good will be done by the user when downloading the ciphertext. As long as the parties (i.e., the cloud and the user) agree on a common source for reliable time, then there will be no dispute of the current time. We stress that assuming that $\mathcal{C}$ and $\mathcal{U}$ agree on a common time is a natural assumption made by most real world systems that we use in everyday life. The Network Time Protocol (NTP) [MMBK,CHMV17] is one example of protocols used for synchronization of the communications over the internet. There has been a lot of work on attacks and defenses for the NTP protocols (see [MG16,MGV+17]), but this problem is orthogonal to the one discussed in this paper. Moreover, we stress that we only need $\mathcal{C}$ and $\mathcal{U}$ to be loosely synchronized, and the parameters of the encryption (i.e., the interval I and $T_{\mathsf{WaitPermission}}$) can be tailored accordingly.

On the Need of State, Obfuscation, Blockchain. We got rid of the clock for the token, by just assuming that the world (the cloud and the user) has a global clock. Can we get rid of the state too by assuming that the world share a global immutable state? If that was possible, we could use a stateless token, or even further, can we replace the token with Indistinguishability Obfuscation [ABG+13,GGH+13,GGHW17,BCP14]. Very recently blockchain technology provides the world with a common state that everyone seems to agree on, without trusting any party. Thus, a possible approach could be for the token to store its state as a transaction in the blockchain, and the cloud can query the token on input the transaction. However, this seems to be challenging since a token could not verify the validity of a transaction without having access to the entire blockchain. Recent work [LKW15,Jag15,KMG17,GG17] show how to construct one-time programs [GKR08] and time-lock encryption leveraging the blockchain (but they are based on witness encryption [GKP+13]). We do not rule out that an interesting solution can be developed using weaker cryptographic assumptions, we leave it as future work to explore this direction.

Other Considerations. For simplicity we assume that the token sent by the user runs the prescribed code (i.e., the user does not embed malicious code into the token). This is only for simplicity of exposition, since standard techniques using zero-knowledge proof could allow us to remove this requirement. We believe that this is a reasonable relaxation, especially for the envisioned application of break-glass encryption, and since this is the first attempt to achieve such security notion. We do not consider side-channel attacks on the token.

On Surveillance and Rational Adversaries. One can argue that this scheme has the undesired effect that it can be used by a government to break the privacy of its citizens (by subpoena the cloud). This is certainly true, but recall that the citizens would detect that their privacy is violated. Therefore, one can be in two cases. Case 1, one lives in a country where the state cares about citizens not being aware that they are monitored. In this case, the state would not use the break functionality to break encryption, but something more subtle. Case 2, one lives in a country where citizens are aware that they are watched. In this case, even if the state imposes the citizens to use a break-glass encryption scheme, then the citizens can still break-glass encrypt a ciphertext (rather than their messages). In this way, even if a break is performed, the perpetrator will only learn more encryptions.

On Refusing to Provide the Service. Just like any client-server system, the cloud can always refuse to provide the service and ignore user's requests. In this case the user will *not* have a *cryptographic proof of cheating* as promised by the break-glass encryption scheme, however, the user can obtain a court order obligating the cloud to release ciphertexts and users' token.

2 Open Problems

The main goal of this work was to introduce the concept of break-glass encryption, and show that in principle is achievable. The proposed solution however is quite impractical and only provides a feasibility result. Several questions are left open: Are (stateful) hardware token necessary to achieve this notion of security? Can we devise a solution that achieves some granularity but it does not require the cloud to continuously update the ciphertexts by querying the token? What are other interesting implementations of $\mathcal{G}_{\mathsf{perm}}$ and can $\mathcal{G}_{\mathsf{perm}}$ have applications in other setting besides break-glass encryption?

3 Related Work

Concurrently and independently from our work, recently the concept of "disposable cryptography" has been introduced by Chung, Georgiou, Lai and Zikas in [CGLZ18]. While sharing some similarity with our work, the aims and the techniques are very different. The goal of this work is to provide an encryption scheme for cloud storage, that can be broken by *anyone* exactly once, in a detectable way. The motivation for break-glass is the case when the *legitimate user* wants to decrypt the data she uploaded to the cloud, but she lost all her secret keys. The goal of [CGLZ18] is to realize trapdoored cryptographic schemes that can be violated once, by a *designated entity* who possesses the trapdoor, which is *not* the legitimate user and without being detected. The motivation for dispensable backdoors is to allow law enforcement to break the scheme exactly once, the envisioned application is breaking into mobile phones undetectably. Somewhat related to the concept of break-glass cryptography is the idea of time-locked encryption [BN00, BGJ+16, BM09, BM17, LPS17]. In time-locked encryption some information is meant to be protected for a certain period time T, thus when the time expires, the cloud will be able to decrypt the information contained in the ciphertext. The difference between break-glass and time-locked encryption is in the fact that our cloud can always break the encryption if she wishes to do so, but at the price of being detected. Our adversarial model is very close in spirit to the covert model [BM09]. In this model the adversary is allowed to cheat and violate the privacy to the parties, but by doing so he will be caught and thus lose reputation.

4 Definitions

4.1 Break the Glass Encryption Scheme

A break-glass encryption is a private-key encryption scheme designed for the cloud storage setting. It provides a procedure called Break which allows a user to decrypt her ciphertexts without knowing the secret key, exactly once. At high-level a break-glass encryption scheme must satisfy the following properties:

- *Completeness.* If the cloud and the user follow the protocol then the user is able to obtain the plaintexts that she encrypted originally, without knowing the key.
- *Confidentiality (Semantic-Security).* If no Break is performed, then the ciphertexts are semantically secure against any PPT malicious cloud.
- *Break-glass Confidentiality.* If break-glass is requested by a legitimate user, the cloud does not learn anything about the broken ciphertexts.
- *Break-glass Detectability.* If break-glass is performed by the cloud without user's permission, the cloud can decrypt each ciphertext exactly once, and each violation is detected by the user (unless the cloud refuses to respond).
- *Break-glass Accountability.* A user should be able to prove that the cloud performed an illegitimate break-glass request.

We provide a simulation-based definition [Gol04, HL10] and capture the above security requirements via an ideal functionality $\mathcal{F}_{\mathsf{break}}$ (Fig. 1). To capture break-glass accountability, $\mathcal{F}_{\mathsf{break}}$ is designed so that it will proceed with an illegitimate break requested by the cloud $\mathcal{C}$, only if $\mathcal{C}$ provides a proof of cheating, that we denote by cheat-proof. $\mathcal{F}_{\mathsf{break}}$ invokes ideal functionalities $\mathcal{G}_{\mathsf{perm}}$ and $\mathcal{G}_{\mathsf{clock}}$ (which are defined as global functionalities). This definitional approach was used in previous work in the (stronger) GUC setting by Badertscher et al. [BMTZ17]. Finally, $\mathcal{F}_{\mathsf{break}}$ captures the real world fact that a cloud can always refuse to provide a service. Thus, every operation on the outsourced messages is fulfilled by $\mathcal{F}_{\mathsf{break}}$ only if the cloud agrees on responding.

Definition 1 (Break-glass encryption scheme). *A scheme Π is a secure break-glass encryption scheme if it realizes the functionality $\mathcal{F}_{\mathsf{break}}$ in the sense of [HL10].*

4.2 The $\mathcal{G}_{\mathsf{perm}}$ Ideal Functionality

The ideal functionality $\mathcal{G}_{\mathsf{perm}}$ is described in Fig. 2 and is inspired by the signature ideal functionality of [Can04]. The purpose of this functionality is to alert the user $\mathcal{U}_i$, registered with alert address $\mathsf{alert\text{-}info}_i$, that a permission request was triggered by a party. The user $\mathcal{U}_i$ can then provide a proof to either legitimate or to invalidate the permission request. This proof is then sent to the cloud $\mathcal{C}_i$ associated to $\mathsf{alert\text{-}info}_i$. If the user fails to provide any proof within time $T_{\mathsf{WaitPermission}}$, then a proof of silence is generated and provided to $\mathcal{C}$.

FUNCTIONALITY $\mathcal{F}_{\mathsf{break}}$.

Participants: The cloud $\mathcal{C}$, a user $\mathcal{U}$, the adversary.

Variables: a boolean *flag*, when $flag = 1$ means that there has been an illegitimate break. A vector $\mathsf{Status} = \mathsf{Status}[1], \ldots, \mathsf{Status}[l]$, with $\mathsf{Status}[i] = b|nlegit$ where $b = 1$ means that the i-th ciphertext was broken; $nlegit = 1$ means that the break was not legitimate. A vector $\mathsf{Cheat\Pi}[1], \ldots, \mathsf{Cheat\Pi}_{\mathsf{cheat}}[l]$ collects proofs of illegitimate break-glass.

External Functionality: $\mathcal{G}_{\mathsf{perm}}$.

Algorithms: $\mathcal{F}_{\mathsf{break}}$ is parameterized by VrfyCheatProof to check the proofs of illegitimate access provided by a corrupted cloud.

Procedure:

▷ **Upload.** Upon receiving $(\mathsf{upload}, \mathsf{sid}, m_1, \ldots, m_l, \mathcal{U})$ from user $\mathcal{U}$, store the vector $M = m_1, \ldots, m_l$. (Ignore any other request of this type). Send $(\mathsf{uploaded}, \mathsf{sid}, l, \mathcal{U})$ to the cloud $\mathcal{C}$ and the adversary.

▷ **Update.** Upon receiving $(\mathsf{update}, \mathsf{sid}, i, m)$ from user $\mathcal{U}$, send $(\mathsf{update}, \mathsf{sid}, i)$ to $\mathcal{C}$. If $\mathcal{C}$ is corrupted, then wait for answer $(\mathsf{ack\text{-}updated}, \mathsf{sid}, \mathcal{U}, resp)$. If $resp = no$ send $(\mathtt{refuse}, \bot)$ to $\mathcal{U}$. Else, update $m_i := m$. Send $(\mathsf{updated}, \mathsf{sid}, i)$ to $\mathcal{U}, \mathcal{C}$.

▷ **Break.** Upon receiving (break, sid, i, perm-proof, cheat-proof) from $\mathcal{C}$.

1. Case 1: User's Request. Parse perm-proof = (alert-info, π_{perm}).
   (a) Validate permission: Send (verify-permission, alert-info, π_{perm}) to $\mathcal{G}_{\mathsf{perm}}$. If the output is `granted`, proceed.
   (b) Send (break-request, sid, i, alert-info, π_{perm}) to $\mathcal{C}$. If $\mathcal{C}$ is corrupted, wait to receive $(\mathsf{ack\text{-}break}, \mathsf{sid}, \mathcal{U}, resp)$. If $resp = no$ send $(\mathtt{refuse}, \bot)$ to $\mathcal{U}$. Else proceed with the break procedure as follows:
   – (Never broken before) if $\mathsf{Status}[i] = 00$ then send $(m_i, flag)$ to $\mathcal{P}$.
   – (Already broken) if $\mathsf{Status}[i] = 1|nlegit$, send ($i$ is `broken`) to $\mathcal{P}$.
2. Case 2. Illegitimate Request. If VrfyCheatProof(cheat-proof) = 1:
   * Set $flag = 1$. Set $\mathsf{Status}[i] = 11$ and send m_i to $\mathcal{C}$.
   * Register $\mathsf{Cheat\Pi}[i]$:=cheat-proof.

▷ **Retrieve.** Upon receiving $(\mathsf{get}, \mathsf{sid}, i, \mathcal{U})$ from $\mathcal{U}$. Send $(\mathsf{retrieve\text{-}request}, \mathsf{sid}, i, \mathcal{U})$ to $\mathcal{C}$. If $\mathcal{C}$ is corrupted, then wait for the command $(\mathsf{ack\text{-}retrieve}, \mathsf{sid}, \mathcal{U}, resp)$; if $resp = no$ send $(\mathtt{refuse}, \bot)$ to $\mathcal{U}$. Else send $(m_i, flag, \mathsf{Status}[i])$ to $\mathcal{U}$.

▷ **Accuse with Proof.** Upon receiving $(\mathsf{accuse}, \mathsf{sid}, j)$ from a party $\mathcal{P}$. Send $(\mathsf{accused}, \mathsf{sid}, \mathcal{P})$ to $\mathcal{C}$ and $\mathsf{Cheat\Pi}[j]$ to $\mathcal{P}$.

Fig. 1. $\mathcal{F}_{\mathsf{break}}$ functionality

4.3 How to Implement $\mathcal{G}_{\mathsf{perm}}$

In this section we informally discuss two possible implementations of $\mathcal{G}_{\mathsf{perm}}$.

Implementation Using a Blockchain. Assuming the existence of a blockchain, $\mathcal{G}_{\mathsf{perm}}$ could be instantiated as follows. Procedure (register, alert-info, $\mathcal{U}_i$) consists in having the user compute keys for a digital signature scheme and send the corresponding public key $\mathsf{vpk}_{\mathcal{U}_i}$ to the cloud. $\mathcal{C}$ will then set alert-info = $\mathsf{vpk}_{\mathcal{U}_i}$.

FUNCTIONALITY $\mathcal{G}_{\mathsf{perm}}$.
$\mathcal{G}_{\mathsf{perm}}$ is parameterized by procedure InfoCheck used to check the validity of the credential provided by the user at registration phase.

Variables. $T_{\mathsf{WaitPermission}}$ is the time allowed to generate a valid permission or to deny a permission. $\mathcal{L}_{\mathcal{U}}$ is the list of registered users.

External Functionality. $\mathcal{G}_{\mathsf{clock}}$

▷ **Register.** Upon receiving $(\mathsf{register}, \mathsf{alert\text{-}info}, \mathcal{U}_i, \mathcal{C}_i)$ from user $\mathcal{U}_i$. If $\mathsf{InfoCheck}(\mathsf{alert\text{-}info}, \mathcal{U}_i) = 1$ then add $(\mathcal{U}_i, \mathsf{alert\text{-}info}, \mathcal{C}_i)$ to the list of registered users $\mathcal{L}_{\mathcal{U}}$ (where $\mathcal{C}_i$ is the party that obtains permissions from $\mathcal{U}_i$) and send it to the adversary.

▷ **Create Permission.** Upon receiving $(\mathsf{CreatePermission}, \mathsf{alert\text{-}info}, \mathcal{U}_i)$ from a party P. If $(\mathcal{U}_i, \mathsf{alert\text{-}info}, \mathcal{C}_i)$ is in $\mathcal{L}_{\mathcal{U}}$, then send $(\mathsf{CreatePermission}, \mathsf{alert\text{-}info})$ to $\mathcal{U}_i$.

- Upon receiving $(\mathsf{ack\text{-}check}, (\mathsf{alert\text{-}info}, \mathcal{U}_i), ans)$ from $\mathcal{U}_i$. Send $(\mathsf{GetProof}, \mathsf{alert\text{-}info}, \mathcal{U}_i, ans)$ to the adversary and obtain π.
- Else, if $T_{\mathsf{WaitPermission}}$ time has elapsed (use $\mathcal{G}_{\mathsf{clock}}$ for this), send $\mathsf{GenSilenceProof}(\mathcal{U}_i, \mathsf{alert\text{-}info}, \mathcal{P})$ to the adversary, and obtain π_ϵ. Set $\pi = \pi_\epsilon$.
- Check that no entry $(\mathsf{alert\text{-}info}, \mathcal{U}_i, \pi, 0)$ is recorded. If it is, output error message to $\mathcal{U}_i$. Else, record $(\mathsf{sid}, \mathsf{alert\text{-}info}, \mathcal{U}_i, \pi, ans, 1)$.
- Finally, send $(\mathsf{Permission}, \mathsf{alert\text{-}info}, \pi, ans)$ to $\mathcal{C}_i$.

▷ **Verify permission.** Upon receiving $(\mathsf{verify\text{-}permission}, \mathsf{alert\text{-}info}, \pi)$ from any party P_j, send $(\mathsf{VerifyPerm}, \mathsf{alert\text{-}info}, \pi, \Phi)$ to the adversary. Then,

1. If there is an entry $(\mathsf{alert\text{-}info}, \mathcal{U}_i, \pi, ans, 1)$ then
   - If $ans = YES$. Send $(\mathsf{alert\text{-}info}, \mathsf{verifiably-granted}, \pi)$ to P_j.
   - Else, if if $ans = NO$ Send $(\mathsf{alert\text{-}info}, \mathsf{verifiably-denied}, \pi)$ to P_j.
2. If there is no entry $(\mathsf{alert\text{-}info}, \mathcal{U}_i, \pi, ans, 1)$ recorded and $\mathcal{U}_i$ is not corrupted, then send $(\mathsf{alert\text{-}info}, \mathsf{notverified}, \pi)$ and record $(\mathsf{alert\text{-}info}, \mathcal{U}_i, \pi, ans, 0)$.
3. Else, if there is an entry $(\mathsf{alert\text{-}info}, \mathcal{U}_i, \pi, ans, 0)$ send $(\mathsf{alert\text{-}info}, \mathsf{notverified}, \pi)$ to P_j.
4. Else, set $(\mathsf{alert\text{-}info}, \mathcal{U}_i, \pi, ans, \Phi)$ and performs checks 1, 2, 3.

Fig. 2. $\mathcal{G}_{\mathsf{perm}}$ functionality

To make a break-glass request, $\mathcal{U}_i$, who potentially lost all the keys, will send a break-glass request to $\mathcal{C}$ (this request can be sent via a website form; to avoid denial of service attack one can enforce that to submit a request the user must pay some small amount of money). Upon receiving the request, $\mathcal{C}$ will look up the alert-info for $\mathcal{U}_i$ and proceed with the CreatePermission procedure.

Procedure $(\mathsf{CreatePermission}, \mathsf{alert\text{-}info}, \mathcal{U}_i)$ is implemented as follows. $\mathcal{C}$ prepares a permission request by posting a transaction $\mathsf{Tx}_{\mathsf{alert}}$ on the blockchain. Such transaction will contain a break-glass request in reference to the tuple $(\mathsf{alert\text{-}info}, \mathcal{C})$. After the transactions has been posted in a block of the blockchain, $\mathcal{C}$ waits $T_{\mathsf{WaitPermission}}$ time (this duration can be agreed on by the parties). Then, $\mathcal{C}$ downloads the blocks of the blockchain that appeared after the transaction $\mathsf{Tx}_{\mathsf{alert}}$ was posted and:

1. If there is no signed transaction that verifies under public key alert-info, then this sequence of $T_{\mathsf{WaitPermission}}$ blocks $(\mathbf{b}_1, \ldots, \mathbf{b}_{T_{\mathsf{WaitPermission}}})$ represents a proof of "silence" $\pi_\epsilon = (\mathbf{b}_1, \ldots, \mathbf{b}_{T_{\mathsf{WaitPermission}}})$ that $\mathcal{C}$ will use when querying the token.
2. Else, if within these blocks there is a transaction π_{ans} signed by alert-info denying $\tau_{\mathsf{alert\text{-}info}}$, this transaction will be the proof of denied permission $\pi = (\tau_{\mathsf{alert\text{-}info}}, \mathbf{b}_1, \ldots, \mathbf{b}_{T_{\mathsf{WaitPermission}}}, \pi_{\mathsf{ans}})$.
3. Else, if transaction π_{ans} is endorsing $\tau_{\mathsf{alert\text{-}info}}$, then such transaction alone will be the proof of permission $\pi = \pi_{\mathsf{ans}}$.

Note that the token is **not** connected to the blockchain, and it does **not** check any transaction. The blockchain transactions are checked only by the parties who will check the permission in case of a dispute. The advantage of a blockchain-based implementation is that it is decentralized, therefore the validity of the permission does not depend on any third party. The downside however is that the permission request must be posted on the blockchain, therefore revealing some information about the fact that a user of a certain cloud $\mathcal{C}$ lost her key.

Implementation with a (Trusted) Email Provider. $\mathcal{G}_{\mathsf{perm}}$ can also be implemented simply using an email system, and it requires the collaboration of the email service provider. In this case, the email provider is a trusted third party between the user and the cloud. Procedure (register, alert-info, $\mathcal{U}_i$) consists in having the user register an email address alert-info that will be used for break-glass communications.

To make a break-glass request, $\mathcal{U}_i$, who potentially lost all the keys, and therefore also the password to access to the email address alert-info, will send to $\mathcal{C}$ a break-glass request (via a web-form, for example, as above).

Procedure (CreatePermission, alert-info, $\mathcal{U}_i$) is implemented by having the cloud sending an email to the address alert-info with the detailed information about the break-glass request received for $\mathcal{U}_i$. If the cloud does not receive any reply after a period of $T_{\mathsf{WaitPermission}}$, it will proceed with the request. The proof π_ϵ for not having received a reply would require the intervention of the email providers of both user and cloud. A proof of valid permission is simply the email sent by address alert-info$_i$ to the cloud, authorizing the procedure. Similarly, a proof of denied permission, is the email sent by address alert-info$_i$ to the cloud, denying the permission.

5 Construction

A break-glass encryption scheme is defined by two procedures: the user's procedure, described in Figs. 3 and 4, and the cloud's procedure, described in Fig. 6. The cloud's procedure consists in interacting with the token $\mathcal{T}$, the token's algorithm is described in Fig. 5. We assume that the token behaves like the ideal token functionality $\mathcal{F}_{\mathsf{wrap}}$ [Kat07] (described in Fig. 10). However, for simplicity of notation we do not use the ideal functionality interface. Also, we assume that all communications are carried over authenticated channels.

In the following we describe user's procedures. $\mathcal{C}$'s procedure and $\mathcal{T}$'s procedure follow naturally.

5.1 User's Procedures

Procedure $\mathsf{Setup}(1^\lambda)$. $\mathcal{U}$'s procedure starts with a one-time initialization step when the token $\mathcal{T}$ is prepared. $\mathcal{U}$ generates a secret key k for the symmetric-key encryption scheme and keys for the signature scheme $(\mathsf{vk}_\mathcal{T}, \mathsf{ssk}_\mathcal{T})$. Key k is used to encrypt the data; the token uses this key to decrypt and re-encrypt the ciphertexts. Signing keys $(\mathsf{vk}_\mathcal{T}, \mathsf{ssk}_\mathcal{T})$ are used by the token to authenticate its outputs. Hence, the token is initialized with secret keys $(k, \mathsf{ssk}_\mathcal{T})$, the current time, and a parameter I denoting the window of time within which the ciphertext is considered valid. In this step, the user also register his alert address alert-info and the identity of the party she wants to authorize (i.e., $\mathcal{C}$) to the $\mathcal{G}_{\mathsf{perm}}$ functionality. Namely $\mathcal{U}$ sends $(\mathsf{register}, \mathsf{alert\text{-}info}, \mathcal{U}, \mathcal{C})$ to $\mathcal{G}_{\mathsf{perm}}$.

Procedure $\mathsf{Upload}()$. The second step for the user is to upload her data. We represent the data as a vector of l blocks (l can be very large). The user will encrypt each block, adding some bookkeeping information. The encryption of the i-th block will have the following format: $\mathsf{ctx}_i = \mathsf{Enc}_k(m_i||\mathsf{bookkeep}||\mathsf{perm})$ where:

- m_i is the message,
- $\mathsf{bookkeep} = [t_i, T_0, T_i]$ contains the bookkeeping information, keeping track of the time of last update, and time of break-glass operations. Specifically:
  - t_i is the time when ciphertext c_i was last updated. This time is used to defeat replay attacks.
  - T_0 is a global value (i.e., it is the same for all ciphertexts) and indicates the time when the first break-glass was performed. Adding this information allows the user to know that a break-glass has happened at least once (without needing to query the token).
  - T_i is the time when the i-th ciphertext was broken. This information allows fine-grained information about which ciphertexts have been compromised and when.
- $\mathsf{perm} = [\mathsf{alert\text{-}info}, \pi_{\mathsf{perm}}, pk, \sigma_\mathcal{C}]$ will contain the info about the break-glass permission (if any) generated by the cloud. This field is empty in normal circumstances. Specifically, $(\mathsf{alert\text{-}info}, \pi_{\mathsf{perm}})$ is the actual proof of permission obtained by the cloud – it can be empty if the cloud performs an illegitimate break-glass; pk is the public key used to encrypt the result of the decryption (when the break is legitimate, this ensures that only the client choosing pk will be able to decrypt the result of the decryption). Finally, $\sigma_\mathcal{C}$ is the signature computed by $\mathcal{C}$. This signature is necessary to hold the cloud accountable of invoking the break-glass procedure.

Procedure $\mathsf{Get}(i, k)$ is used to retrieve the i-th ciphertext. The cloud could refuse to send the ciphertext. If this happens, the user will consider this as a cheating behaviour and will accuse the cloud. The network data can be used as evidence that the cloud received the request but did not fulfill it[2]. If the cloud replies with ciphertext c_i, $\mathcal{U}$ will decrypt it and obtain bookkeeping information: $\mathsf{bookkeep} = [t_i, T_0, T_i]$ and permission information $\mathsf{perm} = (\mathsf{alert\text{-}info}, \pi_{\mathsf{perm}}, pk, \sigma_{\mathcal{C}})$.

$\mathcal{U}$ first checks the following:

1. Case 1. Stale Ciphertext. If $t_i < t - I$, this means that the ciphertext is not updated. Thus, the cloud replied with an older version of the ciphertext, perhaps to hide the fact that the updated ciphertext would have been marked with a information about an illegitimate break. A stale ciphertext triggers a red flag, and the user will use this communication and the network data as an evidence of cheating.
2. Case 2. Unauthorized break. If $T_0 \neq 0$ (recall that T_0 denotes the time the first break occurred) but the user never requested/approved a break-glass procedure then the user $\mathcal{U}$ will us the $\sigma_{\mathcal{C}}$ computed on a wrong or empty π_{perm} information, as a proof of cheating, and she invokes procedure $\mathsf{CloudCheating}(\mathsf{perm}, t)$. (Indeed, since the user did not approve any permission on $\mathcal{G}_{\mathsf{perm}}$ there exists no valid pair $(\mathsf{alert\text{-}info}, \pi_{\mathsf{perm}})$ that could justify the break-glass action performed by $\mathcal{C}$).
3. Case 3. Unauthorized break of i-th ciphertext. If $T_i \neq 0$ (recall that T_i denotes the time when ciphertext c_i was broken) but the user never asked to break ciphertext c_i, $\mathcal{U}$ proceeds as in Step 2.

Else, if none of the conditions above is satisfied, there were no illegitimate breaks, and the user simply outputs the decrypted plaintext m_i.

Procedure $\mathsf{Break}(i, \mathsf{alert\text{-}info})$. This procedure is invoked by *any party* who would like to break ciphertext c_i. A break-glass procedure starts with a party sending a request to the cloud $\mathcal{C}$. The request has the following info: $(\mathsf{break}, i, \mathsf{alert\text{-}info})$ (recall that $\mathsf{alert\text{-}info}$ is the address used to alert user $\mathcal{U}$). On receiving such request, the cloud $\mathcal{C}$ will send a request to $\mathcal{G}_{\mathsf{perm}}$ to obtain a proof of permission. Namely, $\mathcal{C}$ sends $(\mathsf{CreatePermission}, \mathsf{alert\text{-}info}, \mathcal{U})$ to $\mathcal{G}_{\mathsf{perm}}$.

The functionality $\mathcal{G}_{\mathsf{perm}}$ will then send an alert to the actual user $\mathcal{U}$ by sending $(\mathsf{permission\text{-}request}, \mathcal{C})$ to $\mathcal{U}$. At this point the user can entire compute a proof π to endorse/deny the request by sending $(\mathsf{ack\text{-}check}, (\mathsf{alert\text{-}info}, \mathcal{U}_i), yes/no, \pi)$ to $\mathcal{G}_{\mathsf{perm}}$; or she can not respond at all, triggering the generation of a "proof of silence" π_ϵ. The cloud will then obtain $(\mathtt{granted}, \pi_\epsilon)$ or $(\mathtt{granted}, \pi)$ in case the permission is granted, or (denied, π) in case the permission is denied. If granted, the cloud will use proof π_ϵ or π as input to the token T in the break procedure.

Below we provide a table for the notation used in the procedures.

[2] We do not formally cover this cheating case, as it requires formalization of the network interface, which is outside the scope of this work.

I	Maximum time between two updates
$T_{\mathsf{WaitPermission}}$	Time waited before providing a silence proof
T_0	Time when the first Break has been received by $\mathcal{T}$
T_i	Time when c_i was broken
bookkeep	contains t_i, T_0, T_i
perm	contains alert-info, $\pi_{\mathsf{perm}}, pk, \sigma_C$
alert-info	Used to notify a user of a break-glass request
π_{perm}	Equal to either π_ϵ or $\pi_{\mathcal{U}_i}$ or $\perp$
π_ϵ	Proof of silence

6 Security Proof

Theorem 1. *Assume* (KeyGen, Enc, Dec) *is an INT-CTXT NM CPA-secure encryption scheme (Definition in Fig. 9 [BN08]),* (PKGen, PKEnc, PKDec) *is a CPA-secure public key encryption scheme,* (GenSignKey, Sign, Verify) *is a EUF-CMA secure signature scheme; assume that all communications are carried over authenticated channels. Then the scheme described in Figs. 3, 4, 5 and 6 securely realize the $\mathcal{F}_{\mathsf{break}}$ functionality in the $(\mathcal{G}_{\mathsf{perm}}, \mathcal{G}_{\mathsf{clock}}, \mathcal{F}_{\mathsf{wrap}})$-hybrid model.*

6.1 Case Malicious Cloud

The proof consists in showing a PPT simulator Sim that generates the view of a malicious cloud $\mathcal{C}^*$ while only having access to $\mathcal{F}_{\mathsf{break}}$ (Fig. 1), and an indistinguishability proof that the transcript generated by the simulator is indistinguishable from the output generated by the cloud in the real world execution.

Simulator. Sim has blackbox access to $\mathcal{C}^*$ and interacts with $\mathcal{F}_{\mathsf{break}}$ in the ideal world. The ideal functionality $\mathcal{G}_{\mathsf{clock}}$ is used by both the environment and Sim to get the current time, and $\mathcal{G}_{\mathsf{perm}}$ is used to get/validate a permission to break-glass. The simulator also simulates the $\mathcal{F}_{\mathsf{wrap}}$ functionality to $\mathcal{C}^*$. Sim is described in Fig. 7.

Informally, the goal of the simulator is to (1) simulate the ciphertexts without knowing the messages uploaded by the user, and (2) to correctly intercept the break-glass requests coming from the malicious cloud (Sim obtains the legitimate break-glass procedure requests from $\mathcal{G}_{\mathsf{perm}}$ via the command (Permission, alert-info, π)). The ciphertexts are simulated as encryptions of 0. Due to the INT-CTXT NM CPA security property of the underlying encryption scheme, and the tamper-proof property of hardware tokens (modeled as an ideal blackbox by $\mathcal{F}_{\mathsf{wrap}}$) this difference cannot be detected by the malicious cloud. $\mathcal{G}_{\mathsf{perm}}$ guarantees that a permission cannot be fabricated on behalf of $\mathcal{U}_i$ (if $\mathcal{U}_i$ is honest), thus an illegitimate break-glass procedure can be detected by observing the queries made to the token that have an invalid perm-proof field.

User Procedures I

Cryptographic Primitive Used.
$\Pi = (\mathsf{KeyGen}, \mathsf{Enc}, \mathsf{Dec})$: INT-CTXT NM-CPA secure encryption scheme.
$\Sigma = (\mathsf{GenSignKey}, \mathsf{Sign}, \mathsf{Verify})$: a EUF-CMA digital signature scheme.

Parameters.
- I: denotes the frequency with which the ciphertexts need to be updated.
- $\mathsf{vpk}_\mathcal{C}$ is the public key of the cloud $\mathcal{C}$.
- alert-info: **public** alert info used for requesting permission via $\mathcal{G}_{\mathsf{perm}}$.

External Functionalities: $\mathcal{G}_{\mathsf{clock}}$ **and** $\mathcal{G}_{\mathsf{perm}}$.

Procedure $\mathsf{Setup}(1^\lambda)$

- Generate key for encryption of the data: $k \leftarrow \Pi.\mathsf{KeyGen}(1^\lambda)$;
- Generate signature keys for token: $(\mathsf{vk}_\mathcal{T}, \mathsf{ssk}_\mathcal{T}) \leftarrow \Sigma.\mathsf{GenSignKey}(1^\lambda)$.
- Initialize token $\mathcal{T}$ with encryption key k, signature key $\mathsf{ssk}_\mathcal{T}$, cloud's public key $\mathsf{vpk}_\mathcal{C}$, interval I and $\mathsf{mytime} := t$, where t is the current time from $\mathcal{G}_{\mathsf{clock}}$. $\mathcal{T}$'s procedure is described in Figure 5.
- Send $\mathcal{T}$ to the cloud $\mathcal{C}$, publish verification key $\mathsf{vk}_\mathcal{T}$ to a public repository $\mathcal{D}$.
- Register with $\mathcal{G}_{\mathsf{perm}}$: send $(\mathsf{register}, \mathsf{alert\text{-}info}, \mathcal{U}, \mathcal{C})$ to $\mathcal{G}_{\mathsf{perm}}$.

Procedure $\mathsf{Upload}(M)$

- Parse $M = (m_1, \ldots, m_l)$.
- Encrypt each block m_j: $\mathsf{ctx}_j = \mathsf{Enc}_k(m_j||\mathsf{bookkeep}||\mathsf{perm})$ for $j \in \{1, \ldots, l\}$, where $\mathsf{bookkeep} := [t, 0, 0]$ and $\mathsf{perm} = [\bot, \bot, \bot, \bot]$.
- Send $(\mathsf{ctx}_j)_{j\in[l]}$ to $\mathcal{C}$.

Procedure $\mathsf{Get}(i, k)$
Get current time *time* from $\mathcal{G}_{\mathsf{clock}}$.

- (Download ciphertext) Send command $\mathsf{Get}(i, time)$ to $\mathcal{C}$. If $\mathcal{C}$ does not respond, or responds with an invalid ciphertext then output $(\mathtt{refuse}, time)$ and halt.
- Else, let c_i be ciphertext received from $\mathcal{C}$ and let $(m||\mathsf{bookkeep}||\mathsf{perm}) := \mathsf{Dec}(k, c_i)$. Parse $\mathsf{bookkeep} = [t_i||T_0||T_i]$ and $\mathsf{perm} = (v_1, v_2, pk, \sigma_\mathcal{C})$, and perform the following checks.
  1. BAD CASES:
     - (Stale ciphertext) If $t_i < time - I$. This means that the ciphertext was not updated, and considered as potential cheating attempt without immediate proof, hence output $(\mathtt{refuse}, time)$.
     - (Unauthorized Break) . If $(T_0 \neq 0 \wedge \mathsf{Break}(\cdot, \mathsf{alert\text{-}info}))$ was never called before, OR if $(T_i \neq 0 \wedge \mathsf{Break}(i, \mathsf{alert\text{-}info}))$ was never called before, then:
       * If v_1, v_2 is not a valid permission, then set $x = (i, T_i, pk)$ and construct proof $\pi = (x, \sigma_\mathcal{C})$. Call procedure $\mathsf{CloudCheating}(\pi, time)$ (Described in Fig. 4).
       * If v_1, v_2 is a valid permission, then output "$\mathcal{G}_{\mathsf{perm}}$ $\mathtt{failure}$".
  2. GOOD CASE. (No illegitimate break) Else if $t_i \in [time \pm I]$ output m_i.

Fig. 3. User procedures 1

USER PROCEDURES II

Cryptographic Primitive Used.
$\Pi = (\mathsf{PKGen}, \mathsf{PKEnc}, \mathsf{PKDec})$: CPA-secure Public Key encryption scheme.

Procedure $\mathsf{Break}(i, \mathsf{alert\text{-}info})$

Get current time *time* from $\mathcal{G}_{\mathsf{clock}}$. Send $(\mathsf{CreatePermission}, \mathsf{alert\text{-}info}, \mathcal{U}_i)$ to $\mathcal{G}_{\mathsf{perm}}$. Set $\mathsf{T}_{\mathsf{break}} = time$. Then:

- Generate fresh keys $(pk', sk') \leftarrow \mathsf{PKGen}(1^\lambda)$.
- Send break-glass request. Send command $(\mathsf{break}, i, \mathcal{U}, \mathsf{alert\text{-}info}, pk')$ to $\mathcal{C}$. If $\mathcal{C}$ does not respond after more than $T_{\mathsf{WaitPermission}} + \delta$ steps then output $(\mathtt{refuse}, time)$.
- Check authenticity of the answer. Upon receiving $(c_{\mathsf{break}}, input, \sigma_C, \sigma_i)$ from $\mathcal{C}$. For $input = [T_i, \mathsf{alert\text{-}info}, \pi_{\mathsf{perm}}, pk'])$, let $x = (c_{\mathsf{break}}, input, \sigma_C)$. Check that $\mathsf{Verify}_{\mathsf{vk}_\mathcal{T}}(x, \sigma_i) = 1$ and $T_i = time$. If not, output $(\mathtt{refuse}, time)$. Else, recover $(m_i || \mathsf{bookkeep} || \mathsf{VerifyPerm}) \leftarrow \mathsf{PKDec}(sk', c_{\mathsf{break}})$ and proceeds with the checks as in Procedure $\mathsf{Get}(\cdot, \cdot)$.

Procedure $\mathsf{Update}(i, m', k)$

Get current time *time* from $\mathcal{G}_{\mathsf{clock}}$.

- Run $\mathsf{Get}(i, k)$. If the output is OK continue.
- Send the new ciphertext. Send $c_i' = \mathsf{Enc}_k(m' || \mathsf{bookkeep}' || \mathsf{perm}')$ to $\mathcal{C}$, where $\mathsf{bookkeep}' = (time || 0 || 0)$ and $\mathsf{perm}' = (\bot, \bot, \bot, \bot)$.

Procedure $\mathsf{CloudCheating}(\pi, time)$

Parse $\pi = (x, \sigma_C)$. If $\mathsf{Verify}(\mathsf{vpk}_C, x, \sigma_C) = 1$ Accuse $\mathcal{C}$ of cheating with proof $\pi, time$.

Interaction with $\mathcal{G}_{\mathsf{perm}}$

Upon receiving $(\mathsf{CreatePermission}, \mathsf{alert\text{-}info})$ from $\mathcal{G}_{\mathsf{perm}}$. Get current time *time* from $\mathcal{G}_{\mathsf{clock}}$. Let δ a time interval depending on the implementation of $\mathcal{G}_{\mathsf{perm}}$.

- If $time = \mathsf{T}_{\mathsf{break}} \pm \delta$, then endorse request and send $(\mathsf{ack\text{-}check}, (\mathsf{alert\text{-}info}, \mathcal{U}_i), YES)$ to $\mathcal{G}_{\mathsf{perm}}$.
- $time = \mathsf{T}_{\mathsf{break}} \pm \delta$ but secrets are lost do nothing.
- Else, deny the request: send $(\mathsf{ack\text{-}check}, (\mathsf{alert\text{-}info}, \mathcal{U}_i), NO)$ to $\mathcal{G}_{\mathsf{perm}}$.
- If $time \neq \mathsf{T}_{\mathsf{break}} \pm \delta$ but secrets are lost, then output: `Failure to Stop Illegitimate Request`.

Fig. 4. User procedures 2

Indistinguishability Proof. *Overview.* We start by outlining the differences between the view of $\mathcal{C}^*$ in the ideal world and in the real world. The view of $\mathcal{C}^*$ consists in the initial set of ciphertexts $(\mathsf{ctx}_i^0)_{i \in [l]}$, and the output computed by the token $\mathcal{T}$. The crucial differences between the views in the two worlds are:

- Encryptions. In the real world $\mathcal{C}^*$ will observe correct encryptions of messages of the form $(m || \mathsf{bookkeep} || \mathsf{perm})$. Instead, in the ideal world, the ciphertexts are only encryptions of 0. The indistinguishability of the two set of encryptions intuitively follows from the CPA security of the underlying encryption scheme.

TOKEN PROCEDURE $\mathcal{T}$

Hardwired Values. Encryption key k, signing key $\mathsf{ssk}_{\mathcal{T}}$.

Variables.
List of the last κ broken ciphertexts $\mathcal{L}$.
Current time mytime. Set $\sigma_{\mathcal{C}}^{0} = \epsilon$

On input:($\mathsf{CMD}, c, i, \mathsf{external\text{-}time}, \mathsf{perm}'$).

0. Check that i is not in the breaking list: If $i \in \mathcal{L}$ do nothing.

1. Check and Update time.
If $\mathsf{external\text{-}time} \leq \mathsf{mytime}$ output $\perp$ (The cloud is querying with a time that is too far in the past). Else, update current time: set $\mathsf{mytime} := \mathsf{external\text{-}time}$.

2. Decrypt.
Decrypt c using key k and obtain $(m||\mathsf{bookkeep}||\mathsf{perm})$. If decryption fails, do nothing. Let $\mathsf{bookkeep} = (t_i||T_0||T_i)$.

- (Already Broken) If $T_i \neq 0$ then halt and output $\perp$. (This ciphertext is already broken. No re-encryption required)
- (Stale) If $t_i < \mathsf{mytime} - I$ then halt and output $\perp$.
- (Error) If $t_i > \mathsf{mytime} + I$ then halt and output output "Error, someone encrypted under my key?" and stop.

3. Execute Command CMD**.**

Break If $\mathsf{CMD} = \mathtt{break}$.

0. Parse $\mathsf{perm}' = (\mathsf{alert\text{-}info}, \pi_{\mathsf{perm}}, pk, \sigma_{\mathcal{C}})$.
1. Checks: If $\mathsf{Verify}_{\mathsf{vpk}_{\mathcal{C}}}(i||\mathsf{external\text{-}time}||\mathsf{perm}', \sigma_{\mathcal{C}},) = 1$ continues. (Add i to the list of recently broken ciphertext). Unqueue $\mathcal{L}$, then add i to $\mathcal{L}$. Else, ignore the request.
2. Case: First Break. If $T_0 = 0$ then set $T_0 = \mathsf{mytime}$, set $\sigma_{\mathcal{C}}^{0} = \sigma_{\mathcal{C}}$.
3. Re-encrypt using the fresh key pk. $c_{\mathsf{break}} \leftarrow \mathsf{PKEnc}(pk, m_i, \mathsf{bookkeep})$.
4. Authenticate the break-info: $\sigma_{\mathcal{T}} = \mathsf{Sign}_{\mathsf{ssk}_{\mathcal{T}}}(c_{\mathsf{break}}, \mathsf{perm\text{-}proof}, \sigma_{\mathcal{C}})$.
5. Mark the i-th ciphertext as broken.
   (a) Update $\mathsf{bookkeep} = (\mathsf{mytime}, T_0, \mathsf{mytime})$.
   (b) Compute $c_i' = \mathsf{Enc}_k(c_{\mathsf{break}}, \mathsf{bookkeep}, \mathsf{perm}')$. (Note. This ciphertext will never be re-encrypted again).
6. Output $c_{\mathsf{break}}, \mathsf{perm\text{-}proof}, \sigma_{\mathcal{C}}, \sigma_{\mathcal{T}}, c_i'$.

Re-encryption. If $\mathsf{CMD} = \mathtt{Reencrypt}$.
Set $\mathsf{bookkeep} = (\mathsf{mytime}, T_0, 0)$. Set $\mathsf{perm} = (\perp, \perp, \perp, \sigma_{\mathcal{C}}^{0})$.
Output $c_i' = \mathsf{Enc}_k(m||\mathsf{bookkeep}||\mathsf{perm})$.

Fig. 5. The token procedure

- Token's functionality. In the real world, the token will accept any valid encryption provided in input. Namely, on input a ciphertext c, the token will first try to decrypt with its secret key, and if the decryption is successful will proceed with the necessary steps. Instead, in the ideal word, the simulated

CLOUD PROCEDURES

Parameters.
I: denotes the frequency with which the ciphertexts need to be updated.

Private Input. Signing key: $\mathsf{ssk}_{\mathcal{C}}$. **External Functionalities:** $\mathcal{G}_{\mathsf{clock}}$ **and** $\mathcal{G}_{\mathsf{perm}}$.

Setup for user $\mathcal{U}_i$.
Upon receiving $\mathcal{T}_{\mathcal{U}}, \mathsf{vk}_{\mathcal{T}}, (\mathsf{ctx}_i)_{i\in[l]}$ from user $\mathcal{U}$:

- Store ciphertexts $(\mathsf{ctx}_i)_{i\in[l]}$ and user's verification key $\mathsf{vk}_{\mathcal{T}}$.
- Activate Maintenance procedure for $\mathcal{U}$.

Procedure $\mathsf{Maintenance}(\mathsf{ctx}_i, \mathcal{T}_{\mathcal{U}}, \mathsf{vk}_{\mathcal{T}})$
Get *time* from $\mathcal{G}_{\mathsf{clock}}$.
Every I steps: query $\mathcal{T}(c_i, i, \mathtt{Reencrypt}, time, \perp)$ and obtain c_i^{new}. Replace $c_i := c_i^{new}$, $\forall i \in [l]$.

Answering User's requests.

- Get. Upon receiving $\mathsf{Get}(i, t)$. Get current time: $time \leftarrow \mathcal{G}_{\mathsf{clock}}(\mathsf{clockread})$. If $t \in [time \pm \delta]$ then reply with c_i.
- Break. Upon receiving $(\mathsf{break}, i, \mathcal{U}, \mathsf{alert\text{-}info}, pk')$.
  1. Send $(\mathsf{GetPermission}, \mathsf{alert\text{-}info}, \mathcal{U}, \mathcal{C})$ to $\mathcal{G}_{\mathsf{perm}}$. If $\mathcal{G}_{\mathsf{perm}}$ outputs $(\mathtt{granted}, \pi_{\mathsf{perm}})$. compute $\sigma_{\mathcal{C}} = \mathsf{Sign}_{\mathsf{ssk}_{\mathcal{C}}}(i, time, \mathsf{alert\text{-}info}, \pi_{\mathsf{perm}}, pk')$ (else, do nothing).
  2. Query token $\mathcal{T}(\mathsf{Break}, i, c_i, time, \mathsf{perm})$, where $\mathsf{perm}= (\mathsf{alert\text{-}info}, \pi_{\mathsf{perm}}, pk', \sigma_{\mathcal{C}})$ and forward the answer to $\mathcal{U}$.

Fig. 6. Cloud procedure

token accepts only encryptions that were computed by the simulator itself. In other words, if the cloud is able to compute a ciphertext that is valid in the real world and accepted by the real token, this ciphertext will not be accepted by the simulated token. Similarly, in the Get functionality, a real user would accept any valid ciphertext that $\mathcal{C}^*$ provides, instead the simulated user would abort if a valid ciphertext was not computed by the simulated token. The indistinguishability between the two worlds follows from the integrity ciphertext property INT-CTXT NM CPA security defined by Bellare and Namprempre in [BN08], which we report in Fig. 9.
- Break invocation. Recall, there are two types of break requests. The ones generated by the user, and the ones generated by the cloud. The simulator obtains the user requests directly from $\mathcal{F}_{\mathsf{break}}$, and will forward them to the adversary $\mathcal{C}^*$. The main task of the simulator however is to identify the break requests that are *initiated by the cloud.* Since the cloud must interact with the token in order to successfully decrypt a ciphertext[3] the simulator will

[3] To see why, note that, besides the access to the token, a cloud only has a list of ciphertexts. The output of the token is either a ciphertext, or a message m, but no other information about the secret key is given in output. Thus, if a cloud is able to decrypt a ciphertext, without calling the break command, this cloud is violating the CPA-security of the ciphertext.

Simulator Sim

Upload and Initialization. Upon receiving request ($\mathsf{uploaded}, \mathsf{sid}, l, \mathcal{U}$) from $\mathcal{F}_{\mathsf{break}}$ do:

- Generate key for encryption $k \leftarrow \Pi.\mathsf{KeyGen}(1^\lambda)$ and prepare ciphertexts: $[\mathsf{ctx}_1^0, \ldots, \mathsf{ctx}_l^0]$ where $\mathsf{ctx}_i^0 = \mathsf{Enc}_k(0^{p(\lambda)})$.
- Generate signature keys for token: $(\mathsf{vk}_\mathcal{T}, \mathsf{ssk}_\mathcal{T}) \leftarrow \Sigma.\mathsf{GenSignKey}(1^\lambda)$.
- Get the initial time from $\mathcal{G}_{\mathsf{clock}}$ and store it in variable $\mathtt{tkntime}$.
- Initialize matrices $L, \mathcal{L}_{\mathsf{sign}}, \mathcal{B}$. L stores the ciphertexts computed by Sim, $\mathcal{L}_{\mathsf{sign}}$ stores the signatures computed by $\mathsf{Sim}_\mathcal{T}$, $\mathcal{B}$ stores the ciphertexts that have been broken. We denote by $L[i] = (c_0^i, t_0), (c_1^i, t_1), \ldots$ the list of ciphertexts generated for the i-th element. At the beginning, $L[i] := [\mathsf{ctx}_i^0, \mathsf{tkntime}]$ $\mathcal{L}_{\mathsf{sign}}$ contains the signatures computed by the token.
- Send $\mathsf{vk}_\mathcal{T}, [\mathsf{ctx}_1^0, \ldots, \mathsf{ctx}_l^0]$ to $\mathcal{C}^*$.

Update. Upon receiving ($\mathsf{update}, \mathsf{sid}, i$) from $\mathcal{F}_{\mathsf{break}}$. Get current time: $time \leftarrow \mathcal{G}_{\mathsf{clock}}(\mathsf{clockread})$.
First, send $\mathsf{Get}(i, time)$ to $\mathcal{C}^*$. If no response is received then send ($\mathsf{ack\text{-}updated}, \mathsf{sid}, \mathcal{U}, NO$) to $\mathcal{F}_{\mathsf{break}}$. Else, let c_i' be the ciphertext received from $\mathcal{C}^*$. Analyse c_i' as follows:

- Bad Cases.
  1. (Case: Broken ciphertext) If $c_i' \in \mathcal{B}$ then do nothing.
  2. (Case: Wrong ciphertext) If $c_i' \notin L$ and decryption fails, then send ($\mathsf{ack\text{-}updated}, \mathsf{sid}, \mathcal{U}, NO$).
  3. (Case: Stale ciphertext) If there exists a pair $(c_i', t') \in L[i, t']$ but $t' < time - I$ then send ($\mathsf{ack\text{-}updated}, \mathsf{sid}, \mathcal{U}, NO$).
  4. (Failure Case: Good ciphertext not provided by the simulated token) If $c_i' \notin L$ and $\mathsf{Dec}(k, c_i') \neq \bot$ then output `Integrity Encryption Failure` and stop.
- Good cases. If there exists pair $(c_i', t) \in L$ s.t. $t' \in [time - I]$ then send ($\mathsf{ack\text{-}updated}, \mathsf{sid}, \mathcal{U}, yes$) to $\mathcal{F}_{\mathsf{break}}$. Then compute $c'' \leftarrow \mathsf{Enc}_k(0)$, add $(c'', time)$ to $L[i]$ and finally send the updated ciphertext c'' to $\mathcal{C}^*$.

User's Initiated Break Upon receiving ($\mathsf{Permission}, \mathsf{sid}, \mathsf{alert\text{-}info}, \pi, ans$) from $\mathcal{G}_{\mathsf{perm}}$. If $ans = no$, record π in a list of denied permissions $\mathsf{DeniedList}$. Else, if $ans = 1$ continue with the break-glass procedure as an honest user.

1. ($\mathsf{break}, \mathsf{sid}, i, \mathsf{perm\text{-}proof} = \pi, \mathsf{cheat\text{-}proof} = \bot$)
2. Get current time: $time \leftarrow \mathcal{G}_{\mathsf{clock}}(\mathsf{clockread})$. Store ($\mathsf{user\text{-}break}, time$).
3. Generate fresh keys $(pk', sk') \leftarrow \mathsf{PKGen}(1^\lambda)$.
4. Send ($\mathsf{break}, i, \mathsf{alert\text{-}info}, pk'$) to $\mathcal{C}^*$.
5. Upon receiving response ans from $\mathcal{C}^*$ do.
   - $\mathcal{C}^*$ **refuses to collaborate** If $ans = \bot$ then send ($\mathsf{ack\text{-}break}, \mathsf{sid}, \mathcal{U}, NO$) to $\mathcal{F}_{\mathsf{break}}$.
   - $\mathcal{C}^*$ **gives** (x, σ). Parse $x = (c_{\mathsf{break}}, c_i, \mathsf{external\text{-}time}, \mathsf{alert\text{-}info}, \pi, pk, \sigma_C)$.
     (a) Good signature. If $(x, \sigma) \in \mathcal{L}_{\mathsf{sign}}[\mathsf{external\text{-}time}]$ then send ($\mathsf{ack\text{-}break}, \mathsf{sid}, \mathcal{U}, yes$) to $\mathcal{F}_{\mathsf{break}}$
     (b) Forgery. If σ verifies on x, but $(x, \sigma) \notin \mathcal{L}_{\mathsf{sign}}[\mathsf{external\text{-}time}]$ then output `Forgery Failure` and halt.

Retrieve Upon receiving ($\mathsf{retrieve\text{-}request}, \mathsf{sid}, i, \mathcal{U}$) at time $time$, send ($\mathsf{Get}, i, time, \sigma_\mathcal{U}$) to $\mathcal{C}^*$.

- If $\mathcal{C}^*$ sends $\bot$ then send ($\mathsf{ack\text{-}retrieve}, \mathsf{sid}, i, \mathcal{U}, no$).
- Else, let c^* be the ciphertext sent by the cloud. Let $t \in [time - \delta, time + \delta]$.
  - If there exists $(c^*, t) \in L[i]$ then send ($\mathsf{ack} - \mathsf{inquire}, \mathsf{sid}, \mathcal{U}, yes$).
  - Else, send ($\mathsf{ack} - \mathsf{retrieve}, \mathsf{sid}, \mathcal{U}, no$) to $\mathcal{F}_{\mathsf{break}}$.

Fig. 7. Simulator

Token simulation $\mathsf{Sim}_{\mathcal{T}}$.
$\mathcal{B}$ stores the ciphertexts that have been broken.
On input ($\mathsf{CMD}, c, i, \mathsf{alert\text{-}info}, \mathsf{external\text{-}time}, \pi, \sigma_C$):
0. Check broken list If $c \in \mathcal{B}|_{|I|}$ then do nothing.
1. Check time and Ciphertext Validity. If $\mathsf{mytime} < \mathsf{external\text{-}time}$ then update $\mathsf{mytime} = \mathsf{external\text{-}time}$

1. (Stale Ciphertext) If $(c, j) \in L[i]$ but $j \notin [\mathsf{mytime} \pm I]$ then do nothing.
2. (Invalid iphertext c) If there is no $(c, j) \in L[i]$ do nothing.
3. (Forged Ciphertext) If there is no $(c, j) \in L[i]$ but $\mathsf{Dec}_k(c) \neq \perp$ then output `Integrity Encryption Failure` and halts.

Re-encryption If CMD =`Reencrypt`. Compute $c \leftarrow \mathsf{Enc}_k(0)$ and add $L[i] := [c, \mathsf{tkntime}]$. Output c.
Break CMD =`Break`. Verify signature σ_C on input $x = (\mathsf{alert\text{-}info}, \pi, break, i, pk, \mathsf{mytime})$. If check passes do:
1. Detect illegitimate request. If $\pi \neq \perp$ check if it is a legitimate permission by sending ($\mathsf{verify\text{-}permission}, \mathsf{alert\text{-}info}, \pi$) to $\mathcal{G}_{\mathsf{perm}}$. If $\mathcal{G}_{\mathsf{perm}}$ sends ($\mathsf{sid}, \mathsf{alert\text{-}info}, \mathsf{verifiably-denied}, \pi$) or ($\mathsf{sid}, \mathsf{alert\text{-}info}, \mathsf{notverified}, \pi$) then this is a marked as an illegitimate request.
2. Send illegitimate request to $\mathcal{F}_{\mathsf{break}}$. First, set $\mathsf{cheat\text{-}proof} = (\xi, \sigma_C)$ and send ($\mathsf{break}, \mathsf{sid}, i, \perp, \mathsf{cheat\text{-}proof}$) and receive m_i.
   (a) Add i to the list of broken ciphertexts: $\mathcal{B} \leftarrow \mathcal{B} \cup i$.
   (b) Set break time: Record $T_i = \mathsf{tkntime}$; (if $T_0 = 0$) Record $T_0 = \mathsf{tkntime}$, record $\sigma_C^0 = \sigma_C$.
   (c) Compute encryption. Set $c_i = \mathsf{Enc}_k(0^{p(n)})$, add $L[i] = (c_i, \mathsf{tkntime})$.
   (d) Compute token's signature. Set σ_i on input $(m_i||c_i||\mathsf{tkntime}||auth||\pi||\sigma_C)$ add $\sigma_i \mathcal{L}_{\mathsf{sign}}$.
   (e) Return (m_i, c_i) to $\mathcal{C}^*$
3. (Initiated by User.) Else, send ($\mathsf{ack\text{-}break}, \mathsf{sid}, \mathcal{U}, yes$) to $\mathcal{F}_{\mathsf{break}}$. Do steps as above, but instead of outputting m_i, output a dummy encryption $c^* = \mathsf{PKEnc}(pk, 0)$.

Fig. 8. Token simulator

use the simulated token to intercept requests that do not have a valid proof of permission and send them to the ideal functionality. Note that at this step, we are using security of $\mathcal{G}_{\mathsf{perm}}$. Namely, we are assuming that a cloud cannot fabricate a valid permission without the help of the user. If this was not the case the simulator could not use the absence of permission to detect illegitimate break-glass requests.

We will prove the above intuition via a sequence of hybrid games.

Hybrid Arguments Overview. We show the following sequence of hybrid experiments. Hybrid H_0 denotes the real world, in hybrid H_1 all ciphertexts generated by the user and the token are collected in a table, and the user's procedure and the token's procedure will accept only ciphertexts in this table (i.e., valid ciphertexts that are not part of this table are not accepted). Indistinguishability between H_0 and H_1 follows from the INT-CTXT NM CPA Security of the symmetric key encryption scheme. In H_2 and $\bar{H}_2$ we remove the semantic from all the encryptions and simply compute encryptions of 0. Indistinguishability between H_1 and H_2 follows from the CPA security of the underlying symmetric-key encryption scheme. Finally, in H_3 the user accepts only signatures generated by the simulated token, instead of accepting any valid signature. Indistinguishability between H_2 and H_3 follows from the unforgeability of the underlying signature scheme. We assume that all communications between cloud and token are authenticated.

Hybrid H_0. This is the real world experiment. Sim honestly follows the user procedure Figs. 3 and 4, and $\mathcal{T}$'s procedure (Fig. 5).

Hybrid H_1 (Integrity and Non-malleability). This experiment is as H_0 with the only difference that Sim stores the encryptions computed by the user and the token in a matrix L, and token and user accept only encryptions that are in L. If they receive any other encryption that is valid but it is not in L, then the simulated user/token will abort and output `Integrity Encryption Failure`. Note that H_0 and H_1 are different only in the case where $\mathcal{C}^*$ is able to find at a ciphertext c^* that is a valid encryption under secret key k, but it was not computed by the token/user.

In the following lemma we show that probability that $\mathcal{C}^*$ generates such a valid ciphertext is negligible, therefore H_0 and H_1 are computationally indistinguishable.

Lemma 1 (Ciphertext Integrity). *If* (KeyGen, Enc, Dec) *achieves integrity of ciphertext property (INT-CTX, Fig. 9) then event* `Integrity Encryption Failure` *happens with negligible probability.*

Towards a contradiction, assume that there exists a $\mathcal{C}^*$ such that `Integrity Encryption Failure` happens with non-negligible probability $p(\lambda)$. This means that $\mathcal{C}^*$ queried $\mathsf{Sim}_{\mathcal{T}}$ with a valid ciphertext c^* (i.e., a ciphertext that can be correctly decrypted but it was not compute neither by $\mathsf{Sim}_{\mathcal{T}}$ nor by the user). If this is the case, then we can construct an adversary $\mathcal{A}$ that wins the INT-CTXT game with the same probability, as follows.

Reduction INT-CTX Security. $\mathcal{A}$ playing in experiment $\mathsf{Exp}^{\mathsf{INT-CTX}}$ (Fig. 9), has access to encryption oracle and black-box access to $\mathcal{C}^*$. $\mathcal{A}$ simulates real world experiment to $\mathcal{C}^*$:

- (0) $\mathcal{A}$ plays as the honest user and therefore knows all the plaintexts $m_1, \ldots, m_l$.
- (1) Encryption. To generated ciphertexts on behalf of the token and the user, $\mathcal{A}$ uses its oracle access to Enc, provided by the experiment $\mathsf{Exp}^{\mathsf{INT-CTX}}$. $\mathcal{A}$ collects all the ciphertext generated, together with the plaintext used, in a matrix L'. (This matrix is different from the matrix used by the simulator in that the simulator does not need to remember the correspondent plaintexts).

– (2) Decryption. To decrypt a ciphertexts c provided by the cloud, $\mathcal{A}$ will first check if the ciphertexts are contained in the matrix L'. If $c \notin L'$ then $\mathcal{A}$ will call $\mathsf{VF}(c)$ in $\mathsf{Exp}^{\mathsf{INT-CTX}}$ and obtain answer m. If $m \neq \perp$ then $\mathcal{A}$ wins the game and halts. Else, if $m = \perp$, $\mathcal{A}$ simply continues the reduction, following the honest user and token procedure.

Analysis. Note that $\mathcal{A}$ follows the honest user's procedure and honest token's procedure just like in the H_0. $\mathcal{A}$ will interrupt the reduction and deviate from H_0, only if the cloud provides a ciphertext c that is accepted $VF(c)$ in which case $\mathcal{A}$ simply halts, just like the simulator in H_1. Thus the probability that $\mathcal{A}$ wins the game and halts the reduction, it is closely related to the probability that there is a difference between H_0 and H_1. Since the underlying encryption scheme is assumed to be INT-CTX secure, the probability of $\mathcal{A}$ winning is negligible, consequently, the distributions of transcripts in H_0 and H_1 are distinguishable with negligible probability.

Due to Lemma 1, it follows that probability that $\mathcal{C}^*$ generates such a valid ciphertext is negligible, therefore H_0 and H_1 are computationally indistinguishable.

Hybrid H_2^j $j = 1, \dots$ (CPA-security). In this sequence of hybrid experiments we change the value encrypted in the j-th ciphertext. Instead of encrypting the actual information $(m||\mathsf{bookkeep}||\mathsf{perm})$ we will encrypt to 0 (but for the sake of the simulation we will still keep record of the plaintexts that should be instead encrypted.) The difference between H_2^j and H_1^{j-1} is that in H_2^j one more ciphertext is computed as encryption of 0. Assume that there is a distinguisher between the two experiments, we will construct an adversary for CPA-security.

Hybrid $\bar{H}_2^j$ for $j = 1, \dots$ (PK CPA-security). In this sequence of hybrid we replace the encryptions output by the token after a user-triggered break-glass encryption (i.e., c_{break}). Instead of encrypting the actual message m_i, it will encrypt 0. This sequence of hybrid is indistinguishable to the CPA-security of the public key encryption scheme.

Hybrid H_3 (Unforgeability of Token's signature). In this hybrid, the procedure of the simulated user is modified as follows. The simulator (playing as user) accepts only signatures that are in $\mathcal{L}_{\mathsf{sign}}$. When a signature (x^*, σ^*) verifies under $\mathsf{vk}_\mathcal{T}$ but $\sigma^* \notin \mathcal{L}_{\mathsf{sign}}$ then the simulated user will output `Forgery Failure` and abort. Therefore, the difference between H_2 and H_3 is that in H_2 a user would accept any signature σ^* that verifies under $\mathsf{vk}_\mathcal{T}$ (i.e., $\mathsf{Verify}(\mathsf{vk}_\mathcal{T}, x^*, \sigma^*)$), instead in H_3, when a valid signature $\sigma^* \notin \mathcal{L}_{\mathsf{sign}}$ is presented by $\mathcal{C}^*$, the user will abort.

The following lemma shows that the probability that $\mathcal{C}^*$ can compute such a signature is negligible due to the unforgeability of the underlying signature scheme.

Lemma 2. *If* (GenSignKey, Sign, Verify) *is a EUF-CMA digital signature scheme, then event* `Forgery Failure` *happens with negligible probability.*

Assume, towards a contradiction, that there exists an adversary $\mathcal{C}^*$ that is able to generate a signature valid σ^* that was not generated by $\mathsf{Sim}_{\mathcal{T}}$ with probability $p(\lambda)$. Thus, we can construct an adversary $\mathcal{A}$ that computes a forgery with the same probability as follows.

Reduction EUF-CMA Security

$\mathcal{A}$ playing in experiment $\mathsf{Exp}^{\mathsf{forge}}$, has oracle access to $\mathcal{C}^*$ and simulates experiment H_2 to $\mathcal{C}^*$ with the following difference:

1. Token Signatures. When the token is required to compute a signature on a message x, $\mathcal{A}$ will forward x to $\mathsf{Exp}^{\mathsf{forge}}$ and obtain signature σ. Add σ to the list $\mathcal{L}_{\mathsf{sign}}$ and set it as the output of the token.
2. Decision. Upon receiving a signature (x^*, σ^*) from $\mathcal{C}^*$, such that $\sigma^* \notin \mathcal{L}_{\mathsf{sign}}$. If (x^*, σ^*) verifies then send σ^* to $\mathsf{Exp}^{\mathsf{forge}}$ and output win.

Analysis. $\mathcal{A}$ wins the forgery game $\mathsf{Exp}^{\mathsf{forge}}$ with the same probability that $\mathcal{C}^*$ computes a valid σ^* and trigger event `Forgery Failure`. Since by assumption the underlying signature scheme is EUF-CMA secure, then probability that $\mathcal{A}$ trigger the above event is negligible.

6.2 Exculpability in Presence of a Malicious User

In the ideal functionality a user obtains a proof to accuse a cloud only if the cloud actually invoked a break command without permission granted from $\mathcal{G}_{\mathsf{perm}}$. In the ideal world there is nothing that the user can do to trigger an accusation against an honest cloud (without violating $\mathcal{G}_{\mathsf{perm}}$).

Instead in the real world, there are several ways the user could accuse an honest cloud. We divide them in four categories: network attack, permission attack, token attack and forgery attack, which we describe below. We show that three of them can be quickly ruled out by definition, while the implausibility of the fourth one can be ruled out by unforgeability property of the underlying signature scheme.

1. Network Attack. A malicious user could accuse the cloud of not responding. This accusation can be challenged by the cloud by having access to logs on the network traffic that guarantees that a correct answer was correctly and timely delivered to the user.
2. Permission Attack. A malicious user could trigger a break-glass procedure, and then accuse the cloud of having fabricated such permission. Since our protocol works in the $\mathcal{G}_{\mathsf{perm}}$-hybrid model, we assume that the procedure for granting permission cannot be counterfeit by anyone.
3. Token Attack. A malicious user could accuse the cloud of not correctly updating the ciphertext. We note however that accusation is not possible since we assume that the token is trusted and will follow the honest procedure. Thus, the cloud will be able to show updated ciphertexts as a proof of honest behaviour.

4. Forgery Attack. A user could accuse an honest cloud by fabricating a valid signature σ that verifies under $\mathsf{vpk}_{\mathcal{C}}$, on a message that contains the word `break` but does not contain any valid authorization received by $\mathcal{G}_{\mathsf{perm}}$. Let us call this event `Sign Forgery Accusation`. We show in Lemma 3 that this events happen with negligible probability.

Permission attack and Token attack are ruled out, since we are assuming to work in the $\mathcal{G}_{\mathsf{perm}}$-hybrid model, and we assume that the token is trusted. For network attacks, we also implicitly assume that there is a way for the cloud to prove that the messages were timely delivered to the user.

Lemma 3. *If* (GenSignKey, Sign, Verify) *is a EUF-CMA digital signature scheme, then event* `Sign Forgery Accusation` *happens with negligible probability.*

Assume, towards a contradiction, that there exists a malicious user $\mathcal{U}^*$ that is able to accuse $\mathcal{C}$ by generating a valid signature σ^* that was not generated by $\mathcal{C}$ with probability $p(\lambda)$. Thus, we can construct an adversary $\mathcal{A}$ that computes a forgery with the same probability as follows.

Reduction EUF-CMA Security

$\mathcal{A}$ playing in experiment $\mathsf{Exp}^{\mathsf{forge}}$, has oracle access to $\mathcal{U}^*$ and simulate the cloud to $\mathcal{U}^*$.

1. Protocol Execution. $\mathcal{A}$ receives the token from $\mathcal{U}^*$ and fulfills all the requests received by $\mathcal{U}^*$ by simply following the honest cloud procedure and using the Signature oracle provided by $\mathsf{Exp}^{\mathsf{forge}}$.
2. Accuse. When $\mathcal{U}^*$ sends an accusation on input $\pi = (x, \sigma^*)$, if $\mathsf{Verify}(\mathsf{vpk}_{\mathcal{C}}, x, \sigma^*) = 1$ send π to $\mathsf{Exp}^{\mathsf{forge}}$ and output 1.

Analysis. Since by assumption the underlying signature scheme is EUF-CMA secure, probability of event `Sign Forgery Accusation` is negligible.

Acknowledgments. We thank Laurie Williams for the initial discussion on break-glass encryption, as well as many other insightful conversations. We also thank the anonymous reviewers for their useful comments.

A Additional Security Definitions

Ciphertext Integrity INT-CTX [BN08]. The definition of Cipher Integrity INT-CTX, introduced by Bellare et al. in [BN08] is described in Fig. 9.
Ideal Functionality $\mathcal{F}_{\mathsf{wrap}}$. For completeness we report the ideal $\mathcal{F}_{\mathsf{wrap}}$ functionality in Fig. 10.

INT-CTX NM Experiment
Proc Initialize
$K \xleftarrow{\$} \mathsf{Gen}(1^\lambda)$, $S \leftarrow \emptyset$.
Proc Enc (M)
$C \xleftarrow{\$} \mathsf{Enc}_K(M)$. $S \leftarrow S \cup \{C\}$.
Proc VF(C)
$M \leftarrow \mathsf{Dec}_K(C)$.
If $M \neq \bot$ and $C \notin S$ win $\leftarrow$ true.
Return $M \neq \bot$.
Proc Finalize
Return win

Fig. 9. INT-CTX game [BN08]

Ideal Functionality $\mathcal{F}_{\mathsf{wrap}}$.
The functionality is parameterized by a polynomial $p(\cdot)$ and an implicit security parameter λ.

Create: Upon receiving an input (create, sid, C, U, M) from a party C (i.e., the token creator), where U is another party (i.e., the token user) and M is an interactive Turing machine, do: If there is no tuple of the form $\langle C, U, \star, \star, \star\rangle$ stored, store $\langle C, U, M, 0, \emptyset, \rangle$. Send $(create, \langle sid, C, U\rangle)$ to the adversary.

Deliver: Upon receiving (READY, $\langle sid, C, U\rangle$) from the adversary, send (READY, $\langle \mathsf{sid}, C, U\rangle$) to U.

Execute: Upon receiving an input (RUN, $\langle \mathsf{sid}, C, U\rangle, msg$) from U, find the unique stored tuple $\langle C, U, M, i, \mathsf{state}\rangle$. If no such tuple exists, do nothing. Otherwise, do: If M has never been used yet (i.e.,$i = 0$), then choose uniform $\omega \in \{0,1\}^{p(\lambda)}$ and set $\mathsf{state} := \omega$. Run $(\mathsf{out}, \mathsf{state}') := M(msg; \mathsf{state})$ for at most $p(\lambda)$ steps where out is the response and state' is the new state of M (set $\mathsf{out} := \bot$ and $\mathsf{state}' := \mathsf{state}$ if M does not respond in the allotted time). Send (RESPONSE,$\langle \mathsf{sid}, C, U\rangle, \mathsf{out}$) to U. Erase $\langle C, U, M, i, \mathsf{state}\rangle$ and store $\langle C, U, M, i+1, \mathsf{state}'\rangle$.

Fig. 10. $\mathcal{F}_{\mathsf{wrap}}$ functionality [Kat07]

References

[ABG+13] Ananth, P., Boneh, D., Garg, S., Sahai, A., Zhandry, M.: Differing-inputs obfuscation and applications. IACR Cryptology ePrint Archive 2013, p. 689 (2013)

[AL07] Aumann, Y., Lindell, Y.: Security against covert adversaries: efficient protocols for realistic adversaries. In: Vadhan, S.P. (ed.) TCC 2007. LNCS, vol. 4392, pp. 137–156. Springer, Heidelberg (2007). https://doi.org/10.1007/978-3-540-70936-7_8

[BCP14] Boyle, E., Chung, K.-M., Pass, R.: On extractability obfuscation. In: Lindell, Y. (ed.) TCC 2014. LNCS, vol. 8349, pp. 52–73. Springer, Heidelberg (2014). https://doi.org/10.1007/978-3-642-54242-8_3

[BGJ+16] Bitansky, N., Goldwasser, S., Jain, A., Paneth, O., Vaikuntanathan, V., Waters, B.: Time-lock puzzles from randomized encodings. In: Proceedings of the 2016 ACM Conference on Innovations in Theoretical Computer Science, Cambridge, MA, USA, 14–16 January 2016, pp. 345–356 (2016)

[BM09] Barak, B., Mahmoody-Ghidary, M.: Merkle puzzles are optimal—an $O(n^2)$-query attack on any key exchange from a random oracle. In: Halevi, S. (ed.) CRYPTO 2009. LNCS, vol. 5677, pp. 374–390. Springer, Heidelberg (2009). https://doi.org/10.1007/978-3-642-03356-8_22

[BM17] Barak, B., Mahmoody-Ghidary, M.: Merkle's key agreement protocol is optimal: an $o(n^2)$ attack on any key agreement from random oracles. J. Cryptol. **30**(3), 699–734 (2017)

[BMTZ17] Badertscher, C., Maurer, U., Tschudi, D., Zikas, V.: Bitcoin as a transaction ledger: a composable treatment. In: Katz, J., Shacham, H. (eds.) CRYPTO 2017. LNCS, vol. 10401, pp. 324–356. Springer, Cham (2017). https://doi.org/10.1007/978-3-319-63688-7_11

[BN00] Boneh, D., Naor, M.: Timed commitments. In: Bellare, M. (ed.) CRYPTO 2000. LNCS, vol. 1880, pp. 236–254. Springer, Heidelberg (2000). https://doi.org/10.1007/3-540-44598-6_15

[BN08] Bellare, M., Namprempre, C.: Authenticated encryption: relations among notions and analysis of the generic composition paradigm. J. Cryptol. **21**(4), 469–491 (2008)

[Can04] Canetti, R.: Universally composable signature, certification, and authentication. In: 17th IEEE Computer Security Foundations Workshop (CSFW-17 2004), Pacific Grove, CA, USA, 28–30 June 2004, p. 219 (2004)

[CGLZ18] Chung, K.-M., Georgiou, M., Lai, C.-Y., Zikas, V.: Cryptography with dispensable backdoors. IACR Cryptology ePrint Archive 2018, p. 352 (2018)

[CHMV17] Canetti, R., Hogan, K., Malhotra, A., Varia, M.: A universally composable treatment of network time. In: 30th IEEE Computer Security Foundations Symposium, CSF 2017, pp. 360–375 (2017)

[GG17] Goyal, R., Goyal, V.: Overcoming cryptographic impossibility results using blockchains. In: Kalai, Y., Reyzin, L. (eds.) TCC 2017. LNCS, vol. 10677, pp. 529–561. Springer, Cham (2017). https://doi.org/10.1007/978-3-319-70500-2_18

[GGH+13] Garg, S., Gentry, C., Halevi, S., Raykova, M., Sahai, A., Waters, B.: Candidate indistinguishability obfuscation and functional encryption for all circuits. In: 54th Annual IEEE Symposium on Foundations of Computer Science, FOCS 2013, Berkeley, CA, USA, 26–29 October, pp. 40–49 (2013)

[GGHW17] Garg, S., Gentry, C., Halevi, S., Wichs, D.: On the implausibility of differing-inputs obfuscation and extractable witness encryption with auxiliary input. Algorithmica **79**(4), 1353–1373 (2017)

[GKP+13] Goldwasser, S., Kalai, Y.T., Popa, R.A., Vaikuntanathan, V., Zeldovich, N.: How to run turing machines on encrypted data. In: Canetti, R., Garay, J.A. (eds.) CRYPTO 2013. LNCS, vol. 8043, pp. 536–553. Springer, Heidelberg (2013). https://doi.org/10.1007/978-3-642-40084-1_30

[GKR08] Goldwasser, S., Kalai, Y.T., Rothblum, G.N.: One-time programs. In: Wagner, D. (ed.) CRYPTO 2008. LNCS, vol. 5157, pp. 39–56. Springer, Heidelberg (2008). https://doi.org/10.1007/978-3-540-85174-5_3

[GM84] Goldwasser, S., Micali, S.: Probabilistic encryption. J. Comput. Syst. Sci. **28**(2), 270–299 (1984)

[Gol04] Goldreich, O.: The Foundations of Cryptography: Basic Applications, vol. 2. Cambridge University Press, Cambridge (2004)

[HL10] Hazay, C., Lindell, Y.: Efficient Secure Two-Party Protocols: Techniques and Constructions. ISC. Springer, Heidelberg (2010). https://doi.org/10.1007/978-3-642-14303-8

[Jag15] Jager, T.: How to build time-lock encryption. IACR Cryptology ePrint Archive 2015, p. 478 (2015)

[Kat07] Katz, J.: Universally composable multi-party computation using tamper-proof hardware. In: Naor, M. (ed.) EUROCRYPT 2007. LNCS, vol. 4515, pp. 115–128. Springer, Heidelberg (2007). https://doi.org/10.1007/978-3-540-72540-4_7

[KMG17] Kaptchuk, G., Miers, I., Green, M.: Managing secrets with consensus networks: fairness, ransomware and access control. IACR Cryptology ePrint Archive 2017, p. 201 (2017)

[LKW15] Liu, J., Kakvi, S.A., Warinschi, B.: Extractable witness encryption and timed-release encryption from bitcoin. IACR Cryptology ePrint Archive 2015, p. 482 (2015)

[LPS17] Lin, H., Pass, R., Soni, P.: Two-round concurrent non-malleable commitment from time-lock puzzles. IACR Cryptology ePrint Archive 2017, p. 273 (2017)

[MG16] Malhotra, A., Goldberg, S.: Attacking NTP's authenticated broadcast mode. Comput. Commun. Rev. **46**(2), 12–17 (2016)

[MGV+17] Malhotra, A., Van Gundy, M., Varia, M., Kennedy, H., Gardner, J., Goldberg, S.: The security of NTP's datagram protocol. In: Kiayias, A. (ed.) FC 2017. LNCS, vol. 10322, pp. 405–423. Springer, Cham (2017). https://doi.org/10.1007/978-3-319-70972-7_23

[MMBK] Mills, D., Martin, J., Burbank, J., Kasch, W.: RFC 5905: network time protocol version 4: protocol and algorithms specification. Internet Engineering Task Force (IETF). http://tools.ietf.org/html/rfc5905

Registration-Based Encryption from Standard Assumptions

Sanjam Garg[1(✉)], Mohammad Hajiabadi[1,2], Mohammad Mahmoody[2], Ahmadreza Rahimi[2], and Sruthi Sekar[3]

[1] Berkeley, USA
{sanjamg,mdhajiabadi}@berkeley.edu

[2] University of Virginia, Charlottesville, USA
{mohammad,ahmadreza}@virginia.edu

[3] Indian Institute of Science, Bangalore, Bangalore, India
sruthisekar@iisc.ac.in

Abstract. The notion of *Registration-Based Encryption* (RBE) was recently introduced by Garg, Hajiabadi, Mahmoody, and Rahimi [TCC'18] with the goal of removing the private-key generator (PKG) from IBE. Specifically, RBE allows encrypting to identities using a (compact) master public key, like how IBE is used, with the benefit that the PKG is substituted with a weaker entity called "key curator" who has no knowledge of any secret keys. Here individuals generate their secret keys on their own and then publicly *register* their identities and their corresponding public keys to the key curator. Finally, individuals obtain "rare" decryption-key updates from the key curator as the population grows. In their work, they gave a construction of RBE schemes based on the combination of indistinguishability obfuscation and somewhere statistically binding hash functions. However, they left open the problem of constructing RBE schemes based on standard assumptions.

In this work, we resolve the above problem and construct RBE schemes based on standard assumptions (e.g., CDH or LWE). Furthermore, we show a new application of RBE in a novel context. In particular, we show that anonymous variants of RBE (which we also construct under standard assumptions) can be used for realizing abstracts forms of anonymous messaging tasks in simple scenarios in which the parties communicate by writing messages on a shared board in a synchronized way.

S. Garg—Research supported in part from DARPA/ARL SAFEWARE Award W911NF15C0210, AFOSR Award FA9550-15-1-0274, AFOSR YIP Award, DARPA and SPAWAR under contract N66001-15-C-4065, a Hellman Award and research grants by the Okawa Foundation, Visa Inc., and Center for Long-Term Cybersecurity (CLTC, UC Berkeley). The views expressed are those of the author and do not reflect the official policy or position of the funding agencies.

M. Hajiabadi—Supported by NSF award CCF-1350939 and AFOSR Award FA9550-15-1-0274.

M. Mahmoody—Supported by NSF CAREER award CCF-1350939, and two University of Virginia's SEAS Research Innovation Awards.

A. Rahimi—Supported by NSF award CCF-1350939.

D. Lin and K. Sako (Eds.): PKC 2019, LNCS 11443, pp. 63–93, 2019.
https://doi.org/10.1007/978-3-030-17259-6_3

1 Introduction

Identity based encryption, first introduced by Shamir [31], and then realized based on pairings by Boneh and Franklin [7], allows a set of remote parties to communicate secretly by only knowing one single public key and the name of the recipient identity. Despite being a milestone in foundations of cryptography and a powerful tool for simplifying key-management, real-world uses of IBE schemes come with a major caveat: IBE schemes require a *private-key generator* (PKG) who holds the master key and uses it to generate decryption keys for the identities. Therefore, the PKG has the ability to decrypt all cipherexts. This issue, inherent to IBE by design, is known as the *key escrow* problem.

Many previous works tried to rectify the key escrow problem in IBE. These efforts include making the trust de-centralized using multiple PKGs [7], making the PKG *accountable* for distributing the decryption keys to unauthorized users [23,24], making it hard for PKG to find out the receiver identity in a large set of identities [12,14,33], or using Certificateless Public Key Cryptography [1] as a hybrid of IBE and public-key directories. However, none of these efforts resolve the key escrow problem completely. The issue of key escrow was also discussed in [11] in depth and resolving this was left as a major open problem with no good solutions.

Motivated by entirely removing PKGs from IBE schemes, recently Garg, Hajiabadi, Mahmoody, and Rahimi [22] introduced the notion of *registration-based encryption* (RBE for short). In an RBE scheme, the PKG entity is substituted by a much weaker entity called the *key curator* (KC for short). The KC will not posses any secret keys, and all it does is to manage the set of public keys of the *registered* identities. More specifically, in an RBE scheme identities (or, rather the users corresponding to the identities) generate their own public and secret keys, and then they will register their public keys to the KC who maintains and updates a public parameter pp_n where n is the number of parties who have joined the system so far. This public parameter pp_n can be used (now and in the future) to encrypt messages to any of the n identities who have registered so far. The first key efficiency requirement of RBE schemes is that pp_n is *compact*; i.e., $\text{poly}(\kappa, \log n)$ in size where κ is the security parameter. Moreover, RBE requires that the process of "identity registration" is also efficient; i.e., runs in time $\text{poly}(\kappa, \log n)$. In order to connect an updated public parameter pp_n to the previously registered identities, RBE allows the identities to obtain *updates* from the KC, which (together with their own secret keys) can be used as decryption keys. The second efficiency requirement of RBE is that such updates are only needed at most $O(\log n)$ times over the lifetime of the system. In summary, RBE schemes are required to perform both "identity registration" and "update generation" in time *sublinear* in n. In particular, these two operations are required to run in time $\text{poly}(\kappa, \log n)$ where κ is the security parameter.

The work of [22] showed how to construct RBE schemes based on the combination of indistinguishability obfuscation (IO) [3,21] and somewhere statistically binding hash functions (SSBH) [25]. Towards the goal of basing RBE schemes on more standard assumptions, [22] also showed how to construct *weakly effi-*

cient RBE schemes with poly(κ, n) identity registration time based on standard assumptions such as CDH and LWE. The work of [22] left open the question of constructing RBE schemes (with the required registration time poly($\kappa, \log n$)) from standard cryptographic assumptions. This gap leads us to the following question, which is the main question studied in this work:

> *Can we base registration-based encryption on standard cryptographic assumptions?*

Our results. In this work, we resolve the above question affirmatively. Namely, as the main result of this work, we construct RBE schemes with all the required compactness and efficiency requirements based on standard assumptions such as LWE, CDH, or Factoring. In particular, in our RBE scheme (based on CDH or LWE assumptions) the time it takes to register any new identity into the system is only poly($\kappa, \log n$) where κ is the security parameter and n is the number of identities registered into the system so far.

In addition to resolving the question above, in this work we show the usefulness of RBE by demonstrating a connection between an *anonymous* variant of RBE (defined similarly to how anonymous IBE [6] is defined) to an abstract anonymous messaging primitive that we call *anonymous board communication* (ABC for short). At a high level, (anonymous) IBE fails to achieve ABC, exactly because of the key escrow problem, which does not exist in RBE.

1.1 Technical Overview

In this subsection, we will first describe the high level ideas behind our RBE scheme based on standard assumptions. We will then describe how to add the extra property of anonymity to RBE, allowing it to be used for realizing ABC as described above.

Figure 1 shows the high level structure and the roadmap of the primitives that we use (and construct along the way) for achieving RBE from standard assumptions. The features in parentheses (i.e., "blind" and "anonymous") can be added to or removed from the figure. When they are added, Fig. 1 demonstrates the way we obtain *anonymous* RBE.

The big picture. We construct our RBE scheme based on the primitive *hash garbling* which was formally defined in [22] but was used implicitly in some prior works [10,13,19,20], and a new primitive "time-stamp" RBE (T-RBE for short) that we introduce in this work. T-RBE is a special case of RBE, where we use the time-stamp t_{id} of the registration time of each identity instead of their (arbitrary string identity) id. T-RBE also requires the same efficiency and compactness requirements of RBE. Since T-RBE is a special case of RBE, achieving T-RBE from standard assumptions is potentially easier; we leverage this in our approach.

In particular, as depicted in Fig. 1, we first show how T-RBE can be constructed from public-key encryption and hash garbling schemes. Then, having T-RBE, hash garbling, and a red-black Merkle tree we show how to construct an

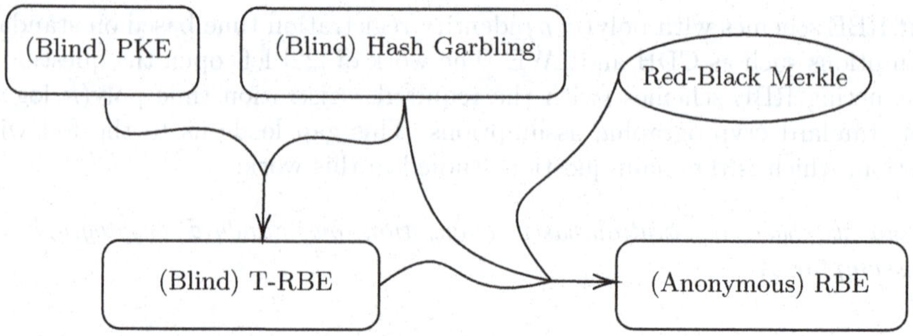

Fig. 1. Roadmap

RBE scheme. This resolves the open question of [22] where they obtained *weakly* efficient RBE schemes. Finally, we show that by substituting each of the used primitives with a "blind" version of them as defined in [10] we can bootstrap our new RBE construction to make it anonymous. Below, we describe each of these steps, their corresponding challenges, and how we resolve them.

The weakly efficient RBE of [22]**.** Before describing our RBE construction, we describe the main challenge in achieving the required registration efficiency, which made the construction of [22] (based on standard assumptions) *weakly efficient.* For that, we need to quickly recall the high level structure of the (weakly-efficient) construction of [22]. At a high level, the registration algorithm in the construction of [22] leads to an auxiliary information stored at the KC that consists of some Merkle trees $\mathsf{Tree}_1, \ldots, \mathsf{Tree}_\eta$ where each of these trees in their leaves contains the ids of the already registered identities, along with their public keys pk. The encryption algorithm of this scheme requires to use the public key corresponding to the specific identity to encrypt the message. To do so, it requires to do a binary search on the tree containing the id (so as to access the corresponding public key), for which it is required that the leaves of the trees are *sorted* according to their labels (i.e., identities) from left to right. This binary search was captured by generation of a sequence of garbled circuits. Now, going back to the registration algorithm, if the execution of the registration algorithm ever leads to two trees with the same size, those two will be merged into one tree, which *again* needs to have the identities sorted. (Merging the trees is necessary to keep the public parameter compact, because the public parameter is basically the concatenation of the roots of theses trees, and so the number of trees shall remain bounded.) Hence, every time a tree merge operation is done in their registration process, the entire tree needs to be restructured based on the *newly sorted* list of the identities in the two trees. This very sorting made the construction of [22] weakly efficient.

Step one: weakening the functionality for sake of efficiency. To overcome the challenge of achieving the required efficiency for RBE, in this work we first introduce a new primitive that we call T-RBE (short form of *time-stamp* RBE) that weakens RBE for the sake of achieving efficient registration. (Looking ahead, we will later bootstrap T-RBE to RBE.) This new primitive has the same functionality as RBE, except that in a T-RBE, the identities do not register with their actual ids, but rather with the corresponding time-stamps of their registration moments. This has the immediate obvious effect that the time-stamp strings already arrive in sorted order, hence removing the need of re-structuring the trees for sorting purposes. Note that since time-stamps are taking the role of the identities, all the algorithms (including the encryption) shall use the time-stamp as the identity's label (instead of the id).

We now describe how T-RBE can indeed overcome the efficiency challenge left open about RBE. Notice that the time-stamps used for registrations are already sorted based on the arrival times. One useful consequence of this phenomenon is that, if we apply the same approach of [22] for weakly-efficient RBE, the resulting T-RBE will have leaves of the trees *automatically sorted* at all times. Hence, when we want to merge two trees, we may simply hash their roots into a new root, with a guarantee that all the leaves in one sub-tree will be larger than all those in the other sub-tree. Hence, by restricting the problem to T-RBE, we would not require to restructure the trees when we merge them. Hence, the T-RBE registration overcomes the main reason for inefficiency in the RBE construction of [22] and turns out to be efficient as required. The other algorithms of the T-RBE scheme are also similar to the corresponding algorithms of the RBE in [22], with some natural changes.

Step two: bootstrapping T-RBE to RBE (using Red-Black Merkle Tree). Recall that T-RBE uses the *time-stamps* of the identities as if they were the actual ids. So, to come up with a construction of RBE with the same efficiency as T-RBE, we somehow need to find a way to connect the actual identities of the parties to their corresponding registration time-stamps. In particular, the encryption algorithm of the RBE scheme, which now takes as input an identity id as opposed to a time-stamp, would need to first obtain the corresponding time-stamp of the given id, and then run the T-RBE encryption algorithm using this time-stamp. Further, we also need to ensure that the registration and update algorithms of this RBE scheme are efficient. At a high level, we achieve this efficiency by using a red-black Merkle tree in addition to the auxiliary input maintained by our T-RBE scheme. Such a tree allows us to (indirectly) obtain the time-stamp corresponding to an identity id in an efficient way (details of which are described below), without having to store the tree in the public parameter (which is prohibitive due to the tree size).

In order to enable this indirect access to the red-black Merkle tree, we will make further use of the hash-garbling primitive. Here we give a high-level description of our RBE scheme which uses T-RBE (and hash garbling) as subroutines together with the help of a red-black Merkle tree. In this scheme, the auxiliary information aux, stored by the key curator consists of η full binary Merkle trees $\mathsf{Tree}_1, \ldots, \mathsf{Tree}_\eta$, as was in the construction of [22]. In addition, aux contains a red-black Merkle tree TimeTree, whose leaves contain pairs of identities/time-stamps, sorted according to the identities. TimeTree is a key part in enabling the efficiency of our registration part.

- **The description of** $\mathsf{TimeTree}$**.** It is a close variant of red-black Merkle tree, where each leaf is of the form $(\mathsf{id}, t_{\mathsf{id}})$ and every non-leaf node in this tree contains the hash of its left child, the largest identity in its left sub-tree and the hash of the right child (all hashes use a hash key generated at the setup and described by a CRS). It differs from just red-black tree in the sense that each internal node also contains the largest identity in its left sub-tree. The choice of this specific data-structure is crucial for our construction. Notice that the leaves are sorted in ascending order of the identities. In addition, every node has another bit of information representing its color, which would be helpful in keeping the tree balanced using the red-black Merkle tree rotation algorithms.
- **How to register (Updating** aux**).** As we use the T-RBE as a subroutine, aux consists of the auxiliary information of T-RBE, $\mathsf{aux}_{\mathcal{T}}$, the $\mathsf{TimeTree}$ and a list of already registered identities. $\mathsf{aux}_{\mathcal{T}}$ itself comprises of the Merkle trees $\mathcal{T} = \{\mathsf{Tree}_1, \cdots, \mathsf{Tree}_\eta\}$, with the time-stamps and their corresponding public keys at the leaf nodes. So to update the aux when somebody registers, we insert their identity id as well as their time-stamp t_{id} to $\mathsf{TimeTree}$, update $\mathsf{aux}_{\mathcal{T}}$ using the T-RBE subroutine and add id to the list of registered identities. Recall that the T-RBE registration process involves creating a new Merkle tree with leaf nodes t_{id} and its corresponding public key pk and the merging the trees in $\mathcal{T}$ which are of same depth (merging only requires hashing the roots of the two trees to obtain a new tree).
- **How to encrypt.** The encryption algorithm takes as input the public parameter pp, a message m, and a receiver's identity id, and outputs a ciphertext, which is obtained by encrypting m using the T-RBE encryption under the time-stamp corresponding to id. To do this, the encryption algorithm requires to first look up id in $\mathsf{TimeTree}$ to obtain its time-stamp and then use it to encrypt m under the T-RBE encryption. However, the encryption algorithm only takes pp as public information, which is too small to contain $\mathsf{TimeTree}$, and so a "direct search" is impossible. To get around this problem, the encryption algorithm "defers" this search process to the time of decryption: Specifically, the encryption algorithm constructs a sequence of (garbled) programs, which enable one to do a binary search on $\mathsf{TimeTree}$ (during the decryption time) to obtain the time-stamp corresponding to id and then to use it to encrypt the message using the T-RBE encryption. The ciphertext then consists of the hash garbling of these programs.
- **How to decrypt.** The decryption algorithm takes as input two paths $u = \mathsf{pth}_1, \mathsf{pth}_2$, a secret key sk and a ciphertext, which contains the garbled programs, and outputs a message (or aborts). Here, pth_1 is the path from the root of $\mathsf{TimeTree}$ to the node that contains the id of the decryptor and its time-stamp t_{id}, and pth_2 is the updated path (obtained using the update algorithm of T-RBE) required for running the T-RBE decryption algorithm. Using pth_1, the decryptor runs the hash garbled programs to obtain the ciphertext under the T-RBE scheme with time-stamp t_{id} as the output of the last program. Then, it runs the decryption algorithm of T-RBE with inputs pth_2, sk and the obtained ciphertext to get the message m.

- **How to update u (the auxiliary information required by decryptor).** With the registration as described above, we can guarantee the efficiency. The updation algorithm requires to only read a path in the TimeTree, which leads to id and its time-stamp t_{id} and further use the updation algorithm of the T-RBE scheme. This would also be efficient. But we also need to guarantee that the number of times an id calls the updation algorithm is at most $\log(n)$ (where n is the number of identities registered so far). This is not guaranteed if we only have a single variant of the TimeTree. This is because, each time an id registers, its addition to the TimeTree modifies the root hash, changing the root-to-leaf path for every other identity registered. We resolve this issue by maintaining a variant of the same TimeTree, at the times corresponding to which each Merkle tree in $\mathcal{T}$ was last updated (which means we maintain at most $\log n$ variants of the TimeTree from different time instances). This guarantees two things: firstly that an identity contained in Tree_i of $\mathcal{T}$ will definitely be contained in the corresponding i-th variant of TimeTree and secondly that this identity only requires to update its root-to-leaf path in the TimeTree, when the tree Tree_i is modified (which happens only when the tree is merged with another tree and the number of times this merger can occur is at most $\log(n)$). These two observations would guarantee that the number of updates (of root to leaf path in TimeTree) required by any user is at most $\log(n)$. Hence, this would give the desired efficiency in number of updates. Note that this is also the reason why we need a combination of the Merkle trees $\mathcal{T}$ and the TimeTree and why we cannot use the TimeTree alone to store the ids and their pks.

Adding anonymity. Adding the anonymity feature to our RBE scheme involves techniques which are in essence same as those used in [10]. We build an RBE scheme achieving the stronger notion of "blindness," which in turn implies the required anonymity property of an anonymous RBE scheme. While the notion of anonymity guarantees that the identity id is hidden along with the message being encrypted (similar to an anonymous IBE), the property of "blindness" gives a stronger guarantee that the ciphertext generated on a uniformly random message looks uniform. The fact that this stronger guarantee is achieved by our scheme and that it implies anonymity is shown in Sect. 5.3.

As shown in the Fig. 1, we can get the blind T-RBE based on blind PKE and blind hash garbling schemes. The construction of the blind T-RBE is exactly the same as the regular T-RBE, except that instead of using a regular PKE scheme and a hash garbling scheme, we will use blind variants of these primitives and separate the corresponding ciphertexts and hash inputs into two parts. Then using blind T-RBE and blind hash garbling, we can get the desired anonymous RBE scheme (which is in fact a blind RBE).

1.2 Potential Applications of Anonymous RBE

Here we describe a possible application of anonymous RBE in scenarios where other seemingly similar and powerful primitives (e.g., anonymous IBE [6,9] or anonymous PKE [4]) seem incapable of.

Anonymous board communication (ABC). In an ABC scheme, a dynamic set of (semi-honest) parties $\{\mathsf{id}_1, \ldots, \mathsf{id}_n\}$ anonymously communicate by writing and reading on a single shared board $\mathbf{B}$ in a synchronized way. More formally, whenever a party joins the system, they update some information on the board $\mathbf{B}$. Also, the communication between $\{\mathsf{id}_1, \ldots, \mathsf{id}_n\}$ is done in synchronized cycles. In cycle t, each identity id_i has a list of messages $\mathsf{m}_{i,1}, \mathsf{m}_{i,2}, \ldots$ to be delivered to some parties $\mathsf{id}_{i,1}, \mathsf{id}_{i,2}, \ldots$. Then at the beginning of the cycle t, all of the parties write some arbitrary messages on the common board $\mathbf{B}$. After all the parties are done with writing, in the second half of the cycle t, all the parties read (their selected parts or all of) the content of the board $\mathbf{B}$. By the end of cycle t, all the parties should be able to obtain the messages intended to be sent to them. Namely, if the message m was sent to identity id (by another identity id'), by the end of cycle t, m should be obtained by id. The security goal is to keep all the senders and receivers anonymous from the perspective of any adversary who can read all the information written on the common board $\mathbf{B}$. The efficiency goal here is have parties write their messages in "small" time. In particular, we require the write time of each party to be $\text{poly}(\kappa, \log n) \cdot k$ where k is the total length of the message to be sent out and κ is the security parameter.

ABC from anonymous IBE? One might try to get ABCs from anonymous IBE as follows. The public key of the anonymous IBE scheme is written on the board, and the parties use it to compose their messages for the desired receivers. During the read part of each cycle, each party will read the whole board $\mathbf{B}$ and try to decrypt messages that are sent to them. This approach provides receiver anonymity and sender efficiency, but the main issue is that the master secret key should be stored somewhere and there is only one place for storing it: on the board $\mathbf{B}$. So, anyone who has full access to the board can decrypt all the messages. On the other hand, one might try to avoid IBE and use a public-key directory storing public-keys of an (anonymous) PKE scheme at the board $\mathbf{B}$. Then the parties can try to use this information and write their messages to the desired recipients on the same board. The problem with this approach is that the writing parties need to read the whole set of public-keys from the board to obtain the desired target public keys.

ABC from anonymous RBE. Interestingly, anonymous RBE directly enables ABC and achieves what anonymous IBE and PKE seem incapable of. In particular, a specific part of the common board $\mathbf{B}$ would be dedicated to store the information required for maintaining the public parameters and the auxiliary information of the KC of the anonymous RBE scheme (and note that no master secret key exists). This way, by reading the public parameter pp_n (after n people have joined), an (anonymous-receiver) message can be composed to any recipient. In particular, if $\mathsf{m}_{i,1}, \mathsf{m}_{i,2}, \ldots$ are to be sent to parties $\mathsf{id}_{i,1}, \mathsf{id}_{i,2}, \ldots$ by party id_i, all id_i does is to generate anonymous-receiver ciphertexts containing the messages and encrypted to the right identities. The anonymity of the sender stems from the fact that RBE can be used like an IBE and anyone (including those in the system) can compose messages to any other identify in a secret way. Finally, the fact that the key curator is transparent (and all it does is curating the keys) allows the parties to join the system freely one by one and update the public parameter as required.

Relation to other works on secure messaging. We emphasize that our ABC primitive is not by any means aiming to capture practical scenarios of secure messaging that have been a source of intense work over recent years [2,5,15–18,30,32]. For example a large body of work (e.g., see [16–18]) explore realistic messaging settings in which a set of distributed parties communicate over a network and aim to message each other in a way that senders, receivers, (and some more specific relations) remain secret despite the messages being sent over the network. Some of these works achieve privacy by using non-colluding servers, while ABC only uses one "server". On the other hand, our ABC occurs in a centralized setting in which all the messages by the parties are directly written to and read from the shared board. In a different direction, many works (e.g., see [5,8,15,26,28] in the context of what is now known as "Ratcheted Key Exchange" study ways to expand shared keys to secure refreshed keys to be used in the future, and so they fundamentally differ from ABC simply because in ABC there are no keys shared between the parties. Thus, we note that the main goal of introducing ABC is to demonstrate a basic abstract messaging scenario with challenges that can be resolved immediately using (anonymous) RBE, while other powerful tools do not seem to be capable of doing the same. While the idea for our ABC scheme requires a more concrete formalization, we introduce it as an attempt to lay down a concrete framework for an anonymous messaging scheme in the "single server" model (see also the discussion in [29]).

2 Preliminary Definitions

In this section we describe the needed definitions. We separate the definitions of variants of RBE into those borrowed from previous work and those that are introduced in this work.

2.1 Previous Definitions About RBE

In this subsection we recall the definition of RBE, taken verbatim from [22].

Definition 1 (Syntax of RBE). *A* registration-based encryption *(RBE for short) scheme consists of PPT algorithms* (Gen, Reg, Enc, Upd, Dec) *working as follows. The* Reg *and* Upd *algorithms are performed by the key curator, which we call KC for short.*

- **Generating common random string.** *Some of the subroutines below will need a common random string* crs*, which could be sampled publicly using some public randomness beacon.* crs *of length* poly(κ) *is sampled at the beginning, for the security parameter* κ.
- **Key generation.** $\text{Gen}(1^\kappa) \to (\mathsf{pk}, \mathsf{sk})$*: The randomized algorithm* Gen *takes as input the security parameter* 1^κ *and outputs a pair of public/secret keys* (pk, sk)*. Note that these are only* public *and* secret *keys, not the* encryption *or* decryption *keys. The key generation algorithm is run by any honest party locally who wants to register itself into the system.*
- **Registration.** $\text{Reg}^{[\mathsf{aux}]}(\mathsf{crs}, \mathsf{pp}, \mathsf{id}, \mathsf{pk}) \to \mathsf{pp}'$*: The deterministic algorithm* Reg *takes as input the common random sting* crs*, current public parameter* pp*, a registering identity* id *and a public key* pk *(supposedly for the identity* id*), and it outputs* pp′ *as the updated public parameters. The* Reg *algorithm uses* read and write *oracle access to* aux *which will be updated into* aux′ *during the process of registration. (The system is initialized with public parameters* pp *and auxiliary information* aux *set to* $\perp$.*)*
- **Encryption.** $\text{Enc}(\mathsf{crs}, \mathsf{pp}, \mathsf{id}, \mathsf{m}) \to \mathsf{ct}$*: The randomized algorithm* Enc *takes as input the common random sting* crs*, a public parameter* pp*, a recipient identity* id *and a plaintext message* m *and outputs a ciphertext* ct.
- **Update.** $\text{Upd}^{\mathsf{aux}}(\mathsf{pp}, \mathsf{id}) \to \mathsf{u}$*: The deterministic algorithm* Upd *takes as input the current information* pp *stored at the KC and an identity* id*, has* read only *oracle access to* aux *and generates an* update *information* u *that can help* id *to decrypt its messages.*
- **Decryption.** $\text{Dec}(\mathsf{sk}, \mathsf{u}, \mathsf{ct})$*: The deterministic decryption algorithm* Dec *takes as input a secret key* sk*, an update information* u*, and a ciphertext* ct*, and it outputs a message* $\mathsf{m} \in \{0,1\}^*$ *or in* $\{\perp, \texttt{GetUpd}\}$*. The special symbol* $\perp$ *indicates a syntax error, while* **GetUpd** *indicates that more recent update information (than* u*) might be needed for decryption.*

Definition 2 (Completeness, compactness, and efficiency of RBE). *For any interactive* computationally unbounded *adversary* Adv *that still has a limited* poly(κ) *round complexity, consider the following game* $\mathit{Comp}_{\mathsf{Adv}}(\kappa)$ *between* Adv *and a challenger* Chal.

1. ***Initialization.*** Chal *sets* $\mathsf{pp} = \perp$, $\mathsf{aux} = \perp$, $\mathsf{u} = \perp$, $\mathsf{ID} = \varnothing$, $\mathsf{id}^* = \perp$, $t = 0$, $\mathsf{crs} \leftarrow U_{\text{poly}(\kappa)}$ *and sends the sampled* crs *to* Adv.
2. *Till* Adv *continues (which is at most* poly(κ) *steps), proceed as follows. At every iteration,* Adv *chooses exactly one of the actions below to be performed.*
   (a) ***Registering new (non-target) identity.*** Adv *sends some* $\mathsf{id} \notin \mathsf{ID}$ *and* pk *to* Chal. Chal *registers* (id, pk) *by letting* $\mathsf{pp} := \text{Reg}^{[\mathsf{aux}]}(\mathsf{crs}, \mathsf{pp}, \mathsf{id}, \mathsf{pk})$ *and* $\mathsf{ID} := \mathsf{ID} \cup \{\mathsf{id}\}$.
   (b) ***Registering the target identity.*** *If* id^* *was chosen by* Adv *already (i.e.,* $\mathsf{id}^* \neq \perp$*), skip this step. Otherwise,* Adv *sends some* $\mathsf{id}^* \notin \mathsf{ID}$ *to* Chal. Chal *then samples* $(\mathsf{pk}^*, \mathsf{sk}^*) \leftarrow \text{Gen}(1^\kappa)$*, updates* $\mathsf{pp} := \text{Reg}^{[\mathsf{aux}]}(\mathsf{crs}, \mathsf{pp}, \mathsf{id}^*, \mathsf{pk}^*)$, $\mathsf{ID} := \mathsf{ID} \cup \{\mathsf{id}^*\}$*, and sends* pk^* *to* Adv.
   (c) ***Encrypting for the target identity.*** *If* $\mathsf{id}^* = \perp$ *then skip this step. Otherwise,* Chal *sets* $t = t + 1$*, then* Adv *sends some* $\mathsf{m}_t \in \{0,1\}^*$ *to*

Chal *who then sets* $\mathsf{m}'_t := \mathsf{m}_t$ *and sends back a corresponding ciphertext* $\mathsf{ct}_t \leftarrow \mathrm{Enc}(\mathsf{crs}, \mathsf{pp}, \mathsf{id}^*, \mathsf{m}_t)$ *to* Adv.

(d) ***Decryption by target identity.*** Adv *sends a* $j \in [t]$ *to* Chal. Chal *then lets* $\mathsf{m}'_j = \mathrm{Dec}(\mathsf{sk}^*, \mathsf{u}, \mathsf{ct}_j)$. *If* $\mathsf{m}'_j = \texttt{GetUpd}$, *then* Chal *obtains the update* $\mathsf{u} = \mathrm{Upd}^{\mathsf{aux}}(\mathsf{pp}, \mathsf{id}^*)$ *and then lets* $\mathsf{m}'_j = \mathrm{Dec}(\mathsf{sk}^*, \mathsf{u}, \mathsf{ct}_j)$.

3. *The adversary* Adv *wins the game if there is some* $j \in [t]$ *for which* $\mathsf{m}'_j \neq \mathsf{m}_j$.

Let $n = |\mathsf{ID}|$ *be the number of identities registered till a specific moment. We require the following properties to hold for any* Adv *(as specified above) and for* all *the moments (and so for all the values of* ID *and* $n = |\mathsf{ID}|$ *as well) during the game* $\mathit{Comp}_{\mathsf{Adv}}(\kappa)$.

- **Completeness.** $\Pr[\mathsf{Adv}$ *wins in* $\mathit{Comp}_{\mathsf{Adv}}(\kappa)] = \mathrm{negl}(\kappa)$.
- **Compactness of public parameters and updates.** $|\mathsf{pp}|, |\mathsf{u}|$ *are both* $\leq \mathrm{poly}(\kappa, \log n)$.
- **Efficiency of runtime of registration and update.** *The running time of each invocation of* Reg *and* Upd *algorithms is at most* $\mathrm{poly}(\kappa, \log n)$. *(This implies the compactness property.)*
- **Efficiency of the number of updates.** *The* total *number of invocations of* Upd *for identity* id^* *in Step 2d of the game* $\mathit{Comp}_{\mathsf{Adv}}(\kappa)$ *is at most* $O(\log n)$ *for every* n *during* $\mathit{Comp}_{\mathsf{Adv}}(\kappa)$.

Definition 3 (WE-RBE). *A* weakly efficient RBE *(or WE-RBE for short) is defined similarly to Definition 2, where the specified* $\mathrm{poly}(\kappa, \log n)$ *runtime efficiency of the registration algorithm is not required anymore, but instead we require the registration time to be* $\mathrm{poly}(\kappa, n)$.

Definition 4 (Security of RBE). *For any interactive PPT adversary* Adv, *consider the following game* $\mathit{Sec}_{\mathsf{Adv}}(\kappa)$ *between* Adv *and a challenger* Chal. *(Steps that are different from the completeness definition are denoted with purple stars* ($\star\star$)*. Specifically, Steps 2c and 2d from Definition 2 are replaced by Step 3 below. Additionally, Step 3 from Definition 2 is replaced by Step 4 below.)*

1. ***Initialization.*** Chal *sets* $\mathsf{pp} = \perp$, $\mathsf{aux} = \perp$, $\mathsf{ID} = \varnothing$, $\mathsf{id}^* = \perp$, $\mathsf{crs} \leftarrow U_{\mathrm{poly}(\kappa)}$ *and sends the sampled* crs *to* Adv.
2. *Till* Adv *continues (which is at most* $\mathrm{poly}(\kappa)$ *steps), proceed as follows. At every iteration,* Adv *chooses exactly one of the actions below to be performed.*
   (a) ***Registering new (non-target) identity.*** Adv *sends some* $\mathsf{id} \notin \mathsf{ID}$ *and* pk *to* Chal. Chal *registers* $(\mathsf{id}, \mathsf{pk})$ *by letting* $\mathsf{pp} := \mathrm{Reg}^{[\mathsf{aux}]}(\mathsf{crs}, \mathsf{pp}, \mathsf{id}, \mathsf{pk})$ *and* $\mathsf{ID} := \mathsf{ID} \cup \{\mathsf{id}\}$.
   (b) ***Registering the target identity.*** *If* id^* *was chosen by* Adv *already (i.e.,* $\mathsf{id}^* \neq \perp$*), skip this step. Otherwise,* Adv *sends some* $\mathsf{id}^* \notin \mathsf{ID}$ *to* Chal. Chal *then samples* $(\mathsf{pk}^*, \mathsf{sk}^*) \leftarrow \mathrm{Gen}(1^\kappa)$, *updates* $\mathsf{pp} := \mathrm{Reg}^{[\mathsf{aux}]}(\mathsf{crs}, \mathsf{pp}, \mathsf{id}^*, \mathsf{pk}^*)$, $\mathsf{ID} := \mathsf{ID} \cup \{\mathsf{id}^*\}$, *and sends* pk^* *to* Adv.
3. ($\star\star$) ***Encrypting for the target identity.*** *If no* id^* *was chosen by* Adv *before (i.e.,* $\mathsf{id}^* = \perp$*) then* Adv *first sends some* $\mathsf{id}^* \notin \mathsf{ID}$ *to* Chal. *Next,* Chal *generates* $\mathsf{ct} \leftarrow \mathrm{Enc}(\mathsf{crs}, \mathsf{pp}, \mathsf{id}^*, b)$, *where* $b \leftarrow \{0, 1\}$ *is a random bit, lets* $\mathsf{ID} = \mathsf{ID} \cup \{\mathsf{id}^*\}$, *and sends* ct *to* Adv.

4. *(⋆⋆) The adversary* Adv *outputs a bit* b' *and wins the game if* $b = b'$.
We call an RBE scheme secure if $\Pr[\mathsf{Adv}$ *wins in* $\mathsf{Sec}_{\mathsf{Adv}}(\kappa)] < \frac{1}{2} + \mathrm{negl}(\kappa)$ *for any PPT* Adv.

2.2 New Definitions About (Anonymous) RBE

In this section we define an anonymity feature for the notion of RBE, and we will show later how to build efficient anonymous RBE from standard assumptions.

Definition 5 (Anonymous RBE). *An anonymous RBE scheme has the same syntax as that of an RBE scheme, with PPT algorithms* (Gen, Reg, Enc, Upd, Dec). *It satisfies the properties of completeness, compactness and efficiency as a RBE scheme and has the following stronger notion of security: For any interactive PPT adversary* Adv*, consider the game* $\mathsf{EXP}^{\mathsf{Anon}}_{\mathsf{Adv}}(\kappa)$ *between* Adv *and a challenger* Chal *as follows.*

1. ***Initialization.*** Chal *sets* $\mathsf{pp} = \bot$, $\mathsf{aux} = \bot$, $\mathsf{ID} = \varnothing$, $\mathsf{id}_0 = \bot$, $\mathsf{id}_1 = \bot$, $\mathsf{crs} \leftarrow U_{\mathrm{poly}(\kappa)}$ *and sends the sampled* crs *to* Adv.
2. *Till* Adv *continues (which is at most* $\mathrm{poly}(\kappa)$ *steps), proceed as follows. At every iteration,* Adv *can perform exactly one of the following actions.*
   (a) ***Registering new (non-target) identity.*** Adv *sends some* $\mathsf{id} \notin \mathsf{ID}$ *and* pk *to* Chal. Chal *registers* $(\mathsf{id}, \mathsf{pk})$ *by getting* $\mathsf{pp} = \mathrm{Reg}^{[\mathsf{aux}]}(\mathsf{crs}, \mathsf{pp}, (\mathsf{id}, \mathsf{pk}))$ *and lets* $\mathsf{ID} = \mathsf{ID} \cup \{\mathsf{id}\}$.
   (b) ***Registering new target identity pair.*** *If* id_0 *or* id_1 *was chosen by* Adv *already (i.e.,* $\mathsf{id}_0 \neq \bot$ *or* $\mathsf{id}_1 \neq \bot$*), skip this step. Otherwise,* Adv *sends challenges* $\mathsf{id}_0, \mathsf{id}_1 \notin \mathsf{ID}$ *to* Chal. Chal *first samples* $(\mathsf{pk}_0, \mathsf{sk}_0) \leftarrow \mathrm{Gen}(1^\kappa)$*, registers* id_0 *by setting* $\mathsf{pp} = \mathrm{Reg}^{[\mathsf{aux}]}(\mathsf{crs}, \mathsf{pp}, (\mathsf{id}_0, \mathsf{pk}_0))$ *and then samples* $(\mathsf{pk}_1, \mathsf{sk}_1) \leftarrow \mathrm{Gen}(1^\kappa)$*, registers* id_1 *by setting* $\mathsf{pp} = \mathrm{Reg}^{[\mathsf{aux}]}(\mathsf{crs}, \mathsf{pp}, (\mathsf{id}_1, \mathsf{pk}_1))$*. Next,* Chal *lets* $\mathsf{ID} = \mathsf{ID} \cup \{\mathsf{id}_0, \mathsf{id}_1\}$ *and sends* $\mathsf{pk}_0, \mathsf{pk}_1$ *to* Adv.
3. ***Encrypting for the challenge identity.*** *If* $\mathsf{id}_0, \mathsf{id}_1$ *was not chosen by* Adv *already (i.e.,* $\mathsf{id}_0 = \bot, \mathsf{id}_1 = \bot$*), then* Adv *first sends some* $\mathsf{id}_0, \mathsf{id}_1 \notin \mathsf{ID}$ *to* Chal *before continuing this step. Next,* Chal *samples a bit* $b \in \{0, 1\}$ *and generates the challenge ciphertext* $\mathsf{ct} \leftarrow \mathrm{Enc}(\mathsf{crs}, \mathsf{pp}, \mathsf{id}_b, b)$*. Further,* Chal *sets* $\mathsf{ID} = \mathsf{ID} \cup \{\mathsf{id}_0, \mathsf{id}_1\}$ *and sends* ct *to* Adv.
4. *The adversary* Adv *outputs a bit* b' *and wins the game if* $b' = b$.

We call an RBE scheme an Anonymous-RBE if $\Pr[\mathsf{Adv}$ *wins in* $\mathsf{EXP}^{\mathsf{Anon}}_{\mathsf{Adv}}(\kappa)] < \frac{1}{2} + \mathrm{negl}(\kappa)$ *for any PPT* Adv.

As a step-stone toward building efficient (anonymous) RBE, we will first show how to build a primitive which we call *timestamp-RBE*. We define this notion formally below.

Definition 6 (T-RBE). *A* timestamp-RBE *(or T-RBE for short) has syntax exactly similar to Definition 1, except for one difference: we now consider the registration algorithm* Reg*, the encryption algorithm* Enc *and the update algorithm*

Upd *to take as input the timestamp* $\mathsf{t_{id}}$ *of an identity* id *(binary representation of the time at which an identity registers) as input instead of the identity* id. *The completeness, compactness of public parameters, the efficiency of runtime of registration and update and the efficiency of the number of updates is exactly similar to Definition 2 and the security guarantee is similar to Definition 4, replacing identity* id *with its timestamp* $\mathsf{t_{id}}$ *in all the appropriate places. For a T-RBE, we define the notion of anonymity exactly as in Definition 5, replacing identity* id *with its timestamp* $\mathsf{t_{id}}$ *in all the appropriate places.*

2.3 Blind Public Key Encryption

In this subsection we define blindness features for several cryptographic primitives, which will be used in our main constructions. We first start with the notion of blind PKE. The notion of blindness for PKE is well-studied with a few prior definitions; see, e.g., [4,27]. Here we give a tailored version of this definition suitable for our later constructions.

Definition 7 (Blind Public Key Encryption). *A blind public key encryption scheme (with public parameters) has algorithms* $(\mathsf{Params}, \mathrm{G}, \mathrm{E}, \mathrm{D})$ *which is IND-CPA secure and satisfies the following additional security property: the function* $\mathrm{E}(\mathsf{pp}, \mathsf{pk}, \mathsf{m}; \mathsf{r})$ *can be expressed as* $\mathrm{E}_1(\mathsf{pp}; \mathsf{r}) || \mathrm{E}_2(\mathsf{pp}, \mathsf{pk}, \mathsf{m}; \mathsf{r})$ *such that the distribution of* $\{(\mathsf{pp}, \mathsf{pk}, \mathsf{sk}, \mathrm{Enc}(\mathsf{pp}, \mathsf{pk}, \mathsf{m}; \mathsf{r})) : \mathsf{pp} \leftarrow \mathsf{Params}(1^\lambda), (\mathsf{pk}, \mathsf{sk}) \leftarrow \mathrm{G}(\mathsf{pp}), \mathsf{m} \xleftarrow{\$} \mathcal{M}, \mathsf{r} \xleftarrow{\$} \{0,1\}^*\}$ *is computationally indistinguishable from* $\{(\mathsf{pp}, \mathsf{pk}, \mathsf{sk}, \mathrm{E}_1(\mathsf{pp}; \mathsf{r}), \mathsf{subct}_2) : \mathsf{pp} \leftarrow \mathsf{Params}(1^\lambda), (\mathsf{pk}, \mathsf{sk}) \leftarrow \mathrm{G}(\mathsf{pp}), m \xleftarrow{\$} \mathcal{M}, \mathsf{r} \xleftarrow{\$} \{0,1\}^*, \mathsf{subct}_2 \xleftarrow{\$} \{0,1\}^L\}$*, where* $L = |\mathrm{E}_2(\mathsf{pp}, \mathsf{pk}, \mathsf{m}; \mathsf{r})|$.

We now define a blindness notion for garbled circuits. Our blindness requirement is the same as that introduced and used by [10].

Definition 8 (Blind Garbled Circuits [10]). *A garbling scheme consists of PPT algorithms* $(\mathsf{Garble}, \mathsf{Eval})$ *and a simulator* $\mathsf{G.Sim}$ *where:*

1. $\mathsf{Garble}(1^\lambda, 1^l, 1^m, \mathrm{C}; \mathsf{state}) := \mathsf{Garble}_1(1^\lambda, 1^l, 1^m; \mathsf{state}) || \mathsf{Garble}_2(1^\lambda, 1^l, 1^m, \mathrm{C}; \mathsf{state})$. Garble_1 *takes as input the security parameter* λ*, the input length* l *and output length* m *for circuit* C *and a random value* $\mathsf{state} \in \{0,1\}^\lambda$ *and outputs the labels for input wire of the Garbled circuit* $\{\mathsf{lab}_{j,b}\}_{j\in[l], b\in\{0,1\}}$*, where* $\mathsf{lab}_{j,b} \in \{0,1\}^\lambda$ *and* Garble_2 *takes the circuit* C *in addition, and outputs the garbled circuit* $\tilde{\mathrm{C}}$.
2. $\mathsf{Eval}(1^\lambda, \tilde{\mathrm{C}}, \tilde{\mathsf{lab}})$ *is a deterministic algorithm that takes as input the garbled circuit* $\tilde{\mathrm{C}}$*, along with a set of* l *labels* $\tilde{\mathsf{lab}} = \{\mathsf{lab}_j\}_{j\in[l]}$ *and outputs a string* $y \in \{0,1\}^m$.
3. $\mathsf{G.Sim}(1^\lambda, 1^{|\mathrm{C}|}, 1^l, y)$ *takes as input the security parameter* λ*, the description length of circuit* C*, the input length* l *and a string* $y \in \{0,1\}^m$ *and outputs a simulated garbled circuit* $\tilde{\mathrm{C}}$ *and labels* $\tilde{\mathsf{lab}}$.

A blind garbling scheme must satisfy the following properties:

1. ***Correctness.*** *For all circuits* C*, inputs* x *and all* $(\tilde{\mathsf{C}}, \{\mathsf{lab}_{j,b}\}_{j\in[l],b\in\{0,1\}}) \leftarrow \mathsf{Garble}(\mathsf{C})$ *and* $\tilde{\mathsf{lab}} = \{\mathsf{lab}_{j,x_j}\}_{j\in[l]}$, *we have* $\mathsf{Eval}(\tilde{\mathsf{C}}, \tilde{\mathsf{lab}}) = \mathsf{C}(x)$.
2. ***Simulation Security.*** *For all circuits* $\mathsf{C} : \{0,1\}^l \to \{0,1\}^m$ *and all inputs* $x \in \{0,1\}^l$, *the following distributions are computationally indistinguishable:*

$$\{(\tilde{\mathsf{C}}, \tilde{\mathsf{lab}}) : (\tilde{\mathsf{C}}, \{\mathsf{lab}_{j,b}\}_{j\in[l],b\in\{0,1\}}) \leftarrow \mathsf{Garble}(\mathsf{C}), \tilde{\mathsf{lab}} = \{\mathsf{lab}_{j,x_j}\}_{j\in[l]}\}$$
$$\stackrel{c}{\approx} \{(\tilde{\mathsf{C}}, \tilde{\mathsf{lab}}) : (\tilde{\mathsf{C}}, \tilde{\mathsf{lab}}) \leftarrow \mathsf{G.Sim}(1^\lambda, 1^{|\mathsf{C}|}, 1^l, \mathsf{C}(x))\}$$

3. ***Blindness.*** $\mathsf{G.Sim}(1^\lambda, 1^{|\mathsf{C}|}, 1^l, U_m) \stackrel{c}{\approx} U$. *The output of the simulator on a completely uniform output is indistinguishable from a uniform bit string.*

We now review the notion of blind batch encryption from [10]. The notion of batch encryption is in turn similar to some notions such as hash encryption and laconic oblivious transfer [13,19].

Definition 9 (Blind Single Batch Encryption [10]**).** *A blind single batch encryption scheme consists of PPT algorithms* (Setup, H, HEnc, HDec)*:*

1. $\mathsf{Setup}(1^\lambda, 1^l)$ *takes as input the security parameter* λ, *a length parameter* l *and outputs a hash key* hk.
2. $\mathsf{H}(\mathsf{hk}, x)$ *takes as input a hash key* hk *and* $x \in \{0,1\}^l$ *and deterministically outputs* $h \in \{0,1\}^\lambda$.
3. $\mathsf{HEnc}(\mathsf{hk}, h, i, M)$ *takes as input the hash key* hk, *hash value* h *and a message matrix* $M \in \{0,1\}^{1\times 2}$ *and outputs a ciphertext* ct, *which can be written as a concatenation of two parts* $\mathsf{ct} = (\mathsf{subct}_1, \mathsf{subct}_2)$.
4. $\mathsf{HDec}(\mathsf{hk}, x, i, \mathsf{ct})$ *takes as input the ciphertext* ct *and outputs an* $m \in \{0,1\}$.

A blind single batch encryption must satisfy the following properties:

1. ***Correctness.*** *Let* $\mathsf{hk} \leftarrow \mathsf{Setup}(1^\lambda, 1^l)$. *For all* x, i, M, *taking* $h = \mathsf{H}(\mathsf{hk}, x)$, $\mathsf{ct} = \mathsf{HEnc}(\mathsf{hk}, h, i, M)$, *it holds that* $\mathsf{HDec}(\mathsf{hk}, x, i, \mathsf{ct}) = M_{x_i}$, *with probability at least* $1/2 + 1/\mathrm{poly}(\lambda)$ *over the randomness of* HEnc.
2. ***Semantic Security.*** *For any PPT adversary* Adv *the probability of winning in the following game between* Adv *and a challenger* Chal *is* $1/2 + \mathrm{negl}(\lambda)$*:*
   (a) Adv *takes as input* 1^λ *and sends* $1^l, x \in \{0,1\}^l, i \in [l]$ *to* Chal.
   (b) Chal *generates* $\mathsf{hk} = \mathsf{Setup}(1^\lambda, 1^l)$ *and sends* hk *to* Adv.
   (c) Adv *sends a pair* $M^{(0)}, M^{(1)}$, *such that* $M^{(0)}_{x_i} = M^{(1)}_{x_i}$, *to* Chal.
   (d) Chal *computes* $h = \mathsf{H}(\mathsf{hk}, x)$, *chooses* $b \in_R \{0,1\}$ *and sends* $\mathsf{ct} = \mathsf{HEnc}(\mathsf{hk}, h, i, M^{(b)})$ *to* Adv.
   (e) Adv *outputs a bit* b' *and wins if* $b' = b$.
3. ***Blindness.*** *The encryption* $\mathsf{HEnc}(\mathsf{hk}, h, i, M; \mathsf{r})$ *can be considered as a concatenation of* $\mathsf{HEnc}_1(\mathsf{hk}; \mathsf{r}) || \mathsf{HEnc}_2(\mathsf{hk}, h, i, M; \mathsf{r})$. *Further, any PPT adversary* Adv *the probability of winning in the following game with a Challenger* Chal *is at most* $1/2 + \mathrm{negl}(\lambda)$*:*
   (a) Adv *takes as input* 1^λ *and sends* $1^l, x, i$ *to* Chal.
   (b) Chal *generates* $\mathsf{hk} = \mathsf{Setup}(1^\lambda, 1^l)$ *and computes* $h = \mathsf{H}(\mathsf{hk}, x)$. *Further it samples a random* $b \in \{0,1\}$, *a random message matrix* $M \in \{0,1\}^{1\times 2}$ *and encrypts* $(\mathsf{subct}_1, \mathsf{subct}_2) \leftarrow \mathsf{HEnc}(\mathsf{hk}, h, i, M)$. *It generates* ct *as:*

- *If* $b = 0$, *the* $\mathsf{ct} = (\mathsf{subct}_1, \mathsf{subct}_2)$.
- *If* $b = 1$, *then pick a random* subct_2' *of same length as* subct_2 *and set* $\mathsf{ct} = (\mathsf{subct}_1, \mathsf{subct}_2')$.

Chal *sends* hk, ct *to* Adv.

(c) Adv *outputs a bit* b' *and wins if* $b' = b$.

3 Blind Hash Garbling

In this section we introduce and build a primitive which we call blind hash garbling, which will later be used as an ingredient in the construction of anonymous T-RBE schemes. We first define this notion below and will then show how to build it using tools defined in the previous sections.

3.1 Definition of Blind Hash Garbling

The notion of hash garbling was defined in [22]; here we review this notion and define a blindness feature for it.

Definition 10 (Blind Hash Garbling). *A blind hash garbling scheme has the following polynomial time algorithms* HGen, Hash, HObf, HInp*:*

- $\mathrm{HGen}(1^\kappa, 1^l) \to \mathsf{hk}$. *It takes as input the security parameter* κ *and an output length parameter* 1^l *for* $l \le \mathrm{poly}(\kappa)$, *and outputs a hash key* hk.
- $\mathrm{Hash}(\mathsf{hk}, x) = y$. *It takes as input* hk *and* $x \in \{0,1\}^l$ *and deterministically outputs* $y \in \{0,1\}^\kappa$.
- $\mathrm{HObf}(\mathsf{hk}, \mathrm{C}, \mathsf{state}) \to \tilde{\mathrm{C}}$. *It takes as input* hk, *a circuit* C, *and a secret state* $\mathsf{state} \in \{0,1\}^\kappa$ *and outputs a circuit* $\tilde{\mathrm{C}}$.
- $\mathrm{HInp}(\mathsf{hk}, y, \mathsf{state}) \to \tilde{y}$. *This takes as input* hk, *a value* $y \in \{0,1\}^\kappa$, *and secret state* state *and outputs* $\tilde{y}$. *Consider* $\tilde{y}$ *as concatenation of two parts* $\tilde{y}_1 || \tilde{y}_2$.

A blind hash garbling scheme must satisfy the following properties:

- ***Correctness.*** *For all* κ, l, *hash key* $\mathsf{hk} \leftarrow \mathrm{HGen}(1^\kappa, 1^l)$, *circuit* C, *input* $x \in \{0,1\}^l$, $\mathsf{state} \in \{0,1\}^\kappa$, $\tilde{\mathrm{C}} \leftarrow \mathrm{HObf}(\mathsf{hk}, \mathrm{C}, \mathsf{state})$ *and* $\tilde{y} \leftarrow \mathrm{HInp}(\mathsf{hk}, \mathrm{Hash}(\mathsf{hk}, x), \mathsf{state})$, *then* $\tilde{\mathrm{C}}(\tilde{y}, x) = \mathrm{C}(x)$.
- ***Security.*** *There exists a PPT simulator* Sim *such that for all* κ, l *and PPT (in* κ*)* Adv *we have that*

$$(\mathsf{hk}, x, \tilde{y}_1, \tilde{\mathrm{C}}, \tilde{y}_2) \stackrel{c}{\approx} (\mathsf{hk}, x, \tilde{y}_1, \mathsf{Sim}(\mathsf{hk}, x, 1^{|\mathrm{C}|}, \mathrm{C}(x))),$$

where $\mathsf{hk} \leftarrow \mathrm{HGen}(1^\kappa, 1^l)$, $(\mathrm{C}, x) \leftarrow \mathsf{Adv}(\mathsf{hk})$, $\mathsf{state} \leftarrow \{0,1\}^\kappa$, $\tilde{\mathrm{C}} \leftarrow \mathrm{HObf}(\mathsf{hk}, \mathrm{C}, \mathsf{state})$ *and* $(\tilde{y}_1, \tilde{y}_2) \leftarrow \mathrm{HInp}(\mathsf{hk}, \mathrm{Hash}(\mathsf{hk}, x), \mathsf{state})$.
- ***Blindness.*** *The function* $\tilde{y} = \mathrm{HInp}(\mathsf{hk}, y, \mathsf{state}; \mathsf{r})$ *can be expressed as the concatenation* $\mathrm{HInp}_1(\mathsf{hk}; \mathsf{r}) || \mathrm{HInp}_2(\mathsf{hk}, y, \mathsf{state}; \mathsf{r}) = \tilde{y}_1 || \tilde{y}_2$ *such that*

$$(\mathsf{hk}, x, \mathrm{HInp}_1(\mathsf{hk}; \mathsf{r}), \mathsf{Sim}(\mathsf{hk}, x, 1^{|\mathrm{C}|}, U_{|\mathrm{C}(x)|})) \stackrel{c}{\approx} (\mathsf{hk}, x, \mathrm{HInp}_1(\mathsf{hk}; \mathsf{r}), U_{|\tilde{\mathrm{C}}|+|\tilde{y}_2|})$$

where $1^l, x \leftarrow \mathsf{Adv}(1^\kappa)$, $\mathsf{hk} \leftarrow \mathrm{HGen}(1^\kappa, 1^l)$. *(It is clear that the distinguisher should not know about the random output value that was used for simulation)*

3.2 Construction of a Blind Hash Garbling Scheme

We require the following building blocks to construct blind hash garbling:

- Blind single batch encryption scheme $(\mathsf{Setup}, \mathsf{H}, \mathsf{HEnc}, \mathsf{HDec})$ as Definition 9.
- Blind garbled circuit scheme $(\mathsf{Garble}, \mathsf{Eval})$ as in Definition 8.

The blind hash garbling scheme is as follows:

1. $\mathrm{HGen}(1^\kappa, 1^l)$: Generate $\mathsf{hk} \leftarrow \mathsf{Setup}(1^\kappa, 1^l)$ and output hk.
2. $\mathrm{Hash}(\mathsf{hk}, x)$: Generate $\mathsf{H}(\mathsf{hk}, x) = y$ and output y.
3. $\mathrm{HObf}(\mathsf{hk}, \mathsf{C}, \mathsf{state})$: Generate $\tilde{\mathsf{C}} \leftarrow \mathsf{Garble}_2(1^\kappa, 1^l, 1^m, \mathsf{C}; \mathsf{state})$ and output $\tilde{\mathsf{C}}[\mathsf{hk}]$ (circuit $\tilde{\mathsf{C}}$ hardwired with hk).
4. $\mathrm{HInp}(\mathsf{hk}, y, \mathsf{state})$:
   - Generate $\{\mathsf{lab}_{j,b}\}_{j\in[l],b\in\{0,1\}} \leftarrow \mathsf{Garble}_1(1^\kappa, 1^l, 1^m; \mathsf{state})$.
   - Generate $\tilde{y} = \{\mathsf{HEnc}(\mathsf{hk}, y, j, [\mathsf{lab}_{j,0}\ \mathsf{lab}_{j,1}])\}_{j\in[l]} = \{\mathsf{subct}_{1,j}, \mathsf{subct}_{2,j}\}_{j\in[l]}$.

   Let $\tilde{y}_1 = \{\mathsf{subct}_{1,j}\}_{j\in[l]}$ and $\tilde{y}_2 = \{\mathsf{subct}_{2,j}\}_{j\in[l]}$. Output $\tilde{y} = (\tilde{y}_1, \tilde{y}_2)$.

Theorem 11. *The above construction* (HGen, Hash, HObf, HInp) *satisfies the correctness, security and blindness properties as given in Definition 10.*

Proof. We now prove the above theorem.

1. **Correctness.** Consider the circuit $\tilde{\mathsf{C}}[\mathsf{hk}](\tilde{y}, x)$:
   - Recovers $\mathsf{lab}_{j,x_j} := \mathsf{HDec}(\mathsf{hk}, x, j, \tilde{y}_j)$ for each $j \in [l]$, where $\tilde{y} = \{\tilde{y}_j\}_{j\in[l]}$.
   - Outputs $\mathsf{Eval}(\tilde{\mathsf{C}}, \{\mathsf{lab}_{j,x_j}\}_{j\in[l]})$.

   Then clearly by correctness of the blind garbling circuit and the correctness of the blind single batch encryption scheme, $\tilde{\mathsf{C}}[\mathsf{hk}](\tilde{y}, x) = \mathsf{C}(x)$.
2. **Security.** We define the simulator Sim as below: $\mathsf{Sim}(\mathsf{hk}, x, 1^{|\mathsf{C}|}, \mathsf{C}(x))$:
   - Evaluate $(\tilde{\mathsf{C}}, \{\mathsf{lab}_j\}_{j\in[l]}) \leftarrow \mathsf{G.Sim}(1^\kappa, 1^{|\mathsf{C}|}, 1^l, \mathsf{C}(x))$.
   - For $j \in [l]$, let $M_j = [M_{j,0}\ M_{j,1}]$, where $M_{j,x_j} = \mathsf{lab}_j$, $M_{j,1-x_j} \in_R \{0,1\}^\kappa$.
   - Evaluate $\tilde{y} = \{\mathsf{HEnc}(\mathsf{hk}, \mathsf{H}(\mathsf{hk}, x), j, M_j)\}_{j\in[l]}$. As expressed in the protocol, $\tilde{y} = (\tilde{y}_1, \tilde{y}_2)$.
   - Output $(\tilde{\mathsf{C}}, \tilde{y}_2)$.

   Then, by simulation security of the blind garbled circuit scheme and the semantic security of the blind single batch encryption scheme, it can be shown through a sequence of hybrids that:

   $$(\mathsf{hk}, x, \tilde{y}_1, \tilde{\mathsf{C}}, \tilde{y}_2) \overset{c}{\approx} (\mathsf{hk}, x, \tilde{y}_1, \mathsf{Sim}(\mathsf{hk}, x, 1^{|\mathsf{C}|}, \mathsf{C}(x))),$$

   where $\mathsf{hk} \leftarrow \mathrm{HGen}(1^\kappa, 1^l)$, $(\mathsf{C}, x) \leftarrow \mathsf{Adv}(\mathsf{hk})$, $\mathsf{state} \leftarrow \{0,1\}^\kappa$, $\tilde{\mathsf{C}} \leftarrow \mathrm{HObf}(\mathsf{hk}, \mathsf{C}, \mathsf{state})$ and $(\tilde{y}_1, \tilde{y}_2) \leftarrow \mathrm{HInp}(\mathsf{hk}, \mathrm{Hash}(\mathsf{hk}, x), \mathsf{state})$.
3. **Blindness.** For the simulator Sim described above, consider the distribution of $\mathsf{Sim}(\mathsf{hk}, x, 1^{|\mathsf{C}|}, U_{|\mathsf{C}(x)|})$ for a uniformly generated output.
   - By the blindness of blind garbled circuit, $\mathsf{G.Sim}(1^\kappa, 1^{|\mathsf{C}|}, 1^l, U_{|\mathsf{C}(x)|}) \overset{c}{\approx} U$.
   - Hence for each $j \in [l]$, $M_j \overset{c}{\approx} U$. Thus, by blindness of the blind single batch encryption, $\tilde{y} = (\tilde{y}_1, \tilde{y}_2)$ (as described in the protocol), where $\tilde{y}_1$ can be expressed as $\mathrm{HInp}_1(\mathsf{hk}; \mathsf{r})$ and $(\mathsf{hk}, x, \tilde{y}_1, \tilde{y}_2) \overset{c}{\approx} (\mathsf{hk}, x, \tilde{y}_1, U)$.

   Hence, it follows that $(\mathsf{hk}, x, \tilde{y}_1, \mathsf{Sim}(\mathsf{hk}, x, 1^{|\mathsf{C}|}, U_{|\mathsf{C}(x)|})) \overset{c}{\approx} (\mathsf{hk}, x, \tilde{y}_1, U)$.

4 Efficient Blind T-RBE

We first define and construct an efficient blind T-RBE and then use it to construct an efficient Anonymous RBE scheme.

4.1 Definition

Definition 12 (Blind T-RBE). *A T-RBE scheme* (TGen, TReg, TEnc, TUpd, TDec) *is said to be blind if, in addition to completeness, compactness, efficiency and security properties, as in Definition 6, it also satisfies the following blindness property: the function* $\mathrm{TEnc}(\mathsf{crs}, \mathsf{pp}, t_{\mathsf{id}}, \mathsf{m}; \mathsf{r})$ *can be expressed as the concatenation* $\mathrm{TEnc}_1(\mathsf{crs}, \mathsf{pp}; \mathsf{r})||\mathrm{TEnc}_2(\mathsf{crs}, \mathsf{pp}, t_{\mathsf{id}}, \mathsf{m}; \mathsf{r})$ *such that for any PPT adversary* Adv, *the probability of winning in the following game with a challenger* Chal *is at most* $1/2 + \mathrm{negl}(\kappa)$*:*

1. ***Initialization.*** Chal *sets* $\mathsf{pp} = \perp$, $\mathsf{aux} = \perp$, $\mathsf{ID} = \varnothing$, $t = 1$, $t^* = \perp$, $\mathsf{id}^* = \perp$, $\mathsf{crs} \leftarrow U_{\mathrm{poly}(\kappa)}$ *and sends the sampled* crs *to* Adv.
2. *Till* Adv *continues (which is at most* $\mathrm{poly}(\kappa)$ *steps), proceed as follows. At every iteration,* Adv *can perform exactly one of the following actions.*
   (a) ***Registering new (non-target) identity.*** Adv *sends some* $\mathsf{id} \notin \mathsf{ID}$ *and* pk *to* Chal. Chal *registers* $(\mathsf{id}, \mathsf{pk})$ *by getting* $\mathsf{pp} = \mathrm{TReg}^{[\mathsf{aux}]}(\mathsf{crs}, \mathsf{pp}, (t, \mathsf{pk}))$ *and sets* $\mathsf{ID} = \mathsf{ID} \cup \{\mathsf{id}\}$ *and* $t = t + 1$.
   (b) ***Registering new target identity pair.*** *If* id^* *was chosen by* Adv *already (i.e.,* $\mathsf{id}^* \neq \perp$*), skip this step. Otherwise,* Adv *sends challenge identities* $\mathsf{id}^* \notin \mathsf{ID}$ *to* Chal. Chal *first samples* $(\mathsf{pk}^*, \mathsf{sk}^*) \leftarrow \mathrm{TGen}(1^\kappa)$*, registers* id^* *by setting* $\mathsf{pp} = \mathrm{TReg}^{[\mathsf{aux}]}(\mathsf{crs}, \mathsf{pp}, (t, \mathsf{pk}^*))$*. Next,* Chal *lets* $\mathsf{ID} = \mathsf{ID} \cup \{\mathsf{id}^*\}$, $t = t^*$ *and* $t = t + 1$*, and sends* $t^*, \mathsf{pk}^*, \mathsf{sk}^*$ *to* Adv. *(Note that unlike the security property, the secret key* is *given to* Adv.*)*
3. ***Encrypting for the challenge identity.*** *If* id^* *was not chosen by* Adv *already (i.e.,* $\mathsf{id}^* \neq \perp$*), then* Adv *first sends some* $\mathsf{id}^* \notin \mathsf{ID}$ *to* Chal *before continuing this step. Next,* Chal *samples a random message* $\mathsf{m} \in_R \mathcal{M}$ *and generates* $(\mathsf{subct}_1, \mathsf{subct}_2) \leftarrow \mathrm{TEnc}(\mathsf{crs}, \mathsf{pp}, t^*, \mathsf{m}; \mathsf{r})$*. It generates a bit* $b \in_R \{0, 1\}$ *and:*
   - *if* $b = 0$*, set* $\mathsf{ct} = (\mathsf{subct}_1, \mathsf{subct}_2)$.
   - *if* $b = 1$*, generate a random* subct_2' *of same length as* subct_2 *and set* $\mathsf{ct} = (\mathsf{subct}_1, \mathsf{subct}_2')$.

   Chal *sends* ct *to* Adv *(Note that the* Adv *does not know the random message* m *being encrypted).*
4. *The adversary* Adv *outputs a bit* b' *and wins the game if* $b' = b$.

4.2 Construction of an Efficient Blind T-RBE Scheme

We construct a blind T-RBE scheme (TGen, TReg, TUpd, TEnc, TDec), as in Definition 12, using the following building blocks:

- Blind Hash Garbling scheme (HGen, Hash, HObf, HInp), where the function HInp is expressible as concatenation of function outputs of HInp_1 and HInp_2 as in Definition 10.
- Blind Public-key Encryption scheme (G, E, D), where the function E is expressible as a concatenation of outputs of E_1 and E_2, as in Definition 7.

The subroutines of the T-RBE scheme are defined as follows:

- $\mathrm{TGen}(1^\kappa)$:
  1. $(\mathsf{pk}, \mathsf{sk}) \leftarrow G(1^\kappa)$
  2. Output $(\mathsf{pk}, \mathsf{sk})$.
- $\mathrm{TReg}^{[\mathsf{aux}]}(\mathsf{pp}, t_{\mathsf{id}}, \mathsf{pk})$:
  1. aux consists of a family of Merkle trees $\mathcal{T} = \{\mathsf{Tree}_1, \cdots, \mathsf{Tree}_\eta\}$ which are constructed through the process of registration described below. It also consists of a list of timestamps corresponding to each tree in $\mathcal{T}$, TID, arranged in ascending order of timestamps of the identities.
  2. Parse $\mathsf{pp} = (\mathsf{hk}, (\mathsf{rt}_1, d_1), \cdots, (\mathsf{rt}_\eta, d_\eta))$, where $\mathsf{hk} \leftarrow \mathrm{HGen}(1^\kappa, 1^{2\kappa+\log n})$ and (rt_i, d_i) represent the root and depth of Tree_i in $\mathcal{T}$.
  3. Updating aux:
     (a) Create $\mathsf{Tree}_{\eta+1}$ with leaves t_{id} and pk and root $\mathsf{rt}_{\eta+1} = \mathsf{Hash}(\mathsf{hk}, t_{\mathsf{id}}||\mathsf{pk}||0^\kappa)$.
     (b) If there are two trees Tree_L and Tree_R in $\mathcal{T}$ of same depth d then proceed as follows:
        - Let t_L and t_R denote the largest timestamps of Tree_L and Tree_R respectively (can be obtained by reading the last leaf of each tree). WLOG, suppose $t_L < t_R$.
        - Merge the trees, with Tree_L on the left and Tree_R on the right[1], with corresponding roots rt_L and rt_R, to obtain Tree with root $\mathsf{rt} = \mathsf{Hash}(\mathsf{hk}, \mathsf{rt}_L||\mathsf{rt}_R||t_L)$.
        - Remove Tree_L and Tree_R from $\mathcal{T}$ and add Tree to it.
     (c) $\mathsf{TID} := \mathsf{TID} \cup \{t_{\mathsf{id}}\}$.
  4. Set $\mathsf{pp}' = (\mathsf{hk}, (\mathsf{rt}_1, d_1), \cdots, (\mathsf{rt}_\zeta, d_\zeta))$, where (rt_i, d_i) represent the root and depth of Tree_i in updated $\mathcal{T}$.
  5. Output pp'.
- $\mathrm{TUpd}^{[\mathsf{aux}]}(\mathsf{pp}, t_{\mathsf{id}})$:
  1. Parse $\mathsf{pp} = (\mathsf{hk}, (\mathsf{rt}_1, d_1), \cdots, (\mathsf{rt}_\eta, d_\eta))$.
  2. Let $\mathsf{u} = \mathsf{pth}$, the Merkle opening from the leaf node t_{id} and its sibling pk to the root rt_i (in Tree_i containing the timestamp t_{id}).
  3. Output u.
- $\mathrm{TEnc}(\mathsf{pp}, t_{\mathsf{id}}, m)$:
  1. Parse $\mathsf{pp} = (\mathsf{hk}, (\mathsf{rt}_1, d_1), \cdots, (\mathsf{rt}_\eta, d_\eta))$.
  2. For each $i = 1, \cdots, \eta$:
     (a) For each $j = 1, \cdots, d_i$:
        - Sample $\mathsf{state}_{i,j} \leftarrow \{0, 1\}^\kappa$

[1] This will guarantee that the leaf nodes are sorted in ascending order of the timestamps of the identities.

  - Generate $\widetilde{\mathrm{P}}_{i,j} \leftarrow \mathrm{HObf}(\mathsf{hk}, \mathrm{P}_{i,j}, \mathsf{state}_{i,j})$

  (b) Obtain $\tilde{y}_{i,1} \leftarrow \mathrm{HInp}(\mathsf{hk}, \mathsf{rt}_i, \mathsf{state}_{i,1})$, where $\tilde{y}_{i,1} = \tilde{y}_{i,1}^{(0)} || \tilde{y}_{i,1}^{(1)}$

  (c) For each $j = 2, \cdots, d_i$, obtain $\tilde{y}_{i,j}^{(0)} = \mathrm{HInp}_1(\mathsf{hk}; \mathsf{r}_{i,j})$

3. Output $\mathsf{ct} = (\mathsf{pp}, \{\widetilde{\mathrm{P}}_{i,j}\}_{i,j}, \{\tilde{y}_{i,j}^{(0)}\}_{i,j}, \{\tilde{y}_{i,1}^{(1)}\}_i, \mathrm{E}_1(\mathsf{r}))$. Let $\mathsf{subct}_1 = (\mathsf{pp}, \{\tilde{y}_{i,j}^{(0)}\}_{i,j}, \mathrm{E}_1(\mathsf{r}))$ and $\mathsf{subct}_2 = (\{\widetilde{\mathrm{P}}_{i,j}\}_{i,j}, \{\tilde{y}_{i,1}^{(1)}\}_i)$. Then $\mathsf{ct} = (\mathsf{subct}_1, \mathsf{subct}_2)$.

The program $\mathrm{P}_{i,j}$ is as defined below:

Hardwired: $t_{\mathsf{id}}, \mathsf{hk}, \mathsf{state}_{i,j+1}, \mathsf{m}, \mathsf{r}_{i,j+1}$ (where $\mathsf{state}_{i,d_i+1} = \bot$, $\mathsf{r}_{i,d_i+1} = \mathsf{r}$).

Input: $a||b||t^*$.

1. If $t^* = 0^\kappa$ and $a = t_{\mathsf{id}}$, output $\mathrm{E}_2(b, \mathsf{m}; \mathsf{r}_{i,j+1})$.
2. If $t^* = 0^\kappa$ and $a \neq t_{\mathsf{id}}$, output $\bot$.
3. If $t_{\mathsf{id}} > t^*$, output $\mathrm{HInp}_2(\mathsf{hk}, b, \mathsf{state}_{i,j+1}; \mathsf{r}_{i,j+1})$. Else, output $\mathrm{HInp}_2(\mathsf{hk}, a, \mathsf{state}_{i,j+1}; \mathsf{r}_{i,j+1})$.

- $\mathrm{TDec}(\mathsf{sk}, \mathsf{u}, \mathsf{ct})$:
  1. Parse ct as $(\mathsf{pp}, \{\widetilde{\mathrm{P}}_{i,j}\}_{i,j}, \{\tilde{y}_{i,j}^{(0)}\}_{i,j}, \{\tilde{y}_{i,1}^{(1)}\}_i, \mathrm{E}_1(\mathsf{r}))$.
  2. Parse u as $\mathsf{pth} = (z_0 = \mathsf{rt}_{i^*}, z_1, \cdots, z_{d_{i^*}} = t_{\mathsf{id}}||\mathsf{pk}||0^\kappa)$, the Merkle opening from leaf t_{id} to the root rt_{i^*} of Tree_{i^*} (containing t_{id}).
  3. For each $j = 1, \cdots, d_{i^*} - 1$ evaluate:
     - $\tilde{y}_{i^*,j+1}^{(1)} \leftarrow \widetilde{\mathrm{P}}_{i^*,j}(\tilde{y}_{i^*,j}, z_j)$
  4. Let $c_2 = \widetilde{\mathrm{P}}_{i^*,d_{i^*}}(\tilde{y}_{i^*,d_{i^*}}, z_{d_{i^*}})$. If $c_2 = \bot$, set $c = \bot$, else set $c = \mathrm{E}_1(\mathsf{r})||c_2$.
  5. If $c = \bot$, output $\mathtt{GetUpd}$, else output $\mathrm{D}(\mathsf{sk}, c)$.

Theorem 13. *The T-RBE construction Sect. 4.2 satisfies the completeness, compactness, efficiency, security and blindness (Definition 12) properties.*

In the following subsections, we prove Theorem 13.

4.3 Proofs of Completeness, Compactness and Efficiency of the T-RBE Construction

Completeness. By the correctness of the hash garbling scheme and the Public-key Encryption scheme, completeness property follows.

Compactness of public parameters and update. Consider the public parameter $\mathsf{pp} = (\mathsf{hk}, (\mathsf{rt}_1, d_1), \cdots, (\mathsf{rt}_\eta, d_\eta))$. We observe that:

- The number of Merkle trees, η, in $\mathcal{T}$ at any time is at most $\log(n)$. This is because the trees are full binary trees and the size of the trees are always different (as we keep merging in the registration process).
- The hash key hk, the root and the depth of each tree are all of size κ each.

Hence, the size of pp is $O(\kappa. \log n)$.

Consider the update $\mathsf{u} = \mathsf{pth}$, the Merkle opening from leaf node t_{id} ad its sibling pk to the root rt_i. The depth of the tree is d_i and hence, there are at most $2.d_i + 1$ nodes in the Merkle opening, where $d_i \leq \kappa$. Hence, the size of u is at most $O((2.\kappa + \log n).\kappa) = O(\mathrm{poly}(\kappa, \log(n)))$.

Efficiency of runtime of registration and update. The registration process involves evaluating a hash value to create a new tree with the new identity and then merging the trees of same depth after this. We observe that:

- The number of merge operations is $O(\log n)$ as the number of trees is always logarithmic.
- Computing each hash costs $O(\kappa)$.

Hence, each invocation of the registration process takes time $O(\kappa.\log n)$. Consider a single invocation of the update. This just involves reading aux to output the Merkle opening required and this takes time $O((2.\kappa + \log n)\kappa) = O(\text{poly}(\kappa, \log n))$.

Efficiency of the number of updates. Each identity would require to invoke Upd, whenever the Merkle opening for the id gets modified. This in turn happens whenever two tress are merged. Since the number of merges is at most $O(\log n)$, the total number of invocations of Upd by each identity is at most $O(\log n)$.

4.4 Proof of Security of the T-RBE Construction

We prove the security assuming that there is only one tree at the time of encryption. The proof for the case of multiple trees will be the same.

Proof. Suppose that at the time of encryption, the underlying tree has root rt and depth d. For simplicity, for each $j \in [d]$, we denote the circuits $\mathrm{P}_{1,j}$ by P_j and the state used for obfuscation, $\mathsf{state}_{1,j}$ by state_j, i.e., for each $j \in [d]$

$$\mathrm{P}_j \equiv \mathrm{P}_{1,j}[t_{\mathsf{id}}, \mathsf{hk}, \mathsf{state}_{j+1}, \mathsf{m}, \mathsf{r}_{1,j+1}]$$

where all the variables are as in the encryption algorithm of the construction.

As in the construction, let the Merkle opening from the leaf node t_{id} and its sibling pk to the root rt be denoted by:

$$\mathsf{pth} = ((t_{\mathsf{id}}, \mathsf{pk}, 0^\kappa), (a_1, b_1, t_1), \cdots, (a_{d-1}, b_{d-1}, t_{d-1}), \mathsf{rt})$$

As in the decryption algorithm of the construction, we denote the hash-obfuscation of the inputs of the circuits by $\tilde{y}_j \equiv \tilde{y}_{1,j} = (\tilde{y}_{1,j}^{(0)}, \tilde{y}_{1,j}^{(1)})$ for each $j \in [d]$. Then, in the actual game, the output of the encryption algorithm is $\mathsf{ct}_0 := (\mathsf{subct}_{0,1}, \mathsf{subct}_{0,2})$, where $\mathsf{subct}_{0,1} = (\mathsf{pp}, \tilde{y}_1^{(0)}, \cdots, \tilde{y}_d^{(0)}, \mathrm{E}_1(\mathsf{r}))$ and $\mathsf{subct}_{0,2} = (\widetilde{\mathrm{P}}_1, \cdots, \widetilde{\mathrm{P}}_d, \tilde{y}_1^{(1)})$ (as in the protocol we have two parts of the ciphertext).

We describe the following sequence of hybrids, where we first replace the garbled versions of the programs P_j and the corresponding garbled inputs $\tilde{y}_j$ by their simulated variants, which do not use state_j, one by one.

- **Hybrid$_0$ (encryption in real game)**: The ciphertext here will be $\mathsf{ct}_0 := (\mathsf{subct}_{0,1}, \mathsf{subct}_{0,2})$, where $\mathsf{subct}_{0,1} = (\mathsf{pp}, \tilde{y}_1^{(0)}, \cdots, \tilde{y}_d^{(0)}, \mathrm{E}_1(\mathsf{r}))$ and $\mathsf{subct}_{0,2} = (\widetilde{\mathrm{P}}_1, \cdots, \widetilde{\mathrm{P}}_d, \tilde{y}_1^{(1)})$, are as described above.

- **Hybrid**$_1$: We replace the first obfuscated program $\tilde{\mathrm{P}}_1$ with its simulated form. $\tilde{\mathrm{P}}_2, \cdots, \tilde{\mathrm{P}}_d$ are sampled as in the construction. Let $\tilde{\mathrm{P}}_{1,\mathsf{sim}}$ and $\tilde{y}_{1,\mathsf{sim}}^{(1)}$ be sampled as:

$$(\tilde{\mathrm{P}}_{1,\mathsf{sim}}, \tilde{y}_{1,\mathsf{sim}}^{(1)}) \leftarrow \mathsf{Sim}(\mathsf{hk}, (a_{d-1}, b_{d-1}, t_{d-1}), 1^{|\mathrm{P}_1|}, \tilde{y}_2^{(1)})$$

Then, the ciphertext in this hybrid is $\mathsf{ct}_1 := (\mathsf{subct}_{1,1}, \mathsf{subct}_{1,2})$, where $\mathsf{subct}_{1,1} = (\mathsf{pp}, \tilde{y}_1^{(0)}, \cdots, \tilde{y}_d^{(0)}, \mathrm{E}_1(\mathsf{r}))$ and $\mathsf{subct}_{1,2} = (\tilde{\mathrm{P}}_{1,\mathsf{sim}}, \tilde{\mathrm{P}}_2, \cdots, \tilde{\mathrm{P}}_d, \tilde{y}_{1,\mathsf{sim}}^{(1)})$.
- **Hybrid**$_i$, for each $i \in [d-1]$: The ciphertext is $\mathsf{ct}_i := (\mathsf{subct}_{i,1}, \mathsf{subct}_{i,2})$, where $\mathsf{subct}_{i,1} = (\mathsf{pp}, \tilde{y}_1^{(0)}, \cdots, \tilde{y}_d^{(0)}, \mathrm{E}_1(\mathsf{r}))$ and $\mathsf{subct}_{i,2} = (\tilde{\mathrm{P}}_{1,\mathsf{sim}}, \cdots, \tilde{\mathrm{P}}_{i,\mathsf{sim}}, \tilde{\mathrm{P}}_{i+1}, \cdots, \tilde{\mathrm{P}}_d, \tilde{y}_{1,\mathsf{sim}}^{(1)})$ where for each $j \in [i]$:

$$(\tilde{\mathrm{P}}_{j,\mathsf{sim}}, \tilde{y}_{j,\mathsf{sim}}^{(1)}) \leftarrow \mathsf{Sim}(\mathsf{hk}, (a_{d-j}, b_{d-j}, t_{d-j}), 1^{|\mathrm{P}_j|}, \tilde{y}_{j+1}^{(1)})$$

- **Hybrid**$_d$: The ciphertext is $\mathsf{ct}_d := (\mathsf{subct}_{d,1}, \mathsf{subct}_{d,2})$, where $\mathsf{subct}_{d,1} = (\mathsf{pp}, \tilde{y}_1^{(0)}, \cdots, \tilde{y}_d^{(0)}, \mathrm{E}_1(\mathsf{r}))$ and $\mathsf{subct}_{d,2} = (\tilde{\mathrm{P}}_{1,\mathsf{sim}}, \cdots, \tilde{\mathrm{P}}_{d,\mathsf{sim}}, \tilde{y}_{1,\mathsf{sim}}^{(1)})$ where for each $j \in [d-1]$

$$(\tilde{\mathrm{P}}_{j,\mathsf{sim}}, \tilde{y}_{j,\mathsf{sim}}^{(1)}) \leftarrow \mathsf{Sim}(\mathsf{hk}, (a_{d-j}, b_{d-j}, t_{d-j}), 1^{|\mathrm{P}_j|}, \tilde{y}_{j+1}^{(1)})$$

and

$$(\tilde{\mathrm{P}}_{d,\mathsf{sim}}, \tilde{y}_{d,\mathsf{sim}}^{(1)}) \leftarrow \mathsf{Sim}(\mathsf{hk}, (t_{\mathsf{id}}, \mathsf{pk}, 0^\kappa), 1^{|\mathrm{P}_d|}, \mathrm{E}_2(\mathsf{pk}, \mathsf{m}; \mathsf{r}))$$

By the simulation security of the hash garbling scheme, we know that, for each $j \in [d-1]$,

$$(\mathsf{hk}, (a_{d-j}, b_{d-j}, t_{d-j}), \tilde{y}_j^{(0)}, \tilde{\mathrm{P}}_j, \tilde{y}_j^{(1)}) \overset{c}{\approx} (\mathsf{hk}, (a_{d-j}, b_{d-j}, t_{d-j}), \tilde{y}_j^{(0)}, \tilde{\mathrm{P}}_{j,\mathsf{sim}}, \tilde{y}_{j,\mathsf{sim}}^{(1)})$$

and

$$(\mathsf{hk}, (t_{\mathsf{id}}, \mathsf{pk}, 0^\kappa), \tilde{y}_d^{(0)}, \tilde{\mathrm{P}}_d, \tilde{y}_d^{(1)}) \overset{c}{\approx} (\mathsf{hk}, (t_{\mathsf{id}}, \mathsf{pk}, 0^\kappa), \tilde{y}_d^{(0)}, \tilde{\mathrm{P}}_{d,\mathsf{sim}}, \tilde{y}_{d,\mathsf{sim}}^{(1)})$$

Hence, it follows that for each $i = 0, \cdots, d-1$, $\mathbf{Hybrid}_i \overset{c}{\approx} \mathbf{Hybrid}_{i+1}$.

Now, let $\mathbf{Hybrid}_i^0$ denote the hybrids described above with use of underlying message m_0 and $\mathbf{Hybrid}_i^1$ for message m_1. By semantic security of the underlying public-key encryption scheme, we get:

$$\mathsf{Sim}(\mathsf{hk}, (t_{\mathsf{id}}, \mathsf{pk}, 0^\kappa), 1^{|\mathrm{P}_d|}, \mathrm{E}_2(\mathsf{pk}, \mathsf{m}_0; \mathsf{r})) \overset{c}{\approx} \mathsf{Sim}(\mathsf{hk}, (t_{\mathsf{id}}, \mathsf{pk}, 0^\kappa), 1^{|\mathrm{P}_d|}, \mathrm{E}_2(\mathsf{pk}, \mathsf{m}_1; \mathsf{r}))$$

Hence, $\mathbf{Hybrid}_d^0 \overset{c}{\approx} \mathbf{Hybrid}_d^1$. Then, it follows that $\mathbf{Hybrid}_0^0 \overset{c}{\approx} \mathbf{Hybrid}_0^1$, which represent the actual security game with use of messages m_0 and m_1 in respective hybrids. Hence, the security of the T-RBE scheme is proved.

4.5 Proof of Blindness of the T-RBE Construction

We prove the blindness of the scheme assuming that there is only one tree at the time of encryption. The proof for the case of multiple trees will be the same.

Proof. Suppose that at the time of encryption, the underlying tree has root rt and depth d. For simplicity, for each $j \in [d]$, we denote the circuits $\mathrm{P}_{1,j}$ by P_j and the state used for obfuscation, $\mathsf{state}_{1,j}$ by state_j, i.e., for each $j \in [d]$

$$\mathrm{P}_j \equiv \mathrm{P}_{1,j}[t_{\mathsf{id}}, \mathsf{hk}, \mathsf{state}_{j+1}, \mathsf{m}, \mathsf{r}_{1,j+1}]$$

where all the variables are as in the encryption algorithm of the construction.

As in the construction, let the Merkle opening from the leaf node t_{id} and its sibling pk to the root rt be denoted by:

$$\mathsf{pth} = ((t_{\mathsf{id}}, \mathsf{pk}, 0^{\kappa}), (a_1, b_1, t_1), \cdots, (a_{d-1}, b_{d-1}, t_{d-1}), \mathsf{rt}).$$

As in the decryption algorithm of the construction, we denote the hash-obfuscation of the inputs of the circuits by $\tilde{y}_j \equiv \tilde{y}_{1,j} = (\tilde{y}_{1,j}^{(0)}, \tilde{y}_{1,j}^{(1)})$ for each $j \in [d]$. Then, in the actual game, where now the message m is chosen at random, the output of the encryption algorithm is $\mathsf{ct}_0 := (\mathsf{subct}_{0,1}, \mathsf{subct}_{0,2})$, where $\mathsf{subct}_{0,1} = (\mathsf{pp}, \tilde{y}_1^{(0)}, \cdots, \tilde{y}_d^{(0)}, \mathrm{E}_1(\mathsf{r}))$ and $\mathsf{subct}_{0,2} = (\tilde{\mathrm{P}}_1, \cdots, \tilde{\mathrm{P}}_d, \tilde{y}_1^{(1)})$ (as in the protocol we have two parts of the ciphertext). Clearly $\mathsf{subct}_{0,1}$ is expressible as $\mathrm{TEnc}_1(\mathsf{pp}; \mathsf{r})$.

We describe the following sequence of hybrids, where we first follow the sequence of hybrids in the security proof of Sect. 4.4 to replace all the garbled versions of the programs P_j and the corresponding garbled inputs $\tilde{y}_j$ by their simulated variants. Then we use the blindness property of the blind hash garbling scheme and the blind public key encryption scheme to replace the simulated garbled circuits with uniform.

- **Hybrid$_0$ (encryption in real blindness game)**: The ciphertext in this hybrid will be $\mathsf{ct}_0 := (\mathsf{subct}_{0,1}, \mathsf{subct}_{0,2})$, where $\mathsf{subct}_{0,1} = (\mathsf{pp}, \tilde{y}_1^{(0)}, \cdots, \tilde{y}_d^{(0)}, \mathrm{E}_1(\mathsf{r}))$ and $\mathsf{subct}_{0,2} = (\tilde{\mathrm{P}}_1, \cdots, \tilde{\mathrm{P}}_d, \tilde{y}_1^{(1)})$, as described above.
- **Hybrid$_1$**: The ciphertext is $\mathsf{ct}_1 := (\mathsf{subct}_{1,1}, \mathsf{subct}_{1,2})$, where $\mathsf{subct}_{1,1} = (\mathsf{pp}, \tilde{y}_1^{(0)}, \cdots, \tilde{y}_d^{(0)}, \mathrm{E}_1(\mathsf{r}))$ and $\mathsf{subct}_{1,2} = (\tilde{\mathrm{P}}_{1,\mathsf{sim}}, \cdots, \tilde{\mathrm{P}}_{d,\mathsf{sim}}, \tilde{y}_{1,\mathsf{sim}}^{(1)})$ where for each $j \in [d-1]$

$$(\tilde{\mathrm{P}}_{j,\mathsf{sim}}, \tilde{y}_{j,\mathsf{sim}}^{(1)}) \leftarrow \mathsf{Sim}(\mathsf{hk}, (a_{d-j}, b_{d-j}, t_{d-j}), 1^{|\mathrm{P}_j|}, \tilde{y}_{j+1}^{(1)})$$

and

$$(\tilde{\mathrm{P}}_{d,\mathsf{sim}}, \tilde{y}_{d,\mathsf{sim}}^{(1)}) \leftarrow \mathsf{Sim}(\mathsf{hk}, (t_{\mathsf{id}}, \mathsf{pk}, 0^{\kappa}), 1^{|\mathrm{P}_d|}, \mathrm{E}_2(\mathsf{pk}, \mathsf{m}; \mathsf{r})).$$

- **Hybrid$_i$** for each $i = 2, \cdots, d$: The ciphertext is $\mathsf{ct}_i := (\mathsf{subct}_{i,1}, \mathsf{subct}_{i,2})$, where $\mathsf{subct}_{i,1} = (\mathsf{pp}, \tilde{y}_1^{(0)}, \cdots, \tilde{y}_d^{(0)}, \mathrm{E}_1(\mathsf{r}))$ and $\mathsf{subct}_{i,2} = (\tilde{\mathrm{P}}_{1,\mathsf{sim}}, \cdots, \tilde{\mathrm{P}}_{d-(i-1),\mathsf{sim}}, U_{|\tilde{\mathrm{P}}_{d-(i-2)}|}, \cdots, U_{|\tilde{\mathrm{P}}_d|}, \tilde{y}_{1,\mathsf{sim}}^{(1)})$.
- **Hybrid$_{d+1}$**: The ciphertext is $\mathsf{ct}_{d+1} := (\mathsf{subct}_{d+1,1}, \mathsf{subct}_{d+1,2})$, where $\mathsf{subct}_{d+1,1} = (\mathsf{pp}, \tilde{y}_1^{(0)}, \cdots, \tilde{y}_d^{(0)}, \mathrm{E}_1(\mathsf{r}))$ and $\mathsf{subct}_{d+1,2} = (U_{|\tilde{\mathrm{P}}_1|+|\tilde{y}_1^{(1)}|}, U_{|\tilde{\mathrm{P}}_2|}, \cdots, U_{|\tilde{\mathrm{P}}_d|})$.

By the proof of security in Sect. 4.4, we know that $\mathbf{Hybrid}_0 \overset{c}{\approx} \mathbf{Hybrid}_1$. Now, by blindness property of the blind public key encryption scheme, we know:

$$(\mathsf{pk}, \mathsf{sk}, \mathrm{E}_1(\mathsf{r}), \mathrm{E}_2(\mathsf{pk}, \mathsf{m}; \mathsf{r})) \overset{c}{\approx} (\mathsf{pk}, \mathsf{sk}, \mathrm{E}_1(\mathsf{r}), U).$$

Hence, by the blindness property of the hash garbling scheme, it follows that:

$$(\mathsf{hk}, (t_{\mathsf{id}}, \mathsf{pk}, 0^\kappa), \mathsf{sk}, \tilde{y}_d^{(0)}, \tilde{\mathrm{P}}_{d,\mathsf{sim}}, \tilde{y}_{d,\mathsf{sim}}^{(1)}) \overset{c}{\approx} (\mathsf{hk}, (t_{\mathsf{id}}, \mathsf{pk}, 0^\kappa), \mathsf{sk}, \tilde{y}_d^{(0)}, U_{|\,\mathrm{P}_d\,| + |\tilde{y}_d^{(1)}|}).$$

Hence, it follows that $\mathbf{Hybrid}_1 \overset{c}{\approx} \mathbf{Hybrid}_2$ even given the secret key sk.

By consecutive use of blindness property of the hash garbling scheme, it would follow that for each $i = 2, \cdots, d$, $\mathbf{Hybrid}_i \overset{c}{\approx} \mathbf{Hybrid}_{i+1}$ which holds even given the secret key sk.

Hence, we have that $\mathbf{Hybrid}_0 \overset{c}{\approx} \mathbf{Hybrid}_{d+1}$, even given the secret key sk, which exactly represents the blindness game. This completes the proof of blindness of the T-RBE scheme.

5 Anonymous Registration-Based Encryption

We now construct an efficient anonymous RBE scheme as in Definition 5.

5.1 Construction of an Efficient Anonymous RBE Scheme

We now construct a RBE scheme (Gen, Reg, Enc, Upd, Dec) using the following building blocks:

- Blind Hash Garbling scheme (HGen, Hash, HObf, HInp), where the function HInp is expressible as concatenation of function outputs of HInp_1 and HInp_2, as in Definition 10.
- Blind T-RBE scheme (TGen, TReg, TEnc, TUpd, TDec), where the function TEnc is expressible as the concatenation of function outputs of TEnc_1 and TEnc_2, as in Definition 12.

The subroutines of our RBE scheme are defined as follows:

- $\mathrm{Gen}(1^\kappa)$:
  1. $(\mathsf{pk}, \mathsf{sk}) \leftarrow \mathrm{TGen}(1^\kappa)$.
  2. Output $(\mathsf{pk}, \mathsf{sk})$.
- $\mathrm{Reg}^{[\mathsf{aux}]}(\mathsf{pp}, \mathsf{id}, \mathsf{pk})$:
  1. aux consists of a Red-black Merkle tree $\mathsf{TimeTree}$ which has the identities (along with their timestamps) at the leaf nodes, sorted according to the identities. $\mathsf{TimeTree}$ is constructed through the process of registration, as described below. aux also consists of the database aux_T required by the T-RBE scheme and a list ID of identities registered so far, in ascending order. Let the Merkle trees contained in aux_T be $\mathcal{T} = \{\mathsf{Tree}_1, \cdots, \mathsf{Tree}_\eta\}$.

2. Parse pp as $(\mathsf{hk}, \mathsf{pp}_T, (\mathsf{rt}_1, d_1), \cdots, (\mathsf{rt}_\eta, d_\eta))$, where $\mathsf{hk} \leftarrow \mathrm{HGen}(1^\kappa, 1^{3\kappa})$, pp_T corresponds to the public parameter of the T-RBE scheme and $(\mathsf{rt}_1, d_1), \cdots, (\mathsf{rt}_\eta, d_\eta)$ are the roots and depth of the same $\mathsf{TimeTree}$ corresponding to the time when $\mathsf{Tree}_1, \cdots, \mathsf{Tree}_\eta$ where last updated respectively.[2]
3. Updating $\mathsf{TimeTree}$:
   (a) $\mathsf{TimeTree}$ is a Red-Black Merkle tree with each non-leaf node containing a hash of its left child, hash of its right child and the largest identity on the left subtree. The leaves of the tree contain the identities (with their timestamps, i.e., a binary representation of when the identity registered). Further, each node has an additional bit of information, indicating if it's colored red or black. The color helps in keeping the tree "approximately" balanced after each insertion[3].
   (b) Evaluate $h_{\mathsf{id}} = \mathrm{Hash}(\mathsf{hk}, \mathsf{id}||0^{2\kappa - \log n}||t_{\mathsf{id}})$.
   (c) To insert the new id at the right location, we first parse the root of $\mathsf{TimeTree}$ as $\mathsf{rt} = h_1||\mathsf{id}^*||h_2$. If $\mathsf{id} > \mathsf{id}^*$, read the right child, else read the left child. Continue traversing the path down the tree to figure out the correct insertion point of id.
   (d) The parent node of $\mathsf{id}||t_{\mathsf{id}}$ contains h_{id} along with the largest identity on its left subtree and the hash of its other child. Re-order the tree, recolor, to keep it balanced. This will take at most $\log n$ time (as it's a red-black tree). Every node that is not a leaf or a parent node of a leaf node, is of the form $h_L||id^*||h_R$, where $h_L = \mathrm{Hash}(\mathsf{hk}, h_1||id_L||h_2)$ and $h_R = \mathrm{Hash}(\mathsf{hk}, h_3||id_R||h_4)$ and id^* is the largest identity on the left subtree of this node.
4. Evaluate $\mathsf{pp}'_T \leftarrow \mathrm{TReg}^{[\mathsf{aux}]}(\mathsf{pp}_T, t_{\mathsf{id}}, \mathsf{pk})$, where t_{id} will be the binary representation of the timestamp corresponding to id (can be obtained by checking ID to see the current number of identities).
5. Suppose the registration process of T-RBE above results in a merge of trees Tree_L and Tree_R and the corresponding root hashes of $\mathsf{TimeTree}$ at the time of last update of these trees be rt_L and rt_R. Remove (rt_L, d_L) and (rt_R, d_R) from pp and add (rt, d), which is the root hash and the depth of $\mathsf{TimeTree}$ at time t_{id}. Suppose the updated root hashes and depth of $\mathsf{TimeTree}$ after all the merges in $\mathcal{T}$ be $(\mathsf{rt}_1, d_1), \cdots, (\mathsf{rt}_\varsigma, d_\varsigma)$.
6. Set $\mathsf{pp}' = (\mathsf{hk}, \mathsf{pp}'_T, (\mathsf{rt}_1, d_1), \cdots, (\mathsf{rt}_\varsigma, d_\varsigma))$.
7. Output pp'.

- $\mathrm{Upd}^{[\mathsf{aux}]}(\mathsf{pp}, \mathsf{id})$:
  1. Parse $\mathsf{pp} = (\mathsf{hk}, \mathsf{pp}_T, (\mathsf{rt}_1, d_1), \cdots, (\mathsf{rt}_\eta, d_\eta))$.
  2. Evaluate $\mathsf{u}_1 \leftarrow \mathrm{TUpd}^{[\mathsf{aux}]}(\mathsf{pp}_T, t_{\mathsf{id}})$.

[2] Looking ahead, we need to store the root hashes of $\mathsf{TimeTree}$ at mulitple times in order to ensure that the number of updates required by each person remains $\log n$.

[3] The main advantage of having a Red-Black Merkle tree is that after each insertion, the depth of the tree does not increase beyond $\log n$, where n is the number of people registered in the system. The balancing is not perfect, but ensures that further insertions, rearrangement after insertion to balance, searches, all take time $O(\log n)$.

3. Set pth to be the path from the leaf node $\mathsf{id}||t_{\mathsf{id}}||0^{2\kappa-\log n}$ to the root hash rt_i of $\mathsf{TimeTree}$ at the time of last modification of the Merkle tree, Tree_i, containing id.[4]
4. Set $\mathsf{u} = (\mathsf{u}_1, \mathsf{pth})$.
5. Output u.

- $\mathrm{Enc}(\mathsf{pp}, \mathsf{id}, \mathsf{m})$:
  1. Parse pp as $(\mathsf{hk}, \mathsf{pp}_T, (\mathsf{rt}_1, d_1), \cdots, (\mathsf{rt}_\eta, d_\eta))$.
  2. For each $i = 1, \cdots, \eta$:
     (a) For each $j = 1, \cdots, d_\eta$:
        i. Sample $\mathsf{state}_{i,j} \leftarrow \{0,1\}^\kappa$.
        ii. Generate $\tilde{\mathrm{Q}}_{i,j} \leftarrow \mathrm{HObf}(\mathsf{hk}, \mathrm{Q}_{i,j}, \mathsf{state}_{i,j})$.
     (b) Parse rt_i as $h_1||\mathsf{id}^*||h_2$.
     (c) If $\mathsf{id} > \mathsf{id}^*$, obtain $\tilde{y}_{i,1} \leftarrow \mathrm{HInp}(\mathsf{hk}, h_2, \mathsf{state}_1)$, where $\tilde{y}_{i,1} = \tilde{y}_{i,1}^{(0)}||\tilde{y}_{i,1}^{(1)}$
     Else obtain $\tilde{y}_{i,1} \leftarrow \mathrm{HInp}(\mathsf{hk}, h_1, \mathsf{state}_1)$, where $\tilde{y}_{i,1} = \tilde{y}_{i,1}^{(0)}||\tilde{y}_{i,1}^{(1)}$.
     (d) For each $j = 2, \cdots, d_i$, obtain $\tilde{y}_{i,j}^{(0)} \leftarrow \mathrm{HInp}_1(\mathsf{hk}; \mathsf{r}_{i,j})$.
  3. Output $\mathsf{ct} = (\mathsf{pp}, \{\tilde{\mathrm{Q}}_{i,j}\}_{i,j}, \{\tilde{y}_{i,j}^{(0)}\}_{i,j}, \{\tilde{y}_{i,1}^{(1)}\}_i, \mathrm{TEnc}_1(\mathsf{pp}_T; \mathsf{r}))$.
  Let $\mathsf{subct}_1 = (\mathsf{pp}, \{\tilde{y}_{i,j}^{(0)}\}_{i,j}, \mathrm{TEnc}_1(\mathsf{pp}_T; \mathsf{r}))$ and $\mathsf{subct}_2 = (\{\tilde{\mathrm{Q}}_{i,j}\}_{i,j}, \{\tilde{y}_{i,1}^{(1)}\}_i)$. Then $\mathsf{ct} = (\mathsf{subct}_1, \mathsf{subct}_2)$.

The program $\mathrm{Q}_{i,j}$ is defined as:
Hardwired: $\mathsf{hk}, \mathsf{state}_{i,j+1}, \mathsf{id}, \mathsf{m}, \mathsf{r}_{i,j+1}, \mathsf{r}, \mathsf{pp}_T$ (for $\mathsf{state}_{i,d_i+1} = \mathsf{r}_{i,d_i+1} = \perp$).
Input: $a||\mathsf{id}^*||b$.
1. If $\mathsf{id}^* = 0^{2\kappa-\log n}$ and $a = \mathsf{id}$, output $\mathrm{TEnc}_2(\mathsf{pp}_T, b, \mathsf{m}; \mathsf{r})$.
2. If $\mathsf{id}^* = 0^{2\kappa-\log n}$ and $a \neq \mathsf{id}$, output $\perp$.
3. If $\mathsf{id} > \mathsf{id}^*$, output $\mathrm{HInp}_2(\mathsf{hk}, b, \mathsf{state}_{i,j+1}; \mathsf{r}_{i,j+1})$.
Else, output $\mathrm{HInp}_2(\mathsf{hk}, a, \mathsf{state}_{i,j+1}; \mathsf{r}_{i,j+1})$.

- $\mathrm{Dec}(\mathsf{sk}, \mathsf{u}, \mathsf{ct})$:
  1. Parse u as $(\mathsf{u}_1, \mathsf{pth})$, where $\mathsf{pth} = (z_0 = \mathsf{rt}_i, z_1, \cdots, z_d = \mathsf{id}||0^{2\kappa-\log n}||t_{\mathsf{id}})$. Here rt_i is the root hash of $\mathsf{TimeTree}$ at the time when Tree_i, the tree containing id, was last updated.
  2. Parse ct as $(\mathsf{pp}, \{\tilde{\mathrm{Q}}_{i,j}\}_{i,j}, \{\tilde{y}_{i,j}^{(0)}\}_{i,j}, \{\tilde{y}_{i,1}^{(1)}\}_i, \mathrm{TEnc}_1(\mathsf{pp}_T; \mathsf{r}))$.
  3. For $j = 1, \cdots, d-1$, evaluate:
     - $\tilde{y}_{i,j+1}^{(1)} \leftarrow \tilde{\mathrm{Q}}_{i,j}(\tilde{y}_{i,j}, z_j)$
  4. Let $c_2 = \tilde{\mathrm{Q}}_{i,d}(\tilde{y}_{i,d}, z_d)$. If $c_2 = \perp$, set $c = \perp$, else set $c = \mathrm{TEnc}_1(\mathsf{pp}_T; \mathsf{r})||c_2$.[5]
  5. If $c = \perp$, output `GetUpd`, else output $\mathrm{TDec}(\mathsf{sk}, \mathsf{u}_1, c)$.

Theorem 14. *The RBE construction Sect. 5.1 satisfies the completeness, compactness, efficiency (Definition 2) and the stronger security notion of an anonymous RBE (Definition 5) properties.*

In the following subsections, we prove Theorem 14.

[4] Note that we must store the versions of the same $\mathsf{TimeTree}$ at times corresponding to last updation of each Tree_i in $\mathcal{T}$. But there would only be $\log n$ such versions.

[5] Alternately, we could have performed these operations for each i, which would be the number of trees in $\mathcal{T}$. Here, we would have obtained a value $\neq \perp$ only for one i.

5.2 Completeness, Compactness and Efficiency of the Construction

Completeness. By the correctness of the hash garbling scheme and the completeness of the T-RBE scheme, completeness property follows.

Compactness of public parameters and update. Consider the public parameter $\mathsf{pp} = (\mathsf{hk}, \mathsf{pp}_{\mathcal{T}}, (\mathsf{rt}_1, d_1), \cdots, (\mathsf{rt}_\eta, d_\eta))$. We observe that:

- The public parameter of T-RBE, $\mathsf{pp}_{\mathcal{T}}$ is of size $O(\text{poly}(\kappa, \log n))$.
- The hash key hk and the depth d_i are each of size κ.
- The root of the time tree rt_i is of size $3.\kappa$.
- η is at any time is atmost $\log(n)$, as the number of trees in $\mathcal{T}$ at any time is at most $\log(n)$.

Hence, the size of pp is $O(\text{poly}(\kappa, \log n))$.

Consider the update $\mathsf{u} = (\mathsf{u}_1, pth)$. By efficiency of T-RBE, size of u_1 is $O(\text{poly}(\kappa, \log n))$. pth is the path of nodes from the leaf $\mathsf{id}||t_{\mathsf{id}}||0^{2\kappa - \log n}$ to the root rt and hence of size at most $\kappa.(3\kappa) = O(\kappa)$. Hence, the size of u is $O(\text{poly}(\kappa, \log n))$.

Efficiency of runtime of registration and update. The registration process involves running the registration of underlying T-RBE, which takes time at most $\text{poly}(\kappa, \log n)$ and inserting the new identity into the Red-black Merkle tree $\mathsf{TimeTree}$, which takes time at most $\log n$. Hence, each invocation of the registration process takes time $O(\text{poly}(\kappa, \log n))$.

Consider a single invocation of the update process. It involves a single invocation of the update algorithm of T-RBE, which takes time at most $\text{poly}(\kappa, \log n)$ and reading a single path from $\mathsf{TimeTree}$ in aux, which takes time $O((3.\kappa).\kappa)$ and an additional $\log(n)$ time to figure out the correct version of $\mathsf{TimeTree}$ to read the path from. Hence a single invocation of the update takes time $O(\text{poly}(\kappa, \log n))$.

Efficiency of the number of updates. Each identity would require to invoke Upd, whenever the Merkle tree in $\mathcal{T}$ containing id gets modified (by a merge). Unless a merge operation occurs, the identities can use the opening in the $\mathsf{TimeTree}$ corresponding to the time its Merkle tree (in $\mathcal{T}$) was last updated (even though $\mathsf{TimeTree}$ gets updated at each registration). Since the number of merges is at most $O(\log(n))$, the number of invocations of Upd by each identity is at most $O(\log n)$.

5.3 Proof of Anonymity and Security of the RBE Construction

We now prove that the RBE scheme satisfies the stronger notion of security of an anonymous RBE (Definition 5).

Proof. We prove the security assuming that there is only one Merkle tree in $\mathcal{T}$ at the time of encryption for simplicity. The proof for the case of multiple trees will be the same. Let $\mathsf{TimeTree}$ have root rt and let the challenge identity id be at depth d in TimeTree, at the time of encryption. For each $j \in [d]$, as in the construction, we have:

$$\mathsf{Q}_j \equiv \mathsf{Q}_{1,j}[\mathsf{hk}, \mathsf{state}_{1,j+1}, \mathsf{id}, \mathsf{m}, \mathsf{r}_{1,j+1}, \mathsf{r}, \mathsf{pp}_T]$$

where all the variables are as in the encryption algorithm of the construction.

As in the construction, let the path from the leaf node $\mathsf{id}||0^{2\kappa-\log n}||t_{\mathsf{id}}$ to the root rt be denoted by:

$$\mathsf{pth} = ((\mathsf{id}, 0^{2\kappa-\log n}, t_{\mathsf{id}}), (a_1, \mathsf{id}_1, b_1), \cdots, (a_{d-1}, \mathsf{id}_{d-1}, b_{d-1}), \mathsf{rt})$$

As in the decryption algorithm of the construction, we denote the hash-garbling of the inputs of the circuits by $\tilde{y}_j = \tilde{y}_{1,j}^{(0)}||\tilde{y}_{1,j}^{(1)}$ for each $j \in [d]$. Then, in the actual game, the output of the encryption algorithm is $\mathsf{ct}_0 := (\mathsf{subct}_{0,1}, \mathsf{subct}_{0,2})$, where $\mathsf{subct}_{0,1} = (\mathsf{pp}, \{\tilde{y}_j^{(0)}\}_j, \mathrm{TEnc}_1(\mathsf{pp}_T; \mathsf{r}))$ and $\mathsf{subct}_{0,2} = (\{\tilde{\mathsf{Q}}_j\}_j, \tilde{y}_1^{(1)})$.

We describe the following sequence of hybrids, *for uniformly drawn message* m, where we first replace the garbled versions of the programs Q_j and the corresponding garbled inputs $\tilde{y}_j$ by their simulated variants, which do not use state_j, one by one. Then, in the subsequent hybrids, we replace the simulated garbled programs and inputs by uniform, one by one. This uses the blindness of the T-RBE scheme and the blind hash garbling scheme.

- **Hybrid$_0$ (encryption in real game)**: The ciphertext in this hybrid is $\mathsf{ct}_0 := (\mathsf{subct}_{0,1}, \mathsf{subct}_{0,2})$, where $\mathsf{subct}_{0,1} = (\mathsf{pp}, \{\tilde{y}_j^{(0)}\}_j, \mathrm{TEnc}_1(\mathsf{pp}_T; \mathsf{r}))$ and $\mathsf{subct}_{0,2} = (\tilde{\mathsf{Q}}_1, \cdots, \tilde{\mathsf{Q}}_d, \tilde{y}_1^{(1)})$, as described above.
- **Hybrid$_1$**: We replace the first obfuscated program $\tilde{\mathsf{Q}}_1$ with its simulated form. $\tilde{\mathsf{Q}}_2, \cdots, \tilde{\mathsf{Q}}_d$ are sampled as in the construction. Let $\tilde{\mathsf{Q}}_{1,\mathsf{sim}}$ and $\tilde{y}_{1,\mathsf{sim}}^{(1)}$ be sampled as:

$$(\tilde{\mathsf{Q}}_{1,\mathsf{sim}}, \tilde{y}_{1,\mathsf{sim}}^{(1)}) \leftarrow \mathsf{Sim}(\mathsf{hk}, (a_{d-1}, \mathsf{id}_{d-1}, b_{d-1}), 1^{|\mathsf{Q}_1|}, \tilde{y}_2^{(1)})$$

  Then, the ciphertext in this hybrid is $\mathsf{ct}_1 := (\mathsf{subct}_{1,1}, \mathsf{subct}_{1,2})$, where $\mathsf{subct}_{1,1} = (\mathsf{pp}, , \{\tilde{y}_j^{(0)}\}_j, \mathrm{TEnc}_1(\mathsf{pp}_T; \mathsf{r}))$ and $\mathsf{subct}_{1,2} = (\tilde{\mathsf{Q}}_{1,\mathsf{sim}}, \cdots, \tilde{\mathsf{Q}}_d, \tilde{y}_{1,\mathsf{sim}}^{(1)})$.
- **Hybrid$_i$**, for each $i \in [d-1]$: The ciphertext is $\mathsf{ct}_i := (\mathsf{subct}_{i,1}, \mathsf{subct}_{i,2})$, where $\mathsf{subct}_{i,1} = (\mathsf{pp}, \{\tilde{y}_j^{(0)}\}_j, \mathrm{TEnc}_1(\mathsf{pp}_T; \mathsf{r}))$ and $\mathsf{subct}_{i,2} = (\tilde{\mathsf{Q}}_{1,\mathsf{sim}}, \cdots, \tilde{\mathsf{Q}}_{i,\mathsf{sim}}, \tilde{\mathsf{Q}}_{i+1}, \cdots, \tilde{\mathsf{Q}}_d, \tilde{y}_{1,\mathsf{sim}}^{(1)})$ where for each $j \in [i]$:

$$(\tilde{\mathsf{Q}}_{j,\mathsf{sim}}, \tilde{y}_{j,\mathsf{sim}}^{(1)}) \leftarrow \mathsf{Sim}(\mathsf{hk}, (a_{d-j}, \mathsf{id}_{d-j}, b_{d-j}), 1^{|\mathsf{Q}_j|}, \tilde{y}_{j+1}^{(1)})$$

- **Hybrid$_d$**: The ciphertext is $\mathsf{ct}_d := (\mathsf{subct}_{d,1}, \mathsf{subct}_{d,2})$, where $\mathsf{subct}_{d,1} = (\mathsf{pp}, \{\tilde{y}_j^{(0)}\}_j, \mathrm{TEnc}_1(\mathsf{pp}_T; \mathsf{r}))$ and $\mathsf{subct}_{d,2} = (\tilde{\mathsf{Q}}_{1,\mathsf{sim}}, \cdots, \tilde{\mathsf{Q}}_{d,\mathsf{sim}}, \tilde{y}_{1,\mathsf{sim}}^{(1)})$ where for each $j \in [d-1]$

$$(\tilde{\mathsf{Q}}_{j,\mathsf{sim}}, \tilde{y}_{j,\mathsf{sim}}^{(1)}) \leftarrow \mathsf{Sim}(\mathsf{hk}, (a_{d-j}, \mathsf{id}_{d-j}, b_{d-j}), 1^{|\mathsf{Q}_j|}, \tilde{y}_{j+1}^{(1)})$$

  and

$$(\tilde{\mathsf{Q}}_{d,\mathsf{sim}}, \tilde{y}_{d,\mathsf{sim}}^{(1)}) \leftarrow \mathsf{Sim}(\mathsf{hk}, (\mathsf{id}, 0^{2\kappa-\log n}, t_{\mathsf{id}}), 1^{|\mathsf{Q}_d|}, \mathrm{TEnc}_2(\mathsf{pp}_T, t_{\mathsf{id}}, \mathsf{m}; \mathsf{r}))$$

- **Hybrid**$_i$ for each $i = d+1, \cdots, 2d-1$: The ciphertext is $\mathsf{ct}_i := (\mathsf{subct}_{i,1}, \mathsf{subct}_{i,2})$, where $\mathsf{subct}_{i,1} = (\mathsf{pp}, \{\tilde{y}_j^{(0)}\}_j, \mathrm{TEnc}_1(\mathsf{pp}_T; \mathsf{r}))$ and $\mathsf{subct}_{i,2} = (\tilde{\mathsf{Q}}_{1,\mathsf{sim}}, \cdots, \tilde{\mathsf{Q}}_{2d-i,\mathsf{sim}}, U_{|\tilde{\mathsf{Q}}_{2d-i+1}|}, \cdots, U_{|\tilde{\mathsf{Q}}_d|}, \tilde{y}^{(1)}_{1,\mathsf{sim}})$
- **Hybrid**$_{2d}$: The ciphertext is $\mathsf{ct}_{2d} := (\mathsf{subct}_{2d,1}, \mathsf{subct}_{2d,2})$, where $\mathsf{subct}_{2d,1} = (\mathsf{pp}, \{\tilde{y}_j^{(0)}\}_j, \mathrm{TEnc}_1(\mathsf{pp}_T; \mathsf{r}))$ and $\mathsf{subct}_{2d,2} = (U_{|\tilde{\mathsf{Q}}_1|+|\tilde{y}_1^{(1)}|}, U_{|\tilde{\mathsf{Q}}_2|}, \cdots, U_{|\tilde{\mathsf{Q}}_d|})$

By the simulation security of the hash garbling scheme, for each $j \in [d-1]$,

$$(\mathsf{hk}, (a_{d-j}, \mathsf{id}_{d-j}, b_{d-j}), \tilde{y}_j^{(0)}, \tilde{\mathsf{Q}}_j, \tilde{y}_j^{(1)}) \overset{c}{\approx} (\mathsf{hk}, (a_{d-j}, \mathsf{id}_{d-j}, b_{d-j}), \tilde{y}_j^{(0)}, \tilde{\mathsf{Q}}_{j,\mathsf{sim}}, \tilde{y}^{(1)}_{j,\mathsf{sim}})$$
$$(\mathsf{hk}, (\mathsf{id}, 0^{2\kappa-\log n}, t_{\mathsf{id}}), \tilde{y}_d^{(0)}, \tilde{\mathsf{Q}}_d, \tilde{y}_d^{(1)}) \overset{c}{\approx} (\mathsf{hk}, (\mathsf{id}, 0^{2\kappa-\log n}, t_{\mathsf{id}}), \tilde{y}_d^{(0)}, \tilde{\mathsf{Q}}_{d,\mathsf{sim}}, \tilde{y}^{(1)}_{d,\mathsf{sim}})$$

Hence, it follows that for each $i = 0, \cdots, d-1$, **Hybrid**$_i \overset{c}{\approx}$ **Hybrid**$_{i+1}$.

Now, as the sequence of hybrids were defined for uniformly drawn message m, by the blindness of underlying T-RBE scheme, we know that:

$$(\mathrm{TEnc}_1(\mathsf{pp}_T; \mathsf{r}), \mathrm{TEnc}_2(\mathsf{pp}_T, t_{\mathsf{id}}, \mathsf{m}; \mathsf{r})) \overset{c}{\approx} (\mathrm{TEnc}_1(\mathsf{pp}_T; \mathsf{r}), U)$$

Hence, by the blindness property of the hash garbling scheme, it follows that:

$$(\mathsf{hk}, (\mathsf{id}, 0^{2\kappa-\log n}, t_{\mathsf{id}}), \tilde{y}_d^{(0)}, \tilde{\mathsf{Q}}_{d,\mathsf{sim}}, \tilde{y}^{(1)}_{d,\mathsf{sim}}) \overset{c}{\approx} (\mathsf{hk}, (\mathsf{id}, 0^{2\kappa-\log n}, t_{\mathsf{id}}), \tilde{y}_d^{(0)}, U_{|\tilde{\mathsf{Q}}_d|+|\tilde{y}_1^{(d)}|})$$

Hence, **Hybrid**$_d \overset{c}{\approx}$ **Hybrid**$_{d+1}$.

Similarly, by consecutive application of the blindness property of the hash garbling scheme, it holds that for each $i = d+1, \cdots, 2d-1$, **Hybrid**$_i \overset{c}{\approx}$ **Hybrid**$_{i+1}$. Hence, we have that, for uniformly drawn message m,

$$\textbf{Hybrid}_0 \overset{c}{\approx} \textbf{Hybrid}_{2d} \tag{1}$$

We now prove that, in fact, indistinguishability in Eq. 1 is stronger than the desired anonymity of the RBE scheme:

For $b = 0, 1$, let $\mathsf{ct}_0^{\mathsf{m}_b,\mathsf{id}_b} = (\mathsf{subct}_{0,1}^{\mathsf{m}_b,\mathsf{id}_b}, \mathsf{subct}_{0,2}^{\mathsf{m}_b,\mathsf{id}_b})$ and $\mathsf{ct}_{2d}^{\mathsf{m}_b,\mathsf{id}_b} = (\mathsf{subct}_{2d,1}^{\mathsf{m}_b,\mathsf{id}_b}, \mathsf{subct}_{2d,2}^{\mathsf{m}_b,\mathsf{id}_b})$ denote the ciphertexts in **Hybrid**$_0$ and **Hybrid**$_{2d}$ respectively for the b-th message, identity pair.

1. By security of T-RBE, it would follow that **Hybrid**$_d^0 \overset{c}{\approx}$ **Hybrid**$_d^1$, where **Hybrid**$_i^\beta$ denote the hybrids described above with use of message m_β. Hence, it follows that **Hybrid**$_0^0 \overset{c}{\approx}$ **Hybrid**$_0^1$.
2. Using the above indistinguishability, it follows that, for a random message m, we have $\mathsf{ct}_0^{\mathsf{m}_0,\mathsf{id}_0} \overset{c}{\approx} \mathsf{ct}_0^{\mathsf{m},\mathsf{id}_0}$.
3. Since **Hybrid**$_0 \overset{c}{\approx}$ **Hybrid**$_{2d}$ for random message m, it then follows that $\mathsf{ct}_0^{\mathsf{m},\mathsf{id}_0} = (\mathsf{subct}_{0,1}^{\mathsf{m},\mathsf{id}_0}, \mathsf{subct}_{0,2}^{\mathsf{m},\mathsf{id}_0}) \overset{c}{\approx} (\mathsf{subct}_{0,1}^{\mathsf{m},\mathsf{id}_0}, U) = \mathsf{ct}_{2d}^{\mathsf{m},\mathsf{id}_0}$.
4. Since $\mathsf{subct}_{0,1}^{\mathsf{m},\mathsf{id}_0} = \mathrm{TEnc}_1(\mathsf{pp}_T; \mathsf{r})$, is independent of identity or the message m, it then follows that $\mathsf{ct}_{2d}^{\mathsf{m},\mathsf{id}_0} \overset{c}{\approx} \mathsf{ct}_{2d}^{\mathsf{m},\mathsf{id}_1}$.

Combining the steps 2, 3 and 4 above, it follows that $\mathsf{ct}_0^{\mathsf{m}_0,\mathsf{id}_0} \overset{c}{\approx} \mathsf{ct}_0^{\mathsf{m}_1,\mathsf{id}_1}$. This exactly represents the stronger security game of the anonymous RBE. Hence, the anonymity and security of the RBE scheme is proved.

References

1. Al-Riyami, S.S., Paterson, K.G.: Certificateless public key cryptography. In: Laih, C.-S. (ed.) ASIACRYPT 2003. LNCS, vol. 2894, pp. 452–473. Springer, Heidelberg (2003). https://doi.org/10.1007/978-3-540-40061-5_29
2. Alexopoulos, N., Kiayias, A., Talviste, R., Zacharias, T.: MCMix: anonymous messaging via secure multiparty computation. In: USENIX Security Symposium, pp. 1217–1234. USENIX Association, Vancouver (2017)
3. Barak, B., et al.: On the (im)possibility of obfuscating programs. In: Kilian, J. (ed.) CRYPTO 2001. LNCS, vol. 2139, pp. 1–18. Springer, Heidelberg (2001). https://doi.org/10.1007/3-540-44647-8_1
4. Bellare, M., Boldyreva, A., Desai, A., Pointcheval, D.: Key-privacy in public-key encryption. In: Boyd, C. (ed.) ASIACRYPT 2001. LNCS, vol. 2248, pp. 566–582. Springer, Heidelberg (2001). https://doi.org/10.1007/3-540-45682-1_33
5. Bellare, M., Singh, A.C., Jaeger, J., Nyayapati, M., Stepanovs, I.: Ratcheted encryption and key exchange: the security of messaging. In: Katz, J., Shacham, H. (eds.) CRYPTO 2017. LNCS, vol. 10403, pp. 619–650. Springer, Cham (2017). https://doi.org/10.1007/978-3-319-63697-9_21
6. Boneh, D., Di Crescenzo, G., Ostrovsky, R., Persiano, G.: Public key encryption with keyword search. In: Cachin, C., Camenisch, J.L. (eds.) EUROCRYPT 2004. LNCS, vol. 3027, pp. 506–522. Springer, Heidelberg (2004). https://doi.org/10.1007/978-3-540-24676-3_30
7. Boneh, D., Franklin, M.: Identity-based encryption from the Weil pairing. In: Kilian, J. (ed.) CRYPTO 2001. LNCS, vol. 2139, pp. 213–229. Springer, Heidelberg (2001). https://doi.org/10.1007/3-540-44647-8_13
8. Borisov, N., Goldberg, I., Brewer, E.: Off-the-record communication, or, why not to use PGP. In: Proceedings of the 2004 ACM Workshop on Privacy in the Electronic Society, pp. 77–84. ACM (2004)
9. Boyen, X., Waters, B.: Anonymous hierarchical identity-based encryption (without random oracles). In: Dwork, C. (ed.) CRYPTO 2006. LNCS, vol. 4117, pp. 290–307. Springer, Heidelberg (2006). https://doi.org/10.1007/11818175_17
10. Brakerski, Z., Lombardi, A., Segev, G., Vaikuntanathan, V.: Anonymous IBE, leakage resilience and circular security from new assumptions. In: Nielsen, J.B., Rijmen, V. (eds.) EUROCRYPT 2018, Part I. LNCS, vol. 10820, pp. 535–564. Springer, Cham (2018). https://doi.org/10.1007/978-3-319-78381-9_20
11. Callas, J.: Identity-based encryption with conventional public-key infrastructure (2005)
12. Cheng, Z., Comley, R., Vasiu, L.: Remove key escrow from the identity-based encryption system. In: Levy, J.-J., Mayr, E.W., Mitchell, J.C. (eds.) TCS 2004. IIFIP, vol. 155, pp. 37–50. Springer, Boston, MA (2004). https://doi.org/10.1007/1-4020-8141-3_6
13. Cho, C., Döttling, N., Garg, S., Gupta, D., Miao, P., Polychroniadou, A.: Laconic oblivious transfer and its applications. In: Katz, J., Shacham, H. (eds.) CRYPTO 2017, Part II. LNCS, vol. 10402, pp. 33–65. Springer, Cham (2017). https://doi.org/10.1007/978-3-319-63715-0_2
14. Chow, S.S.M.: Removing escrow from identity-based encryption. In: Jarecki, S., Tsudik, G. (eds.) PKC 2009. LNCS, vol. 5443, pp. 256–276. Springer, Heidelberg (2009). https://doi.org/10.1007/978-3-642-00468-1_15
15. Cohn-Gordon, K., Cremers, C., Dowling, B., Garratt, L., Stebila, D.: A formal security analysis of the signal messaging protocol. In: 2017 IEEE European Symposium on Security and Privacy (EuroS&P), pp. 451–466. IEEE (2017)

16. Cooper, D.A., Birman, K.P.: Preserving privacy in a network of mobile computers. Technical report, Cornell University (1995)
17. Corrigan-Gibbs, H., Boneh, D., Mazières, D.: Riposte: an anonymous messaging system handling millions of users. arXiv:1503.06115 (2015)
18. Corrigan-Gibbs, H., Ford, B.: Dissent: accountable anonymous group messaging. In: Proceedings of the 17th ACM Conference on Computer and Communications Security, pp. 340–350. ACM (2010)
19. Döttling, N., Garg, S.: Identity-based encryption from the Diffie-Hellman assumption. In: Katz, J., Shacham, H. (eds.) CRYPTO 2017, Part I. LNCS, vol. 10401, pp. 537–569. Springer, Cham (2017). https://doi.org/10.1007/978-3-319-63688-7_18
20. Döttling, N., Garg, S., Hajiabadi, M., Masny, D.: New constructions of identity-based and key-dependent message secure encryption schemes. In: Abdalla, M., Dahab, R. (eds.) PKC 2018, Part I. LNCS, vol. 10769, pp. 3–31. Springer, Cham (2018). https://doi.org/10.1007/978-3-319-76578-5_1
21. Garg, S., Gentry, C., Halevi, S., Raykova, M., Sahai, A., Waters, B.: Candidate indistinguishability obfuscation and functional encryption for all circuits. In: 54th Annual Symposium on Foundations of Computer Science, Berkeley, CA, USA, 26–29 October 2013, pp. 40–49. IEEE Computer Society Press (2013)
22. Garg, S., Hajiabadi, M., Mahmoody, M., Rahimi, A.: Registration-based encryption: removing private-key generator from IBE. In: Beimel, A., Dziembowski, S. (eds.) TCC 2018. LNCS, vol. 11239, pp. 689–718. Springer, Cham (2018). https://doi.org/10.1007/978-3-030-03807-6_25
23. Goyal, V.: Reducing trust in the PKG in identity based cryptosystems. In: Menezes, A. (ed.) CRYPTO 2007. LNCS, vol. 4622, pp. 430–447. Springer, Heidelberg (2007). https://doi.org/10.1007/978-3-540-74143-5_24
24. Goyal, V., Lu, S., Sahai, A., Waters, B.: Black-box accountable authority identity-based encryption. In: Proceedings of the 15th ACM Conference on Computer and Communications Security, pp. 427–436. ACM (2008)
25. Hubacek, P., Wichs, D.: On the communication complexity of secure function evaluation with long output. In: Roughgarden, T. (ed.) ITCS 2015: 6th Conference on Innovations in Theoretical Computer Science, Rehovot, Israel, 11–13 January 2015, pp. 163–172. Association for Computing Machinery (2015)
26. Jaeger, J., Stepanovs, I.: Optimal channel security against fine-grained state compromise: the safety of messaging. In: Shacham, H., Boldyreva, A. (eds.) CRYPTO 2018. LNCS, vol. 10991, pp. 33–62. Springer, Cham (2018). https://doi.org/10.1007/978-3-319-96884-1_2
27. Mohassel, P.: A closer look at anonymity and robustness in encryption schemes. In: Abe, M. (ed.) ASIACRYPT 2010. LNCS, vol. 6477, pp. 501–518. Springer, Heidelberg (2010). https://doi.org/10.1007/978-3-642-17373-8_29
28. Poettering, B., Rösler, P.: Towards bidirectional ratcheted key exchange. In: Shacham, H., Boldyreva, A. (eds.) CRYPTO 2018. LNCS, vol. 10991, pp. 3–32. Springer, Cham (2018). https://doi.org/10.1007/978-3-319-96884-1_1
29. Rogaway, P.: The moral character of cryptographic work. IACR Cryptology ePrint Archive 2015:1162 (2015)
30. Rösler, P., Mainka, C., Schwenk, J.: More is less: on the end-to-end security of group chats in signal, WhatsApp, and Threema (2018)
31. Shamir, A.: Identity-based cryptosystems and signature schemes. In: Blakley, G.R., Chaum, D. (eds.) CRYPTO 1984. LNCS, vol. 196, pp. 47–53. Springer, Heidelberg (1985). https://doi.org/10.1007/3-540-39568-7_5

32. Unger, N., et al.: SoK: secure messaging. In: 2015 IEEE Symposium on Security and Privacy (SP), pp. 232–249. IEEE (2015)
33. Wei, Q., Qi, F., Tang, Z.: Remove key escrow from the BF and Gentry identity-based encryption with non-interactive key generation. Telecommun. Syst. **69**, 253–262 (2018)

Functional Encryption

FE for Inner Products and Its Application to Decentralized ABE

Zhedong Wang[1,2(✉)], Xiong Fan[3], and Feng-Hao Liu[4]

[1] School of Cyber Security, University of Chinese Academy of Sciences, Beijing, China

[2] State Key Laboratory of Information Security, Institute of Information Engineering, Chinese Academy of Sciences, Beijing, China
wangzhedong@iie.ac.cn

[3] Cornell University, Ithaca, NY, USA
xfan@cs.cornell.edu

[4] Florida Atlantic University, Boca Raton, FL, USA
fenghao.liu@fau.edu

Abstract. In this work, we revisit the primitive functional encryption (FE) for inner products and show its application to decentralized attribute-based encryption (ABE). Particularly, we derive an FE for inner products that satisfies a stronger notion, and show how to use such an FE to construct decentralized ABE for the class $\{0,1\}$-LSSS against bounded collusions in the plain model. We formalize the FE notion and show how to achieve such an FE under the LWE or DDH assumption. Therefore, our resulting decentralized ABE can be constructed under the same standard assumptions, improving the prior construction by Lewko and Waters (Eurocrypt 2011). Finally, we also point out challenges to construct decentralized ABE for general functions by establishing a relation between such an ABE and witness encryption for general NP statements.

1 Introduction

In this work, we revisit the functional encryption (FE) for inner products [6] and show its application to decentralized attribute-based encryption [22]. In particular, we identify a stronger notion for FE required in this application, and show how to build such a scheme under the LWE or DDH assumption. Our new analysis improves the parameters of the LWE-based scheme (over [6]) substantially. Next, we show how to build a decentralized ABE against bounded collusion from FE for inner products that satisfies the stronger notion. By combining the instantiation of the FE, we can derive a decentralized ABE against bounded collusion from LWE or DDH, improving the prior work [41] in the perspective of weaker assumptions. Below, we briefly review the contexts and motivation of our study.

Z. Wang—This work was done when the author was visiting Florida Atlantic University.

D. Lin and K. Sako (Eds.): PKC 2019, LNCS 11443, pp. 97–127, 2019.
https://doi.org/10.1007/978-3-030-17259-6_4

1.1 A Brief History and Motivation

We start with the application of decentralized ABE, and then discuss our central tool – FE for inner products.

Attribute-based Encryption. Attribute-based Encryption (ABE) [11,34] generalizes public key encryption to allow fine grained access control on encrypted data. In (ciphertext-policy) attribute-based encryption, a ciphertext ct for message μ is associated with a policy function f, and a secret key sk corresponds to an attribute x. The functionality requires that decryptor learns the underlying message μ if attribute x satisfies the policy function f, and if not, security guarantees that nothing about μ can be learned. In the past decade, significant progress has been made towards constructing attribute-based encryption for advanced functionalities based on various assumptions [5,8,14,17,18,20,26,29,32,33,35,39,42,49,51,54,55].

In 2007, Chase [22] considered an extension called multi-authority (or decentralized) ABE. In almost all ABE proposals listed above, the secret keys are generated by one central authority, who has the ability to verify all attributes for the secret keys it generated. These systems can be utilized to share information according to a policy within a domain or organization, where the central authority is in charge of issuing secret keys. However, in many applications, we wish to share some confidential information associated with a policy function across several different trusted organizations. For instance, in a joint project by two corporations, like Google and Facebook, they both may issue secret keys associated with attributes within their own organizations. This setting is outside the scope of the single authority ABE, as the single authority is not capable to verify attributes from different organizations. In [41], the authors show how to construct a decentralized ABE that captures the desired properties, for a large class of functions. Their solutions are secure against unbounded collusion in the random oracle model, or against bounded collusion in the standard model. For both cases, their proofs of security however, rely on several new computational assumptions on bilinear groups. Moreover, their security model only captures a static corruption where the adversary must commit to a set of corrupted parties at the beginning of the security game. To our knowledge, there is no construction that is based on better studied computational assumptions, such as DDH or LWE, even for the setting of bounded collusion. Thus, we ask:

Can we build a decentralized ABE under standard assumptions, even for some restricted class of functions and against bounded collusion?

Along the way to answer this question, we identify an interesting connection between decentralized ABE and functional encryption for inner products [6]. We first review the context of functional encryption (for inner products), and then elaborate on the connection in the technical overview section below.

Functional Encryption (for Inner Products). In a Functional Encryption (FE) scheme [16,48], a secret key sk_g is associated with a function g, and a ciphertext ct_x is associated with some input x from the domain of g. The functionality of FE requires that the decryption procedure outputs $g(x)$, while security guarantees that nothing more than than $g(x)$ can be learned. Constructing FE for general functions is quite challenging – the only known solutions (supporting unbounded key queries) either rely on indistinguishability obfuscation [25] or multilinear maps [27]. On the other hand, researchers have identified some special classes of functions that already suffice for many interesting applications [3,7]. One of them is the *inner products*, where a ciphertext ct encrypts a vector $\boldsymbol{y} \in D^\ell$ for some domain D, and a secret key for vector $\boldsymbol{x} \in D^\ell$ allows computing $\langle \boldsymbol{x}, \boldsymbol{y} \rangle$ but nothing else. Abdalla et al. [1] constructed a scheme and prove security against *selective* adversaries, who have to declare the challenge messages $(\boldsymbol{y}_0, \boldsymbol{y}_1)$ at the beginning before seeing the master public key mpk. More recently, Agrawal et al. [6] constructed an adaptively secure FE for inner products that removes this restriction, and in particular, their scheme guarantees the indistinguishability-based (IND) security for key queries both before and after the challenge ciphertext. Moreover, Agrawal et al. [6] pointed out that the IND-based security achieves "almost" the best possible security, as it implies the simulation-based (SIM) security (for the case of inner products) without post-challenge-ciphertext key queries. On the other hand, the SIM-based security is in general impossible to achieve even for one post-challenge-ciphertext key query [6,16].

In this work, we observe that the IND-based security does not suffice for our task of constructing decentralized ABE with a stronger security guarantee. Furthermore, the efficiency of the currently best known lattice-based construction (FE for inner products) [6] degrades exponentially with the dimension of the vector $\boldsymbol{y}$. A subsequent work [4] improved the parameters significantly, yet with a tradeoff of weaker security where the adversary can only receive $\mathsf{sk}_{\boldsymbol{x}}$ for random $\boldsymbol{x}$'s before the challenge ciphertext and cannot issue more key queries afterwards. Their scheme [4] is useful in the setting of designing trace-and-revoke systems, but cannot be applied to the decentralized ABE where the adversary can obtain keys of his own choice, both before and after the challenge ciphertext. Thus, the applicability of currently known FE for inner products is still limited. Therefore, we ask the following question:

Can we further generalize the security framework and construct more efficient schemes of FE for inner products?

1.2 Our Results

Below we summarize our answers to the two questions in three folds as below.

1. For the question related to decentralized ABE, we first generalize the security notion of [41] by considering adaptive corruption of parties (in addition to making adaptive key queries). Then we construct a new scheme for $\{0,1\}$-LSSS (a class that captures monotone boolean formula) with the building block – functional encryption for inner products (with a stronger security requirement). Our scheme is in the plain model and the security holds against bounded collusion.

2. We formalize this requirement and instantiate two schemes – one by LWE, and the other by DDH. Our constructions make *essential modifications* of the constructions by [6], and we improve the analysis significantly (especially for the LWE-based construction), resulting in more efficient schemes with stronger security.
3. We show that decentralized ABE for general access structures is somewhat equivalent to witness encryption (WE) for general NP relations. This can be viewed as a challenge in achieving decentralized ABE based on standard assumptions, as we are not aware of any construction of WE for NP relations based on standard assumptions.

By putting (1) and (2) together, we achieve the following informal theorem:

Theorem 1.1 (Informally Stated). *Assume the DDH or LWE assumption. For the function class of* $\{0,1\}$-LSSS*, there exists a decentralized ABE scheme that is secure against adversary who can make adaptive key queries and adaptively corrupt parties, with bounded collusions.*

Our LWE-based construction provides another path to construct decentralized ABE that is potentially secure against quantum computers as long as LWE is quantum hard. Next we compare our DDH construction with that of the prior work [41]. First, both schemes achieve the function class $\{0,1\}$-LSSS. Second, our scheme achieves stronger security against adaptive corruptions of parties, yet the work [41] achieves security against static security where the adversary needs to commit to a subset of corrupted parties at the beginning of the security experiment. Third, our scheme only relies on the DDH assumption without the need of pairings, yet the work [41] requires three new assumptions on bilinear groups. Finally, the work [41] can support an unbounded number of collusions by using random oracle, yet in the plain model, their scheme can only support a bounded number of collusions. On the other hand, our scheme works natively in the plain model and supports a bounded number of collusions. We leave it as an interesting open question whether our scheme can be upgraded in the random oracle model.

1.3 Our Techniques

Decentralized ABE. In this work, one focus is to construct decentralized ABE, following the direction of the prior work [22,41]. We first briefly review the setting. In a decentralized ABE system, anyone can become an authority by simply creating a public key and issuing secret keys to different users for their attributes, without coordinating with (or even being aware of) other authorities. Similarly as in [22,41], we use the concept of global identifiers (GID) to link together secret keys issued by different authorities. Ciphertexts are generated corresponding to some access structure over attributes. The decryptor can recover the message if he holds secret keys from different attributes that have the same GID and satisfy the access structure specified by the ciphertext. In the security model, the adversary can corrupt authorities and query authorities for attributes associated with GID adaptively, with the restrictions that the information learned from these collusion cannot help adversary decrypt challenge ciphertext. For the bounded collusion setting, the number of GID queried by adversary is fixed according to the scheme parameter.

To present our intuition, we first consider a very simple case and then present how we can generalize the idea. Let us assume that there is only one known GID, and there are three parties P_1, P_2, P_3, where each P_i holds only one attribute i. In this case, constructing a decentralized ABE is simple. Each P_i just samples $(\mathsf{pk}_i, \mathsf{sk}_i)$ from a regular encryption scheme, and outputs pk_i as the master public key and keeps sk_i as the master secret key. To issue a key for the attribute i, the party P_i just simply outputs sk_i. To encrypt a message m, the encryptor first secret share $(w_1, w_2, w_3) \leftarrow \mathsf{Share}(m)$ (according to its access structure), and outputs $\mathsf{Enc}_{\mathsf{pk}_1}(w_1), \mathsf{Enc}_{\mathsf{pk}_2}(w_2), \mathsf{Enc}_{\mathsf{pk}_3}(w_3)$ as the ciphertext. Intuitively, if the decryptor holds a set of keys $\{\mathsf{sk}_j\}_{j\in S}$ where S satisfies the access structure, then the decryptor can obtain $\{w_j\}_{j\in S}$ and recover the original message m. On the other hand, if S does not satisfy the structure, then by the security of the secret sharing scheme, the adversary cannot learn any information about m.

To generalize the idea to a larger GID domain, we consider a *new* secret sharing that takes shares over polynomials.[1] Particularly, we let $p_0(x) = m$ be a constant degree polynomial with the coefficient m. The encryptor now shares $(p_1(x), p_2(x), p_3(x)) \leftarrow \mathsf{Share}(p_0(x))$, and outputs the ciphertext as $\left(\mathsf{Enc}_{\mathsf{pk}_1}(p_1(x)), \mathsf{Enc}_{\mathsf{pk}_2}(p_2(x)), \mathsf{Enc}_{\mathsf{pk}_3}(p_3(x))\right)$. Suppose we can achieve the following properties:

1. P_i can issue a secret key $\mathsf{sk}_{i,\mathsf{GID}}$ such that whoever holds the key can learn $p_i(\mathsf{GID})$.
2. Suppose $\left(\{p_i(\mathsf{GID}_1)\}_{i\in S_1}, \{p_i(\mathsf{GID}_2)\}_{i\in S_2}, \ldots, \{p_i(\mathsf{GID}_t)\}_{i\in S_t}\right)$ is given for distinct $\mathsf{GID}_1, \ldots, \mathsf{GID}_t$.
   (a) If there exists some S_j that satisfies the access structure, then one can recover $p_0(\mathsf{GID}_j) = m$.
   (b) If no such S_j exists, then $p_0(x) = m$ remains hidden.

Then it is not hard to see that the scheme also achieves the decentralized ABE, as P_i can issue $\mathsf{sk}_{i,\mathsf{GID}}$ as Property 1, the decryption works by Property 2(a), and intuitively, security is guaranteed by Property 2(b).

Now we elaborate on how to implement the properties in more details. First, we can see that functional encryption (FE) is exactly what we need for Property 1, and in fact, FE for inner products suffices for the functionality. The encryption algorithm can encrypt $\boldsymbol{y} = (c_0, c_1, \ldots, c_k)$ that represents the polynomial $p(x) = \sum_{i=0}^{k} c_i x^i$, and a key for GID can be set as the FE key $\mathsf{sk}_{\boldsymbol{x}}$ for $\boldsymbol{x} = (1, \mathsf{GID}, \mathsf{GID}^2, \ldots, \mathsf{GID}^k)$. By using the FE decryption with the secret key

[1] We will discuss the secret sharing in more details, but let us focus on the high level concepts at this point.

$\mathsf{sk}_{\boldsymbol{x}}$, one can learn $\langle \boldsymbol{x}, \boldsymbol{y} \rangle = p(\mathsf{GID})$. To implement Property 2, we find that we can apply the known $\{0, 1\}$-LSSS sharing scheme [13] over the coefficients of the polynomial, and prove Properties 2(a) and 2(b). If the shares of polynomials are of degree k, then we can tolerate up to $t = k - 1$ distinct GID queries. See our Sect. 4 for further details.

We notice that any FE for inner products can achieve the functionality of Property 1 as stated above, yet connecting security of the FE and security of the decentralized ABE is not obvious. First, the (challenge) messages used in the decentralized ABE come from a distribution (i.e., shares from $\mathsf{Share}(p_0(x))$ form a distribution), yet the IND-based security considered by prior work [1, 6, 16] focuses on two fixed challenge messages $\boldsymbol{y}_0$ and $\boldsymbol{y}_1$. It is not clear how to define two fixed $\boldsymbol{y}_0$ and $\boldsymbol{y}_1$ to capture two distributions of $\mathsf{Share}(p_0(x))$ and $\mathsf{Share}(q_0(x))$ in the decentralized ABE setting, and furthermore, is not clear how to define *admissible* key queries in our setting. SIM-based FE might be helpful, but it is impossible to achieve the notion (for challenge ciphertexts that encrypt a vector of messages) if the adversary is allowed to make post-challenge ciphertext key queries, as pointed out by [6]. We also note that the scheme of Gorbunov, Vaikuntanathan, and Wee [31] cannot be applied to our setting directly, as their SIM adaptive security only holds for challenge ciphertexts that encrypt a single-message.[2] Second, in our decentralized ABE, the adversary is allowed to corrupt parties and make key queries adaptively, i.e., at any time of the game. It is not clear whether the currently functional encryption schemes are secure under adaptive corruption if several ciphertexts under different public keys are given first and then several master secret keys are compromised. Consider the following example: suppose $\mathsf{Enc}_{\mathsf{pk}_1}(\boldsymbol{y}_1), \mathsf{Enc}_{\mathsf{pk}_2}(\boldsymbol{y}_2), \mathsf{Enc}_{\mathsf{pk}_3}(\boldsymbol{y}_3)$ are given first, and then the adversary can corrupt any subset, say sk_1 and sk_2, and make key query to sk_3, what security can we guarantee for the remaining message $\boldsymbol{y}_3$?

Functional Encryption for Inner Products. To handle the issues above, we consider a more generalized security notion of functional encryption. Intuitively, our framework considers encryption over a set of messages from two (challenge) distributions, say $(\boldsymbol{y}_1, \ldots, \boldsymbol{y}_\ell) \leftarrow \mathcal{D}_b^\ell$ for $b \in \{0, 1\}$, under different public keys $(\mathsf{pk}_1, \ldots, \mathsf{pk}_\ell)$, and the ciphertexts $\big(\mathsf{Enc}_{\mathsf{pk}_1}(\boldsymbol{y}_1), \ldots, \mathsf{Enc}_{\mathsf{pk}_\ell}(\boldsymbol{y}_\ell)\big)$ are given to the adversary. The adversary can make (1) a corruption query to any sk_i and (2) a key query $\boldsymbol{x}$ to an uncorrupted sk_j, multiple times before or after the challenge phase. Our security requires that the adversary cannot guess b correctly, as long as the distributions $\mathcal{D}_0^\ell$ and $\mathcal{D}_1^\ell$ remain indistinguishable under the functionalities from (1) and (2). This security notion lies in between the IND-based security and the SIM-based security. We prove that any functional encryption that satisfies the notion can be used to implement the idea above to build a secure decentralized ABE. We present the details in Sect. 4.

Next we turn to the question how to build such a functional encryption scheme. We make *essential* modifications of the DDH and LWE-based

[2] The work [31] can derive an IND adaptively secure scheme for challenge ciphertexts that encrypt a vector of messages, but as we discussed above, IND security seems not sufficient for our application.

constructions from the work [6], and prove that the modified schemes achieve our new security definition. Conceptually, we develop two new techniques: (1) we use a complexity leverage argument (or random guessing [36]) in a clever way that does not affect of the underlying LWE or DDH assumption *at all.* (2) Our LWE-based construction uses a re-randomized technique proposed in the work [37] to avoid the use of multi-hint extended LWE as required by the work [6]. The reduction from multi-hint LWE to LWE incurs a significant security loss, and the standard deviation required by the discrete Gaussian distribution is large. By using our new analysis, we are able to have a direct security proof of the scheme without multi-hint LWE, resulting in an exponential improvement over the parameters. Below we elaborate on more details. As we improve over some subtle but important points of the work [6], for the next paragraph we assume some familiarity of the work [6].

We briefly review the approach of [6]. The master public/secret keys have the form $\mathsf{mpk} = (\mathbf{A}, \mathbf{U})$ and $\mathsf{msk} = \mathbf{Z}$ such that $\mathbf{U} = \mathbf{ZA}$. The ciphertext has the form $\mathsf{Enc}(\boldsymbol{y}) = (c_0, c_1)$ where $c_0 = \mathbf{A}\boldsymbol{s} + \boldsymbol{e}_0$, and $c_1 = \mathbf{U}\boldsymbol{s} + \boldsymbol{e}_1 + K\boldsymbol{y}$ for some appropriate number K. The security proof of [6] proceeds as follows:

- Let H_0 be the original game.
- Hybrid H_1: c_0 remains the same, and $c_1 = \mathbf{Z}(c_0 - \boldsymbol{e}_0) + \boldsymbol{e}_1 + K\boldsymbol{y}$.
- Hybrid H_2: c_0 is switched to the uniform vector, and c_1 remains the same as H_1.

It is quite easy to see that H_1 is just a rephrase of H_0, so the two hybrids are identical. The difference between H_1 and H_2 relies on the multi-hint extended LWE, as we need the hint of $\mathbf{Z}\boldsymbol{e}_0$ in order to simulate c_1 given c_0. Then Agrawal et al. [6] showed that in H_2, the adversary has a negligible winning probability with an information-theoretic argument. This is to say, in H_2, even a computationally unbounded adversary cannot win the game with better than a negligible probability.

To get rid of the use of multi-hint extended LWE, we modify the hybrid 1:

- New H_1': c_0 remains the same as H_0, and $c_1 = \mathsf{ReRand}(\mathbf{Z}, c_0, \alpha q, \sigma^*) + K\boldsymbol{y}$ for some $\alpha q, \sigma^*$.

The algorithm ReRand was proposed in the work by Katsumata et al. [37]. We show that this technique can be used to improve analysis in our setting: by setting $\alpha q, \sigma^*$ appropriately, the output distribution of the ReRand will be statistically close to $\mathbf{U}\boldsymbol{s} + \boldsymbol{e}^*$ where $\boldsymbol{e}^*$ has the same distribution of $\boldsymbol{e}_1$. Consequently, c_1 can be generated independent of $\boldsymbol{e}_0$, and thus we can get rid of the need of the multi-hint LWE.

To prove security of our setting, we need to analyze the success probability of an adversary in H_2. We observe that the proof technique by the work [6] cannot be applied to our setting. Intuitively, the crux of their security proof (in H_2) relies on the following facts: (1) once the adversary submits the challenge messages $\boldsymbol{y}_0, \boldsymbol{y}_1$, the space of key queries in the remaining game is fixed to $\Lambda^{\perp}(\boldsymbol{y}_0 - \boldsymbol{y}_1)$. (2) The adversary cannot distinguish $\boldsymbol{y}_0$ from $\boldsymbol{y}_1$ even if he is given the ciphertext and a set of keys in each dimension of $\Lambda^{\perp}(\boldsymbol{y}_0 - \boldsymbol{y}_1)$ at the same time. (This is captured as $\mathbf{X}_{top}\mathbf{Z}$ in their proof.) (3) Any post-challenge key queries can be derived by a linear combination of the keys obtained in (2), i.e, $\mathbf{X}_{top}\mathbf{Z}$. In our setting however, the fact (1) no longer holds. Given two message distributions, it is not clear whether the space for the remaining key queries is even fixed or not. Therefore, their argument cannot be used in our setting.

Another possible way to handle adaptive queries is to use a complexity leveraging argument (or random guessing according to the work [36]). However, by folklore we know that naively applying the argument will result in an exponential security loss, i.e., $\epsilon_{\mathsf{scheme}} \leq 2^{\lambda} \cdot \epsilon_{\mathsf{LWE}}$. Our new insight to tackle this problem is to apply it cleverly: we only apply the argument in the hybrid H_2 where all the analysis is information-theoretic. In more details, we show that in H_2 the advantage of any adversary who only makes pre-challenge ciphertext key queries is bounded by some ϵ_2, and by the complexity leveraging argument, the advantage of a full adversary is bounded by $2^{\lambda} \cdot \epsilon_2$. By setting the parameters appropriately, we can afford the loss without affecting the hardness of the underlying LWE or DDH assumption. Our overall advantage of the adversary would be $\epsilon_{\mathsf{scheme}} \leq \Delta(H_0, H_1) + \Delta(H_1, H_2) + \mathbf{Adv}(H_2)$. By the property of ReRand, $\Delta(H_0, H_1)$ is negligible; by the security of LWE, $\Delta(H_1, H_2) \leq \epsilon_{\mathsf{LWE}}$; by the above argument $\mathbf{Adv}(H_2) = 2^{\lambda} \cdot \epsilon_2$ can also be set to negligible. Therefore, we have $\epsilon_{\mathsf{scheme}} \leq \epsilon_{\mathsf{LWE}} + \mathsf{negl}(\lambda)$. Details can be found in the full version of the paper.

Can We Achieve Decentralized ABE for General Functions? After achieving decentralized ABE for $\{0,1\}$-LSSS, it is natural to ask whether we can do more. Here we show that any decentralized ABE for general functions implies a witness encryption (WE) for general NP statements. On the other hand, an extractable witness encryption for general NP statements plus signatures implies decentralized ABE, following the argument of the work [29]. The result provides a challenge to construct decentralized ABE for general functions under standard assumptions, as we are not aware of any construction of WE from standard assumptions. We leave it as an interesting open question whether there exists a decentralized ABE for a class between $\{0,1\}$-LSSS and general functions.

1.4 Additional Related Work

Decentralized ABE. The problem of building ABE with multiple authorities was proposed by Sahai and Waters [53], and first considered by Chase [22]. In [22], Chase introduced the concept of using a global identifier to link secret keys together. However, her system relies on a central authority and is limited to express a strict AND policy over a *pre-determined* set of authorities. Müller et al. [46,47] proposed another construction with a centralized authority for any LSSS structure, based on [54], but their construction is secure only against non-adaptive queries. Lin et al. [43] showed a threshold based scheme (somewhat decentralized) against bounded collusions. In their system, the set of authorities is fixed ahead of time, and they must interact during system setup. Chase and

Chow [23] showed how to remove the central authority using a distributed PRF, but the restriction of an AND policy over a pre-determined set of authorities remained. In [41], Lewko and Waters proposed a decentralized ABE system for any LSSS structure from bilinear groups. Their system is secure against adaptive secret key queries and selective authority corruption in random oracle model. Liu et al. [44] proposed a fully secure decentralized ABE scheme in standard model, but there exists multiple central authorities issuing identity-related keys to users.

Functional Encryption for Inner Products. The problem of FE for inner products was first considered by Abdalla et al. [1], where they show constructions against selective adversaries based on standard assumptions, like DDH and LWE. Later on, Bishop et al. [12] consider the same functionality in the secret-key setting with the motivation of achieving function privacy and security against adaptive adversaries. Recently, in work by Agrawal et al. [6], they provide constructions in public key setting based on several standard assumptions that are secure against more realistic adaptive adversaries, where challenge messages are declared in the challenge phase, based on previously collected information. Benhamouda et al. [10] show a CCA-Secure Inner-Product Functional Encryption generically from projective hash functions with homomorphic properties.

For the multi-input version of the inner product functionality, more recently, Abdalla et al. [2] show a construction of multi-input functional encryption scheme (MIFE) for the inner products functionality based on the k-linear assumption in prime-order bilinear groups, which is secure against adaptive adversaries. In [24], Datta et al. describe two non-generic constructions based on bilinear groups of prime order, where one construction can withstand an arbitrary number of encryption slots.

Witness Encryption. Recently, Brakerski et al. [19] proposed a new framework to construct WE via ABE. We note that a result similar to our construction can be obtained from their work.

1.5 Roadmap

The notations and some preliminaries are described in Sect. 2. In Sect. 3, we present our new security definition for FE, and propose an LWE based construction satisfying our new security. Due to the space limitation, we defer the full security proof to the full version of the paper. In Sect. 4, we give a stronger security definition for decentralized ABE and present our construction. Furthermore, we explore the relationship between decentralized ABE and (extratable) witness encryption in Sect. 5. The DDH-based constructions for FE and decentralized ABE can be found in the full version of the paper.

2 Preliminaries

Notations. We use λ to denote security parameter throughout this paper. For an integer n, we write $[n]$ to denote the set $\{1, \ldots, n\}$. We use bold lowercase letters to denote vectors (e.g. $\boldsymbol{v}$) and bold uppercase letters for matrices (e.g. $\mathbf{A}$). For a vector $\boldsymbol{v}$, we let $\|\boldsymbol{v}\|$ denote its ℓ_2 norm. The ℓ_2 norm of a matrix $\mathbf{R} = \{\boldsymbol{r}_1, ..., \boldsymbol{r}_m\}$ is denoted by $\|\mathbf{R}\| = \max_i \|\boldsymbol{r}_i\|$. The spectral norm of $\mathbf{R}$ is denoted by $\mathsf{s}_1(\mathbf{R}) = \mathsf{sup}_{\boldsymbol{x}\in\mathbb{R}^{m+1}} \|\mathbf{R} \cdot \boldsymbol{x}\|$.

We say a function $\mathsf{negl}(\cdot) : \mathbb{N} \to (0, 1)$ is negligible, if for every constant $c \in \mathbb{N}$, $\mathsf{negl}(n) < n^{-c}$ for sufficiently large n. For any set X, we denote by $\mathcal{P}(X)$ as the power set of X. For any $Y, Z \in \{0,1\}^n$, we say that $Y \subseteq Z$ if for each index $i \in [n]$ such that $Y_i = 1$, We have $Z_i = 1$. The statistical distance between two distributions X and Y over a countable domain D is defined to be $\frac{1}{2}\sum_{d\in D} |X(d) - Y(d)|$. We say that two distributions are statistically close if their statistical distance is negligible in λ.

A family of functions $\mathcal{H} = \{h_i : D \to R\}$ from a domain D to range R is called k-wise independent, if for every pairwise distinct $x_1, ..., x_k \in D$ and every $y_1, ..., y_k \in R$,

$$\mathsf{Pr}_{h\leftarrow\mathcal{H}}[h(x_1) = y_1 \wedge ... \wedge h(x_k) = y_k] = 1/|R|^k.$$

Secret Sharing and the $\{0,1\}$-LSSS Access Structure. We briefly describe the syntax of secret sharing and the $\{0,1\}$-LSSS access structure, and refer the full version of the paper for further details. A secret sharing scheme consists of two algorithms as follow: $\mathsf{SS} = (\mathsf{SS.Share}, \mathsf{SS.Combine})$. The share algorithm $\mathsf{SS.Share}$ takes input a secret message k and an access structure $\mathbb{A}$ and output a set of shares $s_1, \ldots, s_t$. The combine algorithm $\mathsf{SS.Combine}$ takes input a subset of shares can recover the secret k if the subset satisfies the access structure $\mathbb{A}$. If not, then the secret k should remain hidden to the algorithm. Briefly speaking, if the combine algorithm just applies a linear combination over shares to recover the message, then the secret sharing scheme is called *linear*, or LSSS in brief. If the coefficients are in $\{0,1\}$, then it is called $\{0,1\}$-LSSS. It is worthwhile pointing out that the $\{0,1\}$-LSSS contains a powerful class called Monotone Boolean Formula (MBF) pointed out by the work [13,41], who showed that any MBF can be expressed as an access structure in $\{0,1\}$-LSSS. In this work, our construction of decentralized ABE achieves the class of $\{0,1\}$-LSSS and thus supports any the class of MBF.

3 Adaptively Secure FE for Chosen Message Distributions

In this section, we define a new security notion of functional encryption, called adaptively secure functional encryption for chosen message distributions. This notion is a generalization of prior adaptively secure functional encryption [6]. We first propose the definition, and then construct an LWE-based scheme that achieves the security notion. Our construction modified the scheme of [6] in an essential way, and our security analysis provides significantly better parameters than the work [6]. The DDH-based construction and its security proof can be analyzed in a similar way as our LWE-based scheme.

3.1 New Security Definition

In functional encryption, a secret key sk_g is associated with a function g, and a ciphertext ct_x is associated with some input x from the domain of g. The functionality of FE requires that the decryption procedure outputs $g(x)$, while security guarantees that nothing more than $g(x)$ can be learned. The formal description of syntax is in the full version of the paper.

Suppose that in a functional encryption scheme, a set of messages can be chosen from two distributions, and we obtain a set of ciphertexts by encrypting each message y_i using different master public keys mpk_i. Before choosing the two message distributions, the adversary is sent a set of master public keys $\{\mathsf{mpk}_i\}_{i\in[t]}$ and can also make two kinds of queries:

- Function queries: For query (f, i), obtain secret key sk_i^f for function f from msk_i.
- Opening queries: For query i, obtain master secret key msk_i.

The natural restrictions we enforce here are (1) the distributions of queried function evaluations for the two message distributions remains indistinguishable, (2) the distributions of opening messages are also indistinguishable. Otherwise, there can be no security as the adversary can trivially distinguish the two message distributions. On the other hand, other additional information such as, the opening messages, queried keys, and the function values, may help the adversary to learn to distinguish the message distributions from the ciphertexts. Our new security notion – *adaptively secure functional encryption for chosen message distributions*, requires that the choice of the message distribution of challenger remains indistinguishable even if the adversary is given the additional information.

We formalize IND-based security definition with respect to *admissible mappings*. For ease of exposition, we first define the query mappings.

Definition 3.1. *Let $t = t(\lambda)$ be an integer and $\mathcal{M}$ be the message space. $\{x_i\}_{i\in[t]} \in \mathcal{M}^t$ is a set of messages, and $f : \mathcal{M} \to \mathcal{K}$ be a function. We define the functions $(i, f) : \mathcal{M}^t \to \mathcal{K}$ as $(i, f)(x_1, ..., x_t) = f(x_i)$, and function $(i, I) : \mathcal{M}^t \to \mathcal{M}$ as $(i, I)(x_1, ..., x_t) = x_i$.*

Definition 3.2 (Admissible mappings). *Let $t = t(\lambda)$ be an integer, $\mathcal{M}$ be the message space, and $\mathcal{M}_0, \mathcal{M}_1$ be two distributions over space $\mathcal{M}^t$. Let subsets $T_1, T_2 \subsetneq [t]$ such that $T_2 \cap T_1 = \emptyset$ and $|T_2 \cup T_1| < t$, and let $\{k_i\}_{i\in T_2}$ be a set of integers. We say that mappings $\{(i, I)\}_{i\in T_1}$ and $\{(i, f_{ij})\}_{i\in T_2, j\in[k_i]}$ are admissible if it holds that*

$$\begin{aligned}&\{\{(i, I)(\mathcal{M}_0)\}_{i\in T_1}, \{(i, f_{ij})(\mathcal{M}_0)\}_{i\in T_2, j\in[k_i]}\}\\ =&\{\{(i, I)(\mathcal{M}_1)\}_{i\in T_1}, \{(i, f_{ij})(\mathcal{M}_1)\}_{i\in T_2, j\in[k_i]}\}\end{aligned}$$

Remark 3.3. The requirement of *admissible mappings* is that the above two distributions are identical. We can also relax the definition by requiring the two distributions are statistically or computationally close.

We define the adaptive security of functional encryption for chosen message distributions through an experiment $\mathbf{Expt}_{\mathcal{A}}^{\mathsf{FE}}(1^\lambda, 1^t)$ between an adversary and challenger:

1. **Setup**: For $i \in [t]$, challenger first computes $(\mathsf{mpk}_i, \mathsf{msk}_i) \leftarrow \mathsf{Setup}(1^\lambda)$, then sends $\{\mathsf{mpk}_i\}_{i\in[t]}$ to adversary $\mathcal{A}$.
2. **Query Phase I**: Proceeding adaptively, adversary can make any polynomial number of queries to the oracle $\mathcal{O}(\{\mathsf{msk}_i\}_{i\in[t]}, \cdot)$ of the following two kinds:
   - Function queries (i, f_{ij}): Challenger sends back $\mathsf{sk}_{f_{ij}} \leftarrow \mathsf{KeyGen}(\mathsf{sk}_i, f_{ij})$.
   - Opening queries (i, I): Challenger sends back msk_i.
3. **Challenge Phase**: Adversary $\mathcal{A}$ sends two message distributions $\mathcal{M}_0$ and $\mathcal{M}_1$ over message space $\mathcal{M}^t$ with the restriction that any queries made in **Query Phase I** are *admissible* with respect to $(\mathcal{M}_0, \mathcal{M}_1)$ (c.f. Definition 3.2). The challenger chooses a random bit $b \in \{0,1\}$, and sends ciphertext $\{\mathsf{ct}_i = \mathsf{Enc}(\mathsf{mpk}_i, x_i)\}_{i\in[t]}$ back to adversary, where $\{x_i\}_{i\in[t]} \leftarrow \mathcal{M}_b$.
4. **Query Phase II**: Adversary $\mathcal{A}$ can continue making queries as specified in **Query Phase I** as long as the queries are admissible.
5. **Guess**: Adversary $\mathcal{A}$ outputs his guess b'.

We define the advantage of adversary $\mathcal{A}$ in the experiment $\mathbf{Expt}_{\mathcal{A}}^{\mathsf{FE}}(1^\lambda, 1^t)$ as

$$\mathbf{Adv}_{\mathcal{A}}(1^\lambda, 1^t) = |\Pr[\mathbf{Expt}_{\mathcal{A}}^{\mathsf{FE}}(1^\lambda, 1^t) = 1] - 1/2|$$

Definition 3.4. *We say a functional encryption scheme Π is adaptively secure for chosen message distributions security if for any polynomial $t = t(\lambda)$, and any* PPT *adversary $\mathcal{A}$, we have $\mathbf{Adv}_{\mathcal{A}}(1^\lambda, 1^t) \le \mathsf{negl}(\lambda)$.*

3.2 Functional Encryption for Inner Products Modulo p

Agrawal et al. [6] show a construction of functional encryption for inner products modulo p assuming the hardness of LWE problem. In this section, we made some *important* modifications of their construction, particularly the encryption and key generation algorithms, and then show that the modified scheme satisfies our new security definition. Our modifications and new analysis provide significantly better parameters as we will discuss below. We first present the construction:

- $\mathsf{Setup}(1^n, 1^\ell, 1^k, p)$: Set integers $m, q = p^e$ for some integer e, and real numbers $\alpha, \alpha' \in (0,1)$. Randomly sample matrices $\mathbf{A} \xleftarrow{\$} \mathbb{Z}_q^{m\times n}$ and $\mathbf{Z}_i \xleftarrow{\$} \mathbb{Z}_p^{\ell\times m}$, for $i = 1, ..., k$. Compute $\mathbf{U}_i = \mathbf{Z}_i \cdot \mathbf{A} \in \mathbb{Z}_q^{\ell\times n}$. Output $\mathsf{mpk} := (\mathbf{A}, \{\mathbf{U}_i\}_{i\in[k]})$ and $\mathsf{msk} := (\{\mathbf{Z}_i\}_{i\in[k]})$.
- $\mathsf{KeyGen}(\mathsf{msk}, \boldsymbol{x})$: On input a vector $\boldsymbol{x} = (\boldsymbol{x}_1, \ldots, \boldsymbol{x}_k)$, where for each $i \in [k]$, $\boldsymbol{x}_i \in \mathbb{Z}_p^\ell$, compute the secret key $\boldsymbol{z}_{\boldsymbol{x}}$ as follows. As $\boldsymbol{x}$ is linearly independent from the key queries have been made so far modulo p, we can compute $\boldsymbol{z}_{\boldsymbol{x}} = \sum_{i=1}^k \boldsymbol{x}_i^T \cdot \mathbf{Z}_i$, and output secret key $\mathsf{sk}_{\boldsymbol{x}} = \boldsymbol{z}_{\boldsymbol{x}}$.
- $\mathsf{Enc}(\mathsf{mpk}, \boldsymbol{y})$: On input $\boldsymbol{y} = (\boldsymbol{y}_1, ..., \boldsymbol{y}_k)$, where for each $i \in [k]$, $\boldsymbol{y}_i \in \mathbb{Z}_p^\ell$, sample $\boldsymbol{s} \xleftarrow{\$} \mathbb{Z}_q^n, \boldsymbol{e}_0 \leftarrow \mathcal{D}_{\mathbb{Z},\alpha q}^m$ and $\{\boldsymbol{e}_i\}_{i\in[k]} \leftarrow \mathcal{D}_{\mathbb{Z},\alpha' q}^\ell$ and compute
$$\boldsymbol{c}_0 = \mathbf{A}\cdot\boldsymbol{s} + \boldsymbol{e}_0 \in \mathbb{Z}_q^m, \quad \boldsymbol{c}_i = \mathbf{U}_i\cdot\boldsymbol{s} + \boldsymbol{e}_i + p^{e-1}\cdot\boldsymbol{y}_i \in \mathbb{Z}_q^\ell, \forall i \in [k]$$
Then, output $\mathsf{ct} = (\boldsymbol{c}_0, \{\boldsymbol{c}_i\}_{i\in[k]})$.

- Dec(mpk, $\mathsf{sk}_{\boldsymbol{x}}$, ct): On input $\mathsf{ct} = (\boldsymbol{c}_0, \{\boldsymbol{c}_i\}_{i\in[k]})$ and a secret key $\mathsf{sk}_{\boldsymbol{x}} = \boldsymbol{z}_{\boldsymbol{x}}$ for $\boldsymbol{x} = (\boldsymbol{x}_1, \ldots, \boldsymbol{x}_k) \in \mathbb{Z}_p^{k\ell}$, compute $\mu' = \sum_{i=1}^{k}\langle \boldsymbol{x}_i, \boldsymbol{c}_i\rangle - \langle \boldsymbol{z}_{\boldsymbol{x}}, \boldsymbol{c}_0\rangle$ and output the value $\mu \in \mathbb{Z}_p$ that minimizes $|p^{e-1} \cdot \mu - \mu'|$.

Decryption Correctness. Correctness derives from the following equation:

$$\mu' = \sum_{i=1}^{k}\langle \boldsymbol{x}_i, \boldsymbol{c}_i\rangle - \langle \boldsymbol{z}_{\boldsymbol{x}}, \boldsymbol{c}_0\rangle = p^{e-1} \cdot \left(\sum_{i=1}^{k}\langle \boldsymbol{x}_i, \boldsymbol{y}_i\rangle \bmod p\right) + \sum_{i=1}^{k}\langle \boldsymbol{x}_i, \boldsymbol{e}_i\rangle - \langle \boldsymbol{z}_{\boldsymbol{x}}, \boldsymbol{e}_0\rangle \bmod q$$

If the magnitude of error term $\sum_{i=1}^{k}\langle \boldsymbol{x}_i, \boldsymbol{e}_i\rangle - \langle \boldsymbol{z}_{\boldsymbol{x}}, \boldsymbol{e}_0\rangle$ is $\leq p^{e-1}/2$ with overwhelming probability, then the correctness holds with overwhelming probability.

Parameters Setting. The parameters in Table 1 are selected in order to satisfy the following constraints. In the table below, $e, c_1, c_2, \delta_1, \delta_2, \delta$ are constants, and $\delta = \delta_1 + \delta_2$

Table 1. Parameter description and simple example setting

Parameters	Description	Setting
λ	security parameter	
n	column of public matrix	λ
m	row of public matrix	$n^{1+\delta}$
p	modulus of inner products	n^{c_1}
e	power of q to p	$> 3 + (\frac{7\delta}{2} + \frac{c_2}{2} + 2)/c_1$
q	modulus of LWE	$n^{c_1 e}$
αq	Gaussian parameter of $\boldsymbol{e}_0$	$\sqrt{n^{c_2+2\delta}} \cdot \log n$
$\alpha' q$	Gaussian parameter of $\boldsymbol{e}_i$	$n^{1+\delta+c_1} \cdot \sqrt{n^{c+2\delta}} \cdot \log n$
t	number of distinct mpk's	n^{c_2}
k	number of $\boldsymbol{x}_i$ in $\boldsymbol{x}$	n^{δ_1}
ℓ	dimension of $\boldsymbol{x}_i$	n^{δ_2}
σ^*	parameter of ReRand algorithm	pm

- To ensure correctness of decryption, we require $p^{e-1} > 2kp^2 m\ell\alpha q(2\sqrt{\ell}+\sqrt{m})$.
- To ensure the correctness of ReRand algorithm, we require $\sigma^* \geq pm$.
- By the property of ReRand algorithm, we have $\alpha' q = 2\sigma^* \alpha q$.
- To ensure small enough reduction loss for the ReRand algorithm, we require $\alpha q > \sqrt{\lambda + tk^2\ell^2 \log p}$.
- To ensure large enough entropy required by Claim (in full version), we require $m \geq 2k\ell + ek\ell(n+1) + 3\lambda$.

Comparison with the Work [4,6]**.** Our analysis shows that the scheme can support a much wider range of parameters than the analysis of Agrawal et al. [6]. For their analysis, the efficiency degrade quickly when the dimension increases, and in particular, the modulus $q \geq p^\ell$. This is why the work [6] sets the dimension $\ell = \Omega(\log n)$. In our analysis, we can build a direct reduction to LWE (without using the intermediate extended LWE), allowing us to choose $\mathbf{Z}_i \leftarrow \mathbf{U}(Z_p^{\ell \times m})$ (instead of using a discrete Gaussian with a very large deviation). This gives us a significant improvement over the parameters: our modulus q does not depend on ℓ in an exponential way, so we can set the dimension to any fixed polynomial, without increasing q significantly.

A subsequent work [4] improved the parameters significantly, yet with a tradeoff of weaker security where the adversary can only receive $\mathsf{sk}_{\boldsymbol{x}}$ for random $\boldsymbol{x}$'s before the challenge ciphertext and cannot issue more key queries afterwards. Their scheme [4] is useful in the setting of designing trace-and-revoke systems, but cannot be applied to the decentralized ABE where the adversary can obtain keys of his own choice, both before and after the challenge ciphertext.

Security Proof. Now we can show the following theorem that under the parameters above, the functional encryption for inner product scheme described above is adaptively secure for chosen message distributions. Due to space limit, we defer the full proof to the full version of the paper.

Theorem 3.5. *Under the* LWE *assumption, the above functional encryption for inner products is adaptively secure for chosen message distributions, assuming for each* msk_i*, the secret key queries to the* msk_i *are linearly independent.*

Remark 3.6. The functionality of the scheme described above is inner products modulo a prime p. In [6], the authors have given an attack for the case that the secret key queries are not linearly independent modulo p but linearly independent over the integers, and they proposed a stateful key generation technique to get rid of the attack. Here we can also use a stateful key generation algorithm to remove the last assumption (i.e., linearly independent queries) in the theorem.

4 Decentralized ABE: Stronger Definition and Construction

In this section, we first describe the syntax of decentralized ABE, following the work [41], and then we define a stronger security notion. Next, we present our construction and security proof, relying on the functional encryption scheme in Sect. 3.2. We first present a basic scheme that supports smaller GID and message spaces (Sect. 4.2), and next we show an improved scheme that supports significantly larger spaces (Sect. 4.3).

4.1 Syntax of Decentralized ABE Scheme and Stronger Security

We first recall the syntax of decentralized ABE as defined in [41] and then present a stronger security definition. Let $\mathcal{F}$ be a function class. A decentralized ABE for $\mathcal{F}$ consists of the following algorithms:

- $\mathsf{Global.Setup}(1^\lambda) \to \mathsf{GP}$ The global setup algorithm takes in the security parameter λ and outputs global parameters GP for the system.
- $\mathsf{Authority.Setup}(\mathsf{GP}) \to (\mathsf{pk}, \mathsf{sk})$ Each authority runs the authority setup algorithm with GP as input to produce its own secret key and the public key pair $(\mathsf{sk}, \mathsf{pk})$.
- $\mathsf{Enc}(\mu, f, \mathsf{GP}, \{\mathsf{pk}\}) \to \mathsf{ct}$ Encryption algorithm takes as inputs a message μ, a function $f \in \mathcal{F}$, a set of public keys for relevant authorities, and the global parameters, and outputs a ciphertext ct.
- $\mathsf{KeyGen}(\mathsf{GID}, \mathsf{GP}, i, \mathsf{sk}) \to \mathsf{k}_{i,\mathsf{GID}}$ The key generation algorithm takes as inputs an identity GID, global parameters GP, an attribute i, and secret key sk for this authority who holds the attribute. It produces a key $\mathsf{k}_{i,\mathsf{GID}}$ for this attribute-identity pair.
- $\mathsf{Dec}(\mathsf{ct}, \mathsf{GP}, \{\mathsf{k}_{i,\mathsf{GID}}\}) \to \mu$ The decryption algorithm takes as inputs the global parameters GP, a ciphertext ct, and a set of keys $\{\mathsf{k}_{i,\mathsf{GID}}\}$ corresponding to attribute-identity pairs. It outputs a message μ, if the set of attributes i satisfies the policy specified by f and all the identities have the same GID. Otherwise, it outputs $\perp$.

Definition 4.1 (Correctness). *We say a decentralized ABE scheme is correct if for any* $\mathsf{GP} \leftarrow \mathsf{Global.Setup}(1^\lambda)$, $f \in \mathcal{F}$, *message* μ, *and* $\{\mathsf{k}_{i,\mathsf{GID}}\}$ *obtained from the key generation algorithm for the same identity* GID *where the attributes satisfy the policy* f, *we have*

$$\Pr[\mathsf{Dec}(\mathsf{Enc}(\mu, f, \mathsf{GP}, \{pk\}), \mathsf{GP}, \{\mathsf{k}_{i,\mathsf{GID}}\}) = \mu] = 1 - \mathsf{negl}(\lambda).$$

Security Definition. We define the notion of *full* security of decentralized ABE schemes. In our setting, the adversary can *adaptively* corrupt authorities, as well as making *adaptive* key queries. In a similar but weaker model defined in [41], the adversary can make adaptive key queries but only *static* corruption queries, i.e., the adversary can only corrupt parties before the global parameter is generated.

Let $t = \mathsf{poly}(\lambda)$ denote the number of authorities, and we consider parties $P_1, P_2, \ldots, P_t$, where each party P_i holds an attribute i. Then we define the security notion via an experiment $\mathbf{Expt}_{\mathcal{A}}^{\mathsf{dabe}}(1^\lambda, 1^t)$ between an adversary and the challenger:

1. Setup: The challenger runs $\mathsf{GP} \leftarrow \mathsf{Global\ Setup}(1^\lambda)$, and then $(\mathsf{pk}_i, \mathsf{sk}_i) \leftarrow \mathsf{Authority\ Setup}(\mathsf{GP})$ for $i \in [t]$. Then the challenger sends $(\mathsf{GP}, \{\mathsf{pk}_i\}_{i\in[t]})$ to the adversary, and keeps $\{\mathsf{sk}_i\}_{i\in[t]}$ secretly.
2. Key Query Phase 1: Proceeding adaptively, adversary can make the two types of queries:

(a) Secret key query (i, GID): $\mathcal{A}$ submits a pair (i, GID) to the challenger, where i is an attribute belonging to an uncorrupted authority P_i and GID is an identity. The challenger runs $\mathsf{k}_{i,\mathsf{GID}} \leftarrow \mathsf{KeyGen}(\mathsf{GID}, \mathsf{GP}, i, \mathsf{sk}_i)$ and forwards the adversary $\mathsf{k}_{i,\mathsf{GID}}$.

(b) Corruption query (i, corr): $\mathcal{A}$ submits (i, corr) to the challenger, where i is an attribute that the adversary want to corrupt. The challenger responds by giving $\mathcal{A}$ the corresponding master secret key msk_i.

3. Challenge Phase: $\mathcal{A}$ specify two messages μ_0, μ_1, and a function f, where function satisfies the following constraint. We let ω_c denote the attributes controlled by the corrupted authorities, and for each GID we let ω_{GID} denote the attributes which the adversary has queried. We require that $f(\omega_c, \omega_{\mathsf{GID}}) \neq 1$ (In other words, the adversary does not hold a set of keys that allow decryption). The challenger flips a random coin $b \in \{0, 1\}$ and sends the adversary an encryption of μ_b under f.
4. Key Query Phase 2: The adversary can further make corruption and key queries as the Key Query Phase 1, under the constraint of f as specified above.
5. Guess: The adversary submits a guess bit b', and wins if $b' = b$. The advantage of adversary in the experiment $\mathbf{Expt}_{\mathcal{A}}^{\mathsf{dabe}}(1^\lambda, 1^t)$ is defined as $\mathbf{Adv}_{\mathcal{A}}(1^\lambda) = |\Pr[b' = b] - 1/2|$.

Definition 4.2. *A decentralized ABE scheme is fully secure if for any* PPT *adversary $\mathcal{A}$, we have $\mathbf{Adv}_{\mathcal{A}}(1^\lambda) \leq \mathsf{negl}(\lambda)$. The scheme is fully secure against k-bounded collusion if we further require that $\mathcal{A}$ can query at most k distinct* GID*'s in the experiment.*

4.2 Our Basic Construction

In the description here, we first present our basic construction of decentralized ABE for $\{0,1\}$-LSSS. The basic construction can only support $\mathsf{GID} \in \mathbf{GF}(p)$ for some fixed prime p, and the message space is also $\mathbf{GF}(p)$. Next we show how to extend the GID domain to $\mathbf{GF}(p^\ell)$ by using the field extension technique.

Our construction uses the following building blocks: (1) a $\{0,1\}$-LSSS scheme SS, and (2) a fully secure functional encryption for inner product modulo p, denoted as FEIP. We can instantiate the $\{0,1\}$-LSSS as definition in [13], and the FEIP as the construction in Sect. 3.2. Then we define our construction $\Pi = (\mathsf{Global.Setup}, \mathsf{Authority.Setup}, \mathsf{Enc}, \mathsf{KeyGen}, \mathsf{Dec})$ as follows:

- $\mathsf{Global.Setup}(1^\lambda)$: On input security parameter λ, the global setup algorithm sets $k = k(\lambda)$ to denote the collusion bound of the scheme and $t = t(\lambda)$ to denote the number of associated attributes. The global setup algorithm also sets an integer $n = n(\lambda)$ and a prime number $p = p(\lambda)$. It outputs $\mathsf{GP} = (k, t, n, p)$ as the global parameter.
- $\mathsf{Authority.Setup}(\mathsf{GP})$: On input GP, for any attribute i belonged to the authority, the authority runs the algorithm $\mathsf{FEIP.Setup}(1^n, 1^\ell, 1^k, p)$ to generate $\mathsf{FEIP.mpk}_i$ and $\mathsf{FEIP.msk}_i$. Then output $\mathsf{pk} = \{\mathsf{FEIP.mpk}_i\}$ as its public key, and keep $\mathsf{sk} = \{\mathsf{FEIP.msk}_i, \forall i\}$ as its secret key. (In the basic scheme, ℓ is set to 1.)

- $\mathsf{Enc}(\mu, (\mathbf{A}, \rho), \mathsf{GP}, \{\mathsf{pk}\})$: On input a message $\mu \in \mathbb{Z}_p$, an access matrix $\mathbf{A} \in \mathbb{Z}_p^{t \times d}$ with ρ mapping its row number x to attributes, the global parameters GP, and the public keys $\{\mathsf{FEIP.mpk}_i\}$ of the relevant authorities. The encryption algorithm invokes k times $\{0,1\}$-LSSS for secret space $\mathcal{K} = \mathbb{Z}_p$ to generate:

$$(u_{1,1}, ...u_{1,t}) \leftarrow \mathsf{SS.Share}(\mu, \mathbf{A}),$$
$$(u_{i,1}, ...u_{i,t}) \leftarrow \mathsf{SS.Share}(0, \mathbf{A}), \forall i \in [2, k].$$

  For each $(u_{1,x}, ..., u_{k,x}) \in \mathbb{Z}_p^k, x \in [t]$ it generates

$$\mathsf{FEIP.ct}_{\rho(x)} \leftarrow \mathsf{FEIP.Enc}(\mathsf{FEIP.mpk}_{\rho(x)}, (u_{1,x}, ..., u_{k,x})).$$

  The ciphertext is $\mathsf{ct} = (\{\mathsf{FEIP.ct}_{\rho(x)}\}_{x=1,...t})$.
- $\mathsf{KeyGen}(\mathsf{GID}, i, \mathsf{sk}, \mathsf{GP})$: On inputs attribute i, global identifier $\mathsf{GID} \in \mathbb{Z}_p$, secret key sk and global parameter GP, the algorithm sets $\mathbf{GID} = (1, \mathsf{GID}, ..., \mathsf{GID}^{k-1})$ and computes

$$\mathsf{FEIP.sk}_{i,\mathsf{GID}} \leftarrow \mathsf{FEIP.KeyGen}(\mathsf{FEIP.msk}_i, \mathbf{GID}),$$

  and outputs $\mathsf{k}_{i,\mathsf{GID}} = \mathsf{FEIP.sk}_{i,\mathsf{GID}}$.
- $\mathsf{Dec}(\{\mathsf{k}_{i,\mathsf{GID}}\}, \mathbf{A}, \mathsf{ct}, \mathsf{GP})$: On input secret keys $\{\mathsf{k}_{\rho(x),\mathsf{GID}}\}$, the access matrix $\mathbf{A}$, ciphertext ct and global parameter GP, the decryptor first checks if $(1, 0, \ldots, 0)$ is in the span of the rows $\{\mathbf{A}_x\}$. If not, the algorithm outputs $\perp$. Otherwise, it computes

$$\eta_{\rho(x)} = \mathsf{FEIP.Dec}\left(\mathsf{FEIP.sk}_{\rho(x),\mathsf{GID}}, \mathsf{FEIP.ct}_{\rho(x)}\right) \text{ for each } \rho(x),$$

  and outputs $\eta = \mathsf{SS.Combine}(\{\eta_{\rho(x)}\})$.

Remark 4.3. We note that for any distinct k GID's, $\mathsf{GID}_1, \ldots, \mathsf{GID}_k$, the vectors $\left\{\mathbf{GID}_i = (1, \mathsf{GID}_i, ..., \mathsf{GID}_i^{k-1})\right\}_{i \in [k]}$ are linearly independent. In our construction above, each $\mathsf{GID} \in \mathbb{Z}_p$ and the vectors can be expressed as a Vandermonde matrix

$$\mathbf{X} = \begin{bmatrix} 1 & \ldots & 1 \\ x_1 & \ldots & x_k \\ \vdots & \ddots & \vdots \\ x_1^{k-1} & \ldots & x_k^{k-1} \end{bmatrix}, \text{ which is full-rank if the elements } \{x_i\}_{i \in [k]} \text{ are distinct.}$$

Therefore, for any less than k distinct GID's, the key queries for these GID's are linearly independent.

Correctness. We show that the scheme above is correct. By correctness of the fully secure functional encryption scheme FEIP, we have that for each $\rho(x)$,

$$\eta_{\rho(x)} = u_{1,\rho(x)} + \sum_{j=1}^{k-1} u_{j+1,\rho(x)} \mathsf{GID}^j \bmod p.$$

Since $(u_{1,1},...u_{1,t})$ is secret sharing of message μ, and $\{(u_{i,1},...u_{i,t})\}_{i=2}^{k}$ is secret sharing of 0, then by correctness of $\{0,1\}$-LSSS scheme, we have that $\eta = \mu \bmod p$. This proves correctness.

Parameter Setting. We can instantiate the scheme FEIP (c.f. Sect. 3.2) by setting $n = \lambda$, $\ell = 1$, $k = \mathsf{poly}(\lambda)$, $t = \mathsf{poly}(\lambda)$ and $p = \mathsf{poly}(\lambda)$, and obtain a decentralized ABE with both the message space and GID space being $\mathbb{Z}_p$. In summary, our basic scheme can support any fixed $\mathsf{poly}(\lambda)$ GID and message spaces, against any fixed $\mathsf{poly}(\lambda)$ bounded collusion.

Security Proof. Next we prove security of the above scheme in the following theorem.

Theorem 4.4. *Assuming that* FEIP *is a functional encryption for inner products and* FEIP *is adaptively secure for chosen message distributions, and* SS *is a* $\{0,1\}$*-LSSS, the decentralized ABE construction* Π *described above is fully secure against* $k-1$ *bounded collusion.*

Proof. We prove the theorem by reduction. Assume that there exists an adversary $\mathcal{A}$ who breaks the scheme with some non-negligible advantage ϵ, then we can construct a reduction $\mathcal{B}$ that breaks the security of FEIP. Given an adversary $\mathcal{A}$, we define $\mathcal{B}$ as follows:

1. $\mathcal{B}$ first receives $\{\mathsf{mpk}_i\}$ from its challenger, and forwards $\{\mathsf{mpk}_i\}$ to $\mathcal{A}$.
2. $\mathcal{B}$ runs $\mathcal{A}$ to simulate the Key Query Phase 1 of the ABE security game. In each round, $\mathcal{B}$ may receive either a corruption query (i, I) or a key query (GID, i).
   - Upon receiving a query (GID, i), $\mathcal{B}$ makes a key query $((1, \mathsf{GID}, ..., \mathsf{GID}^k), i)$ to its challenger, and receives $\mathsf{k}_{i,\mathsf{GID}}$. $\mathcal{B}$ forward $\mathcal{A}$ with the key.
   - Upon receiving a query (i, corr), $\mathcal{B}$ make a query (i, I) to the challenger and receives msk_i. $\mathcal{B}$ just sends $\mathcal{A}$ msk_i.

   $\mathcal{B}$ continue to run this step until $\mathcal{A}$ makes the challenge query.
3. Upon receiving $\mathcal{A}$'s challenge query, which contains an access structure $\mathbb{A}$ and two messages $\mu_0, \mu_1 \in \mathbb{Z}_p$, $\mathcal{B}$ first checks whether all the key queries satisfy the constraint of the security game of decentralized ABE. (This can be efficiently checked in our setting). If not, $\mathcal{B}$ aborts the game and outputs a random guess. Otherwise, $\mathcal{B}$ defines two distributions $\mathcal{M}_0$ and $\mathcal{M}_1$ as follows. For $b \in \{0,1\}$, $\mathcal{M}_b$ is defined as the distribution that first samples k times of the $\{0,1\}$-LSSS procedure

$$(u_{1,1}^{(b)}, ...u_{1,t}^{(b)}) \leftarrow \mathsf{SS.Share}(\mu_b, \mathbf{A})$$

$$(u_{i,1}^{(b)}, ...u_{i,t}^{(b)}) \leftarrow \mathsf{SS.Share}(0, \mathbf{A}), \forall i \in [2, k].$$

   Then $\mathcal{M}_b$ outputs:

$$\left((u_{1,1}^{(b)}, ..., u_{k,1}^{(b)}), ..., (u_{1,t}^{(b)}, ..., u_{k,t}^{(b)})\right).$$

   $\mathcal{B}$ sends the descriptions of $\mathcal{M}_0, \mathcal{M}_1$ (which can be succinctly described, e.g., $(\mu_b, \mathbf{A})$) to the challenger, and then $\mathcal{B}$ forwards $\mathcal{A}$ the challenge ciphertext received from the external FEIP challenger.

4. $\mathcal{B}$ simulates the Key Query Phase 2 in the same way as Step 2.
5. Finally $\mathcal{B}$ outputs $\mathcal{A}$'s guess b'.

Next we are going to analyze the reduction $\mathcal{B}$. Since $\mathcal{B}$ perfectly emulates the FEIP security game for $\mathcal{A}$, $\mathcal{B}$'s advantage is the same as $\mathcal{A}$'s, assuming the queries are admissible in the FEIP security game. Therefore, it suffices to prove the theorem by showing that the queries made by $\mathcal{B}$ are admissible.

The assumption of the theorem requires that $\mathcal{A}$ can query at most $k-1$ different GID's for each msk_i. Let T_1 be the set that $\mathcal{B}$ (and also $\mathcal{A}$ as well) makes corruption queries, and k_i be the number of secret key queries that $\mathcal{B}$ makes to msk_i. Then we need to show that the two distributions defined below are identical, i.e., $\mathcal{D}_0 = \mathcal{D}_1$, where

$$D_b = \left\{ \{(i, I)(\mathcal{M}_b)\}_{i \in T_1}, \{(i, \boldsymbol{x}_{ij})(\mathcal{M}_b)\}_{i \in T_2, j \in [k_i]} \right\},$$

where $\boldsymbol{x}_{ij} = (1, \mathsf{GID}_{ij}, ... \mathsf{GID}_{ij}^{k-1})$, T_1 is the set $\mathcal{B}$ corrupts, and T_2 is the set that $\mathcal{B}$ makes key queries but does not corrupt.

We note that, for an opening query (i, I), $(i, I)(\mathcal{M}_b) = \left(u_{1,i}^{(b)}, ..., u_{k,i}^{(b)}\right)$ can be viewed as coefficients of the polynomial $P_i(x) = u_{1,i}^{(b)} + \sum_{j=2}^{k} u_{j,i}^{(b)} \cdot x^{j-1} \bmod p)$. By the property of Lagrange interpolation formula, the coefficients of a polynomial $P(x)$ of degree k can be uniquely determined given $P(x_1), \ldots, P(x_k)$ for any distinct $(x_1, \ldots, x_k)$. This implies that $(i, I)(\mathcal{M}_b)$ can be simulated by $\{(i, \mathbf{GID}_{ij})(\mathcal{M}_b)\}_{j \in [k]}$ for any distinct $\{\mathsf{GID}_{ij}\}_{j \in [k]}$, where $\mathbf{GID} = (1, \mathsf{GID}, \ldots, \mathsf{GID}^{k-1})$. Therefore, it is without loss of generality to assume that D_b only contains information of the form $\{(i, \mathbf{GID}_{ij})(\mathcal{M}_b)\}$.

As we argue above, all queries are of the form $(i, \boldsymbol{x}_{ij})$, so we can re-write the queries in D_b as $\{q_1, \ldots, q_n\}$, where each q_j is of the form $(i, \boldsymbol{x})$. Denote $\{q_1, \ldots, q_n\}$ as $\overrightarrow{\boldsymbol{q}}$, and then we can further re-write D_b as $\overrightarrow{\boldsymbol{q}}(\mathcal{M}_b)$. Now it suffices to show that for every admissible $\overrightarrow{\boldsymbol{q}}$ and possible values $\boldsymbol{z}$,

$$\Pr[\overrightarrow{\boldsymbol{q}}(\mathcal{M}_0) = \boldsymbol{z}] = \Pr[\overrightarrow{\boldsymbol{q}}(\mathcal{M}_1) = \boldsymbol{z}].$$

$\Pr[\overrightarrow{\boldsymbol{q}}(\mathcal{M}_b) = \boldsymbol{z}]$ can be expanded as

$$\begin{aligned} &\Pr[\overrightarrow{\boldsymbol{q}}(\mathcal{M}_b) = \boldsymbol{z}] \\ =&\Pr[q_1(\mathcal{M}_b) = z_1] \cdot \Pr[q_2(\mathcal{M}_b) = z_2 | q_1(\mathcal{M}_b) = z_1] \cdots \\ &\Pr[q_n(\mathcal{M}_b) = z_n | q_1(\mathcal{M}_b) = z_1 \wedge \ldots \wedge q_{n-1}(\mathcal{M}_b) = z_{n-1}]. \end{aligned}$$

We first observe that the message distribution $\mathcal{M}_b = \left((u_{1,1}^{(b)}, ..., u_{k,1}^{(b)}), ..., (u_{1,t}^{(b)}, ..., u_{k,t}^{(b)})\right)$ can be viewed as coefficients of t degree-k polynomials $(P_1(x), \ldots, P_t(x))$. Since the marginal distribution of $(u_{1,i}^{(b)}, ..., u_{k,i}^{(b)})$ is uniformly random by the $\{0,1\}$-LSSS property, the marginal distribution of any polynomial P_i is uniform, i.e., a random degree-k polynomial in $\mathbb{Z}_p$. Therefore, $\Pr[q_1(\mathcal{M}_b) = x_1] = 1/p$, independent of b.

Next we will show that for any $j \in [n]$,

$$\Pr\left[q_j(\mathcal{M}_b) = z_j \mid q_{j-1}(\mathcal{M}_b) = z_{j-1} \wedge \cdots \wedge q_1(\mathcal{M}_b) = z_1\right] = 1/p,$$

assuming $q_1, \ldots, q_j$ are admissible.

To prove this, we first set up some notations. We assume that $\mathsf{GID}_1, \ldots, \mathsf{GID}_{k-1}$ are the identifiers queried by the adversary. If the adversary corrupts some msk_i, then he will further learn $P_i(\mathsf{GID}_k)$ (for another GID_k) in addition to $P_i(\mathsf{GID}_1), \ldots, P_i(\mathsf{GID}_{k-1})$. We assume that $q_j = (i, \mathbf{GID}_r)$ for some $i \in [t], r \in [k]$. Let S be an arbitrary maximal invalid set that includes all v's with $(v, \mathbf{GID}_r)$ belongs to the queries $\{q_1, \ldots, q_j\}$, according to the access structure $\mathbb{A}$, i.e. $\{v : (v, \mathbf{GID}_r) \in \{q_1, \ldots, q_j\}\} \subseteq S$. Since the queries are admissible, such a set S always exists.

By the privacy guarantee of the LSSS, we know the distributions of the polynomials $P_1(x), \ldots, P_t(x)$ generated in the encryption algorithm is identical to the following process:

- For every $v \in S$, sample $P_v(x)$ (the coefficients) uniformly and independently at random.
- For every $v \notin S$, set $P_v(x) = \mu_b - \sum_{w \in \Gamma_v} P_w(x)$, where $\Gamma_v \subseteq S$ is the reconstruction set that can be efficiently determined given $(v, \mathbb{A})$.

Next, we observe the following facts:

1. Since $P_i(x)$ is a random polynomial (the marginal distribution), we know that the (marginal) distribution $P_i(\mathsf{GID}_r)$ is uniformly random even conditioned on all $\{P_i(\mathsf{GID}_w)\}_{w \in [k] \setminus \{r\}}$ (as a random degree k polynomial is k-wise independent).
2. From the above sampling procedure, we know that $P_i(x)$ is independent of $\{P_v(x)\}_{v \in S \setminus \{i\}}$.
3. From the above two facts, we know that the (marginal) distribution $P_i(\mathsf{GID}_r)$ is still uniformly random even further conditioned on $\{P_v(x)\}_{v \in S \setminus \{i\}}$ and $\{P_i(\mathsf{GID}_w)\}_{w \in [k] \setminus \{r\}}$.
4. For every $v \notin S$, $w \in [k] \setminus \{r\}$, $P_v(\mathsf{GID}_w)$ can be deterministically obtained given the information $\{P_v(x)\}_{v \in S \setminus \{i\}}$ and $\{P_i(\mathsf{GID}_w)\}_{w \in [k] \setminus \{r\}}$. This implies that the conditional distribution $P_i(\mathsf{GID}_r)$ is uniform even further given $\{P_v(\mathsf{GID}_w)\}_{v \in [t] \setminus S, w \in [k] \setminus \{r\}}$ in addition to $\{P_v(x)\}_{v \in S \setminus \{i\}}$ and $\{P_i(\mathsf{GID}_w)\}_{w \in [k] \setminus \{r\}}$.

It is not hard to see that the information of $q_1(\mathcal{M}_b), \ldots, q_{j-1}(\mathcal{M}_b)$ can be obtained given $\{P_v(\mathsf{GID}_w)\}_{v \in [t] \setminus S, w \in [k] \setminus \{r\}}$, $\{P_v(x)\}_{v \in S \setminus \{i\}}$, and $\{P_i(\mathsf{GID}_w)\}_{w \in [k] \setminus \{r\}}$. Therefore, we have showed: for any $j \in [n]$,

$$\Pr\left[q_j(\mathcal{M}_b) = z_j \mid q_{j-1}(\mathcal{M}_b) = z_{j-1} \wedge \cdots \wedge q_1(\mathcal{M}_b) = z_1\right] = 1/p.$$

Then we can conclude that

$$\begin{aligned}
&\mathsf{Pr}[\overrightarrow{\boldsymbol{q}}(\mathcal{M}_0) = \boldsymbol{x}]\\
&= \mathsf{Pr}[q_1(\mathcal{M}_0) = x_1] \cdot \mathsf{Pr}[q_2(\mathcal{M}_0) = x_2 | q_1(\mathcal{M}_0) = x_1] \cdots\\
&\quad \mathsf{Pr}[q_n(\mathcal{M}_0) = x_n | q_1(\mathcal{M}_0) = x_1 \wedge ... \wedge q_{n-1}(\mathcal{M}_0) = x_{n-1}]\\
&= \mathsf{Pr}[q_1(\mathcal{M}_1) = x_1] \cdot \mathsf{Pr}[q_2(\mathcal{M}_1) = x_2 | q_1(\mathcal{M}_1) = x_1] \cdots\\
&\quad \mathsf{Pr}[q_n(\mathcal{M}_1) = x_n | q_1(\mathcal{M}_1) = x_1 \wedge ... \wedge q_{n-1}(\mathcal{M}_1) = x_{n-1}]\\
&= \mathsf{Pr}[\overrightarrow{\boldsymbol{q}}(\mathcal{M}_1) = \boldsymbol{x}].
\end{aligned}$$

This proves that all the queries $\mathcal{B}$ makes during the game are admissible. This means that $\mathcal{B}$ is a legal adversary in the security game of FEIP. Since $\mathcal{B}$ also perfect simulates the challenger of $\mathcal{A}$, the advantage of $\mathcal{B}$ is the same as the advantage of $\mathcal{A}$, a non-negligible quantity. This reaches a contraction, and completes the proof. □

4.3 An Improved Construction for Large Spaces

We can modify our basic construction so that it can support significantly lager GID and message spaces, using the technique of finite field extension to $\mathbf{GF}(p^\ell)$ for some ℓ. In more detail, we consider the embedding technique described in the work [45,56]. Intuitively, we can compute $\mathbf{GF}(p^\ell)$ field operations via projecting $\mathbf{GF}(p^\ell)$ elements to $\mathbb{Z}_p^\ell$ (and $\mathbb{Z}_p^{\ell\times\ell}$), and thus, the field operations can be supported by our FEIP scheme.

Let $p \in \mathbb{N}$ be a prime, $\ell \in \mathbb{N}$, and let $f(x)$ be a monic irreducible polynomial in $\mathbb{Z}_p$ of degree ℓ. Then we define $R = \mathbb{Z}_p[X]/\langle f(x)\rangle$, and note that R is isomorphic to $\mathbf{GF}(p^\ell)$ as p is a prime and $f(x)$ is an irreducible polynomial of degree ℓ. We will use R as the representation of $\mathbf{GF}(p^\ell)$.

We then define two mappings $\phi : R \to \mathbb{Z}_p^\ell$ and $\mathsf{Rot} : R \to \mathbb{Z}_p^{\ell\times\ell}$ by

$$\phi : \theta = a_1 + a_2 x + ... + a_\ell x^{\ell-1} \mapsto (a_1, ..., a_\ell)^\top,$$

$$\mathsf{Rot} : \theta = a_1 + a_2 x + ... + a_\ell x^{\ell-1} \mapsto \left[\phi(\theta)\phi(\theta x)...\phi(\theta x^{\ell-1})\right].$$

We note that $\mathsf{Rot}(\theta) \cdot \phi(\vartheta) = \phi(\theta\vartheta)$, $\mathsf{Rot}(\theta) \cdot \mathsf{Rot}(\vartheta) = \mathsf{Rot}(\theta\vartheta)$, and $\mathsf{Rot}(\theta) + \mathsf{Rot}(\vartheta) = \mathsf{Rot}(\theta + \vartheta)$. This means that Rot is a ring-homomorphism from R to $\mathbb{Z}_p^{\ell\times\ell}$. If $\theta \neq \theta' \in \mathbf{GF}(p^\ell)$, then $\mathsf{Rot}(\theta) - \mathsf{Rot}(\theta') = \mathsf{Rot}(\theta - \theta') \neq 0$.

Now we present our modified construction Π = (Global.Setup, Authority. Setup, Enc, KeyGen, Dec):

- Global.Setup(1^λ): On input the security parameter λ, the global setup algorithm sets $k = k(\lambda)$ to denote the collusion bound of our scheme and $t = t(\lambda)$ to denote the number of associated attributes. The global setup algorithm also sets $n = n(\lambda)$, $\ell = \ell(\lambda)$ and $p = p(\lambda)$ to denote the input parameters of FEIP.Setup. It outputs GP = (k, t, n, ℓ, p) as the global parameter, and sets both the GID and message spaces as $\mathbf{GF}(p^\ell)$.

- $\mathsf{Authority.Setup}(\mathsf{GP})$: On input GP, for attribute i belonged to the authority, the authority runs the algorithm $\mathsf{FEIP.Setup}(1^n, 1^\ell, 1^k, p)$ to generate $\mathsf{FEIP.mpk}_i$ and $\mathsf{FEIP.msk}_i$. Then output $\mathsf{pk} = \{\mathsf{FEIP.mpk}_i\}$ as its public key, and keep $\mathsf{sk} = \{\mathsf{FEIP.msk}_i, \forall i\}$ as its secret key.
- $\mathsf{Enc}(\mu, (\mathbf{A}, \rho), \mathsf{GP}, \{\mathsf{pk}\})$: On input a message $\mu \in \mathbf{GF}(p^\ell)$, an access matrix $\mathbf{A} \in \mathbf{GF}(p^\ell)^{t\times d}$ with ρ mapping its row number x to attributes, the global parameters GP, and the public keys $\{\mathsf{FEIP.mpk}_i\}$ of the relevant authorities. The encryption algorithm invokes k times $\{0,1\}$-LSSS over secret space $\mathbf{GF}(p^\ell)$ to generate

$$(u_{1,1}, ...u_{1,t}) \leftarrow \mathsf{SS.Share}(\mu, \mathbf{A}),$$

$$(u_{i,1}, ...u_{i,t}) \leftarrow \mathsf{SS.Share}(0, \mathbf{A}), \forall i \in [2, k],$$

For each $(u_{1,x}, ..., u_{k,x}) \in \mathbf{GF}(p^\ell)^k, x \in [t]$, the encryption algorithm first computes:

$$(\boldsymbol{u}_{1,x}, ..., \boldsymbol{u}_{k,x}) \leftarrow \phi(u_{1,x}, ..., u_{k,x}),$$

and then generates

$$\mathsf{FEIP.ct}_{\rho(x)} \leftarrow \mathsf{FEIP.Enc}(\mathsf{FEIP.mpk}_{\rho(x)}, (\boldsymbol{u}_{1,x}, ..., \boldsymbol{u}_{k,x})).$$

The ciphertext is $\mathsf{ct} = (\{\mathsf{FEIP.ct}_{\rho(x)}\}_{x=1,...t})$.
- $\mathsf{KeyGen}(\mathsf{GID}, i, \mathsf{sk}, \mathsf{GP})$: On input attribute i, global identifier $\mathsf{GID} \in \mathbf{GF}(p^\ell)$, secret key sk and global parameters GP. To generate a key for GID for attribute i belonging to an authority, the authority first computes k elements $\mathsf{GID}^j \in \mathbf{GF}(p^\ell), \forall j \in [k-1]$, then computes $\mathsf{Rot}(\mathsf{GID}^j), \forall j \in [k-1]$, and denotes the column vectors of $\begin{bmatrix} \mathbf{I} \\ \mathsf{Rot}(\mathsf{GID}) \\ \vdots \\ \mathsf{Rot}(\mathsf{GID}^{k-1}) \end{bmatrix}$ to be $\{\boldsymbol{g}_j\}_{j\in\ell}$, where $\mathbf{I}$ is the identity matrix in $\mathbb{Z}_p^{\ell\times\ell}$, finally sets

$$\mathsf{FEIP.sk}_{i,\mathsf{GID}}^{(j)} \leftarrow \mathsf{FEIP.KeyGen}\left(\mathsf{FEIP.msk}_i, \boldsymbol{g}_j, \mathsf{rand}_i\right), \forall j \in [\ell].$$

Outputs $\mathsf{k}_{i,\mathsf{GID}} = \{\mathsf{FEIP.sk}_{i,\mathsf{GID}}^{(j)}\}_{j\in[\ell]}$.
- $\mathsf{Dec}(\{\mathsf{k}_{i,\mathsf{GID}}\}, \mathbf{A}, \mathsf{ct}, \mathsf{GP})$: On input secret keys $\{\mathsf{k}_{\rho(x),\mathsf{GID}}\}$, the access matrix $\mathbf{A}$, ciphertext ct and global parameters GP, the decryptor first checks if $(1, 0, \ldots, 0)$ is in the span of the rows $\{\mathbf{A}_x\}$ or not. If not, the algorithm outputs $\perp$. Otherwise, it computes

$$\eta_{\rho(x)}^{(j)} = \mathsf{FEIP.Dec}\left(\mathsf{FEIP.sk}_{\rho(x),\mathsf{GID}}^{(j)}, \mathsf{FEIP.ct}_{\rho(x)}\right), \forall j \in [\ell], \text{ for each } \rho(x),$$

and sets $\boldsymbol{\eta}_{\rho(x)} = \left(\eta_{\rho(x)}^{(1)}, ..., \eta_{\rho(x)}^{(\ell)}\right)$, $\theta_{\rho(x)} = \phi^{-1}(\boldsymbol{\eta}_{\rho(x)})$, then outputs $\theta = \mathsf{SS.Combine}(\{\theta_{\rho(x)}\})$.

Correctness. By correctness of the scheme FEIP, we have that for each $\rho(x)$,

$$\begin{aligned}\boldsymbol{\eta}_{\rho(x)} &= \boldsymbol{u}_{1,\rho(x)} + \sum_{j=1}^{k-1} \boldsymbol{u}_{j+1,\rho(x)} \mathsf{Rot}(\mathsf{GID}^j) (\bmod p) \\ &= \phi(u_{1,\rho(x)} + \sum_{j=1}^{k-1} u_{j+1,\rho(x)} \mathsf{GID}^j).\end{aligned}$$

Then $\theta_{\rho(x)} = u_{1,\rho(x)} + \sum_{j=1}^{k-1} u_{j+1,\rho(x)} \mathsf{GID}^j$. By correctness of the $\{0,1\}$-LSSS scheme over $\mathbf{GF}(p^\ell)$, we have that $\theta = \mu$. This proves correctness.

Parameters. We can instantiate the scheme FEIP (c.f. Sect. 3.2) by setting $n = \lambda$, $\ell = \mathsf{poly}(\lambda)$ $k = \mathsf{poly}(\lambda)$, $t = \mathsf{poly}(\lambda)$ and $p = \mathsf{poly}(\lambda)$, and obtain a decentralized ABE with both the message space and GID space being $\mathbf{GF}(p^\ell)$. In summary, our modified scheme can support *exponential-sized* GID and message spaces, against any fixed $\mathsf{poly}(\lambda)$ bounded collusion.

Security. Security of the modified scheme can be proven in the same way as our basic scheme, as the only difference is the underlying finite field. We note that the analysis that the distributions D_b are identical in the proof of Theorem 4.4 works for any underlying finite field (either $\mathbb{Z}_p$ or $\mathbf{GF}(p^\ell)$), so the analysis can be carried to the modified scheme straightforwardly. To avoid repetition, we just state the theorem as follow.

Theorem 4.5. *Assume that* FEIP *is a functional encryption for inner products that is adaptively secure for chosen message distributions, and* SS *is a* $\{0,1\}$-LSSS *over* $\mathbf{GF}(p^\ell)$. *Then the scheme* Π *above is a fully secure decentralized ABE against* $k-1$ *bounded collusion for* $\{0,1\}$-LSSS *over* $\mathbf{GF}(p^\ell)$.

Combining Theorem 4.5 and the instantiation by Theorem 3.5, we obtain the following corollary:

Corollary 4.6. *Assume the LWE assumption. Then there exits a decentralized ABE that is fully secure against* $k-1$ *bounded collusion for any polynomial* k, *for the function class* $\{0,1\}$-LSSS *over* $\mathbb{Z}_p$ *for any polynomial prime* p. *The scheme supports exponential-sized* GID *and message spaces.*

5 Witness Encryption and Decentralized ABE

In this section, we discuss the relation between decentralized ABE and witness encryption, which is introduced by Garg et al. [28]. We first recall the syntax of witness encryption and its security, after that we give a construction of witness construction for NP language using decentralized ABE for general circuits, and then show that extractable witness encryption implies decentralized ABE for general circuits.

5.1 Witness Encryption

We recall the syntax of WE introduced by Garg et al. [28], and also the extractability security defined by Goldwasser et al. [29]. A witness encryption scheme for an NP language L (with corresponding witness relation R) consists of algorithms $\Pi = (\mathsf{Enc}, \mathsf{Dec})$:

- $\mathsf{Enc}(1^\lambda, x, \mu)$: On input the security parameter λ, an unbounded-length string x, and a message $\mu \in \{0,1\}$, the encryption algorithm outputs a ciphertext ct.
- $\mathsf{Dec}(\mathsf{ct}, w)$: On input a ciphertext and an unbounded-length string w, the decryption algorithm outputs a message μ or a special symbol $\perp$.

Definition 5.1 (Witness Encryption). *We say Π described above is a witness encryption, if it satisfies:*

- **Correctness:** *For any security parameter λ, any $\mu \in \{0,1\}$, and $x \in L$ such that $R(x, w) = 1$, we have that*

$$\Pr[\mathsf{Dec}(\mathsf{Enc}(1^\lambda, x, \mu), w) = \mu] = 1$$

- **Soundness Security:** *For any* PPT *adversary $\mathcal{A}$, there exists a negligible function* $\mathsf{negl}(\cdot)$ *such that for any $x \notin L$, we have:*

$$|\Pr[\mathcal{A}(\mathsf{Enc}(1^\lambda, x, 0)) = 1] - \Pr[\mathcal{A}(\mathsf{Enc}(1^\lambda, x, 1)) = 1]| < \mathsf{negl}(\lambda)$$

Definition 5.2 (Extractable security). *A witness encryption scheme for an NP language L is secure if for all* PPT *adversary $\mathcal{A}$, and all poly q, there exist a* PPT *extractor E and a poly p, such that for all auxiliary inputs z and for all $x \in \{0,1\}^*$, the following holds:*

$$\Pr[b \leftarrow \{0,1\}; \mathsf{ct} \leftarrow \mathsf{WE.Enc}(1^\lambda, x, b) : \mathcal{A}(x, \mathsf{ct}, z) = b] \geq 1/2 + 1/q(|x|)$$
$$\Rightarrow \Pr[E(x, z) = \omega : (x, \omega) \in R_L] \geq 1/p(|x|).$$

5.2 Witness Encryption from Decentralized ABE for General Circuit

We first describe a transformation from witness encryption for NP languages from decentralized ABE for general circuits. Intuitively, the witness encryption can use the Decentralized ABE scheme in the following way: the general circuit f is used as the NP verifier such that the decryptor can recover the message if he has the witness ω for the statement x satisfying $f(x, \omega) = 1$.

More specifically, given an NP language L, we present witness encryption scheme $(\mathsf{WE.Enc}, \mathsf{WE.Dec})$ for L as follows:

- $\mathsf{WE.Enc}(1^\lambda, x, \mu)$: The encryption algorithm takes input a string $x \in \{0,1\}^n$ (whose witness has length bounded by m) and message μ. Then the algorithm runs the following procedures:

- It runs $\mathsf{Global.Setup}$ and $\mathsf{Authority.Setup}$ to generate a global parameters GP and public keys $\{\mathsf{pk}_i\}_{i\in[n+m]}$ and secret keys $\mathsf{sk} = \{\mathsf{sk}_i\}_{i\in[n+m]}$.
- Then it invokes KeyGen to generate $\{\mathsf{k}_{i,x_i}\}_{i\in[n]}$ and $\{\mathsf{k}_{j,0}, \mathsf{k}_{j,1}\}_{j=n+1}^{n+m}$.[3]
- It sets $f : \{0,1\}^n \times \{0,1\}^m \to \{0,1\}$ as the NP verifier for L that on input $x \in \{0,1\}^n, \omega \in \{0,1\}^m$ outputs 1 iff ω is a valid witness of x. Then it generates $\mathsf{ct} \leftarrow \mathsf{Enc}(\mu, f, \mathsf{GP}, \{\mathsf{pk}_i\}_{i\in[n+m]})$.
- Finally, it outputs $\mathsf{ct} = \left(x, \{\mathsf{k}_{i,x_i}\}_{i\in[n]}, \{\mathsf{k}_{j,0}, \mathsf{k}_{j,1}\}_{j=n+1}^{n+m}, \{\mathsf{pk}_i\}_{i\in[n+m]}, \mathsf{ct}\right)$.

– $\mathsf{WE.Dec}(1^\lambda, \omega, \mathsf{ct})$: The decryption algorithm takes input a witness $\omega \in \{0,1\}^m$ for the statement $x \in \{0,1\}^n$ and a ciphertex ct for x. Then the algorithm runs the following procedures:
  - It first checks if $f(x,\omega) = 1$ holds, if not, the decryption algorithm outputs $\perp$.
  - Otherwise, for $j = n+1, \ldots, n+m$, the decryption algorithm chooses k_{j,ω_t} from $\{\mathsf{k}_{j,0}, \mathsf{k}_{j,1}\}_{j=n+1}^{n+m}$ (where $\omega_i \in \{0,1\}$ is the i-th bit of ω). Then it outputs

$$\mu = \mathsf{Dec}\left(\mathsf{ct}, \mathsf{GP}, \left\{\{\mathsf{k}_{i,x_i}\}_{i\in[n]}, \{\mathsf{k}_{j,\omega_t}\}_{j=n+1}^{n+m}\right\}\right).$$

Correctness of the witness encryption scheme is straightforward from the correctness of decentralized ABE scheme. Now we can show the following theorem. Due to space limit, we defer the full proof to the full version of the paper.

Theorem 5.3. *Assuming that Π is a secure decentralized ABE scheme for general circuits (against 1-bounded corruption, static corruption of authorities and selective key queries), the witness encryption scheme above is secure.*

Remark 5.4. Bellare et al. [9] has introduced a stronger security of WE which is denoted as adaptive soundness security. However, our construction can not achieve the stronger adaptive soundness security, because the NP language L we defined is not (efficiently) falsifiable.

Remark 5.5. We note that a weaker notion of decentralized ABE (where the adversary makes static corruption at the beginning of security game, and key queries only once) suffices to construct the witness encryption scheme. This demonstrates the hardness to construct decentralized ABE for general circuits.

Remark 5.6. The scheme we construct above makes use of a decentralized ABE scheme for $n+m$ authorities. We can also construct a WE scheme by invoking a decentralized ABE scheme for only two authorities. Intuitively, we set the attribute space as $\{0,1\}^n$. Then the NP statement $x \in \{0,1\}^n$ is the one attribute controlled by the non-corrupt authority, and the witness $\omega \in \{0,1\}^m$ of x is the one attribute controlled by the corrupt authority. We set f as the NP verifier algorithm. And the decryptor of WE scheme can recover the message if he can find the witness ω for x such that $f(x,\omega) = 1$. Then we can obtain the scheme similarly to the scheme above.

[3] In our setting, we consider a general case where there is no GID.

5.3 Decentralized ABE from Extractable Witness Encryption

Next, we show how to construct a decentralized ABE for general circuits from the following two components: (1) an extractable witness encryption scheme $\mathsf{WE} = (\mathsf{WE.Enc}, \mathsf{WE.Dec})$ [29], and (2) an existentially unforgeable signature scheme $\mathsf{SIG} = (\mathsf{SIG.KeyGen}, \mathsf{SIG.Sign}, \mathsf{SIG.Verify})$ [30].

In our construction, we assume that each authority P_i has a polynomial number of distinct attributes $S_i = \{x_j\}$. This is without loss of generality because we can always encode the party's ID in the first several bits of the attributes. Our construction $\Pi = (\mathsf{Authority\ Setup}, \mathsf{Enc}, \mathsf{KeyGen}, \mathsf{Dec})$ (we omit algorithm $\mathsf{Global\ Setup}$, as it does not affect the functionality) is described as follows:

- $\mathsf{Authority\ Setup}(1^\lambda)$ (for party P_j): On input security parameter λ, for each attribute x_i belonged to the authority P_j, i.e., $\boldsymbol{x}_i \in S_j$, the algorithm runs $\mathsf{SIG.KeyGen}(1^\lambda)$ to generate key pair $(\mathsf{svk}_{\boldsymbol{x}_i}, \mathsf{ssk}_{\boldsymbol{x}_i})$. Then it sets $\mathsf{pk} = \{\mathsf{svk}_{\boldsymbol{x}_i}\}_{\boldsymbol{x}_i \in S_j}$ as the public key, and keeps $\mathsf{sk} = \{\mathsf{ssk}_{\boldsymbol{x}_i}\}_{\boldsymbol{x}_i \in S_j}$ as its secret key.
- $\mathsf{Enc}(\{\mathsf{pk}\}, f, \mu)$: On input public key pk, a function f and message μ, the encryption algorithm sets an instance x_f as $x_f = (\{\mathsf{svk}_{\boldsymbol{x}_i}\}, f)$, and defines NP language L such that $x_f \in L$ if and only if there exists n signature pairs $(\sigma_1, (\boldsymbol{x}_1, \mathsf{GID})), \ldots, (\sigma_n, (\boldsymbol{x}_n, \mathsf{GID}))$ such that

$$(\forall i, \mathsf{SIG.Verify}_{\mathsf{svk}_{\boldsymbol{x}_i}}(\sigma_i, (\boldsymbol{x}_i, \mathsf{GID})) = 1) \wedge (f(\boldsymbol{x}_1, ..., \boldsymbol{x}_n) = 1)$$

  Next it computes and outputs $\mathsf{ct} \leftarrow \mathsf{WE.Enc}(x_f, \mu)$.
- $\mathsf{KeyGen}(\boldsymbol{x}_j, \mathsf{GID}, \mathsf{sk}_i)$: On input attribute $\boldsymbol{x}_j$, the authority outputs $\mathsf{k}_{j,\mathsf{GID}} = \sigma_j \leftarrow \mathsf{SIG.Sign}(\mathsf{ssk}_i, (\boldsymbol{x}_j, \mathsf{GID}))$ if $\boldsymbol{x}_j \in S_i$. Otherwise, it outputs $\perp$.
- $\mathsf{Dec}(\{\mathsf{k}_{i,\mathsf{GID}}\}, \mathsf{GP}, \mathsf{ct})$: If the decryptor has a set of keys with the same GID such that $f(\boldsymbol{x}_1, \ldots, \boldsymbol{x}_n) = 1$, and all the signature verifications succeed, then $\{\mathsf{k}_{i,\mathsf{GID}}\}$ servers as witness for x_f, and it calls $\mathsf{WE.Dec}(\omega, \mathsf{ct})$ to recover the message μ. Otherwise, the decryption fails.

It is straightforward that the correctness of the scheme described above comes from the correctness of witness encryption WE and signature scheme SIG.

Next, we are going to show that the construction above achieves a ABE against static corruption. For convenience of our proof, we use the following presentation of definition for security against static corruption. Let $\mathcal{A} = (\mathcal{A}_1, \mathcal{A}_2)$ be an adversary, and T denote the set of authorities.

$\mathsf{Exp}^{\mathsf{dabe}}(1^\lambda)$:

1. $(T', \{\mathsf{pk}_i, \mathsf{sk}_i\}_{i \in T'}) \leftarrow \mathcal{A}_1(1^\lambda)$
2. $\{\mathsf{pk}_j, \mathsf{sk}_j\}_{j \in T \setminus T'} \leftarrow \mathsf{Authority.Setup}(1^\lambda)$
3. $(f, \mathsf{state}) \leftarrow \mathcal{A}_1^{\mathsf{KeyGen}(\mathsf{sk}_j, \cdot)}(\{\mathsf{pk}_k\}_{k \in [T]})$
4. Choose a bit b at random and let $\mathsf{ct} \leftarrow \mathsf{Enc}(\{\mathsf{pk}_k\}_{k \in [T]}, f, b)$
5. $b' \leftarrow \mathcal{A}_2^{\mathsf{KeyGen}(\mathsf{sk}_j, \cdot)}(\mathsf{state}, \mathsf{ct})$
6. If $b = b'$ and for all attributes $\boldsymbol{x}_{go}$ that $\mathcal{A}$ makes key requests to oracle $\mathsf{KeyGen}(\mathsf{sk}_j, .)$ along with the attributes $\boldsymbol{x}_{co}$ controlled by corrupted authorities $(\mathcal{A})$, we have $f(\boldsymbol{x}_{go}, \boldsymbol{x}_{co}) \neq 1$, output 1, else output 0.

We say that the scheme is secure (against static corruption of authorities) if for all PPT adversaries $\mathcal{A}$, the advantage $\mathbf{Adv}_{\mathcal{A}}^{\mathsf{dabe}}$ of $\mathcal{A}$ is negligible. where:

$$\mathbf{Adv}_{\mathcal{A}}^{\mathsf{dabe}} = |\Pr[\mathsf{Exp}_{\mathcal{A}}^{\mathsf{dabe}}(1^{\lambda}) = 1] - 1/2|.$$

Then we can show the following theorem. Due to space limit, we defer the full proof to the full version of the paper.

Theorem 5.7. *Assuming the existence of an extractable witness encryption scheme* WE *and an existentially unforgeable signature scheme* SIG, *then the scheme described above is secure against static corruption of authorities.*

6 Conclusion

We investigated the constructions of LWE-based and DDH-based decentralized ABE, which satisfy stronger security notion that adversary can make corruption queries of parties adaptively in addition to making adaptive key queries. As a building block, we first introduced a functional encryption for inner product functionality with a stronger security requirement, and then we proposed the constructions of FE for inner product with the stronger security by making some modifications of the constructions by [6]. Combining the FE for inner product with the stronger security and a $\{0,1\}$-LSSS scheme, we obtained the constructions of the desired decentralized ABE. Finally, we showed that decentralized ABE for general access structures is somewhat equivalent to witness encryption (WE) for general NP relations.

Our scheme is in the plain model and the security holds against bounded collusion, the work [41] can support an unbounded number of collusions by using random oracle. We leave it as an interesting open question whether our scheme can be upgraded in the random oracle model.

Acknowledgements. We would like to thank Qiang Tang, Mingsheng Wang for their helpful discussions and suggestions. We also thank the anonymous reviewers of PKC 2019 for their insightful advices. Zhedong Wang is supported by the National Key R&D Program of China-2017YFB0802202. Xiong Fan is supported in part by IBM under Agreement 4915013672 and NSF Award CNS-1561209. Feng-Hao Liu is supported by the NSF Award CNS-1657040. Any opinions, findings, and conclusions or recommendations expressed in this material are those of the author(s) and do not necessarily reflect the views of the sponsors.

References

1. Abdalla, M., Bourse, F., De Caro, A., Pointcheval, D.: Simple functional encryption schemes for inner products. In: Katz [38], pp. 733–751
2. Abdalla, M., Gay, R., Raykova, M., Wee, H.: Multi-input inner-product functional encryption from pairings. In: Coron, J.-S., Nielsen, J.B. (eds.) EUROCRYPT 2017, Part I. LNCS, vol. 10210, pp. 601–626. Springer, Cham (2017). https://doi.org/10.1007/978-3-319-56620-7_21

3. Agrawal, S.: Stronger security for reusable garbled circuits, general definitions and attacks. In: Katz and Shacham [40], pp. 3–35
4. Agrawal, S., Bhattacherjee, S., Phan, D.H., Stehlé, D., Yamada, S.: Efficient public trace and revoke from standard assumptions: extended abstract. In: Thuraisingham, B.M., Evans, D., Malkin, T., Xu, D. (eds.) ACM CCS 2017, pp. 2277–2293. ACM Press, New York (2017)
5. Agrawal, S., Freeman, D.M., Vaikuntanathan, V.: Functional encryption for inner product predicates from learning with errors. In: Lee, D.H., Wang, X. (eds.) ASIACRYPT 2011. LNCS, vol. 7073, pp. 21–40. Springer, Heidelberg (2011). https://doi.org/10.1007/978-3-642-25385-0_2
6. Agrawal, S., Libert, B., Stehlé, D.: Fully secure functional encryption for inner products, from standard assumptions. In: Robshaw and Katz [50], pp. 333–362
7. Agrawal, S., Rosen, A.: Functional encryption for bounded collusions, revisited. In: Kalai, Y., Reyzin, L. (eds.) TCC 2017, Part I. LNCS, vol. 10677, pp. 173–205. Springer, Cham (2017). https://doi.org/10.1007/978-3-319-70500-2_7
8. Ananth, P., Fan, X.: Attribute based encryption for RAMs from LWE. Cryptology ePrint Archive, Report 2018/273 (2018). https://eprint.iacr.org/2018/273
9. Bellare, M., Hoang, V.T.: Adaptive witness encryption and asymmetric password-based cryptography. In: Katz [38], pp. 308–331
10. Benhamouda, F., Bourse, F., Lipmaa, H.: CCA-secure inner-product functional encryption from projective hash functions. In: Fehr, S. (ed.) PKC 2017, Part II. LNCS, vol. 10175, pp. 36–66. Springer, Heidelberg (2017). https://doi.org/10.1007/978-3-662-54388-7_2
11. Bethencourt, J., Sahai, A., Waters, B.: Ciphertext-policy attribute-based encryption. In: 2007 IEEE Symposium on Security and Privacy, pp. 321–334. IEEE Computer Society Press, May 2007
12. Bishop, A., Jain, A., Kowalczyk, L.: Function-hiding inner product encryption. In: Iwata, T., Cheon, J.H. (eds.) ASIACRYPT 2015. LNCS, vol. 9452, pp. 470–491. Springer, Heidelberg (2015). https://doi.org/10.1007/978-3-662-48797-6_20
13. Boneh, D., et al.: Threshold cryptosystems from threshold fully homomorphic encryption. Cryptology ePrint Archive, Report 2017/956 (2017). https://eprint.iacr.org/2017/956
14. Boneh, D., et al.: Fully key-homomorphic encryption, arithmetic circuit ABE and compact garbled circuits. In: Nguyen, P.Q., Oswald, E. (eds.) EUROCRYPT 2014. LNCS, vol. 8441, pp. 533–556. Springer, Heidelberg (2014). https://doi.org/10.1007/978-3-642-55220-5_30
15. Boneh, D., Roughgarden, T., Feigenbaum, J. (eds.): 45th ACM STOC. ACM Press, New York (2013)
16. Boneh, D., Sahai, A., Waters, B.: Functional encryption: definitions and challenges. In: Ishai, Y. (ed.) TCC 2011. LNCS, vol. 6597, pp. 253–273. Springer, Heidelberg (2011). https://doi.org/10.1007/978-3-642-19571-6_16
17. Boyen, X.: Attribute-based functional encryption on lattices. In: Sahai, A. (ed.) TCC 2013. LNCS, vol. 7785, pp. 122–142. Springer, Heidelberg (2013). https://doi.org/10.1007/978-3-642-36594-2_8
18. Boyen, X., Li, Q.: Turing machines with shortcuts: efficient attribute-based encryption for bounded functions. In: Manulis, M., Sadeghi, A.-R., Schneider, S. (eds.) ACNS 2016. LNCS, vol. 9696, pp. 267–284. Springer, Cham (2016). https://doi.org/10.1007/978-3-319-39555-5_15

19. Brakerski, Z., Jain, A., Komargodski, I., Passelegue, A., Wichs, D.: Non-trivial witness encryption and null-iO from standard assumptions. Cryptology ePrint Archive, Report 2017/874 (2017). https://eprint.iacr.org/2017/874
20. Brakerski, Z., Vaikuntanathan, V.: Circuit-ABE from LWE: unbounded attributes and semi-adaptive security. In: Robshaw and Katz [50], pp. 363–384
21. Canetti, R., Garay, J.A. (eds.): CRYPTO 2013, Part II. LNCS, vol. 8043. Springer, Heidelberg (2013). https://doi.org/10.1007/978-3-642-40084-1
22. Chase, M.: Multi-authority attribute based encryption. In: Vadhan, S.P. (ed.) TCC 2007. LNCS, vol. 4392, pp. 515–534. Springer, Heidelberg (2007). https://doi.org/10.1007/978-3-540-70936-7_28
23. Chase, M., Chow, S.S.M.: Improving privacy and security in multi-authority attribute-based encryption. In: Al-Shaer, E., Jha, S., Keromytis, A.D. (eds.) ACM CCS 2009, pp. 121–130. ACM Press, New York (2009)
24. Datta, P., Okamoto, T., Tomida, J.: Full-hiding (unbounded) multi-input inner product functional encryption from the k-linear assumption. In: Abdalla, M., Dahab, R. (eds.) PKC 2018, Part II. LNCS, vol. 10770, pp. 245–277. Springer, Cham (2018). https://doi.org/10.1007/978-3-319-76581-5_9
25. Garg, S., Gentry, C., Halevi, S., Raykova, M., Sahai, A., Waters, B.: Candidate indistinguishability obfuscation and functional encryption for all circuits. In: 54th FOCS, pp. 40–49. IEEE Computer Society Press, October 2013
26. Garg, S., Gentry, C., Halevi, S., Sahai, A., Waters, B.: Attribute-based encryption for circuits from multilinear maps. In: Canetti and Garay [21], pp. 479–499
27. Garg, S., Gentry, C., Halevi, S., Zhandry, M.: Functional encryption without obfuscation. In: Kushilevitz, E., Malkin, T. (eds.) TCC 2016, Part II. LNCS, vol. 9563, pp. 480–511. Springer, Heidelberg (2016). https://doi.org/10.1007/978-3-662-49099-0_18
28. Garg, S., Gentry, C., Sahai, A., Waters, B.: Witness encryption and its applications. In: Boneh et al. [15], pp. 467–476
29. Goldwasser, S., Kalai, Y.T., Popa, R.A., Vaikuntanathan, V., Zeldovich, N.: How to run turing machines on encrypted data. In: Canetti and Garay [21], pp. 536–553
30. Goldwasser, S., Micali, S., Rivest, R.L.: A digital signature scheme secure against adaptive chosen-message attacks. SIAM J. Comput. **17**(2), 281–308 (1988)
31. Gorbunov, S., Vaikuntanathan, V., Wee, H.: Functional encryption with bounded collusions via multi-party computation. In: Safavi-Naini and Canetti [52], pp. 162–179
32. Gorbunov, S., Vaikuntanathan, V., Wee, H.: Attribute-based encryption for circuits. In: Boneh et al. [15], pp. 545–554
33. Gorbunov, S., Vaikuntanathan, V., Wee, H.: Predicate encryption for circuits from LWE. In: Gennaro, R., Robshaw, M.J.B. (eds.) CRYPTO 2015, Part II. LNCS, vol. 9216, pp. 503–523. Springer, Heidelberg (2015). https://doi.org/10.1007/978-3-662-48000-7_25
34. Goyal, V., Pandey, O., Sahai, A., Waters, B.: Attribute-based encryption for fine-grained access control of encrypted data. In: Juels, A., Wright, R.N., Vimercati, S. (eds.) ACM CCS 2006, pp. 89–98. ACM Press, October/November 2006. Cryptology ePrint Archive Report 2006/309
35. Green, M., Hohenberger, S., Waters, B.: Outsourcing the decryption of ABE ciphertexts. In: USENIX Security Symposium, vol. 2011 (2011)
36. Jafargholi, Z., Kamath, C., Klein, K., Komargodski, I., Pietrzak, K., Wichs, D.: Be adaptive, avoid overcommitting. In: Katz and Shacham [40], pp. 133–163

37. Katsumata, S., Yamada, S.: Partitioning via non-linear polynomial functions: more compact IBEs from ideal lattices and bilinear maps. In: Cheon, J.H., Takagi, T. (eds.) ASIACRYPT 2016, Part II. LNCS, vol. 10032, pp. 682–712. Springer, Heidelberg (2016). https://doi.org/10.1007/978-3-662-53890-6_23
38. Katz, J. (ed.): PKC 2015. LNCS, vol. 9020. Springer, Heidelberg (2015). https://doi.org/10.1007/978-3-662-46447-2
39. Katz, J., Sahai, A., Waters, B.: Predicate encryption supporting disjunctions, polynomial equations, and inner products. In: Smart, N.P. (ed.) EUROCRYPT 2008. LNCS, vol. 4965, pp. 146–162. Springer, Heidelberg (2008). https://doi.org/10.1007/978-3-540-78967-3_9
40. Katz, J., Shacham, H. (eds.): CRYPTO 2017, Part I. LNCS, vol. 10401. Springer, Cham (2017). https://doi.org/10.1007/978-3-319-63688-7
41. Lewko, A., Waters, B.: Decentralizing attribute-based encryption. In: Paterson, K.G. (ed.) EUROCRYPT 2011. LNCS, vol. 6632, pp. 568–588. Springer, Heidelberg (2011). https://doi.org/10.1007/978-3-642-20465-4_31
42. Lewko, A.B., Okamoto, T., Sahai, A., Takashima, K., Waters, B.: Fully secure functional encryption: attribute-based encryption and (hierarchical) inner product encryption. In: Gilbert, H. (ed.) EUROCRYPT 2010. LNCS, vol. 6110, pp. 62–91. Springer, Heidelberg (2010). https://doi.org/10.1007/978-3-642-13190-5_4
43. Lin, H., Cao, Z., Liang, X., Shao, J.: Secure threshold multi authority attribute based encryption without a central authority. In: Chowdhury, D.R., Rijmen, V., Das, A. (eds.) INDOCRYPT 2008. LNCS, vol. 5365, pp. 426–436. Springer, Heidelberg (2008). https://doi.org/10.1007/978-3-540-89754-5_33
44. Liu, Z., Cao, Z., Huang, Q., Wong, D.S., Yuen, T.H.: Fully secure multi-authority ciphertext-policy attribute-based encryption without random oracles. In: Atluri, V., Diaz, C. (eds.) ESORICS 2011. LNCS, vol. 6879, pp. 278–297. Springer, Heidelberg (2011). https://doi.org/10.1007/978-3-642-23822-2_16
45. Micciancio, D.: Generalized compact knapsacks, cyclic lattices, and efficient one-way functions from worst-case complexity assumptions. In: 43rd FOCS, pp. 356–365. IEEE Computer Society Press, November 2002
46. Müller, S., Katzenbeisser, S., Eckert, C.: Distributed attribute-based encryption. In: Lee, P.J., Cheon, J.H. (eds.) ICISC 2008. LNCS, vol. 5461, pp. 20–36. Springer, Heidelberg (2009). https://doi.org/10.1007/978-3-642-00730-9_2
47. Muller, S., Katzenbeisser, S., Eckert, C.: On multi-authority ciphertext-policy attribute-based encryption. Bull. Korean Math. Soc. **46**(4), 803–819 (2009)
48. O'Neill, A.: Definitional issues in functional encryption. Cryptology ePrint Archive, Report 2010/556 (2010). http://eprint.iacr.org/2010/556
49. Ostrovsky, R., Sahai, A., Waters, B.: Attribute-based encryption with non-monotonic access structures. In: Ning, P., di Vimercati, S.D.C., Syverson, P.F. (eds.) ACM CCS 2007, pp. 195–203. ACM Press, New York (2007)
50. Robshaw, M., Katz, J. (eds.): CRYPTO 2016, Part III. LNCS, vol. 9816. Springer, Heidelberg (2016). https://doi.org/10.1007/978-3-662-53015-3
51. Rouselakis, Y., Waters, B.: Practical constructions and new proof methods for large universe attribute-based encryption. In: Sadeghi, A.-R., Gligor, V.D., Yung, M. (eds.) ACM CCS 2013, pp. 463–474. ACM Press, New York (2013)
52. Safavi-Naini, R., Canetti, R. (eds.): CRYPTO 2012. LNCS, vol. 7417. Springer, Heidelberg (2012). https://doi.org/10.1007/978-3-642-32009-5
53. Sahai, A., Waters, B.R.: Fuzzy identity-based encryption. In: Cramer, R. (ed.) EUROCRYPT 2005. LNCS, vol. 3494, pp. 457–473. Springer, Heidelberg (2005). https://doi.org/10.1007/11426639_27

54. Waters, B.: Ciphertext-policy attribute-based encryption: an expressive, efficient, and provably secure realization. In: Catalano, D., Fazio, N., Gennaro, R., Nicolosi, A. (eds.) PKC 2011. LNCS, vol. 6571, pp. 53–70. Springer, Heidelberg (2011). https://doi.org/10.1007/978-3-642-19379-8_4
55. Waters, B.: Functional encryption for regular languages. In: Safavi-Naini and Canetti [52], pp. 218–235
56. Xagawa, K.: Improved (hierarchical) inner-product encryption from lattices. In: Kurosawa, K., Hanaoka, G. (eds.) PKC 2013. LNCS, vol. 7778, pp. 235–252. Springer, Heidelberg (2013). https://doi.org/10.1007/978-3-642-36362-7_15

Decentralizing Inner-Product Functional Encryption

Michel Abdalla[1,2](✉), Fabrice Benhamouda[3], Markulf Kohlweiss[4], and Hendrik Waldner[4]

[1] DIENS, École normale supérieure, CNRS, PSL University, Paris, France
michel.abdalla@ens.fr
[2] Inria, Paris, France
[3] IBM Research, Yorktown Heights, NY, USA
fabrice.benhamouda@normalesup.org
[4] University of Edinburgh, Edinburgh, UK
{mkohlwei,hendrik.waldner}@ed.ac.uk

Abstract. Multi-client functional encryption (MCFE) is a more flexible variant of functional encryption whose functional decryption involves multiple ciphertexts from different parties. Each party holds a different secret key and can independently and adaptively be corrupted by the adversary. We present two compilers for MCFE schemes for the inner-product functionality, both of which support encryption labels. Our first compiler transforms any scheme with a special key-derivation property into a decentralized scheme, as defined by Chotard et al. (ASIACRYPT 2018), thus allowing for a simple distributed way of generating functional decryption keys without a trusted party. Our second compiler allows to lift an unnatural restriction present in existing (decentralized) MCFE schemes, which requires the adversary to ask for a ciphertext from each party. We apply our compilers to the works of Abdalla et al. (CRYPTO 2018) and Chotard et al. (ASIACRYPT 2018) to obtain schemes with hitherto unachieved properties. From Abdalla et al., we obtain instantiations of DMCFE schemes in the standard model (from DDH, Paillier, or LWE) but without labels. From Chotard et al., we obtain a DMCFE scheme with labels still in the random oracle model, but without pairings.

1 Introduction

Functional encryption (FE) [12,23,24] is a form of encryption that allows fine-grained access control over encrypted data. Besides the classical encryption and decryption procedures, functional encryption schemes consists of a key derivation algorithm, which allows the owner of a master secret key to derive keys with more restricted capabilities. These derived keys sk_f are called functional decryption keys and are associated with a function f. Using the key sk_f for the decryption of a ciphertext $\mathsf{Enc}(x)$ generates the output $f(x)$. During this decryption procedure no more information is revealed about the underlying plaintext than $f(x)$.

In the case of classical functional encryption, the (functional) decryption procedure takes as input a single ciphertext $\mathsf{Enc}(x)$. A natural extension is the

D. Lin and K. Sako (Eds.): PKC 2019, LNCS 11443, pp. 128–157, 2019.
https://doi.org/10.1007/978-3-030-17259-6_5

multi-input setting, where the decryption procedure takes as input n different ciphertexts and outputs a function applied on the n corresponding plaintexts. Such a scheme is called multi-input functional encryption (MIFE) scheme [20]. In a MIFE scheme, each ciphertext can be generated independently (i.e., with completely independent randomness).

An important use case of MIFE considers multiple parties or clients, where each party P_i generates a single ciphertext of the tuple. The ciphertext generated by party P_i is often said to correspond to *position* or *slot* i. In the multi-client setting, it becomes natural to assume that each party has a different secret/encryption key sk_i that can be corrupted by the adversary. We call such a scheme a multi-client functional encryption (MCFE) scheme [15,20].

We remark that the exact terminology varies from paper to paper. Here, a MCFE scheme is always supposed to be secure against corruption of the parties encrypting messages. In a MIFE scheme, on the other hand, all the parties may use the same encryption key and there is no security against corruption.

The multi-input and multi-client settings still require a trusted third party that sets up the encryption keys and holds the master secret key used to derive the functional decryption keys. As a result, the central authority is able to recover every client's private data. This raises the question if it is possible to decentralize the concept of functional encryption and get rid of this trusted entity. In this work, we focus on the notion of decentralized multi-client functional encryption (DMCFE) introduced by Chotard et al. [15]. In DMCFE, the key derivation procedure KeyDer is divided into two procedures $\mathsf{KeyDerShare}$ and $\mathsf{KeyDerComb}$. The KeyDer procedure allows each party P_i to generate a share $\mathsf{sk}_{i,f}$ of the functional key sk_f from its secret key sk_i. The $\mathsf{KeyDerComb}$ procedure is then used to combine these n different shares $\mathsf{sk}_{1,f}, \dots, \mathsf{sk}_{n,f}$ to generate the functional key sk_f. Assuming that the secret key sk_i can also be generated in a distributed way, this makes it possible to get rid of the trusted party and to ensure that every party has complete control over their individual data.

An important property of MIFE and (D)MCFE schemes is whether they are labeled or not. The labeled setting is similar to vanilla multi-input/multi-client functional encryption, but the encryption procedure takes as input a second parameter, a so-called label ℓ. The decryption procedure is restricted in such a way that it is only possible to decrypt ciphertexts that are encrypted under the same label $\mathsf{Enc}(\mathsf{sk}_1, x_1, \ell), \dots, \mathsf{Enc}(\mathsf{sk}_n, x_n, \ell)$. This setting is sometimes desirable in practice as it allows repeated computations over encrypted data that comes from different sources (for example data mining over encrypted data or multi-client delegation of computation [15]).

In the last few years, many multi-input or multi-client functional encryption schemes have been constructed. As noted in [4], these schemes can be split into two main categories: (1) feasibility for general functionalities, and (2) concrete and efficient realizations for more restricted functionalities. Constructions of the first category [6,7,13,20] are based on more unstable assumptions, such as indistinguishable obfuscation or multilinear maps, and tackle the problem of creating schemes for more general functionalities. A few constructions of the second category are provided in the work of Abdalla et al. in [3,4] and Chotard et al. in [15], which consider different types of secret-key constructions for the inner-product functionality. In these schemes, each function is specified by a collection $\boldsymbol{y}$ of n vectors $\boldsymbol{y}_1, \ldots, \boldsymbol{y}_n$ and takes a collection $\boldsymbol{x}$ of n vectors $\boldsymbol{x}_1, \ldots, \boldsymbol{x}_n$ as input. Their output is $f_{\boldsymbol{y}}(\boldsymbol{x}) = \sum_{i=1}^{n} \langle \boldsymbol{x}_i, \boldsymbol{y}_i \rangle = \langle \boldsymbol{x}, \boldsymbol{y} \rangle$. As the original single-input inner-product functionality [2,5,11,17] and their quadratic extensions [8], multi-input or multi-client inner-product functionalities can be quite useful for computing statistics or performing data mining on encrypted databases [4,15].

Currently, the work of Chotard et al. provides the only known DMCFE to our knowledge. However, while their MCFE uses any cyclic group where the Decisional Diffie-Hellman (DDH) assumption holds, their DMCFE scheme requires pairings. Furthermore, the security notion they achieve only guarantees security against an adversary that queries the encryption/challenge oracle for every position i. At first glance, it might seem that more encryption queries would help the adversary, but this does not allow trivial attacks and the adversary is restricted as follows: all functions f for which the adversary has a functional decryption key must evaluate to the same value on all the plaintext tuples queried to the encryption oracle. However, when a position i is not queried, this condition is always satisfied since the function f in principle can never be really evaluated due to a missing input. Hence, requiring the adversary to query the encryption/challenge oracle for every position i actually weakens the achieved security notion.

This leaves open the following problems that we tackle in this paper:

1. Constructing DMCFE schemes without pairings, and even from more general assumptions than discrete-logarithm-based ones.
2. Removing the restriction that the adversary has to query the encryption oracle for every position i.

1.1 Contributions

Our first main contribution is to provide a generic compiler from any MCFE scheme satisfying an extra property called *special key derivation* into an DMCFE scheme. The transformation is purely information-theoretic and does not require any additional assumptions. As the MCFE from Chotard et al. [15] satisfies this extra property, we obtain a *labeled* DMCFE scheme secure under the plain DDH assumption without pairings (in the random oracle model). As in [15], the version of the scheme without labels is secure in the standard model (i.e., without random oracles).

Furthermore, we show as an additional contribution that the MIFE schemes from Abdalla et al. [3] are actually MCFE secure against adaptive corruptions (but without labels). This directly yields the first DMCFE scheme without labels from the LWE assumptions and the Paillier assumptions in the standard model.

Our second main contribution is to provide generic compilers to transform any scheme in the weaker model where the adversary is required to query the encryption oracle at every position i, into a scheme without this restriction. We propose two versions of the compiler: one without labels (in the standard model) which only requires an IND-CPA symmetric encryption scheme, and one with labels in the random oracle model.

These two compilers can be used to lift the security of the previously mentioned constructions of DMCFE to the stronger model. The resulting instantiations from DDH, LWE, and Paillier described above rely on the same assumptions.

1.2 Technical Overview

Contribution 1: A MCFE to DMCFE compiler. The DMCFE construction introduced by Chotard et al. [15] is based on pairings and proven in the random oracle model.

Our first compiler transforms an MCFE scheme into a DMCFE scheme and does not require pairings. It operates on schemes with the special key derivation property, namely whose master secret key can be split into separate secret keys, one for each input, i.e. $\mathsf{msk} = \{\mathsf{sk}_i\}_{i\in[n]}$, and whose functional decryption keys are derived through a combination of local and linear inner-product computations on i, f, sk_i and pp. That is, the functional decryption key sk_f for the function $f : \boldsymbol{x} \mapsto \sum_{i=1}^{n}\langle \boldsymbol{x}_i, \boldsymbol{y}_i\rangle$ can be written as $\mathsf{sk}_f = (\{s(\mathsf{sk}_i, \boldsymbol{y})\}_{i\in[n]}, \sum_{i=1}^{n}\langle u(\mathsf{sk}_i), \boldsymbol{y}_i\rangle)$, where f is defined by the collection $\boldsymbol{y}$ of the vectors $\boldsymbol{y}_1, \ldots, \boldsymbol{y}_n$ and takes as input a collection $\boldsymbol{x}$ of n vectors $\boldsymbol{x}_1, \ldots, \boldsymbol{x}_n$, and where s and u are two public functions.[1] Sums and inner products are computed modulo some integer L which is either prime or hard to factor.

For instance the MCFE scheme of [15], without pairings but supporting labels, has functional decryption keys of the form $\mathsf{sk}_f = (\boldsymbol{y}, \sum_i \mathsf{sk}_i \cdot y_i)$.

Consider first the following straw man compiler. It splits KeyDer into two procedures KeyDerShare and KeyDerComb. The first procedure assumes that each party P_i has access to the i-th share $t_{i,y}$ of a fresh secret sharing of zero $\{t_{i,y}\}_{i\in[n]}$. It then computes $s_{i,y} = s(\mathsf{sk}_i, \boldsymbol{y})$ (which is a local computation) and $\mathsf{dk}_{i,y} = \langle u(\mathsf{sk}_i), \boldsymbol{y}_i\rangle + t_{i,y}$. The output key share is $\mathsf{sk}_{i,y} = (s_{i,y}, \mathsf{dk}_{i,y})$. In the KeyDerComb procedure, the $\mathsf{dk}_{i,y}$ values get summed up to cancel out the $t_{i,y}$ values and to obtain $\sum_i\langle u(\mathsf{sk}_i), \boldsymbol{y}_i\rangle$. The output gets then extended with the values $s(\mathsf{sk}_i, \boldsymbol{y})$ to obtain the complete functional decryption key sk_f. This works but the question on the generation of the fresh secret sharing of zero $\{t_{i,y}\}_{i\in[n]}$ is left out.

One solution consists in generating it as follows: $t_{i,y} = \sum_{j\neq i}(-1)^{j<i} F_{\mathsf{K}_{i,j}}(\boldsymbol{y})$, where $F_{\mathsf{K}_{i,j}}$ is a pseudorandom function with key $\mathsf{K}_{i,j} = \mathsf{K}_{j,i}$ shared between parties P_i and P_j. This yields an DMCFE scheme secure against static corruption. Unfortunately, we do not know how to prove such a scheme secure against adaptive corruptions.

Our full compiler improves this construction in two ways: it allows adaptive corruptions and does not require any pseudorandom function. The procedure

[1] We note that our compiler actually is not restricted to the inner-product functionality. The only requirement is the special key derivation property.

$\mathsf{KeyDerShare}$ of our full compiler uses masking values $\{\boldsymbol{v}_i\}_{i\in[n]}$, $\boldsymbol{v}_i \in \mathbb{Z}_L^{m\cdot n}$, such that $\boldsymbol{v}_n = -\sum_{i=1}^{n-1} \boldsymbol{v}_i$, to derive the key shares $\mathsf{sk}_{i,f} = \langle u(\mathsf{sk}_i), \boldsymbol{y}_i\rangle + \langle \boldsymbol{v}_i, \boldsymbol{y}\rangle$. Here, $\langle \boldsymbol{v}_i, \boldsymbol{y}\rangle$ acts as a kind of information theoretic pseudorandom function with key $\boldsymbol{v}_i$. To make this work, the queried values need to be linearly independent. This allows us to construct an information-theoretic compiler that provides security against adaptive corruptions (see Sect. 3 for details).

The masking of values prevents the combination of key shares for different functions $\boldsymbol{y}$. If one computes shares on different $\boldsymbol{y}$'s, then the sum of these shares will not sum up to 0 and the resulting key will be invalid. The encryption and decryption procedures proceed in the same way as in the MCFE setting.

Contribution 2: A compiler enforcing a single ciphertext query for each position. The standard security property of MIFE/MCFE schemes guarantees that an adversary can only learn a function of the inputs when it is in possession of a ciphertext for every input position i. This property is not satisfied by the schemes of [3,4,15]. Their basic definitions guarantee security *only* when the adversary queries every position at least once. We call a scheme satisfying this property *pos-IND* secure (for positive) while we call the standard property *any-IND* secure.

To overcome this deficiency, Abdalla et al. [4] constructed a compiler that turns any *pos-IND* secure MIFE scheme into an *any-IND* secure MIFE scheme. The compiler uses a symmetric encryption scheme in addition to their MIFE encryption scheme. In more detail, the setup procedure of the compiler samples a key K for the symmetric encryption scheme and splits it into n shares $\mathsf{k}_1, \dots, \mathsf{k}_n$, such that $\mathsf{k}_1 \oplus \cdots \oplus \mathsf{k}_n = \mathsf{K}$. Each party P_i receives its MIFE key sk_i, the symmetric encryption key K, as well as its share of the encryption key k_i. To encrypt, every party first runs the encryption procedure of the MIFE scheme to generate $\mathsf{ct}_i \leftarrow \mathsf{Enc}(\mathsf{sk}_i, \boldsymbol{x}_i)$ and then encrypts the output ct_i using the symmetric encryption scheme to get $\mathsf{ct}'_i \leftarrow \mathsf{Enc}_{\mathsf{SE}}(\mathsf{K}, \mathsf{ct}_i)$. The output of the encryption procedure is $(\mathsf{ct}'_i, \mathsf{k}_i)$. This compiler obviously does not work when we allow corruptions as this would allow the adversary to learn K after corrupting any single party and use it to recover ct_i from ct'_i for all positions i. Consequently, the compiler does not work for (D)MCFE schemes.

In this work, we construct an extension of the compiler described above that works in the multi-client setting by individually having a separate symmetric encryption key for each position. Hence, we increase the number of symmetric encryption keys from 1 to n and the number of the corresponding shares from n to n^2. This allows us to ensure that if the adversary does not ask encryption queries in every uncorrupted position, it does not learn any information about the underlying (D)MCFE ciphertexts.

We describe in more detail how the compiler handles the additional keys. In the setup procedure, every party (or a trusted party) generates its own key K_i and corresponding shares $\mathsf{k}_{i,j}$, such that $\mathsf{k}_{i,1} \oplus \cdots \oplus \mathsf{k}_{i,n} = \mathsf{K}_i$. The share $\mathsf{k}_{i,j}$ gets exchanged with Party P_j afterwards. In the encryption procedure every party encrypts its plaintext in the same way as in the MIFE setting, but using its own key K_i instead of the single symmetric encryption key K. The ciphertext corresponding to slot i of Party P_i is $(\mathsf{ct}'_i, \{\mathsf{k}_{j,i}\}_{j\in[n]})$.

If the adversary does not know all of the shares $\{\mathsf{k}_{i,j}\}_{i,j\in[n]}$, then security relies on the security of the symmetric encryption scheme. If the adversary knows all of the different symmetric encryption keys $\mathsf{K}_i, i \in [n]$, it relies on the security of the multi-client scheme. All of the key shares are only released if an encryption query has been made in every uncorrupted position.

This first compiler is, however, restricted to (D)MCFE schemes without labels. To add support for labels, the first idea is to use fresh keys $\mathsf{k}_{i,j,\ell}$ for each label ℓ. These keys can be locally derived from $\mathsf{k}_{i,j}$ using a pseudorandom function. Unfortunately, we do not know how to prove the security of such a scheme except in a very restricted setting (selective and static corruptions), where the adversary needs to output all its corruption and encryption queries at the beginning of the security experiment. We show how to achieve the standard (adaptive) security notion when the above pseudorandom function as well as the symmetric encryption scheme is implemented using hash functions that can be modeled as random oracles. The use of random oracles allows us to show that the adversary learns absolutely nothing about the inner ciphertexts ct_i until it has queried all the positions (for each given label) and we can then program the random oracles to properly "explain" the previously generated ciphertexts ct'_i.

1.3 Additional Related Work

In [19], Fan and Tang proposed a new notion of distributed public key functional encryption, in which the key generation procedure generates n different shares $\{\mathsf{sk}_i^f\}_{i\in[n]}$ instead of a single functional decryption key sk_f. The decryption of a ciphertext ct (a encryption of a message m) under a function f requires first the decryption under the functional key shares $s_i \leftarrow \mathsf{Dec}(\mathsf{sk}_i^f, \mathsf{ct})$ for all $i \in [n]$. These shares $\{s_i\}_{i\in[n]}$ are then used to reconstruct $f(m)$. In this setting, a trusted third party is still needed to set up the public parameters and to generate the functional keys, which makes it not really decentralized.

In Private Stream Aggregation (PSA), a weighted sum $f(\boldsymbol{x}) \mapsto \sum_i^n x_i$ gets computed. This is similar to DMCFE for the inner-product functionality $f(\boldsymbol{x}) \mapsto \langle \boldsymbol{x}, \boldsymbol{y} \rangle$. PSA was introduced by Shi et al. [25] and allows a set of users to compute the sum of their encrypted data for different time periods. Compared to DMCFE, PSA is more restricted. It only allows computation of simple sums, whereas in principle DMCFE allows the computation of different functions on the input data. Furthermore, research on PSA has mainly focused on achieving new properties or better efficiency [10,14,18,21,22], instead of providing new functionalities.

1.4 Concurrent Work

Concurrently and independently of our work, Chotard et al. [16] proposed new constructions of MCFE schemes for inner products both in the centralized and decentralized settings. Their paper contains three main contributions: (1) A pairing-based compiler that turns any *pos-IND* secure MCFE scheme into an *any-IND* secure MCFE scheme, secure under the decisional Bilinear Diffie-Hellman problem in the random oracle model; (2) A second compiler that turns a *one-IND* secure MCFE scheme into a *pos-IND* secure MCFE scheme; and (3) A compiler that transforms a class of MCFE schemes for inner products into a corresponding DMCFE scheme, based on either the CDH assumption in the random-oracle model or the DDH assumption in the standard model.

While contribution (2) is unrelated and complementary to our work, contributions (1) and (3) are related to our contributions in Sects. 4 and 3, respectively. Regarding (1), their compiler from *pos-IND* to *any-IND* security produces constant-size ciphertexts, but it requires pairings and random oracles. Our compiler in Sect. 4, on the other hand, avoids pairings, requiring either symmetric encryption when applied to schemes without labels or random oracles for schemes with labels, but ciphertext sizes are linear in the number of inputs. Regarding (3), their compiler is similar to the straw man compiler described above. It is based on the DDH assumption and proven secure with respect to static corruptions. Our compiler in Sect. 3, on the other hand, is information-theoretic and achieves adaptive security.

1.5 Organization

The paper is organized as follows. In Sect. 2, we recall classical definitions as well as the definition of MCFE and DMCFE. Section 3 presents our first main contribution: the compiler from MCFE to DMCFE. Our second main contribution, namely our compilers from pos-IND security to any-IND security, is shown in Sect. 4. We conclude our paper by the proof that the MIFE scheme of Abdalla et al. [3] is actually an MCFE scheme that is secure under adaptive corruptions.

2 Definitions and Security Models

Notation. We use $[n]$ to denote the set $\{1, \ldots, n\}$. We write $\boldsymbol{x}$ for vectors and x_i for the i-th element. For security parameter λ and additional parameters n, we denote the winning probability of an adversary $\mathcal{A}$ in a game or experiment G as $\mathsf{Win}_{\mathcal{A}}^{\mathsf{G}}(\lambda, n)$, which is $Pr[\mathsf{G}(\lambda, n, \mathcal{A}) = 1]$. The probability is taken over the random coins of G and $\mathcal{A}$. We define the distinguishing advantage between games G_0 and G_1 of an adversary $\mathcal{A}$ in the following way: $\mathsf{Adv}_{\mathcal{A}}^{\mathsf{G}}(\lambda, n) = \left|\mathsf{Win}_{\mathcal{A}}^{\mathsf{G}_0}(\lambda, n) - \mathsf{Win}_{\mathcal{A}}^{\mathsf{G}_1}(\lambda, n)\right|$.

2.1 Multi-Client Functional Encryption

In this section, we define the notion of MCFE [20].

Definition 2.1 ***(Multi-Client Functional Encryption).*** *Let $\mathcal{F} = \{\mathcal{F}_\rho\}_\rho$ be a family (indexed by ρ) of sets $\mathcal{F}_\rho$ of functions $f\colon \mathcal{X}_{\rho,1} \times \cdots \times \mathcal{X}_{\rho,n_\rho} \to \mathcal{Y}_\rho$.*[2] *Let $\mathsf{Labels} = \{0,1\}^*$ or $\{\bot\}$ be a set of labels. A multi-client functional encryption scheme (MCFE) for the function family $\mathcal{F}$ and the label set Labels is a tuple of five algorithms $\mathsf{MCFE} = (\mathsf{Setup}, \mathsf{KeyGen}, \mathsf{KeyDer}, \mathsf{Enc}, \mathsf{Dec})$:*

$\mathsf{Setup}(1^\lambda, 1^n)$: *Takes as input a security parameter λ and the number of parties n, and generates public parameters pp. The public parameters implicitly define an index ρ corresponding to a set $\mathcal{F}_\rho$ of n-ary functions (i.e., $n = n_\rho$).*

$\mathsf{KeyGen}(\mathsf{pp})$: *Takes as input the public parameters pp and outputs n secret keys $\{\mathsf{sk}_i\}_{i\in[n]}$ and a master secret key msk.*

$\mathsf{KeyDer}(\mathsf{pp}, \mathsf{msk}, f)$: *Takes as input the public parameters pp, the master secret key msk and a function $f \in \mathcal{F}_\rho$, and outputs a functional decryption key sk_f.*

$\mathsf{Enc}(\mathsf{pp}, \mathsf{sk}_i, x_i, \ell)$: *Takes as input the public parameters pp, a secret key sk_i, a message $x_i \in \mathcal{X}_{\rho,i}$ to encrypt, a label $\ell \in \mathsf{Labels}$, and outputs ciphertext $\mathsf{ct}_{i,\ell}$.*

$\mathsf{Dec}(\mathsf{pp}, \mathsf{sk}_f, \mathsf{ct}_{1,\ell}, \ldots, \mathsf{ct}_{n,\ell})$: *Takes as input the public parameters pp, a functional key sk_f and n ciphertexts under the same label ℓ and outputs a value $y \in \mathcal{Y}_\rho$.*

A scheme MCFE is correct, if for all $\lambda, n \in \mathbb{N}$, $\mathsf{pp} \leftarrow \mathsf{Setup}(1^\lambda, 1^n)$, $f \in \mathcal{F}_\rho$, $\ell \in \mathsf{Labels}$, $x_i \in \mathcal{X}_{\rho,i}$, when $(\{\mathsf{sk}_i\}_{i\in[n]}, \mathsf{msk}) \leftarrow \mathsf{KeyGen}(\mathsf{pp})$ and $\mathsf{sk}_f \leftarrow \mathsf{KeyDer}(\mathsf{pp}, \mathsf{msk}, f)$, we have

$$\Pr\left[\mathsf{Dec}(\mathsf{pp}, \mathsf{sk}_f, \mathsf{Enc}(\mathsf{pp}, \mathsf{sk}_1, x_1, \ell), \ldots, \mathsf{Enc}(\mathsf{pp}, \mathsf{sk}_n, x_n, \ell)) = f(x_1, \ldots, x_n)\right] = 1.$$

When ρ is clear from context, the index ρ is omitted. When $\mathsf{Labels} = \{0,1\}^*$, we say that the scheme is *labeled* or *with labels*. When $\mathsf{Labels} = \{\bot\}$, we say that the scheme is *without labels*, and we often omit ℓ.

Remark 2.2. We note that contrary to most definitions, the algorithm Setup only generates public parameters that determine the set of functions for which functional decryption keys can be created. The secret/encryption keys and the master secret keys are generated by another algorithm KeyGen, while the functional decryption keys are generated by KeyDer. This separation between Setup and KeyGen is especially useful when combining multiple MCFE/MIFE schemes as in [3] to ensure that all the MCFE/MIFE instances are using the same modulus. Note that this separation prevents for example the functionality to consist of inner products modulo some RSA modulus $N = pq$ and the master secret key to contain the factorization of N (except if the factorization of the modulus N is public).

---

[2] All the functions inside the same set $\mathcal{F}_\rho$ have the same domain and the same range.

As noted in [15,20], the security model of multi-client functional encryption is similar to the security model of standard multi-input functional encryption, except that instead of a single master secret key msk for encryption, each slot i has a different secret key sk_i and the keys sk_i can be individually corrupted. In addition, one also needs to consider corruptions to handle possible collusions between different parties. In the following, we define security as adaptive left-or-right indistinguishability under both static (sta), and adaptive (adt) corruption. We also consider three variants of these notions (one, any, pos) related to the number of encryption queries asked by the adversary for each slot.

Definition 2.3 ***(Security of MCFE).*** *Let* MCFE *be an MCFE scheme,* $\mathcal{F} = \{\mathcal{F}_\rho\}_\rho$ *a function family indexed by* ρ *and* Labels *a label set. For* $\mathrm{xx} \in \{\mathrm{sta}, \mathrm{adt}\}$, $\mathrm{yy} \in \{\mathrm{one}, \mathrm{any}, \mathrm{pos}\}$, *and* $\beta \in \{0,1\}$, *we define the experiment* $\mathrm{xx\text{-}yy\text{-}}\mathit{IND}_\beta^{\mathsf{MCFE}}$ *in Fig. 1, where the oracles are defined as:*

Corruption oracle $\mathsf{QCor}(i)$: *Outputs the encryption key* sk_i *of slot* i. *We denote by* $\mathcal{CS}$ *the set of corrupted slots at the end of the experiment.*

Encryption oracle $\mathsf{QEnc}(i, x_i^0, x_i^1, \ell)$: *Outputs* $\mathsf{ct}_{i,\ell} = \mathsf{Enc}(\mathsf{pp}, \mathsf{sk}_i, x_i^\beta, \ell)$ *on a query* (i, x_i^0, x_i^1, ℓ). *We denote by* $Q_{i,\ell}$ *the number of queries of the form* $\mathsf{QEnc}(i, \cdot, \cdot, \ell)$.

Key derivation oracle $\mathsf{QKeyD}(f)$: *Outputs* $\mathsf{sk}_f = \mathsf{KeyDer}(\mathsf{pp}, \mathsf{msk}, f)$.

and where Condition (*) *holds if all the following conditions hold:*

- *If* $i \in \mathcal{CS}$ *(i.e., slot* i *is corrupted): for any query* $\mathsf{QEnc}(i, x_i^0, x_i^1, \ell)$, $x_i^0 = x_i^1$.
- *For any label* $\ell \in$ Labels, *for any family of queries* $\{\mathsf{QEnc}(i, x_i^0, x_i^1, \ell)\}_{i \in [n] \setminus \mathcal{CS}}$, *for any family of inputs* $\{x_i \in \mathcal{X}_{\rho,i}\}_{i \in \mathcal{CS}}$, *for any query* $\mathsf{QKeyD}(f)$, *we define* $x_i^0 = x_i^1 = x_i$ *for any slot* $i \in \mathcal{CS}$, $\boldsymbol{x}^b = (x_1^b, \ldots, x_n^b)$ *for* $b \in \{0,1\}$, *and we require that:*
$$f(\boldsymbol{x}^0) = f(\boldsymbol{x}^1).$$
We insist that if one index $i \notin \mathcal{CS}$ *is not queried for the label* ℓ, *there is no restriction.*
- *When* yy = one*: for any slot* $i \in [n]$ *and* $\ell \in$ Labels, $Q_{i,\ell} \in \{0,1\}$, *and if* $Q_{i,\ell} = 1$, *then for any slot* $j \in [n] \setminus \mathcal{CS}$, $Q_{j,\ell} = 1$. *In other words, for any label, either the adversary makes no encryption query or makes exactly one encryption query for each* $i \in [n] \setminus \mathcal{CS}$.
- *When* yy = pos*: for any slot* $i \in [n]$ *and* $\ell \in$ Labels, *if* $Q_{i,\ell} > 0$, *then for any slot* $j \in [n] \setminus \mathcal{CS}$, $Q_{j,\ell} > 0$. *In other words, for any label, either the adversary makes no encryption query or makes at least one encryption query for each slot* $i \in [n] \setminus \mathcal{CS}$.

We define the advantage of an adversary $\mathcal{A}$ *in the following way:*

$$\mathsf{Adv}_{\mathsf{MCFE},\mathcal{A}}^{\mathrm{xx\text{-}yy\text{-}}\mathit{IND}}(\lambda, n) = \big|\Pr[\mathrm{xx\text{-}yy\text{-}IND}_0^{\mathsf{MCFE}}(\lambda, n, \mathcal{A}) = 1] - \Pr[\mathrm{xx\text{-}yy\text{-}IND}_1^{\mathsf{MCFE}}(\lambda, n, \mathcal{A}) = 1]\big|.$$

A multi-client functional encryption scheme MCFE *is* xx-yy-*IND secure, if for any* n, *for any polynomial-time adversary* $\mathcal{A}$, *there exists a negligible function* negl *such that:* $\mathsf{Adv}_{\mathsf{MCFE},\mathcal{A}}^{\mathrm{xx\text{-}yy\text{-}}\mathit{IND}}(\lambda, n) \le \mathrm{negl}(\lambda)$.

$\textbf{sta-yy-IND}_{\beta}^{\mathsf{MCFE}}(\lambda, n, \mathcal{A})$	$\textbf{adt-yy-IND}_{\beta}^{\mathsf{MCFE}}(\lambda, n, \mathcal{A})$
$\mathcal{CS} \leftarrow \mathcal{A}(1^\lambda, 1^n)$ $\mathsf{pp} \leftarrow \mathsf{Setup}(1^\lambda, 1^n)$ $(\{\mathsf{sk}_i\}_{i\in[n]}, \mathsf{msk}) \leftarrow \mathsf{KeyGen}(\mathsf{pp})$ $\alpha \leftarrow \mathcal{A}^{\mathsf{QEnc}(\cdot,\cdot,\cdot,\cdot),\mathsf{QKeyD}(\cdot)}(\mathsf{pp}, \{\mathsf{sk}_i\}_{i\in\mathcal{CS}})$ **Output:** α if Condition (*) is satisfied, or a uniform bit otherwise	$\mathsf{pp} \leftarrow \mathsf{Setup}(1^\lambda, 1^n)$ $(\{\mathsf{sk}_i\}_{i\in[n]}, \mathsf{msk}) \leftarrow \mathsf{KeyGen}(\mathsf{pp})$ $\alpha \leftarrow \mathcal{A}^{\mathsf{QCor}(\cdot),\mathsf{QEnc}(\cdot,\cdot,\cdot,\cdot),\mathsf{QKeyD}(\cdot)}(\mathsf{pp})$ **Output:** α if Condition (*) is satisfied, or a uniform bit otherwise

Fig. 1. Security games for MCFE

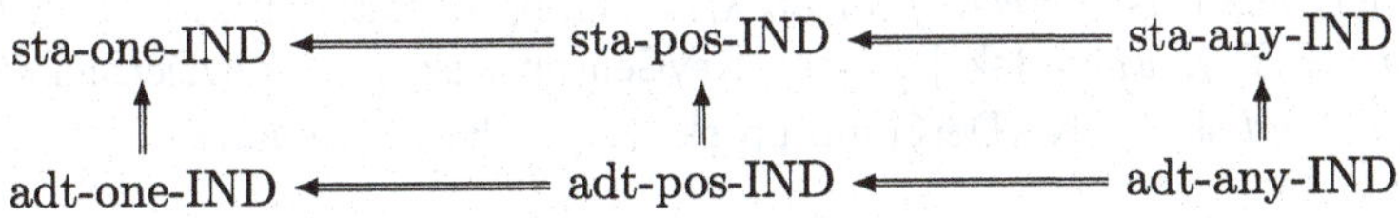

Fig. 2. Relations between the MCFE security notions (arrows indicate implication or being "a stronger security notion than")

We omit n when it is clear from the context. We also often omit $\mathcal{A}$ from the parameter of experiments or games when it is clear from context.

We summarize the relations between the six security notions in Fig. 2. Multi-input functional encryption (MIFE) and functional encryption (FE) are special cases of MCFE. MIFE is MCFE without corruption, and FE is the special case of $n = 1$ (in which case, MIFE and MCFE coincide as there is no non-trivial corruption). Therefore, for single-input FE schemes, sta-any-IND = adt-any-IND = any-IND corresponds to the secret-key version of the standard adaptive indistinguishability notion used in [5]. The security notions considered in [15] are actually xx-pos-IND and so are the MIFE notions of [3]. An xx-one-IND MCFE is also called a one-time secure scheme.

2.2 Decentralized Multi-Client Functional Encryption

Now, we introduce the definition of decentralized multi-client functional encryption (DMCFE) [15]. As for our definition of MCFE, we separate the algorithm Setup which generates public parameters defining in particular the set of functions, from the algorithm KeyGen (see Remark 2.2).

Definition 2.4 ***(Decentralized Multi-Client Functional Encryption).*** *Let $\mathcal{F} = \{\mathcal{F}_\rho\}_\rho$ be a family (indexed by ρ) of sets $\mathcal{F}_\rho$ of functions $f\colon \mathcal{X}_{\rho,1} \times \cdots \times \mathcal{X}_{\rho,n_\rho} \to \mathcal{Y}_\rho$. Let* Labels $= \{0,1\}^*$ *or* $\{\perp\}$ *be a set of labels. A decentralized multi-client functional encryption scheme (DMCFE) for the function family $\mathcal{F}$ and the label set* Labels *is a tuple of six algorithms* DMCFE = (Setup, KeyGen, KeyDerShare, KeyDerComb, Enc, Dec)*:*

$\mathsf{Setup}(1^\lambda, 1^n)$ *is defined as for MCFE in Definition 2.1.*

$\mathsf{KeyGen}(\mathsf{pp})$: *Takes as input the public parameters* pp *and outputs* n *secret keys* $\{\mathsf{sk_i}\}_{i\in[n]}$.

$\mathsf{KeyDerShare}(\mathsf{pp}, \mathsf{sk}_i, f)$: *Takes as input the public parameters* pp*, a secret key* sk_i *from position* i *and a function* $f \in \mathcal{F}_\rho$*, and outputs a partial functional decryption key* $\mathsf{sk}_{i,f}$.

$\mathsf{KeyDerComb}(\mathsf{pp}, \mathsf{sk}_{1,f}, \ldots, \mathsf{sk}_{n,f})$: *Takes as input the public parameters* pp*,* n *partial functional decryption keys* $\mathsf{sk}_{1,f}, \ldots, \mathsf{sk}_{n,f}$ *and outputs the functional decryption key* sk_f.

$\mathsf{Enc}(\mathsf{pp}, \mathsf{sk}_i, x_i, \ell)$ *is defined as for MCFE in Definition 2.1.*

$\mathsf{Dec}(\mathsf{pp}, \mathsf{sk}_f, \mathsf{ct}_{1,\ell}, \ldots, \mathsf{ct}_{n,\ell})$ *is defined as for MCFE in Definition 2.1.*

A scheme DMCFE *is correct, if for all* $\lambda, n \in \mathbb{N}$, $\mathsf{pp} \leftarrow \mathsf{Setup}(1^\lambda, 1^n)$, $f \in \mathcal{F}_\rho$, $\ell \in \mathsf{Labels}$, $x_i \in \mathcal{X}_{\rho,i}$*, when* $\{\mathsf{sk}_i\}_{i\in[n]} \leftarrow \mathsf{KeyGen}(\mathsf{pp})$, $\mathsf{sk}_{i,f} \leftarrow \mathsf{KeyDerShare}(\mathsf{sk}_i, f)$ *for* $i \in [n]$*, and* $\mathsf{sk}_f \leftarrow \mathsf{KeyDerComb}(\mathsf{pp}, \mathsf{sk}_{1,f}, \ldots, \mathsf{sk}_{n,f})$*, we have*

$$\Pr\left[\mathsf{Dec}(\mathsf{pp}, \mathsf{sk}_f, \mathsf{Enc}(\mathsf{pp}, \mathsf{sk}_1, x_1, \ell), \ldots, \mathsf{Enc}(\mathsf{pp}, \mathsf{sk}_n, x_n, \ell)) = f(x_1, \ldots, x_n)\right] = 1.$$

We remark that there is no master secret key msk. Furthermore, similarly to [15], our definition does not explicitly ask the setup to be decentralized. However, all our constructions allow for the setup to be easily decentralized, at least assuming that the original schemes have such a property in the case of our compilers.

We consider a similar security definition for the decentralized multi-client scheme. We point out that contrary to [15], we do not differentiate encryption keys from secret keys. This is without loss of generality, as corruptions in [15] only allow to corrupt both keys at the same time.

Definition 2.5 ***(Security of DMCFE).*** *The* xx-yy-*IND security notion of an DMCFE scheme (*xx $\in$ {sta, adt} *and* yy $\in$ {one, any, pos}*) is similar to the one of an MCFE (Definition 2.3), except that there is no master secret key* msk *and the key derivation oracle is now defined as:*

Key derivation oracle $\mathsf{QKeyD}(f)$: *Computes* $\mathsf{sk}_{i,f} := \mathsf{KeyDerShare}(\mathsf{pp}, \mathsf{sk}_i, f)$ *for* $i \in [n]$ *and outputs* $\{\mathsf{sk}_{i,f}\}_{i\in[n]}$.

2.3 Inner-Product Functionality

We describe the functionalities supported by the constructions in this paper, by considering the index ρ of $\mathcal{F}$ in more detail.

The index of the family is defined as $\rho = (\mathcal{R}, n, m, X, Y)$ where $\mathcal{R}$ is either $\mathbb{Z}$ or $\mathbb{Z}_L$ for some integer L, and n, m, X, Y are positive integers. If X, Y are omitted, then $X = Y = L$ is used (i.e., no constraint).

This defines $\mathcal{F}_\rho = \{f_{y_1,\ldots,y_n} : (\mathcal{R}^m)^n \to \mathcal{R}\}$ where

$$f_{\boldsymbol{y}_1,\ldots,\boldsymbol{y}_n}(\boldsymbol{x}_1, \ldots, \boldsymbol{x}_n) = \sum_{i=1}^{n} \langle \boldsymbol{x}_i, \boldsymbol{y}_i \rangle = \langle \boldsymbol{x}, \boldsymbol{y} \rangle,$$

where the vectors satisfy the following bounds: $\|\boldsymbol{x}_i\|_\infty < X, \|\boldsymbol{y}_i\|_\infty < Y$ for $i \in [n]$, and where $\boldsymbol{x} \in \mathcal{R}^{mn}$ and $\boldsymbol{y} \in \mathcal{R}^{mn}$ are the vectors corresponding to the concatenation of the n vectors $\boldsymbol{x}_1, \ldots, \boldsymbol{x}_n$ and $\boldsymbol{y}_1, \ldots, \boldsymbol{y}_n$ respectively.

2.4 Symmetric Encryption

For our second compiler (Sect. 4.1), we make use of a symmetric encryption scheme $\mathsf{SE} = (\mathsf{Enc}_{\mathsf{SE}}, \mathsf{Dec}_{\mathsf{SE}})$ that is indistinguishable secure under chosen plaintext attacks (IND-CPA) and whose keys are uniform strings in $\{0,1\}^\lambda$ as defined by [9].

$\mathsf{Enc}_{\mathsf{SE}}(\mathsf{K}, x)$: Takes as input a key $\mathsf{K} \in \{0,1\}^\lambda$ and a message x to encrypt, and outputs the ciphertext ct.

$\mathsf{Dec}_{\mathsf{SE}}(\mathsf{K}, \mathsf{ct})$: Takes as input a key K and a ciphertext ct to decrypt, and outputs a message x.

We denote with $\mathsf{Adv}^{\text{IND-CPA}}_{\mathsf{SE},\mathcal{A}}(\lambda)$ the advantage of an adversary guessing β in the following game: the challenger picks $\mathsf{K} \leftarrow \{0,1\}^\lambda$ and gives $\mathcal{A}$ access to an encryption oracle $\mathsf{QEnc}(x_i^0, x_i^1)$ that outputs $\mathsf{ct} = \mathsf{Enc}_{\mathsf{SE}}(\mathsf{K}, x_i^\beta)$ on a query (x^0, x^1).

3 From MCFE to DMCFE

In this section, we describe our first compiler which allows the decentralization of MCFE schemes that satisfy an additional property, called special key derivation. We start by defining this property and showing that existing schemes from [3, 15] satisfy it. Next, we describe the compiler and prove its security when the underlying modulus of the special key derivation property is prime. Finally, we extend the proof to the case where this modulus is a hard-to-factor composite number.

3.1 Special Key Derivation Property

Definition 3.1 (MCFE with Special Key Derivation). *An MCFE scheme* $\mathsf{MCFE} = (\mathsf{Setup}, \mathsf{KeyGen}, \mathsf{KeyDer}, \mathsf{Enc}, \mathsf{Dec})$ *for a family of functions* $\mathcal{F}$ *and a set of labels* Labels *has the special key derivation property modulo* L *if:*[3]

- *Secret keys* sk_i *generated by* KeyGen *have the following form:* $\mathsf{sk}_i = (i, s_i, \{\boldsymbol{u}_i^k\}_{k\in[\kappa]})$, *where* $s_i \in \{0,1\}^*$, *and* $\boldsymbol{u}_i^k \in \mathbb{Z}_L^m$, *and* κ *and* m *are positive integers implicitly depending on the public parameters* pp.
- $\mathsf{sk}_f \leftarrow \mathsf{KeyDer}(\mathsf{pp}, \mathsf{msk}, f)$ *outputs* $\mathsf{sk}_f = (\{s_{i,f}\}_{i\in[n]}, \{\mathsf{dk}_f^k\}_{k\in[\kappa]})$, *where* $s_{i,f}$ *is a (polynomial-time) function of* pp, i, s_i, *and* f, *while:*

$$\mathsf{dk}_f^k = \sum_{i=1}^{n} \langle \boldsymbol{u}_i^k, \boldsymbol{y}_{i,f}^k \rangle = \langle \boldsymbol{u}^k, \boldsymbol{y}_f^k \rangle,$$

[3] The integer L can depend on the public parameters pp.

where $y_{i,f}^k \in \mathbb{Z}_L^m$ *is a (polynomial-time) function of* pp, i, *and* f, *and* $\mathbf{u}^k$ *and* $\boldsymbol{y}_f^k$ *are the vectors in* $\mathbb{Z}_L^{mn}$ *corresponding to the concatenation of the vectors* $\{\boldsymbol{u}_i^k\}_{i\in[n]}$ *and* $\{\boldsymbol{y}_{i,f}^k\}_{i\in[n]}$ *respectively.*

Without loss of generality for MCFE with the special key derivation property, we can suppose that $\mathsf{msk} = \{\mathsf{sk}_i\}_{i\in[n]}$. We also remark that we do not require any property of the family of functions $\mathcal{F}$ and that our compiler could be applicable to more general MCFE than inner-product ones.

3.2 Instantiations

The MCFE construction of Chotard et al. [15, Section 4] satisfies the special key derivation property modulo $L = p$ (the order of the cyclic group), with $\kappa = 2$ and $\boldsymbol{y}_f^k = \boldsymbol{y}$, when $f : \boldsymbol{x} \mapsto \langle \boldsymbol{x}, \boldsymbol{y} \rangle$.

The generic constructions of Abdalla et al. [3, Section 3] (both over $\mathbb{Z}$ and $\mathbb{Z}_L$, see also Sect. 5) satisfy the special key derivation property modulo L (where L is the modulo used for the information-theoretic MIFE/MCFE with one-time security) with $\boldsymbol{y}_f^k = \boldsymbol{y}$. The instantiations from MDDH, LWE, and Paillier [3, Section 4] use $L = p$ the prime order of the cyclic group, $L = q$ the prime modulo for LWE (we need $L = q$ to be prime for our compiler), $L = N = pq$ the modulus used for Paillier respectively.

3.3 Compiler for Prime Moduli

We start by presenting our compiler from MCFE schemes with the special key derivation property modulo a prime L in Fig. 3. Correctness follows directly from the fact that:

$$\begin{aligned}\sum_{i=1}^n \mathsf{dk}_{i,f}^k &= \sum_{i=1}^n \langle \boldsymbol{u}_i^k, \boldsymbol{y}_{i,f}^k \rangle + \sum_{i=1}^n \langle \boldsymbol{v}_i^k, \boldsymbol{y}_f^k \rangle \\ &= \mathsf{dk}_f^k + \langle \sum_{i=1}^n \boldsymbol{v}_i^k, \boldsymbol{y}_f^k \rangle = \mathsf{dk}_f^k + \langle \mathbf{0}, \boldsymbol{y}_f^k \rangle = \mathsf{dk}_f^k.\end{aligned}$$

We insist on the fact that while vectors $\boldsymbol{u}_i^k$ and $\boldsymbol{y}_{i,f}^k$ are m-dimensional, vectors $\boldsymbol{v}_i^k$ and $\boldsymbol{y}_f^k$ are (mn)-dimensional.

We have the following security theorem.

Theorem 3.2. *Let* $\mathsf{MCFE} = (\mathsf{Setup}, \mathsf{KeyGen}, \mathsf{KeyDer}, \mathsf{Enc}, \mathsf{Dec})$ *be an MCFE construction for a family of functions* $\mathcal{F}$ *and a set of labels* Labels. *We suppose that* MCFE *has the special key derivation property modulo a prime L. For any* $\mathrm{xx} \in \{\mathrm{sta}, \mathrm{adt}\}$ *and any* $\mathrm{yy} \in \{\mathrm{one}, \mathrm{pos}, \mathrm{any}\}$, *if* MCFE *is an* xx-yy-*IND-secure MCFE scheme, then the scheme* DMCFE′ *depicted in Fig. 3 is an* xx-yy-*IND-secure DMCFE scheme. Namely, for any PPT adversary* $\mathcal{A}$, *there exist a PPT adversary* $\mathcal{B}$ *such that:*

$$\mathsf{Adv}_{\mathsf{DMCFE}',\mathcal{A}}^{\text{xx-yy-IND}}(\lambda, n) \le \mathsf{Adv}_{\mathsf{MCFE},\mathcal{B}}^{\text{xx-yy-IND}}(\lambda, n).$$

$\underline{\mathsf{Setup}'(1^\lambda, 1^n):}$

Return $\mathsf{Setup}(1^\lambda, 1^n)$

$\underline{\mathsf{KeyGen}'(\mathsf{pp}):}$

$(\{\mathsf{sk}_i\}_{i\in[n]}, \mathsf{msk}) \leftarrow \mathsf{KeyGen}(\mathsf{pp})$

Recall that $\mathsf{sk}_i = (i, s_i, \{\boldsymbol{u}_i^k\}_{k\in[\kappa]})$

For $k \in [\kappa]$:

For $i \in [n-1]$, $\boldsymbol{v}_i^k \leftarrow \mathbb{Z}_L^M$

$$\boldsymbol{v}_n^k := -\sum_{i=1}^{n-1} \boldsymbol{v}_i^k \bmod L$$

Return $\{\mathsf{sk}'_i = (\mathsf{sk}_i, \{\boldsymbol{v}_i^k\}_{k\in[\kappa]})\}_{i\in[n]}$

$\underline{\mathsf{Enc}'(\mathsf{pp}, \mathsf{sk}'_i, x_i, \ell):}$

Parse $\mathsf{sk}'_i = (\mathsf{sk}_i, \{\boldsymbol{v}_i^k\}_{k\in[\kappa]})$

Return $\mathsf{ct}_{i,\ell} \leftarrow \mathsf{Enc}(\mathsf{pp}, \mathsf{sk}_i, x_i, \ell)$

$\underline{\mathsf{KeyDerShare}'(\mathsf{pp}, \mathsf{sk}'_i, f):}$

Parse $\mathsf{sk}'_i = (\mathsf{sk}_i, \{\boldsymbol{v}_i^k\}_{k\in[\kappa]})$

For $k \in [\kappa]$, $\mathsf{dk}_{i,f}^k := \langle \boldsymbol{u}_i^k, \boldsymbol{y}_{i,f}^k \rangle + \langle \boldsymbol{v}_i^k, \boldsymbol{y}_f^k \rangle$

Return $\mathsf{sk}'_{i,f} := (s_{i,f}, \{\mathsf{dk}_{i,f}^k\}_{k\in[\kappa]})$

$\underline{\mathsf{KeyDerComb}'(\mathsf{pp}, \{\mathsf{sk}'_{i,f}\}_{i\in[n]}):}$

Parse $\{\mathsf{sk}'_{i,f} = (s_{i,f}, \{\mathsf{dk}_{i,f}^k\}_{k\in[\kappa]})\}_{i\in[n]}$

For $k \in [\kappa]$, $\mathsf{dk}_f^k := \sum_{i=1}^{n} \mathsf{dk}_{i,f}^k$

Return $\mathsf{sk}'_f = (\{s_{i,f}\}_{i\in[n]}, \{\mathsf{dk}_f^k\}_{k\in[\kappa]})$

$\underline{\mathsf{Dec}'(\mathsf{pp}, \mathsf{sk}'_f, \{\mathsf{ct}_{i,\ell}\}_{i\in[n]}):}$

Return $\mathsf{Dec}(\mathsf{pp}, \mathsf{sk}'_f, \{\mathsf{ct}_{i,\ell}\}_{i\in[n]})$

Fig. 3. Compiler from MCFE to DMCFE$'$: $s_{i,f}$ is a function of pp, i, s_i, f and $\boldsymbol{y}_{i,f}^k$ is a function of pp, i, f, and k. $M = mn$.

Below, we provide a proof sketch of the theorem. The formal proof is in the full version [1].

Proof (Theorem 3.2—sketch). In this sketch, we focus on a setting without corruption and where L is a prime number. For the sake of simplicity, we also suppose that $\kappa = 1$ and $s_{i,f}$ is an empty string, so that we can omit the superscript k and we have $\mathsf{sk}'_{i,f} = \mathsf{dk}_{i,f} = \langle \boldsymbol{u}_i, \boldsymbol{y}_{i,f} \rangle + \langle \boldsymbol{v}_i, \boldsymbol{y}_f \rangle$. We can define $\boldsymbol{u}'_i \in \mathbb{Z}_L$ to be $\boldsymbol{u}_i$ "padded with 0" so that we can write: $\langle \boldsymbol{u}_i, \boldsymbol{y}_{i,f} \rangle = \langle \boldsymbol{u}'_i, \boldsymbol{y}_f \rangle$ (recall that $\boldsymbol{y}_f$ is just the concatenation of the vectors $\boldsymbol{y}_{i,f}$ for $i \in [n]$). Thus we have:

$$\mathsf{sk}'_{i,f} = \mathsf{dk}_{i,f} = \langle \boldsymbol{u}'_i, \boldsymbol{y}_f \rangle + \langle \boldsymbol{v}_i, \boldsymbol{y}_f \rangle = \langle \boldsymbol{u}'_i + \boldsymbol{v}_i, \boldsymbol{y}_f \rangle.$$

Now, we remark that from keys $\mathsf{dk}_{i,g}$ for $g \in \{f_1, \ldots, f_q\}$, one can compute the key $\mathsf{dk}_{i,f}$ for any f such that $\boldsymbol{y}_f$ is in the subspace generated by $\boldsymbol{y}_{f_1}, \ldots, \boldsymbol{y}_{f_q}$. Indeed, if $\boldsymbol{y} = \sum_{j=1}^{q} \mu_j \cdot \boldsymbol{y}_{f_j}$, for some $\mu_1, \ldots, \mu_q \in \mathbb{Z}_L$, then: $\mathsf{dk}_{i,f} = \sum_{j=1}^{q} \mu_j \cdot \mathsf{dk}_{i,f_j}$.

Let S be the set of functions f queried to QKeyD such that the family of vector $\{\boldsymbol{y}_f\}_{f\in S}$ is linearly independent. We compute the $\mathsf{dk}_{i,f}$ of linearly dependent functions as outlined above. We now look at linearly independent functions. As the vectors $\boldsymbol{v}_i$ are uniformly distributed under the constraints $\sum_{i=1}^{n} \boldsymbol{v}_i = \boldsymbol{0}$

(by definition of Setup'), linear algebra ensures that the values $\{\langle \boldsymbol{v}_i, \boldsymbol{y}_f \rangle\}_{i \in [n], f \in S}$ are distributed uniformly under the constraints $\sum_{i=1}^{n} \langle \boldsymbol{v}_i, \boldsymbol{y}_f \rangle = 0$ for $f \in S$. Thus, from Sect. 3.3, we get that for any $f \in S$, $\{\mathsf{dk}_{i,f}\}_{i \in [n]}$ is a fresh additive secret sharing of

$$\sum_{i=1}^{n} \mathsf{dk}_{i,f} = \sum_{i=1}^{n} \langle \boldsymbol{u}'_i, \boldsymbol{y}_f \rangle = \sum_{i=1}^{n} \langle \boldsymbol{u}_i, \boldsymbol{y}_{i,f} \rangle = \mathsf{dk}_f,$$

and hence can be simulated knowing only $\mathsf{dk}_f = \mathsf{KeyDer}(\mathsf{msk}, f)$ (but not the vectors $\boldsymbol{u}_i$ themselves, which are parts of the secret keys sk_i). In other words queries to the oracle $\mathsf{QKeyD}(f)$ in the security game of DMCFE' can be simulated just from $\mathsf{KeyDer}(\mathsf{pp}, \mathsf{msk}, f)$ (or equivalently just from queries to the oracle $\mathsf{QKeyD}(f)$ in the security game of MCFE).

Thus, we have a perfect reduction from the security of DMCFE' to the security of MCFE. □

3.4 Extension to Hard-to-Factor Moduli

We can extend the previous scheme to moduli L which are hard to factor. This is required for the Paillier instantiation from [3, Section 4.3].

Let us provide formal details.

Definition 3.3 (Factorization). *Let* GenL *be a PPT algorithm taking as input the security parameter* 1^λ *and outputing a number* $L \geq 2$. *We define the experiment* $\mathsf{Factor}_{\mathsf{GenL}}(\lambda, \mathcal{A})$ *for an adversary* $\mathcal{A}$ *as follows: it outputs* 1 *if on input* $L \leftarrow \mathsf{GenL}(1^\lambda)$, *the adversary outputs two integers* $L_1, L_2 \geq 2$, *such that* $L_1 \cdot L_2 = L$. *The advantage of* $\mathcal{A}$ *is* $\mathsf{Adv}^{\mathsf{Factor}}_{\mathsf{GenL},\mathcal{A}}(\lambda) = \Pr[\mathsf{Factor}_{\mathsf{GenL}}(\lambda, \mathcal{A})]$. *Factorization is hard for* GenL *if the advantage of any PPT adversary* $\mathcal{A}$ *is negligible in* λ.

We have the following security theorem proven in the full version [1].

Theorem 3.4. *Let* $\mathsf{MCFE} = (\mathsf{Setup}, \mathsf{KeyGen}, \mathsf{KeyDer}, \mathsf{Enc}, \mathsf{Dec})$ *be an MCFE construction for an ensemble of functions* $\mathcal{F}$ *and a set of labels* Labels. *We suppose that* MCFE *has the special key derivation property modulo an integer* L, *which is part of the public parameter* pp *and generated as* $L \leftarrow \mathsf{GenL}(1^\lambda)$ *in the setup, for some polynomial-time algorithm. We assume that factorization is hard for* GenL. *For any* $\mathrm{xx} \in \{\mathrm{sta}, \mathrm{adt}\}$ *and any* $\mathrm{yy} \in \{\mathrm{one}, \mathrm{pos}, \mathrm{any}\}$, *if* MCFE *is an* xx-yy-*IND-secure MCFE scheme, then the scheme* DMCFE' *depicted in Fig. 3 is an* xx-yy-*IND-secure DMCFE scheme. Namely, for any PPT adversary* $\mathcal{A}$, *there exist two PPT adversaries* $\mathcal{B}$ *and* $\mathcal{B}'$ *such that:*

$$\mathsf{Adv}^{\text{xx-yy-IND}}_{\mathsf{DMCFE}',\mathcal{A}}(\lambda, n) \leq \mathsf{Adv}^{\text{xx-yy-IND}}_{\mathsf{MCFE},\mathcal{B}}(\lambda, n) + 2 \cdot \mathsf{Adv}^{\mathsf{Factor}}_{\mathsf{GenL},\mathcal{B}'}(\lambda).$$

4 From xx-pos-IND to xx-any-IND Security

We present two compilers transforming pos-IND-secure MIFE, MCFE, and DMCFE schemes into any-IND schemes. These compilers essentially force the adversary to ask for at least one ciphertext per position i (and per label, for labeled schemes).

The first compiler works for sta-pos-IND and adt-pos-IND-secure schemes without labels ($\mathsf{Labels} = \{\perp\}$) and only requires an IND-CPA symmetric encryption scheme to work. We prove it for the adt-pos-IND case as the proof for sta-pos-IND is simpler. The second compiler supports labeled schemes, but is in the random oracle model. Although our presentation is for DMCFE, the compilers can be adapted to work for MCFE schemes in a straightforward way.

Regarding efficiency, both compilers add $2n-1$ symmetric keys (i.e., λ-bit strings) to each secret key sk_i, and n symmetric keys to each ciphertext ct_i (plus the overhead due to symmetric encryption, which can be as low as λ bits using stream ciphers for example). (Partial) functional decryption keys and public parameters are unchanged. For the first compiler, the computational complexity overhead essentially consists in one symmetric encryption of the original ciphertext for functional encryption, and n symmetric decryptions for functional decryption. The second compiler uses a specific encryption scheme based on hash functions (modeled as random oracles) which requires $2n-1$ hash function evaluations in addition to the encryption algorithm.

4.1 Compiler for DMCFE Schemes Without Labels

The compiler without labels is described in Fig. 4. Where SE is an IND-CPA symmetric-key encryption scheme. We show the following security theorem.

Theorem 4.1. *Let* $\mathsf{DMCFE} = (\mathsf{Setup}, \mathsf{KeyGen}, \mathsf{KeyDerShare}, \mathsf{KeyDerComb}, \mathsf{Enc}, \mathsf{Dec})$ *be an* adt-pos-*IND-secure DMCFE scheme without labels* ($\mathsf{Labels} = \{\perp\}$) *for a family of functions $\mathcal{F}$. Let* $\mathsf{SE} = (\mathsf{Enc}_{\mathsf{SE}}, \mathsf{Dec}_{\mathsf{SE}})$ *be an IND-CPA symmetric-key encryption scheme. Then the DMCFE scheme* $\mathsf{DMCFE}' = (\mathsf{Setup}', \mathsf{KeyGen}', \mathsf{KeyDerShare}', \mathsf{KeyDerComb}', \mathsf{Enc}', \mathsf{Dec}')$ *described in Fig. 4 is an* adt-any-*IND-secure DMCFE scheme. Namely, for any PPT adversary $\mathcal{A}$, there exist PPT adversaries $\mathcal{B}$ and $\mathcal{B}'$ such that:*

$$\mathsf{Adv}^{\text{adt-any-IND}}_{\mathsf{DMCFE}',\mathcal{A}}(\lambda, n) \leq \mathsf{Adv}^{\text{adt-pos-IND}}_{\mathsf{DMCFE},\mathcal{B}}(\lambda, n) + n \cdot \mathsf{Adv}^{\text{IND-CPA}}_{\mathsf{SE},\mathcal{B}'}(\lambda).$$

Proof. An encryption query on the i-th slot is denoted as (x_i^0, x_i^1).

In the proof we need to consider two different cases:

1. In all uncorrupted positions $i \notin \mathcal{CS}$, at least one query has been made, $Q_i \geq 1$.
2. In an uncorrupted position $i \notin \mathcal{CS}$, zero queries have been made, $Q_i = 0$.

We begin our proof by considering the first point.

$\underline{\mathsf{Setup}'(1^\lambda, 1^n):}$

Return $\mathsf{pp} \leftarrow \mathsf{Setup}(1^\lambda, 1^n)$

$\underline{\mathsf{KeyGen}'(\mathsf{pp}):}$

$\{\mathsf{sk}_i\}_{i\in[n]} \leftarrow \mathsf{KeyGen}(\mathsf{pp})$

For $i \in [n]$:

$\quad \mathsf{k}_{i,1}, \ldots, \mathsf{k}_{i,n} \leftarrow \{0,1\}^\lambda$

$\quad \mathsf{K}_i = \oplus_{j\in[n]} \mathsf{k}_{i,j}$

Return $\{\mathsf{sk}'_i = (\mathsf{sk}_i, \mathsf{K}_i, \{\mathsf{k}_{i,j}, \mathsf{k}_{j,i}\}_{j\in[n]})\}_{i\in[n]}$

$\underline{\mathsf{Enc}'(\mathsf{pp}, \mathsf{sk}'_i, x_i):}$

Parse $\mathsf{sk}'_i = (\mathsf{sk}_i, \mathsf{K}_i, \{\mathsf{k}_{i,j}, \mathsf{k}_{j,i}\}_{j\in[n]})$

$\mathsf{ct}_i \leftarrow \mathsf{Enc}(\mathsf{pp}, \mathsf{sk}_i, x_i)$

$\mathsf{ct}'_i \leftarrow \mathsf{Enc}_{\mathsf{SE}}(\mathsf{K}_i, \mathsf{ct}_i)$

Return $(\mathsf{ct}'_i, \{\mathsf{k}_{j,i}\}_{j\in[n]})$

$\underline{\mathsf{KeyDerShare}'(\mathsf{pp}, \mathsf{sk}'_i, f):}$

Parse $\mathsf{sk}'_i = (\mathsf{sk}_i, \mathsf{K}_i, \{\mathsf{k}_{i,j}, \mathsf{k}_{j,i}\}_{j\in[n]})$

Return $\mathsf{sk}'_{i,f} \leftarrow \mathsf{KeyDerShare}(\mathsf{sk}_i, f)$

$\underline{\mathsf{KeyDerComb}'(\mathsf{pp}, \{\mathsf{sk}'_{i,f}\}_{i\in[n]}):}$

$\mathsf{sk}_f := \mathsf{KeyDerComb}(\mathsf{pp}, \{\mathsf{sk}'_{i,f}\}_{i\in[n]})$

Return sk_f

$\underline{\mathsf{Dec}'(\mathsf{pp}, \mathsf{sk}_f, \mathsf{ct}''_1, \ldots, \mathsf{ct}''_n):}$

Parse $\{\mathsf{ct}''_i = (\mathsf{ct}'_i, \{\mathsf{k}_{j,i}\}_{j\in[n]})\}_{i\in[n]}$

For $i \in [n]$:

$\quad \mathsf{K}_i = \oplus_{j\in[n]} \mathsf{k}_{i,j}$

$\quad \mathsf{ct}_i \leftarrow \mathsf{Dec}_{\mathsf{SE}}(\mathsf{K}_i, \mathsf{ct}'_i)$

Return $\mathsf{Dec}(\mathsf{pp}, \mathsf{sk}_f, \mathsf{ct}_1, \ldots, \mathsf{ct}_n)$.

Fig. 4. Compiler from an xx-pos-IND DMCFE DMCFE without labels into an xx-any-IND DMCFE DMCFE′ using an IND-CPA symmetric-key encryption scheme SE

Lemma 4.2. *Let* DMCFE = (Setup, KeyGen, KeyDerShare, KeyDerComb, Enc, Dec) *be an* adt-pos-*IND-secure DMCFE construction without labels (*Labels = $\{\bot\}$*) for a family of functions* $\mathcal{F}$*. Let* SE = ($\mathsf{Enc}_{\mathsf{SE}}, \mathsf{Dec}_{\mathsf{SE}}$) *be a symmetric-key encryption scheme. Then the DMCFE scheme* DMCFE′ = (Setup′, KeyGen′, KeyDerShare′, KeyDerComb′, Enc′, Dec′) *described in Fig. 4 is* adt-any-*IND secure. Namely, for any PPT adversary* $\mathcal{A}$ *restricted to make* $Q_i \geq 1$ *for all* $i \notin \mathcal{CS}$ *there exist a PPT adversary* $\mathcal{B}$ *such that:*

$$\mathsf{Adv}^{\text{adt-any-IND}}_{\mathsf{DMCFE}',\mathcal{A}}(\lambda, n) \leq \mathsf{Adv}^{\text{adt-pos-IND}}_{\mathsf{DMCFE},\mathcal{B}}(\lambda, n).$$

Proof. We construct an adversary $\mathcal{B}$ against the adt-any-IND security of the scheme DMCFE′. $\mathcal{B}$ generates $\mathsf{k}_{i,1}, \ldots, \mathsf{k}_{i,n}$ and K_i for every $i \in [n]$.

If $\mathcal{A}$ ask a query $\mathsf{QCor}'(i)$, $\mathcal{B}$ asks a query $\mathsf{QCor}(i)$ to its own corruption oracle to obtain the key sk_i and uses it to create sk'_i, which gets forwarded to $\mathcal{A}$.

When the adversary $\mathcal{A}$ asks a query $\mathsf{QEnc}'(i, x_i^0, x_i^1)$, $\mathcal{B}$ directly forwards it to its own encryption oracle. It receives $\mathsf{ct}_i \leftarrow \mathsf{Enc}(\mathsf{pp}, \mathsf{sk}_i, x_i^\beta)$ as a result and uses K_i to generate $\mathsf{ct}'_i \leftarrow \mathsf{Enc}_{\mathsf{SE}}(\mathsf{K}_i, \mathsf{ct}_i)$. This ciphertext gets concatenated with the key shares of the symmetric encryption scheme $\{\mathsf{k}_{j,i}\}_{j\in[n]}$ and sent to $\mathcal{A}$ as an answer to the encryption query.

If $\mathcal{A}$ asks a query $\mathsf{QKeyD}'(f)$, $\mathcal{B}$ forwards it to its own oracle to receive $\mathsf{sk}_{i,f}$, which gets forwarded to $\mathcal{A}$.

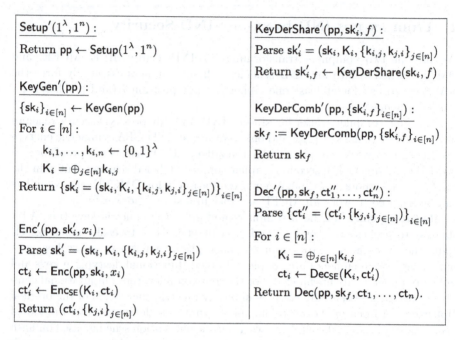

It is straightforward to see that the adversary $\mathcal{B}$ perfectly simulates the security game for DMCFE' to $\mathcal{A}$. Hence, we have:

$$\mathsf{Adv}^{\text{adt-any-IND}}_{\mathsf{DMCFE}',\mathcal{A}}(\lambda, n) \leq \mathsf{Adv}^{\text{adt-pos-IND}}_{\mathsf{DMCFE},\mathcal{B}}(\lambda, n).$$

□

We continue with the consideration of the second point.

Lemma 4.3. *Let* $\mathsf{DMCFE} = (\mathsf{Setup}, \mathsf{KeyGen}, \mathsf{KeyDerShare}, \mathsf{KeyDerComb}, \mathsf{Enc}, \mathsf{Dec})$ *be a DMCFE construction without labels* ($\mathsf{Labels} = \{\perp\}$) *for a family of functions* $\mathcal{F}$. *Let* $\mathsf{SE} = (\mathsf{Enc}_{\mathsf{SE}}, \mathsf{Dec}_{\mathsf{SE}})$ *be an IND-CPA symmetric-key encryption scheme and let* $Q_i = 0$ *for at least one* $i \notin \mathcal{CS}$. *Then the DMCFE scheme* $\mathsf{DMCFE}' = (\mathsf{Setup}', \mathsf{KeyGen}', \mathsf{KeyDerShare}', \mathsf{KeyDerComb}', \mathsf{Enc}', \mathsf{Dec}')$ *described in Fig. 4 is* adt-any-*IND-secure. Namely, for any PPT adversary* $\mathcal{A}$, *there exists an adversary* $\mathcal{B}'$ *such that:*

$$\mathsf{Adv}^{\text{adt-any-IND}}_{\mathsf{DMCFE}',\mathcal{A}}(\lambda, n) \leq n \cdot \mathsf{Adv}^{\text{IND-CPA}}_{\mathsf{SE},\mathcal{B}'}(\lambda).$$

Proof. We prove this part by using a hybrid argument. We define the games $\mathsf{G}_1, \ldots, \mathsf{G}_n$ in Fig. 5.

Due to the definition of the game it holds that: Game G_0 corresponds to the experiment adt-any-$\text{IND}^{\mathsf{DMCFE}'}_{\beta}$ for $\beta = 1$ and G_n to the experiment adt-any-$\text{IND}^{\mathsf{DMCFE}'}_{\beta}$ for $\beta = 1$ therefore using the triangular inequality, we get:

$$\mathsf{Adv}^{\text{adt-any-IND}}_{\mathsf{DMCFE}',\mathcal{A}}(\lambda, n) \leq \sum_{t=1}^{n} |\mathsf{Win}^{\mathsf{G}_{t-1}}_{\mathcal{A}}(\lambda, n) - \mathsf{Win}^{\mathsf{G}_t}_{\mathcal{A}}(\lambda, n)|.$$

We then conclude by showing that for any t, there exists an adversary $\mathcal{B}_t$ such that

$$|\mathsf{Win}^{\mathsf{G}_{t-1}}_{\mathcal{A}}(\lambda, n) - \mathsf{Win}^{\mathsf{G}_t}_{\mathcal{A}}(\lambda, n)| \leq \mathsf{Adv}^{\text{IND-CPA}}_{\mathsf{SE},\mathcal{B}_t}(\lambda).$$

The adversary $\mathcal{B}'$ of the statement then just picks $t \in [n]$ and simulates $\mathcal{B}_t$. The standard details are omitted here. The adversary $\mathcal{B}_t$ against the IND-CPA security of the symmetric encryption scheme behaves in the following way:

In the first step, $\mathcal{B}_t$ generates the keys K_i and also samples sk_i for all $i \in [n] \setminus \{t\}$ by running the key generation algorithm of DMCFE.

We denote by $\mathcal{ES}$ the set of positions i in which encryption queries have been made.

If $\mathcal{A}$ corrupts a position $i \neq t$, the adversary $\mathcal{B}_t$ samples random values $\mathsf{k}_{i,j}$ for all $j \in [n] \setminus (\mathcal{CS} \cup \mathcal{ES})$ such that $\mathsf{K}_i = \oplus_{j \in [n]} \mathsf{k}_{i,j}$. If the position i has not been corrupted before and if no encryption query has been asked in this position (i.e. $i \notin \mathcal{CS} \cup \mathcal{ES}$), then $\mathcal{B}_t$ samples random values $\mathsf{k}_{j,i}$ for all $j \in [n] \setminus (\mathcal{CS} \cup \{i\})$. If the adversary $\mathcal{A}$ asks a corruption query $\mathsf{QCor}'(t)$, the adversary $\mathcal{B}_t$ directly outputs a random value $r \leftarrow \{0, 1\}$. This is due to the fact that, if party t is corrupted the games G_{t-1} and G_t are the same. This results in an advantage equal to 0.

$\underline{\mathsf{G}_t(\lambda, n, \mathcal{A}):}$

$\mathcal{ES} = \{\}$

$\mathsf{pp} \leftarrow \mathsf{Setup}(1^\lambda, 1^n)$

$(\mathsf{sk}_i, \mathsf{K}_i, \{\mathsf{k}_{i,j}, \mathsf{k}_{j,i}\}_{j\in[n]})_{i\in[n]} \leftarrow \mathsf{KeyGen}'(\mathsf{pp})$

$\alpha \leftarrow \mathcal{A}^{\mathsf{QEnc}'(\cdot,\cdot,\cdot),\mathsf{QKeyD}'(\cdot),\mathsf{QCor}'(\cdot)}(\mathsf{pp})$

Output: α

$\mathsf{QEnc}'(i, x_i^0, x_i^1)$

Add i to $\mathcal{ES}$

If $i \notin (\mathcal{CS} \cup \mathcal{ES})$, $\mathsf{k}_{j,i} \leftarrow_R \{0,1\}^\lambda$ for all $j \in [n] \setminus \mathcal{CS}$

If $i \leq t$, return$(\mathsf{Enc}_{\mathsf{SE}}(\mathsf{K}_i, \mathsf{Enc}(\mathsf{pp}, \mathsf{sk}_i', x_i^0)), \{\mathsf{k}_{j,i}\}_{j\in[n]})$

If $i > t$, return$(\mathsf{Enc}_{\mathsf{SE}}(\mathsf{K}_i, \mathsf{Enc}(\mathsf{pp}, \mathsf{sk}_i', x_i^1)), \{\mathsf{k}_{j,i}\}_{j\in[n]})$

$\mathsf{QKeyD}'(y)$

Return $\{\mathsf{sk}_{i,f}' \leftarrow \mathsf{KeyDerShare}(\mathsf{pp}, \mathsf{sk}_i, f)\}_{i\in[n]}$

$\mathsf{QCor}'(i)$

If $i \notin \mathcal{CS}$

$\mathsf{k}_{i,j} \leftarrow_R \{0,1\}^\lambda$ for all $j \in [n] \setminus (\mathcal{CS} \cup \mathcal{ES})$, s.t. $\mathsf{K}_i = \oplus_{j\in[n]} \mathsf{k}_{i,j}$

If $i \notin \mathcal{ES}$

$\mathsf{k}_{j,i} \leftarrow_R \{0,1\}^\lambda$ for all $j \in [n] \setminus (\mathcal{CS} \cup \{i\})$

Return $(\mathsf{sk}_i, \mathsf{K}_i, \{\mathsf{k}_{i,j}, \mathsf{k}_{j,i}\}_{j\in[n]})$

Fig. 5. The description of the hybrid used for the reduction to the symmetric-key encryption scheme in Lemma 4.3.

Whenever $\mathcal{A}$ asks a query $\mathsf{QEnc}'(i, x_i^0, x_i^1)$ we consider three different cases. In the first case, $\mathcal{A}$ queries the encryption oracle for $i < t$, then $\mathcal{B}_t$ generates $\mathsf{Enc}_{\mathsf{SE}}(\mathsf{K}_i, \mathsf{Enc}(\mathsf{pp}, \mathsf{sk}_i, x_i^0))$ using the key K_i. The same happens for queries with $i > t$, but with x_i^1 instead of x_i^0, i.e. $\mathsf{Enc}_{\mathsf{SE}}(\mathsf{K}_i, \mathsf{Enc}(\mathsf{pp}, \mathsf{sk}_i, x_i^1))$. In the case that $\mathcal{A}$ asks a query $\mathsf{QEnc}'(t, x_t^0, x_t^1)$, $\mathcal{B}_t$ generates $(\mathsf{Enc}(\mathsf{pp}, \mathsf{sk}_t, x_t^0), \mathsf{Enc}(\mathsf{pp}, \mathsf{sk}_t, x_t^1))$ and sends it to its own encryption oracle to receive $\mathsf{Enc}_{\mathsf{SE}}(\mathsf{Enc}(\mathsf{pp}, \mathsf{sk}_t, x_t^\beta))$. If no encryption has been asked in the position i before and if i is not corrupted (i.e., $i \notin (\mathcal{CS} \cup \mathcal{ES})$) then we sample $\mathsf{k}_{j,i}$ for all $j \in [n] \setminus \mathcal{CS}$. If $i \in (\mathcal{CS} \cup \mathcal{ES})$ then the values $\mathsf{k}_{j,i}$ have already been sampled for all $j \in [n]$. The ciphertext $\mathsf{Enc}_{\mathsf{SE}}(\mathsf{K}_i, \mathsf{Enc}(\mathsf{pp}, \mathsf{sk}_i, x_i^\beta))$ together with $\mathsf{k}_{j,i}, \forall j \in [n]$ are then sent to $\mathcal{A}$ in the last step.

If $\mathcal{A}$ asks a key derivation query $\mathsf{QKeyD}'(f)$, $\mathcal{B}_t$ uses the public parameters pp and the keys $\{\mathsf{sk}_i, f\}_{i\in[n]}$ to generate $\{\mathsf{sk}'_{i,f} \leftarrow \mathsf{KeyDerShare}(\mathsf{pp}, \mathsf{sk}_i, f)\}_{i\in[n]}$ as a response for $\mathcal{A}$.

The reduction shows that for all $t \in [n]$:

$$|\mathsf{Win}_{\mathcal{A}}^{\mathsf{G}_{t-1}}(\lambda, n) - \mathsf{Win}_{\mathcal{A}}^{\mathsf{G}_t}(\lambda, n)| \leq \mathsf{Adv}_{\mathsf{SE},\mathcal{B}_t}^{\text{IND-CPA}}(\lambda).$$

This results in:

$$\sum_{t=1}^{n} |\mathsf{Win}_{\mathcal{A}}^{\mathsf{G}_{t-1}}(\lambda, n) - \mathsf{Win}_{\mathcal{A}}^{\mathsf{G}_t}(\lambda, n)| \leq \sum_{t=1}^{n} \mathsf{Adv}_{\mathsf{SE},\mathcal{B}_t}^{\text{IND-CPA}}(\lambda).$$

□

Theorem 4.1 follow from the two above lemmas. □

4.2 Compiler for Labeled DMCFE Schemes

We now present the compiler supporting labels in Fig. 6, where $\mathsf{H}_1 : \{0,1\}^* \to \{0,1\}^\lambda$ and $\mathsf{H}_2 : \{0,1\}^* \to \{0,1\}^{|\mathsf{ct}_i|}$ are two hash functions modeled as random oracles in the security proof. We formally prove the following security theorem in the full version [1].

Theorem 4.4. *Let* $\mathsf{DMCFE} = (\mathsf{Setup}, \mathsf{KeyGen}, \mathsf{KeyDerShare}, \mathsf{KeyDerComb}, \mathsf{Enc}, \mathsf{Dec})$ *be an* adt-pos-*IND-secure DMCFE scheme for an ensemble of functions* $\mathcal{F}$ *and set of labels* Labels. *Then the DMCFE scheme* $\mathsf{DMCFE}' = (\mathsf{Setup}', \mathsf{KeyGen}', \mathsf{KeyDerShare}', \mathsf{KeyDerComb}', \mathsf{Enc}', \mathsf{Dec}')$ *described in Fig. 6 is an* adt-any-*IND-secure scheme. Namely, when the hash functions* H_1 *and* H_2 *are modeled as random oracles, for any PPT adversary* $\mathcal{A}$ *there exist a PPT adversary* $\mathcal{B}$ *such that:*

$$\mathsf{Adv}_{\mathsf{DMCFE}',\mathcal{A}}^{\text{adt-any-IND}}(\lambda, n) \leq \mathsf{Adv}_{\mathsf{DMCFE},\mathcal{B}}^{\text{adt-pos-IND}}(\lambda, n) + \frac{2q_{\mathsf{H}_1} + (2n+1)\cdot(q_{\mathsf{H}_2} q_{\mathsf{QEnc}} + q_{\mathsf{QEnc}}^2)}{2^\lambda},$$

where q_{H_1}, q_{H_2}, *and* q_{QEnc} *are the numbers of queries to the oracles* H_1, H_2, *and* QEnc *respectively.*

A high-level overview of the proof of this theorem can be found in Sect. 1.2.

5 Security of the MCFE from Abdalla et al. Against Adaptive Corruptions

In this section, we prove that the MIFE scheme by Abdalla et al. [3] is also secure against adaptive corruptions, when their unique encryption and secret

$\underline{\mathsf{Setup}'(1^\lambda, 1^n):}$	$\underline{\mathsf{KeyDerShare}'(\mathsf{pp}, \mathsf{sk}'_i, f):}$
Return $\mathsf{pp} \leftarrow \mathsf{Setup}(1^\lambda, 1^n)$	Parse $\mathsf{sk}'_i = (\mathsf{sk}_i, \mathsf{K}_i, \{\mathsf{k}_{i,j}, \mathsf{k}_{j,i}\}_{j\in[n]})$
$\underline{\mathsf{KeyGen}'(\mathsf{pp}):}$	Return $\mathsf{sk}'_{i,f} \leftarrow \mathsf{KeyDerShare}(\mathsf{pp}, \mathsf{sk}'_i, f)$
$\{\mathsf{sk}_i\}_{i\in[n]} \leftarrow \mathsf{KeyGen}(\mathsf{pp})$	
For $i \in [n]$:	$\underline{\mathsf{KeyDerComb}'(\mathsf{pp}, \{\mathsf{sk}'_{i,f}\}_{i\in[n]}):}$
$\quad \mathsf{k}_{i,1}, \ldots, \mathsf{k}_{i,n} \leftarrow \{0,1\}^\lambda$	$\mathsf{sk}_f := \mathsf{KeyDerComb}(\mathsf{pp}, \{\mathsf{sk}_{i,f}\}_{i\in[n]})$
Return $\{\mathsf{sk}'_i = (\mathsf{sk}_i, \mathsf{K}_i, \{\mathsf{k}_{i,j}, \mathsf{k}_{j,i}\}_{j\in[n]})\}_{i\in[n]}$	Return sk_f
$\underline{\mathsf{Enc}'(\mathsf{pp}, \mathsf{sk}'_i, x_i, \ell):}$	$\underline{\mathsf{Dec}'(\mathsf{pp}, \mathsf{sk}_f, \mathsf{ct}''_1, \ldots, \mathsf{ct}''_n):}$
Parse $\mathsf{sk}'_i = (\mathsf{sk}_i, \mathsf{K}_i, \{\mathsf{k}_{i,j}, \mathsf{k}_{j,i}\}_{j\in[n]})$	Parse $\{\mathsf{ct}''_i = (\mathsf{ct}'_i, r_i, \{\mathsf{k}_{j,i,\ell}\}_{j\in[n]})\}_{i\in[n]}$
$\mathsf{ct}_i \leftarrow \mathsf{Enc}(\mathsf{pp}, \mathsf{sk}_i, x_i)$	For $i \in [n]$:
For $j \in [n]$:	$\quad \mathsf{K}_{i,\ell} = \oplus_{j\in[n]} \mathsf{k}_{i,j,\ell}$
$\quad \mathsf{k}_{i,j,\ell} := \mathsf{H}_1(\mathsf{k}_{i,j} \| i \| j \| \ell)$	$\quad \mathsf{ct}_i = \mathsf{ct}'_i \oplus \mathsf{H}_2(\mathsf{K}_{i,\ell} \| r_i)$
$\quad \mathsf{k}_{j,i,\ell} := \mathsf{H}_1(\mathsf{k}_{j,i} \| j \| i \| \ell)$	Return $\mathsf{Dec}(\mathsf{pp}, \mathsf{sk}_f, \mathsf{ct}_1, \ldots, \mathsf{ct}_n)$.
$\mathsf{K}_{i,\ell} := \oplus_{j\in[n]} \mathsf{k}_{i,j,\ell}$	
$r_i \leftarrow \{0,1\}^\lambda$; $\mathsf{ct}'_i := \mathsf{ct}_i \oplus \mathsf{H}_2(\mathsf{K}_{i,\ell} \| r_i)$	
Return $(\mathsf{ct}'_i, r_i, \{\mathsf{k}_{j,i,\ell}\}_{j\in[n]})$	

Fig. 6. Compiler from an xx-pos-IND DMCFE DMCFE with labels into an xx-any-IND DMCFE DMCFE′ with labels, where $\mathsf{H}_1 : \{0,1\}^* \to \{0,1\}^\lambda$ and $\mathsf{H}_2 : \{0,1\}^* \to \{0,1\}^{|\mathsf{ct}_i|}$ are two hash functions modeled as random oracles in the security proof.

key is split into individual secret keys for each party in a natural way[4], as described in Figs. 7 and 9.

For simplicity, we focus here on the bounded-norm MIFE case since the construction over $\mathbb{Z}_L$ can be easily adapted from it. Towards this goal, Sect. 5.1 first recalls the definition of FE with two-step decryption and linear encryption. Next, Sect. 5.2 recalls the other building block, an *sta-one-IND-secure* MCFE scheme for $\mathcal{F}_\rho, \rho = (\mathbb{Z}_L, n, m, L, L)$. Finally, Sect. 5.3 recalls the MCFE construction from [3].

5.1 Inner-Product FE with Two-Step Decryption and Linear Encryption

The [3] construction extends a one-time secure MIFE scheme over $\mathbb{Z}_L$ to a many-time secure MIFE scheme over $\mathbb{Z}$. This extension relies on a single-input FE scheme for $\mathcal{F}_\rho, \rho = (\mathbb{Z}, 1, m, X, Y)$ satisfying two properties, called *two-step*

[4] Note that the schemes in [3] were presented as a MIFE scheme with a unique encryption and secret key. It is however straightforward to split the encryption key and secret key into a key sk_i for each party.

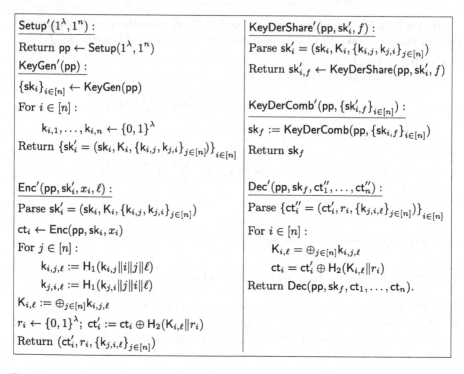

decryption and *linear encryption* [3]. As indicated in [3], the *two-step decryption* property informally says that the FE decryption algorithm can be broken in two steps: one step that uses the secret key to return an encoding of the result and the other step that returns the actual result $\langle \boldsymbol{x}, \boldsymbol{y} \rangle$ as long as the bounds $||\boldsymbol{x}||_\infty < X, ||\boldsymbol{y}||_\infty < Y$ hold. The *linear encryption* property, on the other hand, informally states that the FE encryption algorithm is additively homomorphic. We now recall these definitions more formally.

Definition 5.1 (Two-step decryption [3]). *A secret-key FE scheme* $\mathsf{FE} = (\mathsf{Setup}, \mathsf{KeyGen}, \mathsf{KeyDer}, \mathsf{Enc}, \mathsf{Dec})$ *for the function ensemble* $\mathcal{F}_\rho, \rho = (\mathbb{Z}, 1, m, X, Y)$ *satisfies the* two-step decryption *property if it admits PPT algorithms* $\mathsf{Setup}^\star, \mathsf{Dec}_1, \mathsf{Dec}_2$ *and an encoding function* $\mathcal{E}$ *such that:*

1. *For all* $\lambda \in \mathbb{N}, \mathsf{Setup}^\star(1^\lambda, 1^n)$ *outputs* pp *where* pp *includes* $\rho = (\mathbb{Z}, 1, m, X, Y)$ *and a bound* $B \in \mathbb{N}$*, as well as the description of a group* $\mathbb{G}$ *(with group law* $\circ$*) of order* $L > 2 \cdot n \cdot m \cdot X \cdot Y$*, which defines the encoding function* $\mathcal{E} : \mathbb{Z}_L \times \mathbb{Z} \to \mathbb{G}$.
2. *For all* $\mathsf{msk} \leftarrow \mathsf{KeyGen}(\mathsf{pp}), \boldsymbol{x} \in \mathbb{Z}^m, \mathsf{ct} \leftarrow \mathsf{Enc}(\mathsf{pp}, \mathsf{msk}, \boldsymbol{x}), \boldsymbol{y} \in \mathbb{Z}^m$*, and* $\mathsf{sk} \leftarrow \mathsf{KeyDer}(\mathsf{msk}, \boldsymbol{y})$*, we have*
$$\mathsf{Dec}_1(\mathsf{pp}, \mathsf{sk}, \mathsf{ct}) = \mathcal{E}(\langle \boldsymbol{x}, \boldsymbol{y} \rangle \bmod L, \mathsf{noise}),$$
for some $\mathsf{noise} \in \mathbb{N}$ *that depends on* ct *and* sk*. Furthermore, it holds that* $Pr[\mathsf{noise} < B] = 1 - \mathrm{negl}(\lambda)$*, where the probability is taken over the random coins of* KeyGen *and* KeyDer*. Note that there is no restriction on the norm of* $\langle \boldsymbol{x}, \boldsymbol{y} \rangle$ *here.*
3. *Given any* $\gamma \in \mathbb{Z}_L$*, and* pp*, one can efficiently compute* $\mathcal{E}(\gamma, 0)$.
4. *The encoding* $\mathcal{E}$ *is linear, that is: for all* $\gamma, \gamma' \in \mathbb{Z}_L, \mathsf{noise}, \mathsf{noise}' \in \mathbb{Z}$*, we have*
$$\mathcal{E}(\gamma, \mathsf{noise}) \circ \mathcal{E}(\gamma', \mathsf{noise}') = \mathcal{E}(\gamma + \gamma' \bmod L, \mathsf{noise} + \mathsf{noise}').$$
5. *For all* $\gamma < 2 \cdot n \cdot m \cdot X \cdot Y$*, and* $\mathsf{noise} < n \cdot B, \mathsf{Dec}_2(\mathsf{pp}, \mathcal{E}(\gamma, \mathsf{noise})) = \gamma$.

Definition 5.2 (Linear encryption [3]). *A secret-key FE scheme* $\mathsf{FE} = (\mathsf{Setup}, \mathsf{KeyGen}, \mathsf{KeyDer}, \mathsf{Enc}, \mathsf{Dec})$ *is said to satisfy the linear encryption property if there exists a deterministic algorithm* Add *that takes as input a ciphertext and a message, such that for all* $\boldsymbol{x}, \boldsymbol{x}' \in \mathbb{Z}^m$*, the following are identically distributed:*
$$\mathsf{Add}(\mathsf{Enc}(\mathsf{pp}, \mathsf{msk}, \boldsymbol{x}), \boldsymbol{x}'), \text{ and } \mathsf{Enc}(\mathsf{pp}, \mathsf{msk}, (\boldsymbol{x} + \boldsymbol{x}' \bmod L)).$$
Recall that the value $L \in \mathbb{N}$ *is defined as part of the output of the algorithm* $\mathsf{Setup}^\star$ *(see the two-step decryption property above).*

5.2 One-Time Inner-Product MCFE over $\mathbb{Z}_L$

We recap the one-time secure scheme provided by Abdalla et al. [3] in Fig. 7, to which we made the following modifications. First, our description does not

Define $\mathsf{pp}_{\mathsf{ot}} = (n, m, L)$	$\mathsf{KeyDer}^{\mathsf{ot}}(\mathsf{pp}_{\mathsf{ot}}, \mathsf{msk}, \boldsymbol{y})$:
	Parse $\mathsf{msk} = \{\boldsymbol{u}_i\}_{i\in[n]}, \boldsymbol{y} = (\boldsymbol{y}_1, \dots, \boldsymbol{y}_n)$
$\mathsf{KeyGen}^{\mathsf{ot}}(\mathsf{pp}_{\mathsf{ot}})$:	Return $\mathsf{dk}_{\boldsymbol{y}} := \sum_{i\in[n]} \langle \boldsymbol{u}_i, \boldsymbol{y}_i \rangle$
$\{\boldsymbol{u}_i\}_{i\in[n]} \leftarrow (\mathbb{Z}_L^m)^n$	
Return $\mathsf{msk} := \{\mathsf{msk}_i\}_{i\in[n]} = \{\boldsymbol{u}_i\}_{i\in[n]}$	
	$\mathsf{Dec}^{\mathsf{ot}}(\mathsf{pp}_{\mathsf{ot}}, \mathsf{dk}_{\boldsymbol{y}}, \boldsymbol{y}, \{\mathsf{ct}_i\}_{i\in[n]})$:
$\mathsf{Enc}^{\mathsf{ot}}(\mathsf{pp}_{\mathsf{ot}}, \mathsf{msk}_i, \boldsymbol{x}_i)$:	Parse $\boldsymbol{y} = (\boldsymbol{y}_1, \dots, \boldsymbol{y}_n)$
Parse $\mathsf{msk}_i = \boldsymbol{u}_i$	Return $\sum_{i\in[n]} \langle \mathsf{ct}_i, \boldsymbol{y}_i \rangle - \mathsf{dk}_{\boldsymbol{y}} \bmod L$
Return $\mathsf{ct}_i := \boldsymbol{u}_i + \boldsymbol{x}_i \bmod L$	

Fig. 7. One-Time Inner-Product MCFE over $\mathbb{Z}_L$ (for $\mathcal{F}_{L,n}^m$)

need a setup procedure $\mathsf{Setup}^{\mathsf{ot}}$, which now simply defines (n, m, L). Second, the steps of the original $\mathsf{Setup}^{\mathsf{ot}}$ in Abdalla et al. [3] are now defined in the $\mathsf{KeyGen}^{\mathsf{ot}}$ procedure. When doing so, we also split their unique secret key into individual secret keys for each party. Since these modifications do not impact the correctness of the scheme, we refer to [3] for a proof of correctness. As for its security with respect to adaptive corruptions, we need to modify the proof of Abdalla et al. [3] to account for corruption queries.

Theorem 5.3. *The* $\mathsf{MCFE}^{\mathsf{ot}}$ *scheme in Fig. 7 is* adt-one-IND *secure. Namely, for any adversary* $\mathcal{A}$, $\mathsf{Adv}^{\text{adt-one-IND}}_{\mathsf{MCFE}^{\mathsf{ot}},\mathcal{A}}(\lambda) = 0$.

Proof. Let $\mathcal{A}$ be an adversary against the adt-one-IND security of the $\mathsf{MCFE}^{\mathsf{ot}}$ scheme with advantage $\mathsf{Adv}^{\text{adt-one-IND}}_{\mathsf{MCFE}^{\mathsf{ot}},\mathcal{A}}(\lambda)$. Let sta-one-sel-$\text{IND}^{\mathsf{MCFE}^{\mathsf{ot}}}_{\beta}(\lambda, n, \mathcal{B})$ be a variant of the sta-one-$\text{IND}^{\mathsf{MCFE}^{\mathsf{ot}}}_{\beta}(\lambda, n, \mathcal{B})$ experiment in which the selective adversary $\mathcal{B}$ additionally specifies the encryption challenges $\{\boldsymbol{x}_i^b\}_{i\in[n],b\in\{0,1\}}$ together with the corrupted set at the beginning of the experiment. (Recall that there is a single challenge per slot.)

We use complexity leveraging to transform $\mathcal{A}$ into a selective adversary $\mathcal{B}$ such that:

$$\mathsf{Adv}^{\text{adt-one-IND}}_{\mathsf{MCFE}^{\mathsf{ot}},\mathcal{A}}(\lambda) \leq 2^{-n} \cdot (2X)^{-2nm} \cdot \mathsf{Adv}^{\text{sta-one-sel-IND}}_{\mathsf{MCFE}^{\mathsf{ot}},\mathcal{B}}(\lambda).$$

After adversary $\mathcal{B}$ made its guesses $\{\boldsymbol{x}_i^b\}_{i\in[n],b\in\{0,1\}}$ and determined the set of corrupted parties, it simulates $\mathcal{A}$'s experiment using its own static and selective experiment. When $\mathcal{B}$ receives a challenge or corruption query from $\mathcal{A}$, it checks if the guess was successful: if it was, it continues simulating $\mathcal{A}$'s experiment, otherwise, it returns 0. When the guess is successful, $\mathcal{B}$ perfectly simulates $\mathcal{A}$'s view.

Hence, to prove that $\mathsf{MCFE}^{\mathsf{ot}}$ satisfies perfect adt-one-IND security, we just need to prove that it satisfies perfect sta-one-sel-IND security. In order to prove

$\mathcal{H}_\beta(1^\lambda, \mathcal{B})$	$\mathsf{O_K}(i, \boldsymbol{y})$
$(\mathcal{CS}, \{\boldsymbol{x}_i^b\}_{i\in[n],b\in\{0,1\}}) \leftarrow \mathcal{B}(1^\lambda, 1^n)$ For $i \in [n]$, $\quad \boldsymbol{u}_i \leftarrow \mathbb{Z}_L^m; \mathsf{ct}_i \leftarrow \boldsymbol{u}_i$ $\alpha \leftarrow \mathcal{B}^{\mathsf{O_K}(\cdot)}(\{\boldsymbol{u}_i\}_{i\in\mathcal{CS}}, \{\mathsf{ct}_i\}_{i\in[n]})$ Output α	Parse $\boldsymbol{y} = (\boldsymbol{y}_1, \ldots, \boldsymbol{y}_n)$ $\mathsf{sk}_{\boldsymbol{y}} = \sum_{i\in[n]} \langle \boldsymbol{u}_i - \boldsymbol{x}_i^\beta, \boldsymbol{y}_i \rangle$ Return $\mathsf{sk}_{\boldsymbol{y}}$

Fig. 8. Hybrid experiments for the proof of Theorem 5.3.

$\mathsf{MCFE^{ot}}$ satisfies perfect sta-one-sel-IND security (i.e., $\mathsf{Adv}^{\text{sta-one-sel-IND}}_{\mathsf{MCFE^{ot}},\mathcal{B}}(\lambda) = 0$), we introduce hybrid games $\mathcal{H}_\beta(1^\lambda, \mathcal{B})$, described in Fig. 8.

We prove that for all $\beta \in \{0,1\}$, the hybrid $\mathcal{H}_\beta(1^\lambda, \mathcal{B})$ is identical to the experiment sta-one-sel-$\text{IND}_\beta^{\mathsf{MCFE^{ot}}}(\lambda, n, \mathcal{B})$. This can be seen by using the fact that, in the selective security game, all $\{\boldsymbol{x}_i^\beta \in \mathbb{Z}^m\}_{i\in[n]}$ have identical distributions: $\{\boldsymbol{u}_i \bmod L\}_{i\in[n]}$ and $\{\boldsymbol{u}_i - \boldsymbol{x}_i^\beta \bmod L\}$, with $\boldsymbol{u}_i \leftarrow_R \mathbb{Z}_L^m$. This also holds for the corrupted positions $i \in \mathcal{CS}$, because in this case it holds that $\boldsymbol{x}_i^0 = \boldsymbol{x}_i^1$.

Finally, we show that $\mathcal{B}$'s view in $\mathcal{H}_\beta(1^\lambda, \mathcal{B})$ is independent of β. Indeed, the only information about β that leaks in the experiment is $\langle \boldsymbol{x}_i^\beta, \boldsymbol{y}_i \rangle$, which is independent of β by the definition of the security game. □

5.3 Inner-Product MCFE over $\mathbb{Z}$

In Fig. 9, we recall the construction of [3] of a pos-IND-secure scheme MCFE = $(\mathsf{Setup}, \mathsf{KeyGen}, \mathsf{KeyDer}, \mathsf{Enc}, \mathsf{Dec})$ from the (one-IND-secure) MCFE scheme $\mathsf{MCFE^{ot}} = (\mathsf{KeyGen^{ot}}, \mathsf{KeyDer^{ot}}, \mathsf{Enc^{ot}}, \mathsf{Dec^{ot}})$ described in Sect. 5.2 and from any any-IND-secure scheme $\mathsf{FE} = (\mathsf{Setup^{si}}, \mathsf{KeyGen^{si}}, \mathsf{KeyDer^{si}}, \mathsf{Enc^{si}}, \mathsf{Dec^{si}})$ for a single input. As for the one-time scheme in Sect. 5.2, we also modified the KeyGen procedure in [3] in order to split their unique secret key into individual secret keys for each party. Since these modifications do not impact the correctness of the scheme, we refer to [3] for a proof of the latter. In the following, we show that this construction allows for adaptive corruption.

Lemma 5.4. *Assume that the single-input scheme* FE *is any-IND-secure and the multi-client scheme* $\mathsf{MCFE^{ot}}$ *is adt-one-IND-secure. Then the multi-client scheme* MCFE *is adt-pos-IND-secure. Namely, for any PPT adversary* $\mathcal{A}$, *there exist PPT adversaries* $\mathcal{B}$ *and* $\mathcal{B}'$ *such that*

$$\mathsf{Adv}^{\text{adt-pos-IND}}_{\mathsf{MCFE},\mathcal{A}}(\lambda, n) \leq \mathsf{Adv}^{\text{adt-one-IND}}_{\mathsf{MCFE^{ot}},\mathcal{B}}(\lambda, n) + n \cdot \mathsf{Adv}^{\text{any-IND}}_{\mathsf{FE},\mathcal{B}'}(\lambda, n).$$

Proof. To prove the security of the multi-client inner-product functional encryption scheme, we define a sequence of games, where G_0 is the

$\underline{\mathsf{Setup}(1^\lambda, 1^n):}$

$\mathsf{pp_{si}} \leftarrow \mathsf{Setup^{si}}(1^\lambda, 1^n)$
Set $\mathsf{pp_{ot}} := (n, m, L)$, with $\rho_{\mathsf{si}} = (\mathbb{Z}, 1, m, 3X, Y)$ and L implicitly defined from $\mathsf{pp_{si}}$
Return $\mathsf{pp} = (\mathsf{pp_{si}}, \mathsf{pp_{ot}})$

$\underline{\mathsf{KeyGen}(\mathsf{pp}):}$

$\{\boldsymbol{u}_i\}_{i\in[n]} \leftarrow \mathsf{KeyGen^{ot}}(\mathsf{pp_{ot}})$
For $i \in [n]$, $\mathsf{msk}_i^{\mathsf{si}} \leftarrow \mathsf{KeyGen^{si}}(\mathsf{pp_{si}})$, $\mathsf{sk}_i := (\mathsf{msk}_i^{\mathsf{si}}, \boldsymbol{u}_i)$
Return $\{\mathsf{sk}_i\}_{i\in[n]}$

$\underline{\mathsf{Enc}(\mathsf{pp}, \mathsf{sk}_i, \boldsymbol{x}_i):}$

Parse $\mathsf{sk}_i = (\mathsf{msk}_i^{\mathsf{si}}, \boldsymbol{u}_i)$ and return $\mathsf{ct}_i := \mathsf{Enc^{si}}(\mathsf{pp_{si}}, \mathsf{msk}_i^{\mathsf{si}}, \mathsf{Enc^{ot}}(\mathsf{pp_{ot}}, \boldsymbol{u}_i, \boldsymbol{x}_i))$

$\underline{\mathsf{KeyDer}(\mathsf{pp}, \mathsf{msk}, \boldsymbol{y}):}$

Parse $\mathsf{msk} = \{\mathsf{msk}_i^{\mathsf{si}}, \boldsymbol{u}_i\}_{i\in[n]}, \boldsymbol{y} = (\boldsymbol{y}_1, \ldots, \boldsymbol{y}_n)$
For $i \in [n]$, $\mathsf{sk}_{i,\boldsymbol{y}} \leftarrow \mathsf{KeyDer^{si}}(\mathsf{pp_{si}}, \mathsf{msk}_i^{\mathsf{si}}, \boldsymbol{y}_i)$
$\mathsf{dk}_{\boldsymbol{y}} := \mathsf{KeyDer^{ot}}(\mathsf{pp_{ot}}, \{\boldsymbol{u}_i\}_{i\in[n]}, \boldsymbol{y})$
Return $\mathsf{sk}_{\boldsymbol{y}} := (\{\mathsf{sk}_{i,\boldsymbol{y}}\}_{i\in[n]}, \mathsf{dk}_{\boldsymbol{y}})$

$\underline{\mathsf{Dec}(\mathsf{pp}, \mathsf{sk}_{\boldsymbol{y}}, \{\mathsf{ct}_i\}_{i\in[n]}):}$

Parse $\mathsf{sk}_{\boldsymbol{y}} = (\{\mathsf{sk}_{i,\boldsymbol{y}}\}_{i\in[n]}, \mathsf{dk}_{\boldsymbol{y}})$
For $i \in [n]$, $\mathcal{E}(\langle \boldsymbol{u}_i + \boldsymbol{x}_i, \boldsymbol{y}_i\rangle \bmod L, \mathsf{noise}_i) \leftarrow \mathsf{Dec}_1^{\mathsf{si}}(\mathsf{pp_{si}}, \mathsf{sk}_{i,\boldsymbol{y}}, \mathsf{ct}_i)$
Return $\mathsf{Dec}_2^{\mathsf{si}}(\mathsf{pp_{si}}, \mathcal{E}(\langle \boldsymbol{u}_1 + \boldsymbol{x}_1, \boldsymbol{y}_1\rangle \bmod L, \mathsf{noise}_1)) \circ \ldots$
$\circ\, \mathcal{E}(\langle \boldsymbol{u}_n + \boldsymbol{x}_n, \boldsymbol{y}_n\rangle \bmod L, \mathsf{noise}_n) \circ \mathcal{E}(-\mathsf{dk}_{\boldsymbol{y}}, 0))$

Fig. 9. Inner-Product for $\mathcal{F}_\rho, \rho = (\mathbb{Z}, n, m, X, Y)$ built from $\mathsf{MCFE^{ot}}$ for $\mathcal{F}_{\rho_{\mathsf{ot}}}, \rho_{\mathsf{ot}} = (\mathbb{Z}_L, n, m, L, L)$ and FE for $\mathcal{F}_{\rho_{\mathsf{si}}}, \rho_{\mathsf{si}} = (\mathbb{Z}, 1, m, 3X, Y)$

Game	ct_i^j	justification/remark
G_0	$\mathsf{Enc}(\mathsf{pp}, \mathsf{sk}_i, \boldsymbol{x}_i^{0,j} - \boldsymbol{x}_i^{0,1} + \boldsymbol{x}_i^{0,1})$	
G_1	$\mathsf{Enc}(\mathsf{pp}, \mathsf{sk}_i, \boldsymbol{x}_i^{0,j} - \boldsymbol{x}_i^{0,1} + \boxed{\boldsymbol{x}_i^{1,1}})$	adt-one-IND of $\mathsf{MCFE^{ot}}$
$\mathsf{G}_{1.k}$	$\mathsf{Enc}(\mathsf{pp}, \mathsf{sk}_i, \boxed{\boldsymbol{x}_i^{1,j} - \boldsymbol{x}_i^{1,1}} + \boldsymbol{x}_i^{1,1})$, for $i \le k$ $\mathsf{Enc}(\mathsf{pp}, \mathsf{sk}_i, \boldsymbol{x}_i^{0,j} - \boldsymbol{x}_i^{0,1} + \boldsymbol{x}_i^{1,1})$, for $i > k$	any-IND of FE
G_2	$\mathsf{Enc}(\mathsf{pp}', \mathsf{sk}_i, \boxed{\boldsymbol{x}_i^{1,j}})$	$\mathsf{G}_2 = \mathsf{G}_{1,n}$

Fig. 10. Overview of the games to prove the security of the MCFE scheme.

adt-pos-IND$_0^{\mathsf{MCFE}}(\lambda, n, \mathcal{A})$ game and G_2 the adt-pos-IND$_1^{\mathsf{MCFE}}(\lambda, n, \mathcal{A})$ game. A description of all the different games can be found in Fig. 10. We denote the winning probability of an adversary $\mathcal{A}$ in a game G_i as $\mathsf{Win}_{\mathcal{A}}^{\mathsf{G}_i}(\lambda, n)$, which is $Pr[\mathsf{G}_i(\lambda, n, \mathcal{A}) = 1]$. The probability is taken over the random coins of G_i and $\mathcal{A}$. The encryption query j on the i-th slot is denoted as $(\boldsymbol{x}_i^{0,j}, \boldsymbol{x}_i^{1,j})$.

We start our proof by considering the games G_0 and G_1.

Lemma 5.5. *For any PPT $\mathcal{A}$, there exists a PPT adversary $\mathcal{B}$ such that*

$$|\mathsf{Win}_{\mathcal{A}}^{\mathsf{G}_0}(\lambda, n) - \mathsf{Win}_{\mathcal{A}}^{\mathsf{G}_1}(\lambda, n)| \leq \mathsf{Adv}_{\mathsf{MCFE}^{\mathsf{ot}},\mathcal{B}}^{\text{adt-one-IND}}(\lambda, n).$$

Proof. Compared to G_0, G_1 replaces the encryptions of $\boldsymbol{x}_i^{0,j} - \boldsymbol{x}_i^{0,1} + \boldsymbol{x}_i^{0,1}$ with the encryptions of $\boldsymbol{x}_i^{0,j} - \boldsymbol{x}_i^{0,1} + \boldsymbol{x}_i^{1,1}$ for all of the slots i under adaptive corruptions. This mirrors directly the distribution of the challenge ciphertexts in G_β.

The adversary $\mathcal{B}$ simulates G_β to $\mathcal{A}$ using the adt-one-IND$_\beta^{\mathsf{MCFE}}$ experiment. In the beginning $\mathcal{B}$ generates the parameters $\mathsf{pp} = (\mathsf{pp}_{\mathsf{si}}, \mathsf{pp}_{\mathsf{ot}}) \leftarrow \mathsf{Setup}(1^\lambda, 1^n)$ and the keys $\mathsf{msk}_i^{\mathsf{si}} \leftarrow \mathsf{KeyGen}(\mathsf{pp}_{\mathsf{si}})$ for all the positions $i \in [n]$. Whenever $\mathcal{A}$ asks a query $\mathsf{QKeyD}'(\boldsymbol{y} = (\boldsymbol{y}_1, \ldots, \boldsymbol{y}_n))$, $\mathcal{B}$ uses its own key derivation oracle to get $\mathsf{dk}_{\boldsymbol{y}} = \sum_{i\in[n]}\langle \boldsymbol{u}_i, \boldsymbol{y}_i\rangle$ and computes the keys $\mathsf{sk}_{i,\boldsymbol{y}} \leftarrow \mathsf{KeyDer}^{\mathsf{si}}(\mathsf{pp}_{\mathsf{si}}, \mathsf{msk}_i^{\mathsf{si}}, \boldsymbol{y}_i)$ for all the positions $i \in [n]$ on its own and sends them to $\mathcal{A}$.

For each position $i \in [n]$, the first encryption query $\mathsf{QEnc}'(i, \boldsymbol{x}_i^{0,1}, \boldsymbol{x}_i^{1,1})$ by $\mathcal{A}$ gets forwarded to the challenger. $\mathcal{B}$ receives $\mathsf{ct}_{i,\mathsf{ot}} = \boldsymbol{u}_i + \boldsymbol{x}_i^{\beta,1}$ as an answer, computes $\mathsf{ct}_i^1 = \mathsf{Enc}^{\mathsf{si}}(\mathsf{pp}_{\mathsf{si}}, \mathsf{msk}_i^{\mathsf{si}}, \boldsymbol{u}_i + \boldsymbol{x}_i^{\beta,1})$, and returns it to $\mathcal{A}$. For all further queries $(j > 1)$, $\mathcal{B}$ produces ct_i^j by encrypting $(\boldsymbol{x}_i^{0,j} - \boldsymbol{x}_i^{0,1} + \mathsf{ct}_{i,\mathsf{ot}}) \bmod L$.

When $\mathcal{A}$ asks a query $\mathsf{QCor}'(i)$, it is necessary that $\boldsymbol{x}_i^{0,j} = \boldsymbol{x}_i^{1,j}$ holds for all the corruption queries that $\mathcal{A}$ has asked before. In this case, $\mathcal{B}$ computes $\boldsymbol{u}_i = \mathsf{ct}_{i,\mathsf{ot}} - \boldsymbol{x}_i^{0,1}$ and sends $(\mathsf{msk}_i^{\mathsf{si}}, \mathsf{mpk}_i^{\mathsf{si}}, \boldsymbol{u}_i)$ to $\mathcal{A}$.

Finally, $\mathcal{B}$ outputs 1, if and only if $\mathcal{A}$ outputs 1. By the reasoning above, we can conclude that:

$$|\mathsf{Win}_{\mathcal{A}}^{\mathsf{G}_0}(\lambda, n) - \mathsf{Win}_{\mathcal{A}}^{\mathsf{G}_1}(\lambda, n)| \leq \mathsf{Adv}_{\mathsf{MCFE}^{\mathsf{ot}},\mathcal{B}}^{\text{adt-one-IND}}(\lambda, n).$$

□

In the next step we consider game G_2. In this game, we change the encryption from $\mathsf{Enc}^{\mathsf{si}}(\mathsf{pp}_{\mathsf{si}}, \mathsf{msk}_i^{\mathsf{si}}, \boldsymbol{x}_i^{0,j} - \boldsymbol{x}_i^{0,1} + \boldsymbol{u}_i + \boldsymbol{x}_i^{1,1})$ to $\mathsf{Enc}^{\mathsf{si}}(\mathsf{pp}_{\mathsf{si}}, \mathsf{msk}_i^{\mathsf{si}}, \boldsymbol{x}_i^{1,j} - \boldsymbol{x}_i^{1,1} + \boldsymbol{u}_i + \boldsymbol{x}_i^{1,1})$ for all slots i and all queries j.

To prove that G_1 is indistinguishable from G_2 we need to apply a hybrid argument over the n slots, using the security of the single input FE scheme.

Using the definition of the games in Fig. 11, we can see that

$$|\mathsf{Win}_{\mathcal{A}}^{\mathsf{G}_1}(\lambda, n) - \mathsf{Win}_{\mathcal{A}}^{\mathsf{G}_2}(\lambda, n)| = \sum_{k=1}^{n} |\mathsf{Win}_{\mathcal{A}}^{\mathsf{G}_{1.k-1}}(\lambda, n) - \mathsf{Win}_{\mathcal{A}}^{\mathsf{G}_{1.k}}(\lambda, n)|,$$

where G_1 corresponds to game $\mathsf{G}_{1.0}$ and whereas G_2 is identical to game $\mathsf{G}_{1.n}$.

Now, we can bound the difference between each consecutive pair of games for every k:

Lemma 5.6. *For every $k \in [n]$, there exists a PPT adversary $\mathcal{B}_k$ against the* any-IND *security of the single-input scheme* FE *such that*

$$|\mathsf{Win}_{\mathcal{A}}^{\mathsf{G}_{1.k-1}}(\lambda, n) - \mathsf{Win}_{\mathcal{A}}^{\mathsf{G}_{1.k}}(\lambda, n)| \leq \mathsf{Adv}_{\mathsf{FE},\mathcal{B}_k}^{\text{any-IND}}(\lambda, n).$$

Proof. $\mathsf{G}_{1.k}$ replaces the encryption of $\boldsymbol{x}_i^{0,j} - \boldsymbol{x}_i^{0,1} + \boldsymbol{x}_i^{1,1}$ with encryptions of $\boldsymbol{x}_i^{1,j} - \boldsymbol{x}_i^{1,1} + \boldsymbol{x}_i^{1,1}$ in all slots, for $i \leq k$. As already described in the preliminaries, it must hold that $\langle \boldsymbol{x}_i^{0,j} - \boldsymbol{x}_i^{0,1}, \boldsymbol{y}_i \rangle = \langle \boldsymbol{x}_i^{1,j} - \boldsymbol{x}_i^{1,1}, \boldsymbol{y}_i \rangle$ for all queries. Hence $\langle \boldsymbol{x}_i^{0,j} - \boldsymbol{x}_i^{0,1} + \boldsymbol{x}_i^{1,1}, \boldsymbol{y}_i \rangle = \langle \boldsymbol{x}_i^{1,j} - \boldsymbol{x}_i^{1,1} + \boldsymbol{x}_i^{1,1}, \boldsymbol{y}_i \rangle$, and since $\|\boldsymbol{x}_i^{0,j} - \boldsymbol{x}_i^{0,1} + \boldsymbol{x}_i^{1,1}\|_\infty < 3X$ and $\|\boldsymbol{x}_i^{1,j} - \boldsymbol{x}_i^{1,1} + \boldsymbol{x}_i^{1,1}\|_\infty < 3X$, using the linear encryption property, we can reduce the difference in the winning probability of an adversary $\mathcal{A}$ in games $\mathsf{G}_{1.k-1}$ and $\mathsf{G}_{1.k}$ to the any-IND security of the single-input scheme FE.

More precisely, we build an adversary $\mathcal{B}_k$ that simulates $\mathsf{G}_{1.k-1+\beta}$ to $\mathcal{A}$ when interacting with the underlying any-$\text{IND}_\beta^{\mathsf{FE}}$ experiment. In the beginning of the reduction, $\mathcal{B}_k$ receives the public parameters from the experiment. The received key from the challenge is set to be $\mathsf{mpk}_k^{\mathsf{si}}$, corresponding to the k-th encryption instance. In the next step, $\mathcal{B}_k$ randomly chooses $\boldsymbol{u}_i \in \mathbb{Z}_L^m$ for all $i \in [n]$ and runs the KeyGen procedure to get $\mathsf{msk}_i^{\mathsf{si}}$ for all $i \neq k$.

Whenever $\mathcal{A}$ asks a query $\mathsf{QKeyD}'(\boldsymbol{y})$, $\mathcal{B}_k$ computes $\mathsf{dk}_y = \sum_{i\in[n]} \langle \boldsymbol{u}_i, \boldsymbol{y}_i \rangle$ on its own and generates $\mathsf{sk}_{i,y} \leftarrow \mathsf{KeyGen}^{\mathsf{si}}(\mathsf{pp}_{\mathsf{si}}, \mathsf{msk}_i^{\mathsf{si}}, \boldsymbol{y}_i)$ for all $i \neq k$. To get the functional key $\mathsf{sk}_{k,\boldsymbol{y}}$, $\mathcal{B}_k$ queries its own key derivation oracle on $\boldsymbol{y}_i$ and outputs $(\{\mathsf{sk}_{i,y}\}_{i\in[n]}, \mathsf{dk}_y)$ to $\mathcal{A}$.

For the encryption queries $\mathsf{QEnc}(i, \boldsymbol{x}_i^{0,j}, \boldsymbol{x}_i^{1,j})$, $\mathcal{B}_k$ proceeds in the following way:

- If $i < k$ it computes $\mathsf{Enc}^{\mathsf{si}}(\mathsf{pp}_{\mathsf{si}}, \mathsf{msk}_i^{\mathsf{si}}, \boldsymbol{u}_i + \boldsymbol{x}_i^{1,j})$.
- If $i > k$ it computes $\mathsf{Enc}^{\mathsf{si}}(\mathsf{pp}_{\mathsf{si}}, \mathsf{msk}_i^{\mathsf{si}}, \boldsymbol{x}_i^{0,j} - \boldsymbol{x}_i^{0,1} + \boldsymbol{u}_i + \boldsymbol{x}_i^{1,1})$.
- If $i = k$, $\mathcal{B}_k$ queries the encryption oracle on input $(\boldsymbol{x}_k^{0,j} - \boldsymbol{x}_k^{0,1} + \boldsymbol{x}_k^{1,1}, \boldsymbol{x}_k^{1,j} - \boldsymbol{x}_k^{1,1} + \boldsymbol{x}_k^{1,1})$ to get back the ciphertext $\mathsf{ct}_*^j := \mathsf{Enc}^{\mathsf{si}}(\mathsf{pp}_{\mathsf{si}}, \mathsf{msk}_k^{\mathsf{si}}, \boldsymbol{x}_k^{\beta,j} - \boldsymbol{x}_k^{\beta,1} + \boldsymbol{x}_k^{1,1})$ from the any-$\text{IND}_\beta^{\mathsf{FE}}$ experiment.[5] Then, $\mathcal{B}_k$ computes the ciphertext $\mathsf{ct}_k^j := \mathsf{Add}(\mathsf{ct}_*^j, \boldsymbol{u}_k)$ and forwards it to $\mathcal{A}$.

As in the security proof of the MIFE scheme in [3], we remark that by the two-step property Definition 5.2, ct_k^j is identically distributed to $\mathsf{Enc}^{\mathsf{si}}(\mathsf{pp}_{\mathsf{si}}, \mathsf{msk}_k^{\mathsf{si}}, \boldsymbol{x}_k^{j,\beta} - \boldsymbol{x}_k^{1,\beta} + \boldsymbol{x}_k^{1,1} + \boldsymbol{u}_k \mod L)$, which is itself equal to $\mathsf{Enc}^{\mathsf{si}}(\mathsf{pp}_{\mathsf{si}}, \mathsf{msk}_k^{\mathsf{si}}, \mathsf{Enc}^{\mathsf{ot}}(\boldsymbol{x}_k^{j,\beta} - \boldsymbol{x}_k^{1,\beta} + \boldsymbol{x}_k^{1,1}))$.

In the case that the adversary $\mathcal{A}$ asks a corruption query $\mathsf{QCor}'(k)$ for position k at any time, the adversary $\mathcal{B}_k$ directly outputs a random value $\alpha \leftarrow \{0, 1\}$. This is due to the fact that, if position k is corrupted, then the games $\mathsf{G}_{1.k-1}$ and $\mathsf{G}_{1.k}$ are identical given that $\boldsymbol{x}_k^{1,0} = \boldsymbol{x}_k^{1,1}$. This results in an advantage equal to 0 and Lemma 5.6 trivially holds in this case.

[5] As in [3], note that these vectors have norm less than $3X$, and as such, are a valid input to the encryption oracle. Furthermore, these queries are allowed, since as explained at the beginning of the proof: it holds that $\langle \boldsymbol{x}_i^{0,j} - \boldsymbol{x}_i^{0,1}, \boldsymbol{y}_i \rangle = \langle \boldsymbol{x}_i^{1,j} - \boldsymbol{x}_i^{1,1}, \boldsymbol{y}_i \rangle$.

$\mathsf{G}_0(1^\lambda, \mathcal{A})$, $\boxed{\mathsf{G}_1(1^\lambda, \mathcal{A})}$, $\mathsf{G}_2(1^\lambda, \mathcal{A})$ (dashed box):

$\mathsf{pp} \leftarrow \mathsf{Setup}(1^\lambda, 1^n)$
$\{\mathsf{sk}_i\}_{i\in[n]} \leftarrow \mathsf{KeyGen}(\mathsf{pp})$
$\alpha \leftarrow \mathcal{A}^{\mathsf{QEnc}'(\cdot,\cdot,\cdot),\mathsf{QKeyD}'(\cdot),\mathsf{QCor}'(\cdot)}(\mathsf{pp})$
Output: α

$\mathsf{QEnc}'(i, \boldsymbol{x}^0, \boldsymbol{x}^1)$
Return $\mathsf{Enc}(\mathsf{pp}, \mathsf{sk}_i, \boldsymbol{x}_i^{0,j} - \boldsymbol{x}_i^{0,1} + \boldsymbol{x}_i^{0,1})$
$\boxed{\text{Return } \mathsf{Enc}(\mathsf{pp}, \mathsf{sk}_i, \boldsymbol{x}_i^{0,j} - \boldsymbol{x}_i^{0,1} + \boldsymbol{x}_i^{1,1})}$
Return $\mathsf{Enc}(\mathsf{pp}, \mathsf{sk}_i, \boldsymbol{x}_i^{1,j} - \boldsymbol{x}_i^{1,1} + \boldsymbol{x}_i^{1,1})$ (dashed box)

$\mathsf{QKeyD}'(\boldsymbol{y})$
$\mathsf{dk}_{\boldsymbol{y}} = \sum_{i\in[n]} \langle \boldsymbol{u}_i, \boldsymbol{y}_i \rangle$,
For $i \in [n]$,
$\mathsf{sk}_{i,\boldsymbol{y}} \leftarrow \mathsf{KeyDer}^{\mathsf{si}}(\mathsf{pp}, \mathsf{msk}_i^{\mathsf{si}}, \boldsymbol{y}_i)$
Return $(\{\mathsf{sk}_{i,\boldsymbol{y}}\}_{i\in[n]}, \mathsf{dk}_{\boldsymbol{y}})$

$\mathsf{G}_{1.k}(1^\lambda, \mathcal{A})$:

$\mathsf{pp} \leftarrow \mathsf{Setup}(1^\lambda, 1^n)$
$\{\mathsf{sk}_i\}_{i\in[n]} \leftarrow \mathsf{KeyGen}(\mathsf{pp})$
$\alpha \leftarrow \mathcal{A}^{\mathsf{QEnc}'(\cdot,\cdot,\cdot),\mathsf{QKeyD}'(\cdot),\mathsf{QCor}'(\cdot)}(\mathsf{pp})$
Output: α

$\mathsf{QEnc}'(i, \boldsymbol{x}^0, \boldsymbol{x}^1)$
If $i \leq k$ return
$\mathsf{Enc}(\mathsf{pp}, \mathsf{sk}_i, \boldsymbol{x}_i^{1,j} - \boldsymbol{x}_i^{1,1} + \boldsymbol{x}_i^{1,1})$
If $i > k$ return
$\mathsf{Enc}(\mathsf{pp}, \mathsf{sk}_i, \boldsymbol{x}_i^{0,j} - \boldsymbol{x}_i^{0,1} + \boldsymbol{x}_i^{1,1})$

$\mathsf{QKeyD}'(\boldsymbol{y})$
$\mathsf{dk}_{\boldsymbol{y}} = \sum_{i\in[n]} \langle \boldsymbol{u}_i, \boldsymbol{y}_i \rangle$,
For $i \in [n]$,
$\mathsf{sk}_{i,\boldsymbol{y}} \leftarrow \mathsf{KeyDer}^{\mathsf{si}}(\mathsf{pp}, \mathsf{msk}_i^{\mathsf{si}}, \boldsymbol{y}_i)$
Return $(\{\mathsf{sk}_{i,\boldsymbol{y}}\}_{i\in[n]}, \mathsf{dk}_{\boldsymbol{y}})$

Fig. 11. A more detailed description of how the games work.

In the case that the adversary $\mathcal{A}$ asks a corruption query $\mathsf{QCor}'(i)$ for $i \neq k$, $\mathcal{B}_k$ simply returns $(\mathsf{msk}_i^{\mathsf{si}}, \boldsymbol{u}_i)$ to $\mathcal{A}$.

This covers the simulation of the game $\mathsf{G}_{1.k-1+\beta}$. Finally, $\mathcal{B}_k$ outputs the same bit β' returned by $\mathcal{A}$:

$$|\mathsf{Win}_{\mathcal{A}}^{\mathsf{G}_{1.k-1}}(\lambda, n) - \mathsf{Win}_{\mathcal{A}}^{\mathsf{G}_{1.k}}(\lambda, n)| \leq \mathsf{Adv}_{\mathsf{FE},\mathcal{B}_k}^{\text{any-IND}}(\lambda, n).$$

□

The proof of theorem follows by combining the statements in Lemmas 5.5 and 5.6 and noticing that the adversary $\mathcal{B}'$ in the theorem statement can be obtained by picking $i \in [n]$ and running $\mathcal{B}_i$. The standard details are omitted here. □

Acknowledgments. This work was supported in part by the European Union's Horizon 2020 Research and Innovation Programme under grant agreement 780108 (FENTEC), by the ERC Project aSCEND (H2020 639554), by the French *Programme d'Investissement d'Avenir* under national project RISQ P141580, and by the French FUI project ANBLIC.

References

1. Abdalla, M., Benhamouda, F., Kolhweiss, M., Waldner, H.: Decentralizing inner-product functional encryption. Cryptology ePrint Archive, Report 2019/020 (2019). http://eprint.iacr.org/2019/020
2. Abdalla, M., Bourse, F., De Caro, A., Pointcheval, D.: Simple functional encryption schemes for inner products. In: Katz, J. (ed.) PKC 2015. LNCS, vol. 9020, pp. 733–751. Springer, Heidelberg (2015). https://doi.org/10.1007/978-3-662-46447-2_33
3. Abdalla, M., Catalano, D., Fiore, D., Gay, R., Ursu, B.: Multi-input functional encryption for inner products: function-hiding realizations and constructions without pairings. In: Shacham, H., Boldyreva, A. (eds.) CRYPTO 2018, Part I. LNCS, vol. 10991, pp. 597–627. Springer, Cham (2018). https://doi.org/10.1007/978-3-319-96884-1_20
4. Abdalla, M., Gay, R., Raykova, M., Wee, H.: Multi-input inner-product functional encryption from pairings. In: Coron, J.-S., Nielsen, J.B. (eds.) EUROCRYPT 2017, Part I. LNCS, vol. 10210, pp. 601–626. Springer, Cham (2017). https://doi.org/10.1007/978-3-319-56620-7_21
5. Agrawal, S., Libert, B., Stehlé, D.: Fully secure functional encryption for inner products, from standard assumptions. In: Robshaw, M., Katz, J. (eds.) CRYPTO 2016, Part III. LNCS, vol. 9816, pp. 333–362. Springer, Heidelberg (2016). https://doi.org/10.1007/978-3-662-53015-3_12
6. Ananth, P., Jain, A.: Indistinguishability obfuscation from compact functional encryption. In: Gennaro, R., Robshaw, M.J.B. (eds.) CRYPTO 2015, Part I. LNCS, vol. 9215, pp. 308–326. Springer, Heidelberg (2015). https://doi.org/10.1007/978-3-662-47989-6_15
7. Badrinarayanan, S., Gupta, D., Jain, A., Sahai, A.: Multi-input functional encryption for unbounded arity functions. In: Iwata, T., Cheon, J.H. (eds.) ASIACRYPT 2015, Part I. LNCS, vol. 9452, pp. 27–51. Springer, Heidelberg (2015). https://doi.org/10.1007/978-3-662-48797-6_2
8. Baltico, C.E.Z., Catalano, D., Fiore, D., Gay, R.: Practical functional encryption for quadratic functions with applications to predicate encryption. In: Katz, J., Shacham, H. (eds.) CRYPTO 2017, Part I. LNCS, vol. 10401, pp. 67–98. Springer, Cham (2017). https://doi.org/10.1007/978-3-319-63688-7_3
9. Bellare, M., Desai, A., Jokipii, E., Rogaway, P.: A concrete security treatment of symmetric encryption. In: 38th FOCS, pp. 394–403. IEEE Computer Society Press, October 1997. https://doi.org/10.1109/SFCS.1997.646128
10. Benhamouda, F., Joye, M., Libert, B.: A new framework for privacy-preserving aggregation of time-series data. ACM Trans. Inf. Syst. Secur. **18**(3), 101–1021 (2016). https://doi.org/10.1145/2873069
11. Bishop, A., Jain, A., Kowalczyk, L.: Function-hiding inner product encryption. In: Iwata, T., Cheon, J.H. (eds.) ASIACRYPT 2015, Part I. LNCS, vol. 9452, pp. 470–491. Springer, Heidelberg (2015). https://doi.org/10.1007/978-3-662-48797-6_20
12. Boneh, D., Sahai, A., Waters, B.: Functional encryption: definitions and challenges. In: Ishai, Y. (ed.) TCC 2011. LNCS, vol. 6597, pp. 253–273. Springer, Heidelberg (2011). https://doi.org/10.1007/978-3-642-19571-6_16
13. Brakerski, Z., Komargodski, I., Segev, G.: Multi-input functional encryption in the private-key setting: stronger security from weaker assumptions. J. Cryptol. **31**(2), 434–520 (2018). https://doi.org/10.1007/s00145-017-9261-0

14. Chan, T.-H.H., Shi, E., Song, D.: Privacy-preserving stream aggregation with fault tolerance. In: Keromytis, A.D. (ed.) FC 2012. LNCS, vol. 7397, pp. 200–214. Springer, Heidelberg (2012). https://doi.org/10.1007/978-3-642-32946-3_15
15. Chotard, J., Dufour Sans, E., Gay, R., Phan, D.H., Pointcheval, D.: Decentralized multi-client functional encryption for inner product. In: Peyrin, T., Galbraith, S. (eds.) ASIACRYPT 2018, Part II. LNCS, vol. 11273, pp. 703–732. Springer, Cham (2018). https://doi.org/10.1007/978-3-030-03329-3_24
16. Chotard, J., Dufour Sans, E., Gay, R., Phan, D.H., Pointcheval, D.: Multi-client functional encryption with repetition for inner product. Cryptology ePrint Archive, Report 2018/1021 (2018). http://eprint.iacr.org/2018/1021
17. Datta, P., Dutta, R., Mukhopadhyay, S.: Functional encryption for inner product with full function privacy. In: Cheng, C.-M., Chung, K.-M., Persiano, G., Yang, B.-Y. (eds.) PKC 2016, Part I. LNCS, vol. 9614, pp. 164–195. Springer, Heidelberg (2016). https://doi.org/10.1007/978-3-662-49384-7_7
18. Emura, K.: Privacy-preserving aggregation of time-series data with public verifiability from simple assumptions. In: Pieprzyk, J., Suriadi, S. (eds.) ACISP 2017. LNCS, vol. 10343, pp. 193–213. Springer, Cham (2017). https://doi.org/10.1007/978-3-319-59870-3_11
19. Fan, X., Tang, Q.: Making public key functional encryption function private, distributively. In: Abdalla, M., Dahab, R. (eds.) PKC 2018, Part II. LNCS, vol. 10770, pp. 218–244. Springer, Cham (2018). https://doi.org/10.1007/978-3-319-76581-5_8
20. Goldwasser, S., et al.: Multi-input functional encryption. In: Nguyen, P.Q., Oswald, E. (eds.) EUROCRYPT 2014. LNCS, vol. 8441, pp. 578–602. Springer, Heidelberg (2014). https://doi.org/10.1007/978-3-642-55220-5_32
21. Joye, M., Libert, B.: A scalable scheme for privacy-preserving aggregation of time-series data. In: Sadeghi, A.-R. (ed.) FC 2013. LNCS, vol. 7859, pp. 111–125. Springer, Heidelberg (2013). https://doi.org/10.1007/978-3-642-39884-1_10
22. Li, Q., Cao, G.: Efficient and privacy-preserving data aggregation in mobile sensing. In: 20th IEEE International Conference on Network Protocols, ICNP, pp. 1–10. IEEE Computer Society, Austin (2012). https://doi.org/10.1109/ICNP.2012.6459985
23. O'Neill, A.: Definitional issues in functional encryption. Cryptology ePrint Archive, Report 2010/556 (2010). http://eprint.iacr.org/2010/556
24. Sahai, A., Waters, B.R.: Fuzzy identity-based encryption. In: Cramer, R. (ed.) EUROCRYPT 2005. LNCS, vol. 3494, pp. 457–473. Springer, Heidelberg (2005). https://doi.org/10.1007/11426639_27
25. Shi, E., Chan, T.H.H., Rieffel, E.G., Chow, R., Song, D.: Privacy-preserving aggregation of time-series data. In: NDSS 2011. The Internet Society, February 2011

Non-zero Inner Product Encryption Schemes from Various Assumptions: LWE, DDH and DCR

Shuichi Katsumata[1,2](✉) and Shota Yamada[2]

[1] The University of Tokyo, Tokyo, Japan
shuichi_katsumata@it.k.u-tokyo.ac.jp
[2] National Institute of Advanced Industrial Science and Technology (AIST), Tokyo, Japan
yamada-shota@aist.go.jp

Abstract. In non-zero inner product encryption (NIPE) schemes, ciphertexts and secret keys are associated with vectors and decryption is possible whenever the inner product of these vectors does *not* equal zero. So far, much effort on constructing bilinear map-based NIPE schemes have been made and this has lead to many efficient schemes. However, the constructions of NIPE schemes without bilinear maps are much less investigated. The only known other NIPE constructions are based on lattices, however, they are all highly inefficient due to the need of converting inner product operations into circuits or branching programs.

To remedy our rather poor understanding regarding NIPE schemes without bilinear maps, we provide two methods for constructing NIPE schemes: a direct construction from lattices and a generic construction from schemes for inner products (LinFE). For our first direct construction, it highly departs from the traditional lattice-based constructions and we rely heavily on new tools concerning Gaussian measures over *multi-dimensional lattices* to prove security. For our second generic construction, using the recent constructions of LinFE schemes as building blocks, we obtain the first NIPE constructions based on the DDH and DCR assumptions. In particular, we obtain the first NIPE schemes *without* bilinear maps or lattices.

1 Introduction

1.1 Background

An attribute-based encryption (ABE) scheme is an advanced form of public key encryption where an access control over encrypted data is possible. In an ABE scheme, a ciphertext and a secret key are associated with attributes X and Y, respectively, and the decryption is possible only when they satisfy $R(X, Y) = 1$ for a certain relation R. The concept of ABE was first proposed by Sahai and Waters [SW05]. Since then, many study followed in order to

D. Lin and K. Sako (Eds.): PKC 2019, LNCS 11443, pp. 158–188, 2019.
https://doi.org/10.1007/978-3-030-17259-6_6

improve the scheme in many aspects: security [LOS+10,OT10], expressibility [GPSW06,LW11,GVW13], and efficiency [ALDP11]. While the early constructions of ABE schemes are based on bilinear maps, some of the more recent schemes are based on lattices.

In this paper, we focus on a special form of an ABE scheme called non-zero inner product encryption (NIPE) scheme. In an NIPE scheme, a ciphertext attribute is a vector $\boldsymbol{x}$ and a secret key attribute is a vector $\boldsymbol{y}$, and the relation is defined as $R(\boldsymbol{x}, \boldsymbol{y}) = 1$ iff $\langle \boldsymbol{x}, \boldsymbol{y} \rangle \neq 0$. The notion of NIPE was first introduced in [KSW08]. It was not until Attrapadung and Libert [AL10] who gave the direct first construction of an NIPE scheme using bilinear maps.[1] In their work, they provided interesting applications of NIPE schemes such as identity-based revocation (IBR) schemes, where an IBR scheme is a type of broadcast encryption scheme that allows for efficient revocation of small member size. Since then, many efficient NIPE schemes have been proposed [AL10,ALDP11,OT10,OT15], [YAHK14,CW14,CLR16]. They are all based on number theoretic assumptions on bilinear maps.

On the other hand, the constructions of NIPE schemes without bilinear maps are much less investigated. The only known other constructions are based on lattices. However, unlike in the bilinear map setting, we do not know of any direct constructions of a NIPE scheme in the lattice setting. In more detail, we have ABE schemes for any circuit (i.e. the relation R being general circuits) [GVW13,BGG+14] and any branching programs [GVW13,GV15] from the learning with errors (LWE) assumption. Here, the expressibility of the latter constructions are more limited, however, these schemes can be proven secure under the LWE assumption with polynomial approximation factors unlike the former schemes that require sub-exponential approximation factors, i.e., the required hardness assumption is much weaker. Although we have two lines of works that allow us to indirectly construct lattice-based NIPE schemes, they are both highly inefficient. In particular, we can use the former constructions from circuits to implement an NIPE scheme, however, this would require us to express the computation of the non-zero inner product predicates as a circuit, which would result in a highly inefficient scheme. Furthermore, it would require us to base security on a sub-exponential LWE assumption, which is not desirable both from the efficiency and security stand points. Alternatively, we can use the latter construction for branching programs. To do so, we would first represent the non-zero inner product predicate as an NC^1 circuit, which is possible because arithmetic operations are known to be in NC^1 [BCH86], and then convert it into a branching program using the Barrington's theorem. Using [GVW13] or [GV15], the construction by this approach enjoys security from the standard polynomial LWE assumption. However, the approach is still highly inefficient due to the large overhead incurred by the invocation of the Barrington's theorem [Bar89].

[1] We note that Goyal et al. [GPSW06] propose an ABE scheme for $\mathbf{NC}^1$ circuit, which in turn implies a NIPE scheme, since the computation of inner products can be performed in $\mathbf{NC}^1$. However, the resulting construction is highly inefficient.

More on NIPEs. Although NIPE schemes allows us to construct other cryptographic primitives such as IBR schemes as explained above, it may be more helpful to understand the usefulness of the primitive through its "negating" feature. As the name suggests, NIPE scheme is the counterpart of inner-product encryption (IPE) schemes. It is well known that IPE schemes can be used to construct functional encryption schemes that can handle many practical predicates such as polynomial evaluations, disjunction and/or conjunctions of equality tests, membership tests and so on (for concrete applications see for example [BW07,KSW08]). In brief, NIPE schemes are primitives that can handle the exact opposite of all these predicates. Due to its usefulness in practice, negated policies in the area of ABE have been highlighted in prior works [OSW07,AL10,ABS17].

Furthermore, aside from its practical interest, NIPE schemes are theoretically interesting in its own right, since as we show as one of our results, NIPE schemes can be constructed from much weaker assumptions than one would expect. In particular, we construct NIPE schemes from the DDH or DCR assumption, where it currently seems that stronger assumptions such as the DBDH or DLIN assumption is required to construct its counterpart—IPE schemes. Therefore, although an NIPE scheme may be simply understood as an IPE scheme in the opposite flavor, our result indicates a distinct gap between the two primitives when it comes to concrete constructions. Considering the recent breakthrough in constructing identity-based encryption schemes [DG17] and functional encryption schemes for inner products [ABDCP15,ALS16] from weak assumptions, we hope our work to spark interest to finding the minimum assumption for other ABE-related primitives.

1.2 Our Contributions

To remedy our rather poor understanding regarding NIPE schemes without bilinear maps, we provide two methods for constructing NIPE schemes: a direct construction from lattices and a generic construction from functional encryption schemes for inner products (LinFE)[2]. For the first direct lattice-based approach, we propose two NIPE constructions where the differences lie in where the inner products between attribute and predicate vectors are taken. The first scheme is over $\mathbb{Z}$ whereas the second scheme is over $\mathbb{Z}_p$. For the second generic approach, we show how to generically construct NIPE schemes from any LinFE scheme. In particular, we can use the recent works of [ABDCP15,ALS16] to instantiate various types of NIPE schemes. Concretely, since [ALS16] provides us with LinFE schemes from the LWE assumption, the DDH assumption and the DCR assumption, we obtain NIPE schemes secure under all of these assumptions. Notably, we obtain the first NIPE constructions *without* bilinear maps or lattices.

We give a brief overview on the properties that our NIPE schemes satisfy. As for the first direct approach, we obtain two NIPE schemes with different properties: a selectively secure *stateless* NIPE scheme over $\mathbb{Z}$ and a selectively secure

[2] The term LinFE is borrowed from [ALS16]. It is named as such, since it is a special type of functional encryption scheme restricted to the class of linear functions.

stateful NIPE scheme over $\mathbb{Z}_p$. As for the second generic approach, by using the LinFE schemes provided in [ALS16], which subsumes the work of [ABDCP15], we obtain an adaptively secure *stateless* or *stateful* NIPE scheme over $\mathbb{Z}$ or $\mathbb{Z}_p$, depending on what we use as the underlying LinFE scheme. The main advantage of the first approach is that it leads to a more efficient NIPE scheme in the amortized sense compared with the second approach instantiated with a lattice-based LinFE scheme. In more detail, to encrypt a message of ℓ_M-bit length, the first approach requires $(\ell_M + m + m\ell)$ elements of $\mathbb{Z}_q$ in a ciphertext and the second requires $(m + \ell)\ell_M$. Here, ℓ is the dimension of the predicate vectors in the NIPE scheme and q and m are the modulus size and the number of columns of the LWE matrix involved in the scheme, respectively. The first approach is more efficient than the second one when we encrypt more than $m\ell/(m + \ell)$ bits at once. For a natural setting of $\ell < m, \lambda$ where λ is the security parameter, this encompasses the most interesting case of KEM-DEM settings where one encrypts λ bits of session key. In fact, when we are in the ring setting, since m is $O(\log \lambda)$, the first approach will be more efficient regardless of the size ℓ. Furthermore, for NIPE schemes over $\mathbb{Z}_p$, the first approach would require smaller LWE modulus. Indeed, in certain regime of parameters such as $\ell = \log n / \log\log\log n$ and $p = \log\log n$, the first approach would yield a scheme with polynomial modulus whereas the second requires super-polynomial modulus. However, on the other hand, the advantage of the second approach is that it achieves adaptive security and allows us to instantiate the NIPE scheme with different types of hardness assumptions such as the DDH and DCR assumptions. Below, we give an outline of the techniques we used for constructing our lattice-based NIPE schemes and the generic construction of NIPE schemes from LinFE. We believe the techniques we utilized for the lattice-based direct NIPE construction to be of independent interest.

Lattice-Based Constructions. We propose two NIPE schemes built directly from lattices. At a high level, our two NIPE constructions share many similarities; both constructions highly depart from the previous lattice-based ABE constructions [GVW13, BGG+14, GV15] and they rely heavily on the tools of Gaussian measures over *multi-dimensional lattices* during the security proof. Notably, for both of our constructions: a trapdoor $\mathbf{T}_\mathbf{A} \in \mathbb{Z}^{m \times m}$ for the public matrix $\mathbf{A} \in \mathbb{Z}_q^{n \times m}$ is not required, a secret key for a user is simply a linear combination of the master secret keys, and the algorithm $\mathsf{SampleRight}$ of [ABB10] is used during decryption. To the knowledgeable readers of lattice-based cryptography, this may seem somewhat peculiar, since $\mathsf{SampleRight}$ is an algorithm that customary appears in the security proof for allowing the simulator to sample a short vector $\mathbf{e}$ such that $[\mathbf{A}|\mathbf{B}]\mathbf{e} = \mathbf{u}$ without knowledge of the trapdoor of $\mathbf{A}$, in case $\mathbf{B}$ is in the special form $\mathbf{AR} + t \cdot \mathbf{G} \mod q$, where $t \in \mathbb{Z}_q$ is some invertible element and $\mathbf{G}$ [MP12] is a special matrix with a publicly known trapdoor $\mathbf{T}_\mathbf{G}$.

Below we sketch our construction. We set the master public key MPK and the master secret key MSK as follows:

$$\mathsf{MPK} = (\mathbf{A}, \mathbf{B}_1, \cdots, \mathbf{B}_\ell, \mathbf{u}) \quad \text{and} \quad \mathsf{MSK} = (\mathbf{R}_1, \cdots, \mathbf{R}_\ell),$$

where ℓ denotes the dimension of the vectors, $\{\mathbf{R}_i\}_{i\in[\ell]}$ are random matrices whose columns are sampled from the discrete Gaussian distribution and $\mathbf{B}_i = \mathbf{A}\mathbf{R}_i \mod q$. In the following, we focus on the overview of our first NIPE scheme with inner product space $\mathbb{Z}$. Although the high level construction is the same for our second NIPE scheme with inner product space $\mathbb{Z}_p$, we require some additional technicalities during key generation, which we describe later.

Given the master secret key MSK, our secret key generation algorithm is very simple and does not require any Gaussian sampling as in prior works. Concretely, given a predicate vector $\boldsymbol{y} = (y_1, \cdots, y_\ell) \in \mathbb{Z}^\ell$, we simply return $\mathbf{R}_{\boldsymbol{y}} = \sum_{i=1}^{\ell} y_i \mathbf{R}_i \in \mathbb{Z}^{m\times m}$ as the secret key. To embed an attribute vector $\boldsymbol{x} = (x_1, \cdots, x_\ell) \in \mathbb{Z}^\ell$ into the ciphertext, we use the techniques of [AFV11,BGG+14], and create vectors $\{\mathbf{c}_i = \mathbf{s}^\top(\mathbf{B}_i + x_i \cdot \mathbf{G}) + \mathbf{z}_i\}_{i\in[\ell]}$ along with $\mathbf{c}_0 = \mathbf{s}^\top\mathbf{A} + \mathbf{z}_0$. Here, $\mathbf{s}$ is a randomly sampled vector in $\mathbb{Z}_q^n$ and $\{\mathbf{z}_i\}_{i\in[0,\ell]}$ are short vectors in $\mathbb{Z}^m$ sampled from a particular discrete Gaussian distribution. Then, for decryption, a user with predicate vector $\boldsymbol{y}$ computes the following:

$$\sum_{i=1}^{\ell} y_i \cdot \mathbf{c}_i = \mathbf{s}^\top(\sum_{i=1}^{\ell} y_i \mathbf{B}_i + \langle \boldsymbol{x}, \boldsymbol{y}\rangle \cdot \mathbf{G}) + \mathsf{noise} = \mathbf{s}^\top(\mathbf{A}\mathbf{R}_{\boldsymbol{y}} + \langle \boldsymbol{x}, \boldsymbol{y}\rangle \cdot \mathbf{G}) + \mathsf{noise}.$$

Therefore, if $\langle \boldsymbol{x}, \boldsymbol{y}\rangle \neq 0$ (over $\mathbb{Z}$), we can use the algorithm $\mathsf{SampleRight}$ to sample a short vector $\mathbf{e} \in \mathbb{Z}^{2m}$ such that $[\mathbf{A}|\mathbf{A}\mathbf{R}_{\boldsymbol{y}} + \langle \boldsymbol{x}, \boldsymbol{y}\rangle \cdot \mathbf{G}]\mathbf{e} = \mathbf{u} \mod q$. Here, to take care of the subtle problem that $\langle \boldsymbol{x}, \boldsymbol{y}\rangle$ has to be invertible over $\mathbb{Z}_q$, we require the attribute and predicate vectors to be in some restricted domains.

However, despite the simplicity of our construction, the security proof requires a rather sensitive and technical analysis that calls for new techniques. In particular, building upon the prior works of [BF11], we prepare new tools concerning Gaussian measures over *mulit-dimensional lattices*, which we believe to be of independent interest. Using these tools, we are able to provide a rigorous treatment on the distribution of the secret keys $\mathbf{R}_{\boldsymbol{y}}$ of the real world and the simulated world. In more detail, given a challenge attribute $\boldsymbol{x}^* \in \mathbb{Z}^\ell$ at the outset of the game, the simulator samples random matrices $\{\mathbf{R}_i^{\mathsf{SIM}}\}_{i\in[\ell]}$ as in the real world and sets the public matrices $\mathbf{B}_i$ as $\mathbf{A}\mathbf{R}_i^{\mathsf{SIM}} - x_i^* \cdot \mathbf{G}$. We answer the secret key queries as in the real world, i.e., given a predicate vector $\boldsymbol{y} = (y_1, \cdots, y_\ell) \in \mathbb{Z}^\ell$, we simply return $\mathbf{R}_{\boldsymbol{y}}^{\mathsf{SIM}} = \sum_{i=1}^{\ell} y_i \mathbf{R}_i^{\mathsf{SIM}} \in \mathbb{Z}^{m\times m}$. At first glance this seems completely insecure, since an adversary may query $\boldsymbol{y} = (1, 0, \cdots, 0) \in \mathbb{Z}^\ell$ and recover $\mathbf{R}_1$ or $\mathbf{R}_1^{\mathsf{SIM}}$ depending on which world it is in. Then, the adversary can check whether $\mathbf{B}_1 = \mathbf{A}\mathbf{R}_1$ or $\mathbf{B}_1 = \mathbf{A}\mathbf{R}_1^{\mathsf{SIM}} - x_1^* \cdot \mathbf{G}$ to distinguish between the real world and the simulated world. However, this seemingly acute tactic cannot be used to attack our NIPE scheme. The main observation is that, if $\boldsymbol{y} = (1, 0, \cdots, 0) \in \mathbb{Z}^\ell$ is a valid predicate for the key extraction query, then we must have $\langle \boldsymbol{x}^*, \boldsymbol{y}\rangle = 0$, or in other words $x_1^* y_1 = x_1^* = 0$. Therefore, since $\mathbf{R}_1$ and $\mathbf{R}_1^{\mathsf{SIM}}$ are distributed statistically close, the above attack cannot be used to distinguish between the two worlds. Our security analysis builds on this idea and proves that the distribution of the secret keys the adversary obtains in the two worlds $\{\mathbf{R}_{\boldsymbol{y}^{(j)}}\}_{j\in[Q]}$ and $\{\mathbf{R}_{\boldsymbol{y}^{(j)}}^{\mathsf{SIM}}\}_{j\in[Q]}$ are indeed statistically indistinguishable.

The main technical contribution is developing new tools for Gaussian measures over multi-dimensional lattices, and analyzing the (set of) linear combinations of Gaussian distributions $\{\mathbf{R}_{\boldsymbol{y}^{(j)}} = \sum_{i=1}^{\ell} y_i^{(j)} \mathbf{R}_i\}_{j\in[Q]}$.

Finally, we briefly note on the aforementioned technical issue that arises for our second NIPE construction with inner product space $\mathbb{Z}_p$. Notably, we require our NIPE scheme to be *stateful.* This is similar to an issue that came up in the works of [ALS16] for their LinFE scheme over $\mathbb{Z}_p$. Unlike in the NIPE construction with inner product space $\mathbb{Z}$, the linear dependency of the predicate vectors $\boldsymbol{y} \in \mathbb{Z}_p^{\ell}$ and the secret keys $\mathbf{R}_{\boldsymbol{y}} \in \mathbb{Z}^{m\times m}$ are no longer consistent. In other words, even when an adversary queries for secret keys corresponding to predicate vectors that are linearly dependent over $\mathbb{Z}_p$, the corresponding secret keys may no longer be linearly dependent over $\mathbb{Z}$. Therefore, the adversary can recover the full master secret key $\{\mathbf{R}_i\}_{i\in[\ell]}$ by querying the right predicate vectors. To prevent this from happening, we make the key generation algorithm stateful and pay special attention so as not to give out linearly independent secret keys for linearly dependent predicate vectors. In addition, we also specify how to maintain the state in a clever way. This is because the representation of the state has a direct effect on the required LWE assumption, and if we maintain the state naively, we would have to base our security on the subexponential LWE assumption.

Generic Construction from LinFE. Besides the direct constructions from lattices, we also propose a generic construction of a NIPE scheme from a LinFE scheme. The idea for the generic conversion is inspired by the works of [ABP+17] and is surprisingly simple. To explain the idea, let us first recall that in a LinFE scheme, a ciphertext and a private key are associated with vectors $\boldsymbol{x}$ and $\boldsymbol{y}$, and when we decrypt the ciphertext using the private key, we recover $\langle \boldsymbol{x}, \boldsymbol{y} \rangle$. Given a LinFE scheme, we construct a NIPE scheme as follows. To encrypt a message M for a vector $\boldsymbol{x}$, we encrypt a vector $\mathsf{M} \cdot \boldsymbol{x}$ using the underlying LinFE scheme to obtain a ciphertext. A private key for a vector $\boldsymbol{y}$ in the NIPE scheme is exactly the same as a private key for $\boldsymbol{y}$ in the underlying LinFE scheme. Observe that when we decrypt the ciphertext using the private key, we recover $\langle \mathsf{M} \cdot \boldsymbol{x}, \boldsymbol{y} \rangle = \mathsf{M} \cdot \langle \boldsymbol{x}, \boldsymbol{y} \rangle$. This value corresponds to 0 when $\langle \boldsymbol{x}, \boldsymbol{y} \rangle = 0$ regardless of the value of the message. On the other hand, when $\boldsymbol{x}$ and $\boldsymbol{y}$ are known, M can be recovered by computing $\mathsf{M} \cdot \langle \boldsymbol{x}, \boldsymbol{y} \rangle / \langle \boldsymbol{x}, \boldsymbol{y} \rangle = \mathsf{M}$. That is, the message is recovered if and only if $\langle \boldsymbol{x}, \boldsymbol{y} \rangle \neq 0$. Indeed, this functionality exactly matches that of NIPE schemes.

While the idea is very simple, it leads to interesting consequences. By applying our LinFE-to-NIPE conversion to existing LinFE constructions [ABDCP15, ALS16], we obtain several new NIPE schemes. Notably, we obtain the first NIPE constructions from the DDH and DCR assumptions. In other words, we obtain NIPE constructions without relying on bilinear maps or lattices. This result may be somewhat surprising, since we do not know any other similar primitives to inner product encryption (IPE)[3] schemes that can be constructed without bilinear maps or lattices. In particular, it was not until recently for even a simple primitive such as an identity-based encryption scheme (in the standard model) to be constructed without relying on bilinear maps or lattices [DG17]. Therefore, our result indicates that NIPE schemes may be a primitive quite different from other ABE type primitives in nature.

2 Preliminaries

2.1 Non-zero Inner Product Encryption

Syntax. Let $\mathcal{P}$ and $\mathcal{I}$ denote the predicate space and attribute space, where the inner product between elements (i.e., vectors) from $\mathcal{P}$ and $\mathcal{I}$ are well-defined. Furthermore, let $\mathcal{S}$ denote the space where the inner product is taken. A *stateful* non-zero inner product encryption (NIPE) scheme over $\mathcal{S}$ consists of the following four algorithms:

$\mathsf{Setup}(1^\lambda, 1^\ell) \to (\mathsf{MPK}, \mathsf{MSK}, \mathsf{st})$: The setup algorithm takes as input a security parameter 1^λ and the length ℓ of the vectors in the predicate and attribute spaces, and outputs a master public key MPK, a master secret key MSK and an initial state st.

$\mathsf{KeyGen}(\mathsf{MPK}, \mathsf{MSK}, \mathsf{st}, \boldsymbol{y}) \to (\mathsf{sk}_{\boldsymbol{y}}, \mathsf{st})$: The key generation algorithm takes as input the master public key MPK, the master secret key MSK, the state st and a predicate vector $\boldsymbol{y} \in \mathcal{P}$. It outputs a private key $\mathsf{sk}_{\boldsymbol{y}}$ and a updated state st. We assume that $\boldsymbol{y}$ is implicitly included in $\mathsf{sk}_{\boldsymbol{y}}$.

$\mathsf{Encrypt}(\mathsf{MPK}, \boldsymbol{x}, \mathsf{M}) \to C$: The encryption algorithm takes as input a master public key MPK, an attribute vector $\boldsymbol{x} \in \mathcal{I}$ and a message$\mathsf{M}$. It outputs a ciphertext C.

$\mathsf{Decrypt}(\mathsf{MPK}, \mathsf{sk}_{\boldsymbol{y}}, (\boldsymbol{x}, C)) \to \mathsf{M}$ or $\bot$: The decryption algorithm takes as input the master public key MPK, a private key $\mathsf{sk}_{\boldsymbol{y}}$, and a ciphertext C with an associating attribute vector $\boldsymbol{x}$. It outputs the message M or $\bot$, which means that the ciphertext is not in a valid form.

Correctness. We require correctness of decryption: that is, for all $\lambda, \ell \in \mathbb{N}$, all $\boldsymbol{x} \in \mathcal{I}, \boldsymbol{y} \in \mathcal{P}$, and all M in the specified message space, the following holds:

- if $\langle \boldsymbol{x}, \boldsymbol{y} \rangle \neq 0$, then $\Pr[\mathsf{Dec}(\mathsf{MPK}, \mathsf{sk}_{\boldsymbol{y}}, \mathsf{Enc}(\mathsf{MPK}, \boldsymbol{x}, \mathsf{M})) = \mathsf{M}] = 1 - \mathsf{negl}(\lambda)$
- if $\langle \boldsymbol{x}, \boldsymbol{y} \rangle = 0$, then $\Pr[\mathsf{Dec}(\mathsf{MPK}, \mathsf{sk}_{\boldsymbol{y}}, \mathsf{Enc}(\mathsf{MPK}, \boldsymbol{x}, \mathsf{M})) = \bot] = 1 - \mathsf{negl}(\lambda)$,

where the inner products are taken over $\mathcal{S}$ and the probability is taken over the randomness used in all the algorithms.

[3] IPE is a special kind of ABE where decryption is possible iff the inner product of the vectors corresponding to a ciphertext and a private key is 0. This should not be confused with LinFE, where the decryption is always possible and the decryption result is the inner product itself.

We also define a *stateless* non-zero inner product encryption, where we do not require any state information in the above algorithms.

Security. We define the security of a (stateful) NIPE scheme over $\mathcal{S}$ with predicate space $\mathcal{P}$ and attribute space $\mathcal{I}$ by the following game between a challenger and an adversary $\mathcal{A}$.

- Setup. At the outset of the game, the challenger runs $(\mathsf{MPK}, \mathsf{MSK}, \mathsf{st}) \leftarrow \mathsf{Setup}(1^\lambda, 1^\ell)$ and gives the public parameter MPK to $\mathcal{A}$.

- Phase 1. $\mathcal{A}$ may adaptively make key-extraction queries. If $\mathcal{A}$ submits a predicate vector $\boldsymbol{y} \in \mathcal{P}$ to the challenger, the challenger runs $(\mathsf{sk}_{\boldsymbol{y}}, \mathsf{st}) \leftarrow \mathsf{KeyGen}(\mathsf{MPK}, \mathsf{MSK}, \mathsf{st}, \boldsymbol{y})$ and returns $\mathsf{sk}_{\boldsymbol{y}}$.

- Challenge Phase. At some point, $\mathcal{A}$ outputs messages $\mathsf{M}_0, \mathsf{M}_1$ and an attribute vector $\boldsymbol{x}^* \in \mathcal{I}$ on which it wishes to be challenged, with the restriction that $\langle \boldsymbol{x}^*, \boldsymbol{y} \rangle = 0$ (over $\mathcal{S}$) for all $\boldsymbol{y}$ queried during Phase 1. Then, the challenger picks a random bit $b \in \{0, 1\}$ and returns $C^* \leftarrow \mathsf{Enc}(\mathsf{MPK}, \boldsymbol{x}^*, \mathsf{M}_b)$ to $\mathcal{A}$.

- Phase 2. After the challenge query, $\mathcal{A}$ may continue to make key-extraction queries for predicate vectors $\boldsymbol{y} \in \mathcal{P}$, with the added restriction that $\langle \boldsymbol{x}^*, \boldsymbol{y} \rangle = 0$ (over $\mathcal{S}$).

- Guess. Finally, $\mathcal{A}$ outputs a guess b' for b.

The advantage of $\mathcal{A}$ is defined as $\mathsf{Adv}^{\mathsf{NIPE}}_{\mathcal{A},\mathcal{S}} = \left|\Pr[b' = b] - \frac{1}{2}\right|$. We say that a stateful NIPE scheme with inner product space $\mathcal{S}$ is *adaptively secure*, if the advantage of any PPT $\mathcal{A}$ is negligible. Similarly, we define *selective security* for a stateful NIPE scheme with inner product space $\mathcal{S}$, by modifying the above game so that the adversary $\mathcal{A}$ is forced to declare its challenge attribute vector $\boldsymbol{x}^*$ before **Setup**. Therefore, we also add the restriction that $\langle \boldsymbol{x}^*, \boldsymbol{y} \rangle = 0$ (over $\mathcal{S}$) during **Phase 1**. Finally, we define an analogous security notion for stateless NIPE schemes, where we do not require any state information during the above game.

Remark on the Security Model. In the stateful setting, it may be more natural to consider a security model where the adversary is allowed to request the challenger to create a secret key without actually seeing it. Such a query will change the internal state of KeyGen in a possibly malicious way. In our work, we follow the stateful functional encryption formalization of [ALS16] and do not consider this stronger security model. We leave it open the problem of constructing efficient NIPE scheme satisfying this security notion.

2.2 Lattices

A (full-rank-integer) m-dimensional lattice Λ in $\mathbb{Z}^m$ is a set of the form $\{\sum_{i \in [m]} x_i \mathbf{b}_i | x_i \in \mathbb{Z}\}$, where $\mathbf{B} = \{\mathbf{b}_1, \cdots, \mathbf{b}_m\}$ are m linearly independent vectors in $\mathbb{Z}^m$. We call $\mathbf{B}$ the basis of the lattice Λ. For any positive integers n, m and $q \geq 2$, a matrix $\mathbf{A} \in \mathbb{Z}_q^{n \times m}$ and a vector $\mathbf{u} \in \mathbb{Z}_q^n$, we define$\Lambda^\perp(\mathbf{A}) = \{\mathbf{z} \in \mathbb{Z}^m | \mathbf{A}\mathbf{z} = \mathbf{0} \mod q\}, \Lambda^\perp_{\mathbf{u}}(\mathbf{A}) = \{\mathbf{z} \in \mathbb{Z}^m | \mathbf{A}\mathbf{z} = \mathbf{u} \mod q\}$.

For an m-dimensional lattice $\Lambda \subseteq \mathbb{Z}^m$, define the m-dimensional k-multi lattice Λ^k as $[\Lambda|\cdots|\Lambda] = \{[z_1|\cdots|z_k] | \forall z_i \in \Lambda, \forall i \in [k]\} \subseteq \mathbb{Z}^{m\times k}$. For a matrix $\mathbf{T} = [\mathbf{t}_1|\cdots|\mathbf{t}_k] \in \mathbb{Z}^{m\times k}$, denote $\Lambda^k + \mathbf{T}$ as $[\Lambda + \mathbf{t}_1|\cdots|\Lambda + \mathbf{t}_k] \subseteq \mathbb{Z}^{m\times k}$. For a matrix $\mathbf{M} \in \mathbb{Z}^{k\times \ell}$ define $\Lambda^k \cdot \mathbf{M}$ as the multi lattice $\{\mathbf{VM} | \mathbf{V} \in \Lambda^k\} \subseteq \mathbb{Z}^{m\times \ell}$.

Gaussian Measures. For any vector $\mathbf{c} \in \mathbb{R}^m$ and positive real $\sigma > 0$, the m-dimensional Gaussian function over $\mathbb{R}^m$ centered at $\mathbf{c}$ with parameter s is defined as $\rho_{\sigma,\mathbf{c}}(\mathbf{x}) = \exp(-\pi\|\mathbf{x}-\mathbf{c}\|^2/\sigma^2)$. The continuous Gaussian distribution D_σ over $\mathbb{R}^m$ centered at $\mathbf{c}$ with parameter σ is defined as $D_{\sigma,\mathbf{c}}(\mathbf{x}) = \rho_{\sigma,\mathbf{c}}(\mathbf{x})/\sigma^m$. For an m-dimensional lattice Λ, the discrete Gaussian distribution over Λ with center $\mathbf{c}$ and parameter σ is defined as $D_{\Lambda,\sigma,\mathbf{c}}(\mathbf{x}) = \rho_{\sigma,\mathbf{c}}(\mathbf{x})/\rho_{\sigma,\mathbf{c}}(\Lambda)$ for all $\mathbf{x} \in \Lambda$, where $\rho_{\sigma,\mathbf{c}}(\Lambda) = \sum_{\mathbf{x}\in\Lambda} \rho_{\sigma,\mathbf{c}}(\mathbf{x})$. Finally, for an m-dimensional shifted lattice $\Lambda + \mathbf{t}$, we define the Gaussian distribution $D_{\Lambda+\mathbf{t},\sigma}$ with center $\mathbf{c} = 0$ and parameter σ as the process of adding the vector $\mathbf{t}$ to a sample from $D_{\Lambda,\sigma,-\mathbf{t}}$. We omit the subscripts σ and $\mathbf{c}$ when they are taken to be 1 and $\mathbf{0}$, respectively.

Lemma 1 ([GPV08], **Lem. 5.2, Cor. 5.4 and Adapted from** [ALS16], **Lem. 9).** *Let q be a prime or some power of a prime*[4] *p and let n, m be positive integers such that $m \geq 2n\log q$. Let σ be any positive real such that $\sigma \geq \omega(\sqrt{\log n})$. Then for $\mathbf{A} \leftarrow \mathbb{Z}_q^{n\times m}$ and $\mathbf{e} \leftarrow D_{\mathbb{Z}^m,\sigma}$, the distribution of $\mathbf{u} = \mathbf{Ae} \mod q$ is statistically close to uniform over $\mathbb{Z}_q^n$.*

Furthermore, fix $\mathbf{u} \in \mathbb{Z}_q^n$ and let $\mathbf{t} \in \mathbb{Z}^m$ be an arbitrary solution to $\mathbf{At} = \mathbf{u} \mod q$. Then the conditional distribution of $\mathbf{e} \leftarrow D_{\mathbb{Z}^m,\sigma}$, given $\mathbf{Ae} = \mathbf{u} \mod q$ for a uniformly random $\mathbf{A}$ in $\mathbb{Z}_q^{n\times m}$ is exactly $D_{\Lambda^\perp(\mathbf{A})+\mathbf{t},\sigma}$ with all but negligible probability.

Lemma 2 ([MP12], **Lem. 2.8 and Lem. 2.9).** *Let m, k be positive integers, $\{\sigma_i\}_{i=1}^k$ a set of positive reals and denote $\sigma_{max} = \max_i\{\sigma_i\}$. Let $\mathbf{R} \in \mathbb{Z}^{m\times k}$ be a matrix where its i-th column is sampled from $D_{\mathbb{Z}^m,\sigma_i}$. Then there exists a universal constant $C > 0$ such that we have $s_1(\mathbf{R}) \leq C \cdot \sigma_{max}(\sqrt{m} + \sqrt{k})$ with all but negligible probability in m.*

Lemma 3 ([ABB10], **Lem. 8).** *Let n, m, q be positive integers with $m > n$, $\mathbf{A} \in \mathbb{Z}_q^{n\times m}$ be a matrix, $\mathbf{u} \in \mathbb{Z}_q^n$ be a vector, $\mathbf{T}_\mathbf{A}$ be a basis for $\Lambda^\perp(\mathbf{A})$, and $\sigma > \|\mathbf{T}_\mathbf{A}\| \cdot \omega(\sqrt{\log m})$. Then, if we sample a vector $\mathbf{x} \leftarrow D_{\Lambda_\mathbf{u}^\perp(\mathbf{A}),\sigma}$, we have* $\Pr[\|\mathbf{x}\| > \sqrt{m}\sigma] < \mathsf{negl}(n)$.

Lemma 4 (Noise Rerandomization, [KY16], **Lem. 1).** *Let q, ℓ, m be positive integers and r a positive real satisfying $r > \max\{\omega(\sqrt{\log m}), \omega(\sqrt{\log \ell})\}$. Let $\mathbf{b} \in \mathbb{Z}_q^m$ be arbitrary and $\mathbf{z}$ chosen from $D_{\mathbb{Z}^m,r}$. Then for any $\mathbf{V} \in \mathbb{Z}^{m\times\ell}$ and positive real $\sigma > s_1(\mathbf{V})$, there exists a PPT algorithm* $\mathsf{ReRand}(\mathbf{V}, \mathbf{b}+\mathbf{z}, r, \sigma)$ *that outputs $\mathbf{b}'^\top = \mathbf{b}^\top\mathbf{V} + \mathbf{z}'^\top \in \mathbb{Z}_q^\ell$ where $\mathbf{z}'$ is distributed statistically close to $D_{\mathbb{Z}^\ell,2r\sigma}$.*

Analogously to above, for an m-dimensional k-multi lattice Λ^k, we define the discrete Gaussian distribution over Λ^k with center $\mathbf{C} \in \mathbb{Z}^{m\times k}$ and parameter σ

[4] Note that for the case $q = p^k$ for some $k \in \mathbb{N}$, we set the statistical distance to be $n^{-\omega(1)}$ rather than $2^{-\Omega(n)}$ as in [ALS16], Lem. 9.

denoted as $D_{\Lambda^k,\sigma,\mathbf{C}}$ by the process of sampling a matrix whose i-th column is a sample from $D_{\Lambda,\sigma,\mathbf{C}_i}$ for $i \in [k]$, where $\mathbf{C}_i$ denotes the i-th column of $\mathbf{C}$. This definition extends naturally to shifted multi-lattices as well.

Key Theorem. The following theorem concerning the distribution of the sum of discrete Gaussians plays a central roll in our security proof. The proof of the theorem is given in the full version with a more formal treatment on the output distribution.

Theorem 1. *Let q be a prime or some power of a prime p. Let n, m, ℓ, t be positive integers such that $m \geq 2n \log q$ and $\ell > t$, let $\mathbf{A} \in \mathbb{Z}_q^{n\times m}$ be a random matrix and $\mathbf{T} \in \mathbb{Z}^{m\times \ell}$ be an arbitrary matrix. Let $\mathbf{M} \in \mathbb{Z}^{\ell\times(\ell-t)}$ and $\mathbf{W} \in \mathbb{Z}^{\ell\times t}$ be full rank matrices satisfying $\mathbf{W}^\top\mathbf{M} = \mathbf{0} \in \mathbb{Z}^{t\times(\ell-t)}$. Finally, let σ be a positive real such that $\sigma > \sqrt{s_1(\mathbf{W}^\top\mathbf{W})} \cdot \omega(\sqrt{\log m})$.Notably, if $\mathbf{X} \in \mathbb{Z}^{m\times\ell}$ is distributed as $D_{\Lambda^\perp(\mathbf{A})^\ell+\mathbf{T},\sigma}$, then $\mathbf{X}\mathbf{M} \in \mathbb{Z}^{m\times(\ell-t)}$ is statistically close to a distribution parameterized by $\Lambda^\perp(\mathbf{A}), \sigma, \mathbf{M}, (\mathbf{T}\mathbf{M} \mod \Lambda^\perp(\mathbf{A})^\ell\mathbf{M})$.*

Remark 1. An important observation is that, if we independently sample $\mathbf{X}_0 \leftarrow D_{\Lambda^k+\mathbf{T}_0,\sigma}$ and $\mathbf{X}_1 \leftarrow D_{\Lambda^k+\mathbf{T}_1,\sigma}$, then the distributions of $\mathbf{X}_0\mathbf{M}$ and $\mathbf{X}_1\mathbf{M}$ are statistically close whenever $\mathbf{T}_0\mathbf{M} = \mathbf{T}_1\mathbf{M} \mod \Lambda^k\mathbf{M}$. This is the key insight used in our security proof; in the real world the secret components are sampled as $\mathbf{X}_0$ and in the simulated world they are sampled as $\mathbf{X}_1$. Furthermore, for any matrix $\bar{\mathbf{M}}$, if we let $\mathbf{M}$ be an arbitrary maximal independent subset of the columns of $\bar{\mathbf{M}}$, since all the columns of $\mathbf{X}\bar{\mathbf{M}}$ are linear combinations of the columns of $\mathbf{X}\mathbf{M}$, the distribution of $\mathbf{X}\bar{\mathbf{M}}$ is parameterized solely by the distribution of $\Lambda, \sigma, \mathbf{M}, (\mathbf{T}\mathbf{M} \mod \Lambda^k\mathbf{M})$.

Sampling Algorithms. The following lemma states useful algorithms for sampling short vectors from lattices.

Lemma 5. *Let $n, m, q > 0$ be integers with $m > n$. Then:*

- *([GPV08])* $\mathsf{SamplePre}(\mathbf{A}, \mathbf{u}, \mathbf{T_A}, \sigma) \to \mathbf{e}$: *There exists a randomized algorithm that, given a matrix $\mathbf{A} \in \mathbb{Z}_q^{n\times m}$, a vector $\mathbf{u} \in \mathbb{Z}_q^n$, a basis $\mathbf{T_A}$ for $\Lambda^\perp(\mathbf{A})$, and a Gaussian parameter $\sigma > \|\mathbf{T_A}\|_{\mathsf{GS}} \cdot \omega(\sqrt{\log m})$, outputs a vector $\mathbf{e} \in \mathbb{Z}^m$ sampled from a distribution which is* $\mathsf{negl}(n)$*-close to $D_{\Lambda^\perp_{\mathbf{u}}(\mathbf{A}),\sigma}$.*
- *([ABB10])* $\mathsf{SampleRight}(\mathbf{A}, \mathbf{G}, \mathbf{R}, t, \mathbf{u}, \mathbf{T_G}, \sigma) \to \mathbf{e}$*: There exists a randomized algorithm that, given a full-rank matrix $\mathbf{A}, \mathbf{G} \in \mathbb{Z}_q^{n\times m}$, an invertible element $t \in \mathbb{Z}_q$, a matrix $\mathbf{R} \in \mathbb{Z}^{m\times m}$, a vector $\mathbf{u} \in \mathbb{Z}_q^n$, a basis $\mathbf{T_G}$ for $\Lambda^\perp(\mathbf{G})$, and a Gaussian parameter $\sigma > s_1(\mathbf{R}) \cdot \|\mathbf{T_G}\|_{\mathsf{GS}} \cdot \omega(\sqrt{\log m})$, outputs a vector $\mathbf{e} \in \mathbb{Z}^{2m}$ sampled from a distribution which is* $\mathsf{negl}(n)$*-close to $D_{\Lambda^\perp_{\mathbf{u}}([\mathbf{A}|\mathbf{A}\mathbf{R}+t\mathbf{G}]),\sigma}$.*
- *([MP12]) Let $m \geq n\lceil \log q \rceil$. Then, there exists a fixed full-rank matrix $\mathbf{G} \in \mathbb{Z}_q^{n\times m}$ such that the lattice $\Lambda^\perp(\mathbf{G})$ has publicly known basis $\mathbf{T_G} \in \mathbb{Z}^{m\times m}$ with $\|\mathbf{T_G}\|_{\mathsf{GS}} \leq \sqrt{5}$.*

Observe that even if we are in possession of a "nice" trapdoor matrix $\mathbf{R}$, we can not use the $\mathsf{SampleRight}$ algorithm in case t is not invertible over $\mathbb{Z}_q$.

Below we consider the case where $q = p^d$ for some prime p and positive integer d, and slightly modify SampleRight so that we can sample short vectors from some shifted lattice of $\Lambda^{\perp}([\mathbf{A}|\mathbf{AR} + p^{d-1}t'\mathbf{G}])$ for an invertible element $t' \in \mathbb{Z}_q$. Note that $t = p^{d-1}t'$ is no longer invertible over $\mathbb{Z}_q$. The proof is provided in the full version.

Lemma 6 (Algorithm SampleSkewed). *Let $q = p^d$ for a prime p and positive integer d. Then, there exists a polynomial time algorithm* SampleSkewed *with the following property.*

SampleSkewed$(\mathbf{A}, \mathbf{G}, \mathbf{R}, t, p^{d-1}\mathbf{u}, \mathbf{T_G}) \to \mathbf{e}$: *a randomized algorithm that, given full-rank matrices $\mathbf{A}, \mathbf{G} \in \mathbb{Z}_q^{n\times m}$, a matrix $\mathbf{R} \in \mathbb{Z}^{m\times m}$, a vector $p^{d-1}\mathbf{u} \in \mathbb{Z}_q^n$, and an invertible element $t \in \mathbb{Z}_q$, outputs a vector $\mathbf{e} \in \mathbb{Z}^{2m}$ such that $[\mathbf{A}|\mathbf{AR} + p^{d-1} \cdot t \cdot \mathbf{G}]\mathbf{e} = p^{d-1}\mathbf{u} \mod q$ and $\|\mathbf{e}\| \le s_1(\mathbf{R})\sqrt{m} \cdot \omega(\sqrt{\log n})$ with all but negligible probability.*

Hardness Assumptions. We define the Learning with Errors (LWE) problem first introduced by Regev [Reg05], and further define a variant of LWE called the First-is-Errorless LWE (FE.LWE) problem introduced by [BLP+13]. Both problems are shown to be as hard as approximating the worst-case GapSVP problems. In particular, the FE.LWE problem is proven to be essentially as hard as the LWE problem. Looking ahead, FE.LWE will be used for our lattice-based NIPE construction over $\mathbb{Z}_p$.

Definition 1 (LWE and FE.LWE). *For integers $n = n(\lambda), m = m(n), q = q(n) > 2$, an error distribution over $\chi = \chi(n)$ over $\mathbb{Z}$, and a PPT algorithm $\mathcal{A}$, an advantage $\mathsf{Adv}_{\mathcal{A}}^{\mathsf{LWE}_{n,m,q,\chi}}$ for the* learning with errors problem $\mathsf{LWE}_{n,m,q,\chi}$ *of $\mathcal{A}$ is defined as follows:*

$$\left| \Pr\left[\mathcal{A}(\{\mathbf{a}_i\}_{i=1}^m, \{\mathbf{a}_i^\top \mathbf{s} + x_i\}_{i=1}^m) = 1\right] - \Pr\left[\mathcal{A}(\{\mathbf{a}_i\}_{i=1}^m, \{v_i\}_{i=1}^m) = 1\right] \right|$$

where $\mathbf{a}_i \leftarrow \mathbb{Z}_q^n$, $\mathbf{s} \leftarrow \mathbb{Z}_q^n$, $x_i \leftarrow \chi$, $v_i \leftarrow \mathbb{Z}_q$ for each $i \in [m]$. We say that the LWE *assumption holds if $\mathsf{Adv}_{\mathcal{A}}^{\mathsf{LWE}_{n,m,q,\chi}}$ is negligible for all PPT $\mathcal{A}$.*

In addition, we define the first-is-errorless learning with errors problem $\mathsf{FE.LWE}_{n,m,q,\chi}$, *which is the LWE problem where the first sample is noise free, i.e., we have $x_1 = 0$ instead of $x_1 \leftarrow \chi$. The advantage for the* $\mathsf{FE.LWE}_{n,m,q,\chi}$ *problem of $\mathcal{A}$ is defined analogously to above.*

3 Construction from Lattices with Inner Product over $\mathbb{Z}$

3.1 Constructions

Here we construct a *stateless* NIPE scheme with inner product space $\mathbb{Z}$. We consider the predicate space $\mathcal{P} = \{-P+1, \dots, P-2, P-1\}^\ell \subset \mathbb{Z}^\ell$ and attribute space $\mathcal{I} = \{-I+1, \dots, I-2, I-1\}^\ell \subset \mathbb{Z}^\ell$ for some integers $P = P(n), I = I(n)$, where $\ell = \ell(n)$ is typically taken to be $\mathsf{poly}(n)$, and set the modulus size to be a prime $q = q(n)$ such that the inner products of the predicate and attribute vectors do not wrap around q, i.e., $\ell PI < q$. Other parameters including $m(n), \sigma(n), \alpha(n), \alpha'(n), s(n)$ are specified later. Here, we assume that the message space is $\{0, 1\}$. For the multi-bit variant, we refer Sect. 3.4.

Setup$(1^n, 1^\ell)$: On input $1^n, 1^\ell$, it samples a random matrix $\mathbf{A} \leftarrow \mathbb{Z}_q^{n\times m}$, a random vector $\mathbf{u} \leftarrow \mathbb{Z}_q^n$ and random matrices $\mathbf{R}_i \leftarrow \left(D_{\mathbb{Z}^m,\sigma}\right)^m$ for $i \in [\ell]$. It then sets $\mathbf{B}_i = \mathbf{A}\mathbf{R}_i \mod q$. Finally, it outputs

$$\mathsf{MPK} = (\mathbf{A}, \mathbf{B}_1, \cdots, \mathbf{B}_\ell, \mathbf{u}) \quad \text{and} \quad \mathsf{MSK} = (\mathbf{R}_1, \cdots, \mathbf{R}_\ell).$$

KeyGen(MPK, MSK, $\boldsymbol{y} \in \mathcal{P}$): Given a predicate vector $\boldsymbol{y} = (y_1, \cdots, y_\ell) \in \mathcal{P}$, it computes

$$\mathbf{R}_{\boldsymbol{y}} = \sum_{i=1}^{\ell} y_i \mathbf{R}_i \in \mathbb{Z}^{m\times m}.$$

Then, it returns the secret key $\mathsf{sk}_{\boldsymbol{y}} = \mathbf{R}_{\boldsymbol{y}}$.

Enc(MPK, $\boldsymbol{x} \in \mathcal{I}$, M): To encrypt a message $\mathsf{M} \in \{0,1\}$ for an attribute $\boldsymbol{x} = (x_1, \cdots, x_\ell) \in \mathcal{I}$, it samples $\mathbf{s} \leftarrow \mathbb{Z}_q^n$, $z \leftarrow D_{\mathbb{Z},\alpha q}$ and $\mathbf{z}_i \leftarrow D_{\mathbb{Z}^m,\alpha' q}$ for $i \in [0, \ell]$, and computes

$$\begin{cases} c = \mathbf{u}^\top \mathbf{s} + z + \mathsf{M}\lfloor q/2 \rceil, \\ \mathbf{c}_0 = \mathbf{A}^\top \mathbf{s} + \mathbf{z}_0, \\ \mathbf{c}_i = (\mathbf{B}_i + x_i \mathbf{G})^\top \mathbf{s} + \mathbf{z}_i, \quad (i \in [\ell]). \end{cases}$$

Then, it returns the ciphertext $C = (c, (\mathbf{c}_i)_{i\in[0,\ell]}) \in \mathbb{Z}_q \times (\mathbb{Z}_q^m)^{(\ell+1)}$ with the corresponding attribute $\boldsymbol{x}$.

Dec(MPK, $(\boldsymbol{y}, \mathsf{sk}_{\boldsymbol{y}}), (\boldsymbol{x}, C)$): To decrypt a ciphertext $C = (c, (\mathbf{c}_i)_{i\in[0,\ell]})$ with an associating attribute $\boldsymbol{x} \in \mathcal{I}$ using a secret key $\mathsf{sk}_{\boldsymbol{y}} = \mathbf{R}_{\boldsymbol{y}} = \sum_{i=1}^{\ell} y_i \mathbf{R}_i$ with an associating predicate $\boldsymbol{y} \in \mathcal{P}$, it first computes

$$\mathbf{c}_{\boldsymbol{y}} = \sum_{i=1}^{\ell} y_i \mathbf{c}_i \in \mathbb{Z}_q^m.$$

Next, it samples a short vector $\mathbf{e} \in \mathbb{Z}^{2m}$ by running SampleRight$(\mathbf{A}, \mathbf{G}, \mathbf{R}_{\boldsymbol{y}}, \langle \boldsymbol{x}, \boldsymbol{y} \rangle, \mathbf{u}, \mathbf{T}_{\mathbf{G}}, s)$. Then, it computes $w = c - \mathbf{e}^\top [\mathbf{c}_0^\top | \mathbf{c}_{\boldsymbol{y}}^\top]^\top \in \mathbb{Z}_q$. Finally, it returns 1 if $|w - \lceil q/2 \rceil| < \lceil q/4 \rceil$ and 0 otherwise.

3.2 Correctness and Parameter Selection

Lemma 7 (correctness). *Assume* $\left(\alpha q + \ell P^2 \sigma m \alpha' q\right) \cdot \omega(\sqrt{\log n}) < q/5$ *holds with overwhelming probability. Then the above scheme has negligible decryption error.*

The correctness is omitted to the full version. The main observation is that $\mathbf{c}_{\boldsymbol{y}} = \left(\mathbf{A}\mathbf{R}_{\boldsymbol{y}} + \langle \boldsymbol{x}, \boldsymbol{y} \rangle \mathbf{G}\right)^\top \mathbf{s} + \mathbf{z}'$ for some vector $\mathbf{z}'$ with sufficiently small noise, and we are able to use algorithm SampleRight to sample a short vector $\mathbf{e} \in \mathbb{Z}^{2m}$ such that $[\mathbf{A}|\mathbf{A}\mathbf{R}_{\boldsymbol{y}} + \langle \boldsymbol{x}, \boldsymbol{y} \rangle \mathbf{G}]\mathbf{e} = \mathbf{u}$ if and only if $\langle \boldsymbol{x}, \boldsymbol{y} \rangle \neq 0$ (and invertible).

Parameter Selection. We provide a candidate parameter selection in the full version. Notably, we can base security on the polynomial LWE assumption.

3.3 Security Proof

Theorem 2. *The above NIPE scheme with inner product space* $\mathbb{Z}$ *is selectively secure assuming* $\mathsf{LWE}_{n,m+1,q,\chi}$ *is hard, where* $\chi = D_{\mathbb{Z},\alpha q}$.

Proof. Let $\mathcal{A}$ be a PPT adversary that breaks the selective security of the NIPE scheme. In addition, let $Q = Q(n)$ be the number of key extraction queries $\mathcal{A}$ makes, and denote $\boldsymbol{y}^{(k)} \in \mathcal{P}$ as the k-th predicate vector $\mathcal{A}$ queries, where $k \in [Q]$. Here, we assume that $\mathcal{A}$ always queries for $\ell - 1$ linearly independent predicate vectors, which are all orthogonal to the challenge attribute vector $\boldsymbol{x}^*$ over $\mathbb{Z}$. This can be done without loss of generality, since $\mathcal{A}$ can simply ignore these additional queries. The proof proceeds with a sequence of games that starts with the real game and ends with a game in which $\mathcal{A}$ has negligible advantage. For each game Game_i denote S_i the event that $\mathcal{A}$ wins the game.

Game_0 : This is the real security game. Namely, adversary $\mathcal{A}$ declares its challenge attribute vector $\boldsymbol{x}^* \in \mathcal{I}$ at the beginning of the game. Note that any predicate vector $\boldsymbol{y} \in \mathcal{P}$ queried by $\mathcal{A}$ to the challenger as a key extraction query must satisfy $\langle \boldsymbol{x}^*, \boldsymbol{y} \rangle = 0$ over $\mathbb{Z}$ if $\mathcal{A}$ is a legitimate adversary.

Game_1 : In this game, we change the way the public matrices $\mathbf{B}_1, \cdots, \mathbf{B}_\ell$ are created. On receiving the challenge attribute vector $\boldsymbol{x}^* = (x_1^*, \cdots, x_\ell^*) \in \mathcal{I}$ from adversary $\mathcal{A}$ at the beginning of the game, the challenger samples random matrices $\mathbf{R}_i \leftarrow \left(D_{\mathbb{Z}^m,\sigma}\right)^m$ and sets $\mathbf{B}_i = \mathbf{A}\mathbf{R}_i - x_i^* \mathbf{G} \mod q$ for $i \in [\ell]$. Otherwise, the behavior of the challenger is identical as in Game_0. Namely, the challenger remains to answer the key extraction query for a predicate vector $\boldsymbol{y} \in \mathcal{P}$ as $\mathsf{sk}_{\boldsymbol{y}} = \mathbf{R}_{\boldsymbol{y}} = \sum_{i=1}^{\ell} y_i \mathbf{R}_i$ where $\boldsymbol{y} = (y_1, \cdots, y_\ell)$, and creates the challenge ciphertext as in Game_0.

Before continuing to Game_2, we show that Game_0 is statistically indistinguishable from Game_1; this is the crux of our proof. In particular, we show that the view of the adversary in both games is statistically close. Here, the view of the adversary is completely determined by

$$\left\{ \mathsf{MPK} = \left\{ \mathbf{A}, \{\mathbf{B}_i\}_{i \in [\ell]}, \mathbf{u} \right\}, \quad \{\mathbf{R}_{\boldsymbol{y}^{(k)}}\}_{k \in [Q]}, \quad C^* \right\}$$

where $\{\mathbf{R}_{\boldsymbol{y}^{(k)}}\}_{k \in [Q]}$ is the set of secret keys returned by the challenger during the key extraction query and $C^* \leftarrow \mathsf{Enc}(\mathsf{MPK}, \boldsymbol{x}^*, \mathsf{M}_b)$ is the challenge ciphertext, where b is the random bit chosen by the challenger. Observe that in both games $\mathbf{A}, \mathbf{u}$ are distributed identically. Furthermore, the challenge ciphertext C^* is created using only the terms in MPK (with some extra randomness that are identical in both games). Furthermore, from our assumption on $\mathcal{A}$, we assume that $\{\boldsymbol{y}^{(k)}\}_{k \in [\ell-1]}$ is the set of the $\ell - 1$ linearly independent vectors that $\mathcal{A}$ queries. Then, what we need to consider are only the $\ell - 1$ secret keys $\{\mathbf{R}_{\boldsymbol{y}^{(k)}}\}_{k \in [\ell-1]}$, since all the other secret keys can be created by the linear combinations of $\{\mathbf{R}_{\boldsymbol{y}^{(k)}}\}_{k \in [\ell-1]}$. Therefore, the difference in the views of the adversary in Game_0 and Game_1 is determined solely by the difference in the distribution of

$$\left\{ \{\mathbf{B}_i\}_{i \in [\ell]}, \quad \{\mathbf{R}_{\boldsymbol{y}^{(k)}}\}_{k \in [\ell-1]} \right\}. \tag{1}$$

Hence, we aim at proving that the view of Eq. (1) for the adversary is statistically close in both games. More strictly, we compare the following probability of each game:

$$\Pr\left[\left\{\{\mathbf{B}_i\}_{i\in[\ell]},\quad \{\mathbf{R}_{\boldsymbol{y}^{(k)}}\}_{k\in[\ell-1]}\right\} = \left\{\{\widehat{\mathbf{B}}_i\}_{i\in[\ell]},\quad \{\widehat{\mathbf{R}}_{\boldsymbol{y}^{(k)}}\}_{k\in[\ell-1]}\right\}\right]$$

$$= \underbrace{\Pr\left[\{\mathbf{R}_{\boldsymbol{y}^{(k)}}\}_{k\in[\ell-1]} = \{\widehat{\mathbf{R}}_{\boldsymbol{y}^{(k)}}\}_{k\in[\ell-1]}\ \middle|\ \{\mathbf{B}_i\}_{i\in[\ell]} = \{\widehat{\mathbf{B}}_i\}_{i\in[\ell]}\right]}_{(A)}$$

$$\times \underbrace{\Pr\left[\{\mathbf{B}_i\}_{i\in[\ell]} = \{\widehat{\mathbf{B}}_i\}_{i\in[\ell]}\right]}_{(B)},$$

where the probability is taken over the randomness of $\{\mathbf{R}_i\}_{i\in[\ell]}$ during Setup; recall each $\mathbf{R}_i$ is distributed according to $\left(D_{\mathbb{Z}^m,\sigma}\right)^m$ in both games. Note that in the above we abuse the notation for sets by implicitly assigning an order over the elements, i.e., $\{\mathbf{X},\mathbf{Y}\} \neq \{\mathbf{Y},\mathbf{X}\}$.

We first prove that the value of (B) is negligibly close in both games. Observe that for all $i \in [\ell]$, $\mathbf{AR}_i$ is distributed uniformly at random over $\mathbb{Z}_q^{n\times m}$ with all but negligible probability where $\mathbf{R}_i \leftarrow \left(D_{\mathbb{Z}^m,\sigma}\right)^m$, which follows from Lemma 1 and our parameter selections. Concretely, since $\mathbf{B}_i = \mathbf{AR}_i$ and $\mathbf{B}_i = \mathbf{AR}_i - x_i^*\mathbf{G}$ for Game_0 and Game_1, respectively, we have that in both games $\{\mathbf{B}_i\}_{i\in[\ell]}$ is distributed statistically close to uniform over $\left(\mathbb{Z}_q^{n\times m}\right)^\ell$.

We now proceed to prove that the value of (A) is negligibly close in both games. We first analyze the case for Game_0. Let $\mathbf{B}_{\mathsf{view}} \in \mathbb{Z}_q^{n\times m\ell}$ and $\mathbf{R} \in \mathbb{Z}^{m\times m\ell}$ denote the matrices $[\mathbf{B}_1|\cdots|\mathbf{B}_\ell]$ and $[\mathbf{R}_1|\cdots|\mathbf{R}_\ell]$, respectively. Then we have $\mathbf{B}_{\mathsf{view}} = \mathbf{AR} \mod q$. Furthermore, let $\mathbf{T} = [\mathbf{T}_1|\cdots|\mathbf{T}_\ell] \in \mathbb{Z}^{m\times m\ell}$ be an arbitrary solution to $\mathbf{B}_{\mathsf{view}} = \mathbf{AT} \mod q$. Then, due to Lemma 1, conditioned on $\{\widehat{\mathbf{B}}_i\}_{i\in[\ell]} = \{\mathbf{AR}_i\}_{i\in[\ell]} \pmod q$, the conditional distribution of $\mathbf{R}$ is $D_{\Lambda^\perp(\mathbf{A})^{m\ell}+\mathbf{T},\sigma}$. Now, we are ready to determine the conditional distribution of the secret keys $\{\mathbf{R}_{\boldsymbol{y}^{(k)}}\}_{k\in[\ell-1]}$ obtained by the adversary $\mathcal{A}$. Observe the following equation:

$$\underbrace{[\mathbf{R}_{\boldsymbol{y}^{(1)}}|\mathbf{R}_{\boldsymbol{y}^{(2)}}|\cdots|\mathbf{R}_{\boldsymbol{y}^{(\ell-1)}}]}_{:=\mathbf{R}_{\mathsf{sk}}\ \in\mathbb{Z}^{m\times m(\ell-1)}} = \underbrace{[\mathbf{R}_1|\mathbf{R}_2|\cdots|\mathbf{R}_\ell]}_{=\mathbf{R}\ \in\mathbb{Z}^{m\times m\ell}} \underbrace{\left[\begin{array}{c|c|c|c} y_1^{(1)}\mathbf{I}_m & y_1^{(2)}\mathbf{I}_m & \cdots & y_1^{(\ell-1)}\mathbf{I}_m \\ y_2^{(1)}\mathbf{I}_m & y_2^{(2)}\mathbf{I}_m & \cdots & y_2^{(\ell-1)}\mathbf{I}_m \\ \vdots & \vdots & \cdots & \vdots \\ y_\ell^{(1)}\mathbf{I}_m & y_\ell^{(2)}\mathbf{I}_m & & y_\ell^{(\ell-1)}\mathbf{I}_m \end{array}\right]}_{:=\mathbf{M}=\mathbf{Y}\otimes\mathbf{I}_m\ \in\mathbb{Z}^{m\ell\times m(\ell-1)}}, \tag{2}$$

where $y_j^{(k)}$ is the j-th entry of the k-th predicate vector $\boldsymbol{y}^{(k)}$ and $\mathbf{Y} \in \mathbb{Z}^{\ell\times(\ell-1)}$ is a full rank matrix whose k-th column is $\boldsymbol{y}^{(k)}$. We also denote the left and right hand matrices as $\mathbf{R}_{\mathsf{sk}}$ and $\mathbf{M} \in \mathbb{Z}^{m\ell \times m(\ell-1)}$, respectively. Note that the equality is taken over $\mathbb{Z}$. Now, since $\boldsymbol{x}^{\star\top}\mathbf{Y} = \mathbf{0} \in \mathbb{Z}^{1\times(\ell-1)}$, we have $\mathbf{W}^\top\mathbf{M} = \mathbf{0} \in \mathbb{Z}^{m\times m(\ell-1)}$ where $\mathbf{W} = \boldsymbol{x}^\star \otimes \mathbf{I}_m \in \mathbb{Z}^{m\ell\times m}$ is a full rank matrix. Furthermore, by construction, we have $\sqrt{s_1(\mathbf{W}^\top\mathbf{W})} = \|\boldsymbol{x}^*\|$. Therefore, by Theorem 1 and from the fact that $\mathbf{R}$ is distributed according to $D_{\Lambda^\perp(\mathbf{A})^{m\ell}+\mathbf{T},\sigma}$, for our parameter selection, we have that the distribution of $\mathbf{R}_{\mathsf{sk}} = \mathbf{RM}$ is statistically close to a distribution parameterized by $\Lambda^\perp(\mathbf{A}), \sigma, \mathbf{M}$ and $(\mathbf{TM} \mod \Lambda^\perp(\mathbf{A})^{m\ell}\mathbf{M})$.

We now show that this holds in case for Game_1 as well. Similarly to above, we begin by determining the conditional distribution of $\mathbf{R}$ given $\{\mathbf{B}_i\}_{i\in[\ell]} = \{\mathbf{AR}_i - x_i^*\mathbf{G}\}_{i\in[\ell]}$. Let us denote $\mathbf{G}_{\boldsymbol{x}^*} \in \mathbb{Z}_q^{n\times m\ell}$ as the matrix $[x_1^*\mathbf{G}|x_2^*\mathbf{G}|\cdots|x_\ell^*\mathbf{G}]$. Then, $\mathbf{B}_{\mathsf{view}} + \mathbf{G}_{\boldsymbol{x}^*} = \mathbf{AR} \mod q$. Next, let us chose an arbitrary matrix $\mathbf{E} \in \mathbb{Z}^{m\times m}$ such that $\mathbf{G} = \mathbf{AE} \mod q$, and define $\mathbf{E}_{\boldsymbol{x}^*} \in \mathbb{Z}^{m\times m\ell}$ as the matrix $[x_1^*\mathbf{E}|x_2^*\mathbf{E}|\cdots|x_\ell^*\mathbf{E}]$. Then, we have $\mathbf{G}_{\boldsymbol{x}^*} = \mathbf{AE}_{\boldsymbol{x}^*} \mod q$. Combining this with the $\mathbf{T}$ we have defined above in Game_0, we obtain $\mathbf{B}_{\mathsf{view}} + \mathbf{G}_{\boldsymbol{x}^*} = \mathbf{A}(\mathbf{T} + \mathbf{E}_{\boldsymbol{x}^*}) \mod q$. Therefore, by Lemma 1, the conditional distribution of $\mathbf{R}$ given $\{\mathbf{B}_i\}_{i\in[\ell]}$ is $D_{\Lambda^\perp(\mathbf{A})^{m\ell}+\mathbf{T}+\mathbf{E}_{\boldsymbol{x}^*},\sigma}$. Next, we determine the conditional distribution of the secret keys $\{\mathbf{R}_{\boldsymbol{y}^{(k)}}\}_{k\in[\ell-1]}$ obtained by the adversary $\mathcal{A}$. Observe that equation Eq. (2) holds for Game_1 as well, since we do not change the way we answer the key extraction queries. Concretely, we have $\mathbf{M} = \mathbf{Y} \otimes \mathbf{I}_m$ and $\mathbf{W}^\top\mathbf{M} = \mathbf{0}$ where $\mathbf{W} = \boldsymbol{x}^\star \otimes \mathbf{I}_m$. Hence, by Theorem 1 and the fact that $\mathbf{R}$ is distributed according to $D_{\Lambda^\perp(\mathbf{A})^{m\ell}+\mathbf{T}+\mathbf{E}_{\boldsymbol{x}^*},\sigma}$, we have that the distribution of $\mathbf{R}_{\mathsf{sk}} = \mathbf{RM}$ is statistically close to a distribution parameterized by $\Lambda^\perp(\mathbf{A}), \sigma, \mathbf{M}$ and $(\mathbf{TM} + \mathbf{E}_{\boldsymbol{x}^*}\mathbf{M} \mod \Lambda^\perp(\mathbf{A})^{m\ell}\mathbf{M})$. Finally, it remains to prove that $\mathbf{E}_{\boldsymbol{x}^*}\mathbf{M} = \mathbf{0}$ (over $\mathbb{Z}$) in order to prove equivalence of (A) between Game_0 and Game_1. Observe that

$$
\begin{aligned}
\mathbf{E}_{\boldsymbol{x}^*}\mathbf{M} &= \mathbf{E}\cdot[x_1^*\mathbf{I}_m|x_2^*\mathbf{I}_m|\cdots|x_\ell^*\mathbf{I}_m]
\left[\begin{array}{c|c|c|c}
y_1^{(1)}\mathbf{I}_m & y_1^{(2)}\mathbf{I}_m & & y_1^{(\ell-1)}\mathbf{I}_m \\
y_2^{(1)}\mathbf{I}_m & y_2^{(2)}\mathbf{I}_m & \cdots & y_2^{(\ell-1)}\mathbf{I}_m \\
\vdots & \vdots & \cdots & \vdots \\
y_\ell^{(1)}\mathbf{I}_m & y_\ell^{(2)}\mathbf{I}_m & & y_\ell^{(\ell-1)}\mathbf{I}_m
\end{array}\right] \\
&= \mathbf{E}\cdot[\langle\boldsymbol{x}^*, \boldsymbol{y}^{(1)}\rangle\mathbf{I}_m|\langle\boldsymbol{x}^*, \boldsymbol{y}^{(2)}\rangle\mathbf{I}_m|\cdots|\langle\boldsymbol{x}^*, \boldsymbol{y}^{(\ell-1)}\rangle\mathbf{I}_m] \\
&= \mathbf{0} \in \mathbb{Z}^{m\times m(\ell-1)},
\end{aligned}
$$

since we have $\langle\boldsymbol{x}^*, \boldsymbol{y}^{(k)}\rangle = 0$ over $\mathbb{Z}$ for $k \in [\ell-1]$. Hence, we conclude that the value of (A), i.e., the conditional probability of $\mathbf{R}_{\mathsf{sk}}$ given $\{\mathbf{B}_i\}_{i\in[\ell]}$, in Game_0 and Game_1 are statistically close. Therefore, we have $|\Pr[S_0] - \Pr[S_1]| = \mathsf{negl}(n)$.

Game_2 : In this game, we change the way the challenge ciphertext is created. Recall that in the previous game, the challenge ciphertext was created as

$$
c = \mathbf{u}^\top\mathbf{s} + z + \mathsf{M}_b\lfloor q/2\rceil, \quad \mathbf{c}_0 = \mathbf{A}^\top\mathbf{s} + \mathbf{z}_0, \quad (\mathbf{c}_i = (\mathbf{AR}_i)^\top\mathbf{s} + \mathbf{z}_i)_{i\in[\ell]} \qquad (3)
$$

where $\mathbf{s} \leftarrow \mathbb{Z}_q^n$, $z \leftarrow D_{\mathbb{Z},\alpha q}$, $\mathbf{z}_i \leftarrow D_{\mathbb{Z}^m,\alpha' q}$ for $i \in [0,\ell]$, and $b \leftarrow \{0,1\}$, where the last term follows from the fact that in Game_1 we modified $\mathbf{B}_i$ so that $\mathbf{B}_i = \mathbf{AR}_i - x_i^*\mathbf{G}$, and $\mathsf{M}_0, \mathsf{M}_1$ are the two messages sent by the adversary $\mathcal{A}$. To create the challenge ciphertext in Game_2, the challenger first picks $\mathbf{s} \leftarrow \mathbb{Z}_q^n$ and

$\mathbf{z} \leftarrow D_{\mathbb{Z}^m,\alpha q}$ and computes $\mathbf{v} = \mathbf{A}^\top \mathbf{s} + \mathbf{z} \in \mathbb{Z}_q^m$. It then runs the algorithm

$$\mathsf{ReRand}\Big([\mathbf{I}_m|\mathbf{R}], \mathbf{v}, \alpha q, \frac{\alpha'}{2\alpha}\Big) \rightarrow \mathbf{c} \in \mathbb{Z}_q^{m(\ell+1)}$$

from Lemma 4, and parses $\mathbf{c}$ into $\ell+1$ vectors $(\mathbf{c}_i)_{i\in[\ell+1]}$ in $\mathbb{Z}_q^m$ such that $\mathbf{c}^\top = [\mathbf{c}_0^\top|\mathbf{c}_1^\top|\cdots|\mathbf{c}_\ell^\top] \in \mathbb{Z}_q^{m(\ell+1)}$. Finally, it picks $z \leftarrow D_{\mathbb{Z},\alpha q}$, $b \leftarrow \{0,1\}$ and sets the challenge ciphertext as

$$C^* = \Big(c = v + \mathsf{M}_b\lfloor q/2\rceil, \quad \mathbf{c}_0, \quad (\mathbf{c}_i)_{i\in[\ell]}\Big) \in \mathbb{Z}_q \times \mathbb{Z}_q^m \times (\mathbb{Z}_q^m)^\ell, \qquad (4)$$

where $v = \mathbf{u}^\top \mathbf{s} + z$.

We claim that this change alters the view of $\mathcal{A}$ only negligibly. First, the first term c is distributed identically as in Eq.(3). Next, observe that the input to ReRand is $[\mathbf{I}_m|\mathbf{R}] \in \mathbb{Z}^{m\times m(\ell+1)}$ and $\mathbf{v} = \mathbf{A}^\top\mathbf{s} + \mathbf{z} \in \mathbb{Z}_q^m$. Therefore, due to Lemma 4, for our choices of α and α', the output of ReRand is

$$\begin{aligned}\mathbf{c}^\top &= \big(\mathbf{A}^\top\mathbf{s}\big)^\top [\mathbf{I}_m|\mathbf{R}] + \mathbf{z}'^\top \\ &= \mathbf{s}^\top[\mathbf{A}|\mathbf{AR}] + \mathbf{z}'^\top \quad \in \mathbb{Z}_q^{m(\ell+1)},\end{aligned}$$

where the distribution of $\mathbf{z}'$ is within statistical distance from $\mathbf{z}' \leftarrow D_{\mathbb{Z}^{m(\ell+1)},\alpha' q}$. By parsing $\mathbf{c}$ appropriately as above, it can be seen that it is statistically close to $(\mathbf{c}_i)_{i\in[0,\ell]}$ of Eq.(3). Therefore, the challenge ciphertexts of Game_1 and Game_2 are statistically indistinguishable. Hence, we have $|\Pr[S_1] - \Pr[S_2]| = \mathsf{negl}(n)$.

Game_3 : In this game, we further change the way the challenge ciphertext is created. To create the challenge ciphertext, the challenger first samples $v \leftarrow \mathbb{Z}_q$, $\mathbf{v}' \leftarrow \mathbb{Z}_q^m$ and $\mathbf{z} \leftarrow D_{\mathbb{Z}^m,\alpha q}$, and runs $\mathsf{ReRand}\Big([\mathbf{I}_m|\mathbf{R}], \mathbf{v}, \alpha q, \frac{\alpha'}{2\alpha}\Big) \rightarrow \mathbf{c} \in \mathbb{Z}_q^{m(\ell+1)}$, where $\mathbf{v} = \mathbf{v}' + \mathbf{z}$. Then, the challenge ciphertext is set as in Eq.(4). We show in the full version that we have $|\Pr[S_2] - \Pr[S_3]| = \mathsf{negl}(n)$. Assuming the hardness of $\mathsf{LWE}_{n,m+1,q,\chi}$.

Furthermore, since v is uniformly random over $\mathbb{Z}_q$ and independent of the other values, the term in the challenge ciphertext $c = v + \mathsf{M}_b\lfloor q/2\rceil$ that conveys the information on the message is distributed independently from the value of M_b. Therefore, we have $\Pr[S_3] = 1/2$. Combining everything together, we have $\left|\Pr[S_0] - \frac{1}{2}\right| = \left|\sum_{i=0}^{2}(\Pr[S_i] - \Pr[S_{i+1}]) + \Pr[S_3] - \frac{1}{2}\right| \leq \left|\Pr[S_3] - \frac{1}{2}\right| + \sum_{i=0}^{2}|\Pr[S_i] - \Pr[S_{i+1}]| \leq \mathsf{negl}(n)$. Therefore, the probability that $\mathcal{A}$ wins Game_0 is negligible.

3.4 Multi-bit Variant

Here, we explain how to extend our scheme to a multi-bit variant without increasing much the size of the master public keys, secret keys, and ciphertexts following the techniques of [PVW08, ABB10, Yam16]. To modify the scheme to deal with message space of length ℓ_M, we replace $\mathbf{u} \in \mathbb{Z}_q^n$ in MPK with $\mathbf{U} \in \mathbb{Z}_q^{n\times \ell_M}$.

The component c in the ciphertext is replaced with $\mathbf{c} = \mathbf{U}^\top \mathbf{s} + \mathbf{z} + \mathsf{M}\lceil q/2 \rceil$ where $\mathbf{z} \leftarrow D_{\mathbb{Z}^{\ell_M}, \alpha q}$ and $\mathsf{M} \in \{0,1\}^{\ell_M}$ is the message to be encrypted. When decrypting the message, one samples a matrix $\mathbf{E} \in \mathbb{Z}^{2m \times \ell_M}$ such that $[\mathbf{A}|\mathbf{A}\mathbf{R}_{\boldsymbol{y}} + \langle \boldsymbol{x}, \boldsymbol{y} \rangle \mathbf{G}]\mathbf{E} = \mathbf{U}$, which is possible given $\mathsf{sk}_{\boldsymbol{y}}$ by running SampleRight in a column wise manner. We can prove security for the multi-bit variant from $\mathsf{LWE}_{n,m+\ell_M,q,\chi}$ by naturally extending the proof of Theorem 2. We note that the same parameters as in the single-bit variant work for the multi-bit variant. By this change, the sizes of the master public keys, ciphertexts, and private keys become $\tilde{O}((n^2\ell + n\ell_M)\log q)$,$\tilde{O}((n + \ell + \ell_M)\log q)$, and $\tilde{O}(n^2 \log q)$ from $\tilde{O}(n^2\ell \log q)$, $\tilde{O}((n+\ell)\log q)$, and $\tilde{O}(n^2 \log q)$, respectively. The sizes of the master public keys and ciphertexts will be asymptotically the same as long as $\ell_M = \tilde{O}(n)$. To deal with longer messages, we employ a KEM-DEM approach as suggested in [Yam16]. Namely, we encrypt a random ephemeral key of sufficient length and then encrypt the message by using the ephemeral key.

4 Constructions from Lattices with Inner Product over $\mathbb{Z}_p$

In this section, we construct a *stateful* NIPE scheme with inner product space $\mathbb{Z}_p$ for $p = p(n)$ a prime, where the predicate and attribute spaces are $\mathbb{Z}_p^\ell$.

Overview. We give a more detailed overview on the intuition given in the introduction. First, we need the state to keep track of what kind of predicate vectors $\boldsymbol{y}$ we gave out secret keys to. Unlike in the NIPE construction of Sect. 3, for our NIPE scheme with predicate space $\mathbb{Z}_p$, the linear dependency of the predicate vectors (over $\mathbb{Z}_p$) and the secret keys (over $\mathbb{Z}$) are no longer consistent. Namely, when an adversary queries for linearly dependent predicate vectors over $\mathbb{Z}_p$, the corresponding secret keys may no longer be linearly dependent over $\mathbb{Z}$. For our particular construction, when an adversary obtains secret keys to a linearly independent predicate vectors over $\mathbb{Z}$, the scheme leads to a complete break in security. Therefore, we need to maintain information on the linear span of the predicate vectors (over $\mathbb{Z}_p$ and $\mathbb{Z}$) that it has generated secret keys to, and create a secret key for a new predicate vector $\boldsymbol{y}$ as a $\mathbb{Z}$-linear combination of the previously generated secret keys if $\boldsymbol{y}$ lies in the $\mathbb{Z}_p$-linear span maintained in the state.

Here, we also maintain our state in a unique way, which allows us to base security of our scheme on a weaker polynomial LWE assumption. As already mentioned, the state maintains the information of the linear span of the predicate vectors that it has generated secret keys to. In our scheme, this is expressed by a list of tuples of the form $(\boldsymbol{h}^{(i)}, \mathsf{h}^{(i)}, \mathsf{sk}_{\boldsymbol{h}^{(i)}}) \in \mathbb{Z}_p^\ell \times \mathbb{Z}^\ell \times \mathbb{Z}^{m \times m}$, where $i \in \mathsf{list} \subseteq [\ell]$. Informally, list indicates the distinctive indices that specifies the linear span of the so far queried predicate vectors, and $|\mathsf{list}|$ is the dimension of the linear span. Furthermore, $\boldsymbol{h}^{(i)} \in \mathbb{Z}_p^\ell$ are vectors specifying the linear span of the queried predicate vectors, $\mathsf{h}^{(i)}$ are vectors in $\mathbb{Z}^\ell$ that is in a sense encodings of $\boldsymbol{h}^{(i)}$ that maintain linear dependency over $\mathbb{Z}$, and $\mathsf{sk}_{\boldsymbol{h}^{(i)}}$ are the secret keys corresponding to the predicate vector $\boldsymbol{h}^{(i)}$. When queried a new predicate vector $\boldsymbol{y}$, the algorithm first checks if it lies in the $\mathbb{Z}_p$-linear span of $\{\boldsymbol{h}^{(i)}\}_{i\in\mathsf{list}}$. If so, (informally) it computes secret keys as a $\mathbb{Z}$-linear combination of $\{\mathsf{sk}_{\boldsymbol{h}^{(i)}}\}_{i\in\mathsf{list}}$. If not, it processes $\boldsymbol{y}$ into a new vector $\boldsymbol{h}^{(j)} \in \mathbb{Z}_p^\ell$ that does not lie in the $\mathbb{Z}_p$-linear span of $\{\boldsymbol{h}^{(i)}\}_{i\in\mathsf{list}}$ and adds j to list. Here, in order for us to base security on an LWE assumption with polynomial approximation factor, we need to process $\boldsymbol{y}$ in such a way that the matrix with columns $\{\boldsymbol{h}^{(i)}\}_{i\in\mathsf{list}}$ interpreted as vectors in $\mathbb{Z}^\ell$ has a small singular value. At a high level, this can be achieved by keeping the diagonal elements small, which we can do since we can store any factor of $\boldsymbol{h}^{(i)} \in \mathbb{Z}_p^\ell$ without altering the $\mathbb{Z}_p$-linear span. Here, the crucial observation is that the $\mathbb{Z}_p$-linear dependency of $\{\boldsymbol{h}^{(i)}\}_{i\in\mathsf{list}}$ and the size of the singular values of $\{\boldsymbol{h}^{(i)}\}_{i\in\mathsf{list}}$ interpreted as a matrix over $\mathbb{Z}$ are (almost completely) independent with each other.

Construction. Let $q = p^d$ for some positive integer $d \geq 3$ and let $m(n), \sigma(n), \alpha(n), \alpha'(n), s(n)$ be parameters that are specified later. Here, we assume that the message space is $\{0,1\}$. We can easily extend the scheme to the multi-bit variant similarly to Sect. 3.4.

$\mathsf{Setup}(1^n, 1^\ell)$: On input $1^n, 1^\ell$, it samples a random matrix $\mathbf{A} \leftarrow \mathbb{Z}_q^{n\times m}$, a random vector $\mathbf{u} \leftarrow \mathbb{Z}_q^n$, random matrices $\mathbf{R}_i \leftarrow \left(D_{\mathbb{Z}^m,\sigma}\right)^m$ for $i \in [\ell]$ and sets $\mathbf{B}_i = \mathbf{A}\mathbf{R}_i \mod q$. Furthermore, it initializes a state st that inculdes an empty list $\mathsf{list} \subseteq [\ell]$. Finally, it outputs

$$\mathsf{MPK} = \left(\mathbf{A}, \{\mathbf{B}_i\}_{i\in[\ell]}, \mathbf{u}\right) \quad \text{and} \quad \mathsf{MSK} = \left(\mathsf{st}, \{\mathbf{R}_i\}_{i\in[\ell]}\right).$$

$\mathsf{KeyGen}\,(\mathsf{MPK}, \mathsf{MSK}, \boldsymbol{y} \in \mathbb{Z}_p^\ell, \mathsf{st})$: Given a predicate vector $\boldsymbol{y} \in \mathbb{Z}_p^\ell$ and an internal state st, it computes the secret key $\mathsf{sk}_{\boldsymbol{y}}$ as follows. At any point of the execution, the internal state st contains a list of indices $\mathsf{list} \subseteq [\ell]$ and at most ℓ tuples of the form $(\boldsymbol{h}^{(i)}, \mathsf{h}^{(i)}, \mathsf{sk}_{\boldsymbol{h}^{(i)}}) \in \mathbb{Z}_p^\ell \times \mathbb{Z}^\ell \times \mathbb{Z}^{m\times m}$, where the vectors $\{\boldsymbol{h}^{(i)}\}_{j\in\mathsf{list}}$ form a basis of the $\mathbb{Z}_p$-linear span of the predicate vectors which the key extraction queries has been made so far.

If $\boldsymbol{y} \in \mathbb{Z}_p^\ell$ is linearly independent modulo p from all the $\{\boldsymbol{h}^{(j)}\}_{j\in\mathsf{list}}$ in the state st, it first runs the following procedure. By construction, for all $j \in \mathsf{list}$, we will have $(j = \arg\min_{i\in[\ell]}\{h_i^{(j)} \neq 0\}) \wedge (h_j^{(j)} = 1)$, i.e., the smallest index for which the entry of $\boldsymbol{h}^{(j)}$ is non-zero is j, and at that index it holds that $h_j^{(j)} = 1$. It sets $\boldsymbol{h} = \boldsymbol{y}$, and starting with the smallest index $j \in \mathsf{list}$, it iterates through list in ascending order by updating $\boldsymbol{h} \leftarrow \boldsymbol{h} - h_j \cdot \boldsymbol{h}^{(j)} \mod p$ so that the updated $\boldsymbol{h}$ satisfies $h_j = 0 \mod p$, where h_j denotes the j-th element of $\boldsymbol{h}$. After it runs through all the element in list, it finds the smallest index j' such that $\boldsymbol{h}_{j'} \neq 0$. This always exists since $\boldsymbol{y}$ is linearly independent modulo p from $\{\boldsymbol{h}^{(j)}\}_{j\in\mathsf{list}}$. Then, it updates $\boldsymbol{h}$ once more by $\boldsymbol{h} \leftarrow (1/h_{j'}) \cdot \boldsymbol{h} \mod p$ and sets $\boldsymbol{h}^{(j')} = \boldsymbol{h} \in \mathbb{Z}_p^\ell$. It can be checked that $(j' = \arg\min_{i\in[\ell]}\{h_i^{(j')} \neq 0\}) \wedge (h_{j'}^{(j')} = 1)$. Finally, it sets $\mathsf{h}^{(j')} = \boldsymbol{h}^{(j')}$, interpreted as a vector in $\mathbb{Z}^\ell$, and sets $\mathsf{sk}_{\boldsymbol{h}^{(j')}}$ as

$$\mathbf{R}_{\boldsymbol{h}^{(j')}} = \sum_{i=1}^{\ell} \mathsf{h}_i^{(j')} \mathbf{R}_i \in \mathbb{Z}^{m \times m}, \tag{5}$$

where $\mathsf{h}_i^{(j')}$ is the i-th entry of $\mathbf{h}^{(j')}$. It then adds j' to list and the tuple $(\boldsymbol{h}^{(j')}, \mathbf{h}^{(j')}, \mathsf{sk}_{\boldsymbol{h}^{(j')}})$ to st.[5] Note that after this procedure, the predicate vector $\boldsymbol{y}$ is linearly dependent modulo p with the vectors $\{\boldsymbol{h}^{(j)}\}_{j \in \mathsf{list}}$ in the state st. Furthermore, when ℓ linearly independent queries has been made, we have $\mathsf{list} = [\ell]$ and the set of vectors $\{\boldsymbol{h}^{(j)}\}_{j \in [\ell]}$ forms a lower triangular matrix with ones along the diagonal.

Finally, to construct the secret key for $\boldsymbol{y}$, it sets $\boldsymbol{y} = \sum_{j \in \mathsf{list}} \lambda_j \boldsymbol{h}^{(j)} \mod p$ for some λ_j's in $\mathbb{Z}_p$ and sets $\mathbf{y} = \sum_{j \in \mathsf{list}} \lambda_j \mathbf{h}^{(j)} \in \mathbb{Z}^{\ell}$ where here λ_j is viewed as an element over $\mathbb{Z}$. Finally, it sets $\mathsf{sk}_{\boldsymbol{y}}$ as

$$\mathbf{R}_{\boldsymbol{y}} = \sum_{i=1}^{\ell} \mathsf{y}_i \mathbf{R}_i \in \mathbb{Z}^{m \times m},$$

where y_i is the i-th entry of $\mathbf{y}$, and returns the tuple $(\mathbf{y}, \mathsf{sk}_{\boldsymbol{y}}) \in \mathbb{Z}^{\ell} \times \mathbb{Z}^{m \times m}$ as the secret key.

$\mathsf{Enc}(\mathsf{MPK}, \boldsymbol{x} \in \mathbb{Z}_p^{\ell}, \mathsf{M})$: To encrypt a message $\mathsf{M} \in \{0,1\}$ for an attribute $\boldsymbol{x} = (x_1, \cdots, x_\ell) \in \mathbb{Z}_p^{\ell}$, it samples $\mathbf{s} \leftarrow \mathbb{Z}_q^n$, $\mathbf{z}_0, \mathbf{z}_i \leftarrow D_{\mathbb{Z}^m, \alpha' q}$ for $i \in [\ell]$, and computes

$$\begin{cases} c = p^{d-1} \cdot (\mathbf{u}^\top \mathbf{s} + \mathsf{M} \lfloor p/2 \rceil), \\ \mathbf{c}_0 = \mathbf{A}^\top \mathbf{s} + \mathbf{z}_0, \\ \mathbf{c}_i = (\mathbf{B}_i + p^{d-1} \cdot x_i \mathbf{G})^\top \mathbf{s} + \mathbf{z}_i, \quad (i \in [\ell]), \end{cases}$$

Then, it returns the ciphertext $C = (c, \mathbf{c}_0, (\mathbf{c}_i)_{i \in [\ell]}) \in \mathbb{Z}_q \times (\mathbb{Z}_q^m)^{\ell+1}$ with its corresponding attribute $\boldsymbol{x}$.

$\mathsf{Dec}(\mathsf{MPK}, (\boldsymbol{y}, \mathbf{y}, \mathsf{sk}_{\boldsymbol{y}}), (\boldsymbol{x}, C))$: To decrypt a ciphertext $C = (c, \mathbf{c}_0, (\mathbf{c}_i)_{i \in [\ell]})$ with an associating attribute $\boldsymbol{x} \in \mathbb{Z}_p^{\ell}$, it first computes

$$\mathbf{c}_{\boldsymbol{y}} = \sum_{i=1}^{\ell} \mathsf{y}_i \mathbf{c}_i \mod q \in \mathbb{Z}_q^m,$$

where y_i is the i-th entry of $\mathbf{y}$. Next, it samples a short vector $\mathbf{e} \in \mathbb{Z}^{2m}$ by running $\mathsf{SampleSkewed}(\mathbf{A}, \mathsf{sk}_{\boldsymbol{y}} = \mathbf{R}_{\boldsymbol{y}}, \langle \boldsymbol{x}, \boldsymbol{y} \rangle, p^{d-1}\mathbf{u}, \mathbf{T}_{\mathbf{G}})$. Then, it computes $t = c - \mathbf{e}^\top [\mathbf{c}_0^\top | \mathbf{c}_{\boldsymbol{y}}^\top]^\top \in \mathbb{Z}_q$.
Finally, it returns 1 if $|t - \lceil q/2 \rceil| < \lceil q/4 \rceil$ and 0 otherwise.

[5] Although $\boldsymbol{h}^{(j')} \in \mathbb{Z}_p^{\ell}$ and $\mathbf{h}^{(j')} \in \mathbb{Z}^{\ell}$ are in some sense identical, we intentionally write it redundantly in this form for consistency with the other predicate vectors $\boldsymbol{y}$, i.e., $(\mathbf{h}^{(j')}, \mathsf{sk}_{\boldsymbol{h}^{(j')}})$ acts as a valid secret key for the predicate vector $\boldsymbol{h}^{(j')}$.

4.1 Correctness and Parameter Selection

The correctness of the scheme and a candidate parameter selection is given in the full version. Notably, by setting the parameters appropriately we can base security on the polynomial LWE assumption.

4.2 Security Proof

Theorem 3. *The above NIPE scheme with inner product space* $\mathbb{Z}_p$ *is selectively secure assuming* $\mathsf{FE.LWE}_{n,m+1,q,\chi}$ *is hard, where* $\chi = D_{\mathbb{Z},\alpha q}$.

Proof. Let $\mathcal{A}$ be a PPT adversary that breaks the selective security of the NIPE scheme. Here, assume that $\mathcal{A}$ makes key extraction queries in a way that at the end of the game the state st contains $\ell - 1$ linearly independent (modulo p) predicate vectors $\{\boldsymbol{h}^{(j)}\}_{j\in\mathsf{list}}$ where $|\mathsf{list}| = \ell-1$ (which are all orthogonal modulo p to the challenge attribute vector $\boldsymbol{x}^*$). Note that this assumption can be made without loss of generality, since $\mathcal{A}$ may simply ignore unnecessary additional secret keys, and $\mathcal{A}$ can not obtain no more than $\ell - 1$ linearly independent (modulo p) vectors without violating the $\langle \boldsymbol{x}^*, \boldsymbol{y}\rangle = 0 \mod p$ condition. The proof proceeds with a sequence of games that starts with the real game and ends with a game in which $\mathcal{A}$ has negligible advantage. For each game Game_i denote S_i the event that $\mathcal{A}$ wins the game.

Game_0 : This is the real security game. Namely, adversary $\mathcal{A}$ declares its challenge attribute vector $\boldsymbol{x}^* \in \mathbb{Z}_p^\ell$ at the beginning of the game. Note that any predicate vector $\boldsymbol{y} \in \mathbb{Z}_p^\ell$ queried by $\mathcal{A}$ to the challenger as a key extraction query must satisfy $\langle \boldsymbol{x}^*, \boldsymbol{y}\rangle = 0 \mod p$ if $\mathcal{A}$ is a legitimate adversary.

Game_1 : In this game, we change the way the public matrices $\mathbf{B}_1, \cdots, \mathbf{B}_\ell$ are created. On receiving the challenge attribute vector $\boldsymbol{x}^* = (x_1^*, \cdots, x_\ell^*) \in \mathbb{Z}_p^\ell$ from adversary $\mathcal{A}$ at the beginning of the game, the challenger samples random matrices $\mathbf{R}_i \leftarrow \left(D_{\mathbb{Z}^m,\sigma}\right)^m$ and sets $\mathbf{B}_i = \mathbf{A}\mathbf{R}_i - p^{d-1} \cdot x_i^* \mathbf{G} \mod q$ for $i \in [\ell]$. Otherwise, the behavior of the challenger is identical as in Game_0. Namely, the challenger remains to answer the key extraction query for a predicate vector $\boldsymbol{y} \in \mathbb{Z}_p^\ell$ and creates the challenge ciphertext as in Game_0.

Before moving on to Game_2, we show that Game_0 is *statistically* indistinguishable from Game_1. In particular, we prove that the view of the adversary in both games is statistically close. In doing so, we first show that every secret keys are $\mathbb{Z}$-linear combinations of the secret keys stored in the state st. Namely, let $\{\boldsymbol{h}^{(j)}\}_{j\in\mathsf{list}}$ denote the vectors stored in the state st on time of constructing the secret key for the queried predicate vector $\boldsymbol{y}$, where $\mathsf{list} \subseteq [\ell]$ is the index set contained in st. Then, we want to show that for a predicate vector $\boldsymbol{y}$ of the form $\sum_{j\in\mathsf{list}} \lambda_j \boldsymbol{h}^{(j)} \mod p$ for some λ_j's in $\mathbb{Z}_p$, the corresponding secret key $\mathsf{sk}_{\boldsymbol{y}}\ (= \mathbf{R}_{\boldsymbol{y}})$ is a $\mathbb{Z}$-linear combination of $\{\mathsf{sk}_{\boldsymbol{h}^{(j)}} = \mathbf{R}_{\boldsymbol{h}^{(j)}}\}_{j\in\mathsf{list}}$. To see this let the tuples stored in st be $(\boldsymbol{h}^{(j)}, \mathsf{h}^{(j)}, \mathsf{sk}_{\boldsymbol{h}^{(j)}} = \mathbf{R}_{\boldsymbol{h}^{(j)}}) \in \mathbb{Z}_p^\ell \times \mathbb{Z}^\ell \times \mathbb{Z}^{m\times m}$ for $j \in \mathsf{list}$.

Then, we have the following:

$$\mathbf{R}_y = \sum_{i=1}^{\ell} \mathsf{y}_i \mathbf{R}_i \overset{\text{(i)}}{=} \sum_{i=1}^{\ell} \Big(\sum_{j \in \mathsf{list}} \lambda_j \mathsf{h}_i^{(j)} \Big) \mathbf{R}_i = \sum_{j \in \mathsf{list}} \lambda_j \Big(\sum_{i=1}^{\ell} \mathsf{h}_i^{(j)} \mathbf{R}_i \Big) \overset{\text{(ii)}}{=} \sum_{j \in \mathsf{list}} \lambda_j \mathbf{R}_{\boldsymbol{h}^{(j)}},$$

where $\mathsf{h}_i^{(j)}$ is the i-th entry of $\mathbf{h}^{(j)}$. Equation (i) follows from the definition of y_i and Eq. (ii) follows from Eq. (5)

Therefore the distribution of the secret keys obtained by adversary $\mathcal{A}$ is completely determined by the distribution of the secret keys $\{\mathsf{sk}_{\boldsymbol{h}^{(j)}} = \mathbf{R}_{\boldsymbol{h}^{(j)}}\}_{j \in \mathsf{list}}$ stored in the state st at the end of the game. Therefore, the view of the adversary in both games is determined by

$$\Big\{ \mathsf{MPK} = \big\{ \mathbf{A}, \{\mathbf{B}_i\}_{i \in [\ell]}, \mathbf{u} \big\}, \quad \{\mathbf{R}_{\boldsymbol{h}^{(j)}}\}_{j \in \mathsf{list}}, \quad C^* \Big\},$$

where $C^* \leftarrow \mathsf{Enc}(\mathsf{MPK}, \boldsymbol{x}^*, \mathsf{M}_b)$ is the challenge ciphertext, b is the random bit chosen by the challenger and $|\mathsf{list}| = \ell - 1$ by assumption. Observe that in both games $\mathbf{A}, \mathbf{u}$ are distributed identically and the challenge ciphertext C^* is created using only the terms in MPK (with some extra randomness that are identical in both games). Therefore, the differences in the views of the adversary in Game_0 and Game_1 is solely determined by the difference in the distribution of

$$\Big\{ \{\mathbf{B}_i\}_{i \in [\ell]}, \quad \{\mathbf{R}_{\boldsymbol{h}^{(j)}}\}_{j \in \mathsf{list}} \Big\}. \tag{6}$$

Hence, we aim at proving that the view of Eq.(6) in both games are statistically close to the adversary. More specifically, we compare the following probability of each game:

$$\begin{aligned} &\Pr\Big[\Big\{ \{\mathbf{B}_i\}_{i \in [\ell]}, \{\mathbf{R}_{\boldsymbol{h}^{(j)}}\}_{j \in \mathsf{list}} \Big\} = \Big\{ \{\widehat{\mathbf{B}}_i\}_{i \in [\ell]}, \{\widehat{\mathbf{R}}_{\boldsymbol{h}^{(j)}}\}_{j \in \mathsf{list}} \Big\} \Big] \\ &= \underbrace{\Pr\Big[\{\mathbf{R}_{\boldsymbol{h}^{(j)}}\}_{j \in \mathsf{list}} = \{\widehat{\mathbf{R}}_{\boldsymbol{h}^{(j)}}\}_{j \in \mathsf{list}} \;\Big|\; \{\mathbf{B}_i\}_{i \in [\ell]} = \{\widehat{\mathbf{B}}_i\}_{i \in [\ell]} \Big]}_{\text{(A)}} \cdot \underbrace{\Pr\Big[\{\mathbf{B}_i\}_{i \in [\ell]} = \{\widehat{\mathbf{B}}_i\}_{i \in [\ell]} \Big]}_{\text{(B)}}, \end{aligned}$$

where the probability is taken over the randomness of $\{\mathbf{R}_i\}_{i \in [\ell]}$ during Setup; recall each $\mathbf{R}_i$ is distributed according to $\left(D_{\mathbb{Z}^m,\sigma}\right)^m$ in both games. Note that in the above we abuse the notation for sets by implicitly assigning an order over the elements, i.e., $\{\mathbf{X}, \mathbf{Y}\} \neq \{\mathbf{Y}, \mathbf{X}\}$.

We first prove that the value of (B) is negligibly close in both games. Observe that for all $i \in [\ell]$, $\mathbf{A}\mathbf{R}_i$ is distributed uniformly at random over $\mathbb{Z}_q^{n \times m}$ with all but negligible probability where $\mathbf{R}_i \leftarrow \left(D_{\mathbb{Z}^m,\sigma}\right)^m$, which follows from Lemma 1 and our parameter selections. Concretely, since $\mathbf{B}_i = \mathbf{A}\mathbf{R}_i$ and $\mathbf{B}_i = \mathbf{A}\mathbf{R}_i - p^{d-1} \cdot x_i^* \mathbf{G}$ for Game_0 and Game_1 respectively, we have that in both games $\{\mathbf{B}_i\}_{i \in [\ell]}$ is distributed statistically close to uniform over $\left(\mathbb{Z}_q^{n \times m}\right)^\ell$.

We now proceed to prove that the value of (A) is negligibly close in both games. We first analyze the case for Game_0. Let $\mathbf{B}_{\mathsf{view}} \in \mathbb{Z}_q^{n \times m\ell}$ and $\mathbf{R} \in \mathbb{Z}^{m \times m\ell}$

denote the matrices $[\mathbf{B}_1|\cdots|\mathbf{B}_\ell]$ and $[\mathbf{R}_1|\cdots|\mathbf{R}_\ell]$, respectively. Then, we have $\mathbf{B}_{\mathsf{view}} = \mathbf{AR} \mod q$. Furthermore, let $\mathbf{T} = [\mathbf{T}_1|\cdots|\mathbf{T}_\ell] \in \mathbb{Z}^{m\times m\ell}$ be an arbitrary solution to $\mathbf{B}_{\mathsf{view}} = \mathbf{AT} \mod q$. Then, due to Lemma 1 and the conditions on $\{\widehat{\mathbf{B}}_i\}_{i\in[\ell]} = \{\mathbf{AR}_i\}_{i\in[\ell]}$, the conditional distribution of $\mathbf{R}$ is given by $D_{\Lambda^\perp(\mathbf{A})^{m\ell}+\mathbf{T},\sigma}$. Now, we are ready to determine the conditional distribution of the secret keys $\{\mathbf{R}_{\boldsymbol{h}^{(j)}}\}_{j\in\mathsf{list}}$ obtained by the adversary $\mathcal{A}$. Here, let $j^* \in [\ell]$ denote the index $[\ell]\backslash\mathsf{list}$ where $|\mathsf{list}| = \ell - 1$,and observe that $\mathbf{R}_{\mathsf{sk}} := [\mathbf{R}_{\boldsymbol{h}^{(1)}}|\mathbf{R}_{\boldsymbol{h}^{(2)}}|\cdots|\mathbf{R}_{\boldsymbol{h}^{(\ell-1)}}] \in \mathbb{Z}^{m\times m(\ell-1)}$ is equal to the following

$$\underbrace{[\mathbf{R}_1|\mathbf{R}_2|\cdots|\mathbf{R}_\ell]}_{=\mathbf{R}\,\in\mathbb{Z}^{m\times m\ell}}\underbrace{\begin{bmatrix} \mathsf{h}_1^{(1)}\mathbf{I}_m & \cdots & \mathsf{h}_1^{(j^*-1)}\mathbf{I}_m & \mathsf{h}_1^{(j^*+1)}\mathbf{I}_m & \cdots & \mathsf{h}_1^{(\ell-1)}\mathbf{I}_m \\ \mathsf{h}_2^{(1)}\mathbf{I}_m & \cdots & \mathsf{h}_2^{(j^*-1)}\mathbf{I}_m & \mathsf{h}_2^{(j^*+1)}\mathbf{I}_m & \cdots & \mathsf{h}_2^{(\ell-1)}\mathbf{I}_m \\ \vdots & & \vdots & \vdots & & \vdots \\ \mathsf{h}_\ell^{(1)}\mathbf{I}_m & \cdots & \mathsf{h}_\ell^{(j^*-1)}\mathbf{I}_m & \mathsf{h}_\ell^{(j^*+1)}\mathbf{I}_m & \cdots & \mathsf{h}_\ell^{(\ell-1)}\mathbf{I}_m \end{bmatrix}}_{:=\mathbf{M}\,\in\mathbb{Z}^{m\ell\times m(\ell-1)}}, \quad (7)$$

where $\mathsf{h}_k^{(j)}$ is the k-th entry of $\mathbf{h}^{(j)}$ that is associated with the j-th vector $\boldsymbol{h}^{(j)}$ in st for $j \in \mathsf{list}$. We denote the left and right hand matrices as $\mathbf{R}_{\mathsf{sk}} \in \mathbb{Z}^{m\times m(\ell-1)}$ and $\mathbf{M} \in \mathbb{Z}^{m\ell\times m(\ell-1)}$ respectively. We show in the full versionthat there exists a matrix $\mathbf{W} \in \mathbb{Z}^{m\ell\times m}$ such that $\mathbf{W}^\top\mathbf{M} = \mathbf{0}$ over $\mathbb{Z}$ with a sufficiently small singular value. Therefore, for our parameter selection and the fact that $\mathbf{R}$ is distributed according to $D_{\Lambda^\perp(\mathbf{A})^{m\ell}+\mathbf{T},\sigma}$ we can apply Theorem 1. Namely, the distribution of $\mathbf{R}_{\mathsf{sk}} = \mathbf{RM}$ is statistically close to a distribution parameterized by $\Lambda^\perp(\mathbf{A}), \sigma, \mathbf{M}$ and $(\mathbf{TM} \mod \Lambda^\perp(\mathbf{A})^{m\ell}\mathbf{M})$.

We now show that this holds in case for Game_1 as well. We begin by determining the conditional distribution of $\mathbf{R}$ given $\{\mathbf{B}_i\}_{i\in[\ell]} = \{\mathbf{AR}_i - p^{d-1}\cdot x_i^*\mathbf{G}\}_{i\in[\ell]}$. Let us denote $\mathbf{G}_{\boldsymbol{x}^*} \in \mathbb{Z}_q^{n\times m\ell}$ as the matrix $p^{d-1}\cdot[x_1^*\mathbf{G}|x_2^*\mathbf{G}|\cdots|x_\ell^*\mathbf{G}]$. Then, $\mathbf{B}_{\mathsf{view}} + \mathbf{G}_{\boldsymbol{x}^*} = \mathbf{AR} \mod q$. Next, let us chose an arbitrary matrix $\mathbf{E} \in \mathbb{Z}^{m\times m}$ such that $\mathbf{G} = \mathbf{AE} \mod q$, and define $\mathbf{E}_{\boldsymbol{x}^*} \in \mathbb{Z}^{m\times m\ell}$ as the matrix $p^{d-1}\cdot[x_1^*\mathbf{E}|x_2^*\mathbf{E}|\cdots|x_\ell^*\mathbf{E}]$. Then, we have $\mathbf{G}_{\boldsymbol{x}^*} = \mathbf{AE}_{\boldsymbol{x}^*} \mod q$. Combining this with the $\mathbf{T}$ we have defined above in Game_0, we obtain $\mathbf{B}_{\mathsf{view}}+\mathbf{G}_{\boldsymbol{x}^*} = \mathbf{A}(\mathbf{T}+\mathbf{E}_{\boldsymbol{x}^*}) \mod q$. Therefore, by Lemma 1, the conditional distribution of $\mathbf{R}$ given $\{\mathbf{B}_i\}_{i\in[\ell]}$ is $D_{\Lambda^\perp(\mathbf{A})^{m\ell}+\mathbf{T}+\mathbf{E}_{\boldsymbol{x}^*},\sigma}$. Next, we determine the conditional distribution of the secret keys $\{\mathbf{R}_{\boldsymbol{h}^{(j)}}\}_{j\in\mathsf{list}}$ obtained by the adversary $\mathcal{A}$. Observe that equation Eq.(7) holds for Game_1 as well, since we do not change the way we answer the key extraction query. Hence, following the same argument as above, by Theorem 1 and the fact that $\mathbf{R}$ is distributed according to $D_{\Lambda^\perp(\mathbf{A})^{m\ell}+\mathbf{T}+\mathbf{E}_{\boldsymbol{x}^*},\sigma}$, we have that the distribution of $\mathbf{R}_{\mathsf{sk}} = \mathbf{RM}$ is statistically close to a distribution parameterized by $\Lambda^\perp(\mathbf{A}), \sigma, \mathbf{M}$ and $(\mathbf{TM} + \mathbf{E}_{\boldsymbol{x}^*}\mathbf{M} \mod \Lambda^\perp(\mathbf{A})^{m\ell}\mathbf{M})$.

Finally, we prove that $\mathbf{E}_{\boldsymbol{x}^*}\mathbf{M} \in \Lambda^\perp(\mathbf{A})^{m\ell}\mathbf{M}$ to prove equivalence of the distributions between Game_0 and Game_1. Observe that $\mathbf{E}_{\boldsymbol{x}^*}\mathbf{M}$ is qual to the following:

$$p^{d-1} \cdot \mathbf{E} \cdot [x_1^* \mathbf{I}_m | x_2^* \mathbf{I}_m | \cdots | x_\ell^* \mathbf{I}_m] \cdot \begin{bmatrix} \mathsf{h}_1^{(1)} \mathbf{I}_m & \dots & \mathsf{h}_1^{(j^*-1)} \mathbf{I}_m & \mathsf{h}_1^{(j^*+1)} \mathbf{I}_m & \dots & \mathsf{h}_1^{(\ell-1)} \mathbf{I}_m \\ \mathsf{h}_2^{(1)} \mathbf{I}_m & \dots & \mathsf{h}_2^{(j^*-1)} \mathbf{I}_m & \mathsf{h}_2^{(j^*+1)} \mathbf{I}_m & \dots & \mathsf{h}_2^{(\ell-1)} \mathbf{I}_m \\ \vdots & \dots & \vdots & \vdots & \dots & \vdots \\ \mathsf{h}_\ell^{(1)} \mathbf{I}_m & & \mathsf{h}_\ell^{(j^*-1)} \mathbf{I}_m & \mathsf{h}_\ell^{(j^*+1)} \mathbf{I}_m & & \mathsf{h}_\ell^{(\ell-1)} \mathbf{I}_m \end{bmatrix},$$

$$= p^{d-1} \cdot \mathbf{E} \cdot [\langle \boldsymbol{x}^*, \mathsf{h}^{(1)} \rangle \mathbf{I}_m | \cdots | \langle \boldsymbol{x}^*, \mathsf{h}^{(j^*-1)} \rangle \mathbf{I}_m | \langle \boldsymbol{x}^*, \mathsf{h}^{(j^*+1)} \rangle \mathbf{I}_m | \cdots | \langle \boldsymbol{x}^*, \mathsf{h}^{(\ell-1)} \rangle \mathbf{I}_m]$$
$$= q \cdot \mathbf{E} \cdot [n_1 \mathbf{I}_m | \cdots | n_{j^*-1} \mathbf{I}_m | n_{j^*+1} \mathbf{I}_m | \cdots | n_{\ell-1} \mathbf{I}_m] \in q\mathbb{Z}^{m \times m(\ell-1)},$$

where we set $n_j = \langle \boldsymbol{x}^*, \mathsf{h}^{(j)} \rangle / p \in \mathbb{N}$ for $j \in \mathsf{list}$. Note that this is well-defined since $\langle \boldsymbol{x}^*, \mathsf{h}^{(j)} \rangle = \langle \boldsymbol{x}^*, \boldsymbol{h}^{(j)} \rangle = 0 \mod p$ (See Sect. 4.1) and $q = p^d$. Therefore, to prove $\mathbf{E}_{\boldsymbol{x}^*} \mathbf{M} \in \Lambda^\perp(\mathbf{A})^{m\ell} \mathbf{M}$, it suffices to prove that $q\mathbb{Z}^{m \times m(\ell-1)} \subset \Lambda^\perp(\mathbf{A})^{m\ell} \mathbf{M}$. Namely, we prove that for every $\mathbf{Z} \in q\mathbb{Z}^{m \times m(\ell-1)}$, there exists a matrix $\mathbf{V} \in \Lambda^\perp(\mathbf{A})^{m\ell} \subset \mathbb{Z}^{m \times m\ell}$ such that $\mathbf{VM} = \mathbf{Z}$ (over $\mathbb{Z}$). Here, recall that for the vectors $\{\boldsymbol{h}^{(j)}\}_{j \in \mathsf{list}}$ in the state st, we had $(j = \arg\min_{i \in [\ell]} \{h_i^{(j)} \neq 0\}) \wedge (h_j^{(j)} = 1)$. Namely, the smallest index with a non-zero entry for $\boldsymbol{h}^{(j)}$ is j, and at that index we have $h_j^{(j)} = 1$. Therefore, denoting $\mathbf{H} \in \mathbb{Z}^{\ell \times (\ell-1)}$ as the matrix whose columns are the vectors in $\{h^{(j)}\}_{j \in \mathsf{list}}$, we can properly rearrange the columns and rows of $\mathbf{H}$, or more concretely there exists a permutation matrix $\mathbf{P} \in \{0,1\}^{\ell \times \ell}, \mathbf{Q} \in \{0,1\}^{(\ell-1) \times (\ell-1)}$, such that $\mathbf{H}$ gets transformed into the following matrix:

$$\mathbf{PHQ} = \begin{bmatrix} \star & \cdots & \star & \star \\ \hline 1 & 0 & \cdots\cdots & 0 \\ \star & 1 & \ddots & \vdots \\ \vdots & \star & \ddots & \ddots & \vdots \\ \vdots & & \ddots & 1 & 0 \\ \star & \star & \cdots & \star & 1 \end{bmatrix} = \begin{bmatrix} \mathbf{a}^\top \\ \mathbf{U} \end{bmatrix} \in \mathbb{Z}^{\ell \times (\ell-1)}, \tag{8}$$

where $\star$ denotes an arbitrary element in $\mathbb{Z}$, $\mathbf{a} \in \mathbb{Z}^{\ell-1}$ is some vector and $\mathbf{U} \in \mathbb{Z}^{(\ell-1) \times (\ell-1)}$ is unimodular. Recall that permutation matrices are orthogonal matrices: $\mathbf{Q}^{-1} = \mathbf{Q}^\top$, and that the inverse of a unitary matrix is also unitary: $\mathbf{U}^{-1} \in \mathbb{Z}^{(\ell-1) \times (\ell-1)}$. We now proceed to prove that $\mathbf{V} = [\mathbf{0}_{m \times m} \mid \mathbf{Z} \cdot (\mathbf{QU}^{-1} \otimes \mathbf{I}_m)] \cdot (\mathbf{P} \otimes \mathbf{I}_m) \in \mathbb{Z}^{m \times m\ell}$ satisfies the above condition, i.e., $\mathbf{V} \in \Lambda^\perp(\mathbf{A})^{m\ell}$ and $\mathbf{VM} = \mathbf{Z}$ (over $\mathbb{Z}$). First, it is easy to check that $\mathbf{V} \in \Lambda^\perp(\mathbf{A})^{m\ell}$, since $\mathbf{Z} \in q\mathbb{Z}^{m \times m(\ell-1)}$ and $q\mathbb{Z}^m \subset \Lambda^\perp(\mathbf{A})$. Then, recalling that $\mathbf{M} = \mathbf{H} \otimes \mathbf{I}_m$, we have

$$\mathbf{VM} = \Big([\mathbf{0}_{m \times m} \mid \mathbf{Z} \cdot (\mathbf{QU}^{-1} \otimes \mathbf{I}_m)](\mathbf{P} \otimes \mathbf{I}_m) \Big) \cdot (\mathbf{H} \otimes \mathbf{I}_m)$$
$$= \Big([\mathbf{0}_{m \times m} \mid \mathbf{Z} \cdot (\mathbf{QU}^{-1} \otimes \mathbf{I}_m)](\mathbf{P} \otimes \mathbf{I}_m) \Big) \cdot \left(\mathbf{P}^\top \begin{bmatrix} \mathbf{a}^\top \\ \mathbf{U} \end{bmatrix} \mathbf{Q}^\top \right) \otimes \mathbf{I}_m \tag{9}$$
$$= [\mathbf{0}_{m \times m} \mid \mathbf{Z} \cdot (\mathbf{QU}^{-1} \otimes \mathbf{I}_m)](\mathbf{P} \otimes \mathbf{I}_m)(\mathbf{P}^\top \otimes \mathbf{I}_m) \left(\begin{bmatrix} \mathbf{a}^\top \mathbf{Q}^\top \\ \mathbf{UQ}^\top \end{bmatrix} \otimes \mathbf{I}_m \right) \tag{10}$$
$$= [\mathbf{0}_{m \times m} \mid \mathbf{Z} \cdot (\mathbf{QU}^{-1} \otimes \mathbf{I}_m)] \begin{bmatrix} \mathbf{a}^\top \mathbf{Q}^\top \otimes \mathbf{I}_m \\ \mathbf{UQ}^\top \otimes \mathbf{I}_m \end{bmatrix} \tag{11}$$
$$= \mathbf{Z}, \tag{12}$$

where Eq. (9) follows from Eq. (8), Eq. (10) follows from the fact that $(\mathbf{AB} \otimes \mathbf{I}_m) = (\mathbf{A} \otimes \mathbf{I}_m)(\mathbf{B} \otimes \mathbf{I}_m)$ and Eq. (11), (12) follows from the fact that $\mathbf{P}, \mathbf{Q}$ are orthogonal matrices. Therefore, we have $\mathbf{E}_{\boldsymbol{x}^*}\mathbf{M} \in \Lambda^{\perp}(\mathbf{A})^{m\ell}\mathbf{M}$.

Hence, we conclude that the value of (A), i.e., the conditional probability of $\mathbf{R}_{\mathsf{sk}}$ given $\{\mathbf{B}_i\}_{i\in[\ell]}$ in Game_0 and Game_1 are statistically close. Therefore, we have $|\Pr[S_0] - \Pr[S_1]| = \mathsf{negl}(n)$.

It remains to show that the challenge ciphertext is indistinguishable from random. Since the remaining proof follows closely to Game_2 and Game_3 in the previous proof of Theorem 2, we omit the details to the full version. The main difference is that we use the *first-is-errorless* LWE problem instead of the standard LWE problem to simulate the challenge ciphertext.

5 A Generic Construction of NIPE from LinFE

In this section, we show a generic conversion from a functional encryption scheme for inner products to a NIPE scheme. We note that the former primitive is a special case of the notion of functional encryption schemes where only linear functions are available. Henceforth we call this primitive as LinFE in the following. The idea for the conversion is drawn from the work of Agrawal et al. [ABP+17], who constructed trace and revoke schemes from LinFE.

5.1 Definition of Functional Encryption for Inner Product

Syntax. Let $\mathcal{Q}$ and $\mathcal{J}$ denote the predicate space and attribute spaces, where the inner product between elements (i.e., vectors) from $\mathcal{Q}$ and $\mathcal{J}$ are well-defined. Furthermore, let $\mathcal{D}$ denote the space where the inner product is taken. A *stateful* functional encryption scheme for inner products over $\mathcal{D}$ consists of the following four algorithms:

$\mathsf{Setup}(1^\lambda, 1^\ell) \to (\mathsf{MPK}, \mathsf{MSK}, \mathsf{st})$: The setup algorithm takes as input a security parameter 1^λ and the length ℓ of the vectors in the predicate and an attribute spaces, and outputs a master public key MPK, a master secret key MSK and an initial state st.

$\mathsf{KeyGen}(\mathsf{MPK}, \mathsf{MSK}, \mathsf{st}, \boldsymbol{y}) \to (\mathsf{sk}_{\boldsymbol{y}}, \mathsf{st})$: The key generation algorithm takes as input the master public key MPK, the master secret key MSK, the state st and a predicate vector $\boldsymbol{y} \in \mathcal{Q}$. It outputs a private key $\mathsf{sk}_{\boldsymbol{y}}$ and a updated state st. We assume that $\boldsymbol{y}$ is implicitly included in $\mathsf{sk}_{\boldsymbol{y}}$.

$\mathsf{Encrypt}(\mathsf{MPK}, \boldsymbol{x}) \to C$: The encryption algorithm takes as input a master public key MPK and attribute vector $\boldsymbol{x} \in \mathcal{J}$. It outputs a ciphertext C.

$\mathsf{Decrypt}(\mathsf{MPK}, \mathsf{sk}_{\boldsymbol{y}}, C) \to \langle \boldsymbol{x}, \boldsymbol{y} \rangle$ or $\perp$: The decryption algorithm takes as input the master public key MPK, a private key $\mathsf{sk}_{\boldsymbol{y}}$, and a ciphertext C. It outputs $\langle \boldsymbol{x}, \boldsymbol{y} \rangle$ or $\perp$, which means that the ciphertext is not in a valid form.

Correctness. We require correctness of decryption: that is, for all $\lambda, \ell \in \mathbb{N}$, and all $\boldsymbol{x} \in \mathcal{J}, \boldsymbol{y} \in \mathcal{Q}$, we require

$$\Pr[\mathsf{Dec}(\mathsf{MPK}, \mathsf{sk}_{\boldsymbol{y}}, \mathsf{Enc}(\mathsf{MPK}, \boldsymbol{x}, \mathsf{M})) = \langle \boldsymbol{x}, \boldsymbol{y} \rangle] = 1 - \mathsf{negl}(\lambda)$$

holds, where the probability is taken over the randomness used in $(\mathsf{MPK}, \mathsf{MSK}, \mathsf{st}) \leftarrow \mathsf{Setup}(1^\lambda, 1^\ell)$, $(\mathsf{sk}_{\boldsymbol{y}}, \mathsf{st}) \leftarrow \mathsf{KeyGen}(\mathsf{MPK}, \mathsf{MSK}, \mathsf{st}, \boldsymbol{y})$, and $\mathsf{Enc}(\mathsf{MPK}, \boldsymbol{x})$.

We also define a *stateless* LinFE scheme, where we do not require any state information in the above algorithms.

Security. We define the security of a (stateful) LinFE scheme for inner product space D with predicate space $\mathcal{Q}$ and attribute space $\mathcal{J}$ by the following game between a challenger and an adversary $\mathcal{A}$.

- **Setup.** At the outset of the game, the challenger runs $(\mathsf{MPK}, \mathsf{MSK}, \mathsf{st}) \leftarrow \mathsf{Setup}(1^\lambda, 1^\ell)$ and gives the public parameter MPK to $\mathcal{A}$.

- **Phase 1.** $\mathcal{A}$ may adaptively make key-extraction queries. If $\mathcal{A}$ submits a predicate vector $\boldsymbol{y} \in \mathcal{Q}$ to the challenger, the challenger runs $(\mathsf{sk}_{\boldsymbol{y}}, \mathsf{st}) \leftarrow \mathsf{KeyGen}(\mathsf{MPK}, \mathsf{MSK}, \mathsf{st}, \boldsymbol{y})$ and returns $\mathsf{sk}_{\boldsymbol{y}}$ to $\mathcal{A}$.

- **Challenge Phase.** At some point, $\mathcal{A}$ outputs messages $\boldsymbol{x}_0^*, \boldsymbol{x}_1^*$ on which it wishes to be challenged, with the restriction that $\langle \boldsymbol{x}_0^*, \boldsymbol{y} \rangle = \langle \boldsymbol{x}_1^*, \boldsymbol{y} \rangle$ (over $\mathcal{D}$) for all $\boldsymbol{y}$ queried during Phase 1. Then, the challenger picks a random bit $b \in \{0, 1\}$ and returns $C^* \leftarrow \mathsf{Enc}(\mathsf{MPK}, \boldsymbol{x}_b^*)$ to $\mathcal{A}$.

- **Phase 2.** After the challenge query, $\mathcal{A}$ may continue to make key-extraction queries for predicate vectors $\boldsymbol{y} \in \mathcal{Q}$, with the added restriction that $\langle \boldsymbol{x}_0^*, \boldsymbol{y} \rangle = \langle \boldsymbol{x}_1^*, \boldsymbol{y} \rangle$ (over $\mathcal{D}$).

- **Guess.** Finally, $\mathcal{A}$ outputs a guess b' for b. The advantage of $\mathcal{A}$ is defined as

$$\mathsf{Adv}_{\mathcal{A},\mathcal{D}}^{\mathsf{LinFE}} = \left| \Pr[b' = b] - \frac{1}{2} \right|.$$

We say that an LinFE scheme with inner product space $\mathcal{D}$ is *adaptively secure*, if the advantage of any PPT $\mathcal{A}$ is negligible. Similarly, we define *selective security* for a stateful LinFE scheme with inner product space $\mathcal{D}$, by modifying the above game so that the adversary $\mathcal{A}$ is forced to declare its challenge attribute vectors $\boldsymbol{x}_0^*, \boldsymbol{x}_1^*$ before **Setup**. Finally, we define an analogous security notion for stateless LinFE schemes, where we do not require any state information during the above game.

5.2 Generic Construction of NIPE from LinFE

Here, we show a generic construction of NIPE from LinFE. Specifically, we convert a LinFE scheme with predicate space $\mathcal{Q}$, attribute space $\mathcal{J}$ with inner product space D into an NIPE scheme over D with predicate space $\mathcal{P}$, attribute space $\mathcal{I}$, and message space $\mathcal{M}$. The conversion is possible when the following properties are satisfied:

- We require $\mathcal{P}, \mathcal{Q}, \mathcal{I}, \mathcal{J} \subseteq \mathcal{D}^\ell$ and $\mathcal{M} \subseteq \mathcal{D}$ for some integral domain $\mathcal{D}$.
- We also require $\{ \mathsf{M} \cdot \boldsymbol{x} \mid \mathsf{M} \in \mathcal{M},\ \boldsymbol{x} \in \mathcal{I} \} \subseteq \mathcal{J}$ and $\mathcal{P} = \mathcal{Q}$.
- Division can be efficiently performed over $\mathcal{D}$. More specifically, we require that given $\alpha, \beta \in \mathcal{D}$, it is possible to efficiently compute $\gamma \in \mathcal{D}$ satisfying $\alpha = \beta\gamma$ if such γ exists.

We now show the construction. Note that the conversion works both for the stateless and stateful cases. Let ($\mathsf{Setup}, \mathsf{KeyGen}, \mathsf{Enc}, \mathsf{Dec}$) be the underlying LinFE scheme and ($\mathsf{Setup}', \mathsf{KeyGen}', \mathsf{Enc}', \mathsf{Dec}'$) be the resulting NIPE scheme.

$\mathsf{Setup}'(1^\lambda, 1^\ell)$: It is the same as $\mathsf{Setup}(1^\lambda, 1^\ell)$.
$\mathsf{KeyGen}'(\mathsf{MPK}, \mathsf{MSK}, \boldsymbol{y} \in \mathcal{P}, \mathsf{st})$: It is the same as $\mathsf{KeyGen}(\mathsf{MPK}, \mathsf{MSK}, \boldsymbol{y} \in \mathcal{P}, \mathsf{st})$.
$\mathsf{Enc}'(\mathsf{MPK}, \boldsymbol{x} \in \mathcal{I}, \mathsf{M} \in \mathcal{M})$: To encrypt a message $\mathsf{M} \in \mathcal{M}$ for an attribute $\boldsymbol{x} = (x_1, \cdots, x_\ell) \in \mathcal{I}$, it runs $C \leftarrow \mathsf{Enc}(\mathsf{MPK}, \mathsf{M} \cdot \boldsymbol{x})$ and outputs C.
$\mathsf{Dec}'(\mathsf{MPK}, (\boldsymbol{y}, \mathsf{sk}_{\boldsymbol{y}}), (\boldsymbol{x}, C))$: To decrypt a ciphertext C with an associating attribute $\boldsymbol{x} \in \mathcal{I}$ using a secret key $\mathsf{sk}_{\boldsymbol{y}}$ with an associating predicate $\boldsymbol{y} \in \mathcal{P}$, it first computes $z = \mathsf{Dec}(\mathsf{MPK}, \mathsf{sk}_{\boldsymbol{y}}, C)$. It then computes $\langle \boldsymbol{x}, \boldsymbol{y} \rangle$ and outputs $\perp$ if $\langle \boldsymbol{x}, \boldsymbol{y} \rangle = 0$ over $\mathcal{D}$. Otherwise, it outputs $z / \langle \boldsymbol{x}, \boldsymbol{y} \rangle$. Note that the final step is possible because of the requirement on $\mathcal{D}$.

Correctness. Due to the requirements on the domains, we have $\mathsf{M} \cdot \boldsymbol{x} \subseteq \mathcal{J}$ and $\boldsymbol{y} \in \mathcal{Q} = \mathcal{P}$. Therefore, by the correctness of the underlying LinFE scheme, we have $z = \langle \mathsf{M} \cdot \boldsymbol{x}, \boldsymbol{y} \rangle = \mathsf{M} \cdot \langle \boldsymbol{x}, \boldsymbol{y} \rangle$ with overwhelming probability. Thus, the correctness of the resulting NIPE scheme follows.

Theorem 4. *If the underlying LinFE scheme is adaptively secure, so is the above NIPE scheme.*

Proof. Suppose there exists an adversary $\mathcal{A}$ against the NIPE scheme that has non-negligible advantage. We use $\mathcal{A}$ to construct another adversary $\mathcal{B}$ against the underlying LinFE scheme as follows.

- **Setup.** At the outset of the game, the challenger runs $(\mathsf{MPK}, \mathsf{MSK}, \mathsf{st}) \leftarrow \mathsf{Setup}(1^\lambda, 1^\ell)$ and gives the public parameter MPK to $\mathcal{B}$. $\mathcal{B}$ then passes MPK to $\mathcal{A}$.

- **Phase 1.** When $\mathcal{A}$ makes a key-extraction query for a vector $\boldsymbol{y}$, $\mathcal{B}$ submits the same $\boldsymbol{y}$ to its challenger and is given $\mathsf{sk}_{\boldsymbol{y}}$. Then, it passes the same $\mathsf{sk}_{\boldsymbol{y}}$ to $\mathcal{A}$.

- **Challenge Phase.** When $\mathcal{A}$ outputs the messages $(\mathsf{M}_0, \mathsf{M}_1)$ and the challenge attribute $\boldsymbol{x}^*$ on which it wishes to be challenged, $\mathcal{B}$ submits $(\mathsf{M}_0 \cdot \boldsymbol{x}^*, \mathsf{M}_1 \cdot \boldsymbol{x}^*)$ to its challenger and receives the challenge ciphertext C^*. $\mathcal{B}$ then passes C^* to $\mathcal{A}$.

- **Phase 2.** It is the same as **Phase 1**.

- **Guess.** Finally, $\mathcal{A}$ outputs a guess b'. $\mathcal{B}$ outputs the same bit as its guess.

Analysis. We first show that $\mathcal{B}$ does not violate the restriction of the security game as long as $\mathcal{A}$ does not. To see this, observe that

$$\langle \mathsf{M}_0 \cdot \boldsymbol{x}^*, \boldsymbol{y} \rangle = \mathsf{M}_0 \cdot \langle \boldsymbol{x}^*, \boldsymbol{y} \rangle = 0 = \mathsf{M}_1 \cdot \langle \boldsymbol{x}^*, \boldsymbol{y} \rangle = \langle \mathsf{M}_1 \cdot \boldsymbol{x}^*, \boldsymbol{y} \rangle$$

holds for all $\mathbf{y}$ that is queried during the game. Here, the second and the third equalities follow from the restrictions on the queries posed on $\mathcal{A}$. It is clear that $\mathcal{B}$'s simulation for $\mathcal{A}$ is perfect and $\mathcal{B}$'s advantage is exactly the same as $\mathcal{A}$. This concludes the proof of the theorem.

One may expect that the above proof works also in the selective setting (i.e., if we start from a selectively secure LinFE, we obtain a selectively secure NIPE). However, interestingly we require to modify the proof to work in the selective setting. In particular, in the selective setting, the LinFE adversary $\mathcal{B}$ above has to declare its target $(\mathsf{M}_0\boldsymbol{x}^*, \mathsf{M}_1\boldsymbol{x}^*)$ at the beginning of the game. However, since the NIPE adversary $\mathcal{A}$ only declares $\boldsymbol{x}^*$ at the outset and decides $(\mathsf{M}_0, \mathsf{M}_1)$ later in the game, it is difficult for $\mathcal{B}$ to correctly decide its target. One way to circumvent this problem is to restrict the message space $\mathcal{M}$ to be of polynomial size and change the proof so that $\mathcal{B}$ simply guesses $(\mathsf{M}_0, \mathsf{M}_1)$. The probability of $\mathcal{B}$ correctly guessing the values is noticeable due to the restriction on the size of the message space, which will be enough for our purpose. The drawback of the approach is that we can only encrypt short messages of logarithmic length. To encrypt a longer message, one needs to run the encryption algorithm many times to encrypt each chunk of the message. Formally, we have the following theorem. The proof is omitted to the full version.

Theorem 5. *Let us assume that the size of the message space $\mathcal{M}$ is polynomially bounded. Then, if the underlying LinFE scheme is selectively secure, so is the above NIPE scheme.*

5.3 Instantiations

By applying the conversion to the existing adaptively secure LinFE schemes of [ABDCP15, ALS16], we obtain several new NIPE schemes. Since the result of [ALS16] subsumes that of [ABDCP15] in the sense that the former achieves adaptive security whereas the latter achieves selective security, we discuss new schemes obtained by applying our conversion to the former schemes. This results in new adaptively secure NIPE schemes from the LWE assumption, the DDH assumption, and the DCR assumption. In particular, our DDH and DCR instantiations are the first constructions of NIPE schemes without bilinear maps or lattices. One thing to note is that the resulting scheme obtained by our conversion can only deal with logarithmic-size message space when $\mathcal{D}$ is of polynomial size and in order to encrypt a longer message, one needs to separate the message into chunks and run the encryption algorithm multiple times to encrypt each of them.

Construction from the LWE Assumption. In [ALS16], the authors proposed two LinFE schemes from lattices. One is in the stateless setting where the inner product is taken over $\mathbb{Z}$, and the other one is in the stateful setting where the inner product is taken over $\mathbb{Z}_p$ for some prime p. To apply the conversion to the former scheme, we set $\mathcal{D} = \mathbb{Z}$, $\mathcal{P} = \mathcal{Q} = \{0, \ldots, P-1\}^\ell$, $\mathcal{I} = \{0, \ldots, I-1\}^\ell$, $\mathcal{M} = \{0, \ldots, M-1\}$ and $\mathcal{J} = \{0, \ldots, MI-1\}$ for (polynomially bounded) integers P, I, M. It is straightforward to see that these domains satisfy our conditions for the conversion. This results in a stateless NIPE scheme over $\mathbb{Z}$.To apply the conversion to the latter scheme, we set $\mathcal{D} = \mathbb{Z}_p, \mathcal{P} = \mathcal{Q} = \mathcal{I} = \mathcal{J} = \mathbb{Z}_p^\ell$, and $\mathcal{M} = \mathbb{Z}_p$. It is also easy to see that these domains satisfy our condition for the conversion. This results in a stateful NIPE scheme over $\mathbb{Z}_p$.Since the original scheme is adaptively secure under the LWE assumption with sub-exponential approximation factors, so is our scheme obtained by the conversion.

Here, we compare our direct construction in Sect. 4 with the scheme obtained via the above conversion. To encrypt a message of ℓ_M-bit length, the first approach requires $(\ell_M + m + m\ell)$ elements of $\mathbb{Z}_q$ in a ciphertext and the second requires $(m + \ell)\ell_M$. The first approach is more efficient than the second one when we encrypt more than $m\ell/(m + \ell)$ bits at once. For a natural setting of $\ell < m, \lambda$, this condition encompasses the most interesting case of KEM-DEM settings where one encrypts λ bits of session key. In fact, when we are in the ring setting, since m is $O(\log \lambda)$, the first approach will be more efficient regardless of the size ℓ. Furthermore, for NIPE schemes over $\mathbb{Z}_p$, the first approach would require smaller LWE modulus. Indeed, in certain regime of parameters such as $\ell = \log n / \log\log\log n$ and $p = \log\log n$, the first approach would yield a scheme with polynomial modulus whereas the second requires super-polynomial modulus. However, on the other hand, the advantage of the second approach is that it achieves adaptive security.

Construction from the DDH Assumption. In [ALS16], the authors proposed a stateless LinFE scheme from the DDH assumption. In the scheme, the inner product is taken over $\mathbb{Z}_q$, where q is the order of the underlying group $\mathbb{G}$. One subtlety regarding their scheme is that the decryption algorithm is efficient only when the inner product $\langle \boldsymbol{x}, \boldsymbol{y} \rangle$ is polynomially bounded. This is because the decryption algorithm first recovers $g^{\langle \boldsymbol{x}, \boldsymbol{y} \rangle}$ for the generator g of $\mathbb{G}$ and then retrieves $\langle \boldsymbol{x}, \boldsymbol{y} \rangle$ by solving the discrete logarithm problem. Due to this problem, we cannot apply the conversion in a completely black box manner and some modification is needed. To apply our conversion to their scheme, we set $\mathcal{D} = \mathbb{Z}_q$, $\mathcal{P} = \mathcal{Q} = \mathcal{I} = \mathcal{J} = \mathbb{Z}_q^\ell$, and $\mathcal{M} = \{0, 1, \ldots, M\}$ for polynomially bounded M. Then, $(\mathsf{Setup}', \mathsf{KeyGen}', \mathsf{Enc}')$ are defined as in Sect. 5.2. We slightly modify the decryption algorithm. We run the decryption algorithm of the underlying LinFE scheme to obtain $Z = g^{\mathsf{M} \cdot \langle \boldsymbol{x}, \boldsymbol{y} \rangle}$, but halt it before computing the discrete logarithm $\log_g Z$, which is impossible when $\mathsf{M} \cdot \langle \boldsymbol{x}, \boldsymbol{y} \rangle$ is exponentially large. Instead, we compute $Z^{1/\langle \boldsymbol{x}, \boldsymbol{y} \rangle} = g^{\mathsf{M}}$ and then retrieve the message M by solving the discrete logarithm problem.

The above scheme can encrypt only short messages. We can modify the scheme so that it can encrypt longer messages without degrading the efficiency much. The main idea is that we can use the above scheme as a key encapsulation mechanism (KEM). Namely, we change the above scheme so that the encryption algorithm first encrypts a randomness $s \in \mathbb{Z}_p$ and then encrypt the message M by using the "DEM key" $K = g^s$. The decryption algorithm first retrieves $K = g^s$ and then retrieves the message M using the key K.

Construction from the DCR Assumption. In [ALS16], the authors proposed two LinFE schemes from the DCR assumption. One is in the stateless setting where the inner product is taken over $\mathbb{Z}$, and the other is in the stateful setting where the inner product is taken over $\mathbb{Z}_N$. To apply the conversion to the former scheme, we set $\mathcal{D} = \mathbb{Z}$, $\mathcal{P} = \mathcal{Q} = \{0, \ldots, P-1\}^\ell$, $\mathcal{I} = \{0, \ldots, I-1\}^\ell$, $\mathcal{M} = \{0, \ldots, M-1\}$ and $\mathcal{J} = \{0, \ldots, MI-1\}$ for (possibly exponentially large) integers P, I, M. It is straightforward to see that these domains satisfy our condition for the conversion. This results in a stateless NIPE scheme over $\mathbb{Z}$.To apply the conversion to the latter scheme, we set $\mathcal{D} = \mathbb{Z}_N$,$\mathcal{P} = \mathcal{Q} = \mathcal{I} = \mathcal{J} = \mathbb{Z}_N^\ell$, and $\mathcal{M} = \mathbb{Z}_N$.Rigorously speaking, we cannot apply the conversion because $\mathbb{Z}_N$ is not an integral domain.However, we can treat $\mathbb{Z}_N$ as if it were an integral domain, since any element $x \in \mathbb{Z}_N$ with $\gcd(x, N) \neq 1$ will allow us to factorize N, which contradicts the hardness of the DCR assumption.

Acknowledgement. The first author was partially supported by JST CREST Grant Number JPMJCR1302 and JSPS KAKENHI Grant Number 17J05603. The second author was supported by JST CREST Grant Number JPMJCR1688 and JSPS KAKENHI Grant Number 16K16068.

References

[ABB10] Agrawal, S., Boneh, D., Boyen, X.: Efficient lattice (H)IBE in the standard model. In: Gilbert, H. (ed.) EUROCRYPT 2010. LNCS, vol. 6110, pp. 553–572. Springer, Heidelberg (2010). https://doi.org/10.1007/978-3-642-13190-5_28

[ABDCP15] Abdalla, M., Bourse, F., De Caro, A., Pointcheval, D.: Simple functional encryption schemes for inner products. In: Katz, J. (ed.) PKC 2015. LNCS, vol. 9020, pp. 733–751. Springer, Heidelberg (2015). https://doi.org/10.1007/978-3-662-46447-2_33

[ABP+17] Agrawal, S., Bhattacherjee, S., Phan, D.H., Stehlé, D., Yamada, S.: Efficient trace-and-revoke with public traceability. In: CCS (2017)

[ABS17] Ambrona, M., Barthe, G., Schmidt, B.: Generic transformations of predicate encodings: constructions and applications. In: Katz, J., Shacham, H. (eds.) CRYPTO 2017. LNCS, vol. 10401, pp. 36–66. Springer, Cham (2017). https://doi.org/10.1007/978-3-319-63688-7_2

[AFV11] Agrawal, S., Freeman, D.M., Vaikuntanathan, V.: Functional encryption for inner product predicates from learning with errors. In: Lee, D.H., Wang, X. (eds.) ASIACRYPT 2011. LNCS, vol. 7073, pp. 21–40. Springer, Heidelberg (2011). https://doi.org/10.1007/978-3-642-25385-0_2

[AL10] Attrapadung, N., Libert, B.: Functional encryption for inner product: achieving constant-size ciphertexts with adaptive security or support for negation. In: Nguyen, P.Q., Pointcheval, D. (eds.) PKC 2010. LNCS, vol. 6056, pp. 384–402. Springer, Heidelberg (2010). https://doi.org/10.1007/978-3-642-13013-7_23

[ALDP11] Attrapadung, N., Libert, B., Panafieu, E.D.: Expressive key-policy attribute-based encryption with constant-size ciphertexts. In: Catalano, D., Fazio, N., Gennaro, R., Nicolosi, A. (eds.) PKC 2011. LNCS, vol. 6571, pp. 90–108. Springer, Heidelberg (2011). https://doi.org/10.1007/978-3-642-19379-8_6

[ALS16] Agrawal, S., Libert, B., Stehlé, D.: Fully secure functional encryption for inner products, from standard assumptions. In: Robshaw, M., Katz, J. (eds.) CRYPTO 2016. LNCS, vol. 9816, pp. 333–362. Springer, Heidelberg (2016). https://doi.org/10.1007/978-3-662-53015-3_12

[Bar89] Barrington, D.A.: Bounded-width polynomial-size branching programs recognize exactly those languages in NC1. J. Comput. Syst. Sci. **38**(1), 150–164 (1989)

[BCH86] Beame, P.W., Cook, S.A., Hoover, H.J.: Log depth circuits for division and related problems. SIAM J. Comput. **15**(4), 994–1003 (1986)

[BF11] Boneh, D., Freeman, D.M.: Linearly homomorphic signatures over binary fields and new tools for lattice-based signatures. In: Catalano, D., Fazio, N., Gennaro, R., Nicolosi, A. (eds.) PKC 2011. LNCS, vol. 6571, pp. 1–16. Springer, Heidelberg (2011). https://doi.org/10.1007/978-3-642-19379-8_1

[BGG+14] Boneh, D., et al.: Fully key-homomorphic encryption, arithmetic circuit ABE and compact garbled circuits. In: Nguyen, P.Q., Oswald, E. (eds.) EUROCRYPT 2014. LNCS, vol. 8441, pp. 533–556. Springer, Heidelberg (2014). https://doi.org/10.1007/978-3-642-55220-5_30

[BLP+13] Brakerski, Z., Langlois, A., Peikert, C., Regev, O., Stehlé, D.: Classical hardness of learning with errors. In: STOC (2013)

[BW07] Boneh, D., Waters, B.: Conjunctive, subset, and range queries on encrypted data. In: Vadhan, S.P. (ed.) TCC 2007. LNCS, vol. 4392, pp. 535–554. Springer, Heidelberg (2007). https://doi.org/10.1007/978-3-540-70936-7_29

[CLR16] Chen, J., Libert, B., Ramanna, S.C.: Non-zero inner product encryption with short ciphertexts and private keys. In: Zikas, V., De Prisco, R. (eds.) SCN 2016. LNCS, vol. 9841, pp. 23–41. Springer, Cham (2016). https://doi.org/10.1007/978-3-319-44618-9_2

[CW14] Chen, J., Wee, H.: Doubly spatial encryption from DBDH. Theor. Comput. Sci. **543**, 79–89 (2014)

[DG17] Döttling, N., Garg, S.: Identity-based encryption from the Diffie-Hellman assumption. In: Katz, J., Shacham, H. (eds.) CRYPTO 2017. LNCS, vol. 10401, pp. 537–569. Springer, Cham (2017). https://doi.org/10.1007/978-3-319-63688-7_18

[GPSW06] Goyal, V., Pandey, O., Sahai, A., Waters, B.: Attribute-based encryption for fine-grained access control of encrypted data. In: CCS (2006)

[GPV08] Gentry, C., Peikert, C., Vaikuntanathan, V.: Trapdoors for hard lattices and new cryptographic constructions. In: STOC (2008)

[GV15] Gorbunov, S., Vinayagamurthy, D.: Riding on asymmetry: efficient ABE for branching programs. In: Iwata, T., Cheon, J.H. (eds.) ASIACRYPT 2015. LNCS, vol. 9452, pp. 550–574. Springer, Heidelberg (2015). https://doi.org/10.1007/978-3-662-48797-6_23

[GVW13] Gorbunov, S., Vaikuntanathan, V., Wee, H.: Attribute-based encryption for circuits. In: STOC (2013)

[KSW08] Katz, J., Sahai, A., Waters, B.: Predicate encryption supporting disjunctions, polynomial equations, and inner products. In: Smart, N. (ed.) EUROCRYPT 2008. LNCS, vol. 4965, pp. 146–162. Springer, Heidelberg (2008). https://doi.org/10.1007/978-3-540-78967-3_9

[KY16] Katsumata, S., Yamada, S.: Partitioning via non-linear polynomial functions: more compact IBEs from ideal lattices and bilinear maps. In: Cheon, J.H., Takagi, T. (eds.) ASIACRYPT 2016. LNCS, vol. 10032, pp. 682–712. Springer, Heidelberg (2016). https://doi.org/10.1007/978-3-662-53890-6_23

[LOS+10] Lewko, A., Okamoto, T., Sahai, A., Takashima, K., Waters, B.: Fully secure functional encryption: attribute-based encryption and (hierarchical) inner product encryption. In: Gilbert, H. (ed.) EUROCRYPT 2010. LNCS, vol. 6110, pp. 62–91. Springer, Heidelberg (2010). https://doi.org/10.1007/978-3-642-13190-5_4

[LW11] Lewko, A.B., Waters, B.: Unbounded HIBE and attribute-based encryption. In: Paterson, K.G. (ed.) EUROCRYPT 2011. LNCS, vol. 6632, pp. 547–567. Springer, Heidelberg (2011). https://doi.org/10.1007/978-3-642-20465-4_30

[MP12] Micciancio, D., Peikert, C.: Trapdoors for lattices: simpler, tighter, faster, smaller. In: Pointcheval, D., Johansson, T. (eds.) EUROCRYPT 2012. LNCS, vol. 7237, pp. 700–718. Springer, Heidelberg (2012). https://doi.org/10.1007/978-3-642-29011-4_41

[OSW07] Ostrovsky, R., Sahai, A., Waters, B.: Attribute-based encryption with non-monotonic access structures. In: CCS (2007)

[OT10] Okamoto, T., Takashima, K.: Fully secure functional encryption with general relations from the decisional linear assumption. In: Rabin, T. (ed.) CRYPTO 2010. LNCS, vol. 6223, pp. 191–208. Springer, Heidelberg (2010). https://doi.org/10.1007/978-3-642-14623-7_11

[OT15] Okamoto, T., Takashima, K.: Achieving short ciphertexts or short secret-keys for adaptively secure general inner-product encryption. Des. Codes Cryptogr. **77**(2–3), 725–771 (2015)

[PVW08] Peikert, C., Vaikuntanathan, V., Waters, B.: A framework for efficient and composable oblivious transfer. In: Wagner, D. (ed.) CRYPTO 2008. LNCS, vol. 5157, pp. 554–571. Springer, Heidelberg (2008). https://doi.org/10.1007/978-3-540-85174-5_31

[Reg05] Regev, O.: On lattices, learning with errors, random linear codes, and cryptography. In: STOC (2005)

[SW05] Sahai, A., Waters, B.: Fuzzy identity-based encryption. In: Cramer, R. (ed.) EUROCRYPT 2005. LNCS, vol. 3494, pp. 457–473. Springer, Heidelberg (2005). https://doi.org/10.1007/11426639_27

[YAHK14] Yamada, S., Attrapadung, N., Hanaoka, G., Kunihiro, N.: A framework and compact constructions for non-monotonic attribute-based encryption. In: Krawczyk, H. (ed.) PKC 2014. LNCS, vol. 8383, pp. 275–292. Springer, Heidelberg (2014). https://doi.org/10.1007/978-3-642-54631-0_16

[Yam16] Yamada, S.: Adaptively secure identity-based encryption from lattices with asymptotically shorter public parameters. In: Fischlin, M., Coron, J.-S. (eds.) EUROCRYPT 2016. LNCS, vol. 9666, pp. 32–62. Springer, Heidelberg (2016). https://doi.org/10.1007/978-3-662-49896-5_2

Function Private Predicate Encryption for Low Min-Entropy Predicates

Sikhar Patranabis(✉), Debdeep Mukhopadhyay, and Somindu C. Ramanna

Department of Computer Science and Engineering,
Indian Institute of Technology Kharagpur, Kharagpur, India
sikhar.patranabis@iitkgp.ac.in, {debdeep,somindu}@cse.iitkgp.ac.in

Abstract. In this work, we propose new constructions for zero inner-product encryption (ZIPE) and non-zero inner-product encryption (NIPE) from prime-order bilinear pairings, which are both attribute and function private in the public-key setting.

- Our ZIPE scheme is adaptively attribute private under the standard Matrix DDH assumption for unbounded collusions. It is additionally computationally function private under a min-entropy variant of the Matrix DDH assumption for predicates sampled from distributions with super-logarithmic min-entropy. Existing (statistically) function private ZIPE schemes due to Boneh et al. [Crypto'13, Asiacrypt'13] *necessarily* require predicate distributions with significantly larger min-entropy in the public-key setting.
- Our NIPE scheme is adaptively attribute private under the standard Matrix DDH assumption, albeit for bounded collusions. In addition, it achieves computational function privacy under a min-entropy variant of the Matrix DDH assumption for predicates sampled from distributions with super-logarithmic min-entropy. To the best of our knowledge, existing NIPE schemes from bilinear pairings were neither attribute private nor function private.

Our constructions are inspired by the linear FE constructions of Agrawal et al. [Crypto'16] and the simulation secure ZIPE of Wee [TCC'17]. In our ZIPE scheme, we show a novel way of embedding two different hard problem instances in a single secret key - one for unbounded collusion-resistance and the other for function privacy. For NIPE, we introduce new techniques for simultaneously achieving attribute and function privacy. We further show that the two constructions naturally generalize to a wider class of predicate encryption schemes such as subspace membership, subspace non-membership and hidden-vector encryption.

1 Introduction

Predicate encryption (PE) [5,14,30] is a modern public-key primitive that enables fine-grained role-based access control on encrypted data, which makes it desirable for a number of real-life applications. In a PE scheme, a single master secret key msk is used to derive several secret keys of the form sk_f, where f is

D. Lin and K. Sako (Eds.): PKC 2019, LNCS 11443, pp. 189–219, 2019.
https://doi.org/10.1007/978-3-030-17259-6_7

a Boolean function over Σ. A ciphertext corresponds to an attribute-message pair $(I, M) \in \Sigma \times \mathcal{M}$, where Σ is a pre-defined set of attributes and $\mathcal{M}$ is a set of payload messages. Decryption of a ciphertext corresponding to (I, M) by sk_f reveals M if and only if $f(I) = 1$. Based on the security notion achieved, a PE scheme may be classified into one or more of the categories described below.

Public Attribute PE. In a public attribute PE system, a ciphertext ct on (I, M) leaks no information about the message M to an adversary possessing secret-keys that do not decrypt ct (i.e., sk_f such that $f(I) = 0$). The attribute I, on the other hand, is public. Such schemes are often nomenclatured as *attribute-based encryption* (ABE). Concrete ABE schemes have been proposed for a wide range of Boolean predicates, including equality/identity testing (IBE) [10,24], keyword search [1,9], Boolean formulae [29], regular languages [36], general polynomial-size circuits [11,22,27], and even Turing machines [25].

Attribute Private PE. In an attribute private PE, the ciphertext ct leaks no information about either the attribute I or the message M to an adversary possessing secret-keys that do not decrypt ct. Concrete instantiations of private attribute PE have been achieved for hidden vector encryption (HVE) [14] that supports, in addition to equality, conjunctive, range and subset predicates, and also for zero-inner-product encryption (ZIPE) [30,33]. ZIPE has been realized using bilinear maps [30,33] and also from lattice-based techniques [2,5,6].

In a more recent work [37], Wee demonstrated many new techniques for achieving selectively simulation-secure attribute private PE from prime-order bilinear groups under the standard Matrix DDH assumption. The main result of this work is a partially hiding predicate encryption scheme for functions that compute an arithmetic branching program on public attributes, followed by an inner product predicate on private attributes. In the realm of lattices, Gorbunov et al. [28] showed how to construct attribute private PE for all circuits from the learning with errors (LWE) assumption.

Although attribute privacy has been realized for many different predicates from bilinear pairings, it remains open to construct pairing-based attribute private PE for certain simple predicates such as non-zero inner-product encryption (NIPE) [7] and its natural generalization to a broader class of subspace non-membership encryption (SNME) predicates.

Function Private PE. In a function private PE, a secret-key sk_f reveal no information beyond the absolute minimum about the underlying predicate f. Note that the notions of attribute and function privacy for a PE are mutually exclusive in the sense that one does not necessarily imply the other. In the setting of private-key PE, there already exist function private constructions from pairings for predicates such as ZIPE [8,20]. In fact, using techniques introduced by Brakerski et al. [15], any private-key PE can be made function private in a generic manner. However, in the setting of public-key PE, formalizing a realistic notion of function privacy is significantly more challenging [12,13].

Consider, for example, an adversary against an IBE scheme who is given a secret-key $\mathsf{sk}_{\mathsf{id}}$ corresponding to an identity id. As long as the adversary has some apriori information that id belongs to a set $\mathcal{S}$ such that $|\mathcal{S}|$ is at most polynomial in the security parameter λ, it can fully recover id from $\mathsf{sk}_{\mathsf{id}}$: it can simply resort to encrypting a random message M under each identity in $\mathcal{S}$, and decrypting using $\mathsf{sk}_{\mathsf{id}}$ to check for a correct recovery.

Hence, in the setting of public-key PE, function privacy can only hold under the minimal assumption that each predicate is sampled from a distribution with min-entropy at least super logarithmic in the security parameter λ [12,13]. Under similar assumptions, function private public-key constructions have been reported for IBE [12], ZIPE [3] and subspace membership encryption (SME) [13], which is essentially a generalization of ZIPE. These works throw open several interesting questions. We discuss them below.

1. The PE schemes proposed in [12,13] are inherently restricted to satisfying a *statistical* notion of function privacy. For a vast majority of applications, a relaxed *computational* notion of function privacy suffices. It is currently open to design public-key PE schemes with function privacy in this relaxed computational setting.
2. The function private PE schemes in [12,13] *necessarily* assume predicate distributions with min-entropy $k \geq \lambda$ (where λ is the security parameter).[1] This is a rather stringent assumption in the context of real-world predicates. An interesting question is whether a public-key PE scheme can be function private for predicate distributions with only super-logarithmic min-entropy.

There are several real-world applications that warrant the study of PE schemes which are simultaneously attribute and function private. These include searching on encrypted data, secure information retrieval, secure mail gateways and payment gateways, and many others. The reader is referred to [12] for an elaborate discussion of these applications.

1.1 Our Contributions

We focus on the following questions discussed in the previous section:

Is it possible to design attribute private PE from bilinear maps for the non-zero inner product functionality?

What is a meaningful definition of function privacy against resource-bounded adversaries?

Can the min-entropy requirements on the underlying predicate distributions be restricted to a bare minimum while defining function privacy?

[1] The PE schemes in [12,13] are not function private, even in the weaker computational setting, if the min-entropy requirements are relaxed any further.

Are there constructions for public-key PE that are provably function private, with respect to the relaxed definition, under standard computational assumptions?

In this paper, we answer these questions in the affirmative by first presenting a relaxed definition of function privacy taking into account resource bounded adversaries and restricting the min-entropy requirements of the underlying predicate distributions to $\omega(\log \lambda)$. We then present new pairing-based constructions in the public key setting for subspace membership encryption (SME) and subspace non-membership encryption (SNME) that generalize ZIPE and NIPE respectively. Our constructions are adaptively attribute private and computationally function private in tandem, under variants of the well-known matrix Diffie-Hellman (MDDH) assumption.

Our ZIPE scheme is the first to achieve computational function privacy for predicates with super-logarithmic min-entropy. As already mentioned, existing (statistically) function private ZIPE schemes due to Boneh et al. [13] *necessarily* require predicate distributions with significantly larger min-entropy in the public-key setting. Our NIPE scheme is first to achieve both attribute and function privacy under group-theoretic assumptions, albeit in the bounded collusion setting. Existing constructions for NIPE based on group-theoretic assumptions [7,16] were neither attribute nor function private, even in the bounded collusion setting.

Our key technical contributions may be summarized as follows.

- Relaxing function privacy definition to account for resource-bounded adversaries and underlying predicates sampled from distributions with min-entropy $k = \omega(\log \lambda)$ (λ being the security parameter).
- Introduction of a min-entropy variant of MDDH assumption where the matrix provided in the instance does not have the uniform distribution but guaranteed to have $\omega(\log \lambda)$ min-entropy.
- Simple and efficient constructions for ZIPE and NIPE from prime-order asymmetric bilinear pairings, that are simultaneously attribute and function private under the presumed hardness of matrix DDH and its min-entropy variant, respectively, so long as the predicates are sampled from distributions with super-logarithmic min-entropy.
- Generalizations of the aforementioned constructions to a broader class of predicates, namely SME and SNME.

Our constructions are inspired by the linear FE constructions of Agrawal et al. [6] and the simulation secure ZIPE of Wee [37]. In our SME (and hence ZIPE) scheme, we show a novel way of embedding two different hard problem instances in a single secret key - one for unbounded collusion-resistance and the other for function privacy. With respect to SNME (and hence NIPE), we introduce new techniques for simultaneously achieving attribute and function privacy, albeit in the bounded collusion setting.

1.2 Overview of Results and Techniques

In this section, we briefly explain the core ideas of our attribute private and function private SME/SNME in terms of the simplest cases, namely, ZIPE/NIPE. The security of our constructions follow from different variants of the Matrix DDH assumption over both source groups of a bilinear pairing.

The Matrix DDH assumption in a group $\mathbb{G}$ of prime order q given by a generator g requires distinguishing between two distributions – $(g^{\mathbf{A}}, g^{\mathbf{Ar}})$ and $(g^{\mathbf{A}}, g^{\mathbf{u}})$ – where $\mathbf{A} \in \mathbb{Z}_q^{(k+1)\times k}$, $\mathbf{r} \in \mathbb{Z}_q^k$ and $\mathbf{u} \in \mathbb{Z}_q^{k+1}$ are sampled uniformly and independently from their respective domains (here $k \geq 1$ and it is assumed that $\mathbf{A}$ has full rank with overwhelming probability). For the function privacy proofs we rely on a special form of the MDDH assumption parameterized by (m, n) – an instance (with respect to a group $\mathbb{G} = \langle g \rangle$) consists of $g^{\mathbf{W}}, g^{\mathbf{u}}$ where $\mathbf{W} \xleftarrow{R} \mathbf{V}^*$ for some source distribution $\mathbf{V}^*$ over $\mathbb{Z}_q^{m\times n}$ of min-entropy $\omega(\log \lambda)$ and the task is to determine if $\mathbf{u} = \mathbf{W}^{\mathbf{T}} \cdot \mathbf{y}$ for $\mathbf{y} \xleftarrow{R} \mathbb{Z}_q^m$ or $\mathbf{u}$ is randomly distributed in $\mathbb{Z}_q^n$.

Denote an asymmetric pairing by the 7-tuple $\mathcal{G} = (\mathbb{G}_1, \mathbb{G}_2, \mathbb{G}_T, q, g_1, g_2, e)$ where $|\mathbb{G}_1| = |\mathbb{G}_2| = |\mathbb{G}_T| = q$, g_1, g_2 respectively generate $\mathbb{G}_1, \mathbb{G}_2$ and $e : \mathbb{G}_1 \times \mathbb{G}_2 \to \mathbb{G}_T$ is a non-degenerate, efficiently computable bilinear map. Call $\mathcal{G}$ Matrix DDH-hard if the Matrix DDH assumption holds in both $\mathbb{G}_1$ and $\mathbb{G}_2$.

Zero Inner-Product Encryption (ZIPE). Our attribute and function private ZIPE construction, named Π^{ZIPE}, is inspired by the simulation secure ZIPE scheme of Wee [37]. The public parameters and the master secret key in Π^{ZIPE} are given by

$$\begin{aligned}\mathsf{pp} &= \left(g_1, g_1^{\mathbf{A}}, g_1^{\mathbf{S}_0\cdot\mathbf{A}}, g_1^{\mathbf{S}_1\cdot\mathbf{A}}, \ldots, g_1^{\mathbf{S}_n\cdot\mathbf{A}}, e(g_1, g_2)^{\mathbf{K}\cdot\mathbf{A}}\right),\\ \mathsf{msk} &= (g_2, \mathbf{S}_0, \mathbf{S}_1, \ldots, \mathbf{S}_n, \mathbf{K}, \mathbf{B}_0),\end{aligned}$$

where $\mathbf{A} \xleftarrow{R} \mathbb{Z}_q^{(k+1)\times k}$, $\mathbf{S}_0, \mathbf{S}_1, \ldots, \mathbf{S}_n \xleftarrow{R} \mathbb{Z}_q^{(2k+1)\times(k+1)}$, $\mathbf{K} \xleftarrow{R} \mathbb{Z}_q^{1\times(k+1)}$ and $\mathbf{B}_0 \xleftarrow{R} \mathbb{Z}_q^{(2k+1)\times k}$ are sampled uniformly. A ciphertext ct on attribute vector $\mathbf{x} = (x_1, \ldots, x_n) \in \mathbb{Z}_q^n$ and message M is given by

$$\mathsf{ct} = \left(c_0, \{c_j\}_{j=1}^n, c_{n+1}\right) = \left(g_1^{(\mathbf{A}\cdot\mathbf{r})^{\mathbf{T}}}, \left\{g_1^{((x_j\cdot\mathbf{S}_0+\mathbf{S}_j)\cdot\mathbf{A}\cdot\mathbf{r})^{\mathbf{T}}}\right\}_{j=1}^n, M\cdot e(g_1, g_2)^{(\mathbf{K}\cdot\mathbf{A}\cdot\mathbf{r})^{\mathbf{T}}}\right),$$

for $\mathbf{r} \xleftarrow{R} \mathbb{Z}_q^k$. The secret key $\mathsf{sk}_{\mathbf{w}}$ on a vector $\mathbf{w} = (w_1, \ldots, w_n) \in \mathbb{Z}_q^n$ is defined as

$$\mathsf{sk}_{\mathbf{w}} = \left(h_0, \{h_j\}_{j=1}^n\right) = \left(g_2^{\mathbf{K}+y\sum_{j=1}^n w_j\cdot\mathbf{t}\cdot\mathbf{S}_j}, \left\{g_2^{yw_j\mathbf{t}}\right\}_{j=1}^n\right),$$

where $y \xleftarrow{R} \mathbb{Z}_q$ and $\mathbf{t} = (\mathbf{B}_0 \cdot \mathbf{s})^{\mathbf{T}}$ for $\mathbf{s} \xleftarrow{R} \mathbb{Z}_q^k$.

For correctness, we restrict the message space $\mathcal{M}$ to an exponentially smaller subset of $\mathbb{G}_T$. The decryption algorithm computes

$$M = c_{n+1} \cdot \left(\prod_{j=1}^{n} e(c_j, h_j) \right) \Big/ e(c_0, h_0),$$

which returns the correct message if $\langle \mathbf{x}, \mathbf{w} \rangle = 0$. When $\langle \mathbf{x}, \mathbf{w} \rangle \neq 0$ the message thus computed is uniformly distributed in $\mathbb{G}_T$ and with high probability will be outside $\mathcal{M}$. In such a case, the decryption algorithm may return a symbol $\perp$ indicating failure.

We prove that Π^{ZIPE} is adaptively attribute private assuming the hardness of the decisional MDDH problems in $\mathbb{G}_1$ and $\mathbb{G}_2$. The attribute privacy game asks an adversary to distinguish between encryptions to attribute vectors $\mathbf{x}_0$ and $\mathbf{x}_1$. Or in other words, the adversary is given a challenge ciphertext for $\mathbf{x}_b$ where $b \xleftarrow{R} \{0, 1\}$ and its task is to guess b. Essentially, we need to argue that the components $\{c_j\}_{j=1}^n$ in the challenge ciphertext hide the attribute $\mathbf{x}$.

The proof relies on the dual system proof methodology and proceeds through a sequence of games, each changing the distribution of challenge ciphertext and keys. The key steps in the proof are listed below.

1. The reduction first embeds an instance of MDDH in $\mathbb{G}_1$ in the challenge ciphertext to make it *semi-functional.* At this stage, the exponent of ciphertext component c_0 is no longer correlated to $\mathbf{A}$ and this is consistent with the other components.
2. In a series of subsequent games, we turn each secret key provided to the adversary upon a key extract query to *semi-functional* form by embedding MDDH instances in the group $\mathbb{G}_2$. This step is crucial for unbounded collusion resistance.
3. Once the distribution of all keys are modified, we apply a "change of basis" to the challenge ciphertext, and argue that $\mathbf{x}_b$ is information theoretically hidden from the adversary.

We prove the indistinguishability of each pair of consecutive games by resorting to a set of techniques involving dual bases in prime-order bilinear groups (similar techniques have been used in prior works, notably [17,23,26]). The reader may refer to Sect. 4 and the full version [35] for details of the proof.

For showing function privacy of Π^{ZIPE}, we rely on the min-entropy variant of the MDDH assumption. In the function privacy experiment, the adversary picks two vector distributions, each component of which is an $\omega(\log \lambda)$-source over $\mathbb{Z}_q$. The challenger samples a vector $\mathbf{w}$ according to one of the distributions, computes a secret key $\mathsf{sk}_{\mathbf{w}}$ for vector $\mathbf{w}$ and gives it to the adversary. The adversary's task is to determine the distribution of $\mathbf{w}$ looking at $\mathsf{sk}_{\mathbf{w}}$. To prove that the secret key hides the distribution from which $\mathbf{w}$ was sampled, we embed an instance of the min-entropy variant of the MDDH assumption in the challenge secret key provided to the adversary. If the instance is sampled from the correct distribution, the secret key is well-formed. On the other hand, if the instance is uniformly random, the secret key perfectly hides the distribution from which $\mathbf{w}$ was sampled. The reader may refer to Sect. 4 for the detailed proof.

Note that our ZIPE scheme essentially embeds two different problem instances in the same secret key – an MDDH problem instance over $\mathbb{G}_2$ that is exploited to achieve unbounded collusion-resistance in the attribute privacy experiment, and a min-entropy MDDH instance over $\mathbb{G}_2$, which is the basis for the proof of function privacy. We believe that this "simultaneous embedding" strategy is of independent interest, and may be useful in other applications.

Non-Zero Inner-Product Encryption (NIPE). Our NIPE scheme is inspired by the linear FE construction of Agrawal, Libert and Stehlé [6] referred to as LinFE in what follows. A LinFE ciphertext ct is created by encrypting a vector $\mathbf{x}$ of length n. Decryption of ct by a secret key, generated for a linear function (given by a length n vector $\mathbf{w}$), returns the value of the inner-product $\langle \mathbf{x}, \mathbf{w} \rangle$.

In a NIPE scheme, a ciphertext is associated with a payload message M and a vector $\mathbf{x}$ while a secret key corresponds to a vector $\mathbf{y}$. to be encoded in the ciphertext. Decryption algorithm should be designed to return M iff $\langle \mathbf{x}, \mathbf{w} \rangle \neq 0$. To derive NIPE from LinFE, we use two instantiations of the LinFE with independent master secret keys. The public parameters and master secret key for the resulting scheme would be

$$\mathsf{pp} = \left(g, g^{\mathbf{A}}, g^{\mathbf{S}_1}, g^{\mathbf{S}_2}\right) \quad \mathsf{msk} = (\mathbf{S}_1, \mathbf{S}_2).$$

The ciphertext for $(\mathbf{x}, M)$ will result from encoding $\mathbf{x}$ and $M \cdot \mathbf{x}$ using the two individual schemes as shown below:

$$\mathsf{ct} = \left(g^{\mathbf{A}\mathbf{r}_1}, g^{\mathbf{x}+\mathbf{S}_1\mathbf{A}\mathbf{r}_1}, g^{\mathbf{A}\mathbf{r}_2}, g^{M\cdot\mathbf{x}+\mathbf{S}_2\mathbf{A}\mathbf{r}_2}\right).$$

Here $\mathbf{r}_1, \mathbf{r}_2$ are sampled uniformly at random from $\mathbb{Z}_q^k$. A secret key $\mathsf{sk}_{\mathbf{w}} = (\mathbf{w}^{\mathbf{T}}\mathbf{S}_1, \mathbf{w}^{\mathbf{T}}\mathbf{S}_2)$ helps in recovering $g^{M\langle \mathbf{x}, \mathbf{w} \rangle}$ and $g^{\langle \mathbf{x}, \mathbf{w} \rangle}$ with respect to g. One may recover M by simply computing the discrete logarithm of $g^{M\langle \mathbf{x}, \mathbf{w} \rangle}$ by $g^{\langle \mathbf{x}, \mathbf{w} \rangle}$ which is possible only when $\langle \mathbf{x}, \mathbf{w} \rangle \neq 0$. The restriction on the inner-products now shifts to the messages that is, the messages have to lie in a polynomial-sized subset of $\mathbb{Z}_q$. A similar technique has been previously used in [4] to construct public revocation and traitor-tracing from LinFE and revocation, in particular, can be seen as a special case of NIPE. However, our naive construction is not sufficient to (simultaneously) achieve attribute privacy and function privacy since the secret key already reveals too much information about $\mathbf{w}$.

To circumvent the problem, we adapt the construction to the bilinear map setting. This is because functions are associated with secret keys and a basic step to ensure privacy of the function encoded in the secret key components is to hide them in the exponents of elements coming from a discrete log hard group. Ciphertext components already live in a cyclic group. Decryption requires combining the ciphertext and key components to recover the message which can be facilitated if the two groups are equipped with a pairing/bilinear map.

Furthermore, the secret key is additionally randomized with $y \in \mathbb{Z}_q$ (for the generalized case of SNME, this would be a vector $\mathbf{y} \in \mathbb{Z}_q^m$ where $\mathbf{w}$ is replaced by a matrix $\mathbf{W} \in \mathbb{Z}_q^{m \times n}$). Randomization is essential for the function privacy proof, which exploits the hardness of a min-entropy variant of the MDDH assumption. We now discuss the construction of a NIPE scheme possessing both attribute and function privacy.

Let $\mathcal{G} = (\mathbb{G}_1, \mathbb{G}_2, \mathbb{G}_T, q, g_1, g_2, e)$ denote an asymmetric bilinear map ensemble. The public parameters and master secret key for our modified scheme Π^{NIPE} would be similar to the naive scheme we described earlier except that pp components now live in $\mathbb{G}_1$.

$$\mathsf{pp} = \left(g_1, g_1^{\mathbf{A}}, g_1^{\mathbf{S}_1}, g_1^{\mathbf{S}_2}\right) \quad \mathsf{msk} = (g_2, \mathbf{S}_1, \mathbf{S}_2).$$

Similarly, the ciphertext for $(\mathbf{x}, M)$ for Π^{NIPE} is given by

$$\mathsf{ct} = \left(g_1^{\mathbf{Ar}_1}, g_1^{\mathbf{x}+\mathbf{S}_1\mathbf{Ar}_1}, g_1^{\mathbf{Ar}_2}, g_1^{M\cdot\mathbf{x}+\mathbf{S}_2\mathbf{Ar}_2}\right),$$

where $\mathbf{r}_1, \mathbf{r}_2$ are uniformly distributed in $\mathbb{Z}_q^k$. Secret key for $\mathbf{w}$ would now be defined as

$$\mathsf{sk}_{\mathbf{w}} = \left(g_2^{y\cdot\mathbf{w}}, g_2^{y\cdot\mathbf{w}^{\mathbf{T}}\mathbf{S}_1}, g_2^{y\cdot\mathbf{w}^{\mathbf{T}}\mathbf{S}_2}\right)$$

randomized by y sampled uniformly from $\mathbb{Z}_q$. During decryption, ciphertext and key components are paired to obtained $e(g_1, g_2)^{My\langle\mathbf{x},\mathbf{w}\rangle}$ and $e(g_1, g_2)^{y\langle\mathbf{x},\mathbf{w}\rangle}$. Message M can be recovered by computing the discrete logarithm of the former with respect to the latter, conditioned on $\langle\mathbf{x}, \mathbf{w}\rangle \neq 0$.

Unlike the SME case, we can only prove attribute privacy of our SNME scheme in the bounded collusion model. More precisely, an adversary is allowed to query at most $n - 1$ secret keys, so that the master secret key components $\mathbf{S}_0, \mathbf{S}_1 \ldots, \mathbf{S}_n$ retain sufficient entropy from the adversary's point of view. The proof then proceeds via a sequence of two hybrid experiments, in each of which the proof embeds a fresh MDDH instance in the challenge ciphertext.

We argue that when these instances are sampled from the "random" distribution instead of the "real" distribution, the challenge ciphertext perfectly hides which attribute-message pair among $(\mathbf{x}_0, M_0)$ and $(\mathbf{x}_1, M_1)$ is being encrypted. The argument for perfect hiding relies on hash proof systems [18,19], similar to those used by Agrawal et al. in proving the security of their linear FE scheme [6]. Finally, the scheme is adaptively secure because the reduction knows the master secret key at any time, which allows it to answer all secret key queries without knowing the challenge attributes beforehand. For more details on the proof, the reader may refer to Sect. 5 and the full version [35].

To prove function privacy, we again rely on the min-entropy variant of the MDDH assumption over the group $\mathbb{G}_2$. This proof is technically very similar to the proof of function privacy for our SME scheme. The reader may refer to Sect. 5 for the detailed proof.

Hidden Vector Encryption (HVE). We extend our techniques to construct a hidden vector encryption wherein a secret key for a vector $\mathbf{y} \in (\Sigma \cup \{\star\})^n$ allows decryption of a ciphertext on attribute vector $\mathbf{x} \in \Sigma^n$ if for each $j \in [1, n]$, either $y_j = x_j$ or $y_j = \star$. Although attribute-private HVE is implied by attribute-private SME, the implication does not extend to function privacy. In fact, defining function privacy for HVE itself is tricky given the presence of wildcard characters. We overcome this issue by presenting a weaker notion of function privacy for HVE that allows revealing positions of the *wildcard* ($\star$) characters in a given predicate vector, while hiding the contents of the other "non-wildcard" ositions. Also presented is a construction of HVE that is provably function private in this weaker model from bilinear maps. The construction is quite similar to our SME construction, except for certain minor tweaks to account for the presence of wildcard characters. The proofs of attribute and function privacy (in the weak model) also follow analogously.

1.3 Open Problems

Several interesting questions remain unanswered. The construction of NIPE/SNME we present have a restriction – attribute privacy only holds in the bounded collusions model. It would be interesting to obtain constructions free of this restriction. Another problem is to construct efficient function-private PE for richer functionalities such as Boolean and arithmetic span programs from standard assumptions.

1.4 Organization of the Paper

In Sect. 2, we present the notation, a quick review of bilinear maps and related assumptions followed by definitions of PE and associated security notions. This is followed by a description of min-entropy variants of MDDH assumption required for our proofs. We formalize the relaxed computational notion of function privacy and discuss related issues in Sect. 3. In Sect. 4, we present our SME construction followed by proofs of attribute privacy and function privacy. Section 5 describes our construction of SNME. Due to lack of space, we omit details of the proofs. Interested readers are referred to the full version [35]. The full version also describes a function private hidden vector encryption along with a sketch of its security proof.

2 Background and Preliminary Definitions

In this section, we fix notation, present background material on predicate encryption and recall certain standard computational assumptions in bilinear groups. We also introduce certain *min-entropy* variants of these assumptions useful for our proofs.

2.1 Notation

This section summarizes the notations used throughout the rest of the paper. We write $x \xleftarrow{R} \chi$ to represent that an element x is sampled uniformly at random from a set/distribution $\mathcal{X}$. The output a of a deterministic algorithm $\mathcal{A}$ is denoted by $x = \mathcal{A}$ and the output a' of a randomized algorithm $\mathcal{A}'$ is denoted by $x' \leftarrow \mathcal{A}'$.

We refer to $\lambda \in \mathbb{N}$ as the security parameter, and denote by $\mathsf{exp}(\lambda)$, $\mathsf{poly}(\lambda)$ and $\mathsf{negl}(\lambda)$ any generic (unspecified) exponential function, polynomial function and negligible function in λ respectively. Note that a function $f : \mathbb{N} \rightarrow \mathbb{N}$ is said to be negligible in λ if for every positive polynomial p, $f(\lambda) < 1/p(\lambda)$ when λ is sufficiently large.

For $a, b \in \mathbb{Z}$ such that $a \leq b$, we denote by $[a, b]$ the set of integers lying between a and b (both inclusive). For a finite field $\mathbb{F}_q$ (q being a λ-bit prime) and $m, n \in \mathbb{N}$, we denote by $\mathbb{F}_q^{m\times n}$ the space of all $m \times n$ matrices $\mathbf{W}$ with elements from $\mathbb{F}_q$. We use the short-hand notation $\mathbb{F}_q^m$ to represent the vector space $\mathbb{F}_q^{m\times 1}$. The transpose of a matrix $\mathbf{W} \in \mathbb{F}_q^{m\times n}$ is denoted as $\mathbf{W}^\mathrm{T}$. The symbol $\mathbf{0}$ is used to denote an all-zero matrix of appropriate dimension.

Finally, the min-entropy of a random variable Y is denoted as $\mathbf{H}_\infty(\mathrm{Y})$ and is evaluated as $\mathbf{H}_\infty(\mathrm{Y}) = -\log\left(\max_y \Pr[\mathrm{Y} = y]\right)$. A random variable Y is said to be a k-source if $\mathbf{H}_\infty(\mathrm{Y}) \geq k$.

2.2 Predicate Encryption

Definition 1 (Predicate Encryption). A predicate encryption (PE) scheme for a class of predicates $\mathcal{F}$ over an attribute space Σ and a payload-message space $\mathcal{M}$ is a quadruple of PPT algorithms $\Pi = (\mathsf{Setup}, \mathsf{KeyGen}, \mathsf{Enc}, \mathsf{Dec})$, defined as follows:

- $\mathsf{Setup}(1^\lambda)$: On input the security parameter λ, the setup algorithm generates the public parameter pp and the master secret key msk.
- $\mathsf{KeyGen}(\mathsf{pp}, \mathsf{msk}, f)$: On input the public parameter pp, the master secret key msk and a predicate $f \in \mathcal{F}$, the key-generation algorithm outputs a secret key sk_f.
- $\mathsf{Enc}(\mathsf{pp}, I, M)$: On input the public parameter pp, an attribute $I \in \Sigma$ and a payload message $M \in \mathcal{M}$, the encryption algorithm outputs a ciphertext ct.
- $\mathsf{Dec}(\mathsf{pp}, \mathsf{sk}_f, \mathsf{ct})$: On input the public parameter pp, a ciphertext ct and a secret key sk_f, the decryption algorithm outputs either a payload-message $M \in \mathcal{M}$ or the symbol $\perp$.

Correctness. A PE scheme is said to be functionally correct if for any security parameter $\lambda \in \mathbb{N}$, any predicate $f \in \mathcal{F}$, any attribute $I \in \Sigma$, and any payload message $M \in \mathcal{M}$, letting $(\mathsf{pp}, \mathsf{msk}) \leftarrow \mathsf{Setup}(1^\lambda)$, $\mathsf{sk}_f \leftarrow \mathsf{KeyGen}(\mathsf{pp}, \mathsf{msk}, f)$ and $\mathsf{ct} \leftarrow \mathsf{Enc}(\mathsf{pp}, I, M)$, the following hold:

1. If $f(I) = 1$, $\Pr[\mathsf{Dec}(\mathsf{pp}, \mathsf{ct}, \mathsf{sk}_f) = M] = 1$,
2. If $f(I) = 0$, $\Pr[\mathsf{Dec}(\mathsf{pp}, \mathsf{ct}, \mathsf{sk}_f) = \perp]$ with overwhelmingly large probability,

Experiment $\mathsf{Expt}^{(b)}_{\mathsf{AP},\Pi,\mathcal{A}}(\lambda)$:

1. The challenger samples $(\mathsf{pp}, \mathsf{msk}) \leftarrow \mathsf{Setup}(1^\lambda)$ and provides pp to $\mathcal{A}$.
2. The adversary $\mathcal{A}$ adaptively issues key-generation queries. For each query predicate f, the challenger responds with
$$\mathsf{sk}_f \leftarrow \mathsf{KeyGen}\,(\mathsf{pp}, \mathsf{msk}, f)\,.$$
3. The adversary $\mathcal{A}$ outputs attribute-message pairs (I_0, M_0) and (I_1, M_1), such that for each predicate f queried, it holds that
$$f(I_0) = f(I_1) = 0.$$
The challenger responds to the adversary $\mathcal{A}$ with the ciphertext
$$\mathsf{ct} \leftarrow \mathsf{Enc}\,(\mathsf{pp}, I_b, M_b)\,.$$
4. The adversary $\mathcal{A}$ continues to adaptively issue key-generation queries, subject to the aforementioned restrictions. The challenger responds as above.
5. Eventually, the adversary $\mathcal{A}$ outputs a bit b'.

Fig. 1. The attribute privacy experiment for predicate encryption

where the probabilities are computed over the randomness of the Setup, KeyGen and Enc algorithms.

Attribute Privacy. Define the experiment $\mathsf{Expt}^{(b)}_{\mathsf{AP},\Pi,\mathcal{A}}(\lambda)$ as in Fig. 1 for a PE $\Pi = (\mathsf{Setup}, \mathsf{KeyGen}, \mathsf{Enc}, \mathsf{Dec})$, a security parameter $\lambda \in \mathbb{N}$ and a bit $b \in \{0,1\}$. Let $\mathbf{Adv}^{\mathsf{AP}}_{\Pi,\mathcal{A}}(\lambda)$ denote the advantage of the adversary $\mathcal{A}$ in the aforementioned experiment, defined as

$$\mathbf{Adv}^{\mathsf{AP}}_{\Pi,\mathcal{A}}(\lambda) := \left| \Pr\left[\mathsf{Expt}^{(0)}_{\mathsf{AP},\Pi,\mathcal{A}}(\lambda) = 1\right] - \Pr\left[\mathsf{Expt}^{(1)}_{\mathsf{AP},\Pi,\mathcal{A}}(\lambda) = 1\right] \right| \leq \mathsf{negl}(\lambda).$$

Definition 2 (Attribute Private PE). A PE scheme Π is said to be *attribute private* if for all security parameters $\lambda \in \mathbb{N}$ and for all PPT adversaries $\mathcal{A}$, it holds that $\mathbf{Adv}^{\mathsf{AP}}_{\Pi,\mathcal{A}}(\lambda) \leq \mathsf{negl}(\lambda)$.

2.3 Sub-Classes of Predicate Encryption

In this subsection, we recall definitions of certain sub-classes of predicate encryption that are used in the rest of the paper.

Inner Product Encryption. An inner product encryption (IPE) scheme [30, 33] is a PE over an attribute space $\Sigma = \mathbb{F}_q^n$ (q being a λ-bit prime) and a set of Boolean predicates $f_{\mathbf{y}} : \mathbb{F}_q^n \longrightarrow \{0,1\}$ such that for each $\mathbf{y} \in \mathbb{F}_q^n$ and $\mathbf{x} \in \mathbb{F}_q^n$, we have

$$f_{\mathbf{y}}(\mathbf{x}) = \begin{cases} 1 & \text{if } \langle \mathbf{y}, \mathbf{x} \rangle = 0 \\ 0 & \text{otherwise.} \end{cases}$$

where $\langle \cdot, \cdot \rangle$ denotes the inner product (equivalently, scalar product) of two vectors over $\mathbb{Z}_q$.

Subspace Membership Encryption. Subspace membership encryption (SME) [13] is a generalization of IPE to accommodate general linear subspaces as opposed to only vector spaces. Formally, an SME scheme is is a PE over an attribute space $\Sigma = \mathbb{F}_q^n$ (q being a λ-bit prime) and a set of Boolean predicates $f_{\mathbf{W}} : \mathbb{F}_q^n \longrightarrow \{0,1\}$ such that for each $\mathbf{W} \in \mathbb{F}_q^{m \times n}$ and $\mathbf{x} \in \mathbb{F}_q^n$, we have

$$f_{\mathbf{W}}(\mathbf{x}) = \begin{cases} 1 & \text{if } \mathbf{W} \cdot \mathbf{x} = \mathbf{0} \\ 0 & \text{otherwise.} \end{cases}$$

Non-Zero IPE. Non-zero IPE (NIPE) [7,16] is the dual of IPE in the sense that it is a PE over an attribute space $\Sigma = \mathbb{F}_q^n$ (q being a λ-bit prime) and a set of Boolean predicates $f_{\mathbf{y}} : \mathbb{F}_q^n \longrightarrow \{0,1\}$ such that for each $\mathbf{y} \in \mathbb{F}_q^n$ and $\mathbf{x} \in \mathbb{F}_q^n$, we have

$$f_{\mathbf{y}}(\mathbf{x}) = \begin{cases} 1 & \text{if } \langle \mathbf{y}, \mathbf{x} \rangle \neq 0 \\ 0 & \text{otherwise.} \end{cases}$$

Subspace Non-Membership Encryption. Subspace non-membership encryption (SNME) is a generalization of NIPE and the dual of SME in the sense that it is a PE over an attribute space $\Sigma = \mathbb{F}_q^n$ (q being a λ-bit prime) and a set of Boolean predicates $f_{\mathbf{W}} : \mathbb{F}_q^n \longrightarrow \{0,1\}$ such that for each $\mathbf{W} \in \mathbb{F}_q^{m \times n}$ and $\mathbf{x} \in \mathbb{F}_q^n$, we have

$$f_{\mathbf{W}}(\mathbf{x}) = \begin{cases} 1 & \text{if } \mathbf{W} \cdot \mathbf{x} \neq \mathbf{0} \\ 0 & \text{otherwise.} \end{cases}$$

2.4 Bilinear Maps and Matrix Diffie-Hellman Assumptions

Let $\mathsf{GroupGen}(1^\lambda)$ be a PPT algorithm that takes as input a security parameter λ, and outputs a tuple of the form $(\mathbb{G}_1, \mathbb{G}_2, \mathbb{G}_T, q, g_1, g_2, e)$, where $\mathbb{G}_1$, $\mathbb{G}_2$ and $\mathbb{G}_T$ are distinct cyclic groups of order q (q being a λ-bit prime), g_1 is a generator for $\mathbb{G}_1$, g_2 is a generator for $\mathbb{G}_2$, and $e : \mathbb{G}_1 \times \mathbb{G}_2 \longrightarrow \mathbb{G}_T$ is an efficiently computable non-degenerate asymmetric bilinear map. Also, let $\mathbf{W} \in \mathbb{Z}_q^{m \times n}$ be an $m \times n$ matrix with entries $\{w_{i,j}\}_{i \in [1,m], j \in [1,n]}$. Throughout the paper, we use the following notations:

- $g_1^{\mathbf{W}}$: set of group elements $\{g_1^{w_{i,j}}\}_{i \in [1,m], j \in [1,n]} \in \mathbb{G}_1^{m \times n}$
- $g_2^{\mathbf{W}}$: set of group elements $\{g_2^{w_{i,j}}\}_{i \in [1,m], j \in [1,n]} \in \mathbb{G}_2^{m \times n}$
- $e(g_1, g_2)^{\mathbf{W}}$: set of group elements $\{e(g_1, g_2)^{w_{i,j}}\}_{i \in [1,m], j \in [1,n]} \in \mathbb{G}_T^{m \times n}$

We now review the matrix Diffie-Hellman (MDDH) assumption over the source groups $\mathbb{G}_1$ and $\mathbb{G}_2$ of a bilinear map.

The $\mathcal{D}_{m,n}$-MDDH Assumption. Let $m, n \in \mathbb{N}$ such that $m > n$, and let $\mathcal{D}_{m,n}$ denote a matrix distribution over $Z_q^{m\times n}$ such that a matrix $\mathbf{W} \xleftarrow{R} \mathcal{D}_{m,n}$ has full rank n with overwhelmingly large probability. The $\mathcal{D}_{m,n}$-MDDH assumption [21] holds over the group $\mathbb{G}_i$ (for $i = 1, 2$) if the distribution ensembles:

$$\left\{\left(g_i^{\mathbf{W}}, g_i^{\mathbf{W}\cdot\mathbf{y}}\right)\right\}_{\mathbf{W}\xleftarrow{R}\mathcal{D}_{m,n},\ \mathbf{y}\xleftarrow{R}\mathbb{Z}_q^n} \text{ and } \left\{\left(g_i^{\mathbf{W}}, g_i^{\mathbf{u}}\right)\right\}_{\mathbf{W}\xleftarrow{R}\mathcal{D}_{m,n},\ \mathbf{u}\xleftarrow{R}\mathbb{Z}_q^m}$$

are computationally indistinguishable.

The $\mathcal{U}_{m,n}$-MDDH Assumption. The $\mathcal{U}_{m,n}$-MDDH assumption is a special instance of the $\mathcal{D}_{m,n}$-MDDH assumption where the matrix distribution $\mathcal{D}_{m,n}$ is the uniform distribution over $Z_q^{m\times n}$.

2.5 A "Min-Entropy" Variant of the MDDH Assumption

In this subsection, we introduce another special instance of the $\mathcal{D}_{k_1,k_2}$-MDDH assumption where the matrix distribution $\mathcal{D}_{k_1,k_2}$ is not uniform, but an ordered collection of $m \times n$ independent $\omega(\log \lambda)$-sources over $\mathbb{Z}_q$. We first state and prove the following lemma.

Lemma 2.1. *Let $\mathcal{W}_{k_1,k_2} = \left[\mathrm{W}_{i,j}\right]_{i\in[1,k_1],j\in[1,k_2]}$ be a matrix of independently distributed random variables such that each random variable $\mathrm{W}_{i,j}$ for $i \in [1, k_1]$ and $j \in [1, k_2]$ is an $\omega(\log \lambda)$-source over $\mathbb{Z}_q$. Then, any matrix $\mathbf{W} \xleftarrow{R} \mathcal{W}_{k_1,k_2}$ has full rank n with overwhelmingly large probability.*

Proof. Let $\mathcal{W}_{k_1,k_2} = \left[\mathrm{W}_{i,j}\right]_{i\in[1,k_1],j\in[1,k_2]}$ be a tuple of $(k_1 \times k_2)$ independently distributed random variables such that each random variable $\mathrm{W}_{i,j}$ for $i \in [1, k_1]$ and $j \in [1, k_2]$ is a t-source over $\mathbb{Z}_q$. Let $\mathbf{W} \xleftarrow{R} \mathcal{W}_{k_1,k_2}$, and let $\widetilde{\mathbf{W}}$ be any arbitrary $k_2 \times k_2$ sub-matrix of $\mathbf{W}$. Then, the probability of the event that $\widetilde{\mathbf{W}}$ has a zero determinant may be quantified as:

$$\begin{aligned}\Pr\left[\mathrm{Det}(\widetilde{\mathbf{W}}) = 0\right] &= 1 - \left(\prod_{j=1}^{k_2-1}\left(1 - 2^{-j\cdot t}\right)\right)\\ &\leq 1 - \left(1 - 2^{-t}\right)^{(k_2-1)} \leq (k_2 - 1)\cdot 2^{-t},\end{aligned}$$

which is negligible for $t = \omega(\log \lambda)$. This completes the proof of Lemma 2.1.

The Min-Entropy-MDDH Assumption. Let $k_1, k_2 \in \mathbb{N}$ with $k_1 > k_2$, and let $\mathcal{W}_{k_1,k_2} = \left[\mathrm{W}_{i,j}\right]_{i\in[1,k_1],j\in[1,k_2]}$ be a tuple of *independently distributed* random variables such that each random variable $\mathrm{W}_{i,j}$ for $i \in [1, k_1]$ and $j \in [1, k_2]$ is an $\omega(\log \lambda)$-source over $\mathbb{Z}_q$. The (k_1, k_2)-min-entropy-MDDH assumption holds over the group $\mathbb{G}_i$ (for $i = 1, 2$) if the distribution ensembles:

$$\left\{\left(g_i^{\mathbf{W}}, g_i^{\mathbf{W}\cdot\mathbf{y}}\right)\right\}_{\mathbf{W}\xleftarrow{R}\mathcal{W}_{k_1,k_2},\ \mathbf{y}\xleftarrow{R}\mathbb{Z}_q^n} \text{ and } \left\{\left(g_i^{\mathbf{W}}, g_i^{\mathbf{u}}\right)\right\}_{\mathbf{W}\xleftarrow{R}\mathcal{W}_{k_1,k_2},\ \mathbf{u}\xleftarrow{R}\mathbb{Z}_q^m}$$

are computationally indistinguishable.

All proofs of function privacy for the schemes presented in this paper are based on the $\mathcal{W}_{m,n}$-MDDH assumption over the group $\mathbb{G}_2$.

2.6 Dual Bases

We briefly recall the concept of "dual bases" [16], along with some useful lemmas that are used in the rest of the proof. Fix some integers $k_0, k_1, k_2 \geq 1$, and let $k = k_0 + k_1 + k_2$. We denote by "basis" a uniformly sampled tuple of matrices

$$(\mathbf{B}_0, \mathbf{B}_1, \mathbf{B}_2) \xleftarrow{R} \mathbb{Z}_q^{k \times k_0} \times \mathbb{Z}_q^{k \times k_1} \times \mathbb{Z}_q^{k \times k_2}.$$

The corresponding "dual basis" is the tuple of matrices

$$(\mathbf{B}_0^*, \mathbf{B}_1^*, \mathbf{B}_2^*) \in \mathbb{Z}_q^{k \times k_0} \times \mathbb{Z}_q^{k \times k_1} \times \mathbb{Z}_q^{k \times k_2},$$

such that the following "non-degeneracy" conditions hold:

$$\mathbf{B}_0^{\mathbf{T}} \cdot \mathbf{B}_0^* = \mathbf{I}_0 \mod q, \quad \mathbf{B}_1^{\mathbf{T}} \cdot \mathbf{B}_1^* = \mathbf{I}_1 \mod q, \quad \mathbf{B}_2^{\mathbf{T}} \cdot \mathbf{B}_2^* = \mathbf{I}_2 \mod q,$$

where $\mathbf{I}_0, \mathbf{I}_1$ and $\mathbf{I}_2$ are identity matrices of appropriate dimensions, and the following "orthogonality" conditions hold:

$$\mathbf{B}_i^{\mathbf{T}} \cdot \mathbf{B}_j^* = \mathbf{0} \mod q \quad \text{for } i, j \in \{0, 1, 2\}, i \neq j.$$

We also recall some useful lemmas related to dual bases. These lemmas have been used in many prior works, notably [17,23,26].

Lemma 2.2. *Let* $(\mathbf{B}_0, \mathbf{B}_1, \mathbf{B}_2)$ *be a uniformly sampled basis as described above with corresponding dual basis* $(\mathbf{B}_0^*, \mathbf{B}_1^*, \mathbf{B}_2^*)$. *Any arbitrary vector* $\mathbf{u} \in \mathbb{Z}_q^k$ *may be uniquely decomposed as* $\mathbf{u} = \mathbf{u}_0 + \mathbf{u}_1 + \mathbf{u}_2$ *such that*

$$\mathbf{u}_0 = \mathbf{B}_0^* \cdot \mathbf{s}_0, \quad \mathbf{u}_1 = \mathbf{B}_1^* \cdot \mathbf{s}_1, \quad \mathbf{u}_2 = \mathbf{B}_2^* \cdot \mathbf{s}_2,$$

for $(\mathbf{s}_0, \mathbf{s}_1, \mathbf{s}_2) \in \mathbb{Z}_q^{k_0} \times \mathbb{Z}_q^{k_1} \times \mathbb{Z}_q^{k_2}$. *Additionally, the following holds for each* $i \in \{0, 1, 2\}$:

$$\mathbf{u}^{\mathbf{T}} \cdot \mathbf{B}_i = \mathbf{u}_i^{\mathbf{T}} \cdot \mathbf{B}_i.$$

Lemma 2.3. *Let* $(\mathbf{B}_0, \mathbf{B}_1, \mathbf{B}_2)$ *be a uniformly sampled basis as described above with corresponding dual basis* $(\mathbf{B}_0^*, \mathbf{B}_1^*, \mathbf{B}_2^*)$. *Let a uniform vector* $\mathbf{u} \xleftarrow{R} \mathbb{Z}_q^k$ *be decomposed as* $\mathbf{u} = \mathbf{u}_0 + \mathbf{u}_1 + \mathbf{u}_2$ *such that*

$$\mathbf{u}_0 = \mathbf{B}_0^* \cdot \mathbf{s}_0, \quad \mathbf{u}_1 = \mathbf{B}_1^* \cdot \mathbf{s}_1, \quad \mathbf{u}_2 = \mathbf{B}_2^* \cdot \mathbf{s}_2,$$

for $(\mathbf{s}_0, \mathbf{s}_1, \mathbf{s}_2) \in \mathbb{Z}_q^{k_0} \times \mathbb{Z}_q^{k_1} \times \mathbb{Z}_q^{k_2}$. *Then, for each* $i \in \{0, 1, 2\}$ *and for uniform* $\mathbf{s}'_i \xleftarrow{R} \mathbb{Z}_q^{k_i}$, *it holds that the distributions of the tuples*

$$(\mathbf{u}_i, \{\mathbf{u}_j\}_{j \neq i}) \quad \text{and} \quad ((\mathbf{u}_i + \mathbf{B}_i^* \cdot \mathbf{s}'_i), \{\mathbf{u}_j\}_{j \neq i})$$

are statistically indistinguishable.

To see that the aforementioned lemma holds, fix an arbitrary $i \in \{0, 1, 2\}$, set $\mathbf{u}' = \mathbf{u} + \mathbf{B}_i^* \cdot \mathbf{s}_i'$ for uniform $\mathbf{s}_i' \xleftarrow{R} \mathbb{Z}_q^{k_i}$, decompose $\mathbf{u}' = \mathbf{u}_0' + \mathbf{u}_1' + \mathbf{u}_2'$ and observe that:

- For each $j \in \{0, 1, 2\} \setminus \{i\}$, we have $\mathbf{u}_j' = \mathbf{u}_j$ by the orthogonality property.
- The distributions of $\mathbf{u}_i$ and $(\mathbf{u}_i + \mathbf{B}_i^* \cdot \mathbf{s}_i')$ are statistically indistinguishable whenever the vectors $\mathbf{u}$ and $\mathbf{s}_i'$ are uniformly random.

Lemma 2.4. *Let $(\mathbf{B}_0, \mathbf{B}_1, \mathbf{B}_2)$ be a uniformly sampled basis as described above with corresponding dual basis $(\mathbf{B}_0^*, \mathbf{B}_1^*, \mathbf{B}_2^*)$. Let (i_0, i_1, i_2) be a fixed but arbitrary permutation of the set $\{0, 1, 2\}$. Let $\widehat{\mathbf{B}}_{i_0,i_1}$ be a basis for the span of the matrices $[\mathbf{B}_{i_0}^* \mid \mathbf{B}_{i_1}^*]$ and let $\widehat{\mathbf{B}}_{i_2}$ be a basis for the span of the matrix $\mathbf{B}_{i_2}^*$. Let*

$$\mathbf{t}_0 = (\mathbf{B}_{i_0} \cdot \mathbf{s}_0)^{\mathbf{T}}, \quad \mathbf{t}_1 = (\mathbf{B}_{i_0} \cdot \mathbf{s}_{1,0} + \mathbf{B}_{i_1} \cdot \mathbf{s}_{1,1})^{\mathbf{T}},$$

where $\mathbf{s}_0, \mathbf{s}_{1,0}, \mathbf{s}_{1,1}$ are uniformly sampled vectors of appropriate dimensions. If the $\mathcal{U}_{(k_{i_0}+k_{i_1}),k_{i_0}}$-MDDH assumption holds over the bilinear group $\mathbb{G}_2$, then for all PPT adversaries $\mathcal{A}$, we have

$$\left|\Pr\left[\mathcal{A}\left(D, g_2^{\mathbf{t}_0}\right) = 1\right] - \Pr\left[\mathcal{A}\left(D, g_2^{\mathbf{t}_1}\right) = 1\right]\right| \leq \mathsf{negl}(\lambda),$$

where $D := \left(g_2^{\mathbf{B}_0^*}, g_2^{\mathbf{B}_1^*}, g_2^{\mathbf{B}_2^*}, \widehat{\mathbf{B}}_{i_0,i_1}, \widehat{\mathbf{B}}_{i_2}\right)$.

Note that Lemma 2.4 is essentially the prime-order analog of the well-known subgroup decision assumption over composite order groups, which has classically been used for dual system encryption [32]. The reader may refer to [17] for the proof of this lemma.

3 Function Privacy of SME and SNME

In this section, we define the indistinguishability-based framework for the function privacy of subspace membership encryption (SME) and subspace non-membership encryption (SNME). Let $\Pi = (\mathsf{Setup}, \mathsf{KeyGen}, \mathsf{Enc}, \mathsf{Dec})$ be an SME (equivalently, SNME) scheme. Define the experiment $\mathsf{Expt}_{\mathsf{FP},\Pi,\mathcal{A}}^{(b)}(\lambda)$ as in Fig. 2 for a security parameter $\lambda \in \mathbb{N}$ and a bit $b \in \{0, 1\}$. Let $\mathbf{Adv}_{\Pi,\mathcal{A}}^{\mathsf{FP}}(\lambda)$ denote the advantage of the adversary $\mathcal{A}$ in the aforementioned experiment, defined as

$$\mathbf{Adv}_{\Pi,\mathcal{A}}^{\mathsf{FP}}(\lambda) := \left|\Pr\left[\mathsf{Expt}_{\mathsf{FP},\Pi,\mathcal{A}}^{(0)}(\lambda) = 1\right] - \Pr\left[\mathsf{Expt}_{\mathsf{FP},\Pi,\mathcal{A}}^{(1)}(\lambda) = 1\right]\right| \leq \mathsf{negl}(\lambda).$$

Definition 3 (Function Private SME). An SME scheme Π is said to be *function private* if for all security parameters $\lambda \in \mathbb{N}$ and for all PPT adversaries $\mathcal{A}$, it holds that $\mathbf{Adv}_{\Pi,\mathcal{A}}^{\mathsf{FP}}(\lambda) \leq \mathsf{negl}(\lambda)$.

Definition 4 (Function Private SNME). An SNME scheme Π is said to be *function private* if for all security parameters $\lambda \in \mathbb{N}$ and for all PPT adversaries $\mathcal{A}$, it holds that $\mathbf{Adv}_{\Pi,\mathcal{A}}^{\mathsf{FP}}(\lambda) \leq \mathsf{negl}(\lambda)$.

Experiment $\mathsf{Expt}^{(b)}_{\mathsf{FP},\Pi,\mathcal{A}}(\lambda)$:

1. The challenger samples $(\mathsf{pp}, \mathsf{msk}) \leftarrow \mathsf{Setup}(1^\lambda)$ and provides pp to $\mathcal{A}$.
2. The adversary $\mathcal{A}$ adaptively issues key-generation queries. For each queried predicate matrix $\mathbf{W}$, the challenger responds with
$$\mathsf{sk}_{\mathbf{W}} \leftarrow \mathsf{KeyGen}(\mathsf{pp}, \mathsf{msk}, \mathbf{W}).$$
3. The adversary $\mathcal{A}$ outputs circuits of the form
$$\mathcal{W}_0 = \left[\mathrm{W}^{(0)}_{i,j}\right]_{i\in[1,m],j\in[1,n]}, \quad \mathcal{W}_1 = \left[\mathrm{W}^{(1)}_{i,j}\right]_{i\in[1,m],j\in[1,n]},$$
representing joint distributions over $\mathbb{F}_q^{m\times n}$, with the following restrictions:
   (a) For each $i \in [1,m], j \in [1,n]$ and $\tilde{b} \in \{0,1\}$, $\mathrm{W}^{(\tilde{b})}_{i,j}$ represents an $\omega(\log\lambda)$-source over $\mathbb{F}_q$.
   (b) For each $i, i' \in [1,m], j, j' \in [1,n]$ and $\tilde{b} \in \{0,1\}$, $\mathrm{W}^{(\tilde{b})}_{i,j}$ and $\mathrm{W}^{(\tilde{b})}_{i',j'}$ represent mutually independent distributions.

   The challenger samples $\mathbf{W} \xleftarrow{R} \mathcal{W}_b$ and responds to the adversary $\mathcal{A}$ with the secret-key
$$\mathsf{sk}_{\mathbf{W}} = \mathsf{KeyGen}(\mathsf{msk}, \mathbf{W}).$$
4. The adversary $\mathcal{A}$ continues to adaptively issue key-generation queries. The challenger responds as above.
5. Eventually, the adversary $\mathcal{A}$ outputs a bit b'.

Fig. 2. The function privacy experiment for SME and SNME

The Mutual Independence Condition. Observe that the function privacy experiment requires the adversarially chosen distributions $\mathcal{W}_0$ and $\mathcal{W}_1$ to be constructed such that the individual component distributions are both "mutually independent" and "sufficiently unpredictable". A stronger notion of function privacy could allow these components to be "arbitrarily correlated", so long as they are "individually" sufficiently unpredictable. As shown in [13], such a notion is impossible to satisfy. In other words, if arbitrary correlations were allowed, the adversary $\mathcal{A}$ in the function privacy experiment can always create challenge distributions that satisfy the unpredictability requirement, but secret keys for matrices from these distributions are easily distinguishable. We present a brief illustration here for the sake of completeness.

Consider an IPE scheme (equivalently, an SME scheme of dimension $m = 1$) and an adversary $\mathcal{A}$ in the function privacy experiment that chooses the challenge distributions as:

$$\mathcal{W}_0 = \left[\mathrm{W}^{(0)}_1, 2\mathrm{W}^{(0)}_1, \mathrm{W}^{(0)}_2, \ldots, \mathrm{W}^{(0)}_{n-1}\right], \quad \mathcal{W}_1 = \left[\mathrm{W}^{(1)}_1, \mathrm{W}^{(1)}_2, \ldots, \mathrm{W}^{(1)}_{n-1}, 2\mathrm{W}^{(1)}_{n-1}\right],$$

where for each $j \in [1, n-1]$ and $\tilde{b} \in \{0,1\}$, $\mathrm{W}^{(\tilde{b})}_j$ represents a *uniform* source over $\mathbb{F}_q$. Clearly, each individual distribution has min-entropy $\log q = \omega(\log\lambda)$; yet, secret keys for vectors sampled from $\mathcal{W}_0$ can be distinguished from secret keys for vectors sampled from $\mathcal{W}_1$ with non-negligible advantage as follows: encrypt a message M under two attribute vectors $\mathbf{x}_0$ and $\mathbf{x}_1$ defined as:

$$\mathbf{x}_0 = (2, -1, 0, \ldots, 0), \quad \mathbf{x}_1 = (0, \ldots, 0, 2, -1),$$

and see which of the two ciphertexts decrypts correctly under the challenge secret key. This justifies the mutual independence criteria imposed in the function privacy experiment.

Multi-Challenge vs. Single-Challenge. Observe that the aforementioned function privacy definition for SME/SNME is "single-challenge" in the sense that the function privacy experiment allows the adversary a single challenge query. In fact, as the adversary is also given access to the key-generation oracle, the "single-challenge" definition is polynomially equivalent to a "multi-challenge" variant where the adversary is allowed polynomially many challenge queries. This equivalence may be proved by a hybrid argument (originally proposed in [13]), where the hybrids are constructed such that only one query is forwarded to the function privacy oracle, and all other queries are answered using the key-generation oracle.

4 Function Private SME

In this section, we present the construction of an SME scheme that achieves computational function privacy whenever the predicate matrices are sampled from distributions with min-entropy $\omega(\log \lambda)$. In contrast, the SME scheme of Boneh *et al.* [13] is statistically function private, albeit for predicate matrices sampled from distributions with min-entropy slightly larger than λ.

Attribute and function privacy guarantees of our scheme follow from variants of the general $\mathcal{D}$-MDDH assumption in the standard model. More specifically, attribute privacy can be based on the $\mathcal{U}_{k+1,k}$-MDDH assumption in $\mathbb{G}_1$ and $\mathcal{U}_{2k,k}$-MDDH assumption in $\mathbb{G}_2$, while function privacy follows from the $\mathcal{W}_{m,n}$-MDDH assumption described in Sect. 2.4. The scheme is described below, while the proofs of attribute and function privacy are presented subsequently.

4.1 The Construction

Let $\mathsf{GroupGen}(1^\lambda)$ be a PPT algorithm that takes as input a security parameter $\lambda \in \mathbb{N}$, and outputs the tuple $(\mathbb{G}_1, \mathbb{G}_2, \mathbb{G}_T, q, g_1, g_2, e)$, where $\mathbb{G}_1$, $\mathbb{G}_2$ and $\mathbb{G}_T$ are cyclic groups of prime order q (q being a λ-bit prime), g_1 is a generator for $\mathbb{G}_1$, g_2 is a generator for $\mathbb{G}_2$, and $e : \mathbb{G}_1 \times \mathbb{G}_2 \longrightarrow \mathbb{G}_T$ is an efficiently computable non-degenerate asymmetric bilinear map. Our scheme Π^{SME} is parameterized by $m, n = \mathsf{poly}(\lambda)$ in the sense that it supports predicate matrices of the form $\mathbf{W} \in \mathbb{Z}_q^{m \times n}$, and attribute vectors of the form $\mathbf{x} \in \mathbb{Z}_q^n$. Finally, the payload message space $\mathcal{M}$ is assumed to a "super-polynomially smaller" subset of $\mathbb{G}_T$, namely $|\mathcal{M}| < |\mathbb{G}_T|^{1/2}$. Our scheme works as follows.[2]

- $\mathsf{Setup}(1^\lambda)$: Uniformly sample $(\mathbb{G}_1, \mathbb{G}_2, \mathbb{G}_T, q, g_1, g_2, e) \leftarrow \mathsf{GroupGen}(1^\lambda)$. Also, uniformly sample

$$\mathbf{A} \xleftarrow{R} \mathbb{Z}_q^{(k+1)\times k}, \quad \mathbf{S}_0, \mathbf{S}_1, \ldots, \mathbf{S}_n \xleftarrow{R} \mathbb{Z}_q^{(2k+1)\times(k+1)},$$

$$\mathbf{K} \xleftarrow{R} \mathbb{Z}_q^{1\times(k+1)}, \quad \mathbf{B}_0 \xleftarrow{R} \mathbb{Z}_q^{(2k+1)\times k}$$

for some constant $k > 0$. Output

$$\mathsf{pp} = \left(g_1, g_1^{\mathbf{A}}, g_1^{\mathbf{S}_0\cdot\mathbf{A}}, g_1^{\mathbf{S}_1\cdot\mathbf{A}}, \ldots, g_1^{\mathbf{S}_n\cdot\mathbf{A}}, e(g_1, g_2)^{\mathbf{K}\cdot\mathbf{A}} \right),$$

$$\mathsf{msk} = (g_2, \mathbf{S}_0, \mathbf{S}_1, \ldots, \mathbf{S}_n, \mathbf{K}, \mathbf{B}_0).$$

- $\mathsf{KeyGen}(\mathsf{pp}, \mathsf{msk}, \mathbf{W})$: Parse the predicate matrix $\mathbf{W} \in \mathbb{Z}_q^{m\times n}$ as

$$\mathbf{W} = \left[w_{i,j}\right]_{i\in[1,m], j\in[1,n]}.$$

Uniformly sample $\mathbf{s} \xleftarrow{R} \mathbb{Z}_q^k$ and set $\mathbf{t} = (\mathbf{B}_0 \cdot \mathbf{s})^{\mathbf{T}}$. Finally, pick uniform $y_1, \ldots, y_m \xleftarrow{R} \mathbb{Z}_q$ and output $\mathsf{sk}_{\mathbf{W}} = \left(\{h_j\}_{j\in[0,n]}\right)$ where

$$h_0 = g_2^{\left(\mathbf{K} + \sum_{i=1}^m y_i \cdot \left(\sum_{j=1}^n w_{i,j} \cdot \mathbf{t} \cdot \mathbf{S}_j\right)\right)^{\mathbf{T}}},$$

$$h_j = g_2^{\left(\sum_{i=1}^m y_i \cdot w_{i,j} \cdot \mathbf{t}\right)^{\mathbf{T}}} \quad \textit{for } j \in [1, n].$$

- $\mathsf{Enc}(\mathsf{pp}, \mathbf{x}, M)$: Given an attribute vector $\mathbf{x} = \left[x_1 \ldots x_n\right]^{\mathbf{T}} \in \mathbb{Z}_q^n$ and a message $M \in \mathcal{M} \subset \mathbb{G}_T$, uniformly sample $\mathbf{r} \xleftarrow{R} \mathbb{Z}_q^k$ and output $\mathsf{ct} = \left(\{c_j\}_{j\in[0,n+1]}\right)$ where

$$c_0 = g_1^{(\mathbf{A}\cdot\mathbf{r})^{\mathbf{T}}}$$

$$c_j = g_1^{((x_j\cdot\mathbf{S}_0 + \mathbf{S}_j)\cdot\mathbf{A}\cdot\mathbf{r})^{\mathbf{T}}} \quad \textit{for } j \in [1, n]$$

$$c_{n+1} = M \cdot e(g_1, g_2)^{(\mathbf{K}\cdot\mathbf{A}\cdot\mathbf{r})^{\mathbf{T}}}$$

- $\mathsf{Dec}(\mathsf{pp}, \mathsf{sk}_{\mathbf{W}}, \mathsf{ct})$: Parse the ciphertext as $\mathsf{ct} = \left(\{c_j\}_{j\in[0,n+1]}\right)$ and the secret key as $\mathsf{sk}_{\mathbf{W}} = \left(\{h_j\}_{j\in[0,n]}\right)$. Compute

$$M = \left(c_{n+1} \cdot \prod_{j=1}^{n} e(c_j, h_j) \right) \Big/ e(c_0, h_0).$$

If $M \in \mathcal{M}$, output M. Otherwise, output $\perp$.

[2] The restriction on the size of the message space $\mathcal{M}$ is necessary for correctness as explained subsequently. Note that this restriction does not prevent $\mathcal{M}$ from being exponentially large.

Correctness. To see that the aforementioned scheme is functionally correct, observe the following.

$$\prod_{j=1}^{n} e(c_j, h_j) = \prod_{j=1}^{n} e(g_1, g_2)^{\left(\sum_{i=1}^{m} y_i \cdot w_{i,j} \cdot \mathbf{t} \cdot (x_j \cdot \mathbf{S}_0 + \mathbf{S}_j) \cdot \mathbf{A} \cdot \mathbf{r}\right)^{\mathbf{T}}}$$

$$= e(g_1, g_2)^{\left(\left(\sum_{j=1}^{n} \sum_{i=1}^{m} y_i \cdot w_{i,j} \cdot x_j \cdot \mathbf{t} \cdot \mathbf{S}_0 + \sum_{j=1}^{n} \sum_{i=1}^{m} y_i \cdot w_{i,j} \cdot \mathbf{t} \cdot \mathbf{S}_j\right) \cdot \mathbf{A} \cdot \mathbf{r}\right)^{\mathbf{T}}}$$

$$= e(g_1, g_2)^{\left(\sum_{i=1}^{m} y_i \cdot \sum_{j=1}^{n} w_{i,j} \cdot x_j \cdot \mathbf{t} \cdot \mathbf{S}_0 \cdot \mathbf{A} \cdot \mathbf{r}\right)^{\mathbf{T}}} \cdot e(g_1, g_2)^{\left(\sum_{i=1}^{m} y_i \cdot \left(\sum_{j=1}^{n} w_{i,j} \cdot \mathbf{t} \cdot \mathbf{S}_j\right) \cdot \mathbf{A} \cdot \mathbf{r}\right)^{\mathbf{T}}}$$

$$= e(g_1, g_2)^{\left(\sum_{i=1}^{m} y_i \cdot \sum_{j=1}^{n} w_{i,j} \cdot x_j \cdot \mathbf{t} \cdot \mathbf{S}_0 \cdot \mathbf{A} \cdot \mathbf{r}\right)^{\mathbf{T}}} \cdot e\left(g_1^{(\mathbf{A} \cdot \mathbf{r})^{\mathbf{T}}}, g_2^{\left(\sum_{i=1}^{m} y_i \cdot \left(\sum_{j=1}^{n} w_{i,j} \cdot \mathbf{t} \cdot \mathbf{S}_j\right)\right)^{\mathbf{T}}}\right)$$

$$= M \cdot (c_{n+1})^{-1} \cdot e(c_0, h_0) \cdot e(g_1, g_2)^{((\mathbf{y} \cdot \mathbf{W} \cdot \mathbf{x}) \cdot \mathbf{t} \cdot \mathbf{S}_0 \cdot \mathbf{A} \cdot \mathbf{r})^{\mathbf{T}}}$$

where $\mathbf{y} = \begin{bmatrix} y_1 \ldots y_m \end{bmatrix}$. Hence, when $\mathbf{W} \cdot \mathbf{x} = \mathbf{0} \mod q$, the decryption algorithm recovers M correctly. On the other hand, when $\mathbf{W} \cdot \mathbf{x} \neq \mathbf{0} \mod q$ the distribution of M such that M satisfies the decryption equation is uniformly random over $\mathbb{G}_T$, and hence, with overwhelmingly large probability over the randomness of KeyGen and Enc, the decryption algorithm returns $\perp$.[3]

4.2 Attribute Privacy

We state and prove the following theorem.

Theorem 4.1. *If the $\mathcal{U}_{k+1,k}$-MDDH assumption holds over the group $\mathbb{G}_1$ and the $\mathcal{U}_{2k,k}$-MDDH assumption holds over the group $\mathbb{G}_2$, then for all PPT adversaries $\mathcal{A}$, we have* $\mathbf{Adv}^{\mathsf{AP}}_{\Pi^{\mathrm{SME}},\mathcal{A}}(\lambda) \leq \mathsf{negl}(\lambda)$.

Proof. The proof proceeds through a sequence of experiments, beginning with the "real" attribute privacy experiment and ending with an experiment where the adversary has no advantage. We consider a variant of the "real" attribute privacy experiment where the challenge messages M_0 and M_1 are chosen to be equal by the adversary. One can reduce the case for $M_0 \neq M_1$ to this case by arguing that an encryption of M_b for $b \in \{0,1\}$ is indistinguishable from an encryption of M_0 [16,37]. Hence, it is sufficient to assume that $M_0 = M_1$ in the hybrid experiments presented next.[4]

Expt-0. This is the "real" experiment. In this experiment, the adversary $\mathcal{A}$ is given the public parameter pp. The adversary chooses two (distinct) vector-message pairs $(\mathbf{x}_0, M_0), (\mathbf{x}_1, M_1) \in \mathbb{Z}_q^n \times \mathcal{M}$, such that

$$\mathbf{x}_b = \begin{bmatrix} x_{1,b} & x_{2,b} & \ldots & x_{n,b} \end{bmatrix}^{\mathbf{T}} \quad \text{for each } b \in \{0,1\}.$$

[3] The argument follows from the fact that both $\mathbf{y}$ and $\mathbf{r}$ are uniformly random vectors in $\mathbb{Z}_q^m$ and $\mathbb{Z}_q^k$, respectively, and $|\mathcal{M}| < |\mathbb{G}_T|^{1/2}$.

[4] Due to paucity of space, we only provide brief proof sketches in several cases. We refer the reader to the full version of the paper [35] for the detailed proofs.

and $M_0 = M_1$. In addition, the adversary (adaptively) issues a maximum of Q key generation queries (for some fixed polynomial $Q = Q(\lambda)$) corresponding to predicate matrices the form $\mathbf{W}_1, \ldots, \mathbf{W}_Q \in \mathbb{Z}_q^{m\times n}$, subject to the restriction that

$$(\mathbf{W}_\ell \cdot \mathbf{x}_0 \neq 0 \mod q) \wedge (\mathbf{W}_\ell \cdot \mathbf{x}_1 \neq \mathbf{0} \mod q) \text{ for each } \ell \in [1, Q].$$

It receives in response $(\mathsf{ct}^*, \mathsf{sk}_{\mathbf{W}_1}, \ldots, \mathsf{sk}_{\mathbf{W}_Q})$, where

$$\mathsf{ct}^* \leftarrow \mathsf{Enc}(\mathsf{pp}, \mathbf{x}_b, M_0) \quad \text{for some random } b \xleftarrow{R} \{0,1\},$$
$$\mathsf{sk}_{\mathbf{W}_\ell} \leftarrow \mathsf{KeyGen}(\mathsf{pp}, \mathsf{msk}, \mathbf{W}_\ell) \quad \text{for each } \ell \in [1, Q].$$

Finally, it outputs a bit b'. Let $P_{\mathcal{A},0}$ denote the probability that $b = b'$.

Expt-1. This experiment is identical to Expt-0 except for the manner in which the challenge ciphertext ct^* is generated. Namely, the challenger $\mathcal{B}$ uniformly samples $\mathbf{r} \xleftarrow{R} \mathbb{Z}_q^k$ and uses the master secret key components $\mathbf{S}_0, \mathbf{S}_1, \ldots, \mathbf{S}_n, \mathbf{K}$ to generate the ciphertext $\mathsf{ct}^* = \left(\{c_j\}_{j\in[0,n+1]}\right)$ as

$$c_0 = g_1^{(\mathbf{A}\cdot\mathbf{r})^{\mathbf{T}}}, \quad \left\{c_j = (c_0)^{(x_{j,b}\cdot\mathbf{S}_0+\mathbf{S}_j)^{\mathbf{T}}}\right\}_{j\in[1,n]}, \quad c_{n+1} = M_0 \cdot e\left(c_0, g_2\right)^{\mathbf{K}^{\mathbf{T}}}.$$

Note that for each $j \in [1, n]$, we essentially have $c_j = g_1^{\left(\mathbf{v}_j^{(1)}\right)^{\mathbf{T}}}$, where

$$\mathbf{v}_j^{(1)} = (x_{j,b} \cdot \mathbf{S}_0 + \mathbf{S}_j) \cdot \mathbf{A} \cdot \mathbf{r}.$$

Let $P_{\mathcal{A},1}$ denote the probability that $b = b'$, where b' is the bit output by the adversary $\mathcal{A}$ at the end of Expt-1. Observe that the challenge ciphertext ct^* in Expt-1 has the same distribution as in Expt-0. Hence, we have $P_{\mathcal{A},1} = P_{\mathcal{A},0}$.

Expt-2. This experiment is identical to Expt-1 except for the manner in which the challenge ciphertext ct^* is generated. Namely, the challenger $\mathcal{B}$ uniformly samples $\mathbf{u} \xleftarrow{R} \mathbb{Z}_q^{k+1}$, and generates the ciphertext $\mathsf{ct}^* = \left(\{c_j\}_{j\in[0,n+1]}\right)$ as

$$c_0 = g_1^{\mathbf{u}^{\mathbf{T}}}, \quad \left\{c_j = (c_0)^{(x_{j,b}\cdot\mathbf{S}_0+\mathbf{S}_j)^{\mathbf{T}}}\right\}_{j\in[1,n]}, \quad c_{n+1} = M_0 \cdot e\left(c_0, g_2\right)^{\mathbf{K}^{\mathbf{T}}}.$$

Note that for each $j \in [1, n]$, we essentially have $c_j = g_1^{\left(\mathbf{v}_j^{(2)}\right)^{\mathbf{T}}}$, where

$$\mathbf{v}_j^{(2)} = \boxed{(x_{j,b} \cdot \mathbf{S}_0 + \mathbf{S}_j) \cdot \mathbf{u}}.$$

Let $P_{\mathcal{A},2}$ denote the probability that $b = b'$, where b' is the bit output by the adversary $\mathcal{A}$ at the end of Expt-2. We state the following lemma.

Lemma 4.1. *For all PPT adversaries $\mathcal{A}$, $|P_{\mathcal{A},2} - P_{\mathcal{A},1}| \leq \mathsf{negl}(\lambda)$.*

The proof of this lemma follows directly from the $\mathcal{U}_{k+1,k}$-MDDH assumption over the group $\mathbb{G}_1$. More specifically, given a PPT adversary $\mathcal{A}$ that can distinguish between between its views in Expt-1 and Expt-2 with non-negligible probability, one can construct a PPT algorithm that can distinguish between the ensembles

$$\left\{\left(g_1^{\mathbf{A}}, g_1^{\mathbf{A}\cdot\mathbf{r}}\right)\right\}_{\mathbf{A}\xleftarrow{R}\mathbb{Z}_q^{(k+1)\times k},\mathbf{r}\xleftarrow{R}\mathbb{Z}_q^k} \text{ and } \left\{\left(g_1^{\mathbf{A}}, g_1^{\mathbf{u}}\right)\right\}_{\mathbf{A}\xleftarrow{R}\mathbb{Z}_q^{(k+1)\times k},\ \mathbf{u}\xleftarrow{R}\mathbb{Z}_q^{k+1}}$$

with non-negligible probability. Quite evidently, the existence of such a PPT algorithm violates the $\mathcal{U}_{k+1,k}$-MDDH assumption over the group $\mathbb{G}_1$.

Expt-3. This experiment is identical to Expt-2 except for the manner in which the challenge ciphertext ct^* is generated. Namely, the challenger $\mathcal{B}$ uniformly samples a basis

$$(\mathbf{B}_0, \mathbf{B}_1, \mathbf{B}_2) \in \mathbb{Z}_q^{(2k+1)\times k} \times \mathbb{Z}_q^{(2k+1)\times 1} \times \mathbb{Z}_q^{(2k+1)\times k},$$

with corresponding dual basis $(\mathbf{B}_0^*, \mathbf{B}_1^*, \mathbf{B}_2^*)$, and uses $\mathbf{B}_0$ as part of the master secret key msk. It samples $\mathbf{u} \xleftarrow{R} \mathbb{Z}_q^{k+1}$ and decomposes $\mathbf{S}_0 \cdot \mathbf{u} \in \mathbb{Z}_q^{2k+1}$ as

$$\mathbf{S}_0 \cdot \mathbf{u} = \mathbf{u}_0 + \mathbf{u}_1 + \mathbf{u}_2,$$

such that

$$\mathbf{u}_0 = \mathbf{B}_0^* \cdot \mathbf{s}_0, \quad \mathbf{u}_1 = \mathbf{B}_1^* \cdot s_1, \quad \mathbf{u}_2 = \mathbf{B}_2^* \cdot \mathbf{s}_2 \quad \text{for some } \mathbf{s}_0, \mathbf{s}_2 \in \mathbb{Z}_q^k, s_1 \in \mathbb{Z}_q.$$

Note that such a decomposition always exists by Lemma 2.2. The challenger $\mathcal{B}$ then generates the ciphertext $\mathsf{ct}^* = \left(\{c_j\}_{j\in[0,n+1]}\right)$ as

$$c_0 = g_1^{\mathbf{u}^{\mathbf{T}}}, \quad \left\{c_j = g_1^{\left(\mathbf{v}_j^{(3)}\right)^{\mathbf{T}}}\right\}_{j\in[1,n]}, \quad c_{n+1} = M_0 \cdot e\left(c_0, g_2\right)^{\mathbf{K}^{\mathbf{T}}},$$

where for each $j \in [1, n]$, we have

$$\mathbf{v}_j^{(3)} = x_{j,b} \cdot \mathbf{u}_0 + \boxed{x_{j,1-b} \cdot \mathbf{u}_1} + x_{j,b} \cdot \mathbf{u}_2 + \mathbf{S}_j \cdot \mathbf{u}.$$

Let $P_{\mathcal{A},3}$ denote the probability that $b = b'$, where b' is the bit output by the adversary $\mathcal{A}$ at the end of Expt-3. We state the following lemma.

Lemma 4.2. *For all unbounded adversaries $\mathcal{A}$, $|P_{\mathcal{A},3} - P_{\mathcal{A},2}| \leq \mathsf{negl}(\lambda)$.*

Proof Sketch. To prove Lemma 4.2, it is sufficient to prove that for each $j \in [1, n]$ and for all $\mathbf{x}_0, \mathbf{x}_1 \in \mathbb{Z}_q^n$, the distributions of $\mathbf{v}_j^{(2)}$ and $\mathbf{v}_j^{(3)}$ are statistically close. Informally, the proof is based on the following observations and a simple application of Lemma 2.3.

1. If one were to decompose $\mathbf{S}_j \cdot \mathbf{u}$ for $j \in [1, n]$ as
$$\mathbf{S}_j \cdot \mathbf{u} = \mathbf{u}_{j,0} + \mathbf{u}_{j,1} + \mathbf{u}_{j,2},$$
such that
$$\mathbf{u}_{j,0} = \mathbf{B}_0^* \cdot \mathbf{s}_{j,0}, \quad \mathbf{u}_{j,1} = \mathbf{B}_1^* \cdot s_{j,1}, \quad \mathbf{u}_{j,2} = \mathbf{B}_2^* \cdot \mathbf{s}_{j,2},$$
for some $\mathbf{s}_{j,0}, \mathbf{s}_{j,2} \in \mathbb{Z}_q^k, s_{j,1} \in \mathbb{Z}_q$, then the public parameter pp and the secret keys $\mathsf{sk}_{\mathbf{W}_1}, \ldots, \mathsf{sk}_{\mathbf{W}_Q}$ statistically hide $\mathbf{u}_{j,1}$ for $j \in [1, n]$. In other words, in the view of an unbounded adversary, the distribution of $\mathbf{u}_{j,1}$ is statistically indistinguishable from that of a uniformly random vector in the span of $\mathbf{B}_1^*$. The reasoning behind this observation is detailed in the full version [35].
2. For each $j \in [1, n]$, for all $\mathbf{x}_0, \mathbf{x}_1 \in \mathbb{Z}_q^n$ and for all $\mathbf{u}_1$ in the span of $\mathbf{B}_1^*$, the distributions of
$$(x_{j,b} \cdot \mathbf{u}_1 + \mathbf{u}_{j,1}) \quad \text{and} \quad (x_{j,1-b} \cdot \mathbf{u}_1 + \mathbf{u}_{j,1})$$
are statistically indistinguishable whenever $\mathbf{u}_{j,1}$ is uniform in the span of $\mathbf{B}_1^*$.

Expt-4-ℓ. For each $\ell \in [0, Q]$, the experiment Expt-4-ℓ is identical to Expt-3 except for the manner in which the first ℓ secret key queries are answered by the challenger $\mathcal{B}$. More specifically, $\mathcal{B}$ uniformly samples a basis $(\mathbf{B}_0, \mathbf{B}_1, \mathbf{B}_2)$ with corresponding dual basis $(\mathbf{B}_0^*, \mathbf{B}_1^*, \mathbf{B}_2^*)$, and uses $\mathbf{B}_0$ as part of the master secret key msk. For each $\ell' \in [1, \ell]$, $\mathcal{B}$ uniformly samples $\mathbf{s}_{\ell',0} \xleftarrow{R} \mathbb{Z}_q^k$ and $s_{\ell',1} \xleftarrow{R} \mathbb{Z}_q$, and sets
$$\mathbf{t}_{\ell'} = (\mathbf{B}_0 \cdot \mathbf{s}_{\ell',0} + \mathbf{B}_1 \cdot s_{\ell',1})^{\mathbf{T}}.$$
In other words, the vector $(\mathbf{t}_{\ell'})^{\mathbf{T}}$ now lies in the span of $\left[\mathbf{B}_0 \mid \mathbf{B}_1\right]$ and not in the span of $\mathbf{B}_0$, as in the real experiment. The challenger $\mathcal{B}$ then generates the secret key corresponding to the predicate matrix $\mathbf{W}_{\ell'}$ as $\mathsf{sk}_{\mathbf{W}_{\ell'}} = \left(\{h_{j,\ell'}\}_{j \in [0,n]}\right)$ where
$$h_{0,\ell'} = g_2^{\left(\mathbf{K} + \sum_{i=1}^m y_{\ell',i} \cdot \left(\sum_{j=1}^n w_{i,j} \cdot \mathbf{t}_{\ell'} \cdot \mathbf{S}_j\right)\right)^{\mathbf{T}}},$$
$$h_{j,\ell'} = g_2^{\left(\sum_{i=1}^m y_{\ell',i} \cdot w_{i,j} \cdot \mathbf{t}_{\ell'}\right)^{\mathbf{T}}} \quad \text{for } j \in [1, n].$$
where $y_{\ell',1}, \ldots, y_{\ell',m} \xleftarrow{R} \mathbb{Z}_q$.
Let $P_{\mathcal{A},4,\ell}$ denote the probability that $b = b'$, where b' is the bit output by the adversary $\mathcal{A}$ at the end of Expt-4-ℓ. We state the following lemma.

Lemma 4.3. *For all PPT adversaries $\mathcal{A}$, $\left|P_{\mathcal{A},4,\ell} - P_{\mathcal{A},4,(\ell-1)}\right| \leq \mathsf{negl}(\lambda)$ for each $\ell \in [1, Q]$.*

Proof. The proof proceeds through another sequence of hybrid experiments, beginning with an experiment identical to Expt-4-$(\ell - 1)$ and ending with an experiment identical to Expt-4-ℓ. Each experiment in this sequence differs from its predecessor in one of two ways: either the ℓth secret key sk_ℓ is generated in a different manner, or the challenge ciphertext ct^* is generated in a different manner. The corresponding indistinguishability arguments between pairs of successive experiments rely heavily on Lemmas 2.2, 2.3 and 2.4.

Expt-5. This experiment is identical to Expt-4-Q except for the manner in which the challenge ciphertext ct^* is generated. More specifically, the challenger $\mathcal{B}$ samples $\mathbf{u}, \mathbf{u}', \mathbf{u}'' \xleftarrow{R} \mathbb{Z}_q^{k+1}$ and uses the dual basis to decompose these as

$$\begin{aligned}\mathbf{S}_0 \cdot \mathbf{u} &= (\mathbf{u}_0 + \mathbf{u}_1 + \mathbf{u}_2)\\ \mathbf{S}_0 \cdot \mathbf{u}' &= (\mathbf{u}'_0 + \mathbf{u}'_1 + \mathbf{u}'_2)\\ \mathbf{S}_0 \cdot \mathbf{u}'' &= (\mathbf{u}''_0 + \mathbf{u}''_1 + \mathbf{u}''_2)\end{aligned}$$

It then generates the ciphertext $\mathsf{ct}^* = \left(\{c_j\}_{j\in[0,n+1]}\right)$ as

$$c_0 = g_1^{\mathbf{u}^{\mathbf{T}}}, \quad \left\{c_j = g_1^{\left(\mathbf{v}_j^{(5)}\right)^{\mathbf{T}}}\right\}_{j\in[1,n]}, \quad c_{n+1} = M_0 \cdot e\left(c_0, g_2\right)^{\mathbf{K}^{\mathbf{T}}},$$

where for each $j \in [1, n]$, we have

$$\mathbf{v}_j^{(5)} = \boxed{x_{j,0} \cdot (\mathbf{u}'_0 + \mathbf{u}'_1)} + \boxed{x_{j,1} \cdot (\mathbf{u}''_0 + \mathbf{u}''_1)} + x_{j,b} \cdot \mathbf{u}_2 + \mathbf{S}_j \cdot \mathbf{u}.$$

Let $P_{\mathcal{A},5}$ denote the probability that $b = b'$, where b' is the bit output by the adversary $\mathcal{A}$ at the end of Expt-5. We state and prove the following lemma.

Lemma 4.4. *For all unbounded adversaries* $\mathcal{A}$, $|P_{\mathcal{A},5} - P_{\mathcal{A},4-Q}| \leq \mathsf{negl}(\lambda)$.

Proof Sketch. To prove this lemma, we employ the standard "change of basis" technique used in dual pairing vector spaces [31,33,34]. More specifically, we argue that the distributions of

$$(\mathbf{u}_1, \mathbf{u}_2) \quad \text{and} \quad ((\mathbf{u}'_0 + \mathbf{u}'_1), (\mathbf{u}''_0 + \mathbf{u}''_1))$$

are statistically indistinguishable whenever the vectors $\mathbf{u}, \mathbf{u}', \mathbf{u}''$ and the basis matrices $\mathbf{B}_0, \mathbf{B}_1$ are uniformly random. Informally, the argument follows from the following observations:

- The randomness $\mathbf{t}_i$ in each secret key $\mathsf{sk}_{\mathbf{W}_i}$ for $i \in [1, Q]$ statistically hides the span of $[\mathbf{B}_0 \mid \mathbf{B}_1]$. This allows for an alternative simulation of Expt-4, where the basis matrices $\mathbf{B}_0, \mathbf{B}_1$ are "changed", i.e., replaced by two other specially constructed basis matrices, such that the replacement matrices are also distributed uniformly.
- The alternative simulation of Expt-4 is statistically indistinguishable from the original simulation of Expt-4.
- The alternative simulation of Expt-4 with respect to the changed basis matrices is statistically indistinguishable from the simulation of Expt-5 with respect to the original basis matrices.

Expt-6. This experiment is identical to Expt-5 except for the manner in which the challenge ciphertext ct^* is generated. Namely, the challenger $\mathcal{B}$ uniformly samples $\mathbf{u}, \mathbf{u}', \mathbf{u}'' \xleftarrow{R} \mathbb{Z}_q^{k+1}$ and generates the ciphertext $\mathsf{ct}^* = \left(\{c_j\}_{j\in[0,n+1]}\right)$ as

$$c_0 = g_1^{\mathbf{u}^{\mathbf{T}}}, \quad \left\{c_j = g_1^{\left(\mathbf{v}_j^{(6)}\right)^{\mathbf{T}}}\right\}_{j\in[1,n]}, \quad c_{n+1} = M_0 \cdot e\left(c_0, g_2\right)^{\mathbf{K}^{\mathbf{T}}},$$

where for each $j \in [1, n]$, we have

$$\mathbf{v}_j^{(6)} = \boxed{x_{j,0} \cdot \mathbf{S}_0 \cdot \mathbf{u}' + x_{j,1} \cdot \mathbf{S}_0 \cdot \mathbf{u}''} + \mathbf{S}_j \cdot \mathbf{u}.$$

Let $P_{\mathcal{A},6}$ denote the probability that $b = b'$, where b' is the bit output by the adversary $\mathcal{A}$ at the end of Expt-6. We state and prove the following lemma.

Lemma 4.5. *For all unbounded adversaries $\mathcal{A}$, $|P_{\mathcal{A},6} - P_{\mathcal{A},5}| \leq \mathsf{negl}(\lambda)$.*

Proof. The proof is similar to the proof of indistinguishability of Expt 2 and Expt 3.

Finally, observe that in Expt-6, the adversary $\mathcal{A}$ has no advantage in guessing b, since the ciphertext ct^* is entirely independent of b. In other words, for all PPT adversaries $\mathcal{A}$, we must have $P_{\mathcal{A},6} = 1/2$. This completes the proof of Theorem 4.1. □

4.3 Function Privacy

We state and prove the following theorem.

Theorem 4.2. *If the* (n, m)-min-entropy-MDDH *assumption holds over the group* $\mathbb{G}_2$, *then for all PPT adversaries* $\mathcal{A}$, *we have* $\mathbf{Adv}^{\mathsf{FP}}_{\Pi^{\mathrm{SME}},\mathcal{A}}(\lambda) \leq \mathsf{negl}(\lambda)$.

Proof. The proof proceeds through a sequence of experiments, beginning with the "real" function privacy experiment and ending with an experiment where the adversary has no advantage.

Expt-0. This is the "real" function privacy experiment. In this experiment, the adversary $\mathcal{A}$ is given the public parameter pp. The adversary chooses two circuits corresponding to matrix distributions of the form

$$\mathcal{W}_0 = \left[\mathrm{W}_{i,j}^{(0)}\right]_{i\in[1,m],j\in[1,n]}, \quad \mathcal{W}_1 = \left[\mathrm{W}_{i,j}^{(1)}\right]_{i\in[1,m],j\in[1,n]},$$

representing joint distributions over $\mathbb{Z}_q^{m\times n}$, subject to the following restrictions:

1. For each $i \in [1, m], j \in [1, n]$ and $\tilde{b} \in \{0, 1\}$, $\mathrm{W}_{i,j}^{(\tilde{b})}$ represents an $\omega(\log\lambda)$-source over $\mathbb{F}_q$.
2. For each $i, i' \in [1, m], j, j' \in [1, n]$ and $\tilde{b} \in \{0, 1\}$, $\mathrm{W}_{i,j}^{(\tilde{b})}$ and $\mathrm{W}_{i',j'}^{(\tilde{b})}$ represent mutually independent distributions.

The adversary $\mathcal{A}$ also (adaptively) issues key generation queries corresponding to predicate matrices the form $\mathbf{W}_1, \ldots, \mathbf{W}_Q \in \mathbb{Z}_q^{m\times n}$ for some $Q = \mathsf{poly}(\lambda)$. The challenger samples $\mathbf{W}^* \xleftarrow{R} \mathcal{W}_b$ for some random $b \xleftarrow{R} \{0, 1\}$, where

$$\mathbf{W}^* = \left[w_{i,j}^*\right]_{i\in[1,m],j\in[1,n]},$$

and uses the master secret key $\mathsf{msk} = (g_2, \mathbf{S}_0, \mathbf{S}_1, \ldots, \mathbf{S}_n, \mathbf{K}, \mathbf{B}_0)$ to set the challenge secret key $\mathsf{sk}_{\mathbf{W}^*} = \left(\{h_j\}_{j\in[0,n]}\right)$ where

$$h_0 = g_2^{\left(\mathbf{K}+\sum_{i=1}^{m} y_i\cdot(\sum_{j=1}^{n} w^*_{i,j}\cdot\mathbf{t}\cdot\mathbf{S}_j)\right)^{\mathrm{T}}},$$
$$h_j = g_2^{\left(\sum_{i=1}^{m} y_i\cdot w^*_{i,j}\cdot\mathbf{t}\right)^{\mathrm{T}}} \quad \text{for } j\in[1,n],$$

where $y_1, \ldots, y_m \xleftarrow{R} \mathbb{Z}_q$ and $\mathbf{t} = (\mathbf{B}\cdot\mathbf{s})^{\mathrm{T}}$ for some $\mathbf{s} \xleftarrow{R} \mathbb{Z}_q^k$. The adversary $\mathcal{A}$ receives $(\mathsf{sk}_{\mathbf{W}^*}, \mathsf{sk}_{\mathbf{W}_1}, \ldots, \mathsf{sk}_{\mathbf{W}_Q})$, where

$$\mathsf{sk}_{\mathbf{W}_\ell} \leftarrow \mathsf{KeyGen}(\mathsf{pp}, \mathsf{msk}, \mathbf{W}_\ell) \quad \text{for each } \ell\in[1,Q].$$

Finally, it outputs a bit b'. Let $P_{\mathcal{A},0}$ denote the probability that $b = b'$.

Expt-1. This experiment is identical to Expt-0 except for the manner in which the challenge secret key $\mathsf{sk}_{\mathbf{W}^*}$ is generated. Namely, the challenger $\mathcal{B}$ uniformly samples $u_1, \ldots, u_n \xleftarrow{R} \mathbb{Z}_q$ and sets the challenge secret key $\mathsf{sk}_{\mathbf{W}^*} = \left(\{h_j\}_{j\in[0,n]}\right)$ as follows:

$$h_0 = g_2^{\left(\mathbf{K}+\sum_{j=1}^{n} u_j\cdot\mathbf{t}\cdot\mathbf{S}_j\right)^{\mathrm{T}}},$$
$$h_j = g_2^{(u_j\mathbf{t})^{\mathrm{T}}} \quad \text{for } j\in[1,n],$$

where $\mathbf{t} = (\mathbf{B}\cdot\mathbf{s})^{\mathrm{T}}$ for some $\mathbf{s} \xleftarrow{R} \mathbb{Z}_q^k$. Let $P_{\mathcal{A},1}$ denote the probability that $b = b'$, where b' is the bit output by the adversary $\mathcal{A}$ at the end of Expt-1. By the (n,m)-min-entropy-MDDH assumption, we must have $|P_{\mathcal{A},2} - P_{\mathcal{A},1}| \leq \mathsf{negl}(\lambda)$.

Finally, observe that the challenge secret key $\mathsf{sk}_{\mathbf{W}^*}$ in Expt-1 is independent of the bit b chosen by the challenger. Hence, for all PPT adversaries $\mathcal{A}$, we must have $P_{\mathcal{A},1} = 1/2$. This completes the proof of Theorem 4.2. □

5 Function Private SNME

In this section, we present an SNME scheme that is (computationally) function private whenever the predicate matrices are sampled from distributions with super-logarithmic min-entropy. Similar to the SME scheme, attribute privacy of our SNME scheme can be based on the $\mathcal{U}_{k+1,k}$-MDDH assumption, albeit in the bounded collusion setting, while function privacy follows from the min-entropy-MDDH assumption described in Sect. 2.4.

5.1 The Construction

Let $\mathsf{GroupGen}(1^\lambda)$ be a PPT algorithm that takes as input a security parameter $\lambda \in \mathbb{N}$, and outputs the tuple $(\mathbb{G}_1, \mathbb{G}_2, \mathbb{G}_T, q, g_1, g_2, e)$, where $\mathbb{G}_1$, $\mathbb{G}_2$ and $\mathbb{G}_T$ are cyclic groups of prime order q (q being a λ-bit prime), g_1 is a generator for $\mathbb{G}_1$, g_2 is a generator for $\mathbb{G}_2$, and $e : \mathbb{G}_1 \times \mathbb{G}_2 \longrightarrow \mathbb{G}_T$ is an efficiently computable non-degenerate asymmetric bilinear map. Our scheme Π^{SNME} is parameterized by $m, n = \mathsf{poly}(\lambda)$ in the sense that it supports predicate matrices of the form $\mathbf{W} \in \mathbb{Z}_q^{m\times n}$, and attribute vectors of the form $\mathbf{x} \in \mathbb{Z}_q^n$. The payload message space $\mathcal{M}$ for this scheme is assumed to be a "small" subset of $\mathbb{Z}_q$ such that $|\mathcal{M}| \leq \mathsf{poly}(\lambda)$.

- $\mathsf{Setup}(1^\lambda)$: Uniformly sample $(\mathbb{G}_1, \mathbb{G}_2, \mathbb{G}_T, q, g_1, g_2, e) \leftarrow \mathsf{GroupGen}(1^\lambda)$. Also, uniformly sample $\mathbf{A} \xleftarrow{R} \mathbb{Z}_q^{(k+1)\times k}$ and $\mathbf{S}_1, \mathbf{S}_2 \xleftarrow{R} \mathbb{Z}_q^{n\times(k+1)}$ for some constant $k > 0$. Output

$$\mathsf{pp} = \left(g_1, g_1^{\mathbf{A}}, g_1^{\mathbf{S}_1\cdot\mathbf{A}}, g_1^{\mathbf{S}_2\cdot\mathbf{A}}\right), \quad \mathsf{msk} = \left(g_2, \mathbf{S}_1, \mathbf{S}_2\right).$$

- $\mathsf{KeyGen}(\mathsf{pp}, \mathsf{msk}, \mathbf{W})$: Given a predicate matrix $\mathbf{W} \in \mathbb{Z}_q^{m\times n}$, sample $\mathbf{y} \xleftarrow{R} \mathbb{Z}_q^m$ and output $\mathsf{sk}_{\mathbf{W}} = (h_0, h_1, h_2)$, where

$$h_0 = g_2^{\mathbf{W}^{\mathbf{T}}\cdot\mathbf{y}}, \quad h_1 = g_2^{(\mathbf{W}\cdot\mathbf{S}_1)^{\mathbf{T}}\cdot\mathbf{y}}, \quad h_2 = g_2^{(\mathbf{W}\cdot\mathbf{S}_2)^{\mathbf{T}}\cdot\mathbf{y}}.$$

- $\mathsf{Enc}(\mathsf{pp}, \mathbf{x}, M)$: Given an attribute vector $\mathbf{x} \in \mathbb{Z}_q^n$ and a message $M \in \mathcal{M} \subset \mathbb{Z}_q$, uniformly sample $\mathbf{r}_1, \mathbf{r}_2 \xleftarrow{R} \mathbb{Z}_q^k$ and output $\mathsf{ct} = (c_{1,0}, c_{1,1}, c_{2,0}, c_{2,1})$ where

$$c_{1,0} = g_1^{(\mathbf{A}\cdot\mathbf{r}_1)^{\mathbf{T}}}, \quad c_{1,1} = g_1^{(\mathbf{x}+\mathbf{S}_1\cdot\mathbf{A}\cdot\mathbf{r}_1)^{\mathbf{T}}},$$
$$c_{2,0} = g_1^{(\mathbf{A}\cdot\mathbf{r}_2)^{\mathbf{T}}}, \quad c_{2,1} = g_1^{(M\cdot\mathbf{x}+\mathbf{S}_2\cdot\mathbf{A}\cdot\mathbf{r}_2)^{\mathbf{T}}}.$$

- $\mathsf{Dec}(\mathsf{pp}, \mathsf{sk}_{\mathbf{W}}, \mathsf{ct})$: Parse the ciphertext as $\mathsf{ct} = (c_{1,0}, c_{1,1}, c_{2,0}, c_{2,1})$ and the secret key as $\mathsf{sk}_{\mathbf{W}} = (h_0, h_1, h_2)$. Check if there exists a *unique* $M \in \mathcal{M}$ such that

$$e\left(c_{2,1}, h_0\right) \cdot e\left(c_{2,0}, h_2\right)^{-1} = \left(e\left(c_{1,1}, h_0\right) \cdot e\left(c_{1,0}, h_1\right)^{-1}\right)^M.$$

  If yes, return M. Else return $\perp$.

Correctness. To see that the aforementioned scheme is functionally correct, observe the following.

$$\begin{aligned} e\left(c_{1,1}, h_0\right) \cdot e\left(c_{1,0}, h_1\right)^{-1} &= e\left(g_1, g_2\right)^{\left(\mathbf{y}^{\mathbf{T}}\cdot\mathbf{W}\cdot(\mathbf{x}+\mathbf{S}_1\cdot\mathbf{A}\cdot\mathbf{r}_1) - \mathbf{y}^{\mathbf{T}}\cdot\mathbf{W}\cdot\mathbf{S}_1\cdot\mathbf{A}\cdot\mathbf{r}_1\right)^{\mathbf{T}}} \\ &= e\left(g_1, g_2\right)^{\left(\mathbf{y}^{\mathbf{T}}\cdot\mathbf{W}\cdot\mathbf{x}\right)^{\mathbf{T}}} \\ e\left(c_{2,1}, h_0\right) \cdot e\left(c_{2,0}, h_2\right)^{-1} &= e\left(g_1, g_2\right)^{\left(\mathbf{y}^{\mathbf{T}}\cdot\mathbf{W}\cdot(M\cdot\mathbf{x}+\mathbf{S}_2\cdot\mathbf{A}\cdot\mathbf{r}_2) - \mathbf{y}^{\mathbf{T}}\cdot\mathbf{W}\cdot\mathbf{S}_2\cdot\mathbf{A}\cdot\mathbf{r}_2\right)^{\mathbf{T}}} \\ &= e\left(g_1, g_2\right)^{M\cdot\left(\mathbf{y}^{\mathbf{T}}\cdot\mathbf{W}\cdot\mathbf{x}\right)^{\mathbf{T}}} \end{aligned}$$

When $\mathbf{W}\cdot\mathbf{x} \neq \mathbf{0} \mod q$, we have $\mathbf{y}^{\mathbf{T}}\cdot\mathbf{W}\cdot\mathbf{x} \neq 0 \mod q$ with overwhelmingly large probability over the randomness of KeyGen, and the decryption algorithm correctly recovers the message M. But when $\mathbf{W}\cdot\mathbf{x} = \mathbf{0} \mod q$, the message M cannot be uniquely recovered and the decryption algorithm returns $\perp$.

5.2 Attribute Privacy

We state the following theorem.

Theorem 5.1. *If the* $\mathcal{U}_{k+1,k}$-MDDH *assumption holds over the group* $\mathbb{G}_1$*, then for all PPT adversaries* $\mathcal{A}$ *that issue as most* $(n-1)$ *secret key queries during the attribute privacy experiment, we have* $\mathbf{Adv}^{\mathsf{AP}}_{\Pi^{\mathrm{SNME}},\mathcal{A}}(\lambda) \leq \mathsf{negl}(\lambda)$.

Proof Sketch. Due to lack of space, we only provide a brief proof sketch. We refer the reader to the full version of the paper [35] for the detailed proof.

The proof essentially relies on hash proof systems [18,19], and uses arguments similar to those used by Agrawal et al. in proving the security of their linear FE scheme [6]. The analysis exploits the following fact: given the public parameter pp and no more than $(n-1)$ secret keys, the master secret key components $\mathbf{S}_0, \mathbf{S}_1 \ldots, \mathbf{S}_n$ retain sufficient entropy from an (unbounded) adversary's point of view. This in turn ensures that at some stage, if the challenge ciphertext is generated using the master-secret-key instead of the public parameter, it will perfectly hide which attribute-message pair among $(\mathbf{x}_0, M_0)$ and $(\mathbf{x}_1, M_1)$ is encrypted.

Finally, the scheme is adaptively secure because the reduction knows the master secret key at any time, which allows it to answer all secret key queries without knowing the challenge attributes beforehand. This feature is common to nearly all security proofs relying on hash proof systems [18,19].

5.3 Function Privacy

We state and prove the following theorem.

Theorem 5.2. *If the* (n,m)-min-entropy-MDDH *assumption holds over the group* $\mathbb{G}_2$*, then for all PPT adversaries* $\mathcal{A}$*, we have* $\mathbf{Adv}^{\mathsf{FP}}_{\Pi^{\mathrm{SNME}},\mathcal{A}}(\lambda) \leq \mathsf{negl}(\lambda)$.

Proof. The proof proceeds through a sequence of experiments, beginning with the "real" function privacy experiment and ending with an experiment where the adversary has no advantage.

Expt-0. This is the "real" function privacy experiment. In this experiment, the adversary $\mathcal{A}$ is given the public parameter pp. The adversary chooses two circuits corresponding to matrix distributions of the form

$$\mathcal{W}_0 = \left[\mathrm{W}^{(0)}_{i,j}\right]_{i\in[1,m],j\in[1,n]}, \quad \mathcal{W}_1 = \left[\mathrm{W}^{(1)}_{i,j}\right]_{i\in[1,m],j\in[1,n]},$$

representing joint distributions over $\mathbb{Z}_q^{m\times n}$, subject to the following restrictions:

1. For each $i \in [1,m], j \in [1,n]$ and $\tilde{b} \in \{0,1\}$, $\mathrm{W}^{(\tilde{b})}_{i,j}$ represents an $\omega(\log\lambda)$-source over $\mathbb{F}_q$.
2. For each $i,i' \in [1,m], j,j' \in [1,n]$ and $\tilde{b} \in \{0,1\}$, $\mathrm{W}^{(\tilde{b})}_{i,j}$ and $\mathrm{W}^{(\tilde{b})}_{i',j'}$ represent mutually independent distributions.

The adversary $\mathcal{A}$ also (adaptively) issues key generation queries corresponding to predicate matrices the form $\mathbf{W}_1, \ldots, \mathbf{W}_Q \in \mathbb{Z}_q^{m \times n}$ for some $Q = \mathsf{poly}(\lambda)$. The challenger samples $\mathbf{W}^* \xleftarrow{R} \mathcal{W}_b$ for some random $b \xleftarrow{R} \{0,1\}$, and and uses the master secret key $\mathsf{msk} = \left(\mathbf{S}_1, \mathbf{S}_2\right)$ to set $\mathsf{sk}_{\mathbf{W}^*} = (h_0, h_1, h_2)$, where

$$h_0 = g_2^{(\mathbf{W}^*)^{\mathbf{T}} \cdot \mathbf{y}}, \quad h_1 = g_2^{(\mathbf{W} \cdot \mathbf{S}_1^*)^{\mathbf{T}} \cdot \mathbf{y}}, \quad h_2 = g_2^{(\mathbf{W} \cdot \mathbf{S}_2^*)^{\mathbf{T}} \cdot \mathbf{y}},$$

where $\mathbf{y} \xleftarrow{R} \mathbb{Z}_q^m$. The adversary $\mathcal{A}$ receives $\left(\mathsf{sk}_{\mathbf{W}^*}, \mathsf{sk}_{\mathbf{W}_1}, \ldots, \mathsf{sk}_{\mathbf{W}_Q}\right)$, where

$$\mathsf{sk}_{\mathbf{W}_\ell} \leftarrow \mathsf{KeyGen}(\mathsf{pp}, \mathsf{msk}, \mathbf{W}_\ell) \quad \text{for each } \ell \in [1, Q].$$

Finally, it outputs a bit b'. Let $P_{\mathcal{A},0}$ denote the probability that $b = b'$.

Expt-1. This experiment is identical to Expt-0 except for the manner in which the challenge secret key $\mathsf{sk}_{\mathbf{W}^*}$ is generated. Namely, the challenger $\mathcal{B}$ uniformly samples $\mathbf{u} \xleftarrow{R} \mathbb{Z}_q^n$ and uses the master secret key $\mathsf{msk} = (g_2, \mathbf{S}_1, \mathbf{S}_2)$ to output $\mathsf{sk}_{\mathbf{W}^*} = (h_0, h_1, h_2)$ where

$$h_0 = g_2^{\mathbf{u}}, \quad h_1 = g_2^{(\mathbf{S}_1)^{\mathbf{T}} \cdot \mathbf{u}}, \quad h_2 = g_2^{(\mathbf{S}_2)^{\mathbf{T}} \cdot \mathbf{u}}.$$

Let $P_{\mathcal{A},1}$ denote the probability that $b = b'$, where b' is the bit output by the adversary $\mathcal{A}$ at the end of Expt-1. By the (n, m)-min-entropy-MDDH assumption, we must have $|P_{\mathcal{A},2} - P_{\mathcal{A},1}| \leq \mathsf{negl}(\lambda)$.

Finally, observe that the challenge secret key $\mathsf{sk}_{\mathbf{W}^*}$ in Expt-1 is independent of the bit b chosen by the challenger. Hence, for all PPT adversaries $\mathcal{A}$, we must have $P_{\mathcal{A},1} = 1/2$. This completes the proof of Theorem 5.2. □

Acknowledgments. We thank the anonymous reviewers of PKC 2019 for useful comments. Patranabis and Mukhopadhyay are patially supported by Qualcomm India Innovation Fellowship grant. Mukhopadhyay is partially supported by a DST India Swarnajayanti Fellowship. Ramanna is partially supported by DST India Inspire Faculty award. We stress that the opinions, findings and conclusions expressed in this material are those of the authors and do not necessarily reflect the views of the funding organizations.

References

1. Abdalla, M., et al.: Searchable encryption revisited: consistency properties, relation to anonymous IBE, and extensions. J. Cryptol. **21**, 350–391 (2008)
2. Abdalla, M., Bourse, F., De Caro, A., Pointcheval, D.: Simple functional encryption schemes for inner products. In: Katz, J. (ed.) PKC 2015. LNCS, vol. 9020, pp. 733–751. Springer, Heidelberg (2015). https://doi.org/10.1007/978-3-662-46447-2_33
3. Agrawal, S., Agrawal, S., Badrinarayanan, S., Kumarasubramanian, A., Prabhakaran, M., Sahai, A.: On the practical security of inner product functional encryption. In: Katz, J. (ed.) PKC 2015. LNCS, vol. 9020, pp. 777–798. Springer, Heidelberg (2015). https://doi.org/10.1007/978-3-662-46447-2_35

4. Agrawal, S., Bhattacherjee, S., Phan, D.H., Stehlé, D., Yamada, S.: Efficient public trace and revoke from standard assumptions: extended abstract. In: CCS 2017, pp. 2277–2293 (2017)
5. Agrawal, S., Freeman, D.M., Vaikuntanathan, V.: Functional encryption for inner product predicates from learning with errors. In: Lee, D.H., Wang, X. (eds.) ASIACRYPT 2011. LNCS, vol. 7073, pp. 21–40. Springer, Heidelberg (2011). https://doi.org/10.1007/978-3-642-25385-0_2
6. Agrawal, S., Libert, B., Stehlé, D.: Fully secure functional encryption for inner products, from standard assumptions. In: Robshaw, M., Katz, J. (eds.) CRYPTO 2016. LNCS, vol. 9816, pp. 333–362. Springer, Heidelberg (2016). https://doi.org/10.1007/978-3-662-53015-3_12
7. Attrapadung, N., Libert, B.: Functional encryption for inner product: achieving constant-size ciphertexts with adaptive security or support for negation. In: Nguyen, P.Q., Pointcheval, D. (eds.) PKC 2010. LNCS, vol. 6056, pp. 384–402. Springer, Heidelberg (2010). https://doi.org/10.1007/978-3-642-13013-7_23
8. Bishop, A., Jain, A., Kowalczyk, L.: Function-hiding inner product encryption. In: Iwata, T., Cheon, J.H. (eds.) ASIACRYPT 2015. LNCS, vol. 9452, pp. 470–491. Springer, Heidelberg (2015). https://doi.org/10.1007/978-3-662-48797-6_20
9. Boneh, D., Di Crescenzo, G., Ostrovsky, R., Persiano, G.: Public key encryption with keyword search. In: Cachin, C., Camenisch, J.L. (eds.) EUROCRYPT 2004. LNCS, vol. 3027, pp. 506–522. Springer, Heidelberg (2004). https://doi.org/10.1007/978-3-540-24676-3_30
10. Boneh, D., Franklin, M.K.: Identity-based encryption from the Weil pairing. In: Kilian, J. (ed.) CRYPTO 2001. LNCS, vol. 2139, pp. 213–229. Springer, Heidelberg (2001). https://doi.org/10.1007/3-540-44647-8_13
11. Boneh, D., et al.: Fully key-homomorphic encryption, arithmetic circuit ABE and compact Garbled circuits. In: Nguyen, P.Q., Oswald, E. (eds.) EUROCRYPT 2014. LNCS, vol. 8441, pp. 533–556. Springer, Heidelberg (2014). https://doi.org/10.1007/978-3-642-55220-5_30
12. Boneh, D., Raghunathan, A., Segev, G.: Function-private identity-based encryption: hiding the function in functional encryption. In: Canetti, R., Garay, J.A. (eds.) CRYPTO 2013. LNCS, vol. 8043, pp. 461–478. Springer, Heidelberg (2013). https://doi.org/10.1007/978-3-642-40084-1_26
13. Boneh, D., Raghunathan, A., Segev, G.: Function-private subspace-membership encryption and its applications. In: Sako, K., Sarkar, P. (eds.) ASIACRYPT 2013. LNCS, vol. 8269, pp. 255–275. Springer, Heidelberg (2013). https://doi.org/10.1007/978-3-642-42033-7_14
14. Boneh, D., Waters, B.: Conjunctive, subset, and range queries on encrypted data. In: Vadhan, S.P. (ed.) TCC 2007. LNCS, vol. 4392, pp. 535–554. Springer, Heidelberg (2007). https://doi.org/10.1007/978-3-540-70936-7_29
15. Brakerski, Z., Segev, G.: Function-private functional encryption in the private-key setting. In: Dodis, Y., Nielsen, J.B. (eds.) TCC 2015. LNCS, vol. 9015, pp. 306–324. Springer, Heidelberg (2015). https://doi.org/10.1007/978-3-662-46497-7_12
16. Chen, J., Gay, R., Wee, H.: Improved dual system ABE in prime-order groups via predicate encodings. In: Oswald, E., Fischlin, M. (eds.) EUROCRYPT 2015. LNCS, vol. 9057, pp. 595–624. Springer, Heidelberg (2015). https://doi.org/10.1007/978-3-662-46803-6_20
17. Chen, J., Gong, J., Kowalczyk, L., Wee, H.: Unbounded ABE via bilinear entropy expansion, revisited. In: Nielsen, J.B., Rijmen, V. (eds.) EUROCRYPT 2018. LNCS, vol. 10820, pp. 503–534. Springer, Cham (2018). https://doi.org/10.1007/978-3-319-78381-9_19

18. Cramer, R., Shoup, V.: A practical public key cryptosystem provably secure against adaptive chosen ciphertext attack. In: Krawczyk, H. (ed.) CRYPTO 1998. LNCS, vol. 1462, pp. 13–25. Springer, Heidelberg (1998). https://doi.org/10.1007/BFb0055717
19. Cramer, R., Shoup, V.: Universal hash proofs and a paradigm for adaptive chosen ciphertext secure public-key encryption. In: Knudsen, L.R. (ed.) EUROCRYPT 2002. LNCS, vol. 2332, pp. 45–64. Springer, Heidelberg (2002). https://doi.org/10.1007/3-540-46035-7_4
20. Datta, P., Dutta, R., Mukhopadhyay, S.: Functional encryption for inner product with full function privacy. In: Cheng, C.-M., Chung, K.-M., Persiano, G., Yang, B.-Y. (eds.) PKC 2016. LNCS, vol. 9614, pp. 164–195. Springer, Heidelberg (2016). https://doi.org/10.1007/978-3-662-49384-7_7
21. Escala, A., Herold, G., Kiltz, E., Ràfols, C., Villar, J.L.: An algebraic framework for Diffie-Hellman assumptions. In: Canetti, R., Garay, J.A. (eds.) CRYPTO 2013. LNCS, vol. 8043, pp. 129–147. Springer, Heidelberg (2013). https://doi.org/10.1007/978-3-642-40084-1_8
22. Garg, S., Gentry, C., Halevi, S., Sahai, A., Waters, B.: Attribute-based encryption for circuits from multilinear maps. In: Canetti, R., Garay, J.A. (eds.) CRYPTO 2013. LNCS, vol. 8043, pp. 479–499. Springer, Heidelberg (2013). https://doi.org/10.1007/978-3-642-40084-1_27
23. Gay, R., Hofheinz, D., Kiltz, E., Wee, H.: Tightly CCA-secure encryption without pairings. In: Fischlin, M., Coron, J.-S. (eds.) EUROCRYPT 2016. LNCS, vol. 9665, pp. 1–27. Springer, Heidelberg (2016). https://doi.org/10.1007/978-3-662-49890-3_1
24. Gentry, C., Peikert, C., Vaikuntanathan, V.: Trapdoors for hard lattices and new cryptographic constructions. In: ACM STOC 2008, pp. 197–206 (2008)
25. Goldwasser, S., Kalai, Y.T., Popa, R.A., Vaikuntanathan, V., Zeldovich, N.: How to run turing machines on encrypted data. In: Canetti, R., Garay, J.A. (eds.) CRYPTO 2013. LNCS, vol. 8043, pp. 536–553. Springer, Heidelberg (2013). https://doi.org/10.1007/978-3-642-40084-1_30
26. Gong, J., Dong, X., Chen, J., Cao, Z.: Efficient IBE with tight reduction to standard assumption in the multi-challenge setting. In: Cheon, J.H., Takagi, T. (eds.) ASIACRYPT 2016. LNCS, vol. 10032, pp. 624–654. Springer, Heidelberg (2016). https://doi.org/10.1007/978-3-662-53890-6_21
27. Gorbunov, S., Vaikuntanathan, V., Wee, H.: Attribute-based encryption for circuits. J. ACM **62**(6), 45:1–45:33 (2015)
28. Gorbunov, S., Vaikuntanathan, V., Wee, H.: Predicate encryption for circuits from LWE. In: Gennaro, R., Robshaw, M. (eds.) CRYPTO 2015. LNCS, vol. 9216, pp. 503–523. Springer, Heidelberg (2015). https://doi.org/10.1007/978-3-662-48000-7_25
29. Goyal, V., Pandey, O., Sahai, A., Waters, B.: Attribute-based encryption for fine-grained access control of encrypted data. In: ACM CCS 2006, pp. 89–98 (2006)
30. Katz, J., Sahai, A., Waters, B.: Predicate encryption supporting disjunctions, polynomial equations, and inner products. J. Cryptol. **26**(2), 191–224 (2013)
31. Lewko, A.B.: Tools for simulating features of composite order bilinear groups in the prime order setting. In: Pointcheval, D., Johansson, T. (eds.) EUROCRYPT 2012. LNCS, vol. 7237, pp. 318–335. Springer, Heidelberg (2012). https://doi.org/10.1007/978-3-642-29011-4_20

32. Lewko, A.B., Waters, B.: New techniques for dual system encryption and fully secure HIBE with short ciphertexts. In: Micciancio, D. (ed.) TCC 2010. LNCS, vol. 5978, pp. 455–479. Springer, Heidelberg (2010). https://doi.org/10.1007/978-3-642-11799-2_27
33. Okamoto, T., Takashima, K.: Adaptively attribute-hiding (hierarchical) inner product encryption. In: Pointcheval, D., Johansson, T. (eds.) EUROCRYPT 2012. LNCS, vol. 7237, pp. 591–608. Springer, Heidelberg (2012). https://doi.org/10.1007/978-3-642-29011-4_35
34. Okamoto, T., Takashima, K.: Fully secure unbounded inner-product and attribute-based encryption. In: Wang, X., Sako, K. (eds.) ASIACRYPT 2012. LNCS, vol. 7658, pp. 349–366. Springer, Heidelberg (2012). https://doi.org/10.1007/978-3-642-34961-4_22
35. Patranabis, S., Mukhopadhyay, D., Ramanna, S.C.: Function private predicate encryption for low min-entropy predicates. IACR Cryptology ePrint Archive, p. 1250 (2018)
36. Waters, B.: Functional encryption for regular languages. In: Safavi-Naini, R., Canetti, R. (eds.) CRYPTO 2012. LNCS, vol. 7417, pp. 218–235. Springer, Heidelberg (2012). https://doi.org/10.1007/978-3-642-32009-5_14
37. Wee, H.: Attribute-hiding predicate encryption in bilinear groups, revisited. In: Kalai, Y., Reyzin, L. (eds.) TCC 2017. LNCS, vol. 10677, pp. 206–233. Springer, Cham (2017). https://doi.org/10.1007/978-3-319-70500-2_8

Obfuscation Based Cryptography

Adaptively Single-Key Secure Constrained PRFs for $\mathbf{NC}^1$

Nuttapong Attrapadung[1], Takahiro Matsuda[1], Ryo Nishimaki[2], Shota Yamada[1], and Takashi Yamakawa[2(✉)]

[1] National Institute of Advanced Industrial Science and Technology (AIST), Tokyo, Japan
{n.attrapadung,t-matsuda,yamada-shota}@aist.go.jp

[2] NTT Secure Platform Laboratories, Tokyo, Japan
{ryo.nishimaki.zk,takashi.yamakawa.ga}@hco.ntt.co.jp

Abstract. We present a construction of an adaptively single-key secure constrained PRF (CPRF) for $\mathbf{NC}^1$ assuming the existence of indistinguishability obfuscation (IO) and the subgroup hiding assumption over a (pairing-free) composite order group. This is the first construction of such a CPRF in the standard model without relying on a complexity leveraging argument.

To achieve this, we first introduce the notion of partitionable CPRF, which is a CPRF accommodated with partitioning techniques and combine it with shadow copy techniques often used in the dual system encryption methodology. We present a construction of partitionable CPRF for $\mathbf{NC}^1$ based on IO and the subgroup hiding assumption over a (pairing-free) group. We finally prove that an adaptively single-key secure CPRF for $\mathbf{NC}^1$ can be obtained from a partitionable CPRF for $\mathbf{NC}^1$ and IO.

1 Introduction

1.1 Background

Constrained pseudorandom function (CPRF) [10][1] is a PRF with an additional functionality to "constrain" the ability of a secret key. A constrained key associated with a boolean function f enables us to compute a PRF value on inputs x such that $f(x) = 0$.[2] Security of CPRF roughly requires that for a "challenge input" x^* such that $f(x^*) = 1$, the PRF value on x^* remains pseudorandom given sk_f. There are many applications of CPRFs including broadcast encryption [10], attribute-based encryption (ABE) [2], identity-based non-interactive key exchange [10], and policy-based key distribution [10].

[1] It is also known as delegatable PRF [36] and functional PRF [12].

[2] We note that the role of the constraining function f is "reversed" from the definition by Boneh and Waters [10], in the sense that the evaluation by a constrained key sk_f is possible for inputs x with $f(x) = 1$ in their definition, while it is possible for inputs x for $f(x) = 0$ in our paper. Our treatment is the same as Brakerski and Vaikuntanathan [14].

D. Lin and K. Sako (Eds.): PKC 2019, LNCS 11443, pp. 223–253, 2019.
https://doi.org/10.1007/978-3-030-17259-6_8

Since the proposal of the concept of CPRF, there have been significant progresses in constructing CPRFs [1–3,6,8–14,16,23,30,36,40]. However, most known collusion-resistant[3] CPRFs (e.g., [10]) only satisfy weaker security called "selective-challenge" security, where an adversary must declare a challenge input at the beginning of the security game. In the single-key setting where an adversary is given only one constrained key (e.g., [14]), we often consider "selective-constraint" security where an adversary must declare a constraint for which it obtains a constrained key at the beginning of the security game whereas it is allowed to choose a challenge input later.[4] In a realistic scenario, adversaries should be able to choose a constraint and a challenge input in an arbitrary order. We call such security "adaptive security".

An easy way to obtain an adaptively secure CPRF is converting selective-challenge secure one into adaptively secure one by guessing a challenge input with a standard technique typically called complexity leveraging. However, this incurs an exponential security loss, and thus we have to rely on sub-exponential assumptions. We would like to avoid this to achieve better security. In the random oracle model, Hofheinz, Kamath, Koppula and Waters [32] constructed an adaptively secure collusion-resistant CPRF for all circuits without relying on complexity leveraging based on indistinguishability obfuscation (IO) [4,27], and Attrapadung et al. [2] constructed an adaptively single-key secure CPRF for $\mathbf{NC}^1$ on pairing-free groups. However, the random oracle model has been recognized to be problematic [17].

There are a few number of adaptively secure CPRFs in the standard model. Hohenberger, Koppula, and Waters [34] constructed an adaptively secure puncturable PRF based on IO and the subgroup hiding assumption on a composite order group.[5] Very recently, Davidson et al. [22] constructed an adaptively secure CPRF for bit-fixing functions secure against a constant number of collusion based on one-way functions. However, these schemes only support puncturing functions or bit-fixing functions which are very limited functionalities, and there is no known construction of adaptively secure CPRF for a sufficiently expressive function class (e.g., $\mathbf{NC}^1$ or all polynomial-size circuits) even in the single-key setting and even with IO.

1.2 Our Contribution

In this study, we achieve an adaptively single-key secure CPRF for $\mathbf{NC}^1$ assuming the existence of IO and the subgroup hiding assumption over a (pairing-free) composite order group. This is the first construction of such a CPRF in the standard model without relying on the complexity leveraging technique.

[3] A CPRF is called collusion-resistant if it remains secure even if adversaries are given polynomially many constrained keys.

[4] In previous works, both selective-challenge and selective-constraint security are simply called selective security. We use different names for them for clarity.

[5] More precisely, they also generalized their construction to obtain a CPRF for t-puncturing functions, which puncture the input space on t points for a polynomial t (rather than a single point).

We emphasize that using IO is *not an easy solution* to achieve adaptive security even in the single-key setting, although IO is a strong cryptographic tool (a.k.a. "heavy hammer"). All CPRFs for a sufficiently expressive class based on IO in the standard model do not achieve adaptive security if we do not rely on complexity leveraging [1,9,11,21,23].

1.3 Design Idea and Technical Overview

In this section, we give an overview of our design idea and technique.

Toward adaptive security: partitioning technique. Our construction is based on a technique called the partitioning technique, which has been widely used to achieve adaptive security in the context of signature, identity-based encryption, verifiable random function etc. [7,19,35,44,45]. Roughly speaking, in the partitioning technique, a reduction algorithm partitions the input space into two disjoint spaces, the challenge space and the simulation space, so that it can compute PRF values on all inputs in the simulation space whereas it cannot compute it on any input in the challenge space. More specifically, the input space is partitioned via an *admissible hash function* denoted by $h : \{0,1\}^n \to \{0,1\}^m$ and a *partitioning policy* $u \in \{0,1,\perp\}^m$ where $\{0,1\}^n$ is the input space.[6] We partition the input space $\{0,1\}^n$ so that $x \in \{0,1\}^n$ is in the challenge space if $P_u(h(x)) = 0$ and it is in the simulation space if $P_u(h(x)) = 1$, where P_u is defined by

$$P_u(y) = \begin{cases} 0 & \text{If for all } i \in [m],\ u_i = \perp \ \vee \ y_i = u_i \\ 1 & \text{Otherwise} \end{cases},$$

where y_i and u_i are the i-th bit of y and u, respectively. If we choose u according to an appropriate distribution (depending on the number of evaluation queries), the probability that all evaluation queries fall in the simulation space and a challenge query falls in the challenge space is noticeable, in which case, a reduction algorithm works well. The crucial feature of this technique is that a reduction algorithm need not know a challenge query at the beginning of its simulation.

Though it may seem easy to construct adaptively secure CPRFs based on the above idea, it is not the case because we also have to simulate constrained keys in security proofs of CPRFs. Indeed, Hofheinz et al. [32] observed that the partitioning technique does not seem to work for constructing collusion-resistant CPRFs. Nonetheless, we show that it works in the case of single-key secure CPRFs by using a *partitionable CPRF* which we introduce in this study.

Partitionable CPRF. Intuitively, a partitionable CPRF is a CPRF with an additional functionality that enables us to generate a "merged" key from two independent master keys and a partitioning policy u. The behavior of a merged key

[6] Actually, we use an extended notion called a balanced admissible hash function (Sect. 2.2).

depends on whether an input is in the challenge space or in the simulation space. Namely, if we merge msk_0 and msk_1 with a partitioning policy u to generate a merged key $\mathsf{k}[\mathsf{msk}_0, \mathsf{msk}_1, u]$, then it works similarly to msk_0 for inputs x in the challenge space, and msk_1 for inputs x in the simulation space. We often call msk_0 a real master key, and msk_1 a "shadow" master key because the former is the real master secret key used in actual constructions and the latter is an artificial key that only appears in security proofs.

For a partitionable CPRF, we require two properties. First, we require that it satisfy selective-constraint no-evaluation security as a CPRF, where an adversary must declare its unique constraining query at the beginning of the security game and does not make any evaluation queries. Here, it is important that in this security notion, an adversary is allowed to *adaptively* choose a challenge query. Second, we require a property called the partition-hiding, which means that $\mathsf{k}[\mathsf{msk}_0, \mathsf{msk}_1, u]$ does not reveal u. In particular, $\mathsf{k}[\mathsf{msk}_0, \mathsf{msk}_1, \perp^m]$, which works exactly the same as msk_0, is computationally indistinguishable from $\mathsf{k}[\mathsf{msk}_0, \mathsf{msk}_1, u]$.

Adaptively secure CPRF from partitionable CPRF. Now, we take a closer look at how we construct an adaptively single-key secure CPRF based on a partitionable CPRF and IO. Master secret keys and PRF values of the CPRF are defined to be exactly the same as those of the underlying partitionable CPRF. The only difference between them is the way of generating constrained keys. In the proposed CPRF, a constrained key for a function f is an obfuscated program that computes PRF values on all inputs x such that $f(x) = 0$ with a real master secret key.

The security proof proceeds as follows. First, we remark that if a challenge query is made before the constraining query, then the proof is easy by the standard puncturing technique [11,41]. Thus, in the following, we assume that a challenge query is made after the constraining query. First, we modify the security game so that we use $\mathsf{k}[\mathsf{msk}_0, \mathsf{msk}_1, \perp^m]$ instead of msk_0 where msk_1 is a "shadow" master secret key that is independent from msk_0. This modification causes a negligible difference by the security of IO because $\mathsf{k}[\mathsf{msk}_0, \mathsf{msk}_1, \perp^m]$ works exactly the same as msk_0. Then we replace $\mathsf{k}[\mathsf{msk}_0, \mathsf{msk}_1, \perp^m]$ with $\mathsf{k}[\mathsf{msk}_0, \mathsf{msk}_1, u]$ for a partitioning policy u chosen from an appropriate distribution. This modification causes a negligible difference by the partition-hiding of the underlying partitionable CPRF. Here, suppose that all evaluation queries are in the simulation space, and the challenge query x^* is in the challenge space. Such an event occurs with noticeable probability by the way we choose u. In this case, all evaluation queries can be simulated by using the shadow master secret key msk_1 whereas a challenge value is computed by using the real secret key msk_0. Then we modify a constrained key sk_f associated with a function f so that we hardwire $\mathsf{sk}_f^{\mathsf{real}}$, which is a constrained key associated with the function f derived from msk_0 by the constraining algorithm of the underlying partitionable CPRF, instead of msk_0. This modification causes a negligible difference by the security of IO since $\mathsf{sk}_f^{\mathsf{real}}$ and msk_0 work similarly on inputs x such that $f(x) = 0$. At this point, a PRF value on x^* such that $f(x^*) = 1$ is pseudorandom by the selective-constraint no-evaluation security of the underlying partitionable CPRF (Recall that msk_0 is not used for simulating the evaluation oracle now). This completes the proof of the adaptive single-key security of the CPRF.

Partitionable CPRF for puncturing [34]. What is left is a construction of a partitionable CPRF. First, we observe that the construction of adaptively secure puncturable PRF by Hohenberger et al. [34] can be seen as a construction of a partitionable CPRF for puncturing functions. Their construction is a variant of the Naor-Reingold PRF [39] on a composite order group $\mathbb{G} = \mathbb{G}_p \times \mathbb{G}_q$ of an order $N = pq$. Namely, a master secret key $\mathsf{msk}^{\mathsf{hkw}}$ consists of $s_{i,b} \in \mathbb{Z}_N$ for $i \in [m]$ and $b \in \{0, 1\}$, and their PRF F_{hkw} is defined as

$$F_{\mathsf{hkw}}(\mathsf{msk}^{\mathsf{hkw}}, x) := g^{\prod_{i=1}^{m} s_{i,y_i}}.$$

Here, g is a generator of $\mathbb{G}$ and y_i is the i-th bit of $y := h(x)$, where h is an admissible hash function. A punctured key on the challenge input x^* is an obfuscated program that computes $F_{\mathsf{hkw}}(\mathsf{msk}, x)$ on all inputs $x \neq x^*$. They implicitly proved that the above construction is a partitionable CPRF for puncturing if we define $\mathsf{k}[\mathsf{msk}_0, \mathsf{msk}_1, u]$ to be an obfuscation of a program that computes $F_{\mathsf{hkw}}(\mathsf{msk}_{P_u(x)}, x)$ on an input x.

We remark that we cannot directly reduce the partition-hiding property to the security of IO because the functionality of $\mathsf{k}[\mathsf{msk}_0, \mathsf{msk}_1, \perp^m]$ and $\mathsf{k}[\mathsf{msk}_0, \mathsf{msk}_1, u]$ differ on exponentially many inputs. They overcome this problem by sophisticated use of the subgroup hiding assumption on a composite order group. Namely, we can prove that this construction satisfies the partition-hiding under the security of IO and the subgroup hiding assumption, which claims that random elements of $\mathbb{G}_p$ and $\mathbb{G}$ are computationally indistinguishable. Then if we can prove the above construction is a selective-constraint no-evaluation secure CPRF for a function class $\mathcal{F}$, then we obtain an adaptively single-key secure CPRF for the function class $\mathcal{F}$ as discussed in the previous paragraph. One may think that it is easy to prove that the above construction is selective-constraint no-evaluation secure for all circuits by using the standard puncturing technique with IO [11,41]. However, it is not the case because the selective-constraint security requires security against an adversary that makes a challenge query after making a constraining query. Though IO is quite powerful when considering selective-challenge security where an adversary declares a challenge query at the beginning, it is almost useless for selective-constraint security where an adversary may adaptively choose a challenge query. For the case of puncturable PRF, a challenge input is automatically determined when a constraining query is made, and thus selective-constraint security is equivalent to selective-challenge security. This is why they achieved adaptive security only for a puncturable PRF.

Partitionable CPRF for $\mathbf{NC}^1$. Finally, we explain how to construct a partitionable CPRF for $\mathbf{NC}^1$. Our idea is to combine Hohenberger et al.'s construction as described above and the selective-constraint no-evaluation secure CPRF for $\mathbf{NC}^1$ recently proposed by Attrapadung et al. [2]. The construction of Attrapadung et al.'s CPRF F_{amnyy} (instantiated on a composite order group $\mathbb{G} = \mathbb{G}_p \times \mathbb{G}_q$) is described as follows.

$$F_{\mathsf{amnyy}}(\mathsf{msk}^{\mathsf{amnyy}}, x) = g^{U(\boldsymbol{b},x)/\alpha}$$

where $\mathsf{msk}^{\mathsf{amnyy}} = (\boldsymbol{b} \in \mathbb{Z}_N^z, \alpha \in \mathbb{Z}_N)$ is a master secret key and $U(\cdot)$ is a polynomial that works as a universal circuit for $\mathbf{NC}^1$. We omit a description of constrained keys for this CPRF since this is not important in this overview (See Sect. 3.2 for details). They proved that F_{amnyy} satisfies selective-constraint no-evaluation security under the L-DDHI assumption[7], which can be reduced to the subgroup hiding assumption (See Lemma 2.1). An important fact is that their CPRF is secure against adversaries that adaptively make a challenge query as long as a constraining query is declared at the beginning and they do not make any evaluation queries.

Then we combine F_{amnyy} and F_{hkw} to define F_{ours} as follows:

$$F_{\mathsf{ours}}(\mathsf{msk}^{\mathsf{ours}}, x) = g^{(\prod_{i=1}^{m} s_{i,y_i}) \cdot U(\boldsymbol{b},x)/\alpha},$$

where x is an input, y_i is the i-th bit of $h(x)$, h is an admissible hash function, and $\mathsf{msk}^{\mathsf{ours}} = (\boldsymbol{b}, \alpha, \{s_{i,b}\}_{i \in [m], b \in \{0,1\}})$ is a master secret key. A constrained key for a predicate f consists of that of F_{amnyy} and $\{s_{i,b}\}_{i \in [m], b \in \{0,1\}}$. It is easy to see that this constrained key can be used to evaluate $F_{\mathsf{ours}}(\mathsf{msk}^{\mathsf{ours}}, x)$ for all x such that $f(x) = 0$ since we have

$$F_{\mathsf{ours}}(\mathsf{msk}^{\mathsf{ours}}, x) = F_{\mathsf{amnyy}}(\mathsf{msk}^{\mathsf{amnyy}}, x)^{\prod_{i=1}^{m} s_{i,y_i}}$$

where $\mathsf{msk}^{\mathsf{amnyy}} := (\boldsymbol{b}, \alpha)$. By this equation, it is also easy to see that the selective-constraint no-evaluation security of F_{ours} can be reduced to that of F_{amnyy}. A merged key is an obfuscated circuit that computes $\mathsf{Eval}(\mathsf{msk}_{P_u(h(x))}, x)$ where $\mathsf{msk}_0 = (\boldsymbol{b}, \alpha, \{s_{i,b}\}_{i \in [m], b \in \{0,1\}})$ and $\mathsf{msk}_1 = (\hat{\boldsymbol{b}}, \hat{\alpha}, \{\hat{s}_{i,b}\}_{i \in [m], b \in \{0,1\}})$ are two independent master secret keys and u is a partitioning policy embedded into the merged key.

Now, we look at why the construction satisfies partition-hiding. Intuitively, a partitioning policy u is hidden because it is hardwired in an obfuscated circuit. However, since the functionality of $\mathsf{k}[\mathsf{msk}_0, \mathsf{msk}_1, \perp^m]$ and $\mathsf{k}[\mathsf{msk}_0, \mathsf{msk}_1, u]$ differ on exponentially many inputs, we cannot directly argue indistinguishability of them based on the security of IO. In the following, we explain how to prove it relying on the subgroup hiding assumption. Roughly speaking, this consists of two parts. In the first part, we modify the way of computing PRF values inside a merged key (which is an obfuscated program) so that it uses a different way to compute them on inputs in the challenge space and on those in the simulation space. In the second step, we make a shadow copy of the real master key by using the Chinese remainder theorem.

[7] It assumes that $\{(\mathcal{G}, g, (g^{\beta^i})_{i \in [L]}, g^{1/\beta})\} \approx_{\mathsf{c}} \{(\mathcal{G}, g, (g^{\beta^i})_{i \in [L]}, \psi_1)\}$ holds, where $\mathcal{G} = (N, \mathbb{G}, \mathbb{G}_p, \mathbb{G}_q, g_1, g_2)$, $\mathbb{G}$, $\mathbb{G}_p$, and $\mathbb{G}_q$ are groups of order N, p, and q, respectively, g, g_1, and g_2 are generators of $\mathbb{G}$, $\mathbb{G}_p$, and $\mathbb{G}_q$, respectively, and $\psi_1 \xleftarrow{\mathsf{R}} \mathbb{G}$.

First, to modify the way of computing PRF values inside a merged key, we use the $(m-1)$-DDH assumption, which claims that we have $\{(\mathcal{G}, g, (g^{\beta^i})_{i\in[m-1]}, g^{\beta^m})\} \approx_c \{(\mathcal{G}, g, (g^{\beta^i})_{i\in[m-1]}, \psi_1)\}$, where $\mathcal{G} = (N, \mathbb{G}, \mathbb{G}_p, \mathbb{G}_q, g_1, g_2)$, $\mathbb{G}$, $\mathbb{G}_p$, and $\mathbb{G}_q$ are groups of order N, p, and q, respectively, g, g_1, and g_2 are generators of $\mathbb{G}$, $\mathbb{G}_p$, and $\mathbb{G}_q$, respectively, and $\psi_1 \xleftarrow{\mathsf{R}} \mathbb{G}$. As shown in Lemma 2.1, this assumption can be reduced to the subgroup hiding assumption. Recall that the partitioning policy $P_u(y)$ outputs 0 (i.e., x is in the challenge space) if for all i, $u_i = y_i \vee u_i = \bot$. Here, we set $s_{i,\eta} := \beta s'_{i,\eta} \in \mathbb{Z}_N$ for all (i, η) such that $u_i = \bot$ or $\eta = u_i$, where $s'_{i,\eta}$ is a uniformly random and β comes from the $(m-1)$-DDH instance. The distributions of $s_{i,\eta}$ set as above are statistically close to the original ones. Now, a merged key uses the $(m-1)$-DDH challenge $w \in \mathbb{G}$ (which is g^{β^m} or random) for simulating a PRF value on an input x in the challenge space. That is, it computes the PRF value on x as $w^{(\prod_{i=1}^m s'_{i,y_i})\cdot U(\boldsymbol{b},x)/\alpha}$. On the other hand, on inputs x in the simulation space, it uses the values $(g, g^{\beta}, \ldots, g^{\beta^{m-1}})$ in the $(m-1)$-DDH problem instances as $(g^{\beta^r})^{(\prod_{i=1}^m s'_{i,y_i})\cdot U(\boldsymbol{b},x)/\alpha}$, where $r := |\{i \in [m] \mid u_i = y_i\}| \leq m-1$. If $w = g^{\beta^m}$, then a merged key as modified above correctly computes PRF values on all inputs. Thus, this modification causes a negligible difference by the security of IO. Then we can replace w with a random element in $\mathbb{G}$ by using the $(m-1)$-DDH assumption.

Now, we use the subgroup hiding assumption to make a shadow copy of the real master key. By the subgroup hiding assumption, we can replace $w \in \mathbb{G}$ and $g \in \mathbb{G}$ with $w \in \mathbb{G}_p$ and $g \in \mathbb{G}_q$, respectively, where $\mathbb{G}$ (resp. $\mathbb{G}_p$, $\mathbb{G}_q$) is a group of order $N = pq$ (resp. p, q) and p, q are primes.[8] Then, we can set $\mathsf{msk}_0 := \{s'_{i,b} \bmod p\}_{i,b}$ and $\mathsf{msk}_1 := \{s'_{i,b} \bmod q\}_{i,b}$. Since $w \in \mathbb{G}_p$ and $g^{\beta^j} \in \mathbb{G}_q$ where $j \in \{1, \ldots, m-1\}$, it holds that

$$w^{(\prod s'_{i,y_i})\cdot U(\boldsymbol{b},x)/\alpha} = w^{((\prod s'_{i,y_i})\cdot U(\boldsymbol{b},x)/\alpha \mod p)}$$
$$(g^{\beta^j})^{(\prod s'_{i,y_i})\cdot U(\boldsymbol{b},x)/\alpha} = (g^{\beta^j})^{((\prod s'_{i,y_i})\cdot U(\boldsymbol{b},x)/\alpha \mod q)}$$

and this change is indistinguishable due to the security of IO. Lastly, by the Chinese remainder theorem, msk_0 and msk_1 are independently and uniformly random (that is, msk_1 can be changed into $\{\hat{s}_{i,b} \bmod q\}_{i,b}$ where $\hat{s}_{i,b}$ are independent of $s'_{i,b}$ and uniformly random). Now, the shadow master secret key is used for evaluating PRF values on inputs in the challenge space whereas the real master secret key is used for evaluating those on inputs in the simulation space as desired.

By these techniques, we can obtain a partitionable CPRF for $\mathbf{NC}^1$ based on IO and the subgroup hiding assumption in pairing-free groups though we omit many details for simplicity in this overview.

In summary, we can obtain an adaptively single-key secure CPRF for $\mathbf{NC}^1$ by combining the above partitionable CPRF for $\mathbf{NC}^1$ based on IO and the subgroup

[8] Note that being given both $g_1 \in \mathbb{G}_p$ and $g_2 \in \mathbb{G}_q$ does not lead to a trivial attack since we use "pairing-free" groups.

hiding assumption with the transformation from a partitionable CPRF into an adaptively secure CPRF explained in the paragraph of "Adaptively secure CPRF from partitionable CPRF".

1.4 Discussion

Why subgroup-hiding needed? One may wonder why we need the subgroup hiding assumption as an extra assumption though we rely on IO, which is already a significantly strong assumption. We give two reasons for this below. The first reason is that we do not know how to construct a CPRF with *selective-constraint* security (even in the single-key setting) from IO though we can construct collusion-resistant CRPF with *selective-challenge* security from IO [11]. In the CPRF based on IO, a constrained key is an obfuscated program that evaluates the PRF on inputs that satisfy the constraint. In the security proof, we puncture the obfuscated program on the challenge input by using the security of IO. This argument is crucially based on the fact that the challenge is given before all constraining queries, and cannot be used in the selective-constraint setting where the challenge is chosen after a constrained key is given. Since our security definition of partitionable CPRF requires selective-constraint security, it seems difficult to construct it from IO. We note that selective-constraint security (rather than selective-challenge security) of partitionable CPRF is crucial to prove the adaptive security of our final CPRF. The second reason is specific to the security proof of our partitionable CPRF. Namely, in the proof of the partition-hiding property of our partitionable CPRF, we have to modify outputs of an obfuscated circuit (which is a constrained key) on exponentially many inputs. Since the security of IO only enables us to modify an obfuscated circuit only on one input, it would need an exponential number of hybrids to modify outputs on exponentially many inputs if we just use the security of IO. We overcome this issue by sophisticated use of the subgroup hiding assumption in a similar way to the work by Hohenberger et al. [34]. We note that in this technique, the Chinese remainder theorem is essential, and we cannot replace the assumption with the decisional linear (DLIN) assumption on a prime-order group, though there are some known prime-to-composite-order conversions in some settings [24,31,37,42].

Why single-key security for $\mathbf{NC}^1$? One may wonder why our adaptive CPRF only achieves single-key security rather than collusion-resistance and supports $\mathbf{NC}^1$ rather than all polynomial-size circuits ($\mathbf{P/poly}$) though there seems to be no obvious attack against our CPRF even if an adversary is given multiple constrained keys for constraints possibly outside $\mathbf{NC}^1$.[9] In fact, we can prove that our CPRF is collusion-resistant and supports $\mathbf{P/poly}$ in the selective-challenge setting by the puncturing technique similarly to [11]. However, in the security

[9] We note that even if the underlying partitionable CPRF only supports $\mathbf{NC}^1$, we can naturally define a constrained key for a function outside $\mathbf{NC}^1$ in the CPRF given in Sect. 4 because a function class supported by the partitionable CPRF matters only in the security proof and does not matter for the correctness.

of adaptive security, we crucially rely on the selective-constraint security of the underlying partitionable CPRF, which stems from the CPRF by Attrapadung et al. [2]. Since their CPRF only achieves single-key security and supports $\mathbf{NC}^1$, our CPRF inherits them. Possible alternatives to their CPRF are lattice-based CPRFs [13,14,40] which satisfy selective-constraint single-key security and supports $\mathbf{P/poly}$. If we could use these CPRFs instead of Attrapadung et al.'s scheme, we would obtain adaptively single-key secure CPRFs for $\mathbf{P/poly}$. However, since we use techniques based on the subgroup-hiding assumption in the proof of the partition-hiding property of our partitionable CPRF, we have to rely on group-based CPRFs for compatibility to the technique, and this is the reason why we cannot use lattice-based CPRFs.

Relation with private CPRF. Partitionable CPRF and private CPRF [9] share a similarity that both enable one to modify functionality of a PRF key without revealing inputs on which outputs were manipulated. Actually, a partitionable CPRF can be seen as a private CPRF for the "admissible hash friendly" functionality [30]. On the other hand, the inverse is not true. Private CPRF does not put any restriction on behaviors of a constrained key on inputs that do not satisfy the constraint except that they look random. On the other hand, partitionable CPRF requires behaviors on these inputs should be consistent in the sense that they are PRF values evaluated on another master secret key. This difference makes it more difficult to construct a partitionable CPRF than constructing a private CPRF.

1.5 Other Related Work

Here, we discuss two additional related works that are relevant to adaptively secure CPRFs.

Fuchsbauer, Konstantinov, Pietrazk, and Rao [26] proved that the classical GGM PRF [29] is an adaptively secure puncturable PRF if the underlying PRG is quasi-polynomially secure. We note that quasi-polynomially-secure PRG is a super-polynomial hardness assumption.

Canetti and Chen [15] proposed a lattice-based construction of (constraint-hiding) single-key secure CPRF for $\mathbf{NC}^1$ that achieves a weaker form of adaptive security where adversaries are allowed to send *logarithmically* many evaluation queries before a constraining query as long as it correctly declares if the evaluation query satisfies the constraint to be queried as a constraining query. We note that in the proceedings version [16], they claimed security against adversaries that make an unbounded number of evaluation queries before a constraining query, but they retracted the claim [15, footnotes 1 and 2]. We remark that the adaptive security defined in this paper does not put any restriction on the number of evaluation queries before a constraining query nor require adversaries to declare if the evaluation query satisfies the constraint to be queried as a constraining query.

Organization. The rest of the paper is organized as follows. After introducing notations, security definitions, and building blocks in Sect. 2, we present the definition of partitionable CPRF, our construction of partitionable CPRF for $\mathbf{NC}^1$, and its security proofs in Sect. 3, and our adaptively single-key secure CPRFs for $\mathbf{NC}^1$ and its security proofs in Sect. 4.

2 Preliminaries

In this section, we review the definitions for complexity assumptions, tools, and cryptographic primitives.

2.1 Composite Order Group

In this paper, in a similar manner to Hohenberger et al. [34], we will use a group of composite order in which the subgroup hiding assumption holds. We recall it here.

Let GGen be a PPT algorithm (called the *group generator*) that takes a security parameter 1^λ as input, and outputs $(N, p, q, \mathbb{G}, \mathbb{G}_p, \mathbb{G}_q, g_1, g_2)$, where $p, q \in \Omega(2^\lambda)$, $N = pq$, $\mathbb{G}$ is a cyclic group of order N, $\mathbb{G}_p$ and $\mathbb{G}_q$ are the subgroups of $\mathbb{G}$ of orders p and q respectively, and g_1 and g_2 are generators of $\mathbb{G}_p$ and $\mathbb{G}_q$ respectively. The subgroup hiding assumption with respect to GGen is defined as follows:

Definition 2.1 (Subgroup Hiding Assumption). *Let* GGen *be a group generator. We say that the* subgroup hiding *assumption holds with respect to* GGen*, if for all PPT adversaries* $\mathcal{A}$*, the advantage* $\mathsf{Adv}^{\mathsf{sgh}}_{\mathsf{GGen},\mathcal{A}}(\lambda)$ *defined below is negligible:*

$$\mathsf{Adv}^{\mathsf{sgh}}_{\mathsf{GGen},\mathcal{A}}(\lambda) := \left|\Pr[\mathcal{A}(\mathcal{G}, \psi_0) = 1] - \Pr[\mathcal{A}(\mathcal{G}, \psi_1) = 1]\right|,$$

where $(N, p, q, \mathbb{G}, \mathbb{G}_p, \mathbb{G}_q, g_1, g_2) \xleftarrow{\mathsf{R}} \mathsf{GGen}(1^\lambda)$, $\mathcal{G} := (N, \mathbb{G}, \mathbb{G}_p, \mathbb{G}_q, g_1, g_2)$, $\psi_0 \xleftarrow{\mathsf{R}} \mathbb{G}$*, and* $\psi_1 \xleftarrow{\mathsf{R}} \mathbb{G}_p$.

For our purpose in this paper, it is convenient to introduce the following *L-DDH*[10] and *L-DDHI* assumptions with respect to GGen. These are not additional assumptions since they are implied by the subgroup hiding assumption.

Definition 2.2 (L-DDH & L-DDHI Assumptions). *Let* GGen *be a group generator and* $L = L(\lambda) = \mathrm{poly}(\lambda)$. *We say that the* L-decisional Diffie-Hellman (L-DDH) *assumption holds with respect to* GGen*, if for all PPT adversaries* $\mathcal{A}$*, the advantage* $\mathsf{Adv}^{L\text{-}\mathsf{ddh}}_{\mathsf{GGen},\mathcal{A}}(\lambda)$ *defined below is negligible:*

$$\mathsf{Adv}^{L\text{-}\mathsf{ddh}}_{\mathsf{GGen},\mathcal{A}}(\lambda) := \left|\Pr[\mathcal{A}(\mathcal{G}, g, (g^{\alpha^i})_{i\in[L]}, \psi_0) = 1] - \Pr[\mathcal{A}(\mathcal{G}, g, (g^{\alpha^i})_{i\in[L]}, \psi_1) = 1]\right|,$$

where $(N, p, q, \mathbb{G}, \mathbb{G}_p, \mathbb{G}_q, g_1, g_2) \xleftarrow{\mathsf{R}} \mathsf{GGen}(1^\lambda)$, $\mathcal{G} := (N, \mathbb{G}, \mathbb{G}_p, \mathbb{G}_q, g_1, g_2)$, $g \xleftarrow{\mathsf{R}} \mathbb{G}$, $\alpha \xleftarrow{\mathsf{R}} \mathbb{Z}_N^*$, $\psi_0 := g^{\alpha^{L+1}}$*, and* $\psi_1 \xleftarrow{\mathsf{R}} \mathbb{G}$.

[10] The L-DDH assumption was called *Assumption 2* by Hohenberger et al. [33].

The L-decisional Diffie-Hellman inversion (L-DDHI) assumption with respect to GGen *is defined in the same way as the above, except that "$\psi_0 := g^{\alpha^{L+1}}$" is replaced with "$\psi_0 := g^{1/\alpha}$".*

Lemma 2.1. *Let* GGen *be a group generator. If the subgroup hiding assumption holds with respect to* GGen*, then the L-DDH and L-DDHI assumptions hold with respect to* GGen *for all polynomials $L = L(\lambda)$.*

The proof of Lemma 2.1 can be found in the full version.

2.2 Balanced Admissible Hash Functions and Related Facts

Here, we describe the definition of a balanced admissible hash function (AHF) introduced by Jager [35]. A balanced AHF is an extension of an ordinary AHF [7,19], but with some more properties. Similarly to an ordinary AHF, it partitions the input space in a security proof so that the simulation is possible with a noticeable probability. The reason why we use a balanced AHF instead of an ordinary AHF is that the former simplifies our security proof. We note that the following formalization of a balanced AHF is slightly different from that by Jager [35] and corresponds to a special case of the general notion of "a partitioning function" introduced by Yamada [45].

Definition 2.3 ([35,45]). *Let $n(\lambda)$ and $m(\lambda)$ be polynomials. Furthermore, for $u \in \{0,1,\perp\}^m$, let $P_u : \{0,1\}^m \rightarrow \{0,1\}$ be defined as*

$$P_u(y) = \begin{cases} 0 & \textit{If for all } i \in [m],\ u_i = \perp \ \vee \ y_i = u_i \\ 1 & \textit{Otherwise} \end{cases},$$

where y_i and u_i are the i-th bit of y and u, respectively. We say that an efficiently computable function $h : \{0,1\}^n \rightarrow \{0,1\}^m$ is a balanced admissible hash function (balanced AHF), if there exists an efficient algorithm $\mathsf{AdmSample}(1^\lambda, Q, \delta)$*, which takes as input (Q, δ) where $Q = Q(\lambda) \in \mathbb{N}$ is polynomially bounded and $\delta = \delta(\lambda) \in (0, 1]$ is noticeable, and outputs $u \in \{0,1,\perp\}^m$ such that:*

1. *There exists $\lambda_0 \in \mathbb{N}$ such that*
$$\Pr\left[\, u \xleftarrow{\mathsf{R}} \mathsf{AdmSample}(1^\lambda, Q(\lambda), \delta(\lambda)) \ : \ u \in \{0,1\}^m \,\right] = 1$$
for all $\lambda > \lambda_0$. Here, λ_0 may depend on functions $Q(\lambda)$ and $\delta(\lambda)$.
2. *For $\lambda > \lambda_0$ (defined in Item 1), there exist $\gamma_{\max}(\lambda)$ and $\gamma_{\min}(\lambda)$ that depend on $Q(\lambda)$ and $\delta(\lambda)$ such that for all $x_1, ..., x_Q, x^* \in \{0,1\}^n$ with $x^* \notin \{x_1, ..., x_Q\}$,*
$$\gamma_{\max}(\lambda) \geq \Pr\left[P_u(h(x_1)) = ... = P_u(h(x_Q)) = 1 \wedge P_u(h(x^*)) = 0\right] \geq \gamma_{\min}(\lambda)$$
where $\gamma_{\max}(\lambda)$ and $\gamma_{\min}(\lambda)$ satisfy that the function $\tau(\lambda)$ defined as
$$\tau(\lambda) = \gamma_{\min}(\lambda) \cdot \delta(\lambda) - \frac{\gamma_{\max}(\lambda) - \gamma_{\min}(\lambda)}{2}$$
is noticeable. We note that the probability is taken over the choice of u where $u \xleftarrow{\mathsf{R}} \mathsf{AdmSample}(1^\lambda, Q(\lambda), \delta(\lambda))$.

Remark 2.1. The term $\tau(\lambda)$ defined above may appear very specific. However, as discussed by Jager [35], such a term appears typically in security analyses that follow the approach of Bellare and Ristenpart [5].

As shown by Jager [35], who extended previous works that gave simple constructions of AHF [25,38], a family of codes $h : \{0,1\}^n \to \{0,1\}^m$ with minimal distance mc for a constant c is a balanced AHF. Explicit constructions of such codes are known [28,43,46].

2.3 Constrained Pseudorandom Functions

Here, we recall the syntax and security definitions for a CPRF. We use the same definitions as Attrapadung et al. [2].

Syntax. Let $\mathcal{F} = \{\mathcal{F}_{\lambda,k}\}_{\lambda,k\in\mathbb{N}}$ be a class of functions[11] where each $\mathcal{F}_{\lambda,k}$ is a set of functions with domain $\{0,1\}^k$ and range $\{0,1\}$, and the description size (when represented by a circuit) of every function in $\mathcal{F}_{\lambda,k}$ is bounded by $\mathrm{poly}(\lambda, k)$.

A CPRF for $\mathcal{F}$ consists of the five PPT algorithms ($\mathsf{Setup}, \mathsf{KeyGen}, \mathsf{Eval}, \mathsf{Constrain}, \mathsf{CEval}$) with the following interfaces:

$\mathsf{Setup}(1^\lambda) \xrightarrow{\mathsf{R}} \mathsf{pp}$: This is the setup algorithm that takes a security parameter 1^λ as input, and outputs a public parameter pp,[12] where pp specifies the descriptions of the key space $\mathcal{K}$, the input-length $n = n(\lambda) = \mathrm{poly}(\lambda)$ (that defines the domain $\{0,1\}^n$), and the range $\mathcal{R}$.

$\mathsf{KeyGen}(\mathsf{pp}) \xrightarrow{\mathsf{R}} \mathsf{msk}$: This is the key generation algorithm that takes a public parameter pp as input, and outputs a master secret key $\mathsf{msk} \in \mathcal{K}$.

$\mathsf{Eval}(\mathsf{pp}, \mathsf{msk}, x) =: y$: This is the deterministic evaluation algorithm that takes a public parameter pp, a master secret key $\mathsf{msk} \in \mathcal{K}$, and an element $x \in \{0,1\}^n$ as input, and outputs an element $y \in \mathcal{R}$.

$\mathsf{Constrain}(\mathsf{pp}, \mathsf{msk}, f) \xrightarrow{\mathsf{R}} \mathsf{sk}_f$: This is the constraining algorithm that takes as input a public parameter pp, a master secret key msk, and a function $f \in \mathcal{F}_{\lambda,n}$, where $n = n(\lambda) = \mathrm{poly}(\lambda)$ is the input-length specified by pp. Then, it outputs a constrained key sk_f.

$\mathsf{CEval}(\mathsf{pp}, \mathsf{sk}_f, x) =: y$: This is the deterministic constrained evaluation algorithm that takes a public parameter pp, a constrained key sk_f, and an element $x \in \{0,1\}^n$ as input, and outputs an element $y \in \mathcal{R}$.

Whenever clear from the context, we will drop pp from the inputs of Eval, $\mathsf{Constrain}$, and CEval, and the executions of them are denoted as "$\mathsf{Eval}(\mathsf{msk}, x)$", "$\mathsf{Constrain}(\mathsf{msk}, f)$", and "$\mathsf{CEval}(\mathsf{sk}_f, x)$", respectively.

---

[11] In this paper, a "class of functions" is a set of "sets of functions". Each $\mathcal{F}_{\lambda,k}$ in $\mathcal{F}$ considered for a CPRF is a set of functions parameterized by a security parameter λ and an input-length k.

[12] For clarity, we will define a CPRF as a primitive that has a public parameter. However, this treatment is compatible with the standard syntax in which there is no public parameter, because it can always be contained as part of a master secret key and constrained secret keys.

$$
\begin{array}{l}
\mathsf{Expt}^{\mathsf{cprf}}_{\mathsf{CPRF},\mathcal{F},\mathcal{A}}(\lambda):\\
\quad \mathsf{coin} \xleftarrow{\mathsf{R}} \{0,1\}\\
\quad \mathsf{pp} \xleftarrow{\mathsf{R}} \mathsf{Setup}(1^\lambda)\\
\quad \mathsf{msk} \xleftarrow{\mathsf{R}} \mathsf{KeyGen}(\mathsf{pp})\\
\quad \mathsf{RF}(\cdot) \xleftarrow{\mathsf{R}} \mathsf{Func}(\{0,1\}^n, \mathcal{R})\\
\quad \mathcal{O}_{\mathsf{Chal}}(\cdot) := \begin{cases} \mathsf{Eval}(\mathsf{msk},\cdot) & \text{if } \mathsf{coin} = 1\\ \mathsf{RF}(\cdot) & \text{if } \mathsf{coin} = 0 \end{cases}\\
\quad (f, \mathsf{st}_{\mathcal{A}}) \xleftarrow{\mathsf{R}} \mathcal{A}_1^{\mathcal{O}_{\mathsf{Chal}}(\cdot),\mathsf{Eval}(\mathsf{msk},\cdot)}(\mathsf{pp})\\
\quad \mathsf{sk}_f \xleftarrow{\mathsf{R}} \mathsf{Constrain}(\mathsf{msk}, f)\\
\quad \widehat{\mathsf{coin}} \xleftarrow{\mathsf{R}} \mathcal{A}_2^{\mathcal{O}_{\mathsf{Chal}}(\cdot),\mathsf{Eval}(\mathsf{msk},\cdot)}(\mathsf{sk}_f, \mathsf{st}_{\mathcal{A}})\\
\quad \text{Return } (\widehat{\mathsf{coin}} \stackrel{?}{=} \mathsf{coin}).
\end{array}
$$

Fig. 1. The experiment for defining single-key security for a CPRF.

Correctness. For correctness of a CPRF for a function class $\mathcal{F} = \{\mathcal{F}_{\lambda,k}\}_{\lambda,k\in\mathbb{N}}$, we require that for all $\lambda \in \mathbb{N}$, $\mathsf{pp} \xleftarrow{\mathsf{R}} \mathsf{Setup}(1^\lambda)$ (which specifies the input length $n = n(\lambda) = \mathrm{poly}(\lambda)$), $\mathsf{msk} \xleftarrow{\mathsf{R}} \mathsf{KeyGen}(\mathsf{pp})$, functions $f \in \mathcal{F}_{\lambda,n}$, and inputs $x \in \{0,1\}^n$ satisfying $f(x) = 0$, we have $\mathsf{CEval}(\ \mathsf{Constrain}(\mathsf{msk}, f), x\ ) = \mathsf{Eval}(\mathsf{msk}, x)$. We stress that a constrained key sk_f can compute the PRF if $f(x) = 0$. (This treatment is reversed from the original definition by Boneh and Waters [10].)

Security. Here, we give the security definitions for a CPRF. We only consider CPRFs that are secure in the presence of a single constrained key, for which we consider two flavors of security: *adaptive single-key security* and *selective-constraint no-evaluation security.*[13] The former notion captures security against adversaries $\mathcal{A}$ that may decide the constraining function f any time during the experiment. (That is, $\mathcal{A}$ can specify the constraining function f even after seeing some evaluation results of the CPRF.) In contrast, the latter notion captures security against adversaries that declare a constraining query at the beginning of the security game and have no access to the evaluation oracle. The definition below reflects these differences.

Formally, for a CPRF $\mathsf{CPRF} = (\mathsf{Setup}, \mathsf{KeyGen}, \mathsf{Eval}, \mathsf{Constrain}, \mathsf{CEval})$ (with input-length $n = n(\lambda)$) for a function class $\mathcal{F} = \{\mathcal{F}_{\lambda,k}\}_{\lambda,k\in\mathbb{N}}$ and an adversary $\mathcal{A} = (\mathcal{A}_1, \mathcal{A}_2)$, we define the single-key security experiment $\mathsf{Expt}^{\mathsf{cprf}}_{\mathsf{CPRF},\mathcal{F},\mathcal{A}}(\lambda)$ as described in Fig. 1 where $\mathsf{Func}(\{0,1\}^n, \mathcal{R})$ denotes the set of all functions from $\{0,1\}^n$ to $\mathcal{R}$.

In the security experiment, the adversary $\mathcal{A}$'s single constraining query is captured by the function f included in the first-stage algorithm $\mathcal{A}_1$'s output. Furthermore, $\mathcal{A}_1$ and $\mathcal{A}_2$ have access to the *challenge* oracle $\mathcal{O}_{\mathsf{Chal}}(\cdot)$ and the *evaluation* oracle $\mathsf{Eval}(\mathsf{msk}, \cdot)$, where the former oracle takes $x^* \in \{0,1\}^n$ as

13 Selective-constraint no-evaluation security was simply called no-evaluation security in [2].

input, and returns either the actual evaluation result $\mathsf{Eval}(\mathsf{msk}, x^*)$ or the output $\mathsf{RF}(x^*)$ of a random function, depending on the challenge bit $\mathsf{coin} \in \{0,1\}$.

We say that an adversary $\mathcal{A} = (\mathcal{A}_1, \mathcal{A}_2)$ in the experiment $\mathsf{Expt}^{\mathsf{cprf}}_{\mathsf{CPRF},\mathcal{F},\mathcal{A}}(\lambda)$ is *admissible* if $\mathcal{A}_1$ and $\mathcal{A}_2$ are PPT and respect the following restrictions:

- $f \in \mathcal{F}_{\lambda,n}$.
- $\mathcal{A}_1$ and $\mathcal{A}_2$ never make the same query twice.
- All challenge queries x^* made by $\mathcal{A}_1$ and $\mathcal{A}_2$ satisfy $f(x^*) = 1$, and are distinct from any of the evaluation queries x that they submit to the evaluation oracle $\mathsf{Eval}(\mathsf{msk}, \cdot)$.

Furthermore, we say that $\mathcal{A}$ is a *selective-constraint no-evaluation adversary* if $\mathcal{A}_1$ and $\mathcal{A}_2$ are PPT, and they do not make any queries, except that $\mathcal{A}_2$ is allowed to make only a single challenge query x^* such that $f(x^*) = 1$.

Definition 2.4 (Single-Key Security of CPRF). *We say that a CPRF* CPRF *for a function class* $\mathcal{F}$ *is* adaptively single-key secure, *if for all admissible adversaries* $\mathcal{A}$, *the advantage* $\mathsf{Adv}^{\mathsf{cprf}}_{\mathsf{CPRF},\mathcal{F},\mathcal{A}}(\lambda) := 2 \cdot |\Pr[\mathsf{Expt}^{\mathsf{cprf}}_{\mathsf{CPRF},\mathcal{F},\mathcal{A}}(\lambda) = 1] - 1/2|$ *is negligible.*

We define selective-constraint no-evaluation security *of* CPRF *analogously, by replacing the phrase "all admissible adversaries* $\mathcal{A}$*" in the above definition with "all selective-constraint no-evaluation adversaries* $\mathcal{A}$*".*

Remark 2.2. As noted by Boneh and Waters [10], without loss of generality we can assume that $\mathcal{A}$ makes a challenge query only once, because security for a single challenge query can be shown to imply security for multiple challenge queries via a standard hybrid argument. Hence, in the rest of the paper we only use the security experiment with a single challenge query for simplicity.

2.4 Indistinguishability Obfuscation

Here, we recall the definition of indistinguishability obfuscation (iO) (for all circuits) [4,27].

Definition 2.5 (Indistinguishability Obfuscation). *We say that a PPT algorithm* iO *is a secure* indistinguishability obfuscator *(iO), if it satisfies the following properties:*

Functionality: iO *takes a security parameter* 1^λ *and a circuit* C *as input, and outputs an obfuscated circuit* $\widehat{C}$ *that computes the same function as* C. *(We may drop* 1^λ *from an input to* iO *when* λ *is clear from the context.)*

Security: *For all PPT adversaries* $\mathcal{A} = (\mathcal{A}_1, \mathcal{A}_2)$, *the advantage function* $\mathsf{Adv}^{\mathsf{io}}_{\mathsf{iO},\mathcal{A}}(\lambda)$ *defined below is negligible:*

$$\mathsf{Adv}^{\mathsf{io}}_{\mathsf{iO},\mathcal{A}}(\lambda) := 2 \cdot \left| \Pr\left[\begin{array}{l} (C_0, C_1, \mathsf{st}) \xleftarrow{\mathsf{R}} \mathcal{A}_1(1^\lambda);\ \mathsf{coin} \leftarrow \{0,1\}; \\ \widehat{C} \xleftarrow{\mathsf{R}} \mathsf{iO}(1^\lambda, C_b);\ \widehat{\mathsf{coin}} \xleftarrow{\mathsf{R}} \mathcal{A}_2(\mathsf{st}, \widehat{C}) \end{array} : \widehat{\mathsf{coin}} = \mathsf{coin} \right] - \frac{1}{2} \right|.$$

where it is required that C_0 *and* C_1 *compute the same function and have the same description size.*

3 Partitionable Constrained Pseudorandom Function

In this section, we introduce a concept of Partitionable Constrained Pseudorandom Function (PCPRF), which is used as a building block for constructing our adaptively single-key secure CPRF. Then we construct a PCPRF for $\mathbf{NC}^1$ based on iO and the subgroup hiding assumption.

3.1 Definition

A PCPRF for $\mathcal{F}$ w.r.t. a function $h : \{0,1\}^n \rightarrow \{0,1\}^m$ consists of $(\mathsf{Setup}, \mathsf{KeyGen}, \mathsf{Eval}, \mathsf{Constrain}, \mathsf{CEval}, \mathsf{Merge}, \mathsf{MEval})$ where $(\mathsf{Setup}, \mathsf{KeyGen}, \mathsf{Eval}, \mathsf{Constrain}, \mathsf{CEval})$ forms a CPRF for $\mathcal{F}$. Two additional algorithms Merge and MEval work as follows.

$\mathsf{Merge}(\mathsf{msk}_0, \mathsf{msk}_1, u)$: This is the merging algorithm that takes two master keys $(\mathsf{msk}_0, \mathsf{msk}_1)$ and a partitioning policy $u \in \{0,1,\perp\}^m$, and outputs a merged key $\mathsf{k}[\mathsf{msk}_0, \mathsf{msk}_1, u]$.

$\mathsf{MEval}(\mathsf{k}[\mathsf{msk}_0, \mathsf{msk}_1, u], x)$: This is the evaluation algorithm that takes a merged key $\mathsf{k}[\mathsf{msk}_0, \mathsf{msk}_1, u]$ and $x \in \{0,1\}^n$ as input, and outputs y.

Correctness. In addition to the correctness as a CPRF, we require the following. For all $\lambda \in \mathbb{N}$, $\mathsf{pp} \xleftarrow{R} \mathsf{Setup}(1^\lambda)$ (which specifies the input length $n = n(\lambda) = \mathrm{poly}(\lambda)$), $\mathsf{msk}_0, \mathsf{msk}_1 \xleftarrow{R} \mathsf{KeyGen}(\mathsf{pp})$, $u \in \{0,1,\perp\}^m$, $\mathsf{k}[\mathsf{msk}_0, \mathsf{msk}_1, u] \xleftarrow{R} \mathsf{Merge}(\mathsf{msk}_0, \mathsf{msk}_1, u)$ and inputs $x \in \{0,1\}^n$ we have

$$\mathsf{MEval}(\mathsf{k}[\mathsf{msk}_0, \mathsf{msk}_1, u], x) = \mathsf{Eval}(\mathsf{msk}_{P_u(h(x))}, x)$$

where we recall that P_u is as defined in Definition 2.3.

Security. We define two security requirements for PCPRFs. The first one is the security as a CPRF, and the second one is partition-hiding, which roughly means that a merged key hides the partition policy u with which the merged key is generated.

CPRF security. We say that a PCPRF is selective-constraint no-evaluation secure if $(\mathsf{Setup}, \mathsf{KeyGen}, \mathsf{Eval}, \mathsf{Constrain}, \mathsf{CEval})$ is selective-constraint no-evaluation secure as a CPRF.[14]

Partition-hiding. For all PPT adversaries $\mathcal{A} = (\mathcal{A}_1, \mathcal{A}_2)$, the advantage $\mathsf{Adv}^{\mathsf{ph}}_{\mathsf{PCPRF},\mathcal{A}}(\lambda)$, defined below, is negligible:

$$\mathsf{Adv}^{\mathsf{ph}}_{\mathsf{PCPRF},\mathcal{A}}(\lambda) :=$$
$$\left| 2 \cdot \Pr\left[\begin{array}{l} \mathsf{pp} \xleftarrow{R} \mathsf{Setup}(1^\lambda); \mathsf{msk}_0, \mathsf{msk}_1 \xleftarrow{R} \mathsf{KeyGen}(\mathsf{pp}); \\ (u, \mathsf{st}) \xleftarrow{R} \mathcal{A}_1(\mathsf{pp}); \\ \mathsf{k}_0 \xleftarrow{R} \mathsf{Merge}(\mathsf{msk}_0, \mathsf{msk}_1, \perp^m); \\ \mathsf{k}_1 \xleftarrow{R} \mathsf{Merge}(\mathsf{msk}_0, \mathsf{msk}_1, u); \\ \mathsf{coin} \leftarrow \{0,1\}; \widehat{\mathsf{coin}} \xleftarrow{R} \mathcal{A}_2(\mathsf{st}, \mathsf{k}_{\mathsf{coin}}) \end{array} : \widehat{\mathsf{coin}} = \mathsf{coin} \right] - \frac{1}{2} \right|.$$

[14] Though it is possible to define the adaptive security for PCPRFs in the similar way, we only define the selective-constraint no-evaluation security since we only need it.

We note that k_0 generated by $\mathsf{Merge}(\mathsf{msk}_0, \mathsf{msk}_1, \perp^m)$ works completely identically to msk_0, albeit in the sense that $\mathsf{MEval}(\mathsf{k}_0, x) = \mathsf{Eval}(\mathsf{msk}_0, x)$. This is since we have $P_{\perp^m}(h(x)) = 0$ for all $x \in \{0,1\}^n$.

3.2 Construction

Here, we construct a partition-hiding and selective-constraint no-evaluation secure PCPRF for $\mathbf{NC}^1$ based on iO and the subgroup hiding assumption. Before describing our scheme, we prepare some notations and describe class of functions our scheme supports. Since the function class our scheme supports is exactly the same as that of [2], the following two paragraphs are taken from [2].

Notations. In the following, we will sometimes abuse notation and evaluate a boolean circuit $C(\cdot) : \{0,1\}^\ell \to \{0,1\}$ on input $y \in \mathbb{R}^\ell$ for some ring $\mathbb{R}$. The evaluation is done by regarding $C(\cdot)$ as the arithmetic circuit whose AND gates $(y_1, y_2) \mapsto y_1 \wedge y_2$ being changed to the multiplication gates $(y_1, y_2) \mapsto y_1 y_2$, NOT gates $y \mapsto \neg y$ changed to the gates $y \mapsto 1-y$, and the OR gates $(y_1, y_2) \mapsto y_1 \vee y_2$ changed to the gates $(y_1, y_2) \mapsto y_1 + y_2 - y_1 y_2$. It is easy to observe that if the input is confined within $\{0,1\}^\ell \subseteq \mathbb{R}^\ell$, the evaluation of the arithmetized version of $C(\cdot)$ equals to that of the binary version. (Here, we identify ring elements $0, 1 \in \mathbb{R}$ with the binary bit.) In that way, we can regard $C(\cdot)$ as an ℓ-variate polynomial over $\mathbb{R}$. The degree of $C(\cdot)$ is defined as the maximum of the total degree of all the polynomials that appear during the computation.

Class of Functions. Let $n = \mathrm{poly}(\lambda)$, $z(n) = \mathrm{poly}(n)$, and $d(n) = O(\log n)$ be parameters. The function class that will be dealt with by the scheme is denoted by $\mathcal{F}^{\mathbf{NC}^1} = \{\mathcal{F}^{\mathbf{NC}^1}_{\lambda, n(\lambda)}\}_{\lambda \in \mathbb{N}}$, where $\mathcal{F}^{\mathbf{NC}^1}_{\lambda, n}$ consists of (Boolean) circuits f whose input size is $n(\lambda)$, the description size is $z(n)$, and the depth is $d(n)$. We can set the parameters arbitrarily large as long as they do not violate the asymptotic bounds above, and thus the function class corresponds to $\mathbf{NC}^1$ circuits with bounded size. The following lemma will be helpful when describing our scheme.

Lemma 3.1. *([2, 20]) Let $n = \mathrm{poly}(\lambda)$. There exists a family of universal circuit $\{U_n\}_{n \in \mathbb{N}}$ of degree $D(\lambda) = \mathrm{poly}(\lambda)$ such that $U_n(f, x) = f(x)$ for any $f \in \mathcal{F}^{\mathbf{NC}^1}_{\lambda, n(\lambda)}$ and $x \in \{0,1\}^n$.*

Construction. Let $\mathcal{F}^{\mathbf{NC}^1} = \{\mathcal{F}^{\mathbf{NC}^1}_{\lambda, n}\}_{\lambda, n \in \mathbb{N}}$ be the family of the circuit defined as above and $\{U_n\}_{n \in \mathbb{N}}$ be the family of the universal circuit defined in Lemma 3.1. Let the parameter $D(\lambda)$ be the degree of the universal circuit (chosen as specified in Lemma 3.1). Since we will fix n in the construction, we drop the subscripts and just denote $\mathcal{F}^{\mathbf{NC}^1}$ and U in the following. Let $h : \{0,1\}^n \to \{0,1\}^m$ be any efficiently computable function.[15] The description of our PCPRF $\mathsf{PCPRF} = (\mathsf{Setup}, \mathsf{KeyGen}, \mathsf{Eval}, \mathsf{Constrain}, \mathsf{CEval}, \mathsf{Merge}, \mathsf{MEval})$ is given below.

$\mathsf{Setup}(1^\lambda)$: It obtains the group description $\mathcal{G} = (N, p, q, \mathbb{G}, \mathbb{G}_p, \mathbb{G}_q, g_1, g_2)$ by running $\mathcal{G} \xleftarrow{R} \mathsf{GGen}(1^\lambda)$. It then outputs the public parameter $\mathsf{pp} := (N, \mathbb{G})$.

$\mathsf{KeyGen}(\mathsf{pp})$: It chooses $g \xleftarrow{R} \mathbb{G}$, $(s_{1,0}, s_{1,1}), ..., (s_{m,0}, s_{m,1}) \xleftarrow{R} \mathbb{Z}_N^2$, and $(b_1, ..., b_z) \xleftarrow{R} \mathbb{Z}_N^z$, $\alpha \xleftarrow{R} \mathbb{Z}_N^*$.[16] It outputs $\mathsf{msk} := (g, (s_{1,0}, s_{1,1}), ..., (s_{m,0}, s_{m,1}), b_1, \ldots, b_z, \alpha)$.

$\mathsf{Eval}(\mathsf{msk}, x)$: Given input $x \in \{0,1\}^n$, it computes $y := h(x)$ and outputs

$$X := g^{\prod_{i=1}^m s_{i,y_i} \cdot U((b_1, \ldots, b_z), (x_1, \ldots, x_n))/\alpha}.$$

$\mathsf{Constrain}(\mathsf{msk}, f)$: It first parses $(g, (s_{1,0}, s_{1,1}), ..., (s_{m,0}, s_{m,1}), b_1, \ldots, b_z, \alpha) \leftarrow \mathsf{msk}$. Then it sets

$$b'_i := (b_i - f_i)\alpha^{-1} \mod N \quad \text{for } i \in [z]$$

where f_i is the i-th bit of the binary representation of f. It then outputs

$$\mathsf{sk}_f := ((s_{1,0}, s_{1,1}), ..., (s_{m,0}, s_{m,1}), f, b'_1, \ldots, b'_z, g, g^\alpha, \ldots, g^{\alpha^{D-1}}).$$

$\mathsf{CEval}(\mathsf{sk}_f, x)$: It parses $((s_{1,0}, s_{1,1}), ..., (s_{n,0}, s_{n,1}), f, b'_1, \ldots, b'_z, g, g^\alpha, \ldots, g^{\alpha^{D-1}}) \leftarrow \mathsf{sk}_f$. It can be shown that, from $(b'_1, ..., b'_z)$, f and x, it is possible to efficiently compute $\{c_i\}_{i \in [D]}$ that satisfies

$$U((b_1, \ldots, b_z), (x_1, \ldots, x_n)) = f(x) + \sum_{j=1}^{D} c_j \alpha^j. \tag{1}$$

If $f(x) = 0$, it computes $y = h(x)$ and $X := (\prod_{j=1}^D (g^{\alpha^{j-1}})^{c_j})^{\prod_{i=1}^m s_{i,y_i}}$ and outputs X. Otherwise it outputs $\perp$.

$\mathsf{Merge}(\mathsf{msk}_0, \mathsf{msk}_1, u)$: Let $\mathsf{MergedKey}[\mathsf{msk}_0, \mathsf{msk}_1, u]$ be a program as described in Fig. 2. It computes and outputs

$$\mathsf{k}[\mathsf{msk}_0, \mathsf{msk}_1, u] \xleftarrow{R} \mathsf{iO}(\mathsf{MergedKey}[\mathsf{msk}_0, \mathsf{msk}_1, u]).$$

$\mathsf{MEval}(\mathsf{k}[\mathsf{msk}_0, \mathsf{msk}_1, u], x)$: It computes and outputs $y := \mathsf{k}[\mathsf{msk}_0, \mathsf{msk}_1, u](x)$.

The proof of correctness of PCPRF can be found in the full version.

Theorem 3.1. *If* iO *is a secure indistinguishability obfuscator and the subgroup hiding assumption holds for* GGen, *then* PCPRF *is selective-constraint no-evaluation secure PCPRF for $\mathcal{F}$ and partition-hiding with respect to h.*

---

[15] The construction will be partition-hiding with respect to h. Looking ahead, we will show that PCPRF that is partition-hiding with respect to a balanced AHF is adaptively single-key secure in Sect. 4. There, we will set h to be a balanced AHF. However, in this section, h can be any efficiently computable function.

[16] This can be done by sampling in $\mathbb{Z}_N$; if it is not in $\mathbb{Z}_N^*$, sampling again until it is. This will succeed with an overwhelming probability since N is a composite with two large prime factors.

$\mathsf{MergedKey}[\mathsf{msk}_0, \mathsf{msk}_1, u]$
Input: $x \in \{0,1\}^n$
Constants: $\mathsf{pp} = (N, \mathbb{G})$
$\mathsf{msk}_0 = (g, (s_{1,0}, s_{1,1}), ..., (s_{m,0}, s_{m,1}), b_1, \ldots, b_z, \alpha)$
$\mathsf{msk}_1 = (\widehat{g}, (\widehat{s}_{1,0}, \widehat{s}_{1,1}), ..., (\widehat{s}_{m,0}, \widehat{s}_{m,1}), \widehat{b}_1, \ldots, \widehat{b}_z, \widehat{\alpha})$
$u \in \{0,1,\perp\}^m$
Output $\mathsf{Eval}(\mathsf{msk}_{P_u(h(x))}, x)$

Fig. 2. Description of program $\mathsf{MergedKey}[\mathsf{msk}_0, \mathsf{msk}_1, u]$

3.3 Security of Our Partitionable CPRF

We present the proof of Theorem 3.1 in this section.

Proof sketch of Theorem 3.1. We have to prove that the construction satisfies the selective-constraint no-evaluation security and partition-hiding. From high level, the selective-constraint no-evaluation security is proven similarly to [2], and the partition-hiding is proven similarly to [34]. The selective-constraint no-evaluation security of PCPRF can be reduced to the $(D-1)$-DDHI assumption, which in turn follows from the subgroup hiding assumption similarly to the security proof of the no-evaluation secure CPRF of [2]. Therefore we omit it here, and the proof for this part can be found in the full version. In the following, we give a proof sketch for the partition-hiding.

We want to prove that k generated by $\mathsf{iO}(\mathsf{MergedKey}[\mathsf{msk}_0, \mathsf{msk}_1, \perp^m])$ and generated by $\mathsf{iO}(\mathsf{MergedKey}[\mathsf{msk}_0, \mathsf{msk}_1, u])$ are computationally indistinguishable. The difficulty is that $\mathsf{MergedKey}[\mathsf{msk}_0, \mathsf{msk}_1, \perp^m]$ and $\mathsf{MergedKey}[\mathsf{msk}_0, \mathsf{msk}_1, u]$ do not have the same functionality, and thus we cannot simply use the security of iO to conclude it.[17] Actually, this can be proven by using the subgroup hiding assumption in a sophisticated way as in the work by Hohenberger, Koppula and Waters [34]. Let $\mathcal{A} = (\mathcal{A}_1, \mathcal{A}_2)$ be a PPT adversary against the partition-hiding property. We prove the above theorem by considering the following sequence of games. We underline modifications from the previous one in descriptions of games. In the following, T_i denotes the event that Game i returns 1.

Game 0: This game corresponds to the case of coin $= 0$ in the experiment defining the partition-hiding. More precisely,

1. Let $\mathcal{G} = (N, p, q, \mathbb{G}, \mathbb{G}_p, \mathbb{G}_q, g_1, g_2) \xleftarrow{R} \mathsf{GGen}(1^\lambda)$, Set $\mathsf{pp} := (N, \mathbb{G})$.
2. Compute $(u, \mathsf{st}_\mathcal{A}) \xleftarrow{R} \mathcal{A}_1(\mathsf{pp})$.
3. Choose $g \xleftarrow{R} \mathbb{G}$, $(b_1, ..., b_z) \xleftarrow{R} \mathbb{Z}_N^z$, and $\alpha \xleftarrow{R} \mathbb{Z}_N^*$. Then choose $(s_{1,0}, s_{1,1}), ..., (s_{m,0}, s_{m,1}) \xleftarrow{R} \mathbb{Z}_N^{2m}$. Set $\mathsf{msk}_0 := (g, (s_{1,0}, s_{1,1}), ..., (s_{m,0}, s_{m,1}), b_1, \ldots, b_z, \alpha)$.

[17] If one relies on the technique of "exponential number of hybrids" (e.g., [18]), then we can prove the indistinguishability of these two cases without relying on subgroup hiding. However, the technique requires sub-exponentially secure iO, which we want to avoid.

MergedKey-Zero[msk_0]
Input: $x \in \{0,1\}^n$
Constants: $\mathsf{pp} = (N, \mathbb{G})$
$\mathsf{msk}_0 = (g, (s_{1,0}, s_{1,1}), ..., (s_{m,0}, s_{m,1}), b_1, \ldots, b_z, \alpha)$
Compute $y := h(x)$
Output $g^{\prod_{i=1}^{m} s_{i,y_i} \cdot U((b_1,...,b_z),(x_1,...,x_n))/\alpha}$.

Fig. 3. Description of program MergedKey-Zero[msk_0]

Choose $\widehat{g} \xleftarrow{R} \mathbb{G}$, $(\widehat{b}_1, ..., \widehat{b}_z) \xleftarrow{R} \mathbb{Z}_N^z$ and $\widehat{\alpha} \xleftarrow{R} \mathbb{Z}_N^*$. Then choose $(\widehat{s}_{1,0}, \widehat{s}_{1,1})$, ..., $(\widehat{s}_{m,0}, \widehat{s}_{m,1}) \xleftarrow{R} \mathbb{Z}_N^{2m}$. Set $\mathsf{msk}_1 := (\widehat{g}, (\widehat{s}_{1,0}, \widehat{s}_{1,1}), ..., (\widehat{s}_{m,0}, \widehat{s}_{m,1}), \widehat{b}_1, \ldots, \widehat{b}_z, \widehat{\alpha})$.

4. Compute $\mathsf{k} \xleftarrow{R} \mathsf{iO}(\mathsf{MergedKey}[\mathsf{msk}_0, \mathsf{msk}_1, \perp^m])$
5. Compute $\widehat{\mathsf{coin}} \xleftarrow{R} \mathcal{A}_2(\mathsf{st}_\mathcal{A}, \mathsf{k})$. The game returns $\widehat{\mathsf{coin}}$.

Game 1: In this game, we set k as an obfuscation of MergedKey-Zero[msk_0], which is described in Fig. 3.

1. Let $\mathcal{G} = (N, p, q, \mathbb{G}, \mathbb{G}_p, \mathbb{G}_q, g_1, g_2) \xleftarrow{R} \mathsf{GGen}(1^\lambda)$, Set $\mathsf{pp} := (N, \mathbb{G})$.
2. Compute $(u, \mathsf{st}_\mathcal{A}) \xleftarrow{R} \mathcal{A}_1(\mathsf{pp})$.
3. Choose $g \xleftarrow{R} \mathbb{G}$, $(b_1, ..., b_z) \xleftarrow{R} \mathbb{Z}_N^z$, and $\alpha \xleftarrow{R} \mathbb{Z}_N^*$. Then choose $(s_{1,0}, s_{1,1}), ..., (s_{m,0}, s_{m,1}) \xleftarrow{R} \mathbb{Z}_N^{2m}$. Set $\mathsf{msk}_0 := (g, (s_{1,0}, s_{1,1}), ..., (s_{m,0}, s_{m,1}), b_1, \ldots, b_z, \alpha)$.
4. Compute $\mathsf{k} \xleftarrow{R} \mathsf{iO}(\mathsf{MergedKey\text{-}Zero}[\mathsf{msk}_0])$.
5. Compute $\widehat{\mathsf{coin}} \xleftarrow{R} \mathcal{A}_2(\mathsf{st}_\mathcal{A}, \mathsf{k})$. The game returns $\widehat{\mathsf{coin}}$.

We have $|\Pr[\mathsf{T}_1] - \Pr[\mathsf{T}_0]| = \mathrm{negl}(\lambda)$ by the security of iO.

Game 2: In this game, we generate $(s_{1,0}, s_{1,1}), ..., (s_{m,0}, s_{m,1})$ in a different way.

1. Let $\mathcal{G} = (N, p, q, \mathbb{G}, \mathbb{G}_p, \mathbb{G}_q, g_1, g_2) \xleftarrow{R} \mathsf{GGen}(1^\lambda)$, Set $\mathsf{pp} := (N, \mathbb{G})$.
2. Compute $(u, \mathsf{st}_\mathcal{A}) \xleftarrow{R} \mathcal{A}_1(\mathsf{pp})$.
3. Choose $g \xleftarrow{R} \mathbb{G}$, $(b_1, ..., b_z) \xleftarrow{R} \mathbb{Z}_N^z$, and $\alpha \xleftarrow{R} \mathbb{Z}_N^*$.
   Choose $\beta \xleftarrow{R} \mathbb{Z}_N^*$ and $(s'_{1,0}, s'_{1,1}), ..., (s'_{m,0}, s'_{m,1}) \xleftarrow{R} \mathbb{Z}_N^{2m}$. Set
$$s_{i,\eta} := \begin{cases} \beta \cdot s'_{i,\eta} & \text{If } u_i = \perp \vee \eta = u_i \\ s'_{i,\eta} & \text{Otherwise} \end{cases}.$$
   Set $\mathsf{msk}_0 := (g, (s_{1,0}, s_{1,1}), ..., (s_{m,0}, s_{m,1}), b_1, \ldots, b_z, \alpha)$.
4. Compute $\mathsf{k} \xleftarrow{R} \mathsf{MergedKey\text{-}Zero}[\mathsf{msk}_0]$.
5. Compute $\widehat{\mathsf{coin}} \xleftarrow{R} \mathcal{A}_2(\mathsf{st}_\mathcal{A}, \mathsf{k})$. The game returns $\widehat{\mathsf{coin}}$.

We have $\Pr[\mathsf{T}_2] = \Pr[\mathsf{T}_1]$ since $\{s_{i,\eta}\}_{i \in [m], \eta \in \{0,1\}}$ is uniformly distributed in $\mathbb{Z}_N^{2m}$ in both games.

Game 3: In this game, we set k as an obfuscation of MergedKey-Zero′[$\mathsf{msk}'_0, u, v_0, ..., v_{m-1}, w$]), which is described in Fig. 4.

1. Let $\mathcal{G} = (N, p, q, \mathbb{G}, \mathbb{G}_p, \mathbb{G}_q, g_1, g_2) \xleftarrow{R} \mathsf{GGen}(1^\lambda)$, Set $\mathsf{pp} := (N, \mathbb{G})$.

MergedKey-Zero$'[\mathsf{msk}'_0, u, v_0, ..., v_{m-1}, w]$
Input: $x \in \{0,1\}^n$
Constants: $\mathsf{pp} = (N, \mathbb{G})$
$v_0, ..., v_{m-1}, w \in \mathbb{G}^{m+1}$
$\mathsf{msk}'_0 = ((s'_{1,0}, s'_{1,1}), ..., (s'_{m,0}, s'_{m,1}), b_1, \ldots, b_z, \alpha)$
$u \in \{0, 1, \perp\}^m$
Compute $y := h(x)$
If $P_u(y) = 0$
Output $w^{\prod_{i=1}^m s'_{i,y_i} \cdot U((b_1,...,b_z),(x_1,...,x_n))/\alpha}$.
Else
Compute $r := \|\{i \in [m] \| u_i = y_i\}\|$
Output $v_r^{\prod_{i=1}^m s'_{i,y_i} \cdot U((b_1,...,b_z),(x_1,...,x_n))/\alpha}$.

Fig. 4. Description of program MergedKey-Zero$'[\mathsf{msk}'_0, u, v_0, ..., v_{m-1}, w]$

2. Compute $(u, \mathsf{st}_\mathcal{A}) \xleftarrow{R} \mathcal{A}_1(\mathsf{pp})$.
3. Choose $g \xleftarrow{R} \mathbb{G}$, $(b_1, ..., b_z) \xleftarrow{R} \mathbb{Z}_N^z$, and $\alpha \xleftarrow{R} \mathbb{Z}_N^*$.
   Choose $\beta \xleftarrow{R} \mathbb{Z}_N^*$ and $(s'_{1,0}, s'_{1,1}), ..., (s'_{m,0}, s'_{m,1}) \xleftarrow{R} \mathbb{Z}_N^{2m}$.
   Set $v_j := g^{\beta^j}$ for $j \in \{0, ..., m-1\}$ and $w := g^{\beta^m}$.
   Set $\mathsf{msk}'_0 := ((s'_{1,0}, s'_{1,1}), ..., (s'_{m,0}, s'_{m,1}), b_1, \ldots, b_z, \alpha)$.
4. Compute $\mathsf{k} \xleftarrow{R} \mathsf{iO}(\mathsf{MergedKey\text{-}Zero}'[\mathsf{msk}'_0, u, v_0, ..., v_{m-1}, w])$.
5. Compute $\widehat{\mathsf{coin}} \xleftarrow{R} \mathcal{A}_2(\mathsf{st}_\mathcal{A}, \mathsf{k})$. The game returns $\widehat{\mathsf{coin}}$.

We have $|\Pr[\mathsf{T}_3] - \Pr[\mathsf{T}_2]| = \mathrm{negl}(\lambda)$ by the security of iO.

Game 4: In this game, we randomly choose w from $\mathbb{G}$, which was set to be g^{β^m} in the previous game.

1. Let $\mathcal{G} = (N, p, q, \mathbb{G}, \mathbb{G}_p, \mathbb{G}_q, g_1, g_2) \xleftarrow{R} \mathsf{GGen}(1^\lambda)$, Set $\mathsf{pp} := (N, \mathbb{G})$.
2. Compute $(u, \mathsf{st}_\mathcal{A}) \xleftarrow{R} \mathcal{A}_1(\mathsf{pp})$.
3. Choose $g \xleftarrow{R} \mathbb{G}$, $(b_1, ..., b_z) \xleftarrow{R} \mathbb{Z}_N^z$, and $\alpha \xleftarrow{R} \mathbb{Z}_N^*$.
   Choose $\beta \xleftarrow{R} \mathbb{Z}_N^*$ and $(s'_{1,0}, s'_{1,1}), ..., (s'_{m,0}, s'_{m,1}) \xleftarrow{R} \mathbb{Z}_N^{2m}$.
   Set $v_j := g^{\beta^j}$ for $j \in \{0, ..., m-1\}$. Choose $w \xleftarrow{R} \mathbb{G}$.
   Set $\mathsf{msk}'_0 := ((s'_{1,0}, s'_{1,1}), ..., (s'_{m,0}, s'_{m,1}), b_1, \ldots, b_z, \alpha)$.
4. Compute $\mathsf{k} \xleftarrow{R} \mathsf{iO}(\mathsf{MergedKey\text{-}Zero}'[\mathsf{msk}'_0, u, v_0, ..., v_{m-1}, w])$.
5. Compute $\widehat{\mathsf{coin}} \xleftarrow{R} \mathcal{A}_2(\mathsf{st}_\mathcal{A}, \mathsf{k})$. The game returns $\widehat{\mathsf{coin}}$.

We have $|\Pr[\mathsf{T}_4] - \Pr[\mathsf{T}_3]| = \mathrm{negl}(\lambda)$ by the $(m-1)$-DDH assumption.

Game 5: In this game, we randomly choose g and w from $\mathbb{G}_q$ and $\mathbb{G}_p$, respectively, which are randomly chosen from $\mathbb{G}$ in the previous game.

1. Let $\mathcal{G} = (N, p, q, \mathbb{G}, \mathbb{G}_p, \mathbb{G}_q, g_1, g_2) \xleftarrow{R} \mathsf{GGen}(1^\lambda)$, Set $\mathsf{pp} := (N, \mathbb{G})$.
2. Compute $(u, \mathsf{st}_\mathcal{A}) \xleftarrow{R} \mathcal{A}_1(\mathsf{pp})$.

MergedKey-Alt[$\mathsf{msk}'_0, \mathsf{msk}'_1, u, v_0, ..., v_{m-1}, w$]
Input: $x \in \{0,1\}^n$
Constants: $\mathsf{pp} = (N, \mathbb{G})$
$v_0, ..., v_{m-1}, w \in \mathbb{G}^{m+1}$
$\mathsf{msk}'_0 = ((s'_{1,0}, s'_{1,1}), ..., (s'_{m,0}, s'_{m,1}), b_1, \ldots, b_z, \alpha)$
$\mathsf{msk}'_1 = ((\widehat{s}_{1,0}, \widehat{s}_{1,1}), ..., (\widehat{s}_{m,0}, \widehat{s}_{m,1}), \widehat{b}_1, \ldots, \widehat{b}_z, \widehat{\alpha})$
$u \in \{0,1,\perp\}^m$
Compute $y := h(x)$
If $P_u(y) = 0$
Output $w^{\prod_{i=1}^m s'_{i,y_i} \cdot U((b_1,...,b_z),(x_1,...,x_n))/\alpha}$.
Else
Compute $r := \lvert\{i \in [m] \mid u_i = y_i\}\rvert$
Output $v_r^{\prod_{i=1}^m \widehat{s}_{i,y_i} \cdot U((\widehat{b}_1,...,\widehat{b}_z),(x_1,...,x_n))/\widehat{\alpha}}$.

Fig. 5. Description of program MergedKey-Alt[$\mathsf{msk}'_0, \mathsf{msk}'_1, u, v_0, ..., v_{m-1}, w$]

3. Choose $g \xleftarrow{R} \mathbb{G}_q$, $(b_1, ..., b_z) \xleftarrow{R} \mathbb{Z}_N^z$, and $\alpha \xleftarrow{R} \mathbb{Z}_N^*$.
   Choose $\beta \xleftarrow{R} \mathbb{Z}_N^*$ and $(s'_{1,0}, s'_{1,1}), ..., (s'_{m,0}, s'_{m,1}) \xleftarrow{R} \mathbb{Z}_N^{2m}$.
   Set $v_j := g^{\beta^j}$ for $j \in \{0, ..., m-1\}$. Choose $w \xleftarrow{R} \mathbb{G}_p$.
   Set $\mathsf{msk}'_0 := ((s'_{1,0}, s'_{1,1}), ..., (s'_{m,0}, s'_{m,1}), b_1, \ldots, b_z, \alpha)$.
4. Compute $\mathsf{k} \xleftarrow{R} \mathsf{iO}(\mathsf{MergedKey\text{-}Zero'}[\mathsf{msk}'_0, u, v_0, ..., v_{m-1}, w])$.
5. Compute $\widehat{\mathsf{coin}} \xleftarrow{R} \mathcal{A}_2(\mathsf{st}_\mathcal{A}, \mathsf{k})$. The game returns $\widehat{\mathsf{coin}}$.

We have $\lvert \Pr[\mathsf{T}_5] - \Pr[\mathsf{T}_4] \rvert = \mathrm{negl}(\lambda)$ by the subgroup hiding assumption.

Game 6: In this game, we set k as an obfuscation of MergedKey-Alt[$\mathsf{msk}'_0, \mathsf{msk}'_1, u, v_0, ..., v_{m-1}, w$], which is described in Fig. 5.

1. Let $\mathcal{G} = (N, p, q, \mathbb{G}, \mathbb{G}_p, \mathbb{G}_q, g_1, g_2) \xleftarrow{R} \mathsf{GGen}(1^\lambda)$, Set $\mathsf{pp} := (N, \mathbb{G})$.
2. Compute $(u, \mathsf{st}_\mathcal{A}) \xleftarrow{R} \mathcal{A}_1(\mathsf{pp})$.
3. Choose $g \xleftarrow{R} \mathbb{G}_q$, $(b_1, ..., b_z) \xleftarrow{R} \mathbb{Z}_N^z$, and $\alpha \xleftarrow{R} \mathbb{Z}_N^*$.
   Choose $\beta \xleftarrow{R} \mathbb{Z}_N^*$ and $(s'_{1,0}, s'_{1,1}), ..., (s'_{m,0}, s'_{m,1}) \xleftarrow{R} \mathbb{Z}_N^{2m}$.
   Set $s'_{i,\eta,p} := s'_{i,\eta} \mod p$ and $s'_{i,\eta,q} := s'_{i,\eta} \mod q$ for $i \in [m]$ and $\eta \in \{0,1\}$.
   Set $b_{i,p} := b_i \mod p$ and $b_{i,q} := b_i \mod q$ for $i \in [m]$.
   $\alpha_p := \alpha \mod p$ and $\alpha_q := \alpha \mod q$.
   Set $v_j := g^{\beta^j}$ for $j \in \{0, ..., m-1\}$. Choose $w \xleftarrow{R} \mathbb{G}_p$.
   Set $\mathsf{msk}'_0 := ((s'_{1,0,p}, s'_{1,1,p}), ..., (s'_{m,0,p}, s'_{m,1,p}), b_{1,p}, \ldots, b_{z,p}, \alpha_p)$.
   Set $\mathsf{msk}'_1 := ((s'_{1,0,q}, s'_{1,1,q}), ..., (s'_{m,0,q}, s'_{m,1,q}), b_{1,q}, \ldots, b_{z,q}, \alpha_q)$.
4. Compute $\mathsf{k} \xleftarrow{R} \mathsf{iO}(\mathsf{MergedKey\text{-}Alt}[\mathsf{msk}'_0, \mathsf{msk}'_1, u, v_0, ..., v_{m-1}, w])$.
5. Compute $\widehat{\mathsf{coin}} \xleftarrow{R} \mathcal{A}_2(\mathsf{st}_\mathcal{A}, \mathsf{k})$. The game returns $\widehat{\mathsf{coin}}$.

We have $\lvert \Pr[\mathsf{T}_6] - \Pr[\mathsf{T}_5] \rvert = \mathrm{negl}(\lambda)$ by the security of iO.

Game 7: In this game, we modify how to generate $s'_{i,\eta,q}$, $b_{i,q}$ and α_q.

1. Let $\mathcal{G} = (N, p, q, \mathbb{G}, \mathbb{G}_p, \mathbb{G}_q, g_1, g_2) \xleftarrow{R} \mathsf{GGen}(1^\lambda)$, Set $\mathsf{pp} := (N, \mathbb{G})$.

2. Compute $(u, \mathsf{st}_{\mathcal{A}}) \xleftarrow{R} \mathcal{A}_1(\mathsf{pp})$.
3. Choose $g \xleftarrow{R} \mathbb{G}_q$, $(b_1, ..., b_z) \xleftarrow{R} \mathbb{Z}_N^z$, and $\alpha \xleftarrow{R} \mathbb{Z}_N^*$.
   Choose $\beta \xleftarrow{R} \mathbb{Z}_N^*$ and $(s'_{1,0}, s'_{1,1}), ..., (s'_{m,0}, s'_{m,1}) \xleftarrow{R} \mathbb{Z}_N^{2m}$.
   Choose $(\widehat{b}_1, ..., \widehat{b}_z) \xleftarrow{R} \mathbb{Z}_N^z$, $\widehat{\alpha} \xleftarrow{R} \mathbb{Z}_N^*$, and $(\widehat{s}_{1,0}, \widehat{s}_{1,1}), ..., (\widehat{s}_{m,0}, \widehat{s}_{m,1}) \xleftarrow{R} \mathbb{Z}_N^{2m}$.
   Set $s'_{i,\eta,p} := s'_{i,\eta} \mod p$ and $s'_{i,\eta,q} := \widehat{s}_{i,\eta} \mod q$ for $i \in [m]$, $\eta \in \{0,1\}$.
   Set $b_{i,p} := b_i \mod p$ and $b_{i,q} := \widehat{b}_i \mod q$ for $i \in [m]$.
   Set $\alpha_p := \alpha \mod p$ and $\alpha_q := \widehat{\alpha} \mod q$.
   Set $v_j := g^{\beta^j}$ for $j \in \{0, ..., m-1\}$. Choose $w \xleftarrow{R} \mathbb{G}_p$.
   Set $\mathsf{msk}'_0 := ((s'_{1,0,p}, s'_{1,1,p}), ..., (s'_{m,0,p}, s'_{m,1,p}), b_{1,p}, \ldots, b_{z,p}, \alpha_p)$.
   Set $\mathsf{msk}'_1 := ((s'_{1,0,q}, s'_{1,1,q}), ..., (s'_{m,0,q}, s'_{m,1,q}), b_{1,q}, \ldots, b_{z,q}, \alpha_q)$.
4. Compute $\mathsf{k} \xleftarrow{R} i\mathcal{O}(\mathsf{MergedKey\text{-}Alt}[\mathsf{msk}'_0, \mathsf{msk}'_1, u, v_0, ..., v_{m-1}, w])$.
5. Compute $\widehat{\mathsf{coin}} \xleftarrow{R} \mathcal{A}_2(\mathsf{st}_{\mathcal{A}}, \mathsf{k})$. The game returns $\widehat{\mathsf{coin}}$.

We have $\Pr[\mathsf{T}_7] = \Pr[\mathsf{T}_6]$ by the Chinese remainder theorem.

Game 8: In this game, we modify the way to set msk'_0 and msk'_1.

1. Let $\mathcal{G} = (N, p, q, \mathbb{G}, \mathbb{G}_p, \mathbb{G}_q, g_1, g_2) \xleftarrow{R} \mathsf{GGen}(1^\lambda)$, Set $\mathsf{pp} := (N, \mathbb{G})$.
2. Compute $(u, \mathsf{st}_{\mathcal{A}}) \xleftarrow{R} \mathcal{A}_1(\mathsf{pp})$.
3. Choose $g \xleftarrow{R} \mathbb{G}_q$, $(b_1, ..., b_z) \xleftarrow{R} \mathbb{Z}_N^z$, and $\alpha \xleftarrow{R} \mathbb{Z}_N^*$.
   Choose $\beta \xleftarrow{R} \mathbb{Z}_N^*$ and $(s'_{1,0}, s'_{1,1}), ..., (s'_{m,0}, s'_{m,1}) \xleftarrow{R} \mathbb{Z}_N^{2m}$.
   Choose $(\widehat{b}_1, ..., \widehat{b}_z) \xleftarrow{R} \mathbb{Z}_N^z$, $\widehat{\alpha} \xleftarrow{R} \mathbb{Z}_N^*$, and $(\widehat{s}_{1,0}, \widehat{s}_{1,1}), ..., (\widehat{s}_{m,0}, \widehat{s}_{m,1}) \xleftarrow{R} \mathbb{Z}_N^{2m}$.
   Set $v_j := g^{\beta^j}$ for $j \in \{0, ..., m-1\}$. Choose $w \xleftarrow{R} \mathbb{G}_p$.
   Set $\mathsf{msk}'_0 := ((s'_{1,0}, s'_{1,1}), ..., (s'_{m,0}, s'_{m,1}), b_1, \ldots, b_z, \alpha)$.
   Set $\mathsf{msk}'_1 := ((\widehat{s}_{1,0}, \widehat{s}_{1,1}), ..., (\widehat{s}_{m,0}, \widehat{s}_{m,1}), \widehat{b}_1, \ldots, \widehat{b}_z, \widehat{\alpha})$.
4. Compute $\mathsf{k} \xleftarrow{R} i\mathcal{O}(\mathsf{MergedKey\text{-}Alt}[\mathsf{msk}'_0, \mathsf{msk}'_1, u, v_0, ..., v_{m-1}, w])$.
5. Compute $\widehat{\mathsf{coin}} \xleftarrow{R} \mathcal{A}_2(\mathsf{st}_{\mathcal{A}}, \mathsf{k})$. The game returns $\widehat{\mathsf{coin}}$.

We have $|\Pr[\mathsf{T}_8] - \Pr[\mathsf{T}_7]| = \mathsf{negl}(\lambda)$ by the security of $i\mathcal{O}$.

Game 9: In this game, we set k to be an obfuscation of $\mathsf{MergedKey}[\mathsf{msk}_0, \mathsf{msk}_1, u]$, which is described in Fig. 2. For clarity, we give more concrete description of $\mathsf{MergedKey}[\mathsf{msk}_0, \mathsf{msk}_1, u]$ in Fig. 6.

1. Let $\mathcal{G} = (N, p, q, \mathbb{G}, \mathbb{G}_p, \mathbb{G}_q, g_1, g_2) \xleftarrow{R} \mathsf{GGen}(1^\lambda)$, Set $\mathsf{pp} := (N, \mathbb{G})$.
2. Compute $(u, \mathsf{st}_{\mathcal{A}}) \xleftarrow{R} \mathcal{A}_1(\mathsf{pp})$.
3. Choose $g \xleftarrow{R} \mathbb{G}_q$, $(b_1, ..., b_z) \xleftarrow{R} \mathbb{Z}_N^z$, and $\alpha \xleftarrow{R} \mathbb{Z}_N^*$.
   Choose $\beta \xleftarrow{R} \mathbb{Z}_N^*$ and $(s'_{1,0}, s'_{1,1}), ..., (s'_{m,0}, s'_{m,1}) \xleftarrow{R} \mathbb{Z}_N^{2m}$.
   Set
   $$s_{i,\eta} := \begin{cases} \beta \cdot s'_{i,\eta} & \text{If } u_i = \bot \vee \eta = u_i \\ s'_{i,\eta} & \text{Otherwise} \end{cases}.$$
   Choose $(\widehat{b}_1, ..., \widehat{b}_z) \xleftarrow{R} \mathbb{Z}_N^z$, $\widehat{\alpha} \xleftarrow{R} \mathbb{Z}_N^*$, and $(\widehat{s}_{1,0}, \widehat{s}_{1,1}), ..., (\widehat{s}_{m,0}, \widehat{s}_{m,1}) \xleftarrow{R} \mathbb{Z}_N^{2m}$.

MergedKey[$\mathsf{msk}_0, \mathsf{msk}_1, u$]
Input: $x \in \{0,1\}^n$
Constants: $\mathsf{pp} = (N, \mathbb{G})$
$v_0, ..., v_{m-1}, w \in \mathbb{G}^{m+1}$
$\mathsf{msk}_0' = (g, (s_{1,0}, s_{1,1}), ..., (s_{m,0}, s_{m,1}), b_1, \ldots, b_z, \alpha)$
$\mathsf{msk}_1' = (\widehat{g}, (\widehat{s}_{1,0}, \widehat{s}_{1,1}), ..., (\widehat{s}_{m,0}, \widehat{s}_{m,1}), \widehat{b}_1, \ldots, \widehat{b}_z, \widehat{\alpha})$
$u \in \{0,1,\perp\}^m$
Compute $y := h(x)$
If $P_u(y) = 0$
Output $g^{\prod_{i=1}^m s_{i,y_i} \cdot U((b_1,\ldots,b_z),(x_1,\ldots,x_n))/\alpha}$.
Else
Output $\widehat{g}^{\prod_{i=1}^m \widehat{s}_{i,y_i} \cdot U((\widehat{b}_1,\ldots,\widehat{b}_z),(x_1,\ldots,x_n))/\widehat{\alpha}}$.

Fig. 6. Description of program MergedKey[$\mathsf{msk}_0, \mathsf{msk}_1, u$], more concretely

Choose $w \xleftarrow{R} \mathbb{G}_p$.
Set $\mathsf{msk}_0 := (w, (s_{1,0}, s_{1,1}), ..., (s_{m,0}, s_{m,1}), b_1, \ldots, b_z, \alpha)$.
Set $\mathsf{msk}_1 := (g, (\widehat{s}_{1,0}, \widehat{s}_{1,1}), ..., (\widehat{s}_{m,0}, \widehat{s}_{m,1}), \widehat{b}_1, \ldots, \widehat{b}_z, \widehat{\alpha})$.

4. Compute $\mathsf{k} \xleftarrow{R} \mathsf{iO}(\mathsf{MergedKey}[\mathsf{msk}_0, \mathsf{msk}_1, u])$.
5. Compute $\widehat{\mathsf{coin}} \xleftarrow{R} \mathcal{A}_2(\mathsf{st}_{\mathcal{A}}, \mathsf{k})$. The game returns $\widehat{\mathsf{coin}}$.

We have $|\Pr[\mathsf{T}_9] - \Pr[\mathsf{T}_8]| = \mathrm{negl}(\lambda)$ by the security of iO.

Game 10: In this game, we modify the way to set $s_{i,\eta}$.

1. Let $\mathcal{G} = (N, p, q, \mathbb{G}, \mathbb{G}_p, \mathbb{G}_q, g_1, g_2) \xleftarrow{R} \mathsf{GGen}(1^\lambda)$, Set $\mathsf{pp} := (N, \mathbb{G})$.
2. Compute $(u, \mathsf{st}_{\mathcal{A}}) \xleftarrow{R} \mathcal{A}_1(\mathsf{pp})$.
3. Choose $g \xleftarrow{R} \mathbb{G}_q$, $(b_1, ..., b_z) \xleftarrow{R} \mathbb{Z}_N^z$, and $\alpha \xleftarrow{R} \mathbb{Z}_N^*$.
   Choose $\beta \xleftarrow{R} \mathbb{Z}_N^*$ and $(s_{1,0}, s_{1,1}), ..., (s_{m,0}, s_{m,1}) \xleftarrow{R} \mathbb{Z}_N^{2m}$.
   Choose $(\widehat{b}_1, ..., \widehat{b}_z) \xleftarrow{R} \mathbb{Z}_N^z$, $\widehat{\alpha} \xleftarrow{R} \mathbb{Z}_N^*$, and $(\widehat{s}_{1,0}, \widehat{s}_{1,1}), ..., (\widehat{s}_{m,0}, \widehat{s}_{m,1}) \xleftarrow{R} \mathbb{Z}_N^{2m}$.
   Choose $w \xleftarrow{R} \mathbb{G}_p$.
   Set $\mathsf{msk}_0 := (w, (s_{1,0}, s_{1,1}), ..., (s_{m,0}, s_{m,1}), b_1, \ldots, b_z, \alpha)$.
   Set $\mathsf{msk}_1 := (g, (\widehat{s}_{1,0}, \widehat{s}_{1,1}), ..., (\widehat{s}_{m,0}, \widehat{s}_{m,1}), \widehat{b}_1, \ldots, \widehat{b}_z, \widehat{\alpha})$.
4. Compute $\mathsf{k} \xleftarrow{R} \mathsf{iO}(\mathsf{MergedKey}[\mathsf{msk}_0, \mathsf{msk}_1, u])$.
5. Compute $\widehat{\mathsf{coin}} \xleftarrow{R} \mathcal{A}_2(\mathsf{st}_{\mathcal{A}}, \mathsf{k})$. The game returns $\widehat{\mathsf{coin}}$.

We have $\Pr[\mathsf{T}_{10}] = \Pr[\mathsf{T}_9]$ since $\{s_{i,\eta}\}_{i \in [m], \eta \in \{0,1\}}$ is uniformly distributed in $\mathbb{Z}_N^{2m}$ in both games.

Game 11: In this game, we randomly choose g and w from $\mathbb{G}$, which are chosen from $\mathbb{G}_q$ and $\mathbb{G}_p$ in the previous game.

1. Let $\mathcal{G} = (N, p, q, \mathbb{G}, \mathbb{G}_p, \mathbb{G}_q, g_1, g_2) \xleftarrow{R} \mathsf{GGen}(1^\lambda)$, Set $\mathsf{pp} := (N, \mathbb{G})$.
2. Compute $(u, \mathsf{st}_{\mathcal{A}}) \xleftarrow{R} \mathcal{A}_1(\mathsf{pp})$.

3. Choose $\underline{g \xleftarrow{R} \mathbb{G}}$, $(b_1, ..., b_z) \xleftarrow{R} \mathbb{Z}_N^z$, and $\alpha \xleftarrow{R} \mathbb{Z}_N^*$.
   Choose $\beta \xleftarrow{R} \mathbb{Z}_N^*$ and $(s_{1,0}, s_{1,1}), ..., (s_{m,0}, s_{m,1}) \xleftarrow{R} \mathbb{Z}_N^{2m}$.
   Choose $(\widehat{b}_1, ..., \widehat{b}_z) \xleftarrow{R} \mathbb{Z}_N^z$, $\widehat{\alpha} \xleftarrow{R} \mathbb{Z}_N^*$, and $(\widehat{s}_{1,0}, \widehat{s}_{1,1}), ..., (\widehat{s}_{m,0}, \widehat{s}_{m,1}) \xleftarrow{R} \mathbb{Z}_N^{2m}$.
   Choose $\underline{w \xleftarrow{R} \mathbb{G}}$.
   Set $\mathsf{msk}_0 := (w, (s_{1,0}, s_{1,1}), ..., (s_{m,0}, s_{m,1}), b_1, \ldots, b_z, \alpha)$.
   Set $\mathsf{msk}_1 := (g, (\widehat{s}_{1,0}, \widehat{s}_{1,1}), ..., (\widehat{s}_{m,0}, \widehat{s}_{m,1}), \widehat{b}_1, \ldots, \widehat{b}_z, \widehat{\alpha})$.
4. Compute $\mathsf{k} \xleftarrow{R} \mathsf{iO}(\mathsf{MergedKey}[\mathsf{msk}_0, \mathsf{msk}_1, u])$.
5. Compute $\widehat{\mathsf{coin}} \xleftarrow{R} \mathcal{A}_2(\mathsf{st}_\mathcal{A}, \mathsf{k})$. The game returns $\widehat{\mathsf{coin}}$.

We have $|\Pr[\mathsf{T}_{11}] - \Pr[\mathsf{T}_{10}]| = \mathsf{negl}(\lambda)$ by the subgrup hiding assumption.

Game 12: This game is the same as the previous game except that we rename g and w by $\widehat{g}$ and g.

1. Let $\mathcal{G} = (N, p, q, \mathbb{G}, \mathbb{G}_p, \mathbb{G}_q, g_1, g_2) \xleftarrow{R} \mathsf{GGen}(1^\lambda)$, Set $\mathsf{pp} := (N, \mathbb{G})$.
2. Compute $(u, \mathsf{st}_\mathcal{A}) \xleftarrow{R} \mathcal{A}_1(\mathsf{pp})$.
3. Choose $\underline{\widehat{g} \xleftarrow{R} \mathbb{G}}$, $(b_1, ..., b_z) \xleftarrow{R} \mathbb{Z}_N^z$, and $\alpha \xleftarrow{R} \mathbb{Z}_N^*$.
   Choose $\beta \xleftarrow{R} \mathbb{Z}_N^*$ and $(s_{1,0}, s_{1,1}), ..., (s_{m,0}, s_{m,1}) \xleftarrow{R} \mathbb{Z}_N^{2m}$.
   Choose $(\widehat{b}_1, ..., \widehat{b}_z) \xleftarrow{R} \mathbb{Z}_N^z$, $\widehat{\alpha} \xleftarrow{R} \mathbb{Z}_N^*$, and $(\widehat{s}_{1,0}, \widehat{s}_{1,1}), ..., (\widehat{s}_{m,0}, \widehat{s}_{m,1}) \xleftarrow{R} \mathbb{Z}_N^{2m}$.
   Choose $\underline{g \xleftarrow{R} \mathbb{G}}$.
   Set $\mathsf{msk}_0 := (g, (s_{1,0}, s_{1,1}), ..., (s_{m,0}, s_{m,1}), b_1, \ldots, b_z, \alpha)$.
   Set $\mathsf{msk}_1 := (\widehat{g}, (\widehat{s}_{1,0}, \widehat{s}_{1,1}), ..., (\widehat{s}_{m,0}, \widehat{s}_{m,1}), \widehat{b}_1, \ldots, \widehat{b}_z, \widehat{\alpha})$.
4. Compute $\mathsf{k} \xleftarrow{R} \mathsf{iO}(\mathsf{MergedKey}[\mathsf{msk}_0, \mathsf{msk}_1, u])$.
5. Compute $\widehat{\mathsf{coin}} \xleftarrow{R} \mathcal{A}_2(\mathsf{st}_\mathcal{A}, \mathsf{k})$. The game returns $\widehat{\mathsf{coin}}$.
   We have $\Pr[\mathsf{T}_{12}] = \Pr[\mathsf{T}_{11}]$ since we just renamed g and w by $\widehat{g}$ and g. This game corresponds to the case of $\mathsf{coin} = 1$ in the experiment defining the partition-hiding.

Game 0 and Game 12 correspond to the cases of $\mathsf{coin} = 0$ and $\mathsf{coin} = 1$ in the experiment defining the partition-hiding, and we proved $|\Pr[\mathsf{T}_{12}] - \Pr[\mathsf{T}_0]| = \mathsf{negl}(\lambda)$. This completes the proof of the constraint-hiding. More detailed analysis of the above sequence of games can be found in the full version.

This completes the proof of Theorem 3.1. ■

4 Adaptively Single-Key Secure CPRF

In this section, we construct an adaptively single-key secure CPRF based on iO and a partition-hiding no-evaluation secure PCPRF. By instantiating the latter with our construction of PCPRF in Sect. 3.2, we obtain the first adaptively single-key secure CPRF for $\mathbf{NC}^1$ in the standard model.

4.1 Construction

Let PCPRF = (Setup, KeyGen, Eval, Constrain, CEval, Merge, MEval) be a partition-hiding and selective-constraint no-evaluation secure PCPRF for function

$\mathsf{ConstrainedKey}[\mathsf{msk}, f]$
Input: $x \in \{0,1\}^n$
Constants: pp, msk, f
If $f(x) = 0$
Output $\mathsf{Eval}(\mathsf{msk}, x)$
Else
Output $\perp$

Fig. 7. Description of program $\mathsf{ConstrainedKey}[\mathsf{msk}, f]$

class $\mathcal{F}$. Then we construct CPRF $\mathsf{CPRF} = (\mathsf{Setup}', \mathsf{KeyGen}', \mathsf{Eval}', \mathsf{Constrain}', \mathsf{CEval}')$ for the same function class as follows.

$\mathsf{Setup}'(1^\lambda)$: This algorithm is completely identical to $\mathsf{Setup}(1^\lambda)$.
$\mathsf{KeyGen}'(\mathsf{pp})$: This algorithm is completely identical to $\mathsf{KeyGen}(\mathsf{pp})$.
$\mathsf{Eval}'(\mathsf{msk}, x)$: This algorithm is completely identical to $\mathsf{Eval}(\mathsf{msk}, x)$.
$\mathsf{Constrain}'(\mathsf{msk}, f)$: It computes and outputs $\mathsf{sk}_f \xleftarrow{\mathsf{R}} i\mathcal{O}(\mathsf{ConstrainedKey}[\mathsf{msk}, f])$ where $\mathsf{ConstrainedKey}[\mathsf{msk}, f]$ is a program described in Fig. 7.
$\mathsf{CEval}'(\mathsf{sk}_f, x)$: It computes and outputs $\mathsf{sk}_f(x)$.

We note that the program $\mathsf{ConstrainedKey}[\mathsf{msk}, f]$ is padded so that the size of it is the same size as the programs that appear in the security proof. See also Remark 4.1.

The following theorem addresses the security of the above construction. We require $\mathcal{F}$ to contain some basic functions in the theorem. However, this restriction is very mild. Indeed, the requirement for the function class is satisfied in our construction of PCPRF in Sect. 3.2.

Theorem 4.1. *Let $\mathcal{F}$ be a function class that contains constant functions and punctured function $g_y : \{0,1\}^n \to \{0,1\}$ defined as $g_y(x) = (x \stackrel{?}{=} y)$ for all $y \in \{0,1\}^n$. If* iO *is a secure indistinguishability obfuscator and* PCPRF *is both partition-hiding with respect to a balanced AHF $h : \{0,1\}^n \to \{0,1\}^m$ and selective-constraint no-evaluation secure PCPRF for $\mathcal{F}$, then* CPRF *constructed above is an adaptively single-key secure CPRF for $\mathcal{F}$.*

By combining Theorems 3.1 and 4.1, we obtain the following theorem.

Theorem 4.2. *If there exists a secure indistinguishability obfuscator and a group generator for which the subgroup hiding assumption holds, then there exists an adaptively single-key secure CPRF for the function class $\mathcal{F}^{\mathbf{NC}^1}$, which is defined in Sect. 3.*

Proof. Let $\mathcal{A}$ be a PPT adversary that breaks adaptive single-key security of the scheme. In addition, let $\epsilon = \epsilon(\lambda)$ and $Q = Q(\lambda)$ be its advantage and the upper bound on the number of evaluation queries, respectively. By assumption, $Q(\lambda)$ is polynomially bounded and there exists a noticeable function $\epsilon_0(\lambda)$ such that

$\epsilon(\lambda) \geq \epsilon_0(\lambda)$ holds for infinitely many λ. By the property of the balanced AHF (Definition 2.3, Item 1), $\Pr[u \xleftarrow{R} \mathsf{AdmSample}(1^\lambda, Q(\lambda), \epsilon_0(\lambda)) : u \in \{0,1\}^m] = 1$ for all sufficiently large λ. Therefore, in the following, we assume that this condition always holds. We show the security of the scheme via the following sequence of games. In the following, T_i denotes the event that Game i returns 1, and we denote the master secret key of the scheme by msk_0 for notational convenience.

Game 0: This is the real single-key security experiment $\mathsf{Expt}^{\mathsf{cprf}}_{\mathsf{CPRF},\mathcal{F},\mathcal{A}}(\lambda)$ against an admissible adversary $\mathcal{A} = (\mathcal{A}_1, \mathcal{A}_2)$. Namely,

$\mathsf{coin} \xleftarrow{R} \{0,1\}$
$\mathsf{pp} \xleftarrow{R} \mathsf{Setup}(1^\lambda)$
$\mathsf{msk}_0 \xleftarrow{R} \mathsf{KeyGen}(\mathsf{pp})$
$X^* \xleftarrow{R} \mathcal{R}$
$(f, \mathsf{st}_\mathcal{A}) \xleftarrow{R} \mathcal{A}_1^{\mathcal{O}_{\mathsf{Chal}}(\cdot), \mathsf{Eval}(\mathsf{msk}_0, \cdot)}(\mathsf{pp})$
$\mathsf{sk}_f \xleftarrow{R} \mathsf{iO}(\mathsf{ConstrainedKey}[\mathsf{msk}, f])$
$\widehat{\mathsf{coin}} \xleftarrow{R} \mathcal{A}_2^{\mathcal{O}_{\mathsf{Chal}}(\cdot), \mathsf{Eval}(\mathsf{msk}_0, \cdot)}(\mathsf{sk}_f, \mathsf{st}_\mathcal{A})$
Return $(\widehat{\mathsf{coin}} \stackrel{?}{=} \mathsf{coin})$

where the challenge oracle $\mathcal{O}_{\mathsf{Chal}}(\cdot)$ is described below.

$\mathcal{O}_{\mathsf{Chal}}(x^*)$: Given $x^* \in \{0,1\}^n$ as input, it returns $\mathsf{Eval}(\mathsf{msk}_0, x^*)$ if $\mathsf{coin} = 1$ and X^* if $\mathsf{coin} = 0$.

We recall that $\mathcal{O}_{\mathsf{Chal}}(\cdot)$ is queried at most once during the game.

Game 1: In this game, we change Game 0 so that the game performs the following additional step at the end of the experiment. First, the game samples $u \xleftarrow{R} \mathsf{AdmSample}(1^\lambda, Q, \epsilon_0)$ and checks whether the following condition holds:

$$P_u(h(x_1)) = \cdots = P_u(h(x_Q)) = 1 \ \wedge \ P_u(h(x^*)) = 0, \tag{2}$$

where $x_1, \ldots, x_Q$ are inputs to the PRF for which $\mathcal{A}$ called the evaluation oracle $\mathsf{Eval}(\mathsf{msk}_0, \cdot)$. If it does not hold, the game ignores the output $\widehat{\mathsf{coin}}$ of $\mathcal{A}$, and replace it with a fresh random coin $\widehat{\mathsf{coin}} \xleftarrow{R} \{0,1\}$. In this case, we say that the game aborts.

By using the property of AHF, we can prove that the probability that the game does not abort is noticeable. More precisely, if $|\Pr[\mathsf{T}_0] - 1/2|$ is non-negligible, so is $|\Pr[\mathsf{T}_1] - 1/2|$ (See the full version for details).

Game 2: In this game, we change the way sk_f is generated and the oracles return answers. At the beginning of the game, we sample $\mathsf{msk}_0 \xleftarrow{R} \mathsf{KeyGen}(\mathsf{pp})$ and $\mathsf{msk}_1 \xleftarrow{R} \mathsf{KeyGen}(\mathsf{pp})$, and compute $\mathsf{k}[\mathsf{msk}_0, \mathsf{msk}_1, \bot^m] \xleftarrow{R} \mathsf{Merge}[\mathsf{msk}_0, \mathsf{msk}_1, \bot^m]$. We then set $C := \mathsf{MEval}(\mathsf{k}[\mathsf{msk}_0, \mathsf{msk}_1, \bot^m], \cdot)$. Furthermore, sk_f given to $\mathcal{A}_2$ is generated as $\mathsf{sk}_f \xleftarrow{R} \mathsf{iO}(\mathsf{ConstrainedKeyAlt}[C, f])$ instead of $\mathsf{sk}_f \xleftarrow{R} \mathsf{iO}(\mathsf{ConstrainedKey}[\mathsf{msk}, f])$, where the circuit $\mathsf{ConstrainedKeyAlt}[C, f]$ is depicted in Fig. 8. We also replace the evaluation oracle $\mathsf{Eval}(\mathsf{msk}_0, \cdot)$ and the challenge oracle $\widetilde{\mathcal{O}}_{\mathsf{Chal}}(\cdot)$ with the following oracles.

$\widetilde{\mathsf{Eval}}(C, \cdot)$: Given $x \in \{0,1\}^n$ as input, it returns $C(x)$.

$\widetilde{\mathcal{O}}_{\mathsf{Chal}}(C, \cdot)$: Given x^* as input, it returns $C(x^*)$ if $\mathsf{coin} = 1$ and X^* if $\mathsf{coin} = 0$.

ConstrainedKeyAlt$[C, f]$
Input: $x \in \{0,1\}^n$
Constants: pp, C, and f
If $f(x) = 0$
Output $C(x)$
Else
Output $\perp$

Fig. 8. Description of program ConstrainedKeyAlt$[C, f]$

We have $|\Pr[\mathsf{T}_2] - \Pr[\mathsf{T}_1]| = \mathrm{negl}(\lambda)$ by the security of iO.

Game 3: Recall that in Game 2, it is checked whether the abort condition Eq. (2) holds or not at the end of the game. In this game, we change the game so that it samples u at the beginning of the game and aborts and outputs a random bit as soon as the abort condition becomes true.
We have $\Pr[\mathsf{T}_3] = \Pr[\mathsf{T}_2]$ since the change is conceptual and nothing is changed from the adversary's view.

Game 4: In this game, we further change the way C is generated. At the beginning of the game, the game samples $\mathsf{k}[\mathsf{msk}_0, \mathsf{msk}_1, u] \xleftarrow{\mathsf{R}} \mathsf{Merge}[\mathsf{msk}_0, \mathsf{msk}_1, u]$ and then set $C := \mathsf{MEval}(\mathsf{k}[\mathsf{msk}_0, \mathsf{msk}_1, u], \cdot)$ instead of $C := \mathsf{MEval}(\mathsf{k}[\mathsf{msk}_0, \mathsf{msk}_1, \perp^m], \cdot)$.
We have $|\Pr[\mathsf{T}_4] - \Pr[\mathsf{T}_3]| = \mathrm{negl}(\lambda)$ by the partition-hiding property of PCPRF.

Game 5: In this game, we replace $\widetilde{\mathsf{Eval}}(C, \cdot)$ and $\widetilde{\mathcal{O}}_{\mathsf{Chal}}(C, \cdot)$ with the following oracles.
$\mathsf{Eval}(\mathsf{msk}_1, \cdot)$: Given $x \in \{0,1\}^n$ as input, it returns $\mathsf{Eval}(\mathsf{msk}_1, x)$.
$\bar{\mathcal{O}}_{\mathsf{Chal}}(\mathsf{msk}_0, \cdot)$: Given $x^* \in \{0,1\}^n$ as input, it returns $\mathsf{Eval}(\mathsf{msk}_0, x^*)$ if $\mathsf{coin} = 1$ and X^* if $\mathsf{coin} = 0$.
We have $\Pr[\mathsf{T}_5] = \Pr[\mathsf{T}_4]$ since as soon as $\mathcal{A}$ makes an evaluation or challenge query that makes a difference for the response by the oracles, these games abort.

Game 6: In this game, we change the way sk_f is generated when $\mathcal{A}_1$ makes the call to $\mathcal{O}_{\mathsf{Chal}}$ (namely, the challenge query is made before f is chosen by $\mathcal{A}$). Let x^* be the challenge query made by $\mathcal{A}_1$. We set the function $g_{x^*} : \{0,1\}^n \to \{0,1\}$ as $g_{x^*}(x) = (x \stackrel{?}{=} x^*)$. To generate sk_f, we first sample $\mathsf{sk}_{0,g_{x^*}} \xleftarrow{\mathsf{R}} \mathsf{Constrain}(\mathsf{msk}_0, g_{x^*})$ and set $sk_f \xleftarrow{\mathsf{R}} \mathsf{iO}(\widetilde{C}[\mathsf{sk}_{0,g_{x^*}}, \mathsf{msk}_1, f, u])$, where $\widetilde{C}[\mathsf{sk}_{0,g}, \mathsf{msk}_1, f, u]$ is depicted in Fig. 9. Note that if $\mathcal{A}_1$ does not make the challenge query, we do not change the way sk_f is generated.
We have $|\Pr[\mathsf{T}_6] - \Pr[\mathsf{T}_5]| = \mathrm{negl}(\lambda)$ by the security of iO.

Game 7: In this game, we change the way sk_f is generated when $\mathcal{A}_1$ stops without making challenge query (namely, the challenge query will be made after $\mathcal{A}$ chooses f). In such a case, we first sample $\mathsf{sk}_{0,f} \xleftarrow{\mathsf{R}} \mathsf{Constrain}(\mathsf{msk}_0, f)$ and set $sk_f \xleftarrow{\mathsf{R}} \mathsf{iO}(\widetilde{C}[\mathsf{sk}_{0,f}, \mathsf{msk}_1, f, u])$.
We have $|\Pr[\mathsf{T}_7] - \Pr[\mathsf{T}_6]| = \mathrm{negl}(\lambda)$ by the security of iO.

$\widetilde{C}[\mathsf{sk}_{0,g}, \mathsf{msk}_1, f, u]$
Input: $x \in \{0,1\}^n$
Constants: pp, $\mathsf{sk}_{0,g}$, msk_1, f, u
If $f(x) = 0 \wedge P_u(h(x)) = 0$
  Output $\mathsf{CEval}(\mathsf{sk}_{0,g}, x)$
If $f(x) = 0 \wedge P_u(h(x)) = 1$
  Output $\mathsf{Eval}(\mathsf{msk}_1, x)$
Else
  Output $\perp$

Fig. 9. Description of program $\widetilde{C}[\mathsf{sk}_{0,g}, \mathsf{msk}_1, f, u]$

Finally, we observe that we have $|\Pr[\mathsf{T}_7] - 1/2| = \mathrm{negl}(\lambda)$ by the selective-constraint no-evaluation security of PCPRF. The above completes the proof of Theorem 4.1. More detailed analysis of the above sequence of games can be found in the full version. ■

Remark 4.1. As one may notice, in the hybrids, we obfuscate a program that contains a merged key $\mathsf{k}[\mathsf{msk}_0, \mathsf{msk}_1, u]$ that itself is also an obfuscation of some program in our construction. Therefore when generating a constrained key, $\mathsf{ConstrainedKey}[\mathsf{msk}, f]$ should be padded to the maximum size of an obfuscated program that appears in the hybrids, and thus the size of sk_f is the size of an obfuscation of an obfuscation. Actually, this "obfuscation of obfuscation" blowup could be avoided if we directly construct an adaptively secure CPRF based on iO and the subgroup hiding assumption. However, we believe that the abstraction of PCPRF makes it easier to understand our security proof, and there should be further applications of it.

Acknowledgments. We would like to thank Yilei Chen for the valuable discussion about adaptive security of the LWE-based constraint-hiding CPRFs. The first, second, and fourth authors were supported by JST CREST Grant Number JPMJCR1688, Japan.

References

1. Abusalah, H., Fuchsbauer, G., Pietrzak, K.: Constrained PRFs for unbounded inputs. In: Sako, K. (ed.) CT-RSA 2016. LNCS, vol. 9610, pp. 413–428. Springer, Cham (2016). https://doi.org/10.1007/978-3-319-29485-8_24
2. Attrapadung, N., Matsuda, T., Nishimaki, R., Yamada, S., Yamakawa, T.: Constrained PRFs for NC^1 in traditional groups. In: Shacham, H., Boldyreva, A. (eds.) CRYPTO 2018, Part II. LNCS, vol. 10992, pp. 543–574. Springer, Cham (2018). https://doi.org/10.1007/978-3-319-96881-0_19
3. Banerjee, A., Fuchsbauer, G., Peikert, C., Pietrzak, K., Stevens, S.: Key-homomorphic constrained pseudorandom functions. In: Dodis, Y., Nielsen, J.B. (eds.) TCC 2015, Part II. LNCS, vol. 9015, pp. 31–60. Springer, Heidelberg (2015). https://doi.org/10.1007/978-3-662-46497-7_2

4. Barak, B., Goldreich, O., Impagliazzo, R., Rudich, S., Sahai, A., Vadhan, S.P., Yang, K.: On the (im)possibility of obfuscating programs. J. ACM **59**(2), 6:1–6:48 (2012)
5. Bellare, M., Ristenpart, T.: Simulation without the artificial abort: simplified proof and improved concrete security for Waters' IBE scheme. In: Joux, A. (ed.) EUROCRYPT 2009. LNCS, vol. 5479, pp. 407–424. Springer, Heidelberg (2009). https://doi.org/10.1007/978-3-642-01001-9_24
6. Bitansky, N.: Verifiable random functions from non-interactive witness-indistinguishable proofs. In: Kalai, Y., Reyzin, L. (eds.) TCC 2017, Part II. LNCS, vol. 10678, pp. 567–594. Springer, Cham (2017). https://doi.org/10.1007/978-3-319-70503-3_19
7. Boneh, D., Boyen, X.: Secure identity based encryption without random oracles. In: Franklin, M. (ed.) CRYPTO 2004. LNCS, vol. 3152, pp. 443–459. Springer, Heidelberg (2004). https://doi.org/10.1007/978-3-540-28628-8_27
8. Boneh, D., Kim, S., Montgomery, H.W.: Private puncturable PRFs from standard lattice assumptions. In: Coron, J.-S., Nielsen, J.B. (eds.) EUROCRYPT 2017, Part I. LNCS, vol. 10210, pp. 415–445. Springer, Cham (2017). https://doi.org/10.1007/978-3-319-56620-7_15
9. Boneh, D., Lewi, K., Wu, D.J.: Constraining pseudorandom functions privately. In: Fehr, S. (ed.) PKC 2017, Part II. LNCS, vol. 10175, pp. 494–524. Springer, Heidelberg (2017). https://doi.org/10.1007/978-3-662-54388-7_17
10. Boneh, D., Waters, B.: Constrained pseudorandom functions and their applications. In: Sako, K., Sarkar, P. (eds.) ASIACRYPT 2013, Part II. LNCS, vol. 8270, pp. 280–300. Springer, Heidelberg (2013). https://doi.org/10.1007/978-3-642-42045-0_15
11. Boneh, D., Zhandry, M.: Multiparty key exchange, efficient traitor tracing, and more from indistinguishability obfuscation. In: Garay, J.A., Gennaro, R. (eds.) CRYPTO 2014, Part I. LNCS, vol. 8616, pp. 480–499. Springer, Heidelberg (2014). https://doi.org/10.1007/978-3-662-44371-2_27
12. Boyle, E., Goldwasser, S., Ivan, I.: Functional signatures and pseudorandom functions. In: Krawczyk, H. (ed.) PKC 2014. LNCS, vol. 8383, pp. 501–519. Springer, Heidelberg (2014). https://doi.org/10.1007/978-3-642-54631-0_29
13. Brakerski, Z., Tsabary, R., Vaikuntanathan, V., Wee, H.: Private constrained PRFs (and More) from LWE. In: Kalai, Y., Reyzin, L. (eds.) TCC 2017, Part I. LNCS, vol. 10677, pp. 264–302. Springer, Cham (2017). https://doi.org/10.1007/978-3-319-70500-2_10
14. Brakerski, Z., Vaikuntanathan, V.: Constrained key-homomorphic PRFs from standard lattice assumptions - or: how to secretly embed a circuit in your PRF. In: Dodis, Y., Nielsen, J.B. (eds.) TCC 2015, Part II. LNCS, vol. 9015, pp. 1–30. Springer, Heidelberg (2015). https://doi.org/10.1007/978-3-662-46497-7_1
15. Canetti, R., Chen, Y.: Constraint-hiding constrained PRFs for NC1 from LWE. Cryptology ePrint Archive, Report 2017/143 (2017)
16. Canetti, R., Chen, Y.: Constraint-hiding constrained PRFs for NC^1 from LWE. In: Coron, J.-S., Nielsen, J.B. (eds.) EUROCRYPT 2017, Part I. LNCS, vol. 10210, pp. 446–476. Springer, Cham (2017). https://doi.org/10.1007/978-3-319-56620-7_16
17. Canetti, R., Goldreich, O., Halevi, S.: The random oracle methodology, revisited. J. ACM **51**(4), 557–594 (2004)
18. Canetti, R., Lin, H., Tessaro, S., Vaikuntanathan, V.: Obfuscation of probabilistic circuits and applications. In: Dodis, Y., Nielsen, J.B. (eds.) TCC 2015, Part II. LNCS, vol. 9015, pp. 468–497. Springer, Heidelberg (2015). https://doi.org/10.1007/978-3-662-46497-7_19

19. Cash, D., Hofheinz, D., Kiltz, E., Peikert, C.: Bonsai trees, or how to delegate a lattice basis. J. Cryptol. **25**(4), 601–639 (2012)
20. Cook, S.A., Hoover, H.J.: A depth-universal circuit. SIAM J. Comput. **14**(4), 833–839 (1985)
21. Datta, P., Dutta, R., Mukhopadhyay, S.: Constrained pseudorandom functions for unconstrained inputs revisited: achieving verifiability and key delegation. In: Fehr, S. (ed.) PKC 2017, Part II. LNCS, vol. 10175, pp. 463–493. Springer, Heidelberg (2017). https://doi.org/10.1007/978-3-662-54388-7_16
22. Davidson, A., Katsumata, S., Nishimaki, R., Yamada, S.: Constrained PRFs for bit-fixing from OWFs with constant collusion resistance, IACR Cryptology ePrint Archive 2018/982 (2018)
23. Deshpande, A., Koppula, V., Waters, B.: Constrained pseudorandom functions for unconstrained inputs. In: Fischlin, M., Coron, J.-S. (eds.) EUROCRYPT 2016, Part II. LNCS, vol. 9666, pp. 124–153. Springer, Heidelberg (2016). https://doi.org/10.1007/978-3-662-49896-5_5
24. Freeman, D.M.: Converting pairing-based cryptosystems from composite-order groups to prime-order groups. In: Gilbert, H. (ed.) EUROCRYPT 2010. LNCS, vol. 6110, pp. 44–61. Springer, Heidelberg (2010). https://doi.org/10.1007/978-3-642-13190-5_3
25. Freire, E.S.V., Hofheinz, D., Paterson, K.G., Striecks, C.: Programmable hash functions in the multilinear setting. In: Canetti, R., Garay, J.A. (eds.) CRYPTO 2013, Part I. LNCS, vol. 8042, pp. 513–530. Springer, Heidelberg (2013). https://doi.org/10.1007/978-3-642-40041-4_28
26. Fuchsbauer, G., Konstantinov, M., Pietrzak, K., Rao, V.: Adaptive security of constrained PRFs. In: Sarkar, P., Iwata, T. (eds.) ASIACRYPT 2014, Part II. LNCS, vol. 8874, pp. 82–101. Springer, Heidelberg (2014). https://doi.org/10.1007/978-3-662-45608-8_5
27. Garg, S., Gentry, C., Halevi, S., Raykova, M., Sahai, A., Waters, B.: Candidate indistinguishability obfuscation and functional encryptionfor all circuits. SIAM J. Comput. **45**(3), 882–929 (2016)
28. Goldreich, O.: Computational Complexity - A Conceptual Perspective. Cambridge University Press, Cambridge (2008)
29. Goldreich, O., Goldwasser, S., Micali, S.: How to construct random functions. J. ACM **33**(4), 792–807 (1986)
30. Goyal, R., Hohenberger, S., Koppula, V., Waters, B.: A generic approach to constructing and proving verifiable random functions. In: Kalai, Y., Reyzin, L. (eds.) TCC 2017, Part II. LNCS, vol. 10678, pp. 537–566. Springer, Cham (2017). https://doi.org/10.1007/978-3-319-70503-3_18
31. Herold, G., Hesse, J., Hofheinz, D., Ràfols, C., Rupp, A.: Polynomial spaces: a new framework for composite-to-prime-order transformations. In: Garay, J.A., Gennaro, R. (eds.) CRYPTO 2014, Part I. LNCS, vol. 8616, pp. 261–279. Springer, Heidelberg (2014). https://doi.org/10.1007/978-3-662-44371-2_15
32. Hofheinz, D., Kamath, A., Koppula, V., Waters, B.: Adaptively secure constrained pseudorandom functions. In: FC 2019 (2019, to appear)
33. Hohenberger, S., Koppula, V., Waters, B.: Adaptively secure puncturable pseudorandom functions in the standard model. Cryptology ePrint Archive, Report 2014/521 (2014)
34. Hohenberger, S., Koppula, V., Waters, B.: Adaptively secure puncturable pseudorandom functions in the standard model. In: Iwata, T., Cheon, J.H. (eds.) ASIACRYPT 2015, Part I. LNCS, vol. 9452, pp. 79–102. Springer, Heidelberg (2015). https://doi.org/10.1007/978-3-662-48797-6_4

35. Jager, T.: Verifiable random functions from weaker assumptions. In: Dodis, Y., Nielsen, J.B. (eds.) TCC 2015, Part II. LNCS, vol. 9015, pp. 121–143. Springer, Heidelberg (2015). https://doi.org/10.1007/978-3-662-46497-7_5
36. Kiayias, A., Papadopoulos, S., Triandopoulos, N., Zacharias, T.: Delegatable pseudorandom functions and applications. In: ACM CCS 2013, pp. 669–684 (2013)
37. Lewko, A.: Tools for simulating features of composite order bilinear groups in the prime order setting. In: Pointcheval, D., Johansson, T. (eds.) EUROCRYPT 2012. LNCS, vol. 7237, pp. 318–335. Springer, Heidelberg (2012). https://doi.org/10.1007/978-3-642-29011-4_20
38. Lysyanskaya, A.: Unique signatures and verifiable random functions from the DH-DDH separation. In: Yung, M. (ed.) CRYPTO 2002. LNCS, vol. 2442, pp. 597–612. Springer, Heidelberg (2002). https://doi.org/10.1007/3-540-45708-9_38
39. Naor, M., Reingold, O.: Number-theoretic constructions of efficient pseudo-random functions. J. ACM **51**(2), 231–262 (2004)
40. Peikert, C., Shiehian, S.: Privately constraining and programming PRFs, the LWE way. In: Abdalla, M., Dahab, R. (eds.) PKC 2018, Part II. LNCS, vol. 10770, pp. 675–701. Springer, Cham (2018). https://doi.org/10.1007/978-3-319-76581-5_23
41. Sahai, A., Waters, B.: How to use indistinguishability obfuscation: deniable encryption, and more. In: 46th ACM STOC, pp. 475–484 (2014)
42. Seo, J.H., Cheon, J.H.: Beyond the limitation of prime-order bilinear groups, and round optimal blind signatures. In: Cramer, R. (ed.) TCC 2012. LNCS, vol. 7194, pp. 133–150. Springer, Heidelberg (2012). https://doi.org/10.1007/978-3-642-28914-9_8
43. Sipser, M., Spielman, D.A.: Expander codes. IEEE Trans. Inf. Theor. **42**(6), 1710–1722 (1996)
44. Waters, B.: Efficient identity-based encryption without random oracles. In: Cramer, R. (ed.) EUROCRYPT 2005. LNCS, vol. 3494, pp. 114–127. Springer, Heidelberg (2005). https://doi.org/10.1007/11426639_7
45. Yamada, S.: Asymptotically compact adaptively secure lattice IBEs and verifiable random functions via generalized partitioning techniques. In: Katz, J., Shacham, H. (eds.) CRYPTO 2017, Part III. LNCS, vol. 10403, pp. 161–193. Springer, Cham (2017). https://doi.org/10.1007/978-3-319-63697-9_6
46. Zémor, G.: On expander codes. IEEE Trans. Inf. Theor. **47**(2), 835–837 (2001)

Obfuscating Simple Functionalities from Knowledge Assumptions

Ward Beullens[1](✉) and Hoeteck Wee[2]

[1] imec-COSIC, KU Leuven, Leuven, Belgium
ward.beullens@esat.kuleuven.be
[2] CNRS, ENS and PSL, Paris, France
wee@di.ens.fr

Abstract. This paper shows how to obfuscate several simple functionalities from a new Knowledge of OrthogonALity Assumption (KOALA) in cyclic groups which is shown to hold in the Generic Group Model. Specifically, we give simpler and stronger security proofs for obfuscation schemes for point functions, general-output point functions and pattern matching with wildcards. We also revisit the work of Bishop et al. (CRYPTO 2018) on obfuscating the pattern matching with wildcards functionality. We improve upon the construction and the analysis in several ways:

- attacks and stronger guarantees: We show that the construction achieves virtual black-box security for a simulator that runs in time roughly $2^{n/2}$, as well as distributional security for larger classes of distributions. We give attacks that show that our results are tight.
- weaker assumptions: We prove security under KOALA.
- better efficiency: We also provide a construction that outputs $n+1$ instead of $2n$ group elements.

We obtain our results by first obfuscating a simpler "big subset functionality", for which we establish full virtual black-box security; this yields a simpler and more modular analysis for pattern matching. Finally, we extend our distinguishing attacks to a large class of simple linear-in-the-exponent schemes.

1 Introduction

Program obfuscation is a powerful cryptographic primitive where an *obfuscator* $\mathcal{O}$ takes the description of a program as input and outputs an obfuscated program that has the same input-output behavior as the original program while hiding how the program works internally. The first theoretic investigation of obfuscation was made in the work of Barak et al. [1,14] that defined the Virtual Black Box (VBB) security definition, and showed that this strong definition can not be satisfied for general circuits. This has sparked a line of research, starting from [12], into trying to realize the weaker notion of indistinguishability obfuscation for general circuits. There have been many candidate IO for circuits, but they all rely on non-standard and poorly understood assumptions

D. Lin and K. Sako (Eds.): PKC 2019, LNCS 11443, pp. 254–283, 2019.
https://doi.org/10.1007/978-3-030-17259-6_9

Security	General Output	self-composable	Assumption	Reference
VBB	✗	✗	Nonstandard DDH	[7]
VBB	✓	✓	ROM	[15]
VBB	✓	✗	Strong OWP	[16]
VBB	✓	✓	Perfect OWF	[8]
VGB	✓	✓	Nonstandard DDH	[4]
VBB	✓	✓	KOALA	This work

Fig. 1. Security for obfuscation of point functions.

several of which have been broken. In contrast, there is a different line of work to achieve the full VBB obfuscation for more restricted functionalities. Work in this direction has shown that one can VBB obfuscate simple functionalities such as point functions [4,7,8,15,16] and hyperplane membership testing [9]. Obfuscating the pattern matching with wildcards functionality (also called conjunctions) was shown to be possible from LWE and variants [5,6,13,17]. A pattern is specified by a string ρ in $\{0,1,\star\}^n$ and matches an input $\mathbf{x} \in \{0,1\}^n$ if $\rho_i = x_i$ or $\rho_i = \star$ for all $i \in [n]$. Recently at CRYPTO 2018 Bishop et al. presented a simple and efficient method for obfuscating pattern matching with wildcards [3] where the obfuscated pattern compromises of $2n$ elements in a cyclic group, and showed that the construction achieves distributional VBB (DVBB) security for the uniform distribution over patterns containing a fixed number of wildcards up to $0.75n$.

1.1 Our Results

We introduce a knowledge assumption that is weaker than the generic group model. The knowledge assumption is a natural decisional analogue of Damgard's KEA assumption [10], and asserts that given any adversary that distinguishes $g^{\mathbf{Mr}}$ for any $\mathbf{M}$ and a random $\mathbf{r}$ from the uniform distribution, there exists another adversary (sometimes referred to as an "extractor") that outputs a non-trivial vector $\mathbf{z}$ such that $\mathbf{zM} = \mathbf{0}$. We refer to this as the Knowledge of OrthogonALity Assumption (KOALA). The assumption can also be viewed as a natural decisional analogue of the recent algebraic group model [11], which essentially asserts that the only way an adversary can *compute* a new group element is to take a linear combination of previous ones.

To showcase the power of KOALA we give a simple proof for the VBB security of the point function obfuscator of [7]. Moreover, we also give the first proof of the self composability of this obfuscator and we extend the construction to VBB obfuscation of point functions with general output. Prior work on obfuscating point functions is summarized in Fig. 1.

We improve on the work of Bishop et al. in a number of directions. First we explain that it is possible to, given an obfuscation of a pattern ρ, learn if the first half of ρ consists of wildcards. Since it is not possible to learn this efficiently through black box access only, this attack shows that the construction is not VBB

Class of Patterns	Distribution	Security	Assumption	Reference
$\{0,1,\star\}^n$, exactly w $\star$'s	uniform, $w \leq 0.75n$	DVBB	generic group	[3]
	uniform, $w \leq n - \omega(\log n)$	DVBB	generic group	[2]
	uniform, $w \leq n - \omega(\log n)$	DVBB	KOALA	Thm. 10
$\{0,1,\star\}^n$	–	$2^{0.5n}$-VBB	KOALA	Thm. 8
	–	**not** $2^{0.499n}$-VBB	–	Thm. 6
	min-entropy $\geq n + \omega(\log n)$	DVBB	KOALA	Thm. 9
	min-entropy $\leq n - \omega(\log n)$	**not** DVBB	–	Lem. 4

Fig. 2. Security for obfuscation of pattern matching with wildcards in cyclic groups [3]. Note that the KOALA knowledge assumption holds in the generic group model. The (independent) work of [2] also proved DVBB results for the class of patterns with exactly w $\star$'s in the high min-entropy setting.

secure. Moreover, the attack shows that there are high entropy distributions for which the scheme is not DVBB secure. On the other hand we prove stronger security claims by proving the scheme to be VBB secure with simulators that run in time roughly $2^{n/2}$. We also give optimal min-entropy bounds such that any distribution that has this amount of min-entropy is automatically DVBB secure. More precisely, we prove that any distribution over $\{0,1,\star\}^n$ with $n + \omega(\log n)$ bits of min-entropy is distributional VBB secure. We give a similar result for distributions with a fixed number of wildcards. Previous works only showed DVBB security for certain specific distributions, namely uniform distributions with a fixed number of wildcards $\leq 3n/4$. These distributions have min-entropy at least $1.06n$ for sufficiently large n and therefore DVBB security for these distributions follows as a special case of our DVBB result for high min-entropy distributions. Another advantage of our security proofs is that they only rely on the KOALA, rather than on the full generic group model (Fig. 2).

In our security proof we show that the construction of Bishop et al. is essentially built around an obfuscator for a new *Big Subset*-functionality that could be of independent interest. For input size n, the functions of this functionality are parametrized by a subset $Y \subset [n]$ and a threshold value $0 \leq t \leq n$. The function $f_{Y,n,t} : \mathcal{P}([n]) \to \{0,1\}$ takes a subset $X \subset [n]$ as input and outputs 1 if and only if X is a big enough subset of Y (i.e. $|X| \geq t$). The key result is that the big subset functionality can be obfuscated with VBB security assuming KOALA. The security guarantees for the pattern matching functionality follow from this result by embedding the pattern matching functionality into the big subset functionality.

The scheme of [3] uses only linear operations which are hidden in the exponent of a cryptographic group. We formulate the framework for linear-in-the-exponent obfuscation schemes in the hope of finding more efficient and more secure constructions. On the positive side we find a more efficient construction whose obfuscated programs are represented by $n+1$ group elements rather than $2n$ group elements while having at least the same security as the construction of [3]. On the negative side we prove that our distinguishing attack extends to a wide family of "natural" linear-in-the-exponent obfuscation schemes.

1.2 Technical Overview

We provide a brief overview of our obfuscation construction for the "big subset functionality", which is implicit in [3], and then explain how this relates to obfuscating pattern matching with wildcards.

Obfuscating "big subset". The functionality $f_{Y,n,t}$ is parametrized by (Y, n, t) where $Y \subseteq [n], t \leq n$, and given an input $X \subseteq [n]$,

$$f_{Y,n,t}(X) = 1 \Leftrightarrow |X| \geq t \text{ and } X \subseteq Y\,.$$

The obfuscation of $f_{Y,n,t}$ comprises n group elements $[v_1]_g, \ldots, [v_n]_g$ (we use $[\cdot]_g$ to denote group exponentiation) where

- $\{v_i : i \in Y\}$ are random Shamir shares of 0, that is, the evaluations of a random degree $t-1$ polynomial whose constant term is 0, and
- the remaining v_i's, $i \notin Y$ are chosen uniformly at random.

To evaluate the obfuscated program on input X, we simply return 1 if and only if reconstruction "in the exponent" over the shares corresponding to X returns $[0]_g$.

To prove VBB security, we adopt a "random or learn" strategy similar to that in [7,9,16]. Given an adversary $\mathcal{A}$, we try to simulate its view by feeding it n random group elements. Suppose this simulation fails, which means $\mathcal{A}$ distinguishes an obfuscation of $f_{Y,n,t}$ from uniformly random group elements. Then, by our KOALA assumption, then we can "extract" from $\mathcal{A}$ a vector $\mathbf{z}$ from which we can efficiently compute an X such that $f_{Y,n,t}(X) = 1$. In fact, X simply corresponds to the indices of $\mathbf{z}$ that are non-zero; $X \subseteq Y$ follows from the fact that v_i's outside Y are uniformly random, and $|X| \geq t$ follows from the secrecy of Shamir's secret-sharing scheme. Finally, we show that given oracle access to $f_{Y,n,t}$ and an X such that $f_{Y,n,t}(X) = 1$, we can efficiently recover Y, t, upon which we can simulate the view of the adversary perfectly.

We mention here that the actual simulation is a bit more complex, since the KOALA assumption only guarantees extraction with inverse polynomial probability. Therefore, we will need to "extract" multiple $\mathbf{z}$'s and run the above simulation of each of these $\mathbf{z}$; the number of samples we need and thus the running time of the simulator is inverse polynomial in the simulation accuracy. We also note that the same approach also yields a much easier proof for the VBB security of Canetti's point function obfuscator (which outputs just two group elements). Moreover, we can also give a proof for the self-composability of Canetti's obfuscator.

Obfuscating pattern matching with wildcards. To go from obfuscating the "big subset functionality" to obfuscating pattern-matching with wildcards, we observe that there is a simple embedding of $\{0, 1, \star\}^n$ into $(\mathcal{P}([2n]), 2n, n)$ where we replace the i'th symbol with either $2i-1, 2i$ or both. Indeed, this was the approach (implicitly) taken in [3]. Unfortunately, this embedding also allows an adversary to check whether any subset of $n/2$ positions of a pattern correspond to wildcards, which is the basis for our distinguishing attack. As mentioned earlier in the introduction, we show that

- this construction achieves VBB security with roughly $2^{n/2}$-time simulation. This essentially follows from the fact that we can simulate any query to big subset oracle with $2^{n/2}$ queries to the pattern matching oracle.
- this construction achieves D-VBB security for any distribution over $\{0,1,\star\}^n$ with min-entropy at least $n + \omega(\log n)$. This essentially follows from the fact that any distribution over $(\mathcal{P}([2n]), 2n, n)$ for big subset with min-entropy $n+\omega(\log n)$ is evasive. The latter in turn follows from the fact that any $X \subseteq [2n]$ of size n is an accepting input for at most 2^n patterns in $(\mathcal{P}([2n]), 2n, n)$.
- the construction is not D-VBB secure for some distribution over $\{0,1,\star\}^n$ with min-entropy $n - \omega(\log n)$. In particular, take any $a = \omega(\log n)$ and consider the distribution where the first a positions is uniform over $\{0,1\}^a$, the next a positions are $\star$'s, and the last $n - 2a$ positions are uniform over $\{0,\star\}^{n-2a}$. This distribution is evasive, and yet we can distinguish obfuscation of this distribution from that of the uniform distribution over $\{0,1,\star\}^n$.

Prior analysis only considers restricted distributions, namely the uniform distribution over patterns with a fixed number of wildcards; we note that our techniques are fairly general and also provide matching results for these restricted distributions.

In the last section of the paper, we explore the possibility of achieving VBB obfuscation for pattern matching with wildcards via some "natural" generalization of the above constructions. Our results here are mostly negative. Along the way, we also present a compression technique that allows us to reduce the output of the obfuscator from $2n$ to $n+1$ group elements.

Open problems. We conclude with a number of open problems on efficient obfuscation using cyclic groups:

- Construct simple obfuscation schemes for simple functionalities beyond "big subset".
- Prove or disprove: for every $\delta > 0$, there exists an efficient obfuscation scheme for pattern matching with wildcards that is D-VBB for any distribution over $\{0,1,\star\}$ with min-entropy δn (alternatively, VBB secure with $2^{\delta n}$-time simulation).

Roadmap. The rest of the paper consists of the following: In Sect. 2 we state the definitions of VBB, T-VBB and DVBB secure obfuscation schemes. We also prove that T-VBB security implies DVBB security for T-elusive distributions. In Sect. 3 we describe the construction of [3] for obfuscating pattern matching with wildcards. In Sect. 4 we introduce the KOALA knowledge assumption and we prove that it holds in the generic group model. We also showcase the power of the KOALA by giving a simple proof of the VBB security of the point function obfuscator of Canetti [7], and giving the first proof of its self composability. In Sect. 5 we introduce the big subset functionality, we show that it can be obfuscated with VBB security and we prove that certain distributions of big subset functions are elusive. In Sect. 6 we give our security analysis including a family of attacks and new security proofs. In Sect. 7 we describe and study linear-in-the-exponent obfuscation schemes for pattern matching with wildcards. We find more efficient schemes, but we prove that there are no VBB secure obfuscators in a broad class of constructions that follow this paradigm.

Independent work. We clarify here that an independent work of Bartusek, et al. [2] achieved a subset of our results (in addition to other results not in this work): the overlap are the construction with $n+1$ group elements, as well as distributional VBB for the uniform distribution over patterns with exactly w wildcards for any $w = \omega(\log n)$ in the generic group model.

2 Preliminaries

Notation. Throughout the paper we use $[n]$ to denote the set $\{1, \cdots, n\}$. We write vectors in boldface (e.g. $\mathbf{x}$) and their entries in plain text (e.g. x_1). We also use the implicit representation of group elements: If G is a cyclic group of order p with generator g, then for $a \in \mathbb{Z}_p$ we use $[a]_g$ to denote the group element g^a. If $\mathbf{v} \in \mathbb{Z}_p^n$ is a vector mod p, then $[\mathbf{v}]_g$ denotes the tuple of n group elements $\{g^{v_i}\}_{i \in [n]}$.

2.1 Security Definitions

In this section we define Virtual Black Box [1] (VBB) and Distributional Virtual Black Box [5] (DVBB) security. We also introduce T-VBB security, which is a variant of VBB security where the simulator is allowed to run in super-polynomial time $O(T)$. We prove that T-VBB security implies distributional VBB security for distributions that are T-evasive (even with simulators that make no black box queries).

Let $\mathcal{F} = \{\mathcal{F}_n\}_{n \in \mathbb{N}}$ be a sequence of function families where $\mathcal{F}_n$ is a set of functions that takes n bits as input. A PPT algorithm $\mathcal{O}$ is said to be an *Obfuscator* for $\mathcal{F}$ if it takes an input length n (in unary representation) and a function $f \in \mathcal{F}_n$ as input, and outputs an obfuscated program $\mathcal{O}(1^n, f)$ that:

1. preserves functionality: For any n, $f \in \mathcal{F}_n$ and $\mathbf{x} \in \{0,1\}^n$ we have that $\mathcal{O}(1^n, f)(\mathbf{x}) = f(\mathbf{x})$ with a probability that is overwhelming as a parameter of n.
2. has only polynomial slowdown: For any n and $f \in \mathcal{F}_n$ the obfuscated program $\mathcal{O}(1^n, f)$ runs in time that is *poly*$(n, T(f))$, where $T(f)$ is the run time of f.

To ease notation, we don't explicitly write the input length n as an input to the obfuscator $\mathcal{O}$ in the rest of the paper.

Virtual Black Box Security (VBB). If an obfuscator reveals no more information about the function $f \in \mathcal{F}_n$ than what can by learned from black box access the obfuscator is said to be Virtual Black Box (VBB) secure. More formally, we have the following definition.

Definition 1 (VBB Security). *An obfuscator $\mathcal{O}$ for the functionality $\{\mathcal{F}_n\}_{n\in\mathbb{N}}$ is said to be VBB secure if for any PPT Adversary $\mathcal{A}$ and polynomial $p(n)$, there exists a PPT simulator $\mathcal{S}$ that has black box access to a function in $\mathcal{F}$ and an n_0 such that for any $n \geq n_0$ and any $f \in \mathcal{F}_n$*

$$\left| \Pr_{\mathcal{O},\mathcal{A}}[\mathcal{A}(\mathcal{O}(f)) = 1] - \Pr_{\mathcal{S}}[\mathcal{S}^f(1^n) = 1] \right| \leq \frac{1}{p(n)}.$$

Remark 1. In our definition (and in our definition of T-VBB security below), the simulator $\mathcal{S}$ is allowed to depend on the required simulator accuracy $p(n)$. This is slightly weaker than the original definition of [1].

One can relax the condition that $\mathcal{S}$ runs in polynomial time to obtain a weaker security notion. An obfuscator satisfying this relaxed security notion reveals nothing about the function it obfuscated beyond what can be learned with *a lot* of black box queries.

Definition 2 (T-VBB Security). *An obfuscator $\mathcal{O}$ for the functionality $\mathcal{F}$ is said to be T-VBB secure if for any PPT Adversary $\mathcal{A}$ and any polynomial $p(n)$, there exists a simulator $\mathcal{S}$ that has black box access to a function in $\mathcal{F}$ that runs in time $O(T * \mathrm{poly}(n))$ and an n_0 such that for any $n \geq n_0$ and $f \in \mathcal{F}_n$*

$$\left| \Pr_{\mathcal{O},\mathcal{A}}[\mathcal{A}(\mathcal{O}(f)) = 1] - \Pr_{\mathcal{S}}[\mathcal{S}^f(1^n) = 1] \right| \leq \frac{1}{p(n)}.$$

Distributional Virtual Black Box security ($\mathcal{D}$- DVBB). A weaker notion of Obfuscator security is that of Distributional VBB security (also called Average-Case VBB). In the distributional setting, there is a sequence of distributions $\mathcal{D} = \{\mathcal{D}_n\}_{n\in\mathbb{N}}$ that the function f to be obfuscated is drawn from. If an obfuscator $\mathcal{O}$ reveals nothing about functions randomly drawn from $\mathcal{D}$ beyond what can be learned from black box access, the obfuscator $\mathcal{O}$ is said to be $\mathcal{D}$-DVBB secure. This is captured by the following definition:

Definition 3 ($\mathcal{D}$-DVBB Security). *Let $\mathcal{D} = \{\mathcal{D}_n\}_{n\in\mathbb{N}}$ be a sequence of distributions on $\mathcal{F}$, and $\mathcal{O}$ an obfuscator for the $\mathcal{F}$ functionality. Then $\mathcal{O}$ is said to be $\mathcal{D}$-DVBB secure if for any adversary $\mathcal{A}$ and any sequence of predicates $P = \{P_n : \mathcal{F}_n \to \{0,1\}\}$ there exists a PPT Simulator $\mathcal{S}$ such that*

$$\left| \Pr_{f\leftarrow\mathcal{D}_n,\mathcal{O},\mathcal{A}}[\mathcal{A}(\mathcal{O}(f)) = P_n(f)] - \Pr_{f\leftarrow\mathcal{D}_n,\mathcal{S}}[\mathcal{S}^f(1^n) = P_n(f)] \right| = \mathrm{negl}(n).$$

The fact that VBB security implies distributional VBB security for any arbitrary distribution is trivial. However, we prove that VBB security also implies DVBB security with simulators that don't make black-box queries for distributions that are evasive. It is also the case that T-VBB implies DVBB with simulators that make no black-box queries for distributions which are T-evasive.

Definition 4 (evasive, T-evasive). *A sequence $\{\mathcal{D}_n\}_{n\in\mathbb{N}}$ of distributions on $\{\mathcal{F}_n\}_{n\in\mathbb{N}}$ is evasive if there is a negligible function $\mu(n)$ such that for all $\mathbf{x} \in \{0,1\}^n$ we have*

$$\Pr_{f\leftarrow\mathcal{D}_n}[f(\mathbf{x}) \neq 0] < \mu(n).$$

A the sequence of distributions is said to be T-evasive if there is a negligible function $\mu(n)$ such that for all $\mathbf{x} \in \{0,1\}^n$ we have

$$\Pr_{f\leftarrow\mathcal{D}_n}[f(\mathbf{x}) \neq 0] < \frac{\mu(n)}{T(n)}.$$

Lemma 1 (VBB implies DVBB without black-box queries for evasive distributions). *Suppose $\mathcal{O}$ is a VBB secure (resp. T-VBB secure) obfuscator for the functionality $\{\mathcal{F}_n\}_{n\in\mathbb{N}}$ and let $\mathcal{D} = \{\mathcal{D}_n\}_{n\in\mathbb{N}}$ be an evasive (resp. T-evasive) sequence of distributions that can be sampled from efficiently, then $\mathcal{O}$ is $\mathcal{D}$-DVBB secure with a simulator that does not make any black box queries.*

Proof. Let $\mathcal{O}, \{\mathcal{F}_n\}_{n\in\mathbb{N}}$ and $\{\mathcal{D}_n\}_{n\in\mathbb{N}}$ be as in the statement of the theorem. Let $\mathcal{A}$ be an adversary and P a predicate on $\mathcal{F}$. We define a simulator $\mathcal{S}$ that draws a function f from $\mathcal{D}_n$ and outputs $\mathcal{A}(\mathcal{O}(f))$. It is clear that this simulator makes no black box queries to f. We now prove that $\mathcal{S}$ has negligible simulation error.

Fix any polynomial $p(n)$ and let $\mathcal{S}_{\text{VBB}}$ be a simulator that runs in polynomial time (resp. $O(T * poly(n))$) with a simulation error that is eventually less than $\frac{1}{3p(n)}$. This is guaranteed to exist because of the VBB (resp T-VBB) property of $\mathcal{O}$. Then we have for large enough n that

$$\left|\Pr_{f\leftarrow\mathcal{D}_n}[\mathcal{A}(\mathcal{O}(f)) = P(f)] - \Pr_{f\leftarrow\mathcal{D}_n}[\mathcal{S}^f_{\text{VBB}}(1^n) = P(f)]\right| \leq \tag{1}$$
$$\sum_{f\in\mathcal{F}_n} \Pr[D_n = f]\left|\Pr[\mathcal{A}(\mathcal{O}(f)) = 1] - \Pr[\mathcal{S}^f_{\text{VBB}}(1^n) = 1]\right| \leq \frac{1}{3p(n)}.$$

Since $\mathcal{S}_{\text{VBB}}$ makes at most polynomially many (resp. $O(T * poly(n))$) queries to f and since the sequence $\mathcal{D}$ is evasive (resp. T-evasive) we have

$$\left|\Pr_{f\leftarrow\mathcal{D}_n}[\mathcal{S}^f_{\text{VBB}}(1^n) = P(f)] - \Pr_{f\leftarrow\mathcal{D}_n}[\mathcal{S}^0_{\text{VBB}}(1^n) = P(f)]\right| \leq negl(n), \tag{2}$$

and similarly we have

$$\left|\Pr_{f\leftarrow\mathcal{D}_n}[\mathcal{S}^0_{\text{VBB}}(1^n) = P(f)] - \Pr_{f_1,f_2\leftarrow\mathcal{D}_n}[\mathcal{S}^{f_1}_{\text{VBB}}(1^n) = P(f_2)]\right| \leq negl(n). \tag{3}$$

Finally, similar to Eq. 1 we have for large enough n that

$$\left|\Pr_{f_1,f_2\leftarrow\mathcal{D}_n}[\mathcal{S}^{f_1}_{\text{VBB}}(1^n) = P(f_2)] - \Pr_{f_1,f_2\leftarrow\mathcal{D}_n}[\mathcal{A}(\mathcal{O}(f_1)) = P(f_2)]\right| \leq \tag{4}$$
$$\sum_{f_1\in\mathcal{F}_n} \Pr[\mathcal{D}_n = f_1]\left|\Pr[\mathcal{S}^{f_1}_{\text{VBB}}(1^n) = 1] - \Pr[\mathcal{A}(\mathcal{O}(f_1)) = 1]\right| \leq \frac{1}{3p(n)}.$$

Putting these four inequalities together we have for large enough n that

$$\left| \Pr_{f \leftarrow \mathcal{D}_n}[\mathcal{A}(\mathcal{O}(f)) = P(f)] - \Pr_{f_1, f_2 \leftarrow \mathcal{D}_n}[\mathcal{A}(\mathcal{O}(f_1)) = P(f_2)] \right| \le \frac{2}{3p(n)} + negl(n),$$

which shows that the simulator error is eventually lower than $\frac{1}{p(n)}$ for any $p(n)$. □

3 Obfuscation for Pattern Matching with Wildcards

The class of functions for the pattern matching with wildcards functionality it parametrized by length n strings over the alphabet $\{0, 1, \star\}$. For a pattern $\rho = (\rho_i)_{i \in [n]}$ in $\{0, 1, \star\}^n$ we define the pattern matching function f_ρ that takes a binary string $\mathbf{x} = (x_i)_{i \in [n]}$ as input, and outputs whether the string matches the pattern ρ. More precisely we have

$$f_\rho(\mathbf{x}) = \begin{cases} 1 & \text{if for all } i \text{ either } \rho_i = x_i \text{ or } \rho_i = \star \\ 0 & \text{otherwise} \end{cases}$$

A simple and efficient construction. The work of Bishop et al. [3] gives a simple obfuscation scheme for the pattern matching with wildcards functionality. The obfuscation of a pattern ρ consists of $2n$ elements $\{v_{i,j}\}_{(i,j) \in [n] \times 1,2}$ of a cyclic group G of prime order p with generator g. This obfuscation is produced by picking a random degree $n-1$ polynomial $h(x) = a_1 x + \cdots + a_{n-1} x^{n-1}$ with $h(0) = 0$ and defining

$$v_{i,j} = \begin{cases} h(2i - j) & \text{if } \rho_i = \star \text{ or } \rho_i = j \\ r_{i,j} & \text{otherwise} \end{cases},$$

where the $r_{i,j}$ are chosen uniformly at random. The obfuscation $\mathcal{O}(\rho)$ then consists of the $2n$ group elements $[\{v_{i,j}\}_{(i,j) \in [n] \times \{0,1\}}]_g$.

To evaluate the obfuscated program on input $\mathbf{x}$, the evaluator computes the polynomial interpolation coefficients

$$C_a = \prod_{\substack{b \in [n], \\ b \neq a}} \frac{-2b - x_b}{2a + x_a - 2b - x_b},$$

and computes $h_0 = [\sum_{i \in [n]} C_i v_{i,x_i}]_g$. If the pattern ρ accepts $\mathbf{x}$ then all the v_{i,x_i} are of the form $[h(2i - j)]_g$ and the polynomial interpolation will work in the exponent such that $h_0 = [h(0)]_g = [0]_g$. If $h_0 = [0]_g$ the obfuscated program accepts the input $\mathbf{x}$ and otherwise it rejects. If the pattern ρ does not accept $\mathbf{x}$ at least one uniformly random group element enters into h, so that the obfuscated program will only accept a bad input with probability $1 - \frac{1}{p}$.

Prior analysis in [3]. The construction of [3] is proven to be Distributional VBB secure (Definition 3) in the generic group model for uniform distributions of patterns with a fixed number up to $\frac{3n}{4}$ wildcards. More strongly, it is proven that the result of obfuscating a uniformly random pattern in $\{0,1,\star\}^n$ with a fixed number up to $\frac{3n}{4}$ wildcards is indistinguishable from $2n$ uniformly chosen group elements.

4 A New Knowledge Assumption: KOALA

We introduce a new assumption, the Knowledge of OrthogonALity Assumption (KOALA), that is valid in the generic group model and based on which we will prove the security of the Obfuscation scheme. The assumption says that an adversary can only distinguish $[\mathbf{v}]_g$ for vectors $\mathbf{v}$ drawn uniformly at random from a subspace $V \subset \mathbb{Z}_p^n$ from $[\mathbf{u}]_g$ for uniformly random vectors $\mathbf{u} \in \mathbb{Z}_p^n$ if it can also produce a non-zero vector orthogonal to V in the clear.

Definition 5 (KOALA). *A sequence of cyclic groups $\{G_n\}_{n \in \mathbb{N}}$ of order $p_n \in [2^n, 2^{n+1})$ satisfies the knowledge of orthogonality assumption if for every PPT adversary $\mathcal{A}$, there exists a polynomial $s(n)$ and a PPT algorithm $\mathcal{A}'$ that outputs nonzero vectors such that for every subspace $V \subset \mathbb{Z}_p^n$, if $\mathcal{A}$ distinguishes uniform samples of $[V]_g$ from random with advantage*

$$\mathsf{Adv}_{\mathcal{A},V} = \left| \Pr_{\mathbf{v} \leftarrow V}[\mathcal{A}([\mathbf{v}]_g) = 1] - \Pr_{\mathbf{u} \leftarrow \mathbb{Z}_p^n}[\mathcal{A}([\mathbf{u}]_g) = 1] \right|,$$

then $\mathcal{A}'(1^n)$ is orthogonal to V with probability

$$\Pr[\mathcal{A}'(1^n) \in V^\perp \setminus \{\mathbf{0}\}] \geq \frac{\mathsf{Adv}_{\mathcal{A},V}}{s(n)}.$$

4.1 KOALA Is Weaker Than Generic Group Model

Although KOALA is quite a strong assumption, it is weaker than the generic group model:

Theorem 1 (Generic groups satisfy KOALA). *A sequence of cyclic groups $\{G_{p_n}\}_{n \in \mathbb{N}}$ of order $p_n \in [2^n, 2^{n+1})$ satisfies KOALA in the generic group model.*

Proof. Given an adversary $\mathcal{A}$, we construct an extractor $\mathcal{E}^{\mathcal{A}}$ that satisfies the condition of Definition 5. The extractor runs $\mathcal{A}$ on a list of n generic group elements $\mathbf{e} = \{e_i\}_{i \in [n]}$, then by looking at how $\mathcal{A}$ interacts with the group oracle $\mathcal{E}$ records all the vectors $\mathbf{v}$ for which $\mathcal{A}$ has computed $\mathbf{v} \cdot \mathbf{e}$. When $\mathcal{A}$ terminates, $\mathcal{E}$ chooses two distinct vectors that it has collected and outputs their difference.

More formally the extractor $\mathcal{E}^{\mathcal{A}}$ works as follows: $\mathcal{E}^{\mathcal{A}}$ simulates a group oracle $\mathcal{G}_2$ that gives randomly encoded access to the group $\mathbb{Z}_p^n$. He does this by maintaining a table $\{(\mathbf{q}_i, h_i)\}_{i \in I} \subset \mathbb{Z}_p^n \times \{0,1\}^n$ mapping vectors of $\mathbb{Z}_p^n$ to random handles that he updates on the fly when new vectors are discovered. Initially he populates the table with random handles for the n unit vectors e_i for $i \in [n]$. Then it runs $\mathcal{A}^{\mathcal{G}_2}$ with the handles of the n unit vectors as input. When $\mathcal{A}$ terminates the extractor picks two distinct vectors $\mathbf{q}_i, \mathbf{q}_j$ from the group oracle table and outputs $\mathbf{q}_i - \mathbf{q}_j$.

We now fix a subspace $V \subset \mathbb{Z}_p^n$ with basis $\{\mathbf{v}_1, \cdots, \mathbf{v}_k\}$ and we show that if $\mathcal{A}$ makes Q queries to the group oracle and distinguishes $[V]_g$ from $[\mathbb{Z}_p^n]_g$ with probability

$$\mathsf{Adv}_{\mathcal{A},V} = \left| \Pr_{\mathbf{v} \leftarrow V}[\mathcal{A}([\mathbf{v}]_g) = 1] - \Pr_{\mathbf{u} \leftarrow \mathbb{Z}_p^n}[\mathcal{A}([\mathbf{u}]_g) = 1] \right|,$$

then the extractor will output a nonzero vector orthogonal to V with probability

$$\Pr[\mathcal{A}'(1^n) \in V^{\perp} \setminus \{\mathbf{0}\}] \geq \frac{\mathsf{Adv}_{\mathcal{A},V}}{(Q+2n)^2} - \frac{2}{p},$$

so the extractor satisfies the requirement in Definition 5. We show this through a sequence of four games.

1. In the first game $\mathcal{A}$ is given access to the group oracle $\mathcal{G}_1$ for G_p, and it is given the encoding of $[\mathbf{u}]_g$, for $\mathbf{u}$ a random vector from $\mathbb{Z}_p^n$ as input.

$$\mathsf{Game}_1 = \mathbf{u} \leftarrow \mathbb{Z}_p^n;\ \mathsf{Return}\ \mathcal{A}^{\mathcal{G}_1}(\mathbf{u}));$$

2. In the second game $\mathcal{A}$ is given a group oracle $\mathcal{G}_2$ for the group $\mathbb{Z}_p^n$. Let $\mathbf{e}_i \in \mathbb{Z}_p^n$ for $i \in [n]$ be the unit vectors of $\mathbb{Z}_p^n$. The input to $\mathcal{A}$ is a random encoding of these n unit vectors.

$$\mathsf{Game}_2 = \mathsf{Return}\ \mathcal{A}^{\mathcal{G}_2}(\{\mathbf{e}_i\}_{i \in [n]});$$

3. In the third game $\mathcal{A}$ is given access to a group oracle $\mathcal{G}_3$ for $\mathbb{Z}_p^k$. Let $\mathbf{e}'_i \in \mathbb{Z}_p^k$ for $i \in [k]$ be the unit vectors of $\mathbb{Z}_p^k$. The input to $\mathcal{A}$ is the encoding of n vectors $\{\mathbf{m}_i\}_{i \in [n]}$, where $\mathbf{m}_i = \sum_{j=1}^k (\mathbf{v}_i)_j \mathbf{e}'_j$.

$$\mathsf{Game}_3 = \mathsf{Return}\ \mathcal{A}^{\mathcal{G}_3}(\{\mathbf{m}_i\}_{i \in [n]});$$

4. In the last game $\mathcal{A}$ is given access to the group oracle $\mathcal{G}_1$ for G_p again, and it is given the encoding of $[\mathbf{v}]_g$, for $\mathbf{v}$ a random vector from V as input.

$$\mathsf{Game}_4 = \mathbf{v} \leftarrow V;\ \mathsf{Return}\ \mathcal{A}^{\mathcal{G}_1}(\mathbf{v}));$$

Game_1 and Game_2 are close. Consider the map $\phi_1 : \mathbb{Z}_p^n \to G_p : \mathbf{x} \mapsto [\mathbf{x} \cdot \mathbf{u}]_g$, where $\mathbf{u}$ is the vector chosen uniformly from $\mathbb{Z}_p^n$ in the first game. Now consider a group oracle $\mathcal{G}_1 \circ \phi_1$ that maintains a table $\{(\mathbf{q}_i, [\mathbf{q}_i \cdot \mathbf{u}]_g, h_i)\}_{i \in I}$ of vectors that were queried, their images under ϕ_1, and random encodings of the images $\phi_1(\mathbf{q}_i)$. As long as no two queries q_i,q_j map to the same element of G_p this is an honest implementation of the group oracle G_2. Moreover, ϕ_1 maps the inputs to $\mathcal{A}$ in Game_2 to the inputs of $\mathcal{A}$ in Game_1, so unless $\mathcal{A}$ queries $\mathcal{G}_2$ at two vectors that are mapped to the same group element by ϕ_1 the views of $\mathcal{A}$ in Game_1 and Game_2 are identical. After Q group oracle queries the table contains $Q+2n$ entries. For each pair of distinct vectors $(\mathbf{q}_i, \mathbf{q}_j)$ the probability that $\phi_1(\mathbf{q}_i) = \phi_1(\mathbf{q}_j)$ is $1/p$, so a union bound yields

$$|\Pr[\mathsf{Game}_1() = 1] - \Pr[\mathsf{Game}_2() = 1]| < (Q + 2n)^2/p$$

Game_2 and Game_3 are close unless nonzero vectors orthogonal to V are found. Now, consider the map $\phi_2 : \mathbb{Z}_p^n \to \mathbb{Z}_p^k$, defined on the unit vectors as

$$\phi_2(\mathbf{e}_i) = \sum_{j=1}^{k} (\mathbf{v}_i)_j \mathbf{e}'_j\,,$$

and extended to all of $\mathbb{Z}_p^n$ by linearity. Notice that the vectors orthogonal to V are precisely the vectors in the kernel of ϕ_2 because the i-th component of $\phi_2(\mathbf{u})$ is $\mathbf{u} \cdot \mathbf{v}_i$. Now consider the group oracle $G_3 \circ \phi_2$ that maintains the table $\{(\mathbf{q}_i, \phi_2(\mathbf{q}_i), h_i)\}_{i \in I}$. This is an honest implementation of G_2 as long as it is not queried on two different vectors $\mathbf{q}_i, \mathbf{q}_j$ that are mapped to the same vector by ϕ_2. The connecting map ϕ_2 maps the inputs to $\mathcal{A}$ in Game_2 to the inputs of $\mathcal{A}$ in Game_3. Therefore we have

$$|\Pr[\mathsf{Game}_2() = 1] - \Pr[\mathsf{Game}_3() = 1]| \leq \mathsf{Collision}\,,$$

where $\mathsf{Collision}$ is the probability that two vectors in the table of $\mathcal{G}_3 \circ \phi_2$ have the same image under ϕ_2.

Game_3 and Game_4 are close. The proof of this transition is very similar to that of the first transition, with the connecting map $\phi_3 : \mathbb{Z}_p^k \to G_p : \mathbf{x} \mapsto [\mathbf{x} \cdot \mathbf{c}]_g$, where $\mathbf{c} \in \mathbb{Z}_p^k$ is the unique vector such that $\mathbf{v} = \sum_{i=1}^k c_i \mathbf{v}_i$. The map ϕ_3 sends the input of $\mathcal{A}$ in Game_3 to the input of $\mathcal{A}$ in Game_4, so like in the first transition, the view of $\mathcal{A}$ is identical in Game_3 and Game_4 as long as no two queries to $\mathcal{G}_1 \circ \phi_3$ are mapped to the same group element by ϕ. This happens with probability bounded by $(Q + 2n)^2/p$, so we have

$$|\Pr[\mathsf{Game}_3() = 1] - \Pr[\mathsf{Game}_4() = 1]| < (Q + 2n)^2/p$$

Putting everything together. Combining the previous results with the triangle inequality we get

$$|\Pr[\mathsf{Game}_1() = 1] - \Pr[\mathsf{Game}_4() = 1]| < \mathsf{Collision} + 2(Q + 2n)^2/p\,.$$

Here the left hand side is exactly the distinguishing advantage $\mathsf{Adv}_{\mathcal{A},V}$, so we get

$$\mathsf{Collision} > \mathsf{Adv}_{\mathcal{A},V} - \frac{2(Q + 2n)^2}{p}\,.$$

The extractor outputs the difference of two randomly chosen vectors out of the $Q + 2n$ vectors in the table of $\mathcal{G}_2$. Therefore, since the kernel of ϕ_2 is exactly the set of vectors orthogonal to V we know that $\mathcal{E}$ outputs a vector in $V^{\perp} \setminus \{\mathbf{0}\}$ with probability at least $\frac{\mathsf{Collision}}{(Q+2n)^2}$, which finishes the proof. □

4.2 Obfuscating Point Functions from KOALA

To demonstrate the power of KOALA, we prove the VBB security of the simple point function obfuscator of [7]. To obfuscate the function that tests whether an input $x \in \mathbf{Z}_p$ is equal to x_0 the obfuscator simply outputs $[r]_g, [-x_0 r]_g$, where $[r]_g$ is a uniformly random group element. On input $x \in \mathbb{Z}_p$, the evaluator simply computes $[xr - x_0 r]$ and outputs 1 if and only if this is equal to $[0]_g$.

Theorem 2 (Obfuscating point functions from KOALA). *The point function obfuscator from [7] using a sequence of groups $\{G_n\}_{n\in\mathbb{N}}$ that satisfies KOALA is VBB secure.*

Proof. Given an adversary $\mathcal{A}$ and required simulator accuracy of $\frac{1}{p(n)}$, let $\mathcal{A}'$ and $s(n)$ be the PPT algorithm and polynomial that are guaranteed to exists because of KOALA. We construct a simulator $\mathcal{S}$ that on input $[\mathbf{v}]_g = ([v_1]_g, [v_2]_g)$ calls $\mathcal{A}'(1^n)$ to get output $\mathbf{o} = (o_1, o_2)$, if $o_2 = 0$ then $\mathcal{S}$ discards $\mathbf{o}$ and otherwise it makes a black box query to the point function on input $\frac{o_1}{o_2}$. The simulator $\mathcal{S}$ repeats this a total of $s(n)p(n)$ times. Then there are two cases:

A All of the black box queries return 0. In this case $\mathcal{S}$ picks a uniformly random vector $\mathbf{u} \in \mathbb{Z}_p^2$ and outputs $\mathcal{A}([\mathbf{u}]_g)$.
B A black box query with input x_0 returns 1. In this case $\mathcal{S}$ outputs $\mathcal{A}(\mathcal{O}(x_0))$.

In case of event **B** the simulation of $\mathcal{S}$ is perfect, so the simulation error of $\mathcal{S}$ is

$$\Pr[\mathbf{A}] \cdot \left| \Pr_{r \leftarrow \mathbf{Z}_p}[\mathcal{A}([r]_g, [xr]_g) = 1] - \Pr_{r_1, r_2 \leftarrow \mathbb{Z}_p}[\mathcal{A}([r_1]_g, [r_2]_g) = 1] \right| = \Pr[\mathbf{A}] \mathsf{Adv}_{\mathcal{A}, \langle (1,-x) \rangle}.$$

Event **A** only occurs if none of the outputs of $\mathcal{A}'$ are orthogonal to $\langle (1, -x) \rangle$, so using KOALA we get that the simulation error is bounded by

$$\Pr[\mathcal{A}(1^n)^{\perp} \cdot (1,-x) \neq 0]^{s(n)p(n)} \mathsf{Adv}_{\mathcal{A}, \langle (1,-x) \rangle} \leq \left(1 - \frac{\mathsf{Adv}_{\mathcal{A}, \langle (1,-x) \rangle}}{s(n)}\right)^{s(n)p(n)} \cdot \mathsf{Adv}_{\mathcal{A}, \langle (1,-x) \rangle}.$$

Using $1 - x \leq e^{-x}$ and $e^{-x} \leq \frac{1}{x}$ for $x > 0$ this means that the simulation error is bounded by

$$e^{-\mathsf{Adv}_{\mathcal{A}, \langle (1,-x) \rangle} p(n)} \cdot \mathsf{Adv}_{\mathcal{A}, \langle (1,-x) \rangle} \leq \frac{1}{p(n)},$$

as required. □

Definition 6 (Array of functions). *Let $f_1, \cdots, f_k : D \to R$ be a sequence of k functions on the same domain D, then we define a new function $[\![f_1, \cdots, f_k]\!] : [k] \times D \to R$ by*

$$[\![f_1, \cdots, f_k]\!](i, x) = f_i(x).$$

Definition 7 (VBB Self composability). *A VBB secure obfuscator $\mathcal{O}$ for a function family $\mathcal{F}$ is said to be VBB self composable if $\mathcal{O}' : (f_1, \cdots, f_k) \in \mathcal{F}^* \to (\mathcal{O}(f_1), \cdots, \mathcal{O}(f_k))$ is a VBB secure obfuscator for the function family*

$$\{[\![f_1, \cdots, f_k]\!] | (f_1, \cdots, f_k) \in \mathcal{F}^k\}$$

Remark 2. This definition is stronger than the one of [15] because it works simultaneously for all (polynomially bounded) k, rather than a fixed value of k.

Theorem 3. *The point function obfuscator from [7] using a sequence of groups $\{G_n\}_{n\in\mathbb{N}}$ that satisfies KOALA is VBB self composable.*

Proof. Let $\mathcal{A}$ be an adversary and let $p(n)$ be a polynomial such that $\frac{1}{p(n)}$ is the desired simulator accuracy. We then construct a simulator $\mathcal{S}$ that works in two phases. On input $(\mathcal{O}(\mathbf{x}_1), \cdots, \mathcal{O}(\mathbf{x}_k))$ the simulator $\mathcal{S}$ starts with a learning phase $\mathcal{S}$ in which it tries to recover as many of the $\mathbf{x}_i$ as possible. Then in the simulation phase it outputs $\mathcal{A}(u_1, \cdots, u_k)$, where

$$u_i = \begin{cases} \mathcal{O}(x_i) & \text{if } \mathcal{S} \text{ has learned } \mathbf{x}_i \\ [\mathbf{r}_i]_g & \text{if } \mathcal{S} \text{ has not learned } \mathbf{x}_i \end{cases},$$

where the $\mathbf{r}_i$ are uniformly random vectors in $\mathbb{Z}_p^2$.

Learning phase: The learning phase starts with a empty set $L = \{\}$ of learned $\mathbf{x}_i$'s. Let $\mathcal{A}_1'$ and $s(n)$ be the PPT algorithm and the polynomial given by the KOALA assumption. Then, like in the proof of Theorem 2, we call $\mathcal{A}_0()$ a total of $ks(n)p(n)$ times to get an output $\mathbf{o} = ((o_{1,1}, o_{1,2}), \cdots, (o_{k,1}, o_{k,2}))$. For all $i \in [k]$, if $o_{i,2} \neq 0$, then $\mathcal{S}$ queries the black box oracle for f_i at input $\frac{o_{i,1}}{o_{i,2}}$. If all the queries return False, the learning phase ends and $\mathcal{S}$ moves on to the Simulation phase. Conversely, if the query $f_i(\mathbf{x}_i)$ returns True, then $(i, \mathbf{x}_i)$ is added to L.

If the learning phase has not ended in the first iteration (i.e. if $\mathbf{x}_i$ are discovered), then we construct a new adversary $\mathcal{A}_2$ that accepts $k - |L|$ obfuscated programs as input. The adversary $\mathcal{A}_2$ computes an obfuscation $\mathcal{O}(\mathbf{x}_i)$ for each $\mathbf{x}_i$ that it has learned, and plugs it into the slots of $\mathcal{A} = \mathcal{A}_1$. The $k - |L|$ inputs are plugged into the remaining slots and then $\mathcal{A}_2$ calls $\mathcal{A}$ with these inputs and returns the output of $\mathcal{A}$. The KOALA guarantees there exist a PPT algorithm $\mathcal{A}_2'$ and polynomial $s_2(n)$. Then $\mathcal{S}$ calls $\mathcal{A}_2'()$ a total of $ks_2(n)p(n)$ times to get outputs $\mathbf{o} = ((o_{1,1}, o_{1,2}), \cdots, (o_{k,1}, o_{k,2}))$. Again, if $o_{i,2} \neq 0$, then $\mathcal{S}$ queries the black box oracle for f_i at input $\frac{o_{i,1}}{o_{i,2}}$. If all the queries return False, the learning phase ends and $\mathcal{S}$ moves on to the Simulation phase. Conversely, if the query $f_i(\mathbf{x}_i)$ returns True, then $(i, \mathbf{x}_i)$ is added to L.

This process continues with $\mathcal{A}_i + 1$ the algorithm that calculates $\mathcal{O}(\mathbf{x}_i)$ for the newly discovered $\mathbf{x_i}$ and plugging it into $\mathcal{A}_i$. After at most k iterations no new inputs are learned and the Learning phase terminates.

Simulation phase: After the Learning phase the simulator $\mathcal{S}$ computes $u_i = \mathcal{O}(\mathbf{x}_i)$ for all $(i, \mathbf{x}_i)$ in L. Then it fixes the remaining u_i to $[\mathbf{r}_i]_g$ for $\mathbf{r}_i$ random vectors in $\mathbb{Z}_p^2$ and outputs $\mathbf{A}(\mathbf{u}_1, \cdots, \mathbf{u}_k)$. In other words, $\mathcal{S}$ calls the last iteration $\mathcal{A}_i$ of the adversary constructed in the Learning phase on uniformly random input, and return the result.

Now we analyze the simulation error of this simulator $\mathcal{S}$. Let $I = \{i | \exists \mathbf{x}_i s.t. (i, \mathbf{x}_i) \in L\}$ be the set of indices of the $\mathbf{x}_i$ that are learned at the end of the learning phase. Now, for $X \subset [k]$ Let $u_{X,i}$ be the distribution defined as

$$u_{X,i} = \begin{cases} \mathcal{O}(\mathbf{x}_i) & \text{if } i \text{ in X} \\ [U(\mathbb{Z}_p^2)]_g & \text{else} \end{cases}$$

Then we have that the output of $\mathcal{S}$ is equal to $\mathcal{A}(u_{I,1}, \cdots, u_{I,k})$, so the simulation error of $\mathcal{S}$ is bounded by

$$\left| \Pr[\mathcal{A}(\mathcal{O}(f_{\mathbf{x}_1}), \cdots, \mathcal{O}(f_{\mathbf{x}_k})) = 1] - \Pr[\mathcal{S}^{[\![f_{\mathbf{x}_1}, \cdots, f_{\mathbf{x}_k}]\!]}(1^{kn}) = 1 \right| \leq$$

$$\sum_{X \subset [k]} \Pr[X = I] \left| \Pr[\mathcal{A}(\mathcal{O}(f_{\mathbf{x}_1}), \cdots, \mathcal{O}(f_{\mathbf{x}_k})) = 1] - \Pr[\mathcal{A}(u_{X,1}, \cdots, u_{X,k}) = 1] \right| =$$

$$\sum_{X \subset [k]} \Pr[X = I] \cdot \mathsf{Adv}_{\mathcal{A},X} \,,$$

where $\mathsf{Adv}_{\mathcal{A},X}$ denotes the advantage of $\mathcal{A}$ for distinguishing $\mathcal{O}(f_{\mathbf{x}_1}), \cdots, \mathcal{O}(f_{\mathbf{x}_k})$ from $u_{X,1}, \cdots, u_{X,k}$.

The probability $\Pr[X = I]$ is equal to $\Pr[\text{reach } X] \Pr[\text{stay at } X | \text{ reach } X]$, where $\Pr[\text{reach } X]$ is the probability that $\mathcal{S}$ reaches a state where the indices of the learned $\mathbf{x}_i$ is exactly X, and $\Pr[\text{stay at } X | \text{ reach } X]$ is the probability that $\mathcal{S}$ does not leave this state, given that this state is reached. So, $\Pr[\text{stay at } X | \text{ reach } X]$ is bounded by the probability that none of vectors outputted by A'_i is nonzero and orthogonal to the $2(k - |X|)$ dimensional space of obfuscations of the $k - |X|$ point functions that are not learned. According the KOALA this implies

$$\Pr[\text{ stay at } X | \text{ reach } X] \leq \left(1 - \frac{\mathsf{Adv}_{\mathcal{A},X}}{s_i(n)}\right)^{ks_i(n)p(n)} \leq \frac{1}{k\mathsf{Adv}_{\mathcal{A},X}p(n)} \,.$$

Plugging this in to the upper bound for the simulator error shows that it is bounded by

$$\sum_{X \subset [k]} \Pr[\text{reach } X] \cdot \frac{1}{kp(n)} \,.$$

Now, since there are at most k iterations in the learning phase (each new iteration increases $|L|$, and $|L| \leq k$) we know that $\sum_{X \subset [k]} \Pr[\text{reach } X]$ is bounded by k, so the simulation error of $\mathcal{S}$ is bounded by $\frac{1}{p(n)}$, as required. □

Definition 8 (multi-bit output point functions). *Point functions with multi-bit output are parametrized by two bitstrings* $\mathbf{a} \in \{0,1\}^n$ *and* $\mathbf{b} \in \{0,1\}^l$. *The function* $f_{\mathbf{x},\mathbf{y}}$ *is defined as*

$$f_{\mathbf{a},\mathbf{b}}(\mathbf{x}) = \begin{cases} \mathbf{b} & \textit{if } \mathbf{x} = \mathbf{a} \\ \bot & \textit{else} \end{cases}$$

Theorem 4 (Obfuscating multi-bit output point functions). *Suppose* $\mathcal{O}$ *is a VBB self-composable obfuscator for point functions, then there exists a VB self-composable obfuscator* $\mathcal{O}'$ *for point functions with multi-bit output*

Proof. On input $(\mathbf{a}, \mathbf{b}) \in \{0,1\}^n \times \{0,1\}^l$ the obfuscator $\mathcal{O}'$ simply computes and outputs l obfuscated programs $\mathcal{O}(\mathbf{a}||b_1), \cdots, \mathcal{O}(\mathbf{a}||b_l)$. To evaluate $\mathcal{O}'(\mathbf{a}, \mathbf{b})$ at input $\mathbf{x}$, one simply evaluates all the obfuscations at $\mathbf{x}||0$ and $\mathbf{x}||1$. If for some of the obfuscations neither $\mathbf{x}||0$ nor $\mathbf{x}||1$ is accepted, then the evaluator returns $\bot$, otherwise the evaluator returns $\mathbf{y}$ defined as

$$y_i = \begin{cases} 0 & \text{if } i\text{-th obfuscated program accepts } \mathbf{x}||0 \\ 1 & \text{if } i\text{-th obfuscated program accepts } \mathbf{x}||1 \end{cases}$$

Correctness and poly-time slowdown of this obfuscator $\mathcal{O}'$ follows immediately from the correctness and poly-time slowdown of $\mathcal{O}$.

Now we show that the construction is VBB secure for compositions of k multi-bit output point functions. Let $\mathcal{A}$ be an adversary and let $\frac{1}{p(n)}$ be the desired simulator accuracy. Then the VBB self-composability property of $\mathcal{O}$ immediately implies there is a PPT simulator $\mathcal{S}$ with the desired simulator accuracy that makes black box queries to the $k \times l$ point functions $f_{\mathbf{a_1}||b_{11}}, \cdots, f_{\mathbf{a_1}||b_{1l}}, \cdots, f_{\mathbf{a_k}||b_{k1}}, \cdots, f_{\mathbf{a_k}||b_{kl}}$. We can answer these queries because we have black box access to $f_{\mathbf{a_1}||\mathbf{b_1}}, \cdots, f_{\mathbf{a}_k||\mathbf{b}_k}$. To answer a query to $f_{\mathbf{a}_i||b_{ij}}$ with input $\mathbf{x}, b$ we first query the black box oracle for $f_{\mathbf{a}_i||\mathbf{b}_i}(\mathbf{x})$. If this returns $\bot$, we answer the query with False, otherwise if $f_{\mathbf{a}_i||\mathbf{b}_i}(\mathbf{x}) = \mathbf{b}_i \in \{0,1\}^l$, then we answer the query with $b_{ij} = b$. □

5 Obfuscating Big Subset Functionality

The obfuscator for pattern matching with wildcards of [3] contains an obfuscator for a different functionality, we call this other functionality the *big subset* functionality. We show that there is an embedding of the pattern matching with wildcards functionality into the big subset functionality and hence, that any obfuscator for the big subset functionality can be transformed generically into an obfuscator for pattern matching with wildcards. This transformation preserves VBB security at the cost of a slowdown of the simulator by a factor $2^{n/2}$. The transformation also preserves distributional VBB security with simulators that make no black box queries without slowing down the simulator. Since the obfuscator of [3] is an instantiation of this transformation this will ultimately allow us to prove its VBB security with super-polynomial simulator and Distributional VBB security for a wide variety of distributions.

Definition 9 (Big Subset Functionality). *For each $n \in \mathbb{N}$, we define the class of functions parametrized by (Y, n, t), where Y is a subset of $[n]$ and t is a threshold value with $0 \leq t \leq n$. We define $f_{Y,n,t} : P([n]) \rightarrow \{0,1\}$ that on input a subset X outputs*

$$f_{Y,n,t}(X) = \begin{cases} 1 & \textit{if } |X| \geq t \textit{ and } X \subset Y \\ 0 & \textit{otherwise} \end{cases} .$$

5.1 VBB Secure Obfuscation of Big Subset Functionality

The following construction is implicit in [3]: To obfuscate the function $f_{Y,n,t}$ the obfuscator picks a random degree $t-1$ polynomial $h(x) = a_1 x + \cdots + a_{t-1}x^{t-1}$ with coefficients in $\mathbb{Z}_p$ such that $h(0) = 0$. Then it outputs n group elements $[\mathbf{v}]_g$ defined as

$$v_i = \begin{cases} h(i) \text{ if } i \in Y \\ r_i \text{ otherwise} \end{cases} ,$$

where the $r_i \in \mathbb{Z}_p$ are chosen uniformly at random. To evaluate the function at input $X \subset [n]$ we use polynomial interpolation in the exponent to check if the points $\{(i, o_i) \,|\, i \in X\}$ lie on a degree $|X| - 1$ polynomial h_x with $h_x(0) = 0$.

We now prove that under KOALA this construction is a VBB secure obfuscator.

Theorem 5 ($\mathcal{O}$ is VBB secure). *Let $\mathcal{O}$ be the obfuscator for the big subset functionality defined above, using a family of cyclic groups that satisfies KOALA. Then $\mathcal{O}$ is VBB secure.*

Proof. Let $\mathcal{A}$ be an adversary and $p(n)$ the polynomial such that $\frac{1}{p(n)}$ is the desired simulator accuracy. Then we construct a simulator $\mathcal{S}$ that runs in time $O(p(n)*poly(n))$ such that for any (Y, n, t) with sufficiently large n the simulation error

$$\left| \Pr_{\mathcal{O},\mathcal{A}}[\mathcal{A}(\mathcal{O}(Y,n,t)) = 1] - \Pr_{\mathcal{S}}[\mathcal{S}^{f_{Y,n,t}}(1^n) = 1] \right| \leq \frac{1}{p(n)} .$$

The simulator $\mathcal{S}$ is constructed as follows: According to KOALA, there exists a PPT algorithm $\mathcal{A}'$ that samples vectors in $\mathbb{Z}_p^n$ that are likely to be orthogonal to any subspace V such that $\mathcal{A}$ can distinguish $[\mathbf{v}]_g \leftarrow [V]_g$ from $[\mathbf{u}]_g \leftarrow [\mathbb{Z}]_g$. Now $\mathcal{S}$ repeatedly calls $\mathbf{x} \leftarrow \mathcal{A}'$ and queries the $f_{Y,n,t}$ oracle on $\mathrm{Sup}(\mathbf{x})$ for a total of $R(n)$ times (for R some polynomial to be determined later). Now there are two possibilities:

- **A. All of the $f_{Y,n,t}$ queries return 0.** In this case $\mathcal{S}$ just picks a uniformly random vector $\mathbf{u} \in \mathbb{Z}_p^n$ and outputs $\mathcal{A}([\mathbf{u}]_g)$.
- **B. One of the queries $f_{Y,n,t}(X)$ returns 1.** In this case $\mathcal{S}$ makes $n - |X|$ additional queries to $f_{Y,n,t}$ on the inputs $X \cup \{i\}$ for $i \notin X$ in order to learn the set Y. Once $\mathcal{S}$ knows Y it queries $f_{Y,n,t}$ on subsets of Y of increasing size until it gets an accept in order to learn the threshold value t. Then $\mathcal{S}$ outputs $\mathcal{A}(\mathcal{O}(Y, n, t))$.

The intuition to why this simulator works is that either $\mathcal{A}$ can distinguish $\mathcal{O}(Y,n,t)$ from randomness, in which case we can show that $\mathbf{B}$ occurs with overwhelming probability, or $\mathcal{A}$ cannot distinguish $\mathcal{O}(Y,n,t)$ from $[\mathbf{u}]_g$ in which case the event $\mathbf{A}$ can happen with non-negligible probability, but this is not a problem because then $\mathcal{S}$ outputs $\mathcal{A}([\mathbf{u}]_g)$ which is close enough to $\mathcal{A}(\mathcal{O}(Y,n,t))$.

Let $s(n)$ be the polynomial from the KOALA assumption (Definition 5) such that for any subspace $V \subset \mathbb{Z}_p^n$

$$\Pr[\mathcal{A}'(1^n) \in V^{\perp} \setminus \{\mathbf{0}\}] \geq \frac{\mathsf{Adv}_{\mathcal{A},V}}{s(n)} .$$

The remainder of the proof shows that the simulation error of $\mathcal{S}$ is bounded by $\frac{s(n)}{R(n)}$, so by taking $R(n) = s(n)p(n)$, we get that the simulation error of $\mathcal{S}$ is less than $\frac{1}{p(n)}$, as required.

Let $V_{Y,n,t}$ be the set of exponent vectors of possible obfuscations of $f_{Y,n,t}$. This is a vector space that can be written as $V_{Y,n,t} = C + E$, where C is

$$C = \{\{h(i)\}_{i\in[n]} \mid h \text{ a degree } t-1 \text{ polynomial with } h(0) = 0\ \} ,$$

and E is the subspace with basis $\{\mathbf{e}_i \mid i \notin Y\}$. C is the column space of the (almost Vandermonde) n-by-$(t-1)$ matrix

$$\begin{pmatrix} 1 & 1 & \cdots & 1 \\ 2 & 2^2 & \cdots & n^{t-1} \\ \vdots & \vdots & \ddots & \vdots \\ n & n^2 & \cdots & n^{t-1} \end{pmatrix}$$

Any $(t-1)$-by-$(t-1)$ submatrix of this matrix is invertible, which means that elements in $C^{\perp}$ are either 0 or have more than $(t-1)$ nonzero entries. So for any $\mathbf{x} \in (V_{Y,n,t}^{\perp} \setminus \{\mathbf{0}\}) \subset (C^{\perp} \setminus \{0\})$ we have $|\operatorname{Sup}(\mathbf{x})| \geq t$. Also, $\mathbf{x} \in E^{\perp}$, which implies that $\operatorname{Sup}(\mathbf{x}) \subset Y$. Therefore, $x \in V_{Y,n,t}^{\perp} \setminus \{\mathbf{0}\}$ implies $f_{Y,n,t}(\operatorname{Sup}(\mathbf{x})) = 1$.

So the event $\mathbf{A}$ that the support of none of the vectors sampled by $\mathcal{A}'$ is accepted by the $f_{Y,n,t}$ oracle is less probable than the event that none of the vectors sampled by $\mathcal{A}'$ is orthogonal to $V_{Y,n,t}$. Because of KOALA this means

$$\Pr[\mathbf{A}] \leq \left(1 - \Pr[\mathcal{A}'(1^n) \in V^{\perp} \setminus \{\mathbf{0}\}]\right)^{R(n)} \leq \left(1 - \frac{\mathsf{Adv}_{\mathcal{A},V}}{s(n)}\right)^{R(n)} . \quad (5)$$

The simulator returns the output $\mathcal{A}$ on random input or on input $\mathcal{O}(Y,n,t)$ in case of event $\mathbf{A}$ or event $\mathbf{B}$ respectively, so

$$\Pr[\mathcal{S}^{f_{Y,n,t}}(1^n) = 1] = \Pr[\mathbf{A}] \cdot \Pr_{\mathbf{u} \leftarrow \mathbb{Z}_p^n}[\mathcal{A}([\mathbf{u}]_g) = 1] + \Pr[\mathbf{B}] \cdot \Pr[\mathcal{A}(\mathcal{O}(Y,n,t)) = 1] ,$$

so the simulation error of $\mathcal{S}$ is equal to

$$\Pr[\mathbf{A}] \cdot \left| \Pr[\mathcal{A}(\mathcal{O}(V,n,t)) = 1] - \Pr_{\mathbf{u} \leftarrow \mathbb{Z}_p^n}[\mathcal{A}([\mathbf{u}]_g) = 1] \right| = \Pr[\mathbf{A}] \cdot \mathsf{Adv}_{\mathcal{A},V_{Y,n,t}} .$$

Combining this with Eq. 5 says that the simulation error of $\mathcal{S}$ is at most

$$\left(1-\frac{\mathsf{Adv}_{\mathcal{A},V_{Y,n,t}}}{s(n)}\right)^{R(n)}\cdot \mathsf{Adv}_{\mathcal{A},V_{Y,n,t}} \leq \exp\left[\frac{\mathsf{Adv}_{\mathcal{A},V_{Y,n,t}}R(n)}{s(n)}\right]\mathsf{Adv}_{\mathcal{A},V_{Y,n,t}} \leq \frac{s(n)}{R(n)},$$

where for the first inequality we use $1-x \leq \exp(-x)$, and for the second inequality we use $\exp(-x) \leq \frac{1}{x}$ for $x > 0$. □

5.2 Evasive Distributions

We describe several evasive distributions for the big subset functionality, which will come in handy later for analyzing pattern matching with wildcards.

Lemma 2 (Evasive distributions for big subset). *Let $\mathcal{D} = \{\mathcal{D}_n\}_{n\in\mathbb{N}}$ be a sequence of distributions and $t_0(n), t_1(n)$ functions with $0 \leq t_0(n) \leq t_1(n) \leq n$. Then we have*

1. *If $\mathcal{D}_n$ outputs (Y, n, t) with $t \geq t_0$, and the min-entropy of $\mathcal{D}_n$ is $n - t_o(n) + \omega(\log n)$, then $\mathcal{D}$ is evasive.*
2. *If $\mathcal{D}_n$ outputs $(Y, n, t_0(n))$ with $|Y| = t_1(n)$, and the min-entropy of $\mathcal{D}_n$ is $\log(\binom{n-t_0(n)}{t_1(n)-t_0(n)}) + \omega(\log n)$, then $\mathcal{D}$ is $\mathcal{D}$ evasive.*

Proof. Suppose $\mathcal{D}$ and t_0 satisfy the assumptions of 1 and let m_n be the min-entropy of $\mathcal{D}_n$. Take any n and $X \subset [n]$. Now we prove that

$$\Pr_{(Y,n,t)\leftarrow\mathcal{D}_n}[f_{Y,n,t}(X) = 1] \leq (n - t_0(n))2^{n-t_0(n)-m_n}.$$

If $|X| \leq t_0(n)$, then clearly this probability is zero, because we have $|X| \leq t$ with probability 1. So suppose $|X| \geq t_0(n)$. Then there are at most $2^{n-t_0(n)}$ values of Y such that $X \subset Y$ and at most $(n - t_0(n))$ values of t such that $|X| \leq t$. This makes a total of $(n-t_0(n))2^{n-t_0(n)}$ triples (Y, n, t) such that $f_{Y,n,t}(X) = 1$. Since each of these triples occurs with probability at most 2^{-m_n} the inequality above follows.

This shows that if the min-entropy of $\mathcal{D}_n$ is $n - t_o(n) + \omega(\log n)$, then

$$\Pr_{(Y,n,t)\leftarrow\mathcal{D}_n}[f_{Y,n,t}(X) = 1] \leq (n - t_0(n))2^{-\omega(\log n)},$$

which is a negligible function of n, so $\mathcal{D}$ is evasive.

The argument to prove 2 is very similar, the only difference being that $t = t_o(n)$ and $|Y| = t_1(n)$ reduces the number of triples (Y, n, t) such that $f_{Y,n,t}(X) = 1$. If $|X| < t_0(n)$, then there are no accepting triples. If $|X| \geq t_0$ the number of Y of size $t_1(n)$ such that $X \subset Y$ is $\binom{n-t_0(n)}{t_1(n)-t_0(n)}$, so

$$\Pr_{(Y,n,t)\leftarrow\mathcal{D}_n}[f_{Y,n,t}(X) = 1] \leq \binom{n-t_0(n)}{t_1(n)-t_0(n)}2^{-m_n}.$$

The rest of the argument is the same as in the proof of 1. □

6 Obfuscating Pattern Matching with Wildcards, Revisited

In this section, we further investigate the security of the obfuscation scheme of [3]. On the negative side we introduce an attack that allows an adversary to learn if the first half of the pattern consists of wildcards. This proves the scheme is not VBB secure, and even that the scheme is not DVBB secure for some high entropy distributions. On the positive side however, we prove that the scheme is VBB secure if we allow for a super-polynomial simulator.

We also show that any distribution of patterns that has at least $n+\omega(\log n)$ bits of min-entropy is automatically secure. We give similar bounds for distributions that output patterns with a fixed number of wildcards. Our attacks match these min-entropy bounds and hence they show that the bounds are nearly optimal. The bounds immediately prove that the scheme is DVBB secure for uniform patterns and uniform patterns with a fixed number of wildcards up to $n-\omega(\log n)$. This is stronger than the result of [3] that only proves DVBB security for uniform distributions of up to $\frac{3n}{4}$ wildcards. Having up to $n-\omega(\log n)$ wildcards is optimal, because for $n-O(\log n)$ wildcards a pattern can be recovered through black box queries in polynomial time and VBB security is trivial. Indeed, if there are only $O(\log n)$ non wildcards, then after polynomially many black box queries at random inputs we will get an accepting input. Once an accepting input $\mathbf{x} \in \{0,1\}^n$ is found we can learn the entire pattern with n additional black box queries on the n inputs that differ from $\mathbf{x}$ at exactly one position.

6.1 The Construction of [3] Is Not VBB Secure

By looking at an obfuscation of a pattern ρ it is possible to check whether the first half consists of wildcards. This is done by simply doing polynomial interpolation in the exponent in the values $v_{i,j}$ for $(i,j) \in [\lceil n/2 \rceil] \times \{0,1\}$. Determining whether the first half of a pattern consists of wildcards is not efficiently possible with only black box access, so this attack breaks VBB security. Moreover, this breaks DVBB security for high entropy distributions.

Let $[\mathbf{v}]_g = [\{v_{i,j}\}_{(i,j)\in[n]\times\{0,1\}}]_g$ be the obfuscation of a pattern ρ. To simplify the notation we assume that n is even. The $[v_{i,j}]_g$ are of the form $[p(2i-j)]_g$ for all $(i,j) \in [n/2] \times \{0,1\}$ if and only if the first half of the pattern ρ consist of wildcards. Therefore we can compute the polynomial interpolation coefficients

$$C_{i,j} = \prod_{\substack{(a,b)\in[n/2]\times\{0,1\},\\ (a,b)\neq(i,j)}} \frac{-2a+b}{2i-j-2a+b}$$

and then $h = [\sum_{(i,j)\in[n/2]\times\{0,1\}} C_{i,j} v_{i,j}]_g$ will be equal to $[p(0)]_g = [0]_g$ if the first half of ρ consist of wildcards. If the first half does not consist of wildcards, then a random group element enters in the calculation of h and then $h \neq [0]_g$ with overwhelming probability $1-1/p$.

Lemma 3 (A very evasive insecure distribution). *There exists a sequence of distributions* $\{\mathcal{D}_n\}_{n\in\mathbb{N}}$ *that is* $2^{n/2}n^{-\omega(1)}$*-evasive such that the obfuscation scheme of [3] is not* $\mathcal{D}$*-DVBB secure.*

Proof. Let $\mathcal{D}_n$ be the distribution that tosses a fair coin and on tails outputs a uniformly random pattern without wildcards and on heads outputs a uniformly random pattern with wildcards in the first half but no wildcards in the second half. Clearly for any $\mathbf{x}$ the probability

$$\Pr_{\rho\leftarrow D_n}[f_\rho(\mathbf{x})=1] < 2^{-n/2},$$

so this sequence of distributions is $2^{n/2}n^{-\omega(1)}$-evasive. Let $\mathcal{A}$ the adversary that executes the attack of the previous paragraph and outputs 1 if $h=[0]_g$ and 0 otherwise. Let P be the predicate of the first half of a pattern being wildcards and let $\mathcal{S}$ be a PPT simulator. Since our distribution is evasive we have

$$\left|\Pr_{\rho\leftarrow\mathcal{D}_n,\mathcal{S}}[\mathcal{S}^{f_\rho}(1^n)=P(\rho)] - \Pr_{\rho\leftarrow\mathcal{D}_n,\mathcal{S}}[\mathcal{S}^{0}(1^n)=P(\rho)]\right| = negl(n).$$

Now we can bound the simulation error of $\mathcal{S}$:

$$\left|\Pr_{\rho\leftarrow\mathcal{D}_n}[\mathcal{A}(\mathcal{O}(\rho))=P(\rho)] - \Pr_{\rho\leftarrow\mathcal{D}_n,\mathcal{S}}[\mathcal{S}^{f_\rho}(1^n)=P(\rho)]\right| \leq$$

$$\left|\Pr_{\rho\leftarrow\mathcal{D}_n}[\mathcal{A}(\mathcal{O}(\rho))=P(\rho)] - \Pr_{\rho\leftarrow\mathcal{D}_n,\mathcal{S}}[\mathcal{S}^{0}(1^n)=P(\rho)]\right| - negl(n) =$$

$$\left|\left(1-\frac{1}{2p}\right)-\frac{1}{2}\right| - negl(n).$$

which is clearly not negligible. This proves the obfuscation scheme is not distributional VBB secure for this scheme. □

Theorem 6 ($\mathcal{O}$ is not $2^{0.5n}n^{-\omega(1)}$-VBB secure.). *Let* $\mathcal{O}$ *be the obfuscation scheme for pattern matching with wildcards from [3], then* $\mathcal{O}$ *is not* $2^{0.5n}n^{-\omega(1)}$*-VBB secure.*

Proof. This follows immediately from Lemma 1 combined with Lemma 3. □

The distribution of Lemma 3 has $n/2+1$ bits of min-entropy, but the attack can be generalized to showcase distributions that are not DVBB with even more min-entropy. If a pattern has wildcards in the first $a \leq n/2$ positions, 0 or $\star$ in the next $n-2a$ positions and 0,1 or $\star$ in the last a positions, then an attacker can do polynomial interpolation on the $(n-a)+a$ values $\{[v_{i,0}]_g\}_{i\in[n-a]}\cup\{[v_{i,1}]_g\}_{i\in[a]}$ to detect this. If we pick $a=\omega(\log n)$ and we sample from these patterns uniformly we get an evasive distribution. So, similar to the proof of Lemma 3 this leads to an insecure distribution.

Lemma 4 (Insecure distribution with high min-entropy). *There exists a sequence of distributions* $\{\mathcal{D}_n\}_{n\in\mathbb{N}}$ *with* $n-2a+\log(3)a+1$ *bits of min-entropy such that the obfuscation scheme of [3] is not* $\mathcal{D}$*-DVBB secure if* $a=\omega(\log n)$.

We showed that the construction is not VBB secure because by looking at $\mathcal{O}(\rho)$ it is possible to learn something about ρ in polynomial time that would take $O(2^{n/2})$ black box queries to learn otherwise. Later, we will prove that this is essentially the best attack (assuming KOALA). Specifically, we prove that anything that can be learned from an obfuscation of f can also be learned from roughly $2^{n/2}$ black box queries to f_ρ (see Theorem 8).

6.2 Pattern Matching from Big Subset

Next, we show how to derive an obfuscation scheme for pattern matching starting with that for big subset.

Theorem 7 (Pattern matching with wildcards obfuscator from big subset obfuscator). *For an obfuscation scheme $\mathcal{O}$ for the big subset functionality, there exists an obfuscator $\mathcal{O}'$ for the pattern matching with wildcards functionality such that:*

1. *If $\mathcal{O}$ is T-VBB secure with simulators making Q black box queries, then $\mathcal{O}'$ is $(T + Q2^{n/2})$-VBB secure.*
2. *If $\mathcal{O}$ is T-VBB secure with simulators making Q black box queries, then $\mathcal{O}'$ is $(T + Q(2^w + n))$-VBB secure for pattern matching with up to w wildcards.*
3. *For a sequence of distributions $\{\mathcal{D}'_n\}_{n\in\mathbb{N}}$ of length n patterns, let $\mathcal{D}_n = (Y_{\mathcal{D}'_n}, 2n, n)$, where for pattern ρ, the subset Y_ρ is defined as*

$$2i - j \in Y_\rho \Leftrightarrow \rho_i = \star \text{ or } \rho_i = j\,.$$

Then, if $\mathcal{O}$ is $\mathcal{D}$-DVBB secure with simulators that don't make black box queries, then $\mathcal{O}'$ is $\mathcal{D}'$-DVBB secure with simulators that don't make black box queries.

Proof. The obfuscator $\mathcal{O}'$ works as follows:

- To obfuscate a pattern $\rho \in \{0, 1, \star\}^n$ the obfuscator $\mathcal{O}'$ simply outputs $\mathcal{O}(Y_\rho, n, 2n)$.
- To evaluate the Obfuscated program at input $\mathbf{x} \in \{0,1\}^n$, one simply outputs $\mathcal{O}(Y_\rho, 2n, n)(X_\mathbf{x})$, where

$$X_\mathbf{x} = \{2i - j \mid (i,j) \in [n] \times \{0,1\} \text{ s.t. } x_i = j\}\,.$$

To prove 1, assume that $\mathcal{A}$ is an adversary against the $\mathcal{O}'$ obfuscator, and that $\frac{1}{p(n)}$ is the desired simulator accuracy. We can use $\mathcal{A}$ as an adversary to $\mathcal{O}$, so if $\mathcal{O}$ is T-VBB secure there exists a simulator $\mathcal{S}$, running in time $O(T * \mathit{poly}(n))$, such that for sufficiently large n we have

$$\left|\Pr_{\mathcal{O},\mathcal{A}}[\mathcal{A}(\mathcal{O}(Y_\rho, 2n, n)) = 1] - \Pr_{\mathcal{S}}[\mathcal{S}^{f_{Y_\rho,2n,2}}(1^n) = 1]\right| \le \frac{1}{p(n)}\,.$$

So $\mathcal{S}$ is almost a good simulator to prove T-VBB security for $\mathcal{O}'$, the only problem is that $\mathcal{S}$ makes black box queries to $f_{Y_\rho,2n,n}$ instead of to f_ρ. To solve this problem it suffices to prove that one can answer queries to $f_{Y_\rho,2n,n}$ using at most $O(2^{n/2})$ queries to f_ρ.

If $f_{Y_\rho,2n,n}$ is queried on input X with $|X| < n$ we can return 0 without making any queries to f_ρ. We define

$$\begin{aligned}\mathsf{Wildcards} &= \{i \mid 2i \in X \text{ and } 2i-1 \in X\},\\ \mathsf{Zeros} &= \{i \mid 2i \in X \text{ and } 2i-1 \notin X\} \text{ and}\\ \mathsf{Ones} &= \{i \mid 2i \notin X \text{ and } 2i-1 \in X\}.\end{aligned}$$

Since $2|\mathsf{Wildcards}| + |\mathsf{Ones}| + |\mathsf{Zeros}| = |X| \geq n$ we have $|\mathsf{Wildcards}| + |\mathsf{Ones}| + |\mathsf{Zeros}| \geq n/2$. This means there are at most $2^{n/2}$ inputs $\mathbf{x}$ that are zero at the indices of $\mathsf{Wildcards} \cup \mathsf{Zeros}$ and one at the indices in Ones. We query f_ρ at each of these inputs. If each of these queries returns 0 we know that $X \not\subset Y_\rho$, so we return 0. If one of the queries returns a 1 we can do n additional black box queries to f_ρ to recover the entire pattern ρ and we output 1 only if $X \subset Y_\rho$.

This shows that there is a simulator $\mathcal{S}'$ for $\mathcal{O}'$ with negligible simulation error that runs in time $O(T * poly(n) + Q2^{n/2})$, which proves 1. For 2 we observe that if ρ has at most w wildcards, then $|\mathsf{Wildcards}| \leq w$ which implies $|\mathsf{Wildcards}| + |\mathsf{Ones}| + |\mathsf{Zeros}| \geq n - w$. Therefore we can answer each query to $f_{Y_{\rho,2n,n}}$ in time $O(2^w + n)$ which proves 2.

To prove 3, assume $\mathcal{A}$ is an adversary against the $\mathcal{O}'$ obfuscator and $\{P'_n\}_{n\in\mathbb{N}}$ a sequence of predicates. Define a sequence of predicates P_n : $\{P([2n], 2n, [2n])\} \to \{0,1\}$ such that $P_n((Y_\rho, 2n, n)) = P'_n(\rho)$ for all $\rho \in 0, 1^*$ and with arbitrary behavior on other inputs. By assumption there exists a simulator $\mathcal{S}$ for $(\mathcal{A}, P)$ that makes no black box queries and with negligible simulation error

$$\left| \Pr_{(Y_\rho,2n,n)\leftarrow\mathcal{D}_n} [\mathcal{A}(\mathcal{O}(Y_\rho, 2n, n)) = P_n(Y_\rho, 2n, n)] - \Pr_{(Y_\rho,2n,n)\leftarrow\mathcal{D}_n} [\mathcal{S}(1^n) = P_n(Y_\rho, 2n, n)] \right| .$$

But this simulation error is exactly equal to

$$\left| \Pr_{\rho\leftarrow\mathcal{D}'_n} [\mathcal{A}(\mathcal{O}'(\rho)) = P'_n(\rho)] - \Pr_{(\rho\leftarrow\mathcal{D}'_n} [\mathcal{S}(1^n) = P'_n(\rho)] \right| ,$$

so $\mathcal{S}$ is also a good simulator for $(\mathcal{A}, P')$, which proves that $\mathcal{O}'$ is $\mathcal{D}'$-DVBB secure. □

6.3 Security Guarantees for Construction of [3]

Since the obfuscator of [3] is an instantiation of the transformation of Theorem 7 with the big subset obfuscator whose VBB security we prove in Theorem 5 we can now derive security guarantees. In particular we derive the $2^{n/2}$-VBB security of the obfuscator and we prove that a sequence of distributions that has enough min-entropy is automatically DVBB secure. We prove one statement for distributions that output (Y, n, t) with $t \geq t_0$ for a certain t_0, and one statement for distributions that output (Y, n, t) with a fixed $t = t_0$, and a fixed size of Y equal to t_1. The following follows immediately from combining Theorem 7 with Theorem 5 (note that VBB security is equivalent to 1-VBB security, because the T-VBB security definition hides polynomial factors in the runtime of the simulators).

Theorem 8 ($\mathcal{O}$ is $2^{n/2}$- VBB secure and 2^w-VBB secure). *The obfuscator for pattern matching with wildcards from [3] is $2^{n/2}$-VBB secure. If the functionality is restricted to patterns with at most $w(n)$ wildcards, the obfuscator is 2^w-VBB secure.*

The DVVB security of the pattern matching obfuscator for a wide variety of distributions also follows.

Theorem 9 (DVBB security for min-entropy distributions). *Let $\mathcal{D} = \{\mathcal{D}_n\}_{n\in\mathbb{N}}$ be a sequence of distributions over $\{0, 1, \star\}^n$ and let $w(n)$ be a function with $0 \leq w(n) \leq n$, then*

1. *If the min-entropy of $\mathcal{D}_n$ is $n + \omega(\log n)$, then the obfuscation scheme is $\mathcal{D}$-DVBB secure with simulators that make no black box queries.*
2. *If $\mathcal{D}_n$ is supported on patterns with $w(n)$ wildcards, and its min-entropy is $\log(\binom{n}{w(n)}) + \omega(\log n)$, then the obfuscation scheme is $\mathcal{D}$-DVBB secure with simulators that make no black box queries.*

Proof. The embedding of pattern matching instances into big subset instances $\rho \mapsto (Y_\rho, 2n, n)$ is injective so it preserves min-entropy. Now point 1 of Lemma 2 with $t_0(2n) = n$ says that if the min-entropy of $\mathcal{D}' = (Y_\rho, 2n, n)$ is $n + \omega(\log n)$, then the obfuscation scheme for the big subset functionality is $\mathcal{D}'$-DVBB secure with a simulator that makes no black box queries. From this, Theorem 7 says that the obfuscation scheme for pattern matching is $\mathcal{D}$-VBB secure with simulators that make no black box queries.

To prove 2, we use point 2 of Lemma 2 with $t_0(2n) = n$ and $t_1(2n) = n + w(n)$. This tells us that if the min-entropy of $\mathcal{D}_n$ is $\log(\binom{n}{w(n)}) + \omega(\log n)$ then the big subset-obfuscator is DVBB secure. From this, Theorem 7 says that the pattern matching-obfuscator is $\mathcal{D}$-DVVB secure. □

The min-entropy bounds of Theorem 9 are almost optimal. The generalized attack of Lemma 4 gives a distribution which has min-entropy larger than $n - \omega(\log n)$. Similarly, we can construct distributions of functions with exactly $w(n)$ wildcards for which the scheme is not DVBB secure that have min-entropy at least $\log(\binom{n}{w(n)}) - \omega(\log n)$.

From the min-entropy criteria it follows immediately that the obfuscator of [3] is DVVB secure for uniform distributions, and uniform distributions with a fixed number of wildcards.

Theorem 10 (DVBB security for uniform distributions). *Let $\mathcal{O}$ be the obfuscator from [3], and let $w(n)$ be a function with $n \leq w(n) \leq n$, such that $n - w(n)$ is $\omega(\log n)$ then*

1. *$\mathcal{O}$ is DVBB secure for the sequence of uniform distributions of patterns of length n, and*
2. *$\mathcal{O}$ is DVBB secure for the sequence of uniform distributions of length n patterns with $w(n)$ wildcards.*

Proof. There are 3^n patterns of length n, so the min-entropy of the uniform distributions is $\log(3)n$, which is clearly $n + \omega(\log n)$. The claim now follows from Theorem 9.

For 2, there are $\binom{n}{w(n)}2^{n-w(n)}$ patterns, so the min-entropy of the distribution is $\log(\binom{n}{w(n)}) + n - w(n)$, so again the claim follows from Theorem 9. □

Remark 3. The condition that $n - w(n)$ is $\omega(\log n)$ is essentially optimal, because if the number of non-wildcards is $O(\log n)$, then an adversary can find an accepting input in polynomial time and recover the entire pattern with n additional black box queries.

7 Generalizing the Scheme

A natural question is whether we can generalize the scheme of [3] to create a scheme that is fully VBB secure. For example, one could hope to introduce some extra error terms to the scheme to prevent the attack of Sect. 6.1 and get a fully VBB secure scheme. However, we formulate a big class of generalizations of the scheme and show that all these schemes suffer from an attack similar the one in Sect. 6.1. On the positive side we give a variant of the scheme of [3] which has exactly the same security, but where the obfuscation only consists of $n+1$ group elements instead of $2n$.

7.1 Framework

At a high level, the construction of [3] consist of a mapping $\mathbf{u} : \{0,1\}^n \rightarrow \mathbb{Z}_p^m$ that maps an input $\mathbf{x}$ to a vector $\mathbf{u_x}$ of length m (In the construction we have $m = 2n$), and a mapping V that assigns a vector space V_ρ to each pattern ρ in $\{0,1,\star\}^n$. An obfuscation of the pattern ρ is then $[\mathbf{v}]_g$, where $\mathbf{v}$ is a vector, chosen uniformly from V_ρ. To evaluate the obfuscated program at input $\mathbf{x}$ the evaluator computes $[\mathbf{u_x}^\top \cdot \mathbf{v}]_g$. If this inner product is $[0]_g$ the evaluator outputs 1, otherwise it outputs 0. For correctness, we require that $\mathbf{u_x}$ is orthogonal to V_ρ if and only $f_\rho(\mathbf{x}) = 1$. This ensures that the obfuscated program outputs 1 if $f_\rho(\mathbf{x}) = 1$ with probability 1, and 0 if $f_\rho(\mathbf{x}) = 0$ with overwhelming probability $1 - 1/p$.

Definition 10 (Linear-in-the-exponent obfuscation scheme). *A linear-in-the-exponent obfuscation scheme (for pattern matching with wildcards) is a tuple $(\mathbf{u}, V, m(n), \mathcal{O})$, where $\mathbf{u}$ is a mapping $\{0,1\}^n \rightarrow \mathbb{Z}_p^{m(n)}$ and V is a mapping that sends patterns in $\{0,1,\star\}^n$ to subspaces of $\mathbb{Z}_p^{m(n)}$ such that*

$$\mathbf{u_x} \in V_\rho^\perp \Leftrightarrow f_\rho(\mathbf{x}) = 1,$$

and $\mathcal{O}$ is the obfuscation scheme that in input ρ outputs $[v]_g$, for a uniformly chosen vector $v \in V_\rho$. Note that $m(n)$ has to be bounded by a polynomial, because otherwise $\mathcal{O}$ does not have a polynomial slowdown.

Concretely, in the construction of [3] the mapping $\mathbf{u}$ assigns to input $\mathbf{x} \in \{0,1\}^n$ the length-$2n$ vector $\mathbf{u_x}$ whose $(2i-j)$-th component is the correct polynomial interpolation coefficient if $\mathbf{x}_i = j$, and 0 otherwise. For a pattern ρ, the vector space $V_\rho = C + E_\rho$, where

$$C = \{\{h(i)\}_{i\in[n]} \,|h \text{ a degree } t-1 \text{ polynomial with } h(0) = 0 \ \}\ ,$$

and E_ρ is the subspace with basis $\{\mathbf{e}_{2i-j} \,|\, \rho_i \neq \star \text{ and } \rho_i \neq j\}$. We have correctness because $\mathbf{u_x}$ is orthogonal to C regardless of $\mathbf{x}$, and orthogonal to E if and only if $f_\rho(\mathbf{x}) = 1$.

7.2 Compression

We observed that $\mathbf{u_x}$ is orthogonal to C, regardless of $\mathbf{x}$. This is because $\mathbf{u_x} \cdot \mathbf{v}$ corresponds to looking at certain coefficients of $\mathbf{u}$ and doing polynomial interpolation on them at 0, while the entries of $\mathbf{u} \in C$ are precisely the evaluation of a low degree polynomial h with $h(0) = 0$. This shows that $\mathbf{u}$ sends all the inputs $\mathbf{x}$ to a vector in $C^\perp$, which is a subspace of dimension $n+1$. So the scheme is not using the additional $n-1$ dimensions of $\mathbf{Z}_p^{2n}$, which is wasteful. We can "cut out" these extra dimensions to get a scheme $(\mathbf{u}', V')$ which has more compact obfuscated programs consisting of $n+1$ group elements instead of $2n$, but still has the same security. This compression can be performed for any linear-in-the-exponent obfuscation scheme $(\mathbf{u}, V)$ if $\langle \mathbf{u_x} \,|\, \mathbf{x} \in \{0,1\}^n \rangle \neq \mathbb{Z}_p^m$.

Theorem 11 (Compressing linear-in-the-exponent schemes). *Let $(\mathbf{u}, V, m, \mathcal{O})$ be a linear-in-the-exponent obfuscation scheme, then there exists a scheme $(\mathbf{u}', V', m', \mathcal{O}')$ such that*

$$m'(n) = \dim(\langle \mathbf{u_x} \,|\, \mathbf{x} \in \{0,1\}^n \rangle) = \dim(\langle \mathbf{u'_x} \,|\, \mathbf{x} \in \{0,1\}^n \rangle).$$

Let T be a function and $\{\mathcal{D}_n\}_{n\in\mathrm{N}}$ be a sequence of distributions of length-n patterns. If $\mathcal{O}$ is VBB, T-VBB or $\mathcal{D}$-DVBB secure then $\mathcal{O}'$ is VBB, T-VBB or $\mathcal{D}$-DVBB secure respectively.

Proof. For any n, let $U_n = \langle \mathbf{u_x} \,|\, \mathbf{x} \in \{0,1\}^n \rangle$ be the space spanned by the $\mathbf{u_x}$. Let $m'(n) = \dim(U_n)$ and let $\mathbf{u}_1, \cdots, \mathbf{u}_{m'(n)}$ be a basis for U and extend this to a basis $u_1, \cdots, u_n$ for all of $\mathbb{Z}_p^{m(n)}$. Let M be the matrix whose columns are the u_i, and $\overline{M^\top}$ and $\overline{M^{-1}}$ the first $m'(n)$ rows of $M^\top$ and M^{-1} respectively. Now we define $\mathbf{u}'_\mathbf{x} = \overline{M^{-1}}\mathbf{u_x}$ and $V'_\rho = \overline{M^\top} V_\rho$. Let $\mathbf{u}$ be a vector from V_ρ and $\mathbf{v}' = \overline{M^\top}\mathbf{v}$, then we have

$$\mathbf{u}_\mathbf{x}'^\top \cdot \mathbf{v}' = \mathbf{u}_\mathbf{x}^\top \cdot \overline{M^{-1}}^\top \cdot \overline{M^\top} \cdot \mathbf{v} = \mathbf{u}_\mathbf{x}^\top \cdot \mathbf{v}\,.$$

This shows that the new linear-in-the-exponent obfuscation scheme $(\mathbf{u}', V', m', \mathcal{O}')$ is correct if the original scheme is.

To prove that the compression preserves security, let $\mathcal{A}'$ be an adversary that breaks VBB, T-VBB or $\mathcal{D}$-DVBB security of $\mathcal{O}'$, then it is easy to see that the adversary $\mathcal{A}$ that on input $[v]_g$ computes $[\overline{M^\top \mathbf{v}}]_g$ and outputs $\mathcal{A}'([\overline{M^\top \mathbf{v}}]_g)$ is an adversary that breaks VBB, T-VBB or $\mathcal{D}$-DVBB security of $\mathcal{O}$ respectively. □

7.3 Impossibility Result

We have proven that the construction of [3] is essentially only $2^{n/2}$-VBB secure. So constructing a simple, efficient and fully VBB secure construction is still an open problem. A priori, one can hope to find another construction that follows the linear-in-the-exponent paradigm which is fully VBB secure, or perhaps something that is $2^{\sqrt{n}}$-VBB secure. Unfortunately we show that our attack on the construction of [3] generalizes to a wide class of "natural" linear-in-the exponent constructions. Recall that our attack on the scheme of [3] allowed to check whether the first half of an obfuscated pattern consists of wildcards. This was done by interpolating on the first n values. In the language of the linear-in-the-exponent framework this means there is a vector $\mathbf{o}$ (which corresponds to polynomial interpolation) that is orthogonal to V_ρ for every pattern ρ that has wildcards in the first $n/2$ positions. So, given an obfuscated program $\mathcal{O}(\rho) = [\mathbf{v}]_g$, one can test if the first half of the obfuscated pattern ρ consists of wildcards by checking if $[\mathbf{o}^\top \cdot \mathbf{v}]_g = [0]_g$. One crucial element here for the attack work is that $[\mathbf{o}^\top \cdot \mathbf{v}]_g \neq [0]_g$ with a large probability if $[\mathbf{v}]_g$ is the obfuscation of a pattern that does have non-wildcard characters in the first half of the pattern. For the construction of [3] this is obviously true.

The same thing happens for general linear-in-the-exponent obfuscation schemes. We show in Lemma 5 that if $a \leq \frac{n}{\log(m)}$, then there exist a subset $A \subset [n]$ of size a and a non-zero attack vector $\mathbf{o}$ such that $\mathbf{o}$ is orthogonal to V_ρ for every pattern ρ that has only wildcards outside of A. If $\mathbf{o}$ is not orthogonal to obfuscations of uniformly chosen patterns with a non-negligible probability, then this breaks VBB security (and even $2^{\frac{n}{\omega(\log n)}}$-VBB security). Note that without loss of generality we can assume that no vector is orthogonal to *every* V_ρ, because otherwise we can use the compression trick to obtain a more efficient and equally secure scheme. Schemes for which each vector is not orthogonal to a significant fraction of the V_ρ are called natural. We then prove that there are no natural linear-in-the-exponent obfuscation schemes.

Definition 11 (Natural linear-in-the-exponent schemes). *A linear-in-the-exponent obfuscation scheme* $(\mathbf{u}, V, m, \mathcal{O})$ *is called* natural *if there exists a polynomial* $p(n)$ *such that for all vectors* $\mathbf{o}$

$$\Pr_{\rho \leftarrow \{0,1,\star\}^n}[\mathbf{o} \notin V_\rho^\perp] \geq \frac{1}{p(n)}\,.$$

Remark 4. All schemes where $m(n) = n + 1$ are natural.

Lemma 5 (There exist vectors orthogonal to patterns with wildcards at fixed positions). *Let* $(\mathsf{u}, V, m, \mathcal{O})$ *be a linear-in-the-exponent obfuscation scheme for pattern matching with wildcards. Then if* $a(n) \leq \frac{n}{\log(m(n))}$ *then there exist subsets* $A_n \subset [n]$ *of size* $|A_n| = a(n)$ *and non-zero vectors* $\mathbf{o}_n$ *such that* $\mathbf{o}_n$ *is orthogonal to* V_ρ *for any pattern* ρ *that has wildcards outside of* A_n.

Proof. Suppose $(\mathsf{u}, V, m, \mathcal{O})$ is a linear-in-the-exponent obfuscation scheme for pattern matching with wildcards. Let $a(n)$ be a function such that $2^{\lfloor \frac{n}{a(n)} \rfloor} > m(n)$ then we will prove that there is a subset $A \subset [n]$ of size $|A| = a$ together with a non-zero vector $\mathbf{o}$ such that $\mathbf{o}$ is orthogonal to V_ρ for all patterns ρ such that $\rho_i = \star$ for all i outside of A. It suffices to show this in the case that the V_ρ are maximal given the correctness constraints, i.e.

$$V_\rho = \langle \mathbf{u_x} \,|\, \mathbf{x} \in \{0,1\}^n : \rho(\mathbf{x}) = 1 \rangle^\perp .$$

Clearly, if we prove there exists a vector $\mathbf{o}$ that is orthogonal to the maximal V_ρ, than this $\mathbf{o}$ will also be orthogonal to whatever the V_ρ are in any other linear-in-the-exponent obfuscation scheme with the same $\mathbf{u}$ map.

For $i \in [n]$ and $j \in \{0, 1, \star\}$ let $e_{i,j}$ be the pattern that has the character j at position i and wildcards at all other positions. Then we have for a general pattern ρ that $f_\rho(\mathbf{x}) = 1$ if and only if $f_{e_{i,\rho_j}}(\mathbf{x}) = 1$ for all $i \in [n]$. Therefore we have that

$$\begin{aligned} V_\rho &= \langle \mathbf{u_x} \,|\, \mathbf{x} \in \{0,1\}^n : f_{e_{i,\rho_i}}(\mathbf{x}) = 1 \ \forall i \in [n] \rangle^\perp \\ &= \sum_{i=1}^{n} \langle \mathbf{u_x} \,|\, \mathbf{x} \in \{0,1\}^n : f_{e_{i,\rho_i}}(\mathbf{x}) = 1 \rangle^\perp = \sum_{i=1}^{n} V_{e_{i,\rho_i}} . \end{aligned}$$

Working towards a contradiction, suppose no $A \subset [n]$ of size $|A| = a$ and $\mathbf{o}$ exists. This means that for every set $A \subset [n]$ of size $|A| = a$ we have

$$\cap \{ V_\rho^\perp \,|\, \rho : \rho_i = \star \forall i \notin A \} = \{0\} ,$$

which is equivalent to $\sum \{ V_\rho \,|\, \rho : \rho_i = \star \forall i \notin A \} = \mathbb{Z}_p^{m(n)}$. Using the fact that $V_\rho = \sum_{i=0}^{n} V_{e_{i,\rho_i}}$ this is the same as

$$\left(\sum_{i \in A} V_{e_{i,0}} \right) + \left(\sum_{i \in A} V_{e_{i,1}} \right) = \mathbb{Z}_p^{m(n)} . \tag{6}$$

Pick $\lceil \frac{n}{a} \rceil$ disjoint subsets $A_1, \cdots, A_k$, each of size a, and define the vector spaces

$$V_i^j = \sum_{i \in A_i} V_{e_{i,j}} .$$

Then Eq. 6 says that for any i we have $V_i^0 + V_i^1 = \mathbb{Z}_p^{m(n)}$. At the same time we have for any $\mathbf{y} \in \{0,1\}^k$ that

$$V_\mathbf{y} = \sum_{i=1}^{k} V_i^{\mathbf{y}_i} \neq \mathbb{Z}_p^n ,$$

because if ρ is the pattern such that $\rho_i = \mathbf{y}_j$ if $i \in A_j$ and $\rho_i = \star$ otherwise, then $V_\rho = \sum_{i=1}^{k} V_i^{y_i}$, and V_ρ is not equal to $\mathbb{Z}_p^m(n)$ because by correctness it is orthogonal to $\mathbf{x}$ for any $\mathbf{x}$ that is accepted by ρ.

Now we show that the 2^k none of the spaces $V_{\mathbf{y}}^{\perp}$ are included in the sum of the other $2^k - 1$ ones. Indeed, suppose $V_{\mathbf{y}}^{\perp} \subset \sum_{\mathbf{y}' \neq \mathbf{y}} V_{\mathbf{y}'}^{\perp}$, which is equivalent to $V_{\mathbf{y}} \supset \bigcap_{\mathbf{y}' \neq \mathbf{y}} V_{\mathbf{y}'}$, then after adding $V_{\mathbf{y}}$ to both sides we get

$$V_{\mathbf{y}} \supset \bigcap_{\mathbf{y}' \neq \mathbf{y}} (V_{\mathbf{y}'} + V_{\mathbf{y}}) .$$

But this is a contradiction because the left hand side is not equal to $\mathbb{Z}_p^{m(n)}$ while each space in the intersection is equal to $\mathbb{Z}_p^{m(n)}$ because if $\mathbf{y}_i \neq \mathbf{y}'_i$, then $V_{\mathbf{y}'} + V_{\mathbf{y}}$ contains $V_i^0 + V_i^1 = \mathbb{Z}_p^{m(n)}$. The fact that none of 2^k subspaces of $\mathbb{Z}_p^{m(n)}$ is included in the sum of the other $2^k - 1$ ones implies that $m(n) \geq 2^k = 2^{\lfloor \frac{n}{a} \rfloor}$, which contradicts the assumption that $m(n) < 2^{\lfloor \frac{n}{a} \rfloor}$. □

The following theorem follows readily from Lemma 5 and the discussion above.

Theorem 12 (Limitations of linear-in-the-exponent obfuscation). *There are no natural linear-in-the-exponent obfuscation schemes that are $2^{\frac{n}{\omega(\log n)}}$-VBB secure.*

Since every scheme with the minimal dimensionality of $m = n+1$ is automatically natural, this implies that no VBB secure constructions with $m(n) = n+1$ exist.

Proof. Let $a(n) = \frac{n}{\log(m(n))} - 1$. Then Lemma 3 says that there exists an A_n of size $a(n)$ and vectors $\mathbf{o}_n$ such that $\mathbf{o}$ is orthogonal to V_ρ for all patterns ρ that have wilcards outside of A_n. Sampling uniformly from patterns that have wildcards outside of A_n and no wildcards at locations in A_n are $2^{a(n)}n^{-\omega(1)}$-elusive. But obfuscations of these patterns can be efficiently distinguished from obfuscations of uniformly random patterns (which are also elusive) with the vectors $\mathbf{o}_n$, because the former are orthogonal to $\mathbf{o}$, and the latter are not with non negligible probability (because of the naturality assumption). Then it follows from Lemma 1 that the scheme is not $2^{a(n)}n^{-\omega(1)}$-VBB secure. The claim follows because $2^{a(n)}n^{-\omega(1))}$ is eventually bigger than $2^{n/f(n)}$ for every $f(n)$ that is $\omega(\log n)$. □

Acknowledgements. This work started at ENS over the summer; we thank Luke Kowalczyk for telling us about [3], as well as Michel Abdalla, Georg Fuchsbauer and Hendrik Waldner for helpful discussions. This work was supported in part by the Research Council KU Leuven: C16/15/058, C14/18/067 and STG/17/019. In addition, this work was supported by the European Commission through the Horizon 2020 research and innovation programme under grant agreement H2020-DS-LEIT-2017-780108 FENTEC, by the Flemish Government through FWO SBO project SNIPPET and by the IF/C1 on Cryptanalysis of post-quantum cryptography. Ward Beullens is funded by an FWO fellowship. Hoeteck Wee is supported by ERC Project aSCEND (H2020 639554).

References

1. Barak, B., et al.: On the (im)possibility of obfuscating programs. In: Kilian, J. (ed.) CRYPTO 2001. LNCS, vol. 2139, pp. 1–18. Springer, Heidelberg (2001). https://doi.org/10.1007/3-540-44647-8_1
2. Bartusek, J., Lepoint, T., Ma, F., Zhandry, M.: New techniques for obfuscating conjunctions. Cryptology ePrint Archive, Report 2018/936 (2018). https://eprint.iacr.org/2018/936
3. Bishop, A., Kowalczyk, L., Malkin, T., Pastro, V., Raykova, M., Shi, K.: A simple obfuscation scheme for pattern-matching with wildcards. In: Shacham, H., Boldyreva, A. (eds.) CRYPTO 2018. LNCS, vol. 10993, pp. 731–752. Springer, Cham (2018). https://doi.org/10.1007/978-3-319-96878-0_25
4. Bitansky, N., Canetti, R.: On strong simulation and composable point obfuscation. In: Rabin, T. (ed.) CRYPTO 2010. LNCS, vol. 6223, pp. 520–537. Springer, Heidelberg (2010). https://doi.org/10.1007/978-3-642-14623-7_28
5. Brakerski, Z., Rothblum, G.N.: Obfuscating conjunctions. In: Canetti, R., Garay, J.A. (eds.) CRYPTO 2013, Part II. LNCS, vol. 8043, pp. 416–434. Springer, Heidelberg (2013). https://doi.org/10.1007/978-3-642-40084-1_24
6. Brakerski, Z., Vaikuntanathan, V., Wee, H., Wichs, D.: Obfuscating conjunctions under entropic ring LWE. In: ITCS, pp. 147–156. ACM (2016)
7. Canetti, R.: Towards realizing random oracles: hash functions that hide all partial information. In: Kaliski, B.S. (ed.) CRYPTO 1997. LNCS, vol. 1294, pp. 455–469. Springer, Heidelberg (1997). https://doi.org/10.1007/BFb0052255
8. Canetti, R., Dakdouk, R.R.: Obfuscating point functions with multibit output. In: Smart, N. (ed.) EUROCRYPT 2008. LNCS, vol. 4965, pp. 489–508. Springer, Heidelberg (2008). https://doi.org/10.1007/978-3-540-78967-3_28
9. Canetti, R., Rothblum, G.N., Varia, M.: Obfuscation of hyperplane membership. In: Micciancio, D. (ed.) TCC 2010. LNCS, vol. 5978, pp. 72–89. Springer, Heidelberg (2010). https://doi.org/10.1007/978-3-642-11799-2_5
10. Damgård, I.: Towards practical public key systems secure against chosen ciphertext attacks. In: Feigenbaum, J. (ed.) CRYPTO 1991. LNCS, vol. 576, pp. 445–456. Springer, Heidelberg (1992). https://doi.org/10.1007/3-540-46766-1_36
11. Fuchsbauer, G., Kiltz, E., Loss, J.: The algebraic group model and its applications. In: Shacham, H., Boldyreva, A. (eds.) CRYPTO 2018. LNCS, vol. 10992, pp. 33–62. Springer, Cham (2018). https://doi.org/10.1007/978-3-319-96881-0_2
12. Garg, S., Gentry, C., Halevi, S., Raykova, M., Sahai, A., Waters, B.: Candidate indistinguishability obfuscation and functional encryption for all circuits. SIAM J. Comput. **45**(3), 882–929 (2016)
13. Goyal, R., Koppula, V., Waters, B.: Lockable obfuscation. In: FOCS, pp. 612–621 (2017)
14. Hada, S.: Zero-knowledge and code obfuscation. In: Okamoto, T. (ed.) ASIACRYPT 2000. LNCS, vol. 1976, pp. 443–457. Springer, Heidelberg (2000). https://doi.org/10.1007/3-540-44448-3_34
15. Lynn, B., Prabhakaran, M., Sahai, A.: Positive results and techniques for obfuscation. In: Cachin, C., Camenisch, J.L. (eds.) EUROCRYPT 2004. LNCS, vol. 3027, pp. 20–39. Springer, Heidelberg (2004). https://doi.org/10.1007/978-3-540-24676-3_2
16. Wee, H.: On obfuscating point functions. In: STOC, pp. 523–532. ACM (2005)
17. Wichs, D., Zirdelis, G.: Obfuscating compute-and-compare programs under LWE. In: FOCS, pp. 600–611 (2017)

Re-encryption Schemes

What About Bob? The Inadequacy of CPA Security for Proxy Reencryption

Aloni Cohen(✉)

MIT, Cambridge, MA, USA
aloni@mit.edu

Abstract. In the simplest setting of proxy reencryption, there are three parties: Alice, Bob, and Polly (the proxy). Alice keeps some encrypted data that she can decrypt with a secret key known only to her. She wants to communicate the data to Bob, but not to Polly (nor anybody else). Using proxy reencryption, Alice can create a *reencryption key* that will enable Polly to reencrypt the data for Bob's use, but which will not help Polly learn anything about the data.

There are two well-studied notions of security for proxy reencryption schemes: security under chosen-plaintext attacks (CPA) and security under chosen-ciphertext attacks (CCA). Both definitions aim to formalize the security that Alice enjoys against both Polly and Bob.

In this work, we demonstrate that CPA security guarantees much less security against Bob than was previously understood. In particular, CPA security does not prevent Bob from learning Alice's secret key after receiving a single honestly reencrypted ciphertext. As a result, CPA security provides scant guarantees in common applications.

We propose security under honest reencryption attacks (HRA), a strengthening of CPA security that better captures the goals of proxy reencryption. In applications, HRA security provides much more robust security. We identify a property of proxy reencryption schemes that suffices to amplify CPA security to HRA security and show that two existing proxy reencryption schemes are in fact HRA secure.

Keywords: Proxy reencryption · Definitions · Public-key cryptography

1 Introduction

Consider three parties: Alice, Bob, and Polly Proxy. Alice keeps encrypted data (created with a public key) that she can decrypt with a secret key known only to her. She wants to communicate some of the data to Bob, but not to Polly

Supported by Facebook Fellowship 2018, NSF GRFP, NSF MACS CNS-1413920, DARPA IBM W911NF-15-C-0236, and Simons Investigator Award Agreement Dated 6-5-12. We would like to thank Rio LaVigne, Akshay Degwekar, Shafi Goldwasser, Vinod Vaikuntanathan, and anonymous reviewers for their helpful feedback.

D. Lin and K. Sako (Eds.): PKC 2019, LNCS 11443, pp. 287–316, 2019.
https://doi.org/10.1007/978-3-030-17259-6_10

(nor anybody else). Assuming Alice and Polly know Bob's public key, how can she communicate the data to him?

If she is willing to entrust Bob with all her secrets, past and future, Alice might try to tell Bob her secret decryption key by encrypting it using Bob's public key. We call this the *Trivial Scheme*. If she does not have such trust in Bob, Alice can instead decrypt the data, and reencrypt it using Bob's public key. But what if Alice does not want to do the work of decrypting and reencrypting large amounts of data?

Proxy reencryption (PRE) provides an elegant solution: Alice creates and gives to Polly a *reencryption key* that will enable Polly to reencrypt her data under Bob's public key for his use, but that will not reveal the data to Polly. Proxy reencryption guarantees that Bob can recover the data uncorrupted (correctness) and that Polly cannot learn anything about Alice's data (security). The most widely-studied model of security for proxy reencryption is called *CPA security*, named after the corresponding notion from standard encryption on which it is based.

But what about Bob? As already observed, if we do not require any security against Bob, proxy reencryption is trivial: Alice uses the Trivial Scheme, simply sending Bob her encrypted secret key. This is undesirable, unsatisfying, and insufficient for a number of supposed applications of proxy reencryption (Sect. 2).

Surprisingly, *the Trivial Scheme is a CPA secure proxy reencryption scheme* when the public key encryption scheme used is circularly secure [6]! Bob completely learns Alice's secret key, and circular security is used only to prove security against a malicious Polly. Furthermore, the CPA-security of any proxy reencryption scheme remains uncompromised if Polly attaches the reencryption key to every reencrypted ciphertext sent to Bob, even though this would enable Bob to decrypt messages encrypted under Alice's public key (Sect. 3.1).

These "constructions" of CPA-secure proxy reencryption—original to this work—demonstrate the inadequacy of CPA security for proxy reencryption. If they had been observed previously, perhaps CPA security would not have gained the traction that it has.

Throughout this work, we use CPA (respectively, CCA and HRA) to refer to the security notion for proxy reencryption, and Enc-CPA (resp., Enc-CCA) to refer to the security notion for standard encryption. We restrict our attention to *unidirectional* proxy reencryption, where the reencryption key allows Alice's ciphertexts to be reencrypted to Bob's key, but not the reverse. In a bidirectional scheme, Bob—using his own secret key and Alice's public key—is able compute the Alice-to-Bob reencryption key himself; thus a lack of security against Bob is inherent.

1.1 CPA and CCA Security of Proxy Reencryption

First considered by Blaze, Bleumer, and Strauss [5], proxy reencryption has received significant and continuous attention in the last decade, including definitions [4,10,22,28], number-theoretical constructions [3,12,26], lattice-based constructions [2,17,19,30], implementations [8,20,25,31], and early success in program obfuscation [11,21].

Adapting notions from standard encryption, this literature considers two main indistinguishability-based security notions for proxy reencryption: security under *chosen plaintext attacks (CPA)* [3] and *chosen ciphertext attacks (CCA)* [10]. While CCA security is considered the gold-standard, CPA security has received significant attention [3,4,21], especially in latticed-based constructions [2,19,30,31]. CPA security has been used as a testing ground for new techniques for proxy reencryption and in settings where efficiency concerns make the added security of CCA undesirable.

We now briefly describe the definitions of CPA and CCA security for proxy reencryption, with the goal of communicating the underlying intuition. For this informal description, we restrict our attention to the limited three party setting of Alice, Bob, and Polly and strip away many of the complexities of the full definition. For a full definitions of CPA and CCA security, see Definition 3 and the full version of this article [13], respectively.

Both notions are typically defined using a security game between an adversary and a challenger in which the adversary's task is to distinguish between encryptions of two messages. Both notions allow the adversary to corrupt either Bob (learning $\mathsf{sk}_{\mathsf{bob}}$) or Polly (learning the reencryption key rk). CCA and CPA security differ in the additional power granted to the adversary.

CCA security grants the adversary access to two oracles:

- $\mathcal{O}_{\mathsf{Dec}}$: The decryption oracle takes as input a ciphertext along with the public key of either Alice or Bob, and outputs the decryption of the ciphertext using the corresponding secret key.
- $\mathcal{O}_{\mathsf{ReEnc}}$: The reencryption oracle takes as input a ciphertext $\mathsf{ct}_{\mathsf{alice}}$ and outputs a reencrypted ciphertext $\mathsf{ct}_{\mathsf{bob}}$.

These oracles come with restrictions to prevent the adversary from simply reencrypting or decrypting the challenge ciphertext, adapting replayable chosen-ciphertext security of standard encryption (Enc-CCA) in the natural way.

CPA security of proxy reencryption, however, removes both oracles.[1] Why? First, to adapt chosen-plaintext security from standard encryption (Enc-CPA) to proxy reencryption, we must of course do away with $\mathcal{O}_{\mathsf{Dec}}$. Secondly, it seems we must also remove $\mathcal{O}_{\mathsf{ReEnc}}$: otherwise, by corrupting Bob it seems that the adversary can use the combination of $\mathcal{O}_{\mathsf{ReEnc}}$ and $\mathsf{sk}_{\mathsf{bob}}$ to simulate $\mathcal{O}_{\mathsf{Dec}}$. Removing both decryption and reencryption oracles, according to [3], naturally extends the Enc-CPA security to proxy reencryption, yielding CPA security.

As we observe in this work, a natural definition is not always a good definition. Not only is the above intuition for removing $\mathcal{O}_{\mathsf{ReEnc}}$ false (see full version

[1] This description is an oversimplification. In the many party setting, the adversary has access to a reencryption oracle which will reencrypt ciphertexts between two uncorrupted parties or between two corrupted parties, but not from an honest party to a corrupted party.

[13]), but CPA security as defined above guarantees little against a honest-but-curious Bob, even under *normal operation.* The definition only requires that the adversary will not win the game as long as it never sees any reencrypted ciphertexts. It guarantees nothing if Bob sees even a single reencrypted ciphertext. This vulnerability is not purely theoretical: in the CPA secure scheme of [31], Bob can recover Alice's secret key with significant probability from a single reencrypted ciphertext (Theorem 4).

This makes CPA security ill-suited for the most commonly cited applications of proxy reencryption, including forwarding of encrypted email and single-writer, many-reader encrypted storage (Sect. 2). CPA security is inadequate for proxy reencryption and must be replaced.

1.2 Security Against Honest Reencryption Attacks

What minimal guarantees should proxy reencryption provide? First, it should offer security against a dishonest proxy Polly when Alice and Bob are honest and using the proxy reencryption as intended. Polly's knowledge of a reencryption key from Alice to Bob (or vice versa) should not help her learn anything about the messages underlying ciphertexts encrypted under $\mathsf{pk}_{\mathsf{alice}}$ or $\mathsf{pk}_{\mathsf{bob}}$. Such security against the corrupted proxy is guaranteed by CPA.

Second, proxy reencryption should offer security against a dishonest receiver Bob when Alice and Polly are honest and using the proxy reencryption as intended. Bob's knowledge of *honestly reencrypted ciphertexts* (that were honestly generated to begin with) should not help him learn anything about the messages underlying other ciphertexts encrypted under $\mathsf{pk}_{\mathsf{alice}}$ that have not been reencrypted. As we show in this work, such security against the corrupted receiver is not guaranteed by CPA.

Generalizing these dual guarantees to many possibly colluding parties, we want security as long as the adversary only sees honestly reencrypted ciphertexts. In Sect. 4, we formalize this notion as proxy reencryption security against *honest reencryption attacks (HRA).* Recall that CCA security provides the adversary with both $\mathcal{O}_{\mathsf{Dec}}$ and $\mathcal{O}_{\mathsf{ReEnc}}$ while CPA provides neither oracle. In contrast, HRA security provides the adversary with a restricted reencryption oracle which will only reencrypt honestly generated ciphertexts.

By guaranteeing security of both kinds described above, HRA is a strengthening of CPA security that better captures our intuitions for security of proxy reencryption. Furthermore, HRA guarantees more meaningful security in the most common applications of proxy reencryption (Sect. 4.1). HRA security is an appropriate goal when developing new techniques for proxy reencryption and in settings where full CCA security is undesirable or out of reach.

Security of Existing Schemes. Can we construct a proxy reencryption scheme that is HRA secure? HRA security is a strict strengthening of CPA security, so it is not immediately clear that any existing constructions are HRA secure without redoing the proofs from scratch. Indeed, the CPA secure scheme of [31] is not HRA secure (Theorem 4).

In Sect. 5, we identify a property—*reencryption simulatablity*—which is sufficient to boost CPA security to HRA security. Very roughly, reencryption simulatability means that reencrypted ciphertexts resulting from computing $\mathsf{ReEnc}(\mathsf{rk}_{\mathsf{alice}\to\mathsf{bob}}, \mathsf{ct}_{\mathsf{alice}})$ can be simulated without knowledge of the secret key $\mathsf{sk}_{\mathsf{alice}}$ (but with knowledge of the plaintext message $\mathbf{m}$). Reencryption simulatability allows a reduction with access to the CPA oracles to efficiently implement the honest reencryption oracle, thereby reducing HRA security to CPA security.

We the examine the simple construction of proxy reencryption from any fully-homomorphic encryption [19], and the pairing-based construction of [4]. In the first case, if the fully-homomorphic encryption secure is circuit private, then the resulting proxy reencryption scheme is reencryption simulatable. In the second case, rerandomizing reencrypted ciphertexts suffices for reencryption simulation.[2]

1.3 Related Work

The below mentioned works are just the most directly relevant. There is by now an extensive research literature on proxy reencryption, presenting a zoo of definitions. There have been three main approaches to defining security: CPA, CCA, and (to a much lesser extent) obfuscation-based. The CPA notion, in one form or another, is by far the most well studied. In this work, we make the deliberate choice to address the core CPA definition, not to present an ultimate definition of security for proxy reencryption nor to address the vast array of different criticisms or strengthenings of CPA security that have been or may be considered. We hope that doing so will make these ideas more understandable and adaptable.

RIND-CPA Security. In concurrent and independent work defining and constructing forward-secure proxy reencryption, Derler, Krenn, Lorünser, Ramacher, Slamanig, and Striecks identify the same problem with CPA security as discussed in this work [14, Definition 14]. As in our work, they address the problem with CPA security by defining a new security notion—RIND-CPA security—which expands the power of the adversary. They additionally separate RIND-CPA and CPA security with a construction that is essentially our Concatenation Scheme.

However, this is where the resemblance between [14] and our work ends. In the RIND-CPA game offered by [14], the adversary gets access to an reencryption oracle that works on all inputs (not just honestly generated ones), but only before the challenge ciphertext is generated.[3] In contrast, HRA allows reencryption both before and after the challenge, but only for honestly generated ciphertexts.

[2] While we don't examine every pairing-based construction of proxy reencryption, we suspect that rerandomizing reencryption will suffice for reencryption simulation in many, if not all.

[3] The full version [13] discusses the related definition of $\mathsf{IND\text{-}CCA}_{0,1}$ security from [28].

RIND-IND is inadequate as a replacement for CPA security in the research literature: its usefulness in applications is unclear, and it appears too strong to provide a useful testing ground for the development of new techniques for constructing proxy reencryption.

In the course of normal operation of a proxy reencryption in applications, an adversarial party will typically see many reencrypted ciphertexts. These ciphertexts may come at any time—both before and after other ciphertexts whose contents should remain secret. HRA is meaningful in many such applications—many more than CPA security. But because RIND-CPA restricts the reencryption oracle to the period before the challenge ciphertext, its usefulness in applications is not clear.

The challenge of proving CCA security for encryption (proxy or otherwise) is demonstrating that an adversary cannot use dishonestly generated, malformed ciphertexts to win in the security game. In this respect, RIND-CPA security is much more akin to CCA security than to CPA security. HRA, on the other hand, makes minimal assumptions about the distribution of plaintext messages by allowing the adversary to choose messages itself, just as in Enc-CPA for standard encryption.

Appendix B discusses RIND-CPA security in more depth, expanding on the arguments above and proving that RIND-CPA and HRA security are incomparable.

Subsequent Work. Two subsequent works continue the study of HRA secure proxy reencryption. Fuchsbauer, Kamath, Klein, and Pietrzak study CPA and HRA secure proxy reencryption in an adaptive corruption model [18]. As in our work, they prove the HRA security of their construction by first proving CPA security and then lifting it to full HRA security using a version of reencryption simulatability.

More recently, Dottling and Nishimaki study the problem of converting ciphertexts between different public-key encryption schemes, a problem they call universal proxy reencryption [15]. They define security by extending HRA security to the universal setting. [15] extends Theorem 5 to show that a computational version of reencryption simulatability suffices to lift CPA to HRA security. However, they prove HRA security directly rather, finding that proving computational reencryption simulatability is not much more simple than proving HRA security itself.

Other Related Work. Our dual-guarantee conception of proxy reencryption security mirrors the security requirements of what Ivan and Dodis call CPA security [22]. Their notion differs substantially from what is now referred to by that name. The [22] conception of CPA security is only defined in a proof in the appendix of that work and seems to have been completely overlooked by the later works proposing the modern notion of CPA security (beginning with [4] and then in its present form in [3]). If, however, Ivan and Dodis had undertaken to revisit proxy reencryption after [3], they might have proposed a security definition similar to HRA.

In [28], Nuñez, Agudo, and Lopez provide a parameterized family of CCA-type attack models for proxy reencryption. Their weakest model corresponds to CPA security and their strongest to full CCA security. That work is partially a response to a claimed construction of CCA-1 secure proxy reencryption in a security model that does not allow reencryption queries. [28] provide an attack on the construction in the presence of a reencryption oracle consisting of carefully constructed, dishonestly generated queries which leak the reencryption key. They do not consider restricting the reencryption oracle in the security game to honestly generated ciphertexts. We discuss [28] further in the full version [13].

Finally, a parallel line of work initiated by Hohenberger, Rothblum, Shelat, Vaikuntanathan which studies proxy reencryption using an obfuscation-based definition that is incomparable to CPA security [21]. Their definition requires that the functionality of the obfuscated reencryption circuit be statistically close to that of the ideal reencryption functionality: namely, that $\mathsf{ReEnc}(\mathsf{rk}_{i\to j}, \mathsf{Enc}(\mathsf{pk}_i, \mathbf{m})) \approx_s \mathsf{Enc}(\mathsf{pk}_j, \mathbf{m})$. Thus the definition of [21] (and even the relaxed correctness found in [11]) imply *reencryption simulatability* defined in Sect. 5.

1.4 Organization

We begin by discussing applications of proxy reencryption and identifying the weaknesses of CPA security in those applications (Sect. 2). Then we present the existing CPA security definition and further demonstrate its weaknesses with two new schemes: the Trivial Scheme and Concatentation Scheme (Sect. 3). We propose a new security notion to overcome those weaknesses: security against honest reenecryption attacks (HRA) (Sect. 4). We examine the relationship between CPA and HRA security and the HRA security (or insecurity) of existing reencryption schemes (Sect. 5). The appendix provides additional discussion of the Trivial Scheme (Appendix A) and comparison between HRA and RIND-CPA security (Appendix B). The full version provides additional discussion of CCA security [13].

2 Insufficiency of CPA Security for Applications

In Sect. 3, we recall the definition of CPA security of proxy reencryption from [3] and formalize the Trivial Scheme from the introduction satisfying the notion. In the Trivial Scheme, Bob learns Alice's secret key after receiving a single reencrypted ciphertext.

We are faced with a choice: accept the existing definition of CPA security, or reject it and seek a definition that better captures our intuitions. In support of the latter, we describe a number of applications of proxy reencryption proposed in the literature for which CPA security (as implemented by the Trivial Scheme) is potentially unsatisfactory, but for which full CCA security may not always be necessary.[4] We revisit these applications in Sect. 4.1 after proposing our new security notion.

Encrypted Email Forwarding [4,5,23]. Forwarding of encrypted email without requiring the sender's participation might be desirable for temporary delegation during a vacation [23] or for spam filtering [4]. Does the Trivial Scheme suffice? The Trivial Scheme enables Bob, the receiver of Alice's forwarded (and reencrypted) email, to recover Alice's secret key. If Alice trusts Bob enough to use the Trivial Scheme, she could instead reveal her secret key. The Trivial Scheme might be preferable in very specific trust or interaction models, but it does not offer meaningful security against Bob if Alice only wishes to forward a subset of emails (for example, from particular senders or during a specific time period).

Key Escrow [22]. Similar to email forwarding, Ivan and Dodis describe the application of key escrow as follows: "The problem is to allow the law enforcement agency to read messages encrypted for a set of users, for a limited period of time, without knowing the users secrets. The solution is to locate a key escrow agent between the users and the law enforcement agency, such that it controls which messages are read by the law enforcement agencies." As in email forwarding, the "for a limited period of time" requirement suggests that Ivan and Dodis would not have been satisfied with the Trivial Scheme.[5]

Single-Writer, Many-Reader Encrypted Storage [4,24,25,31]. Under different monikers (including DRM and publish/subscribe systems), these works describe systems in which a single privileged writer encrypts data and determines an access control policy for readers. A semi-honest proxy server is entrusted with reencryption keys and is tasked with enforcing the access control policy. Whether the Trivial Scheme suffices for these applications depends on what sort of access control policies are envisioned. If the access is *all or nothing* (i.e., all readers may access all data), the Trivial Scheme suffices; if the access is *fine grained* (i.e., each reader may access only a specific subset of the data), then it does not. Existing works are often unclear on which is envisioned.

[4] We might also appeal for support to [22], the only paper in the proxy reencryption literature of which we are aware adopting a security definition providing a reencryption oracle without a decryption oracle. One could look to the originators of proxy reencryption for guidance, but the shortcoming we identify does not manifest in the original setting of [5] (there is only Alice and Bob; there is no Proxy). It is therefore of little help.

[5] Note that Ivan and Dodis do not adopt the CPA definition used elsewhere, but a definition much closer to our own. There is no gap between their security guarantees and the requirements of their briefly-described application.

Though primarily focused on the setting where the key escrow agent enforces the limited time requirement by eventually refusing to reencrypt, [22] considers the possibility of dividing time into epochs and enforcing the time limitation technically. Such a proxy reencryption is called *temporary* in [4]. We do not discuss temporary proxy reencryption further.

For completeness, we mention that CPA security does suffice for two important applications of proxy reencryption: namely, key rotation for encrypted cloud storage [7,16] and fully homomorphic encryption [19].

3 Security Against Chosen Plaintext Attacks

In this section, we recall the definition of CPA security for proxy reencryption and illustrate its shortcomings. We begin with the definitions of syntax, correctness, and CPA security from [3, Definition 2.2] (with minor changes in notation and presentation, and the change noted in Remark 1 at the end of this subsection). The syntax and correctness requirements are common to CPA, HRA, and CCA security.

For the sake of concreteness, simplicity, and brevity, we restrict the discussion to unidirectional, single-hop schemes. In multi-hop schemes, reencryption keys $\mathsf{rk}_{A\to B}$ and $\mathsf{rk}_{B\to C}$ can be used to reencrypt a ciphertext ct_A from pk_A to pk_C. In single-hop schemes, they cannot. Single-hop or multi-hop schemes each have their benefits and drawbacks, and works typically focus on one or the other notion.[6] To the best of our knowledge, our observations and results can all be adapted to the multi-hop setting.

Definition 1 (Proxy Reencryption: Syntax [3]**).** *A proxy reencryption scheme for a message space $\mathcal{M}$ is a tuple of algorithms* $\mathsf{PRE} = (\mathsf{Setup}, \mathsf{KeyGen}, \mathsf{ReKeyGen}, \mathsf{Enc}, \mathsf{ReEnc}, \mathsf{Dec})$*:*

$\mathsf{Setup}(1^\lambda) \to \mathsf{pp}$. *On input security parameter 1^λ, the* setup *algorithm outputs the public parameters* pp.

$\mathsf{KeyGen}(\mathsf{pp}) \to (\mathsf{pk}, \mathsf{sk})$. *On input public parameters, the* key generation *algorithm outputs a public key* pk *and a secret key* sk. *For ease of notation, we assume that both* pk *and* sk *include* pp *and refrain from including* pp *as input to other algorithms.*

$\mathsf{ReKeyGen}(\mathsf{sk}_i, \mathsf{pk}_j) \to \mathsf{rk}_{i\to j}$. *On input a secret key* sk_i *and a public key* pk_j*, where $i \neq j$, the* reencryption key generation *algorithm outputs a reencryption key* $\mathsf{rk}_{i\to j}$.

[6] The literature is divided about whether "single-hop" is merely a correctness property (i.e., able to reencrypt at least once, but agnostic about whether reencrypting more than once is possible) or if it is also a security property (i.e., a ciphertext can be reencrypted once, but never twice). This distinction manifests in the security definition. In works that consider only single-hop correctness [3,4,21,28], the oracle $\mathcal{O}_{\mathsf{ReKeyGen}}$ in the security game will not accept queries from honest users to corrupted users (i.e., (i, j) such that $i \in \mathsf{Hon}$ and $j \in \mathsf{Cor}$). We adopt this formalism in Definitions 3 and 5 for simplicity of presentation only.

In works that consider single-hop security [12,17,26], the oracle will answer such queries, but the challenge ciphertext must be encrypted under the key of an honest user i^* for which no such reencryption key was generated (which can be formalized in a number of ways).

This work adopts the simplest model, requiring only one hope of correctness, but neither requiring nor forbidding additional functionality.

$\mathsf{Enc}(\mathsf{pk}_i, \mathbf{m}) \rightarrow \mathsf{ct}_i$. *On input a public key* pk_i *and a message* $\mathbf{m} \in \mathcal{M}$, *the* encryption algorithm *outputs a ciphertext* ct_i.

$\mathsf{ReEnc}(\mathsf{rk}_{i\to j}, \mathsf{ct}_i) \rightarrow \mathsf{ct}_j$. *On input a reencryption key from i to j* $\mathsf{rk}_{i\to j}$ *and a ciphertext* ct_i, *the* reencryption algorithm *ouputs a ciphertext* ct_j *or the error symbol* $\perp$.

$\mathsf{Dec}(\mathsf{sk}_j, \mathsf{ct}_j) \rightarrow \mathbf{m}$. *Given a secret key* sk_j *and a ciphertext* ct_j, *the* decryption *algorithm outputs a message* $\mathbf{m} \in \mathcal{M}$ *or the error symbol* $\perp$.

Definition 2 (Proxy Reencryption: Correctness [3]**).** *A proxy reencryption scheme* PRE *is correct with respect to message space* $\mathcal{M}$ *if for all* $\lambda \in \mathbb{N}$, $\mathsf{pp} \leftarrow \mathsf{Setup}(1^\lambda)$, *and* $\mathbf{m} \in \mathcal{M}$:

1. *for all* $(\mathsf{pk}, \mathsf{sk}) \leftarrow \mathsf{KeyGen}(\mathsf{pp})$:

$$\mathsf{Dec}(\mathsf{sk}, \mathsf{Enc}(\mathsf{pk}, \mathbf{m})) = \mathbf{m}.$$

2. *for all* $(\mathsf{pk}_i, \mathsf{sk}_i), (\mathsf{pk}_j, \mathsf{sk}_j) \leftarrow \mathsf{KeyGen}(\mathsf{pp})$, $\mathsf{rk}_{i\to j} \leftarrow \mathsf{ReKeyGen}(\mathsf{sk}_i, \mathsf{pk}_j)$:

$$\mathsf{Dec}(\mathsf{sk}_j, \mathsf{ReEnc}(\mathsf{rk}_{i\to j}, \mathsf{Enc}(\mathsf{pk}_i, \mathbf{m}))) = \mathbf{m}.$$

Security is modeled by a game played by an adversary $\mathcal{A}$. $\mathcal{A}$ has the power to corrupt a set of users Cor (learning their secret keys) while learning only the public keys for a set of honest users Hon. Additionally, $\mathcal{A}$ may reencrypt ciphertexts (either by getting a reencryption key or calling a reencryption oracle) between pairs of users in Hon or in Cor, or from Cor to Hon, but not from Hon to Cor. This is in contrast to the simplified three-party setting discussed in the introduction, where the $\mathcal{A}$ could not reencrypt whatsoever.

Definition 3 (Proxy Reencryption: Security Game for Chosen Plaintext Attacks (CPA) [3]**).** *Let* λ *be the security parameter and* $\mathcal{A}$ *be an oracle Turing machine. The CPA game consists of an execution of* $\mathcal{A}$ *with the following oracles. The game consists of three phases, which are executed in order. Within each phase, each oracle can be executed in any order,* poly(λ) *times, unless otherwise specified.*

Phase 1:

Setup: *The public parameters are generated and given to* $\mathcal{A}$. *A counter* numKeys *is initialized to 0, and the sets* Hon *(of honest, uncorrupted indices) and* Cor *(of corrupted indices) are initialized to be empty. This oracle is executed first and only once.*

Uncorrupted Key Generation: *Obtain a new key pair* $(\mathsf{pk}_{\mathsf{numKeys}}, \mathsf{sk}_{\mathsf{numKeys}}) \leftarrow \mathsf{KeyGen}(\mathsf{pp})$ *and give* $\mathsf{pk}_{\mathsf{numKeys}}$ *to* $\mathcal{A}$. *The current value of* numKeys *is added to* Hon *and* numKeys *is incremented.*

Corrupted Key Generation: *Obtain a new key pair* $(\mathsf{pk}_{\mathsf{numKeys}}, \mathsf{sk}_{\mathsf{numKeys}}) \leftarrow \mathsf{KeyGen}(\mathsf{pp})$ *and given to* $\mathcal{A}$. *The current value of* numKeys *is added to* Cor *and* numKeys *is incremented.*

Phase 2: For each pair $i, j \leq \mathsf{numKeys}$, *compute the reencryption key* $\mathsf{rk}_{i \to j} \leftarrow \mathsf{ReKeyGen}(\mathsf{sk}_i, \mathsf{pk}_j)$.

Reencryption Key Generation $\mathcal{O}_{\mathsf{ReKeyGen}}$: *On input* (i, j) *where* $i, j \leq \mathsf{numKeys}$, *if* $i = j$ *or if* $i \in \mathsf{Hon}$ *and* $j \in \mathsf{Cor}$, *output* $\perp$. *Otherwise return the reencryption key* $\mathsf{rk}_{i \to j}$.

Reencryption $\mathcal{O}_{\mathsf{ReEnc}}$: *On input* (i, j, ct_i) *where* $i, j \leq \mathsf{numKeys}$, *if* $i = j$ *or if* $i \in \mathsf{Hon}$ *and* $j \in \mathsf{Cor}$, *output* $\perp$. *Otherwise return the reencrypted ciphertext* $\mathsf{ReEnc}(\mathsf{rk}_{i \to j}, \mathsf{ct}_i)$.

Challenge Oracle: *On input* $(i, \mathbf{m}_0, \mathbf{m}_1)$ *where* $i \in \mathsf{Hon}$ *and* $\mathbf{m}_0, \mathbf{m}_1 \in \mathcal{M}$, *sample a bit* $b \leftarrow \{0, 1\}$ *uniformly at random, and return the challenge ciphertext* $\mathsf{ct}^* \leftarrow \mathsf{Enc}(\mathsf{pk}_i, \mathbf{m}_b)$. *This oracle can only be queried once.*

Phase 3:

Decision: *On input a bit* $b' \in \{0, 1\}$, *return* win *if* $b = b'$.

The CPA advantage *of* $\mathcal{A}$ *is defined as*

$$\mathsf{Adv}_{\mathsf{cpa}}^{\mathcal{A}}(\lambda) = \Pr[\mathsf{win}],$$

where the probability is over the randomness of $\mathcal{A}$ *and the oracles in the CPA game.*

Definition 4 (Proxy Reencryption: CPA Security[3]). *Given a security parameter* 1^λ, *a proxy reencryption scheme is CPA secure if for all probabilistic polynomial-time adversaries* $\mathcal{A}$, *there exists a negligible function* negl *such that*

$$\mathsf{Adv}_{\mathsf{cpa}}^{\mathcal{A}}(\lambda) < \frac{1}{2} + \mathsf{negl}(\lambda)$$

Remark 1. Another definitional subtlety of proxy reencryption worth discussing affects not just CPA security, but HRA and CCA security as well. Consider the specification of $\mathcal{O}_{\mathsf{ReKeyGen}}$ and $\mathcal{O}_{\mathsf{ReEnc}}$ in Definition 3. As defined, the reencryption keys $\mathsf{rk}_{i \to j}$ are *persistent*: the same key is used each time a pair (i, j) is queried. This follows [3, Definition 2.5] and [2,17], though we find our formalization somewhat simpler.

Contrast this with [3, Definition 2.2] in which reencryption keys are *ephemeral*: they are generated afresh each time either oracle is invoked on the same pair (i, j). [7,10,30] similarly use ephemeral keys in their definitions. In the remaining papers we examined, it was less clear whether reencryption keys were ephemeral or persistent.

Neither definition implies the other; any scheme secure with persistent keys can be modified into one that is insecure with ephemeral keys, and vice-versa. The definitions, however, are not in serious tension; any scheme secure with persistent keys and having deterministic ReKeyGen is also secure with ephemeral keys, and ReKeyGen can in general be derandomized using pseudorandom functions. Of course, one can easily define a hybrid notion stronger than both by allowing the adversary to specify for each query whether it wants to use reencryption keys that are new or old.

We adopt the persistent formalization as it better captures 'typical' use. To the best of our knowledge, all claims in this work can be adapted to the ephemeral setting.

Remark 2. The power of the adversary above can be strengthened by allowing *adaptive* corruptions instead of dividing the game into phases. Our definitions of CPA and HRA security follow the convention of [3] primarily because it is most common in the research literature. For an examination of CPA and HRA security in the adaptive setting, see the subsequent work of Fuchsbauer, Kamath, Klein, and Pietrzak [18]. Adaptive-secure, bidirectional, CCA secure proxy reencryption has been studied in [10,28].

3.1 Concatenation Scheme and Trivial Scheme

The weakness of CPA security lies in the specification of $\mathcal{O}_{\mathsf{ReEnc}}$, which does not reencrypt any ciphertexts from honest to corrupt users. Said another way, $\mathcal{O}_{\mathsf{ReEnc}}$ reencrypts between only those pairs keys for which $\mathcal{O}_{\mathsf{ReKeyGen}}$ outputs a reencryption key (rather than returning $\perp$). We now describe two schemes that are CPA secure, but are insecure against a dishonest receiver of reencrypted ciphertexts. In both schemes, a single ciphertext reencrypted from an honest index to a corrupted index enables the decryption of messages encrypted under the honest index's public key.

Concatenation Scheme. Let $\mathsf{PRE} = (\mathsf{Setup}, \mathsf{KeyGen}, \mathsf{Enc}, \mathsf{Dec}, \mathsf{ReKeyGen}, \mathsf{ReEnc})$ be a CPA-secure proxy reencryption scheme. Define a new scheme by modifying only reencryption and decryption:

$$\mathsf{ReEnc}'(\mathsf{rk}, \mathsf{ct}) := \mathsf{ReEnc}(\mathsf{rk}, \mathsf{ct}) \| \mathsf{rk}$$

$$\mathsf{Dec}'(\mathsf{sk}, \mathsf{ct}) := \begin{cases} \mathsf{Dec}(\mathsf{sk}, \mathsf{ct}^1) & \text{if } \mathsf{ct} = \mathsf{ct}^1 \| \mathsf{ct}^2 \\ \mathsf{Dec}(\mathsf{sk}, \mathsf{ct}) & \text{otherwise} \end{cases}$$

Theorem 1. *Let* $\mathsf{PRE} = (\mathsf{Setup}, \mathsf{KeyGen}, \mathsf{Enc}, \mathsf{Dec}, \mathsf{ReKeyGen}, \mathsf{ReEnc})$ *be a CPA-secure proxy reencryption scheme. The corresponding Concatenation Scheme* $\mathsf{PRE}' = (\mathsf{Setup}, \mathsf{KeyGen}, \mathsf{Enc}, \mathsf{Dec}', \mathsf{ReKeyGen}, \mathsf{ReEnc}')$ *is a CPA-secure proxy reencryption scheme.*

Proof. For any probabilistic, polynomial-time algorithm $\mathcal{A}'$ (the CPA adversary against PRE'), we construct an efficient algorithm $\mathcal{A}$ such that $\mathsf{Adv}^{\mathcal{A}}_{\mathsf{cpa}} = \mathsf{Adv}^{\mathcal{A}'}_{\mathsf{cpa}}$. By the CPA security of PRE, this advantage is negligible, completing the proof.

$\mathcal{A}$ runs $\mathcal{A}'$ and simulates the CPA security game for PRE' (if $\mathcal{A}'$ does not follow the specification of the game, $\mathcal{A}$ simply aborts). Except for calls to $\mathcal{O}_{\mathsf{ReEnc}}$, all oracle calls by $\mathcal{A}'$ are passed along unaltered by $\mathcal{A}$, along with their responses.

$\mathcal{A}$ begins Phase 2 by requesting all admissible reencryption keys $\mathsf{rk}_{i \to j}$ from its own reencryption key generation oracle. To answer oracle calls from $\mathcal{A}'$ to

$\mathcal{O}_{\mathsf{ReEnc}}$, $\mathcal{A}$ first queries its own reencryption oracle, which returns ct^1. If $\mathsf{ct}^1 = \bot$, then $\mathcal{A}'$ returns $\bot$. Otherwise, $\mathcal{A}'$ concatenates the appropriate reencryption key rk to form the new ciphertext $\mathsf{ct} = \mathsf{ct}^1 \| \mathsf{rk}$. This is possible because if $\mathsf{ct}^1 \neq \bot$, then $\mathcal{A}$ is able to get the corresponding reencryption key at the beginning of Phase 2.

$\mathcal{A}$ perfectly implements the CPA security game for PRE', and $\mathcal{A}'$ wins that game if and only if $\mathcal{A}$ wins the corresponding game for PRE. Therefore, $\mathsf{Adv}^{\mathcal{A}}_{\mathsf{cpa}} = \mathsf{Adv}^{\mathcal{A}'}_{\mathsf{cpa}}$. Finally, the running time of $\mathcal{A}$ is polynomially related to that of $\mathcal{A}'$.

While the Concatenation Scheme builds upon any CPA-secure proxy reencryption scheme, the Trivial Scheme presented next makes use of public-key encryption enjoying *circular security.* Informally, circular security guarantees that encryptions of messages that are a function of the secret key(s) are as secure as encryptions of messages that are independent of the secret key(s), a security property that does not follow from standard semantic security.

In the Trivial Scheme, the reencryption key from party i to j is simply $\mathsf{rk}_{i\to j} = \mathsf{Enc}(\mathsf{pk}_j, \mathsf{sk}_i)$. CPA security of the resulting proxy reencryption scheme requires security against an adversary who has both $\mathsf{rk}_{i\to j}$ and $\mathsf{rk}_{j\to i}$. This requires that the underlying encryption scheme is circular secure.

Because existing definitions and constructions of circular secure encryption schemes based on standard assumptions (e.g., [6] from DDH) require a bound on the total number of public keys n, the corresponding Trivial Scheme will only satisfy a bounded-key variant of CPA security. Any circular secure encryption scheme without this limitation would yield a Trivial Scheme secure according to Definition 4. We defer the definitions of circular security, bounded-key CPA security, and the proof of Theorem 2 to Appendix A.

Trivial Scheme. Let $(\mathsf{KeyGen}_{\mathsf{circ}}, \mathsf{Enc}_{\mathsf{circ}}, \mathsf{Dec}_{\mathsf{circ}})$ be an n-way circular-secure encryption scheme. Let $\mathsf{Setup} \equiv \bot$, $\mathsf{KeyGen} \equiv \mathsf{KeyGen}_{\mathsf{circ}}$; $\mathsf{Enc} \equiv \mathsf{Enc}_{\mathsf{circ}}$;

$$\mathsf{ReKeyGen}(\mathsf{sk}_i, \mathsf{pk}_j) := \mathsf{Enc}_{\mathsf{circ}}(\mathsf{pk}_j, \mathsf{sk}_i)$$

$$\mathsf{ReEnc}(\mathsf{rk}_{i\to j}, \mathsf{ct}_i) := \mathsf{ct}_i \| \mathsf{rk}_{i\to j}$$

$$\mathsf{Dec}(\mathsf{sk}, \mathsf{ct}) := \begin{cases} \mathsf{Dec}_{\mathsf{circ}}(\mathsf{Dec}_{\mathsf{circ}}(\mathsf{sk}, \mathsf{ct}^2), \mathsf{ct}^1) & \text{if } \mathsf{ct} = \mathsf{ct}^1 \| \mathsf{ct}^2 \\ \mathsf{Dec}_{\mathsf{circ}}(\mathsf{sk}, \mathsf{ct}) & \text{otherwise} \end{cases}.$$

Theorem 2. *Let* $(\mathsf{KeyGen}_{\mathsf{circ}}, \mathsf{Enc}_{\mathsf{circ}}, \mathsf{Dec}_{\mathsf{circ}})$ *be an n-way circular-secure encryption scheme. The corresponding Trivial Scheme* PRE *is an n-way CPA secure proxy reencryption scheme.*

4 Security Against Honest Reencryption Attacks

We seek a definition of security which holds as long as the adversary only sees honestly reencrypted ciphertexts, unless the set of corrupt parties can trivially violate security (by some chain of reencryption keys from an uncorrupted public key to a corrupted public key).

We term this notion security against *honest reencryption attacks (HRA)*. To formalize it, we model the ability of an adversary to see honest reencryptions by granting it access to a modified reencryption oracle $\mathcal{O}_{\mathsf{ReEnc}}$. Instead of taking a ciphertext as input, the modified $\mathcal{O}_{\mathsf{ReEnc}}$ takes as input a reference to a previously generated ciphertext (either as the output of $\mathcal{O}_{\mathsf{Enc}}$ or $\mathcal{O}_{\mathsf{ReEnc}}$ itself).

To implement such an oracle, we introduce to the security game a key-value store C as additional state: the values are ciphertexts ct which are keyed by a pair of integers (i, k), where i denotes the index of the key pair $(\mathsf{pk}_i, \mathsf{sk}_i)$ under which ct was (re)encrypted, and k is a unique index assigned to ct.

As described, this new $\mathcal{O}_{\mathsf{ReEnc}}$ admits a trivial attack: simply reencrypt the challenge ciphertext to a corrupted key and decrypt. To address this issue, we adapt an idea from [10] definition of CCA security: we rule out the trivial attack by storing a set Deriv of ciphertexts derived from the challenge by reencrypting, and rejecting queries to $\mathcal{O}_{\mathsf{ReEnc}}$ for ciphertexts in Deriv and a corrupted target key. We might have instead chosen to forbid any reencryptions of the challenge ciphertext, even between uncorrupted keys. Though this would have simplified the definition, it would have been unsatisfactory. For example, in the single-writer, many-reader encrypted storage application the contents of a message $\mathbf{m}$ that gets reencrypted from Alice to Charlie should be hidden from Bob.

We now present the honest reencryption attacks security game. The game is similar to the CPA security game with some modifications to Setup, Challenge, and $\mathcal{O}_{\mathsf{ReEnc}}$, and the addition of an Enc oracle $\mathcal{O}_{\mathsf{Enc}}$ to Phase 2. $\mathcal{O}_{\mathsf{Enc}}$ may be executed poly(λ) times and in any order relative to the other oracles in Phase 2. For the sake of clarity we reproduce the full game below and mark the modified oracles with a $\star$.

Definition 5 (Proxy Reencryption: Security Game for Honest Reencryption Attacks (HRA)). *Let λ be the security parameter and $\mathcal{A}$ be an oracle Turing machine. The HRA game consists of an execution of $\mathcal{A}$ with the following oracles.*

Phase 1:

$\star$ Setup: *The public parameters are generated and given to $\mathcal{A}$. A counter* $\mathsf{numKeys}$ *is initialized to 0, and the sets* Hon *(of honest, uncorrupted indices) and* Cor *(of corrupted indices) are initialized to be empty.*
Additionally the following are initialized: a counter numCt *to 0, a key-value store* C *to empty, and a set* Deriv *to be empty. This oracle is executed first and only once.*

Uncorrupted Key Generation: *Obtain a new key pair* $(\mathsf{pk}_{\mathsf{numKeys}}, \mathsf{sk}_{\mathsf{numKeys}}) \leftarrow \mathsf{KeyGen}(\mathsf{pp})$ *and give* $\mathsf{pk}_{\mathsf{numKeys}}$ *to $\mathcal{A}$. The current value of* $\mathsf{numKeys}$ *is added to* Hon *and* $\mathsf{numKeys}$ *is incremented.*

Corrupted Key Generation: *Obtain a new key pair* $(pk_{\mathsf{numKeys}}, \mathsf{sk}_{\mathsf{numKeys}}) \leftarrow \mathsf{KeyGen}(\mathsf{pp})$ *and given to $\mathcal{A}$. The current value of* $\mathsf{numKeys}$ *is added to* Cor *and* $\mathsf{numKeys}$ *is incremented.*

Phase 2: For each pair $i, j \leq \mathsf{numKeys}$*, compute the reencryption key* $\mathsf{rk}_{i \to j} \leftarrow \mathsf{ReKeyGen}(\mathsf{sk}_i, \mathsf{pk}_j)$.

Reencryption Key Generation $\mathcal{O}_{\mathsf{ReKeyGen}}$: *On input* (i, j) *where* $i, j \leq \mathsf{numKeys}$*, if* $i = j$ *or if* $i \in \mathsf{Hon}$ *and* $j \in \mathsf{Cor}$*, output* $\perp$*. Otherwise return the reencryption key* $\mathsf{rk}_{i \to j}$.

- $\star$ Encryption $\mathcal{O}_{\mathsf{Enc}}$: *On input* $(i, \mathbf{m})$*, where* $i \leq \mathsf{numKeys}$*, compute* $\mathsf{ct} \leftarrow \mathsf{Enc}(\mathsf{pk}_i, \mathbf{m})$ *and increment* numCt*. Store the value* ct *in* $\mathcal{C}$ *with key* (i, numCt)*. Return* $(\mathsf{numCt}, \mathsf{ct})$.
- $\star$ Challenge Oracle: *On input* $(i, \mathbf{m}_0, \mathbf{m}_1)$ *where* $i \in \mathsf{Hon}$ *and* $\mathbf{m}_0, \mathbf{m}_1 \in \mathcal{M}$*, sample a bit* $b \leftarrow \{0, 1\}$ *uniformly at random, compute the challenge ciphertext* $\mathsf{ct}^* \leftarrow \mathsf{Enc}(\mathsf{pk}_i, \mathbf{m}_b)$*, and increment* numCt*. Add* numCt *to the set* Deriv*. Store the value* ct^* *in* $\mathcal{C}$ *with key* (i, numCt)*. Return* $(\mathsf{numCt}, \mathsf{ct}^*)$*. This oracle can only be queried once.*
- $\star$ Reencryption $\mathcal{O}_{\mathsf{ReEnc}}$: *On input* (i, j, k) *where* $i, j \leq \mathsf{numKeys}$ *and* $k \leq \mathsf{numCt}$*, if* $j \in \mathsf{Cor}$ *and* $k \in \mathsf{Deriv}$ *return* $\perp$*. If there is no value in* $\mathcal{C}$ *with key* (i, k)*, return* $\perp$.
  Otherwise, let ct_i *be that value in* $\mathcal{C}$*, let* $\mathsf{ct}_j \leftarrow \mathsf{ReEnc}(\mathsf{rk}_{i \to j}, \mathsf{ct}_i)$*, and increment* numCt*. Store the value* ct_j *in* $\mathcal{C}$ *with key* (j, numCt)*. If* $k \in \mathsf{Deriv}$*, add* numCt *to the set* Deriv.
  Return $(\mathsf{numCt}, \mathsf{ct}_j)$.

Phase 3:

Decision: *On input a bit* $b' \in \{0, 1\}$*, return* win *if* $b = b'$.

The HRA advantage *of* $\mathcal{A}$ *is defined as*

$$\mathsf{Adv}^{\mathcal{A}}_{\mathsf{hra}}(\lambda) = \Pr[\mathsf{win}],$$

where the probability is over the randomness of $\mathcal{A}$ *and the oracles in HRA game.*

Definition 6 (Proxy Reencryption: HRA Security). *Given a security parameter* 1^λ*, a proxy reencryption scheme is HRA secure if for all probabilistic polynomial-time adversaries* $\mathcal{A}$*, there exists a negligible function* negl *such that*

$$\mathsf{Adv}^{\mathcal{A}}_{\mathsf{hra}}(\lambda) < \frac{1}{2} + \mathsf{negl}(\lambda)$$

The Concatenation Scheme demonstrates that CPA security does not necessarily imply HRA security. Together with following theorem, we see that HRA security is a strict strengthening of CPA security.

Theorem 3. *Let* PRE *be an HRA secure proxy reencryption scheme. Then* PRE *is CPA secure.*

Proof. From any probabilistic, polynomial-time algorithm $\mathcal{A}$ (the CPA adversary), we construct an efficient algorithm $\mathcal{A}'$ such that $\mathsf{Adv}^{\mathcal{A}'}_{\mathsf{hra}} = \mathsf{Adv}^{\mathcal{A}}_{CPA}$. By the HRA security of PRE this advantage is negligible, completing the proof.

$\mathcal{A}'$ runs $\mathcal{A}$ and simulates the CPA security game (if $\mathcal{A}$ does not follow the specification of the CPA security game, $\mathcal{A}'$ simply aborts). Except for calls to $\mathcal{O}_{\mathsf{ReEnc}}$, all oracle calls by $\mathcal{A}'$ are passed along unaltered by $\mathcal{A}$ to the corresponding HRA oracles, along with their responses.

$\mathcal{A}'$ begins Phase 2 by requesting all (admissible) reencryption keys $\mathsf{rk}_{i \to j}$ from $\mathcal{O}_{\mathsf{ReKeyGen}}$. racle calls from $\mathcal{A}$ to $\mathcal{O}_{\mathsf{ReEnc}}$ are answered by $\mathcal{A}'$ by computing the reencryption using the appropriate reencryption key; this is possible because $\mathcal{O}_{\mathsf{ReEnc}}$ returns $\perp$ if and only if $\mathcal{A}'$ is unable to get the corresponding reencryption key.

$\mathcal{A}'$ prefectly implements the CPA security game, and $\mathcal{A}$ wins that game if and only if $\mathcal{A}'$ wins the HRA security game. Therefore $\mathsf{Adv}^{\mathcal{A}'}_{\mathsf{hra}} = \mathsf{Adv}^{\mathcal{A}}_{CPA}$. Finally, the running time of $\mathcal{A}'$ is polynomially related to the that of $\mathcal{A}$.

4.1 Sufficiency of HRA Security for Applications

Returning to the applications of proxy reencryption described in Sect. 2, we observe that HRA security provides substantially stronger security guarantees.

Encrypted Email Forwarding. Using proxy reencryption with HRA security, Alice can forward encrypted email to Bob for a short period of time (during a vacation, say) and be sure that Bob cannot read her email after she returns.

Key Escrow. Similar to encrypted email forwarding, proxy reencryption with HRA can be used to enable law enforcement to read certain encrypted messages without compromising the secrecy of documents outside the scope of a search warrant or subpoena, for example.

Single-Writer, Many-Reader Encrypted Storage. Whereas proxy reencryption with CPA security can only support all or nothing access (i.e., all readers may access all data), HRA security can support fine grained access control (i.e., each reader may access only a specific subset of the data).

There is no question that HRA does not provide as much security as CCA, and that CCA-secure proxy reencryption would yield more robust applications. HRA security, however, can provide meaningful guarantees in the above applications.

Encrypted Email Forwarding. If Alice is forwarding all emails to Bob, then Bob could certainly mount an attack outside the honest reencryption model. On the other hand, if Alice is forwarding only those emails from a third-party sender Charlie, then such an attack is impossible without the involvement of Charlie (supposing of course that the sender of an email can be authenticated).

Key Escrow. The hypothetical legal regime that establishes the government's power of exceptional access by way of key escrow could additionally prohibit the government from mounting chosen-ciphertext attacks. In the United States, a Constitutional argument could perhaps be made that law-enforcement use of chosen-ciphertext attacks must be limited.

Single-Writer, Many-Reader Encrypted Storage. The only ciphertexts being reencrypted are those uploaded by the single-writer to the proxy server (hence the name). It is by no means a stretch to require that the proxy server does not allow writes by unauthorized parties (i.e., the readers). If the honest writer only uploads honestly generated ciphertexts, HRA is appropriate.

5 Security of Existing Proxy Reencryption Schemes

Can we construct HRA-secure proxy reencryption? The most natural place to begin is with existing schemes.

We begin by demonstrating that the CPA secure scheme of [31] is not HRA secure. Although CPA security is strictly weaker than HRA security, we might hope that the existing CPA secure schemes already satisfy the more stringent definition. To this end, we identify a natural property—*reencryption simulatability*—sufficient to boost CPA security to HRA security.[7]

We examine the simple construction of CPA secure proxy reencryption from any fully-homomorphic encryption (FHE) presented in [19]. While the resulting proxy reencryption may not be HRA secure in general, if the FHE is *circuit private*—a property Gentry imbues into his FHE by rerandomization—the same construction will be HRA secure. We then examine pairing-based schemes, finding there too that rerandomization provides a direct path to HRA security.[8]

Remark 3. It may seem that CCA security should imply HRA security, but unfortunately the situation is not so clear. Intuitively, CCA security allows the adversary to make relatively unrestricted queries to both $\mathcal{O}_{\mathsf{ReEnc}}$ and $\mathcal{O}_{\mathsf{Dec}}$, whereas HRA restricts the adversary to making only honest reencryption queries to $\mathcal{O}_{\mathsf{ReEnc}}$.

However the oracles in the CCA definition are restricted in a way that stymies a naive attempt at a reduction. The CCA definition prevents reencryptions or decryptions of all ciphertexts that could in principle be derived from the challenge (including by rerandomization). On the other hand, the HRA security game restricts reencryption queries only when the ciphertext is actually a derivative of the challenge. The adversary may reencrypt other encryptions of the challenge messages, so long as those encryptions were honestly generated independently from the challenge ciphertext.

We do not resolve the question of whether CCA security implies HRA security. By Theorem 5, any CCA secure proxy reencryption scheme satisfying reencryption simulatability is also HRA secure. See the full version of this article [13] for further discussion.

[7] Some existing notions in the proxy reencryption literature seem powerful enough to elevate CPA security to HRA security, including proxy invisibility [4], unlinkability [17], and punctured security [1]. However, these notions are not sufficiently well defined to draw any concrete conclusions. The notion of key-privacy [3] does not in general suffice for HRA security.

[8] While we do not examine every pairing-based construction of proxy reencryption, we suspect that rerandomizing reencryption will suffice for reencryption simulation in many, if not all.

5.1 HRA Insecurity of [31]

Though it is easy to construct CPA secure encryption schemes that are not HRA secure, the question remains whether any previously proposed schemes fail to satisfy HRA security. In this section, we show that the construction of Polyakov, Rohloff, Sahu, and Vaikuntanathan [31, Sect. 5] is one such scheme. Their construction is based on a public key encryption scheme of Brakerski and Vaikuntanathan [9] and is CPA secure assuming the hardness of Ring Learning With Errors (RLWE).

As with the Trivial and Concatenation schemes, the HRA attack is simple yet severe: any single honestly generated ciphertext enables the recipient Bob to recover the sender Alice's secret key with significant probability.

Theorem 4. *The proxy reencryption scheme of [31, Sect. 5] is not HRA secure.*

Proof. Except where noted, the notation used below is consistent with [31]; we restrict our description to those facts necessary to describe the HRA attack.

For n a power of 2 and prime $q \equiv 1 \mod 2n$, let $R_q = \mathbb{Z}_q[x]/(x^n + 1)$ be a ring of degree $(n-1)$ polynomials with coefficients in $\mathbb{Z}_q$. The sender Alice's secret key is s, and the recipient Bob's secret key is s^*. Bob's public key includes $O(\log q) = \text{poly}(n)$ RLWE samples $\theta_i^* = \beta_i \cdot s^* + pe_i$, where p is a public prime and the β_i and e_i are ring elements sampled by Bob.[9] Ciphertexts are pairs of ring elements $(c_0, c_1) \in R_q^2$. By [9, Lemma 4], the distribution of c_1 is statistically close to uniform over R_q. By [27, Lemma 2.25], c_1 is invertible with probability at least $e^{-1} - \mathsf{negl}(n)$. The result of reencrypting (c_0, c_1) is a pair (c_0', c_1') such that $c_0' - s^* \cdot c_1' = c_0 - s \cdot c_1 + pE_1$, where E_i is computable given c_1 and the e_i. This fact is used by [31] to prove the correctness of their scheme. Rearranging the above, we see that

$$s \cdot c_1 = c_0 + pE_1 - c_0' + s^* \cdot c_1'.$$

Given any ciphertext (c_0, c_1) and its reencryption (c_0', c_1'), Bob can evaluate the above and compute $s \cdot c_1$. With probability at least $e^{-1} - \mathsf{negl}(n)$, c_1 is invertible and Bob can recover the secret s.

5.2 Reencryption Simulatability

While HRA is a strictly stronger security notion than CPA, we now show that if a CPA secure proxy reencryption scheme has an additional property we call *reencryption simulatability*, then it must also be HRA secure. Very roughly, reencryption simulatability means that ciphertexts resulting from computing $\mathsf{ReEnc}(\mathsf{rk}_{i \to j}, \mathsf{ct}_i)$ can be simulated without knowledge of the sender's secret key sk_i (but with knowledge of the plaintext message $\mathbf{m}$ and the recipient's secret key sk_j). Note that ReEnc uses $\mathsf{rk}_{i \to j}$ which is a function of sk_i.

[9] [31] separate the computation of θ_i^* from Bob's public key, but this is only a matter of presentation.

Reencryption simulatability allows an algorithm with access to the CPA oracles to efficiently implement the honest reencryption oracle. For intuition, consider the following approach to reducing HRA security to CPA security. Suppose there existed an adversary $\mathcal{A}_{\mathsf{hra}}$ violating the HRA security of a scheme; the reduction plays the roles of both the CPA adversary and the challenger in the HRA security game, and attempts to violate CPA security. To succeed, the reduction must be able to answer honest reencryption queries from uncorrupted keys to corrupted keys. Though the reduction knows the messages being reencrypted, it does not know the appropriate reencryption key. However, if it could indistinguishably simulate these reencryptions then it could indeed leverage $\mathcal{A}_{\mathsf{hra}}$ to violate CPA security.

We emphasize that the goal of Definition 7 is to capture a large swath of possible schemes while still enabling very simple proofs of simulatability (and thus of HRA security for existing CPA secure schemes). It is not intended to be the only avenue for proving HRA security of new or existing constructions. Reencryption simulatability is not necessary for HRA security of proxy reencryption. In particular, analogous versions of Theorem 5 hold with computational simulatability guarantees, but are more complicated [15, Foonote 7 and Appendix A].

Definition 7 (Reencryption Simulatability). *A proxy reencryption scheme* PRE *is* reencryption simulatable *if there exists a probabilistic, polynomial-time algorithm* ReEncSim *such that with high probability over* aux, *for all* $\mathbf{m} \in \mathcal{M}$*:*

$$(\mathsf{ReEncSim}(\mathsf{aux}), \mathsf{aux}) \approx_s (\mathsf{ReEnc}(\mathsf{rk}_{a \to b}, \mathsf{ct}_a), \mathsf{aux}),$$

where $\approx_s$ *denotes statistical indistinguishability, and* ct_a *and* aux *are sampled according to*

$$\begin{aligned}
&\mathsf{pp} \leftarrow \mathsf{Setup}(1^\lambda),\\
&(\mathsf{pk}_a, \mathsf{sk}_a) \leftarrow \mathsf{KeyGen}(\mathsf{pp}),\\
&(\mathsf{pk}_b, \mathsf{sk}_b) \leftarrow \mathsf{KeyGen}(\mathsf{pp}),\\
&\mathsf{rk}_{a \to b} \leftarrow \mathsf{ReKeyGen}(\mathsf{sk}_a, \mathsf{pk}_b),\\
&\mathsf{ct}_a \leftarrow \mathsf{Enc}(\mathsf{pk}_a, \mathbf{m}),\\
&\mathsf{aux} = (\mathsf{pp}, \mathsf{pk}_a, \mathsf{pk}_b, \mathsf{sk}_b, \mathsf{ct}_a, \mathbf{m}).
\end{aligned}$$

A special case of the above is when $\mathsf{ReEncSim}(\mathsf{aux}) = \mathsf{Enc}(\mathsf{pk}_b, \mathbf{m})$ simply computes a fresh encryption of the message. That is, if reencrypted ciphertexts are distributed like fresh ciphertexts, then the scheme is reencryption simulatable.

Theorem 5. *Let* PRE *be an CPA secure, reencryption simulatable, proxy reencryption scheme. Then* PRE *is HRA secure.*

Proof (Outline). The proof proceeds according to the intuition above. From any probabilistic, polynomial-time algorithm $\mathcal{A} = \mathcal{A}_{\mathsf{hra}}$ (the HRA adversary), we construct an algorithm $\mathcal{A}' = \mathcal{A}_{\mathsf{cpa}}$ such that $\mathsf{Adv}^{\mathcal{A}'}_{\mathsf{cpa}}(\lambda) \geq \mathsf{Adv}^{\mathcal{A}}_{\mathsf{hra}}(\lambda) - \mathsf{negl}(\lambda)$; by the CPA security of PRE this advantage is negligible, completing the proof.

$\mathcal{A}_{\mathsf{cpa}}$ runs $\mathcal{A}_{\mathsf{hra}}$ and simulates the HRA security game (if $\mathcal{A}_{\mathsf{hra}}$ does not follow the specification of the HRA security game, $\mathcal{A}_{\mathsf{cpa}}$ simply aborts). To answer oracle calls by $\mathcal{A}_{\mathsf{hra}}$ to any oracle other than $\mathcal{O}_{\mathsf{ReEnc}}$, $\mathcal{A}_{\mathsf{cpa}}$ simply passes the calls and answers unaltered to the corresponding CPA oracles.

To answer oracle calls to $\mathcal{O}_{\mathsf{ReEnc}}$ between two uncorrupted keys or two corrupted keys, $\mathcal{A}_{\mathsf{cpa}}$ uses the corresponding reencryption key. On the other hand, for calls to $\mathcal{O}_{\mathsf{ReEnc}}$ from an uncorrupted key to a corrupted key, $\mathcal{A}_{\mathsf{cpa}}$ simulates the reencryption using ReEncSim. This is possible because $\mathcal{A}_{\mathsf{cpa}}$ knows the underlying $\mathbf{m}$ (along with the other information in aux).

Reencryption simulatability implies that the views of $\mathcal{A}_{\mathsf{hra}}$ in the real security game (using the real $\mathcal{O}_{\mathsf{ReEnc}}$) and the simulated security game (using ReEncSim) are statistically close. $\mathcal{A}_{\mathsf{cpa}}$ wins the CPA security game if and only if $\mathcal{A}_{\mathsf{hra}}$ wins in the simulated HRA game described above.

5.3 Fully Homomorphic Encryption and Proxy Reencryption

There is an intimate connection between FHE and proxy reencryption: a sufficiently powerful somewhat homomorphic encryption scheme implies CPA secure proxy reencryption, which can be used to "bootstrap" the scheme to achieve fully homomorphic encryption [19]. For the relevant FHE definitions, see [19, Sect. 2].

Let $\mathsf{FHE} = (\mathsf{Setup}_{\mathsf{FHE}}, \mathsf{KeyGen}_{\mathsf{FHE}}, \mathsf{Enc}_{\mathsf{FHE}}, \mathsf{Dec}_{\mathsf{FHE}}, \mathsf{Eval}_{\mathsf{FHE}})$ be an FHE scheme. Proxy reencryption can be constructed as follows (compare to the Trivial Scheme):

$\mathsf{KeyGen}_{\mathsf{PRE}}$, $\mathsf{Enc}_{\mathsf{PRE}}$ and $\mathsf{Dec}_{\mathsf{PRE}}$ are identical to their FHE counterparts.

$\mathsf{ReKeyGen}_{\mathsf{PRE}}(\mathsf{sk}_i, \mathsf{pk}_j) = \mathsf{Enc}_{\mathsf{FHE}}(\mathsf{pk}_j, \mathsf{sk}_i) \| \mathsf{pk}_j$. The reencryption key $\mathsf{rk}_{i \to j}$ is an encryption under pk_j of sk_i, along with the target public key pk_j.

$\mathsf{ReEnc}_{\mathsf{PRE}}(\mathsf{rk}_{i \to j}, \mathsf{ct}_i)$: Let $\mathsf{ct}_{i \to j} \leftarrow \mathsf{Enc}_{\mathsf{FHE}}(\mathsf{pk}_j, \mathsf{ct}_i)$. Homomorphically compute the FHE decryption function $\mathsf{Dec}_{\mathsf{FHE}}(\mathsf{sk}_i, \mathsf{ct}_i)$ using the corresponding ciphertexts $\mathsf{rk}_{i \to j}$ and $\mathsf{ct}_{i \to j}$ (under pk_j). Namely, $\mathsf{ct}_j = \mathsf{Eval}_{\mathsf{FHE}}(\mathsf{pk}_j, \mathsf{Dec}_{\mathsf{FHE}}, \mathsf{rk}_{i \to j}, \mathsf{ct}_{i \to j})$.

The correctness of the FHE implies the correctness of the resulting proxy reencryption:

$$\mathsf{Dec}_{\mathsf{PRE}}(\mathsf{sk}_j, \mathsf{ct}_j) = \mathsf{Dec}_{\mathsf{FHE}}(\mathsf{sk}_j, \mathsf{ct}_j) = \mathsf{Dec}_{\mathsf{FHE}}(\mathsf{sk}_i, \mathsf{ct}_i) = \mathsf{Dec}_{\mathsf{PRE}}(\mathsf{sk}_i, \mathsf{ct}_i).$$

Furthermore, the proxy reencryption scheme is CPA secure.

To demonstrate that the construction might not be HRA secure, consider the following fully homomorphic encryption scheme FHE' constructed from any existing scheme FHE. The only modification made in FHE' is to $\mathsf{Eval}_{\mathsf{FHE}'}$:

$$\mathsf{Eval}_{\mathsf{FHE}'}(\mathsf{pk}_j, C, \mathsf{ct}_1, \mathsf{ct}_2) := \mathsf{Eval}_{\mathsf{FHE}}(\mathsf{pk}_j, C, \mathsf{ct}_1, \mathsf{ct}_2) \| \mathsf{ct}_1.$$

Note that FHE' does not violate FHE compactness if ct_1 (in the proxy reencryption construction, $\mathsf{rk}_{i \to j}$) is always of some size bounded by a polynomial in the security parameter of the FHE scheme; this suffices for our purpose. Instantiating the proxy reencryption construction with FHE' essentially results in the Concatenation Scheme, which is not HRA secure.

Circuit Privacy. An FHE scheme is *circuit private* if ciphertexts resulting from FHE evaluations are statistically indistinguishable from fresh ciphertexts [19]. Namely, if for any circuit C and any ciphertexts $\mathsf{ct}_1,\ldots,\mathsf{ct}_t$:

$$\mathsf{Enc}_{\mathsf{FHE}}(\mathsf{pk}, C(\mathsf{ct}_1,\ldots,\mathsf{ct}_t)) \approx_s \mathsf{Eval}_{\mathsf{FHE}}(\mathsf{pk}, C, \mathsf{ct}_1,\ldots,\mathsf{ct}_t).$$

In [19], an FHE scheme without circuit privacy is modified to be circuit private by rerandomizing the ciphertexts resulting from $\mathsf{Eval}_{\mathsf{FHE}}$.

While our proxy reencryption construction above is not in general HRA secure, it is easy to see that if the underlying FHE is circuit private, then the proxy reencryption is reencryption simulatable (Definition 7). By Theorem 5, the resulting scheme is therefore HRA secure.

5.4 Pairing-Based Proxy Reencryption

Many constructions of proxy reencryption are based on the hardness of Diffie-Hellman-type problems over certain bilinear groups, including [3,4,10,21,26].

A prototypical construction is that of [4], which itself is based on the original scheme of [5]. For every λ, let G_1 and G_2 be groups of prime order $q = \Theta(2^\lambda)$, and let g be a generator of G_1. Let e be a non-degenerate bilinear map $e : G_1 \times G_1 \to G_2$ (i.e., for all $h \in G_1$ and $a, b \in \mathbb{Z}_q$, $e(h^a, h^b) = e(h,h)^{ab}$, and for all generators g of G_1, $e(g,g) \neq 1$). Let $Z = e(g,g)$. The message-space of the scheme is G_2.

$\mathsf{Setup}(1^\lambda)$: Output $\mathsf{pp} = (q, g, G_1, G_2, e)$.
$\mathsf{KeyGen}(\mathsf{pp})$: Sample $a \leftarrow \mathbb{Z}_q$ uniformly at random. Output $\mathsf{sk} = a$ and $\mathsf{pk} = g^a$.
$\mathsf{Enc}(\mathsf{pk}, \mathbf{m})$: Sample $k \leftarrow \mathbb{Z}_q$ uniformly at random. Output $\mathsf{ct} = (\mathsf{pk}^k, \mathbf{m}Z^k) = (g^{ak}, \mathbf{m}Z^k)$.
$\mathsf{ReKeyGen}(\mathsf{sk}_A = a, \mathsf{pk}_B = g^b)$: Output $\mathsf{rk}_{A\to B} = g^{b/a}$.
$\mathsf{ReEnc}(\mathsf{rk}_{A\to B}, \mathsf{ct}_A)$: Let $\mathsf{ct}_A = (\alpha_1, \alpha_2)$. Output

$$\mathsf{ct}_B = (e(\alpha_1, \mathsf{rk}_{A\to B}), \alpha_2) = (e(g^{ak}, g^{b/a}), \mathbf{m}Z^k) = (Z^{bk}, \mathbf{m}Z^k).$$

$\mathsf{Dec}(\mathsf{sk}, \mathsf{ct})$: Let $\mathsf{ct} = (\alpha_1, \alpha_2)$. If $\alpha_1 \in G_2$ (i.e., if it is the result of ReEnc), then output $\alpha_2/\alpha_1^{1/a} = \mathbf{m}Z^k/Z^k = \mathbf{m}$. Otherwise $\alpha_1 \in G_1$ (i.e., it is a fresh ciphertext); output $\alpha_2/e(\alpha_1, g)^{1/a} = \mathbf{m}Z^k/e(g^{ak}, g)^{1/a} = \mathbf{m}Z^k/Z^k = \mathbf{m}$.

Is this scheme HRA secure? It is tempting to say that the scheme is reencryption simulatable; after all, given a message $\mathbf{m}$ it is indeed straightforward to sample $(Z^{bk}, \mathbf{m}Z^k)$ for random $k \leftarrow \mathbb{Z}_q$. However $\mathsf{ct}_A = (g^{ak}, \mathbf{m}Z^k)$ and $\mathsf{ct}_B = \mathsf{ReEnc}(\mathsf{rk}_{A\to B}, \mathsf{ct}_A) = (Z^{bk}, \mathbf{m}Z^k)$ share the randomness k. Given $\mathsf{ct}_A = (g^{ak}, \mathbf{m}Z^k)$ and $\mathbf{m}$, it is not clear how to output $(g^{bk}, \mathbf{m}Z^k)$.

Rerandomization. A minor modification to the scheme above guarantees reencryption simulatability and therefore HRA security. Replace ReEnc above with ReEnc′:

ReEnc′($\mathsf{rk}_{A\to B}, \mathsf{ct}_A$): Compute $(Z^{bk}, \mathbf{m}Z^k) = \mathsf{ReEnc}(\mathsf{rk}_{A\to B}, \mathsf{ct}_A)$. Sample $k' \leftarrow \mathbb{Z}$ uniformly at random, and output $(Z^{bk} \cdot e(g^b, g^{k'}), \mathbf{m}Z^k \cdot e(g, g^{k'})) = (Z^{b(k+k')}, \mathbf{m}Z^{k+k'})$.

The resulting proxy reencryption scheme maintains the CPA security of the original, as the only modification is the rerandomization of reencrypted ciphertexts (which can be done by anyone with knowledge of the public parameters).

Furthermore, the scheme is now reencryption simulatable. To see why, observe that the resulting reencrypted ciphertexts are uniformly distributed in $\{(\mathsf{ct}_1, \mathsf{ct}_2) \in G_2 \times G_2 : \mathsf{ct}_2/\mathsf{ct}_1^{1/b} = \mathbf{m}\}$, independent of all other keys and ciphertexts. Such ciphertexts are easily sampled with knowledge of pp, $\mathsf{pk}_B = g^b$ and $\mathbf{m}$ as follows.

ReEncSim($\mathsf{pp}, \mathsf{pk}_B, \mathbf{m}$): Sample $k' \leftarrow \mathbb{Z}_q$ uniformly at random, and and output $(e(\mathsf{pk}_B, g^{k'}), \mathbf{m} \cdot e(g, g^{k'})) = (Z^{bk'}, \mathbf{m}Z^{bk'})$.

Thus, by Theorem 5, the modified scheme is HRA secure. Observe that rerandomization was the key to achieving circuit privacy (and thereby HRA security) in the FHE-based proxy reencryption construction as well.

The pairing-based schemes of [3] and [21] already incorporate rerandomization during reencryption. In the former case, it is used to achieve "key privacy;" in the latter, to achieve obfuscation of the reencryption functionality. In each, it is straightforward to show that the schemes are also reencryption simulatable and therefore HRA secure.

References

1. Ananth, P., Cohen, A., Jain, A.: Cryptography with updates. In: Coron, J.-S., Nielsen, J.B. (eds.) EUROCRYPT 2017. LNCS, vol. 10211, pp. 445–472. Springer, Cham (2017). https://doi.org/10.1007/978-3-319-56614-6_15
2. Aono, Y., Boyen, X., Phong, L.T., Wang, L.: Key-private proxy re-encryption under LWE. In: Paul, G., Vaudenay, S. (eds.) INDOCRYPT 2013. LNCS, vol. 8250, pp. 1–18. Springer, Cham (2013). https://doi.org/10.1007/978-3-319-03515-4_1
3. Ateniese, G., Benson, K., Hohenberger, S.: Key-private proxy re-encryption. In: Fischlin, M. (ed.) CT-RSA 2009. LNCS, vol. 5473, pp. 279–294. Springer, Heidelberg (2009). https://doi.org/10.1007/978-3-642-00862-7_19
4. Ateniese, G., Fu, K., Green, M., Hohenberger, S.: Improved proxy re-encryption schemes with applications to secure distributed storage. ACM Trans. Inf. Syst. Secur. (TISSEC) **9**(1), 1–30 (2006)
5. Blaze, M., Bleumer, G., Strauss, M.: Divertible protocols and atomic proxy cryptography. In: Nyberg, K. (ed.) EUROCRYPT 1998. LNCS, vol. 1403, pp. 127–144. Springer, Heidelberg (1998). https://doi.org/10.1007/BFb0054122

6. Boneh, D., Halevi, S., Hamburg, M., Ostrovsky, R.: Circular-secure encryption from decision Diffie-Hellman. In: Wagner, D. (ed.) CRYPTO 2008. LNCS, vol. 5157, pp. 108–125. Springer, Heidelberg (2008). https://doi.org/10.1007/978-3-540-85174-5_7
7. Boneh, D., Lewi, K., Montgomery, H., Raghunathan, A.: Key homomorphic PRFs and their applications. In: Canetti, R., Garay, J.A. (eds.) CRYPTO 2013. LNCS, vol. 8042, pp. 410–428. Springer, Heidelberg (2013). https://doi.org/10.1007/978-3-642-40041-4_23
8. Borcea, C., Polyakov, Y., Rohloff, K., Ryan, G., et al.: PICADOR: end-to-end encrypted publish-subscribe information distribution with proxy re-encryption. Future Gener. Comput. Syst. **71**, 177–191 (2017)
9. Brakerski, Z., Vaikuntanathan, V.: Fully homomorphic encryption from ring-LWE and security for key dependent messages. In: Rogaway, P. (ed.) CRYPTO 2011. LNCS, vol. 6841, pp. 505–524. Springer, Heidelberg (2011). https://doi.org/10.1007/978-3-642-22792-9_29
10. Canetti, R., Hohenberger, S.: Chosen-ciphertext secure proxy re-encryption. In: Proceedings of the 14th ACM Conference on Computer and Communications Security, pp. 185–194. ACM (2007)
11. Chandran, N., Chase, M., Liu, F.-H., Nishimaki, R., Xagawa, K.: Re-encryption, functional re-encryption, and multi-hop re-encryption: a framework for achieving obfuscation-based security and instantiations from lattices. In: Krawczyk, H. (ed.) PKC 2014. LNCS, vol. 8383, pp. 95–112. Springer, Heidelberg (2014). https://doi.org/10.1007/978-3-642-54631-0_6
12. Chow, S.S.M., Weng, J., Yang, Y., Deng, R.H.: Efficient unidirectional proxy re-encryption. In: Bernstein, D.J., Lange, T. (eds.) AFRICACRYPT 2010. LNCS, vol. 6055, pp. 316–332. Springer, Heidelberg (2010). https://doi.org/10.1007/978-3-642-12678-9_19
13. Cohen, A.: What about Bob? The inadequacy of CPA security for proxy reencryption. Cryptology ePrint Archive, Report 2017/785 (2017). https://eprint.iacr.org/2017/785
14. Derler, D., Krenn, S., Lorünser, T., Ramacher, S., Slamanig, D., Striecks, C.: Revisiting proxy re-encryption: forward secrecy, improved security, and applications. In: Abdalla, M., Dahab, R. (eds.) PKC 2018. LNCS, vol. 10769, pp. 219–250. Springer, Cham (2018). https://doi.org/10.1007/978-3-319-76578-5_8
15. Dttling, N., Nishimaki, R.: Universal proxy re-encryption. Cryptology ePrint Archive, Report 2018/840 (2018). https://eprint.iacr.org/2018/840
16. Everspaugh, A., Paterson, K., Ristenpart, T., Scott, S.: Key rotation for authenticated encryption. In: Katz, J., Shacham, H. (eds.) CRYPTO 2017. LNCS, vol. 10403, pp. 98–129. Springer, Cham (2017). https://doi.org/10.1007/978-3-319-63697-9_4
17. Fan, X., Liu, F.H.: Proxy re-encryption and re-signatures from lattices (2017)
18. Fuchsbauer, G., Kamath, C., Klein, K., Pietrzak, K.: Adaptively secure proxy re-encryption. Cryptology ePrint Archive, Report 2018/426 (2018). https://eprint.iacr.org/2018/426
19. Gentry, C.: A Fully Homomorphic Encryption Scheme. Stanford University (2009)
20. He, Y.J., Hui, L.C., Yiu, S.M.: Avoid illegal encrypted DRM content sharing with non-transferable re-encryption. In: 2011 IEEE 13th International Conference on Communication Technology (ICCT), pp. 703–708. IEEE (2011)
21. Hohenberger, S., Rothblum, G.N., Shelat, A., Vaikuntanathan, V.: Securely obfuscating re-encryption. In: Vadhan, S.P. (ed.) TCC 2007. LNCS, vol. 4392, pp. 233–252. Springer, Heidelberg (2007). https://doi.org/10.1007/978-3-540-70936-7_13

22. Ivan, A.A., Dodis, Y.: Proxy cryptography revisited. In: NDSS (2003)
23. Jakobsson, M.: On quorum controlled asymmetric proxy re-encryption. In: Imai, H., Zheng, Y. (eds.) PKC 1999. LNCS, vol. 1560, pp. 112–121. Springer, Heidelberg (1999). https://doi.org/10.1007/3-540-49162-7_9
24. Khurana, H., Heo, J., Pant, M.: From proxy encryption primitives to a deployable secure-mailing-list solution. In: Ning, P., Qing, S., Li, N. (eds.) ICICS 2006. LNCS, vol. 4307, pp. 260–281. Springer, Heidelberg (2006). https://doi.org/10.1007/11935308_19
25. Lee, S., Park, H., Kim, J.: A secure and mutual-profitable DRM interoperability scheme. In: 2010 IEEE Symposium on Computers and Communications (ISCC), pp. 75–80. IEEE (2010)
26. Libert, B., Vergnaud, D.: Unidirectional chosen-ciphertext secure proxy re-encryption. In: Cramer, R. (ed.) PKC 2008. LNCS, vol. 4939, pp. 360–379. Springer, Heidelberg (2008). https://doi.org/10.1007/978-3-540-78440-1_21
27. Lyubashevsky, V., Peikert, C., Regev, O.: A toolkit for ring-LWE cryptography. In: Johansson, T., Nguyen, P.Q. (eds.) EUROCRYPT 2013. LNCS, vol. 7881, pp. 35–54. Springer, Heidelberg (2013). https://doi.org/10.1007/978-3-642-38348-9_3
28. Nunez, D., Agudo, I., Lopez, J.: A parametric family of attack models for proxy re-encryption. In: 2015 IEEE 28th Computer Security Foundations Symposium (CSF), pp. 290–301. IEEE (2015)
29. Oz, F., Murray, B., Dreyfuss, R.: What About Bob. Touchstone Pictures (1991)
30. Phong, L., Wang, L., Aono, Y., Nguyen, M., Boyen, X.: Proxy re-encryption schemes with key privacy from LWE. Technical report, Cryptology ePrint Archive, Report 2016/327 (2016). http://eprint.iacr.org/2016/327
31. Polyakov, Y., Rohloff, K., Sahu, G., Vaikuntanathan, V.: Fast proxy re-encryption for publish/subscribe systems. ACM Trans. Priv. Secur. (TOPS) **20**(4), 14 (2017)

A The Trivial Scheme

The following description and definition of circular security is adapted with slight modification from [6].

Let $(\mathsf{KeyGen}, \mathsf{Enc}, \mathsf{Dec})$ be a public-key encryption scheme with key space $\mathcal{K}$ and message space $\mathcal{M}$ such that $\mathcal{K} \subseteq \mathcal{M}$. Let $n > 0$ be an integer and let $\mathcal{C}$ be the set of functions $\mathcal{C} = \{f : \mathcal{K}^n \to \mathcal{M}\}$ consisting of

- all $|\mathcal{M}|$ constant functions $f_m(z) = m$ for all $z \in \mathcal{K}^n$, and
- all n selector functions $f_i(x_1, \ldots, x_n) = x_i$ for $1 \leq i \leq n$.

We define circular security using the following game between a challenger and an adversary $\mathcal{A}$. For an integer $n > 0$ and a security parameter λ, the game proceeds as follows:

Initialization: The challenger chooses a random bit $b \leftarrow \{0,1\}$. It generates $(\mathsf{pk}_1, \mathsf{sk}_1), \ldots, (\mathsf{pk}_n, \mathsf{sk}_n)$ by running $\mathsf{KeyGen}(1^\lambda)$ n times, and sends $(\mathsf{pk}_1, \ldots, \mathsf{pk}_n)$ to $\mathcal{A}$.

Queries: The adversary repeatedly issues queries where each query is of the form (i, f) with $1 \leq i \leq n$ and $f \in \mathcal{C}$. The challenger responds by setting $y = f(\mathsf{sk}_1, \ldots, \mathsf{sk}_n)$ and

$$\mathsf{ct} \leftarrow \begin{cases} \mathsf{Enc}(\mathsf{pk}_i, y) & \text{if } b = 0 \\ \mathsf{Enc}(\mathsf{pk}_i, 0^{|y|}) & \text{if } b = 1 \end{cases}$$

and sends ct to $\mathcal{A}$.

Finish: Finally, the adversary outputs a bit $b' \in \{0,1\}$.

We say that $\mathcal{A}$ wins the game if $b = b'$. Let win be the event that $\mathcal{A}$ wins the game and define $\mathcal{A}$'s advantage as

$$\mathsf{Adv}^{\mathcal{A}}_{\mathsf{circ},n}(\lambda) = \Pr[\mathsf{win}].$$

Definition 8 (n-Circular Security). *We say that a public-key encryption scheme* (KeyGen, Enc, Dec) *is n-way* circular secure *if for all probabilistic polynomial time adversaries $\mathcal{A}$, there exists a negligible function* negl *such that*

$$\mathsf{Adv}^{\mathcal{A}}_{\mathsf{circ},n}(\lambda) < \frac{1}{2} + \mathsf{negl}(\lambda).$$

Because existing constructions of circularly secure encryption schemes based on standard assumptions require a bound on the total number of public keys n, the corresponding Trivial Scheme will only satisfy a bounded-key variant of CPA security, defined next.

Definition 9 (Proxy Reencryption: n-CPA Security). *For $n \in \mathbb{N}$, the n-CPA security game is identical to the CPA security game in Definition 3 except for the following underlined modifications. Recall that* numKeys *is initialized to 0 and is incremented after every key generation call in the security game.*

Uncorrupted Key Generation: *If* numKeys $= n$*, return* $\perp$*. Otherwise, obtain a new key pair* $(\mathsf{pk}_i, \mathsf{sk}_i) \leftarrow \mathsf{KeyGen}(\mathsf{pp})$. *$\mathcal{A}$ is given* pk_i. *The current value of* numKeys *is added to* Hon *and* numKeys *is incremented.*

Corrupted Key Generation: *If* numKeys $= n$*, return* $\perp$*. Otherwise, obtain a new key pair* $(pk_i, \mathsf{sk}_i) \leftarrow \mathsf{KeyGen}(\mathsf{pp})$. *$\mathcal{A}$ is given* $(\mathsf{pk}_i, \mathsf{sk}_i)$. *The current value of* numKeys *is added to* Cor *and* numKeys *is incremented.*

*The corresponding n-*CPA *advantage of $\mathcal{A}$ is denoted* $\mathsf{Adv}^{\mathcal{A}}_{\mathsf{cpa},n}(\lambda)$. *A proxy reencryption scheme is n-*CPA secure *if for all probabilistic polynomial-time adversaries $\mathcal{A}$, there exists a negligible function* negl *such that*

$$\mathsf{Adv}^{\mathcal{A}}_{\mathsf{cpa},n}(\lambda) < \frac{1}{2} + \mathsf{negl}(\lambda)$$

Trivial Scheme. Let $(\mathsf{KeyGen}_{\mathsf{circ}}, \mathsf{Enc}_{\mathsf{circ}}, \mathsf{Dec}_{\mathsf{circ}})$ be an n-way circular secure encryption scheme. Let $\mathsf{Setup} \equiv \perp$, $\mathsf{KeyGen} \equiv \mathsf{KeyGen}_{\mathsf{circ}}$; $\mathsf{Enc} \equiv \mathsf{Enc}_{\mathsf{circ}}$;

$$\mathsf{ReKeyGen}(\mathsf{sk}_i, \mathsf{pk}_j) := \mathsf{Enc}_{\mathsf{circ}}(\mathsf{pk}_j, \mathsf{sk}_i)$$

$$\mathsf{ReEnc}(\mathsf{rk}_{i\to j}, \mathsf{ct}_i) := \mathsf{ct}_i \| \mathsf{rk}_{i \to j}$$

$$\mathsf{Dec}(\mathsf{sk}, \mathsf{ct}) := \begin{cases} \mathsf{Dec}_{\mathsf{circ}}(\mathsf{Dec}_{\mathsf{circ}}(\mathsf{sk}, \mathsf{ct}^2), \mathsf{ct}^1) & \text{if } \mathsf{ct} = \mathsf{ct}^1 \| \mathsf{ct}^2 \\ \mathsf{Dec}_{\mathsf{circ}}(\mathsf{sk}, \mathsf{ct}) & \text{otherwise} \end{cases}.$$

Theorem 2 states that if $(\mathsf{KeyGen}_{\mathsf{circ}}, \mathsf{Enc}_{\mathsf{circ}}, \mathsf{Dec}_{\mathsf{circ}})$ is an n-way circular secure encryption scheme, then the corresponding Trivial Scheme PRE is an n-CPA secure proxy reencryption scheme. In fact, the proof below extends the case when there are n uncorrupted keys and any number of corrupted keys.

Proof (of Theorem 2). For all $n \in \mathbb{N}$ and any probabilistic, polynomial-time algorithm $\mathcal{A}$ (the adversary against the trivial scheme), we construct an efficient algorithm $\mathcal{A}_{\mathsf{circ}}$ such that $\mathsf{Adv}^{\mathcal{A}_{\mathsf{circ}}}_{\mathsf{circ},n} = \frac{1}{2} \cdot \mathsf{Adv}^{\mathcal{A}}_{\mathsf{cpa},n}$. By the hypothesis, this advantage is negligible, completing the proof.

At the beginning of the game, the circular security challenger picks a random bit b. If $b = 0$, then the Queries oracle encrypts all messages correctly; if $b = 1$, then the Queries oracle encrypts only the message 0. $\mathcal{A}_{\mathsf{circ}}$ runs $\mathcal{A}$ and simulates the CPA security game for PRE (if $\mathcal{A}$ does not follow the specification of the game, $\mathcal{A}_{\mathsf{circ}}$ simply aborts).

At the start of Phase 1, $\mathcal{A}_{\mathsf{circ}}$ calls its Initialization oracle in the circular security game. In return it receives the public keys $(\mathsf{pk}^{\mathsf{circ}}_1, \ldots, \mathsf{pk}^{\mathsf{circ}}_n)$. To answer an Uncorrupted Key Generation query, $\mathcal{A}_{\mathsf{circ}}$ gives to $\mathcal{A}$ the first unused public key $\mathsf{pk}^{\mathsf{circ}}_i$ from this list. To answer a Corrupted Key Generation query, $\mathcal{A}_{\mathsf{circ}}$ generates a new key pair $(\mathsf{pk}, \mathsf{sk}) \leftarrow \mathsf{KeyGen}$ and gives $(\mathsf{pk}, \mathsf{sk})$ to the adversary.

$\mathcal{A}$ begins Phase 2 by using its Queries oracle to learn the reencryption keys for all pairs of uncorrupted keys generated. Using its knowledge of the corrupted secret keys, it also computes reencryption keys for all the pairs of corrupted keys generated. Oracle calls from $\mathcal{A}$ to $\mathcal{O}_{\mathsf{ReKeyGen}}$ are answered with the corresponding reencryption key (or with $\perp$). To answer oracle calls from $\mathcal{A}$ to $\mathcal{O}_{\mathsf{ReEnc}}$, computes the appropriate response; namely, it concatenates the reencryption key to the ciphertext (or returns $\perp$).

At some point, $\mathcal{A}$ queries the Challenge oracle with an honest key index i and a pair of messages $(\mathbf{m}_0, \mathbf{m}_1)$. $\mathcal{A}_{\mathsf{circ}}$ chooses a random one of the messages $\mathbf{m}$ and queries its own Queries oracle with the pair $(i, \mathbf{m})$, returning the resulting ciphertext to $\mathcal{A}$.

Finally, $\mathcal{A}$ guesses whether $\mathbf{m} = \mathbf{m}_0$ or $\mathbf{m}_1$. If $\mathcal{A}$ guesses correctly, $\mathcal{A}_{\mathsf{circ}}$ guesses the bit $b' = 0$. Otherwise, $\mathcal{A}_{\mathsf{circ}}$ guesses a random $b' \leftarrow \{0, 1\}$. Conditioned on $b = 0$, $\mathcal{A}_{\mathsf{circ}}$ perfectly simulates the PRE security game, and guesses $b' = 0$ with probability $\mathsf{Adv}^{\mathcal{A}}_{\mathsf{cpa},n}$. It follows that $\mathsf{Adv}^{\mathcal{A}_{\mathsf{circ}}}_{\mathsf{circ},n} = \frac{1}{2} \cdot \mathsf{Adv}^{\mathcal{A}}_{\mathsf{cpa},n}$.

B Comparison to RIND-CPA

The concurrent work of Derler, Krenn, Lorünser, Ramacher, Slamanig, and Striecks identify the same problem with CPA security as discussed [14]. They define a new security notion—RIND-CPA security—as an additional property that proxy reencryptions schemes should guarantee.

The key feature of RIND-CPA security is that the adversary gets access to an unrestricted ReEnc oracle, but only before seeing the challenge ciphertext. The definition is similar to $\mathsf{IND\text{-}CCA}_{0,1}$ of [28]. The definition of the RIND-CPA security experiment is from [14, Experiment 8].

Definition 10 (RIND-CPA Security Experiment).

$\mathsf{pp} \leftarrow \mathsf{Setup}(1^\lambda), (\mathsf{pk}, \mathsf{sk}) \leftarrow \mathsf{KeyGen}(\mathsf{pp}), b \leftarrow \{0, 1\}$
$(\mathsf{pk}^*, \mathsf{st}) \leftarrow \mathcal{A}(\mathsf{pp}, \mathsf{pk})$
$\mathsf{rk} \leftarrow \mathsf{ReKeyGen}(\mathsf{sk}, \mathsf{pk}^*)$

$(\mathbf{m}_0, \mathbf{m}_1, \mathsf{st}) \leftarrow \mathcal{A}^{\{\mathsf{ReEnc}(\mathsf{rk},\cdot)\}}(\mathsf{st})$
$b^* \leftarrow \mathcal{A}(\mathsf{st}, \mathsf{Enc}(\mathsf{pk}, \mathbf{m}_b))$
if $b = b^*$ *return 1, else return 0.*

RIND-CPA security requires that for all efficient adversaries, the probability of outputting 1 in the experiment is $\frac{1}{2} \pm \mathsf{negl}(\lambda)$.

In this section, we compare the approach of [14] with ours. We begin by describing RIND-CPA security as defined by [14]. Next, we compare RIND-CPA with HRA security informally, arguing that HRA provides the better generalization of Enc-CPA security to the PRE setting. Finally, we show that HRA and RIND-CPA security are incomparable notions.

B.1 Informal Comparison

RIND-CPA is less suitable than HRA as a replacement for CPA security of proxy reencryption. First and most importantly, HRA better captures the intuitive guarantees of Enc-CPA security for standard encryption. Second, access to an unrestricted ReEnc oracle makes it a more useful as a testing ground for the development of new techniques. Finally, two idiosyncrasies of the [14] formulation of RIND-CPA security present additional issues.

Capturing Enc-CPA security. In Enc-CPA security for standard encryption, the adversary is able to arbitrarily affect the distribution of plaintext messages. One way of viewing this aspect of the definition is that Enc-CPA requires security while being agnostic as to the true distribution over messages (except that it is efficiently sampleable). Other than choosing the distribution over messages, the adversary is only allowed to see publicly-available information (i.e. public keys and parameters) and honestly encrypted ciphertexts. Informally, the Enc-CPA guarantee is that security should hold under normal operating conditions against eavesdropping parties without making distributional assumptions on plaintext messages. However, Enc-CPA makes no guarantees about dishonestly generated or malformed ciphertexts.

HRA security captures this intuitive guarantee better than RIND-CPA. In the course of normal operation of a proxy reencryption, an adversarial party will see reencrypted ciphertexts. These ciphertexts may come at any time—both before and after other ciphertexts whose contents should remain secret. While HRA allows reencryption both before and after the challenge, RIND-CPA restricts the reencryption oracle to the period before the challenge.

HRA makes minimal assumptions about the distribution of plaintext messages by allowing the adversary to choose messages itself, just as in Enc-CPA. RIND-CPA goes further by making requirements in the face of malformed or dishonestly generated ciphertexts.

A testing ground for new techniques. For classical encryption, Enc-CCA security is strictly stronger than Enc-CPA security. In fact, there are many settings where Enc-CPA security is demonstrably insufficient. Why then does the cryptography community continue to study it? There are many answers to this question, but we mention only two. First, although insufficient for some applications, Enc-CPA is useful in others. Second, it is useful as an intermediate goal because it seems to capture a sort of hard core of the general problem of encryption and spurs the development of new techniques.

HRA security enjoys these same features; RIND-CPA does not. As for usefulness for applications, HRA is meaningful in many of the envisioned applications of proxy reencryption—many more than CPA security. Because RIND-CPA restricts the reencryption oracle to the period before the challenge ciphertext, its usefulness in applications is less clear.

The challenge of constructing CCA secure proxy reencryption is the same as the challenge of Enc-CCA secure encryption: namely, dealing with dishonestly generated, possibly malformed ciphertexts. RIND-CPA, by allowing malformed ciphertexts, presents similar challenges as full CCA security.

As for the usefulness of HRA as an intermediate goal towards CCA security, the historical development of proxy reencryption is proof itself. This sounds paradoxical: how can this be true if the notion has only just been introduced in this work? Many of cryptographers that were targeting CPA security developed schemes that achieve HRA security with only minimal modification. The techniques developed in these constructions were later adapted to achieve CCA security. This suggests that cryptographers' intuitions for the hard core of reencryption were not flawed, only the formalization of these intuitions as CPA security. HRA security is a better formalization for these intuitions and thus an appropriate intermediate goal for reencryption research.

Idiosyncrasies of the RIND-CPA definition. We mention two unusual properties of the [14] definition. Unlike the adversary's access to a ReEnc oracle, these properties are not inherent in the RIND-CPA concept. It would be easy to propose a modified RIND-CPA definition that did not have these properties (e.g., $\mathsf{IND\text{-}CCA}_{0,1}$ in [28]).

First, the definition only considers the two party setting. Much like the informal description of proxy reencryption in Sect. 1, there is only a single uncorrupted key and a single corrupted key. It is easy to show that security in the two party setting does not imply security in a many party setting.

Second, not only are inputs to ReEnc allowed to be malformed, but the corrupted public key pk^* can be malformed as well. The adversary outputs pk^* itself and it needs not be honestly generated. This makes RIND-CPA security as defined in [14] formally incomparable to all other definitions of proxy reencryption security we know of, including the $\mathsf{IND\text{-}CCA}_{0,1}$ of [28].

These drawbacks of the [14] definition do not affect the proof of Theorem 7, but neither does the proof depend on them.

B.2 Separating RIND-CPA and HRA Security

The following pair of theorems support the conclusion that HRA security and RIND-CPA security are incomparable.

Theorem 6. *If there exists an HRA secure PRE scheme, then there exists a PRE scheme that is HRA secure but not RIND-CPA secure.*

Proof. Suppose PRE is HRA secure, and let $\top$ be a special symbol that is not a valid ciphertext. Define a new scheme PRE′ by modifying reencryption as follows:

$$\mathsf{ReEnc}'(\mathsf{rk}, \mathsf{ct}) := \begin{cases} \mathsf{ReEnc}(\mathsf{rk}, \mathsf{ct}) & \text{if } \mathsf{ct} \neq \top \\ \mathsf{rk} & \text{if } \mathsf{ct} = \top \end{cases}.$$

PRE′ is still HRA secure: $\mathcal{O}_{\mathsf{ReEnc}'}$ is functionally equivalent to $\mathcal{O}_{\mathsf{ReEnc}}$ when restricted to honestly generated ciphertexts.

PRE′ is not RIND-CPA secure: a single call to $\mathcal{O}_{\mathsf{ReEnc}'}(i, j, \top)$ (made before the challenge) allows the adversary to learn the reencryption key $\mathsf{rk}_{i\to j}$ and thereby decrypt the challenge ciphertext.

Theorem 7. *Under the assumptions stated below, there exists a PRE scheme that is RIND-CPA secure but not HRA secure.*

The claim assumes the existence of pair of encryption schemes, PRE and FHE with the following properties. PRE is a RIND-CPA secure proxy reencryption scheme with a ciphertext space $\mathcal{C}_{\mathsf{inner}}$. FHE is a circuit private fully homomorphic encryption scheme with message space $\mathcal{M}_{\mathsf{fhe}} = \mathcal{C}_{\mathsf{inner}}$. The message spaces and ciphertext spaces of the two schemes are all disjoint and efficiently decidable. Finally, the additional proxy reencryption scheme $\mathsf{PRE}_{\mathsf{FHE}}$ corresponding to the FHE scheme (see Sect. 5.3) is RIND-CPA secure.[10] For simplicity, we also assume perfect correctness of reencryption (for both schemes) and of homomorphic evaluation.

Below we present a intuition for the proof of Theorem 7. The proof is included in the full version [13].

Proof Intuition for Theorem 7. Recall that RIND-CPA security allows the adversary access to an unrestricted ReEnc oracle, but only before the challenge ciphertext is generated. The main difficulty in separating RIND-CPA and HRA security is the restriction in the HRA reencryption oracle to honestly generated ciphertexts.

The first idea in our construction is the observation that separating RIND-CPA and HRA security would be easy if it were possible to use Enc oracle to generate a fresh, honest encryption of the challenge plaintext. This fresh encryption could be reencrypted by the HRA reencryption oracle to a corrupted key, revealing the challenge plaintext.

The second idea is to have two layers of encryption, where the message space of the outer layer is equal to the ciphertext space of the inner layer. If the

[10] The proof requires that an encryption scheme be both fully homomorphic and support proxy reencryption with RIND-CPA security. For concreteness, we have chosen to assume that there exists an FHE scheme whose corresponding PRE is RIND-CPA secure, but a different construction would suffice. We do not further explore the underlying cryptographic assumptions needed to instantiate this encryption scheme.

challenge ciphertext comes from the inner layer, then it can be used as input to the Enc oracle to generate a new *outer ciphertext* containing information about the challenge plaintext—namely, an encryption of the challenge ciphertext. The outer ciphertext is honestly generated and can be reencrypted to a corrupt party and decrypted. But it seems we are no better off; decrypting the outer ciphertext only returns the challenge ciphertext still encrypted under the key of an honest party.

The third idea is to modify ReEnc—using fully homomorphic encryption—to reencrypt both the outer ciphertext and the inner challenge ciphertext. In addition to the usual reencrypted ciphertext, we augment ReEnc to output an additional, *doubly reencrypted* ciphertext, where both the outer and inner ciphertexts have been reencrypted. If the recipient of the resulting ciphertext is corrupt, the adversary can decrypt both layers and recover the challenge plaintext, violating HRA security.

We now describe the intuition for how to perform double reencryption. Suppose the proxy reencryption scheme used for the outer layer of encryption is also fully homomorphic. Such a scheme can be constructed from any FHE scheme (see Sect. 5.3). Given input an outer layer ciphertext $\mathsf{ct}_{\mathsf{outer}} = \mathsf{Enc}(\mathsf{ct}_{\mathsf{inner}})$, ReEnc will homomorphically evaluate $\mathsf{Eval}_{\mathsf{fhe}}(\mathsf{ReEnc}, \mathsf{ct}_{\mathsf{outer}})$. The result is an (non-reencrypted) outer ciphertext containing a reencrypted inner ciphertext. Then, ReEnc reencrypts that outer ciphertext. This produces a reencrypted outer ciphertext containing a reencrypted inner ciphertext.

Violating HRA security is simple: the adversary encrypts the challenge ciphertexts, reencrypts it to a corrupted key, then decrypts the doubly-reencrypted component twice to recover the challenge message.

It remains to prove that the constructed PRE scheme is RIND-CPA secure. The homomorphic double reencryption functionality can be simulated by a sequence of calls to Enc, Dec and $\mathcal{O}_{\mathsf{ReEnc}}$, allowing us to analyze the two-layered scheme without the double-reencryption modification to ReEnc. The RIND-CPA security of that scheme follows directly from the RIND-CPA security of the PRE scheme underlying the two layers.

Adaptively Secure Proxy Re-encryption

Georg Fuchsbauer[1(✉)], Chethan Kamath[2], Karen Klein[2], and Krzysztof Pietrzak[2]

[1] Inria, ENS and PSL University, Paris, France
georg.fuchsbauer@ens.fr
[2] IST Austria, Klosterneuburg, Austria
{ckamath,karen.klein,pietrzak}@ist.ac.at

Abstract. A proxy re-encryption (PRE) scheme is a public-key encryption scheme that allows the holder of a key pk to derive a re-encryption key for any other key pk'. This re-encryption key lets anyone transform ciphertexts under pk into ciphertexts under pk' without having to know the underlying message, while transformations from pk' to pk should not be possible (unidirectional). Security is defined in a multi-user setting against an adversary that gets the users' public keys and can ask for re-encryption keys and can corrupt users by requesting their secret keys. Any ciphertext that the adversary cannot trivially decrypt given the obtained secret and re-encryption keys should be secure.

All existing security proofs for PRE only show *selective* security, where the adversary must first declare the users it wants to corrupt. This can be lifted to more meaningful *adaptive* security by guessing the set of corrupted users among the n users, which loses a factor exponential in n, rendering the result meaningless already for moderate n.

Jafargholi et al. (CRYPTO'17) proposed a framework that in some cases allows to give adaptive security proofs for schemes which were previously only known to be selectively secure, while avoiding the exponential loss that results from guessing the adaptive choices made by an adversary. We apply their framework to PREs that satisfy some natural additional properties. Concretely, we give a more fine-grained reduction for several unidirectional PREs, proving adaptive security at a much smaller loss. The loss depends on the graph of users whose edges represent the re-encryption keys queried by the adversary. For trees and chains the loss is quasi-polynomial in the size and for general graphs it is exponential in their depth and indegree (instead of their size as for previous reductions). Fortunately, trees and low-depth graphs cover many, if not most, interesting applications.

Our results apply e.g. to the bilinear-map based PRE schemes by Ateniese et al. (NDSS'05 and CT-RSA'09), Gentry's FHE-based scheme (STOC'09) and the LWE-based scheme by Chandran et al. (PKC'14).

Keywords: Proxy reencryption · Adaptive security · Tightness

The full version of this paper can be found on the IACR eprint archive: [FKKP18].

D. Lin and K. Sako (Eds.): PKC 2019, LNCS 11443, pp. 317–346, 2019.
https://doi.org/10.1007/978-3-030-17259-6_11

1 Introduction

A proxy re-encryption (PRE) scheme is a public-key encryption scheme with an additional functionality: Alice and Bob, who have key pairs $(\mathtt{pk}_A, \mathtt{sk}_A)$ and $(\mathtt{pk}_B, \mathtt{sk}_B)$, respectively, can generate a re-encryption key (re-key, for short) $\mathtt{rk}_{A,B}$ that allows its holder, say Peggy, to act as a proxy; that is, she can transform ciphertexts under $\mathtt{pk}_A$ to ciphertexts under $\mathtt{pk}_B$ without having to know the underlying message. A trivial way to accomplish this would be for Alice to hand her secret key $\mathtt{sk}_A$ to Peggy, who can then decrypt ciphertexts under $\mathtt{pk}_A$, encrypt them under $\mathtt{pk}_B$ and send them to Bob. Alice's secret key acts thus as the re-key and de- and encryption algorithms are used for re-encryption. However, this approach requires Alice to reveal her secret key to Peggy and therefore place complete trust on her. The more interesting cases are when the parties are mutually distrustful.

Bidirectional vs. unidirectional. In the above setting, if the re-key $\mathtt{rk}_{A,B}$ allows Peggy to also transform ciphertexts under $\mathtt{pk}_B$ to $\mathtt{pk}_A$, the PRE scheme is called "bidirectional". For such schemes the re-key is necessarily a function of both $\mathtt{sk}_A$ and $\mathtt{sk}_B$. In this paper we are interested in the more interesting case of "unidirectional" PRE schemes where the re-key $\mathtt{rk}_{A,B}$ can only transform ciphertexts from $\mathtt{pk}_A$ to $\mathtt{pk}_B$, and not vice-versa, and ciphertexts under $\mathtt{pk}_B$ remain secure even given $\mathtt{sk}_A$ and $\mathtt{rk}_{A,B}$. (Henceforth we will always assume PREs to be unidirectional.) As opposed to bidirectional PREs, the re-key generation algorithm in a unidirectional PRE takes as input "source" keys $(\mathtt{pk}_A, \mathtt{sk}_A)$ and only the "target" public key $\mathtt{pk}_B$.

Single hop vs. multiple hops. Suppose a third user, Charlie, holding keys $(\mathtt{pk}_C, \mathtt{sk}_C)$, enters the picture and suppose Peggy obtains the re-key $\mathtt{rk}_{B,C}$ that allows her to transform ciphertexts under Bob's public key to ciphertexts under Charlie's public key. Peggy can, by definition, transform a ciphertext c_A under $\mathtt{pk}_A$ to a ciphertext c_B under $\mathtt{pk}_B$ using her re-key $\mathtt{rk}_{A,B}$. If it allows Peggy to transform ciphertext c_B, which has already been re-encrypted once, to a ciphertext c_C under $\mathtt{pk}_C$ using the re-key $\mathtt{rk}_{B,C}$ then we say that the PRE scheme allows two "hops". In a similar manner, one can consider multiple hops of re-encryptions. Such a scheme is termed "multi-hop" as opposed to a "single-hop" scheme (which does not allow re-encryptions of already re-encrypted ciphertexts).

1.1 Modelling Security

The basic notion of security for unidirectional PREs is that of indistinguishability under chosen-plaintext attack (CPA). There are n users and, at the beginning of the game, the adversary gets their public keys $\mathtt{pk}_1, \ldots, \mathtt{pk}_n$ from the challenger. In the first phase, the adversary can corrupt users of its choice by requesting their secret keys; in the second phase, it can obtain re-keys $\mathtt{rk}_{i,j}$ and re-encryptions for ciphertexts of its choice. The scheme is CPA-secure if it is infeasible for the adversary to distinguish encryptions of two messages under a key that the adversary has not corrupted either directly or indirectly (through a re-key or re-encryption query to a corrupted user).

Just as in standard public-key encryption, the above security definition can be strengthened to chosen-ciphertext attack (CCA) by allowing the adversary access to a decryption oracle which, on input a ciphertext and a public key $\mathtt{pk}_i$ returns the decryption of the ciphertext under $\mathtt{sk}_i$. The conditions to ensure non-triviality have to be altered accordingly.

We note that both definitions are *selective* in nature: the adversary must choose the set of players it corrupts before issuing any queries.

1.2 Prior Work

Bidirectional PREs were introduced as "atomic proxy cryptography" by Blaze, Bleumer and Strauss [BBS98], who constructed a multi-hop scheme under the decisional Diffie-Hellman assumption. Unidirectional PREs were introduced later by Ateniese et al. [AFGH05]. Their main motivation was to limit the amount of trust placed on the proxy, as required by their application to access control for distributed storage. Since the notion of security for unidirectional PRE is different from a bidirectional PRE, they also reformulated the notion of CPA (for the single-hop setting). Assuming hardness of certain problems on bilinear groups, they constructed CPA-secure schemes that are single-hop and unidirectional.

The definition of CCA security for single-hop bidirectional schemes is due to Canetti and Hohenberger [CH07] and is more involved than previous definitions, mainly because the adversary is allowed adaptive corruption. They gave a scheme satisfying their notion under the standard decisional bilinear Diffie-Hellman assumption. The definition of CCA security in the unidirectional setting is due to Libert and Vergnaud [LV08], who instantiate it under a slightly non-standard assumption on bilinear groups.

The earlier constructions of multi-hop, unidirectional schemes were based on program obfuscation [HRsV07,CCV12]. In his seminal paper, Gentry [Gen09] gave a generic construction of PREs from fully homomorphic encryption. The first construction (with succinct ciphertexts) based on a standard assumption is due to Chandran et al. [CCL+14]: their scheme is CPA-secure assuming decisional learning with errors. Phong et al. [PWA+16] followed up with a construction that, in addition, enjoys a security property called "key-privacy". The only construction of a CCA-secure multi-hop, unidirectional scheme is due to Fan and Liu [FL17]. In their paper, they also rigorously defined the security models (CPA and CCA) for the multi-hop setting.

Cohen [Coh17] has recently argued that CPA security might be too weak for some applications and introduced *indistinguishability against honest-reencryption attack* (HRA), a notion that lies between CPA and CCA. He also showed that if a PRE satisfies a property called "source-hiding", which several existing CPA-secure schemes do, then HRA security reduces to CPA security.

1.3 Our Contribution

Our starting point is the observation that, unlike bidirectional PREs, the security definitions for unidirectional PREs (that is, CPA, HRA and CCA) are all *selective* in nature: the adversary must choose the set of parties it corrupts before issuing any queries. A more meaningful notion would be *adaptive* security, where the adversary is allowed to corrupt users at any time during the game. However, modelling this turns out to be as tricky as in the bidirectional setting. In this paper, we lift the definitions for CPA and HRA to the adaptive setting.

1.3.1 First Contribution: Modelling Adaptive Corruption. The main problem that arises when we allow the adversary to adaptively corrupt users is that we must ensure that the adversary cannot trivially win the security game. For bidirectional PREs this was handled in [CH07] by defining a relation that keeps track of the dependency between the re-keys and re-encryptions that were issued during the game. Our approach is similar in spirit: the security game maintains a "recoding graph" that has n nodes, and whose edges are derived from the re-keys and re-encryptions issued to the adversary. The exact definitions of the recoding graph for adaptive CPA and for adaptive HRA differ slightly, but in both cases it is defined so that no corrupt key is reachable from the challenge key. That is, the adversary is forbidden from making *any* re-key or re-encryption queries to a corrupt user that is reachable from the challenge key. The recoding graph now allows to ensure non-triviality of the adversary's actions by checking a few basic graph properties.

1.3.2 Second Contribution: The Reduction. Proving adaptive security can be reduced to showing selective security by initially guessing the set of users that will be corrupted. However, this reduction loses an exponential factor in n, rendering the reduction meaningless already for moderate n. As our main contribution, we give a more fine-grained reduction from adaptive to selective security which in many practical settings and for several existing schemes (or minor variants) implies adaptive security at much smaller (quasi-polynomial, or even polynomial) loss. More precisely, the loss in our reduction depends on the structure of the recoding graph: for trees and chains we get a quasi-polynomial $n^{O(\log n)}$ loss, whereas for general graphs the loss is exponential in their depth. Fortunately, trees, chains, and low-depth graphs cover many, if not most, interesting applications.

Security assumptions. A key step in our search for a tighter reduction was the identification of the basic security assumptions on a PRE that we required in our arguments. For the case of CPA, it turned out to be ciphertext indistinguishability and *weak* key-privacy, both fairly standard security requirements already explored in some of the previous works.

As the name suggests, a PRE is ciphertext-indistinguishable (or, for short, indistinguishable) if the underlying encryption is. Since the syntax of the encryption algorithm for a PRE is slightly different from that of a standard public-key encryption, the definition of indistinguishability has to be slightly changed. To be precise, the encryption algorithm for a PRE takes also a "level" as input, and we require that the ciphertexts are indistinguishable *on all levels.* It is not hard, therefore, to see that any selectively CPA-secure PRE has to trivially satisfy indistinguishability.

The notion of key-privacy was introduced in a strong form in [ABH09]. We require the PRE to satisfy a much weaker property, namely that a re-key $\mathtt{rk}_{A,B}$ looks pseudorandom given just the source and target public keys $\mathtt{pk}_A$ and $\mathtt{pk}_B$. Existing PRE schemes that satisfy the stronger key privacy as defined in [ABH09] are therefore candidates for our reduction.

To apply our reduction to HRA-secure PRE, we need a third assumption to hold: source-hiding. This is the same property that allowed Cohen [Coh17] to lift a CPA-secure PRE to a HRA-secure one. Informally, a PRE is source-hiding if ciphertexts that result from re-encryptions are distributed close to fresh encryptions (at the corresponding level).

For PRE satisfying these assumptions, we show that the framework of Jafargholi et al. [JKK+17], who gave an abstraction of the techniques from [FKPR14], can be applied. This framework has been used to show adaptive security of a variety of cryptographic protocols (e.g., secret sharing, garbled circuits etc.) in the "symmetric-key" setting while avoiding an exponential loss that typically results from the guessing step when going from selective to adaptive security. Its application to PREs in this work is the first in the "public-key" setting. We describe their framework in more detail below.

The [JKK+17] **framework.** A standard way to prove adaptive security is to first define a "selective" variant that requires the adversary to commit to some of its choices (e.g., whom to corrupt, or on what input to be challenged at the end) at the beginning of the game. Let $\mathcal{W}$ denote the set of all possible choices.

Consider a selective security notion defined as two games H^0 and H^1 being indistinguishable. A security proof often uses a hybrid argument: one defines a sequence of hybrid games $(\mathsf{H}_0, \ldots, \mathsf{H}_\tau)$ where the first and last games correspond to the original selective games (i.e., $\mathsf{H}^0 = \mathsf{H}_0$ and $\mathsf{H}^1 = \mathsf{H}_\tau$). One then proves that any two consecutive hybrids (H_t and H_{t+1}) are ϵ-indistinguishable. As indistinguishability satisfies the triangle inequality, the extreme games H_0 and H_τ are $(\epsilon \cdot \tau)$-indistinguishable.

Now to prove security against an adaptive adversary (who will not reveal its choices at the beginning), one defines a new reduction that just guesses the adversary's future choices at random from the set $\mathcal{W}$ and then follows the selective reduction. Conditioned on the guess being correct, this reduction has the same success probability as the selective one.

Unfortunately, the overall loss in security of this second step is as large as the size of $\mathcal{W}$, which is typically exponential (e.g., exponential in the number of parties that can be corrupted). Thus, if the selective reduction implied ϵ-indistinguishability (based on some underlying assumption), the adaptive reduction will only imply $(\epsilon \cdot |\mathcal{W}|)$-indistinguishability, which in most cases will be meaningless.

The key observation in [JKK+17] was that in many selective reductions as above, only a highly compressed version $h(w)$ of the information $w \in \mathcal{W}$ that the adversary commits to is actually used in the simulation of intermediate hybrids. Jafargholi et al. called these "partially selective" hybrids, as opposed to the original hybrids, which are "fully selective". They show that the security loss in such cases is only exponential in the length of $h(w)$ (its the longest value for any two consecutive hybrids), and not exponential in the length of the entire w.

In all the instances to which the [JKK+17] framework has been applied the simulation of the security game depends on some underlying graph (e.g., the access structure in secret sharing or the Boolean circuit in case of garbling) and the hybrid games involve incremental changes to the simulation *depending* on the structure of this graph. Jafargholi et al. managed to decouple the particulars of the simulation from the design of the hybrids by using a pebbling game on the graph (the graph must thus be directed and acyclic). To be more precise, they associated the simulation of a hybrid (H_t) to a pebbling configuration ($\mathcal{P}_t$), and therefore the incremental changes in the simulation to the pebbling sequence ($\mathcal{P}_0, \ldots, \mathcal{P}_\tau$). In particular, if a vertex carries a pebble then the part of simulation of the hybrid that is dependent on the vertex is carried out in a different manner (e.g., in garbling using Yao's scheme the ciphertexts in the garbled table for a gate are all bogus). The rules of the simulation is what then determines the pebbling rules, i.e., when exactly a pebble can be placed on or removed from a vertex. The extreme hybrids correspond to the initial and final pebbling configurations, and the immediate goal is to show that two hybrids that differ by a pebble are indistinguishable to an adversary. Indistinguishability of the original games then follows by transitivity of indistinguishability.

In the fully selective games of the above examples, the adversary commits to the whole graph; but, as explained above, knowledge of the vertices that are pebbled suffices to simulate the intermediate hybrids. Therefore, in the partially selective game the adversary "commits" to some pebbling configuration. Since we have established a correspondence between the simulation and a pebbling configuration, the task of designing a better sequence of hybrids has been reduced to finding a better pebbling sequence. In particular, the fewer pebbles are on the graph at any particular time, the more concisely we can describe this configuration, and thus the smaller the incurred security loss.

Designing the hybrids. The graph that underlies the simulation in adaptive CPA and HRA is precisely the recoding graph. (Strictly speaking, it suffices to consider the subgraph that is reachable from the challenge vertex, which we will call the "challenge graph".) The presence (or not) of a pebble on a vertex dictates how the re-encryption and re-key queries outgoing from that vertex are simulated. Therefore in the fully selective games, the adversary commits to the recoding graph (which is different from the original selective game in which the adversary committed to the set of corrupt users), whereas in the partially selective games it "commits" just to a pebbling configuration.

Let us first consider adaptive CPA: the edges of the recoding graph correspond to the re-key and re-encryption queries made by the adversary during the game. For simplicity, assume that the recoding graph has a single source vertex i^* that is also the vertex the adversary wants to be challenged on. Once it has made all the queries, the adversary receives its challenge, which is the encryption of either m_0^* or m_1^* under $\mathtt{pk}_{i^*}$; let CPA^0 and CPA^1 denote the respective games. In case there are no outgoing edges from i^*, indistinguishability of CPA^0 and CPA^1 follows from ciphertext indistinguishability (the first assumption): The reduction embeds the challenge public key (of the indistinguishability game) as the i^*-th key, relays (m_0^*, m_1^*) to its challenger and forwards the challenge ciphertext it receives to the adversary. As there are no outgoing re-keys from i^*, the simulation does not require the secret key $\mathtt{sk}_{i^*}$.

In case i^* does have outgoing edges, the idea is to use a sequence of hybrids to reach a game where knowledge of $\mathtt{sk}_{i^*}$ is not required for simulation, just like above. To argue indistinguishability of hybrids, we use weak key-privacy, which guarantees that a re-key looks pseudorandom given the source and target public keys. Weak key-privacy allows the simulator to fake the outgoing edges from a vertex, after which the secret key for this vertex is not required for simulation anymore. However, the simulator cannot fake edges right away: it has to fake all children of a vertex first, before it can rely on weak key-privacy. Consequently, the pebbling must obey the following rule: in a move, a pebble can be placed on or removed from a vertex only if all its children carry pebbles.

To be precise, in game H_t^b, for each pebbled vertex in $\mathcal{P}_t$ all queried re-keys outgoing from that vertex are faked. Observe that as the secret key corresponding to a vertex is used only for the generation of the re-keys outgoing from that vertex, the simulation of a hybrid can be carried out *without* knowledge of the secret key corresponding to the pebbled vertices. Thus, a pebbling sequence describes a sequence of hybrids.

Main result. Our main result bounds the security loss for arbitrary recoding graphs in terms of their space and time complexity, where a graph is said to have space complexity σ and time complexity τ if there exists a valid pebbling strategy for that graph that uses at most σ pebbles and requires at most τ moves. More generally, a class of graphs has space complexity σ and time complexity τ if this is the case for every graph in that class.

Theorem 1 (Informal Theorem 5). *Let $\mathcal{G}(n)$ denote a family of graphs on n vertices with space-complexity σ and time-complexity τ. Then a PRE that is ciphertext-indistinguishable and weakly key-private for computationally bounded adversaries is also adaptively CPA-secure against computationally bounded adversaries for recoding graphs in $\mathcal{G}$ with a loss in security of $\approx \tau \cdot n^\sigma$. If the PRE is also statistically source-hiding then it is also adaptively HRA-secure.*

In many applications, the underlying recoding graph has a very particular structure like trees (or even paths) and low-depth graphs, which cover many interesting applications. For paths, or fixed-arity trees, our reduction only loses a quasi-polynomial factor. For low-depth graphs, the loss is exponential only in the depth (and thus polynomial for fixed depth-graphs). Below, we mention two such applications.

Table 1. PRE schemes we prove adaptively CPA and HRA secure (see Sect. 5 and the full version [FKKP18] for the definitions of the assumptions).

Scheme	Setting	Assumption(s)	Hops
[CCL+14] (Constr. 2, Section 5)	Lattices	LWE	Multiple
[AFGH05] ([FKKP18, Constr. 4])	Bilinear maps	eDBDH and XDH	Single
[ABH09] ([FKKP18, Constr. 6])	Bilinear maps	eDBDH and DLin	Single
[Gen09] ([FKKP18, Constr. 5])	–	FHE	Multiple

1. In *key rotation* for encrypted cloud storage, a client has its data encrypted on a server, and occasionally wants to re-encrypt it (say, to restore security after key leakage). As the client does not trust the server, it will not want to hand it the decryption key. When using PRE, the client can simply send a re-key to the server, which enables it to locally re-encrypt all ciphertexts to the new key. In this application the recoding graph is simply a chain.
2. Another common application is *forwarding of encrypted email* without involving the receiver, say, for delegation during vacation or for filtering spam emails. In most cases the underlying delegation structure will be captured by simple graphs. For example, if delegation only happens to subordinates, the depth of the recoding graph is bounded by the depth of the hierarchy of the organisation.

1.3.3 Third Contribution: Adaptively-Secure PREs. Finally, we show that the aforementioned three properties are satisfied by several existing constructions or by minor variants thereof, and thus Theorem 1 can be applied to them. An overview of these schemes is given in Table 1. We consider the most interesting corollary to our results the adaptive security of the LWE-based scheme by Chandran et al. [CCL+14]:

Theorem 2 (Informal Theorem 6). *The quasi-polynomially secure decisional LWE problem implies multi-hop, unidirectional adaptively CPA/HRA-secure PRE for chains or complete binary trees.*

2 Formal Definitions

Notation. We use $[a, b]$ to denote $\{a, a+1, \ldots, b\}$ and $[b]$ as a shorthand for $[1, b]$. We will only consider logarithms to the base 2 (i.e., $\log := \log_2$). For two sets $\mathcal{X}, \mathcal{Y}$ we write $\mathcal{X} \Delta \mathcal{Y}$ for the symmetric difference. We write $x \leftarrow \mathcal{X}$ for sampling an element x uniformly at random from the set $\mathcal{X}$; analogously, $x_1, \ldots, x_n \leftarrow \mathcal{X}$ denotes sampling $x_1, \ldots, x_n$ independently and uniformly at random from the set $\mathcal{X}$. To indicate sampling according to a distribution X on $\mathcal{X}$, we write $x \leftarrow X$. By $[X]$ we denote the support of X, i.e., the values with positive probability.

For two distributions X, Y, $\Delta(X, Y)$ denotes their statistical distance. We write $X \equiv Y$ if X has the same input/output distribution as Y. Two distributions $X = \{X_\kappa\}_{\kappa \in \mathbb{N}}$ and $\{Y_\kappa\}_{\kappa \in \mathbb{N}}$ are (s, ϵ)-indistinguishable, denoted $X \approx_{(s,\epsilon)} Y$, if for every adversary A of size at most s

$$|\mathbb{P}[\mathsf{A}(X) = 1] - \mathbb{P}[\mathsf{A}(Y) = 1]| \leq \epsilon.$$

Throughout the paper, we will repeatedly use the following lemma concerning the transitivity of the indistinguishability relation $\approx$:

Lemma 1. *Let X, Y, Z be distributions on a set $\mathcal{X}$. If $X \approx_{(s_1,\epsilon_1)} Y$ and $Y \approx_{(s_2,\epsilon_2)} Z$, then $X \approx_{(\min(s_1,s_2),\epsilon_1+\epsilon_2)} Z$.*

For indistinguishability-based security games, we use $\langle \mathsf{G}, \mathsf{A} \rangle$ to denote the bit output by the challenger G at the end of its interaction with the adversary A. We say that two games G^0 and G^1 are (s, ϵ)-indistinguishable, denoted $\mathsf{G}^0 \approx_{(s,\epsilon)} \mathsf{G}^1$, if for every adversary A of size at most s

$$|\mathbb{P}[\langle \mathsf{G}^0, \mathsf{A} \rangle = 1] - \mathbb{P}[\langle \mathsf{G}^1, \mathsf{A} \rangle = 1]| \leq \epsilon.$$

For an algorithm A, we use s_{A} to denote its size; in a similar manner, for a set $\mathcal{X}$, we use $s_{\mathcal{X}}$ to denote the complexity of sampling from $\mathcal{X}$ uniformly at random.

Notation for graphs. We let $G = (\mathcal{V}, \mathcal{E})$ denote a directed graph with vertices $\mathcal{V}$ (usually $\mathcal{V} = [n]$ for some $n \in \mathbb{N}$) and edges $\mathcal{E} \subseteq \mathcal{V}^2$. The indegree (resp., outdegree) of a vertex is defined as the number of edges coming in to (resp., going out of) that vertex. The indegree (resp., outdegree) of the graph is the maximum indegree (resp., outdegree) over all the vertices. A vertex with indegree (resp., outdegree) zero is called a source (resp., sink). A vertex i is *connected* to another vertex j (or alternatively j is reachable from i) if there is a directed path from i to j in G.

2.1 Proxy Reencryption: Formal Definitions

Definition 1 (Multi-hop, unidirectional PRE). *A multi-hop, unidirectional PRE scheme for a message space $\mathcal{M}$ consists of the six-tuple of algorithms* $(\mathsf{S}, \mathsf{K}, \mathsf{RK}, \mathsf{E}, \mathsf{D}, \mathsf{RE})$, *which are explained below.*

$\mathsf{S}(1^\kappa, 1^\lambda) \to \mathtt{pp}$: *On input the security parameter κ and the maximum level λ (both in unary) supported by the scheme,* **setup** *outputs the public parameters* $\mathtt{pp}$. *We assume that* $\mathtt{pp}$ *is implicit in other function calls.*

$\mathsf{K}(\mathtt{pp}) \to (\mathtt{pk}, \mathtt{sk})$: **Key generation** *returns a public key* $\mathtt{pk}$ *and the corresponding secret key* $\mathtt{sk}$.

$\mathsf{RK}((\mathtt{pk}_i, \mathtt{sk}_i), \mathtt{pk}_j) \to \mathtt{rk}_{i,j}$: *On input a source key pair* $(\mathtt{pk}_i, \mathtt{sk}_i)$ *and a target public key* $\mathtt{pk}_j$, **re-key generation** *generates a unidirectional re-encryption key (rekey, for short)* $\mathtt{rk}_{i,j}$.

$\mathsf{E}(\mathtt{pk}, (m, \ell)) \to (c, \ell)$: **Encryption** *takes as input the public key* $\mathtt{pk}$*, a message* m *and a level* $\ell \in [\lambda]$*, and outputs a level-*ℓ *ciphertext* (c, ℓ).

$\mathsf{D}(\mathtt{sk}, (c, \ell)) \to m$: *On input a ciphertext* (c, ℓ) *and the secret key* $\mathtt{sk}$, **decryption** *outputs a message* m*, or the symbol* $\perp$ *(if the ciphertext is invalid).*

$\mathsf{RE}(\mathtt{rk}_{i,j}, \mathtt{pk}_i, \mathtt{pk}_j, (c_i, \ell)) \to (c_j, \ell + 1)$: **Reencryption** *takes a re-key* $\mathtt{rk}_{i,j}$*, a source public key* $\mathtt{pk}_i$*, a target public key* $\mathtt{pk}_j$ *and a level-*ℓ *ciphertext* c_i *under* $\mathtt{pk}_i$ *and transforms it to a level-*$(\ell + 1)$ *ciphertext* c_j *under* $\mathtt{pk}_j$*. Only ciphertexts belonging to levels* $\ell \in [\lambda - 1]$ *can be re-encrypted. In constructions where arguments* $\mathtt{pk}_i$ *and/or* $\mathtt{pk}_j$ *are optional, we simply drop them.*

Definition 1 differs slightly from the definition of multi-hop unidirectional PRE in [FL17]. Here, the re-keys are level-agnostic: the same re-key can be used to re-encrypt a ciphertext belonging to any level. In [FL17], however, a re-key associated to a level *cannot* be used to re-encrypt a ciphertext from a different level. We require the PRE to satisfy the following two correctness properties.

Definition 2 (Correctness [ABH09]**).** *A proxy re-encryption scheme (as in Definition 1) is correct w.r.t. the message space* $\mathcal{M}$ *if the following two properties hold:*

1. *Correctness of encryption:* $\forall \kappa, \lambda \in \mathbb{N}\ \forall \mathsf{pp} \in [\mathsf{S}(1^\kappa, 1^\lambda)]\ \forall (\mathtt{pk}, \mathtt{sk}) \in [\mathsf{K}(\mathsf{pp})]\ \forall (m, \ell) \in \mathcal{M} \times [\lambda]$*:*

$$\mathbb{P}[\mathsf{D}(\mathtt{sk}, \mathsf{E}(\mathtt{pk}, (m, \ell))) \neq m] = \mathsf{negl}(\kappa, \lambda),$$

where the probability is over the random coins of E.

2. *Correctness of re-encryption:* $\forall \kappa, \lambda \in \mathbb{N}\ \forall \mathsf{pp} \in [\mathsf{S}(1^\kappa, 1^\lambda)]\ \forall (\mathtt{pk}_i, \mathtt{sk}_i), (\mathtt{pk}_j, \mathtt{sk}_j) \in [\mathsf{K}(\mathsf{pp})]\ \forall \mathtt{rk}_{i,j} \in [\mathsf{RK}((\mathtt{pk}_i, \mathtt{sk}_i), \mathtt{pk}_j)]\ \forall (m, \ell) \in \mathcal{M} \times [\lambda - 1]$*:*

$$\mathbb{P}[\mathsf{D}(\mathtt{sk}_j, \mathsf{RE}(\mathtt{rk}_{i,j}, \mathtt{pk}_i, \mathtt{pk}_j, \mathsf{E}(\mathtt{pk}_i, (m, \ell)))) \neq m] = \mathsf{negl}(\kappa, \lambda),$$

where the probability is over the random coins of E *and* RE.

2.2 Modelling Security

2.2.1 Selective Corruption. The selective security of a multi-hop, unidirectional PRE scheme against a chosen-plaintext attack is modelled using the security game given in Game 1. It is an extension of the security model for single-hop PRE from [ABH09] to the multi-hop setting.[1] The limiting feature of the model is that the adversary has to fix, beforehand in Phase 1 (see Game 1), the honest and corrupt public keys. Its goal is to distinguish an encryption of m_0 from an encryption of m_1 (for m_0, m_1 of its choice) under a key of its choice. The game aborts if the adversary does one of the following:

- query the challenge oracle on a corrupt public key ($\mathtt{abort}_1$);

[1] [FL17] formalised security differently; we stick to the definition from [ABH09].

- request a re-key from an honest key to a corrupt key ($\texttt{abort}_2$); or
- query a re-encryption from an honest to a corrupt key ($\texttt{abort}_3$).

Challenger $\mathsf{sCPA}^b(1^\kappa, 1^\lambda, n)$
Set $\mathcal{C} = \emptyset$ ▷ Stores the corrupt public keys
$\texttt{pp} \leftarrow \mathsf{PRE.S}(1^\kappa, 1^\lambda)$, $(\texttt{pk}_1, \texttt{sk}_1), \ldots, (\texttt{pk}_n, \texttt{sk}_n) \leftarrow \mathsf{PRE.K}(\texttt{pp})$ ▷ Generate keys
$\forall i, j \in [n], i \neq j : \texttt{rk}_{i,j} \leftarrow \mathsf{PRE.RK}((\texttt{pk}_i, \texttt{sk}_i), \texttt{pk}_j)$ ▷ Generate re-keys
$\texttt{state} \leftarrow \mathsf{A}_1^{(\texttt{corrupt},\cdot)}(\texttt{pp})$ ▷ Phase 1
$b' \leftarrow \mathsf{A}_2^{(\texttt{rekey},\cdot,\cdot),(\texttt{reencrypt},\cdot,\cdot,\cdot),(\texttt{challenge},\cdot,\cdot,\cdot)}(\texttt{pk}_1, \ldots, \texttt{pk}_n, \texttt{state})$ ▷ Phase 2
return b'

Oracle $(\texttt{corrupt}, i)$
Add i to $\mathcal{C}$
return $\texttt{sk}_i$

Oracle $(\texttt{rekey}, i, j)$
if $i \notin \mathcal{C}$ and $j \in \mathcal{C}$ **then** HALT **end if** ▷ $\texttt{abort}_2$
return $\texttt{rk}_{i,j}$

Oracle $(\texttt{reencrypt}, i, j, (c_i, \ell))$
if $i \notin \mathcal{C}$ and $j \in \mathcal{C}$ **then** HALT **end if** ▷ $\texttt{abort}_3$
return $(c_j, \ell + 1) \leftarrow \mathsf{PRE.RE}(\texttt{rk}_{i,j}, \texttt{pk}_i, \texttt{pk}_j, (c_i, \ell))$

Oracle $(\texttt{challenge}, i^*, (m_0^*, m_1^*), \ell^*)$ ▷ Single access
if $i^* \in \mathcal{C}$ **then** HALT **end if** ▷ $\texttt{abort}_1$
return $(c_{i^*}, \ell^*) \leftarrow \mathsf{PRE.E}(\texttt{pk}_{i^*}, (m_b^*, \ell^*))$

Game 1: sPRE-CPA

Definition 3 (sPRE-CPA-security). *A PRE scheme is (s, ϵ)-selectively secure against chosen-plaintext attack if* $\mathsf{sCPA}^0 \approx_{(s,\epsilon)} \mathsf{sCPA}^1$, *where* sCPA^b *is defined in Game 1.*

Security against honest-reencryption attack. A stronger security definition was introduced in [Coh17] to address some of the restrictions that sPRE-CPA imposes on the adversary. The idea is to allow re-encryptions from honest to corrupt keys, if the ciphertexts to re-encrypt were honestly generated. The adversary can obtain such honest ciphertexts via an `encrypt` oracle, which stores them in a list. The `reencrypt` oracle now takes the index of an honestly generated ciphertext. It was shown in [Coh17] that (selective) HRA-security implies (selective) CPA-security and also that if the PRE scheme is re-encryption-simulatable (a generalisation of Definition 9) then (selective) CPA-security implies (selective) HRA-security. In sPRE-HRA, which we formally define in Game 2, $\texttt{abort}_3$ is relaxed to

- $\texttt{abort}_3^*$: The adversary queries the re-encryption of a ciphertext that is the result of a chain of re-encryptions of the challenge ciphertext from an honest to a corrupt key.

Definition 4 (sPRE-HRA-security). *A PRE scheme is (s, ϵ)-selectively secure against honest-reencryption attack if* $\mathsf{sHRA}^0 \approx_{(s,\epsilon)} \mathsf{sHRA}^1$, *where* sHRA^b *is defined in Game 2.*

Challenger $\mathsf{sHRA}^b(1^\kappa, 1^\lambda, n)$

Set $\mathcal{C}, \mathcal{E} = \emptyset$ ▷ Stores corrupt keys and issued re-keys and re-encryptions
Set $C = 0$ ▷ Counts ciphertexts generated
Set $\mathcal{L}, \mathcal{L}^* = \emptyset$ ▷ Stores honest ciphertexts and which derived from challenge
$\mathtt{pp} \leftarrow \mathsf{PRE.S}(1^\kappa, 1^\lambda)$, $(\mathtt{pk}_1, \mathtt{sk}_1), \ldots, (\mathtt{pk}_n, \mathtt{sk}_n) \leftarrow \mathsf{PRE.K}(\mathtt{pp})$ ▷ Generate keys
$\forall i, j \in [n], i \neq j : \mathtt{rk}_{i,j} \leftarrow \mathsf{PRE.RK}((\mathtt{pk}_i, \mathtt{sk}_i), \mathtt{pk}_j)$ ▷ Generate re-keys
$\mathsf{state} \leftarrow \mathsf{A}_1^{(\mathtt{corrupt},\cdot)}(\mathtt{pp})$ ▷ Phase 1
$b' \leftarrow \mathsf{A}_2^{(\mathtt{encrypt},\cdot,\cdot),(\mathtt{rekey},\cdot,\cdot),(\mathtt{reencrypt},\cdot,\cdot,\cdot),(\mathtt{challenge},\cdot,\cdot,\cdot)}(\mathtt{pk}_1, \ldots, \mathtt{pk}_n, \mathsf{state})$ ▷ Phase 2
return b'

Oracles `corrupt` and `rekey` are defined like in Game 1.

Oracle $(\mathtt{encrypt}, i, (m, \ell))$
$(c, \ell) \leftarrow \mathsf{PRE.E}(\mathtt{pk}_i, (m, \ell))$
Increment C and add $(C, i, m, (c, \ell))$ to $\mathcal{L}$
return (c, ℓ)

Oracle $(\mathtt{reencrypt}, i, j, k)$
Retrieve $(k, i, m, (c_i, \ell))$ from $\mathcal{L}$ and increment C
$(c_j, \ell + 1) \leftarrow \mathsf{PRE.RE}(\mathtt{rk}_{i,j}, \mathtt{pk}_i, \mathtt{pk}_j, (c_i, \ell))$
if $k \in \mathcal{L}^*$ **then** ▷ The ciphertext is derived from the challenge
  if $j \in \mathcal{C}$ **then** HALT **else** add C to $\mathcal{L}^*$ ▷ $\mathtt{abort}_3^*$ **end if**
end if
Add $(C, j, m, (c_j, \ell + 1))$ to $\mathcal{L}$
return $(c_j, \ell + 1)$

Oracle $(\mathtt{challenge}, i^*, (m_0^*, m_1^*), \ell^*)$ ▷ Single access
Compute $(c_{i^*}, \ell^*) \leftarrow \mathsf{PRE.E}(\mathtt{pk}_{i^*}, (m_b^*, \ell^*))$ and increment C
if $i^* \in \mathcal{C}$ **then** HALT **else** add C to $\mathcal{L}^*$ ▷ $\mathtt{abort}_1$ **end if**
Add $(C, i^*, m_b^*, (c_{i^*}, \ell^*))$ to $\mathcal{L}$
return (c_{i^*}, ℓ^*)

Game 2: sPRE-HRA

2.2.2 Modelling Adaptive Corruption. The adaptive security games corresponding to Games 1 and 2 are given in Games 3 and 4, respectively. To model adaptive corruption, we think of the game being played on a directed graph $G = (\mathcal{V}, \mathcal{E})$ called the "recoding" graph. The vertices of the recoding graph correspond to the public keys, i.e., $\mathcal{V} = [n]$. The edges are derived from the re-keys and re-encryptions issued to the adversary in the security game, and their purpose is to ensure that the adversary does not win the game in a trivial manner. In particular, the recoding graph is defined so that *no* corrupt key is reachable from the challenge key. To be precise, in CPA an edge (i, j) is added to $\mathcal{E}$ if the adversary made either a $(\mathtt{rekey}, i, j)$ or $(\mathtt{reencrypt}, i, j, \cdot)$ query (see Game 3 and Fig. 1). Consequently, the adversary is forbidden from making *any* re-key or re-encryption queries to a corrupt user that is reachable from the challenge key.[2]

[2] The selective CPA notion (Game 1) is in fact more restrictive in that it does not allow re-keys and re-encryptions from *any* honest user to a corrupt user.

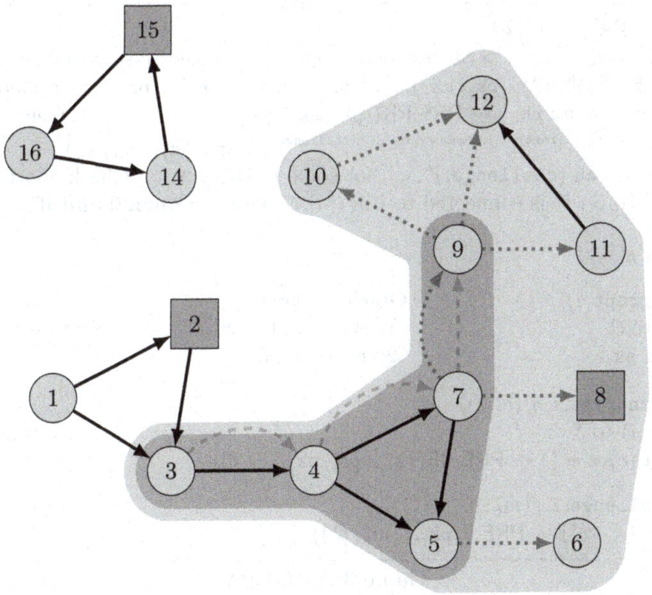

Fig. 1. Recoding graph. The (round) green nodes represent the honest users, whereas the (square) red nodes are the corrupted ones. The edges denote the recoding information. In particular, the (solid) black edges are the re-keys, the (dashed) orange edges are the re-encryptions related to the challenge ciphertext (therefore, 3 is the challenge vertex) and (dotted) blue edges represent the remaining re-encryptions. For CPA, all the edges are counted, but for HRA the blue (dotted) edges are *not* counted. The subgraph of the recoding graph that forms the challenge graph (cf. Sect. 4) is shaded: the darker inner shading for HRA, whereas the lighter outer shading is the challenge graph for CPA. Note that the edge $(7, 8)$ is valid in the case of HRA, but invalid for CPA (and therefore the CPA challenger would abort at the end of such an execution.) (Color figure online)

For HRA, on the other hand, (i, j) is added to $\mathcal{E}$ if the adversary made either a $(\texttt{rekey}, i, j)$ query or a $(\texttt{reencrypt}, i, j, k)$ query where the k-th ciphertext is a re-encryption of the challenge ciphertext (see Game 4 and Fig. 1). This is less restrictive than in CPA: the adversary can make re-encryption queries to a corrupt user that is reachable from the challenge key *unless* it is related to the challenge ciphertext.

For comparison we have reformulated the selective notions defined in Games 1 and 2 using a recoding graph instead of explicit aborts. Games 9 and 10 in the full version define the exact same notions as Games 1 and 2, respectively.

Definition 5 (PRE-CPA-security). *A PRE scheme is* (s, ϵ)*-adaptively secure against chosen-plaintext attack if* $\mathsf{CPA}^0 \approx_{(s,\epsilon)} \mathsf{CPA}^1$, *where* CPA^b *is defined in Game 3.*

Challenger $\mathsf{CPA}^b(1^\kappa, 1^\lambda, n)$

Set $\mathcal{C}, \mathcal{E} = \emptyset$ ▷ Stores corrupt keys and issued re-keys and re-encryptions
$\mathtt{pp} \leftarrow \mathsf{PRE.S}(1^\kappa, 1^\lambda)$, $(\mathtt{pk}_1, \mathtt{sk}_1), \ldots, (\mathtt{pk}_n, \mathtt{sk}_n) \leftarrow \mathsf{PRE.K}(\mathtt{pp})$ ▷ Generate keys
$\forall i, j \in [n], i \neq j : \mathtt{rk}_{i,j} \leftarrow \mathsf{PRE.RK}((\mathtt{pk}_i, \mathtt{sk}_i), \mathtt{pk}_j)$ ▷ Generate re-keys
$b' \leftarrow \mathsf{A}^{(\mathtt{corrupt},\cdot),(\mathtt{rekey},\cdot,\cdot),(\mathtt{reencrypt},\cdot,\cdot,\cdot),(\mathtt{challenge},\cdot,\cdot,\cdot)}(\mathtt{pp}, \mathtt{pk}_1, \ldots, \mathtt{pk}_n)$
if A made call $(\mathtt{challenge}, i^*, \cdot, \cdot)$ for some i^* **then** ▷ Check abort conditions
    if $\exists i \in \mathcal{C} : i^*$ is connected to i in $([n], \mathcal{E})$ **then return** 0 **end if**
end if
return b'

Oracle $(\mathtt{corrupt}, i)$
Add i to $\mathcal{C}$
return $\mathtt{sk}_i$

Oracle $(\mathtt{rekey}, i, j)$
Add (i, j) to $\mathcal{E}$ ▷ Add to recoding graph
return $\mathtt{rk}_{i,j}$

Oracle $(\mathtt{reencrypt}, i, j, (c_i, \ell))$
Add (i, j) to $\mathcal{E}$ ▷ Add to recoding graph
return $(c_j, \ell + 1) \leftarrow \mathsf{PRE.RE}(\mathtt{rk}_{i,j}, \mathtt{pk}_i, \mathtt{pk}_j, (c_i, \ell))$

Oracle $(\mathtt{challenge}, i^*, (m_0^*, m_1^*), \ell^*)$ ▷ Single access
return $(c_{i^*}, \ell^*) \leftarrow \mathsf{PRE.E}(\mathtt{pk}_{i^*}, (m_b^*, \ell^*))$

Game 3: PRE-CPA

Definition 6 (PRE-HRA-security). *A PRE scheme is (s, ϵ)-adaptively secure against honest-reencryption attack if* $\mathsf{HRA}^0 \approx_{(s,\epsilon)} \mathsf{HRA}^1$, *where* HRA^b *is defined in Game 4.*

3 Preliminaries

This section provides the background necessary for the main results in Sect. 4. We start with the security assumptions on PREs that allow us to prove adaptive security (Sect. 3.1) and then give an overview of the framework of [JKK+17] (Sect. 3.2), the description of the pebbling game that is used in the design of the hybrids (Sect. 3.3).

3.1 Security Assumptions on PRE

We describe the three security properties of PRE schemes that allow us to prove adaptive security: indistinguishability, key-privacy and source-hiding.

Indistinguishability of ciphertexts. For proxy re-encryption, we require the notion of indistinguishability, as defined for public-key encryption, to hold on *all* levels:

Definition 7 (Indistinguishability). *A proxy re-encryption scheme* PRE *has (s, ϵ)-indistinguishable ciphertexts if* $\mathsf{IND}^0 \approx_{(s,\epsilon)} \mathsf{IND}^1$ *with* IND *as in Game 5.*

Challenger $\mathsf{HRA}^b(1^\kappa, 1^\lambda, n)$

Set $\mathcal{C}, \mathcal{L}, \mathcal{L}^* = \emptyset$ and $C = 0$ ▷ $\mathcal{L}$ stores honest enc's, $\mathcal{L}^*$ marks challenge reenc's
$\mathcal{E} = \emptyset$ ▷ The edges of the recoding graph
$\mathsf{pp} \leftarrow \mathsf{PRE.S}(1^\kappa, 1^\lambda)$, $(\mathsf{pk}_1, \mathsf{sk}_1), \ldots, (\mathsf{pk}_n, \mathsf{sk}_n) \leftarrow \mathsf{PRE.K}(\mathsf{pp})$ ▷ Generate keys
$\forall i, j \in [n], i \neq j : \mathtt{rk}_{i,j} \leftarrow \mathsf{PRE.RK}((\mathsf{pk}_i, \mathsf{sk}_i), \mathsf{pk}_j)$ ▷ Generate re-keys
$b' \leftarrow \mathsf{A}^{(\mathtt{corrupt},\cdot),(\mathtt{rekey},\cdot,\cdot),(\mathtt{encrypt},\cdot,\cdot),(\mathtt{reencrypt},\cdot,\cdot,\cdot),(\mathtt{challenge},\cdot,\cdot,\cdot)}(\mathsf{pp}, \mathsf{pk}_1, \ldots, \mathsf{pk}_n)$
if A made call $(\mathtt{challenge}, i^*, \cdot, \cdot)$ for some i^* **then** ▷ Check abort conditions
  if $\exists i \in \mathcal{C} : i^*$ is connected to i **then return** 0 **end if**
end if
return b'

Oracle $(\mathtt{corrupt}, i)$
Add i to $\mathcal{C}$
return sk_i

Oracle $(\mathtt{rekey}, i, j)$
Add (i, j) to $\mathcal{E}$ ▷ Add to recoding graph
return $\mathtt{rk}_{i,j}$

Oracle $(\mathtt{encrypt}, i, (m, \ell))$
$c \leftarrow \mathsf{PRE.E}(\mathsf{pk}_i, (m, \ell))$, increment C and add $(C, i, m, (c, \ell))$ to $\mathcal{L}$
return c

Oracle $(\mathtt{reencrypt}, i, j, k)$
Retrieve $(k, i, m, (c_i, \ell))$ from $\mathcal{L}$
$(c_j, \ell + 1) \leftarrow \mathsf{PRE.RE}(\mathtt{rk}_{i,j}, \mathsf{pk}_i, \mathsf{pk}_j, (c_i, \ell))$
Increment C and add $(C, j, m, (c_j, \ell + 1))$ to $\mathcal{L}$
if $k \in \mathcal{L}^*$ **then** ▷ c_j derived from challenge
  Add C to $\mathcal{L}^*$ and add (i, j) to $\mathcal{E}$ ▷ Add to recoding graph
end if
return $(c_j, \ell + 1)$

Oracle $(\mathtt{challenge}, i^*, (m_0^*, m_1^*), \ell^*)$ ▷ Single access
Compute $(c_{i^*}, \ell^*) \leftarrow \mathsf{PRE.E}(\mathsf{pk}_{i^*}, (m_b^*, \ell^*))$
Increment C, add $(C, i^*, m_b^*, (c_{i^*}, \ell^*))$ to $\mathcal{L}$ and C to $\mathcal{L}^*$
return (c_{i^*}, ℓ^*)

Game 4: PRE-HRA

Challenger $\mathsf{IND}^b(1^\kappa, 1^\lambda)$
$\mathsf{pp} \leftarrow \mathsf{PRE.S}(1^\kappa, 1^\lambda)$, $(\mathsf{pk}, \mathsf{sk}) \leftarrow \mathsf{PRE.K}(\mathsf{pp})$
return $b' \leftarrow \mathsf{A}^{(\mathtt{challenge},\cdot,\cdot)}(\mathsf{pp}, \mathsf{pk})$

Oracle $(\mathtt{challenge}, (m_0^*, m_1^*), \ell^*)$
return $\mathsf{PRE.E}(\mathsf{pk}, (m_b^*, \ell^*))$

Game 5: Security game IND for ciphertext indistinguishability

Key-Privacy. The original notion of key-privacy for PREs, which we refer to as "strong" key-privacy, was introduced in [ABH09]. It is modelled by a security game similar to sPRE-CPA: the adversary has access to corrupt, rekey and reencrypt oracles, but as a challenge it has to distinguish a real re-key from a re-key sampled *uniformly at random* from the support of re-keys. We refer the readers to [ABH09] for the details.

We only need a weaker definition stating that re-keys should hide the source keys. That is, the re-key $\mathtt{rk}_{0,1}$ from source $(\mathsf{pk}_0, \mathsf{sk}_0)$ to a target key pk_1 should be indistinguishable from a random source to pk_1. In addition, we need this property to hold with respect to multiple re-keys. More formally, the security game for weak key-privacy is given in Game 6 where the simulator RK^* is defined as

$$\mathsf{RK}^*(\mathtt{pp}, \mathtt{pk}_1) := \mathsf{RK}((\mathtt{pk}_0, \mathtt{sk}_0), \mathtt{pk}_1) : (\mathtt{pk}_0, \mathtt{sk}_0) \leftarrow \mathsf{K}(\mathtt{pp}).$$

Definition 8 (Weak key-privacy). *Let $\delta \in \mathbb{N}$. A proxy re-encryption scheme* PRE *is (s, ϵ, δ)-weakly key-private if* $\mathsf{KP}^0 \approx_{(s,\epsilon)} \mathsf{KP}^1$ *with* KP *as in Game 6.*

Source-hiding. Source-hiding is a special case of re-encryption-simulatability, a notion that was introduced in [Coh17]. It requires that re-encryptions can be simulated without knowledge of the secret key. In particular, the simulated re-encryptions should be indistinguishable from re-encrypted ciphertexts even when given the secret keys for the source and target public keys, as well as the re-key that was used for re-encryption (hence the notion of indistinguishability is at least that of statistical indistinguishability). A PRE scheme is called *source-hiding* if re-encrypted ciphertexts have the same distribution as "fresh" ciphertexts, i.e., the encryption algorithm can be used as a simulator for re-encryption.

Definition 9 (Source-hiding). *A proxy re-encryption scheme* PRE *is (s, ϵ)-source-hiding if* $\mathsf{SH}^0 \approx_{(s,\epsilon)} \mathsf{SH}^1$*, with* SH *as defined in Game 7.*

3.2 Overview of [JKK+17]

Random guessing. A standard way to prove adaptive security is to first show security in a "selective" version of the adaptive game, in which the adversary commits to some of its future choices, and then use random guessing of the adversary's commitment to reduce adaptive security to selective security. For instance, consider the indistinguishability game for identity-based encryption: in the selective counterpart the adversary commits to the challenge identity at the start of the game, and the adaptive to selective reduction then works by guessing the challenge identity. More formally, let G^0 and G^1 denote the two adaptive games. For some function $g\colon \{0,1\}^* \to \mathcal{W}$ we define below the selective games $\mathsf{H}^0 = \mathsf{SEL}_{\mathcal{W}}[\mathsf{G}^0, g]$ and $\mathsf{H}^1 = \mathsf{SEL}_{\mathcal{W}}[\mathsf{G}^1, g]$ where the adversary commits to some information $w \in \mathcal{W}$ – for the case of IBE, $\mathcal{W}$ is the set of all identities. Note that the selective game gets a commitment w from the adversary but essentially ignores it during the rest of the game. It checks that the commitment matches what actually happened during the game only at the very end of the game; whether w matches is defined via the function g.

Definition 10 (Fully selectivised game [JKK+17]**).** *Given an (adaptive) game* G *and some function $g\colon \{0,1\}^* \to \mathcal{W}$, the selectivised game* $\mathsf{H} = \mathsf{SEL}_{\mathcal{W}}[\mathsf{G}, g]$ *is defined as follows. The adversary* A *first sends a commitment $w \in \mathcal{W}$ to* H*. Then* H *runs the challenger* G *against* A*, at the end of which* G *outputs a bit $\hat{b}$. Let* `transcript` *denote all communication exchanged between* G *and* A*. If $g(\mathtt{transcript}) = w$ then* H *outputs the bit $\hat{b}$ and else it outputs* 0.

Challenger $\mathsf{KP}^b(1^\kappa, 1^\lambda)$
$\mathsf{pp} \leftarrow \mathsf{PRE.S}(1^\kappa, 1^\lambda)$, $(\mathbf{pk}_0, \mathbf{sk}_0), \ldots, (\mathbf{pk}_\delta, \mathbf{sk}_\delta) \leftarrow \mathsf{K}(\mathsf{pp})$
$\forall j \in [\delta] : \mathbf{rk}_{0,j}^{(0)} \leftarrow \mathsf{RK}((\mathbf{pk}_0, \mathbf{sk}_0), \mathbf{pk}_j)$
$\quad \mathbf{rk}_{0,j}^{(1)} \leftarrow \mathsf{RK}^*(\mathsf{pp}, \mathbf{pk}_j)$
return $b' \leftarrow \mathsf{A}(\mathsf{pp}, \mathbf{pk}_0, \ldots, \mathbf{pk}_\delta, \mathbf{rk}_{0,1}^{(b)}, \ldots, \mathbf{rk}_{0,\delta}^{(b)})$

Game 6: Security game KP for weak key-privacy

Challenger $\mathsf{SH}^b(1^\kappa, 1^\lambda)$
$\mathsf{pp} \leftarrow \mathsf{PRE.S}(1^\kappa, 1^\lambda)$
$(\mathbf{pk}_0, \mathbf{sk}_0), (\mathbf{pk}_1, \mathbf{sk}_1) \leftarrow \mathsf{PRE.K}(\mathsf{pp})$
$\mathbf{rk}_{0,1} \leftarrow \mathsf{PRE.RK}((\mathbf{pk}_0, \mathbf{sk}_0), \mathbf{pk}_1)$
$b' \leftarrow \mathsf{A}^{(\mathtt{challenge},\cdot,\cdot)}(\mathsf{pp}, (\mathbf{pk}_0, \mathbf{sk}_0), (\mathbf{pk}_1, \mathbf{sk}_1), \mathbf{rk}_{0,1})$
return b'

Oracle $(\mathtt{challenge}, m^*, \ell^*)$ $\quad \triangleright\ \ell^* \in [\lambda - 1]$
$c_0 \leftarrow \mathsf{PRE.E}(\mathbf{pk}_0, (m^*, \ell^*))$
$c_1^{(0)} \leftarrow \mathsf{PRE.RE}(\mathbf{rk}_{0,1}, \mathbf{pk}_0, \mathbf{pk}_1, c_0)$ $\quad \triangleright$ Real re-encryption
$c_1^{(1)} \leftarrow \mathsf{PRE.E}(\mathbf{pk}_1, (m^*, \ell^* + 1))$ $\quad \triangleright$ Simulate re-encryption
return $(c_0, c_1^{(b)})$

Game 7: Security game SH for source hiding

Next, suppose that the selective security is proved using a hybrid argument. That is, to show the indistinguishability of H^0 and H^1 suppose we have a sequence of $\tau + 1$ (selective) hybrid games $\mathsf{H}^0 = \mathsf{H}_0, \mathsf{H}_1, \ldots, \mathsf{H}_\tau = \mathsf{H}^1$ (see Fig. 2). If we only assume that neighbouring hybrids $\mathsf{H}_i, \mathsf{H}_{i+1}$ are indistinguishable, then by combining the hybrid argument and random guessing we get that G^0 and G^1 are indistinguishable with a loss in distinguishing advantage of $\tau \cdot |\mathcal{W}|$. The factor of $|\mathcal{W}|$ is the cost of the random guessing, whereas the factor of τ is due to the hybrid argument. This is stated in the following (recall that $s_\mathcal{W}$ denotes the complexity of sampling from $\mathcal{W}$):

Theorem 3 **([BB04, JKK+17]).** *Assume we have two games defined via (adaptive) challengers* G^0 *and* G^1 *respectively. Let* $g\colon \{0,1\}^* \to \mathcal{W}$ *be an arbitrary function and define the selectivised games* $\mathsf{H}^b = \mathsf{SEL}_\mathcal{W}[\mathsf{G}^b, g]$ *for* $b \in \{0,1\}$*. Also assume that for each* $i \in [\tau]$*, the games* $\mathsf{H}_{i-1}, \mathsf{H}_i$ *are* (s, ϵ)*-indistinguishable. Then,* G^0 *and* G^1 *are* $(s - s_\mathcal{W},\ \epsilon \cdot \tau \cdot |\mathcal{W}|)$*-indistinguishable.*

The framework. In some cases only *part* of the information that the adversary commits to is used in simulating the intermediate hybrids, but when considering all the hybrids the whole commitment is being used. For example, the simulation of an intermediate hybrid in the case of IBE could rely on only certain bits of the challenge identity. It is shown in [JKK+17] that the security loss in such cases can be limited to the maximum size of the information used across any two successive hybrids.

More formally, [JKK+17] makes a stronger assumption: not only are neighbouring hybrids $\mathsf{H}_i, \mathsf{H}_{i+1}$ indistinguishable, but they are "selectivised" versions,

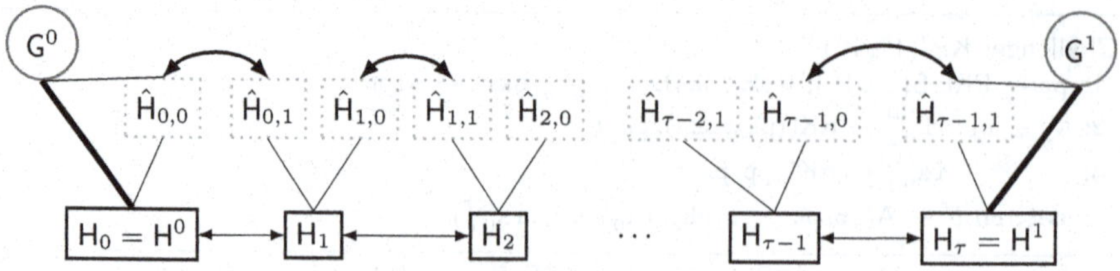

Fig. 2. A schematic diagram showing the relationship between adaptive, fully selective and partially selective hybrids. The adaptive games G^0 and G^1 are in green (circles); the fully selective games $\mathsf{H}_0, \ldots, \mathsf{H}_\tau$ are in solid black (boxes); and the partially selective games $\hat{\mathsf{H}}_{0,0}, \hat{\mathsf{H}}_{0,1}, \ldots, \hat{\mathsf{H}}_{\tau-1,0}, \hat{\mathsf{H}}_{\tau-1,1}$ are in (dotted) blue boxes. The arrows indicate indistinguishability. (Color figure online)

of "partially" selective games $\hat{\mathsf{H}}_{i,0}, \hat{\mathsf{H}}_{i,1}$ which are already indistinguishable. In particular, for each pair of neighbouring hybrids $\mathsf{H}_i, \mathsf{H}_{i+1}$ there exists a pair of partially selective hybrids $\hat{\mathsf{H}}_{i,0}, \hat{\mathsf{H}}_{i,1}$ (see Fig. 2) in which the adversary commits to much less information $h_i(w) \in \mathcal{U}$ instead of $w \in \mathcal{W}$. The selectivised game essentially ignores w and only relies on the partial information $u = h_i(w)$ during the course of the game but at the very end it still checks that the full commitment w matches what actually happened during the game.

Definition 11 (Partially selectivised game [JKK+17]**).** *Assume $\hat{\mathsf{H}}$ is a game which expects to receive some commitment $u \in \mathcal{U}$ from the adversary in the beginning. Given functions $g\colon \{0,1\}^* \to \mathcal{W}$ and $h\colon \mathcal{W} \to \mathcal{U}$ the partially selectivised game $\mathsf{H} = \mathsf{SEL}_{\mathcal{U}\to\mathcal{W}}[\hat{\mathsf{H}}, g, h]$ is defined as follows. The adversary A first sends a commitment $w \in \mathcal{W}$ to H and H begins running $\hat{\mathsf{H}}$ and passes it $u = h(w)$. It then continues running the game between $\hat{\mathsf{H}}$ and A at the end of which $\hat{\mathsf{H}}$ outputs a bit $\hat{b}$. Let* `transcript` *denote all communication exchanged between $\hat{\mathsf{H}}$ and A. If $g(\texttt{transcript}) = w$ then H outputs the bit $\hat{b}$ and else it outputs* 0.

Note that different pairs of partially selective hybrids $\hat{\mathsf{H}}_{i,0}, \hat{\mathsf{H}}_{i,1}$ might rely on completely different partial information $h_i(w)$ about the adversary's choices. The partially selective hybrid associated to each H_i can thus be different when we compare $\mathsf{H}_{i-1}, \mathsf{H}_i$ (in which case it is $\hat{\mathsf{H}}_{i-1,1}$) and when we compare H_i and H_{i+1} (in which case it is $\hat{\mathsf{H}}_{i,0}$) – see Fig. 2. The next theorem shows that we only incur a security loss proportional to $|\mathcal{U}|$ rather than $|\mathcal{W}|$ if we can define a sequence of partially selective hybrids which only require commitments from $\mathcal{U}$.

Theorem 4 ([JKK+17])**.** *Let G^0 and G^1 be two adaptive games. For some function $g\colon \{0,1\}^* \to \mathcal{W}$ we define the selectivised games $\mathsf{H}^0 = \mathsf{SEL}_{\mathcal{W}}[\mathsf{G}^0, g]$, $\mathsf{H}^1 = \mathsf{SEL}_{\mathcal{W}}[\mathsf{G}^1, g]$. Let $\mathsf{H}^0 = \mathsf{H}_0, \mathsf{H}_1, \ldots, \mathsf{H}_\tau = \mathsf{H}^1$ be some sequence of hybrid games. Assume that for each $i \in [0, \tau-1]$, there exists a function $h_i\colon \mathcal{W} \to \mathcal{U}$ and games $\hat{\mathsf{H}}_{i,0}, \hat{\mathsf{H}}_{i,1}$ such that*

$$\mathsf{H}_i \equiv \mathsf{SEL}_{\mathcal{U}\to\mathcal{W}}[\hat{\mathsf{H}}_{i,0}, g, h_i] \quad \textit{and} \quad \mathsf{H}_{i+1} \equiv \mathsf{SEL}_{\mathcal{U}\to\mathcal{W}}[\hat{\mathsf{H}}_{i,1}, g, h_i]. \qquad (1)$$

Furthermore, if $\hat{\mathsf{H}}_{i,0}, \hat{\mathsf{H}}_{i,1}$ *are* (s, ϵ)*-indistinguishable for all* $i \in [0, \tau - 1]$*, then* G^0 *and* G^1 *are* $(s - s_{\mathcal{U}}, \epsilon \cdot \tau \cdot |\mathcal{U}|)$*-indistinguishable.*

3.3 Pebbling Games

The reversible pebbling game on DAGs was introduced in [Ben89] to model reversible computation. We define a variant in which the pebbling rules have been adapted for application to PREs. In particular, the rule is the opposite of that in [Ben89]: a pebble can be placed on or removed from a vertex if all its *children* carry a pebble.[3]

Definition 12. *A reversible pebbling of a directed acyclic graph* $G = (\mathcal{V}, \mathcal{E})$ *with a unique source vertex* i^* *is a sequence* $\mathcal{P} := (\mathcal{P}_0, \ldots, \mathcal{P}_\tau)$ *of pebbling configurations* $\mathcal{P}_t \subseteq \mathcal{V}$*. Two subsequent configurations differ only in one vertex and the following rule is respected in a move: a pebble can be placed on or removed from a vertex iff all its children carry a pebble. That is,* $\mathcal{P}$ *is a valid sequence iff*

$$\forall t \in [\tau]\ \exists!\, i \in \mathcal{P}_{t-1} \triangle \mathcal{P}_t \ \text{ and } \ \mathsf{children}(i, G) \subseteq \mathcal{P}_{t-1}.$$

Starting with an empty graph (i.e., $\mathcal{P}_0 = \emptyset$*), the goal of the game is to place a pebble on the source (i.e.,* $i^* \in \mathcal{P}_\tau$*).*

For a DAG G, let $\mathcal{P}_G$ denote the set of all valid reversible pebbling sequences (as per Definition 12) for G. The *time complexity* of a *particular* sequence $\mathcal{P} = (\mathcal{P}_0, \ldots, \mathcal{P}_\tau)$ for a DAG G is defined as $\tau_G(\mathcal{P}) := \tau$, whereas its space complexity is defined as

$$\sigma_G(\mathcal{P}) := \max_{t \in [0,\tau]} |\mathcal{P}_t|.$$

Definition 13 (Space- and time-complexity of a class of DAGs). *We say that a class of DAGs* $\mathcal{G}$ *has time complexity* τ *and space complexity* σ *if*

$$\forall G \in \mathcal{G}\ \exists \mathcal{P} \in \mathcal{P}_G : \tau_G(\mathcal{P}) \leq \tau \wedge \sigma_G(\mathcal{P}) \leq \sigma.$$

Concrete Bounds. The pebbling complexity for the pertinent classes of *single-source* graphs on n vertices are listed in Table 2. These bounds are proved in Lemmata 2 through 4 in the full version.

[3] Alternatively, one can think of the pebbling game in Definition 12 as the classical reversible pebbling game played on a DAG whose edges have their direction flipped.

Table 2. Space and time complexity for different classes of DAGs. These bounds are proved in Lemmata 2 through 4 in the full version.

Family	Bounds	
	Space (σ)	Time (τ)
DAGs with outdegree δ and depth d $\mathcal{G}(n,\delta,d)$	$(\delta+1)\cdot d$	$(2\delta)^d$
Complete binary trees of size n $\mathcal{B}(n)$	$\log n$	n^2
Chains of length $\mathcal{C}(n)$	$\log n + 1$	$3^{\log n}$

4 Framework for Adaptive Security

In this section we demonstrate, using the framework of [JKK+17], how adaptive security can be achieved for PREs. We focus on CPA, and the analogous result for HRA is given in the full version [FKKP18]. As for the applications given in [JKK+17], we use pebbling games on DAGs to design the hybrid games. Each pebbling configuration uniquely determines a hybrid game bridging the two real games CPA^0 and CPA^1. The DAG that we pebble in the proof is the subgraph of the recoding graph that is reachable from the challenge i^* (via the edges $\mathcal{E}$ defined during the game); it is thus a subgraph of the recoding graph with one unique source i^*, which we call the *challenge graph.* A pebble on a vertex allows the simulation of the hybrid to be carried out *without* the knowledge of the secret key associated with that vertex. The pebbling rules will ensure that hybrids corresponding to two successive pebbling configurations can be proven indistinguishable assuming key-privacy.

4.1 Adaptive Security Against Chosen-Plaintext Attack

We first show how a pebbling sequence on the challenge graph defines a sequence of fully selective hybrids (Lemma 2), and then prove that these hybrids are partially selectivised (Lemma 3).

4.1.1 Fully Selective Hybrids. In the fully selectivised version of PRE-CPA (Game 3), A first makes a commitment $\hat{G}$ to the challenge graph. Any correct commitment $\hat{G}$ must therefore have one unique source, which we denote by $\hat{\imath}$. The selective challenger is thus $\mathsf{SEL}_{\mathcal{G}}[\mathsf{CPA}^b, g]$, where g is the function that extracts the recoding graph G and the challenge user i^* from the transcript and returns the challenge graph, i.e., the subgraph of G reachable from i^*. Note that this is fundamentally different from the original selective game (i.e., sCPA in Game 1) where the adversary commits, beforehand, to *the set of corrupt public keys.*

Each hybrid is associated with a pebbling configuration $\mathcal{P}_t$ and a bit b, and we consider the sequence of hybrids $\mathsf{H}_0^0, \ldots, \mathsf{H}_\tau^0, \mathsf{H}_\tau^1, \ldots, \mathsf{H}_0^1$. The pebbling state of a vertex dictates how the outgoing re-key and re-encrypt queries are simulated, whereas the bit determines how the challenge query is answered. To be precise, in game H_t^b, for each pebbled vertex in $\mathcal{P}_t$ all used re-keys outgoing from that vertex are faked, and the challenge query is answered by an encryption of m_b^*. (Rekeys outgoing from pebbled vertices that are not used for any queries are defined as real re-keys). Observe that the secret key corresponding to a vertex is used only for the generation of the re-keys outgoing from that vertex; the simulation of a hybrid can thus be carried out *without* knowledge of the secret keys corresponding to the pebbled vertices (as the non-queried re-keys need not be generated).

Since the initial pebbling configuration is the empty set, H_0^0 and H_0^1 correspond to the (fully selectivised) games $\mathsf{SEL}_{\mathcal{G}}[\mathsf{CPA}^0, g]$ and $\mathsf{SEL}_{\mathcal{G}}[\mathsf{CPA}^1, g]$, respectively. Now, consider the middle hybrids H_τ^0 and H_τ^1: they are the same except for the response to the challenge query which is the encryption of m_0^* in the former and the encryption of m_1^* in the latter. Since the pebbling configuration $\mathcal{P}_\tau$, by definition, contains a pebble on the challenge vertex i^*, the simulation of this hybrid can be carried out without knowledge of the secret key corresponding to i^*. This means we can reduce indistinguishability of the PRE to the indistinguishability of these two hybrids. To be precise, the reduction embeds the challenge public key at $\hat{\imath}$, which is defined by the commitment $\hat{G}$ and replies to the challenge query (in the CPA game) by sending the challenge ciphertext (of the indistinguishability game). Note that if $i^* \neq \hat{\imath}$, that is, the commitment $\hat{G}$ doesn't coincide with the transcript of the CPA game, then the hybrid returns 0 anyway. The reduction is formally defined in Algorithm 2.

Next, consider any two hybrids H_t^b and H_{t+1}^b, $t \in [0, \tau - 1]$ and $b \in \{0, 1\}$. Also, assume $\mathcal{P}_{t+1}$ results from $\mathcal{P}_t$ by placing a pebble on the vertex i_0 (the case when a pebble is removed can be argued analogously). The simulation of H_t^b and H_{t+1}^b is the same except for the (used) re-keys outgoing from i_0: in H_t^b they are all real whereas in H_{t+1}^b they are all fake. By the rules of the pebbling game, the children of i_0 all carry pebbles in the configurations $\mathcal{P}_t$ and $\mathcal{P}_{t+1}$; therefore the simulation need not know the corresponding secret keys. This means that we can prove indistinguishability of H_t^b and H_{t+1}^b from weak key-privacy: the reduction embeds the (key-privacy) challenge public keys $\mathtt{pk}_0, \ldots, \mathtt{pk}_\delta$ at i_0 and its children, and uses the challenge re-keys $\mathtt{rk}_{0,1}, \ldots, \mathtt{rk}_{0,\delta}$ to simulate the re-key oracle for queries from i_0 to its children. The reduction is formally defined in Algorithm 3. (Note that the simulation of the reduction in Algorithm 3 is perfect: if the commitment $\hat{G}$ does not match with the transcript, it returns 0; else, we have $\hat{\imath} = i^*$ and by definition of the pebbling, i_0 is reachable from $\hat{\imath} = i^*$ and so are its children $i_1, \ldots, i_\delta$. If the adversary corrupts any of these, then the game returns 0.)

In summary, we get a sequence of hybrids $\mathsf{SEL}_{\mathcal{G}}[\mathsf{CPA}^0, g] = \mathsf{H}_0^0, \ldots, \mathsf{H}_\tau^0, \mathsf{H}_\tau^1, \ldots, \mathsf{H}_0^1 = \mathsf{SEL}_{\mathcal{G}}[\mathsf{CPA}^1, g]$, where each pair of subsequent hybrids can be proved indistinguishable. Security in the fully selectivised CPA game follows by Lemma 1. We state this formally in Lemma 2 below.

Hybrid $\mathsf{H}_t^b(1^\kappa, 1^\lambda, n)$

Obtain the challenge graph $\hat{G} \in \mathcal{G}(n, \delta, d)$ from A

Compute $\mathcal{P}_t \leftarrow \mathsf{P}(\hat{G}, t)$ ▷ The t-th pebbling configuration

Set $\mathcal{C}, \mathcal{E} = \emptyset$ ▷ Stores corrupt keys and issued re-keys and re-encryptions

$\mathtt{pp} \leftarrow \mathsf{PRE.S}(1^\kappa, 1^\lambda)$, $(\mathtt{pk}_1, \mathtt{sk}_1), \ldots, (\mathtt{pk}_n, \mathtt{sk}_n) \leftarrow \mathsf{PRE.K}(\mathtt{pp})$

$\forall i \in \mathcal{P}_t, \forall j \in \mathsf{children}(i, \hat{G})$: $\mathtt{rk}_{i,j} \leftarrow \mathsf{RK}^*(\mathtt{pp}, \mathtt{pk}_j)$ ▷ Fake re-keys

$\forall i \in \mathcal{P}_t, \forall j \in [n] \setminus \{\mathsf{children}(i, \hat{G}) \cup i\}$: $\mathtt{rk}_{i,j} \leftarrow \mathsf{PRE.RK}((\mathtt{pk}_i, \mathtt{sk}_i), \mathtt{pk}_j)$ ▷ Real re-keys

$\forall i \in [n] \setminus \mathcal{P}_t, \forall j \neq i$: $\mathtt{rk}_{i,j} \leftarrow \mathsf{PRE.RK}((\mathtt{pk}_i, \mathtt{sk}_i), \mathtt{pk}_j)$ ▷ Real re-keys

$b' \leftarrow \mathsf{A}^{(\mathtt{corrupt},\cdot),(\mathtt{rekey},\cdot,\cdot),(\mathtt{reencrypt},\cdot,\cdot,\cdot),(\mathtt{challenge},\cdot,\cdot,\cdot)}(\mathtt{pp}, \mathtt{pk}_1, \ldots, \mathtt{pk}_n)$

if A made call $(\mathtt{challenge}, i^*, \cdot, \cdot)$ for some i^* **then** ▷ Check abort conditions

  if $\exists i \in \mathcal{C} : i^*$ is connected to i in $([n], \mathcal{E})$ **then return** 0 **end if**

end if

if $\hat{G}$ is the subgraph of $([n], \mathcal{E})$ reachable from i^* **then return** b' **end if**

return 0

Algorithm 1: Template for generating fully selective PRE-CPA hybrids given a pebbling configuration. All the oracles are defined like in Game 3.

Lemma 2 (Security against fully selectivised PRE-CPA). *Consider the sequence of hybrids* $\mathsf{H}_0^0, \ldots, \mathsf{H}_\tau^0, \mathsf{H}_\tau^1, \ldots, \mathsf{H}_0^1$, *where* H_t^b *is defined in Algorithm 1 using the pebbling configuration* $\mathcal{P}_t$. H_0^b *is the fully selectivised game of* CPA^b*: i.e.,* $\mathsf{H}_0^b = \mathsf{SEL}_{\mathcal{G}}[\mathsf{CPA}^b, g]$ *where* g *extracts the challenge graph (subgraph reachable from the challenge vertex) from a transcript. Moreover, if the adversary makes at most* Q_{RE} *re-encryption queries, then a PRE scheme that is* (s_1, ϵ_1)*-indistinguishable and* $(s_2, \epsilon_2, \delta)$*-weakly key-private is* (s, ϵ)*-secure against fully selectivised PRE-CPA restricted to challenge graphs in* $\mathcal{G}(n, \delta, d)$ *with*

$$s := \min(s_1, s_2) - s_{\mathsf{CPA}} \quad \text{and} \quad \epsilon := \epsilon_1 + 2\tau \cdot \epsilon_2,$$

where $s_{\mathsf{CPA}} \approx O(s_{\mathsf{P}} + n^2 \cdot s_{\mathsf{RK}} + Q_{\mathsf{RE}} \cdot s_{\mathsf{RE}})$ *denotes the complexity of simulating the CPA game.*

PRE-CPA-security follows from random guessing (Theorem 3) but with a security loss of 2^{n^2}, where n^2 is an upper bound on the number of bits required to encode the challenge subgraph:

Corollary 1 (PRE-CPA-security by random guessing). *A PRE scheme that is* (s_1, ϵ_1)*-indistinguishable and* $(s_2, \epsilon_2, \delta)$*-weakly key-private is* (s, ϵ)*-secure against PRE-CPA restricted to challenge graphs in* $\mathcal{G}(n, \delta, d)$*, where*

$$s := \min(s_1, s_2) - s_{\mathsf{CPA}} - s_{\mathcal{G}} \quad \text{and} \quad \epsilon := (\epsilon_1 + 2\tau \cdot \epsilon_2) \cdot 2^{n^2}.$$

4.1.2 Partially Selective Hybrids. In hybrid H_t^b described in Algorithm 1, we observe that not all information on the committed recoding graph $\hat{G}$ is actually required for the simulation. In fact, only the pebbling configuration $\mathcal{P}_t$ is required to simulate the hybrid: re-keys are only required once a corresponding re-key or a re-encrypt query is issued; for a pebbled node, such queries lead to an edge added in $\mathcal{E}$; thus the re-key is simulated (while the "not-queried" re-keys are never used during the experiment).

Reduction $\mathsf{R}_\tau^{(\mathtt{IND.challenge},\cdot,\cdot)}(\mathtt{pp}^*, \mathtt{pk}^*)$ ▷ $\mathtt{pk}^*$ denotes the challenge public key

Obtain the challenge graph $\hat{G} \in \mathcal{G}(n, \delta, d)$ from A

Compute $\mathcal{P}_\tau \leftarrow \mathsf{P}(\hat{G}, \tau)$ ▷ The τ-th pebbling configuration

Set $\mathcal{C}, \mathcal{E} = \emptyset$ ▷ Stores corrupt keys and issued re-keys and re-encryptions

$(\mathtt{pk}_1, \mathtt{sk}_1), \ldots, (\mathtt{pk}_{\hat{\imath}-1}, \mathtt{sk}_{\hat{\imath}-1}), (\mathtt{pk}_{\hat{\imath}+1}, \mathtt{sk}_{\hat{\imath}+1}), \ldots, (\mathtt{pk}_n, \mathtt{sk}_n) \leftarrow \mathsf{PRE.K}(\mathtt{pp}^*)$

Let $\hat{\imath}$ be the source of $\hat{G}$, set $\mathtt{pk}_{\hat{\imath}} := \mathtt{pk}^*$ ▷ Embed challenge public key

$\forall i \in \mathcal{P}_\tau, \forall j \in \mathsf{children}(i, \hat{G})$: $\mathtt{rk}_{i,j} \leftarrow \mathsf{RK}^*(\mathtt{pp}, \mathtt{pk}_j)$ ▷ Fake re-keys

$\forall i \in [n] \setminus \mathcal{P}_\tau, \forall j \in \mathsf{children}(i, \hat{G})$: $\mathtt{rk}_{i,j} \leftarrow \mathsf{PRE.RK}((\mathtt{pk}_i, \mathtt{sk}_i), \mathtt{pk}_j)$ ▷ Real re-keys

$\forall i \in \mathcal{P}_\tau, \forall j \in [n] \setminus \{\mathsf{children}(i, \hat{G}) \cup i\}$: $\mathtt{rk}_{i,j} \leftarrow \mathsf{PRE.RK}((\mathtt{pk}_i, \mathtt{sk}_i), \mathtt{pk}_j)$ ▷ Real re-keys

$\forall i \in [n] \setminus \mathcal{P}_\tau, \forall j \neq i$: $\mathtt{rk}_{i,j} \leftarrow \mathsf{PRE.RK}((\mathtt{pk}_i, \mathtt{sk}_i), \mathtt{pk}_j)$ ▷ Real re-keys

$b' \leftarrow \mathsf{A}^{(\mathtt{corrupt},\cdot),(\mathtt{rekey},\cdot,\cdot),(\mathtt{reencrypt},\cdot,\cdot,\cdot),(\mathtt{challenge},\cdot,\cdot,\cdot)}(\mathtt{pp}^*, \mathtt{pk}_1, \ldots, \mathtt{pk}_n)$

if A made call $(\mathtt{challenge}, i^*, \cdot, \cdot)$ for some i^* **then** ▷ Check abort conditions

  if $\exists i \in \mathcal{C} : i^*$ is connected to i in $([n], \mathcal{E})$ **then return** 0 **end if**

end if

if $\hat{G}$ is the subgraph of $([n], \mathcal{E})$ reachable from i^* **then return** b' **end if**

return 0

Oracles $\mathtt{rekey}$ and $\mathtt{reencrypt}$ are defined like in Game 3.

Oracle $(\mathtt{corrupt}, i)$

if $i = \hat{\imath}$ **then** HALT: R_τ returns 0 **end if** ▷ Commitment $\hat{G}$ doesn't match or...

Add i to $\mathcal{C}$ and **return** $\mathtt{sk}_i$ ▷ ... i^* corrupted

Oracle $(\mathtt{challenge}, i^*, (m_0^*, m_1^*), \ell^*)$ ▷ Single access

$(c_{i^*}, \ell^*) \leftarrow \mathsf{IND.challenge}((m_0^*, m_1^*), \ell^*)$ ▷ Embed challenge ciphertext

return (c_{i^*}, ℓ^*)

Algorithm 2: The reduction showing that the hybrids H_τ^0 and H_τ^1 are indistinguishable by indistinguishability of ciphertexts.

In addition to the pebbling configuration $\mathcal{P}_\tau$, the reduction from ciphertext indistinguishability (cf. Algorithm 2) also needs to know the challenge vertex $\hat{\imath}$ in order to embed the challenge public key. The reduction from weak key-privacy (cf. Algorithm 3) requires, in addition to $\mathcal{P}_t$, the vertex that is pebbled or unpebbled in $\mathcal{P}_{t+1}$ (i.e., the vertex i_0) and its children, so it can embed its challenge public keys and re-keys.

To sum up, two consecutive hybrids H_t^b and H_{t+1}^b can be shown to be indistinguishable using a lot less information than what the adversary commits to. We thus have the following:

Lemma 3 (Partially selectivised hybrids). *Let $\mathcal{P}_0, \ldots, \mathcal{P}_\tau$ and $\mathsf{H}_0^0, \ldots, \mathsf{H}_\tau^0$, $\mathsf{H}_\tau^1, \ldots, \mathsf{H}_0^1$ be defined as in Lemma 2, and let σ denote the space complexity of the pebbling sequence. Then, for $t \in [0, \tau - 1]$ and $b, \beta \in \{0, 1\}$,*

$$\mathsf{H}_{t+\beta}^b \equiv \mathsf{SEL}_{\mathcal{U} \to \mathcal{G}}[\hat{\mathsf{H}}_{t,\beta}^b, g, h_t] \;\; \textit{and} \;\; \mathsf{H}_\tau^b \equiv \mathsf{SEL}_{\mathcal{U} \to \mathcal{G}}[\hat{\mathsf{H}}_{\tau,0}^b, g, h_\tau],$$

Reduction $\mathsf{R}_t^b(\mathtt{pp}^*, \mathtt{pk}_0^*, \ldots, \mathtt{pk}_\delta^*, \mathtt{rk}_{0,1}^*, \ldots, \mathtt{rk}_{0,\delta}^*)$

Obtain the challenge graph $\hat{G} \in \mathcal{G}(n, \delta, d)$ from A
Compute $\mathcal{P}_t \leftarrow \mathsf{P}(\hat{G}, t)$, $\mathcal{P}_{t+1} \leftarrow \mathsf{P}(\hat{G}, t+1)$ ▷ The t-th and $(t+1)$-th configurations
Set $\mathcal{C}, \mathcal{E} = \emptyset$ ▷ Stores corrupt keys and issued re-keys and re-encryptions
$i_0 := \mathcal{P}_t \Delta \mathcal{P}_{t+1}$, $i_1, \ldots, i_\delta := \mathsf{children}(i_0, \hat{G})$ ▷ i_0 denotes pebbled/unpebbled vertex
$\forall k \in [0, \delta]$: $\mathtt{pk}_{i_k} := \mathtt{pk}_k^*$ ▷ Embed the challenge public keys
$\forall k \in [n] \setminus \{i_0, \ldots, i_\delta\}$: $(\mathtt{pk}_k, \mathtt{sk}_k) \leftarrow \mathsf{PRE.K}(\mathtt{pp}^*)$ ▷ Real keys
$\forall k \in [\delta] : \mathtt{rk}_{i_0, i_k} := \mathtt{rk}_{0,k}^*$ ▷ Embed challenge re-keys
$\forall i \in \mathcal{P}_t \setminus \{i_0\}, \forall j \in \mathsf{children}(i, \hat{G})$: $\mathtt{rk}_{i,j} \leftarrow \mathsf{RK}^*(\mathtt{pp}^*, \mathtt{pk}_j)$ ▷ Fake re-keys
$\forall i \in \mathcal{P}_t, \forall j \in [n] \setminus \{\mathsf{children}(i, \hat{G}) \cup i\}$: $\mathtt{rk}_{i,j} \leftarrow \mathsf{PRE.RK}((\mathtt{pk}_i, \mathtt{sk}_i), \mathtt{pk}_j)$ ▷ Real re-keys
$\forall i \in [n] \setminus (\mathcal{P}_t \cup \{i_0\}), \forall j \neq i$: $\mathtt{rk}_{i,j} \leftarrow \mathsf{PRE.RK}((\mathtt{pk}_i, \mathtt{sk}_i), \mathtt{pk}_j)$ ▷ Real re-keys
$b' \leftarrow \mathsf{A}^{(\mathtt{corrupt},\cdot),(\mathtt{rekey},\cdot,\cdot),(\mathtt{reencrypt},\cdot,\cdot,\cdot),(\mathtt{challenge},\cdot,\cdot,\cdot)}(\mathtt{pp}^*, \mathtt{pk}_1, \ldots, \mathtt{pk}_n)$
if A made call $(\mathtt{challenge}, i^*, \cdot, \cdot)$ for some i^* **then** ▷ Check abort conditions
    if $\exists i \in \mathcal{C} : i^*$ is connected to i in $([n], \mathcal{E})$ **then return** 0 **end if**
end if
if $\hat{G}$ is the subgraph of $([n], \mathcal{E})$ reachable from i^* **then return** b' **end if**
return 0

Oracles $\mathtt{rekey}$, $\mathtt{reencrypt}$ and $\mathtt{challenge}$ are defined like in Game 3.

Oracle $(\mathtt{corrupt}, i)$
if $i \in \{i_0, \ldots, i_\delta\}$ **then** HALT: R_τ returns 0 **end if** ▷ Commitment $\hat{G}$ doesn't match
Add i to $\mathcal{C}$ and **return** $\mathtt{sk}_i$ ▷ ...or i reachable from i^*

Algorithm 3: The reduction showing that the hybrids H_t^b and H_{t+1}^b, for $t \in [0, \tau - 1]$ and $b \in \{0, 1\}$, are indistinguishable by weak key-privacy.

where $\hat{\mathsf{H}}_{t,\beta}^b$ *is defined in Algorithm 4 (see also Fig. 3), g extracts the challenge graph from the transcript (as in Lemma 2). For* $t \in [0, \tau - 1]$, h_t *is the function that extracts the pebbling configuration* $\mathcal{P}_t$*, the pebbled/unpebbled vertex in* $\mathcal{P}_{t+1}$ *and its children;* h_τ *extracts the pebbling configuration* $\mathcal{P}_\tau$ *and the challenge node* i^**. Thus,* $\mathcal{U}$ *corresponds to the set* $\mathcal{V}^{\sigma+\delta+1}$.

The tighter bound for PRE-CPA-security now results by applying Theorem 4:

Theorem 5 (main, PRE-CPA security). *Let* σ *and* τ *denote, respectively, the pebbling space and time complexity for the class* $\mathcal{G}(n, \delta, d)$*. Then a PRE scheme that is* (s_1, ϵ_1)*-indistinguishable and* $(s_2, \epsilon_2, \delta)$*-weakly key-private is* (s, ϵ)*-PRE-CPA-secure restricted to challenge graphs in* $\mathcal{G}(n, \delta, d)$*, where*

$$s := \min(s_1, s_2) - s_{\mathsf{CPA}} - s_{\mathcal{G}} \quad \text{and} \quad \epsilon := (\epsilon_1 + 2\tau \cdot \epsilon_2) \cdot n^{\sigma+\delta+1}.$$

4.2 Corollaries

Finally, we calculate concrete bounds to Theorem 5 for the families of recoding graphs listed in Table 2. The approximate security loss (assuming $\epsilon_1 = \epsilon_2 = \epsilon'$) that results when substituting these bounds for CPA in Theorem 5 are $n^{O(d \cdot \delta)}$ for $\mathcal{G}(n, \delta, d)$, $n^{O(\log n)}$ for $\mathcal{B}(n)$ and $n^{O(\log n)}$ for $\mathcal{C}(n)$. The same bounds hold for

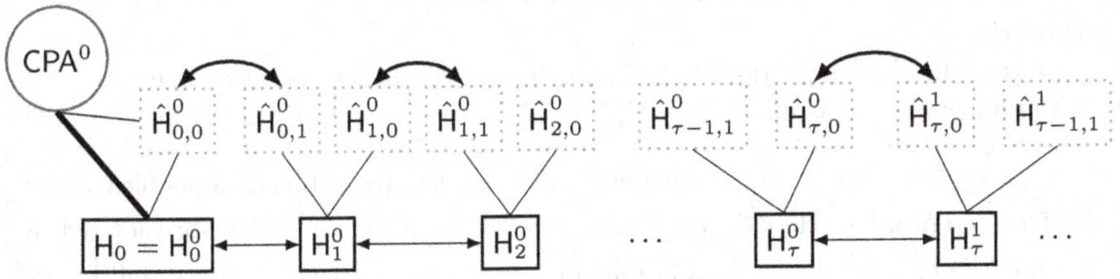

Fig. 3. Diagram showing the partially selectivised hybrids for PRE-CPA.

HRA if one assumes that Q_{RE} and Q_{E} (i.e., number of queries) are polynomial and $\epsilon_3 = 2^{-\kappa}$ (i.e., the PRE scheme is *statistically* source-hiding): see the full version for the details.

5 Lattice-Based Multi-hop Scheme

Here, we describe the lattice-based unidirectional multi-hop PRE scheme from [CCL+14]. The remainder of the schemes—viz. the pairing-based schemes from [AFGH05] and [ABH09] and Gentry's FHE-based construction—are given in the full version [FKKP18]. We note that being based directly on the decision LWE (DLWE) problem this scheme achieves better parameters than the construction from FHE.

5.1 [CCL+14] Scheme

In [CCL+14], Chandran et al. propose two lattice-based unidirectional multi-hop proxy re-encryption schemes. The schemes are built upon Regev's encryption [Reg05] and its dual version [GPV07], respectively. Here, we will describe the former one, which is inspired by the fully homomorphic encryption scheme of [BV11]. Security can be proven assuming the hardness of the decisional learning with errors (DLWE) problem (cf. Definition 14 below).

We recall Regev's encryption scheme in Construction 1. We can now define the PRE scheme from [CCL+14] using RGV in Construction 2.a. To achieve source-hiding, Chandran et al. propose the variant given as Construction 2.b.

In both schemes, the LWE error will grow with each re-encryption and the level bound λ needs to be chosen appropriately so that correctness of decryption is still guaranteed (with overwhelming probability). The second variant achieves the stronger notion of PRE-HRA-security (see below) at the cost of worse parameters; only a small number λ of re-encryptions is supported by this scheme and the underlying security assumption is very strong.

Hybrid $\mathsf{H}^b_{t+\beta}$

Obtain the challenge graph $\hat{G} \in \mathcal{G}(n, \delta, d)$ from A and let $\hat{\imath}$ be its source
Compute $\mathcal{P}_t \leftarrow \mathsf{P}(\hat{G}, t)$, $\mathcal{P}_{t+1} \leftarrow \mathsf{P}(\hat{G}, t+1)$ ▷ The t-th and $(t+1)$-th configurations
$i_0 := \mathcal{P}_t \Delta \mathcal{P}_{t+1}$, $i_1, \ldots, i_\delta := \mathsf{children}(i_0, \hat{G})$ ▷ i_0 denotes pebbled/unpebbled vertex
if $t < \tau$ **then** $\hat{b} \leftarrow \hat{\mathsf{H}}^b_{t,\beta}(\mathcal{P}_t, \{i_0, \ldots, i_\delta\})$ ▷ Key-privacy hybrid
else $\hat{b} \leftarrow \hat{\mathsf{H}}^b_{\tau,0}(\mathcal{P}_\tau, \{\hat{\imath}, \perp, \ldots, \perp\})$ **end if** ▷ $t = \tau$, $\beta = 0$: ind hybrid
if $\hat{G}$ is subgraph of $([n], \mathcal{E})$ reachable from i^* **then return** b' **end if**
return 0

$\hat{\mathsf{H}}^b_{t,\beta}(\mathcal{P}_t, \{i_0, \ldots, i_\delta\})$

Set $\mathcal{C}, \mathcal{E} = \emptyset$ ▷ Stores corrupt keys and issued re-keys and re-encryptions
if $t < \tau$ **then**
  if $i_0 \in \mathcal{P}_t$ **then** $\mathcal{P}_{t+1} := \mathcal{P}_t \setminus \{i_0\}$ **else** $\mathcal{P}_{t+1} := \mathcal{P}_t \cup \{i_0\}$ **end if**
end if
$\mathtt{pp} \leftarrow \mathsf{PRE.S}(1^\kappa, 1^\lambda)$, $(\mathtt{pk}_1, \mathtt{sk}_1), \ldots, (\mathtt{pk}_n, \mathtt{sk}_n) \leftarrow \mathsf{PRE.K}(\mathtt{pp})$
$\forall i, j \in [n], i \neq j : \mathtt{rk}_{i,j} = \perp$ ▷ Delay re-key generation till the query
$b' \leftarrow \mathsf{A}^{(\mathtt{corrupt},\cdot),(\mathtt{rekey},\cdot,\cdot),(\mathtt{reencrypt},\cdot,\cdot,\cdot),(\mathtt{challenge},\cdot,\cdot,\cdot)}(\mathtt{pp}, \mathtt{pk}_1, \ldots, \mathtt{pk}_n)$
if A made call $(\mathtt{challenge}, i^*, \cdot, \cdot)$ for some i^* **then** ▷ Check abort conditions
  if $\exists i \in \mathcal{C} : i^*$ is connected to i in $([n], \mathcal{E})$ **then return** 0 **end if**
end if
return b'

Oracles $\mathtt{corrupt}$ and $\mathtt{challenge}$ are defined like in Game 3.

Oracle $(\mathtt{rekey}, i, j)$

if $\mathtt{rk}_{i,j} = \perp$ **then** ▷ Re-key not generated
  if $i \in \mathcal{P}_{t+\beta}$ **then** $\mathtt{rk}_{i,j} \leftarrow \mathsf{RK}^*(\mathtt{pp}, \mathtt{pk}_j)$ ▷ Fake re-key
  else $\mathtt{rk}_{i,j} \leftarrow \mathsf{RK}((\mathtt{pk}_i, \mathtt{sk}_i), \mathtt{pk}_j)$ **end if** ▷ Real re-key
end if
Add (i, j) to $\mathcal{E}$ ▷ Add to recoding graph
return $\mathtt{rk}_{i,j}$

Oracle $(\mathtt{reencrypt}, i, j, (c_i, \ell))$

if $\mathtt{rk}_{i,j} = \perp$ **then** ▷ Re-key not generated
  if $i \in \mathcal{P}_{t+\beta}$ **then** $\mathtt{rk}_{i,j} \leftarrow \mathsf{RK}^*(\mathtt{pp}, \mathtt{pk}_j)$ ▷ Fake re-key
  else $\mathtt{rk}_{i,j} \leftarrow \mathsf{RK}((\mathtt{pk}_i, \mathtt{sk}_i), \mathtt{pk}_j)$ **end if** ▷ Real re-key
end if
Add (i, j) to $\mathcal{E}$ ▷ Add to recoding graph
return $(c_j, \ell + 1) \leftarrow \mathsf{PRE.RE}(\mathtt{rk}_{i,j}, \mathtt{pk}_i, \mathtt{pk}_j, (c_i, \ell))$

Algorithm 4: Partially selectivised hybrids. For $t \in [0, \tau - 1]$ and $b, \beta \in \{0, 1\}$: $\mathsf{H}^b_{t+\beta} = \mathsf{SEL}_{\mathcal{U} \to \mathcal{G}}[\hat{\mathsf{H}}^b_{t,\beta}, g, h_t]$ and $\mathsf{H}^b_\tau = \mathsf{SEL}_{\mathcal{U} \to \mathcal{G}}[\hat{\mathsf{H}}^b_{\tau,0}, g, h_\tau]$. Moreover, $\mathcal{U}$ is the set $\mathcal{V}^{\sigma+\delta+1}$. Note that the sampling of the re-keys has been deferred to the actual calls.

Security. The PRE scheme in Construction 2.a can be proven secure assuming the hardness of decisional learning with errors (DLWE). We will first show PRE-CPA-security of Construction 2.a and then consider PRE-HRA-security of Construction 2.b.

1. $\mathsf{S}(1^\kappa)$: Pick lattice parameters N, M, $q \in \mathbb{N}$ and a B-bounded error distribution χ on $\mathbb{Z}_q^M$. Sample $\boldsymbol{A} \leftarrow \mathbb{Z}_q^{M \times N}$ uniformly at random and return the public parameters $\mathsf{pp} = (\boldsymbol{A}, N, M, q, \chi)$.
2. $\mathsf{K}(\mathsf{pp})$: Sample $\boldsymbol{s} \leftarrow \mathbb{Z}_q^N$ uniformly at random and compute $\boldsymbol{b} = \boldsymbol{A} \cdot \boldsymbol{s} + \boldsymbol{e}$, where $\boldsymbol{e} \leftarrow \chi$. Set $\mathtt{pk} := \boldsymbol{b}$ as the public key and $\mathtt{sk} := \boldsymbol{s}$ as the secret key. Return $(\mathtt{pk}, \mathtt{sk})$.
3. $\mathsf{E}(\mathtt{pk}, m)$: On input $\mathtt{pk} \in \mathbb{Z}_q^M$ and a message bit $m \in \{0,1\}$, sample $\boldsymbol{r} \leftarrow \{0,1\}^M$ and output
$$\boldsymbol{c} := \boldsymbol{r}^T(\boldsymbol{A}, \boldsymbol{b}) + (0^N, m \cdot \lceil q/2 \rfloor) \in \mathbb{Z}_q^{N+1}.$$
4. $\mathsf{D}(\mathtt{sk}, \boldsymbol{c})$: On input a secret key $\mathtt{sk} = \boldsymbol{s} \in \mathbb{Z}_q^N$ and a ciphertext $\boldsymbol{c} = (\boldsymbol{\alpha}, \beta) \in \mathbb{Z}_q^N \times \mathbb{Z}_q$, output 0 if $\beta - \langle \boldsymbol{\alpha}, \boldsymbol{s} \rangle$ is closer to 0 than to $\lceil q/2 \rfloor$, else output 1.

Construction 1: Regev's Encryption scheme RGV [Reg05].

1. $\mathsf{S}(1^\kappa)$: Get parameters $\mathsf{pp}' \leftarrow \mathsf{RGV.S}(1^\kappa)$, level bound λ and $\boxed{\text{“blurring error” bound } E_\ell}$ for each level $\ell \in [\lambda]$. Return the parameters $\mathsf{pp} = (\mathsf{pp}', \lambda, (E_\ell)_{\ell \in [\lambda]})$.
2. $\mathsf{K}(\mathsf{pp})$: Run $\mathsf{RGV.K}(\mathsf{pp}')$ and output the result.
3. $\mathsf{E}(\mathtt{pk}, (m, \ell))$: Compute $\boldsymbol{c} = \mathsf{RGV.E}(\mathtt{pk}, m) + \boxed{(0^N, f_\ell)}$, where $\boxed{f_\ell \leftarrow [-E_\ell, E_\ell] \cap \mathbb{Z}}$, and return the level-$\ell$ ciphertext $(\boldsymbol{c}, \ell)$.
4. $\mathsf{RK}((\mathtt{pk}_i, \mathtt{sk}_i), \mathtt{pk}_j)$: Parse $\mathtt{sk}_i$ as $\boldsymbol{s}_i = (s_{i,1}, \ldots, s_{i,N}) \in \mathbb{Z}_q^N$. For $k \in [N]$ and $l \in [\lceil \log q \rceil]$, compute $K_{k,l} \leftarrow \mathsf{RGV.E}(\mathtt{pk}_j, 0) + (0^N, s_{i,k} \cdot 2^l)$. Return the re-key:
$$\mathtt{rk}_{i,j} := \{K_{k,l}\}_{k \in [N], l \in [\lceil \log q \rceil]}.$$
5. $\mathsf{RE}(\mathtt{rk}_{i,j}, \mathtt{pk}_i, \mathtt{pk}_j, (\boldsymbol{c}_i, \ell)) \rightarrow (c_j, \ell+1)$: If $\ell \geq \lambda$, abort. Otherwise, parse the level-ℓ ciphertext $\boldsymbol{c}_i$ as $(\boldsymbol{\alpha}, \beta) \in \mathbb{Z}_q^N \times \mathbb{Z}_q$ and $\mathtt{rk}_{i,j}$ as $\{K_{k,l}\}_{k \in [N], l \in [\lceil \log q \rceil]}$. Denote by α_k the k-th component of $\boldsymbol{\alpha}$, and denote the bit decomposition of α_k as $\{\alpha_{k,l}\}_{l \in [\lceil \log q \rceil]}$, i.e., $\alpha_k = \sum_{l \in [\lceil \log q \rceil]} \alpha_{k,l} 2^l$, where each $\alpha_{k,l} \in \{0,1\}$. Compute
$$\boldsymbol{c}_j = (0^N, \beta) + \sum_{k,l} \alpha_{k,l} \cdot K_{k,l} + \mathsf{RGV.E}(\mathtt{pk}_j, 0) + \boxed{(0^N, f_{\ell+1})},$$
where $\boxed{f_{\ell+1} \leftarrow [-E_{\ell+1}, E_{\ell+1}] \cap \mathbb{Z}}$, and return $(\boldsymbol{c}_j, \ell+1)$.
6. $\mathsf{D}(\mathtt{sk}, (\boldsymbol{c}, \ell))$: Run $\mathsf{RGV.D}(\mathtt{sk}, \boldsymbol{c})$ and output the result.

Construction 2: $\boxed{\text{source-hiding}}$ unidirectional multi-hop PRE from [CCL+14]. We refer to the construction without the blurring (ignoring the boxes) by Construction 2.a and the construction with blurring (including the boxes) by Construction 2.b.

Definition 14 (DLWE [Reg05]**).** *Let N, M, $q \in \mathbb{N}$. For a matrix $\boldsymbol{A} \leftarrow \mathbb{Z}_q^{M \times N}$ and a secret vector $\boldsymbol{s} \leftarrow \mathbb{Z}_q^N$, each sampled uniformly at random, and a vector $\boldsymbol{e} \leftarrow \chi$ for an error distribution χ on $\mathbb{Z}_q^M$, the decisional LWE problem $\mathrm{DLWE}_{N,M,q,\chi}$ is to distinguish $(\boldsymbol{A}, \boldsymbol{A} \cdot \boldsymbol{s} + \boldsymbol{e})$ from $(\boldsymbol{A}, \boldsymbol{b})$ for a uniformly random sample $\boldsymbol{b} \leftarrow \mathbb{Z}_q^M$.*

To prove adaptive security for the two variants of Construction 2, we will need the following lemma [BV11].

Lemma 4 (matrix-vector leftover hash lemma). *Let* $\kappa, N, q \in \mathbb{N}$, *and* $M \geq N \cdot \log q + 2\kappa$. *For* $\boldsymbol{A} \leftarrow \mathbb{Z}_q^{M \times N}$, $\boldsymbol{r} \leftarrow \{0,1\}^M$, *and* $\boldsymbol{y} \leftarrow \mathbb{Z}_q^N$ *each sampled uniformly at random, it holds* $\Delta((\boldsymbol{A}, \boldsymbol{A}^T\boldsymbol{r}), (\boldsymbol{A}, \boldsymbol{y})) \leq 2^{-\kappa}$.

Assuming the computational hardness of $\mathrm{DLWE}_{N,M,q,\chi}$ for appropriate parameters, by the above lemma we get for any $\mathsf{pp} = (\boldsymbol{A}, N, M, q, \chi, \lambda)$, $\mathsf{pk} = \boldsymbol{b}$ and $m \in \{0,1\}$: $\mathsf{RGV.E}(\mathsf{pk}, m) = \boldsymbol{r}^T(\boldsymbol{A}, \boldsymbol{b}) + (0^N, m \cdot \lceil q/2 \rfloor)$ is computationally indistinguishable from $\boldsymbol{r}^T(\boldsymbol{A}, \boldsymbol{b}') + (0^N, m \cdot \lceil q/2 \rfloor)$, where $\boldsymbol{r} \leftarrow \{0,1\}^M$ and $\boldsymbol{b}' \leftarrow \mathbb{Z}_q^M$. The latter distribution is, in turn, statistically close to the uniform distribution on $\mathbb{Z}_q^{N+1}$. Informally, since $\mathsf{RGV.E}(\mathsf{pk}, 0)$ is computationally indistinguishable from uniformly random, ciphertexts, re-keys and re-encrypted ciphertexts all look uniformly random; in particular Construction 2.a satisfies indistinguishability of ciphertexts as well as δ-weak key privacy.

Lemma 5. *Assuming* $\mathrm{DLWE}_{N,M,q,\chi}$ *is* (s_1, ϵ_1)*-hard for parameters* N, M, q *as in Lemma 4, Construction 2.a satisfies* $(s_1 - s_{\mathsf{E}}, 2(\epsilon_1 + 2^{-\kappa}))$*-indistinguishability and* $(s_1 - O(\delta\, N \lceil \log q \rceil\, (s_{\mathbb{Z}_q^{N+1}} + s_{\mathsf{RGV.E}})), \delta N \lceil \log q \rceil \epsilon_1, \delta)$*-weak key-privacy.*

Theorem 6 (PRE-CPA-security of Construction 2.a). *Let* σ *and* τ *denote the space and time complexity for the class* $\mathcal{G} = \mathcal{G}(n, \delta, d)$. *Assume the* $\mathrm{DLWE}_{N,M,q,\chi}$ *problem is* (s_1, ϵ_1)*-hard for parameters* N, M, q *as in Lemma 4. Then Construction 2.a is* (s, ϵ)*-PRE-CPA-secure restricted to challenge graphs in* $\mathcal{G}$*, where*

$$s := s_1 - O(\delta\, N \lceil \log q \rceil\, (s_{\mathbb{Z}_q^{N+1}} + s_{\mathsf{RGV.E}})) - s_{\mathsf{CPA}} - s_{\mathcal{G}} \quad \text{and}$$
$$\epsilon := (2\tau \cdot \delta N \lceil \log q \rceil + 1) \cdot \epsilon_1 \cdot n^{\sigma+\delta+1}.$$

Construction 2.a clearly does not satisfy source-hiding and, thus cannot be proven PRE-HRA-secure using our results. Fortunately, Construction 2.b solves this issue, but at the cost of only allowing for a constant level bound λ. The additional uniform error $f_\ell \leftarrow [-E_\ell, E_\ell] \cap \mathbb{Z}$ added in E and RE in Construction 2.b is used to "blur out" the different errors caused by encryption or re-encryption, respectively. Choosing the error bounds E_ℓ appropriately guarantees the source-hiding property of the scheme while still preserving correctness.[4] Chandran et al. refer to this rerandomisation technique as *strong blurring*; a more detailed analysis can be found in [DS16, Sect. 4.1], where the same method for rerandomization of Regev ciphertexts is used to discuss sanitizability of the FHE scheme from [BV11].

To prove PRE-HRA-security of Construction 2.b, note that, as above, semantic security and δ-weak key-privacy of (E, D) directly follow by the security of Regev's encryption scheme. We get a result similar to Lemma 5.

Lemma 6. *For large enough (see Footnote 4) error ranges* E_ℓ, $\ell \in [\lambda]$, *Construction 2.b is (statistically) source-hiding.*

[4] In fact, we need to choose the error bounds $(E_\ell)_{\ell \in [\lambda]}$ exponentially large, eg., $E_1 \geq (M+1)B2^\kappa$. Thus, to provide correctness of the scheme, one needs to choose the modulus q to be of size $\exp(O(\kappa))$ and the level bound λ of size $O(1)$.

Theorem 7 (PRE-HRA-security of Construction 2.b). *Let ϵ be as in Theorem 6 and let σ and τ denote the space and time complexity for $\mathcal{G} = \mathcal{G}(n, \delta, d)$. If* $\mathrm{DLWE}_{N,M,q,\chi}$ *is (s_1, ϵ_1)-hard for parameters N, M, q as in Lemma 4 and E_ℓ ($\ell \in [\lambda]$), λ are chosen appropriately, then Construction 2.b is (s', ϵ')-PRE-HRA-secure restricted to challenge graphs in $\mathcal{G}$, where*

$$s' := s_1 - O(\delta N \lceil \log q \rceil (s_{\mathbb{Z}_q^{N+1}} + s_{\mathsf{RGV.E}})) - s_{\mathsf{HRA}} - s_{\mathcal{G}}, \quad \textit{and}$$
$$\epsilon' := 2n(n-1)(Q_{\mathsf{E}} + Q_{\mathsf{RE}})Q_{\mathsf{RE}} \cdot 2^{-\kappa} + \epsilon.$$

6 Open Problems

We leave as open problems to find adaptively secure PREs (either via the [JKK+17] framework or using a new technique) for more general settings, which includes unidirectional PREs on general graphs, bidirectional PREs and CCA-secure PRE (the schemes above only satisfy CPA, and the slightly stronger HRA security notion).

Acknowledgements. The first author is supported by the French ANR EfTrEC project (ANR-16-CE39-0002). The remaining authors are supported by the European Research Council, ERC consolidator grant TOCNeT (682815).

References

[ABH09] Ateniese, G., Benson, K., Hohenberger, S.: Key-private proxy re-encryption. In: Fischlin, M. (ed.) CT-RSA 2009. LNCS, vol. 5473, pp. 279–294. Springer, Heidelberg (2009). https://doi.org/10.1007/978-3-642-00862-7_19

[AFGH05] Ateniese, G., Fu, K., Green, M., Hohenberger, S.: Improved proxy re-encryption schemes with applications to secure distributed storage. In: 2005 Proceedings of the Network and Distributed System Security Symposium, NDSS, San Diego, California. The Internet Society, USA (2005)

[BB04] Boneh, D., Boyen, X.: Secure identity based encryption without random oracles. In: Franklin, M. (ed.) CRYPTO 2004. LNCS, vol. 3152, pp. 443–459. Springer, Heidelberg (2004). https://doi.org/10.1007/978-3-540-28628-8_27

[BBS98] Blaze, M., Bleumer, G., Strauss, M.: Divertible protocols and atomic proxy cryptography. In: Nyberg, K. (ed.) EUROCRYPT 1998. LNCS, vol. 1403, pp. 127–144. Springer, Heidelberg (1998). https://doi.org/10.1007/BFb0054122

[Ben89] Bennett, C.H.: Time/space trade-offs for reversible computation. SIAM J. Comput. **18**(4), 766–776 (1989)

[BV11] Brakerski, Z., Vaikuntanathan, V.: Efficient fully homomorphic encryption from (standard) LWE. In: 2011 IEEE 52nd Annual Symposium on Foundations of Computer Science, pp. 97–106, October 2011

[CCL+14] Chandran, N., Chase, M., Liu, F.-H., Nishimaki, R., Xagawa, K.: Re-encryption, functional re-encryption, and multi-hop re-encryption: a framework for achieving obfuscation-based security and instantiations from lattices. In: Krawczyk, H. (ed.) PKC 2014. LNCS, vol. 8383, pp. 95–112. Springer, Heidelberg (2014). https://doi.org/10.1007/978-3-642-54631-0_6

[CCV12] Chandran, N., Chase, M., Vaikuntanathan, V.: Functional re-encryption and collusion-resistant obfuscation. In: Cramer, R. (ed.) TCC 2012. LNCS, vol. 7194, pp. 404–421. Springer, Heidelberg (2012). https://doi.org/10.1007/978-3-642-28914-9_23

[CH07] Canetti, R., Hohenberger, S.: Chosen-ciphertext secure proxy re-encryption. In: Proceedings of the 14th ACM Conference on Computer and Communications Security, CCS 2007, pp. 185–194. ACM (2007)

[Coh17] Cohen, A.: What about Bob? The inadequacy of CPA security for proxy reencryption. Cryptology ePrint Report 2017/785 (2017). https://ia.cr/2017/785

[DS16] Ducas, L., Stehlé, D.: Sanitization of FHE ciphertexts. In: Fischlin, M., Coron, J.-S. (eds.) EUROCRYPT 2016. LNCS, vol. 9665, pp. 294–310. Springer, Heidelberg (2016). https://doi.org/10.1007/978-3-662-49890-3_12

[FKKP18] Fuchsbauer, G., Kamath, C., Klein, K., Pietrzak, K.: Adaptively secure proxy re-encryption. Cryptology ePrint Archive, Report 2018/426. https://ia.cr/2018/426

[FKPR14] Fuchsbauer, G., Konstantinov, M., Pietrzak, K., Rao, V.: Adaptive security of constrained PRFs. In: Sarkar, P., Iwata, T. (eds.) ASIACRYPT 2014. LNCS, vol. 8874, pp. 82–101. Springer, Heidelberg (2014). https://doi.org/10.1007/978-3-662-45608-8_5

[FL17] Fan, X., Liu, F.-H.: Proxy re-encryption and re-signatures from lattices. Cryptology ePrint Report 2017/456. https://ia.cr/2017/456

[Gen09] Gentry, C.: Fully homomorphic encryption using ideal lattices. In: Proceedings of the Forty-first Annual ACM Symposium on Theory of Computing, STOC 2009, pp. 169–178. ACM (2009)

[GPV07] Gentry, C., Peikert, C., Vaikuntanathan, V.: Trapdoors for hard lattices and new cryptographic constructions. Electronic Colloquium on Computational Complexity (ECCC), 14(133), 2007

[HRsV07] Hohenberger, S., Rothblum, G.N., Shelat, A., Vaikuntanathan, V.: Securely obfuscating re-encryption. In: Vadhan, S.P. (ed.) TCC 2007. LNCS, vol. 4392, pp. 233–252. Springer, Heidelberg (2007). https://doi.org/10.1007/978-3-540-70936-7_13

[JKK+17] Jafargholi, Z., Kamath, C., Klein, K., Komargodski, I., Pietrzak, K., Wichs, D.: Be adaptive, avoid overcommitting. In: Katz, J., Shacham, H. (eds.) CRYPTO 2017. LNCS, vol. 10401, pp. 133–163. Springer, Cham (2017). https://doi.org/10.1007/978-3-319-63688-7_5

[LV08] Libert, B., Vergnaud, D.: Unidirectional chosen-ciphertext secure proxy re-encryption. In: Cramer, R. (ed.) PKC 2008. LNCS, vol. 4939, pp. 360–379. Springer, Heidelberg (2008). https://doi.org/10.1007/978-3-540-78440-1_21

[PWA+16] Trieu Phong, L., Wang, L., Aono, Y., Nguyen, M.H., Boyen, X.: Proxy re-encryption schemes with key privacy from LWE. Cryptology ePrint Report 2016/327 (2016). https://ia.cr/2016/327

[Reg05] Regev, O.: On lattices, learning with errors, random linear codes, and cryptography. In: Proceedings of the 37th Annual ACM Symposium on Theory of Computing, STOC 2005, pp. 84–93. ACM (2005)

Fundamental Primitives (II)

Generic Constructions of Robustly Reusable Fuzzy Extractor

Yunhua Wen[1,2], Shengli Liu[1,2,3](✉), and Dawu Gu[1]

[1] Department of Computer Science and Engineering, Shanghai Jiao Tong University, Shanghai 200240, China
{happyle8,slliu,dwgu}@sjtu.edu.cn
[2] State Key Laboratory of Cryptology, P.O. Box 5159, Beijing 100878, China
[3] Westone Cryptologic Research Center, Beijing 100070, China

Abstract. Robustly reusable Fuzzy Extractor (rrFE) considers reusability and robustness simultaneously. We present two approaches to the generic construction of rrFE. Both of approaches make use of a secure sketch and universal hash functions. The first approach also employs a special pseudo-random function (PRF), namely unique-input key-shift (ui-ks) secure PRF, and the second uses a key-shift secure auxiliary-input authenticated encryption (AIAE). The ui-ks security of PRF (resp. key-shift security of AIAE), together with the homomorphic properties of secure sketch and universal hash function, guarantees the reusability and robustness of rrFE. Meanwhile, we show two instantiations of the two approaches respectively. The first instantiation results in the first rrFE from the LWE assumption, while the second instantiation results in the first rrFE from the DDH assumption over non-pairing groups.

Keywords: Fuzzy extractor · Reusability · Robustness

1 Introduction

In cryptographic applications, the underlying secret keys are required to be uniformly sampled and reproducible. Uniformity of the secret keys is necessary for the security of cryptographic algorithms, and reproducibility is responsible for the correctness of the algorithms. In reality, there exist many noisy random sources of high entropy, which are neither uniformly distributed nor reproducible. For instance, biometrics [19,20] (like fingerprint, iris, voice, etc), physical unclonable functions [22,23] in electronic devices, and quantum bits generated from quantum devices [4,5]. In fact, the readings of the same source are rarely identical and noises are inevitably introduced in each reading. An interesting topic is research on converting such random sources into uniform and reproducible strings so that they can serve as secret keys for cryptographic systems. The topic was highlighted by Dodis et al. [11] who proposed the concept of Fuzzy Extractor.

Fuzzy extractor (FE) is able to turn a noisy variable of high entropy into a stable, uniformly distributed string. More precisely, it consists of two efficient

D. Lin and K. Sako (Eds.): PKC 2019, LNCS 11443, pp. 349–378, 2019.
https://doi.org/10.1007/978-3-030-17259-6_12

algorithms (Gen, Rep). The generation algorithm Gen on input a reading w from a noisy source W outputs a public helper string P together with an extracted string R. The security of FE requires that R is (pseudo-)random if W has enough entropy. The reproduction algorithm Rep on input w' which is close to w will reproduce R with the help of the public helper string P.

Reusable Fuzzy Extractor. It should be noted that fuzzy extractor only allows one extraction from a noisy source. This feature limits the usability of fuzzy extractor. In fact, a user may like to use his/her fingerprint to generate several keys for different cryptographic applications. To this end, reusable fuzzy extractor was proposed by Boyen [6]. Generally, reusable fuzzy extractor guarantees the security of multiple keys extracted from a single noisy source. More precisely, $\mathsf{R}_1, \mathsf{R}_2, \cdots, \mathsf{R}_Q$ are all pseudorandom even conditioned on $(\mathsf{P}_1, \mathsf{P}_2, \cdots, \mathsf{P}_Q)$ where $(\mathsf{P}_j, \mathsf{R}_j) \leftarrow \mathsf{Gen}(w_j)$, $j \in \{1, \cdots, Q\}$ and w_j is the j-th reading of a noisy source.

In [6], Boyen proposed a reusable FE scheme based on the random oracle. In the security model, it assumes the exclusive OR of two readings of the same source reveals no information of the noisy source W. Wen et al. [27] constructed a reusable FE from the Decisional Diffie-Hellman (DDH) assumption, and the security model assumes that the difference of two readings of the same source does not reveal too much information of the random source.

Canetti et al. [8] constructed a reusable FE from a powerful tool named "digital locker". In the security model, no assumption is made on how multiple readings are correlated. However, existing instantiations of digital locker rely their security either on random oracles or non-standard assumptions. Their work was upgraded by Alamélou et al. [1] to tolerate linear fraction of errors, but still rely on "digital locker".

Apon et al. [2] proposed a reusable FE from the learning with errors (LWE) assumption, but it can only tolerate logarithmic fraction of errors. Later, Wen et al. [24] constructed a new reusable FE from LWE assumption tolerating linear fraction of errors. In both works, it assumes that the differences between two readings of the same source are controlled by a probabilistic polynomial-time (PPT) adversary.

Robust Fuzzy Extractor. Fuzzy extractor does not consider active adversaries. If the public helper string P is modified by an active adversary, the correctness of fuzzy extractor might not be guaranteed. Boyen et al. [7] first highlighted this issue and introduced the concept of robust fuzzy extractor. Robustness of fuzzy extractor concerns the integrity of P, and requires that the reproduction algorithm of FE will output $\perp$ with overwhelming probability if P is modified.

Boyen et al. [7] proposed a generic way of transforming a fuzzy extractor to a robust one based on random oracles. Dodis et al. [10] showed that robustness of information-theoretic fuzzy extractor is not achievable in the *plain model* if the entropy rate of the source is less than 1/2 and they constructed a fuzzy extractor with post-application robustness which applies to sources of entropy rate larger than 2/3. Later, Kanukurthi et al. [16] introduced an improved robust FE, which relaxes entropy rates of sources to be larger than 1/2. With the help of *common reference string* (CRS), Cramer et al. [9] proposed a robust FE and breaks the 1/2 entropy rate barrier in the CRS model.

Robustly Reusable Fuzzy Extractor. Most recently, Wen et al. [25] proposed the concept of robustly reusable Fuzzy Extractor (rrFE), which considers robustness and reusability simultaneously in the CRS model.

According to [25], the reusability of rrFE asks the pseudorandomness of R_j even conditioned on $(\mathsf{R}_1, \cdots, \mathsf{R}_{j-1}, \mathsf{R}_{j+1}, \cdots, \mathsf{R}_Q, \mathsf{P}_1, \cdots, \mathsf{P}_Q)$ where $(\mathsf{P}_j, \mathsf{R}_j) \leftarrow \mathsf{Gen}(w_j = w + \delta_j)$, $j \in [Q]$ ($[Q] := \{1, \cdots, Q\}$) and δ_j is controlled by the adversary. In formula, $(\mathsf{R}_1, \cdots, \mathsf{R}_j, \cdots, \mathsf{R}_Q, \mathsf{P}_1, \cdots, \mathsf{P}_Q) \approx_c (\mathsf{R}_1, \cdots, \mathsf{U}_j, \cdots, \mathsf{R}_Q, \mathsf{P}_1, \cdots, \mathsf{P}_Q)$, where U_j denotes a uniform distribution. In fact, a stronger version requires $(\mathsf{R}_1, \cdots, \mathsf{R}_Q, \mathsf{P}_1, \cdots, \mathsf{P}_Q) \approx_c (\mathsf{U}_1, \cdots, \mathsf{U}_Q, \mathsf{P}_1, \cdots, \mathsf{P}_Q)$. The robustness of rrFE requires that for any PPT adversary, its forged public helper string and reading shift (P^*, δ^*) cannot pass the reproduction algorithm of rrFE except with negligible probability, even if the adversary sees $(\mathsf{P}_j, \mathsf{R}_j)_{j\in[Q]}$. Here $(\mathsf{P}_j, \mathsf{R}_j) \leftarrow \mathsf{Gen}(w_j = w + \delta_j)$. Moreover, $\{\delta_j\}_{j\in[Q]}, (\mathsf{P}^*, \delta^*) \notin \{(\mathsf{P}_j, \mathsf{R}_j)\}_{j\in[Q]}$ are adaptively chosen by the adversary.

In [25], the first robustly reusable fuzzy extractor was constructed based on the DDH and DLIN assumptions in the CRS model. We stress that the DLIN assumption is over pairing-friendly groups, since a core building block of their construction, namely homomorphic lossy algebraic filter (LAF) [15], has only one instantiation, which is over (symmetric) pairing-friendly groups. Though the construction is elegant, the instantiation of LAF introduces big public helper string, and complicated computations over symmetric pairing groups in rrFE.

Question. Is there any other approaches to rrFE? Is it possible to obtain a more efficient rrFE? Is it possible to construct a rrFE from the LWE assumption?

1.1 Our Contribution

We answer the above questions in the affirmative.

- We provide two generic constructions of rrFE. Namely,

$$\mathsf{SS} + \mathcal{H}_\mathcal{I} + \mathsf{ui\text{-}ks\text{-}PRF} \Rightarrow \mathsf{rrFE},$$
$$\mathsf{SS} + \mathcal{H}_\mathcal{I} + \mathsf{AIAE} \Rightarrow \mathsf{rrFE},$$

  where SS is a homomorphic Secure Sketch with linearity property, $\mathcal{H}_\mathcal{I}$ is a family of homomorphic universal hash functions, $\mathsf{ui\text{-}ks\text{-}PRF}$ is a pseudorandom function with unique-input key-shift security, and AIAE is an auxiliary-input authenticated encryption with key-shift security.
- Our construction is simple and can be instantiated with standard assumptions. Both SS and $\mathcal{H}_\mathcal{I}$ have information-theoretic instantiations, and $\mathsf{ui\text{-}ks\text{-}PRF}$ and AIAE have available instantiations from standard assumptions.
  - When instantiating $\mathsf{ui\text{-}ks\text{-}PRF}$ with the PRF constructed in [18], we obtain the first post-quantum rrFE from the LWE assumption.

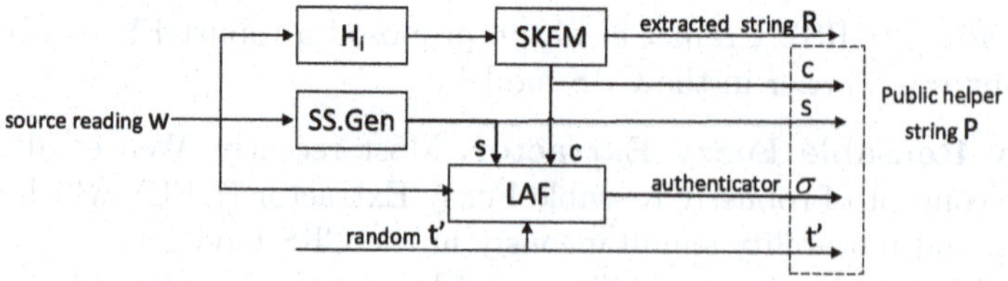

Fig. 1. The generation algorithm of the robustly reusable Fuzzy Extractor in [25].

- When instantiating AIAE with the AIAE scheme from [14], we obtain the first efficient rrFE from the DDH assumption over pairing-free groups.

1.2 Our Approaches

We provide two new approaches to rrFE. Following the security model in [25], the adversary controls the differences between any two different readings of the source W.

First, we recall the generation algorithm of rrFE in [25] in Fig. 1. The source reading w is served as inputs for three building blocks, i.e., universal hash function $\mathsf{H_i}$, secure sketch scheme $\mathsf{SS} = (\mathsf{SS.Gen}, \mathsf{SS.Rec})$ and lossy algebraic filter LAF. With $\mathsf{H_i}$, a string k is extracted from source w and used as a key in the symmetric KEM $\mathsf{SKEM} = (\mathsf{SKEM.Enc}, \mathsf{SKEM.Dec})$, which in turn encapsulates the final extracted string R; with $\mathsf{SS.Gen}$, a secure sketch s is generated from w to help eliminate noises in the reproduction algorithm of rrFE; with LAF, w is used as an authentication key to authenticate the ciphertext c generated by $\mathsf{SKEM.Gen}$, the secure sketch s and a random tag t'. The output σ of LAF can be regarded as an authenticator. The final public helper string is $\mathsf{P} = (\mathsf{c}, \mathsf{s}, \mathsf{t}', \sigma)$.

Differences Between Ours and [25]. Different from the rrFE in [25], we explore a different structure with different primitives. As for primitive, we use pseudorandom function (PRF) or auxiliary-input authentication encryption (AIAE), instead of LAF+SKEM. As for structure, rrFE in [25] uses LAF for authentication of $(\mathsf{c}, \mathsf{s}, \mathsf{t}')$ and SKEM for pseudo-randomness of R, while ours employs only a single primitive $\mathsf{ui\text{-}ks\text{-}PRF}$(or AIAE) to achieve both authentication and pseudo-randomness. Moreover, we do not use w directly as authentication key. Instead, we input w to $\mathsf{H_i}$ to obtain a key k for $\mathsf{ui\text{-}ks\text{-}PRF}/\mathsf{AIAE}$. We expect $\mathsf{ui\text{-}ks\text{-}PRF}/\mathsf{AIAE}$ to provide both pseudorandomness of R and authentication of the public helper string P. In fact, the security of the PRF $\mathsf{ui\text{-}ks\text{-}PRF}/\mathsf{AIAE}$ helps us to obtain reusability and robustness of rrFE. See Figs. 2 and 3.

The First Approach. In the first approach, we resort to a special PRF, namely $\mathsf{ui\text{-}ks\text{-}PRF}$. Taking the output k from $\mathsf{H_i}$ as its key, and the output s from SS and a random t as its input, $\mathsf{ui\text{-}ks\text{-}PRF}$ outputs a string which is further divided into R and v. Here R is the final extracted string, while v behaves as an authenticator. The public helper string is $\mathsf{P} = (\mathsf{s}, \mathsf{t}, \mathsf{v})$.

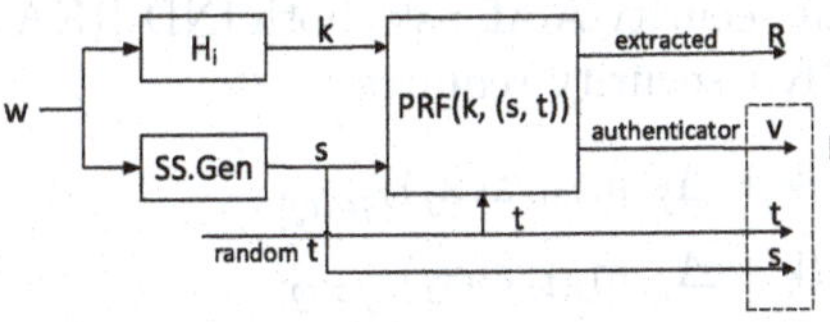

Fig. 2. Gen of the first approach.

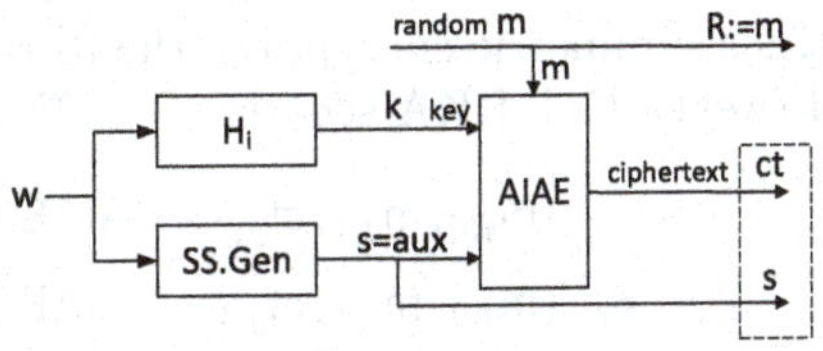

Fig. 3. Gen of the second approach.

The reusability and robustness of rrFE can be reduced to the Unique-Input Key-Shift (ui-ks) security of ui-ks-PRF, with the help of the homomorphic properties of $\mathsf{H_i}$ and SS (and also the linearity property of SS). Informally, the security of the PRF ui-ks-PRF requires

$$(x_j, \mathsf{PRF}(\mathsf{k} + \Delta_j, x_j))_{j\in[Q]} \approx_c (x_j, \mathsf{U}_j)_{j\in[Q]}$$

for all PPT adversaries, where k, U_j are uniformly distributed, PRF is the evaluation algorithm of ui-ks-PRF, inputs $\{x_j\}_{j\in[Q]}$ are distinct, and $\{x_j\}_{j\in[Q]}$ $\{\Delta_j\}_{j\in[Q]}$ are adaptively chosen by the adversary.

Now we outline the high-level idea of proving the reusability and robustness of our first rrFE in Fig. 2.

(i) Due to the homomorphic properties of SS and $\mathsf{H_i}$, it holds that $\mathsf{H_i}(w_j) = \mathsf{H_i}(w+\delta_j) = \mathsf{H_i}(w)+\mathsf{H_i}(\delta_j)$ and $\mathsf{SS.Gen}(w_j) = \mathsf{SS.Gen}(w+\delta_j) = \mathsf{SS.Gen}(w)+\mathsf{SS.Gen}(\delta_j)$. Then the view of the adversary can be considered as the randomized function of $\mathsf{k}(:= \mathsf{H_i}(w))$, $\mathsf{s}(:= \mathsf{SS.Gen}(w))$. The output s from SS only leaks limited amount of information of W. By the leftover hash lemma, the output k from universal hash function $\mathsf{H_i}$ is uniform and independent of s.

(ii) The key of ui-ks PRF is given by $\mathsf{k}_j = \mathsf{H_i}(w_j) = \mathsf{H_i}(w + \delta_j) = \mathsf{k} + \mathsf{H_i}(\delta_j)$, which can be regarded as a key shifted $\Delta_j := \mathsf{H_i}(\delta_j)$ from k. The inputs of ui-ks PRF are $(\mathsf{s}_j, \mathsf{t}_j)_{j\in[Q]}$, which are distinct with each other due to the randomness of t_j. Given that k is uniform and independent of s, key shift Δ_j is determined by δ_j, and all input $(\mathsf{s}_j, \mathsf{t}_j)$ are distinct, it is ready for us to implement the security reduction of rrFE to ui-ks security of ui-ks PRF. The security reduction is non-trivial (see Sect. 4 for details).

(iii) The ui-ks security of ui-ks PRF implies the pseudo-randomness of $(\mathsf{R}_j, \mathsf{v}_j)$ and $(\mathsf{R}^*, \mathsf{v}^*)$ for $\mathcal{A}$, which immediately implies reusability of rrFE. The robustness of rrFE follows as well, since the adversary cannot guess the correct authenticator v^* with non-negligible probability. The security reduction is non-trivial (see Sect. 4 for details).

The Second Approach. In the second approach, we use a special authenticated encryption scheme, namely auxiliary-input authenticated encryption (AIAE). Taking $\mathsf{k} := \mathsf{H_i}(w)$ as its key and $\mathsf{s} := \mathsf{SS.Gen}(w)$ as its auxiliary input, AIAE encrypts a random string R and outputs a ciphertext ct. Then R serves as the final extracted string, while $\mathsf{P} = (\mathsf{s}, \mathsf{ct})$ as the public helper string.

As a symmetric encryption, the Key-Shift security AIAE asks both IND-RKA and (weak) INT-RKA security. The IND-RKA security requires

$$\begin{aligned}&(\mathsf{m}_{j,0}, \mathsf{m}_{j,1}, \mathsf{ct}_{j,0} \leftarrow \mathsf{AIAE.Enc}(\mathsf{k}+\Delta_j, \mathsf{m}_{j,0}, \mathsf{aux}_j))_{j\in[Q]}\\ \approx_c\ &(\mathsf{m}_{j,0}, \mathsf{m}_{j,1}, \mathsf{ct}_{j,1} \leftarrow \mathsf{AIAE.Enc}(\mathsf{k}+\Delta_j, \mathsf{m}_{j,1}, \mathsf{aux}_j))_{j\in[Q]},\end{aligned}$$

where $(\mathsf{m}_{j,0}, \mathsf{m}_{j,1}), \Delta_j$ are adaptively chosen by PPT adversaries. It implies that

$$(\mathsf{R}_j, \mathsf{ct}_j)_{j\in[Q]} \approx_c (\mathsf{R}_j, \mathsf{ct}'_j)_{j\in[Q]},$$

where $\mathsf{R}_j, \mathsf{R}'_j$ are uniformly chosen and $\mathsf{ct}_j \leftarrow \mathsf{AIAE.Enc}(\mathsf{k}+\Delta_j, \mathsf{R}_j, \mathsf{aux}_j)$, $\mathsf{ct}'_j \leftarrow \mathsf{AIAE.Enc}(\mathsf{k}+\Delta_j, \mathsf{R}'_j, \mathsf{aux}_j)$. The weak INT-RKA security requires that given $\mathsf{ct}_j \leftarrow \mathsf{AIAE.Enc}(\mathsf{k}+\Delta_j, \mathsf{m}_j, \mathsf{aux}_j)$ with $(\Delta_j, \mathsf{m}_j, \mathsf{aux}_j)$ chosen by the adversary, it is hard for the PPT adversary to forge a new tuple $(\mathsf{aux}^*, \mathsf{ct}^*, \Delta^*)$ such that $\mathsf{AIAE.Dec}(\mathsf{k}+\Delta^*, \mathsf{ct}^*, \mathsf{aux}^*) \neq \perp$. Here a special rule is imposed: $\Delta^* = \Delta_j$ if $\mathsf{aux}^* = \mathsf{aux}_j$.

The reusability and robustness of rrFE can be reduced to the Key-Shift security of AIAE, thanks to the homomorphic properties of $\mathsf{H_i}$ and SS and the linearity property of SS.

(i)' With the same reason as in (i), $\mathsf{H_i}(w)$ outputs a uniform key k, which is independent of s.

(ii)' The key of AIAE is $\mathsf{k}_j = \mathsf{H_i}(w_j) = \mathsf{H_i}(w+\delta_j) = \mathsf{k}+\mathsf{H_i}(\delta_j)$, which can be regarded as a key shifted $\Delta_j := \mathsf{H_i}(\delta_j)$ from k. The message of AIAE is a random string R, the auxiliary input is $\mathsf{s}_j := \mathsf{s}+\mathsf{SS.Gen}(\delta_j)$ and the corresponding ciphertext is $\mathsf{ct}_j := \mathsf{AIAE.Enc}(\mathsf{k}+\Delta_j, \mathsf{R}, \mathsf{s}_j)$. Given that k is uniform and independent of s, key shift Δ_j is determined by δ_j, it is ready for us to implement the reusability security reduction of rrFE to IND-RKA security of AIAE. The IND-RKA security of AIAE guarantees that $(\mathsf{R}_j, \mathsf{ct}_j)_{j\in[Q]} \approx_c (\mathsf{R}_j, \mathsf{ct}'_j)_{j\in[Q]}$, where $\mathsf{R}_j, \mathsf{R}'_j$ are uniformly chosen and $\mathsf{ct}_j \leftarrow \mathsf{AIAE.Enc}(\mathsf{k}+\Delta_j, \mathsf{R}_j, \mathsf{aux}_j)$, $\mathsf{ct}'_j \leftarrow \mathsf{AIAE.Enc}(\mathsf{k}+\Delta_j, \mathsf{R}'_j, \mathsf{aux}_j)$. This suggests that the extracted string R_j's are pseudo-random, hence reusability of rrFE follows. The security reduction is non-trivial (see Sect. 5 for details).

(iii)' As for robustness, let $(\mathsf{P}^* = (\mathsf{s}^*, \mathsf{ct}^*), \delta^*)$ be the forged pair by a PPT adversary. If $\mathsf{aux}^* = \mathsf{s}^* = \mathsf{s}_j = \mathsf{aux}_j$, then the correctness of SS means $w^* = w_j$, hence the keys $\mathsf{k}^* = \mathsf{H_i}(w^*) = \mathsf{H_i}(w+\delta^*) = \mathsf{H_i}(w_j) = \mathsf{H_i}(w+\delta_j) = \mathsf{k}_j$, i.e., $\Delta^* = \Delta_j$. As a result, the special rule is satisfied. The secure sketch scheme SS is required to be linear so that there exists an efficient function g to compute $\widetilde{\delta^*} = g(\mathsf{s} = \mathsf{SS.Gen}(\mathsf{w}), \mathsf{s}^*, \delta^*)$ such that $\Delta^* := \mathsf{H_i}(\widetilde{\delta^*})$. Now that k is uniform and independent of s, key shift Δ_j, Δ^* are determined by $\delta_j, \delta^*, \mathsf{s}, \mathsf{s}^*$, and the special rule is satisfied. It is ready for us to implement the robustness security reduction of rrFE to INT-RKA security of AIAE. According to the weak INT-RKA security of AIAE, the probability that $\mathsf{AIAE.Dec}(\mathsf{k}+\Delta^*, \mathsf{ct}^*, \mathsf{aux}^* = \mathsf{s}^*) \neq \perp$ is negligible. Hence robustness of rrFE follows. The security reduction is non-trivial (see Sect. 5 for details).

Table 1. Comparison with known FE schemes. "Robustness?" asks whether the scheme achieves robustness. "Reusability?" asks whether the scheme achieves reusability. "Standard Assumption?" asks whether the scheme is based on standard assumptions. "Linear Errors?" asks whether the scheme tolerates linear fraction of errors. "Free of Pairing?" asks whether the scheme is free of pairing. "–" represents the scheme is an information theoretical one.

FE Schemes	Robustness?	Reusability?	Standard Assumption?	Linear Errors?	Free of Pairing?
DRS04[11]	✗	✗	–	✔	✔
FMR13[12]	✗	✗	✔	✗	✔
BDKOS05[7]	✔	✗	✗	✔	✔
DKRS06[10], KR08[16], CDFPW08[9]	✔	✗	–	✔	✔
CFPRS16[8]	✗	✔	✗	✗	✔
Boyen04[6] ABCCFGS18[1]	✗	✔	✗	✔	✔
ACEK17[2]	✗	✔	✔	✗	✔
WL18[24],WLH18[27]	✗	✔	✔	✔	✔
Wen-Liu18[25]	✔	✔	✔	✔	✗
Ours rrFE from ui-ks PRF	✔	✔	✔	✗	✔
Ours rrFE from AIAE	✔	✔	✔	✔	✔

1.3 Comparison

The instantiation of our first approach results in a rrFE based on the LWE assumption, and the instantiation of our second approach results in a rrFE based on the DDH assumption over non-pairing groups. In Table 1, we compare our instantiations with the related works.

The rrFE from the LWE assumption supports sub-linear fraction of errors, due to the parameter choice of ui-ks PRF, but it serves as the first post-quantum rrFE.

The rrFE from the DDH assumption supports linear fraction of errors, just like the Wen-Liu18 rrFE in [25]. The advantages of this rrFE over [25] are as follows.

- Our rrFE is free of pairing, since the underlying building block AIAE is built over non-pairing groups. However, Wen-Liu18 rrFE heavily relies on pairings since its building block LAF is built over symmetric pairing groups[1].
- The crs and the public helper string P of our rrFE are much shorter than that of Wen-Liu18 rrFE [25]. Recall that in the Wen-Liu18 rrFE [25], the reading w is directly input to the building block LAF as an authentication key. This makes the length of the public key (a part of crs), the length of the tag (a part of P) and the evaluation complexity of LAF closely related to the length of w ($|w|$). Our rrFE avoids this problem since our approach has a different frame structure.
- Our rrFE is more efficient than Wen-Liu18 [25]. Due to the complicated pairing operations and the number of pairings depending on $|w|$, Wen-Liu18 rrFE suffers from high computational complexities in the generation and reproduction algorithms. In contrast, our rrFE is much efficient since the underlying building block AIAE is built over a simple group.

[1] As noted by Galbraith [13], the symmetric pairings (i.e., Type 1 pairings) are now essentially dead and it would be better in future to design protocols that do not require Type 1 pairings.

Precise comparison between our DDH-based rrFE and the Wen-Liu18 rrFE is shown in Table 2.

Table 2. Efficiency comparison of our instantiation of rrFE from AIAE and the Wen-Liu18 rrFE in [25]. "Exp/Gen" and "Pairing/Gen" represent the numbers of exponentiations and pairings over groups per generation respectively. "Exp/Rep" and "Pairing/Rep" represent the numbers of exponentiations and pairings over groups per reproduction respectively. The Wen-Liu18 rrFE [25] relies on the DDH assumption over a group $\mathbb{G}$ and the DLIN assumption over a group $\hat{\mathbb{G}}$ of order p' which admits symmetric pairing $e : \hat{\mathbb{G}} \times \hat{\mathbb{G}} \to \mathbb{G}_T$. Define $\mathsf{des}(\hat{\mathbb{G}}, \mathbb{G}_T, e)$ the description of the symmetric pairing group. H_{pk} describes the chameleon hash. $|R_{ch}|$ is the bit-length of the randomness used in chameleon hash function. Meanwhile, $\mathsf{H_i}$, $\mathsf{H_{i_2}}$ describe universal hash functions, and $\mathsf{H_{i_1}}$ a collision-resistant hash function. Define $|\mathsf{des}(\hat{\mathbb{G}}, \mathbb{G}_T, e)|, |H_{pk}|, |\mathsf{H_i}|, |\mathsf{H_{i_1}}|$ and $|\mathsf{H_{i_2}}|$ the bit-lengths of the descriptions respectively. Define $\mathfrak{n} := |w|/\log p'$ (it is necessary that $\mathfrak{n} \geq 2$), where $|w|$ is the bit-length of the source reading w. Define $|a\mathbb{G}|$ as the bit-length of a elements in group $\mathbb{G}$. $|s|$ is the bit-length of secure sketch. $\bar{\mathbb{N}}$ is a prime of $4\lambda + 1$, and $\mathbb{QR}_{\bar{\mathbb{N}}}$ is a subgroup of quadratic residues of $\mathbb{Z}^*_{\bar{\mathbb{N}}}$.

rrFE Schemes	Bit-length of crs	Bit-length of P	Exp/Gen	Exp/Rep	Pairing/Gen	Pairing/Rep	Assumptions
Wen-Liu18 [25]	$\lvert\mathsf{des}(\hat{\mathbb{G}}, \mathbb{G}_T, e)\rvert + \lvert(\lambda+\mathfrak{n})\hat{\mathbb{G}}\rvert + \lvert\mathbb{G}\rvert + \lvert H_{pk}\rvert + \lvert\mathsf{H_i}\rvert = O(\lambda^2)$	$\lvert s\rvert + \lambda + \lvert R_{ch}\rvert + \lvert(1+\mathfrak{n}+\mathfrak{n}^2)\hat{\mathbb{G}}\rvert$	$\mathfrak{n}^2$ (over $\hat{\mathbb{G}}$) +2 (over $\mathbb{G}$)	$\mathfrak{n}^2$ (over $\hat{\mathbb{G}}$) +1 (over $\mathbb{G}$)	$4\mathfrak{n}^2$	$4\mathfrak{n}^2$	DDH (over $\mathbb{G}$)+DLIN (over sym. pairing $\hat{\mathbb{G}}$)
Our rrFE from AIAE	$20\lambda + 3 + \lvert\mathsf{H_i}\rvert + \lvert\mathsf{H_{i_1}}\rvert + \lvert\mathsf{H_{i_2}}\rvert = O(\lambda)$	$\lvert s\rvert + 10\lambda + 2$	4 (over $\mathbb{QR}_{\bar{\mathbb{N}}}$)	2 (over $\mathbb{QR}_{\bar{\mathbb{N}}}$)	0	0	DDH (over $\mathbb{QR}_{\bar{\mathbb{N}}}$)

2 Preliminaries

For an integer, denote $\{1, 2, \cdots, n\}$ by $[n]$. For a set $\mathcal{X}$, let $x \leftarrow_\$ \mathcal{X}$ denote randomly choosing an element x from set $\mathcal{X}$. For a random variable X, let $x \leftarrow X$ denote sampling x according to X. For two random variables X and Y, let $H_\infty(X)$ denote the min-entropy of X, the conditional min-entropy is defined by $H_\infty(X|Y) = -\log(\mathbb{E}_{y \leftarrow Y}\left[2^{-H_\infty(X|Y=y)}\right])$, and the statistical distance between X and Y is defined by $\mathsf{SD}(X, Y) = \frac{1}{2}\sum_{x \in \mathcal{X}} |\Pr[X = x] - \Pr[Y = x]|$. Let $X \overset{c}{\approx}_\epsilon Y$ denote that for any PPT adversary, its advantage to distinguish X and Y is no more than ϵ, and $X \approx_c Y$ denote that distributions X and Y are computationally indistinguishable.

A family of functions $F : \mathcal{K} \times \mathcal{X} \to \mathcal{Y}$ takes a key $k \in \mathcal{K}$ and input $x \in \mathcal{X}$, and returns an output $F(k, x) \in \mathcal{Y}$. Let $\mathsf{FF}(\mathcal{K}, \mathcal{X}, \mathcal{Y})$ be the set of all families of functions $F : \mathcal{K} \times \mathcal{X} \to \mathcal{Y}$. For sets $\mathcal{X}, \mathcal{Y}$, let $\mathsf{Fun}(\mathcal{X}, \mathcal{Y})$ be the set of all functions mapping $\mathcal{X}$ to $\mathcal{Y}$.

For a real number x, let $\lceil x \rfloor$ denote rounding x to the closest integer, and $\lfloor x \rfloor$ denote rounding x to the largest integer which does not exceed it. For a string x, let $|x|$ denote the bit length of x. For integers q, p, y where $q \geq p \geq 2$, we define the function $\lfloor y \rfloor_p : \mathbb{Z}_q \to \mathbb{Z}_p$ as $\lfloor y \rfloor_p = i$, where $i \cdot \lfloor q/p \rfloor$ is the largest multiple of $\lfloor q/p \rfloor$ that does not larger than y. For a vector $\mathbf{y} \in \mathbb{Z}_q^m$, we define $\lfloor \mathbf{y} \rfloor_p$ as the vector in $\mathbb{Z}_p^m$ obtained by rounding each coordinate of the vector individually.

For a primitive XX and a security notion YY, by $\mathsf{Exp}^{\mathrm{YY}}_{\mathcal{A},\mathrm{XX}}(\lambda) \Rightarrow 1$, we mean that the security experiment outputs 1 after interacting with an adversary $\mathcal{A}$. By $\mathsf{Adv}^{\mathrm{YY}}_{\mathcal{A},\mathrm{XX}}(\lambda)$, we denote the advantage of a PPT adversary $\mathcal{A}$ and define $\mathsf{Adv}^{\mathrm{YY}}_{\mathrm{XX}}(\lambda) := \max_{\mathrm{PPT}\mathcal{A}} \mathsf{Adv}^{\mathrm{YY}}_{\mathcal{A},\mathrm{XX}}(\lambda)$.

2.1 Universal Hash Functions

Definition 1 (Universal Hash Functions). *A family of hash functions $\mathcal{H}_{\mathcal{I}} = \{\mathsf{H_i} : \mathcal{X} \to \mathcal{Y}\}_{\mathsf{i}\in\mathcal{I}}$ is universal, if for all distinct $x, x' \in \mathcal{X}$, it holds that*

$$\Pr[\mathsf{H_i} : \mathsf{H_i}(x) = \mathsf{H_i}(x')] \le 1/|\mathcal{Y}|,$$

where i is uniformly chosen from $\mathcal{I}$.

Lemma 1 (Generalized Leftover Hash Lemma). *Let $\mathcal{H}_{\mathcal{I}} = \{\mathsf{H_i} : \mathcal{X} \to \mathcal{Y}\}$ be a family of universal hash functions. Then for any two random variables X, Z,*

$$\mathsf{SD}((\mathsf{H}_I(X), I, Z), (U, I, Z)) \le \frac{1}{2}\sqrt{|\mathcal{Y}| \cdot 2^{-\tilde{H}_\infty(X|Z)}}$$

holds, where I and U are uniform distributions over $\mathcal{I}$ and $\mathcal{Y}$, respectively.

Definition 2 (Homomorphic Universal Hash Functions). *Let $\mathcal{H}_{\mathcal{I}} = \{\mathsf{H_i} : \mathcal{X} \to \mathcal{Y}\}_{\mathsf{i}\in\mathcal{I}}$ be a family of universal hash functions. $\mathcal{H}_{\mathcal{I}}$ is homomorphic if for all $i \in \mathcal{I}$,*

$$\mathsf{H_i}(x + x') = \mathsf{H_i}(x) + \mathsf{H_i}(x').$$

See the full version [26] for a concrete construction of homomorphic universal hash functions.

2.2 Secure Sketch

Definition 3 (Secure Sketch). *An $(\mathcal{M}, m, \tilde{m}, t)$-secure sketch* (SS) *consists of a pair of PPT algorithms* (SS.Gen, SS.Rec) *with the following specifications:*

- SS.Gen(w) *on input* $\mathsf{w} \in \mathcal{M}$ *outputs a sketch* $\mathsf{s} \in \mathcal{S}$.
- SS.Rec(w′, s) *on input* $\mathsf{w}' \in \mathcal{M}$ *and a sketch* s *outputs* $\widetilde{\mathsf{w}}$.

It also satisfies the following properties:

Correctness. *If* $\mathsf{dis}(\mathsf{w}, \mathsf{w}') \le t$, *then* $\mathsf{w} = \mathsf{SS.Rec}(\mathsf{w}', \mathsf{SS.Gen}(\mathsf{w}))$.
Privacy. *For any distribution W over $\mathcal{M}$, if $H_\infty(W) \ge m$, then* $\widetilde{H}_\infty(W|\mathsf{SS.Gen}(W)) \ge \tilde{m}$.

Definition 4 (Secure Sketch Linearity Property) [9]. *Let* SS = (SS.Gen, SS.Rec) *be an $(\mathcal{M}, m, \tilde{m}, t)$-secure sketch. For any $\mathsf{w} \in \mathcal{M}$, $\tilde{\mathsf{s}} \in \mathcal{S}$ and δ such that $\mathsf{dis}(\delta) \le t$, let $\mathsf{s} := \mathsf{SS.Gen}(\mathsf{w})$, $\widetilde{\mathsf{w}} := \mathsf{SS.Rec}(\mathsf{w} + \delta, \tilde{\mathsf{s}})$ and $\widetilde{\delta} := \widetilde{\mathsf{w}} - \mathsf{w}$, then* SS *is linear if there exists a deterministic and efficiently computable function g such that $\widetilde{\delta} = g(\delta, \mathsf{s}, \tilde{\mathsf{s}})$.*

Definition 5 (Homomorphic Secure Sketch). *Let* $\mathsf{SS} = (\mathsf{SS.Gen}, \mathsf{SS.Rec})$ *be an* $(\mathcal{M}, m, \tilde{m}, t)$*-secure sketch.* SS *is homomorphic if*

$$\mathsf{SS.Gen}(\mathsf{w} + \mathsf{w}') = \mathsf{SS.Gen}(\mathsf{w}) + \mathsf{SS.Gen}(\mathsf{w}').$$

In this paper, we will employ a homomorphic secure sketch with linearity property. An instantiation of such SS is the syndrome-based secure sketch [9]. See the full version [26] for the concrete construction of the syndrome-based SS.

2.3 Pseudorandom Functions

Informally, a pseudorandom function (PRF) is an efficiently computable function $F : \mathcal{K} \times \mathcal{X} \rightarrow \mathcal{Y}$ such that no PPT adversary can distinguish the function from a truly random function given only black-box access. We review the definition of pseudorandom functions (PRF) [18] which considers the PRF with public parameters pp.

Definition 6 (PRF). *An efficiently computable function* $F_{\mathsf{pp}} : \mathcal{K} \times \mathcal{X} \rightarrow \mathcal{Y}$ *is a secure* PRF *if for any PPT adversary* $\mathcal{A}$, $\mathsf{Adv}^{\mathsf{prf}}_{\mathcal{A},F_{\mathsf{pp}}}(\lambda) := |\Pr[\mathsf{Exp}^{\mathsf{prf}}_{\mathcal{A},F_{\mathsf{pp}}}(\lambda) \Rightarrow 1] - 1/2|$ *is negligible in* λ*, where the game* $\mathsf{Exp}^{\mathsf{prf}}_{\mathcal{A},F_{\mathsf{pp}}}(\lambda)$ *is defined in Fig. 4. Here* $\mathsf{pp} \leftarrow \mathsf{PRF.Setup}(1^\lambda)$*,* $\mathcal{K}$ *is the key space,* $\mathcal{X}$ *is the domain, and* $\mathcal{Y}$ *is the range of the function.*

Procedure INITIALIZE:	Procedure QUE(x):
$\mathsf{pp} \leftarrow \mathsf{PRF.Setup}(1^\lambda)$, $b \leftarrow_{\$} \{0,1\}$.	Return $f(x)$.
If $b = 0$, $f(\cdot) \leftarrow_{\$} \mathsf{Fun}(\mathcal{X}, \mathcal{Y})$.	
Else, $\mathsf{k} \leftarrow_{\$} \mathcal{K}$, set $f(\cdot) := F_{\mathsf{pp}}(k, \cdot)$.	Procedure FINALIZE(b^*)
Return pp.	If $b^* = b$, Return 1.
	Else, Return 0.

Fig. 4. The experiment for defining the game $\mathsf{Exp}^{\mathsf{prf}}_{\mathcal{A},F_{\mathsf{pp}}}(\lambda)$ for PRF, where $\mathsf{Fun}(\mathcal{X}, \mathcal{Y})$ is the set of all functions mapping $\mathcal{X}$ to $\mathcal{Y}$.

Definition 7 (Φ-RKA-PRF). PRF $F_{\mathsf{pp}} : \mathcal{K} \times \mathcal{X} \rightarrow \mathcal{Y}$ *is* Φ*-RKA-secure w.r.t. a class of related-key deriving functions* $\Phi = \{\phi : \mathcal{K} \rightarrow \mathcal{K}\}$*, if for any PPT adversary* $\mathcal{A}$, $\mathsf{Adv}^{\mathsf{rka\text{-}prf}}_{\mathcal{A},F_{\mathsf{pp}}}(\lambda) = |\Pr[\mathsf{Exp}^{\mathsf{rka\text{-}prf}}_{\mathcal{A},F_{\mathsf{pp}}}(\lambda) \Rightarrow 1] - 1/2|$ *is negligible in* λ*, where the game* $\mathsf{Exp}^{\mathsf{rka\text{-}prf}}_{\mathcal{A},F_{\mathsf{pp}}}(\lambda)$ *is defined in Fig. 5.*

Remark 1. We will make use the fact that $\mathsf{Adv}^{\mathsf{rka\text{-}prf}}_{\mathcal{A},F_{\mathsf{pp}}}(\lambda) = |\Pr[\mathsf{Exp}^{\mathsf{rka\text{-}prf}}_{\mathcal{A},F_{\mathsf{pp}}}(\lambda) \Rightarrow 1] - 1/2| = \frac{1}{2}|\Pr[\mathcal{A} \Rightarrow 1 \mid f(\cdot,\cdot) = F_{\mathsf{pp}}(\mathsf{k}, \cdot)] - \Pr[\mathcal{A} \Rightarrow 1 \mid f(\cdot,\cdot) \text{ is random}]|$, where $\mathcal{A} \Rightarrow 1$ means that the adversary $\mathcal{A}$ returns 1 to FINALIZE.

Procedure INITIALIZE:	**Procedure** RKQUE($\phi \in \Phi, x$):
pp ← PRF.Setup(1^λ), $b \leftarrow_\$ \{0,1\}$.	Return $f(\phi(\mathsf{k}), x)$.
$\mathsf{k} \leftarrow_\$ \mathcal{K}$.	
If $b = 0$, $f(\cdot,\cdot) \leftarrow_\$ \mathsf{FF}(\mathcal{K}, \mathcal{X}, \mathcal{Y})$	**Procedure** FINALIZE(b^*)
Else, set $f(\cdot,\cdot) := F_{\mathsf{pp}}(\cdot,\cdot)$,	If $b^* = b$, Return 1.
Return pp.	Else, Return 0.

Fig. 5. The experiment for defining the Φ-RKA game $\mathsf{Exp}^{\mathsf{rka\text{-}prf}}_{\mathcal{A},F_{\mathsf{pp}}}$ for PRF, where $\mathsf{FF}(\mathcal{K}, \mathcal{X}, \mathcal{Y})$ is the set of all functions $f : \mathcal{K} \times \mathcal{X} \to \mathcal{Y}$.

Definition 8 (Unique-Input RKA Security). *An adversary is a unique-input adversary if the input queries $(\phi_1, x_1), \cdots, (\phi_Q, x_Q)$ are such that $x_i \neq x_j$ in the game $\mathsf{Exp}^{\mathsf{rka\text{-}prf}}_{\mathcal{A},F}(\lambda)$. A PRF F_{pp} is* unique-input Φ-RKA-*secure if it is* Φ-RKA-*secure against unique-input adversaries.*

Define the shift function family $\Phi_\Delta := \{\phi_a : \mathcal{K} \to \mathcal{K} \mid \phi_a(\mathsf{k}) = \mathsf{k} + a\}_{a \in \mathcal{K}}$. The unique-input Φ_Δ-RKA-security of PRF is also named *unique-input key-shift* (ui-ks) security. In this paper, ui-ks security of PRF is sufficient for our construction in Sect. 4.

2.4 Auxiliary-Input Authenticated Encryption

We recall the definition of auxiliary-input authenticated encryption scheme [14].

Definition 9 (AIAE). *An auxiliary-input authenticated encryption scheme consists of three PPT algorithms:*

- AIAE.Setup(1^λ) *on input the security parameter λ outputs the system parameter* pp, *which is an implicit input to* AIAE.Enc *and* AIAE.Dec. *The system parameter* pp *implicitly defines the key space $\mathcal{K}$, the message space $\mathcal{M}_{\mathsf{AIAE}}$ and the auxiliary input space $\mathcal{AUX}$.*
- AIAE.Enc(k, m, aux) *on input a key* $\mathsf{k} \in \mathcal{K}$, *a message* $\mathsf{m} \in \mathcal{M}_{\mathsf{AIAE}}$ *and an auxiliary input* $\mathsf{aux} \in \mathcal{AUX}$ *outputs a ciphertext* ct.
- AIAE.Dec(k, ct, aux) *on input a key* k, *a ciphertext* ct *and an auxiliary input* aux *outputs a message* m *or a rejection symbol* $\perp$.

Correctness. For all pp ← AIAE.Setup(1^λ), all $k \in \mathcal{K}$, all $\mathsf{m} \in \mathcal{M}_{\mathsf{AIAE}}$ and all ct ← AIAE.Enc(k, m, aux), it holds that m = AIAE.Dec(k, ct, aux).

Definition 10 (IND-Φ-RKA and Weak INT-Φ-RKA Securities for AIAE). *For a class of related-key deriving functions $\Phi = \{\phi : \mathcal{K} \to \mathcal{K}\}$, an* AIAE *scheme is* IND-Φ-RKA *and* weak INT-Φ-RKA *secure, if for any PPT adversary $\mathcal{A}$, both $\mathsf{Adv}^{\mathsf{ind\text{-}rka}}_{\mathcal{A},\mathsf{AIAE}}(\lambda) = |\Pr[\mathsf{Exp}^{\mathsf{ind\text{-}rka}}_{\mathcal{A},\mathsf{AIAE}}(\lambda) \Rightarrow 1] - 1/2|$ and $\mathsf{Adv}^{\mathsf{int\text{-}rka}}_{\mathcal{A},\mathsf{AIAE}}(\lambda) = \Pr[\mathsf{Exp}^{\mathsf{int\text{-}rka}}_{\mathcal{A},\mathsf{AIAE}}(\lambda) \Rightarrow 1]$ are negligible, where games $\mathsf{Exp}^{\mathsf{ind\text{-}rka}}_{\mathcal{A},\mathsf{AIAE}}(\lambda)$ and $\mathsf{Exp}^{\mathsf{int\text{-}rka}}_{\mathcal{A},\mathsf{AIAE}}(\lambda)$ are depicted in Fig. 6.*

If AIAE is IND-Φ_Δ-RKA and Weak INT-Φ_Δ-RKA secure, then it is also called a *Key-Shift secure* AIAE.

Procedure INITIALIZE: $\mathsf{pp} \leftarrow \mathsf{AIAE.Setup}(1^\lambda)$, $\mathsf{k} \leftarrow_\$ \mathcal{K}$. $b \leftarrow_\$ \{0,1\}$. Return pp. **Procedure** LR$(\mathsf{m}_0, \mathsf{m}_1, \mathsf{aux}, \phi \in \Phi)$: If $\lvert\mathsf{m}_0\rvert \neq \lvert\mathsf{m}_1\rvert$, Return $\perp$. $\mathsf{ct} \leftarrow \mathsf{AIAE.Enc}(\phi(\mathsf{k}), \mathsf{m}_b, \mathsf{aux})$. Return ct. **Procedure** FINALIZE(b^*) If $b = b^*$, Return 1. Else, Return 0.	**Procedure** INITIALIZE: $\mathsf{pp} \leftarrow \mathsf{AIAE.Setup}(1^\lambda)$, $\mathsf{k} \leftarrow_\$ \mathcal{K}$. $\mathcal{Q}_{enc} = \mathcal{Q}_{aux} = \emptyset$. Return pp. **Procedure** ENC$(\mathsf{m}, \mathsf{aux}, \phi \in \Phi)$: $\mathsf{ct} \leftarrow \mathsf{AIAE.Enc}(\phi(\mathsf{k}), \mathsf{m}, \mathsf{aux})$. $\mathcal{Q}_{enc} := \mathcal{Q}_{enc} \cup \{(\mathsf{aux}, \phi, \mathsf{ct})\}$. $\mathcal{Q}_{aux} := \mathcal{Q}_{aux} \cup \{(\mathsf{aux}, \phi)\}$. Return ct. **Procedure** FINALIZE$(\mathsf{aux}^*, \phi^* \in \Phi, \mathsf{ct}^*)$ If $(\mathsf{aux}^*, \phi^* \in \Phi, \mathsf{ct}^*) \in \mathcal{Q}_{enc}$, Return 0. If there exsits $(\mathsf{aux}, \phi) \in \mathcal{Q}_{aux}$, such that $\mathsf{aux}^* = \mathsf{aux}$ but $\phi^* \neq \phi$, Return 0. Return $(\mathsf{AIAE.Dec}(\phi^*(\mathsf{k}), \mathsf{ct}^*, \mathsf{aux}^*) \neq \perp)$.

Fig. 6. Left: The experiment for defining the IND-Φ-RKA game $\mathsf{Exp}^{\mathsf{int\text{-}rka}}_{\mathcal{A},\mathsf{AIAE}}$ for AIAE. Right: The experiment for defining the weak INT-Φ-RKA game $\mathsf{Exp}^{\mathsf{ind\text{-}rka}}_{\mathcal{A},\mathsf{AIAE}}$ for AIAE.

3 Robustly Reusable Fuzzy Extractor

Definition 11 (Fuzzy Extractor). *An* $(\mathcal{M}, m, \mathcal{R}, t, \varepsilon)$-fuzzy extractor (FE) *consists of three PPT algorithms* $\mathsf{FE} = (\mathsf{Init}, \mathsf{Gen}, \mathsf{Rep})$ *with the following properties:*

- $\mathsf{Init}(1^\lambda)$ *on input the security parameter* λ*, outputs the common reference string* crs.
- $\mathsf{Gen}(\mathsf{crs}, \mathsf{w})$ *on input the common reference string* crs *and an element* $w \in \mathcal{M}$*, outputs a public helper string* P *and an extracted string* $\mathsf{R} \in \mathcal{R}$.
- $\mathsf{Rep}(\mathsf{crs}, \mathsf{w}', \mathsf{P})$ *on input the common reference string* crs*, an element* $w' \in \mathcal{M}$ *and the public helper string* P*, outputs an extracted string* R *or* $\perp$.
- **Correctness.** *If* $\mathsf{dis}(\mathsf{w}, \mathsf{w}') \leq t$*, then for all* $\mathsf{crs} \leftarrow \mathsf{Init}(1^\lambda)$ *and* $(\mathsf{P}, \mathsf{R}) \leftarrow \mathsf{Gen}(\mathsf{crs}, \mathsf{w})$*, we have* $\mathsf{R} = \mathsf{Rep}(\mathsf{crs}, \mathsf{w}', \mathsf{P})$.
- **Security.** *For any distribution* W *over* $\mathcal{M}$ *such that* $H_\infty(W) \geq m$*,* R *is pseudorandom even conditioned on* P *and* crs*, where* $(\mathsf{P}, \mathsf{R}) \leftarrow \mathsf{Gen}(\mathsf{crs}, W)$ *and* $\mathsf{crs} \leftarrow \mathsf{Init}(1^\lambda)$.

Definition 12 (Robustly Reusable Fuzzy Extractor). *A* $\mathsf{FE} = (\mathsf{Init}, \mathsf{Gen}, \mathsf{Rep})$ *is called an* $(\mathcal{M}, m, \mathcal{R}, t, \varepsilon_1, \varepsilon_2)$-robustly reusable Fuzzy Extractor (rrFE)*, if for any PPT adversary* $\mathcal{A}$ *and any distribution* W *over* $\mathcal{M}$ *such that* $H_\infty(W) \geq m$*, it holds that* $\mathsf{Adv}^{\mathsf{reu}}_{\mathcal{A},\mathsf{FE}}(\lambda) = \lvert \Pr[\mathsf{Exp}^{\mathsf{reu}}_{\mathcal{A},\mathsf{FE}}(\lambda) \Rightarrow 1] - 1/2 \rvert \leq \varepsilon_1$ *and* $\mathsf{Adv}^{\mathsf{rob}}_{\mathcal{A},\mathsf{FE}}(\lambda) = \Pr[\mathsf{Exp}^{\mathsf{rob}}_{\mathcal{A},\mathsf{FE}}(\lambda) \Rightarrow 1] \leq \varepsilon_2$*, where games* $\mathsf{Exp}^{\mathsf{reu}}_{\mathcal{A},\mathsf{FE}}(\lambda)$ *and* $\mathsf{Exp}^{\mathsf{rob}}_{\mathcal{A},\mathsf{FE}}(\lambda)$ *are specified in Fig. 7.*

Procedure INITIALIZE: $\mathsf{crs} \leftarrow \mathsf{Init}(1^\lambda)$. $b \leftarrow_\$ \{0,1\}$. $\mathsf{w} \leftarrow W$. Return crs. **Procedure** CHALLENGE(δ): If $\mathsf{dis}(\delta) > t$, Return $\perp$. $(\mathsf{P},\mathsf{R}) \leftarrow \mathsf{Gen}(\mathsf{crs}, \mathsf{w}+\delta)$. If $b=1$, Return (P,R). Else, $\mathsf{U} \leftarrow_\$ \mathcal{R}$, Return (P,U). **Procedure** FINALIZE(b^*): If $b = b^*$, Return 1. Else, Return 0.	**Procedure** INITIALIZE: $\mathsf{crs} \leftarrow \mathsf{Init}(1^\lambda)$. $\mathsf{w} \leftarrow W$. $\mathcal{Q} = \emptyset$. Return crs. **Procedure** GENERATION(δ): If $\mathsf{dis}(\delta) > t$, Return $\perp$. $(\mathsf{P},\mathsf{R}) \leftarrow \mathsf{Gen}(\mathsf{crs}, \mathsf{w}+\delta)$. $\mathcal{Q} = \mathcal{Q} \cup \{\mathsf{P}\}$. Return (P,R). **Procedure** FINALIZE(P^*, δ^*): If $\mathsf{dis}(\delta^*) > t$, Return 0. If $\mathsf{P}^* \in \mathcal{Q}$, Return 0. Return $(\mathsf{Rep}(\mathsf{crs}, \mathsf{w}+\delta^*, \mathsf{P}^*) \neq \perp)$.

Fig. 7. Left: The experiment for defining the reusability game $\mathsf{Exp}^{\mathsf{reu}}_{\mathcal{A},\mathsf{FE}}(\lambda)$ for a FE. Right: The experiment for defining the robustness game $\mathsf{Exp}^{\mathsf{rob}}_{\mathcal{A},\mathsf{FE}}(\lambda)$ for a FE.

Remark 2. The definition of reusability is not identical to but implies the reusability defined in [25]. In [25], a fuzzy extractor is reusable if for all PPT adversary it is hard to distinguish $(\mathsf{U}_1, \mathsf{R}_2, \cdots, \mathsf{R}_Q, \mathsf{P}_1, \cdots, \mathsf{P}_Q)$ from $(\mathsf{R}_1, \mathsf{R}_2, \cdots, \mathsf{R}_Q, \mathsf{P}_1, \cdots, \mathsf{P}_Q)$, where $\mathsf{U}_1 \leftarrow_\$ \mathcal{R}$, $(\mathsf{P}_i, \mathsf{R}_i) \leftarrow \mathsf{Gen}(\mathsf{crs}, \mathsf{w} + \delta_i)$ and δ_i is chosen by the adversary. In our definition, a fuzzy extractor is reusable if for all PPT adversary, it is hard to distinguish the tuple $(\mathsf{U}_1, \mathsf{U}_2, \cdots, \mathsf{U}_Q, \mathsf{P}_1, \cdots, \mathsf{P}_Q)$ from $(\mathsf{R}_1, \mathsf{R}_2, \cdots, \mathsf{R}_Q, \mathsf{P}_1, \cdots, \mathsf{P}_Q)$. In fact, we can show if $(\mathsf{U}_1, \mathsf{U}_2, \cdots, \mathsf{U}_Q, \mathsf{P}_1, \cdots, \mathsf{P}_Q) \overset{c}{\approx}_\epsilon (\mathsf{R}_1, \mathsf{R}_2, \cdots, \mathsf{R}_Q, \mathsf{P}_1, \cdots, \mathsf{P}_Q)$, then $(\mathsf{U}_1, \mathsf{U}_2, \cdots, \mathsf{U}_Q, \mathsf{P}_1, \cdots, \mathsf{P}_Q) \overset{c}{\approx}_\epsilon (\mathsf{U}_1, \mathsf{R}_2, \cdots, \mathsf{R}_Q, \mathsf{P}_1, \cdots, \mathsf{P}_Q)$, by a hybrid argument we get that $(\mathsf{R}_1, \mathsf{R}_2, \cdots, \mathsf{R}_Q, \mathsf{P}_1, \cdots, \mathsf{P}_Q) \overset{c}{\approx}_{2\epsilon} (\mathsf{U}_1, \mathsf{R}_2, \cdots, \mathsf{R}_Q, \mathsf{P}_1, \cdots, \mathsf{P}_Q)$. This means that if a fuzzy extractor is ϵ-reusable in our definition, then it is 2ϵ-reusable in [25].

4 Construction of rrFE from Unique-Input RKA-PRF

We introduce a generic construction of robustly reusable fuzzy extractor (rrFE) from a unique-input key-shift (Φ_Δ-RKA) secure PRF, a Secure Sketch and a family of universal hash functions, as shown in Fig. 8.

$\mathsf{crs} \leftarrow \mathsf{Init}(1^\lambda)$: $\mathsf{i} \leftarrow_\$ \mathcal{I}$ (i.e., $\mathsf{H_i} \leftarrow_\$ \mathcal{H_I}$). $\mathsf{pp} \leftarrow \mathsf{PRF.Setup}(1^\lambda)$. $\mathsf{crs} = (\mathsf{H_i}, \mathsf{pp})$. Return crs.	$(\mathsf{P},\mathsf{R}) \leftarrow \mathsf{Gen}(\mathsf{crs}, \mathsf{w})$: $\mathsf{s} \leftarrow \mathsf{SS.Gen}(\mathsf{w})$. $\mathsf{k} \leftarrow \mathsf{H_i}(\mathsf{w})$. $\mathsf{t} \leftarrow_\$ \mathcal{T}$. $(\mathsf{r}, \mathsf{v}) \leftarrow F_{\mathsf{pp}}(\mathsf{k}, (\mathsf{s}, \mathsf{t}))$. $\mathsf{P} := (\mathsf{s}, \mathsf{t}, \mathsf{v})$, $\mathsf{R} := \mathsf{r}$.	$\mathsf{R} \leftarrow \mathsf{Rep}(\mathsf{crs}, \mathsf{P}, \mathsf{w}')$: Parse $\mathsf{P} = (\mathsf{s}, \mathsf{t}, \mathsf{v})$. $\tilde{\mathsf{w}} \leftarrow \mathsf{SS.Rec}(\mathsf{w}', \mathsf{s})$. $\tilde{\mathsf{k}} \leftarrow \mathsf{H_i}(\tilde{\mathsf{w}})$. $(\tilde{\mathsf{r}}, \tilde{\mathsf{v}}) \leftarrow F_{\mathsf{pp}}(\tilde{\mathsf{k}}, (\mathsf{s}, \mathsf{t}))$. If $\tilde{\mathsf{v}} = \mathsf{v}$, Return $\mathsf{R} := \tilde{\mathsf{r}}$. Else, Return $\perp$.

Fig. 8. Construction of $\mathsf{rrFE_{PRF}}$ from unique-input key-shift secure PRF.

Theorem 1. *The fuzzy extractor* $\mathsf{rrFE}_{\mathsf{PRF}}$ *in Fig. 8 is an* $(\mathcal{M}, m, \mathcal{R}, t, \varepsilon_1, \varepsilon_2)$*-robustly reusable fuzzy extractor with* $\varepsilon_1 = 2\mathsf{Adv}^{\mathsf{rka}}_{\mathsf{PRF}}(\lambda) + 2^{-\omega(\log\lambda)}$ *and* $\varepsilon_2 = 2\mathsf{Adv}^{\mathsf{rka}}_{\mathsf{PRF}}(\lambda) + 2^{-\omega(\log\lambda)}$*, if the underlying building blocks satisfies the following properties.*

- $\mathsf{SS} = (\mathsf{SS.Gen}, \mathsf{SS.Rec})$ *is a homomorphic* $(\mathcal{M}, m, \tilde{m}, 2t)$*-secure sketch with linearity property.*
- $\mathcal{H}_{\mathcal{I}} = \{\mathsf{H_i} : \mathcal{M} \to \mathcal{K}\}_{i\in\mathcal{I}}$ *is a family of homomorphic universal hash functions such that* $\tilde{m} - \log|\mathcal{K}| \geq \omega(\log\lambda)$.
- $F_{\mathsf{pp}}(\mathcal{K}, \mathcal{X}, \mathcal{Y})$ *is a unique-input key-shift secure PRF such that* $\mathcal{X} = \mathcal{U} \times \mathcal{T}$, $\mathcal{S} \subseteq \mathcal{U}$, $\mathcal{Y} = \mathcal{R} \times \mathcal{V}$, $\log|\mathcal{T}| \geq \omega(\log\lambda)$ *and* $\log|\mathcal{V}| \geq \omega(\log\lambda)$.

The correctness of $\mathsf{rrFE}_{\mathsf{PRF}}$ follows from the correctness of the underlying SS, since w can be correctly recovered from the public helper string P if $\mathsf{dis}(\mathsf{w}, \mathsf{w}') \leq t$. The reusability and robustness are shown in Lemmas 2 and 3 respectively.

Lemma 2. *The construction of* rrFE *in Fig. 8 is* ε_1*-reusable with*

$$\varepsilon_1 = 2\mathsf{Adv}^{\mathsf{rka\text{-}prf}}_{\mathsf{PRF}}(\lambda) + 2^{-\omega(\log\lambda)}.$$

Proof. We will prove the reusability of rrFE via a series of games, as shown in Fig. 9. Game $\mathbf{G}_j$ denotes a variant of reusability game played between a PPT adversary $\mathcal{A}$ and a challenger who provides Procedures INITIALIZE and CHALLENGE for $\mathcal{A}$. Denote by $\Pr[\mathbf{G}_j]$ the probability that $\mathcal{A}$ wins, i.e., FINALIZE returns 1, in game $\mathbf{G}_j$. Obviously, $\mathcal{A}$ wins iff $b = b^*$.

Game $\mathbf{G}_0$. $\mathbf{G}_0$ is just the reusability game. More precisely, in Procedures INITIALIZE, the challenger chooses $b \leftarrow_{\$} \{0,1\}$, samples $\mathsf{w} \leftarrow W$, and generates $\mathsf{crs} = (\mathsf{H_i}, \mathsf{pp})$. Upon receiving the j-th CHALLENGE query δ_j from $\mathcal{A}$, the challenger answers $\mathcal{A}$'s CHALLENGE query as follows:

Procedure INITIALIZE: // Games $\mathbf{G}_0$, $\mathbf{G}_1$, $\boxed{\mathbf{G}_2, \mathbf{G}_3}$	**Procedure** CHALLENGE(δ_j): // Games $\mathbf{G}_0$, $\mathbf{G}_1$, $\boxed{\mathbf{G}_2, \mathbf{G}_3}$
$\mathsf{i} \leftarrow_{\$} \mathcal{I}$ (i.e., $\mathsf{H_i} \leftarrow_{\$} \mathcal{H}_{\mathcal{I}}$).	If $\mathsf{dis}(\delta_j) > t$, Return $\perp$.
$\mathsf{pp} \leftarrow \mathsf{PRF.Setup}(1^\lambda)$.	$\mathsf{s}_j \leftarrow \mathsf{SS.Gen}(\mathsf{w} + \delta_j)$.
$\mathsf{crs} = (\mathsf{H_i}, \mathsf{pp})$.	$\mathsf{s}_j = \mathsf{SS.Gen}(\mathsf{w}) + \mathsf{SS.Gen}(\delta_j)$.
$b \leftarrow_{\$} \{0,1\}$.	$\mathsf{k}_j \leftarrow \mathsf{H_i}(\mathsf{w} + \delta_j)$.
$\mathsf{w} \leftarrow W$.	$\mathsf{k}_j = \mathsf{H_i}(\mathsf{w}) + \mathsf{H_i}(\delta_j)$.
$\boxed{\mathsf{k} \leftarrow_{\$} \mathcal{K}.}$	$\boxed{\mathsf{k}_j = \mathsf{k} + \mathsf{H_i}(\delta_j).}$
Return crs.	$\mathsf{t}_j \leftarrow_{\$} \mathcal{T}$.
	$(\mathsf{r}_j, \mathsf{v}_j) \leftarrow F_{\mathsf{pp}}(\mathsf{k}_j, (\mathsf{s}_j, \mathsf{t}_j))$.
Procedure FINALIZE(b^*): // Games $\mathbf{G}_0$-$\mathbf{G}_3$	$(\mathsf{r}_j, \mathsf{v}_j) \leftarrow_{\$} \mathcal{R} \times \mathcal{V}$.
If $b = b^*$, Return 1.	$\mathsf{P}_j := (\mathsf{s}_j, \mathsf{t}_j, \mathsf{v}_j)$, $\mathsf{R}_j := \mathsf{r}_j$.
Else, Return 0.	If $b = 1$, Return $(\mathsf{P}_j, \mathsf{R}_j)$.
	Else, $\mathsf{U}_j \leftarrow_{\$} \mathcal{R}$, Return $(\mathsf{P}_j, \mathsf{U}_j)$.

Fig. 9. Game $\mathbf{G}_0$–$\mathbf{G}_3$ for the security proof of Lemma 2.

1. If $\mathsf{dis}(\delta_j) > t$, then return $\perp$.
2. Compute sketch $\mathsf{s}_j = \mathsf{SS.Gen}(\mathsf{w} + \delta_j)$ and hash value $\mathsf{k}_j = \mathsf{H_i}(\mathsf{w} + \delta_j)$.
3. Choose $\mathsf{t}_j \leftarrow_\$ \mathcal{T}$, compute $(\mathsf{r}_j, \mathsf{v}_j) \leftarrow F_{\mathsf{pp}}(\mathsf{k}_j, (\mathsf{s}_j, \mathsf{t}_j))$ and set $\mathsf{P}_j := (\mathsf{s}_j, \mathsf{t}_j, \mathsf{v}_j)$, $\mathsf{R}_j := \mathsf{r}_j$.
4. If $b = 1$, return $(\mathsf{P}_j, \mathsf{R}_j)$, else choose $\mathsf{U}_j \leftarrow_\$ \mathcal{R}$ and return $(\mathsf{P}_j, \mathsf{U}_j)$.

Clearly,

$$\mathsf{Adv}^{\mathsf{reu}}_{\mathcal{A},\mathsf{FE}}(\lambda) = |\Pr[\mathbf{G}_0] - 1/2|. \tag{1}$$

Game $\mathbf{G}_1$: $\mathbf{G}_1$ is identical to $\mathbf{G}_0$, except for some conceptual changes of the generations of secure sketch s_j and hash value k_j. More precisely, step 2 is changed to step 2′.

2′. Compute $\mathsf{s}_j = \mathsf{SS.Gen}(\mathsf{w}) + \mathsf{SS.Gen}(\delta_j)$ and $\mathsf{k}_j = \mathsf{H_i}(\mathsf{w}) + \mathsf{H_i}(\delta_j)$.

By the homomorphic properties of secure sketch and hash function, we have that

$$\Pr[\mathbf{G}_0] = \Pr[\mathbf{G}_1]. \tag{2}$$

Game $\mathbf{G}_2$. $\mathbf{G}_2$ is the same as $\mathbf{G}_1$, except for two changes.

The first change is to add $\mathsf{k} \leftarrow_\$ \mathcal{K}$ in Initialize of $\mathbf{G}_2$. The second change is the generation of k_j in Challenge. In $\mathbf{G}_2$, instead of computing $\mathsf{k}_j := \mathsf{H_i}(\mathsf{w}) + \mathsf{H_i}(\delta_j)$, the challenger computes $\mathsf{k}_j = \mathsf{k} + \mathsf{H_i}(\delta_j)$. More precisely, step 2′ is changed to step 2″.

2″ Compute $\mathsf{s}_j = \mathsf{SS.Gen}(\mathsf{w}) + \mathsf{SS.Gen}(\delta_j)$ and $\mathsf{k}_j = \mathsf{k} + \mathsf{H_i}(\delta_j)$.

Claim 1 $|\Pr[\mathbf{G}_1] - \Pr[\mathbf{G}_2]| \leq 2^{-\omega(\log\lambda)}$.

Proof. Recall that $H_\infty(W) \geq m$. Then by the privacy of secure sketch, it follows that $H_\infty(W|\mathsf{SS.Gen}(W)) \geq \tilde{m}$. According to the Leftover Hash Lemma (see Lemma 1), we have

$$\mathsf{SD}((\mathsf{H_i}(\mathsf{w}), \mathsf{i}, \mathsf{s} = \mathsf{SS.Gen}(\mathsf{w}), (U, \mathsf{i}, \mathsf{s} = \mathsf{SS.Gen}(\mathsf{w}))) \leq \frac{1}{2}\sqrt{|\mathcal{K}| \cdot 2^{-\tilde{m}}}, \tag{3}$$

where $U \leftarrow_\$ \mathcal{K}$. This implies that for all powerful (not necessarily PPT) algorithm $\mathcal{B}$, it is impossible for $\mathcal{B}$ to tell $(\mathsf{H_i}(\mathsf{w}), \mathsf{i}, \mathsf{s} = \mathsf{SS.Gen}(\mathsf{w}))$ from $(U, \mathsf{i}, \mathsf{s} = \mathsf{SS.Gen}(\mathsf{w})))$ with probability more than $\frac{1}{2}\sqrt{|\mathcal{K}| \cdot 2^{-\tilde{m}}}$. In formula,

$$|\Pr[\mathcal{B}(U, \mathsf{i}, \mathsf{s} = \mathsf{SS.Gen}(\mathsf{w})) \Rightarrow 1] - \Pr[\mathcal{B}(\mathsf{H_i}(\mathsf{w}), \mathsf{i}, \mathsf{s} = \mathsf{SS.Gen}(\mathsf{w})) \Rightarrow 1]| \leq \frac{1}{2}\sqrt{|\mathcal{K}| \cdot 2^{-\tilde{m}}}. \tag{4}$$

Now we show that

$$|\Pr[\mathbf{G}_1] - \Pr[\mathbf{G}_2]| \leq \frac{1}{2}\sqrt{|\mathcal{K}| \cdot 2^{-\tilde{m}}} \leq 2^{-\omega(\log\lambda)}. \tag{5}$$

We prove (5) by constructing a powerful algorithm $\mathcal{B}$ who aims to distinguish $(\mathsf{H_i}(\mathsf{w}), \mathsf{i}, \mathsf{s} = \mathsf{SS.Gen}(\mathsf{w}))$ from $(U, \mathsf{i}, \mathsf{s} = \mathsf{SS.Gen}(\mathsf{w}))$. Given $(X, \mathsf{i}, \mathsf{s} = \mathsf{SS.Gen}(\mathsf{w}))$, where X is either $\mathsf{H_i}(\mathsf{w})$ or a uniform U, $\mathcal{B}$ simulates $\mathbf{G}_1/\mathbf{G}_2$ for $\mathcal{A}$ as follows.

- To simulate Procedure INITIALIZE, $\mathcal{B}$ randomly chooses a bit $b \leftarrow_{\$} \{0,1\}$, then determines $\mathsf{crs} = (\mathsf{H_i}, \mathsf{pp})$ for $\mathcal{A}$ by determining $\mathsf{H_i}$ with i and invoking $\mathsf{pp} \leftarrow \mathsf{PRF.Setup}(1^\lambda)$.
- To answer $\mathcal{A}$'s query δ_j, $\mathcal{B}$ simulates Procedure CHALLENGE(δ_j) as follows.
  - If $\mathsf{dis}(\delta_j) > t$, return $\perp$.
  - $\mathsf{s}_j = \mathsf{s} + \mathsf{SS.Gen}(\delta_j)$.
  - $\mathsf{k}_j = X + \mathsf{H_i}(\delta_j)$.
  - $\mathsf{t}_j \leftarrow_{\$} \mathcal{T}$.
  - $(\mathsf{r}_j, \mathsf{v}_j) \leftarrow F_{\mathsf{pp}}(\mathsf{k}_j, (\mathsf{s}_j, \mathsf{t}_j))$.
  - $\mathsf{P}_j := (\mathsf{s}_j, \mathsf{t}_j, \mathsf{v}_j)$, $\mathsf{R}_j := \mathsf{r}_j$.
  - If $b = 1$, return $(\mathsf{P}_j, \mathsf{R}_j)$. Else, $\mathsf{U}_j \leftarrow_{\$} \mathcal{R}$, return $(\mathsf{P}_j, \mathsf{U}_j)$.
- Finally $\mathcal{A}$ outputs a guessing bit b^*. If $b = b^*$ (i.e., $\mathcal{A}$ wins), then $\mathcal{B}$ outputs 1, otherwise $\mathcal{B}$ outputs 0.

If $X = \mathsf{H_i}(\mathsf{w})$, $\mathcal{B}$ perfectly simulates $\mathbf{G}_1$ for $\mathcal{A}$; if $X = U$, $\mathcal{B}$ perfectly simulates $\mathbf{G}_2$ for $\mathcal{A}$. Consequently,

$$\begin{aligned} &|\Pr[\mathcal{B}(\mathsf{H_i}(\mathsf{w}), \mathsf{i}, \mathsf{s} = \mathsf{SS.Gen}(\mathsf{w})) \Rightarrow 1] - \Pr[\mathcal{B}((U, \mathsf{i}, \mathsf{s} = \mathsf{SS.Gen}(\mathsf{w})) \Rightarrow 1]| \\ &= |\Pr[\mathbf{G}_1] - \Pr[\mathbf{G}_2]|. \end{aligned} \quad (6)$$

Obviously, Eq. (5) follows from Eqs. (4), (6) and the fact of $\widetilde{m} - \log|\mathcal{K}| \geq \omega(\log\lambda)$. The claim follows. □

Game $\mathbf{G}_3$. $\mathbf{G}_3$ is the same as $\mathbf{G}_2$, except that $(\mathsf{r}_j, \mathsf{v}_j)$ is randomly chosen in $\mathbf{G}_3$. More precisely, step 3 is replaced with 3′ in Procedure CHALLENGE(δ_j) of $\mathbf{G}_3$.

3′ $\mathsf{t}_j \leftarrow_{\$} \mathcal{T}$, $(\mathsf{r}_j, \mathsf{v}_j) \leftarrow_{\$} \mathcal{R} \times \mathcal{V}$ and set $\mathsf{P}_j := (\mathsf{s}_j, \mathsf{t}_j, \mathsf{v}_j)$, $\mathsf{R}_j := \mathsf{r}_j$.

Claim 2 $|\Pr[\mathbf{G}_2] - \Pr[\mathbf{G}_3]| \leq 2\mathsf{Adv}^{\mathsf{rka\text{-}prf}}_{\mathsf{PRF}}(\lambda) + 2^{-\omega(\log\lambda)}$.

Proof. Suppose that $\mathcal{A}$ makes Q challenge queries. Let Bad denote the event that there exist $i, j \in [Q]$ such that $\mathsf{t}_i = \mathsf{t}_j$. Note that t_j is randomly chosen from $\mathcal{T}$, so $\Pr[\mathsf{Bad}] = Q(Q-1)/(2|\mathcal{T}|)$. Let $\overline{\mathsf{Bad}}$ denote the event that Bad does not happen. Then

$$\Pr[\mathbf{G}_2] = \Pr[\mathbf{G}_2 \wedge \mathsf{Bad}] + \Pr[\mathbf{G}_2 \wedge \overline{\mathsf{Bad}}],$$

$$\Pr[\mathbf{G}_3] = \Pr[\mathbf{G}_3 \wedge \mathsf{Bad}] + \Pr[\mathbf{G}_3 \wedge \overline{\mathsf{Bad}}],$$

$$\begin{aligned} |\Pr[\mathbf{G}_3] - \Pr[\mathbf{G}_2]| &\leq |\Pr[\mathbf{G}_3 \wedge \mathsf{Bad}] - \Pr[\mathbf{G}_3 \wedge \mathsf{Bad}]| + |\Pr[\mathbf{G}_2 \wedge \overline{\mathsf{Bad}}] - \Pr[\mathbf{G}_3 \wedge \overline{\mathsf{Bad}}]| \\ &\leq \Pr[\mathsf{Bad}] + |\Pr[\mathbf{G}_2 \wedge \overline{\mathsf{Bad}}] - \Pr[\mathbf{G}_3 \wedge \overline{\mathsf{Bad}}]| \\ &= \frac{Q(Q-1)}{2|\mathcal{T}|} + |\Pr[\mathbf{G}_2 \wedge \overline{\mathsf{Bad}}] - \Pr[\mathbf{G}_3 \wedge \overline{\mathsf{Bad}}]|. \end{aligned} \quad (7)$$

Next we show that

$$|\Pr[\mathbf{G}_2 \wedge \overline{\mathsf{Bad}}] - \Pr[\mathbf{G}_3 \wedge \overline{\mathsf{Bad}}]| \leq 2\mathsf{Adv}^{\mathsf{rka\text{-}prf}}_{\mathsf{PRF}}(\lambda). \quad (8)$$

by constructing a PPT algorithm $\mathcal{A}'$ against the unique-input key-shift security of PRF F_{pp}. Recall that in the unique-input key-shift security game $\mathsf{Exp}^{\mathsf{rka\text{-}prf}}_{\mathcal{A},F_{\mathsf{pp}}}$, $\mathcal{A}'$ obtains the public parameter pp which is generated via $\mathsf{pp} \leftarrow \mathsf{PRF.Setup}(1^\lambda)$ by Procedure INITIALIZE. Meanwhile, $\mathcal{A}'$ is able to query (ϕ_Δ, x) and Procedure RKQUE will reply $\mathcal{A}'$ with the function value of $f(\mathsf{k}+\Delta, x)$. The aim of $\mathcal{A}'$ is to tell whether $f(\mathsf{k},\cdot)$ is $F_{\mathsf{pp}}(\mathsf{k},\cdot)$ or a random function. Now $\mathcal{A}'$ simulates $\mathbf{G}_2/\mathbf{G}_3$ for $\mathcal{A}$ as follows.

- To simulate Procedure INITIALIZE of $\mathbf{G}_2/\mathbf{G}_3$, $\mathcal{A}'$ samples $\mathsf{w} \leftarrow W$, chooses $b \leftarrow_\$ \{0,1\}$ and an index $\mathsf{i} \leftarrow_\$ \mathcal{I}$ (hence $\mathsf{H_i}$), then sends $\mathsf{crs} = (\mathsf{H_i}, \mathsf{pp})$ to $\mathcal{A}$.
- $\mathcal{A}'$ initializes a set $\mathcal{Q}_t = \emptyset$. To answer $\mathcal{A}$'s query δ_j, $\mathcal{A}'$ simulates Procedure CHALLENGE(δ_j) as follows.
  - If $\mathsf{dis}(\delta_j) > t$, return $\perp$.
  - Compute $\mathsf{s}_j := \mathsf{SS.Gen}(\mathsf{w}) + \mathsf{SS.Gen}(\delta_j)$ and sample $\mathsf{t}_j \leftarrow_\$ \mathcal{T}$. If $\mathsf{t}_j \in \mathcal{Q}_t$, i.e., Bad happens, then $\mathcal{A}'$ aborts the game. Otherwise, $\mathcal{Q}_t := \mathcal{Q}_t \cup \{\mathsf{t}_j\}$.
  - $\mathcal{A}'$ queries $(\phi_{\mathsf{H_i}(\delta_j)}, (\mathsf{s}_j, \mathsf{t}_j))$ to its Procedure RKQUE, then RKQUE returns $(\mathsf{r}_j, \mathsf{v}_j)$ to $\mathcal{A}'$.
  - $\mathcal{A}'$ defines $\mathsf{P}_j := (\mathsf{s}_j, \mathsf{t}_j, \mathsf{v}_j)$ and $\mathsf{R}_j := \mathsf{r}_j$.
  - If $b = 1$, return $(\mathsf{P}_j, \mathsf{R}_j)$. Else, $\mathsf{U}_j \leftarrow_\$ \mathcal{R}$, return $(\mathsf{P}_j, \mathsf{U}_j)$.
- Finally $\mathcal{A}$ outputs a guessing bit b^* for FINALIZE. If $b = b^*$ (i.e., $\mathcal{A}$ wins), then $\mathcal{A}'$ outputs 1, otherwise $\mathcal{A}'$ outputs 0.

If Bad does not happen, then $\mathcal{A}'$ is a unique-input adversary. There are two cases.

- If $f(\mathsf{k},\cdot) = F_{\mathsf{pp}}(\mathsf{k},\cdot)$, then RKQUE computes $(\mathsf{r}_j, \mathsf{v}_j)$ via $(\mathsf{r}_j, \mathsf{v}_j) \leftarrow F_{\mathsf{pp}}(\mathsf{k} + \mathsf{H_i}(\delta_j), (\mathsf{s}_j, \mathsf{t}_j))$. In this case, $\mathcal{A}'$ can perfectly simulate $\mathbf{G}_2 \wedge \overline{\mathsf{Bad}}$ for $\mathcal{A}$.
- If $f(\mathsf{k},\cdot)$ is a random function and RKQUE takes the value of the random function $f(\mathsf{k}+\mathsf{H_i}(\delta_j), (\mathsf{s}_j, \mathsf{t}_j))$ as $(\mathsf{r}_j, \mathsf{v}_j)$. In this case, $\mathcal{A}'$ can perfectly simulates $\mathbf{G}_3 \wedge \overline{\mathsf{Bad}}$ for $\mathcal{A}$.

Now we consider the advantage of $\mathcal{A}'$

$$\mathsf{Adv}^{\mathsf{rka\text{-}prf}}_{\mathcal{A}',\mathsf{PRF}}(\lambda) = |\Pr[\mathsf{Exp}^{\mathsf{rka\text{-}prf}}_{\mathcal{A}',F_{\mathsf{pp}}}(\lambda) \Rightarrow 1] - \frac{1}{2}|$$

$$= \frac{1}{2}|\Pr[\mathcal{A}' \Rightarrow 1 \mid f(\cdot,\cdot) = F_{\mathsf{pp}}(\mathsf{k},\cdot)] - \Pr[\mathcal{A}' \Rightarrow 1 \mid f(\cdot,\cdot) \text{ is random}]|$$

$$= \frac{1}{2}|\Pr[\mathcal{A} \text{ wins} \wedge \overline{\mathsf{Bad}} \mid f(\cdot,\cdot) = F_{\mathsf{pp}}(\mathsf{k},\cdot)] - \Pr[\mathcal{A} \text{ wins} \wedge \overline{\mathsf{Bad}} \mid f(\cdot,\cdot) \text{ is random}]|$$

$$= \frac{1}{2}|\Pr[\mathbf{G}_2 \wedge \overline{\mathsf{Bad}}] - \Pr[\mathbf{G}_3 \wedge \overline{\mathsf{Bad}}]|. \tag{9}$$

The claim follows from Eqs. (7), (8) and the fact that $\log(|\mathcal{T}|) \geq \omega(\log \lambda)$. □

Observe that in $\mathbf{G}_3$, $(\mathsf{P}_j, \mathsf{R}_j)$ is generated in the same way, no matter whether $b = 0$ or $b = 1$. Therefore,

$$\Pr[\mathbf{G}_3] = 1/2. \tag{10}$$

Taking Eqs. (1), (2), Claims 1, 2 and Eq. (10) together, Lemma 2 follows. ∎

Procedure INITIALIZE: // Games $\mathbf{G}_0$, $\mathbf{G}_1$, $\boxed{\mathbf{G}_2, \mathbf{G}_3}$ $\mathsf{i} \leftarrow_{\$} \mathcal{I}$ (i.e., $\mathsf{H_i} \leftarrow_{\$} \mathcal{H}_{\mathcal{I}}$). $\mathsf{pp} \leftarrow \mathsf{PRF.Setup}(1^\lambda)$. $\mathsf{crs} = (\mathsf{H_i}, \mathsf{pp})$. $\mathsf{w} \leftarrow \mathcal{W}$. $\mathcal{Q} := \emptyset$. $\boxed{\mathsf{k} \leftarrow_{\$} \mathcal{K}.}$ Return crs.	**Procedure** GENERATION(δ_j): // Games $\mathbf{G}_0$, $\mathbf{G}_1$, $\boxed{\mathbf{G}_2, \mathbf{G}_3}$ If $\mathsf{dis}(\delta_j) > t$, return $\perp$. $\mathsf{s}_j \leftarrow \mathsf{SS.Gen}(\mathsf{w} + \delta_j)$. $\mathsf{s}_j = \mathsf{SS.Gen}(\mathsf{w}) + \mathsf{SS.Gen}(\delta_j)$. $\mathsf{k}_j \leftarrow \mathsf{H_i}(\mathsf{w} + \delta_j)$. $\mathsf{k}_j = \mathsf{H_i}(\mathsf{w}) + \mathsf{H_i}(\delta_j)$. $\boxed{\mathsf{k}_j = \mathsf{k} + \mathsf{H_i}(\delta_j).}$ $\mathsf{t}_j \leftarrow_{\$} \mathcal{T}$. $(\mathsf{r}_j, \mathsf{v}_j) \leftarrow \mathcal{F}_{\mathsf{pp}}(\mathsf{k}_j, (\mathsf{s}_j, \mathsf{t}_j))$. $(\mathsf{r}_j, \mathsf{v}_j) \leftarrow_{\$} \mathcal{R} \times \mathcal{V}$. $\mathsf{P}_j := (\mathsf{s}_j, \mathsf{t}_j, \mathsf{v}_j)$, $\mathsf{R}_j := \mathsf{r}_j$. $\mathcal{Q} := \mathcal{Q} \cup \{\mathsf{P}_j\}$. Return $(\mathsf{P}_j, \mathsf{R}_j)$.	**Procedure** FINALIZE(P^*, δ^*): // Games $\mathbf{G}_0$, $\mathbf{G}_1$, $\boxed{\mathbf{G}_2, \mathbf{G}_3}$ If $\mathsf{dis}(\delta^*) > t$, Return 0. If $\mathsf{P}^* \in \mathcal{Q}$, Return 0. Parse $\mathsf{P}^* = (\mathsf{s}^*, \mathsf{t}^*, \mathsf{v}^*)$. $\tilde{\mathsf{w}} \leftarrow \mathsf{SS.Rec}(\mathsf{w} + \delta^*, \mathsf{s}^*)$. $\widetilde{\delta^*} = g(\mathsf{SS.Gen}(\mathsf{w}), \mathsf{s}^*, \delta^*)$. $\tilde{\mathsf{k}} \leftarrow \mathsf{H_i}(\tilde{\mathsf{w}})$. $\tilde{\mathsf{k}} = \mathsf{H_i}(\mathsf{w}) + \mathsf{H_i}(\widetilde{\delta^*})$. $\boxed{\tilde{\mathsf{k}} = \mathsf{k} + \mathsf{H_i}(\widetilde{\delta^*}).}$ $(\tilde{\mathsf{r}}, \tilde{\mathsf{v}}) \leftarrow \mathcal{F}_{\mathsf{pp}}(\tilde{\mathsf{k}}, (\mathsf{s}^*, \mathsf{t}^*))$. $(\tilde{\mathsf{r}}, \tilde{\mathsf{v}}) \leftarrow_{\$} \mathcal{R} \times \mathcal{V}$. If $\tilde{\mathsf{v}} = \mathsf{v}^*$, Return 1. Else, Return 0.

Fig. 10. Game $\mathbf{G}_0$–$\mathbf{G}_3$ for the security proof of Lemma 3.

Lemma 3. *The construction in Fig. 8 is ε_2-robust, with*

$$\varepsilon_2 = 2\mathsf{Adv}_{\mathsf{PRF}}^{\mathsf{rka\text{-}prf}}(\lambda) + 2^{-\omega(\log \lambda)}. \tag{11}$$

Proof. We prove the robustness of fuzzy extractor by a sequence of games as shown in Fig. 10. Denote by $\Pr[\mathbf{G}_j]$ the probability that $\mathcal{A}$ wins in $\mathbf{G}_j$.

Game $\mathbf{G}_0$: $\mathbf{G}_0$ is the robustness game played between the challenger and a PPT adversary $\mathcal{A}$. More precisely, the challenger generates $\mathsf{crs} = (\mathsf{H_i}, \mathsf{pp}_{\mathsf{AIAE}})$, samples $\mathsf{w} \leftarrow \mathcal{W}$, sets $\mathcal{Q} = \emptyset$, and returns crs to $\mathcal{A}$. Upon receiving the j-th generation query δ_j from $\mathcal{A}$, the challenger answers $\mathcal{A}$'s GENERATION query δ_j as follows:

1. If $\mathsf{dis}(\delta_j) > t$, then return $\perp$.
2. Compute the sketch $\mathsf{s}_j = \mathsf{SS.Gen}(\mathsf{w} + \delta_j)$ and the hash value $\mathsf{k}_j = \mathsf{H_i}(\mathsf{w} + \delta_j)$.
3. Sample $\mathsf{t}_j \leftarrow_{\$} \mathcal{T}$, compute $(\mathsf{r}_j, \mathsf{v}_j) \leftarrow \mathcal{F}_{\mathsf{pp}}(\mathsf{k}_j, (\mathsf{s}_j, \mathsf{t}_j))$, set $\mathsf{P}_j := (\mathsf{s}_j, \mathsf{t}_j, \mathsf{v}_j)$, $\mathsf{R}_j := \mathsf{r}_j$, $\mathcal{Q} := \mathcal{Q} \cup \{\mathsf{P}_j\}$, and return $(\mathsf{P}_j, \mathsf{R}_j)$ to $\mathcal{A}$.

In FINALIZE, upon receiving (P^*, δ^*) from $\mathcal{A}$, if $\mathsf{dis}(\delta^*) \geq t$ or $\mathsf{P}^* \in \mathcal{Q}$, the challenger returns 0. Else, it parses $\mathsf{P}^* = (\mathsf{s}^*, \mathsf{t}^*, \mathsf{v}^*)$, then computes $\tilde{\mathsf{w}} = \mathsf{SS.Rec}(\mathsf{w} + \delta^*, \mathsf{s}^*)$, $\tilde{\mathsf{k}} = \mathsf{H_i}(\tilde{\mathsf{w}})$ and $(\tilde{\mathsf{r}}, \tilde{\mathsf{v}}) \leftarrow \mathcal{F}_{\mathsf{pp}}(\tilde{\mathsf{k}}, (\mathsf{s}^*, \mathsf{t}^*))$. If $\tilde{\mathsf{v}} = \mathsf{v}^*$, it returns 1, else, it returns 0.

We have that

$$\mathsf{Adv}_{\mathcal{A},\mathsf{FE}}^{\mathsf{rob}}(\lambda) = \Pr[\mathbf{G}_0]. \tag{12}$$

Game $\mathbf{G}_1$: $\mathbf{G}_1$ is the same as $\mathbf{G}_0$, except for the following changes.

- When answering a generation query δ_j from $\mathcal{A}$, step 2 in GENERATION(δ_j) is changed into step 2′:
  2′. Compute $\mathsf{s}_j = \mathsf{SS.Gen}(\mathsf{w}) + \mathsf{SS.Gen}(\delta_j)$ and $\mathsf{k}_j = \mathsf{H_i}(\mathsf{w}) + \mathsf{H_i}(\delta_j)$.
- In FINALIZE, the generation of $\tilde{\mathsf{k}}$ is changed. Instead of computing $\tilde{\mathsf{k}} := \mathsf{H_i}(\tilde{\mathsf{w}})$ with $\tilde{\mathsf{w}} := \mathsf{SS.Rec}(\mathsf{w} + \delta^*, \mathsf{s}^*)$, now $\tilde{\mathsf{k}} := \mathsf{H_i}(\mathsf{w}) + \mathsf{H_i}(\widetilde{\delta^*})$ with $\widetilde{\delta^*} = g(\mathsf{SS.Gen}(\mathsf{w}), \mathsf{s}^*, \delta^*)$, where g is defined in Definition 4.

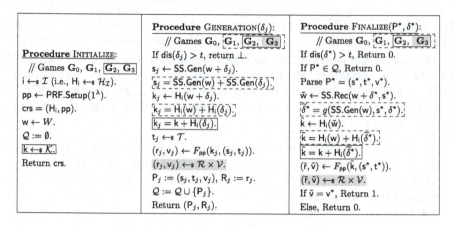

By the linearity property of the secure sketch and the homomorphic properties of secure sketch and hash function, the changes are just conceptual. Hence

$$\Pr[\mathbf{G}_0] = \Pr[\mathbf{G}_1]. \tag{13}$$

Game $\mathbf{G}_2$: $\mathbf{G}_2$ is the same as $\mathbf{G}_1$, except for the generation of k_j and $\tilde{k}$. Instead of computing $\mathsf{k}_j := \mathsf{H_i}(\mathsf{w}) + \mathsf{H_i}(\delta_j)$, now the challenger computes $\mathsf{k}_j := \mathsf{k} + \mathsf{H_i}(\delta_j)$ in $\text{GENERATION}(\delta_j)$ of $\mathbf{G}_2$. Instead of computing $\tilde{\mathsf{k}} = \mathsf{H_i}(\mathsf{w}) + \mathsf{H_i}(\widetilde{\delta^*})$, now the challenger computes $\tilde{\mathsf{k}} = \mathsf{k} + \mathsf{H_i}(\widetilde{\delta^*})$ in $\text{FINALIZE}(\mathsf{P}^*, \delta^*)$ of $\mathbf{G}_2$. Here k is randomly chosen (once and for all in INITIALIZE). More precisely,

- In INITIALIZE, add $\mathsf{k} \leftarrow_{\$} \mathcal{K}$.
- When answering the generation queries from $\mathcal{A}$, step $2'$ in $\text{GENERATION}(\delta_j)$ is changed into step $2''$.
  $2''$. Compute $\mathsf{s}_j = \mathsf{SS.Gen}(\mathsf{w}) + \mathsf{SS.Gen}(\delta_j)$ and $\mathsf{k}_j = \mathsf{k} + \mathsf{H_i}(\delta_j)$.
- In $\text{FINALIZE}(\mathsf{P}^*, \delta^*)$, the challenger computes $\tilde{\mathsf{k}} = \mathsf{k} + \mathsf{H_i}(\widetilde{\delta^*})$ instead of $\tilde{\mathsf{k}} = \mathsf{H_i}(\mathsf{w}) + \mathsf{H_i}(\widetilde{\delta^*})$.

Claim 3 $|\Pr[\mathbf{G}_1] - \Pr[\mathbf{G}_2]| \le 2^{-\omega(\log\lambda)}$.

Proof. The proof is similar to that of Claim 1 in the reusability proof, so we omit it here. See the full version [26] for details. □

Game $\mathbf{G}_3$: $\mathbf{G}_3$ is the same as $\mathbf{G}_2$, except that $(\mathsf{r}_j, \mathsf{v}_j)$ in $\text{CHALLENGE}(\delta_j)$ and $(\tilde{\mathsf{r}}, \tilde{\mathsf{v}})$ in FINALIZE are randomly chosen in $\mathbf{G}_3$. More precisely,

- In $\text{CHALLENGE}(\delta_j)$, step 3 is replaced with $3'$.
  $3'$. $\mathsf{t}_j \leftarrow_{\$} \mathcal{T}$ and $(\mathsf{r}_j, \mathsf{v}_j) \leftarrow_{\$} \mathcal{R} \times \mathcal{V}$, set $\mathsf{P}_j := (\mathsf{s}_j, \mathsf{t}_j, \mathsf{v}_j)$, $\mathsf{R}_j := \mathsf{r}_j$, $\mathcal{Q} := \mathcal{Q} \cup \{\mathsf{P}_j\}$, and return $(\mathsf{P}_j, \mathsf{R}_j)$ to $\mathcal{A}$.
- In FINALIZE, upon receiving a (P^*, δ^*) from $\mathcal{A}$, if $\mathsf{dis}(\delta^*) \ge t$ or $\mathsf{P}^* \in \mathcal{Q}$, the challenger returns 0. Else, it parses $\mathsf{P}^* = (\mathsf{s}^*, \mathsf{t}^*, \mathsf{v}^*)$, and samples $(\tilde{\mathsf{r}}, \tilde{\mathsf{v}}) \leftarrow_{\$} \mathcal{R} \times \mathcal{V}$. If $\tilde{\mathsf{v}} = \mathsf{v}^*$, it returns 1, else, it returns 0.

Observe that in $\mathbf{G}_3$, $\tilde{\mathsf{v}}$ is randomly chosen from $\mathcal{V}$, the probability of $\tilde{\mathsf{v}} = \mathsf{v}^*$ is bounded by $1/|\mathcal{V}|$. Note that $\log|\mathcal{V}| \ge \omega(\log\lambda)$, so we have that

$$\Pr[\mathbf{G}_3] \le 2^{-\omega(\log\lambda)}. \tag{14}$$

Claim 4 $|\Pr[\mathbf{G}_2] - \Pr[\mathbf{G}_3]| \le 2\mathsf{Adv}^{\mathsf{rka\text{-}prf}}_{\mathsf{PRF}}(\lambda) + 2^{-\omega(\log\lambda)}$.

Proof. The proof is similar to that of Claim 2.

Let Q denote the number of generation queries by $\mathcal{A}$. Let Bad denote the event that there exist $i, j \in [Q]$ such that $\mathsf{t}_i = \mathsf{t}_j$. Let Bad' denote the event that $\exists j \in [Q]$ such that $(\mathsf{s}^*, \mathsf{t}^*) = (\mathsf{s}_j, \mathsf{t}_j)$. Similar to Eq. (7), we have

$$
\begin{aligned}
&|\Pr[\mathbf{G}_2] - \Pr[\mathbf{G}_3]| \\
\leq\ &|\Pr[\mathbf{G}_2 \wedge (\mathsf{Bad} \vee \mathsf{Bad}')] - \Pr[\mathbf{G}_3 \wedge (\mathsf{Bad} \vee \mathsf{Bad}')]| \\
&+ |\Pr[\mathbf{G}_2 \wedge \overline{\mathsf{Bad}} \wedge \overline{\mathsf{Bad}'}] - \Pr[\mathbf{G}_3 \wedge \overline{\mathsf{Bad}} \wedge \overline{\mathsf{Bad}'}]| \\
=\ &|\Pr[\mathbf{G}_2 \wedge \mathsf{Bad}] - \Pr[\mathbf{G}_3 \wedge \mathsf{Bad}]| \\
&+ |\Pr[\mathbf{G}_2 \wedge \overline{\mathsf{Bad}} \wedge \overline{\mathsf{Bad}'}] - \Pr[\mathbf{G}_3 \wedge \overline{\mathsf{Bad}} \wedge \overline{\mathsf{Bad}'}]| \qquad (15) \\
\leq\ &\frac{Q(Q-1)}{2|\mathcal{T}|} + |\Pr[\mathbf{G}_2 \wedge \overline{\mathsf{Bad}} \wedge \overline{\mathsf{Bad}'}] - \Pr[\mathbf{G}_3 \wedge \overline{\mathsf{Bad}'} \wedge \overline{\mathsf{Bad}}]|. \qquad (16)
\end{aligned}
$$

Equation (15) is due to

$$\Pr[\mathbf{G}_2 \wedge \mathsf{Bad}'] = \Pr[\mathbf{G}_3 \wedge \mathsf{Bad}'] = 0, \qquad (17)$$

and Eq. (16) is due to $|\Pr[\mathbf{G}_2 \wedge \mathsf{Bad}] - \Pr[\mathbf{G}_3 \wedge \mathsf{Bad}]| \leq \Pr[\mathsf{Bad}] = \frac{Q(Q-1)}{2|\mathcal{T}|}$.

Equation (17) means that it is impossible for $\mathcal{A}$ to win if Bad' happens, say $(\mathsf{s}^*, \mathsf{t}^*) = (\mathsf{s}_j, \mathsf{t}_j)$. The reason is as follows. Recall that $(\mathsf{s}^*, \mathsf{t}^*)$ is from $\mathsf{P}^* = (\mathsf{s}^*, \mathsf{t}^*, \mathsf{v}^*)$ and $(\mathsf{s}_j, \mathsf{t}_j)$ is from $\mathsf{P}_j = (\mathsf{s}_j, \mathsf{t}_j, \mathsf{v}_j)$. Note that $\mathsf{dis}(\delta^*) \leq t$, $\mathsf{dis}(\delta_j) \leq t$ and $\mathsf{s}^* = \mathsf{s}_j = \mathsf{SS.Gen}(\mathsf{w} + \delta_j)$, so we have that $\mathsf{w} + \delta_j = \mathsf{SS.Rec}(\mathsf{w} + \delta^*, \mathsf{s}^*)$ by the correctness of $(\mathcal{M}, m, \widetilde{m}, 2t)$-secure sketch. Meanwhile, by the linearity property we have $\mathsf{SS.Rec}(\mathsf{w} + \delta^*, \mathsf{s}^*) = \mathsf{w} + \widetilde{\delta}^*$, where $\widetilde{\delta}^* = g(\delta^*, \mathsf{SS.Gen}(\mathsf{w}), \mathsf{s}^*)$. As a result, $\delta_j = \widetilde{\delta}^*$ and $\mathsf{k}_j = \phi_{\mathsf{H_i}(\delta_j)}(\mathsf{k}) = \mathsf{k} + \mathsf{H_i}(\delta_j) = \mathsf{k} + \mathsf{H_i}(\widetilde{\delta}^*) = \phi_{\mathsf{H_i}(\widetilde{\delta}^*)}(\mathsf{k}) = \tilde{\mathsf{k}}$. Now that $(\tilde{\mathsf{k}}, (\mathsf{s}^*, \mathsf{t}^*) = (\mathsf{k}_j, \mathsf{s}_j, \mathsf{t}_j)$, hence $F_{\mathsf{pp}}(\tilde{\mathsf{k}}, (\mathsf{s}^*, \mathsf{t}^*)) = F_{\mathsf{pp}}(\mathsf{k}_j, (\mathsf{s}_j, \mathsf{t}_j))$, i.e., $(\tilde{\mathsf{r}}, \tilde{\mathsf{v}}) = (\mathsf{r}_j, \mathsf{v}_j)$. If $\mathsf{v}^* = \mathsf{v}_j$, then $\mathsf{P}^* = \mathsf{P}_j$; otherwise $\tilde{\mathsf{v}} \neq \mathsf{v}^*$. Either case results in the failure of $\mathcal{A}$ in $\mathbf{G}_2/\mathbf{G}_3$.

Next we will prove

$$|\Pr[\mathbf{G}_2 \wedge \overline{\mathsf{Bad}} \wedge \overline{\mathsf{Bad}'}] - \Pr[\mathbf{G}_3 \wedge \overline{\mathsf{Bad}} \wedge \overline{\mathsf{Bad}'}]| \leq 2\mathsf{Adv}^{\mathsf{rka\text{-}prf}}_{\mathsf{PRF}}(\lambda) \qquad (18)$$

by constructing a PPT algorithm $\mathcal{A}'$ against the unique-input key-shift security of PRF F_{pp}, just like the proof of Eq. (8).

Recall that in the unique-input key-shift security game $\mathsf{Exp}^{\mathsf{rka\text{-}prf}}_{\mathcal{A}, F_{\mathsf{pp}}}(\lambda)$, $\mathcal{A}'$ obtains the public parameter pp from its own Initialize. Meanwhile, $\mathcal{A}'$ is able to query (ϕ_Δ, x) to RKQue and obtain the value of $f(\mathsf{k} + \Delta, x)$. The aim of $\mathcal{A}'$ is to tell whether $f(\mathsf{k}, \cdot)$ is $F_{\mathsf{pp}}(\mathsf{k}, \cdot)$ or a random function. Now $\mathcal{A}'$ simulates $\mathbf{G}_2/\mathbf{G}_3$ for $\mathcal{A}$ as follows.

- To simulate Initialize of $\mathbf{G}_2/\mathbf{G}_3$, $\mathcal{A}'$ samples $\mathsf{w} \leftarrow W$, chooses $b \leftarrow_{\$} \{0,1\}$ and an index $\mathsf{i} \leftarrow_{\$} \mathcal{I}$, then sends $\mathsf{crs} = (\mathsf{H_i}, \mathsf{pp})$ for $\mathcal{A}$. And $\mathcal{A}'$ sets $\mathcal{Q} = \mathcal{Q}_t = \emptyset$.
- To answer $\mathcal{A}$'s query δ_j, $\mathcal{A}'$ simulates Procedure Challenge(δ_j) as follows.
  - If $\mathsf{dis}(\delta_j) > t$, return $\perp$.
  - $\mathsf{s}_j := \mathsf{SS.Gen}(\mathsf{w}) + \mathsf{SS.Gen}(\delta_j)$ and $\mathsf{t}_j \leftarrow_{\$} \mathcal{T}$. If $\mathsf{t}_j \in \mathcal{Q}_t$, i.e., Bad happens, then $\mathcal{A}'$ aborts the game. Otherwise, $\mathcal{Q}_t := \mathcal{Q}_t \cup \{\mathsf{t}_j\}$.
  - $\mathcal{A}'$ queries $(\phi_{\mathsf{H_i}(\delta_j)}, (\mathsf{s}_j, \mathsf{t}_j))$ to its Procedure RKQue, then RKQue returns $(\mathsf{r}_j, \mathsf{v}_j)$ to $\mathcal{A}'$.
  - $\mathcal{A}'$ defines $\mathsf{P}_j := (\mathsf{s}_j, \mathsf{t}_j, \mathsf{v}_j)$, $\mathsf{R}_j := \mathsf{r}_j$ and $\mathcal{Q} := \mathcal{Q} \cup \{\mathsf{P}_j\}$.
  - Return $(\mathsf{P}_j, \mathsf{R}_j)$.

– Finally, $\mathcal{A}$ sends (P^*, δ^*) to FINALIZE.
  - If $\mathsf{dis}(\delta^*) \geq t$ or $\mathsf{P}^* \in \mathcal{Q}$, $\mathcal{A}'$ returns 0 to its own challenger.
  - If $\exists j \in [Q]$ such that $(\mathsf{s}^*, \mathsf{t}^*) = (\mathsf{s}_j, \mathsf{t}_j)$, $\mathcal{A}'$ returns 0 to its own challenger.
  - $\mathcal{A}'$ parses $\mathsf{P}^* = (\mathsf{s}^*, \mathsf{t}^*, \mathsf{v}^*)$ and computes $\widetilde{\delta}^* = g(\mathsf{SS.Gen}(\mathsf{w}), \mathsf{s}^*, \delta^*)$. Then $\mathcal{A}'$ queries $((\phi_{\mathsf{H_i}(\widetilde{\delta}^*)}, \mathsf{s}^*, \mathsf{t}^*)$ to RKQUE and receives $\tilde{y} = f(\mathsf{k} + \mathsf{H_i}(\widetilde{\delta}^*), (\mathsf{s}^*, \mathsf{t}^*))$ from RKQUE. $\mathcal{A}'$ parses $\tilde{y} = (\tilde{\mathsf{r}}, \tilde{\mathsf{v}})$. If $\tilde{\mathsf{v}} = \mathsf{v}^*$, $\mathcal{A}'$ returns 1, else $\mathcal{A}'$ returns 0 to its own challenger.

Suppose that neither Bad nor Bad′ happens. Then

- $\mathcal{A}'$ perfectly simulates $\mathbf{G}_2 \wedge \overline{\mathsf{Bad}} \wedge \overline{\mathsf{Bad}'}$ for $\mathcal{A}$ if $f(k, \cdot) = F_{\mathsf{pp}}(k, \cdot)$;
- $\mathcal{A}'$ perfectly simulates $\mathbf{G}_3 \wedge \overline{\mathsf{Bad}} \wedge \overline{\mathsf{Bad}'}$ for $\mathcal{A}$ if $f(k, \cdot)$ is a random function.

Then the advantage of $\mathcal{A}'$ is given by

$$\begin{aligned}
\mathsf{Adv}^{\mathsf{rka\text{-}prf}}_{\mathcal{A}',\mathsf{PRF}}(\lambda) &= |\Pr[\mathsf{Exp}^{\mathsf{rka\text{-}prf}}_{\mathcal{A}',F_{\mathsf{pp}}}(\lambda) \Rightarrow 1] - \frac{1}{2}| \\
&= \frac{1}{2} |\Pr\left[\mathcal{A}' \Rightarrow 1 \mid f(\cdot,\cdot) = F_{\mathsf{pp}}(k,\cdot)\right] - \Pr\left[\mathcal{A}' \Rightarrow 1 \mid f(\cdot,\cdot) \text{ is random}\right]| \\
&= \frac{1}{2} \Big|\Pr\left[\mathcal{A} \text{ wins} \wedge \overline{\mathsf{Bad}} \wedge \overline{\mathsf{Bad}'} \mid f(\cdot,\cdot) = F_{\mathsf{pp}}(k,\cdot)\right] \qquad (19) \\
&\quad - \Pr\left[\mathcal{A} \text{ wins} \wedge \overline{\mathsf{Bad}} \wedge \overline{\mathsf{Bad}'} \mid f(\cdot,\cdot) \text{ is random}\right]\Big| \\
&= \frac{1}{2} |\Pr\left[\mathbf{G}_2 \wedge \overline{\mathsf{Bad}} \wedge \overline{\mathsf{Bad}'}\right] - \Pr\left[\mathbf{G}_3 \wedge \overline{\mathsf{Bad}} \wedge \overline{\mathsf{Bad}'}\right]|. \qquad (20)
\end{aligned}$$

This completes the proof of Eq. (18).

The claim follows from Eqs. (16), (18) and the fact that $\log(|\mathcal{T}|) \geq \omega(\log \lambda)$. □

Taking Eqs. (12), (13), Claims 3, 4 and Eq. (14) together, Lemma 3 follows. ∎

5 Construction of rrFE from AIAE

In this section we propose a generic construction of robustly reusable fuzzy extractor $\mathsf{rrFE} = (\mathsf{Init}, \mathsf{Gen}, \mathsf{Rep})$ from a key-shift secure AIAE, a secure sketch and a family of universal hash functions as shown in Fig. 11.

$\underline{\mathsf{crs} \leftarrow \mathsf{Init}(1^\lambda)}$: $\mathsf{i} \leftarrow_{\$} \mathcal{I}$ (i.e., $\mathsf{H_i} \leftarrow_{\$} \mathcal{H_I}$). $\mathsf{pp_{AIAE}} \leftarrow \mathsf{AIAE.Setup}(1^\lambda)$. $\mathsf{crs} = (\mathsf{H_i}, \mathsf{pp_{AIAE}})$. Return crs.	$\underline{(\mathsf{P}, \mathsf{R}) \leftarrow \mathsf{Gen}(\mathsf{crs}, \mathsf{w})}$: $\mathsf{s} \leftarrow \mathsf{SS.Gen}(\mathsf{w})$. $\mathsf{k} \leftarrow \mathsf{H_i}(\mathsf{w})$. $\mathsf{m} \leftarrow_{\$} \mathcal{M}_{\mathsf{AIAE}}$. $\mathsf{ct} \leftarrow \mathsf{AIAE.Enc}(\mathsf{k}, \mathsf{m}, \mathsf{s})$. $\mathsf{P} := (\mathsf{s}, \mathsf{ct}), \mathsf{R} := \mathsf{m}$.	$\underline{\mathsf{R} \leftarrow \mathsf{Rep}(\mathsf{crs}, \mathsf{P}, \mathsf{w}')}$: Parse $\mathsf{P} = (\mathsf{s}, \mathsf{ct})$. $\tilde{\mathsf{w}} \leftarrow \mathsf{SS.Rec}(\mathsf{w}', \mathsf{s})$. $\tilde{\mathsf{k}} \leftarrow \mathsf{H_i}(\tilde{\mathsf{w}})$. $\tilde{\mathsf{m}}/\perp \leftarrow \mathsf{AIAE.Dec}(\tilde{\mathsf{k}}, \mathsf{ct}, \mathsf{s})$. Return $\tilde{\mathsf{m}}/\perp$.

Fig. 11. Construction of $\mathsf{rrFE_{AIAE}}$ from key-shift secure AIAE.

Theorem 2. *The fuzzy extractor* $\mathsf{rrFE}_{\mathsf{AIAE}}$ *in Fig. 11 is an* $(\mathcal{M}, m, \mathcal{M}_{\mathsf{AIAE}}, t, \varepsilon_1, \varepsilon_2)$*-robustly reusable fuzzy extractor where* $\varepsilon_1 = \mathsf{Adv}^{\mathsf{ind\text{-}rka}}_{\mathsf{AIAE}}(\lambda) + 2^{-\omega(\log \lambda)}$ *and* $\varepsilon_2 = \mathsf{Adv}^{\mathsf{int\text{-}rka}}_{\mathsf{AIAE}}(\lambda) + 2^{-\omega(\log \lambda)}$*, if the building blocks satisfy the following properties.*

- $\mathsf{SS} = (\mathsf{SS.Gen}, \mathsf{SS.Rec})$ *is a homomorphic* $(\mathcal{M}, m, \tilde{m}, 2t)$*-secure sketch with linearity property.*
- $\mathcal{H}_{\mathcal{I}} = \{\mathsf{H_i} : \mathcal{M} \to \mathcal{K}\}_{i \in \mathcal{I}}$ *is a family of homomorphic universal hash functions such that* $\tilde{m} - \log |\mathcal{K}| \geq \omega(\log \lambda)$.
- AIAE *is key-shift secure (IND-*Φ_Δ*-RKA and* weak *INT-*Φ_Δ*-RKA secure) with key space* $\mathcal{K}$*, message space* $\mathcal{M}_{\mathsf{AIAE}}$ *and auxiliary input space* $\{0,1\}^*$.

The correctness follows from the correctness of the underlying SS and AIAE. More precisely, if $\mathsf{dis}(\mathsf{w}, \mathsf{w}') \leq t$, then by the correctness of secure sketch, w can be correctly recovered, so is the secret key $\mathsf{k}(= \mathsf{H_i}(\mathsf{w}))$. Then by the correctness of AIAE, the message m, i.e., R can be precisely reproduced. The reusability and robustness of $\mathsf{rrFE}_{\mathsf{AIAE}}$ are shown in Lemmas 4 and 5 respectively.

Procedure INITIALIZE: // Games $\mathbf{G}_0$, $\mathbf{G}_1$, $\mathbf{G}_2$	Procedure CHALLENGE(δ_j): // Games $\mathbf{G}_0$, $\boxed{\mathbf{G}_1, \mathbf{G}_2}$
$\mathsf{i} \leftarrow_\$ \mathcal{I}$ (i.e., $\mathsf{H_i} \leftarrow_\$ \mathcal{H}_{\mathcal{I}}$).	If $\mathsf{dis}(\delta_j) > t$, Return $\perp$.
$\mathsf{pp}_{\mathsf{AIAE}} \leftarrow \mathsf{AIAE.Setup}(1^\lambda)$.	$\mathsf{s}_j \leftarrow \mathsf{SS.Gen}(\mathsf{w} + \delta_j)$.
$\mathsf{crs} = (\mathsf{H_i}, \mathsf{pp}_{\mathsf{AIAE}})$.	$\boxed{\mathsf{s}_j = \mathsf{SS.Gen}(\mathsf{w}) + \mathsf{SS.Gen}(\delta_j).}$
$b \leftarrow_\$ \{0,1\}$.	$\mathsf{k}_j \leftarrow \mathsf{H_i}(\mathsf{w} + \delta_j)$.
$\mathsf{w} \leftarrow W$.	$\boxed{\mathsf{k}_j = \mathsf{H_i}(\mathsf{w}) + \mathsf{H_i}(\delta_j).}$
$\mathsf{k} \leftarrow_\$ \mathcal{K}$.	$\mathsf{k}_j = \mathsf{k} + \mathsf{H_i}(\delta_j)$.
Return crs.	$\mathsf{m}_j \leftarrow_\$ \mathcal{M}_{\mathsf{AIAE}}$.
	$\mathsf{ct}_j \leftarrow \mathsf{AIAE.Enc}(\mathsf{k}_j, \mathsf{m}_j, \mathsf{s}_j)$.
Procedure FINALIZE(b^*): // Games $\mathbf{G}_0$-$\mathbf{G}_2$	$\mathsf{P}_j := (\mathsf{s}_j, \mathsf{ct}_j), \mathsf{R} := \mathsf{m}_j$.
If $b = b^*$, Return 1.	If $b = 1$, Return $(\mathsf{P}_j, \mathsf{R}_j)$.
Else, Return 0.	Else, $\mathsf{U}_j \leftarrow_\$ \mathcal{M}_{\mathsf{AIAE}}$, Return $(\mathsf{P}_j, \mathsf{U}_j)$.

Fig. 12. Game $\mathbf{G}_0$, $\mathbf{G}_1$ and $\mathbf{G}_2$ for the security proof of Lemma 4.

Lemma 4. *The fuzzy extractor* $\mathsf{rrFE}_{\mathsf{AIAE}}$ *in Fig. 11 is* ε_1*-reusable with* $\varepsilon_1 = \mathsf{Adv}^{\mathsf{ind\text{-}rka}}_{\mathsf{AIAE}}(\lambda) + 2^{-\omega(\log \lambda)}$.

Proof. We will prove the reusability of our construction via a series of games as shown in Fig. 12. By $\Pr[\mathbf{G}_j]$ we denote the probability that $\mathcal{A}$ wins in game $\mathbf{G}_j$.

Game $\mathbf{G}_0$: $\mathbf{G}_0$ is the reusability game played between the challenger and a PPT adversary $\mathcal{A}$. More precisely, in Procedures INITIALIZE, the challenger chooses $b \leftarrow_\$ \{0,1\}$, samples $\mathsf{w} \leftarrow W$, generates $\mathsf{crs} = (\mathsf{H_i}, \mathsf{pp}_{\mathsf{AIAE}})$, and returns crs to $\mathcal{A}$. Upon receiving the j-th CHALLENGE query δ_j from $\mathcal{A}$, the challenger answers $\mathcal{A}$'s query as follows:

1. If $\mathsf{dis}(\delta_j) > t$, then return $\perp$.
2. Compute the sketch $\mathsf{s}_j = \mathsf{SS.Gen}(\mathsf{w} + \delta_j)$ and the hash value $\mathsf{k}_j = \mathsf{H_i}(\mathsf{w} + \delta_j)$.
3. Randomly choose a message $\mathsf{m}_j \leftarrow_\$ \mathcal{M}_{\mathsf{AIAE}}$, compute $\mathsf{ct}_j \leftarrow \mathsf{AIAE.Enc}(\mathsf{k}_j, \mathsf{m}_j, \mathsf{s}_j)$, set $\mathsf{P}_j = (\mathsf{s}_j, \mathsf{ct}_j)$ and $\mathsf{R}_j = \mathsf{m}_j$.
4. If $b = 1$, return $(\mathsf{P}_j, \mathsf{R}_j)$, else randomly choose $\mathsf{U}_j \leftarrow_\$ \mathcal{M}_{\mathsf{AIAE}}$ and return $(\mathsf{P}_j, \mathsf{U}_j)$.

We have that

$$\mathsf{Adv}^{\mathsf{reu}}_{\mathcal{A},\mathsf{FE}}(\lambda) = |\Pr[\mathbf{G}_0] - 1/2|. \tag{21}$$

Game $\mathbf{G}_1$: Game $\mathbf{G}_1$ is identical to $\mathbf{G}_0$, except the conceptual changes of the generations of the secure sketch and the hash value. More precisely, step 2 is changed to step 2′ in CHALLENGE(δ_j).

2′. compute the sketch $\mathsf{s}_j = \mathsf{SS.Gen}(\mathsf{w}) + \mathsf{SS.Gen}(\delta_j)$ and the hash value $\mathsf{k}_j = \mathsf{H_i}(\mathsf{w}) + \mathsf{H_i}(\delta_j)$.

By the homomorphic properties of secure sketch and hash function, we have

$$\Pr[\mathbf{G}_0] = \Pr[\mathbf{G}_1]. \tag{22}$$

Game $\mathbf{G}_2$: Game $\mathbf{G}_2$ is identical to $\mathbf{G}_1$, except that instead of computing $\mathsf{k}_j = \mathsf{H_i}(\mathsf{w}) + \mathsf{H_i}(\delta_j)$, the challenger randomly chooses an element k from $\mathcal{K}$ in INITIALIZE and computes $\mathsf{k}_j := \mathsf{k} + \mathsf{H_i}(\delta_j)$ in CHALLENGE(δ_j) of $\mathbf{G}_2$. More precisely,

- In INITIALIZE, add $\mathsf{k} \leftarrow_\$ \mathcal{K}$.
- When answering the generation queries from $\mathcal{A}$, step 2′ in CHALLENGE(δ_j) is changed into step 2″.
  2″. Compute $\mathsf{s}_j = \mathsf{SS.Gen}(\mathsf{w}) + \mathsf{SS.Gen}(\delta_j)$ and $\mathsf{k}_j = \mathsf{k} + \mathsf{H_i}(\delta_j)$.

Claim 5 $|\Pr[\mathbf{G}_1] - \Pr[\mathbf{G}_2]| \leq 2^{-\omega(\log\lambda)}$.

Proof. This proof is essentially the same as the proof of Claim 1. We omit it here (See the full version [26] for details). □

Claim 6 $|\Pr[\mathbf{G}_2] - 1/2| \leq \mathsf{Adv}^{\mathsf{ind\text{-}rka}}_{\mathsf{AIAE}}(\lambda)$.

Proof. We will reduce the IND-Φ_Δ-RKA security of AIAE to the altered reusability game as described in Game $\mathbf{G}_2$. To this end, we assume a PPT adversary $\mathcal{A}$ winning $\mathbf{G}_2$ and show how to construct a PPT IND-Φ_Δ-RKA adversary $\mathcal{B}$. On input $\mathsf{pp}_{\mathsf{AIAE}}$, $\mathcal{B}$ samples $\mathsf{w} \leftarrow W$ and $\mathsf{i} \leftarrow_\$ \mathcal{I}$ (i.e., $\mathsf{H_i} \leftarrow_\$ \mathcal{H_I}$), sets $\mathsf{crs} = (\mathsf{H_i}, \mathsf{pp}_{\mathsf{AIAE}})$ and returns crs to $\mathcal{A}$. Upon receiving the i-th challenge query δ_j from $\mathcal{A}$, adversary $\mathcal{B}$ simulates CHALLENGE(δ_j) for $\mathcal{A}$ as follows:

1. If $\mathsf{dis}(\delta_j) > t$, then return $\perp$.
2. Compute the sketch $\mathsf{s}_j = \mathsf{SS.Gen}(\mathsf{w}) + \mathsf{SS.Gen}(\delta_j)$ and the hash value $\Delta_j = \mathsf{H_i}(\delta_j)$.

3. Randomly choose two messages $(\mathsf{m}_{j0}, \mathsf{m}_{j1}) \leftarrow_{\$} \mathcal{M}_{\mathsf{AIAE}}$, and send $(\mathsf{m}_{j0}, \mathsf{m}_{j1}, \mathsf{aux}_j = \mathsf{s}_j, \phi_{\Delta_j})$ to its own challenger.
4. Upon receiving ct_j from its own challenger, set $\mathsf{P}_j = (\mathsf{s}_j, \mathsf{ct}_j)$, and return $(\mathsf{P}_j, \mathsf{m}_{j1})$.

Finally, $\mathcal{A}$ outputs a guessing bit b^*, then $\mathcal{B}$ forwards b^* to its own challenger. It is straightforward to see that $\mathcal{B}$ simulates game $\mathbf{G}_2$ perfectly. More precisely,

- If $\mathsf{ct}_j = \mathsf{AIAE.Enc}(\phi_{\Delta_j}, m_{j0}, \mathsf{aux})$, then $\mathcal{B}$ perfectly simulates for the case $b = 0$ in $\mathbf{G}_2$.
- If $\mathsf{ct}_j = \mathsf{AIAE.Enc}(\phi_{\Delta_j}, m_{j1}, \mathsf{aux})$, then $\mathcal{B}$ perfectly simulates for the case $b = 1$ in $\mathbf{G}_2$.

Clearly, $\mathcal{B}$ wins if and only if $\mathcal{A}$ wins. This yields $|\Pr[\mathbf{G}_2] - 1/2| = \mathsf{Adv}^{\mathsf{ind\text{-}rka}}_{\mathcal{B},\mathsf{AIAE}}(\lambda) \leq \mathsf{Adv}^{\mathsf{ind\text{-}rka}}_{\mathsf{AIAE}}(\lambda)$. □

Taking Eq. (21), Eq. (22), Claim 5 and Claim 6 together, we have $\mathsf{Adv}^{\mathsf{reu}}_{\mathsf{FE}}(\lambda) \leq \mathsf{Adv}^{\mathsf{ind\text{-}rka}}_{\mathsf{AIAE}}(\lambda) + 2^{-\omega(\log \lambda)}$, and Lemma 4 follows. ∎

Procedure Initialize:
// Games $\mathbf{G}_0$, $\mathbf{G}_1$, $\mathbf{G}_2$
$\mathsf{i} \leftarrow_{\$} \mathcal{I}$ (i.e., $\mathsf{H_i} \leftarrow_{\$} \mathcal{H}_{\mathcal{I}}$).
$\mathsf{pp}_{\mathsf{AIAE}} \leftarrow \mathsf{AIAE.Setup}(1^{\lambda})$.
$\mathsf{crs} = (\mathsf{H_i}, \mathsf{pp}_{\mathsf{AIAE}})$.
$\mathsf{w} \leftarrow W$.
$\mathcal{Q} := \emptyset$.
$\mathsf{k} \leftarrow_{\$} \mathcal{K}$.
Return crs.

Procedure Generation(δ_j):
// Games $\mathbf{G}_0$, $\mathbf{G}_1$, $\mathbf{G}_2$
If $\mathsf{dis}(\delta_j) > t$, Return $\perp$.
$\mathsf{s}_j \leftarrow \mathsf{SS.Gen}(\mathsf{w} + \delta_j)$.
$\mathsf{s}_j = \mathsf{SS.Gen}(\mathsf{w}) + \mathsf{SS.Gen}(\delta_j)$.
$\mathsf{k}_j \leftarrow \mathsf{H_i}(\mathsf{w} + \delta_j)$.
$\mathsf{k}_j = \mathsf{H_i}(\mathsf{w}) + \mathsf{H_i}(\delta_j)$.
$\mathsf{k}_j = \mathsf{k} + \mathsf{H_i}(\delta_j)$.
$\mathsf{m}_j \leftarrow_{\$} \mathcal{M}_{\mathsf{AIAE}}$.
$\mathsf{ct}_j \leftarrow \mathsf{AIAE.Enc}(\mathsf{k}_j, \mathsf{m}_j, \mathsf{s}_j)$.
$\mathsf{P}_j := (\mathsf{s}_j, \mathsf{ct}_j)$, $\mathsf{R} := \mathsf{m}_j$.
$\mathcal{Q} = \mathcal{Q} \cup \{\mathsf{P}_j\}$.
Return $(\mathsf{P}_j, \mathsf{R}_j)$.

Procedure Finalize(P^*, δ^*):
// Games $\mathbf{G}_0$, $\mathbf{G}_1$, $\mathbf{G}_2$
If $\mathsf{dis}(\delta^*) > t$, Return 0.
If $\mathsf{P}^* \in \mathcal{Q}$, Return 0.
Parse $\mathsf{P}^* = (\mathsf{s}^*, \mathsf{ct}^*)$.
$\tilde{\mathsf{w}} \leftarrow \mathsf{SS.Rec}(\mathsf{w} + \delta^*, \mathsf{s}^*)$.
$\tilde{\delta}^* = g(\mathsf{SS.Gen}(\mathsf{w}), \mathsf{s}^*, \delta^*)$.
$\tilde{\mathsf{k}} \leftarrow \mathsf{H_i}(\tilde{\mathsf{w}})$.
$\tilde{\mathsf{k}} = \mathsf{H_i}(\mathsf{w}) + \mathsf{H_i}(\tilde{\delta}^*)$.
$\tilde{\mathsf{k}} = \mathsf{k} + \mathsf{H_i}(\tilde{\delta}^*)$.
Return $(\mathsf{AIAE.Dec}(\tilde{\mathsf{k}}, \mathsf{ct}^*, \mathsf{s}^*) \neq \perp)$.

Fig. 13. Game $\mathbf{G}_0$-$\mathbf{G}_2$ for the security proof of Lemma 5.

Lemma 5. *The fuzzy extractor* $\mathsf{rrFE}_{\mathsf{AIAE}}$ *in Fig. 11 is* ε_2*-robust with* $\varepsilon_2 = \mathsf{Adv}^{\mathsf{ind\text{-}rka}}_{\mathsf{AIAE}}(\lambda) + 2^{-\omega(\log \lambda)}$.

Proof. We prove the robustness of reusable fuzzy extractor by a sequence of games as shown in Fig. 13. By $\Pr[\mathbf{G}_j]$ we denote the probability that $\mathcal{A}$ wins in game $\mathbf{G}_j$.

Game $\mathbf{G}_0$: $\mathbf{G}_0$ is the original robustness game. More precisely, let $\mathsf{crs} = (\mathsf{H_i}, \mathsf{pp}_{\mathsf{AIAE}})$, $\mathcal{Q} = \emptyset$ and $\mathsf{w} \leftarrow W$. Upon receiving the j-th Generation query δ_j from $\mathcal{A}$, the challenger answers $\mathcal{A}$'s query as follows:

1. If $\mathsf{dis}(\delta_j) > t$, then return $\perp$.

2. Compute the sketch $\mathsf{s}_j = \mathsf{SS.Gen}(\mathsf{w} + \delta_j)$ and the hash value $\mathsf{k}_j = \mathsf{H_i}(\mathsf{w} + \delta_j)$.
3. Randomly choose a message $\mathsf{m}_j \leftarrow_\$ \mathcal{M}_{\mathsf{AIAE}}$, compute $\mathsf{ct}_j \leftarrow \mathsf{AIAE.Enc}(\mathsf{k}_j, \mathsf{m}_j, \mathsf{s}_j)$, set $\mathsf{P}_j = (\mathsf{s}_j, \mathsf{ct}_j)$, $\mathsf{R}_j = \mathsf{m}_j$ and $\mathcal{Q} = \mathcal{Q} \cup \{\mathsf{P}_j\}$, and return $(\mathsf{P}_j, \mathsf{R}_j)$ to $\mathcal{A}$.

In FINALIZE, upon receiving a (P^*, δ^*) from $\mathcal{A}$, if $\mathsf{dis}(\delta^*) \geq t$ or $\mathsf{P}^* \in \mathcal{Q}$, the challenger returns 0. Else, it parses $\mathsf{P}^* = (\mathsf{s}^*, \mathsf{ct}^*)$, then computes $\tilde{\mathsf{w}} = \mathsf{SS.Rec}(\mathsf{w} + \delta^*, \mathsf{s}^*)$ and $\tilde{\mathsf{k}} = \mathsf{H_i}(\tilde{\mathsf{w}})$. If $\mathsf{AIAE.Dec}(\tilde{\mathsf{k}}, \mathsf{ct}^*, \mathsf{s}^*) = \perp$, then return 0, otherwise return 1. We have that

$$\mathsf{Adv}^{\mathsf{rob}}_{\mathcal{A},\mathsf{FE}}(\lambda) = \Pr[\mathbf{G}_0]. \tag{23}$$

Game $\mathbf{G}_1$: $\mathbf{G}_1$ is the same as $\mathbf{G}_0$, except for the following changes.

- When answering a generation query δ_j from $\mathcal{A}$, step 2 in GENERATION(δ_j) is changed into step 2′:
  2′. Compute $\mathsf{s}_j = \mathsf{SS.Gen}(\mathsf{w}) + \mathsf{SS.Gen}(\delta_j)$ and $\mathsf{k}_j = \mathsf{H_i}(\mathsf{w}) + \mathsf{H_i}(\delta_j)$.
- In FINALIZE, the generation of $\tilde{\mathsf{k}}$ is changed. Instead of computing $\tilde{\mathsf{k}} := \mathsf{H_i}(\tilde{\mathsf{w}})$ with $\tilde{\mathsf{w}} := \mathsf{SS.Rec}(\mathsf{w} + \delta^*, \mathsf{s}^*)$, now $\tilde{\mathsf{k}} := \mathsf{H_i}(\mathsf{w}) + \mathsf{H_i}(\widetilde{\delta^*})$ with $\widetilde{\delta^*} = g(\mathsf{SS.Gen}(\mathsf{w}), \mathsf{s}^*, \delta^*)$, where g is defined in Definition 4.

By the linearity property of the secure sketch and the homomorphic properties of secure sketch and hash function, the changes are just conceptual. Hence

$$\Pr[\mathbf{G}_0] = \Pr[\mathbf{G}_1]. \tag{24}$$

Game $\mathbf{G}_2$: Game $\mathbf{G}_2$ is identical to $\mathbf{G}_1$, except that the challenger replaces $\mathsf{H_i}(\mathsf{w})$ by a randomly choosen k from $\mathcal{K}$. More precisely,

- In INITIALIZE, challenger will additionally sample $\mathsf{k} \leftarrow_\$ \mathcal{K}$.
- When the challenger answers the generation queries, step 2′ is changed into step 2″:
  2″. compute the sketch $\mathsf{s}_j = \mathsf{SS.Gen}(\mathsf{w}) + \mathsf{SS.Gen}(\delta_j)$ and the hash value $\mathsf{k}_j = \mathsf{k} + \mathsf{H_i}(\delta_j)$.
- In FINALIZE, the challenger computes $\tilde{\mathsf{k}} = \mathsf{k} + \mathsf{H_i}(\widetilde{\delta^*})$ instead of $\tilde{\mathsf{k}} = \mathsf{H_i}(\mathsf{w}) + \mathsf{H_i}(\widetilde{\delta^*})$.

Claim 7 $|\Pr[\mathbf{G}_1] - \Pr[\mathbf{G}_2]| \leq 2^{-\omega(\log \lambda)}$.

Proof. This proof is similar to that of Claim 3. We omit it here (See the full version [26] for details).

Claim 8 $\Pr[\mathbf{G}_2] \leq \mathsf{Adv}^{\mathsf{int\text{-}rka}}_{\mathsf{AIAE}}(\lambda)$.

Proof. We will reduce the INT-Φ_Δ-RKA security of AIAE to the altered robustness game as described in Game $\mathbf{G}_2$. To this end, we assume a PPT adversary $\mathcal{A}$ winning $\mathbf{G}_2$ and show how to construct a PPT weak INT-Φ_Δ-RKA adversary $\mathcal{B}$. On input $\mathsf{pp}_{\mathsf{AIAE}}$, adversary $\mathcal{B}$ samples $\mathsf{w} \leftarrow W$ and $\mathsf{i} \leftarrow_\$ \mathcal{I}$ (i.e., $\mathsf{H_i} \leftarrow_\$ \mathcal{H_I}$), sets $\mathcal{Q} = \emptyset$ and $\mathsf{crs} = (\mathsf{H_i}, \mathsf{pp}_{\mathsf{AIAE}})$, and returns crs to $\mathcal{A}$. Upon receiving the j-th GENERATION query δ_j from $\mathcal{A}$, adversary $\mathcal{B}$ answers $\mathcal{A}$'s query as follows:

1. If $\mathsf{dis}(\delta_j) > t$, then return $\perp$.
2. Compute the sketch $\mathsf{s}_j = \mathsf{SS.Gen}(\mathsf{w}) + \mathsf{SS.Gen}(\delta_j)$ and the hash value $\Delta_j = \mathsf{H_i}(\delta_j)$.
3. Randomly choose a messages $\mathsf{m}_j \leftarrow_\$ \mathcal{M}_{\mathsf{AIAE}}$, and send $(\mathsf{m}_j, \mathsf{aux}_j = \mathsf{s}_j, \phi_{\Delta_j})$ to its own challenger.
4. Upon receiving ct_j from its own challenger, set $\mathsf{P}_j = (\mathsf{s}_j, \mathsf{ct}_j)$, $\mathcal{Q} = \mathcal{Q} \cup \{\mathsf{P}_j\}$ and return $(\mathsf{P}_j, \mathsf{m}_j)$.

Finally $\mathcal{A}$ will output (P^*, δ^*) for FINALIZE. If $\mathsf{dis}(\delta^*) \geq t$ or $\mathsf{P}^* \in \mathcal{Q}$, $\mathcal{B}$ aborts. Else, $\mathcal{B}$ parses $\mathsf{P}^* = (\mathsf{s}^*, \mathsf{ct}^*)$, then computes $\widetilde{\delta}^* = g(\mathsf{SS.Gen}(\mathsf{w}), \mathsf{s}^*, \delta^*)$ and $\Delta^* = \mathsf{H_i}(\widetilde{\delta}^*)$. Finally, $\mathcal{B}$ takes $(\mathsf{aux}^* = \mathsf{s}^*, \phi_{\Delta^*}, \mathsf{ct}^*)$ as its own forgery and sends the forgery to its own challenger.

Note that $\mathcal{B}$ simulates game $\mathbf{G}_2$ perfectly. As long as the forgery satisfies the additional special rule required for the weak INT-Φ_Δ-RKA security, $\mathcal{B}$ wins if and only if $\mathcal{A}$ wins.

We show that the forgery always satisfies the special rule, i.e., if $\mathsf{aux}^* = \mathsf{s}^* = \mathsf{s}_j = \mathsf{aux}_j$ for some $j \in [Q]$, then $\phi_{\Delta_j} = \phi_{\Delta^*}$.

Note that $\mathsf{dis}(\delta^*) \leq t$, $\mathsf{dis}(\delta_j) \leq t$ and $\mathsf{s}^* = \mathsf{s}_j = \mathsf{SS.Gen}(\mathsf{w} + \delta_j)$, so we have that $\mathsf{w}+\delta_j = \mathsf{SS.Rec}(\mathsf{w}+\delta^*, \mathsf{s}^*)$ by the correctness of $(\mathcal{M}, m, \widetilde{m}, 2t)$-secure sketch. Meanwhile, by the linearity property we have $\mathsf{SS.Rec}(\mathsf{w}+\delta^*, \mathsf{s}^*) = \mathsf{w} + \widetilde{\delta}^*$, where $\widetilde{\delta}^* = g(\delta^*, \mathsf{SS.Gen}(\mathsf{w}), \mathsf{s}^*)$. As a result, $\delta_j = \widetilde{\delta}^*$ and $\Delta_j = \mathsf{H_i}(\delta_j) = \mathsf{H_i}(\widetilde{\delta}^*) = \Delta^*$. Hence the key deriving function $\phi_{\Delta_j} = \phi_{\Delta^*}$, and the special rule is satisfied.

As a result $\Pr[\mathbf{G}_2] = \mathsf{Adv}^{\mathsf{int\text{-}rka}}_{\mathcal{B},\mathsf{AIAE}}(\lambda) \leq \mathsf{Adv}^{\mathsf{int\text{-}rka}}_{\mathsf{AIAE}}(\lambda)$. The claim follows. □

Taking Eq. (23), Eq. (24), Claim 7 and Claim 8 together, we have $\mathsf{Adv}^{\mathsf{reu}}_{\mathcal{A},\mathsf{FE}}(\lambda) \leq \mathsf{Adv}^{\mathsf{int\text{-}rka}}_{\mathsf{AIAE}}(\lambda) + 2^{-\omega(\log\lambda)}$. Lemma 5 follows. ▮ □

6 Instantiations

6.1 Instantiation of $\mathsf{rrFE}_{\mathsf{prf}}$

We recall the unique-input $\Phi_{\mathsf{ln\text{-}aff}}$-RKA-secure PRF for an affine class $\Phi_{\mathsf{ln\text{-}aff}}$ in [18]. For $\mathfrak{m}, p, q \in \mathbb{N}$ such that $p|q$, the public parameters $\mathsf{pp}_{\mathsf{PRF}}$ is a pair of matrices of the form $\mathbf{A}_0, \mathbf{A}_1 \in \mathbb{Z}_q^{\mathfrak{m}\times\mathfrak{m}}$, where each row of $\mathbf{A}_0$ and $\mathbf{A}_1$ is sampled uniformly from $\{0,1\}^{\mathfrak{m}}$. The secret key $\mathbf{K}$ is a matrix in $\mathbb{Z}_q^{\mathfrak{m}\times\mathfrak{m}}$. Pseudo-random function $F_{\mathsf{LWE}} : \mathbb{Z}_q^{\mathfrak{m}\times\mathfrak{m}} \times \{0,1\}^l \rightarrow \mathbb{Z}_p^{\mathfrak{m}\times\mathfrak{m}}$ is defined as

$$F_{\mathsf{LWE}}(\mathbf{K}, x) := \left\lfloor \mathbf{K} \cdot \prod_{i=1}^{l} \mathbf{A}_{x_i} \right\rfloor_p . \quad (25)$$

Its security is based on the LWE assumption [21].

Theorem 3 ([18]). *Let $q = O(\sqrt{\lambda}/\alpha)$, $\mathfrak{m} = \lceil \lambda \log q \rceil$, $l = \lambda^\epsilon / \log\lambda$, $0 < \epsilon < 1$, $p = 2^{\lambda^\epsilon - \omega(\log\lambda)}$, $\alpha = 2^{-\lambda^\epsilon}$, $c, B > 0$ such that the quantity $(2\mathfrak{m})^l cBp/q$ is negligible in the security parameter λ. Under the $(\mathbb{Z}_q, \lambda, \Psi_\alpha)$-LWE assumption, the PRF defined in Eq. (25) is $\Phi_{\mathsf{ln\text{-}aff}}$-RKA-secure against unique-input adversaries for the class $\Phi_{\mathsf{ln\text{-}aff}} := \{\phi_{\mathbf{C},\mathbf{B}} : \phi_{\mathbf{C},\mathbf{B}}(\mathbf{K}) = \mathbf{C}\mathbf{K} + \mathbf{B} \mid \mathbf{C} \in [-c, c]^{\mathfrak{m}\times\mathfrak{m}}, \mathbf{B} \in \mathbb{Z}_q^{\mathfrak{m}\times\mathfrak{m}}\}$.*

$\underline{\mathsf{crs} \leftarrow \mathsf{Init}(1^\lambda):}$	$\underline{(\mathsf{P},\mathsf{R}) \leftarrow \mathsf{Gen}(\mathsf{crs},\mathsf{w}):}$	$\underline{\mathsf{R} \leftarrow \mathsf{Rep}(\mathsf{crs},\mathsf{P},\mathsf{w}'):}$
$\mathsf{i} \leftarrow_{\$} \mathcal{I}$ (i.e., $\mathsf{H_i} \leftarrow_{\$} \mathcal{H}_{\mathcal{I}}$).	$\mathsf{s} \leftarrow \mathsf{SS.Gen}(\mathsf{w})$.	Parse $\mathsf{P} = (\mathsf{s},\mathsf{t},\mathsf{v})$.
$\mathbf{A}_0, \mathbf{A}_1 \leftarrow \mathsf{Sample}(\mathbb{Z}_q^{\mathsf{m}\times\mathsf{m}})$.	$\mathbf{K} \leftarrow \mathsf{H_i}(\mathsf{w})$.	$\tilde{\mathsf{w}} \leftarrow \mathsf{SS.Rec}(\mathsf{w}',\mathsf{s})$.
$\mathsf{crs} = (\mathsf{H_i}, \mathbf{A}_0, \mathbf{A}_1)$.	$\mathsf{t} \leftarrow_{\$} \mathcal{T}$, $x = (\mathsf{s},\mathsf{t})$.	$\tilde{\mathbf{K}} \leftarrow \mathsf{H_i}(\tilde{\mathsf{w}})$, $x = (\mathsf{s},\mathsf{t})$.
Return crs.	$F_{\mathsf{LWE}}(\mathsf{k}, x) := \left\lfloor \mathbf{K} \cdot \prod_{i=1}^{l} \mathbf{A}_{x_i} \right\rfloor_p = (\mathsf{r},\mathsf{v})$.	$F_{\mathsf{LWE}}(\tilde{\mathbf{K}}, x) = (\tilde{\mathsf{r}}, \tilde{\mathsf{v}})$.
	$\mathsf{P} := (\mathsf{s},\mathsf{t},\mathsf{v})$, $\mathsf{R} := \mathsf{r}$.	If $\tilde{\mathsf{v}} = \mathsf{v}$, Return $\mathsf{R} := \tilde{\mathsf{r}}$.
		Else, Return $\perp$.

Fig. 14. Instantiation of $\mathsf{rrFE_{prf}}$ from F_{LWE}: $\mathsf{rrFE}_{\mathsf{prf_{lwe}}}$.

Obviously, $\Phi_{\mathsf{ln\text{-}aff}}$ covers the key shift function set $\Phi_\Delta := \{\phi_\Delta : \phi_\Delta(\mathbf{K}) = \mathbf{K} + \Delta \mid \Delta \in \mathbb{Z}_q^{\mathsf{m}\times\mathsf{m}}\}$. Hence, F_{LWE} is a unique-input key-shift secure PRF.

Let $\mathbf{A}_0, \mathbf{A}_1 \leftarrow \mathsf{Sample}(\mathbb{Z}_q^{\mathsf{m}\times\mathsf{m}})$ denote sampling two matrices $\mathbf{A}_0, \mathbf{A}_1 \in \mathbb{Z}_q^{\mathsf{m}\times\mathsf{m}}$, where each row of $\mathbf{A}_0$ and $\mathbf{A}_1$ is sampled uniformly from $\{0,1\}^{\mathsf{m}}$. By instantiating the PRF F_{pp} in Fig. 8 with F_{LWE}, the SS with the syndrome-based secure sketch scheme (see the full version [26] for its construction) and $\mathcal{H}_{\mathcal{I}} = \{\mathsf{H_i} : \mathcal{M} \rightarrow \mathbb{Z}_q^{\mathsf{m}\times\mathsf{m}}\}_{i\in\mathcal{I}}$ with a homomorphic universal hash function (see the full version [26] for its concrete construction), and by setting $\mathcal{T} = \{0,1\}^{\omega(\log\lambda)}$, $l = \omega(\log\lambda)$, $|s| = |t| = \frac{l}{2}$, $\mathcal{R} = \mathbb{Z}_p^{\mathsf{m}\times(\mathsf{m}-1)}$, $\mathcal{V} = \mathbb{Z}_p^{\mathsf{m}}$, we get a concrete construction of $\mathsf{rrFE_{prf}}$ from the $(\mathbb{Z}_q, \lambda, \Psi_\alpha)$-LWE assumption.

Corollary 1. *Scheme* $\mathsf{rrFE}_{\mathsf{prf_{lwe}}}$ *in Fig. 14 is a robustly reusable fuzzy extractor based on the LWE assumption.*

The computational complexities of Gen and Rep of $\mathsf{rrFE_{prf}}$ are dominated by the computation of the underlying PRF. According to [3], the best known running time of F_{LWE} is $O(\mathsf{m}\lambda^5)$ per output bit. There are totally $\mathsf{m}^2 \log p$ output bits, so the complexity is $O(\lambda^{11})$.

The length of P is given by $|P| = l + \mathsf{m}\log p$, while the length of R is $|R| = \mathsf{m}(\mathsf{m}-1)\log p$.

Note that $|s| = \omega(\log\lambda)$, and this limits the error tolerance of SS. As a result, $\mathsf{rrFE}_{\mathsf{prf_{lwe}}}$ can only support sub-linear fraction of errors.

6.2 Instantiation of $\mathsf{rrFE_{AIAE}}$

We recall the construction of AIAE from one-time (OT) secure AE and the DDH assumption in [14]. Let $(\bar{N}, N, p, q) \leftarrow \mathsf{GenN}(1^\lambda)$ be a group generation algorithm, where p, q are 2λ-bit safe primes such that $\bar{N} = 2pq + 1$ is also a prime and $N = pq$. Let $\mathcal{H}_{\mathcal{I}_1} = \{\mathsf{H_{i_1}} : \{0,1\}^* \rightarrow \mathbb{Z}_N\}_{\mathsf{i_1}\in\mathcal{I}_1}$ and $\mathcal{H}_{\mathcal{I}_2} = \{\mathsf{H_{i_2}} : \mathbb{QR}_{\bar{N}} \rightarrow \mathcal{K}_{\mathsf{AE}}\}_{\mathsf{i_2}\in\mathcal{I}_2}$ be two families of hash functions, where $\mathbb{QR}_{\bar{N}}$ is the subgroup of quadratic residues of $\mathbb{Z}_{\bar{N}}^*$. Let $\mathsf{AE} = (\mathsf{AE.Enc}, \mathsf{AE.Dec})$ be a OT-secure authenticated encryption scheme with key space $\mathcal{K}_{\mathsf{AE}}$ and message space $\mathcal{M}$. The scheme $\mathsf{AIAE} = (\mathsf{AIAE.Setup}, \mathsf{AIAE.Enc}, \mathsf{AIAE.Dec})$ in [14] is described as follows.

$\mathsf{pp}_{\mathsf{AIAE}} \leftarrow \mathsf{AIAE.Setup}(1^\lambda)$:	$(c_1, c_2, \chi) \leftarrow \mathsf{AIAE.Enc}(\mathsf{k}, \mathsf{m}, \mathsf{aux})$:	$\mathsf{m}/\bot\mathsf{AIAE.Dec}(\mathsf{k}, (c_1, c_2, \chi), \mathsf{aux})$:
$(\bar{N}, N, p, q) \leftarrow \mathsf{GenN}(1^\lambda)$. $g_1, g_2 \leftarrow \mathbb{QR}_{\bar{N}}$. $\mathsf{H}_{\mathsf{i}_1} \leftarrow_\$ \mathcal{H}_{\mathcal{I}_1}, \mathsf{H}_{\mathsf{i}_2} \leftarrow_\$ \mathcal{H}_{\mathcal{I}_2}$. $\mathsf{pp}_{\mathsf{AIAE}} := (\bar{N}, N, p, q, g_1, g_2, \mathsf{H}_{\mathsf{i}_1}, \mathsf{H}_{\mathsf{i}_2})$. Return $\mathsf{pp}_{\mathsf{AIAE}}$.	Parse $\mathsf{k} = (k_1, k_2, k_3, k_4) \in (\mathbb{Z}_N)^4$. $\alpha \leftarrow_\$ \mathbb{Z}_N \setminus \{0\}$. $(c_1, c_2) := (g_1^\alpha, g_2^\alpha) \in \mathbb{QR}_{\bar{N}}^2$. $\beta := \mathsf{H}_{\mathsf{i}_1}(c_1, c_2, \mathsf{aux}) \in \mathbb{Z}_N$. $\kappa := \mathsf{H}_{\mathsf{i}_2}(c_1^{k_1+k_3\beta} \cdot c_2^{k_2+k_4\beta}) \in \mathcal{K}_{\mathsf{AE}}$. $\chi \leftarrow \mathsf{AE.Enc}(\kappa, \mathsf{m})$. Return (c_1, c_2, χ).	Parse $\mathsf{k} = (k_1, k_2, k_3, k_4) \in (\mathbb{Z}_N)^4$. If $(c_1, c_2) \notin \mathbb{QR}_{\bar{N}}^2 \vee (c_1, c_2) = (1, 1)$, Return $\bot$. $\beta := \mathsf{H}_{\mathsf{i}_1}(c_1, c_2, \mathsf{aux}) \in \mathbb{Z}_N$. $\kappa := \mathsf{H}_{\mathsf{i}_2}(c_1^{k_1+k_3\beta} \cdot c_2^{k_2+k_4\beta}) \in \mathcal{K}_{\mathsf{AE}}$. $\mathsf{m}/\bot \leftarrow \mathsf{AE.Dec}(\kappa, \chi)$. Return $\mathsf{m}/\bot$.

Fig. 15. Construction of DDH-based $\mathsf{AIAE}_{\mathsf{ddh}}$ from OT-secure AE.

$\mathsf{crs} \leftarrow \mathsf{Init}(1^\lambda)$:	$(\mathsf{P}, \mathsf{R}) \leftarrow \mathsf{Gen}(\mathsf{crs}, \mathsf{w})$:	$\mathsf{R} \leftarrow \mathsf{Rep}(\mathsf{crs}, \mathsf{P}, \mathsf{w}')$:
$\mathsf{i} \leftarrow_\$ \mathcal{I}$ (i.e., $\mathsf{H}_\mathsf{i} \leftarrow_\$ \mathcal{H}_\mathcal{I}$). $(\bar{N}, N, p, q) \leftarrow \mathsf{Gen}(1^\lambda)$. $g_1, g_2 \leftarrow \mathbb{QR}_{\bar{N}}$. $\mathsf{H}_{\mathsf{i}_1} \leftarrow_\$ \mathcal{H}_{\mathcal{I}_1}, \mathsf{H}_{\mathsf{i}_2} \leftarrow_\$ \mathcal{H}_{\mathcal{I}_2}$. $\mathsf{pp}_{\mathsf{AIAE}} := (\bar{N}, N, p, q, g_1, g_2, \mathsf{H}_{\mathsf{i}_1}, \mathsf{H}_{\mathsf{i}_2})$. $\mathsf{crs} = (\mathsf{H}_\mathsf{i}, \mathsf{pp}_{\mathsf{AIAE}})$. Return crs.	$\mathsf{s} \leftarrow \mathsf{SS.Gen}(\mathsf{w})$. $\mathsf{k} \leftarrow \mathsf{H}_\mathsf{i}(\mathsf{w})$. $\mathsf{m} \leftarrow_\$ \mathcal{M}_{\mathsf{AIAE}}$. Parse $\mathsf{k} = (k_1, k_2, k_3, k_4) \in (\mathbb{Z}_N)^4$. $\alpha \leftarrow_\$ \mathbb{Z}_N \setminus \{0\}$. $(c_1, c_2) := (g_1^w, g_2^w) \in \mathbb{QR}_{\bar{N}}^2$. $t := \mathsf{H}_{\mathsf{i}_1}(c_1, c_2, \mathsf{s}) \in \mathbb{Z}_N$. $\kappa := \mathsf{H}_{\mathsf{i}_2}(c_1^{k_1+k_3t} \cdot c_2^{k_2+k_4t}) \in \mathcal{K}_{\mathsf{AE}}$. $\chi \leftarrow \mathsf{AE.Enc}(\kappa, \mathsf{m})$. $\mathsf{P} := (\mathsf{s}, c_1, c_2, \chi), \mathsf{R} := \mathsf{m}$.	Parse $\mathsf{P} = (\mathsf{s}, c_1, c_2, \chi)$. $\tilde{\mathsf{w}} \leftarrow \mathsf{SS.Rec}(\mathsf{w}', \mathsf{s})$. $\tilde{\mathsf{k}} \leftarrow \mathsf{H}_\mathsf{i}(\tilde{\mathsf{w}})$. Parse $\tilde{\mathsf{k}} = (\tilde{k}_1, \tilde{k}_2, \tilde{k}_3, \tilde{k}_4) \in (\mathbb{Z}_N)^4$. If $(c_1, c_2) \notin \mathbb{QR}_{\bar{N}}^2 \vee (c_1, c_2) = (1, 1)$, Return $\bot$. $\beta := \mathsf{H}_{\mathsf{i}_1}(c_1, c_2, \mathsf{s}) \in \mathbb{Z}_N$. $\kappa := \mathsf{H}_{\mathsf{i}_2}(c_1^{\tilde{k}_1+\tilde{k}_3\beta} \cdot c_2^{\tilde{k}_2+\tilde{k}_4\beta}) \in \mathcal{K}_{\mathsf{AE}}$. $\tilde{\mathsf{m}}/\bot \leftarrow \mathsf{AE.Dec}(\kappa, \chi)$. Return $\tilde{\mathsf{m}}/\bot$.

Fig. 16. Instantiation of $\mathsf{rrFE}_{\mathsf{AIAE}}$ from $\mathsf{AIAE}_{\mathsf{ddh}}$: $\mathsf{rrFE}_{\mathsf{AIAE}_{\mathsf{ddh}}}$.

Theorem 4 [14]. *If the underlying* AE *is OT-secure, the DDH assumption holds w.r.t.* GenN *over* $\mathbb{QR}_{\bar{N}}$, $\mathcal{H}_{\mathcal{I}_1}$ *is collision resistant and* $\mathcal{H}_{\mathcal{I}_2}$ *is universal, then* $\mathsf{AIAE}_{\mathsf{ddh}}$ *in Fig. 15 is IND-*Φ_{raff}*-RKA and weak INT-*Φ_{raff}*-RKA secure, where* $\Phi_{\mathsf{raff}} := \{\phi_{\mathsf{a},\mathsf{b}} : (k_1, k_2, k_3, k_4) \in \mathbb{Z}_N^4 \mapsto (ak_1 + b_1, ak_2 + b_2, ak_3 + b_3, ak_4 + b_4) \in \mathbb{Z}_N^4 \mid a \in \mathbb{Z}_N^*, \mathsf{b} = (b_1, b_2, b_3, b_4) \in \mathbb{Z}_N^4\}$.

Clearly, the key deriving function set Φ_{raff} contains the key-shift function set $\Phi_\Delta := \{\phi_\Delta : (k_1, k_2, k_3, k_4) \in \mathbb{Z}_N^4 \mapsto (k_1+b_1, k_2+b_2, k_3+b_3, k_4+b_4) \in \mathbb{Z}_N^4 \mid \Delta = (b_1, b_2, b_3, b_4) \in \mathbb{Z}_N^4\}$. So the $\mathsf{AIAE}_{\mathsf{ddh}}$ in Fig. 15 is Key-Shift secure. In $\mathsf{AIAE}_{\mathsf{ddh}}$, the building block AE can be instantiated with OT-secure AE [17], where $\kappa = (\kappa_1, \kappa_2, \kappa_3) \in \{0,1\}^{3\lambda}$, $\mathcal{M}_{\mathsf{AE}} = \{0,1\}^\lambda$ and $\chi \in \{0,1\}^{2\lambda}$. The definition of OT-secure AE and the construction in [17] are presented in our full paper [26].

By instantiating the AIAE in Fig. 11 with $\mathsf{AIAE}_{\mathsf{ddh}}$, the SS with the syndrome-based secure sketch scheme (see the full version [26]) and $\mathcal{H}_\mathcal{I} = \{\mathsf{H}_\mathsf{i} : \mathcal{M} \to \mathbb{Z}_N^4\}_{i \in \mathcal{I}}$ with the universal hash function (see the full version [26]), we get a concrete construction of $\mathsf{rrFE}_{\mathsf{AIAE}}$ from the DDH assumption (see Fig. 16).

Corollary 2. *Scheme* $\mathsf{rrFE}_{\mathsf{AIAE}_{\mathsf{ddh}}}$ *in Fig. 16 is a robustly reusable fuzzy extractor based on the DDH assumption.*

The computational complexities of Gen and Rep are dominated by the encryption and decryption algorithms of the underlying $\mathsf{AIAE}_{\mathsf{ddh}}$. Consequently, the complexity of Gen is dominated by four modular exponentiations while that of Rep by two modular exponentiations over $\mathbb{QR}_{\bar{N}}$.

Observe that the ciphertext ct of $\mathsf{AIAE}_{\mathsf{ddh}}$ in Fig. 15 is of size $(4\lambda+1)+(4\lambda+1)+2\lambda = 10\lambda+2$. So the public string P of $\mathsf{rrFE}_{\mathsf{AIAE}_{\mathsf{ddh}}}$ in Fig. 16 has $|s|+10\lambda+2$ bits, where $|s|$ depend on the maximal number of errors t. Note that $\mathsf{AIAE}_{\mathsf{ddh}}$ is very efficient, so this instantiation $\mathsf{rrFE}_{\mathsf{AIAE}_{\mathsf{ddh}}}$ in Fig. 16 is very efficient as well.

Since the syndrome-based secure sketch can correct linear fraction of errors and there is no further limits on the length of s, the resulting $\mathsf{rrFE}_{\mathsf{AIAE}_{\mathsf{ddh}}}$ in Fig. 16 can support linear fraction of errors.

Acknowledgements. We would like to thank the reviewers for their valuable comments. Yunhua Wen and Shengli Liu are supported by the National Natural Science Foundation of China (Grant No. 61672346). Dawu Gu is sponsored by the Natural Science Foundation of China (Grant No. 61472250) and Program of Shanghai Academic Research Leader (16XD1401300).

References

1. Alamélou, Q., et al.: Pseudoentropic isometries: a new framework for fuzzy extractor reusability. In: Kim, J., Ahn, G., Kim, S., Kim, Y., López, J., Kim, T. (eds.) AsiaCCS 2018, pp. 673–684. ACM (2018). https://doi.org/10.1145/3196494.3196530
2. Apon, D., Cho, C., Eldefrawy, K., Katz, J.: Efficient, reusable fuzzy extractors from LWE. In: Dolev, S., Lodha, S. (eds.) CSCML 2017. LNCS, vol. 10332, pp. 1–18. Springer, Cham (2017). https://doi.org/10.1007/978-3-319-60080-2_1
3. Banerjee, A., Peikert, C.: New and improved key-homomorphic pseudorandom functions. In: Garay, J.A., Gennaro, R. (eds.) CRYPTO 2014. LNCS, vol. 8616, pp. 353–370. Springer, Heidelberg (2014). https://doi.org/10.1007/978-3-662-44371-2_20
4. Bennett, C.H., DiVincenzo, D.P.: Quantum information and computation. Nature **404**(6775), 247–255 (2000)
5. Bennett, C.H., Shor, P.W.: Quantum information theory. IEEE Trans. Inf. Theory **44**(6), 2724–2742 (1998). https://doi.org/10.1109/18.720553
6. Boyen, X.: Reusable cryptographic fuzzy extractors. In: Atluri, V., Pfitzmann, B., McDaniel, P.D. (eds.) CCS 2004, pp. 82–91. ACM (2004). https://doi.org/10.1145/1030083.1030096
7. Boyen, X., Dodis, Y., Katz, J., Ostrovsky, R., Smith, A.D.: Secure remote authentication using biometric data. In: Cramer, R. (ed.) EUROCRYPT 2005. LNCS, vol. 3494, pp. 147–163. Springer, Heidelberg (2005). https://doi.org/10.1007/11426639_9
8. Canetti, R., Fuller, B., Paneth, O., Reyzin, L., Smith, A.: Reusable fuzzy extractors for low-entropy distributions. In: Fischlin, M., Coron, J. (eds.) EUROCRYPT 2016. LNCS, vol. 9665, pp. 117–146. Springer, Heidelberg (2016). https://doi.org/10.1007/978-3-662-49890-3_5
9. Cramer, R., Dodis, Y., Fehr, S., Padró, C., Wichs, D.: Detection of algebraic manipulation with applications to robust secret sharing and fuzzy extractors. In: Smart, N.P. (ed.) EUROCRYPT 2008. LNCS, vol. 4965, pp. 471–488. Springer, Heidelberg (2008). https://doi.org/10.1007/978-3-540-78967-3_27
10. Dodis, Y., Katz, J., Reyzin, L., Smith, A.D.: Robust fuzzy extractors and authenticated key agreement from close secrets. In: Dwork, C. (ed.) CRYPTO 2006. LNCS, vol. 4117, pp. 232–250. Springer, Heidelberg (2006). https://doi.org/10.1007/11818175_14
11. Dodis, Y., Reyzin, L., Smith, A.D.: Fuzzy extractors: how to generate strong keys from biometrics and other noisy data. In: Cachin, C., Camenisch, J. (eds.) EUROCRYPT 2004. LNCS, vol. 3027, pp. 523–540. Springer, Heidelberg (2004). https://doi.org/10.1007/978-3-540-24676-3_31

12. Fuller, B., Meng, X., Reyzin, L.: Computational fuzzy extractors. In: Sako, K., Sarkar, P. (eds.) ASIACRYPT 2013. LNCS, vol. 8269, pp. 174–193. Springer, Heidelberg (2013). https://doi.org/10.1007/978-3-642-42033-7_10
13. Galbraith, S.: New discrete logarithm records, and the death of type 1 pairings. https://ellipticnews.wordpress.com/2014/02/01/new-discrete-logarithm-records-and-the-death-of-type-1-pairings/
14. Han, S., Liu, S., Lyu, L.: Efficient KDM-CCA secure public-key encryption for polynomial functions. In: Cheon, J.H., Takagi, T. (eds.) ASIACRYPT 2016. LNCS, vol. 10032, pp. 307–338. Springer, Heidelberg (2016). https://doi.org/10.1007/978-3-662-53890-6_11
15. Hofheinz, D.: Circular chosen-ciphertext security with compact ciphertexts. In: Johansson, T., Nguyen, P.Q. (eds.) EUROCRYPT 2013. LNCS, vol. 7881, pp. 520–536. Springer, Heidelberg (2013). https://doi.org/10.1007/978-3-642-38348-9_31
16. Kanukurthi, B., Reyzin, L.: An improved robust fuzzy extractor. In: Ostrovsky, R., De Prisco, R., Visconti, I. (eds.) SCN 2008. LNCS, vol. 5229, pp. 156–171. Springer, Heidelberg (2008). https://doi.org/10.1007/978-3-540-85855-3_11
17. Kurosawa, K., Desmedt, Y.: A new paradigm of hybrid encryption scheme. In: Franklin, M. (ed.) CRYPTO 2004. LNCS, vol. 3152, pp. 426–442. Springer, Heidelberg (2004). https://doi.org/10.1007/978-3-540-28628-8_26
18. Lewi, K., Montgomery, H.W., Raghunathan, A.: Improved constructions of PRFs secure against related-key attacks. In: Boureanu, I., Owesarski, P., Vaudenay, S. (eds.) ACNS 2014. LNCS, vol. 8479, pp. 44–61. Springer, Cham (2014). https://doi.org/10.1007/978-3-319-07536-5_4
19. Li, S.Z., Jain, A.K. (eds.): Handbook of Face Recognition, 2nd edn. Springer, London (2011). https://doi.org/10.1007/978-0-85729-932-1
20. Marasco, E., Ross, A.: A survey on antispoofing schemes for fingerprint recognition systems. ACM Comput. Surv. **47**(2), 28:1–28:36 (2014). https://doi.org/10.1145/2617756
21. Regev, O.: On lattices, learning with errors, random linear codes, and cryptography. In: Gabow, H.N., Fagin, R. (eds.) STOC 2005, pp. 84–93. ACM (2005). https://doi.org/10.1145/1060590.1060603
22. Rührmair, U., Sehnke, F., Sölter, J., Dror, G., Devadas, S., Schmidhuber, J.: Modeling attacks on physical unclonable functions. In: CCS 2010, pp. 237–249 (2010). https://doi.org/10.1145/1866307.1866335
23. Suh, G.E., Devadas, S.: Physical unclonable functions for device authentication and secret key generation. In: Proceedings of the 44th Annual Design Automation Conference, pp. 9–14 (2007)
24. Wen, Y., Liu, S.: Reusable fuzzy extractor from LWE. In: Susilo, W., Yang, G. (eds.) ACISP 2018. LNCS, vol. 10946, pp. 13–27. Springer, Cham (2018). https://doi.org/10.1007/978-3-319-93638-3_2
25. Wen, Y., Liu, S.: Robustly reusable fuzzy extractor from standard assumptions. In: Peyrin, T., Galbraith, S. (eds.) ASIACRYPT 2018. LNCS, vol. 11274, pp. 459–489. Springer, Cham (2018). https://doi.org/10.1007/978-3-030-03332-3_17
26. Wen, Y., Liu, S., Gu, D.: Generic constructions of robustly reusable fuzzy extractor. Cryptology ePrint Archive, Report 2019/018 (2019). https://eprint.iacr.org/2019/018
27. Wen, Y., Liu, S., Han, S.: Reusable fuzzy extractor from the decisional Diffie-Hellman assumption. Des. Codes Crypt. **86**(11), 2495–2512 (2018). https://doi.org/10.1007/s10623-018-0459-4

Safety in Numbers: On the Need for Robust Diffie-Hellman Parameter Validation

Steven Galbraith[1], Jake Massimo[2(✉)], and Kenneth G. Paterson[2]

[1] University of Auckland, Auckland, New Zealand
s.galbraith@auckland.ac.nz

[2] Royal Holloway, University of London, Egham, UK
{jake.massimo.2015,kenny.paterson}@rhul.ac.uk

Abstract. We consider the problem of constructing Diffie-Hellman (DH) parameters which pass standard approaches to parameter validation but for which the Discrete Logarithm Problem (DLP) is relatively easy to solve. We consider both the finite field setting and the elliptic curve setting.

For finite fields, we show how to construct DH parameters (p, q, g) for the safe prime setting in which $p = 2q + 1$ is prime, q is relatively smooth but fools random-base Miller-Rabin primality testing with some reasonable probability, and g is of order q mod p. The construction involves modifying and combining known methods for obtaining Carmichael numbers. Concretely, we provide an example with 1024-bit p which passes OpenSSL's Diffie-Hellman validation procedure with probability 2^{-24} (for versions of OpenSSL prior to 1.1.0i). Here, the largest factor of q has 121 bits, meaning that the DLP can be solved with about 2^{64} effort using the Pohlig-Hellman algorithm. We go on to explain how this parameter set can be used to mount offline dictionary attacks against PAKE protocols. In the elliptic curve case, we use an algorithm of Bröker and Stevenhagen to construct an elliptic curve E over a finite field $\mathbb{F}_p$ having a specified number of points n. We are able to select n of the form $h \cdot q$ such that h is a small co-factor, q is relatively smooth but fools random-base Miller-Rabin primality testing with some reasonable probability, and E has a point of order q. Concretely, we provide example curves at the 128-bit security level with $h = 1$, where q passes a single random-base Miller-Rabin primality test with probability 1/4 and where the elliptic curve DLP can be solved with about 2^{44} effort. Alternatively, we can pass the test with probability 1/8 and solve the elliptic curve DLP with about $2^{35.5}$ effort. These ECDH parameter sets lead to similar attacks on PAKE protocols relying on elliptic curves.

Our work shows the importance of performing proper (EC)DH parameter validation in cryptographic implementations and/or the wisdom of relying on standardised parameter sets of known provenance.

D. Lin and K. Sako (Eds.): PKC 2019, LNCS 11443, pp. 379–407, 2019.
https://doi.org/10.1007/978-3-030-17259-6_13

1 Introduction

In a recent paper, Albrecht *et al.* [AMPS18] conducted a systematic study of primality testing "in the wild". They found flaws in primality tests implemented in several cryptographic libraries, for example a reliance on fixed-base Miller-Rabin primality testing, or the use of too few rounds of the Miller-Rabin test when testing numbers of unknown provenance. They studied the implications of their work for Diffie-Hellman (DH) in the finite field case, showing how to generate DH parameter sets of the form (p, q, g) in which $p = kq + 1$ for some k, p is prime, q is composite but passes a Miller-Rabin primality test with some probability, yet q is sufficiently smooth that the Discrete Logarithm Problem (DLP) is relatively easy to solve using the Pohlig-Hellman algorithm in the order q subgroup generated by g. Such a parameter set (p, q, g) might pass DH parameter validation with non-negligible probability in a cryptographic library that performs "naive" primality testing on p and q, e.g. one carrying out just a few iterations of Miller-Rabin on each number. If such a parameter set were used in a cryptographic protocol like TLS, then it would also allow an attacker to recover all the keying material and thence break the protocol's security, cf. [Won16]. Albrecht *et al.* [AMPS18] posited this as a plausible attack scenario when, for example, a malicious developer hard-codes the DH parameters into the protocol.

It is notable that the methods of [AMPS18] for producing malicious DH parameters do not work in the safe prime setting, wherein $p = 2q + 1$. This is because Albrecht *et al.* need flexibility in choosing k to arrange p to be prime. It is also because their methods can only produce q with 2 or 3 prime factors, meaning that q needs to be relatively small so that the Pohlig-Hellman algorithm applies (recall that Pohlig-Hellman runs in time $O(B^{1/2})$ where B is a bound on the largest prime factor of q; if q has only 3 prime factors and we want an algorithm requiring 2^{64} effort, then q can have at most 384 bits). Yet requiring safe primes is quite common for DH in the finite field setting. This is because it helps to avoid known attacks, such as small subgroup attacks [LL97, VAS+17], and because it ostensibly makes parameter validation easier. For example, OpenSSL's Diffie-Hellman validation routine `DH_check`[1] insists on the safe prime setting by default. Indeed, it was left as an open problem in [AMPS18] to find a large, sufficiently smooth, composite q passing a primality test with high probability such that $p = 2q + 1$ is also prime or passes a primality test.

Interestingly, more than a decade ago, Bleichenbacher [Ble05] addressed a closely related problem: the construction of malicious DH parameters (p, q, g) for which p and q pass *fixed-base* Miller-Rabin primality tests. This was motivated by his observation that, at this time, the GNU Crypto library was using such a test, with the bases being the first 13 primes $a = 2, 3, \ldots, 41$. He produced a number q having 1095 bits and 27 prime factors, the largest of which has 53

[1] See https://www.openssl.org/docs/man1.1.1/man3/DH_check.html for a description and https://github.com/openssl/openssl/blob/master/crypto/dh/dh_check.c for source code.

bits, such that q *always* passed the primality test of GNU Crypto, and such that $p = 2q + 1$ is prime. His q has very special form: it is a Carmichael number obtained using a modified version of the Erdös method [Erd56]. Of course, his DH parameter set (p, q, g) would not stand up to the more commonly used random-base Miller-Rabin testing, but his construction is nevertheless impressive. Bleichenbacher also showed how such a parameter set could be used to break the SRP Password Authenticated Key Exchange (PAKE) protocol: he showed that a client that accepts bad DH parameters in the SRP protocol can be subject to an offline dictionary attack on its password. Here, the attacker impersonates the server in a run of the SRP protocol, sending the client malicious DH parameters, and inducing the client to send a password-dependent protocol message. It is the attacker's ability to solve the DLP that then enables the offline password recovery. Thus Bleichenbacher had already given a realistic and quite standard attack scenario where robust DH (and ECDH) parameter validation is crucial: PAKE protocols in which an attacker impersonating one of the parties can dictate (EC)DH parameters.

1.1 Our Contributions

In this paper, we address the problem left open from [AMPS18] of finding malicious DH parameters in the safe prime setting. We also study the analogous problem in the elliptic curve setting.

Finite Field Setting: As a flavour of the results to come, we exhibit a DH parameter set $(p = 2q+1, q, g)$ in which p has 1024 bits and q is a composite with 9 prime factors, each at most 121 bits in size, which passes a single random-base Miller-Rabin test with probability 2^{-8}. We show that no number with this many factors can achieve a higher passing probability. Because of the 121-bit bound on the factors of q, the DLP in the subgroup of order q generated by g can be solved with about 2^{64} effort using the Pohlig-Hellman algorithm. When OpenSSL's DH validation routine `DH_check` is used in its default configuration, this parameter set is declared valid with probability 2^{-24} for versions of OpenSSL prior to 1.1.0i (released 14th August 2018). This is because OpenSSL uses the size of q to determine how many rounds of Miller-Rabin to apply, and adopts non-adversarial bounds suitable for average case primality testing derived from [DLP93]. These dictate using 3 rounds of testing for 1023-bit q for versions of OpenSSL prior to 1.1.0i, and 5 rounds in later versions (the increase was made in an effort to achieve a 128-bit security level). We also give a DH parameter set $(p = 2q+1, q, g)$ in which p is a 1024 bit prime and q has 11 prime factors, each at most 100 bits in size, which passes a single random-base Miller-Rabin test with probability 2^{-10}. This parameter set is declared valid with a lower probability of 2^{-30} for versions of OpenSSL prior to 1.1.0i, however the DLP in the subgroup of order q generated by g can be solved using the Pohlig-Hellman algorithm with less effort, in about 2^{54} operations.

The probability of 2^{-24} or 2^{-30} for passing DH validation may not seem very large, and indeed can be seen as a vindication of using safe primes for DH. On the other hand, Bleichenbacher-style attacks against PAKEs can be carried out over many sessions and against multiple users, meaning that the success probability of an overall password recovery attack can be boosted. We exemplify this in the context of J-PAKE, a particular PAKE protocol that was supported in OpenSSL until recently (but we stress that the attack is not specific to J-PAKE).

Obtaining such malicious DH parameter sets in the finite field setting requires some new insights. In particular, we are interested in numbers q that are relatively smooth (having all prime factors less than some pre-determined bound B, say), but which pass random-base Miller-Rabin primality tests with probability as high as possible. We therefore investigate the relationship between the number of prime factors m of a number n and the number of Miller-Rabin non-witnesses $S(n)$ for n, this being the number of bases a for which the Miller-Rabin test fails to declare n composite. We are able to prove that $S(n) \leq \varphi(n)/2^{m-1}$ where $\varphi(\cdot)$ is the Euler function. Since for large n we usually have $\varphi(n) \approx n$, this shows that the highest probability a malicious actor can achieve for passing a single, random-base Miller-Rabin test is (roughly) 2^{1-m}. (This already shows that an adversary can only have limited success, especially if multiple rounds of Miller-Rabin are used.) We are also able to completely characterise those numbers achieving equality in this bound for $m \geq 3$: they are exactly the Carmichael numbers having m prime factors that are all congruent to 3 mod 4.

This characterisation then motivates us to develop constructions for such Carmichael numbers with a controlled number of prime factors. We show how to modify the existing Erdös method [Erd56] and the method of Granville and Pomerance [GP02] for constructing Carmichael numbers, and how to combine them, to obtain cryptographically-sized q with the required properties.

However, this only partly solves our problem, since we also require that $p = 2q + 1$ should pass primality tests (or even be prime). We explore further modifications of our approach so as to avoid trivial arithmetic conditions that prevent p from being prime (the prime 3 is particularly troublesome in this regard). We are also able to show that the probability that p is prime is higher than would be expected for a random choice of p by virtue of properties of the Granville-Pomerance construction: essentially, the construction ensures that p cannot be divisible by certain small primes; we tweak the construction further to enhance this property. Combining all of these steps leads to a detailed procedure by which our example DH parameter set $(p = 2q + 1, q, g)$ described above was obtained. This procedure is amenable to parallelisation. The computation of our particular example required 136 core-days of computation using a server with 3.2 GHz processors.

Elliptic Curve Setting: While the main focus of our work is on the finite field setting, we also briefly study the elliptic curve setting. Here ECDH parameters (p, E, P, q, h) consist of a prime p defining a field (we focus on prime fields, $\mathbb{F}_p$), a curve E over that field defined in some standard form (for example, short Weierstrass form), a point P, the (claimed) order q of P, and a co-factor h such that $\#E(\mathbb{F}_p) = h \cdot q$. Parameter validation should verify the primality of p and

q, and check that P does have order q on E by computing $[q]P$ and comparing the result to the point at infinity.

Bröker and Stevenhagen [BS05] gave a reasonably efficient algorithm to construct an elliptic curve E over a prime field $\mathbb{F}_p$ having a specified number of points n, given the factorisation of n as an input. Their algorithm is sensitive to the number of prime factors of n – fewer is better. We use their algorithm with n being one of our specially constructed Carmichael numbers q passing Miller-Rabin primality testing with highest possible probability, or a small multiple of such a q.

Since $p \approx q$ in the elliptic curve setting and we only need these numbers to have, say, 256 bits to achieve a 128-bit security level, the task of constructing q is much easier than in the finite field setting considered above. Indeed, we could employ a Carmichael number q with 3 prime factors to pass Miller-Rabin with probability 1/4 per iteration. At the 128-bit security level, q then has 3 prime factors each of roughly 85 bits, and the Pohlig-Hellman algorithm would solve the ECDLP on the constructed curve in about 2^{44} steps. Using a Carmichael q with 4 prime factors each of exactly 64 bits, we would pass Miller-Rabin with probability 1/8 per iteration and solve the ECDLP with only 2^{34} effort. We give concrete examples of curves having such properties.

These malicious ECDH parameters (p, E, P, q, h) lead to attacks on PAKEs running over elliptic curves, as well as more traditional ECDH key exchanges. These attacks are fully analogous to those in the finite field setting. They highlight the importance of careful validation of ECDH parameters that may originate from potentially malicious sources, especially in the case of bespoke parameter sets sent as part of a cryptographic protocol. For example, the specification of the TLS extension for elliptic curve cryptography [BWBG+06] caters for the use of custom elliptic curves, though this option does not seem to be widely supported in implementations at present. Our work shows that robust checking of any such parameters would be highly advisable.

1.2 Further Related Work

In the light of the Snowden revelations, a body of work examining methods by which the security of cryptographic algorithms and protocols can be deliberately undermined has been developed. Our work can be seen as fitting into that theme (though we stress that the application of our work to PAKE protocols shows that there are concerns in the "standard" cryptographic setting too).

Young and Yung laid the foundations of kleptography, that is, cryptography designed with malicious intent, see for example [YY97]. Bellare *et al.* [BPR14] studied the problem of how to subvert symmetric encryption algorithms, and how to protect against such subversions.

Fried *et al.* [FGHT17] followed up on early work of Gordon [Gor93] to examine how to backdoor the DLP in the finite field setting. These works showed how to construct large primes p for which the Special Number Field Sieve makes solving the DLP possible if one is in possession of trapdoor information about how p was generated. This provides another avenue to subverting the security of DH parameters. It appears that the 1024-bit example in [FGHT17] is not in the safe-prime setting, however.

The NIST DualEC generator was extensively analysed [CNE+14] and found to be used in Juniper's ScreenOS operating system in an exploitable way [CMG+16]. This inspired more theoretical follow-up work on backdoored RNGs [DGG+15] and PRNGs [DPSW16].

Bernstein *et al.* [BCC+15] extensively discuss the problem of certifying that elliptic curve parameter sets are free of manipulation during generation.

The dangers of allowing support for old algorithms and protocol versions, especially those allowing export-grade cryptography, are made manifest by the FREAK [BBD+15], Logjam [ABD+15] and DROWN [ASS+16] attacks on SSL and TLS.

2 Miller-Rabin Primality Testing and Pseudoprimes

Suppose $n > 1$ is an odd integer to be tested for primality. We first write $n = 2^e d + 1$ where d is odd. If n is prime, then for any integer a with $1 \le a < n$, we have:

$$a^d = 1 \mod n \quad \text{or} \quad a^{2^i d} = -1 \bmod n \text{ for some } 0 \le i < e.$$

The Miller-Rabin test then consists of checking the above conditions for some value a, declaring a number to be composite if both conditions fail and to be (probably) prime if either of the two conditions hold. If one condition holds, then we say n is a *pseudoprime to base* a, or that a is a *non-witness to the compositeness of* n (since n may be composite, but a does not demonstrate this fact).

We begin by exploring the relationship between a composite number n and the number of non-witnesses this number possesses, denoted $S(n)$. Since in this work we are interested in constructing numbers n that fool the Miller-Rabin test with as high a probability as possible for random bases a, our main interest is in constructing n for which $S(n)$ is as large as possible. However, since we are also interested in solving discrete logarithm problems in subgroups of order n, we will also want n to be relatively smooth.

The following theorem can be used to calculate the exact number of non-witnesses that some composite n has:

Theorem 1 ([Mon80], Proposition 1). *Let n be an odd composite integer. Suppose that $n = 2^e \cdot d + 1$ where d is odd. Also suppose that n has prime factorisation $n = \prod_{i=1}^{m} p_i^{q_i}$ where each prime p_i can be expressed as $2^{e_i} \cdot d_i + 1$ with each d_i odd. Then:*

$$S(n) = \left(\frac{2^{\min(e_i) \cdot m} - 1}{2^m - 1} + 1 \right) \prod_{i=1}^{m} \gcd(d, d_i). \tag{1}$$

A general upper-bound on $S(n)$ is given by results of [Mon80, Rab80]:

Theorem 2 (Monier-Rabin Bound). *Let $n \neq 9$ be odd and composite. Then*

$$S(n) \leq \frac{\varphi(n)}{4}$$

where φ denotes the Euler totient function.

It is known from [Mon80] that the bound in Theorem 2 is met with equality for numbers n of the form $n = (2x+1)(4x+1)$ with $2x+1, 4x+1$ prime and x odd. It is also known that the bound is met with equality for numbers n that are Carmichael numbers with three prime factors, $n = p_1 p_2 p_3$, and where each factor p_i is congruent to 3 mod 4.

Definition 1 (Carmichael numbers). *Let n be an odd composite number. Then n is said to be a Carmichael number if $a^{n-1} = 1 \bmod n$ for all a co-prime to n.*

Note that Carmichael numbers are those for which the Fermat primality test fails to identify n as composite for all co-prime bases a.

Theorem 3 (Korselt's Criterion). *Let n be odd and composite. Then n is a Carmichael number if and only if n is square-free and for all prime divisors p of n, we have $p - 1 \mid n - 1$.*

For a proof of this theorem, see [Mon80]. It is also known that Carmichael numbers must have at least 3 distinct prime factors.

2.1 On the Relationship Between $S(n)$ and m, the Number of Prime Factors of n

The following result is central to our work.

Theorem 4 (Factor Bound on $S(n)$). *Let n be an odd composite integer with prime factorisation $n = \prod_{i=1}^{m} p_i^{q_i}$. Write $n = 2^e d + 1$ where d is odd and $p_i = 2^{e_i} d_i + 1$ where each d_i is odd. Then $S(n) \leq \frac{\varphi(n)}{2^{m-1}}$, where $\varphi(\cdot)$ denotes Euler's function, with equality if and only if n is square-free and, for all i, $e_i = 1$ and $d_i \mid d$.*

Proof. We have:

$$\begin{aligned}
\frac{\frac{2^{\min(e_i)\cdot m} - 1}{2^m - 1} + 1}{2^{\min(e_i)\cdot m}} &= \frac{1}{2^m - 1} + \left(\frac{1}{2^{\min(e_i)\cdot m}}\right)\left(1 - \frac{1}{2^m - 1}\right) \\
&\leq \frac{1}{2^m - 1} + \left(\frac{1}{2^m}\right)\left(1 - \frac{1}{2^m - 1}\right) \\
&= \frac{2(2^m - 1)}{(2^m)(2^m - 1)} \\
&= \frac{1}{2^{m-1}}.
\end{aligned}$$

Therefore, using Theorem 1, we have:

$$S(n) = \left(\frac{2^{\min(e_i)\cdot m} - 1}{2^m - 1} + 1\right)\prod_{i=1}^{m}\gcd(d, d_i) \leq \frac{1}{2^{m-1}}\cdot 2^{\min(e_i)\cdot m}\prod_{i=1}^{m}\gcd(d, d_i) \tag{2}$$

$$\leq \frac{1}{2^{m-1}}\prod_{i=1}^{m}(2^{e_i}\cdot d_i) \tag{3}$$

$$= \frac{1}{2^{m-1}}\prod_{i=1}^{m}(p_i - 1)$$

$$\leq \frac{1}{2^{m-1}}\varphi(n). \tag{4}$$

We obtain equality in Eq. (2) above when $\min(e_i) = 1$ and in Eq. (3) when $e_1 = e_2 = \cdots = e_m$ and $\gcd(d, d_i) = d_i$ for all i (which is equivalent to $d_i \mid d$). We obtain equality in Eq. (4) when $\varphi(n) = \prod_{i=1}^{m}(p_i - 1)$. This occurs if and only n is square free. The result follows.

Remark: For the case $m = 2$, the bound of Theorem 4 can be strengthened to $S(n) \leq \varphi(n)/4$, that is, the Monier-Rabin bound. As mentioned above, Monier [Mon80] remarked that the bound is met in this case for numbers of the form $n = (2x + 1)(4x + 1)$ with $2x + 1, 4x + 1$ prime and x odd, see also [Nar14]. This form was exploited extensively in [AMPS18], but will be less useful in our work because we require numbers n of cryptographic size that satisfy a smaller smoothness bound. For example, we will be interested in constructing 1024-bit n in which each prime factor has at most 128 bits, meaning n will have at least 8 prime factors.

We now go on to show that, when $m \geq 3$, the bound in the above theorem is attained if and only if n is a Carmichael number of special form.

Theorem 5. *Let n be a Carmichael number with $m \geq 3$ prime factors that are all congruent to* 3 mod 4. *Then $S(n) = \frac{\varphi(n)}{2^{m-1}}$. Conversely, if n has $m \geq 3$ prime factors and $S(n) = \frac{\varphi(n)}{2^{m-1}}$, then n is a Carmichael number whose prime factors are all congruent to* 3 mod 4.

Proof. By Korselt's criterion we know that n is square-free. Write $n = p_1 \cdots p_m$ where the p_i are prime and, by assumption, $p_i = 3 \bmod 4$ for each i. As before, we write $n = 2^e d + 1$ where d is odd and $p_i = 2^{e_i} d_i + 1$ where each d_i is odd. Since $p_i = 3 \bmod 4$ for each i, it is immediate that $e_i = 1$ for each i. Moreover, by Korselt's criterion, we have $2^{e_i} d_i | 2^e d$, and hence $d_i | d$, for each i. The result follows from the converse part of Theorem 4.

For the converse, let $n = \prod_{i=1}^{m} p_i^{q_i}$. Suppose $p_i = 2^{e_i} d_i + 1$ where d_i is odd and $n = 2^e d + 1$ where d is odd. Necessarily, $e \geq 1$. By Theorem 4, since $S(n) = \frac{\varphi(n)}{2^{m-1}}$, we have that n is square free, $e_i = 1$ for all i and $d_i \mid d$ for all i. Since $e_i = 1$ $\forall i$, we have that $p_i = 3 \bmod 4$ and $2^{e_i} \mid 2^e$ for all i. Also, since $d_i \mid d$ for all i, it follows that $2_i^e d_i \mid 2^e d$ for all i, and thus $p_i - 1 \mid n - 1$ for all i. Hence, n satisfies Korselt's criterion, and n is a Carmichael number.

Example 1. Table 1 gives, for each $3 \leq m \leq 10$, the smallest number with m prime factors achieving the bound of Theorem 4. In the light of Theorem 5, these are all Carmichael numbers whose prime factors are all congruent to 3 mod 4. These are obtained from data made available by Pinch and reported in [Pin08]. Of course, these examples are all much too small for cryptographic use.

Table 1. The smallest number C_m with m prime factors that meets the upper bound of $\varphi(C_m)/2^{m-1}$ on $S(C_m)$.

m	C_m	$S(C_m)$
3	$7 \cdot 19 \cdot 67$	$\varphi(C_m)/4$
4	$7 \cdot 19 \cdot 67 \cdot 199$	$\varphi(C_m)/8$
5	$7 \cdot 11 \cdot 19 \cdot 103 \cdot 9419$	$\varphi(C_m)/16$
6	$7 \cdot 11 \cdot 31 \cdot 47 \cdot 163 \cdot 223$	$\varphi(C_m)/32$
7	$19 \cdot 23 \cdot 31 \cdot 67 \cdot 71 \cdot 199 \cdot 271$	$\varphi(C_m)/64$
8	$11 \cdot 31 \cdot 43 \cdot 47 \cdot 71 \cdot 139 \cdot 239 \cdot 271$	$\varphi(C_m)/128$
9	$19 \cdot 31 \cdot 43 \cdot 67 \cdot 71 \cdot 103 \cdot 239 \cdot 307 \cdot 631$	$\varphi(C_m)/256$
10	$7 \cdot 11 \cdot 19 \cdot 31 \cdot 47 \cdot 79 \cdot 139 \cdot 163 \cdot 271 \cdot 2347$	$\varphi(C_m)/512$

3 Generating Large Carmichael Numbers

The results in the previous section motivate the search for cryptographically-sized Carmichael numbers with a chosen number of prime factors, with each factor congruent to 3 mod 4. In this section, we discuss two existing constructions for Carmichael numbers: the Erdös method [Erd56] and the method of Granville and Pomerance [GP02]. We show how to combine these two methods to produce large examples. We also show how to modify the constructions to improve the probability that they will succeed in constructing large examples meeting our additional congruence requirements.

3.1 The Erdös Method

Erdös [Erd56] gave a method to construct Carmichael numbers with many prime factors. The method starts with a highly composite number L and then considers the set $\mathcal{P}(L) = \{p : p \text{ prime}, p - 1 \mid L, p \nmid L\}$. If for some subset $p_1, p_2, \ldots, p_m$ of $\mathcal{P}(L)$, we have $p_1 p_2 \cdots p_m = 1 \bmod L$, then $n = p_1 p_2 \cdots p_m$ is a Carmichael number, by Korselt's criterion. This is easy to see: by construction, $p_i - 1 \mid L$; the condition $n = 1 \bmod L$ implies that $L \mid n - 1$; it follows that $p_i - 1 \mid n - 1$, and n is evidently square-free.

Example 2. If $L = 120 = 2^3 \cdot 3 \cdot 5$, then $\mathcal{P}(L) = \{7, 11, 13, 31, 41, 61\}$. If we examine all the subsets of $\mathcal{P}(L)$, we find that $41040 = 7 \cdot 11 \cdot 13 \cdot 41$, $172081 = 7 \cdot 13 \cdot 31 \cdot 61$ and $852841 = 11 \cdot 31 \cdot 41 \cdot 61$ are all 1 mod 120, and so are all Carmichael numbers.

The Erdös method lends itself to a computational approach to generating Carmichael numbers with a chosen number of prime factors m for moderate values of L. For a given L, the set $\mathcal{P}(L)$ can be quickly generated by considering each factor f of the selected L and testing the primality of $f + 1$. One can then examine all m-products of distinct elements from $\mathcal{P}(L)$ and test the product n against the condition $n = 1 \bmod L$.

Alternatively, as pointed out in [Ble05], one can employ a time-memory trade-off (TMTO): for some k, build a table of all k-products $p_1 \cdots p_k$ from $\mathcal{P}(L)$, and look for collisions in that table with the inverses of $(m-k)$-products $(p_{k+1} \cdots p_m)^{-1} \bmod L$ from $\mathcal{P}(L)$. Such a collision gives an equation

$$p_1 \cdots p_k = (p_{k+1} \cdots p_m)^{-1} \bmod L$$

and hence

$$p_1 \cdots p_k p_{k+1} \cdots p_m = 1 \bmod L.$$

Of course, one needs to take care to avoid repeated primes in such an approach. For the L we use later, the direct approach suffices, and so we did not explore this direction further.

3.2 The Selection of L in the Erdös Method

Clearly, L must be even, otherwise the integers p satisfying $p - 1 \mid L$ will all be even. We can ensure that all primes p in $\mathcal{P}(L)$ satisfy $p = 3 \bmod 4$ by setting the maximum power of 2 in L to be 1, i.e. by setting $L = 2 \bmod 4$. For then each factor f of L must be 2 mod 4, and hence $p = f + 1 = 3 \bmod 4$. As we shall see later, other conditions can be imposed on L as needed.

Note that since $2 \mid L$, $p = 3$ is a candidate for inclusion in $\mathcal{P}(L)$. However, if 3 is also a factor of L then it is excluded because of the additional condition $p \nmid L$ on elements of $\mathcal{P}(L)$; this condition is needed in general, since if $p \mid L$, then any product $p_1 p_2 \cdots p_m$ including p as a factor would be 0 mod L instead of the required 1 mod L.

For the Erdös method to be successful in producing a Carmichael number with m prime factors, we need to find a product p_i such that $p_1 p_2 \cdots p_m = 1 \bmod L$. One can see that the number of possible products that can be considered is $\binom{|\mathcal{P}(L)|}{m}$. Let us make the heuristic assumption that the values of $p_1 p_2 \cdots p_m$ are uniformly distributed amongst the odd numbers modulo the even integer L. Then we need to ensure that:

$$\binom{|\mathcal{P}(L)|}{m} \gtrapprox L/2$$

for the method to have a reasonable chance of success.

Table 2. For a given L_{bound} (column 1), the value L_{best} (column 2) gives the value of $L \leq L_{bound}$ resulting in the largest set of primes $\mathcal{P}(L)$, subject to the additional restriction that $p = 3 \bmod 4$ for all $p \in \mathcal{P}(L)$.

L_{bound}	L_{best}	$\lvert\mathcal{P}(L_{best})\rvert$
2^{20}	$810810 = 2 \cdot 3^4 \cdot 5 \cdot 7 \cdot 11 \cdot 13$	39
2^{21}	$2088450 = 2 \cdot 3^3 \cdot 5^2 \cdot 7 \cdot 13 \cdot 17$	50
2^{22}	$4054050 = 2 \cdot 3^4 \cdot 5^2 \cdot 7 \cdot 11 \cdot 13$	58
2^{23}	$7657650 = 2 \cdot 3^2 \cdot 5^2 \cdot 7 \cdot 11 \cdot 13 \cdot 17$	65
2^{24}	$13783770 = 2 \cdot 3^4 \cdot 5 \cdot 7 \cdot 11 \cdot 13 \cdot 17$	73
2^{25}	$22972950 = 2 \cdot 3^3 \cdot 5^2 \cdot 7 \cdot 11 \cdot 13 \cdot 17$	89
2^{26}	$53603550 = 2 \cdot 3^2 \cdot 5^2 \cdot 7^2 \cdot 11 \cdot 13 \cdot 17$	93

Thus it is desirable to find L such that $|\mathcal{P}(L)|$ is as large as possible. In turn, this heuristically depends on L being as smooth as possible, since such an L has many factors f and therefore many possible candidates $p = f + 1$ that, if prime, can be included in $\mathcal{P}(L)$. This analysis of course depends on the primality of the different values $f + 1$ being in some sense independent for the different factors f of L; this is a reasonable assumption given standard heuristics on the distribution of primes.

For various bounds L_{bound}, we have computed the value of $L \leq L_{bound}$ giving the largest set $\mathcal{P}(L)$, where we impose the restriction $L = 2 \bmod 4$ to ensure the primes in $\mathcal{P}(L)$ are all 3 mod 4. The results are shown in Table 2, and bear out our heuristic analysis suggesting that smooth L make the best choices.

Example 3. Suppose $L = 53603550$. Then $|\mathcal{P}(L)| = 93$ with:

$$\begin{aligned}\mathcal{P}(L) = \{&19, 23, 31, 43, 67, 71, 79, 103, 127, 131, 151, 199, 211, 239, 307, 331, 443,\\ &463, 491, 547, 631, 859, 883, 911, 991, 1051, 1123, 1171, 1327, 1471, 1531,\\ &1667, 1871, 1951, 2003, 2143, 2311, 2551, 2731, 3571, 3823, 3851, 4951,\\ &4999, 5851, 6007, 7151, 7351, 8191, 9283, 10711, 11467, 11551, 16831,\\ &17851, 19891, 22051, 23563, 26951, 27847, 28051, 33151, 34651, 41651,\\ &42043, 43759, 46411, 50051, 53551, 54979, 57331, 72931, 77351, 91631\\ &102103, 117811, 124951, 126127, 150151, 232051, 242551, 286651,\\ &324871, 350351, 450451, 824671, 1051051, 1093951, 1191191, 1624351,\\ &2144143, 4873051, 10720711\}.\end{aligned}$$

As representative examples, the following Carmichael numbers with, respectively 8 and 16 prime factors, can then be obtained by running a simple search algorithm over subsets of $\mathcal{P}(L)$ to find subsets whose products are 1 mod L:

$$C_8 = 19 \cdot 23 \cdot 43 \cdot 239 \cdot 859 \cdot 9283 \cdot 11467 \cdot 242551$$
$$C_{16} = 19 \cdot 23 \cdot 31 \cdot 43 \cdot 67 \cdot 71 \cdot 79 \cdot 103 \cdot 127 \cdot 131 \cdot 491 \cdot 1531 \cdot 3851 \cdot 7151 \cdot 11467 \cdot 33151$$

Here

$$C_8 = 9960524081137300040370 1$$

and

$$C_{16} = 2952075740383473675231403915547850874801.$$

Our SAGE [S+18] implementation of the Erdös method running on a 3.3 GHz processor took 4.83 s to find C_8 and 1.78 s to find C_{16}. The code used to generate these examples can be found in the full version [GMP19].

It would be tempting to think that this method could easily be scaled-up to numbers of cryptographic size. However, this is not so easy. To illustrate, suppose we wanted to construct a 1024-bit n with, say, $m = 8$ prime factors, all having about 128 bits. This would necessitate using an L substantially larger than 2^{128}, which would make the direct approach of finding a product $p_1 \cdots p_8 = 1 \bmod L$ infeasible; even the TMTO version would require prohibitive time and memory, on the order of 2^{64} of each.

3.3 The Method of Granville and Pomerance

The second method of generating Carmichael numbers that we consider is due to Granville and Pomerance [GP02]. This takes a small Carmichael number with m (known) factors and produces from it a larger Carmichael number, also with m factors. It is based on the following theorem.

Theorem 6 (Granville and Pomerance [GP02]**).** *Let* $n = p_1 p_2 \cdots p_m$ *be a Carmichael Number. Let* $L = \mathrm{lcm}(p_i - 1)$ *and let* M *be any integer with* $M \equiv 1 \bmod L$. *Set* $q_i = 1 + M(p_i - 1)$. *Then* $N = q_1 \cdots q_m$ *is a Carmichael number whenever each* q_i *is prime.*

Recall that we are interested in Carmichael numbers N in which all prime factors are congruent to 3 mod 4. Fortunately, as the following lemma shows, the method of Granville and Pomerance 'preserves' this property.

Lemma 1. *With notation as in Theorem 6, suppose* $p_i \equiv 3 \pmod 4$. *Then* $q_i = 3 \pmod 4$.

Proof. The integer L is even as it is the least common multiple of even integers $p_i - 1$. But $M \equiv 1 \pmod L$ implies that M is odd; write $M = 2s + 1$. Moreover, since $p_i = 3 \bmod 4$, we have $p_i - 1 = 2d_i$ with d_i odd; write $d_i = 2t_i + 1$. Then $q_i = 1 + M(p_i - 1) = 1 + (2s+1)(4t_i + 2) = 3 + 4(2st_i + s + t_i)$, which is evidently 3 mod 4.

There are two important choices of variable in this method: M and the starting Carmichael number n.

Clearly, the properties of the resulting Carmichael number N are dependent on n, for example the value of each prime factor mod 4 (as seen in Lemma 1) and the number m of these factors.

The effects of M are more subtle. In particular, we need to select an M such that all the resulting $q_i = 1 + M(p_i - 1)$ are prime. Using the heuristic that the values q_i are as likely to be prime as random choices of odd q_i of the same size, the probability that a random choice of M yields m primes is approximately $(2/\ln(B))^m$ where B is a bound on the q_i. This probability drops very quickly for N of cryptographic size and even moderate m. For example, with B of 128 bits and $m = 8$ (so that the target N has 1024 bits), we obtain $(2/\ln(B))^m \approx 2^{-43.77}$. Clearly then, simply making random choices of M is unlikely to yield candidates of cryptographically interesting sizes in a reasonable amount of time. We therefore turn to investigating methods for improving the probability that the q_i are all prime by careful choice of M.

3.4 The Selection of M in the Method of Granville and Pomerance

The only requirement on M coming from Theorem 6 is that $M \equiv 1 \pmod{L}$, where $L = \text{lcm}(p_i - 1)$. However, by a careful choice of M we can both ensure that this is true, and that the resulting values $q_i = 1+M(p_i-1)$ are more likely to be prime than if M was chosen at random.

Our approach is inspired by techniques originally introduced in [JPV00, JP06] for generating primes on low-end processors. There, one considers numbers of the form $p = kH + \delta$ where H is smooth (say, H is the product of the first h primes, $H = \prod_{i=1}^{h} s_i$), δ is chosen to be co-prime to H, and k is a free parameter. Then p is guaranteed to be divisible by each of $s_1, \ldots, s_h$, since $p = \delta \neq 0 \bmod s_i$. By choosing different values of k, one can generate different candidates for p, and test them for primality. Numbers p generated in this way have a higher probability of being prime than uniformly random candidates, since they are effectively guaranteed to pass trial divisions by each of the small primes dividing H. We refer to this process as 'sieving' by the primes $s_1, s_2, \ldots, s_h$. An analysis using the inclusion-exclusion principle can be used to evaluate the increase in probability that can be achieved by this means; a factor of 5 increase is typical even for moderate values of h, since many small divisors can be eliminated.

We present an adaptation of this method to generate candidates for M in the method of Granville and Pomerance, such that the resulting q_i are guaranteed to be indivisible by many small primes.

Since $M = 1 \pmod{L}$, we can write $M = kL + 1$, where k now becomes the free parameter in the construction method. Then

$$q_i - 1 = M(p_i - 1) = (kL + 1)(p_i - 1) = kLp_i + p_i - kL - 1.$$

Rearranging, we get:

$$q_i = kLp_i + p_i - kL = kL(p_i - 1) + p_i.$$

Note that, typically, many small primes will divide L because L is the least common multiple of the $p_i - 1$. This is especially so if we use the Erdös method to generate the starting Carmichael number n, since it starts with a smooth number which all the $p_i - 1$ will divide.

Now none of the primes dividing L can be a p_i (again, because L is the least common multiple of the $p_i - 1$). For each such prime p, we have:

$$q_i = p_i \neq 0 \bmod p.$$

Hence, we are assured that q_i is not divisible by any of the prime divisors of L: we achieve 'free' sieving on q_i for every such divisor.

Now we consider other primes (not equal to any of the p_i, and not dividing L). Let s denote such a prime, and suppose we choose k such that s divides k. Recalling that $M = kL + 1$, then we get:

$$q_i = kL(p_i - 1) + p_i = p_i \neq 0 \bmod s.$$

Hence, by choosing k so that it is divisible by a product of primes s_j that do not equal any of the p_i nor any of the divisors of L, we also obtain sieving on all the s_j. Of course, we can include an additional factor when building k to ensure that the resulting q_i are of any desired bit-size and that there are sufficiently many choices for k (and thence M). In what follows, we write $k = k' \prod_j s_j$ for some collection of primes s_j subject to the above constraints; k' now replaces k as the free parameter in the construction.

The overall sieving effectiveness will be determined by the collection of prime factors present in L and the s_j. Let us denote the complete set of primes from these two sources as $\{s_1, \ldots, s_h\}$. Then the fraction of non-prime candidates for each q_i that are removed by the sieving can be calculated using the formula:

$$\sigma = 1 - \prod_{i=1}^{h} \left(1 - \frac{1}{s_i}\right). \tag{5}$$

This means that the prime values of q_i are now concentrated in a fraction $1-\sigma$ of the initial set of candidates, so that a random selection from this reduced set is $1/(1-\sigma)$ times more likely to result in a prime. Notice that the effect here is multiplicative across all m of the q_i – they all benefit from the sieving on the s_i. Note too how powerful the prime $s = 3$ is in sieving, contributing a factor $2/3$ to the product term determining σ.

The overall effect is to improve the success probability for each trial of the modified Granville-Pomerance construction (involving a choice of k') from $(2/\ln(B))^m$ to $(2/(1-\sigma)\ln(B))^m$.

Example 4. Using a C implementation of the modified Granville-Pomerance construction, with the Carmichael number C_8 of Example 3 as the starting value n and $L = 53603550$, we found that choosing

$$k = 7891867750444302551322686487$$

produces the 8-factor, 1024-bit Carmichael number $N = q_1 \cdots q_8$ where:

$$
\begin{aligned}
q_1 &= 7614578295977916492449157442324119319 \\
q_2 &= 9306706806195231268548970207285034723 \\
q_3 &= 17767349357281805149048034032089611743 \\
q_4 &= 100681646357930229177938859515174466539 \\
q_5 &= 362961565441614019473409838084116354159 \\
q_6 &= 3926584207959278937939615521091804194983 \\
q_7 &= 48504863745379328056901132907604640055 67 \\
q_8 &= 1026064425383024247357523965353175078100 51.
\end{aligned}
$$

Here, q_8, the largest prime factor, has 137 bits.

As pointed out in Sect. 3.3, with B of 128 bits and $m = 8$ (so that the target N has 1024 bits), we estimate the standard Granville-Pomerance construction to have a success rate of $(2/\ln(B))^m \approx 2^{-43.8}$ per trial, so that the expected number of trials would be about $2^{43.8}$. With our modified version of the Granville-Pomerance construction we obtain sieving on each of the q_i by the primes $3, 5, 7, 11, 13, 17$ that divide L (in this case, we did not add any more primes to k to improve the sieving further). This gives us $\sigma = 0.6393$ and therefore reduces the expected number of trials by a factor of about $1/(1-\sigma)^m \approx 2^{11.8}$ to roughly 2^{32} trials. Finding the above N using our 'C' implementation actually took $2^{31.51}$ trials and less than one core-hour running on 3.3 GHz CPUs.

The above example illustrates that we can generate numbers that are of cryptographically interesting size, have a controlled number of prime factors (and therefore achieve a given smoothness bound), achieve the upper bound of Theorem 4 on the number of Miller-Rabin non-witnesses, and hence maximise the probability of passing random-base Miller-Rabin primality tests.

4 Fooling Diffie-Hellman Parameter Validation in the Safe-Prime Setting

In this section, we target the problem of producing Diffie-Hellman parameters for the prime order setting, where the parameters are able to pass validity tests on the parameters but where the relevant Discrete Logarithm Problem (DLP) is relatively easy.

A Diffie-Hellman (DH) parameter set (p, q, g) in the prime order setting is formed of a prime p with $g \in \mathbb{Z}_p$ generating a group of prime order q, where $q \mid p - 1$. As explained in the introduction, validating the correctness of DH parameters is vital in ensuring the subsequent security of the DH key exchange. As also explained there, Bleichenbacher [Ble05] provided an extreme example of this in the context of Password Authenticated Key Exchange (PAKE): he showed that a client that accepts bad DH parameters in the SRP protocol can be subject to an offline dictionary attack on its password. Here, the attacker impersonates the server in a run of the SRP protocol, and induces the client to send a password-dependent protocol message; the attacker's ability to solve the DLP is what enables the offline password recovery.

DH validation checks should consist of primality tests on both p and q as well as a verification that $p = kq + 1$ for some integer k. The checks should also ensure that the given generator g generates the subgroup of order q. The security is based in part on size of q: it must still be large enough to thwart the Pohlig-Hellman algorithm for solving the DLP. For prime q, this algorithm runs in time $O(\sqrt{q})$.

Albrecht *et al.* [AMPS18] already showed how to subvert DH parameters in the case where k is permitted to be large and where a weak primality test based on Miller-Rabin with a small number of rounds is permitted. For example, they selected q to be of the form $(2x+1)(4x+1)$ with both factors prime, and then tried k of a suitable size until $kq + 1$ was prime. This gives an $O(q^{1/4})$ algorithm using the Pohlig-Hellman algorithm in the subgroups of orders $2x+1$ and $4x + 1$, with q passing t rounds of random-base Miller-Rabin testing with the best possible probability 4^{-t} (this coming from the Monier-Rabin bound).

However, many implementations insist on using DH parameters in which p is a safe prime; that is, they require $p = 2q + 1$, in which case g must have order q or $2q$ if it is not equal to ± 1. OpenSSL in its default setting is a good example of such a library. Insisting on safe primes to a large extent eliminates small subgroup attacks. It is also a good option in the context of protocols like SSL/TLS in which a server following the specification only provides p and g but not q.[2] As noted in the introduction, the techniques of [AMPS18] do not extend to the safe-prime setting, since they need the flexibility in k to force $p = kq + 1$ to be prime. The resulting q would also be too large and have too few prime factors to make the Pohlig-Hellman algorithm effective.

This leaves open the problem of fooling DH parameter validation when random-base Miller-Rabin tests are used for checking p and q (as should be the case in practice, in light of the work of [Arn95] and [Ble05]).

4.1 Generating Carmichael Numbers q Such that $p = 2q + 1$ Is Prime

To summarise the above discussion, we wish to construct a number q such that q and $p = 2q+1$ both pass random-base Miller-Rabin primality testing, and such that q is sufficiently smooth that the Pohlig-Hellman algorithm can be used to solve the DLP in some subgroup mod p.

Our approach parallels that of [Ble05]: we construct q as a large Carmichael number with m prime factors that are all 3 mod 4 using the techniques from the previous section. Then q will pass random-base Miller-Rabin primality tests

2 For if p is not a safe prime, then the client is forced to blindly accept the parameters or to do an expensive computation to factorise $p - 1$ and then test g for different possible orders arising as factors of $p - 1$. We know of no cryptographic library that does the latter.

with the highest possible probability amongst all integers with m prime factors. After constructing a candidate q, we test $2q+1$ for primality (using a robust primality test), rejecting q if this test fails, and stopping if it passes. If $2q+1$ is prime, then the DLP in the subgroup of order q can be solved with $O(mB^{1/2})$ effort where B is an upper bound on the prime factors of q.

The approach just described will fail in practice. The first reason is that it is unlikely that $2q+1$ will happen to be prime by chance (the probability is about $1/\ln q$ by standard density estimates for primes). The second reason is that there may be arithmetic reasons why $2q+1$ can *never* be prime. We investigate and resolve these issues next.

Sieving for $2q+1$: We begin by examining the method of Granville and Pomerance and its consequences for the values of $2q+1$ modulo small primes.

Assume we have some starting Carmichael number $n = p_1 \cdots p_m$, and we apply the method of Granville and Pomerance, setting $q_i = M(p_i - 1) + 1$ where $M = 1 + kL$ and $L = \mathrm{lcm}(p_i - 1)$. We assume k is such that the q_i are all prime, and we write $q = q_1 \cdots q_m$ for the resulting Carmichael number.

Lemma 2. *With notation as above, for all primes s dividing kL, we have that* $2q+1 = 2n+1 \pmod{s}$.

Proof. Since $q_i = M(p_i - 1) + 1 = (1 + kL)(p_i - 1) + 1$, it follows that for any prime s with $s \mid kL$ we have $q_i = p_i \pmod{s}$, therefore $2q+1 \equiv 2n+1 \pmod{s}$.

The importance of the above lemma is that we can determine at the outset, based only on the small starting Carmichael number n, whether $2q+1$ will be divisible by each of the primes s or not. In particular, we should just ignore any n for which $2n+1 \equiv 0 \pmod{s}$ for any of the primes s dividing L or k, since then $2q+1$ can never be prime. Typically, there are many such primes s, since L is usually rather smooth, arising as the least common multiple of the $p_i - 1$. This is particularly so when the Erdös method is used to construct n.

The Prime 3: The prime 3 plays a particularly important role when applying our sieving trick in the method of Granville and Pomerance: it contributes a factor $2/3$ to the product term $\prod_{i=1}^{h}\left(1 - \frac{1}{s_i}\right)$ when computing σ. It is therefore desirable to keep 3 as a factor of kL in the construction. On the other hand, the above lemma then imposes the necessary condition $2n+1 \neq 0 \bmod 3$ for $2q+1$ to be prime; this in turn requires $n = 0 \bmod 3$ or $n = 2 \bmod 3$.

We consider the two cases $n = 0 \bmod 3$ and $n = 2 \bmod 3$.

The case $n = 0 \bmod 3$: In this case, we have $3 \mid n$, and so we can set $p_1 = 3$. Recall that, in our approach, $n = p_1 \cdots p_m$ will be obtained using the Erdös method, in which case $p_1 = 3$ is contained in the set $\mathcal{P}(L^*)$ (henceforth L^* denotes the smooth number used in the Erdös method; we use L^* to distinguish it from $L = \mathrm{lcm}(p_i - 1)$ in the method of Granville and Pomerance – they are often equal but need not be so). From the conditions on $\mathcal{P}(L^*)$, we deduce that $3 \nmid L^*$. Since each prime in $\mathcal{P}(L^*)$ is constructed by adding 1 to a factor of

L^*, we deduce that $p = 2 \bmod 3$ for every $p \in \mathcal{P}(L^*) \setminus \{3\}$. Since we will also have $p = 3 \bmod 4$ by choice of L^*, we deduce that $p = 11 \bmod 12$ for every $p \in \mathcal{P}(L^*) \setminus \{3\}$.

Hence, in the case where 3 appears as a factor in the starting Carmichael number n, and n is obtained via the Erdös method, then the remaining primes arising as factors of n must all be 11 mod 12. This happens automatically in the Erdös method simply by ensuring $3 \nmid L^*$.

The case $n = 2 \bmod 3$: In this case, we can show that $p_i = 2 \bmod 3$ for all primes p_i arising as factors of n. For suppose that $p_i = 1 \bmod 3$ for some i. This implies $3 \mid p_i - 1$. By Korselt's criterion, we deduce that $3 \mid n - 1$, and hence $n = 1 \bmod 3$. This contradicts our starting assumption on n.

Moreover, it is easy to see that we must take m, the number of prime factors of n, to be odd in this case. For $n = \prod_{i=1}^{m} p_i = 2^m \bmod 3$, and so $n = 2 \bmod 3$ if and only if m is odd.

Hence, in the case where $n = 2 \bmod 3$, we are forced to use a starting Carmichael number with m odd in which $p_i = 2 \bmod 3$ for each prime factor p_i (whether or not we use the Erdös method). This may sound overly restrictive. But, fortunately, we have already seen how to arrange this for the Erdös method: we simply need to ensure that $3 \nmid L^*$, where L^* denotes the smooth number used in that construction, and then all but one of the primes $p \in \mathcal{P}(L^*)$ will satisfy this requirement. We then remove $p = 3$ from $\mathcal{P}(L^*)$ when running the last step in the Erdös method.

Other Primes: Of course, Lemma 2 imposes a single condition on n for every other prime s dividing kL, but these conditions are much less restrictive than that in the case $s = 3$, and so we do not investigate the implications for the p_i any further here.

Completing the Construction: We have now assembled all the tools necessary to produce a suitable Carmichael number n such that when the method of Granville and Pomerance is applied to produce q from n, then $2q+1 \neq 0 \bmod 3$; moreover q will attain the bound of Theorem 4 on $S(q)$, the number of Miller-Rabin non-witnesses for q, namely $S(q) = \varphi(q)/2^{m-1}$. Our procedure is as follows:

1. We use the first step of the Erdös method with an L^* such that $2 \mid L^*$, $4 \nmid L^*$, $3 \nmid L^*$. This ensures that the resulting set $\mathcal{P}(L^*)$ contains the prime 3, and a collection of other primes that are all 11 mod 12.[3]
2. We remove 3 from $\mathcal{P}(L^*)$ and run the second step of the Erdös method with an odd m to find a subset of primes $p_1, \ldots, p_m$ such that $n := p_1 \cdots p_m = 1 \pmod{L}$; n is then a Carmichael number with m prime factors that are all 11 mod 12 and therefore both 3 mod 4 and 2 mod 3.

[3] Of course, one could choose not to restrict L^* in this way and just filter the resulting set $\mathcal{P}(L^*)$ for primes that are 11 mod 12, but this involves wasted computation and the use of larger L^* than is necessary.

3. We set $L = \text{lcm}(p_i - 1)$ and test the condition $2n + 1 \neq 0 \bmod s$ for each prime factor s of L (cf. Lemma 2). If any test fails, we go back to the previous step and generate another n.
4. Integer n is then used in the method of Granville and Pomerance to produce candidates for q (in which the q_i are all prime). By construction of the p_i, we will have $3 \nmid L$ in the Granville-Pomerance method, but we desire $3 \mid kL$ in view of the power of sieving by 3 in that method. We therefore set $k = 3k'$ for k' of suitable size when running this step, introducing the prime 3 in k.
5. Finally, we test $2q + 1$ for primality. By choice of n, we are guaranteed that $2q + 1 \neq 0 \bmod 3$ and $2q + 1 \neq 0 \bmod s$ for each prime divisor s of L, so we are assured that $2q + 1$ will not be divisible by certain (small) primes.

Note that the procedure as described focusses on the case $n = 2 \bmod 3$. An alternative procedure could be developed for the case $n = 0 \bmod 3$. The procedure can be enhanced by setting k at step 4 to contain additional prime factors s beyond 3 not already found in L, to increase the effect of sieving. Of course, in view of Lemma 2, certain bad choices of s should be avoided at this stage.

4.2 Examples of Cryptographic Size

Using the method described above, we now give two examples of Carmichael numbers q such that $p = 2q + 1$ is a 1024-bit prime. In the first example q is the product of 9 prime factors, which by construction will pass a random-base Miller-Rabin primality test with probability approximately $1/2^8$. Since the largest factor of q is 121 bits in size, the DLP in the subgroup of order q mod p for this parameter set can be solved in approximately $9 \cdot 2^{60.5} \approx 2^{64}$ operations. In the second example, q is the product of 11 prime factors, which by construction will pass a random-base Miller-Rabin primality test with probability approximately $1/2^{10}$. However, because the q with 11 factors is smoother, with largest factor 100 bits in size, the DLP in the subgroup of order q mod p for this parameter set can be solved in approximately $11 \cdot 2^{50} \approx 2^{54}$ operations. We give both these examples to illustrate the trade off between the probability of a parameter set being accepted and the work required to solve the DLP for that parameter set.

Example 5. Using SAGE [S+18] we examined all $L^* < 2^{30}$ such that $2 \mid L^*$, $4 \nmid L^*$, $3 \nmid L^*$. We found the largest set of primes $\mathcal{P}(L^*)$ was produced when $L = 565815250 = 2 \cdot 5^3 \cdot 7^2 \cdot 11 \cdot 13 \cdot 17 \cdot 19$. Here, $|\mathcal{P}(L^*)| = 53$ (including the prime 3).

Then, using the Erdös method with $L^* = 565815250$ we generated the 9-factor Carmichael number

$$\begin{aligned} n &= 17129693949608879425349215875722 51 \\ &= 71 \cdot 131 \cdot 647 \cdot 1871 \cdot 4523 \cdot 4751 \cdot 46751 \cdot 350351 \cdot 432251. \end{aligned}$$

Using the procedure described above, we found $k = 3k'$ with

$$k' = 1844674409176776955124$$

produced a 9-factor, 1023-bit Carmichael number q such that $n = 2q + 1$ is a 1024-bit prime.

To generate a target q with 1023 bits, with $m = 9$ factors each around 114 bits in size, we estimate the standard Granville-Pomerance construction to have a success rate of $(2/\ln(B))^m \approx 2^{-47.73}$ per trial, so that the expected number of trials would be about $2^{47.7}$. With our modified version of the Granville-Pomerance construction we obtain sieving on each of the q_i by the primes $5, 7, 11, 13, 17, 19$ that divide L and the prime 3 since it divides k. This gives us $\sigma = 0.658$ and therefore reduces the expected number of trials by about $1/(1 - \sigma)^m \approx 2^{13.9}$ to roughly $2^{33.8}$ trials. We then need to consider the probability that the q produced is such that $p = 2q + 1$ is also prime. By Lemma 2 we know that we obtain sieving on $2q+1$ from all primes $s \mid kL$, hence a success rate of $(2/(1 - \sigma)\ln(2^{1024})) \approx 2^{-6.9}$. Therefore we expect to require $2^{33.8+6.9} = 2^{40.7}$ total trials. Finding the above q such that $p = 2q + 1$ is prime actually took $2^{38.15}$ trials, so we were somewhat lucky. Our implementation is in 'C' and ran for 136 core-days on 3.2 GHz CPUs.

The factors of this q are:

$$q_1 = 21918643151936167288212221 6610071$$
$$q_2 = 4070605156788145353525126 87990131$$
$$q_3 = 2022777639450109152597870741858647$$
$$q_4 = 5855408956302947546993836358011871$$
$$q_5 = 1415944347615076406818509 5193010523$$
$$q_6 = 1487336499595668494557257 8984254751$$
$$q_7 = 1463852239075736886748459 08950296751$$
$$q_8 = 1097028089754405172775021694133400351$$
$$q_9 = 1353476214632058330047104687567182251.$$

Since $2^q \equiv 1 \pmod{p}$ we can set a generator $g = 2$ to obtain a complete set of DH parameters (p, q, g). By construction q will pass a random-base Miller-Rabin primality test with probability approximately $1/2^8$. Since q_9, the largest factor of q, is 121 bits in size, the DLP in the subgroup of order $q \bmod p$ for this parameter set can be solved in approximately $9 \cdot 2^{60.5} \approx 2^{64}$ operations. The C code used to generate this example can be found in the full version [GMP19].

Example 6. Again, using the Erdös method with $L^* = 565815250$ we generated the 11-factor Carmichael number

$$n = 96647594591145401276131753609264751$$
$$= 23 \cdot 71 \cdot 191 \cdot 419 \cdot 491 \cdot 3851 \cdot 4523 \cdot 4751 \cdot 9311 \cdot 17291 \cdot 113051.$$

Using the procedure described above, we found $k = 3k'$ with

$$k' = 3994916512074331$$

produced a 11-factor, 1023-bit Carmichael number q such that $p = 2q + 1$ is a 1024-bit prime.

To generate a target q with 1023 bits, with $m = 11$ factors each around 93 bits in size, we estimate the standard Granville-Pomerance construction to have a success rate of $(2/\ln(B))^m \approx 2^{-55.11}$ per trial, so that the expected number of trials would be about $2^{55.1}$. Again, using our modified version of the Granville-Pomerance construction we sieve as in the previous example to reduce the expected number of trials by about $1/(1-0.658)^m \approx 2^{17}$ to roughly $2^{38.1}$ trials. Then again by considering the probability that the q produced is such that $2q+1$ is also prime we expect to require $2^{38.1+6.9} = 2^{45}$ total trials. Finding the above q such that $2q+1$ was prime took $2^{44.83}$ trials. The computation using our 'C' implementation ran for 1680 core-days on 3.3GHz CPUs.

The factors of this q are:

$$
\begin{aligned}
q_1 &= 149185389210558730480951523\\
q_2 &= 474680783851777778803027571\\
q_3 &= 1288419270454825399608217691\\
q_4 &= 2834522395000615879138078919\\
q_5 &= 3322765486962444451621192991\\
q_6 &= 26107443111847777834166516351\\
q_7 &= 30664378636824844510675581023\\
q_8 &= 32210481761370634990205442251\\
q_9 &= 63132544252286444580802666811\\
q_{10} &= 117246153611389111364347809791\\
q_{11} &= 766609465920621112766889525551.
\end{aligned}
$$

Since $2^q \equiv 1 \pmod{p}$ we can set a generator $g = 2$ to obtain a complete set of DH parameters (p, q, g). By construction q will pass a random-base Miller-Rabin primality test with probability approximately $1/2^{10}$. Since q_{11}, the largest factor of q, is 100 bits in size, the DLP in the subgroup of order q mod p for this parameter set can be solved in approximately $11 \cdot 2^{50} \approx 2^{54}$ operations.

4.3 Application to OpenSSL and PAKE Protocols

OpenSSL provides the DH parameter verification function `DH_check` in `dh_check.c`. This function takes a DH parameter set (p, q, g) and performs primality testing on both p and q. A safe-prime setting is enforced by default, and if q is not provided then it is calculated from p via $q = (p-1)/2$. For this reason, Albrecht *et al.* [AMPS18] were not able to create malicious DH parameter sets passing OpenSSL's testing.

The primality test that OpenSSL uses is BN_is_prime_ex; this performs t rounds of random-base Miller-Rabin testing, where t is determined by the bit-size of p and q. Since p and q are 1024 and 1023 bits respectively, $t = 3$ rounds of Miller-Rabin are performed, at least in versions prior to OpenSSL 1.1.0i (released 14th August 2018). From version 1.1.0i onwards, t was increased to 5, with the aim of achieving 128 bits of security instead of 80 bits.[4] This change was made independently of our work and does not appear to have been influenced by the results of [AMPS18]: the numbers 3 and 5 were selected based on estimates for the average case performance of Miller-Rabin primality testing, with the OpenSSL developers implicitly assuming that p and q are generated randomly rather than maliciously.

For the DH parameter set given in Example 5, we know that q has $\varphi(q)/2^8$ Miller-Rabin non-witnesses, and thus a probability of approximately $1/2^8$ of being declared prime by a single round of Miller-Rabin testing. Hence this DH parameter set will be accepted by DH_check as being valid with probability approximately 2^{-24} (and the lower probability of 2^{-40} since version 1.1.0i of OpenSSL).

This may seem like a small probability, and indeed it is in a scenario where, say, malicious DH parameters are hard-coded into a server by a developer with the hope of later compromising honestly established TLS sessions between a client and a server: only 1 in 2^{24} sessions would be successfully established, and the malicious DH parameters would be quickly spotted if ever careful validation were to be carried out.

Consider instead a PAKE scenario like that envisaged by Bleichenbacher [Ble05]. Here, a client and server use some hypothetical PAKE protocol which relies on DH parameters as part of the protocol, with the server supplying the DH parameters. Assume OpenSSL's DH parameter validation is used by the client. Then an attacker impersonating the server to the client has a 1 in 2^{24} chance of fooling the client into using a weak set of DH parameters. For specific PAKE protocols, this may allow the client's password to be recovered thereafter. For example, this is the case for SRP [Wu00, TWMP07], as seen in [Ble05]. It is also true of J-PAKE [Hao17]: in this protocol, the client in a first flow sends values $g_1 = g^{x_1}, g_2 = g^{x_2}$, while the server sends $g_3 = g^{x_3}, g_4 = g^{x_4}$ (along with proofs of knowledge of the exponents). In the second flow in J-PAKE, the client sends $(g_1 g_3 g_4)^{x_2 s}$ where s is the password or a derivative of it. At this point, the attacker aborts the protocol, and uses its ability to solve the DLP to recover x_2 from the first flow and then again to recover $x_2 s$ and thence s from the second flow.

We pick SRP and J-PAKE here only as illustrative examples; many other protocols would be similarly affected. We also note that the specification for using SRP in TLS [TWMP07] makes careful mention of the need to use trusted DH parameters, and gives examples of suitable parameter sets. However, [TWMP07]

[4] Interestingly, the last time these iteration counts were changed was in February 2000 (OpenSSL version 0.9.5), before which they were all 2, independent of the bit-size of the number being tested.

states that *clients SHOULD only accept group parameters that come from a trusted source*, leaving open the possibility for implementations to use parameters from untrusted sources (to remove that possibility the IETF reserved term "MUST" should have been used). Meanwhile J-PAKE [Hao17] just assumes that the DH parameters are agreed in advance and suggests some methods and sources for obtaining parameters. This does not remove the possibility of the parties using bad parameters and side-steps the important problem of parameter verification.

The power of the attack in the PAKE scenario is that the client has a secret that an attacker would like to learn; the attacker then gains an advantage by impersonating the server in a standard attack scenario. This is different from a protocol like TLS where there is no such static secret and the server is usually authenticated and therefore hard to impersonate; there we require a "malicious developer" attack scenario.

The attack can be carried out repeatedly to boost its success probability, and it can be done across a large population of users in a stealthy manner. Thus even a small per-attempt success probability of 2^{-24} may represent a significant weakness in practice.

As remediation, we recommend that OpenSSL and other cryptographic libraries modify their DH parameter testing code to carry out stronger primality tests – as our analysis shows, 3 rounds of random-base Miller-Rabin testing is insufficient; 5 rounds is better in that it reduces the success probability of our attack to 2^{-40}, but this is still far from the 128-bit security level that the OpenSSL developers have targeted.

5 The Elliptic Curve Setting

An elliptic curve over a prime field $\mathbb{F}_p$ in short Weierstrass form is the set of solutions $(x, y) \in \mathbb{F}_p \times \mathbb{F}_p$ satisfying an equation of the type $y^2 = x^3 + ax + b$, where $a, b \in \mathbb{F}_p$ satisfy $4a^3 + 27b^2 \neq 0$, together with the point at infinity $\mathcal{O}$. When using a scheme such as Elliptic Curve Diffie-Hellman (ECDH), one typically transmits a description of the used curve via a set of domain parameters as part of the protocol, uses hard-coded parameters, or uses a standardised 'named' curve. An ECDH parameter set is typically composed of (p, E, P, q, h), where E is a description of the elliptic curve equation (typically represented by a and b), P is a base point that generates a subgroup of order q on the curve and h is the cofactor of this subgroup.

Analogously to our attacks on the parameter sets on finite field DH, we can create malicious ECDH parameter sets. The idea is to first construct a composite number q that is designed to be declared 'probably prime' by a target implementation of a probabilistic primality test but which is actually reasonably smooth, then retroactively construct a curve of suitable order $n = h \cdot q$. This can be done using the algorithm of Bröker and Stevenhagen [BS05].

Depending on the specific structure of n, a composite order will expose ECDH to attacks like Lim-Lee style small subgroup attacks as in [LL97], or may aid in solving the Elliptic Curve Discrete Logarithm Problem (ECDLP) in the order q subgroup. For this we would use the Pohlig-Hellman algorithm to solve ECDLP in time $O(B^{1/2})$ where B is an upper bound on the largest prime factor of q. For example, we could produce a 256-bit q with 4 prime factors, and hope to use the algorithm of Bröker and Stevenhagen to find a suitable curve over a 256-bit prime p of order $n = h \cdot q$ possibly even with $h = 1$. During parameter validation, q would pass a single round of the Miller-Rabin test with probability 1/8. And the ECDLP could be solved with effort approximately $4 \cdot 2^{32} = 2^{34}$ group operations.

5.1 The Algorithm of Bröker and Stevenhagen

For completeness, we give a short exposition of the algorithm of Bröker and Stevenhagen [BS05].

An elliptic curve E over $\mathbb{F}_p$ has $\#E(\mathbb{F}_p) = p + 1 - t$ points where $|t| < 2\sqrt{p}$. The endomorphism ring of E contains $\mathbb{Z}[\sqrt{t^2 - 4p}]$, which is a subring of the imaginary quadratic field $K = \mathbb{Q}(\sqrt{t^2 - 4p})$. Conversely, if E is an elliptic curve over a number field whose endomorphism ring is the ring of integers of K, then (by the Complex Multiplication theory of elliptic curves) the reduction modulo p of E is an elliptic curve over $\mathbb{F}_p$ and, by taking a suitable isomorphism (a twist), we may ensure that the reduced curve has $p + 1 - t$ points.

The algorithm of Bröker and Stevenhagen exploits these ideas. Given an integer n, the first step is to construct a prime p and an integer t such that $p+1-t = n$ and such that $\mathbb{Q}(\sqrt{t^2 - 4p})$ has small discriminant D. Once this is done, the curve E is constructed using standard tools in Complex Multiplication (namely the Hilbert class polynomial).

We now briefly sketch the first step of the algorithm. The input is an integer n, and we wish to construct an elliptic curve with n points.

Let $D < 0$ be a discriminant of an imaginary quadratic field. We will try to find (p, t) such that $t^2 - 4p = f^2 D$ for some $f \in \mathbb{N}$. We also need $p + 1 - t = n$ and so $p = n + t - 1$. If $t^2 - 4p = f^2 D$ then

$$(t-2)^2 - f^2 D = t^2 - f^2 D - 4t + 4 = 4(p - t + 1) = 4n.$$

Hence, to construct a curve with n points it suffices to choose a discriminant D, solve the equation $w^2 - f^2 D = 4n$, and then check whether $n + (w + 2) - 1 = n + w + 1$ is prime. Note that if $\ell \mid n$ then $w^2 - f^2 D \equiv 0 \pmod{\ell}$ and so $(\frac{D}{\ell}) \neq -1$.

An important ingredient is Cornacchia's algorithm, which solves the equation $w^2 - f^2 D = 4n$ (note that $D < 0$, so the left hand side is positive definite and the equation only has finitely many solutions). Cornacchia's algorithm starts by taking as input an integer x_0 such that $x_0^2 \equiv D \pmod{4n}$.

Putting everything together, the algorithm is as follows (we refer to [BS05] for the full details). Let $n = \ell_1 \cdots \ell_k$ be the target group order. Search over all $D < 0$ such that $D \equiv 0, 1 \pmod{4}$, up to some bound $|D| < D_{\text{bound}}$. Ensure that $(\frac{D}{\ell_i}) \geq 0$ for all $\ell_i \mid n$. Determine all solutions $x_0 \in \mathbb{Z}/4n\mathbb{Z}$ such that $x_0^2 \equiv D$

(mod $4n$) and run Cornacchia's algorithm for each. Whenever we find an integer solution $w^2 - f^2 D = 4n$ check whether $p = n + w + 1$ is prime. If so, output (p, t).

Note that the algorithm is not guaranteed to succeed for a given integer n, because we are restricting to $|D| < D_{\text{bound}}$. In our application this is not a serious problem, because we are able to generate many viable choices for n.

In practice one usually desires elliptic curves of order q (supposed to be prime) or whose group order is $4q$ (Edwards and Montgomery curves have group order divisible by 4). We make one remark about the case when $n = 4q$ is even. If D is odd then any solution (w, f) to $w^2 - f^2 D = 4n$ has w odd, and so t is odd. If n is odd then this means $p = n + w + 1$ is odd, which is all good, whereas if n is even then p cannot be prime when D is odd, so when n is odd we must use odd discriminants D. On the other hand, when n is even then we can take D even (so that w and t will be even and so $p = n + w + 1$ will be odd).

5.2 Examples

We implemented the algorithm of Bröker and Stevenhagen [BS05] in SAGE, and ran it with q that are 256-bit Carmichael numbers with 3 and 4 prime factors, all congruent to 3 mod 4. These were generated using methods described in Sect. 3. By design, these values of q pass random-base Miller-Rabin primality testing with probability 1/4 and 1/8 per iteration, respectively. We used an early abort strategy for each q and estimate a success probability of roughly 1/4 for each q we tried. When successful, the computations took less than a minute on a laptop. The SAGE code for the first stage (finding p, t) of the 3-prime case can be found in the full version [GMP19].

Example 7. Set $q = q_1 q_2 q_3$ where:

$$\begin{aligned} q_1 &= 1209693204168095495869377 1 \\ q_2 &= 36290796125042864876081311 \\ q_3 &= 133066252458490504545631471 \end{aligned}$$

Then q is a Carmichael number with 3 prime factors that are all congruent to 3 mod 4, so q passes random-base Miller-Rabin primality testing with probability 1/4 per iteration. Using the algorithm of Bröker and Stevenhagen, we obtain the elliptic curve $E(\mathbb{F}_p)$ defined by $y^2 = x^3 + 5$, where

$$p = 58417055476151343628013443570006259007184622249466895656635947464036346655953$$

such that $\#E(\mathbb{F}_p) = q$ and p has 256 bits. Every point P on this curve satisfies $[q]P = \mathcal{O}$, the point at infinity, so any point can be used as a generator (of course such points may not have order q, but if q is accepted as being prime then this will not matter). The Pohlig-Hellman algorithm can be used to solve the ECDLP on this curve using about $3 \cdot 2^{42.5}$ group operations, since the largest prime factor of q has 85 bits.

Example 8. Set $q = q_1 q_2 q_3 q_4$ where:

$$q_1 = 27587362503824782 63$$

$$q_2 = 82762087511474347 87$$

$$q_3 = 30346098754207260883$$

$$q_4 = 91038296262621782647$$

Then q is a Carmichael number with 4 prime factors that are all congruent to 3 mod 4, so q passes random-base Miller-Rabin primality testing with probability 1/8 per iteration. Using the algorithm of Bröker and Stevenhagen, we obtain the elliptic curve $E(\mathbb{F}_p)$ defined by $y^2 = x^3 + 2$, where

$$p = 63076648027364534028465951740325404957612973168788427535105160157981242952139$$

such that $q = \#E(\mathbb{F}_p)$ and p has 256 bits. Every point P on this curve satisfies $[q]P = \mathcal{O}$, the point at infinity, so any point can be used as a generator. The Pohlig-Hellman algorithm can be used to solve the ECDLP on this curve using about $4 \cdot 2^{33.5}$ group operations, since the largest prime factor of q has 67 bits.

The two examples above both construct examples of order q. We were also able to construct examples of order $4q$, compatible with applications that use Montgomery or Edwards curves, see for example [BL07, BCLN16].

We have not attempted to do it, but we see no reason why similar examples could not be constructed where q passes fixed-base Miller-Rabin primality tests with probability 1, as per [Ble05].

These examples illustrate the necessity for careful parameter validation, in particular robust primality testing of q, when accepting bespoke curves in cryptographic applications.

6 Conclusion and Recommendations

The best countermeasure to malicious DH and ECDH parameter sets is for protocols and systems to use only widely vetted sets of parameters, and to eliminate any options for using bespoke parameters. This is already widely done in the elliptic curve setting, not necessarily because parameter validation is hard, but because suitable parameter generation is non-trivial in the first place, and because safe and efficient implementation is much easier with a limited and well-understood set of curves. Nevertheless, issues can still arise with the provenance of parameter sets. In short, it is difficult to eliminate suspicion that a curve may have a hidden backdoor unless the generation process is fully explained and has demonstrably little opportunity for manipulation; see [BCC+15] for an extensive treatment. Similar concerns apply in the finite field setting, in the light of [Gor93, FGHT17].

On the flip-side is the argument that, in the finite field setting, using a common set of DH parameters may be inadvisable because, with the best known algorithms for finding discrete logarithms, the cost of solving many logarithms can be amortised over the cost of a large pre-computation, making commonly used DH parameter an even more attractive target. This was a crucial factor in assessing the impact of the Logjam attack on 512-bit DH arising in export cipher suites in TLS [ABD+15].

Our work adds to the weight of argument in favour of using only limited sets of carefully vetted DH parameters even in the finite field setting. This approach was recently adopted in TLS 1.3, for example, which in contrast to earlier versions of the protocol only supports a small set of DH and ECDH parameter sets, with the allowed DH parameters being specified in [Gil16].

If bespoke parameters must be used, then implementations should employ robust primality testing as part of parameter validation, using, for example, at least 64 rounds of Miller-Rabin tests, or the Baillie-PSW primality test for which there are no known pseudoprimes, cf. [AMPS18].

Acknowledgements. Massimo was supported by the EPSRC and the UK government as part of the Centre for Doctoral Training in Cyber Security at Royal Holloway, University of London (EP/K035584/1). Paterson was supported by EPSRC grants EP/M013472/1, EP/K035584/1, and EP/P009301/1.

We thank Matilda Backendal for comments on the paper and Richard G.E. Pinch for providing the data on Carmichael numbers used in Table 1.

References

[ABD+15] Adrian, D., et al.: Imperfect forward secrecy: how Diffie-Hellman fails in practice. In: Ray, I., Li, N., Kruegel, C. (eds.) ACM CCS 2015, pp. 5–17. ACM Press, October 2015

[AMPS18] Albrecht, M.R., Massimo, J., Paterson, K.G., Somorovsky, J.: Prime and prejudice: primality testing under adversarial conditions. In: Proceedings of the 2018 ACM SIGSAC Conference on Computer and Communications Security, Toronto, Canada, 15–19 October 2018 (2018)

[Arn95] Arnault, F.: Constructing Carmichael numbers which are strong pseudoprimes to several bases. J. Symb. Comput. **20**(2), 151–161 (1995)

[ASS+16] Aviram, N., et al.: DROWN: breaking TLS using SSLv2. In: Holz, T., Savage, S. (eds.) 25th USENIX Security Symposium, USENIX Security 2016, Austin, TX, USA, 10–12 August 2016, pp. 689–706. USENIX Association (2016)

[BBD+15] Beurdouche, B., et al.: A messy state of the union: taming the composite state machines of TLS. In: 2015 IEEE Symposium on Security and Privacy, pp. 535–552. IEEE Computer Society Press, May 2015

[BCC+15] Bernstein, D.J., et al.: How to manipulate curve standards: a white paper for the black hat `http://bada55.cr.yp.to`. In: Chen, L., Matsuo, S. (eds.) SSR 2015. LNCS, vol. 9497, pp. 109–139. Springer, Cham (2015). https://doi.org/10.1007/978-3-319-27152-1_6

[BCLN16] Bos, J.W., Costello, C., Longa, P., Naehrig, M.: Selecting elliptic curves for cryptography: an efficiency and security analysis. J. Crypt. Eng. **6**(4), 259–286 (2016)

[BL07] Bernstein, D.J., Lange, T.: Faster addition and doubling on elliptic curves. In: Kurosawa, K. (ed.) ASIACRYPT 2007. LNCS, vol. 4833, pp. 29–50. Springer, Heidelberg (2007). https://doi.org/10.1007/978-3-540-76900-2_3

[Ble05] Bleichenbacher, D.: Breaking a cryptographic protocol with pseudoprimes. In: Vaudenay, S. (ed.) PKC 2005. LNCS, vol. 3386, pp. 9–15. Springer, Heidelberg (2005). https://doi.org/10.1007/978-3-540-30580-4_2

[BPR14] Bellare, M., Paterson, K.G., Rogaway, P.: Security of symmetric encryption against mass surveillance. In: Garay, J.A., Gennaro, R. (eds.) CRYPTO 2014, Part I. LNCS, vol. 8616, pp. 1–19. Springer, Heidelberg (2014). https://doi.org/10.1007/978-3-662-44371-2_1

[BS05] Bröker, R., Stevenhagen, P.: Constructing elliptic curves in almost polynomial time. arXiv:math/0511729 (2005)

[BWBG+06] Blake-Wilson, S., Bolyard, N., Gupta, V., Hawk, C., Moeller, B.: Elliptic Curve Cryptography (ECC) Cipher Suites for Transport Layer Security (TLS). RFC 4492 (Informational), May 2006. Obsoleted by RFC 8422, updated by RFCs 5246, 7027, 7919

[CMG+16] Checkoway, S., et al.: A systematic analysis of the juniper dual EC incident. In: Weippl, E.R., Katzenbeisser, S., Kruegel, C., Myers,A.C., Halevi, S. (eds.) ACM CCS 2016, pp. 468–479. ACM Press, October 2016

[CNE+14] Checkoway, S., et al.: On the practical exploitability of dual EC in TLS implementations. In: Fu, K., Jung, J. (eds.) Proceedings of the 23rd USENIX Security Symposium, San Diego, CA, USA, 20–22 August 2014, pp. 319–335. USENIX Association (2014)

[DGG+15] Dodis, Y., Ganesh, C., Golovnev, A., Juels, A., Ristenpart, T.: A formal treatment of backdoored pseudorandom generators. In: Oswald, E., Fischlin, M. (eds.) EUROCRYPT 2015, Part I. LNCS, vol. 9056, pp. 101–126. Springer, Heidelberg (2015). https://doi.org/10.1007/978-3-662-46800-5_5

[DLP93] Damgård, I., Landrock, P., Pomerance, C.: Average case error estimates for the strong probable prime test. Math. Comput. **61**(203), 177–194 (1993)

[DPSW16] Degabriele, J.P., Paterson, K.G., Schuldt, J.C.N., Woodage, J.: Backdoors in pseudorandom number generators: possibility and impossibility results. In: Robshaw, M., Katz, J. (eds.) CRYPTO 2016, Part I. LNCS, vol. 9814, pp. 403–432. Springer, Heidelberg (2016). https://doi.org/10.1007/978-3-662-53018-4_15

[Erd56] Erdös, P.: On pseudoprimes and Carmichael numbers. Publ. Math. Debrecen **4**, 201–206 (1956)

[FGHT17] Fried, J., Gaudry, P., Heninger, N., Thomé, E.: A kilobit hidden SNFS discrete logarithm computation. In: Coron, J.-S., Nielsen, J.B. (eds.) EUROCRYPT 2017, Part I. LNCS, vol. 10210, pp. 202–231. Springer, Cham (2017). https://doi.org/10.1007/978-3-319-56620-7_8

[Gil16] Gillmor, D.: Negotiated Finite Field Diffie-Hellman Ephemeral Parameters for Transport Layer Security (TLS). RFC 7919 (Proposed Standard), August 2016

[GMP19] Galbraith, S., Massimo, J., Paterson, K.G.: Safety in Numbers: On the Need for Robust Diffie-Hellman Parameter Validation. Cryptology ePrint Archive, Report 2019/032 (2019). https://eprint.iacr.org/2019/032

[Gor93] Gordon, D.M.: Designing and detecting trapdoors for discrete log cryptosystems. In: Brickell, E.F. (ed.) CRYPTO 1992. LNCS, vol. 740, pp. 66–75. Springer, Heidelberg (1993). https://doi.org/10.1007/3-540-48071-4_5

[GP02] Granville, A., Pomerance, C.: Two contradictory conjectures concerning Carmichael numbers. Math. Comput. **71**(238), 883–908 (2002)

[Hao17] Hao, F. (ed.): J-PAKE: Password-Authenticated Key Exchange by Juggling. RFC 8236 (Informational), September 2017

[JP06] Joye, M., Paillier, P.: Fast generation of prime numbers on portable devices: an update. In: Goubin, L., Matsui, M. (eds.) CHES 2006. LNCS, vol. 4249, pp. 160–173. Springer, Heidelberg (2006). https://doi.org/10.1007/11894063_13

[JPV00] Joye, M., Paillier, P., Vaudenay, S.: Efficient generation of prime numbers. In: Koç, Ç.K., Paar, C. (eds.) CHES 2000. LNCS, vol. 1965, pp. 340–354. Springer, Heidelberg (2000). https://doi.org/10.1007/3-540-44499-8_27

[LL97] Lim, C.H., Lee, P.J.: A key recovery attack on discrete log-based schemes using a prime order subgroup. In: Kaliski, B.S. (ed.) CRYPTO 1997. LNCS, vol. 1294, pp. 249–263. Springer, Heidelberg (1997). https://doi.org/10.1007/BFb0052240

[Mon80] Monier, L.: Evaluation and comparison of two efficient probabilistic primality testing algorithms. Theor. Comput. Sci. **12**(1), 97–108 (1980)

[Nar14] Narayanan, S.: Improving the Speed and Accuracy of the Miller-Rabin Primality Test. MIT PRIMES-USA (2014). https://math.mit.edu/research/highschool/primes/materials/2014/-Narayanan.pdf

[Pin08] Pinch, R.G.E.: The Carmichael numbers up to 10^{21}. In: Proceedings Conference on Algorithmic Number Theory, vol. 46. Turku Centre for Computer Science General Publications (2008)

[Rab80] Rabin, M.O.: Probabilistic algorithm for testing primality. J. Number Theory **12**(1), 128–138 (1980)

[S+18] Stein, W., et al.: Sage Mathematics Software Version 8.3. The Sage Development Team (2018). http://www.sagemath.org

[TWMP07] Taylor, D., Wu, T., Mavrogiannopoulos, N., Perrin, T.: Using the Secure Remote Password (SRP) Protocol for TLS Authentication. RFC 5054 (Informational), November 2007

[VAS+17] Valenta, L., et al.: Measuring small subgroup attacks against Diffie-Hellman. In: NDSS 2017. The Internet Society, February/March 2017

[Won16] Wong, D.: How to backdoor Diffie-Hellman. Cryptology ePrint Archive, Report 2016/644 (2016). https://eprint.iacr.org/2016/644

[Wu00] Wu, T.: The SRP Authentication and Key Exchange System. RFC 2945 (Proposed Standard), September 2000

[YY97] Young, A., Yung, M.: Kleptography: using cryptography against cryptography. In: Fumy, W. (ed.) EUROCRYPT 1997. LNCS, vol. 1233, pp. 62–74. Springer, Heidelberg (1997). https://doi.org/10.1007/3-540-69053-0_6

Hunting and Gathering – Verifiable Random Functions from Standard Assumptions with Short Proofs

Lisa Kohl(✉)

Karlsruhe Institute of Technology, Karlsruhe, Germany
Lisa.Kohl@kit.edu

Abstract. A *verifiable random function (VRF)* is a pseudorandom function, where outputs can be *publicly verified*. That is, given an output value together with a proof, one can check that the function was indeed correctly evaluated on the corresponding input. At the same time, the output of the function is computationally indistinguishable from random for all non-queried inputs.

We present the first construction of a VRF which meets the following properties at once: It supports an exponential-sized input space, it achieves full adaptive security based on a non-interactive constant-size assumption and its proofs consist of only a logarithmic number of group elements for inputs of arbitrary polynomial length.

Our construction can be instantiated in symmetric bilinear groups with security based on the decision linear assumption. We build on the work of Hofheinz and Jager (TCC 2016), who were the first to construct a verifiable random function with security based on a non-interactive constant-size assumption. Basically, their VRF is a matrix product in the exponent, where each matrix is chosen according to one bit of the input. In order to allow verification given a symmetric bilinear map, a proof consists of all intermediary results. This entails a proof size of $\Omega(L)$ group elements, where L is the bit-length of the input.

Our key technique, which we call *hunting and gathering*, allows us to break this barrier by rearranging the function, which – combined with the partitioning techniques of Bitansky (TCC 2017) – results in a proof size of ℓ group elements for arbitrary $\ell \in \omega(1)$.

1 Introduction

A *pseudorandom function* is, roughly speaking, a function that can be efficiently evaluated if provided a key, but - given only black-box access - is computationally indistinguishable from a truly random function. Since introduced by Goldreich, Goldwasser and Micali [16] in 1986, pseudorandom functions have been proven

Supported by ERC Project PREP-CRYPTO (724307), by DFG grant HO 4534/2-2 and by a DAAD scholarship. This work was done in part while visiting the FACT Center at IDC Herzliya, Israel.

D. Lin and K. Sako (Eds.): PKC 2019, LNCS 11443, pp. 408–437, 2019.
https://doi.org/10.1007/978-3-030-17259-6_14

useful in many applications. Nevertheless, their security guarantee is somewhat one-sided, as by definition a receiver not knowing the key cannot be sure that indeed he obtained the output value of the pseudorandom function.

To open doors to a wider range of applications, in 1999 Micali, Rabin and Vadhan [28] introduced the concept of *verifiable random functions*. A verifiable random function is a pseudorandom function, for which the key holder – in addition to the image – provides a proof of correct evaluation. The security requirement is *unique provability*, i.e. for each preimage there exists a valid proof for at most one function value. Verifiable random functions are applicable in many contexts, like [4,6,24,26,29,30].

In order to achieve unique provability, the key holder has to publish a *verification key*, which can be viewed as a commitment to the function, such that *even a maliciously chosen verification key* commits to at most one function.

At first glance, employing a pseudorandom function together with a zero-knowledge proof seems promising. But, aiming for a non-interactive construction, the following problem arises. As proven in [17], non-interactive zero knowledge proofs require a common reference string. Letting a possibly malicious key holder choose this common reference string compromises soundness.

Recent generic constructions [5,7,18] choose a similar approach and build verifiable random functions based on non-interactive witness-indistinguishable proofs, which by [19] exist without trusted set-up based on standard assumptions. All of them, though, lack efficient instantiations.

At the birth of verifiable random functions, [28] took a different path. Namely, theirs and the following constructions build on functions which have an *implicit* and an *explicit* representation. While the implicit representation serves as the commitment to the function which can be published without compromising pseudorandomness, the explicit representation allows efficient evaluation. For instance, given a function with image in $\mathbb{Z}_p$, one can think of the function values in the exponent of some suitable group as an implicit representation, from which the function cannot be computed efficiently, but which commits the key holder to exactly one function.

A number of constructions [1,11,12,27] followed this line of work, but up until the work of Hohenberger and Waters in 2010 [21] all of them come with some limitation: Either they are based on an interactive assumption, or they only allow polynomial-sized input space, or they do not achieve full adaptive security. In the following we only consider verifiable random functions which suffer from none of those limitations (so-called verifiable random functions *with all desired properties*). While there are many constructions of VRFs with all desired properties (see Fig. 1), they all come at a cost: Either they have to rely on a non-constant-size assumption (i.e. an assumption depending on the security parameter and/or on some quantity of the adversary), or require large proofs. Thus, the following question was left open:

Open question. Do verifiable random functions with all desired properties exist such that further

Reference	$\|vk\|$	$\|\pi\|$	Assumption	Security loss
[HW10] [21]	$\mathcal{O}(L)$	$\mathcal{O}(L)$	$\mathcal{O}(L \cdot Q)$ - DDHE	$L \cdot Q/\varepsilon$
[BMR10] [9]	$\mathcal{O}(L)$	$\mathcal{O}(L)$	$\mathcal{O}(L)$ - DDH	L
[Jag15] [23]	$\mathcal{O}(L)$	$\mathcal{O}(L)$	$\mathcal{O}(\log(Q/\varepsilon))$ - DDH	$Q^\gamma/\varepsilon^{\gamma+1}$
[HJ16] [20]	$\mathcal{O}(L)$	$\mathcal{O}(L)$	DLIN	$L \log\lambda \cdot Q^{2/\mu}/\varepsilon^3$
[Ros17] [33]	$\mathcal{O}(L)$	$\mathcal{O}(L)$	DLIN	$L \log\lambda \cdot Q^{2/\mu}/\varepsilon^3$
[Yam17] [35]	$\omega(L\log\lambda)$	$\omega(\log\lambda)$	$\omega(L\log\lambda)$ - DDH	$Q^\gamma/\varepsilon^{\gamma+1}$
[Kat17] [25]	$\omega(\sqrt{L}\log\lambda)$	$\omega(\log\lambda)$	$\omega(\log^2\lambda)$ - DDH	$Q^\gamma/\varepsilon^{\gamma+1}$
This work	$\omega(L\log\lambda)$	$\omega(\log\lambda)$	DLIN	$\|\pi\| \log\lambda \cdot Q^{2/\mu}/\varepsilon^3$
	$\omega(L^{2+2\eta})$	$\omega(1)$	DLIN	$\|\pi\| \log\lambda \cdot Q^{2+2/\eta}/\varepsilon^3$

Fig. 1. Comparison with previous efficient constructions of VRFs with all desired properties. The **second and third column** give an overview of the sizes of the verification key and the proof *in number of group elements*, respectively. Throughout, by λ we denote the security parameter, by L the input length (a canonical choice is $L = \lambda$) and by $0 < \eta \leq 1$ an arbitrary constant (representing a trade-off between size of the verification key and security loss). In the **fourth column** we provide the underlying assumption. DDHE refers to the decisional Diffie-Hellman exponent assumption (see [21]), and DDH and DLIN to the decisional Diffie-Hellman and the decision linear assumption respectively. In the **last column** we give an overview of the security loss (in $\mathcal{O}$-notation). Here, $\varepsilon \geq 1/\mathsf{poly}(\lambda)$ and $Q \leq \mathsf{poly}(\lambda)$ refer to the advantage and the number of evaluation queries of the adversary, respectively. The constructions [20,23,25,33,35] and our first construction require an error correcting code $\{0,1\}^L \to \{0,1\}^n$ with minimal distance $n\mu$. For the security loss of [23,25,35] we refer to [35], Table 2 (in the eprint version) and [25], Table 1 (in the eprint version). There, γ is such that $\mu = 1 - 2^{-1/\gamma}$. Note that γ can be chosen as close to 1 as desired by choosing $\mu < 1/2$ and n large enough (see [15], Appendix E.1). For [20,33] and our first construction, the admissible hash function is instantiated with [27], where μ is constant and $n \in \mathcal{O}(L)$. Note that the security loss stems from using the *artifical abort technique* by [34]. For our second construction we use the admissible hash function of [7]. We only give the most efficient instantiation of [35] and [25] regarding the proof size, as this is the focus of our work. As the generic constructions [5,7,18] do not come with efficient instantiations, they are omitted in the overview.

(A) the VRF security can be based on a standard *constant-size* assumption AND
(B) the proof consists of $o(L)$ group elements, where L is the bit-length of the input?

While previously only either part on its own was tackled ((A) by Hofheinz and Jager [20] and (B) by Yamada [35] and Katsumata [25]), our work answers this question affirmatively. Further, to our knowledge our construction constitutes the only verifiable random function with all desired properties that requires only ℓ group elements in the proof, where $\ell \in \omega(1)$ arbitrary. We achieve this at the price of larger verification keys and a larger security loss in the reduction to the underlying assumption.

Additionally, we give an instantiation which achieves the same efficiency (regarding the size of the verification key and proofs) as the recent work of Yamada [35], but based on a constant-size assumption.

We leave it as an open question to construct verifiable random functions with all desired properties that have short proofs and a short verification key. It is worth mentioning that, when allowing the input space to be polynomial-sized, even constructions with constant key and proof size (in number of group elements) exist [12].

Why constructing verifiable random functions is difficult. The main source of difficulty in constructing adaptively secure verifiable random functions is the requirement of unique provability. To see this, consider the reduction of pseudorandomness of the VRF to the underlying assumption. While the reduction has to answer all evaluation queries x with the *unique* function value y together with a corresponding proof, the reduction hopes to solve the underlying problem with the function value $y^\star$ corresponding to the challenge value $x^\star$. This imposes the following challenges in addressing the stated open question.

(A) In order to explain why many previous approaches rely on *non-constant-size* assumptions, we take [27] as a starting point. The core of the construction is simply the Naor-Reingold pseudorandom function [3], which, given a secret key $(a_{i,j})_{i \in \{1,\ldots,L\}, j \in \{0,1\}}$ of randomly chosen exponents and an input $x \in \{0,1\}^L$, evaluates to

$$g^{\prod_{i=1}^{L} a_{i,x_i}}.$$

To reduce the security of the pseudorandom function to the decisional Diffie-Hellman assumption, Naor and Reingold [31] employ a hybrid argument, where they gradually randomize images given to the adversary. Using the same proof technique in order to prove VRF security, the reduction would have to provide proofs for random values. Recall that by unique provability even for a verification key which is set up maliciously there exists at most one function value for every preimage which has a validating proof. The reduction has thus no possibility to simulate proofs. As the result of employing a different proof strategy, the security of the verifiable random function has to be based on a non-constant-size computational assumption depending on the input length L of the VRF. Namely, given oracle access to $g^{\prod_{i \in S'} z_i}$ for every proper subset $S' \subsetneq S := \{z_1, \ldots, z_L\}$, it is assumed to be difficult to compute $g^{\prod_{i \in S} z_i}$.

As non-constant-size assumptions become stronger with increasing input length (or even worse depend on the number of adversarial queries [21]), basing the VRF security on constant-size assumptions is desirable.

The only work overcoming the described difficulty and achieving security based on a constant-size assumption so far is [20], who use a more complex underlying function, allowing them to again employ a hybrid argument in the proof of security. Their work will be the starting point of our construction.

(B) As the adversary is allowed to choose the evaluation and the challenge query *adaptively*, the reduction has to partition the input space ahead of time,

such that with noticeable probability it embeds the underlying problem in the challenge query $x^\star$, but is at the same time able to answer all evaluation queries $x^{(1)}, \ldots, x^{(Q)}$.
A common strategy to achieve this is via admissible hash functions [3,8, 10,14,20,23,27] for partitioning. A function (or encoding) $\{0,1\}^L \to \Sigma^n$ (for some $n \in \mathbb{N}$ and alphabet Σ) is called *admissible hash function*, if there exists an efficient sampling algorithm returning a word $Y \in \Sigma^n$ and a subset of indices $I \subseteq \{1, \ldots, n\}$, such that for any choice of $x^{(1)}, \ldots, x^{(Q)}$ and $x^\star \notin \{x^{(1)}, \ldots, x^{(Q)}\}$ with noticeable probability we have

$$x^\star \in \mathcal{Y} := \{x \in \{0,1\}^L \mid \forall i \in I \colon \mathsf{AHF}(x)_i = Y_i\}$$

and

$$\{x^{(1)}, \ldots, x^{(Q)}\} \subseteq \mathcal{Z} := \{0,1\}^L \backslash \mathcal{Y}.$$

Therefore, the reduction can embed the underlying problem into all elements of $\mathcal{Y}$, while being able to answer all evaluation queries in $\mathcal{Z}$. The choice of the encoding is crucial, as an adversary may try to minimize the probability of successful partitioning by maliciously choosing the queries. The most efficient instantiation [14,27] achieve $n = \Theta(L)$ for $\Sigma = \{0,1\}$ by employing a suitable error correcting code with sufficiently large minimal distance.
In most constructions employing admissible hash functions, the reduction embeds Y in some way into the public parameters, leading to parameter sizes of at least $n \cdot |\Sigma|$ [2,8–10,20,23]. In constructions of verifiable random functions a larger verification key often affects the proof size. This is due to the fact that the proof typically consists of intermediate results in order to make the output value verifiable (e.g. by employing a bilinear map). For this reason most previous constructions inherently require proofs to consist of $\Omega(L)$ group elements.

Strategies to achieve short proofs. Recall that an admissible hash function $\mathsf{AHF} : \{0,1\}^L \to \Sigma^n$ partitions a space into $\mathcal{Y} := \{x \in \{0,1\}^L \mid \forall i \in I \colon \mathsf{AHF}(x)_i = Y_i\}$ and $\mathcal{Z} := \{0,1\}^L \setminus \mathcal{Y}$. Note that the relevant information in Y (which has to be embedded into the public parameters in some way) only consists of $|I|$ bits (which is typically logarithmic in Q, where Q is the number of evaluation queries). Yamada [35] achieves shorter proofs by encoding the relevant information of Y into a bitstring consisting of only $\omega(\log Q)$ components and employing an admissible hash function based on the shorter bitstring. Katsumata [25] follows a similar approach and can be viewed as a combination of [35] and [23] to achieve security based on a weaker assumption.

While we build on the same observation, we follow a different strategy. Namely, we remove the dependency of the proof size on n and $|\Sigma|$ by rearranging the underlying pseudorandom function. As a result, our proof size only depends on the number of chosen indices $|I|$.

The instantiation of admissible hash functions by Lysyanskaya [27] (so-called *substring matching*), which is also employed in [20], yields $|I| \in \mathcal{O}(\log Q)$

(= $\mathcal{O}(\log \lambda)$ for $Q \in \mathsf{poly}(\lambda)$). This results in a proof size of $\omega(\log \lambda)$ and a verification key size of $\omega(\lambda \log \lambda)$ (in number of group elements).

We observe that we can reduce the proof size even further to $\omega(1)$ group elements, by using the admissible hash function of Bitansky [7] (so-called *substring matching over polynomial alphabet*). This entails verification keys of $\omega(\lambda^{2+2\eta})$ group elements (where $0 < \eta \leq 1$ is an arbitrary constant influencing the security loss). The reason for the larger verification is that the underlying encoding function has to satisfy stronger properties in order to achieve $|I| \in \omega(1)$ and comes thus with larger parameters n and $|\Sigma|$.

Note that the efficiency gain in our approach (and similar in [25,35]) crucially relies on the restriction to adversaries that ask a *polynomially bounded* number of evaluation queries Q. One could thus consider the construction of [20] with input size $L = \omega(\log \lambda)$ (where λ is the security parameter), thereby obtaining a verifiable random function with proofs consisting of $o(\lambda)$ group elements. We want to emphasize that in this approach, proofs still consist of $\Omega(L)$ group elements and are thus linear regarding the input size. We, on the other hand, achieve proof size $o(\lambda)$ in number of group elements *independent of the input size* (assuming the length of the input to be polynomially bounded).

Restricting to polynomial size adversaries, one could also achieve proofs of size $o(L)$ (in number of group elements) by evaluating the VRF on $H(x)$ for a collision resistant hash function $H\colon \{0,1\}^L \to \{0,1\}^{\omega(\log \lambda)}$. This approach, however, requires an exponential assumption, whereas we obtain short proofs solely relying on the decision linear assumption.

1.1 Technical Overview

In the following we want to give an overview on how we achieve proofs consisting of $\omega(1)$ group elements. Roughly, our strategy is to rearrange the function from [20]. Recall that the raw-VRF of [20] is a matrix product in the exponent, where each factor depends on one bit of a suitable encoding of the input. Instead, we will have each factor depend on *all* bits of the encoding, and only take a product over $|I|$ factors, where I is the index set stemming from partitioning via an admissible hash function AHF. For $|I| \in \omega(1)$, we employ the instantiation of admissible hash functions by Bitansky [7].

It is worth noting that instantiating [20] with the admissible hash function of [7] would, on the contrary, yield larger proofs of size $\omega(L)$, as the technique of Bitansky requires $n \in \omega(L)$ for the output dimension of the encoding, which determines the proof size of [20].

We start by presenting the concept of verifiable vector hash functions (VVHF) introduced in [20], which can be seen as a pre-step of a VRF. Next, we give an overview of partitioning via admissible hash functions. This technique is employed by [20] and this work to construct an *adaptively programmable* VVHF, which in turn yields an *adaptively* secure VRF (via a generic transformation of [20]). As we build on the techniques of [20], we start with an overview of their approach, before presenting our construction.

Verifiable vector hash functions. Let $\mathbb{G}$ be a group of prime-order p with generator g. For a vector $\mathbf{v} = (v_1, v_2, v_3) \in \mathbb{Z}_p^3$ we employ the notation of [13] and write $g^{\mathbf{v}}$ to denote $(g^{v_1}, g^{v_2}, g^{v_3}) \in \mathbb{G}^3$ (and accordingly for matrices). A VVHF takes an evaluation key ek and an input x and outputs a vector $g^{\mathbf{v}} \in \mathbb{G}^3$ and a proof π (which can be verified given a verification key vk), such that the following holds:

- *Unique provability:* As for VRFs, there exists *at most one* image vector $g^{\mathbf{v}} \in \mathbb{G}^3$, for which a valid proof π exists (even for maliciously chosen verification keys).

Instead of pseudorandomness, the security property we require from a VVHF is *adaptive programmability (AP)*. That is, given a basis $\{g^{\mathbf{b}_1}, g^{\mathbf{b}_2}, g^{\mathbf{b}_3}\}$ of $\mathbb{G}^3$, there exists an alternative way of generating a verification key vk together with a trapdoor td (in the following referred to as *trapdoor key generation*), which allows evaluating the VVHF "in the given basis", i.e. given a trapdoor td and an input x, one can efficiently generate coefficients $c_1^x, c_2^x, c_3^x \in \mathbb{Z}_p^3$ together with a proof π, such that π is a valid proof for the output $g^{\mathbf{v}} := g^{\sum_{i=1}^{3} c_i^x \mathbf{b}_i}$. Further, we require the following:

- *Indistinguishability:* The *trapdoor* verification keys are indistinguishable from *real* verification keys.
- *Well-distributed outputs:* With noticeable probability (that is with probability at least $1/\mathsf{poly}(\lambda)$), for any polynomially bounded number of input values $x^{(1)}, \ldots, x^{(Q)}$ and any designated input $x^\star$ with $x^\star \notin \{x^{(1)}, \ldots, x^{(Q)}\}$, we have $c_3^{x^{(\nu)}} = 0$ for all $\nu \in \{1, \ldots, Q\}$ and $c_3^{x^\star} \neq 0$ (where c_3^x is the third coefficient of the trapdoor evaluation on input x and trapdoor td). In other words, with noticeable probability the image vectors of all input values *except the designated one* lie in the 2-dimensional subspace of $\mathbb{G}^3$ generated by $g^{\mathbf{b}_1}$ and $g^{\mathbf{b}_2}$.

As shown in [20], this property together with the decision linear assumption in $\mathbb{G}$ suffices to construct verifiable random functions. The idea is to embed a part of the challenge of the decision linear assumption in $g^{\mathbf{b}_3}$.

Partitioning via admissible hash functions. In order to achieve well-distributed outputs one has to partition the preimage space into a set $\mathcal{Y}$ and a set $\mathcal{Z} := \{0,1\}^L \backslash \mathcal{Y}$, such that for any polynomially bounded number of input values $x^{(1)}, \ldots, x^{(Q)}$ and any designated input $x^\star$ with $x^\star \notin \{x^{(1)}, \ldots, x^{(Q)}\}$, we have $x^\star \in \mathcal{Y}$ and $x^{(\nu)} \in \mathcal{Z}$ for all $\nu \in \{1, \ldots, Q\}$ with noticeable probability. Then, one can set up the trapdoor key generation algorithm such that for all $x \in \mathcal{Z}$ it holds $c_3^x = 0$, and for all $x \in \mathcal{Y}$ it holds $c_3^x \neq 0$ (where c_3^x is the third coefficient of the trapdoor evaluation on input x).

Recall that admissible hash functions partition the space by employing a suitable encoding $\mathsf{AHF}\colon \{0,1\}^L \to \Sigma^n$ for some polynomial-sized alphabet Σ and $n \in \mathbb{N}$. To choose a partitioning, a subset of the indices $I \subseteq \{1, \ldots, n\}$ of suitable size and a word $Y \leftarrow_R \Sigma^n$ are drawn at random. The partitioning is chosen as

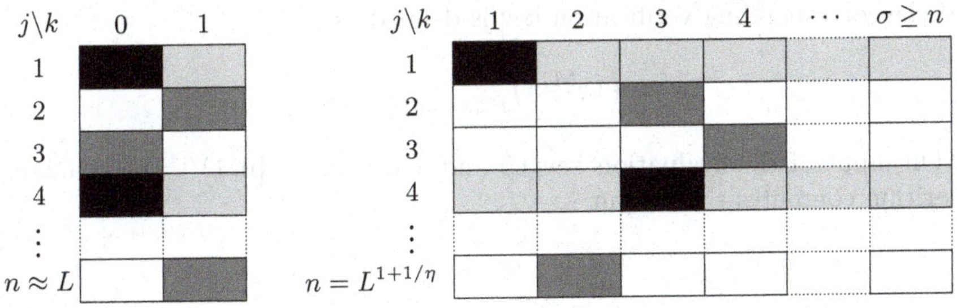

Fig. 2. A graphic representation of *partitioning via substring matching* and *partitioning via substring matching over a polynomial alphabet* $\Sigma = \{1, \ldots, \sigma\}$. In both cases we chose $I = \{1, 4\}$ (marked in light gray) and further $Y = (0, 0, 1, 0, \ldots, 1) \in \{0, 1\}^n$ and $Y' = (1, 3, 4, 3, \ldots, 2) \in \Sigma^n$ (marked in gray and black). A word x lies in the set $\mathcal{Y}$ if and only if $\mathsf{AHF}(x)$ agrees with Y on the entries in black (and for Y' accordingly). Note that only the information in the light gray rows is necessary for partitioning. Recall that L is the bit-length of the input and $0 < \eta \leq 1$ an arbitrary constant.

$$\mathcal{Y} := \{x \in \{0,1\}^L \mid \forall i \in I \colon \mathsf{AHF}(x)_i = Y_i\}.$$

For a graphic representation we refer to Fig. 2. On the left-hand side the partioning via substring matching of [27] is depicted, whereas on the right-hand side we present the partioning via substring matching over a polynomial alphabet by [7]. Note that for the probability of successful partitioning, the underlying code and the index set size $|I|$ are crucial. The instantiation [27] achieves noticeable probability employing an error correcting code with minimal distance μn (for some constant $\mu < 1$) and $|I| \in \omega(\log \lambda)$. Error correcting codes satisfying this requirement exist with $n = \Omega(L)$ and $\Sigma = \{0, 1\}$.

To get by with $|I| \in \omega(1)$, [7] requires larger minimal distance of the underlying code for the following reason. An adversary could fix $x^\star$ and then choose $x^{(1)}, \ldots, x^{(Q)}$ such that $\mathsf{AHF}(x^\star)$ and $\mathsf{AHF}(x^{(\nu)})$ are "close" (for each $\nu \in \{1, \ldots, Q\}$). The smaller $|I|$ is, the more likely it gets that one of the $\mathsf{AHF}(x(\nu))$ agrees with $\mathsf{AHF}(x^\star)$ on all indices in I, and thus the more likely it gets that partitioning is not successful. This requirement on the encoding results in $n = L^{1+1/\eta}$ and increased alphabet size of $\sigma := |\Sigma| \geq n$. Here, $0 < \eta \leq 1$ is an arbitrary constant influencing the probability of successful partitioning.

The VVHF of Hofheinz and Jager [20]**.** The VVHF of [20] can be seen as a multi-dimensional version of the Naor-Reingold pseudorandom function. In order to achieve adaptive programmability, input values are first encoded using a suitable admissible hash function. To set up the evaluation and verification key, the key generation algorithm draws matrices $(\mathbf{M}_{j,k})_{j \in \{1,\ldots,n\}, k \in \Sigma}$ in $\mathbb{Z}_p^{3\times3}$ and a vector $\mathbf{u} \in \mathbb{Z}_p^3$ at random. Note that this can be viewed as choosing a matrix for every cell of the partitioning table (as depicted in Fig. 2). The evaluation key is

$$ek := \left((\mathbf{M}_{j,k})_{j \in \{1,\ldots,n\}, k \in \Sigma}, \mathbf{u}\right)$$

and the corresponding verification key is defined as

$$vk := \left(\left(g^{\mathbf{M}_{j,k}} \right)_{j \in \{1,\dots,n\}, k \in \Sigma}, g^{\mathbf{u}} \right).$$

On input of the evaluation key ek and a value $x \in \{0,1\}^L$, the evaluation algorithm computes the output

$$g^{\left(\prod_{j=1}^{n} \mathbf{M}_{j,\mathsf{AHF}(x)_j}\right)^\top \cdot \mathbf{u}},$$

i.e. the representation of $\mathsf{AHF}(x)$ decides which matrices are used.The corresponding proof $\pi := (\pi_1, \dots, \pi_{n-1})$ consists of all intermediate values

$$\pi_\iota := g^{\left(\prod_{j=1}^{\iota} \mathbf{M}_{j,\mathsf{AHF}(x)_j}\right)^\top \cdot \mathbf{u}}$$

for $\iota \in \{1, \dots, n-1\}$ and has thus linear size. Given the verification key, a proof can be verified employing a symmetric bilinear map.

For trapdoor key generation, the following property of a matrix product is employed in [20]: Let $\mathcal{U}_0, \dots, \mathcal{U}_n$ be 2-dimensional subspaces of $\mathbb{Z}_p^3$ and for all $j \in \{1, \dots, n\}$, $k \in \Sigma$ let $\mathbf{M}_{j,k}$ be such that $\mathbf{M}_{j,k}^\top \cdot \mathcal{U}_{j-1} = \mathcal{U}_j$.[1] Then:

(i) If there exists a $j^\star \in \{1, \dots, n\}$ such that $\mathbf{M}_{j^\star,\mathsf{AHF}(x)_{j^\star}}$ is of rank 2, then $(\prod_{j=1}^{n} \mathbf{M}_{j,\mathsf{AHF}(x)_j})^\top$ maps $\mathbb{Z}_p^3$ (and thus in particular $\mathbb{Z}_p^3 \setminus \mathcal{U}_0$) to $\mathcal{U}_n$.
(ii) If for all $j \in \{1, \dots, n\}$ the matrix $\mathbf{M}_{j,\mathsf{AHF}(x)_j}$ is of rank 3, then the product $(\prod_{j=1}^{n} \mathbf{M}_{j,\mathsf{AHF}(x)_j})^\top$ maps $\mathbb{Z}_p^3 \setminus \mathcal{U}_0$ to $\mathbb{Z}_p^3 \setminus \mathcal{U}_n$.

Let $I \subsetneq \{1, \dots, n\}$ and $Y \in \Sigma^n$ constitute a partitioning of $\{0,1\}^L$ with $\mathcal{Y} := \{x \in \{0,1\}^L \mid \forall i \in I \colon \mathsf{AHF}(x)_i = Y_i\}$ and $\mathcal{Z} = \{0,1\}^L \backslash \mathcal{Y}$. Recall that to achieve *well-distributed outputs*, the goal is to set up trapdoor key generation such that $x \in \mathcal{Z} \Leftrightarrow c_3^x = 0$.

In [20] this is achieved as follows. Given a basis $\{g^{\mathbf{b}_1}, g^{\mathbf{b}_2}, g^{\mathbf{b}_3}\}$ of $\mathbb{G}^3$, the trapdoor key generation algorithm chooses vector spaces $\mathcal{U}_0, \dots, \mathcal{U}_{n-1} \subseteq \mathbb{Z}_p^3$ and a vector $\mathbf{u} \leftarrow_R \mathbb{Z}_p^3 \backslash \mathcal{U}_0$ at random. Further, it defines $\mathcal{U}_n$ as the subspace generated by $\mathbf{b}_1$ and $\mathbf{b}_2$, and chooses $\mathbf{M}_{j,k}$ at random (subject to $\mathbf{M}_{j,k}^\top \cdot \mathcal{U}_{j-1} = \mathcal{U}_j$) of rank 2, whenever $j \in I$ and $k \neq Y_j$ (and of full-rank otherwise). In other words, it chooses all matrices corresponding to light gray cells in Fig. 2 of rank 2, and all matrices corresponding to white, gray or black cells of rank 3. This implies that at least one matrix of rank 2 is part of the evaluation if and only if $x \in \mathcal{Z}$ (as in this case at least for one light gray line a matrix corresponding to the non-black cell is hit). And, by the choice of $\mathbf{u}$, $\mathcal{U}_n$ together with (i), we have $c_3^x = 0$ whenever at least one of the matrices in the product is of rank 2.

Note that, as $g^{\mathbf{b}_1}, g^{\mathbf{b}_2}$ and thus $\mathcal{U}_n$ are only known in the exponent, the trapdoor key generation algorithm can only compute $g^{\mathbf{M}_{n,k}}$ in the exponent (for

[1] For matrix $\mathbf{M} \in \mathbb{Z}_p^3$ and subspaces $\mathcal{U}, \mathcal{V} \subseteq \mathbb{Z}_p^3$, by $\mathbf{M}^\top \cdot \mathcal{U} = \mathcal{V}$ we denote the property that for all $\mathbf{u} \in \mathcal{U}$ we have $\mathbf{M}^\top \mathbf{u} \in \mathcal{V}$ and for each $\mathbf{v} \in \mathcal{V}$ there exists a $\mathbf{u}$ with $\mathbf{M}^\top \mathbf{u} = \mathbf{v}$.

all $k \in \Sigma$). This does not hinder evaluation, as all matrices $\mathbf{M}_{j,k}$ for $j < n, k \in \Sigma$ are known in $\mathbb{Z}_p^{3\times 3}$.

Note that the strategy of [20] requires the product to be taken over *all indices* of $\mathsf{AHF}(x)$. As the proof has to comprise all intermediate steps of the product in order to be verifiable with a symmetric pairing, the proof size is inherently linear in n and thus in L. We now explain how to overcome this barrier.

Towards our construction. Observe that hypothetically in order to achieve well-distributed outputs it would suffice to multiply all matrices with $j \in I$ (in other words to skip all white rows in Fig. 2), thereby allowing much shorter proofs. The problem is, of course, that evaluation has to be independent of I.

We resolve this issue by setting up the underlying function in a different way. First of all, in order to be independent of I, the function evaluation has to be dependent on all indices of $\mathsf{AHF}(x)$ (and not only the ones in a fixed index set I). To this end, we first pretend $|I| = 1$. The idea is to replace the product by a sum, which can be evaluated directly given the verification key without requiring a pairing. More precisely, the prototype of our VVHF is of the form

$$g^{(\sum_{j=1}^{n} \mathbf{M}_{j,\mathsf{AHF}(x)_j})^\top \mathbf{u}}.$$

The key in our proof of adaptive programmability are two observations concerning the sum of matrices. Namely, let $\mathcal{U}_0$, $\mathcal{U}_1$ be 2-dimensional subspaces of $\mathbb{Z}_p^3$ and for all j,k let $\mathbf{M}_{j,k}$ be such that $\mathbf{M}_{j,k}^\top \cdot \mathcal{U}_0 = \mathcal{U}_1$. Then:

(iii) If $\mathbf{M}_{j,\mathsf{AHF}(x)_j}$ is of rank 2 for all j, $(\sum_{j=1}^{n} \mathbf{M}_{j,\mathsf{AHF}(x)_j})^\top$ maps $\mathbb{Z}_p^3$ (and thus in particular $\mathbb{Z}_p^3 \setminus \mathcal{U}_0$) to $\mathcal{U}_1$.
(iv) If there exists exactly one $j^\star \in \{1,\dots,n\}$ such that $\mathbf{M}_{j^\star,\mathsf{AHF}(x)_{j^\star}}$ is of full rank (and the rest of the matrices are of rank at most 2), then the sum $(\sum_{j=1}^{n} \mathbf{M}_{j,\mathsf{AHF}(x)_j})^\top$ maps $\mathbb{Z}_p^3 \setminus \mathcal{U}_0$ to $\mathbb{Z}_p^3 \setminus \mathcal{U}_1$. (This is due to the fact that for any $\mathbf{z} \in \mathbb{Z}_p^3 \setminus \mathcal{U}_0$ it holds $(\sum_{j=1, j\neq j^\star}^{n} \mathbf{M}_{j,\mathsf{AHF}(x)_j})^\top \cdot \mathbf{z} \in \mathcal{U}_1$ and $\mathbf{M}_{j^\star,\mathsf{AHF}(x)_{j^\star}} \cdot \mathbf{z} \in \mathbb{Z}_p^3 \setminus \mathcal{U}_1$.)

Now, given a basis $\{g^{\mathbf{b}_1}, g^{\mathbf{b}_2}, g^{\mathbf{b}_3}\}$ of $\mathbb{G}^3$, the trapdoor key generation algorithm chooses a random 2 dimensional vector space $\mathcal{U}_0 \subseteq \mathbb{Z}_p^3$, defines $\mathcal{U}_1$ as the vector space generated by $\mathbf{b}_1$ and $\mathbf{b}_2$. Further, the algorithm chooses a vector $\mathbf{u} \in \mathbb{Z}_p^3 \setminus \mathcal{U}_0$ at random, and chooses $\mathbf{M}_{j,k}$ of rank 3 if $j \in I$ and $k = Y_j$, and of rank 2 otherwise. This corresponds to choosing the matrix corresponding to the single black cell in the partitioning table in Fig. 2 of rank 3, and all other matrices (corresponding to gray, light gray and white cells) of rank 2. We have

$$x \in \mathcal{Z} \Rightarrow \forall j \in \{1,\dots,n\} \colon \mathbf{M}_{j,\mathsf{AHF}(x)_j} \text{ is of rank } 2 \overset{\text{(iii)}}{\Rightarrow} \sum_{j=1}^{n} \mathbf{M}_{j,\mathsf{AHF}(x)_j}^\top \cdot \mathbf{u} \in \mathcal{U}_1,$$

$$x \in \mathcal{Y} \Rightarrow \mathbf{M}_{j^\star,\mathsf{AHF}(x)_{j^\star}} \text{ is of rank 3 for } j^\star \in I \overset{\text{(iv)}}{\Rightarrow} \sum_{j=1}^{n} \mathbf{M}_{j,\mathsf{AHF}(x)_j}^\top \cdot \mathbf{u} \in \mathbb{Z}_p^3 \setminus \mathcal{U}_1.$$

Our construction of a VVHF with short proofs. For $|I| > 1$, the idea is to repeat this strategy for every $i \in I$ and multiply the results. Note that in order to have evaluation completely oblivious to I (which may vary in size), we employ an upper bound ℓ on the size of I. (Recall that for the instantiation of Bitansky [7], we can choose any $\ell \in \omega(1)$.)

We can now present our final construction. For every $i \in \{1, \ldots, \ell\}$ we choose a fresh set of matrices $(\mathbf{M}_{i,j,k})_{j\in\{1,\ldots,n\},k\in\Sigma}$, each uniformly at random from $\mathbb{Z}_p^{3\times 3}$ and further a vector $\mathbf{u} \leftarrow_R \mathbb{Z}_p^3$. Our evaluation key is of the form

$$ek := \left((\mathbf{M}_{i,j,k})_{i\in\{1,\ldots,\ell\},j\in\{1,\ldots,n\},k\in\Sigma}, \mathbf{u}\right)$$

and the verification key is defined as

$$vk := \left(\left(g^{\mathbf{M}_{i,j,k}}\right)_{i\in\{1,\ldots,\ell\},j\in\{1,\ldots,n\},k\in\Sigma}, g^{\mathbf{u}}\right).$$

To evaluate our VVHF on input x, we compute

$$g^{\left(\prod_{i=1}^{\ell}\sum_{j=1}^{n}\mathbf{M}_{i,j,\mathsf{AHF}(x)_j}\right)^\top \mathbf{u}}$$

and publish the proof $\pi := (\pi_1, \ldots, \pi_{\ell-1})$ consisting of the intermediate steps in computing the product, that is

$$\pi_\iota := g^{\left(\prod_{i=1}^{\iota}\sum_{j=1}^{n}\mathbf{M}_{i,j,\mathsf{AHF}(x)_j}\right)^\top \mathbf{u}}$$

for all $\iota \in \{1, \ldots, \ell - 1\}$.

Trapdoor key generation proceeds as follows. For $i \in \{1, \ldots, |I|\}$, let j_i refer to the i-th index in I. On input of a basis $\{g^{\mathbf{b}_1}, g^{\mathbf{b}_2}, g^{\mathbf{b}_3}\}$ of $\mathbb{G}^3$, we choose vector spaces $\mathcal{U}_0, \ldots, \mathcal{U}_{\ell-1} \subseteq \mathbb{Z}_p^3$ of dimension 2 and define $\mathcal{U}_\ell$ to be the vector space generated by $\mathbf{b}_1, \mathbf{b}_2$. Further, we choose $\mathbf{u} \in \mathbb{Z}_p^3 \setminus \mathcal{U}_0$ and matrices $\mathbf{M}_{i,j,k}$ subject to $\mathbf{M}_{i,j,k} \cdot \mathcal{U}_{i-1} = \mathcal{U}_i$ as follows:

- For all $i \in \{1, \ldots, |I|\}$, we choose $\mathbf{M}_{i,j_i,Y_{j_i}}$ of *rank* 3.
- For all $i \in \{|I| + 1, \ldots, \ell\}$ and all $k \in \Sigma$, we choose $\mathbf{M}_{i,1,k}$ of *rank* 3. (These matrices constitute *dummy matrices* in order to make evaluation oblivious to $|I|$.)
- For all other indices i, j, k we choose $\mathbf{M}_{i,j,k}$ of *rank* 2.

To go back to Fig. 2, this can be viewed as setting up ℓ copies of the partitioning table, where for $i \in \{1, \ldots, |I|\}$ we choose *only* the matrix corresponding to the black cell in row j_i (i.e. in the i-th light gray row) of rank 3 and all other matrices of rank 2. For $i \in \{|I| + 1, \ldots, \ell\}$, we choose all matrices corresponding to the first row of rank 3 (and all other matrices of rank 2). During evaluation, for each $i \in \{1, \ldots, \ell\}$, we sum up all matrices corresponding to the cells $(j, \mathsf{AHF}(x)_j)$ for $j \in \{1, \ldots, n\}$. Whenever $x \in \mathcal{Y}$, we hit exactly one matrix of rank 3 for all $i \in \{1, \ldots, \ell\}$, as for $i \leq |I|$ we hit the matrix corresponding to (j_i, Y_{j_i}) and for $i > |I|$ we always hit one matrix in the first row. Therefore, by (iv) and (ii) the output will be an element of $\mathbb{Z}_p^3 \setminus \mathcal{U}_\ell$. For all $x \in \mathcal{Z}$, on the other hand, there exists at least one $i \in \{1, \ldots, |I|\}$ for which the matrix of rank 3 is not part of the sum. Thus, by (iii) and (i) the output will be an element of $\mathcal{U}_\ell$.

Note that similar to [20] the trapdoor key generation algorithm can only compute $g^{\mathbf{M}_{\ell,j,k}}$ in the exponent for all $j \in \{1, \ldots, n\}, k \in \Sigma$, which is sufficient as all other matrices are known in $\mathbb{Z}_p^{3\times 3}$.

Similar to [20], *indistinguishability* of verification keys generated by the trapdoor key generation from real verification keys can be proven via a hybrid argument, employing the decision linear assumption (or more precisely, the 3-*rank assumption*), which states that it is computationally indistinguishable whether a matrix was drawn uniformly at random from $\{g^{\mathbf{M}} \in \mathbb{G}^{3\times 3} \mid \mathbf{M} \text{ has rank } 3\}$ or from $\{g^{\mathbf{M}} \in \mathbb{G}^{3\times 3} \mid \mathbf{M} \text{ has rank } 2\}$.

We call our approach *hunting and gathering*, as our strategy is to *hunt* out all values $\mathsf{AHF}(x)$ disagreeing with Y on at least one index in I. We do so by setting up ℓ sets of matrices and *gathering* the matrices corresponding to the characters of $\mathsf{AHF}(x)$ for each of these sets. If $\mathsf{AHF}(x)$ disagrees with Y on the i-th index of I, then this will show up in the sum of matrices corresponding to the i-th set.

2 Preliminaries

We will use the following notation throughout this paper. By $\lambda \in \mathbb{N}$ we denote the security parameter. By $L := L(\lambda) \in \mathbb{N}$ we denote the input length, a canonical choice is $L = \lambda$. Further, by the constant $d \geq 3$ we denote the parameter of our assumption. We implicitly assume all other parameters to depend on λ. For an arbitrary set $\mathcal{S}$, by $x \leftarrow_R \mathcal{S}$ we denote the process of sampling an element x from $\mathcal{S}$ uniformly at random. Throughout, $p \in \mathbb{N}$ will be prime. We interpret vectors $\mathbf{v} \in \mathbb{Z}_p^d$ as column-vectors, i.e. $\mathbf{v} \in \mathbb{Z}_p^{d\times 1}$. Further, by v_j we denote the j-th entry of $\mathbf{v}$ for $j \in \{1, \ldots, d\}$. We say that a function is *negligible in* λ if its inverse vanishes asymptotically faster than any polynomial in λ. We say that $\mathcal{A}$ is *probabilistic polynomial time* (PPT), if $\mathcal{A}$ is a probabilistic algorithm with running time polynomial in λ. We use $y \leftarrow \mathcal{A}(x)$ to denote that y is assigned the output of $\mathcal{A}$ running on input x.

In order to formally treat *uniqueness* of proofs, we take the notion of *certified bilinear group generators* from [20]. Note that in the following all numbered references refer to the eprint version [22] of [20].

Definition 1 (Certified bilinear group generator [22, Definition 2.1/2.2]**).** *A* bilinear group generator *is a PPT algorithm* $\mathsf{BG.Gen}$ *that on input* 1^λ *outputs* $\mathcal{G} = (p, \mathbb{G}, \mathbb{G}_T, \circ, \circ_T, e, \varphi, \varphi_T) \leftarrow \mathsf{BG.Gen}(1^\lambda)$ *such that the following are satisfied*

- *p is a 2λ-bit prime*
- *$\mathbb{G}$ and $\mathbb{G}_T$ are subsets of $\{0,1\}^\lambda$, defined by algorithmic descriptions of maps $\varphi \colon \mathbb{Z}_p \to \mathbb{G}$ and $\varphi_T \colon \mathbb{Z}_p \to \mathbb{G}_T$*
- *$\circ$ and $\circ_T$ are algorithmic descriptions of efficiently computable maps $\rho \colon \mathbb{G} \times \mathbb{G} \to \mathbb{G}$ and $\rho_T \colon \mathbb{G}_T \times \mathbb{G}_T \to \mathbb{G}_T$, such that the following hold*
  i. $(\mathbb{G}, \circ)$ and $(\mathbb{G}_T, \circ_T)$ form algebraic groups

ii. φ *is a group isomorphism from* $(\mathbb{Z}_p, +)$ *to* $(\mathbb{G}, \circ)$
iii. φ_T *is a group isomorphism from* $(\mathbb{Z}_p, +)$ *to* $(\mathbb{G}_T, \circ_T)$

– *e is the description of an efficiently computable non-degenerate bilinear map* $e\colon \mathbb{G} \times \mathbb{G} \to \mathbb{G}_T$, *that is*
  i. $e(\varphi(1), \varphi(1)) \neq \varphi_T(0)$
  ii. for all $a \in \mathbb{Z}_p$: $e(\varphi(a), \varphi(1)) = e(\varphi(1), \varphi(a)) = \varphi_T(a)$

In the following we will only include $\varphi(1)$ *in the description of* $\mathcal{G}$. *Note that this suffices, as* $\varphi(1)$ *uniquely determines* φ *and* φ_T.

We say a group generator is certified, *if there exists a deterministic polynomial time algorithm* $\mathsf{BG.Vfy} = (\mathsf{BG.Vfy}_1, \mathsf{BG.Vfy}_2)$ *with the following properties*

Parameter validation. *Given a string* $\mathcal{G}$, *the algorithm* $\mathsf{BG.Vfy}_1(\mathcal{G})$ *outputs* 1 *if and only if* $\mathcal{G}$ *has the form* $\mathcal{G} = (p, \mathbb{G}, \mathbb{G}_T, \circ, \circ_T, e, \varphi(1)) \leftarrow \mathsf{BG.Gen}(1^\lambda)$ *and all requirements from above are satisfied.*

Recognition and unique representation of elements in $\mathbb{G}$. *Further, we require that each element in* $\mathbb{G}$ *has unique representation, which can be efficiently recognized. That is, on input of two strings* Π *and* s, $\mathsf{BG.Vfy}_2(\Pi, s)$ *outputs* 1 *if and only if* $\mathsf{BG.Vfy}_1(\Pi) = 1$ *and it holds that* $s = \varphi(x)$ *for some* $x \in \mathbb{Z}_p$.

Let $\mathcal{G} = (p, \mathbb{G}, \mathbb{G}_T, \circ, \circ_T, e, \varphi(1)) \leftarrow \mathsf{BG.Gen}(1^\lambda)$ be a bilinear group. We use the representation of group elements introduced in [13]. Namely, for $a \in \mathbb{Z}_p$, define $[a] := \varphi(a) \in \mathbb{G}$ as the *implicit representation* of a in $\mathbb{G}$. More generally, for any $n, m \in \mathbb{N}$ and any matrix $\mathbf{A} = (a_{ij}) \in \mathbb{Z}_p^{n \times m}$ we define $[\mathbf{A}]$ as the implicit representation of $\mathbf{A}$ in $\mathbb{G}$:

$$[\mathbf{A}] := \begin{pmatrix} \varphi(a_{11}) & \dots & \varphi(a_{1m}) \\ \vdots & & \vdots \\ \varphi(a_{n1}) & \dots & \varphi(a_{nm}) \end{pmatrix} \in \mathbb{G}^{n \times m}$$

Note that from $[a] \in \mathbb{G}$ it is hard to compute the value a if the Discrete Logarithm assumption holds in $\mathbb{G}$. Obviously, given $[a], [b] \in \mathbb{G}$ and a scalar $x \in \mathbb{Z}_p$, one can efficiently compute $[ax] \in \mathbb{G}$ and $[a + b] \in \mathbb{G}$.

We give the $(d-1)$-linear assumption in a similar form as provided in [20]. This is equivalent to the standard formulation in [13].

Definition 2 (**$(d-1)$-linear assumption** [22, Assumption 5.3]). *Let* $\mathcal{G} \leftarrow \mathsf{BG.Gen}(1^\lambda)$ *be the description of a bilinear group. The* $(d-1)$-linear assumption *over* $\mathcal{G}$ *states that for all PPT adversaries* $\mathcal{A}$ *the advantage*

$$\begin{aligned} \mathsf{Adv}_{\mathcal{G},\mathcal{A}}^{(d-1)\text{-lin}} := \Big| &\Pr[\mathcal{A}(1^\lambda, \mathcal{G}, [\mathbf{c}], [\mathbf{d}], [\sum_{i=1}^{d-1} d_i/c_i]) \mid \mathbf{c}, \mathbf{d} \leftarrow_R \mathbb{Z}_p^{d-1}] \\ &- \Pr[\mathcal{A}(1^\lambda, \mathcal{G}, [\mathbf{c}], [\mathbf{d}], [r]) \mid \mathbf{c}, \mathbf{d} \leftarrow_R \mathbb{Z}_p^{d-1}, r \leftarrow_R \mathbb{Z}_p] \Big| \end{aligned}$$

is negligible in λ.

For $d = 2$, *this corresponds to the* decisional Diffie-Hellman assumption (DDH).

For $d = 3$, *this corresponds to the* decision linear assumption (DLIN).

Note that given a bilinear group with symmetric pairing, the decisional Diffie-Hellman assumption does not hold. For the most efficient instantiation, we thus choose $d = 3$ for this work.

The following assumption can be viewed as a relaxation of the $(d-1)$-linear assumption.

Definition 3 (d-rank assumption [22, Assumption 4.1]**).** *Again, let $\mathcal{G} \leftarrow \mathsf{BG.Gen}(1^\lambda)$ be the description of a bilinear group. The* d-rank assumption *over $\mathcal{G}$ states that for all PPT adversaries $\mathcal{A}$ the advantage*

$$\begin{aligned}\mathsf{Adv}^{d\mathsf{-rank}}_{\mathcal{G},\mathcal{A}} := \big| &\Pr[\mathcal{A}(1^\lambda, \mathcal{G}, [\mathbf{M}]) \mid \mathbf{M} \leftarrow_R \mathbb{Z}_p^{d\times d} \text{ of rank } d-1] \\ &- \Pr[\mathcal{A}(1^\lambda, \mathcal{G}, [\mathbf{M}]) \mid \mathbf{M} \leftarrow_R \mathbb{Z}_p^{d\times d} \text{ of rank } d]\big|\end{aligned}$$

is negligible in λ.

By $e\colon \mathbb{G}^{d\times d} \times \mathbb{G}^d \to \mathbb{G}_T^d$ we denote the natural componentwise extension of e to $\mathbb{G}^{d\times d} \times \mathbb{G}^d$, that is let $\mathbf{M} = (m_{i,j})_{i,j} \in \mathbb{Z}_p^{d\times d}$ be a matrix and $\mathbf{x} = (x_i)_i \in \mathbb{Z}_p^d$ be a vector, then

$$e\colon \mathbb{G}^{d\times d} \times \mathbb{G}^d \to \mathbb{G}_T^d,\ ([\mathbf{M}], [\mathbf{x}]) \mapsto \begin{pmatrix} e([m_{1,1}], [x_1]) \circ_T \cdots \circ_T e([m_{1,d}], [x_d]) \\ \vdots \\ e([m_{d,1}], [x_1]) \circ_T \cdots \circ_T e([m_{d,d}], [x_d]) \end{pmatrix}.$$

2.1 Verifiable Vector Hash Functions and Verifiable Random Functions

Basically, verifiable vector hash functions (VVHF) are a pre-stage of verifiable random functions, where the image is a vector space. Further, instead of pseudorandomness of the output, VVHFs are required to be *adaptively programmable.* An adaptively programmable VVHF has a trapdoor key generation algorithm which is indistinguishable from standard key generation and further meets *well-distributed outputs*, which allows transforming it to a verifiable random function via the generic transformation [20] whenever the decision linear assumption holds in the underlying group. In the following we will recall the definition of adaptively programmable VVHFs from [20], recall the definition of a verifiable random function (VRF) and present the generic transformation from an adaptively programmable VVHF to a VRF (without proof).

Definition 4 (Verifiable vector hash function (VVHF) [22, Definition 3.1]**).** *Let* $\mathsf{BG.Gen}$ *be a bilinear group generator and let $d \in \mathbb{N}$. A* verifiable vector hash function (VVHF) *for* $\mathsf{BG.Gen}$ *with domain $\{0,1\}^L$ and range $\mathbb{G}^d$ is a tuple of PPT algorithms* $\mathsf{VVHF} := (\mathsf{VVHF.Gen}, \mathsf{VVHF.Eval}, \mathsf{VVHF.Vfy})$ *with the following properties.*

- $\mathsf{VVHF.Gen}(\mathcal{G})$ *for $\mathcal{G} \leftarrow \mathsf{BG.Gen}$, outputs a verification key vk and an evaluation key ek.*

- $\mathsf{VVHF.Eval}(ek, x)$ *for an evaluation key ek and* $x \in \{0,1\}^L$, *outputs a function value* $[\mathbf{v}] \in \mathbb{G}^d$ *and a corresponding proof of correctness* π.
- $\mathsf{VVHF.Vfy}(vk, [\mathbf{v}], \pi, x)$ *is a deterministic algorithm that outputs a bit* $b \in \{0,1\}$.

Further, we require the following to hold.

Correctness. *We say that* VVHF *is* correct, *if for all* λ, *all* $\mathcal{G}$ *in the image of* $\mathsf{BG.Gen}(1^\lambda)$, *all* (vk, ek) *in the image of* $\mathsf{VVHF.Gen}(\mathcal{G})$, *all* $x \in \{0,1\}^L$ *and all* $([\mathbf{v}], \pi)$ *in the image of* $\mathsf{VVHF.Eval}(ek, x)$ *we have*

$$\mathsf{VVHF.Vfy}(vk, [\mathbf{v}], \pi, x) = 1.$$

Unique provability. *We say that a verifiable vector hash function* VVHF *satisfies* unique provability, *if for all possible vk (not necessarily created by* VVHF.Gen*), all* $x \in \{0,1\}^L$, *all* $[\mathbf{v}_0], [\mathbf{v}_1] \in \mathbb{G}^d$ *and all possible proofs* π_0, π_1 *we have*

$$\mathsf{VVHF.Vfy}(vk, [\mathbf{v}_0], \pi_0, x) = \mathsf{VVHF.Vfy}(vk, [\mathbf{v}_1], \pi_1, x) = 1 \implies [\mathbf{v}_0] = [\mathbf{v}_1].$$

In other words, for any $x \in \{0,1\}^L$ *there exists a valid proof for at most one function value.*

Note that the following definition slightly differs from the notion of adaptive programmability in [20]. Namely, we additionally provide the algorithm VVHF.TrapGen with the parameter Q in the experiment for well-distributed outputs. Note that employing admissible hash functions to achieve full-adaptive security, in [20] VVHF.TrapGen already implicitly depends on Q to achieve well-distributed outputs. This does not affect the generic transformation from a verifiable vector hash function to a verifiable random function, as for this transformation the existence of a suitable tuple of trapdoor algorithms (VVHF.TrapGen, VVHF.TrapEval) suffices (without requiring explicit knowledge of Q).

Definition 5 (Adaptive programmability [22, Definition 3.3]**).** *We say that a verifiable vector hash function* (VVHF.Gen, VVHF.Eval, VVHF.Vfy) *is* adaptively programmable (AP), *if an additional tuple of algorithms* (VVHF.TrapGen, VVHF.TrapEval) *with the following properties exist.*

- $\mathsf{VVHF.TrapGen}(\mathcal{G}, Q, [\mathbf{B}])$ *for a bilinear group* $\mathcal{G} \leftarrow_R \mathsf{BG.Gen}(1^\lambda)$, *a parameter* Q *which is polynomially bounded in* λ *and a matrix* $[\mathbf{B}] \in \mathbb{G}^{d \times d}$, *outputs a verification key vk and a trapdoor td.*
- $\mathsf{VVHF.TrapEval}(td, x)$ *for a trapdoor td and* $x \in \{0,1\}^L$, *outputs a vector* $\mathbf{c} \in \mathbb{Z}_p^d$ *and a proof* π.

Further, we require the following.

$\mathsf{Exp}^{\mathsf{vhf-ind}}_{\mathsf{VVHF},(\mathsf{VVHF.TrapGen},\mathsf{VVHF.TrapEval}),\mathcal{A},Q}(\lambda)$:	$\mathcal{O}_0(x)$:
$\mathcal{G} \leftarrow \mathsf{BG.Gen}(1^\lambda)$	$([\mathbf{v}],\pi) \leftarrow \mathsf{VVHF.Eval}(vk, x)$
$(vk_0, ek) \leftarrow \mathsf{VVHF.Gen}(\mathcal{G})$	**return** $([\mathbf{v}],\pi)$
$\mathbf{B} \leftarrow_R \mathbb{Z}_p^{d\times d}$ of rank d	
$(vk_1, td) \leftarrow \mathsf{VVHF.TrapGen}(\mathcal{G}, Q, [\mathbf{B}])$	$\mathcal{O}_1(x)$:
$b \leftarrow_R \{0,1\}$	$(\mathbf{c},\pi) \leftarrow \mathsf{VVHF.TrapEval}(td, x)$
$b' \leftarrow \mathcal{A}^{\mathcal{O}_b(\cdot),\mathcal{O}_{\mathsf{check}}(\cdot)}(vk_b)$	$[\mathbf{v}] := [\mathbf{B}]\cdot\mathbf{c}$
if $b = b'$ **return 1**	**return** $([\mathbf{v}],\pi)$
else return 0	
	$\mathcal{O}_{\mathsf{check}}(x)$:
	$(\mathbf{c},\pi) \leftarrow \mathsf{VVHF.TrapEval}(td, x)$
	if $c_d \neq 0$ **return** 1
	else return 0

Fig. 3. VVHF Indistinguishability experiment. Note that $\mathcal{O}_{\mathsf{check}}$ always uses td and VVHF.TrapEval, independently of bit b.

Correctness. *We say that* (VVHF.TrapGen, VVHF.TrapEval) *satisfies* correctness *respective to* VVHF.Vfy, *if for all* $\lambda \in \mathbb{N}$, *for all bilinear groups* $\mathcal{G}$ *in the image of* $\mathsf{BG.Gen}(1^\lambda)$, *for all* Q *that are polynomially bounded in* λ, *for all* $[\mathbf{B}] \in \mathbb{G}^{d\times d}$, *for all* $x \in \{0,1\}^L$ *for all* (vk, td) *in the image of* $\mathsf{VVHF.TrapGen}(\mathcal{G}, Q, [\mathbf{B}])$, *for all* $(\mathbf{c},\pi)$ *in the image of* $\mathsf{VVHF.TrapEval}(td, x)$ *and for all* $[\mathbf{v}] := [\mathbf{B}]\cdot\mathbf{c}$ *it holds*

$$\mathsf{VVHF.Vfy}(vk, [\mathbf{v}], \pi, x) = 1.$$

Indistiguishability. *We define an indistinguishability experiment in Fig. 3. We say that* (VVHF.TrapGen, VVHF.TrapEval) *satisfies* indistinguishability, *if for all* Q *polynomial in* λ *and all PPT adversaries* $\mathcal{A}$ *we have that*

$$\mathsf{Adv}^{\mathsf{vhf-ind}}_{\mathsf{VVHF},(\mathsf{VVHF.TrapGen},\mathsf{VVHF.TrapEval}),\mathcal{A},Q}(\lambda) := \left|\Pr[\mathsf{Exp}^{\mathsf{vhf-ind}}_{\mathsf{VVHF},(\mathsf{VVHF.TrapGen},\mathsf{VVHF.TrapEval}),\mathcal{A},Q}(\lambda) = 1] - \frac{1}{2}\right|$$

is negligible in λ. *In other words, we require that verification keys generated by* VVHF.TrapGen *are indistinguishable from verification keys generated by* VVHF.Gen.

Well-distributed outputs. *Let* Q *be polynomial in* λ *and let* $x^{(1)}, \dots, x^{(Q)}$, $x^\star \in \{0,1\}^L$ *arbitrary with* $x^\star \notin \{x^{(1)}, \dots, x^{(Q)}\}$. *Let* $\mathcal{G} \leftarrow \mathsf{BG.Gen}(1^\lambda)$, $\mathbf{B} \leftarrow_R \mathbb{Z}_p^{d\times d}$ *of rank* d *and* $(vk, td) \leftarrow \mathsf{VVHF.TrapGen}(\mathcal{G}, Q, [\mathbf{B}])$. *Further, for all* $\nu \in \{1, \dots, Q\}$ *let* $(\mathbf{c}^{(\nu)}, \pi) \leftarrow_R \mathsf{VVHF.TrapEval}(td, x^{(\nu)})$ *and* $(\mathbf{c}^\star, \pi) \leftarrow_R \mathsf{VVHF.TrapEval}(td, x^\star)$. *Let* $\Pr^{\mathsf{well-distr}}_{(\mathsf{VVHF.TrapGen},\mathsf{VVHF.TrapEval}),\lambda,Q}(\{x^{(\nu)}\}_\nu, x^\star)$ *be the probability that* $c_d^{(\nu)} = 0$ *for all* $\nu \in \{1, \dots, Q\}$ *and* $c_d^\star \neq 0$ *(where the probability is taken over the random coins of* BG.Gen, VVHF.TrapGen, VVHF.TrapEval *and the random choice of* $\mathbf{B}$*).*

$\mathsf{Exp}^{\mathsf{vrf}}_{\mathsf{VRF},\mathcal{A}=(\mathcal{A}_1,\mathcal{A}_2)}(\lambda)$:	$\mathcal{O}_{\mathsf{eval}}(x)$:
$(vk, sk) \leftarrow \mathsf{VRF.Gen}(1^\lambda)$	**if** $x = x^\star$ **return** $\perp$
$(x^\star, \mathsf{state}) \leftarrow \mathcal{A}_1^{\mathcal{O}_{\mathsf{eval}}(\cdot)}(vk)$	$(y, \pi) \leftarrow \mathsf{VRF.Eval}(vk, x)$
$(y_0, \pi) \leftarrow \mathsf{VRF.Eval}(sk, x^\star)$	**return** (y, π)
$y_1 \leftarrow_R \mathcal{S}$	
$b \leftarrow_R \{0,1\}$	
$b' \leftarrow \mathcal{A}_2^{\mathcal{O}_{\mathsf{eval}}(\cdot)}(\mathsf{state}, y_b)$	
if $b = b'$ **return 1**	
else return 0	

Fig. 4. The VRF security experiment.

We say that (VVHF.TrapGen, VVHF.TrapEval) *satisfies* well-distributed outputs, *if for all* Q *polynomial in* λ *and all* $x^{(1)}, \ldots, x^{(Q)}, x^\star \in \{0,1\}^L$ *with* $x^\star \notin \{x^{(1)}, \ldots, x^{(Q)}\}$ *we have*

$$\Pr^{\mathsf{well-distr}}_{(\mathsf{VVHF.TrapGen},\mathsf{VVHF.TrapEval}),\lambda,Q}(\{x^{(\nu)}\}_\nu, x^\star) \geq \frac{1}{\mathsf{poly}(\lambda)}.$$

Definition 6 (Verifiable random functions [27], **Notation** [22, Definition 5.1]**).** *Let* $\mathsf{VRF} := (\mathsf{VRF.Gen}, \mathsf{VRF.Eval}, \mathsf{VRF.Vfy})$ *be a tuple of polynomial-time algorithms of the following form.*

- $\mathsf{VRF.Gen}(1^\lambda)$ *outputs a secret key* sk *and a verification key* vk.
- $\mathsf{VRF.Eval}(sk, x)$ *for a secret key* sk *and an input* $x \in \{0,1\}^L$, *outputs a function value* $y \in \mathcal{S}$ *(where* $\mathcal{S}$ *is a finite set) and a proof* π.
- $\mathsf{VRF.Vfy}(vk, x, y, \pi)$ *is a deterministic algorithm that for a verification key* vk, *an input* $x \in \{0,1\}^L$, *an output* $y \in \mathcal{S}$ *and a proof* π, *outputs a bit* $b \in \{0,1\}$.

We say VRF *is a* verifiable random function, *if the following properties hold.*

Correctness. *For all* $\lambda \in \mathbb{N}$, *for all* (vk, sk) *in the image of* $\mathsf{VVHF.Gen}(1^\lambda)$, *for all* $x \in \{0,1\}^L$ *and for all* (y, π) *in the image of* $\mathsf{VVHF.Eval}(sk, x)$ *it holds*

$$\mathsf{VRF.Vfy}(vk, x, y, \pi) = 1.$$

Unique provability. *We say that a verifiable random function* VRF *satisfies* unique provability, *if for all possible* vk *(not necessarily created by* VRF.Gen*), all* $x \in \{0,1\}^L$, *all* $y_0, y_1 \in \mathcal{S}$ *and all possible proofs* π_0, π_1 *we have*

$$\mathsf{VRF.Vfy}(vk, x, y_0, \pi_0) = \mathsf{VRF.Vfy}(vk, x, y_1, \pi_1) = 1 \implies y_0 = y_1.$$

In other words, for any $x \in \{0,1\}^L$ *there exists a valid proof for at most one function value.*

Pseudorandomness. *We define a VRF security experiment in Fig. 4. We say that a verifiable random function* VRF *is* pseudorandom, *if for all PPT adversaries* $\mathcal{A} = (\mathcal{A}_1, \mathcal{A}_2)$ *we have that*

$$\mathsf{Adv}^{\mathsf{vrf}}_{\mathsf{VRF},\mathcal{A}}(\lambda) := \left| \Pr[\mathsf{Exp}^{\mathsf{vrf}}_{\mathsf{VRF},\mathcal{A}}(\lambda) = 1] - \frac{1}{2} \right|$$

is negligible in λ. *In other words, we require that the output of* VRF.Eval *is indistinguishable from random values in* $\mathcal{S}$.

Given a verifiable vector hash function with adaptive programmability, one can obtain a verifiable random function via the generic construction of [20]. As we will employ this generic transformation, we want to recall it in the following.

Let BG.Gen be a certified bilinear group generator according to Definition 1. Let VVHF := (VVHF.Gen, VVHF.Eval, VVHF.Vfy) be a vector hash function according to Definition 4. Let VRF := (VRF.Gen, VRF.Eval, VRF.Vfy) be defined as follows.

- $\mathsf{VRF.Gen}(1^\lambda)$ runs $\mathcal{G} \leftarrow \mathsf{BG.Gen}(1^\lambda)$ and $(ek, vk') \leftarrow \mathsf{VVHF.Gen}(\mathcal{G})$. Further, it chooses a random vector $\mathbf{w} \leftarrow_R (\mathbb{Z}_p^\star)^d$, defines $sk := (\mathcal{G}, ek, \mathbf{w})$ and $vk := (\mathcal{G}, vk', [\mathbf{w}])$ and outputs (vk, sk).
- $\mathsf{VRF.Eval}(sk, x)$ for $sk = (\mathcal{G}, ek, \mathbf{w})$ and $x \in \{0,1\}^L$ first runs

$$([\mathbf{v}], \pi') \leftarrow \mathsf{VVHF.Eval}(ek, x).$$

Then, VRF.Eval computes the function value y and an additional proof $[\mathbf{z}] \in \mathbb{G}^d$ as

$$y := \prod_{i=1}^{d} \left[\frac{v_i}{w_i} \right] \text{ and } [\mathbf{z}] := \left[\left(\frac{v_1}{w_1}, \frac{v_2}{w_2}, \ldots, \frac{v_d}{w_d} \right)^\top \right],$$

where, $\prod$ corresponds to the $\circ$ operation over $\mathbb{G}$. Finally, VRF.Eval sets $\pi := ([\mathbf{v}], \pi', [\mathbf{z}])$ and outputs (y, π).
- $\mathsf{VRF.Vfy}(vk, x, y, \pi)$ outputs 1 if and only if all of the following properties are satisfied:
  - The verification key vk has the form $vk = (\mathcal{G}, vk', [\mathbf{w}])$ such that $[\mathbf{w}] \in \mathbb{Z}_p^d$ and the bilinear group parameters and the group elements contained in vk are valid, which can be checked by running $\mathsf{BG.Vfy}_1$ and $\mathsf{BG.Vfy}_2$.
  - The input x is an element of $\{0,1\}^L$.
  - The proof π has the form $\pi = ([\mathbf{v}], \pi', [\mathbf{z}])$ with $\mathsf{VVHF.Vfy}(vk', [\mathbf{v}], \pi', x) = 1$ and both vectors $[\mathbf{v}]$ and $[\mathbf{z}]$ contain only validly-encoded group elements, which can be checked by running $\mathsf{BG.Vfy}_2$.
  - It holds that $[z_i] = [v_i/w_i]$ for all $i \in \{1, \ldots, d\}$ and $y = [\sum_{i=1}^{d} v_i/w_i]$. This can be checked by testing

$$e([z_i], [w_i]) \stackrel{?}{=} e([v_i], [1]) \; \forall i \in \{1, \ldots, d\} \text{ and } y \stackrel{?}{=} \prod_{i=1}^{k} [z_i].$$

By the following theorem this construction yields a verifiable random function. For a proof we refer to [20].

Theorem 1 ([22, Theorem 5.2/5.4]). *If the $(d-1)$-linear assumption holds relative to* BG.Gen *and if the tuple* $\mathsf{VVHF} := (\mathsf{VVHF.Gen}, \mathsf{VVHF.Eval}, \mathsf{VVHF.Vfy})$ *is an adaptively programmable hash function, then* $\mathsf{VRF} := (\mathsf{VRF.Gen}, \mathsf{VRF.Eval}, \mathsf{VRF.Vfy})$ *is a verifiable vector hash function satisfying all requirements of Definition 6.*

2.2 Partitioning Based on Admissible Hash Functions

In order to achieve verifiable random functions with adaptive security, we have to partition the input space into $\mathcal{Y}$ and $\mathcal{Z}$ such that with noticeable probability all evaluation queries are in $\mathcal{Z}$ while the challenge query is in $\mathcal{Y}$.

One commonly used method for partitioning are *admissible hash functions*, a concept first formalized in [8]. As [14] we allow the output space to consist of vectors over a alphabet Σ of polynomial size.

Definition 7 (Admissible hash functions, [8,14]**).** *Let n be polynomial in λ and Σ an alphabet of size $\sigma := |\Sigma|$ polynomial in λ. Let*

$$\mathsf{AHF}\colon \{0,1\}^L \to \Sigma^n,$$

$Y \in \Sigma^n$ and $I \subseteq \{1,\ldots,n\}$ define the partitioning

$$\mathcal{Y} := \left\{x \in \{0,1\}^L \mid \mathsf{AHF}(x)_j = Y_j \text{ for all } j \in I\right\} \text{ and } \mathcal{Z} := \{0,1\}^L \setminus \mathcal{Y}.$$

We say that AHF *is* Q-admissible, *if there exists a PPT algorithm* AHF.Part *that on input $(1^\lambda, Q)$ returns a value $Y \in \Sigma^n$ and a set of indices $I \subseteq \{1,\ldots,n\}$, such that for any $x^{(1)},\ldots,x^{(Q)},x^\star \in \{0,1\}^L$ with $x^\star \notin \{x^{(1)},\ldots,x^{(Q)}\}$ we have*

$$\Pr^{\mathsf{part}}_{\mathsf{AHF},\mathsf{AHF.Part},\lambda,Q}(\{x^{(\nu)}\}_\nu, x^\star) := \Pr[x^\star \in \mathcal{Y} \wedge x^{(\nu)} \in \mathcal{Z}\ \forall \nu \in \{1,\ldots,Q\}] \geq 1/\mathsf{poly}(\lambda),$$

where the probability is taken over the random coins of AHF.Part. *We say that* AHF *is an* admissible hash function (AHF) *if* AHF *is Q-admissible for all Q that are polynomially bounded in λ.*

For our construction we will employ two instantiations of admissible hash functions. The first is the so-called *substring matching* by [27]. In [7] this partitioning method is generalized to polynomial output alphabets. This allows us to shrink the proof size even to $\omega(1)$ group elements.

Note that a common problem arising using partitioning techniques is that the abort probability of the security experiment might depend on the sequence of queries of the adversary. While in [7] this issue is resolved by requiring so-called *balanced* partitioning as proposed in [23], in [20] the *artificial abort* technique from [34] is employed going from verifiable vector hash functions to verifiable random functions. As we apply the transformation of [20] in a black-box way, for our purposes the concept of admissible hash functions is sufficient.

Substring matching. In the following we give the instantiation of admissible hash function from Lysyanskaya [27]. To this aim let $\mathsf{Enc}\colon \{0,1\}^L \to \{0,1\}^n$ be an error correcting code with minimal distance μn for a constant μ (i.e. any two codewords differ in at least μn positions). Note that there exist efficient instantiations of Enc with $n \in \mathcal{O}(L)$. For a proof of the following lemma we refer to [14], Theorem 2.

Lemma 1 **([7,14,27]).** *Let* $\mathsf{AHF}\colon \{0,1\}^L \to \{0,1\}^n$ *be an error correcting code with minimal distance* μn *for a constant* μ*. Then there exists an algorithm* $\mathsf{AHF.Part}$ *such that* AHF *is an admissible hash function. In particular, for any* $x^{(1)}, \ldots, x^{(Q)}, x^\star \in \{0,1\}^L$ *we have*

$$\Pr^{\mathsf{part}}_{\mathsf{AHF},\mathsf{AHF.Part},\lambda,Q}(\{x^{(\nu)}\}_\nu, x^\star) \geq (2Q)^{-1/(\mu \log e)}/2$$

Further, the size of the set I *returned by* $\mathsf{AHF.Part}(1^\lambda, Q)$ *is logarithmic in* λ *for any* Q *which is polynomially bounded in* λ.

Substring matching over polynomial alphabets. The original instantiation by Bitansky [7] requires $n \in \Omega(L^2)$ and an error correcting code with minimum distance $n - L + 1$. To achieve a smaller verification key, we observe that it is actually sufficient to choose a code with $n \in \Omega(L^{1+\eta})$ for some constant $\eta > 0$ with minimum distance at least $n - L + 1$. A suitable instantiation for both is the following code from [32]. We only give the encoding function, as it is sufficient for our purposes.

Remark 1 (Reed-Solomon-Code). Let $\sigma \geq n$ such that σ is a prime-power and let $\Sigma := \mathbb{F}_\sigma$ be the finite field consisting of σ elements. Let $u_1, \ldots, u_n \in \mathbb{F}_\sigma$ be n pairwise different elements and for $x \in \{0,1\}^L$ let $p_x \in \mathbb{F}_\sigma[\mathsf{X}]$ be defined via $p_x[\mathsf{X}] := \sum_{i=0}^{L-1} x_i \mathsf{X}^i$. Then

$$\mathsf{Enc}\colon \{0,1\}^L \to \Sigma^n, x \mapsto (p_x(u_1), \ldots, p_x(u_n))$$

defines a code. Further, for $x \neq y \in \{0,1\}^L$ the polynomial $p_x - p_y \neq 0$ has degree at most $L - 1$. The code has thus minimal distance $n - L + 1$ as required.

As the following lemma slightly deviates from the original lemma in [7], we provide a proof.

Lemma 2 **([7] Section 4.1.1 (in the eprint version)).** *Let* $0 < \eta \leq 1$ *be a constant and let* $n, \sigma \in \mathcal{O}\left(L^{1+\eta}\right)$ *such that* $\mathsf{AHF}\colon \{0,1\}^L \to \Sigma^n$ *is an error correcting code with minimal distance* $n - L + 1$ *and alphabet size* $|\Sigma| = \sigma$*. Then, there exists an algorithm* $\mathsf{AHF.Part}$ *such that* AHF *is an admissible hash function such that for any* $x^{(1)}, \ldots, x^{(Q)}, x^\star \in \{0,1\}^L$ *we have*

$$\Pr^{\mathsf{part}}_{\mathsf{AHF},\mathsf{AHF.Part},\lambda,Q}(\{x^{(\nu)}\}_\nu, x^\star) \geq (2Q)^{-1-1/\eta-\mathcal{O}(1/\log\lambda)}/2$$

Further, the size of the set I *returned by* $\mathsf{AHF.Part}(1^\lambda, Q)$ *is constant for any* Q *which is polynomially bounded in* λ.

Proof. We define AHF.Part as the algorithm that on input $(1^\lambda, Q)$ chooses a random value $Y \leftarrow_R \Sigma^n$, sets $c := \log(2Q)/(\eta \log \lambda)$, and returns Y together with random subset $I \subseteq \{1, \ldots, n\}$ of size c.

Let $i_1, \ldots, i_\iota \in \{1, \ldots, n\}$. Then by $i_{[\iota]}$ we denote the set $\{i_1, \ldots, i_\iota\}$. First, assume $S := \{x^{(1)}, \ldots, x^{(Q)}\}$ and $x^\star$ to be fixed. Then, for any $x^{(\nu)} \in S$, we have

$$\Pr_{I \subset \{1,\ldots,n\}, |I|=c}\left[\mathsf{AHF}(x^{(\nu)})\big|_I = \mathsf{AHF}(x^\star)\big|_I\right]$$

$$= \prod_{j=1}^{c} \Pr_{i_j \notin i_{[j-1]}}\left[\mathsf{AHF}(x^{(\nu)})_{i_j} = \mathsf{AHF}(x^\star)_{i_j} \,\Big|\, \mathsf{AHF}(x^{(\nu)})\big|_{i_{[j-1]}} = \mathsf{AHF}(x^\star)\big|_{i_{[j-1]}}\right]$$

$$\leq \prod_{j=1}^{c}\left(\frac{L-j}{n}\right) \leq \prod_{j=1}^{c}\frac{1}{L^\eta} = L^{-c\eta},$$

where the first inequality follows from the fact that two codewords of AHF have at most $L-1$ bits in common and the second inequality from $n = L^{1+\eta}$. Further, for any fixed $x^\star, I$, we have

$$\Pr_{Y \leftarrow \Sigma^n}[\mathsf{AHF}(x^\star)\big|_I = Y\big|_I] = \sigma^{-c}.$$

Via a union bound we obtain

$$\Pr^{\mathsf{part}}_{\mathsf{AHF},\mathsf{AHF.Part},\lambda,Q}(\{x^{(\nu)}\}_\nu, x^\star) \geq \sigma^{-c} \cdot (1 - Q \cdot L^{-c\eta})$$
$$\geq (2Q)^{-1-1/\eta-\log C/(\eta \log \lambda)}/2,$$

where C is a constant with $\sigma \leq C \cdot n^{1+\eta}$.

Further, we have $|I| = c \in \mathcal{O}(1)$ as η constant and $\log(2Q) \in \mathcal{O}(\log \lambda)$ for any Q which is polynomially bounded in λ.

3 Verifiable Random Function with Short Proofs

In this section we present our construction of an adaptively programmable verifiable vector hash function, which can be seen as a rearrangement of the VVHF of [20]. Via our technique of *hunting and gathering* we achieve significantly shorter proofs. Applying the generic transformation of [20] (see Theorem 1) finally yields an adaptively secure verifiable random function. For the resulting sizes of verification key and proofs for different instantiations of the admissible hash function, we refer to Remark 2 subsequent to our construction.

Definition 8. *Let* AHF: $\{0,1\}^L \to \Sigma^n$ *together with* AHF.Part *be an admissible hash function and* ℓ *be an upper bound on the set* $I \subseteq \{1, \ldots, n\}$ *output by* AHF.Part$(1^\lambda, Q)$ *(for* Q *polynomial in* λ*). Let* BG.Gen *be a certified bilinear group generator and let* $\mathcal{G} \leftarrow_R$ BG.Gen(1^λ)*. We define a verifiable vector hash function* VVHF := (VVHF.Gen, VVHF.Eval, VVHF.Vfy) *as follows.*

- VVHF.Gen *is a probabilistic algorithm that on input of group parameters* $\mathcal{G}$ *samples matrices* $\mathbf{M}_{i,j,k} \leftarrow_R \mathbb{Z}_p^{d \times d}$ *for all* $i \in \{1, \ldots, \ell\}$, $j \in \{1, \ldots, n\}$ *and* $k \in \Sigma$ *uniformly at random. Further the algorithm samples a vector* $\mathbf{u} \leftarrow_R \mathbb{Z}_p^d \backslash \{0\}$ *and outputs the evaluation key*

$$ek := \left((\mathbf{M}_{i,j,k})_{i \in \{1,\ldots,\ell\}, j \in \{1,\ldots,n\}, k \in \Sigma}, \mathbf{u} \right)$$

and the verification key

$$vk := \left([\mathbf{M}_{i,j,k}]_{i \in \{1,\ldots,\ell\}, j \in \{1,\ldots,n\}, k \in \Sigma}, [\mathbf{u}] \right).$$

- VVHF.Eval *is an algorithm that on input of an evaluation key ek and a preimage* $x \in \{0,1\}^L$ *first computes the admissible hash value* $X := \mathsf{AHF}(x) \in \Sigma^n$ *of* x *and further, for each* $\iota \in \{1, \ldots, \ell\}$, *the vector*

$$\mathbf{v}_\iota := \left(\prod_{i=1}^{\iota} \sum_{j=1}^{n} \mathbf{M}_{i,j,X_j} \right)^\top \mathbf{u}. \tag{1}$$

Finally, VVHF.Eval *outputs the image*

$$[\mathbf{v}] := [\mathbf{v}_\ell]$$

and the proof

$$\pi := [\mathbf{v}_1, \ldots, \mathbf{v}_{\ell-1}].$$

- VVHF.Vfy *is an algorithm that on input of a verification key vk, a preimage* x *with image* $\mathsf{AHF}(x) = X = (X_1, \ldots, X_n) \in \Sigma^n$, *an image* $[\mathbf{v}] = [\mathbf{v}_\ell]$ *and a proof* $\pi = [\mathbf{v}_1, \ldots, \mathbf{v}_{\ell-1}]$ *checks whether for all* $\iota \in \{1, \ldots, \ell\}$ *and* $[\mathbf{v}_0] := [\mathbf{u}]$ *it holds*

$$e([\mathbf{1}_d], [\mathbf{v}_\iota]) = e(\sum_{j=1}^{n} [\mathbf{M}_{\iota,j,X_j}]^\top, [\mathbf{v}_{\iota-1}]) \tag{2}$$

and returns 1 *if and only if this is the case.*

Remark 2. Recall that we consider inputs of arbitrary polynomial length L. The following numbers correspond to $d = 3$ (i.e. security based on the decision linear assumption).

The admissible hash function by Lysyanskaya [27] (see Lemma 1) has parameters $\ell \in \omega(\log L)$, $n \in \mathcal{O}(L)$ and $|\Sigma| = 2$. Therefore, instantiating our construction with this AHF and applying the generic transformation of [20] yields a verifiable random function with proofs of size $3(\ell + 1) \in \omega(\log \lambda)$ and a verification key of size $18\ell n + 6 \in \omega(L \log \lambda)$ (in number of group elements).

Alternatively, the admissible hash function by Bitansky [7] (see Lemma 2) comes with parameters $\ell \in \omega(1)$ and $n, |\Sigma| \in \mathcal{O}(L^{1+\eta})$ for an arbitrary constant $\eta > 0$. Employing this instantiation (together with the generic transformation of [20]) thus yields a verifiable random function with proofs consisting of

$3(\ell+1) \in \omega(1)$ group elements and a verification key comprising $18\ell n + 6 \in \omega(L^{2+2\eta})$ group elements.

Note that the additional $3 \cdot 2$ group elements in the proofs and the additional 3 group elements in the verification key stem from the generic transformation (see Theorem 1).

Lemma 3 (Correctness and unique provability). *The tuple* VVHF *given in Definition 8 is a verifiable vector hash function.*

Proof. **Correctness.** Let ek and vk as in Definition 8. Let $x \in \{0,1\}^L$ and $X := \mathsf{AHF}(x)$. Let $[\mathbf{v}] = [\mathbf{v}_\ell]$ be an image and $\pi = [\mathbf{v}_1, \ldots, \mathbf{v}_{\ell-1}]$ be a corresponding proof computed by the algorithm VVHF.Eval on input ek, x. Let $[\mathbf{v}_0] := [\mathbf{u}]$. For all $\iota \in \{1, \ldots, \ell\}$ we have

$$\mathbf{v}_\iota = \left(\prod_{i=1}^{\iota} \sum_{j=1}^{n} \mathbf{M}_{i,j,X_j}\right)^\top \mathbf{u} = \sum_{j=1}^{n} \mathbf{M}_{\iota,j,X_j}^\top \cdot \underbrace{\left(\prod_{i=1}^{\iota-1} \sum_{j=1}^{n} \mathbf{M}_{i,j,X_j}\right)^\top \mathbf{u}}_{=\mathbf{v}_{\iota-1}}$$

by (1), and thus (2) follows.

Unique provability. For each $\iota \in \{1, \ldots, \ell\}$ there exists exactly one $\mathbf{v}_\iota$ satisfying (2) respective to the verification key and $\mathbf{v}_0, \ldots, \mathbf{v}_{\iota-1}$. As the group described by $\mathcal{G}$ satisfies recognition and unique representation of group elements, unique provability follows.

Lemma 4 (Adaptive Programmability). *If the d-rank assumption holds relative to* BG.Gen, *then the verifiable vector hash function* VVHF $=$ (VVHF.Gen, VVHF.Eval, VVHF.Vfy) *given in Definition 8 satisfies adaptive programmability. More precisely, there exist a tuple of trapdoor algorithms* (VVHF.TrapGen, VVHF.TrapEval), *such that the following hold.*

Correctness. (VVHF.TrapGen, VVHF.TrapEval) *satisfies correctness respective to* VVHF.Vfy.

Indistinguishability. *For any Q polynomially bounded in λ and any PPT adversaries $\mathcal{A}$ with running time $t_{\mathcal{A}}$, there exists a PPT adversary $\mathcal{B}$ with running time $t_{\mathcal{B}} \approx t_{\mathcal{A}}$ such that*

$$\mathsf{Adv}^{\mathsf{vhf-ind}}_{\mathsf{VVHF},(\mathsf{VVHF.TrapGen},\mathsf{VVHF.TrapEval}),\mathcal{A},Q}(\lambda) \le \ell \cdot \mathsf{Adv}^{d-\mathsf{rank}}_{\mathcal{G},\mathcal{B}}(\lambda) + \mathcal{O}\left(\frac{\ell n \sigma}{p}\right).$$

Well-distributed outputs. *For any polynomial Q in λ and for any $x^{(1)}, \ldots, x^{(Q)}, x^\star \in \{0,1\}^L$ with $x^\star \notin \{x^{(1)}, \ldots, x^{(Q)}\}$ it holds*

$$\Pr^{\mathsf{well-distr}}_{(\mathsf{VVHF.TrapGen},\mathsf{VVHF.TrapEval}),\lambda,Q}(\{x^{(\nu)}\}_\nu, x^\star) = \Pr^{\mathsf{part}}_{\mathsf{AHF},\mathsf{AHF.Part},\lambda,Q}(\{x^{(\nu)}\}_\nu, x^\star) \ge \frac{1}{\mathrm{poly}(\lambda)}.$$

Proof. We define the following tuple of algorithms:

– VVHF.TrapGen is a probabilistic algorithm that on input of the group parameters $\mathcal{G}$, a parameter Q (which is required to be polynomially bounded in λ) and a matrix $[\mathbf{B}] \in \mathbb{Z}_p^{d\times d}$ proceeds as follows.
First, VVHF.TrapGen samples for each $i \in \{0,\dots,\ell-1\}$ a subspace $\mathcal{U}_i$ of dimension $d-1$ independently and uniformly at random. $\mathcal{U}_\ell$ is defined to be the subspace spanned by the first $d-1$ unit vectors. Further, the algorithm chooses $\mathbf{u} \leftarrow_R \mathbb{Z}_p^d \backslash \mathcal{U}_0$.
Next, VVHF.TrapGen runs AHF.Part to obtain $(Y,I) \leftarrow \mathsf{AHF.Part}(1^\lambda, Q)$ and samples $\mathbf{T}_{i,j,k} \in \mathbb{Z}_p^{d\times d}$ for each $i \in \{1,\dots,\ell\}, j \in \{1,\dots,n\}, k \in \Sigma$ as follows.
  - Let j_i be the i-th value in I. Then, for each $i \in \{1,\dots,|I|\}$, the algorithm samples a matrix $\mathbf{T}_{i,j_i,Y_{j_i}} \in \mathbb{Z}_p^{d\times d}$ uniformly *of rank* d subject to

$$\mathbf{T}_{i,j_i,Y_{j_i}}^\top \cdot \mathcal{U}_{i-1} = \mathcal{U}_i.$$

  - Further, for each $i \in \{|I|+1,\dots,\ell\}$ and all $k \in \Sigma$, again the algorithm samples a matrix $\mathbf{T}_{i,1,k} \in \mathbb{Z}_p^{d\times d}$ uniformly *of rank* d subject to

$$\mathbf{T}_{i,1,k}^\top \cdot \mathcal{U}_{i-1} = \mathcal{U}_i.$$

  - For the remaining $i \in \{1,\dots,\ell\}$, $j \in \{1,\dots,n\}$ and $k \in \Sigma$ the algorithm samples $\mathbf{T}_{i,j,k} \in \mathbb{Z}_p^{d\times d}$ uniformly *of rank* $d-1$ subject to

$$\mathbf{T}_{i,j,k}^\top \cdot \mathbb{Z}_p^d = \mathcal{U}_i.$$

Finally, the algorithm sets

$$[\mathbf{M}_{i,j,k}] := \begin{cases} [\mathbf{T}_{i,j,k}] & \text{if } i \in \{1,\dots,\ell-1\} \\ \mathbf{T}_{i,j,k} \cdot [\mathbf{B}]^\top & \text{if } i = \ell \end{cases}$$

for all $i \in \{1,\dots,\ell\}, j \in \{1,\dots,n\}$ and $k \in \Sigma$ and outputs the trapdoor

$$td := \left((\mathbf{T}_{i,j,k})_{i\in\{1,\dots,\ell\},j\in\{1,\dots,n\},k\in\Sigma}, \mathbf{u}, [\mathbf{B}]\right)$$

and the verification key

$$vk := \left([\mathbf{M}_{i,j,k}]_{i\in\{1,\dots,\ell\},j\in\{1,\dots,n\},k\in\Sigma}, [\mathbf{u}]\right).$$

– VVHF.TrapEval is a probabilistic algorithm that on input of a trapdoor td and a preimage $x \in \{0,1\}^L$ first computes the admissible hash value $X := \mathsf{AHF}(x) \in \Sigma^n$ of x and further, for each $\iota \in \{1,\dots,\ell\}$, the vector

$$\mathbf{v}_\iota := \left(\prod_{i=1}^{\iota}\sum_{j=1}^{n} \mathbf{T}_{i,j,X_j}\right)^\top \mathbf{u}. \tag{3}$$

Finally, VVHF.TrapEval outputs the vector

$$\mathbf{c} := \mathbf{v}_\ell$$

and the proof

$$\pi := [\mathbf{v}_1,\dots,\mathbf{v}_{\ell-1}].$$

In the following we prove that the tuple (VVHF.TrapGen, VVHF.TrapEval) meets the required properties.

Correctness. Let (td, vk) be the output of VVHF.TrapGen on input $(\mathcal{G}, Q, [\mathbf{B}])$. Let $x \in \{0,1\}^L$ be an input value and let $X := \mathsf{AHF}(x)$ its encoding. Let $\mathbf{c} = \mathbf{v}_\ell$ and $\pi = [\mathbf{v}_1, \ldots, \mathbf{v}_{\ell-1}]$ be provided by VVHF.TrapEval on input $[\mathbf{B}]$. Then, for $\iota \in \{1, \ldots, \ell - 1\}$ Eq. (3) yields

$$\mathbf{v}_\iota = \left(\prod_{i=1}^{\iota} \sum_{j=1}^{n} \mathbf{T}_{i,j,X_j} \right)^\top \mathbf{u} = \left(\prod_{i=1}^{\iota} \sum_{j=1}^{n} \mathbf{M}_{i,j,X_j} \right)^\top \mathbf{u}$$

and for $\iota = \ell$ we have

$$\mathbf{B} \cdot \mathbf{c} = \mathbf{B} \cdot \left(\prod_{i=1}^{\ell} \sum_{j=1}^{n} \mathbf{T}_{i,j,X_j} \right)^\top \mathbf{u} = \sum_{j=1}^{n} \underbrace{\mathbf{B} \cdot \mathbf{T}_{\ell,j,X_j}^\top}_{=\mathbf{M}_{\ell,j,X_j}^\top} \cdot \left(\prod_{i=1}^{\ell-1} \sum_{j=1}^{n} \underbrace{\mathbf{T}_{i,j,X_j}}_{=\mathbf{M}_{i,j,X_j}} \right)^\top \mathbf{u}.$$

Thus, correctness follows from the correctness of VVHF.Eval.

Indistinguishability. The proof strategy follows the one of Lemma 4.6 in [22] closely. For $\kappa \in \{1, \ldots, \ell\}$ we define the following algorithm $\mathsf{VVHF.TrapGen}^{(\kappa)}$.

- First, the algorithm $\mathsf{VVHF.TrapGen}^{(\kappa)}$ samples $(d-1)$-dimensional subspaces $\mathcal{U}_0, \ldots, \mathcal{U}_\kappa \subseteq \mathbb{Z}_p^d$ and a vector $\mathbf{u} \leftarrow_R \mathbb{Z}_p^d \setminus \mathcal{U}_0$ uniformly at random.
- Second, the algorithm calls AHF.Part on input $(1^\lambda, Q)$ to obtain Y and I.
- For all $i \leq \kappa$, the algorithm chooses $\mathbf{T}_{i,j,k}$ according to VVHF.TrapGen and sets $\mathbf{M}_{i,j,k} := \mathbf{T}_{i,j,k}$ for all $j \in \{1, \ldots, n\}, k \in \Sigma$.
- For all $i > \kappa$, the algorithm chooses $\mathbf{M}_{i,j,k} \leftarrow_R \mathbb{Z}_p^{d \times d}$ for all $j \in \{1, \ldots, n\}, k \in \Sigma$.

We define the following series of games. We consider the indistinguishability experiment of Definition 4. In game $\mathbf{G}_0$ the verification key is generated by the VVHF.Gen algorithm and in game $\mathbf{G}_2$ the verification key is generated by the VVHF.TrapGen algorithm. We prove the indistinguishability of $\mathbf{G}_0$ and $\mathbf{G}_2$ by a series of games. We define game $\mathbf{G}_{1.\kappa}$ to be the game where VVHF.Gen is replaced by $\mathsf{VVHF.TrapGen}^{(\kappa)}$, respectively. By ε_κ we denote the probability that an adversary $\mathcal{A}$ outputs 1 in $\mathbf{G}_i$, that is $\varepsilon_\kappa := \Pr[\mathcal{A} \text{ outputs } 1]$. It remains to show that for every PPT adversary $\mathcal{A}$, $|\varepsilon_0 - \varepsilon_2|$ is negligible.

Transition $\mathbf{G}_0 \rightsquigarrow \mathbf{G}_{1.0}$: In game $\mathbf{G}_{1.0}$ the vector $\mathbf{u}$ is chosen uniformly at random from $\mathbb{Z}_p^d \backslash \mathcal{U}_0$ for a random subspace $\mathcal{U}_0$ instead of uniformly random from $\mathbb{Z}_p^d \setminus \{0\}$. As the view of $\mathcal{A}$ is independent of $\mathcal{U}_0$ we obtain $\varepsilon_1 = \varepsilon_0$.

Transition $\mathbf{G}_{1.\kappa-1} \rightsquigarrow \mathbf{G}_{1.\kappa}$: Given an adversary $\mathcal{A}$, we construct an adversary $\mathcal{B}$ on the d-rank problem as follows. Let $[\mathbf{A}]$ be the input to $\mathcal{B}$. Then $\mathcal{B}$ sets up the verification key as follows

- First, $\mathcal{B}$ samples $(d-1)$-dimensional subspaces $\mathcal{U}_0, \ldots, \mathcal{U}_{\kappa-1} \subseteq \mathbb{Z}_p^d$ and a vector $\mathbf{u} \leftarrow_R \mathbb{Z}_p^d \setminus \mathcal{U}_0$ uniformly at random.

- Next, the algorithm calls AHF.Part on input $(1^\lambda, Q)$ to obtain Y and I.
- For all $i \leq \kappa - 1, j \in \{1, \ldots, n\}, k \in \Sigma$, $\mathcal{B}$ chooses $\mathbf{T}_{i,j,k}$ according to VVHF.TrapGen and sets $\mathbf{M}_{i,j,k} := \mathbf{T}_{i,j,k}$.
- For $i = \kappa, j \in \{1, \ldots, n\}, k \in \Sigma$, the adversary proceeds as follows. Whenever VVHF.TrapGen would choose a matrix $\mathbf{T}_{\kappa,j,k}$ of rank $d-1$, $\mathcal{B}$ chooses a fresh $\mathbf{R}_{j,k} \leftarrow_R \mathbb{Z}_p^{d\times d}$ and sets $[\mathbf{M}_{\kappa,j,k}] := [\mathbf{T}_{\kappa,j,k}] := \mathbf{R}_{j,k} \cdot [\mathbf{A}]^\top$. Whenever VVHF.TrapGen would choose a matrix $\mathbf{T}_{\kappa,j,k}$ of rank d, $\mathcal{B}$ chooses a fresh basis $\{\mathbf{c}_1^{j,k}, \ldots, \mathbf{c}_{d-1}^{j,k}\}$ of $\mathcal{U}_{\kappa-1}$ (this is efficiently computable as $\mathcal{B}$ chooses $\mathcal{U}_{\kappa-1}$ itself) and further $d-1$ vectors $[\mathbf{d}_1^{j,k}], \ldots, [\mathbf{d}_{d-1}^{j,k}]$ in the image of $[\mathbf{A}]$. Further, $\mathcal{B}$ chooses $\mathbf{c}_d^{j,k}, \mathbf{d}_d^{j,k} \leftarrow_R \mathbb{Z}_p^d$, such that $\mathbf{C}_{j,k} := \left(\mathbf{c}_1^{j,k} | \cdots | \mathbf{c}_d^{j,k}\right)$ is invertible. Finally, $\mathcal{B}$ sets $[\mathbf{D}_{j,k}] := \left[\mathbf{d}_1^{j,k} | \cdots | \mathbf{d}_d^{j,k}\right]$ and $[\mathbf{M}_{\kappa,j,k}] := [\mathbf{T}_{\kappa,j,k}] := ([\mathbf{D}_{j,k}] \cdot \mathbf{C}_{j,k}^{-1})^\top$.
- For all $i > \kappa$, $\mathcal{B}$ chooses $\mathbf{M}_{i,j,k} \leftarrow_R \mathbb{Z}_p^{d\times d}$ for all $j \in \{1, \ldots, n\}, k \in \Sigma$.

Now, $\mathcal{B}$ forwards the verification key to $\mathcal{A}$. To answer evaluation queries, for $\iota \geq \kappa$ the adversary $\mathcal{B}$ can compute $[\mathbf{v}_\iota]$ as

$$[\mathbf{v}_\iota] = \left(\prod_{i=\iota}^{\kappa+1} \sum_{j=1}^{n} \mathbf{M}_{i,j,\mathsf{AHF}(x)_j}^\top [\mathbf{M}_{\kappa,j,\mathsf{AHF}(x)_j}]^\top \prod_{i=\kappa-1}^{1} \sum_{j=1}^{n} \mathbf{M}_{i,j,\mathsf{AHF}(x)_j}^\top \right) \mathbf{u}.$$

(Note that the factors are multiplied in reverse order, as we moved the transpose into the product in the above equation.)
It remains to prove that if $\mathbf{A}$ has rank $d-1$, then $\mathcal{B}$ simulates game $\mathbf{G}_{\kappa-1}$ and $\mathbf{G}_\kappa$ otherwise. We first consider the case that $\mathbf{A}$ has rank $d-1$. Let $\mathcal{U}_\kappa := [\mathbf{A}] \cdot \mathbb{Z}_p^d$ be the $d-1$-dimensional image of $[\mathbf{A}]$. Then the following holds

- For all $j \in \{1, \ldots, n\}, k \in \Sigma$ the matrix $\mathbf{R}_{j,k} \cdot [\mathbf{A}]^\top$ is of rank $d-1$ with $([\mathbf{A}] \cdot \mathbf{R}_{j,k}^\top) \cdot \mathbb{Z}_p^d = [\mathbf{A}] \cdot \mathbb{Z}_p^d = \mathcal{U}_\kappa$. Further, note that for every j, k, $\mathbf{T}_{\kappa,j,k} := \mathbf{R}_{j,k} \cdot [\mathbf{A}]^\top$ is distributed independently and uniformly at random conditioned on $\mathbf{T}_{\kappa,j,k} \cdot \mathbb{Z}_p^d = \mathcal{U}_\kappa$.
- For all $j \in \{1, \ldots, n\}, k \in \Sigma$ the vectors $[\mathbf{d}_1^{j,k}], \ldots, [\mathbf{d}_{d-1}^{j,k}]$ form a basis of $\mathcal{U}_\kappa$ and further $\mathbf{D}_{j,k}$ is full rank with overwhelming probability[2]. In this case $([\mathbf{D}_{j,k}] \cdot \mathbf{C}_{j,k}^{-1})^\top$ is full rank with

$$([\mathbf{D}_{j,k}] \cdot \mathbf{C}_{j,k}^{-1}) \cdot \mathcal{U}_{\kappa-1} = [\mathbf{D}_{j,k}] \cdot \underbrace{(\mathbf{C}_{j,k}^{-1} \cdot \mathcal{U}_{\kappa-1})}_{=\{\mathbf{z}\in\mathbb{Z}_p^d | z_d = 0\}} = \mathcal{U}_\kappa.$$

Again, note that for every j, k, $\mathbf{T}_{\kappa,j,k} := ([\mathbf{D}_{j,k}] \cdot \mathbf{C}_{j,k}^{-1})^\top$ is distributed independently and uniformly at random conditioned on $\mathbf{T}_{\kappa,j,k} \cdot \mathcal{U}_{\kappa-1} = \mathcal{U}_\kappa$.

[2] More precisely, with probability at least $1 - (d-1)/p - 1/p = 1 - d/p$.

We now assume that $\mathbf{A}$ is full rank. Due to the invertibility of $\mathbf{A}$, for all $j \in \{1, \ldots, n\}, k \in \Sigma$ the matrix $\mathbf{R}_{j,k} \cdot [\mathbf{A}]^\top$ is distributed uniformly at random over $\mathbb{G}^{d \times d}$. As further $[\mathbf{D}_{j,k}]$ is distributed uniformly at random over $\mathbb{G}^{d \times d}$, the same holds for $([\mathbf{D}_{j,k}] \cdot \mathbf{C}_{j,k}^{-1})^\top$.
Finally, on input b from $\mathcal{A}$, $\mathcal{B}$ outputs "**rank** $d-1$" if $b=0$ and "**rank** d" otherwise. Altogether, we obtain

$$|\varepsilon_{i.\kappa} - \varepsilon_{i.\kappa-1}| \leq \mathsf{Adv}_{\mathcal{G},\mathcal{B}}^{d\text{-rank}}(\lambda) + \mathcal{O}(n\sigma/p).$$

Transition $\mathbf{G}_{1.\ell} \rightsquigarrow \mathbf{G}_2$: In game $\mathbf{G}_2$ the subspace $\mathcal{U}_\ell$ is the subspace spanned by the first $d-1$ unit vectors (instead of chosen uniformly at random). Further, $\mathbf{M}_{\ell,j,k}$ is defined to equal $\mathbf{T}_{\ell,j,k} \cdot [\mathbf{B}]^\top$. Recall that $\mathbf{B} \leftarrow_R \mathbb{Z}_p^{d \times d}$ is chosen uniformly at random from all invertible matrices. Now, in both games $\mathbf{G}_{1.\ell}$ and game $\mathbf{G}_2$, $\mathbf{M}_{\ell,j,k}^\top$ maps $\mathcal{U}_{\ell-1}$ to a uniform $d-1$ dimensional subspace (namely, in game $\mathbf{G}_2$ to the space spanned by the first $d-1$ column vectors of $\mathbf{B}$). We have thus

$$\varepsilon_2 = \varepsilon_{1.\ell}.$$

Finally, we obtain

$$\begin{aligned}
\mathsf{Adv}^{\mathsf{vhf-ind}}_{\mathsf{VVHF},(\mathsf{VVHF.TrapGen},\mathsf{VVHF.TrapEval}),\mathcal{A},Q}(\lambda) &= |\varepsilon_2 - \varepsilon_0| \\
&= |\varepsilon_{1.\ell} - \varepsilon_{1.0}| \\
&\leq \sum_{\kappa=1}^{\ell} |\varepsilon_{1.\kappa} - \varepsilon_{1.\kappa-1}| \\
&\leq \ell \cdot \mathsf{Adv}_{\mathcal{G},\mathcal{B}}^{d\text{-rank}}(\lambda) + \mathcal{O}(\ell n\sigma/p).
\end{aligned}$$

Well-distributed outputs. Let $x^{(1)}, \ldots, x^{(Q)}, x^\star \in \{0,1\}^L$ be arbitrary with $x \notin \{x^{(1)}, \ldots, x^{(Q)}\}$. Recall that by Definition 7 choosing Y and I partitions the preimage space into sets

$$\mathcal{Y} := \{x \in \{0,1\}^L \mid \mathsf{AHF}(x)_j = Y_j \text{ for all } j \in I\} \text{ and } \mathcal{Z} := \{0,1\}^L \setminus \mathcal{Y}.$$

We hope that we have $x^\star \in \mathcal{Y}$ and $x^{(\nu)} \in \mathcal{Z}$ for all $\nu \in \{1, \ldots, Q\}$. As AHF is an admissible hash function, this is the case at least with probability

$$\Pr^{\mathsf{part}}_{\mathsf{AHF},\mathsf{AHF.Part},\lambda,Q}(\{x^{(i)}\}_i, x^\star) \geq \frac{1}{\mathrm{poly}(\lambda)}.$$

Let $\mathbf{c}^x$ the output vector of $\mathsf{VVHF.TrapEval}$ on input $x \in \{0,1\}^L$. To prove well-distributed outputs by previous considerations it suffices to show

$$c_d^x = 0 \Leftrightarrow x \in \mathcal{Z}.$$

Note that by construction of the subspace $\mathcal{U}_\ell$ we have $c_d^x = 0 \Leftrightarrow \mathbf{c}^x \in \mathcal{U}_\ell$. For all $x \in \{0,1\}^L$, $\iota \in \{1, \ldots, \ell\}$ let

$$\mathbf{v}_\iota^x := \left(\prod_{i=1}^{\iota} \sum_{j=1}^{n} \mathbf{T}_{i,j,\mathsf{AHF}(x)_j}\right)^\top \mathbf{u}. \tag{4}$$

Recall that $\mathbf{u} \in \mathbb{Z}_p^d \backslash \mathcal{U}_0$ and that for all $\mathbf{T}_{i,j,k}$ we have $\mathbf{T}_{i,j,k}^\top \cdot \mathcal{U}_{\iota-1} = \mathcal{U}_\iota$. Therefore, it holds $\mathbf{v}_\iota^x \in \mathcal{U}_\iota$ if

$$\mathbf{v}_{\iota-1}^x \in \mathcal{U}_{\iota-1} \text{ OR } \sum_{j=1}^{n} \mathbf{T}_{\iota,j,\mathsf{AHF}(x)_j}^\top \cdot (\mathbb{Z}_p^d \backslash \mathcal{U}_{\iota-1}) \subseteq \mathcal{U}_\iota.$$

In order to prove the claim it thus suffices to show
(i) $x \in \mathcal{Z} \Rightarrow \exists \iota \in \{1, \dots, \ell\}$: $\sum_{j=1}^n \mathbf{T}_{\iota,j,\mathsf{AHF}(x)_j}^\top \cdot (\mathbb{Z}_p^d \backslash \mathcal{U}_{\iota-1}) \subseteq \mathcal{U}_\iota$ and
(ii) $x \in \mathcal{Y} \Rightarrow \forall \iota \in \{1, \dots, \ell\}$: $\sum_{j=1}^n \mathbf{T}_{\iota,j,\mathsf{AHF}(x)_j}^\top \cdot (\mathbb{Z}_p^d \backslash \mathcal{U}_{\iota-1}) \subseteq \mathbb{Z}_p^d \backslash \mathcal{U}_\iota$.
Let j_ι be the ι-th index in I. For all $x \in \mathcal{Z}$ there exist a $\iota \in \{1, \dots, |I|\}$ with $\mathsf{AHF}(x)_{j_\iota} \neq Y_{j_\iota}$. By construction for this ι we have $\mathbf{T}_{\iota,j,\mathsf{AHF}(x)_j}^\top \cdot \mathbb{Z}_p^d = \mathcal{U}_\iota$ for all $j \in \{1, \dots, n\}$. This implies in particular $\sum_{j=1}^n \mathbf{T}_{\iota,j,\mathsf{AHF}(x)_j}^\top \cdot (\mathbb{Z}_p^d \backslash \mathcal{U}_{\iota-1}) \subseteq \mathcal{U}_\iota$ as required. We thus have $x \in \mathcal{Z} \implies c_d^x = 0$.
For all $x \in \mathcal{Y}$ and for all $\iota \in \{1, \dots, |I|\}$ it holds $\mathsf{AHF}(x)_{j_\iota} = Y_{j_\iota}$. By construction we have $\mathbf{T}_{\iota,j_\iota,Y_{j_\iota}}^\top \cdot (\mathbb{Z}_p^d \backslash \mathcal{U}_{\iota-1}) = \mathbb{Z}_p^d \backslash \mathcal{U}_\iota$. For all $\iota \in \{1, \dots, |I|\}$, $\mathbf{u}_{\iota-1} \in \mathbb{Z}_p^d \backslash \mathcal{U}_{\iota-1}$ we thus have

$$\sum_{j=1}^{n} \mathbf{T}_{\iota,j,\mathsf{AHF}(x)_j}^\top \cdot \mathbf{u}_{\iota-1} = \underbrace{\mathbf{T}_{\iota,j_\iota,\mathsf{AHF}(x)_{j_\iota}}^\top \cdot \mathbf{u}_{\iota-1}}_{\in \mathbb{Z}_p^d \backslash \mathcal{U}_\iota} + \underbrace{\sum_{j \neq j_\iota} \mathbf{T}_{\iota,j,\mathsf{AHF}(x)_j}^\top \cdot \mathbf{u}_{\iota-1}}_{\in \mathcal{U}_\iota} \in \mathbb{Z}_p^d \backslash \mathcal{U}_\iota.$$

Further, for all $\iota > |I|$ we have $\mathbf{T}_{\iota,j,k}$ uniform of rank d (subject to $\mathbf{T}_{\iota,j,k}^\top \cdot \mathcal{U}_{\iota-1} = \mathcal{U}_\iota$) if and only if $j = 1$. For all $\iota > |I|$, $\mathbf{u}_{\iota-1} \in \mathbb{Z}_p^d \backslash \mathcal{U}_{\iota-1}$ it thus holds

$$\sum_{j=1}^{n} \mathbf{T}_{\iota,j,\mathsf{AHF}(x)_j}^\top \cdot \mathbf{u}_{\iota-1} = \underbrace{\mathbf{T}_{\iota,1,\mathsf{AHF}(x)_1}^\top \cdot \mathbf{u}_{\iota-1}}_{\in \mathbb{Z}_p^d \backslash \mathcal{U}_\iota} + \underbrace{\sum_{j=2}^{n} \mathbf{T}_{\iota,j,\mathsf{AHF}(x)_j}^\top \cdot \mathbf{u}_{\iota-1}}_{\in \mathcal{U}_\iota} \in \mathbb{Z}_p^d \backslash \mathcal{U}_\iota.$$

Altogether, we obtain $x \in \mathcal{Y} \implies c_d^x \neq 0$.

Acknowledgments. I would like to thank the anonymous reviewers of TCC 2018 and PKC 2019 for their helpful comments. Further, I would like to thank my advisor Dennis Hofheinz for his support and helpful feedback.

References

1. Abdalla, M., Catalano, D., Fiore, D.: Verifiable random functions from identity-based key encapsulation. In: Joux, A. (ed.) EUROCRYPT 2009. LNCS, vol. 5479, pp. 554–571. Springer, Heidelberg (2009). https://doi.org/10.1007/978-3-642-01001-9_32
2. Abdalla, M., Catalano, D., Fiore, D.: Verifiable random functions: relations to identity-based key encapsulation and new constructions. J. Cryptol. **27**(3), 544–593 (2014). https://doi.org/10.1007/s00145-013-9153-x

3. Abdalla, M., Fiore, D., Lyubashevsky, V.: From selective to full security: semi-generic transformations in the standard model. In: Fischlin, M., Buchmann, J., Manulis, M. (eds.) PKC 2012. LNCS, vol. 7293, pp. 316–333. Springer, Heidelberg (2012). https://doi.org/10.1007/978-3-642-30057-8_19
4. Au, M.H., Susilo, W., Mu, Y.: Practical compact E-Cash. In: Pieprzyk, J., Ghodosi, H., Dawson, E. (eds.) ACISP 2007. LNCS, vol. 4586, pp. 431–445. Springer, Heidelberg (2007). https://doi.org/10.1007/978-3-540-73458-1_31
5. Badrinarayanan, S., Goyal, V., Jain, A., Sahai, A.: A note on VRFs from verifiable functional encryption. Cryptology ePrint Archive, Report 2017/051 (2017). http://eprint.iacr.org/2017/051
6. Belenkiy, M., Chase, M., Kohlweiss, M., Lysyanskaya, A.: Compact E-Cash and simulatable VRFs revisited. In: Shacham, H., Waters, B. (eds.) Pairing 2009. LNCS, vol. 5671, pp. 114–131. Springer, Heidelberg (2009). https://doi.org/10.1007/978-3-642-03298-1_9
7. Bitansky, N.: Verifiable random functions from non-interactive witness-indistinguishable proofs. In: Kalai, Y., Reyzin, L. (eds.) TCC 2017, Part II. LNCS, vol. 10678, pp. 567–594. Springer, Cham (2017). https://doi.org/10.1007/978-3-319-70503-3_19
8. Boneh, D., Boyen, X.: Secure identity based encryption without random oracles. In: Franklin, M. (ed.) CRYPTO 2004. LNCS, vol. 3152, pp. 443–459. Springer, Heidelberg (2004). https://doi.org/10.1007/978-3-540-28628-8_27
9. Boneh, D., Montgomery, H.W., Raghunathan, A.: Algebraic pseudorandom functions with improved efficiency from the augmented cascade. In: Al-Shaer, E., Keromytis, A.D., Shmatikov, V. (eds.) ACM CCS 2010. ACM Press, October 2010, pp. 131–140 (2010). https://doi.org/10.1145/1866307.1866323
10. Cash, D., Hofheinz, D., Kiltz, E., Peikert, C.: Bonsai trees, or how to delegate a lattice basis. In: Gilbert, H. (ed.) EUROCRYPT 2010. LNCS, vol. 6110, pp. 523–552. Springer, Heidelberg (2010). https://doi.org/10.1007/978-3-642-13190-5_27
11. Dodis, Y.: Efficient construction of (distributed) verifiable random functions. In: Desmedt, Y.G. (ed.) PKC 2003. LNCS, vol. 2567, pp. 1–17. Springer, Heidelberg (2003). https://doi.org/10.1007/3-540-36288-6_1
12. Dodis, Y., Yampolskiy, A.: A verifiable random function with short proofs and keys. In: Vaudenay, S. (ed.) PKC 2005. LNCS, vol. 3386, pp. 416–431. Springer, Heidelberg (2005). https://doi.org/10.1007/978-3-540-30580-4_28
13. Escala, A., Herold, G., Kiltz, E., Ràfols, C., Villar, J.: An algebraic framework for Diffie-Hellman assumptions. In: Canetti, R., Garay, J.A. (eds.) CRYPTO 2013, Part II. LNCS, vol. 8043, pp. 129–147. Springer, Heidelberg (2013). https://doi.org/10.1007/978-3-642-40084-1_8
14. Freire, E.S.V., Hofheinz, D., Paterson, K.G., Striecks, C.: Programmable hash functions in the multilinear setting. In: Canetti, R., Garay, J.A. (eds.) CRYPTO 2013, Part I. LNCS, vol. 8042, pp. 513–530. Springer, Heidelberg (2013). https://doi.org/10.1007/978-3-642-40041-4_28
15. Goldreich, O.: Computational complexity: a conceptual perspective. ACM Sigact News **39**(3), 35–39 (2008)
16. Goldreich, O., Goldwasser, S., Micali, S.: How to construct random functions. J. ACM **33**(4), 792–807 (1986)
17. Goldreich, O., Oren, Y.: Definitions and properties of zero-knowledge proof systems. J. Cryptol. **7**(1), 1–32 (1994)
18. Goyal, R., Hohenberger, S., Koppula, V., Waters, B.: A generic approach to constructing and proving verifiable random functions. Cryptology ePrint Archive, Report 2017/021 (2017). http://eprint.iacr.org/2017/021

19. Groth, J., Ostrovsky, R., Sahai, A.: New techniques for noninteractive zero-knowledge. J. ACM **59**(3), 11:1–11:35 (2012). https://doi.org/10.1145/2220357.2220358. ISSN 0004-5411
20. Hofheinz, D., Jager, T.: Verifiable random functions from standard assumptions. In: Kushilevitz, E., Malkin, T. (eds.) TCC 2016, Part I. LNCS, vol. 9562, pp. 336–362. Springer, Heidelberg (2016). https://doi.org/10.1007/978-3-662-49096-9_14
21. Hohenberger, S., Waters, B.: Constructing verifiable random functions with large input spaces. In: Gilbert, H. (ed.) EUROCRYPT 2010. LNCS, vol. 6110, pp. 656–672. Springer, Heidelberg (2010). https://doi.org/10.1007/978-3-642-13190-5_33
22. Hofheinz, D., Jager, T.: Verifiable random functions from standard assumptions. Cryptology ePrint Archive, Report 2015/1048 (2015). http://eprint.iacr.org/2015/1048
23. Jager, T.: Verifiable random functions from weaker assumptions. In: Dodis, Y., Nielsen, J.B. (eds.) TCC 2015, Part II. LNCS, vol. 9015, pp. 121–143. Springer, Heidelberg (2015). https://doi.org/10.1007/978-3-662-46497-7_5
24. Jarecki, S., Shmatikov, V.: Handcuffing big brother: an abuse-resilient transaction escrow scheme. In: Cachin, C., Camenisch, J.L. (eds.) EUROCRYPT 2004. LNCS, vol. 3027, pp. 590–608. Springer, Heidelberg (2004). https://doi.org/10.1007/978-3-540-24676-3_35
25. Katsumata, S.: On the untapped potential of encoding predicates by arithmetic circuits and their applications. In: Takagi, T., Peyrin, T. (eds.) ASIACRYPT 2017, Part III. LNCS, vol. 10626, pp. 95–125. Springer, Cham (2017). https://doi.org/10.1007/978-3-319-70700-6_4
26. Liskov, M.: Updatable zero-knowledge databases. In: Roy, B. (ed.) ASIACRYPT 2005. LNCS, vol. 3788, pp. 174–198. Springer, Heidelberg (2005). https://doi.org/10.1007/11593447_10
27. Lysyanskaya, A.: Unique signatures and verifiable random functions from the DH-DDH separation. In: Yung, M. (ed.) CRYPTO 2002. LNCS, vol. 2442, pp. 597–612. Springer, Heidelberg (2002). https://doi.org/10.1007/3-540-45708-9_38
28. Micali, S., Rabin, M.O., Vadhan, S.P.: Verifiable random functions. In: 40th FOCS. IEEE Computer Society Press, pp. 120–130, October 1999. https://doi.org/10.1109/SFFCS.1999.814584
29. Micali, S., Reyzin, L.: Soundness in the public-key model. In: Kilian, J. (ed.) CRYPTO 2001. LNCS, vol. 2139, pp. 542–565. Springer, Heidelberg (2001). https://doi.org/10.1007/3-540-44647-8_32
30. Micali, S., Rivest, R.L.: Micropayments revisited. In: Preneel, B. (ed.) CT-RSA 2002. LNCS, vol. 2271, pp. 149–163. Springer, Heidelberg (2002). https://doi.org/10.1007/3-540-45760-7_11
31. Naor, M., Reingold, O.: Number-theoretic constructions of efficient pseudo-random functions. J. ACM **51**(2), 231–262 (2004)
32. Reed, I.S., Solomon, G.: Polynomial codes over certain finite fields. J. Soc. Ind. Appl. Math. **8**(2), 300–304 (1960)
33. Roşie, R.: Adaptive-secure VRFs. Cryptology ePrint Archive, Report 2017/750 (2017). http://eprint.iacr.org/2017/750
34. Waters, B.: Efficient identity-based encryption without random oracles. In: Cramer, R. (ed.) EUROCRYPT 2005. LNCS, vol. 3494, pp. 114–127. Springer, Heidelberg (2005). https://doi.org/10.1007/11426639_7
35. Yamada, S.: Asymptotically compact adaptively secure lattice IBEs and verifiable random functions via generalized partitioning techniques. In: Katz, J., Shacham, H. (eds.) CRYPTO 2017, Part III. LNCS, vol. 10403, pp. 161–193. Springer, Cham (2017). https://doi.org/10.1007/978-3-319-63697-9_6

Post Quantum Cryptography

Lattice-Based Revocable (Hierarchical) IBE with Decryption Key Exposure Resistance

Shuichi Katsumata[1,2], Takahiro Matsuda[2], and Atsushi Takayasu[1,2(✉)]

[1] The University of Tokyo, Tokyo, Japan
[2] National Institute of Advanced Industrial Science and Technology, Tokyo, Japan
takayasu@mist.i.u-tokyo.ac.jp

Abstract. *Revocable* identity-based encryption (RIBE) is an extension of IBE that supports a key revocation mechanism, which is an indispensable feature for practical cryptographic schemes. Due to this extra feature, RIBE is often required to satisfy a strong security notion unique to the revocation setting called *decryption key exposure resistance* (DKER). Additionally, *hierarchal* IBE (HIBE) is another orthogonal extension of IBE that supports key delegation functionalities allowing for scalable deployments of cryptographic schemes. So far, R(H)IBE constructions with DKER are only known from bilinear maps, where all constructions rely heavily on the so-called *key re-randomization* property to achieve the DKER and/or hierarchal feature. Since lattice-based schemes seem to be inherently ill-fit with the key re-randomization property, no construction of lattice-based R(H)IBE schemes with DKER are known.

In this paper, we propose the first lattice-based RHIBE scheme with DKER *without* relying on the key re-randomization property, departing from all the previously known methods. We start our work by providing a generic construction of RIBE schemes with DKER, which uses as building blocks any two-level standard HIBE scheme and (weak) RIBE scheme *without* DKER. Based on previous lattice-based RIBE constructions *without* DKER, our result implies the first lattice-based RIBE scheme *with* DKER. Then, building on top of our generic construction, we construct the first lattice-based RHIBE scheme with DKER, by further exploiting the algebraic structure of lattices. To this end, we prepare a new tool called the *level conversion keys*, which enables us to achieve the hierarchal feature without relying on the key re-randomization property.

1 Introduction

Identity-based encryption (IBE) is an advanced form of public key encryption, where an arbitrary string can be used as user's public keys. One extension of IBE is *hierarchical* IBE (HIBE), which further supports a key delegation functionality; an attractive feature for scalable deployments of IBE. However, as opposed to ordinary public key encryption, (H)IBE does not support a key/user

D. Lin and K. Sako (Eds.): PKC 2019, LNCS 11443, pp. 441–471, 2019.
https://doi.org/10.1007/978-3-030-17259-6_15

revocation mechanism due to the absence of the public key infrastructures and there are no trivial ways to drive malicious users out from an ordinary (H)IBE system. Therefore, adding a key revocation mechanism to (H)IBE is considered to be one of the important research themes when considering practical deployments of (H)IBE. For instance, Boneh and Franklin [7] proposed a method for adding a simple revocation mechanism to any IBE system. However, the bottleneck of their proposal was its efficiency. The number of keys generated for every time period was proportional to the number of all users in the IBE system and the scheme did not scale if the number of users became too large. Since then, constructing an (H)IBE scheme with a scalable revocation mechanism has been a sought-after goal. Below, we refer to (H)IBE that allows for such a scalable revocation mechanism as *revocable (H)IBE.*

The first revocable IBE (RIBE) scheme was proposed by Boldyreva et al. [6]. RIBE requires three types of keys: a *secret key*, a *key update*, and a *decryption key*. As in IBE, each user is issued a secret key that is associated with his identity. However, in order to achieve the key revocation mechanism, each user's secret key itself does not allow them to decrypt ciphertexts. To allow the users to decrypt, the key generation center (KGC) broadcasts *key updates* for every time period through a public channel. Roughly, the key update incorporates public information of the users that are currently allowed in the system. Specifically, although the key update is meaningless information to revoked users, it allows non-revoked users to combine with their secret keys to derive a *decryption key*, which effectively enables them to properly decrypt ciphertexts. To achieve a scalable revocation mechanism, Boldyreva et al. utilized a subset cover framework called the complete subtree (CS) method [25], so that the size of the key update sent by the KGC in each time period will be logarithmic in the number of system users. The work of Boldyreva et al. [6] attracted numerous followup works [15,18,20,33,37] and their RIBE construction was also extended to revocable *hierarchical* IBE (RHIBE) which simultaneously support scalable key revocation and key delegation functionalities [13,17,19,32,34,35].

Considering that RIBE and RHIBE were introduced by envisioning the real-world use of (H)IBE systems, their security definitions should take into account as many realistic threats and attack scenarios as possible. For example, leakage of decryption keys due to social/cyber attacks or unexpected human errors are common incidents in practice. Motivated by this, Seo and Emura [33,35] introduced a security notion unique to R(H)IBE called *decryption key exposure resistance* (DKER). Roughly speaking, this security notion guarantees that an exposure of a user's decryption key at some time period will not compromise the confidentiality of ciphertexts that are encrypted for different time periods—a clearly desirable security guarantee in practice. After the introduction of the new security notion DKER, it has quickly become one of the default security requirements for R(H)IBE and attracted many followup works concerning R(H)IBE schemes with DKER [13,15,17–19,23,28,29,32,35,37]. So far constructions of R(H)IBE schemes with DKER are all based on bilinear or multilinear maps.

State of affairs of Lattice-based R(H)IBE. Lattice-based cryptography has been paid much attention in the last decade, however, construction of R(H)IBE schemes with DKER has been rather elusive. In 2012, Chen et al. [10] proposed the first lattice-based RIBE scheme *without* DKER; a work before the now default security notion of DKER was formalized by Seo and Emura [33], building on top of the standard IBE constructions of [1,8]. The only followup work was done recently by Takayasu and Watanabe [36] who partially solved the problem of achieving RIBE with DKER by proposing a variant of [10]. Unfortunately, their scheme only satisfies *bounded* DKER, a strictly weaker notion than DKER, which only allows a bounded number of decryption keys to be leaked. Therefore, constructing an RIBE scheme with (unbounded) DKER based on lattices still remains an unsolved problem. This is in sharp contrast with the bilinear map setting where many constructions are known [13,15,17–19,32,33,35,37]. Moreover, extending the RIBE scheme of Chen et al. [10] to the hierarchal setting seems to be highly non-trivial since no construction of lattice-based RHIBEs are known regardless of the scheme being DKER or not.

One of the main reasons why constructing R(H)IBE schemes with DKER in the lattice-setting has been difficult is because the algebraic structure of lattices seems to be ill-fit with the so-called *key re-randomization* property. So far, all RIBE schemes [15,18,23,29,33,37] and RHIBE schemes with DKER [13,17,19,28,32,35] are based on number theoretical assumptions, e.g., bilinear maps and multilinear maps, which all rely heavily on this key re-randomization property. At a high level, this is the property with which each user can re-randomize their key so that the re-randomized key is distributed identically to (or at least statistically close to) a key generated using a fresh randomness. In essence, this is the central property that enables DKER. Furthermore, this property is also heavily utilized when generating the children's secret keys for fixed randomness without using any secret information, hence, achieving the hierarchal feature. However, unfortunately, due to the difference in the algebraic structure of bilinear, multilinear maps and lattices, we are currently unaware of any way of achieving the key re-randomization property from lattices.[1] Therefore, to construct lattice-based R(H)IBE schemes with DKER, it seems that we must deviate from prior methodologies and develop new techniques.

Our Contributions. In this paper, we propose the first lattice-based R(H)IBE scheme with DKER secure under the learning with errors (LWE) assumption. The techniques used in this work highly depart from previous works that rely on the key re-randomization property for achieving DKER and the key delegation functionality. Specifically, we show a generic construction of an RIBE scheme with DKER from any two-level standard HIBE scheme and RIBE scheme without DKER, thus bypassing the necessity of the key re-randomization property.

---

[1] A knowledgeable reader familiar with lattice-based cryptography may wonder why the existing RIBE schemes [10,36] cannot be easily modified to support the property by using short trapdoor bases. We provide detailed discussions on why this simple modification is insufficient in Sect. 2.

Then, building on top of the idea of our generic construction, we further exploit the algebraic structure of lattices to construct an RHIBE scheme with DKER. We provide a brief summary of our work below and refer the detailed technical overview to Sect. 2.

Our first contribution is a generic construction of RIBE *with* DKER from any RIBE *without* DKER and two-level HIBE. The new tools we introduce to circumvent the necessity of the key re-randomization property are called *leveled ciphertexts* and *leveled decryption keys*. At a high level, each "level" for the leveled ciphertexts and decryption keys is associated to the RIBE scheme without DKER and the two-level HIBE scheme, respectively; one level is responsible for achieving the revocation mechanism and the other is responsible for the key re-randomization mechanism. Therefore, informally, our leveled structure allows for a *partial* key re-randomization mechanism. Using the lattice-based RIBE scheme without DKER of Chen et al. [10] and any lattice-based HIBE scheme, e.g., [1,8], our result implies the first lattice-based RIBE scheme with DKER. Furthermore, since any IBE schemes can be converted to an HIBE scheme [12] (in the selective-identity model) and any RIBE scheme without DKER implies an IBE scheme, our result also implies a generic conversion of any RIBE scheme without DKER into an RIBE scheme with DKER.

Our second contribution is the construction of the first lattice-based RHIBE scheme with DKER. It is built on top of the idea of our generic construction and further exploits the algebraic structure unique to lattices. Namely, to achieve the key delegation functionality, i.e., hierarchal feature, we additionally introduce a tool called *level conversion keys*. In essence, this tool enables a user to convert his (secret) decryption key to a (public) key update for users of different hierarchal levels. In other words, the level conversion key allows one to delegate his key to its children without re-randomizing his key. Although the idea is simple, the concrete machinery to blend the level conversion keys securely into the construction is rather contrived and we refer the details to Sect. 2.

Finally, we state some side contributions worth highlighting in our paper. Firstly, we re-formalize the syntax and security definitions for R(H)IBE. For instance, since previous security definitions [6,33–35] had some ambiguity (e.g. in some cases it is not clear when the values such as secret keys and key updates are generated during the security game), it was up to the readers to interpret the definitions and the proofs. Therefore, in our work we provide a refined security definition for R(H)IBE which in particular is a more rigorous and explicit treatment than the previous definitions. Secondly, we provide a formal treatment on an implicit argument that has been frequently adopted in the R(H)IBE literature. In particular, we introduce a simple yet handy "strategy-dividing lemma", which helps us simplify the security proofs for R(H)IBE schemes in general. For the details, see Sect. 4.

Related Works. Boldyreva et al. [6] proposed the first RIBE scheme that achieved selective-identity security from bilinear maps and Libert and Vergnaud [20] extended their results to the adaptive setting. The first lattice-based RIBE scheme was proposed by Chen et al. [10] and the first RHIBE scheme was proposed by Seo and Emura [34] based on bilinear maps. Recently, Chang et al. [9] proposed an RIBE scheme from codes with rank metric in the random oracle model.

After Seo and Emura [33] introduced the security notion of DKER and proposed the first RIBE scheme with DKER, several improvements and variants have been proposed. These works consist of RIBE [15,18,37] and RHIBE [13, 17,19,35] from bilinear maps, and those from multilinear maps [23,28,29]. From lattices, Takayasu and Watanabe [36] proposed an RIBE scheme with bounded DKER; a strictly weaker notion then DKER.

Server-aided RIBE [11,26,30] is a variant of RIBE where most of the computation of the users are delegated to an untrusted server. The revocation mechanism we study in this paper is sometimes referred to as indirect revocation. A direct revocation mechanism does not require key updates and has been discussed for attribute-based encryption [4,5] and predicate encryption [27]. Recently, Ling et al. proposed the first lattice-based directly revocable predicate encryption scheme [21] and its server-aided variant [22].

Roadmap. In Sect. 2, we provide an overview of our constructions. In Sect. 3, we recall basic tools for lattice-based cryptography. In Sect. 4, we introduce formal definitions for RHIBE. In Sect. 5, we show a generic construction of RIBE with DKER. Finally, in Sect. 6, we show our main result concerning the first lattice-based RHIBE scheme with DKER.

Notations. Before diving into the technical details, we prepare some notations. Let $\mathbb{N}$ be the set of all natural numbers. For non-negative integers $n, n' \in \mathbb{N}$ with $n \leq n'$, we define $[n, n'] := \{n, n+1, \ldots, n'\}$, and we extend the definition for $n > n'$ by $[n, n'] = \emptyset$. For notational convenience, for $n \in \mathbb{N}$, we define $[n] := [1, n]$. Throughout the paper, $\lambda \in \mathbb{N}$ denotes the security parameter.

As usual in the literature of (R)HIBE, an identity ID of a user at level ℓ in the hierarchy in an RHIBE scheme is expressed as a length-ℓ vector $\mathsf{ID} = (\mathsf{id}_1, \cdots, \mathsf{id}_\ell)$. In order not to mix up with an identity $\mathsf{ID} = (\mathsf{id}_1, \mathsf{id}_2, \ldots)$ treated in an RHIBE scheme and its element id_i, we sometimes call the former a *hierarchical identity* and the latter an *element identity.* We refer to the set of all element identities as the *element identity space* and denote it by $\mathcal{ID}$. We assume the element identity space is determined only by the security parameter λ. Thus, for example, the space to which level-ℓ identities belong is expressed as $(\mathcal{ID})^\ell$. For notational convenience, for $\ell \in \mathbb{N}$ we define $(\mathcal{ID})^{\leq \ell} := \bigcup_{i \in [\ell]} (\mathcal{ID})^i$, and the hierarchal identity space $\mathcal{ID}_\mathtt{h} := (\mathcal{ID})^{\leq L}$. We denote by "$\mathsf{kgc}$" the special hierarchical identity for the level-0 user, i.e., the key generation center (KGC).

Like an ordinary vector, we consider a prefix of hierarchical identities. For example, for a level-ℓ hierarchical identity $\mathsf{ID} = (\mathsf{id}_1, \ldots, \mathsf{id}_\ell)$ and $t \leq \ell$, $\mathsf{ID}_{[t]}$ represents the length-t prefix of ID, i.e., $\mathsf{ID}_{[t]} = (\mathsf{id}_1, \ldots, \mathsf{id}_t)$. We denote by "$\mathsf{pa}(\mathsf{ID})$" the identity of its parent (i.e. the direct ancestor), namely, if $\mathsf{ID} \in (\mathcal{ID})^\ell$, then $\mathsf{pa}(\mathsf{ID}) := \mathsf{ID}_{[\ell-1]} = (\mathsf{id}_1, \ldots, \mathsf{id}_{\ell-1})$, and $\mathsf{pa}(\mathsf{ID})$ for a level-1 identity $\mathsf{ID} \in \mathcal{ID}$ is defined to be kgc. Furthermore, we denote by "$\mathsf{prefix}(\mathsf{ID})$" the set consisting of itself and all of its ancestors, namely, $\mathsf{prefix}(\mathsf{ID}) := \{\mathsf{ID}_{[1]}, \mathsf{ID}_{[2]}, \ldots, \mathsf{ID}_{[|\mathsf{ID}|]} =$

$\mathsf{ID}\}$. Also, for $\mathsf{ID} \in (\mathcal{ID})^{\ell}$, we denote by "$\mathsf{ID}\|\mathcal{ID}$" as the subset of $(\mathcal{ID})^{\ell+1}$ that contains all the members who have ID as its parent.

2 Technical Overview

In this section, we provide the technical overview of our results. In order to make the lattice-based RHIBE overview easier to follow, we present the details of our generic construction of RIBE with DKER using lattice terminologies. The general idea presented below translates naturally to our generic construction. To this end, we first prepare two standard hash functions used in lattice-based cryptography: one for the users $\mathsf{ID} \in \mathcal{ID}_{\mathsf{h}} = \mathcal{ID}^{\leq L}$, where each element identity space is defined by $\mathcal{ID} = \mathbb{Z}_q^n \setminus \{\mathbf{0}_n\}$, and another for the time period[2] $\mathsf{t} \in \mathcal{T} \subset \mathbb{Z}_q^n \setminus \{\mathbf{0}_n\}$. In particular, for a user $\mathsf{ID} = (\mathsf{id}_1, \dots, \mathsf{id}_\ell) \in (\mathbb{Z}_q^n \setminus \{\mathbf{0}_n\})^{\leq L}$ and time period $\mathsf{t} \in \mathbb{Z}_q^n \setminus \{\mathbf{0}_n\}$ we use the following hash functions $\mathbf{E}(\cdot)$ and $\mathbf{F}(\cdot)$:

$$\begin{aligned} \mathbf{E}(\mathsf{ID}) &:= [\mathbf{B}_1 + H(\mathsf{id}_1)\mathbf{G}|\cdots|\mathbf{B}_\ell + H(\mathsf{id}_\ell)\mathbf{G}] \in \mathbb{Z}_q^{n\times \ell m}, \\ \mathbf{F}(\mathsf{t}) &:= \mathbf{B}_{L+1} + H(\mathsf{t})\mathbf{G} \in \mathbb{Z}_q^{n\times m}, \end{aligned} \tag{1}$$

where $(\mathbf{B}_j)_{j\in[L+1]}$ are random matrices in $\mathbb{Z}_q^{n\times m}$ chosen at setup of the scheme and $\mathbf{G}$ is the gadget matrix [24]. Here, $H : \mathbb{Z}_q^n \to \mathbb{Z}_q^{n\times n}$ is a specific hash function used to encode an identity to a matrix, and its definition is provided in Sect. 3. Notice that for any $\mathsf{ID} \in (\mathbb{Z}_q^n \setminus \{\mathbf{0}_n\})^{\ell}$ and $\mathsf{id}_{\ell+1} \in \mathbb{Z}_q^n \setminus \{\mathbf{0}_n\}$, we have $\mathbf{E}(\mathsf{ID}\|\mathsf{id}_{\ell+1}) = [\mathbf{E}(\mathsf{ID})|\mathbf{B}_{\ell+1} + H(\mathsf{id}_{\ell+1})\mathbf{G}]$. Finally, we define $\mathbf{E}(\mathsf{kgc}) := \emptyset$.

Review of RIBE *without* DKER. We first recall Chen et al.'s lattice-based RIBE scheme *without* DKER [10] in Fig. 1. Here, $\mathbf{A}$ and $\mathbf{u}$ in the master public key PP are a matrix in $\mathbb{Z}_q^{n\times m}$ and a vector in $\mathbb{Z}_q^n$, respectively, and $\mathbf{T_A}$ is the trapdoor associated with $\mathbf{A}$. Other terms will be explained as we proceed with our technical overview. Below, we see why the scheme realizes the revocation mechanism while it does not satisfy DKER. One feature of RIBE construction is that the KGC maintains a binary tree where each user is assigned to a randomly

$\mathsf{PP} := (\mathbf{A}, \mathbf{u}, \text{hash functions } \mathbf{E}(\cdot), \mathbf{F}(\cdot))$,	$\mathsf{sk}_{\mathsf{kgc}} := \mathbf{T_A}$
$\mathsf{ct} := (c_0 := \mathbf{u}^\top \mathbf{s} + \mathsf{noise} + \mathsf{M}\lfloor \frac{q}{2} \rfloor, \mathbf{c}_1 := [\mathbf{A}|\mathbf{E}(\mathsf{ID})|\mathbf{F}(\mathsf{t})]^\top \mathbf{s} + \mathsf{noise})$	
$\mathsf{sk}_{\mathsf{ID}} := (\mathbf{e}_{\mathsf{ID},\theta})_\theta$	s.t. $[\mathbf{A}|\mathbf{E}(\mathsf{ID})]\mathbf{e}_{\mathsf{ID},\theta} = \mathbf{u}_\theta$
$\mathsf{ku}_{\mathsf{t}} := (\mathbf{e}_{\mathsf{t},\theta})_\theta$	s.t. $[\mathbf{A}|\mathbf{F}(\mathsf{t})]\mathbf{e}_{\mathsf{t},\theta} = \mathbf{u} - \mathbf{u}_\theta$
$\mathsf{dk}_{\mathsf{ID},\mathsf{t}} := \mathbf{d}_{\mathsf{ID},\mathsf{t}}$	s.t. $[\mathbf{A}|\mathbf{E}(\mathsf{ID})|\mathbf{F}(\mathsf{t})]\mathbf{d}_{\mathsf{ID},\mathsf{t}} = \mathbf{u}$

Fig. 1. Chen et al.'s RIBE scheme

[2] As we will show in Sect. 4, the time period space is a set of natural numbers $\{1, 2, \dots\}$. Here, we assume that there is an efficient hash function that maps each natural number to a distinct vector in $\mathbb{Z}_q^n \setminus \{\mathbf{0}_n\}$.

selected leaf. Furthermore, a random vector $\mathbf{u}_\theta \in \mathbb{Z}_q^n$ is uniquely assigned to each node θ of the binary tree. Below, we explain the three types of keys which are core tools to realize the revocation mechanism: A *secret key* for a user ID is a tuple of short vectors $\mathsf{sk}_{\mathsf{ID}} = (\mathbf{e}_{\mathsf{ID},\theta})_\theta$, where each *short* vector $\mathbf{e}_{\mathsf{ID},\theta} \in \mathbb{Z}^{2m}$ is associated to a random vector $\mathbf{u}_\theta$ such that

$$[\mathbf{A}|\mathbf{E}(\mathsf{ID})]\mathbf{e}_{\mathsf{ID},\theta} = \mathbf{u}_\theta.$$

Since $\mathbf{u}_\theta$ is an independent random vector and the ciphertext c_0 only depends on $\mathbf{u}$, the vector $\mathbf{e}_{\mathsf{ID},\theta}$ in $\mathsf{sk}_{\mathsf{ID}}$ itself is useless for decrypting a ciphertext ct. Hence, in each time period the KGC broadcasts a *key update* which is also a tuple of short vectors $\mathsf{ku}_{\mathsf{t}} = (\mathbf{e}_{\mathsf{t},\theta})_\theta$, where each short vector $\mathbf{e}_{\mathsf{t},\theta}$ is associated to a random vector $\mathbf{u}_\theta$ such that

$$[\mathbf{A}|\mathbf{F}(\mathsf{t})]\mathbf{e}_{\mathsf{t},\theta} = \mathbf{u} - \mathbf{u}_\theta.$$

Similarly to above, $\mathbf{e}_{\mathsf{t},\theta}$ in ku_{t} itself is useless for decrypting a ciphertext ct. Now, we explain how the revocation mechanism works. By utilizing the complete subtree (CS) method [25], the KGC is able to broadcast key updates so that there is no common node θ in ku_{t} and $\mathsf{sk}_{\mathsf{ID}}$ of *revoked* IDs, while there is at least one common node θ in ku_{t} and $\mathsf{sk}_{\mathsf{ID}}$ of *non-revoked* IDs. Then, $\mathbf{e}_{\mathsf{ID},\theta}$ in $\mathsf{sk}_{\mathsf{ID}}$ and $\mathbf{e}_{\mathsf{t},\theta}$ in ku_{t} of the common node θ enable a non-revoked ID to derive a well-formed *decryption key* $\mathbf{d}_{\mathsf{ID},\mathsf{t}} \in \mathbb{Z}^{3m}$ which is a *short* vector satisfying

$$[\mathbf{A}|\mathbf{E}(\mathsf{ID})|\mathbf{F}(\mathsf{t})]\mathbf{d}_{\mathsf{ID},\mathsf{t}} = \mathbf{u}.$$

It can be easily checked that $\mathbf{d}_{\mathsf{ID},\mathsf{t}}$ can be obtained by simply adding $\mathbf{e}_{\mathsf{ID},\theta}$ and $\mathbf{e}_{\mathsf{t},\theta}$ in a component-wise fashion. Note that if $\mathbf{e}_{\mathsf{ID},\theta}$ and $\mathbf{e}_{\mathsf{t},\theta}$ are short vectors, then so is $\mathbf{d}_{\mathsf{ID},\mathsf{t}}$. Then, the vector enables us to recover the plaintext by computing

$$c_0 - \mathbf{c}_1^\top \mathbf{d}_{\mathsf{ID},\mathsf{t}} \approx \mathsf{M}\left\lfloor \frac{q}{2} \right\rfloor.$$

The main insight of this construction is that only non-revoked users can use the key updates to eliminate the random factor $\mathbf{u}_\theta$ to obtain a short vector $\mathbf{d}_{\mathsf{ID},\mathsf{t}}$ that is bound to the public matrix $[\mathbf{A}|\mathbf{E}(\mathsf{ID})|\mathbf{F}(\mathsf{t})]$ and public vector $\mathbf{u}$ with which a ciphertexts ct is created.

Although the scheme is proven to be a secure RIBE scheme *without* DKER, it clearly does not satisfy DKER. Indeed, there is a concrete attack even with a single decryption key query (i.e., decryption key exposure) on the target ID^*. The attack is as follows: assume that the adversary obtains a decryption key $\mathsf{dk}_{\mathsf{ID}^*,\mathsf{t}}$ for the target ID^* and a time period $\mathsf{t} \neq \mathsf{t}^*$. Since key updates are publicly broadcast, the adversary also obtains ku_{t} and $\mathsf{ku}_{\mathsf{t}^*}$. Since user ID^* will not be revoked unless $\mathsf{sk}_{\mathsf{ID}^*}$ was revealed to the adversary, the key updates ku_{t} and $\mathsf{ku}_{\mathsf{t}^*}$ will share a common node θ^* with the secret key.[3] Therefore, recalling that $\mathsf{dk}_{\mathsf{ID}^*,\mathsf{t}}$

[3] To be more precise, there are cases ku_{t} and $\mathsf{ku}_{\mathsf{t}^*}$ might not share a common node, however, $\mathcal{A}$ can always adaptively revoke other users so that this holds.

was a simple component-wise addition of $\mathbf{e}_{\mathsf{ID}^*,\theta^*}$ in $\mathsf{sk}_{\mathsf{ID}^*}$ and $\mathbf{e}_{\mathsf{t},\theta^*}$ in ku_{t}, $\mathcal{A}$ can first recover the secret key component $\mathbf{e}_{\mathsf{ID}^*,\theta^*}$ from $(\mathsf{dk}_{\mathsf{ID}^*,\mathsf{t}}, \mathbf{e}_{\mathsf{t},\theta^*})$, which he can then combine it with $\mathbf{e}_{\mathsf{t}^*,\theta^*}$ in $\mathsf{ku}_{\mathsf{t}^*}$ to create the decryption key $\mathbf{d}_{\mathsf{ID}^*,\mathsf{t}^*}$ for the challenge time period t^*. Specifically, this decryption key allows the adversary to completely break the scheme. In reality, this corresponds to the fact that once a decryption key for a certain time period is exposed to an adversary, then all the messages of distinct time periods may also be compromised. In essence, this attack relies on the fact that the decryption key leaks partial information on the secret key, which can then be used to construct decryption keys of all distinct time periods.

In all the previous bilinear map-based constructions, the above problem was circumvented by relying on the so-called *key re-randomization property.* Informally, this property allows one to re-randomize the decryption key, hence even if the decryption key is leaked, it would be impossible to restore the original secret key. In the above construction, this idea would correspond to re-sampling a short random vector $\bar{\mathbf{d}}_{\mathsf{ID},\mathsf{t}}$ such that

$$[\mathbf{A}|\mathbf{E}(\mathsf{ID})|\mathbf{F}(\mathsf{t})]\bar{\mathbf{d}}_{\mathsf{ID},\mathsf{t}} = \mathbf{u}$$

using his original decryption key $\mathbf{d}_{\mathsf{ID},\mathsf{t}}$. Indeed, if the distribution of $\bar{\mathbf{d}}_{\mathsf{ID},\mathsf{t}}$ is independent of the original decryption key $\mathbf{d}_{\mathsf{ID},\mathsf{t}}$, this modification would prevent the above attack, since the adversary will not be able to recover the secret key component $\mathbf{e}_{\mathsf{ID}^*,\theta^*}$ anymore using the above strategy. However, such a re-sampling procedure is computationally infeasible, since otherwise we would be able to trivially solve the small integer solution (SIS) problem.

Readers familiar with lattice-based constructions of (non-revocable) HIBE may think that we could achieve the key re-randomization property by simply using a short trapdoor basis as the secret key instead of a vector. Indeed, if we add a short trapdoor basis $\mathbf{T}_{[\mathbf{A}|\mathbf{E}(\mathsf{ID})]}$ as a part of the secret key $\mathsf{sk}_{\mathsf{ID}}$, the user ID will be able to sample a short vector $\bar{\mathbf{d}}_{\mathsf{ID},\mathsf{t}} \neq \mathbf{d}_{\mathsf{ID},\mathsf{t}}$, since anybody can efficiently extend the trapdoor basis $\mathbf{T}_{[\mathbf{A}|\mathbf{E}(\mathsf{ID})]}$ to $\mathbf{T}_{[\mathbf{A}|\mathbf{E}(\mathsf{ID})|\mathbf{F}(\mathsf{t})]}$ and thus sample a random vector $\bar{\mathbf{d}}_{\mathsf{ID},\mathsf{t}}$ such that $[\mathbf{A}|\mathbf{E}(\mathsf{ID})|\mathbf{F}(\mathsf{t})]\bar{\mathbf{d}}_{\mathsf{ID},\mathsf{t}} = \mathbf{u}$. However, this approach does not mesh well with the above revocation mechanism, since now the user ID can derive decryption keys $\mathbf{d}_{\mathsf{ID},\mathsf{t}}$ for every time period without requiring the key updates ku_{t}. Therefore, adding a short trapdoor basis to the secret key provides too much flexibility to the users and we completely lose the mechanism for supporting revocation.

Constructing RIBE *with* DKER. To summarize so far, the main bottleneck of Chen et al.'s RIBE scheme without DKER is that it satisfies the key revocation mechanism, but seems challenging to extend it to satisfy DKER. On the other hand, adding a short trapdoor basis would definitely be useful for achieving DKER, however, it seems to contradict with the revocation mechanism. In the following, we show that we can carefully combine these two seemingly conflicting ideas together. The concrete construction of our lattice-based RIBE scheme *with* DKER is illustrated in Fig. 2. The boxed items denote the changes made from the previous figure.

$$\mathsf{PP} := (\mathbf{A}, \boxed{\bar{\mathbf{A}}}, \mathbf{u}, \text{hash functions } \mathbf{E}(\cdot), \mathbf{F}(\cdot)), \qquad \mathsf{sk_{kgc}} := (\mathbf{T_A}, \boxed{\mathbf{T}_{\bar{\mathbf{A}}}})$$

$$\mathsf{ct} := \left(\begin{array}{c} c_0 := \mathbf{u}^\top(\mathbf{s} + \boxed{\bar{\mathbf{s}}}) + \mathsf{noise} + \mathsf{M} \left\lfloor \frac{q}{2} \right\rfloor, \\ \mathbf{c}_1 := [\mathbf{A}|\mathbf{E}(\mathsf{ID})|\mathbf{F}(\mathsf{t})]^\top \mathbf{s} + \mathsf{noise}, \ \boxed{\bar{\mathbf{c}}_1 := [\bar{\mathbf{A}}|\mathbf{E}(\mathsf{ID})|\mathbf{F}(\mathsf{t})]^\top \bar{\mathbf{s}} + \mathsf{noise}} \end{array} \right)$$

$$\mathsf{sk_{ID}} := \left((\mathbf{e}_{\mathsf{ID},\theta})_\theta, \boxed{\mathbf{T}_{[\bar{\mathbf{A}}|\mathbf{E}(\mathsf{ID})]}}\right) \quad \text{s.t. } [\mathbf{A}|\mathbf{E}(\mathsf{ID})]\mathbf{e}_{\mathsf{ID},\theta} = \mathbf{u}_\theta$$

$$\mathsf{ku_t} := (\mathbf{e}_{\mathsf{t},\theta})_\theta \quad \text{s.t. } [\mathbf{A}|\mathbf{F}(\mathsf{t})]\mathbf{e}_{\mathsf{t},\theta} = \mathbf{u} - \mathbf{u}_\theta$$

$$\mathsf{dk_{ID,t}} := \left(\mathbf{d}_{\mathsf{ID,t}}, \boxed{\bar{\mathbf{d}}_{\mathsf{ID,t}}}\right) \quad \text{s.t. } [\mathbf{A}|\mathbf{E}(\mathsf{ID})|\mathbf{F}(\mathsf{t})]\mathbf{d}_{\mathsf{ID,t}} = \mathbf{u}, \ \boxed{[\bar{\mathbf{A}}|\mathbf{E}(\mathsf{ID})|\mathbf{F}(\mathsf{t})]\bar{\mathbf{d}}_{\mathsf{ID,t}} = \mathbf{u}}$$

Fig. 2. Our RIBE scheme with DKER

Our construction relies on a tool we call *leveled ciphertexts* and *leveled decryption keys*; the terminology should become more intuitive and helpful in the hierarchical setting that we explain later. Here, we call an element associated with a matrix $\mathbf{A}$ and $\bar{\mathbf{A}}$ level-1 and level-2, respectively. In particular, $\mathbf{c}_1, \bar{\mathbf{c}}_1$ and $\mathbf{d}_{\mathsf{ID,t}}, \bar{\mathbf{d}}_{\mathsf{ID,t}}$ in Fig. 2 are the level-1, level-2 ciphertexts and decryption keys, respectively. Here, the level-1 components $\mathbf{c}_1$ and $\mathbf{d}_{\mathsf{ID,t}}$ correspond to Chen et al.'s RIBE scheme without DKER and are responsible for achieving the revocation mechanism. On the other hand, the level-2 components $\bar{\mathbf{c}}_1$ and $\bar{\mathbf{d}}_{\mathsf{ID,t}}$ are the newly introduced elements that will help us achieve DKER. Since the two decryption keys for levels-1 and 2 are in one-to-one correspondence with the ciphertexts $(\mathbf{c}_1, \bar{\mathbf{c}}_1)$ for levels-1 and 2, both of the decryption keys are required to recover the underlying message as follows:

$$c_0 - \underbrace{\mathbf{c}_1^\top \mathbf{d}_{\mathsf{ID,t}}}_{\text{level-1 component}} - \underbrace{\bar{\mathbf{c}}_1^\top \bar{\mathbf{d}}_{\mathsf{ID,t}}}_{\text{level-2 component}} \approx \mathsf{M} \left\lfloor \frac{q}{2} \right\rfloor.$$

In particular, if either level of the decryption key is missing, the message cannot be recovered. Separating the role of the decryption keys is the main idea that allows us to associate the two seemingly conflicting properties of revocation and key re-randomization to each level of the decryption keys.

First, we observe that the above RIBE scheme achieves the revocation mechanism since it simply inherits this property from the underlying Chen et al.'s RIBE scheme without DKER. Furthermore, we achieve DKER by incorporating the aforementioned trapdoor idea; we add a trapdoor $\mathbf{T}_{[\bar{\mathbf{A}}|\mathbf{E}(\mathsf{ID})]}$ to the secret key $\mathsf{sk_{ID}}$. Using this short trapdoor basis $\mathbf{T}_{[\bar{\mathbf{A}}|\mathbf{E}(\mathsf{ID})]}$, we can now sample a level-2 decryption key $\bar{\mathbf{d}}_{\mathsf{ID,t}}$ for each time period independently from the previous time periods. Namely, using $\mathbf{T}_{[\bar{\mathbf{A}}|\mathbf{E}(\mathsf{ID})]}$, we can sample a short vector $\bar{\mathbf{d}}_{\mathsf{ID,t}}$ such that

$$[\bar{\mathbf{A}}|\mathbf{E}(\mathsf{ID})|\mathbf{F}(\mathsf{t})]\bar{\mathbf{d}}_{\mathsf{ID,t}} = \mathbf{u},$$

where $\bar{\mathbf{d}}_{\mathsf{ID,t}}$ leaks no information of the secret key $\mathsf{sk_{ID}}$. Hence, although we are not able to completely re-randomize the decryption key $\mathsf{dk_{ID,t}} = (\mathbf{d}_{\mathsf{ID,t}}, \bar{\mathbf{d}}_{\mathsf{ID,t}})$, we can *partially* re-randomize the decryption key by sampling a new level-2 decryption key $\bar{\mathbf{d}}_{\mathsf{ID},\mathsf{t}}$ for each time period; even if $\mathsf{dk}_{\mathsf{ID},\mathsf{t}}$ is compromised, this alone will not be sufficient for constructing decryption keys for other time periods. Indeed, we show that this partial key re-randomization property is sufficient to prove the DKER security.

In Sect. 5, we formalize and prove the above idea by providing a generic construction of RIBE with DKER, using as building blocks any RIBE without DKER and 2-level HIBE. At a high level, the 2-level HIBE scheme is responsible for the key re-randomization property and is the core component that allows us to convert non-DKER secure RIBE schemes into DKER secure RIBE schemes.

Constructing RHIBE from Lattices. Next, we show an overview of our lattice-based RHIBE construction. For simplicity of presentation and since we can add DKER via the above idea, we do not take into account DKER in the following RHIBE construction. Specifically, we explain how to construct an RHIBE scheme *without* DKER by modifying Chen et al.'s RIBE scheme.

Before getting into detail, we prepare some notations used for the hierarchal setting. In the following, let L be the maximum depth of the hierarchy, where we treat the KGC as level-0. In RHIBE, all level-i users ID for $i \in [0, L-1]$, including the KGC, maintain a binary tree $\mathsf{BT}_{\mathsf{ID}}$ to manage their children users in $\mathsf{ID} \| \mathcal{ID}$. Furthermore, a random vector $\mathbf{u}_{\mathsf{ID},\theta} \in \mathbb{Z}_q^n$ is uniquely assigned to each node θ of the binary tree $\mathsf{BT}_{\mathsf{ID}}$. The level-$(\ell-1)$ user $\mathsf{pa}(\mathsf{ID})$ creates the secret key $\mathsf{sk}_{\mathsf{ID}}$ of the level-ℓ user ID, and the user ID derives his own decryption key $\mathsf{dk}_{\mathsf{ID},\mathsf{t}}$ by combining his own secret key $\mathsf{sk}_{\mathsf{ID}}$ and the key updates $\mathsf{ku}_{\mathsf{pa}(\mathsf{ID}),\mathsf{t}}$ that are broadcast by the parent user $\mathsf{pa}(\mathsf{ID})$. Throughout the overview, we assume ID represents an level-ℓ user.

<u>Introducing Leveled Secret Keys</u>: Due to the complex nature of our scheme, we believe it to be helpful to provide the intuition of our scheme following a series of modifications, where our final scheme without DKER is depicted in Fig. 6. Our starting point is illustrated in Fig. 3, where as before, the box indicates the changes made from the prior scheme.

$$\mathsf{PP} := \left(\boxed{(\mathbf{A}_i)_{i\in[L]}}, \mathbf{u}, \text{hash functions } \mathbf{E}(\cdot), \mathbf{F}(\cdot)\right), \qquad \mathsf{sk}_{\mathsf{kgc}} := \boxed{(\mathbf{T}_{\mathbf{A}_i})_{i\in[L]}}$$

$$\mathsf{ct} := \left(c_0 := \mathbf{u}^\top \mathbf{s} + \mathsf{noise} + \mathsf{M}\left\lfloor \tfrac{q}{2} \right\rfloor, \mathbf{c}_1 := [\boxed{\mathbf{A}_\ell} | \mathbf{E}(\mathsf{ID}) | \mathbf{F}(\mathsf{t})]^\top \mathbf{s} + \mathsf{noise}\right)$$

$$\mathsf{sk}_{\mathsf{ID}} := \left((\mathbf{e}_{\mathsf{ID},\theta})_\theta, \boxed{(\mathbf{T}_{[\mathbf{A}_i | \mathbf{E}(\mathsf{ID})]})_{i\in[\ell+1,L]}}\right) \quad \text{s.t. } [\boxed{\mathbf{A}_\ell} | \mathbf{E}(\mathsf{ID})] \mathbf{e}_{\mathsf{ID},\theta} = \mathbf{u}_{\mathsf{pa}(\mathsf{ID}),\theta}$$

$$\mathsf{ku}_{\mathsf{pa}(\mathsf{ID}),\mathsf{t}} := (\mathbf{e}_{\mathsf{pa}(\mathsf{ID}),\mathsf{t},\theta})_\theta \quad \text{s.t. } [\boxed{\mathbf{A}_\ell} | \mathbf{E}(\mathsf{pa}(\mathsf{ID})) | \mathbf{F}(\mathsf{t})] \mathbf{e}_{\mathsf{pa}(\mathsf{ID}),\mathsf{t},\theta} = \mathbf{u} - \mathbf{u}_{\mathsf{pa}(\mathsf{ID}),\theta}$$

$$\mathsf{dk}_{\mathsf{ID},\mathsf{t}} := \mathbf{d}_{\mathsf{ID},\mathsf{t}} \quad \text{s.t. } [\boxed{\mathbf{A}_\ell} | \mathbf{E}(\mathsf{ID}) | \mathbf{F}(\mathsf{t})] \mathbf{d}_{\mathsf{ID},\mathsf{t}} = \mathbf{u}$$

Fig. 3. Leveled secret key and i-leveled ciphertext

Toward resolving the incompatibility of the key delegation property and the key revocation mechanism, the scheme in Fig. 3 utilizes leveled ciphertexts as done in the prior non-hierarchal scheme in Fig. 2. Furthermore, we introduce a new tool called *leveled secret keys* in this scheme. Here, we call an element associated with a matrix $\mathbf{A}_i$ level-i, respectively. In particular, the ciphertext ct of a level-ℓ user ID is a level-ℓ ciphertext since $\mathbf{c}_1$ is associated with $\mathbf{A}_\ell$. The main trick of the scheme in Fig. 3 is that a secret key $\mathsf{sk}_{\mathsf{ID}}$ for a level-ℓ user consists of level-i secret keys for $i \in [\ell, L]$, where the level-ℓ secret key $(\mathbf{e}_{\mathsf{ID},\theta})_\theta$ and the other level-i secret keys $\mathbf{T}_{[\mathbf{A}_i|\mathbf{E}(\mathsf{ID})]}$ for $i \in [\ell+1, L]$ serve a different purpose. The level-ℓ secret key in $\mathsf{sk}_{\mathsf{ID}}$ is a tuple of short vectors of the form $(\mathbf{e}_{\mathsf{ID},\theta})_\theta$ each of which satisfies

$$[\mathbf{A}_\ell|\mathbf{E}(\mathsf{ID})]\mathbf{e}_{\mathsf{ID},\theta} = [\mathbf{A}_\ell|\mathbf{E}(\mathsf{pa}(\mathsf{ID}))|\mathbf{B}_\ell + H(\mathsf{id}_\ell)\mathbf{G}]\mathbf{e}_{\mathsf{ID},\theta} = \mathbf{u}_{\mathsf{pa}(\mathsf{ID}),\theta}, \tag{2}$$

and serves the same purpose as the original Chen et al.'s RIBE scheme. Namely, the level-ℓ secret key of a level-ℓ user is used for decrypting its own level-ℓ ciphertext, where the detailed procedure will be explained later. The remaining level-i secret keys in $\mathsf{sk}_{\mathsf{ID}}$ for $i \in [\ell+1, L]$ are trapdoors of the form $\mathbf{T}_{[\mathbf{A}_i|\mathbf{E}(\mathsf{ID})]}$ in $\mathsf{sk}_{\mathsf{ID}}$ and serves the purpose of delegation. Concretely, using the trapdoor $\mathbf{T}_{[\mathbf{A}_i|\mathbf{E}(\mathsf{ID})]}$ for $i \in [\ell+1, L]$, the level-ℓ user ID can sample all level-i secret keys for his children $\mathsf{ID}\|\mathsf{id}_{\ell+1} \in \mathsf{ID}\|\mathcal{ID}$; a set of short vectors $(\mathbf{e}_{\mathsf{ID}\|\mathsf{id}_{\ell+1},\theta})_\theta$ such that $[\mathbf{A}_i|\mathbf{E}(\mathsf{ID}\|\mathsf{id}_{\ell+1})]\mathbf{e}_{\mathsf{ID}\|\mathsf{id}_{\ell+1},\theta} = \mathbf{u}_{\mathsf{ID},\theta}$ and trapdoors $\mathbf{T}_{[\mathbf{A}_i|\mathbf{E}(\mathsf{ID}\|\mathsf{id}_{\ell+1})]}$ for $i \in [\ell+2, L]$. In addition, the level-ℓ user ID can also use the level-$(\ell+1)$ trapdoor $\mathbf{T}_{[\mathbf{A}_{\ell+1}|\mathbf{E}(\mathsf{ID})]}$ in $\mathsf{sk}_{\mathsf{ID}}$ to derive key updates $\mathsf{ku}_{\mathsf{ID},\mathsf{t}}$. Here, a level-$(\ell-1)$ user $\mathsf{pa}(\mathsf{ID})$'s key update $\mathsf{ku}_{\mathsf{pa}(\mathsf{ID}),\mathsf{t}}$ is a tuple of short vectors $(\mathbf{e}_{\mathsf{pa}(\mathsf{ID}),\mathsf{t},\theta})_\theta$ such that

$$[\mathbf{A}_\ell|\mathbf{E}(\mathsf{pa}(\mathsf{ID}))|\mathbf{F}(\mathsf{t})]\mathbf{e}_{\mathsf{pa}(\mathsf{ID}),\mathsf{t},\theta} = \mathbf{u} - \mathbf{u}_{\mathsf{pa}(\mathsf{ID}),\theta}. \tag{3}$$

Then, from Eqs. (2) and (3), the level-ℓ user ID can derive a well-formed decryption key $\mathsf{dk}_{\mathsf{ID},\mathsf{t}}$ which is a short vector of the form $\mathbf{d}_{\mathsf{ID},\mathsf{t}}$ satisfying

$$[\mathbf{A}|\mathbf{E}(\mathsf{ID})|\mathbf{F}(\mathsf{t})]\mathbf{d}_{\mathsf{ID},\mathsf{t}} = [\mathbf{A}|\mathbf{E}(\mathsf{pa}(\mathsf{ID}))|\mathbf{B}_\ell + H(\mathsf{id}_\ell)\mathbf{G}|\mathbf{F}(\mathsf{t})]\mathbf{d}_{\mathsf{ID},\mathsf{t}} = \mathbf{u}.$$

Hence, the scheme in Fig. 3 properly supports the key delegation functionality.

Furthermore, at first glance, the scheme also supports the key revocation mechanism. Since the level-ℓ secret key $(\mathbf{e}_{\mathsf{ID},\theta})_\theta$ of the level-ℓ user ID is exactly the same as the secret key used by user ID in Chen et al.'s RIBE scheme, it simply inherits the revocation mechanism. In particular, user ID will not be able to decrypt his level-ℓ ciphertext without his parent's key update $\mathsf{ku}_{\mathsf{pa}(\mathsf{ID}),\mathsf{t}}$, which will no longer be provided once user ID is revoked. However, unfortunately, this scheme is trivially flawed and does not meet the security notion of RHIBE. In RHIBE, we require the user ID to be revoked once any of his ancestors $\mathsf{ID}_{[i]} \in \mathsf{prefix}(\mathsf{ID})$ for $i \in [\ell-1]$ is revoked. In other words, once a user is revoked from the system, then all of its descendants must also be revoked. It can be easily checked that this requirement is not met by our above RHIBE scheme. Since the level-ℓ user ID has the full trapdoor $\mathbf{T}_{[\mathbf{A}_i|\mathbf{E}(\mathsf{ID})]}$ for $i \in [\ell+1, L]$ as part of its secret key, nothing is preventing user ID from continuing on generating secret keys and key updates for his children.

Introducing Leveled Decryption Keys: To fix the above issue concerning key revocation, we further modify the scheme as in Fig. 4. From now on, we further modify the definition of level-i ciphertext, and call a tuple

$$(\mathbf{u}^\top \mathbf{s}_i + \mathsf{noise}, \quad \mathbf{c}_i = [\mathbf{A}_i|\mathbf{E}(\mathsf{ID}_{[i]})|\mathbf{F}(\mathsf{t})]^\top \mathbf{s}_i + \mathsf{noise})$$

$$\mathsf{PP} := ((\mathbf{A}_i)_{i\in[L]}, \mathbf{u}, \text{hash functions } \mathbf{E}(\cdot), \mathbf{F}(\cdot)), \qquad \mathsf{sk_{kgc}} := (\mathbf{T}_{\mathbf{A}_i})_{i\in[L]}$$

$$\mathsf{ct} := \left(\begin{array}{l} c_0 := \mathbf{u}^\top \boxed{(\mathbf{s}_1 + \cdots + \mathbf{s}_\ell)} + \mathsf{noise} + \mathsf{M}\left\lfloor \frac{q}{2} \right\rfloor, \\ \boxed{(\mathbf{c}_i := [\mathbf{A}_i|\mathbf{E}(\mathsf{ID}_{[i]})|\mathbf{F}(\mathsf{t})]^\top \mathbf{s}_i + \mathsf{noise})_{i\in[\ell]}} \end{array} \right)$$

$$\mathsf{sk_{ID}} := ((\mathbf{e}_{\mathsf{ID},\theta}), (\mathbf{T}_{[\mathbf{A}_i|\mathbf{E}(\mathsf{ID})]})_{i\in[\ell+1,L]}) \quad \text{s.t. } [\mathbf{A}_\ell|\mathbf{E}(\mathsf{ID})]\mathbf{e}_{\mathsf{ID},\theta} = \mathbf{u}_\theta$$

$$\mathsf{ku_{pa(ID),t}} := ((\mathbf{e}_{\mathsf{pa(ID)},\mathsf{t},\theta}), \boxed{(\mathbf{f}_{\mathsf{ID}_{[i]},\mathsf{t}})_{i\in[\ell-1]}}) \quad \text{s.t. } [\mathbf{A}_\ell|\mathbf{E}(\mathsf{pa(ID)})|\mathbf{F}(\mathsf{t})]\mathbf{e}_{\mathsf{pa(ID)},\mathsf{t},\theta} = \mathbf{u} - \mathbf{u}_\theta,$$

$$\boxed{[\mathbf{A}_i|\mathbf{E}(\mathsf{ID}_{[i]})|\mathbf{F}(\mathsf{t})]\mathbf{f}_{\mathsf{ID}_{[i]},\mathsf{t}} = \mathbf{u}}$$

$$\mathsf{dk_{ID,t}} := (\mathbf{d}_{\mathsf{ID},\mathsf{t}}, \boxed{(\mathbf{f}_{\mathsf{ID}_{[i]},\mathsf{t}})_{i\in[\ell-1]}}) \quad \text{s.t. } [\mathbf{A}_\ell|\mathbf{E}(\mathsf{ID})|\mathbf{F}(\mathsf{t})]\mathbf{d}_{\mathsf{ID},\mathsf{t}} = \mathbf{u}$$

Fig. 4. Multiple leveled ciphertext and key update

a level-i ciphertext since $\mathbf{c}_i$ is associated with the public matrix $\mathbf{A}_i$ and both components are associated with the same secret vector $\mathbf{s}_i$. In this scheme, we modify the ciphertext for a level-ℓ user ID to contain all the level-i ciphertexts for $i \in [\ell]$, where each level-i ciphertext is associated with the public matrix $\mathbf{A}_i$ and an identity $\mathsf{ID}_{[i]}$. The idea behind this modification is to revoke any user ID whose ancestors were revoked by including some information specific to the ancestors in the ciphertext. In particular, if some ancestor at level $i \in [\ell - 1]$ were to be revoked, then the level-i ciphertext $\mathbf{c}_i$ should become undecryptable, hence maintaining the secrecy of the plaintext M. To make this idea work, we must now provide user ID with new components to allow decryption of the level-i ciphertexts for $i \in [\ell - 1]$. We achieve this by introducing a new tool called *leveled decryption keys*. A leveled decryption key for a level-ℓ user ID consists of level-i decryption keys for $i \in [\ell]$. Similarly to leveled secret keys, the level-ℓ decryption key $\mathbf{d}_{\mathsf{ID},\mathsf{t}}$ and the other level-i decryption keys $\mathbf{f}_{\mathsf{ID}_{[i]},\mathsf{t}}$ for $i \in [\ell - 1]$ serve a different purpose. The level-ℓ decryption key denoted as $\mathbf{d}_{\mathsf{ID},\mathsf{t}}$ in $\mathsf{dk_{ID,t}}$ serves the same purpose as in the previous schemes. The level-i decryption key for $i \in [\ell - 1]$ denoted as $\mathbf{f}_{\mathsf{ID}_{[i]},\mathsf{t}}$ in $\mathsf{dk_{ID,t}}$ is the actual decryption key used by its ancestor at level-i. Although we use a different notation, $\mathbf{f}_{\mathsf{ID}_{[i]},\mathsf{t}}$ is equivalent to $\mathbf{d}_{\mathsf{ID}_{[i]},\mathsf{t}}$ such that

$$[\mathbf{A}_i|\mathbf{E}(\mathsf{ID}_{[i]})|\mathbf{F}(\mathsf{t})]\mathbf{f}_{\mathsf{ID}_{[i]},\mathsf{t}} = [\mathbf{A}_i|\mathbf{E}(\mathsf{ID}_{[i]})|\mathbf{F}(\mathsf{t})]\mathbf{d}_{\mathsf{ID}_{[i]},\mathsf{t}} = \mathbf{u}. \tag{4}$$

In particular, each ancestor at level-i for $i \in [\ell - 1]$ broadcasts their own decryption key $\mathbf{f}_{\mathsf{ID}_{[i]},\mathsf{t}}$ (See $\mathsf{ku_{pa(ID),t}}$ in Fig. 4) and the user ID sets the level-i decryption key for $i \in [\ell - 1]$ as $\mathbf{f}_{\mathsf{ID}_{[i]},\mathsf{t}}$. It can be easily verified that user ID can correctly decrypt his ciphertext as follows:

$$c_0 - \underbrace{\mathbf{c}_\ell^\top \mathbf{d}_{\mathsf{ID},\mathsf{t}}}_{\text{level-}\ell\text{ component}} - \sum_{i=1}^{\ell-1} \underbrace{\mathbf{c}_i^\top \mathbf{f}_{\mathsf{ID}_{[i]},\mathsf{t}}}_{\text{level-}i\text{ component}} \approx \mathsf{M}\left\lfloor \frac{q}{2} \right\rfloor.$$

$$
\begin{aligned}
&\mathsf{PP} := ((\mathbf{A}_i)_{i\in[L]}, \boxed{(\mathbf{u}_k)_{k\in[L]}}, \text{hash functions } \mathbf{E}(\cdot), \mathbf{F}(\cdot)), \quad \mathsf{sk}_{\mathsf{kgc}} := (\mathbf{T}_{\mathbf{A}_i})_{i\in[L]} \\
&\mathsf{ct} := \begin{pmatrix} c_0 := \boxed{\mathbf{u}_\ell}^\top (\mathbf{s}_1 + \cdots \mathbf{s}_\ell) + \mathsf{noise} + \mathsf{M} \left\lfloor \frac{q}{2} \right\rfloor, \\ (\mathbf{c}_i := [\mathbf{A}_i | \mathbf{E}(\mathsf{ID}_{[i]}) | \mathbf{F}(\mathsf{t})]^\top \mathbf{s}_i + \mathsf{noise})_{i\in[\ell]} \end{pmatrix} \\
&\mathsf{sk}_{\mathsf{ID}} := ((\mathbf{e}_{\mathsf{ID},\theta}), (\mathbf{T}_{[\mathbf{A}_i|\mathbf{E}(\mathsf{ID})]})_{i\in[\ell+1,L]}) \qquad \text{s.t. } [\mathbf{A}_\ell | \mathbf{E}(\mathsf{ID})] \mathbf{e}_{\mathsf{ID},\theta} = \mathbf{u}_\theta, \\
&\mathsf{ku}_{\mathsf{pa}(\mathsf{ID}),\mathsf{t}} := ((\mathbf{e}_{\mathsf{pa}(\mathsf{ID}),\mathsf{t},\theta}), \boxed{(\mathbf{f}_{\mathsf{ID}_{[i]},\mathsf{t},k})_{i\in[\ell-1],k\in[\ell,L]}}) \\
&\qquad \text{s.t. } [\mathbf{A}_\ell | \mathbf{E}(\mathsf{pa}(\mathsf{ID})) | \mathbf{F}(\mathsf{t})] \mathbf{e}_{\mathsf{pa}(\mathsf{ID}),\mathsf{t},\theta} = \mathbf{u}_\ell - \mathbf{u}_\theta, \qquad \boxed{[\mathbf{A}_i | \mathbf{E}(\mathsf{ID}_{[i]}) | \mathbf{F}(\mathsf{t})] \mathbf{f}_{\mathsf{ID}_{[i]},\mathsf{t},k} = \mathbf{u}_k} \\
&\mathsf{dk}_{\mathsf{ID},\mathsf{t}} := (\mathbf{d}_{\mathsf{ID},\mathsf{t}}, \boxed{(\mathbf{f}_{\mathsf{ID}_{[i]},\mathsf{t},\ell})_{i\in[\ell-1]}}) \qquad \text{s.t. } [\mathbf{A}_\ell | \mathbf{E}(\mathsf{ID}) | \mathbf{F}(\mathsf{t})] \mathbf{d}_{\mathsf{ID},\mathsf{t}} = \boxed{\mathbf{u}_\ell}
\end{aligned}
$$

Fig. 5. (k, i)-leveled ciphertext and decryption key

However, this scheme is obviously insecure, since the level-i ancestors are required to publicly broadcast their level-i decryption key $\mathbf{f}_{\mathsf{ID}_{[i]},\mathsf{t}} (= \mathbf{d}_{\mathsf{ID}_{[i]},\mathsf{t}})$, which can in turn be used by anybody to decrypt the level-i ciphertexts of that particular ancestor.

Making the Levels Two-Dimensional: For the scheme in Fig. 4 to be secure, decryption keys of the ancestors should not be made public via the key updates. Specifically, a ciphertext aimed for a user should not contain the same level as of his ancestors, since otherwise the decryption keys of the ancestors must be made public. For the purpose, we further modify the scheme as in Fig. 5. To this end, we incorporate multiple public vectors $(\mathbf{u}_k)_{k\in[L]}$, and redefine the notion of leveled ciphertexts and leveled decryption keys to be *two-dimensional*. Here, we refer to an element associated with a vector $\mathbf{u}_k$ and a matrix $\mathbf{A}_i$ as level-(k, i), respectively. For example, we call a tuple

$$(\mathbf{u}_k^\top \mathbf{s}_i + \mathsf{noise}, \quad \mathbf{c}_i = [\mathbf{A}_i | \mathbf{E}(\mathsf{ID}_{[i]}) | \mathbf{F}(\mathsf{t})]^\top \mathbf{s}_i + \mathsf{noise})$$

a level-(k, i) ciphertext since the first component is associated with the public vector $\mathbf{u}_k$, and the latter component $\mathbf{c}_i$ is associated with the public matrix $\mathbf{A}_i$, and both components are associated with the same secret vector $\mathbf{s}_i$. In particular, a ciphertext for a level-ℓ user ID consists of level-(ℓ, i) ciphertexts for $i \in [\ell]$. Accordingly, we must provide user ID with a redefined leveled decryption key to allow decryption of the two-dimensional leveled ciphertexts. Specifically, we provide a level-ℓ user ID with level-(ℓ, i) decryption keys for $i \in [\ell]$, where again the level-(ℓ, ℓ) decryption key $\mathbf{d}_{\mathsf{ID},\mathsf{t}}$ and the other level-(ℓ, i) decryption keys $\mathbf{f}_{\mathsf{ID}_{[i]},\mathsf{t},\ell}$ for $i \in [\ell - 1]$ serve a different purpose. The level-(ℓ, ℓ) decryption key denoted as $\mathbf{d}_{\mathsf{ID},\mathsf{t}}$ is constructed and serves the exact same purpose as in the previous scheme. The level-(ℓ, i) decryption keys for $i \in [\ell - 1]$ are denoted as $\mathbf{f}_{\mathsf{ID}_{[i]},\mathsf{t},\ell}$. As before, these decryption keys $\mathbf{f}_{\mathsf{ID}_{[i]},\mathsf{t},\ell}$ are broadcast as part of the parent's key updates $\mathsf{ku}_{\mathsf{pa}(\mathsf{ID}),\mathsf{t}}$, however, the way they are defined is slightly different from the previous scheme. Namely, the level-(ℓ, i) decryption key $\mathbf{f}_{\mathsf{ID}_{[i]},\mathsf{t},\ell}$ satisfies

$$[\mathbf{A}_i | \mathbf{E}(\mathsf{ID}_{[i]}) | \mathbf{F}(\mathsf{t})] \mathbf{f}_{\mathsf{ID}_{[i]},\mathsf{t},\ell} = \mathbf{u}_\ell,$$

Note that it is $\mathbf{u}_\ell$ and not $\mathbf{u}$ as in Eq. (4). Using this, a level-ℓ user ID can decrypt its ciphertext as follows:

$$c_0 - \underbrace{\mathbf{c}_\ell^\top \mathbf{d}_{\mathsf{ID},\mathsf{t}}}_{\text{level-}(\ell,\ell)\text{ component}} - \sum_{i=1}^{\ell-1} \underbrace{\mathbf{c}_i^\top \mathbf{f}_{\mathsf{ID}_{[i]},\mathsf{t},\ell}}_{\text{level-}(\ell,i)\text{ component}} \approx \mathsf{M} \left\lfloor \frac{q}{2} \right\rfloor,$$

where each level of the ciphertext and decryption keys are in one-to-one correspondence with each other. Note that the level-ℓ user ID uses only level-(ℓ, i) decryption keys $\mathbf{f}_{\mathsf{ID}_{[i]},\mathsf{t},\ell}$ for $i \in [\ell-1]$ provided in the key update $\mathsf{ku}_{\mathsf{pa}(\mathsf{ID}),\mathsf{t}}$ to decrypt his own ciphertext. He simply forwards the remaining level-(k, i) decryption keys $\mathbf{f}_{\mathsf{ID}_{[i]},\mathsf{t},k}$ for $(k, i) \in [\ell+1, L] \times [\ell-1]$ as part of his key update $\mathsf{ku}_{\mathsf{ID},\mathsf{t}}$.

One can see that the problem in the previous scheme of Fig. 4 is now resolved, since the public term $\mathbf{f}_{\mathsf{ID}_{[i]},\mathsf{t},\ell}$ can only be used in combination with the level-(ℓ, i) ciphertext. In other words, due to the two-dimensional level, $\mathbf{f}_{\mathsf{ID}_{[i]},\mathsf{t},\ell}$ is only useful for decrypting ciphertexts of level-ℓ users. Furthermore, since the level-(ℓ,ℓ) decryption key $\mathbf{d}_{\mathsf{ID},\mathsf{t}}$ still remains secret, the publicly broadcast decryption keys $\mathbf{f}_{\mathsf{ID}_{[i]},\mathsf{t},\ell}$ for $i \in [\ell-1]$ alone are insufficient for decrypting the ciphertexts sent to user ID. The remaining problem with this approach is that there is currently no way for the level-$(\ell-1)$ ancestors $\mathsf{pa}(\mathsf{ID})$ to create the level-$(k, \ell-1)$ decryption keys $(\mathbf{f}_{\mathsf{ID}_{[\ell-1]},\mathsf{t},k})_{k\in[\ell,L]}$ which they must broadcast as part of the key updates $\mathsf{ku}_{\mathsf{pa}(\mathsf{ID}),\mathsf{t}}$. Specifically, since they do not have the trapdoor $\mathbf{T}_{[\mathbf{A}_{\ell-1}|\mathbf{E}(\mathsf{ID}_{[\ell-1]})]}$, they cannot simply sample the level-$(k, \ell-1)$ decryption keys $(\mathbf{f}_{\mathsf{ID}_{[\ell-1]},\mathsf{t},k})_{k\in[\ell,L]}$ for every time period.

Introducing Level Conversion Keys: Finally, we arrive at our proposed RHIBE scheme (without DKER) illustrated in Fig. 6. We overcome our final obstacle by introducing a tool called *level conversion keys*. In the scheme of Fig. 5, a level-ℓ parent user ID is able to create his level-(ℓ,ℓ) decryption key $\mathbf{d}_{\mathsf{ID},\mathsf{t}}$ by himself although he cannot compute the level-(k,ℓ) decryption keys $(\mathbf{f}_{\mathsf{ID},\mathsf{t},k})_{k\in[\ell+1,L]}$ in the key updates $\mathsf{ku}_{\mathsf{ID},\mathsf{t}}$ (which corresponds to $(\mathbf{f}_{\mathsf{ID}_{[\ell-1]},\mathsf{t},k})_{k\in[\ell,L]}$ in $\mathsf{ku}_{\mathsf{pa}(\mathsf{ID}),\mathsf{t}}$ of level-$(\ell-1)$ users in the figure). To overcome the issue, we define a level-$[\ell, k]$ conversion key $(\mathbf{f}_{\mathsf{ID},k})_{k\in[\ell+1,L]}$ of a level-ℓ user ID satisfying

$$\mathsf{PP} := ((\mathbf{A}_i)_{i\in[L]}, (\mathbf{u}_k)_{k\in[L]}, \text{hash functions } \mathbf{E}(\cdot), \mathbf{F}(\cdot)), \qquad \mathsf{sk}_{\mathsf{kgc}} := (\mathbf{T}_{\mathbf{A}_i})_{i\in[L]}$$

$$\mathsf{ct} := \begin{pmatrix} c_0 := \mathbf{u}_\ell^\top(\mathbf{s}_1 + \cdots \mathbf{s}_\ell) + \mathsf{noise} + \mathsf{M}\left\lfloor \frac{q}{2} \right\rfloor, \\ (\mathbf{c}_i := [\mathbf{A}_i | \mathbf{E}(\mathsf{ID}_{[i]}) | \mathbf{F}(\mathsf{t})]^\top \mathbf{s}_i + \mathsf{noise})_{i\in[\ell]} \end{pmatrix}$$

$$\mathsf{sk}_{\mathsf{ID}} := ((\mathbf{e}_{\mathsf{ID},\theta}), \boxed{(\mathbf{f}_{\mathsf{ID},k})_{k\in[\ell+1,L]}}, (\mathbf{T}_{[\mathbf{A}_i|\mathbf{E}(\mathsf{ID})]})_{i\in[\ell+1,L]}) \ \text{ s.t. } [\mathbf{A}_\ell | \mathbf{E}(\mathsf{ID})]\mathbf{e}_{\mathsf{ID},\theta} = \mathbf{u}_\theta, \quad \boxed{[\mathbf{A}_\ell | \mathbf{E}(\mathsf{ID})]\mathbf{f}_{\mathsf{ID},k} = \mathbf{u}_k - \mathbf{u}_\ell}$$

$$\mathsf{ku}_{\mathsf{pa}(\mathsf{ID}),\mathsf{t}} := ((\mathbf{e}_{\mathsf{pa}(\mathsf{ID}),\mathsf{t},\theta}), (\mathbf{f}_{\mathsf{ID}_{[i]},\mathsf{t},k})_{i\in[\ell-1],k\in[\ell,L]})$$
$$\text{s.t. } [\mathbf{A}_\ell | \mathbf{E}(\mathsf{pa}(\mathsf{ID})) | \mathbf{F}(\mathsf{t})]\mathbf{e}_{\mathsf{pa}(\mathsf{ID}),\mathsf{t},\theta} = \mathbf{u}_\ell - \mathbf{u}_\theta, \qquad [\mathbf{A}_i | \mathbf{E}(\mathsf{ID}_{[i]}) | \mathbf{F}(\mathsf{t})]\mathbf{f}_{\mathsf{ID}_{[i]},\mathsf{t},k} = \mathbf{u}_k$$

$$\mathsf{dk}_{\mathsf{ID},\mathsf{t}} := (\mathbf{d}_{\mathsf{ID},\mathsf{t}}, (\mathbf{f}_{\mathsf{ID}_{[i]},\mathsf{t},\ell})_{i\in[\ell-1]}) \qquad \text{s.t. } [\mathbf{A}_\ell | \mathbf{E}(\mathsf{ID}) | \mathbf{F}(\mathsf{t})]\mathbf{d}_{\mathsf{ID},\mathsf{t}} = \mathbf{u}_\ell$$

Fig. 6. Level conversion key

$$[\mathbf{A}_\ell|\mathbf{E}(\mathsf{ID})]\mathbf{f}_{\mathsf{ID},k} = \mathbf{u}_k - \mathbf{u}_\ell.$$

To compute level-(k,ℓ) decryption keys $(\mathbf{f}_{\mathsf{ID},\mathsf{t},k})_{k\in[\ell+1,L]}$ in key updates $\mathsf{ku}_{\mathsf{ID},\mathsf{t}}$, the level-$[\ell,k]$ conversion key allows the user ID to convert his *secret* level-(ℓ,ℓ) decryption key $\mathbf{d}_{\mathsf{ID},\mathsf{t}}$ which satisfies

$$[\mathbf{A}_\ell|\mathbf{E}(\mathsf{ID})|\mathbf{F}(\mathsf{t})]\mathbf{d}_{\mathsf{ID},\mathsf{t}} = \mathbf{u}_\ell$$

into a *public* level-(k,ℓ) decryption key $\mathbf{f}_{\mathsf{ID},\mathsf{t},k}$ which satisfies

$$[\mathbf{A}_\ell|\mathbf{E}(\mathsf{ID})|\mathbf{F}(\mathsf{t})]\mathbf{f}_{\mathsf{ID},\mathsf{t},k} = \mathbf{u}_k,$$

where the conversion is a simple component-wise addition. Since the scheme supports both the key delegation functionality and the key revocation mechanism, it can be shown to be a secure RHIBE scheme *without* DKER.

Adding DKER to the Construction: To make the above lattice-based RHIBE scheme in Fig. 6 satisfy DKER, we will use the same idea incorporated in our generic construction of RIBE with DKER. Specifically, we add one more level to the above scheme and wrap a standard HIBE scheme around it to manage the partial key re-randomization property. The concrete construction appears in Sect. 6.

3 Preliminaries

In this section, we briefly summarize the basic tools used in lattice-based cryptography. We treat vectors in their column form. For a vector $\mathbf{v} \in \mathbb{R}^n$, denote $\|\mathbf{v}\|$ as the standard Euclidean norm. For a matrix $\mathbf{R} \in \mathbb{R}^{n\times n}$, denote $\|\mathbf{R}\|_{\mathrm{GS}}$ as the longest column of the Gram-Schmidt orthogonalization of $\mathbf{R}$ and denote $\|\mathbf{R}\|_2$ as the largest singular value. We denote $\mathbf{I}_m$ as the $m \times m$ identity matrix and $\mathbf{0}_{n\times m}$ as the $n \times m$ zero matrix. We sometimes simply write $\mathbf{0}_n$ to denote (column) zero vectors.

Lattices. A (full-rank-integer) m-dimensional lattice Λ in $\mathbb{Z}^m$ is a set of the form $\{\sum_{i\in[m]} x_i\mathbf{b}_i | x_i \in \mathbb{Z}\}$, where $\mathbf{B} = \{\mathbf{b}_1, \cdots, \mathbf{b}_m\}$ are m linearly independent vectors in $\mathbb{Z}^m$. We call $\mathbf{B}$ the basis of the lattice Λ. For any positive integers n, m and $q \geq 2$, a matrix $\mathbf{A} \in \mathbb{Z}_q^{n\times m}$ and a vector $\mathbf{u} \in \mathbb{Z}_q^n$, we define $\Lambda_q^\perp(\mathbf{A}) = \{\mathbf{z} \in \mathbb{Z}^m | \mathbf{A}\mathbf{z} = \mathbf{0}_n \mod q\}$ and $\Lambda_q^{\mathbf{u}}(\mathbf{A}) = \{\mathbf{z} \in \mathbb{Z}^m | \mathbf{A}\mathbf{z} = \mathbf{u} \mod q\}$.

Gaussian Measures. Let $\mathcal{D}_{\Lambda,\sigma}$ denote the standard discrete Gaussian distribution over Λ with a Gaussian parameter σ. We summarize some basic properties of discrete Gaussian distributions.

Lemma 1 ([14]). *Let Λ be an m-dimensional lattice. Let $\mathbf{T}$ be a basis for Λ, and suppose $\sigma \geq \|\mathbf{T}\|_{\mathrm{GS}} \cdot \omega(\sqrt{\log m})$. Then* $\Pr[\|\mathbf{x}\|_2 > \sigma\sqrt{m} : \mathbf{x} \leftarrow \mathcal{D}_{\Lambda,\sigma}] \leq \mathsf{negl}(m)$.

Lemma 2 ([14]). *Let n, m, q be positive integers such that $m \geq 2n \log q$ and q a prime. Let σ be any positive real such that $\sigma \geq \omega(\sqrt{\log n})$. Then for $\mathbf{A} \leftarrow \mathbb{Z}_q^{n \times m}$ and $\mathbf{e} \leftarrow D_{\mathbb{Z}^m,\sigma}$, the distribution of $\mathbf{u} = \mathbf{Ae} \bmod q$ is statistically close to uniform over $\mathbb{Z}_q^n$. Furthermore, for a fixed $\mathbf{u} \in \mathbb{Z}_q^n$, the conditional distribution of $\mathbf{e} \leftarrow D_{\mathbb{Z}^m,\sigma}$, given $\mathbf{Ae} = \mathbf{u} \bmod q$ for a uniformly random $\mathbf{A}$ in $\mathbb{Z}_q^{n \times m}$ is $D_{\Lambda_q^{\mathbf{u}}(\mathbf{A}),\sigma}$ with all but negligible probability.*

Sampling Algorithms. We review some of the algorithms for sampling short vectors from a given lattice.

Lemma 3. *Let $n, m, \bar{m}, q > 0$ be positive integers with $m \geq 2n\lceil \log q \rceil$ and q a prime. Then, we have the following polynomial time algorithms:*

$\mathsf{TrapGen}(1^n, 1^m, q) \rightarrow (\mathbf{A}, \mathbf{T_A})$ *([2,3,24]): a randomized algorithm that outputs a full rank matrix $\mathbf{A} \in \mathbb{Z}_q^{n \times m}$ and a basis $\mathbf{T_A} \in \mathbb{Z}^{m \times m}$ for $\Lambda_q^{\perp}(\mathbf{A})$ such that $\mathbf{A}$ is statistically close to uniform and $\|\mathbf{T_A}\|_{\mathrm{GS}} = O\left(\sqrt{n \log q}\right)$ with overwhelming probability in n.*

$\mathsf{SampleLeft}(\mathbf{A}, \mathbf{F}, \mathbf{u}, \mathbf{T_A}, \sigma) \rightarrow \mathbf{e}$*([1,24]): a randomized algorithm that, given as input a full rank matrix $\mathbf{A} \in \mathbb{Z}_q^{n \times m}$, a matrix $\mathbf{F} \in \mathbb{Z}_q^{n \times \bar{m}}$, a vector $\mathbf{u} \in \mathbb{Z}_q^n$, a basis $\mathbf{T_A} \in \mathbb{Z}^{m \times m}$ of $\Lambda_q^{\perp}(\mathbf{A})$, and a Gaussian parameter $\sigma \geq \|\mathbf{T_A}\|_{\mathrm{GS}} \cdot \omega\left(\sqrt{\log m}\right)$, outputs a vector $\mathbf{e} \in \mathbb{Z}^{m+\bar{m}}$ sampled from a distribution statistically close to $\mathcal{D}_{\Lambda_q^{\mathbf{u}}([\mathbf{A}|\mathbf{F}]),\sigma}$.*

([24]): There exists a fixed full rank matrix $\mathbf{G} \in \mathbb{Z}_q^{n \times m}$ such that the lattice $\Lambda_q^{\perp}(\mathbf{G})$ has a publicly known basis $\mathbf{T_G} \in \mathbb{Z}^{m \times m}$ with $\|\mathbf{T_G}\|_{\mathrm{GS}} \leq \sqrt{5}$.

For simplicity, we omit the $\mathsf{SamplePre}$ algorithm of [1], since in our paper it will be used as a public algorithm to sample from the lattice $\mathbb{Z}^m$. The following algorithms allow one to securely delegate a trapdoor of a lattice to an arbitrary higher-dimensional extension, with a slight loss in quality. It can be obtained by combining the works of [8] and [1] in a straightforward manner.

Lemma 4. *Let $n, m, \bar{m}, q > 0$ be positive integers with $m > n$ and q a prime. Then, we have the following polynomial time algorithms:*

$\mathsf{ExtRndLeft}(\mathbf{A}, \mathbf{F}, \mathbf{T_A}, \sigma) \rightarrow \mathbf{T}_{[\mathbf{A}|\mathbf{F}]}$: *a randomized algorithm that, given as input matrices $\mathbf{A} \in \mathbb{Z}_q^{n \times m}, \mathbf{F} \in \mathbb{Z}_q^{n \times \bar{m}}$, a basis $\mathbf{T_A}$ of $\Lambda_q^{\perp}(\mathbf{A})$, and a Gaussian parameter $\sigma \geq \|\mathbf{T_A}\|_{\mathrm{GS}} \cdot \omega(\sqrt{\log n})$, outputs a matrix $\mathbf{T}_{[\mathbf{A}|\mathbf{F}]} \in \mathbb{Z}^{(m+\bar{m}) \times (m+\bar{m})}$ distributed statistically close to $(\mathcal{D}_{\Lambda_q^{\perp}([\mathbf{A}|\mathbf{F}]),\sigma})^{m+\bar{m}}$.*

$\mathsf{ExtRndRight}(\mathbf{A}, \mathbf{G}, \mathbf{R}, \mathbf{T_G}, \sigma) \rightarrow \mathbf{T}_{[\mathbf{A}|\mathbf{AR}+\mathbf{G}]}$: *a randomized algorithm that, given as input full rank matrices $\mathbf{A}, \mathbf{G} \in \mathbb{Z}_q^{n \times m}$, a matrix $\mathbf{R} \in \mathbb{Z}^{m \times m}$, a basis $\mathbf{T_G}$ of $\Lambda_q^{\perp}(\mathbf{G})$, and a Gaussian parameter $\sigma \geq \|\mathbf{R}\|_2 \cdot \|\mathbf{T_G}\|_2 \cdot \omega(\sqrt{\log n})$ outputs a matrix $\mathbf{T}_{[\mathbf{A}|\mathbf{AR}+\mathbf{G}]} \in \mathbb{Z}^{2m \times 2m}$ distributed statistically close to $(\mathcal{D}_{\Lambda_q^{\perp}([\mathbf{A}|\mathbf{AR}+\mathbf{G}]),\sigma})^{2m}$.*

We use the standard map to encode identities as matrices in $\mathbb{Z}_q^{n \times n}$.

Definition 1 ([1]). *Let n, q be positive integers with q a prime. We say that a function $H : \mathbb{Z}_q^n \to \mathbb{Z}_q^{n \times n}$ is a full-rank difference (FRD) map if: for all distinct $\mathsf{ID}, \mathsf{ID}' \in \mathbb{Z}_q^n$, the matrix $H(\mathsf{ID}) - H(\mathsf{ID}') \in \mathbb{Z}_q^{n \times n}$ is full rank, and H is computable in polynomial time in $n \log q$.*

Hardness Assumption. The security of our RIBE scheme is reduced to the learning with errors (LWE) assumption introduced by Regev [31].

Assumption 1 (Learning with Errors). *For integers n, m, a prime q, a real $\alpha \in (0, 1)$ such that $\alpha q > 2\sqrt{n}$, and a PPT algorithm $\mathcal{A}$, the advantage for the learning with errors problem $\mathsf{LWE}_{n,m,q,\mathcal{D}_{\mathbb{Z}^m,\alpha q}}$ of $\mathcal{A}$ is defined as $\left|\Pr\left[\mathcal{A}(\mathbf{A}, \mathbf{A}^\top \mathbf{s} + \mathbf{x}) = 1\right] - \Pr\left[\mathcal{A}(\mathbf{A}, \mathbf{v} + \mathbf{x}) = 1\right]\right|$, where $\mathbf{A} \leftarrow \mathbb{Z}^{n \times m}$, $\mathbf{s} \leftarrow \mathbb{Z}^n$, $\mathbf{x} \leftarrow \mathcal{D}_{\mathbb{Z}^m,\alpha q}$, $\mathbf{v} \leftarrow \mathbb{Z}^m$. We say that the LWE assumption holds if the above advantage is negligible for all PPT $\mathcal{A}$.*

4 Formal Definitions for Revocable Hierarchical Identity-Based Encryption and a Supporting Lemma

In this section, we give formal definitions for RHIBE in Sect. 4.1. Then, in Sect. 4.2, we explain a simple and yet handy lemma that we call the "strategy-dividing lemma", which helps us simplify security proofs of R(H)IBE schemes in general.

4.1 Revocable Hierarchical Identity-Based Encryption

As mentioned in the introduction, we re-formalize the syntax of RHIBE. Compared to the existing works on RHIBE, our syntax of RHIBE treats each user's secret key, state information, and revocation list in a simplified manner. Thus, we first explain our treatments of them, and then proceed to introducing the formal syntax and security definitions.

On the Role of a Secret Key. In the literature of R(H)IBE, typically, the entity who has the power to derive a secret key for lower-level users (i.e., the KGC in RIBE, and non-leaf users in RHIBE), is modeled as a stateful entity, and is supposed to maintain a so-called "state", in addition to its own secret key. The state information typically contains the information with which the revocation mechanism is realized, and needs to be treated confidentially. Since it is after all another type of secret information, in our syntax, we merge the roles of the state information and a secret key. Hence, in our model, each user is supposed to maintain its own secret key that is generated by its parent, and it could be updated after performing the key generation algorithm (for generating a secret key for its child) and the key update information generation algorithm.

On the Treatment of Revocation Lists. Note that unlike in standard revocable (non-hierarchical) IBE, the key update information and revocation lists of users are maintained individually by their corresponding parent users in RHIBE.

In our syntax of R(H)IBE, we treat a revocation list just as a subset of (the corresponding children's) identity space. More specifically, the revocation list of a user with identity $\mathsf{ID} \in (\mathcal{ID})^{\ell}$ contains identities that belong to the set $\mathsf{ID}\|\mathcal{ID} \subseteq (\mathcal{ID})^{\ell+1}$.

In the literature, for R(H)IBE, it is typical to consider the "revoke" algorithm whose role is to add an identity of a user to be revoked into the revocation list. We do not explicitly introduce such an algorithm as part of our syntax, since it is a simple operation of appending revoked users to a list.

Syntax. An RHIBE scheme Π consists of the six algorithms ($\mathsf{Setup}, \mathsf{Encrypt}, \mathsf{GenSK}, \mathsf{KeyUp}, \mathsf{GenDK}, \mathsf{Decrypt}$) with the following interface:

$\mathsf{Setup}(1^{\lambda}, L) \to (\mathsf{PP}, \mathsf{sk_{kgc}})$: This is the *setup* algorithm that takes the security parameter 1^{λ} and the maximum depth of the hierarchy $L \in \mathbb{N}$ as input, and outputs a public parameter PP and the KGC's secret key $\mathsf{sk_{kgc}}$ (also called a master secret key).
We assume that the plaintext space $\mathcal{M}$, the time period space $\mathcal{T} := \{1, 2, \ldots, \mathsf{t_{max}}\}$, where $\mathsf{t_{max}}$ is polynomial in λ, the element identity space $\mathcal{ID}$, and the hierarchical identity space $\mathcal{ID}_{\mathsf{h}} := (\mathcal{ID})^{\leq L}$ are determined only by the security parameter λ, and their descriptions are contained in PP.

$\mathsf{Encrypt}(\mathsf{PP}, \mathsf{ID}, \mathsf{t}, \mathsf{M}) \to \mathsf{ct}$: This is the *encryption* algorithm that takes a public parameter PP, an identity ID, a time period t, and a plaintext M as input, and outputs a ciphertext ct.

$\mathsf{GenSK}(\mathsf{PP}, \mathsf{sk_{pa(ID)}}, \mathsf{ID}) \to (\mathsf{sk_{ID}}, \mathsf{sk'_{pa(ID)}})$: This is the *secret key generation* algorithm that takes a public parameter PP, a parent's secret key $\mathsf{sk_{pa(ID)}}$, and an identity $\mathsf{ID} \in \mathcal{ID}_{\mathsf{h}}$ as input, and may update the parent's secret key $\mathsf{sk_{pa(ID)}}$. Then, it outputs a secret key $\mathsf{sk_{ID}}$ for the identity ID and also the parent's "updated" secret key $\mathsf{sk'_{pa(ID)}}$.

$\mathsf{KeyUp}(\mathsf{PP}, \mathsf{t}, \mathsf{sk_{ID}}, \mathsf{RL_{ID,t}}, \mathsf{ku_{pa(ID),t}}) \to (\mathsf{ku_{ID,t}}, \mathsf{sk'_{ID}})$: This is the *key update information generation* algorithm that takes a public parameter PP, a time period t, a secret key $\mathsf{sk_{ID}}$ (of a user with $\mathsf{ID} \in (\mathcal{ID})^{\leq L-1} \cup \{\mathsf{kgc}\}$), a revocation list $\mathsf{RL_{ID,t}} \subseteq \mathsf{ID}\|\mathcal{ID}$, and a parent's key update $\mathsf{ku_{pa(ID),t}}$ as input, and may update the secret key $\mathsf{sk_{ID}}$. Then, it outputs a key update $\mathsf{ku_{ID,t}}$ and also the "updated" secret key $\mathsf{sk'_{ID}}$.
In the special case $\mathsf{ID} = \mathsf{kgc}$, we define $\mathsf{ku_{pa(kgc),t}} := \bot$ for all $\mathsf{t} \in \mathcal{T}$, i.e., a key update is not needed for generating the KGC's key update $\mathsf{ku_{kgc,t}}$.

$\mathsf{GenDK}(\mathsf{PP}, \mathsf{sk_{ID}}, \mathsf{ku_{pa(ID),t}}) \to \mathsf{dk_{ID,t}}$ or $\bot$: This is the *decryption key generation* algorithm that takes a public parameter PP, a secret key $\mathsf{sk_{ID}}$ (of a user with $\mathsf{ID} \in (\mathcal{ID})^{\leq L}$), and a parent's key update $\mathsf{ku_{pa(ID),t}}$ as input, and outputs a decryption key $\mathsf{dk_{ID,t}}$ for time period t or the special "invalid" symbol $\bot$ indicating that ID or some of its ancestor has been revoked.

$\mathsf{Decrypt}(\mathsf{PP}, \mathsf{dk_{ID,t}}, \mathsf{ct}) \to \mathsf{M}$: This is the *decryption* algorithm that takes a public parameter PP, a decryption key $\mathsf{dk_{ID,t}}$, and a ciphertext ct as input, and outputs the decryption result M.

Correctness. We require the following to hold for an RHIBE scheme. Informally, we require a ciphertext corresponding to a user ID for time t to be properly decrypted by user ID if the user or any of its ancestor is not revoked on time t. To fully capture this, we consider all the possible scenarios of creating the secret key for user ID. Namely, for all $\lambda \in \mathbb{N}$, $L \in \mathbb{N}$, $(\mathsf{PP}, \mathsf{sk}_{\mathsf{kgc}}) \leftarrow \mathsf{Setup}(1^\lambda, L)$, $\ell \in [L]$, $\mathsf{ID} \in (\mathcal{ID})^\ell$, $\mathsf{t} \in \mathcal{T}$, $\mathsf{M} \in \mathcal{M}$, $\mathsf{RL}_{\mathsf{kgc},\mathsf{t}} \subseteq \mathcal{ID}$, $\mathsf{RL}_{\mathsf{ID}_{[1]},\mathsf{t}} \subseteq \mathsf{ID}_{[1]} \| \mathcal{ID}, \ldots, \mathsf{RL}_{\mathsf{ID}_{[\ell-1]},\mathsf{t}} \subseteq \mathsf{ID}_{[\ell-1]} \| \mathcal{ID}$, if $\mathsf{ID}' \notin \mathsf{RL}_{\mathsf{pa}(\mathsf{ID}'),\mathsf{t}}$ holds for all $\mathsf{ID}' \in \mathsf{prefix}(\mathsf{ID})$, then we require $\mathsf{M}' = \mathsf{M}$ to hold after executing the following procedures:

(1) $(\mathsf{ku}_{\mathsf{kgc},\mathsf{t}}, \mathsf{sk}_{\mathsf{kgc}}) \leftarrow \mathsf{KeyUp}(\mathsf{PP}, \mathsf{t}, \mathsf{sk}_{\mathsf{kgc}}, \mathsf{RL}_{\mathsf{kgc},\mathsf{t}}, \perp)$.
(2) For all $\mathsf{ID}' \in \mathsf{prefix}(\mathsf{ID})$ (in the short-to-long order), execute (2.1) and (2.2):
  (2.1) $(\mathsf{sk}_{\mathsf{ID}'}, \mathsf{sk}'_{\mathsf{pa}(\mathsf{ID}')}) \leftarrow \mathsf{GenSK}(\mathsf{PP}, \mathsf{sk}_{\mathsf{pa}(\mathsf{ID}')}, \mathsf{ID}')$.
  (2.2) $(\mathsf{ku}_{\mathsf{ID}',\mathsf{t}}, \mathsf{sk}'_{\mathsf{ID}'}) \leftarrow \mathsf{KeyUp}(\mathsf{PP}, \mathsf{t}, \mathsf{sk}_{\mathsf{ID}'}, \mathsf{RL}_{\mathsf{ID}',\mathsf{t}}, \mathsf{ku}_{\mathsf{pa}(\mathsf{ID}'),\mathsf{t}})$.[4]
(3) $\mathsf{dk}_{\mathsf{ID},\mathsf{t}} \leftarrow \mathsf{GenDK}(\mathsf{PP}, \mathsf{sk}_{\mathsf{ID}}, \mathsf{ku}_{\mathsf{pa}(\mathsf{ID}),\mathsf{t}})$.[5]
(4) $\mathsf{ct} \leftarrow \mathsf{Encrypt}(\mathsf{PP}, \mathsf{ID}, \mathsf{t}, \mathsf{M})$.
(5) $\mathsf{M}' \leftarrow \mathsf{Decrypt}(\mathsf{PP}, \mathsf{dk}_{\mathsf{ID},\mathsf{t}}, \mathsf{ct})$.

We note that, the most stringent way to define correctness would be to also capture the fact that the secret keys $\mathsf{sk}_{\mathsf{ID}}$ can be further updated after executing GenSK. In particular, the output of KeyUp, which takes as input the secret key $\mathsf{sk}_{\mathsf{ID}}$, may differ in general before and after GenSK is run. Therefore, to be more precise, we should also allow an arbitrary (polynomial) number of executions of GenSK in between steps (2.1) and (2.2). However, we defined correctness as above for the sake of simplicity and readability. We note that our scheme satisfies the more stringent correctness (which will be obvious from the construction).

Security Definition. Here, we give a formal security definition for RHIBE.

It seems to us that since the previous security definitions [6,33–35] have some ambiguous treatment in the security game, it was up to the readers to interpret the definitions and the proofs. Therefore, in our work, we provide a refined security definition for RHIBE which in particular is a more rigorous and explicit treatment than the previous definitions.

Specifically, we explicitly separate the secret key generation and secret key reveal queries, so that we can capture a situation where some $\mathsf{sk}_{\mathsf{ID}}$ has been generated but not revealed to an adversary. Furthermore, we combine the "revoke" and "key update" queries in the previous definitions into the single "revoke & key update" query, and introduce the notion of the "current time period" $\mathsf{t}_{\mathsf{cu}} \in \mathcal{T}$ which is coordinated with the adversary's revoke & key update query. These make all the key updates of non-revoked users to be well-defined throughout the security game.

Formally, let Π = ($\mathsf{Setup}, \mathsf{Encrypt}, \mathsf{GenSK}, \mathsf{KeyUp}, \mathsf{GenDK}, \mathsf{Decrypt}$) be an RHIBE scheme. We will only consider selective-identity security, which is defined via a game between an adversary $\mathcal{A}$ and the challenger $\mathcal{C}$. The game is parameterized by the security parameter λ and a polynomial $L = L(\lambda)$ representing the maximum depth of the identity hierarchy. Moreover, the game has the global counter t_{cu}, initialized with 1, that denotes the "current time period" with which $\mathcal{C}$'s responses to $\mathcal{A}$'s queries are controlled. The game proceeds as follows:

[4] If $|\mathsf{ID}'| = L$, then this step is skipped.
[5] Here, $\mathsf{sk}_{\mathsf{ID}}$ is the latest secret key that is the result of the step (2).

At the beginning, $\mathcal{A}$ sends the challenge identity/time period pair $(\mathsf{ID}^*, \mathsf{t}^*) \in (\mathcal{ID})^{\leq L} \times \mathcal{T}$ to $\mathcal{C}$. Next, $\mathcal{C}$ runs $(\mathsf{PP}, \mathsf{sk}_{\mathsf{kgc}}) \leftarrow \mathsf{Setup}(1^\lambda, L)$, and prepares a list $\mathtt{SKList}$ that initially contains $(\mathsf{kgc}, \mathsf{sk}_{\mathsf{kgc}})$, and into which identity/secret key pairs $(\mathsf{ID}, \mathsf{sk}_{\mathsf{ID}})$ generated during the game will be stored. From this point on, whenever a new secret key is generated or an existing secret key is updated for an identity $\mathsf{ID} \in (\mathcal{ID})^{\leq L} \cup \{\mathsf{kgc}\}$ due to the execution of GenSK or KeyUp, $\mathcal{C}$ will store $(\mathsf{ID}, \mathsf{sk}_{\mathsf{ID}})$ or update the corresponding entry $(\mathsf{ID}, \mathsf{sk}_{\mathsf{ID}})$ in $\mathtt{SKList}$, and we will not explicitly mention this addition/update. Then, $\mathcal{C}$ executes $(\mathsf{ku}_{\mathsf{kgc},1}, \mathsf{sk}'_{\mathsf{kgc}}) \leftarrow \mathsf{KeyUp}(\mathsf{PP}, \mathsf{t}_{\mathsf{cu}} = 1, \mathsf{sk}_{\mathsf{kgc}}, \mathsf{RL}_{\mathsf{kgc},1} = \emptyset, \perp)$ for generating a key update for the initial time period $\mathsf{t}_{\mathsf{cu}} = 1$. After that, $\mathcal{C}$ gives PP and $\mathsf{ku}_{\mathsf{kgc},1}$ to $\mathcal{A}$.

From this point on, $\mathcal{A}$ may adaptively make the following five types of queries to $\mathcal{C}$:

Secret Key Generation Query: Upon a query $\mathsf{ID} \in (\mathcal{ID})^{\leq L}$ from $\mathcal{A}$, $\mathcal{C}$ checks if $(\mathsf{ID}, *) \notin \mathtt{SKList}$ and $(\mathsf{pa}(\mathsf{ID}), \mathsf{sk}_{\mathsf{pa}(\mathsf{ID})}) \in \mathtt{SKList}$ for some $\mathsf{sk}_{\mathsf{pa}(\mathsf{ID})}$, and returns $\perp$ to $\mathcal{A}$ if this is *not* the case. Otherwise, $\mathcal{C}$ executes $(\mathsf{sk}_{\mathsf{ID}}, \mathsf{sk}'_{\mathsf{pa}(\mathsf{ID})}) \leftarrow \mathsf{GenSK}(\mathsf{PP}, \mathsf{sk}_{\mathsf{pa}(\mathsf{ID})}, \mathsf{ID})$. If $\mathsf{ID} \in (\mathcal{ID})^{\leq L-1}$, then $\mathcal{C}$ furthermore executes $(\mathsf{ku}_{\mathsf{ID},\mathsf{t}_{\mathsf{cu}}}, \mathsf{sk}'_{\mathsf{ID}}) \leftarrow \mathsf{KeyUp}(\mathsf{PP}, \mathsf{t}_{\mathsf{cu}}, \mathsf{sk}_{\mathsf{ID}}, \mathsf{RL}_{\mathsf{ID},\mathsf{t}_{\mathsf{cu}}} = \emptyset, \mathsf{ku}_{\mathsf{pa}(\mathsf{ID}),\mathsf{t}_{\mathsf{cu}}})$. Then, $\mathcal{C}$ returns $\mathsf{ku}_{\mathsf{ID},\mathsf{t}_{\mathsf{cu}}}$ to $\mathcal{A}$ if $\mathsf{ID} \in (\mathcal{ID})^{\leq L-1}$, or returns nothing to $\mathcal{A}$ if $\mathsf{ID} \in (\mathcal{ID})^{L}$.[6]

We require that all identities ID appearing in the following queries (except the challenge query) be "activated", in the sense that $\mathsf{sk}_{\mathsf{ID}}$ is generated via this query and hence $(\mathsf{ID}, \mathsf{sk}_{\mathsf{ID}}) \in \mathtt{SKList}$.

Secret Key Reveal Query: Upon a query $\mathsf{ID} \in (\mathcal{ID})^{\leq L}$ from $\mathcal{A}$, $\mathcal{C}$ checks if the following condition is satisfied:

- If $\mathsf{t}_{\mathsf{cu}} \geq \mathsf{t}^*$ and $\mathsf{ID}' \notin \mathsf{RL}_{\mathsf{pa}(\mathsf{ID}'),\mathsf{t}^*}$ for all $\mathsf{ID}' \in \mathsf{prefix}(\mathsf{ID}^*)$, then $\mathsf{ID} \notin \mathsf{prefix}(\mathsf{ID}^*)$.[7]

If this condition is *not* satisfied, then $\mathcal{C}$ returns $\perp$ to $\mathcal{A}$. Otherwise, $\mathcal{C}$ finds $\mathsf{sk}_{\mathsf{ID}}$ from $\mathtt{SKList}$, and returns it to $\mathcal{A}$.

Revoke & Key Update Query: Upon a query $\mathsf{RL} \subseteq (\mathcal{ID})^{\leq L}$ (which denotes the set of identities that are going to be revoked in the next time period) from $\mathcal{A}$, $\mathcal{C}$ checks if the following conditions are satisfied simultaneously:

- $\mathsf{RL}_{\mathsf{ID},\mathsf{t}_{\mathsf{cu}}} \subseteq \mathsf{RL}$ for all $\mathsf{ID} \in \mathcal{ID}^{\leq L-1} \cup \{\mathsf{kgc}\}$ that appear in $\mathtt{SKList}$.[8]
- For all identities ID such that $(\mathsf{ID}, *) \in \mathtt{SKList}$ and $\mathsf{ID}' \in \mathsf{prefix}(\mathsf{ID})$, if $\mathsf{ID}' \in \mathsf{RL}$ then $\mathsf{ID} \in \mathsf{RL}$.[9]

---

6 We stress that just making this query does not give the secret key $\mathsf{sk}_{\mathsf{ID}}$ to $\mathcal{A}$. It is captured by the "Secret Key Reveal Query" explained next. Furthermore, we provide the key updates to $\mathcal{A}$ unconditionally, since they are typically broadcast via an insecure channel and are not meant to be secret.

7 In other words, this check ensures that if ID^* or any of its ancestors was *not* revoked before the challenge time period t^*, then $\mathsf{sk}_{\mathsf{ID}}$ will not be revealed for any $\mathsf{ID} \in \mathsf{prefix}(\mathsf{ID}^*)$. Without this condition, there is a trivial attack on any RHIBE scheme.

8 This check ensures that the identities that have already been revoked will remain revoked in the next time period.

9 In other words, this check ensures that if some ID is revoked, then all of its descendants are also revoked.

- If $\mathsf{t_{cu}} = \mathsf{t}^* - 1$ and $\mathsf{sk_{ID'}}$ for some $\mathsf{ID'} \in \mathsf{prefix}(\mathsf{ID}^*)$ has already been revealed by the secret key reveal query $\mathsf{ID'}$, then $\mathsf{ID'} \in \mathsf{RL}$.[10]

If these conditions are *not* satisfied, then $\mathcal{C}$ returns $\perp$ to $\mathcal{A}$.
Otherwise $\mathcal{C}$ increments the current time period by $\mathsf{t_{cu}} \leftarrow \mathsf{t_{cu}} + 1$. Then, $\mathcal{C}$ executes the following operations (1) and (2) for all "activated" and non-revoked identities ID, i.e., $\mathsf{ID} \in (\mathcal{ID})^{\leq L-1} \cup \{\mathsf{kgc}\}$, $(\mathsf{ID}, *) \in \mathtt{SKList}$, and $\mathsf{ID} \notin \mathsf{RL}$, in the breadth-first order in the identity hierarchy:
(1) Set $\mathsf{RL_{ID,t_{cu}}} \leftarrow \mathsf{RL} \cap (\mathsf{ID} \| \mathcal{ID})$, where we define $\mathsf{kgc} \| \mathcal{ID} := \mathcal{ID}$.
(2) Run $(\mathsf{ku_{ID,t_{cu}}}, \mathsf{sk'_{ID}}) \leftarrow \mathsf{KeyUp}(\mathsf{PP}, \mathsf{t_{cu}}, \mathsf{sk_{ID}}, \mathsf{RL_{ID,t_{cu}}}, \mathsf{ku_{pa(ID),t_{cu}}})$, where $\mathsf{ku_{pa(kgc),t_{cu}}} := \perp$.

Finally, $\mathcal{C}$ returns all the generated key updates $\{\mathsf{ku_{ID,t_{cu}}}\}_{(\mathsf{ID},*) \in \mathtt{SKList}}$ to $\mathcal{A}$.

Decryption Key Reveal Query: Upon a query $(\mathsf{ID}, \mathsf{t}) \in (\mathcal{ID})^{\leq L} \times \mathcal{T}$ from $\mathcal{A}$, $\mathcal{C}$ checks if the following conditions are simultaneously satisfied:
- $\mathsf{t} \leq \mathsf{t_{cu}}$.
- $\mathsf{ID} \notin \mathsf{RL_{pa(ID),t}}$
- $(\mathsf{ID}, \mathsf{t}) \neq (\mathsf{ID}^*, \mathsf{t}^*)$.[11]

If these conditions are *not* satisfied, then $\mathcal{C}$ returns $\perp$ to $\mathcal{A}$. Otherwise, $\mathcal{C}$ finds $\mathsf{sk_{ID}}$ from $\mathtt{SKList}$, runs $\mathsf{dk_{ID,t}} \leftarrow \mathsf{GenDK}(\mathsf{PP}, \mathsf{sk_{ID}}, \mathsf{ku_{pa(ID),t}})$, and returns $\mathsf{dk_{ID,t}}$ to $\mathcal{A}$.[12]

Challenge Query: $\mathcal{A}$ is allowed to make this query only once. Upon a query $(\mathsf{M_0}, \mathsf{M_1})$ from $\mathcal{A}$, where it is required that $|\mathsf{M_0}| = |\mathsf{M_1}|$, $\mathcal{C}$ picks the challenge bit $b \in \{0,1\}$ uniformly at random, runs $\mathsf{ct}^* \leftarrow \mathsf{Encrypt}(\mathsf{PP}, \mathsf{ID}^*, \mathsf{t}^*, \mathsf{M}_b)$, and returns the challenge ciphertext ct^* to $\mathcal{A}$.

At some point, $\mathcal{A}$ outputs $b' \in \{0,1\}$ as its guess for b and terminates.

The above completes the description of the game. In this game, $\mathcal{A}$'s selective-identity security advantage $\mathsf{Adv}^{\mathtt{RHIBE\text{-}sel}}_{\Pi,L,\mathcal{A}}(\lambda)$ is defined by $\mathsf{Adv}^{\mathtt{RHIBE\text{-}sel}}_{\Pi,L,\mathcal{A}}(\lambda) := 2 \cdot |\Pr[b' = b] - 1/2|$.

Definition 2. *We say that an RHIBE scheme Π with depth L satisfies* selective-identity security, *if the advantage $\mathsf{Adv}^{\mathtt{RHIBE\text{-}sel}}_{\Pi,L,\mathcal{A}}(\lambda)$ is negligible for all PPT adversaries $\mathcal{A}$.*

---

[10] In other words, this check is to ensure that if the secret key $\mathsf{sk_{ID'}}$ of some ancestor $\mathsf{ID'}$ of ID^* (or ID^* itself) has been revealed to $\mathcal{A}$, then $\mathsf{ID'}$ is revoked in the next time period.

[11] In previous works [33,35], $\mathcal{A}$ is disallowed to obtain not only $\mathsf{dk_{ID^*,t^*}}$ (which is clearly necessary to avoid a trivial attack), but also decryption keys $\mathsf{dk_{ID',t^*}}$ for all $\mathsf{ID'} \in \mathsf{prefix}(\mathsf{ID}^*)$. Our relaxed condition here makes the defined security stronger since $\mathcal{A}$ is able to obtain additional information without any restrictions.

[12] Note that $\mathsf{ku_{pa(ID),t}}$ must have been already generated at this point due to the condition $\mathsf{t} \leq \mathsf{t_{cu}}$.

4.2 Strategy-Dividing Lemma

In the literature of R(H)IBE, a typical security proof for an R(H)IBE scheme goes as follows:

(1) classify an adversary's strategies into multiple pre-determined types, say Type-1 to Type-n for some $n \in \mathbb{N}$ that cover all possible strategies, and
(2) for each $i \in [n]$, prove that any adversary that is promised to follow the Type-i strategy (and never break the promise) has negligible advantage in attacking the considered scheme.

Here, it is implicitly assumed that the above mentioned "type-classification-based" security proof is sufficient for proving security against arbitrary adversaries that may decide their attack strategies adaptively during the game.

For completeness, we formalize the above implicit argument as a simple yet handy "strategy-dividing lemma", which helps us simplify security proofs for R(H)IBE schemes in general. Since this is an implicit argument that has been frequently adopted in the R(H)IBE literatures, we provide it in the full version.

5 Generic Construction of RIBE with DKER

In this section, we show a "security-enhancing" generic construction for RIBE. Namely, we show how to construct an RIBE scheme with DKER by combining an RIBE scheme without DKER and a 2-level (non-revocable) HIBE scheme.

Let $\mathsf{r}.\Pi = (\mathsf{r.Setup}, \mathsf{r.Encrypt}, \mathsf{r.GenSK}, \mathsf{r.KeyUp}, \mathsf{r.GenDK}, \mathsf{r.Decrypt})$ be an RIBE scheme (without DKER) with identity space $\mathsf{r}.\mathcal{ID}$, plaintext space $\mathsf{r}.\mathcal{M}$, and time period space $\mathsf{r}.\mathcal{T}$. Let $\mathsf{h}.\Pi = (\mathsf{h.Setup}, \mathsf{h.Encrypt}, \mathsf{h.GenSK}, \mathsf{h.Delegate}, \mathsf{h.Decrypt})$ be a 2-level HIBE scheme with element identity space $\mathsf{h}.\mathcal{ID}$ and plaintext space $\mathsf{h}.\mathcal{M}$. We assume $\mathsf{r}.\mathcal{ID} = \mathsf{h}.\mathcal{ID}$, $\mathsf{r}.\mathcal{M} = \mathsf{h}.\mathcal{M}$, and $\mathsf{r}.\mathcal{T} \subseteq \mathsf{h}.\mathcal{ID}$. Furthermore, we assume that the plaintext space is finite and forms an abelian group with the addition "+" as the group operation.

Using these ingredients, we construct an RIBE scheme $\Pi = (\mathsf{Setup}, \mathsf{Encrypt}, \mathsf{GenSK}, \mathsf{KeyUp}, \mathsf{GenDK}, \mathsf{Decrypt})$ with DKER as follows. The identity space $\mathcal{ID}$, the plaintext space $\mathcal{M}$, and the time period space $\mathcal{T}$ of the constructed RIBE scheme Π are, respectively, $\mathcal{ID} = \mathsf{r}.\mathcal{ID} = \mathsf{h}.\mathcal{ID}$, $\mathcal{M} = \mathsf{r}.\mathcal{M} = \mathsf{h}.\mathcal{M}$, and $\mathcal{T} = \mathsf{r}.\mathcal{T} \subseteq \mathsf{h}.\mathcal{ID}$.

$\mathsf{Setup}(1^\lambda) \to (\mathsf{PP}, \mathsf{sk_{kgc}})$: It takes the security parameter 1^λ as input, and runs $(\mathsf{r.PP}, \mathsf{r.sk_{kgc}}) \leftarrow \mathsf{r.Setup}(1^\lambda)$ and $(\mathsf{h.PP}, \mathsf{h.sk_{kgc}}) \leftarrow \mathsf{h.Setup}(1^\lambda)$. Then, it outputs a public parameter $\mathsf{PP} := (\mathsf{r.PP}, \mathsf{h.PP})$ and the KGC's secret key $\mathsf{sk_{kgc}} := (\mathsf{r.sk_{kgc}}, \mathsf{h.sk_{kgc}})$.

$\mathsf{Encrypt}(\mathsf{PP}, \mathsf{ID}, \mathsf{t}, \mathsf{M}) \to \mathsf{ct}$: It takes a public parameter $\mathsf{PP} = (\mathsf{r.PP}, \mathsf{h.PP})$, an identity $\mathsf{ID} \in \mathcal{ID}$, a time period $\mathsf{t} \in \mathcal{T}$, and a plaintext $\mathsf{M} \in \mathcal{M}$ as input, and samples a pair $(\mathsf{r.M}, \mathsf{h.M}) \in \mathcal{M}^2$ uniformly at random, subject to $\mathsf{r.M} + \mathsf{h.M} = \mathsf{M}$. Then, it runs $\mathsf{r.ct} \leftarrow \mathsf{r.Encrypt}(\mathsf{r.PP}, \mathsf{ID}, \mathsf{t}, \mathsf{r.M})$ and $\mathsf{h.ct} \leftarrow \mathsf{h.Encrypt}(\mathsf{h.PP}, (\mathsf{ID}, \mathsf{t}), \mathsf{h.M})$. Finally, it outputs a ciphertext $\mathsf{ct} := (\mathsf{r.ct}, \mathsf{h.ct})$.

$\mathsf{GenSK}(\mathsf{PP}, \mathsf{sk}_{\mathsf{kgc}}, \mathsf{ID}) \rightarrow (\mathsf{sk}_{\mathsf{ID}}, \mathsf{sk}'_{\mathsf{kgc}})$: It takes a public parameter $\mathsf{PP} = (\mathsf{r.PP}, \mathsf{h.PP})$, the KGC's secret key $\mathsf{sk}_{\mathsf{kgc}} = (\mathsf{r.sk}_{\mathsf{kgc}}, \mathsf{h.sk}_{\mathsf{kgc}})$, and an identity $\mathsf{ID} \in \mathcal{ID}$ as input, and runs $(\mathsf{r.sk}_{\mathsf{ID}}, \mathsf{r.sk}'_{\mathsf{kgc}}) \leftarrow \mathsf{r.GenSK}(\mathsf{r.PP}, \mathsf{r.sk}_{\mathsf{kgc}}, \mathsf{ID})$ and $\mathsf{h.sk}_{\mathsf{ID}} \leftarrow \mathsf{h.GenSK}(\mathsf{h.PP}, \mathsf{h.sk}_{\mathsf{kgc}}, \mathsf{ID})$. Then, it outputs a secret key $\mathsf{sk}_{\mathsf{ID}} := (\mathsf{r.sk}_{\mathsf{ID}}, \mathsf{h.sk}_{\mathsf{ID}})$ for the identity ID and also the KGC's updated secret key $\mathsf{sk}'_{\mathsf{kgc}} := (\mathsf{r.sk}'_{\mathsf{kgc}}, \mathsf{h.sk}_{\mathsf{kgc}})$.

$\mathsf{KeyUp}(\mathsf{PP}, \mathsf{t}, \mathsf{sk}_{\mathsf{kgc}}, \mathsf{RL}_{\mathsf{t}}) \rightarrow (\mathsf{ku}_{\mathsf{t}}, \mathsf{sk}'_{\mathsf{kgc}})$: It takes a public parameter $\mathsf{PP} = (\mathsf{r.PP}, \mathsf{h.PP})$, a time period $\mathsf{t} \in \mathcal{T}$, the KGC's secret key $\mathsf{sk}_{\mathsf{kgc}} = (\mathsf{r.sk}_{\mathsf{kgc}}, \mathsf{h.sk}_{\mathsf{kgc}})$, and a revocation list $\mathsf{RL}_{\mathsf{t}} \subseteq \mathcal{ID}$ as input, and, runs $(\mathsf{r.ku}_{\mathsf{t}}, \mathsf{r.sk}'_{\mathsf{kgc}}) \leftarrow \mathsf{r.KeyUp}(\mathsf{r.PP}, \mathsf{t}, \mathsf{r.sk}_{\mathsf{kgc}}, \mathsf{RL}_{\mathsf{t}})$. Then, it outputs a key update $\mathsf{ku}_{\mathsf{t}} := \mathsf{r.ku}_{\mathsf{t}}$ and also the KGC's updated secret key $\mathsf{sk}'_{\mathsf{kgc}} := (\mathsf{r.sk}'_{\mathsf{kgc}}, \mathsf{h.sk}_{\mathsf{kgc}})$.

$\mathsf{GenDK}(\mathsf{PP}, \mathsf{sk}_{\mathsf{ID}}, \mathsf{ku}_{\mathsf{t}}) \rightarrow \mathsf{dk}_{\mathsf{ID,t}}$ or $\perp$: It takes a public parameter $\mathsf{PP} = (\mathsf{r.PP}, \mathsf{h.PP})$, a secret key $\mathsf{sk}_{\mathsf{ID}} = (\mathsf{r.sk}_{\mathsf{ID}}, \mathsf{h.sk}_{\mathsf{ID}})$, and a key update $\mathsf{ku}_{\mathsf{t}} = \mathsf{r.ku}_{\mathsf{t}}$ as input, and runs $\mathsf{r.dk}_{\mathsf{ID,t}} \leftarrow \mathsf{r.GenDK}(\mathsf{r.PP}, \mathsf{r.sk}_{\mathsf{ID}}, \mathsf{r.ku}_{\mathsf{t}})$ and $\mathsf{h.sk}_{\mathsf{ID,t}} \leftarrow \mathsf{h.Delegate}(\mathsf{h.PP}, \mathsf{h.sk}_{\mathsf{ID}}, \mathsf{t})$. Then, it outputs a decryption key $\mathsf{dk}_{\mathsf{ID,t}} := (\mathsf{r.dk}_{\mathsf{ID,t}}, \mathsf{h.sk}_{\mathsf{ID,t}})$ for time period t, except that if $\mathsf{r.dk}_{\mathsf{ID,t}} = \perp$, then it returns the special "invalid" symbol $\perp$ indicating that ID has been revoked.

$\mathsf{Decrypt}(\mathsf{PP}, \mathsf{dk}_{\mathsf{ID,t}}, \mathsf{ct}) \rightarrow \mathsf{M}$: It takes a public parameter $\mathsf{PP} = (\mathsf{r.PP}, \mathsf{h.PP})$, a decryption key $\mathsf{dk}_{\mathsf{ID,t}} = (\mathsf{r.dk}_{\mathsf{ID,t}}, \mathsf{h.sk}_{\mathsf{ID,t}})$, and a ciphertext $\mathsf{ct} = (\mathsf{r.ct}, \mathsf{h.ct})$ as input, and then runs $\mathsf{r.M} \leftarrow \mathsf{r.Decrypt}(\mathsf{r.PP}, \mathsf{r.dk}_{\mathsf{ID,t}}, \mathsf{r.ct})$ and $\mathsf{h.M} \leftarrow \mathsf{h.Decrypt}(\mathsf{h.PP}, \mathsf{h.sk}_{\mathsf{ID,t}}, \mathsf{h.ct})$. If $\mathsf{r.M} = \perp$ or $\mathsf{h.M} = \perp$, then it returns $\perp$. Otherwise, it outputs the decryption result $\mathsf{M} := \mathsf{r.M} + \mathsf{h.M}$.

It is immediate to see that the correctness of the constructed RIBE scheme Π follows from that of the building blocks. The security of Π is guaranteed by the following theorem.

Theorem 1. *If the underlying RIBE scheme* $\mathsf{r}.\Pi$ *satisfies weak selective-identity (resp. weak adaptive-identity) security and the underlying 2-level HIBE scheme* $\mathsf{h}.\Pi$ *satisfies selective-identity (resp. adaptive-identity) security, then the resulting RIBE scheme* Π *satisfies selective-identity (resp. adaptive-identity) security.*

Proof Overview. Here, we explain an overview of the proof. In the actual proof, we consider the following two attack strategies of an adversary against the RIBE scheme Π that are mutually exclusive and cover all possibilities:

- Type-I: The adversary issues a valid secret key reveal query on ID^*.
- Type-II: The adversary does not issue a valid secret key reveal query on ID^*.

Whether an adversary has deviated from one strategy is easy to detect. Due to the strategy-dividing lemma, it suffices to show that for each type of adversary (that is promised to follow the attack strategy), its advantage is negligible. In particular, we show that the security of the RIBE scheme Π against Type-I (resp. Type-II) adversary is guaranteed by the security of the underlying RIBE scheme $\mathsf{r}.\Pi$ (resp. 2-level HIBE scheme $\mathsf{h}.\Pi$).

6 RHIBE from Lattices

In this section, we first explain our treatment on binary trees, the CS method, and the parameters used in the scheme. Then, we show our proposed scheme in Sect. 6.1 and discuss the security in Sect. 6.2.

On the Treatment of Binary Trees and the CS Method. Every user ID such that $|\mathsf{ID}| \leq L-1$ (including KGC) maintains a binary tree $\mathsf{BT}_{\mathsf{ID}}$ as part of his secret key $\mathsf{sk}_{\mathsf{ID}}$. We assume that auxiliary information such as user identities ID and vectors in $\mathbb{Z}_q^n$ can be stored in the nodes of binary trees. The binary tree along with the CS method is the mechanism used by the parent to manage its children, i.e., keep track whether a child is revoked or not. We use θ to denote a node in a binary tree. We use η when we emphasize that the node θ is a leaf node. Let $\mathsf{Path}(\mathsf{BT}_{\mathsf{pa(ID)}}, \eta_{\mathsf{ID}})$ denote the set of nodes which are on the path along the root of $\mathsf{BT}_{\mathsf{pa(ID)}}$ to the leaf η_{ID}. Note that the size of $\mathsf{Path}(\mathsf{BT}_{\mathsf{pa(ID)}}, \eta_{\mathsf{ID}})$ is $O(\log N)$. We define the CS method by the following four algorithms:

$\mathsf{CS.SetUp}(N) \rightarrow \mathsf{BT}_{\mathsf{pa(ID)}}$: It takes the number of users N as input, and outputs a binary tree $\mathsf{BT}_{\mathsf{pa(ID)}}$ with at least N and at most $2N$ leaves.

$\mathsf{CS.Assign}(\mathsf{BT}_{\mathsf{pa(ID)}}, \mathsf{ID}) \rightarrow (\eta_{\mathsf{ID}}, \mathsf{BT}_{\mathsf{pa(ID)}})$: It takes a binary tree $\mathsf{BT}_{\mathsf{pa(ID)}}$ and an identity ID as inputs, and randomly assigns the user identity ID to a leaf node η_{ID}, to which no other IDs have been assigned yet. Then, it outputs a leaf η_{ID} and an "updated" binary tree $\mathsf{BT}_{\mathsf{pa(ID)}}$.

$\mathsf{CS.Cover}(\mathsf{BT}_{\mathsf{pa(ID)}}, \mathsf{RL}_{\mathsf{pa(ID)},t}) \rightarrow \mathsf{KUNode}(\mathsf{BT}_{\mathsf{pa(ID)}}, \mathsf{RL}_{\mathsf{pa(ID)},t})$: It takes a binary tree $\mathsf{BT}_{\mathsf{pa(ID)}}$ and a revocation list $\mathsf{RL}_{\mathsf{pa(ID)},t}$ as inputs, and outputs a set of nodes $\mathsf{KUNode}(\mathsf{BT}_{\mathsf{pa(ID)}}, \mathsf{RL}_{\mathsf{pa(ID)},t})$. Here, the subtrees with root $\theta \in \mathsf{KUNode}(\mathsf{BT}_{\mathsf{pa(ID)}}, \mathsf{RL}_{\mathsf{pa(ID)},t})$ cover all leaves η_{ID} in $\mathsf{BT}_{\mathsf{pa(ID)}}$ for $\mathsf{ID} \notin \mathsf{RL}_{\mathsf{pa(ID)},t}$ and do not cover any leaves η_{ID} for $\mathsf{ID} \in \mathsf{RL}_{\mathsf{pa(ID)},t}$.

$\mathsf{CS.Match}(\mathsf{Path}(\mathsf{BT}_{\mathsf{pa(ID)}}, \eta_{\mathsf{ID}}), \mathsf{KUNode}(\mathsf{BT}_{\mathsf{pa(ID)}}, \mathsf{RL}_{\mathsf{pa(ID)},t})) \rightarrow \theta$ or $\emptyset$: It takes $\mathsf{Path}(\mathsf{BT}_{\mathsf{pa(ID)}}, \eta_{\mathsf{ID}})$ and $\mathsf{KUNode}(\mathsf{BT}_{\mathsf{pa(ID)}}, \mathsf{RL}_{\mathsf{pa(ID)},t})$ as inputs, and outputs an arbitrary node $\theta \in \mathsf{Path}(\mathsf{BT}_{\mathsf{pa(ID)}}, \eta_{\mathsf{ID}}) \cap \mathsf{KUNode}(\mathsf{BT}_{\mathsf{pa(ID)}}, \mathsf{RL}_{\mathsf{pa(ID)},t})$ if it exists. Otherwise, it outputs $\emptyset$.

Looking ahead, at a high level, all parents maintain the children to whom it has generated secret keys by the binary tree $\mathsf{BT}_{\mathsf{pa(ID)}}$. The secret keys $\mathsf{sk}_{\mathsf{ID}}$ will include some (partial) secret information that are associated with a node in $\mathsf{Path}(\mathsf{BT}_{\mathsf{pa(ID)}}, \eta_{\mathsf{ID}})$. To revoke a set of users $\mathsf{RL}_{\mathsf{pa(ID)},t}$, the parent constructs the key update $\mathsf{ku}_{\mathsf{pa(ID)},t}$ by running $\mathsf{CS.Cover}$ and generates a set of nodes $\mathsf{KUNode}(\mathsf{BT}_{\mathsf{pa(ID)}}, \mathsf{RL}_{\mathsf{pa(ID)},t})$, which represents the set of users that are *not* revoked. Similarly to above, each node in $\mathsf{KUNode}(\mathsf{BT}_{\mathsf{pa(ID)}}, \mathsf{RL}_{\mathsf{pa(ID)},t})$ will include some (partial) secret information. We note that the size of $\mathsf{KUNode}(\mathsf{BT}_{\mathsf{pa(ID)}}, \mathsf{RL}_{\mathsf{pa(ID)},t})$ is $O(R \log(N/R))$, where $R = |\mathsf{RL}_{\mathsf{pa(ID)},t}|$. Notably, the size of the key update $\mathsf{ku}_{\mathsf{pa(ID)},t}$ will be logarithmic in N. Then, any user ID who is not revoked can run the $\mathsf{CS.Match}$ algorithm to obtain a node θ which is included both in $\mathsf{Path}(\mathsf{BT}_{\mathsf{pa(ID)}}, \eta_{\mathsf{ID}})$ and $\mathsf{KUNode}(\mathsf{BT}_{\mathsf{pa(ID)}}, \mathsf{RL}_{\mathsf{pa(ID)},t})$. Combining the two partial secret information embedded in the nodes, user ID will be able to construct the decryption key $\mathsf{dk}_{\mathsf{ID},t}$ which allows him to decrypt the ciphertext.

Parameters. Let L denote the maximum depth of the hierarchy and N denote the maximum number of children each parent manages. Furthermore, let n, m, q be positive integers such that q is a prime and $\alpha, \alpha', (\sigma_i)_{i=0}^{L}$ be positive reals denoting the Gaussian parameters. Finally, we set the plaintext space as $\mathcal{M} = \{0,1\}$, the element identity space as $\mathcal{ID} = \mathbb{Z}_q^n \setminus \{\mathbf{0}_n\}$, and the hierarchal identity space as $\mathcal{ID}_{\mathtt{h}} := (\mathbb{Z}_q^n \setminus \{\mathbf{0}_n\})^{\leq L}$. We also encode the time period space $\mathcal{T} = \{1, 2, \cdots, \mathsf{t}_{\max}\}$ into a polynomial sized subset of $\mathbb{Z}_q^n$. In the following, for readability, we may simply address each space $\mathcal{ID}, \mathcal{ID}_{\mathtt{h}}, \mathcal{T}$ as $\mathcal{T} = \mathcal{ID} = \mathbb{Z}_q^n \setminus \{\mathbf{0}_n\}, \mathcal{ID}_{\mathtt{h}} = (\mathbb{Z}_q^n \setminus \{\mathbf{0}_n\})^{\leq L}$, unless stated otherwise.

6.1 Construction

We provide our RHIBE scheme below. The intuition of the construction follows the explanation given in Sect. 2. Due to the complex nature of our scheme, we encourage readers to go back to Sect. 2 whenever needed.

$\mathsf{Setup}(1^n, L) \to (\mathsf{PP}, \mathsf{sk}_{\mathsf{kgc}})$: The setup algorithm is run by the KGC. It takes the security parameter 1^n and the maximum depth of the hierarchy L as input, and runs $(\mathbf{A}_i, \mathbf{T}_{\mathbf{A}_i}) \leftarrow \mathsf{TrapGen}(1^n, 1^m, q)$ for $i \in [L+1]$. It also samples uniformly random matrices $(\mathbf{B}_j)_{j \in [L+1]} \leftarrow (\mathbb{Z}_q^{n \times m})^{(L+1)}$ and vectors $(\mathbf{u}_k)_{k \in [L]} \leftarrow (\mathbb{Z}_q^n)^L$. Finally, it creates a binary tree by running $\mathsf{BT}_{\mathsf{kgc}} \leftarrow \mathsf{CS.SetUp}(N)$ and outputs

$$\mathsf{PP} := \Big((\mathbf{A}_i)_{i \in [L+1]}, (\mathbf{B}_j)_{j \in [L+1]}, (\mathbf{u}_k)_{k \in [L]} \Big), \quad \mathsf{sk}_{\mathsf{kgc}} := \Big(\mathsf{BT}_{\mathsf{kgc}}, (\mathbf{T}_{\mathbf{A}_i})_{i \in [L+1]} \Big).$$

Recall here that the matrices $\mathbf{B}_j$ define the hash functions $\mathbf{E}(\cdot)$ and $\mathbf{F}(\cdot)$ stated in Eq. (1) in Sect. 2.

$\mathsf{Encrypt}(\mathsf{PP}, \mathsf{ID} = (\mathsf{id}_1, \ldots, \mathsf{id}_\ell), \mathsf{t}, \mathsf{M}) \to \mathsf{ct}$: On input an identity $\mathsf{ID} \in (\mathbb{Z}_q^n)^\ell$ at depth $\ell \in [L]$ and time period $\mathsf{t} \in \mathbb{Z}_q^n$, it first samples $\ell + 1$ uniformly random vectors $(\mathbf{s}_i)_{i \in [\ell]}, \mathbf{s}_{L+1} \in \mathbb{Z}_q^n$. Then it samples $x \leftarrow D_{\mathbb{Z}, \alpha q}, \mathbf{x}_i \leftarrow D_{\mathbb{Z}^{(i+2)m}, \alpha' q}$ for $i \in [\ell]$ and $\mathbf{x}_{L+1} \leftarrow D_{\mathbb{Z}^{(\ell+2)m}, \alpha' q}$, and sets

$$\begin{cases} c_0 = \mathbf{u}_\ell^\top (\mathbf{s}_1 + \cdots + \mathbf{s}_\ell + \mathbf{s}_{L+1}) + x + \mathsf{M} \left\lfloor \frac{q}{2} \right\rfloor, \\ \mathbf{c}_i = [\mathbf{A}_i | \mathbf{E}(\mathsf{ID}_{[i]}) | \mathbf{F}(\mathsf{t})]^\top \mathbf{s}_i + \mathbf{x}_i \quad \text{for } i \in [\ell], \\ \mathbf{c}_{L+1} = [\mathbf{A}_{L+1} | \mathbf{E}(\mathsf{ID}) | \mathbf{F}(\mathsf{t})]^\top \mathbf{s}_{L+1} + \mathbf{x}_{L+1}. \end{cases}$$

Finally, it outputs a ciphertext $\mathsf{ct} := (c_0, \mathbf{c}_1, \ldots, \mathbf{c}_\ell, \mathbf{c}_{L+1}) \in \mathbb{Z}_q \times \mathbb{Z}_q^{3m} \times \cdots \times \mathbb{Z}_q^{(\ell+2)m} \times \mathbb{Z}_q^{(\ell+2)m}$.

$\mathsf{GenSK}(\mathsf{PP}, \mathsf{sk}_{\mathsf{pa(ID)}}, \mathsf{ID}) \to (\mathsf{sk}_{\mathsf{ID}}, \mathsf{sk}'_{\mathsf{pa(ID)}})$: The secret key generation algorithm is run by a parent user $\mathsf{pa(ID)}$ at level $\ell - 1$, where $1 \leq \ell \leq L$, to create a secret key for its child ID.[13] It first runs $(\mathsf{BT}_{\mathsf{pa(ID)}}, \eta_{\mathsf{ID}}) \leftarrow \mathsf{CS.Assign}(\mathsf{BT}_{\mathsf{pa(ID)}}, \mathsf{ID})$.

[13] Recall that a user at level 0 corresponds to the kgc, i.e., for any level-1 user $\mathsf{ID} \in \mathbb{Z}_q^n \setminus \{\mathbf{0}_n\}$, $\mathsf{pa(ID)} = \mathsf{kgc}$.

Then, for each node $\theta \in \mathsf{Path}(\mathsf{BT}_{\mathsf{pa(ID)}}, \eta_{\mathsf{ID}})$, it checks whether a vector $\mathbf{u}_{\mathsf{pa(ID)},\theta} \in \mathbb{Z}_q^n$ has already been assigned. If not, pick a uniformly random vector $\mathbf{u}_{\mathsf{pa(ID)},\theta} \in \mathbb{Z}_q^n$ and update $\mathsf{sk}_{\mathsf{pa(ID)}}$ by storing $\mathbf{u}_{\mathsf{pa(ID)},\theta}$ in node $\theta \in \mathsf{BT}_{\mathsf{pa(ID)}}$. Next, it samples vectors $\mathbf{e}_{\mathsf{ID},\theta}, \mathbf{f}_{\mathsf{ID},k} \in \mathbb{Z}^{(\ell+1)m}$ for $\theta \in \mathsf{Path}(\mathsf{BT}_{\mathsf{pa(ID)}}, \eta_{\mathsf{ID}}), k \in [\ell+1, L]$, respectively, such that $[\mathbf{A}_\ell | \mathbf{E}(\mathsf{ID})]\mathbf{e}_{\mathsf{ID},\theta} = \mathbf{u}_{\mathsf{pa(ID)},\theta}$, $[\mathbf{A}_\ell | \mathbf{E}(\mathsf{ID})]\mathbf{f}_{\mathsf{ID},k} = \mathbf{u}_k - \mathbf{u}_\ell$ by running $\mathsf{SampleLeft}(\cdot)$ with trapdoor $\mathbf{T}_{[\mathbf{A}_\ell|\mathbf{E}(\mathsf{pa(ID)})]}$[14] and Gaussian parameter σ_ℓ. Then, it extends its bases by running the following algorithm for $i \in [\ell+1, L+1]$: $\mathbf{T}_{[\mathbf{A}_i|\mathbf{E}(\mathsf{ID})]} \leftarrow \mathsf{ExtRndLeft}([\mathbf{A}_i|\mathbf{E}(\mathsf{pa(ID)})], \mathbf{B}_\ell + H(\mathsf{id}_\ell)\mathbf{G}, \mathbf{T}_{[\mathbf{A}_i|\mathbf{E}(\mathsf{pa(ID)})]}, \sigma_{\ell-1})$, where $\mathbf{T}_{[\mathbf{A}_i|\mathbf{E}(\mathsf{ID})]} \in \mathbb{Z}^{(\ell+1)m \times (\ell+1)m}$. Here, recall that $\mathbf{E}(\mathsf{ID}) = [\mathbf{E}(\mathsf{pa(ID)}) | \mathbf{B}_\ell + H(\mathsf{id}_\ell)\mathbf{G}]$. Finally, it runs $\mathsf{BT}_{\mathsf{ID}} \leftarrow \mathsf{CS.SetUp}(N)$ and outputs,

$$\mathsf{sk}_{\mathsf{ID}} = \begin{pmatrix} \mathsf{BT}_{\mathsf{ID}}, \mathsf{Path}(\mathsf{BT}_{\mathsf{pa(ID)}}, \eta_{\mathsf{ID}}), \ (\mathbf{e}_{\mathsf{ID},\theta})_{\theta \in \mathsf{Path}(\mathsf{BT}_{\mathsf{pa(ID)}}, \eta_{\mathsf{ID}})}, \\ (\mathbf{f}_{\mathsf{ID},k})_{k \in [\ell+1, L]}, \ (\mathbf{T}_{[\mathbf{A}_i|\mathbf{E}(\mathsf{ID})]})_{i \in [\ell+1, L+1]} \end{pmatrix}$$

along with its updated secret key $\mathsf{sk}'_{\mathsf{pa(ID)}}$.

$\mathsf{KeyUp}(\mathsf{PP}, \mathsf{t}, \mathsf{sk}_{\mathsf{ID}}, \mathsf{RL}_{\mathsf{ID},\mathsf{t}}, \mathsf{ku}_{\mathsf{pa(ID)},\mathsf{t}}) \rightarrow (\mathsf{ku}_{\mathsf{ID},\mathsf{t}}, \mathsf{sk}'_{\mathsf{ID}})$: The key update information generation algorithm is run by user ID at level ℓ, where $0 \leq \ell \leq L-1$, to create a key update $\mathsf{ku}_{\mathsf{ID},\mathsf{t}}$ for time period t for its children. It first runs $\mathsf{KUNode}(\mathsf{BT}_{\mathsf{ID}}, \mathsf{RL}_{\mathsf{ID},\mathsf{t}}) \leftarrow \mathsf{CS.Cover}(\mathsf{BT}_{\mathsf{ID}}, \mathsf{RL}_{\mathsf{ID},\mathsf{t}})$, and checks whether $\mathbf{u}_{\mathsf{ID},\theta}$ is defined for each node $\theta \in \mathsf{KUNode}(\mathsf{BT}_{\mathsf{ID}}, \mathsf{RL}_{\mathsf{ID},\mathsf{t}})$. If not, it picks a random $\mathbf{u}_{\mathsf{ID},\theta} \in \mathbb{Z}_q^n$ and updates $\mathsf{sk}_{\mathsf{ID}}$ by storing $\mathbf{u}_{\mathsf{ID},\theta}$ in the node $\theta \in \mathsf{BT}_{\mathsf{ID}}$. Then, for each node θ, it samples $\mathbf{e}_{\mathsf{ID},\mathsf{t},\theta} \in \mathbb{Z}^{(\ell+2)m}$ such that $[\mathbf{A}_{\ell+1} | \mathbf{E}(\mathsf{ID}) | \mathbf{F}(\mathsf{t})]\mathbf{e}_{\mathsf{ID},\mathsf{t},\theta} = \mathbf{u}_{\ell+1} - \mathbf{u}_{\mathsf{ID},\theta}$ by running $\mathsf{SampleLeft}(\cdot)$ with trapdoor $\mathbf{T}_{[\mathbf{A}_{\ell+1}|\mathbf{E}(\mathsf{ID})]}$ and Gaussian parameter $\sigma_{\ell+1}$.

At this point, the algorithm behaves differently depending on $\ell \geq 1$ or $\ell = 0$ (i.e., $\mathsf{ID} = \mathsf{kgc}$). In case $\ell \geq 1$, it computes its own decryption key $\mathsf{dk}_{\mathsf{ID},\mathsf{t}}$, which includes a vector $\mathbf{d}_{\mathsf{ID},\mathsf{t}} \in \mathbb{Z}^{(\ell+2)m}$, using the decryption key generation algorithm $\mathsf{GenDK}(\mathsf{PP}, \mathsf{sk}_{\mathsf{ID}}, \mathsf{ku}_{\mathsf{pa(ID,t)}})$ defined below, and computes the following vectors for $k \in [\ell+1, L]$: $\mathbf{f}_{\mathsf{ID},\mathsf{t},k} = \mathbf{d}_{\mathsf{ID},\mathsf{t}} + [\mathbf{f}_{\mathsf{ID},k} \| \mathbf{0}_m] \in \mathbb{Z}^{(\ell+2)m}$. Here, $[\cdot\|\cdot]$ denotes vertical concatenation of vectors.

Finally, it extracts $(\mathbf{f}_{\mathsf{ID}_{[i]},\mathsf{t},k} \in \mathbb{Z}^{(i+2)m})_{(i,k) \in [\ell-1] \times [\ell+1, L]}$ from its ancestor's key update information $\mathsf{ku}_{\mathsf{pa(ID)},\mathsf{t}}$ and outputs

$$\mathsf{ku}_{\mathsf{ID},\mathsf{t}} = \begin{pmatrix} \mathsf{KUNode}(\mathsf{BT}_{\mathsf{ID}}, \mathsf{RL}_{\mathsf{ID},\mathsf{t}}), (\mathbf{e}_{\mathsf{ID},\mathsf{t},\theta})_{\theta \in \mathsf{KUNode}(\mathsf{BT}_{\mathsf{ID}}, \mathsf{RL}_{\mathsf{ID},\mathsf{t}})}, \\ (\mathbf{f}_{\mathsf{ID}_{[i]},\mathsf{t},k})_{(i,k) \in [\ell] \times [\ell+1, L]} \end{pmatrix}$$

and the possibly updated $\mathsf{sk}'_{\mathsf{ID}}$.

In case $\ell = 0$, it skips all the above procedures and simply outputs

$$\mathsf{ku}_{\mathsf{ID},\mathsf{t}} = (\mathsf{KUNode}(\mathsf{BT}_{\mathsf{ID}}, \mathsf{RL}_{\mathsf{ID},\mathsf{t}}), (\mathbf{e}_{\mathsf{ID},\mathsf{t},\theta})_{\theta \in \mathsf{KUNode}(\mathsf{BT}_{\mathsf{ID}}, \mathsf{RL}_{\mathsf{ID}})})$$

[14] There are two exceptions for this algorithm. In the special case $\mathsf{ID} = \mathsf{kgc}$, recall that we set $\mathbf{T}_{[\mathbf{A}_1|\mathbf{E}(\mathsf{kgc})]}$ as $\mathbf{T}_{\mathbf{A}_1}$, which is included in the $\mathsf{sk}_{\mathsf{kgc}}$. In the other special case when $\ell = L$, we no longer sample $\mathbf{f}_{\mathsf{ID},k}$, since this vector is only required for delegating key updates to its children, which users at level L do not have.

and the possibly updated $\mathsf{sk}'_{\mathsf{ID}}$.[15]

$\mathsf{GenDK}(\mathsf{PP}, \mathsf{sk}_{\mathsf{ID}}, \mathsf{ku}_{\mathsf{pa(ID)},\mathsf{t}}) \to \mathsf{dk}_{\mathsf{ID},\mathsf{t}}$ or $\perp$: The decryption key generation algorithm is run by user ID at level ℓ, where $1 \leq \ell \leq L$. It extracts $\mathsf{Path}(\mathsf{BT}_{\mathsf{pa(ID)}}, \eta_{\mathsf{ID}})$ in $\mathsf{sk}_{\mathsf{ID}}$ and $\mathsf{KUNode}(\mathsf{BT}_{\mathsf{pa(ID)}}, \mathsf{RL}_{\mathsf{pa(ID)},\mathsf{t}})$ in $\mathsf{ku}_{\mathsf{pa(ID)},\mathsf{t}}$, and runs $\theta/\emptyset \leftarrow \mathsf{CS.Match}(\mathsf{Path}(\mathsf{BT}_{\mathsf{pa(ID)}}, \eta_{\mathsf{ID}}), \mathsf{KUNode}(\mathsf{BT}_{\mathsf{pa(ID)}}, \mathsf{RL}_{\mathsf{pa(ID)},\mathsf{t}}))$. If the output is $\emptyset$, it outputs $\perp$. Otherwise, it extracts $\mathbf{e}_{\mathsf{ID},\theta}, \mathbf{e}_{\mathsf{pa(ID)},\mathsf{t},\theta} \in \mathbb{Z}^{(\ell+1)m}$ in $\mathsf{sk}_{\mathsf{ID}}, \mathsf{ku}_{\mathsf{pa(ID)},\mathsf{t}}$, respectively, and parses it as

$$\mathbf{e}_{\mathsf{ID},\theta} = [\mathbf{e}^{\mathsf{L}}_{\mathsf{ID},\theta} \| \mathbf{e}^{\mathsf{R}}_{\mathsf{ID},\theta}], \ \mathbf{e}_{\mathsf{pa(ID)},\mathsf{t},\theta} = [\mathbf{e}^{\mathsf{L}}_{\mathsf{pa(ID)},\mathsf{t},\theta} \| \mathbf{e}^{\mathsf{R}}_{\mathsf{pa(ID)},\mathsf{t},\theta}],$$

where $\mathbf{e}^{\mathsf{L}}_{\mathsf{ID},\theta}, \mathbf{e}^{\mathsf{L}}_{\mathsf{pa(ID)},\mathsf{t},\theta} \in \mathbb{Z}^{\ell m}$ and $\mathbf{e}^{\mathsf{R}}_{\mathsf{ID},\theta}, \mathbf{e}^{\mathsf{R}}_{\mathsf{pa(ID)},\mathsf{t},\theta} \in \mathbb{Z}^{m}$. Then, it computes

$$\mathbf{d}_{\mathsf{ID},\mathsf{t}} = [\mathbf{e}^{\mathsf{L}}_{\mathsf{ID},\theta} + \mathbf{e}^{\mathsf{L}}_{\mathsf{pa(ID)},\mathsf{t},\theta} \| \mathbf{e}^{\mathsf{R}}_{\mathsf{ID},\theta} \| \mathbf{e}^{\mathsf{R}}_{\mathsf{pa(ID)},\mathsf{t},\theta}] \in \mathbb{Z}^{(\ell+2)m}.$$

It further samples $\mathbf{g}_{\mathsf{ID},\mathsf{t}} \in \mathbb{Z}^{(\ell+2)m}$ such that $[\mathbf{A}_{L+1}|\mathbf{E}(\mathsf{ID})|\mathbf{F}(\mathsf{t})]\mathbf{g}_{\mathsf{ID},\mathsf{t}} = \mathbf{u}_{\ell}$ by running $\mathsf{SampleLeft}(\cdot)$ with trapdoor $\mathbf{T}_{[\mathbf{A}_{L+1}|\mathbf{E}(\mathsf{ID})]}$ and Gaussian parameter σ_{ℓ}.

Finally, in case $\ell \geq 2$, it extracts $(\mathbf{f}_{\mathsf{ID}_{[i]},\mathsf{t},\ell})_{i \in [\ell-1]}$ from $\mathsf{ku}_{\mathsf{pa(ID)},\mathsf{t}}$ and outputs $\mathsf{dk}_{\mathsf{ID},\mathsf{t}} = (\mathbf{d}_{\mathsf{ID},\mathsf{t}}, (\mathbf{f}_{\mathsf{ID}_{[i]},\mathsf{t},\ell})_{i \in [\ell-1]}, \mathbf{g}_{\mathsf{ID},\mathsf{t}})$. Otherwise, in case $\ell = 1$, it simply outputs $\mathsf{dk}_{\mathsf{ID},\mathsf{t}} = (\mathbf{d}_{\mathsf{ID},\mathsf{t}}, \mathbf{g}_{\mathsf{ID},\mathsf{t}})$.

$\mathsf{Decrypt}(\mathsf{PP}, \mathsf{dk}_{\mathsf{ID},\mathsf{t}}, \mathsf{ct}) \to \mathsf{M}$: The decryption algorithm is run by user ID at level ℓ, where $1 \leq \ell \leq L$. It first parses the ciphertext ct as $(c_0, \mathbf{c}_1, \cdots, \mathbf{c}_{\ell}, \mathbf{c}_{L+1})$. Then, in case $\ell \geq 2$, it uses its decryption key $\mathsf{dk}_{\mathsf{ID},\mathsf{t}} = (\mathbf{d}_{\mathsf{ID},\mathsf{t}}, (\mathbf{f}_{\mathsf{ID}_{[i]},\mathsf{t},\ell})_{i \in [\ell-1]}, \mathbf{g}_{\mathsf{ID},\mathsf{t}})$ and computes

$$c' = c_0 - \sum_{i=1}^{\ell-1} \mathbf{f}^{\top}_{\mathsf{ID}_{[i]},\mathsf{t},\ell}\mathbf{c}_i - \mathbf{d}^{\top}_{\mathsf{ID},\mathsf{t}}\mathbf{c}_{\ell} - \mathbf{g}^{\top}_{\mathsf{ID},\mathsf{t}}\mathbf{c}_{L+1} \in \mathbb{Z}_q. \tag{5}$$

Otherwise, in case $\ell = 1$, it uses its decryption key $\mathsf{dk}_{\mathsf{ID},\mathsf{t}} = (\mathbf{d}_{\mathsf{ID},\mathsf{t}}, \mathbf{g}_{\mathsf{ID},\mathsf{t}})$ and computes

$$c' = c_0 - \mathbf{d}^{\top}_{\mathsf{ID},\mathsf{t}}\mathbf{c}_1 - \mathbf{g}^{\top}_{\mathsf{ID},\mathsf{t}}\mathbf{c}_{L+1} \in \mathbb{Z}_q.$$

Finally, it compares c' and $\lfloor \frac{q}{2} \rfloor$ treating them as integers in $\mathbb{Z}$, and outputs 1 in case $|c' - \lfloor \frac{q}{2} \rfloor| < \lfloor \frac{q}{4} \rfloor$ and 0 otherwise.

Correctness. Let a ciphertext be aimed for user ID and time period t. To check correctness, we only need to consider the case where all the ancestors of ID are not revoked. In other words, we check that user ID will be able to obtain all the required components to construct the decryption key $\mathbf{d}_{\mathsf{ID},\mathsf{t}}$ when provided with all the key updates $\mathsf{ku}_{\mathsf{ID}',\mathsf{t}}$ from $\mathsf{ID}' \in \mathsf{prefix}(\mathsf{ID}) \backslash \{\mathsf{ID}\}$.

Lemma 5. *Assume $O((\alpha + mL^2\sigma_L\alpha')q) \leq q/5$ holds with overwhelming probability. Then the above scheme has negligible decryption error.*

[15] The branch in the algorithm is due to the fact that for the special case $\ell = 0$, i.e., $\mathsf{ID} = \mathsf{kgc}$, we have $\mathsf{ku}_{\mathsf{pa(ID)},\mathsf{t}} = \perp$ for all T and there exists no decryption key $\mathsf{dk}_{\mathsf{ID},\mathsf{t}}$.

Remarks. Note that for simplicity we defined correctness of RHIBE to hold with probability one in Sect. 4. Therefore, to be consistent with our definition, we can use standard techniques to modify our lattice-based construction to have no decryption error by considering a bound on the secret/noise vectors.

6.2 Security

Theorem 2. *The above RHIBE scheme Π is selective-identity secure assuming the hardness of the* $\mathsf{LWE}_{n,m+1,q,\chi}$ *problem, where* $\chi = D_{\mathbb{Z}^{m+1},\alpha q}$.

Proof Overview. Here, we provide an overview of the proof. Let $\mathcal{A}$ be a PPT adversary that attacks the selective-identity security of the RHIBE scheme Π with non-negligible advantage. In addition, let $(\mathsf{ID}^* = (\mathsf{id}_1^*, \ldots, \mathsf{id}_{\ell^*}^*), \mathsf{t}^*)$ be the challenge identity/time period pair that $\mathcal{A}$ sends to the challenger at the beginning of the game. Similarly to the RIBE adversary in Sect. 5, the strategy taken by $\mathcal{A}$ can be divided into the following two types that are mutually exclusive, where the first type can be further divided into ℓ types of strategies that are mutually exclusive:

- Type-I: $\mathcal{A}$ issues secret key reveal queries on at least one $\mathsf{ID} \in \mathsf{prefix}(\mathsf{ID}^*)$.
  - Type-I-i^*: $\mathcal{A}$ issues a secret key reveal query on $\mathsf{ID}_{[i^*]}^*$ but not on any $\mathsf{ID} \in \mathsf{prefix}(\mathsf{ID}_{[i^*-1]}^*)$.
- Type-II: $\mathcal{A}$ does not issue secret key reveal queries on any $\mathsf{ID} \in \mathsf{prefix}(\mathsf{ID}^*)$.

Due to the strategy-dividing lemma, it suffices to prove security against each type of adversary independently. In our proof we provide two types of security reduction: one for when $\mathcal{A}$ follows the Type-I-i^* $(1 \le i^* \le \ell^*)$ strategy and another for when $\mathcal{A}$ follows the Type-II strategy. Let us provide a brief overview of the reduction when we are against a Type-I-i^* adversary $\mathcal{A}$. The general idea holds for Type-II adversaries as well.

Our goal is to modify the challenger through a sequence of games so that in the end he would be able to simulate the game against the Type-I-i^* adversary $\mathcal{A}$ using only the trapdoors $\{\mathbf{T_A}\}_{i\in[L+1]\backslash\{i^*\}}$. At a high level, this allows the challenger to embed his LWE challenge into the matrix $\mathbf{A}_{i^*}$ included in the public parameter PP. The following Table 1 depicts all the possible scenarios where the challenger requires the trapdoor $\mathbf{T}_{\mathbf{A}_{i^*}}$, either implicitly or explicitly, in the real game to respond to $\mathcal{A}$'s queries. For readers familiar with the RIBE

Table 1. Items for which the challenger requires $\mathbf{T}_{\mathbf{A}_{i^*}}$ to construct.

	$\mathsf{ID} \in (\mathcal{ID})^{i^*}$	$\mathsf{ID} \in (\mathcal{ID})^{i^*-1}$	(In case $i^* \ge 3$) $\mathsf{ID} \in (\mathcal{ID})^{\le i^*-2}$
Secret Key Generation ($\mathsf{sk}_{\mathsf{ID}}$)	$(\mathbf{e}_{\mathsf{ID},\theta})_{\theta\in\mathsf{Path}(\mathsf{BT}_{\mathsf{pa}(\mathsf{ID})},\eta_{\mathsf{ID}})}$ $(\mathbf{f}_{\mathsf{ID},k})_{k\in[i^*+1,L]}$	$\mathbf{T}_{[\mathbf{A}_{i^*}\mid\mathbf{E}(\mathsf{ID})]}$	$\mathbf{T}_{[\mathbf{A}_{i^*}\mid\mathbf{E}(\mathsf{ID})]}$
Revoke & Key Update ($\mathsf{ku}_{\mathsf{ID},\mathsf{t}}$)	$(\mathbf{f}_{\mathsf{ID},\mathsf{t},k})_{k\in[i^*+1,L]}$	$(\mathbf{e}_{\mathsf{ID},\mathsf{t},\theta})_{\theta\in\mathsf{KUNode}(\mathsf{BT}_{\mathsf{ID}},\mathsf{RL}_{\mathsf{ID},\mathsf{t}})}$	–
Decryption Key Reveal ($\mathsf{dk}_{\mathsf{ID},\mathsf{t}}$)	$\mathbf{d}_{\mathsf{ID},\mathsf{t}}$	–	–

scheme without DKER of Chen et al. [10], it may be helpful to point out that the way we modify the challenger so that he no longer requires $\mathbf{T}_{\mathbf{A}_{i^*}}$ to construct $(\mathbf{e}_{\mathsf{ID},\theta})_\theta$ in the secret key generation query and $(\mathbf{e}_{\mathsf{ID},\mathsf{t},\theta})_\theta$ in the revoke & key update query is very similar to the technique used in [10]. This is mainly because these components are those responsible for achieving the revocation mechanism. Our proof deviates from prior works when we modify the challenger so that he no longer requires $\mathbf{T}_{\mathbf{A}_{i^*}}$ to construct $(\mathbf{f}_{\mathsf{ID},k})_k$ in the secret key generation query and $(\mathbf{f}_{\mathsf{ID},\mathsf{t},k})_k$ in the revoke & key update query, since these are the newly added components for achieving DKER.

Acknowledgement. The first author was partially supported by JST CREST Grant Number JPMJCR1302 and JSPS KAKENHI Grant Number 17J05603. The second author was partially supported by JST CREST Grant Number JPMJCR1688. The third author was partially supported by JST CREST Grant Number JPMJCR14D6.

References

1. Agrawal, S., Boneh, D., Boyen, X.: Efficient lattice (H)IBE in the standard model. In: Gilbert, H. (ed.) EUROCRYPT 2010. LNCS, vol. 6110, pp. 553–572. Springer, Heidelberg (2010). https://doi.org/10.1007/978-3-642-13190-5_28
2. Ajtai, M.: Generating hard instances of the short basis problem. In: Wiedermann, J., van Emde Boas, P., Nielsen, M. (eds.) ICALP 1999. LNCS, vol. 1644, pp. 1–9. Springer, Heidelberg (1999). https://doi.org/10.1007/3-540-48523-6_1
3. Alwen, J., Peikert, C.: Generating shorter bases for hard random lattices. Theory Comput. Syst. **48**(3), 535–553 (2011)
4. Attrapadung, N., Imai, H.: Attribute-based encryption supporting direct/indirect revocation modes. In: Parker, M.G. (ed.) IMACC 2009. LNCS, vol. 5921, pp. 278–300. Springer, Heidelberg (2009). https://doi.org/10.1007/978-3-642-10868-6_17
5. Attrapadung, N., Imai, H.: Conjunctive broadcast and attribute-based encryption. In: Shacham, H., Waters, B. (eds.) Pairing 2009. LNCS, vol. 5671, pp. 248–265. Springer, Heidelberg (2009). https://doi.org/10.1007/978-3-642-03298-1_16
6. Boldyreva, A., Goyal, V., Kumar, V.: Identity-based encryption with efficient revocation. In: CCS 2008, pp. 417–426. ACM (2008)
7. Boneh, D., Franklin, M.K.: Identity-based encryption from the weil pairing. SIAM J. Comput. **32**(3), 586–615 (2003)
8. Cash, D., Hofheinz, D., Kiltz, E., Peikert, C.: Bonsai trees, or how to delegate a lattice basis. J. Cryptol. **25**(4), 601–639 (2012)
9. Chang, D., Chauhan, A.K., Kumar, S., Sanadhya, S.K.: Revocable identity-based encryption from codes with rank metric. In: Smart, N.P. (ed.) CT-RSA 2018. LNCS, vol. 10808, pp. 435–451. Springer, Cham (2018). https://doi.org/10.1007/978-3-319-76953-0_23
10. Chen, J., Lim, H.W., Ling, S., Wang, H., Nguyen, K.: Revocable identity-based encryption from lattices. In: Susilo, W., Mu, Y., Seberry, J. (eds.) ACISP 2012. LNCS, vol. 7372, pp. 390–403. Springer, Heidelberg (2012). https://doi.org/10.1007/978-3-642-31448-3_29
11. Cui, H., Deng, R.H., Li, Y., Qin, B.: Server-aided revocable attribute-based encryption. In: Askoxylakis, I., Ioannidis, S., Katsikas, S., Meadows, C. (eds.) ESORICS 2016. LNCS, vol. 9879, pp. 570–587. Springer, Cham (2016). https://doi.org/10.1007/978-3-319-45741-3_29

12. Döttling, N., Garg, S.: From selective IBE to full IBE and selective HIBE. In: Kalai, Y., Reyzin, L. (eds.) TCC 2017. LNCS, vol. 10677, pp. 372–408. Springer, Cham (2017). https://doi.org/10.1007/978-3-319-70500-2_13
13. Emura, K., Seo, J.H., Youn, T.: Semi-generic transformation of revocable hierarchical identity-based encryption and its DBDH instantiation. IEICE Trans. **99–A**(1), 83–91 (2016)
14. Gentry, C., Peikert, C., Vaikuntanathan, V.: Trapdoors for hard lattices and new cryptographic constructions. In: STOC 2008, pp. 197–206. ACM (2008)
15. Ishida, Y., Shikata, J., Watanabe, Y.: CCA-secure revocable identity-based encryption schemes with decryption key exposure resistance. IJACT **3**(3), 288–311 (2017)
16. Katsumata, S., Yamada, S.: Partitioning via non-linear polynomial functions: more compact IBEs from ideal lattices and bilinear maps. In: Cheon, J.H., Takagi, T. (eds.) ASIACRYPT 2016. LNCS, vol. 10032, pp. 682–712. Springer, Heidelberg (2016). https://doi.org/10.1007/978-3-662-53890-6_23
17. Lee, K.: Revocable hierarchical identity-based encryption with adaptive security. IACR Cryptology ePrint Archive 2016, 749 (2016)
18. Lee, K., Lee, D.H., Park, J.H.: Efficient revocable identity-based encryption via subset difference methods. Des. Codes Cryptogr. **85**(1), 39–76 (2017)
19. Lee, K., Park, S.: Revocable hierarchical identity-based encryption with shorter private keys and update keys. IACR Cryptology ePrint Archive 2016, 460 (2016)
20. Libert, B., Vergnaud, D.: Adaptive-ID secure revocable identity-based encryption. In: Fischlin, M. (ed.) CT-RSA 2009. LNCS, vol. 5473, pp. 1–15. Springer, Heidelberg (2009). https://doi.org/10.1007/978-3-642-00862-7_1
21. Ling, S., Nguyen, K., Wang, H., Zhang, J.: Revocable predicate encryption from lattices. In: Okamoto, T., Yu, Y., Au, M.H., Li, Y. (eds.) ProvSec 2017. LNCS, vol. 10592, pp. 305–326. Springer, Cham (2017). https://doi.org/10.1007/978-3-319-68637-0_19
22. Ling, S., Nguyen, K., Wang, H., Zhang, J.: Server-aided revocable predicate encryption: formalization and lattice-based instantiation. CoRR abs/1801.07844 (2018)
23. Mao, X., Lai, J., Chen, K., Weng, J., Mei, Q.: Efficient revocable identity-based encryption from multilinear maps. Secur. Commun. Netw. **8**(18), 3511–3522 (2015)
24. Micciancio, D., Peikert, C.: Trapdoors for lattices: simpler, tighter, faster, smaller. In: Pointcheval, D., Johansson, T. (eds.) EUROCRYPT 2012. LNCS, vol. 7237, pp. 700–718. Springer, Heidelberg (2012). https://doi.org/10.1007/978-3-642-29011-4_41
25. Naor, D., Naor, M., Lotspiech, J.: Revocation and tracing schemes for stateless receivers. In: Kilian, J. (ed.) CRYPTO 2001. LNCS, vol. 2139, pp. 41–62. Springer, Heidelberg (2001). https://doi.org/10.1007/3-540-44647-8_3
26. Nguyen, K., Wang, H., Zhang, J.: Server-aided revocable identity-based encryption from lattices. In: Foresti, S., Persiano, G. (eds.) CANS 2016. LNCS, vol. 10052, pp. 107–123. Springer, Cham (2016). https://doi.org/10.1007/978-3-319-48965-0_7
27. González-Nieto, J.M., Manulis, M., Sun, D.: Fully private revocable predicate encryption. In: Susilo, W., Mu, Y., Seberry, J. (eds.) ACISP 2012. LNCS, vol. 7372, pp. 350–363. Springer, Heidelberg (2012). https://doi.org/10.1007/978-3-642-31448-3_26
28. Park, S., Lee, D.H., Lee, K.: Revocable hierarchical identity-based encryption from multilinear maps. CoRR abs/1610.07948 (2016)
29. Park, S., Lee, K., Lee, D.H.: New constructions of revocable identity-based encryption from multilinear maps. IEEE Trans. Inf. Forensics Secur. **10**(8), 1564–1577 (2015)

30. Qin, B., Deng, R.H., Li, Y., Liu, S.: Server-aided revocable identity-based encryption. In: Pernul, G., Ryan, P.Y.A., Weippl, E. (eds.) ESORICS 2015. LNCS, vol. 9326, pp. 286–304. Springer, Cham (2015). https://doi.org/10.1007/978-3-319-24174-6_15
31. Regev, O.: On lattices, learning with errors, random linear codes, and cryptography. In: STOC 2005, pp. 84–93. ACM (2005)
32. Ryu, G., Lee, K., Park, S., Lee, D.H.: Unbounded hierarchical identity-based encryption with efficient revocation. In: Kim, H., Choi, D. (eds.) WISA 2015. LNCS, vol. 9503, pp. 122–133. Springer, Cham (2016). https://doi.org/10.1007/978-3-319-31875-2_11
33. Seo, J.H., Emura, K.: Revocable identity-based encryption revisited: security model and construction. In: Kurosawa, K., Hanaoka, G. (eds.) PKC 2013. LNCS, vol. 7778, pp. 216–234. Springer, Heidelberg (2013). https://doi.org/10.1007/978-3-642-36362-7_14
34. Seo, J.H., Emura, K.: Revocable hierarchical identity-based encryption. Theor. Comput. Sci. **542**, 44–62 (2014)
35. Seo, J.H., Emura, K.: Revocable hierarchical identity-based encryption via history-free approach. Theor. Comput. Sci. **615**, 45–60 (2016)
36. Takayasu, A., Watanabe, Y.: Lattice-based revocable identity-based encryption with bounded decryption key exposure resistance. In: Pieprzyk, J., Suriadi, S. (eds.) ACISP 2017. LNCS, vol. 10342, pp. 184–204. Springer, Cham (2017). https://doi.org/10.1007/978-3-319-60055-0_10
37. Watanabe, Y., Emura, K., Seo, J.H.: New revocable IBE in prime-order groups: adaptively secure, decryption key exposure resistant, and with short public parameters. In: Handschuh, H. (ed.) CT-RSA 2017. LNCS, vol. 10159, pp. 432–449. Springer, Cham (2017). https://doi.org/10.1007/978-3-319-52153-4_25

Towards Non-Interactive Zero-Knowledge for NP from LWE

Ron D. Rothblum[1], Adam Sealfon[2], and Katerina Sotiraki[2(✉)]

[1] Technion, Haifa, Israel
rothblum@cs.technion.ac.il
[2] MIT, Cambridge, USA
{asealfon,katesot}@mit.edu

Abstract. Non-interactive zero-knowledge (NIZK) is a fundamental primitive that is widely used in the construction of cryptographic schemes and protocols. Despite this, general purpose constructions of NIZK proof systems are only known under a rather limited set of assumptions that are either number-theoretic (and can be broken by a quantum computer) or are not sufficiently well understood, such as obfuscation. Thus, a basic question that has drawn much attention is whether it is possible to construct general-purpose NIZK proof systems based on the *learning with errors* (LWE) assumption.

Our main result is a reduction from constructing NIZK proof systems for all of **NP** based on LWE, to constructing a NIZK proof system for a particular computational problem on lattices, namely a decisional variant of the Bounded Distance Decoding (BDD) problem. That is, we show that assuming LWE, *every* language $L \in \mathbf{NP}$ has a NIZK proof system if (and only if) the decisional BDD problem has a NIZK proof system. This (almost) confirms a conjecture of Peikert and Vaikuntanathan (CRYPTO, 2008).

To construct our NIZK proof system, we introduce a new notion that we call *prover-assisted oblivious ciphertext sampling* (POCS), which we believe to be of independent interest. This notion extends the idea of *oblivious ciphertext sampling*, which allows one to sample ciphertexts without knowing the underlying plaintext. Specifically, we augment the oblivious ciphertext sampler with access to an (untrusted) prover to help

R. D. Rothblum—This research was conducted in part while the author was at MIT and Northeastern University. Research supported in part by the Israeli Science Foundation (Grant No. 1262/18). Research also supported in part by NSF Grants CNS-1413920 and CNS-1350619, by the Defense Advanced Research Projects Agency (DARPA) and the U.S. Army Research Office under contracts W911NF-15-C-0226 and W911NF-15-C-0236, the Simons Investigator award agreement dated 6-5-12 and the Cybersecurity and Privacy Institute at Northeastern University.

A. Sealfon—Research supported in part by a DOE CSGF fellowship, NSF MACS CNS-1413920, DARPA/NJIT Palisade 491512803, Sloan/NJIT 996698, MIT/IBM W1771646, NSF Center for Science of Information (CSoI) CCF-0939370, and the Simons Investigator award agreement dated 6-5-12.

K. Sotiraki—Research supported in part by NSF grants CNS-1350619, CNS-1718161, CNS-1414119.

D. Lin and K. Sako (Eds.): PKC 2019, LNCS 11443, pp. 472–503, 2019.
https://doi.org/10.1007/978-3-030-17259-6_16

it accomplish this task. We show that the existence of encryption schemes with a POCS procedure, as well as some additional natural requirements, suffices for obtaining NIZK proofs for **NP**. We further show that such encryption schemes can be instantiated based on LWE, assuming the existence of a NIZK proof system for the decisional BDD problem.

1 Introduction

The *learning with errors* (LWE) problem, introduced by Regev [Reg09], has had a profound impact on cryptography. The goal in LWE is to find a solution to a set of *noisy* linear equations modulo a large integer q, where the noise is typically drawn from a discrete Gaussian distribution. The assumption that LWE cannot be broken in polynomial time can be based on *worst-case* hardness of lattice problems [Reg09, Pei09] and has drawn immense interest in recent years.

Immediately following its introduction, LWE was shown to imply the existence of many important cryptographic primitives such as public-key encryption [Reg09], circular secure encryption [ACPS09], oblivious transfer [PVW08], chosen ciphertext security [PW08, Pei09], etc. Even more remarkably, in recent years LWE has been used to achieve schemes and protocols above and beyond what was previously known from other assumptions. Notable examples include fully homomorphic encryption [BV14], predicate encryption and certain types of functional encryption (see, e.g., [AFV11, GKP+13, GVW15]), and even obfuscation of certain expressive classes of computations [WZ17, GKW17].

Despite this amazing list of applications, one major primitive that has resisted all LWE based attempts is general purpose *Non-Interactive Zero-Knowledge* (NIZK) *proof systems* for **NP**.[1] A NIZK proof system for a language $L \in \mathbf{NP}$, as introduced by Blum *et al.* [BFM88], is a protocol between a probabilistic polynomial-time prover P and verifier V in the *Common Random String* (CRS) model. The prover, given an instance $x \in L$, a witness w, and the random string r, produces a proof string π which it sends to the verifier. Based only on x, the random string r and the proof π, the verifier can decide whether $x \in L$. Furthermore, the protocol is zero-knowledge: the proof π reveals nothing to the verifier beyond the fact that $x \in L$.

Non-interactive zero-knowledge proofs have been used extensively in cryptography, with applications ranging from chosen ciphertext security and non-malleability [NY90, DDN03, Sah99], multi-party computation with a small number of rounds (see, e.g., [MW16]), low-round witness-indistinguishability [DN07] to various types of signatures (e.g. [BMW03, BKM06]) and beyond.

Currently, general purpose NIZK proof systems (i.e., NIZK proof systems for all of **NP**) are only known based on number theoretic assumptions (e.g., the hardness of factoring integers [FLS99] or the decisional linear assumption or symmetric external Diffie-Hellman assumption over bilinear groups [GOS12]) or from indistinguishability obfuscation [SW14, BP15] (see Sect. 1.2 for further

[1] As a matter of fact, resolving this question carries a symbolic cash prize; see https://simons.berkeley.edu/crypto2015/open-problems.

discussion). We remark that the former class of assumptions can be broken by a quantum computer [Sho99] whereas the assumption that indistinguishability obfuscation exists is not yet well understood. Thus, the following basic question remains open:

Can we construct NIZK *proofs for all of* **NP** *based on* LWE?

1.1 Our Results

Our main result is a completeness theorem reducing the foregoing question to that of constructing a NIZK proof system for one particular computational problem. Specifically, we will consider a decisional variant of the *bounded distance decoding* (BDD) problem.

Recall that in the BDD problem, the input is a lattice basis and a target vector which is very close to the lattice. The problem is to find the nearby lattice point. This is very similar to the *closest vector problem* CVP except that here the vector is guaranteed to be within the λ_1 radius of the lattice, where λ_1 denotes the length of the shortest non-zero lattice vector (more specifically, the problem is parameterized by $\alpha \geq 1$ and the guarantee is that the point is at distance λ_1/α from the lattice). BDD can also be viewed as a worst-case variant of LWE and is known to be (up to polynomial factors) equivalent to the shortest-vector problem (more precisely, GapSVP) [LM09].

In this work, we consider a decisional variant of BDD, which we denote by dBDD. The $\mathsf{dBDD}_{\alpha,\gamma}$ problem, is a promise problem, parameterized by $\alpha \geq 1$ and $\gamma \geq 1$, where the input is a basis $\mathbf{B}$ of a lattice L and a point $\mathbf{t}$. The goal is to distinguish between pairs $(L, \mathbf{t})$ such that the point $\mathbf{t}$ has distance at most $\frac{\lambda_1(L)}{\alpha}$ from the lattice L from tuples in which $\mathbf{t}$ has distance at least $\gamma \cdot \frac{\lambda_1(L)}{\alpha}$ from L.

Our main result can be stated as follows:

Theorem 1 (Informal; see Theorem *2*).
Suppose that LWE *holds and that* $\mathsf{dBDD}_{\alpha,\gamma}$ *has a* NIZK *proof system (where* α *and* γ *depend on the* LWE *parameters). Then, every language in* **NP** *has a* NIZK *proof system.*

Since dBDD is a special case of the well studied GapCVP problem, a NIZK for GapCVP would likewise suffice for obtaining NIZKs for all of **NP** based on LWE.

Relation to [PV08]. Theorem 1 (almost) confirms a conjecture of Peikert and Vaikuntanathan [PV08]. More specifically, [PV08] conjectured that a NIZK proof-system for a specific computational problem related to lattices would imply a NIZK proof-system for *every* **NP** language. The problem that Peikert and Vaikuntanathan consider is GapSVP whereas the problem that we consider is the closely related dBDD problem. While BDD is known to be no harder than GapSVP [LM09] (and the same can be shown for dBDD, see Proposition 1), these results are shown by *Cook* reductions and so a NIZK for one problem does not necessarily yield a NIZK for the other. In particular, we do not know how to extend Theorem 1 to hold with respect to GapSVP.

Tradeoff Between the Modulus and Gap. The tradeoff between α and γ and the LWE parameters is quantified precisely in the technical sections (see Theorem 2). Roughly speaking, we need both α and γ to be small relative to $1/\beta$, where β is the magnitude of the LWE error divided by the LWE modulus q. This tradeoff allows us to obtain NIZK proof systems for **NP** from a variety of parameter regimes. In particular, given a NIZK proof system for $\mathsf{dBDD}_{\alpha,\gamma}$ where α and γ are polynomial in the security parameter, we can instantiate Theorem 1 even assuming LWE with a polynomial-size modulus. On the other hand, it suffices to have a NIZK for $\mathsf{dBDD}_{\alpha,\gamma}$ with respect to a super-polynomial or even subexponential α or γ, assuming LWE with a super-polynomial or subexponential modulus.

Furthermore, we emphasize that it suffices for us that $\mathsf{dBDD}_{\alpha,\gamma}$ has a non-interactive *computational* zero-knowledge proof-system under the LWE assumption. However, it is entirely plausible that $\mathsf{dBDD}_{\alpha,\gamma}$ has an (unconditional) non-interactive *statistical* zero-knowledge proof system (NISZK).

1.2 Related Works

Non-Interactive Zero-Knowledge. Non-interactive zero-knowledge proofs were first introduced by Blum, Feldman and Micali [BFM88], who also constructed a NIZK proof system for all of **NP** based on the Quadratic Residuocity assumption. Later work by Feige, Lapidot and Shamir [FLS99] gave a construction under (an idealized version of) trapdoor permutations. Together with additional contributions of Bellare and Yung [BY96] and Goldreich [Gol11], this yields NIZK proofs for **NP** based on factoring (using a variant of Rabin's [Rab79] trapdoor permutation collection).

Groth, Ostrovsky and Sahai [GOS12] construct a more efficient general purpose NIZK proof-system based on hardness assumptions on groups equipped with bilinear maps. Groth and Sahai [GS08] also construct a NIZK proof system for *specific problems* related to such bilinear groups. Groth [Gro10] constructs highly efficient NIZK proofs assuming certain "knowledge of exponent" assumptions (which in particular are not falsifiable, in the sense of [Nao03]). More recently, constructions of NIZK arguments and proofs based on indistinguishability obfuscation were given by Sahai and Waters [SW14] and Bitansky and Paneth [BP15].

Another method for constructing non-interactive zero-knowledge proofs is via the *Fiat-Shamir* heuristic [FS86], for reducing interaction in (public-coin) interactive proofs. Loosely speaking, the Fiat-Shamir heuristic uses a cryptographic hash-function to compute the verifier's messages, and the resulting protocol is known to be secure in the random-oracle model [BR93]. However, replacing the random oracle with a concrete hash function may lead to an insecure protocol [CGH04,GK03], and so it is highly desirable to construct NIZK protocols whose security does not depend on random oracles. In recent works, Kalai *et al.* [KRR17] and Canetti *et al.* [CCRR18] construct hash functions for which the Fiat-Shamir heuristic is sound when applied to interactive *proofs* (i.e., with statistical soundness). However, they use very strong assumptions such as the existence of encryption schemes in which the success probability of a key-dependent message (KDM) key recovery attack succeeds only with *exponentially* small probability.

As mentioned above, Peikert and Vaikuntanathan [PV08] conjecture that a NIZK proof-system for GapSVP would suffice to obtain NIZK for all of **NP** based on LWE. [PV08] also suggest that one approach to proving this conjecture is to translate the prior approach of Blum *et al.* [BDSMP91], which referred to the quadratic residuosity problem, to lattices. Our approach differs from that suggested by [PV08] and is more similar to the [FLS99] paradigm.

Recently, Kim and Wu [KW18] showed a construction of multi-theorem NIZK argument for NP from standard lattice assumptions in the preprocessing model. In the preprocessing multi-theorem model, a trusted setup algorithm produces proving and verification keys, which are reusable for an unbounded number of theorems.

Zero-Knowledge Proofs for Specific Lattice Problems. Highly relevant to our assumption of a NIZK proof system for $\mathsf{dBDD}_{\alpha,\gamma}$ are several works on zero-knowledge of lattice problems. Goldreich and Goldwasser [GG00] show that the *complement* of GapSVP_γ and GapCVP_γ, with parameter $\gamma = \Theta(\sqrt{n}/\log n)$, has an honest-verifier SZK protocol. Combined with results on the structure of SZK (see [Vad99]), this implies that GapSVP_γ and GapCVP_γ themselves are in SZK. Subsequently, Micciancio and Vadhan [MV03] show that GapSVP_γ and GapCVP_γ are in SZK for the same approximation factor even with an efficient prover (given the shortest or closest lattice point, resp., as an auxiliary input). Building on the protocol of [MV03], Goldwasser and Kharchenko [GK05] use the connection between Atjai-Dwork ciphertexts and GapCVP to construct a proof of plaintext knowledge.

Peikert and Vaikuntanathan [PV08] construct *non-interactive* statistical zero-knowledge (NISZK) protocols for a variety of lattice problems and in particular leave the question of whether GapSVP_γ has a NISZK proof system as an open problem. Most recently, Alamati *et al.* [APSD17] construct NISZK and SZK protocols for approximating the smoothing parameter of a lattice.

Lastly, we mention that starting with the work of Stern *et al.* [Ste96], several works [KTX08,Lyu08,LNSW13,LLM+16,dPL17] have constructed zero-knowledge proofs for lattice problems in the context of identification schemes.

1.3 Technical Overview

Let $L \in \mathbf{NP}$ be an arbitrary **NP** language. Our goal is to construct a NIZK proof system for L. The starting point for our construction is an (unconditional) NIZK proof system for L in the *hidden-bits model*, a framework introduced by Feige *et al.* [FLS99] and made explicit by Goldreich [Gol01]. In the hidden-bits model, the prover P has access to a string of uniformly random bits $r \in \{0,1\}^N$. Given the input x and a witness w, the prover can decide to reveal some subset

$I \subset [N]$ of the bits to the verifier, and in addition sends a proof-string π. The verifier, given only the input x, the *revealed* bits r_I, and the proof π, decides whether $x \in L$. Note that the unrevealed bits remain entirely hidden from the verifier. A hidden-bits proof is *zero-knowledge* if there exists a simulator S that generates a view that is indistinguishable from that of the verifier (including in particular the revealed bits r_I).

Feige *et al.* [FLS99] show that every **NP** language has a NIZK proof system in the hidden bits model. Furthermore, they show how to implement the hidden bits model, in a computational sense, using *(doubly enhanced) trapdoor permutations,*[2] thereby obtaining a NIZK proof system for **NP** under the same assumption.

Following Goldreich's presentation, we shall also aim to enforce the hidden-bits model using cryptography. In contrast to [FLS99, Gol01], however, rather than using trapdoor permutations, we shall use an encryption scheme that satisfies some strong yet natural properties. The main technical challenge will be in constructing an LWE-based encryption scheme that satisfies these properties.

We begin by describing the two most intuitive properties that we would like from our public-key encryption scheme (G, E, D).

1. **Oblivious Sampling of Ciphertexts:** Firstly, we require the ability to sample ciphertexts while remaining entirely oblivious to the underlying messages. More precisely, we assume that there exists an algorithm Sample that, given a public key pk, samples a random ciphertext $c \leftarrow \mathsf{Sample}(\mathsf{pk})$ such that the plaintext value $\sigma = D_{\mathsf{sk}}(c)$ is hidden, *even given the random coins used to sample c.*[3] Encryption schemes that have oblivious ciphertext sampling or OCS procedures are known in the literature (see, e.g., [GKM+00, GR13]).
2. **NIZK proof for Plaintext Value:** Secondly, we require a NIZK proof for a specific task, namely proving that a given ciphertext $c = E_{\mathsf{pk}}(\sigma)$ is an encryption of the bit σ (with respect to the public-key pk). Note that this is indeed an **NP** task, since the secret key sk is a witness to the fact that c is an encryption of σ.[4] In particular, we require that the honest prover strategy can be implemented efficiently given access to this witness (i.e., the secret key sk).

With these two ingredients in hand we can describe the high-level strategy for implementing the hidden-bits model. The idea is that the common random string will contain N sequences $\rho_1, \ldots, \rho_N$ of random coins for the OCS procedure. Our NIZK prover chooses a public-key/secret-key pair $(\mathsf{pk}, \mathsf{sk})$ and generates the ciphertexts $c_1, \ldots, c_N$, where $c_i = \mathsf{Sample}(\mathsf{pk}; \rho_i)$ (i.e., an obliviously sampled ciphertext with respect to the public key pk and randomness ρ_i).

[2] *Doubly enhanced* trapdoor permutations were actually introduced in [Gol11] (with the motivation of implementing the hidden-bits model). See further discussion in [GR13, CL17].

[3] In particular, the naive algorithm that chooses at random $b \in \{0, 1\}$ and outputs $E_{\mathsf{pk}}(b)$ is *not* oblivious since its random coins fully reveal b.

[4] For simplicity, we focus for now on schemes with perfect correctness.

The prover further computes the corresponding plaintext bits $\sigma_1, \ldots, \sigma_N$, where $\sigma_i = \mathsf{Dec}_{\mathsf{sk}}(c_i)$ (which it can compute efficiently, since it knows the secret key sk). The prover now runs the hidden-bits prover with respect to the random bit sequence $(\sigma_1, \ldots, \sigma_N)$ and obtains in return a subset $I \subseteq [N]$ of coordinates and a proof-string π. To reveal the coordinates $(\sigma_i)_{i \in I}$, we use the second ingredient: our NIZK proof for proving the plaintext value of the ciphertexts $(c_i)_{i \in I}$. Intuitively, the OCS guarantee allows the other bits $(\sigma_i)_{i \notin I}$ to remain hidden.

Certifying Public Keys. An issue that we run into when trying to implement the blueprint above is that a cheating prover may choose to specify a public key pk that is not honestly generated. Given such a key, it is not clear a priori that the prover cannot control the distribution of the hidden bits, or even equivocate by being able to claim that a single ciphertext c_i is both an encryption of the bit 0 and an encryption of the bit 1. This leads to actual attacks that entirely break the soundness of the NIZK proof system.

A closely related issue actually affects the [FLS99] NIZK construction (based on doubly enhanced trapdoor permutations) and was pointed out by Bellare and Yung [BY96].[5] More specifically, in the [FLS99] protocol the prover needs to specify the index of a permutation (which is analogous to the public key in our setting). However, [BY96] observed that if the prover specifies a function that is *not* a permutation, then it can violate soundness. They resolved this issue by constructing a NIZK proof system for proving that the index indeed specifies a permutation[6].

We follow the [BY96] approach by requiring conditions (1) and (2) above, as well as a NIZK proof for certifying public keys. Thus, our NIZK prover also supplies a NIZK proof that the public key that it provides is valid.

Instantiating our Approach with LWE. So far the approach outlined is basically the [FLS99] implementation of the hidden bits model (where we replace the trapdoor permutations with a suitable encryption scheme). However, when trying to instantiate it using LWE, we encounter significant technical challenges.

For our encryption scheme, we will use Regev's [Reg09] scheme which uses n-dimensional vectors over the integer ring $\mathbb{Z}_q$. The public key in this scheme consists of (1) a matrix $\mathbf{A} \leftarrow \mathbb{Z}_q^{n \times m}$, where $m = \Theta(n \cdot \log(q))$, and (2) a vector $\mathbf{b}^T = \mathbf{s}^T \cdot \mathbf{A} + \mathbf{e}^T$, where $\mathbf{s} \leftarrow \mathbb{Z}_q^n$ is the secret key, and $\mathbf{e}$ is drawn from an n-dimensional discrete Gaussian.

To instantiate the approach outlined above we require three procedures: (1) an oblivious ciphertext sampler (OCS), (2) a NIZK proof system for plaintext values, and (3) a NIZK proof system for certifying public keys. We discuss these three requirements in increasing order of complexity.

[5] Further related issues were recently uncovered by Canetti and Lichtenberg [CL17].

[6] Actually, the [BY96] protocol only certifies that the index specifies a function that is *close* to a permutation (i.e., they provide a *non-interactive* zero-knowledge proof of proximity, a notion recently formalized by Berman *et al.* [BRV17]) which suffices in this context.

NIZK *proof for Validating Public Keys.* Recall that a public key in this encryption scheme is of the form $(\mathbf{A}, \mathbf{b}) \in \mathbb{Z}_q^{n \times m} \times \mathbb{Z}_q^m$, where $\mathbf{b}^T = \mathbf{s}^T \cdot \mathbf{A} + \mathbf{e}^T$ for error vector $\mathbf{e} \in \mathbb{Z}_q^m$ drawn from a discrete Gaussian and in particular having bounded entries (with all but negligible probability). To validate the public key we shall construct a NIZK proof system that proves that for the input public key $(\mathbf{A}, \mathbf{b})$, there exists a vector $\mathbf{s} \in \mathbb{Z}_q^n$ such that $\mathbf{s}^T \cdot \mathbf{A}$ is very close to $\mathbf{b}^T$[7].

Producing such a NIZK proof system is where we need (for the first time) our additional assumption that dBDD has a NIZK proof-system. Indeed, proving that there exists $\mathbf{s} \in \mathbb{Z}_q^n$ such that $\mathbf{s}^T \cdot \mathbf{A}$ is very close to $\mathbf{b}^T$ is a dBDD instance: we must show that the distance of the vector $\mathbf{b}$ from the lattice spanned by the rows of $\mathbf{A}$ is a lot smaller than the length of the shortest non-zero vector of this lattice. We note that since the matrix $\mathbf{A}$ is random (it will part of the CRS), we know that (with very high probability) the length of the shortest non-zero vector is large.

NIZK *proof for Plaintext Value.* The second procedure that we need is a NIZK proof-system that certifies that a given ciphertext encrypts a bit σ. To see how we obtain this, we first need to recall the encryption procedure in Regev's [Reg09] scheme. To encrypt a bit $\sigma \in \{0,1\}$, one selects at random $\mathbf{r} \leftarrow \{0,1\}^m$ and outputs the ciphertext $(\mathbf{c}, \omega)$, where $\mathbf{c} = \mathbf{A} \cdot \mathbf{r}$ and $\omega = \mathbf{b}^T \cdot \mathbf{r} + \sigma \cdot \lfloor \frac{q}{2} \rfloor$.

Thus, given an alleged public key $(\mathbf{A}, \mathbf{b}) \in \mathbb{Z}_q^{n \times m} \times \mathbb{Z}_q^m$ and ciphertext $(\mathbf{c}, \omega) \in \mathbb{Z}_q^n \times \mathbb{Z}_q$, we basically want to ensure that there exists a vector $\mathbf{s} \in \mathbb{Z}_q^n$ such that $\mathbf{b}^T \approx \mathbf{s}^T \cdot \mathbf{A}$ and $\omega + \sigma \cdot \lfloor \frac{q}{2} \rfloor \approx \mathbf{s}^T \cdot \mathbf{c}$, where $\sigma \in \{0,1\}$ is the alleged plaintext value. Put differently, we want to ensure that the vector $\left[\mathbf{b}, (\omega + \sigma \cdot \lfloor \frac{q}{2} \rfloor)\right]$ is *close* to the lattice spanned by the rows of $[\mathbf{A}, \mathbf{c}]$. Thus, this problem can also be reduced to an instance of dBDD.

Oblivious Sampling of Ciphertexts. The last ingredient that we need is a procedure for obliviously sampling ciphertexts in Regev's encryption scheme. This is the main technical challenge in our construction.

A first idea for such an OCS procedure is simply to generate a random pair $(\mathbf{c}, \omega)$, where $\mathbf{c} \leftarrow \mathbb{Z}_q^n$ and $\omega \leftarrow \mathbb{Z}_q$. Intuitively, this pair corresponds to a high noise encryption of a random bit. The problem though is precisely the fact that $(\mathbf{c}, \omega)$ is a *high noise* ciphertext. That is, $\mathbf{s}^T \cdot \mathbf{c} - \omega$ will be close to neither 0 nor $\lfloor q/2 \rfloor$. In particular, the above NIZK proof for certifying plaintext values only works for *low noise* ciphertexts.

This issue turns out to be a key one which we do not know how to handle directly. Instead, we shall bypass it by introducing and considering a generalization of OCS in which the (untrusted) prover is allowed to assist the verifier to perform the sampling. We refer to this procedure (or rather protocol) as a

[7] Actually, it is important for us to also establish that $\mathbf{s}$ is *unique*. We enforce this by having the matrix $\mathbf{A}$ be specified as part of the CRS (rather than by the prover). Indeed, it is not too difficult to show that a lattice spanned by a *random* matrix $\mathbf{A}$ does not have short vectors and therefore $\mathbf{b}$ cannot be close to two different lattice points.

prover-assisted oblivious ciphertext sampler (POCS). Thus, a POCS is a protocol between a sampler S, which is given the secret key (and will be run by the prover in our NIZK proof), and a checker C which is given the public key (and will be run by the verifier). The common input to the protocol is a *random* string ρ. The sampler basically generates a sampled ciphertext c and sends it to the checker, who runs some consistency checks. If the sampler behaves honestly and ρ is sampled randomly, then the sampled ciphertext c should correspond to an encryption of a random bit σ and the checker's validation process should pass. Furthermore, the protocol should satisfy the following (loosely stated) requirements:

- **(Computational) Hiding:** The value $\sigma = \mathsf{Dec}_{\mathsf{sk}}(c)$ is computationally hidden from the checker. That is, it is computationally infeasible to predict the value of σ from c and pk, even given the random coins ρ.
- **(Statistical) Binding:** For any value of ρ there exists a *unique* value σ such that *for every* (possibly cheating) sampler strategy S^*, with high probability either the checker rejects or the generated ciphertext c corresponds to an encryption of σ.

With some care, such a POCS procedure can replace the OCS procedure (which did not use a prover) in our original outline. The key step therefore is constructing a POCS procedure for Regev's encryption scheme, which we describe next.

A POCS *Procedure for Regev's Encryption Scheme.* Fix a public key $(\mathbf{A}, \mathbf{b})$ and let $\mathbf{s}$ be the corresponding secret key. The random input string for our POCS procedure consists of a vector $\boldsymbol{\rho} \in \mathbb{Z}_q^n$ and a value $\tau \in \mathbb{Z}_q$. The pair $(\boldsymbol{\rho}, \tau)$ should be thought of as a (high noise) Regev encryption. Denote by $e = \tau - \mathbf{s}^T \cdot \boldsymbol{\rho}$ the noise in this ciphertext.

As discussed above, since $(\boldsymbol{\rho}, \tau)$ corresponds to a high noise ciphertext, we cannot have the sampler just output it as is. Rather we will have the sampler output a value $\tau' = \mathbf{s}^T \cdot \boldsymbol{\rho} + e' + \sigma' \cdot \lfloor \frac{q}{2} \rfloor$, where e' is drawn from the same noise distribution as fresh encryptions (i.e., low noise), and the value of the encrypted bit σ' will be specified next. Observe that $(\boldsymbol{\rho}, \tau')$ corresponds to a *fresh* encryption of σ', and so we will need to make sure that σ' is random and that the hiding and binding properties hold.

To do so, we will define σ' as follows: If $|e' - e| \leq q/4$, then set $\sigma' = 0$, and otherwise set $\sigma' = 1$. Observe that in either case it must be that

$$\left| e' + \sigma' \cdot \left\lfloor \frac{q}{2} \right\rfloor - e \right| \leq q/4 . \tag{1}$$

We would like our checker to enforce that Eq. (1) holds. Initially this seems problematic since our checker has access to none of e, e', and σ'. However, the checker does have access to τ and τ', and it holds that:

$$|\tau' - \tau| = \left| \mathbf{s}^T \cdot \boldsymbol{\rho} + e' + \sigma' \cdot \left\lfloor \frac{q}{2} \right\rfloor - \mathbf{s}^T \cdot \boldsymbol{\rho} - e \right| = \left| e' + \sigma' \cdot \left\lfloor \frac{q}{2} \right\rfloor - e \right|$$

and so we simply have our checker verify that $|\tau' - \tau| \leq q/4$.

It is not too hard to see that σ' is an unbiased bit in this construction. Moreover, it is unbiased even conditioned on $\boldsymbol{\rho}$ (since its value is entirely undetermined until τ is chosen). Thus, the checker only sees a fresh encryption of a random bit σ' which, by the hardness of LWE, hides the value of σ'.

To see that the scheme is binding, observe that for most choices of $\boldsymbol{\rho}$ and τ the (cheating) sampler cannot equivocate to two values τ' and τ'' which correspond to different plaintext bits, as long as both have small noise. Hence, the sampler *cannot* equivocate to two different valid ciphertexts. This concludes the overview of our construction.

1.4 Organization

In Sect. 2 we provide definitions and notation used throughout this work (defining in particular NIZK and the hidden bits model, as well as giving sufficient background on lattices). In Sect. 3 we formalize our abstraction of "prover-assisted oblivious ciphertext sampling" (POCS) and show that encryption schemes admitting such a procedure (as well as some specific NIZK proof systems) imply NIZKs for **NP**. Finally, in Sect. 4 we show how to instantiate the foregoing framework using LWE.

2 Preliminaries

We follow the notation and definitions as in [Gol01].

For a distribution μ, we use $x \leftarrow \mu$ to denote that x is sampled from the distribution μ, and for a set S we use $x \leftarrow S$ to denote that x is sampled uniformly at random from the set S. We use $X \overset{c}{\approx} Y$, $X \overset{s}{\approx} Y$ and $X \equiv Y$ to denote that the distributions X and Y are computationally indistinguishable, statistically close and identically distributed, respectively (where in the case of computational indistinguishability we actually refer to ensembles of distributions parameterized by a security parameter).

2.1 Public-Key Encryption with Public Randomness

For simplicity we restrict our attention to bit-encryption schemes (where messages consist of single bits). We will define a variant of public-key encryption in which all algorithms, including the adversary, have access to some public randomness. We emphasize that this public randomness is an additional input to the key generation algorithm and is revealed also to the adversary. In addition to the public randomness, the key generation algorithm is allowed to toss additional *private* random coins that are not revealed. To avoid cluttering notation, we will assume that the public key includes the public randomness.

Definition 1 (Public-Key Encryption with Public Randomness). *A* public-key encryption scheme with public randomness *is a triple of PPT algorithms* (Gen, Enc, Dec) *such that:*

1. *The* key-generation algorithm $\mathsf{Gen}(1^\kappa, \rho_{\mathsf{pk}})$ *on input* public randomness ρ_{pk} *(and while tossing additional private random coins) outputs a pair of keys* $(\mathsf{pk}, \mathsf{sk})$*, where* pk *includes* ρ_{pk}.
2. *The* encryption algorithm $\mathsf{Enc}(\mathsf{pk}, \sigma)$*, where* $\sigma \in \{0,1\}$*, outputs a ciphertext* c*. We denote this output by* $c = \mathsf{Enc}_{\mathsf{pk}}(\sigma)$.
3. *The deterministic* decryption algorithm $\mathsf{Dec}(\mathsf{sk}, c)$ *outputs a message* σ'*. We denote this output by* $\sigma' = \mathsf{Dec}_{\mathsf{sk}}(c)$.

We require that for every $\sigma \in \{0,1\}$*, except with negligible probability over the public randomness* ρ_{pk}*, the keys* $(\mathsf{pk}, \mathsf{sk}) \leftarrow \mathsf{Gen}(1^\kappa, \rho_{\mathsf{pk}})$ *and the randomness of the encryption scheme, we have that* $\mathsf{Dec}_{\mathsf{sk}}(\mathsf{Enc}_{\mathsf{pk}}(\sigma)) = \sigma$.

Semantic security [GM84] is defined as follows:

Definition 2 (Semantic Security with Public Randomness). *A public-key encryption scheme with public randomness is* semantically secure *if the distributions* $(\mathsf{pk}, E_{\mathsf{pk}}(0))$ *and* $(\mathsf{pk}, E_{\mathsf{pk}}(1))$ *are computationally indistinguishable, where* $\rho_{\mathsf{pk}} \leftarrow \{0,1\}^{\mathrm{poly}(\kappa)}$ *and* $(\mathsf{pk}, \mathsf{sk}) \leftarrow \mathsf{Gen}(1^\kappa, \rho_{\mathsf{pk}})$.

Note that, clearly, any public-key encryption scheme is also a public-key scheme with public randomness, where ρ_{pk} is null. Nevertheless, this notion will be useful in our constructions.

2.2 Non-Interactive Zero-Knowledge Proofs

Non-interactive Zero-knowledge Proofs are a fundamental cryptographic primitive introduced by Blum *et al.* [BFM88].

Definition 3 (NIZK). *A* non-interactive (computational) zero-knowledge proof system *(*NIZK*) for a language* L *is a pair of probabilistic polynomial-time algorithms* (P, V) *such that:*

- **Completeness:** *For every* $x \in L$ *and witness* w *for* x*, we have*

$$\Pr_R\left[V(x, R, P(x, R, w)) = 1\right] > 1 - \mathrm{negl}(|x|)$$

  where $R \leftarrow \{0,1\}^{\mathrm{poly}(|x|)}$*. If the foregoing condition holds with probability* 1*, then we say that the* NIZK *has* perfect completeness.
- **Soundness:** *For every* $x \notin L$ *and every (possibly inefficient) cheating prover* P^**, we have*

$$\Pr_R\left[V(x, R, P^*(x, R)) = 1\right] < \mathrm{negl}(|x|)$$

  where $R \leftarrow \{0,1\}^{\mathrm{poly}(|x|)}$.
- **Zero-Knowledge:** *There exists a probabilistic polynomial-time simulator* S *such that the ensembles* $\{(x, R, P(x, R, w))\}_{x \in L}$ *and* $\{S(x)\}_{x \in L}$ *are computationally indistinguishable, where* $R \leftarrow \{0,1\}^{\mathrm{poly}(|x|)}$.

The random input R *received by both* P *and* V *is referred to as the* common random string *or* CRS.

We extend the definition of NIZK to *promise problems* in the natural way.

We can further define a NIZK proof system with adaptive soundness by allowing the cheating prover to specify the input x as well as the purported witness w.

Definition 4 (Adaptive Soundness for NIZK). *A* NIZK *proof system* (P, V) *is* adaptively sound *if it satisfies the following property. For any* $\kappa \in \mathbb{N}$ *and any (possibly inefficient) cheating prover* P^* *producing output* $(x, w) \in \{0,1\}^\kappa$, *we have*

$$\Pr_{\substack{R, \\ (x,w) \leftarrow P^*(1^\kappa, R)}} [V(x, R, w) = 1 \text{ and } x \notin L] < \text{negl}(\kappa) .$$

Remark 1 (Achieving Adaptive Soundness). By standard amplification techniques, any ordinary NIZK proof may be transformed into one which is adaptively sound (see, e.g. [Gol01, Chapter 4]).

The Hidden Bits Model. The hidden-bits model was introduced by Goldreich [Gol01, Section 4.10.2] as an appealing abstraction of the NIZK proof system of Feige, Lapidot and Shamir [FLS99].

Definition 5 (Hidden Bits Proof-System). *A* hidden-bits proof system *for a language* L *is a pair of PPT algorithms* (P, V) *such that the following conditions hold:*

- *(Completeness) For all* $x \in L$ *and witnesses* w *for* x,
$$\Pr[V(x, R_I, I, \pi) = 1] > 1 - \text{negl}(|x|) ,$$
where R *is a uniformly random string of bits (of length* $\text{poly}(|x|)$*),* $(I, \pi) \leftarrow P(x, R, w)$ *for* I *a subset of the indices of* R, *and* R_I *is the substring of* R *corresponding to the indices in* I.
- *(Soundness) For all* $x \notin L$ *and any computationally unbounded cheating prover* P^*, *we have*
$$\Pr[V(x, R_I, I, \pi) = 1] < \text{negl}(|x|)$$
where R *again is a uniformly random string of bits and* $(I, \pi) \leftarrow P^*(x, R)$.
- *(Zero-knowledge) There exists a probabilistic polynomial-time simulator* S *such that the ensembles* $\{(x, R_I, I, \pi)\}_{x \in L}$ *and* $\{S(x)\}_{x \in L}$ *are computationally indistinguishable, where* R *is a uniformly random string of bits and* $(I, \pi) \leftarrow P(x, R)$.

Feige et al. [FLS99] and Goldreich [Gol01] showed that *every* **NP** language has a hidden-bits proof system *unconditionally* (where the hidden-bits string is of polynomial length and the prover strategy is implemented efficiently given the **NP** witness).

Lemma 1 (See [Gol01, Section 4.10.2]). *For any language* $L \in$ **NP**, *there exists a zero-knowledge hidden-bits proof system for* L. *Moreover, the proof-system has perfect completeness.*

2.3 Lattices and Learning with Errors

In this section we give some basic definitions and lemmata about lattices and the Learning With Errors (LWE) assumption.

Standard Notation. We let the elements of the ring $\mathbb{Z}_q$ be identified with the representatives $\{-\lfloor\frac{q}{2}\rfloor,\ldots,\lceil\frac{q}{2}\rceil-1\}$.

We denote by $[x, y]$ the concatenation of vectors or matrices. For example, if $\mathbf{x} \in \mathbb{Z}_q^n$ and $y \in \mathbb{Z}_q$, then $[\mathbf{x}, y]$ is a vector in $\mathbb{Z}_q^{n+1}$, whose first n components correspond to the n components of $\mathbf{x}$ and whose last component is y. Similarly, if $\mathbf{X} \in \mathbb{Z}_q^{n\times m}$ and $\mathbf{y} \in \mathbb{Z}_q^n$, then $[\mathbf{X}, \mathbf{y}]$ is a matrix in $\mathbb{Z}_q^{n\times(m+1)}$, whose last column is $\mathbf{y}$.

For $x \in \mathbb{Z}_q$, we denote by $|x|$ the value in $[0, \lfloor\frac{q}{2}\rfloor]$ such that $|x| = x$ if $x < q/2$ and $|x| = q - x$ otherwise. Namely, $|x|$ is the distance from 0 in $\mathbb{Z}_q$. Similarly, for $\mathbf{x} \in \mathbb{Z}_q^n$ we denote by $\|\mathbf{x}\|$ the ℓ_2 norm, namely $\|\mathbf{x}\| = \sqrt{\sum |x_i|^2}$, where x_i are the coordinates of $\mathbf{x}$ and $|\cdot|$ is as defined above.

Lastly, we denote by $\lfloor\cdot\rceil_q : \mathbb{Z}_q \to \{0, 1\}$ the function:

$$\lfloor x\rceil_q = \begin{cases} 0 & \text{if } x \in [-\lfloor q/4\rfloor, \lceil q/4\rceil] \\ 1 & \text{otherwise} \end{cases}.$$

Lattices. A lattice Λ is an additive subgroup of $\mathbb{Z}^m$. Every lattice is finitely generated as all integer linear combinations of a set of *linearly independent row vectors*[8] $\mathbf{B}$. We call this set a basis for the lattice and its cardinality the rank of the lattice. We denote by $\Lambda(\mathbf{A})$ the lattice that is generated by the *rows* of $\mathbf{A}$ (which might or might not be a basis) and by $\mathbf{B}(\mathbf{A})$ a basis of the lattice $\Lambda(\mathbf{A})$. We denote by $\lambda_1(\Lambda)$ the length of the shortest nonzero lattice vector:

$$\lambda_1(\Lambda) = \min_{\mathbf{x}\in\Lambda\setminus\{\mathbf{0}\}} \|\mathbf{x}\|.$$

We note the following standard lemma about lattice bases.

Lemma 2. *Let* $\mathbf{A} \in \mathbb{Z}^{n\times m}$ *with* $m \geq n$, *there is an efficient algorithm to compute* $\mathbf{B}(\mathbf{A})$. *Namely, given a generating set of a lattice, we can efficiently compute a basis for the same lattice.*

A special family of lattices with numerous applications in cryptographic is the family of q-ary lattices.

Definition 6. *A lattice* Λ *is called a* q-ary lattice *if* $q\mathbb{Z}^m \subseteq \Lambda$. *Equivalently,* Λ *is* q*-ary if* $\mathbf{x} \in \Lambda$ *if and only if* $(\mathbf{x} \bmod q) \in \Lambda$.

We denote a q-ary lattice by Λ_q. More specifically, if $\mathbf{A} \in \mathbb{Z}_q^{n\times m}$ then we denote by $\Lambda_q(\mathbf{A})$ the lattice:

$$\Lambda_q(\mathbf{A}) = \{\mathbf{y} \in \mathbb{Z}^m : \exists \mathbf{s} \in \mathbb{Z}_q^n \text{ s.t. } \mathbf{y}^T = \mathbf{s}^T\mathbf{A}\} + q\mathbb{Z}^m.$$

[8] In the literature, typically $\mathbf{B}$ is defined as a set of column vectors. However, for our applications it is more convenient to use row vectors.

Decisional Bounded Distance Decoding Problem. We define some well-studied lattice problems as well as the *decisional Bounded Distance Decoding* (dBDD) variant which we use extensively in this work. We also present a reduction from dBDD to the GapSVP problem, showing that dBDD is (up to polynomial loss in the parameters) at most as hard as GapSVP.

Definition 7. *For a given parameter* $\gamma > 1$, *the promise problem* $\mathsf{GapSVP}_\gamma = (\mathsf{YES}, \mathsf{NO})$ *with input a basis* $\mathbf{B} \in \mathbb{Z}^{n \times m}$ *and parameter* $r > 0$ *is defined as:*

- $(B, r) \in \mathsf{YES}$ *if* $\lambda_1(\Lambda(\mathbf{B})) < r$, *and*
- $(B, r) \in \mathsf{NO}$ *if* $\lambda_1(\Lambda(\mathbf{B})) > \gamma r$.

Definition 8. *For a given parameter* $\alpha \geq 1$, *the promise search problem* BDD_α *with input a basis* $\mathbf{B} \in \mathbb{Z}^{n \times m}$, *a target vector* $\mathbf{t} \in \mathbb{R}^m$ *such that* $\mathrm{dist}(\Lambda(\mathbf{B}), \mathbf{t}) < \frac{\lambda_1(\mathbf{B})}{\alpha}$ *outputs a lattice vector* $\mathbf{v} \in \Lambda(\mathbf{B})$ *such that* $\|\mathbf{t} - \mathbf{v}\| = \mathrm{dist}(\Lambda(\mathbf{B}), \mathbf{t})$.

We define a decisional version of the BDD_α problem.

Definition 9. *For two given parameters* $\alpha \geq 1$ *and* $\gamma > 1$, *the promise problem* $\mathsf{dBDD}_{\alpha,\gamma} = (\mathsf{YES}, \mathsf{NO})$ *with input a basis* $\mathbf{B} \in \mathbb{Z}^{n \times m}$ *and a target vector* $\mathbf{t} \in \mathbb{R}^m$ *is defined as:*

- $(\mathbf{B}, \mathbf{t}) \in \mathsf{YES}$ *if* $\mathrm{dist}(\mathbf{t}, \Lambda(\mathbf{B})) \leq \frac{\lambda_1(\Lambda(\mathbf{B}))}{\alpha}$; *and*
- $(\mathbf{B}, \mathbf{t}) \in \mathsf{NO}$ *if* $\mathrm{dist}(\mathbf{t}, \Lambda(\mathbf{B})) > \gamma \cdot \frac{\lambda_1(\Lambda(\mathbf{B}))}{\alpha}$.

In order to establish the complexity of the dBDD problem, we show that it is at most as hard as the well studied lattice problem GapSVP.

Proposition 1. *The problem* $\mathsf{dBDD}_{\alpha,\gamma}$ *is Cook-reducible to* $\mathsf{GapSVP}_{\min(\sqrt{\gamma}, \alpha/2)}$ *where* γ *and* α *are polynomially-bounded.*

Proof. Let $(\mathbf{B}, \mathbf{t})$ be an input of $\mathsf{dBDD}_{\alpha,\gamma}$. First, using binary search and a $\mathsf{GapSVP}_{\sqrt{\gamma}}$ oracle, we compute an r such that $\frac{\lambda_1(\mathbf{B})}{\sqrt{\gamma}} \leq r \leq \sqrt{\gamma} \cdot \lambda_1(\mathbf{B})$.

From [LM09], BDD_α is reducible to $\mathsf{GapSVP}_{\alpha/2}$ with α polynomially-bounded. Therefore, the $\mathsf{GapSVP}_{\alpha/2}$ oracle returns an alleged closest vector $\mathbf{v}$ to $\mathbf{t}$. If $\mathbf{v} \in \Lambda(\mathbf{B})$ and $\|\mathbf{t} - \mathbf{v}\| \leq \sqrt{\gamma} \cdot \frac{r}{\alpha}$, we output 1. Else, we output 0.

Indeed, if $\mathsf{dBDD}_{\alpha,\gamma}(\mathbf{B}, \mathbf{t}) \in \mathsf{YES}$, then there is a vector $\mathbf{v} \in \Lambda(\mathbf{B})$ such that $\|\mathbf{t} - \mathbf{v}\| \leq \frac{\lambda_1(\mathbf{B})}{\alpha} \leq \sqrt{\gamma} \cdot \frac{r}{\alpha}$ and $\mathsf{GapSVP}_{\alpha/2}$ returns this vector. On the other hand, if $\mathsf{dBDD}_{\alpha,\gamma}(\mathbf{B}, \mathbf{t}) \in \mathsf{NO}$, then for every vector $\mathbf{v} \in \Lambda(\mathbf{B})$ it holds that $\|\mathbf{t} - \mathbf{v}\| > \gamma \cdot \frac{\lambda_1(\mathbf{B})}{\alpha} \geq \sqrt{\gamma} \cdot \frac{r}{\alpha}$, so there is no vector $\mathbf{v}$ for which we output 1.

We remark that even though there is a reduction from dBDD to GapSVP, a NIZK proof system for GapSVP does not automatically imply a NIZK proof system for dBDD since it is a *Cook* reduction (rather than a Karp reduction). In particular, we do not know if a NIZK for GapSVP implies a NIZK for dBDD.

Learning with Errors. We proceed to define the main cryptographic assumption we use: Learning With Errors (LWE). First, we define the (one-dimensional) discrete Gaussian distribution:

Definition 10. *For $q \in \mathbb{N} \setminus \{0\}$ and parameter $\beta > 0$, the* discrete Gaussian probability distribution χ_β *is simply the Gaussian distribution restricted to $\mathbb{Z}_q$:*

$$\chi_\beta(x) \propto \begin{cases} \exp(-\pi|x|^2/(\beta q)^2) & \text{if } x \in [-\lfloor q/2 \rfloor, \lceil q/2 \rceil] \cap \mathbb{Z} \\ 0 & \text{otherwise} \end{cases}$$

With the definition of the Discrete Gaussian distribution in hand, we are ready to define LWE:

Definition 11. *The* (Decisional) Learning With Error (LWE) assumption *with parameters n, q, β, denoted by $\mathsf{LWE}_{n,q,\beta}$, states that:*

$$(\mathbf{A}, \mathbf{b}) \overset{c}{\approx} (\mathbf{A}, \mathbf{r})$$

where $\mathbf{A} \leftarrow \mathbb{Z}_q^{n \times m}$ with $m = \mathrm{poly}(n, \log(q))$, $\mathbf{b}^T = \mathbf{s}^T\mathbf{A} + \mathbf{e}^T$, $\mathbf{s} \leftarrow \mathbb{Z}_q^n$, $\mathbf{e} \leftarrow \chi_\beta^m$ and $\mathbf{r} \leftarrow \mathbb{Z}_q^m$.

We utilize the fact that if $\mathbf{A} \leftarrow \mathbb{Z}_q^{n \times m}$ with m large enough, then there is a *unique* $\mathbf{s}$ such that $\mathbf{b}^T \approx \mathbf{s}^T\mathbf{A}$. The proof of this fact follows from bounding the shortest vector in the lattice and observing that if $\mathbf{s}_1, \mathbf{s}_2$ are such that $\mathbf{s}_1^T\mathbf{A} \approx \mathbf{s}_2^T\mathbf{A}$, then $(\mathbf{s}_1^T - \mathbf{s}_2^T)\mathbf{A} \approx \mathbf{0}$. The following lemma can be shown by a standard argument with a union bound over all nonzero vectors $\mathbf{s} \in \mathbb{Z}_q^n$.

Lemma 3. *Let $n, q \in \mathbb{N}$, and $m \geq 2n\log(q)$. Then*

$$\Pr_{\mathbf{A} \leftarrow \mathbb{Z}_q^{n \times m}} \left[\lambda_1(\Lambda_q(\mathbf{A})) \leq q/4 \right] \leq q^{-n}.$$

3 From Prover-Assisted Oblivious Sampling to NIZKs

In this section we introduce the abstraction of a prover-assisted procedure for oblivious ciphertext sampling (POCS) for a public-key encryption scheme (as outlined in the introduction), and show how to combine this notion with NIZK proofs of the validity of public keys and plaintext values to obtain NIZK proofs for any **NP** language.

3.1 Definitions: Valid Public Keys, Ciphertexts and POCS

The first definition we consider is the notion of a *valid* set $\mathcal{PK}$ of public keys. Intuitively, we would like this set to correspond precisely to public keys in the support of the key-generation algorithm. However, due to specifics of our instantiation with LWE, we need to be more lenient and allow public keys that are not quite in the support of the key-generation algorithm but are nevertheless sufficiently well-formed (e.g., keys with a higher level noise).

Loosely speaking, a *valid* public key pk is associated with two sets $C_{\mathsf{pk}}^{(0)}$ and $C_{\mathsf{pk}}^{(1)}$, which correspond to "valid" ciphertexts with respect to that key of messages 0 and 1, respectively. We first require that honestly sampled public keys be valid. We further require that for all valid public keys (i.e., even those not in the support of the key generation algorithm), the associated sets $C_{\mathsf{pk}}^{(0)}$ and $C_{\mathsf{pk}}^{(1)}$ are disjoint (i.e. no ciphertext is a valid encryption both of 0 and of 1)[9].

Definition 12 (Valid Public Keys). *Let* $(\mathsf{Gen}, \mathsf{Enc}, \mathsf{Dec})$ *be a public-key encryption scheme with public randomness. For a given security parameter* κ*, let* $\mathcal{VPK} = (\mathcal{VPK}_\kappa)_{\kappa \in \mathbb{N}}$ *be an ensemble of sets, where for each* $\kappa \in \mathbb{N}$*, each* $\mathsf{pk} \in \mathcal{VPK}_\kappa$ *is associated with a pair of sets* $\left(C_{\mathsf{pk}}^{(0)}, C_{\mathsf{pk}}^{(1)}\right)$ *and public randomness* ρ_{pk}*. We say that* $\mathcal{VPK}$ *is* valid *if it satisfies the following properties.*

1. *For all* $(\mathsf{pk}, \mathsf{sk}) \in \mathsf{Gen}(1^\kappa, \cdot)$*, we have* $\mathsf{pk} \in \mathcal{VPK}_\kappa$*.*
2. *For every* $b \in \{0, 1\}$ *we have that* $c_b \in C_{\mathsf{pk}}^{(b)}$ *with all but negligible probability over the choice of public randomness* ρ_{pk}*, keys* $(\mathsf{pk}, \mathsf{sk}) \leftarrow \mathsf{Gen}(1^\kappa, \rho_{\mathsf{pk}})$*, and ciphertext* $c_b \leftarrow \mathsf{Enc}_{\mathsf{pk}}(b)$*.*
3. *With all but negligible probability over the public randomness* ρ_{pk}*, for all* $\mathsf{pk} \in \mathcal{VPK}_\kappa$ *with public randomness* ρ_{pk}*, it holds that* $C_{\mathsf{pk}}^{(0)} \cap C_{\mathsf{pk}}^{(1)} = \emptyset$*.*

We next formalize the notion of a *prover-assisted oblivious ciphertext sampler* (POCS). This is an extension of oblivious ciphertext samplers (OCS), which (to the best of our knowledge) were introduced by Gertner *et al.* [GKM+00]. An OCS procedure allows one to sample a ciphertext so that the underlying plaintext remains hidden. In this work we introduce a relaxation of this notion in which the sampling is assisted by an *untrusted* prover.

More specifically, a POCS protocol consists of two procedures, a *sampler* and a *checker*, which both have access to a shared random string ρ. The sampler also receives as input the secret-key of the scheme and generates a ciphertext c. The checker receives c, as well as the random string ρ and the public-key (but not the secret-key) and performs a test to ensure that c encodes an unbiased bit depending on the randomness ρ. Jumping ahead, we remark that the role of the sampler is played by the *prover* in our NIZK, whereas the role of the *checker* is played by the verifier.

We require that the POCS procedure satisfy the following loosely stated properties:

1. For honestly sampled ciphertexts c, the checker should accept with overwhelming probability.
2. Given pk, ρ and an honestly sampled ciphertext c, the corresponding plaintext bit $\mathsf{Dec}_{\mathsf{sk}}(c)$ is computationally hidden.

---

[9] Note that in the actual definition we only require the latter to hold *with high probability over the choice of the public randomness* for every valid public key. The notion of encryption schemes with public randomness is discussed in Sect. 2.1.

3. For a given random string ρ, except with a small probability there should not exist both an encryption c_0 of 0 and an encryption c_1 of 1 that pass the checker's test. Thus, for any given ciphertext (even a maliciously generated one) that passes the test, the corresponding plaintext bit is almost always fully determined.
4. The sampled plaintext bit should be (close to) unbiased. The latter should hold even with respect to a *malicious* sampler. In our actual instantiation of POCS (via LWE, see Sect. 4), the plaintext bit will have a small but noticeable (i.e., inverse polynomial) bias. Thus, our definition of POCS leaves the bias as a parameter, which we denote by ϵ.
5. The procedure satisfies the following "zero-knowledge like" simulation property: given only the public-key pk and plaintext bit σ, it should be possible to generate the distribution (ρ, c) of the sampling procedure, conditioned on $\mathsf{Dec}_{\mathsf{sk}}(c) = \sigma$. This property is captured by the EncryptAndExplain procedure below. In our actual formalization we only require that this property holds in a computational sense (i.e., the simulated distribution should only be computationally indistinguishable from the actual sampling procedure). While a statistical requirement may seem like a more natural choice here, we use a computational notion due to a technical consideration in the LWE instantiation. See Sect. 4.3 for details.

We proceed to the formal definition of a POCS encryption scheme.

Definition 13 (Prover-assisted Oblivious Ciphertext Sampler (POCS)). *For a parameter* $\epsilon = \epsilon(\kappa) \in [0, 1]$, *a* $(1 - \epsilon(\kappa))$*-binding* prover-assisted oblivious ciphertext sampler (POCS), *with respect to a* valid *set of public keys* $\mathcal{VPK} = \{\mathcal{VPK}_\kappa\}_{\kappa\in\mathbb{N}}$ *for an encryption scheme* (Gen, Enc, Dec) *with public randomness, is a triple of PPT algorithms* Sample, Check, *and* EncryptAndExplain *satisfying the following properties:*

- **Complete:**

$$\Pr_{\substack{\rho_{\mathsf{pk}},\rho\leftarrow\{0,1\}^{\mathrm{poly}(\kappa)}\\(\mathsf{pk},\mathsf{sk})\leftarrow\mathsf{Gen}(1^\kappa,\rho_{\mathsf{pk}})}}\left[\mathsf{Check}(\mathsf{pk}, \rho, \mathsf{Sample}(\mathsf{sk}, \rho)) = 1\right] > 1 - \mathrm{negl}(\kappa).$$

- **Unbiased:** *For any* $\kappa \in \mathbb{N}$, $\mathsf{pk} \in \mathcal{VPK}_\kappa$ *and any* $b \in \{0, 1\}$, *we have that:*

$$\Pr_{\rho\leftarrow\{0,1\}^{\mathrm{poly}(\kappa)}}\left[\exists c \in C^{(b)}_{\mathsf{pk}} \text{ such that } \mathsf{Check}(\mathsf{pk}, \rho, c) = 1\right] \geq 1/2 - \mathrm{negl}(\kappa).$$

- **Statistically binding:** *With probability* $1 - \mathrm{negl}(\kappa)$ *over the public randomness* ρ_{pk}, *we have for all* $\mathsf{pk} \in \mathcal{VPK}_\kappa$ *with public randomness* ρ_{pk} *that*

$$\Pr_{\rho\leftarrow\{0,1\}^{\mathrm{poly}(\kappa)}}\left[\exists c_0 \in C^{(0)}_{\mathsf{pk}}, c_1 \in C^{(1)}_{\mathsf{pk}} \text{ s.t. } \begin{array}{l}\mathsf{Check}(\mathsf{pk}, \rho, c_0) = 1 \text{ and}\\ \mathsf{Check}(\mathsf{pk}, \rho, c_1) = 1\end{array}\right] < \epsilon(\kappa).$$

We emphasize that $\epsilon(\kappa)$ *is a parameter and is not necessarily negligible.*

- **Simulatable:** *For every* $N = \text{poly}(\kappa)$ *it holds that:*

$$\left(\mathsf{pk}, (\rho_i)_{i=1}^N, (c_i)_{i=1}^N, (\sigma_i)_{i=1}^N\right) \overset{c}{\approx} \left(\mathsf{pk}, (\rho_i')_{i=1}^N, (c_i')_{i=1}^N, (\sigma_i')_{i=1}^N\right),$$

where $\rho_{\mathsf{pk}} \leftarrow \{0,1\}^{\text{poly}(\kappa)}$, $(\mathsf{pk}, \mathsf{sk}) \leftarrow \mathsf{Gen}(1^\kappa, \rho_{\mathsf{pk}})$, *and for every* $i \in [N]$, *it holds that* $\rho_i \leftarrow \{0,1\}^{\text{poly}(\kappa)}$, $c_i \leftarrow \mathsf{Sample}(\mathsf{sk}, \rho_i)$, *and* $\sigma_i = \mathsf{Dec}_{\mathsf{sk}}(c_i)$, $\sigma_i' \leftarrow \{0,1\}$ *and* $(\rho_i', c_i') \leftarrow \mathsf{EncryptAndExplain}(\mathsf{pk}, \sigma')$.
- **Computationally hiding:** *Let* $\rho_{\mathsf{pk}}, \rho \leftarrow \{0,1\}^{\text{poly}(\kappa)}$, $(\mathsf{pk}, \mathsf{sk}) \leftarrow \mathsf{Gen}(1^\kappa, \rho_{\mathsf{pk}})$, *and* $c \leftarrow \mathsf{Sample}(\mathsf{sk}, \rho)$. *Then, for all probabilistic polynomial-time adversaries* $\mathcal{A}$,

$$\Pr\left[\mathcal{A}(\mathsf{pk}, \rho, c) = \mathsf{Dec}_{\mathsf{sk}}(c)\right] \leq \frac{1}{2} + \text{negl}(\kappa).$$

Remark 2 (Relaxing the Hiding Property). We remark that for our construction of NIZK a weaker hiding property suffices, in which the adversary is only given the random string ρ (but not the ciphertext c). Although this definition is strictly weaker, we find it less natural and choose to define the hiding property as specified above.

We next prove two useful propositions showing that the computational hiding property of the POCS implies a hiding property resembling semantic security for the EncryptAndExplain sampling algorithm. Specifically, we show that the encrypted bit remains hidden given both the ciphertext and the explaining randomness produced by the EncryptAndExplain algorithm. The intuition is analogous to the usage of the *double enhancement* property of trapdoor permutations in the construction of NIZKs (see, e.g., [GR13]).

Proposition 2. *Suppose* (Gen, Enc, Dec) *has a* $(1-\epsilon)$*-binding* POCS *with respect to an ensemble of valid public keys* $\mathcal{VPK}$. *Then, for all probabilistic polynomial-time adversaries* $\mathcal{A}$,

$$\Pr\left[\mathcal{A}(\mathsf{pk}, \rho, c) = \sigma\right] \leq \frac{1}{2} + \text{negl}(\kappa),$$

where $\rho_{\mathsf{pk}}, \rho \leftarrow \{0,1\}^{\text{poly}(\kappa)}$, $(\mathsf{pk}, \mathsf{sk}) \leftarrow \mathsf{Gen}(1^\kappa, \rho_{\mathsf{pk}})$, $\sigma \in \{0,1\}$, *and* $(\rho, c) \leftarrow \mathsf{EncryptAndExplain}(\mathsf{pk}, \sigma)$.

Proof. This follows immediately from the simulatable and computationally hiding properties of the POCS.

Proposition 3. *Suppose* (Gen, Enc, Dec) *has a* $(1-\epsilon)$*-binding* POCS *with respect to an ensemble of public keys* $\mathcal{VPK}$. *It holds that*

$$(\mathsf{pk}, \rho_0, c_0) \overset{c}{\approx} (\mathsf{pk}, \rho_1, c_1),$$

where the public randomness $\rho_{\mathsf{pk}} \leftarrow \{0,1\}^{\text{poly}(\kappa)}$, *the keys* $(\mathsf{pk}, \mathsf{sk}) \leftarrow \mathsf{Gen}(1^\kappa, \rho_{\mathsf{pk}})$, $(\rho_0, c_0) \leftarrow \mathsf{EncryptAndExplain}(\mathsf{pk}, 0)$ *and* $(\rho_1, c_1) \leftarrow \mathsf{EncryptAndExplain}(\mathsf{pk}, 1)$.

Proof. This follows from Proposition 2 by a standard argument, similar to the equivalence of semantic security and indistinguishability of encryptions (see, e.g. [Gol04]).

We now define two promise problems for which we will later assume the existence of suitable NIZKs. The first problem that we consider is that of distinguishing public keys which are in the support of the key-generation algorithm (i.e., were honestly generated) from ones which are invalid (i.e., not in the set of valid public keys).

Let $(\mathsf{Gen}, \mathsf{Enc}, \mathsf{Dec})$ be a public-key encryption scheme and let us denote by $\mathcal{VPK}$ an ensemble of valid public-keys. We define the promise problem $\mathsf{GoodPK} = (\mathsf{GoodPK}_{\mathsf{Yes}}, \mathsf{GoodPK}_{\mathsf{No}})$ where:

$$\mathsf{GoodPK}_{\mathsf{Yes}} = \left\{ \mathsf{pk} : \mathsf{pk} \in \bigcup_{\kappa} \mathsf{Gen}(1^{\kappa}) \right\}$$

$$\mathsf{GoodPK}_{\mathsf{No}} = \left\{ \mathsf{pk} : \mathsf{pk} \notin \bigcup_{\kappa} \mathcal{VPK}_{\kappa} \right\}.$$

We also define a related promise problem GoodCT, which corresponds to triplets containing a public key, ciphertext and a single-bit message. Formally, the problem is defined as $\mathsf{GoodCT} = (\mathsf{GoodCT}_{\mathsf{Yes}}, \mathsf{GoodCT}_{\mathsf{No}})$, where:

$$\mathsf{GoodCT}_{\mathsf{Yes}} = \left\{ (\mathsf{pk}, c, b) : \mathsf{pk} \in \bigcup_{\kappa} \mathsf{Gen}(1^{\kappa}) \text{ and } c \in \mathsf{Enc}_{\mathsf{pk}}(b) \right\}$$

$$\mathsf{GoodCT}_{\mathsf{No}} = \left\{ (\mathsf{pk}, c, b) : \mathsf{pk} \in \bigcup_{\kappa} \mathcal{VPK}_{\kappa} \text{ and } c \notin C_{\mathsf{pk}}^{(b)} \right\}.$$

3.2 From POCS to NIZK

In this section we state and prove our transformation of encryption schemes that support POCS and suitable NIZKs for GoodPK and GoodCT, to general purpose NIZKs for **NP**. This is captured by the following lemma:

Lemma 4. *Let* $(\mathsf{Gen}, \mathsf{Enc}, \mathsf{Dec})$ *be a public-key encryption scheme with public randomness, and* $\mathcal{VPK}$ *be a valid set of public keys (as in Definition 12). Suppose the following conditions hold.*

- $(\mathsf{Gen}, \mathsf{Enc}, \mathsf{Dec})$ *has a* $(1-\epsilon)$*-binding* POCS *with respect to* $\mathcal{VPK}$*, for some sufficiently small* $\epsilon = 1/\mathrm{poly}(\kappa)$.
- *There is a* NIZK *for* GoodPK.
- *There is a* NIZK *for* GoodCT.

Then, there exists a NIZK *for every language* $L \in \mathbf{NP}$.

Proof. Let $L \in \mathbf{NP}$. By Lemma 1, there exists a hidden-bits zero knowledge proof system $(P_{\mathsf{hb}}, V_{\mathsf{hb}})$ for L (with perfect completeness). We shall use this proof-system to construct a NIZK for L, using the assumptions in the theorem's statement.

We first give a proof system satisfying a weak notion of soundness. Specifically, we shall weaken soundness by assuming that the cheating prover is constrained to choose a public-key pk before reading the CRS. To be more precise, since the public randomness of the pk comes from the CRS, the prover must choose the public key pk before reading any *other* part of the CRS. Also, the verifier is only required to reject inputs $x \notin L$ only with inverse polynomial probability (rather than with all but negligible probability). Using standard amplification techniques, we will subsequently transform this into a full-fledged NIZK (achieving the standard notion of soundness).

We assume without loss of generality that the NIZK proof systems that we have for GoodPK and GoodCT have *adaptive* soundness (see Remark 1). Our base NIZK protocol, achieving only the aforementioned weak soundness notion, is given in Protocol 1.

Protocol 1 *Let $L \in \mathbf{NP}$. Let $(P_{\mathsf{pk}}, V_{\mathsf{pk}})$ and $(P_{\mathsf{ct}}, V_{\mathsf{ct}})$ be adaptively sound* NIZK *proof systems for the promise problems* GoodPK *and* GoodCT, *respectively, and let $(P_{\mathsf{hb}}, V_{\mathsf{hb}})$ be a hidden-bits proof system for L that uses $N = N(n)$ hidden bits for inputs of length $n \in \mathbb{N}$. Consider the following non-interactive proof system.*

- *Input $x \in \{0,1\}^n$.*
- *Common random string $\rho = (\rho_{\mathsf{pk}}, r_{\mathsf{pk}}, \rho_1, \dots, \rho_N, r_1, \dots, r_N)$.*
- *Prover's witness $w \in \{0,1\}^{\mathrm{poly}(n)}$.*
- *Prover P, given x, w and ρ, performs the following:*
  1. *Let $(\mathsf{pk}, \mathsf{sk}) \leftarrow \mathsf{Gen}(1^n, \rho_{\mathsf{pk}})$.*
  2. *Let $\pi_{\mathsf{pk}} \leftarrow P_{\mathsf{pk}}(\mathsf{pk}, r_{\mathsf{pk}}, \mathsf{sk})$.*
  3. *For $i \in [N]$, let $c_i \leftarrow \mathsf{Sample}(\mathsf{sk}, \rho_i)$ and let $b_i = \mathsf{Dec}_{\mathsf{sk}}(c_i)$*[10]*.*
  4. *Let $(I, \pi_{\mathsf{hb}}) \leftarrow P_{\mathsf{hb}}(x, (b_1, \dots, b_m), w)$.*
  5. *For $i \in I$, let $\pi_i \leftarrow P_{\mathsf{ct}}((\mathsf{pk}, c_i, b_i), r_i, \mathsf{sk})$.*
  6. *Let $c_I = (c_i)_{i \in I}, b_I = (b_i)_{i \in I}, \pi_I = (\pi_i)_{i \in I}$.*
  7. *Output $\pi = (\mathsf{pk}, I, \pi_{\mathsf{pk}}, \pi_{\mathsf{hb}}, c_I, b_I, \pi_I)$.*
- *Verifier V performs the following:*
  1. *Verify* NIZK *proofs by running $V_{\mathsf{pk}}(\mathsf{pk}, r_{\mathsf{pk}}, \pi_{\mathsf{pk}})$ and $V_{\mathsf{ct}}((\mathsf{pk}, c_i, b_i), r_i, \pi_i)$ for every $i \in I$. Reject if any of these tests rejects.*
  2. *Check that $\mathsf{Check}(\mathsf{pk}, \rho_i, c_i) = 1$ for every $i \in I$. Reject if any of these checks fail.*
  3. *Invoke $V_{\mathsf{hb}}(x, b_I, I, \pi_{\mathsf{hb}})$, and accept if and only if it accepts.*

Observe that both the verifier and prover are PPT algorithms. Thus, to show that Protocol 1 is a (weak) NIZK, we need to establish completeness, (weak) soundness and zero-knowledge.

[10] Jumping ahead, we note that for our final NIZK protocol, achieving standard soundness, we will need to repeat steps 3–6 for $\ell = \mathrm{poly}(\kappa)$ times for the same pk to amplify soundness.

Completeness. From the completeness of the NIZKs $(P_{\mathsf{pk}}, V_{\mathsf{pk}})$ and $(P_{\mathsf{ct}}, V_{\mathsf{ct}})$, we have that the verifiers V_{pk} and V_{ct} (for each $i \in [N]$) accept with all but negligible probability. By the completeness property of the POCS, we have that with all but negligible probability, the verifier's invocation of Check outputs 1 for each $i \in I$.

By the perfect completeness of the hidden-bits proof system, verifier V_{hb} accepts for $x \in L$.[11] Consequently, with probability $1-\mathrm{negl}(n)$, all of the verifier's tests pass for $x \in L$ and a proof produced by the honest prover.

Zero-Knowledge. We first define the simulator S. Let S_{hb} be the simulator for the hidden bits proof-system $(P_{\mathsf{hb}}, V_{\mathsf{hb}})$, let S_{pk} be the simulator for the NIZK $(P_{\mathsf{pk}}, V_{\mathsf{pk}})$, and let S_{ct} be the simulator for the NIZK $(P_{\mathsf{ct}}, V_{\mathsf{ct}})$. On input $x \in \{0,1\}^n$, simulator S performs the following.

1. Sample public randomness ρ_{pk}, and let $(\mathsf{pk}, \mathsf{sk}) \leftarrow \mathsf{Gen}(1^n, \rho_{\mathsf{pk}})$.
2. Sample $(\pi_{\mathsf{pk}}, r_{\mathsf{pk}}) \leftarrow S_{\mathsf{pk}}(\mathsf{pk})$ (recall that π_{pk} is the simulated proof string and r_{pk} is the simulated CRS).
3. Sample $(I, \pi_{\mathsf{hb}}, b_I) \leftarrow S_{\mathsf{hb}}(x)$, where $b_I = (b_i)_{i \in I}$. Set $b_i = 0$ for every $i \in [N] \setminus I$.
4. For $i \in [N]$, sample $(\rho_i, c_i) \leftarrow \mathsf{EncryptAndExplain}(\mathsf{pk}, b_i)$.
5. For $i \in I$, sample $(\pi_i, r_i) \leftarrow S_{\mathsf{ct}}(\mathsf{pk}, c_i, b_i)$.
6. For $i \in [N] \setminus I$, let $r_i \leftarrow \{0,1\}^{\mathsf{poly}(n)}$.
7. Let $c_I = (c_i)_{i \in I}, \pi_I = (\pi_i)_{i \in I}$
8. Output simulated proof $\pi = (\mathsf{pk}, I, \pi_{\mathsf{pk}}, \pi_{\mathsf{hb}}, c_I, b_I, \pi_I)$ and simulated common random string $\rho = (\rho_{\mathsf{pk}}, r_{\mathsf{pk}}, \rho_1, \ldots, \rho_N, r_1, \ldots, r_N)$.

Due to lack of space, we defer the proof of indistinguishability of the real and simulated distributions to the full version [RSS18].

Weak soundness. We first prove a weak notion of soundness with respect to provers that are constrained to choose the public key pk before reading the CRS, other than the public randomness for generating the public-key. Subsequently we will apply an amplification argument to achieve full soundness.

Let us fix $x \notin L$ and a cheating prover P^*, and let us sample a CRS $\rho = (\rho_{\mathsf{pk}}, r_{\mathsf{pk}}, \rho_1, \ldots, \rho_N, r_1, \ldots, r_N)$. Let $\pi = (\mathsf{pk}, I, \pi_{\mathsf{pk}}, \pi_{\mathsf{hb}}, c_I, b_I, \pi_I)$ be the proof produced by P^* on input ρ, where P^* is first given only ρ_{pk} and produces pk, and subsequently is given the full CRS ρ and produces the rest of the proof π. By the adaptive soundness of the NIZKs $(P_{\mathsf{pk}}, V_{\mathsf{pk}})$ and $(P_{\mathsf{ct}}, V_{\mathsf{ct}})$, unless $\mathsf{pk} \in \mathcal{VPK}$ and $c_i \in C_{\mathsf{pk}}^{(b_i)}$ for each $i \in I$, the verifier V will reject with all-but-negligible probability. Additionally, with all-but-negligible probability, the public randomness ρ_{pk} in the CRS is such that the statistical binding property of the POCS holds. In the sequel we condition on these events occurring.

---

[11] Here we are utilizing the fact that the hidden-bits proof-system has *perfect* completeness to save us the effort of arguing that the hidden bits are indeed (sufficiently) unbiased.

For a given valid public key $\mathsf{pk} \in \mathcal{VPK}$ and $\sigma \in \{0,1\}$, define $U_{\mathsf{pk}}^{(\sigma)}$ to be the set of randomnesses ρ (for the POCS procedure) that correspond to a ciphertext $c \in C_{\mathsf{pk}}^{(\sigma)}$ but no ciphertext in $C_{\mathsf{pk}}^{(1-\sigma)}$. That is,

$$U_{\mathsf{pk}}^{(\sigma)} = \left\{\rho \in \{0,1\}^{\mathrm{poly}(\kappa)} : \exists c \in C_{\mathsf{pk}}^{(\sigma)} \text{ s.t. } \mathsf{Check}(\mathsf{pk}, \rho, c) = 1 \text{ and } \forall c' \in C_{\mathsf{pk}}^{(1-\sigma)}, \mathsf{Check}(\mathsf{pk}, \rho, c') = 0\right\}.$$

The set $U_{\mathsf{pk}}^{(\sigma)}$ consists of randomness that can be uniquely interpreted as an encryption of σ and not of $1-\sigma$. Consequently, we have that $U_{\mathsf{pk}}^{(0)} \cap U_{\mathsf{pk}}^{(1)} = \emptyset$. By the unbiased and stastically binding properties of the POCS, we have that

$$\Pr_{\rho}\left[\rho \in U_{\mathsf{pk}}^{(\sigma)}\right] \geq 1/2 - \epsilon - \mathrm{negl}(\kappa),$$

where $\epsilon = \epsilon(\kappa)$ is the binding parameter of the POCS.

Note that $U_{\mathsf{pk}}^{(0)} \cap U_{\mathsf{pk}}^{(1)} = \emptyset$. Arbitrarily fix a set U_{pk} consisting half of elements of $U_{\mathsf{pk}}^{(0)}$ and half of elements of $U_{\mathsf{pk}}^{(1)}$ such that

$$\Pr_{\rho}\left[\rho \in U_{\mathsf{pk}}\right] \geq 1 - 2\epsilon - \mathrm{negl}(\kappa).$$

Recall that we first constrain the prover to choosing pk before reading any part of the CRS other than the public randomness ρ_{pk}. Let U_{pk} be the set defined above. Then, with probability $1 - 2\epsilon N$ the strings $\rho_1, \ldots, \rho_N$ are all in U_{pk}. Conditioning on this event, we have that the sequence $b_1, \ldots, b_N$ is unbiased and uniquely determined by $\rho_1, \ldots, \rho_N$. Consequently, by the soundness of the hidden bits proof system $(P_{\mathsf{hb}}, V_{\mathsf{hb}})$ we have that with all but negligible probability, in this event V_{hb} will reject since $x \notin L$. Therefore, it follows that the verifier V will reject with probability at least $1 - 2\epsilon N - \mathrm{negl}(n)$, which is at least $1/3 - \mathrm{negl}(n)$ for $\epsilon = 1/N^2$.

Amplification. We now transform Protocol 1 into a protocol with full soundness.

We modify Protocol 1 as follows. After choosing the public key pk, the prover runs steps 3–6 of Protocol 1 $\ell = \mathrm{poly}(n)$ times on different portions of the CRS, generating ℓ independently sampled $(I, \pi_{\mathsf{hb}}, C_I, b_I, \pi_I)$. The verifier checks each of these separately, rejecting if any test fails.

Completeness and zero-knowledge of the new protocol follow immediately from the same argument as before. It remains to prove (full-fledged) soundness. As before, we have that the verifier will reject with probability $1 - \mathrm{negl}(n)$ unless $\mathsf{pk} \in \mathcal{VPK}$ and the public randomness ρ_{pk} in the CRS satisfies the statistical binding property of the POCS, so we can condition on these events. For a fixed pk, we have from the soundness of Protocol 1 that on a single iteration of steps 3–6, the verifier will reject with probability at least $1/3 - \mathrm{negl}(n)$ on $x \notin L$. Since the public key pk has polynomial size, applying a union bound over public keys, we can take $\ell = \mathrm{poly}(n)$ sufficiently large that with probability $1 - \mathrm{negl}(n)$, the verifier will reject for every public key.[12] Consequently soundness holds in the amplified protocol.

[12] The argument here resembles the standard argument for obtaining adaptively sound NIZKs from NIZKs that only have non-adaptive soundness.

4 Instantiating with LWE

In this section we show that, assuming the hardness of LWE and the existence of a NIZK proof system for dBDD, Regev's [Reg09] LWE-based encryption scheme satisfies the conditions of Lemma 4 and therefore yields NIZK proof-systems for *all* of **NP**:

Theorem 2. *Let κ be the security parameter. Let $n = n(\kappa) \in \mathbb{N}$, $q = q(\kappa) \in \mathbb{N}$, $\beta = \beta(\kappa)$, $\alpha = \alpha(\kappa) \geq 1$ and $\gamma = \gamma(\kappa) > 1$, such that $n = \mathrm{poly}(\kappa)$ and $\beta = o\left(\frac{1}{\log(\kappa)\max(\alpha,\gamma)\sqrt{n\log(q)}}\right)$. Assume that the following conditions hold:*

- *The $\mathsf{LWE}_{n,q,\beta}$ assumption holds; and*
- *There exists a NIZK proof system for $\mathsf{dBDD}_{\alpha,\gamma}$.*

Then, there exists a NIZK proof system for every language $L \in \mathbf{NP}$.

Section Organization. In Sect. 4.1, we present Regev's [Reg09] encryption scheme. In Sect. 4.2, we present the NIZK proof systems for certifying public keys and plaintext values for this encryption scheme (based on the NIZK proof system for dBDD in the hypothesis of Theorem 2). In Sect. 4.3, we show that Regev's encryption has a POCS procedure. Finally, in Sect. 4.4, we use the tools developed in the prior subsections to prove Theorem 2.

4.1 Regev's Encryption Scheme

A public-key encryption scheme based on the LWE assumption was introduced in [Reg09]. We present the scheme of [Reg09], phrased as an encryption scheme with public randomness in the sense of Definition 1.

Construction 5. *Let κ be the security parameter. Let $n = n(\kappa) \in \mathbb{N}$, $q = q(\kappa) \in \mathbb{N}$, $m = 2n\log(q)$, $\beta = \beta(\kappa) \in [0,1]$ such that $n = \mathrm{poly}(\kappa)$ and $\beta = o(1/\sqrt{m})$. We define the encryption scheme* (Gen, Enc, Dec) *with public randomness as follows:*

- **Public Randomness:** *The public randomness is a matrix $\mathbf{A} \leftarrow \mathbb{Z}_q^{n\times m}$. We assume without loss of generality that $\lambda_1(\mathbf{A}) > q/4$*[13]*.*
- **Key Generation** $\mathsf{Gen}(1^\kappa, \mathbf{A})$: *Sample $\mathbf{s} \leftarrow \mathbb{Z}_q^n \backslash \{0\}$, and $\mathbf{e} \leftarrow \chi_\beta^m$, where χ_β is a discrete Gaussian with parameter β (see Definition 10). Let $\mathbf{b}^T = \mathbf{s}^T \cdot \mathbf{A} + \mathbf{e}^T$. We assume without loss of generality that $\left\|\mathbf{s}^T \cdot \mathbf{A} - \mathbf{b}^T\right\| = \left\|\mathbf{e}^T\right\| \leq \ell\sqrt{m}\beta q$, where $\ell = \omega(\log(\kappa))$*[14]*. Set the public key to be $(\mathbf{A}, \mathbf{b})$ and the secret key to be $\mathbf{s}$.*

[13] From Lemma 3 this happens with overwhelming probability.

[14] Since the complementary event happens with negligible probability in κ, in case it does happen we choose the public-keys to have zero noise.

- **Encryption** $\mathsf{Enc}_{(\mathbf{A},\mathbf{b})}(\sigma)$: *On input a message* $\sigma \in \{0,1\}$*, sample* $\mathbf{r} \leftarrow \{0,1\}^m$ *and output* $(\mathbf{c}, \omega)$*, where* $\mathbf{c} = \mathbf{A} \cdot \mathbf{r}$ *and* $\omega = \mathbf{b}^T \cdot \mathbf{r} + \sigma \cdot \lfloor \frac{q}{2} \rfloor$*. We assume without loss of generality*[15] *that*

$$\left\| \mathbf{s}^T \cdot [\mathbf{A}, \mathbf{c}] - \left[\mathbf{b}, \left(\omega - \sigma \cdot \left\lfloor \frac{q}{2} \right\rfloor \right) \right]^T \right\| \leq 2\ell\sqrt{m}\beta q,$$

where $\ell = \omega(\log(\kappa))$*.*
- **Decryption** $\mathsf{Dec}_{\mathbf{s}}((\mathbf{c}, \omega))$: *Output* $\sigma = \lfloor \mathbf{s}^T \cdot \mathbf{c} - \omega \rceil_q$*.*

Regev [Reg09] proved that a variant of this scheme is semantically secure (under the LWE assumption).

Proposition 4. (c.f. [Reg09]). *Let* $n = n(\kappa) \in \mathbb{N}$*,* $q = q(\kappa) \in \mathbb{N}$ *and* $\beta = \beta(\kappa) \in [0,1]$ *such that* $\beta = o(1/\sqrt{m})$ *and* $n = \mathrm{poly}(\kappa)$*. If the* $\mathsf{LWE}_{n,q,\beta}$ *assumption holds, then Construction 5 is semantically secure.*

In order to use the results of Sect. 3, we need to show that Construction 5 admits a POCS procedure. As our first step, we define a valid set of public keys. Later, we shall show NIZK proofs for the related promise problems GoodPK and GoodCT as well as a POCS procedure for Construction 5.

Fix a security parameter κ. Let $n = \mathrm{poly}(\kappa)$, $q = q(\kappa)$, and $\beta = \beta(\kappa)$ be parameters and set $m = 2n\log(q)$. In the sequel, we omit κ from the notation to avoid cluttering. In addition, we set $\ell = \omega(\log(\kappa))$, $\mathrm{e}_{\max} = \ell\sqrt{m}\beta q$, $1 \leq \alpha < \frac{q}{8\mathrm{e}_{\max}}$ and $\gamma > 1$. We assume that the following hold:

- $\beta < \frac{1}{16\ell\gamma\sqrt{m}}$;
- the $\mathsf{LWE}_{n,q,\beta}$ assumption holds; and
- there exists a NIZK proof system for $\mathsf{dBDD}_{\alpha,\gamma/4}$.

Now, we define a set (of alleged public keys) $\mathcal{VPK}$ for (Gen, Enc, Dec). Later we will argue that it is in fact a *valid* set of public keys as per Definition 12. Let

$$\mathcal{VPK} = \left\{ (\mathbf{A}, \mathbf{b}) \in \mathbb{Z}_q^{n \times m} \times \mathbb{Z}_q^m \; : \; \exists \mathbf{s} \in \mathbb{Z}_q^n \text{ s.t. } \left\| \mathbf{s}^T \cdot \mathbf{A} - \mathbf{b}^T \right\| \leq \gamma \mathrm{e}_{\max} \right\}. \quad (2)$$

We note that the noise level allowed in Eq. (2) is *larger* by a multiplicative γ factor than the noise level that exists in honestly generated public keys.

For each $\mathsf{pk} = (\mathbf{A}, \mathbf{b}) \in \mathcal{VPK}$ and $\sigma \in \{0,1\}$, define $C_{\mathsf{pk}}^{(\sigma)} \subseteq \mathbb{Z}_q^n \times \mathbb{Z}_q$ as:

$$C_{\mathsf{pk}}^{(\sigma)} = \left\{ (\mathbf{c}, \omega) : \exists \mathbf{s}' \in \mathbb{Z}_q^n \text{ s.t. } \left\| \mathbf{s}'^T \cdot [\mathbf{A}, \mathbf{c}] - \left[\mathbf{b}, \left(\omega - \sigma \cdot \left\lfloor \frac{q}{2} \right\rfloor \right) \right]^T \right\| \leq 2\gamma \mathrm{e}_{\max} \right\} \quad (3)$$

The noise level allowed in Eq. (3) is also *larger* by a multiplicative γ factor than the noise level that exists in honestly generated ciphertexts.

[15] Again, the complementary event happens with negligible probability, in which case we can output a ciphertext with zero noise.

Remark 3. As noted in the introduction, we would like for $\mathcal{VPK}$ to contain only the honestly generated public keys and $C_{\mathsf{pk}}^{(\sigma)}$ to contain only the honestly generated encryptions of σ with respect to pk. However, introducing a gap in the definitions allows us to rely on NIZKs for suitable *approximation* problems.

We conclude this section by showing that $\mathcal{VPK}$ is indeed a valid set of public keys.

Proposition 5. *The set $\mathcal{VPK}$ is a valid set of public keys.*

Due to lack of space, we defer the proof to the full version [RSS18].

4.2 NIZKs for Validating Keys and Ciphertexts

Now that we have defined a valid set of public keys $\mathcal{VPK}$, we prove that Construction 5 satisfies the conditions of Lemma 4. To do so we assume the existence of a NIZK proof system for dBDD. Using this NIZK, we obtain NIZK proof systems for the promise problems GoodPK and GoodCT (with respect to $\mathcal{VPK}$).

Lemma 6. *Assume there exists a* NIZK *proof system for* $\mathsf{dBDD}_{\alpha,\gamma/4}$. *Then, there exists a* NIZK *proof system for the promise problem* GoodPK *(with respect to $\mathcal{VPK}$).*

Lemma 7. *Assume there exists a* NIZK *proof system for* $\mathsf{dBDD}_{\alpha,\gamma/4}$. *Then, there exists a* NIZK *proof system for the promise problem* GoodCT *(with respect to $\mathcal{VPK}$).*

We defer the proofs of Lemmas 6 and 7 to the full version [RSS18].

4.3 A POCS Procedure for Regev's Scheme

The last and most challenging condition that we need is to prove that Construction 5 has a POCS procedure.

Lemma 8. *Construction 5 has a $(1 - 4\gamma\ell\sqrt{m}\beta)$-binding* POCS *procedure with respect to $\mathcal{VPK}$.*

The rest of Sect. 4.3 is devoted to the proof of Lemma 8.

Proof. (Proof of Lemma 8).

For technical convenience and simplicity, we assume for now that $q \equiv 2 \pmod 4$. The case that $q \not\equiv 2 \pmod 4$ adds some mild complications in order to avoid introducing a small, but noticeable bias (i.e., roughly $1/q$) in the obliviously sampled bits. We describe how to extend our approach to general q in the full version [RSS18][16].

[16] Alternatively, we could reduce the bias to be negligible using Von Neumann's trick [VN61] for transforming a biased source to an almost unbiased source.

Let us first describe the algorithms Sample and Check. The Sample algorithm takes as input a secret key $\mathsf{sk} = \mathbf{s}$ and randomness $(\boldsymbol{\rho}, \tau) \in \mathbb{Z}_q^n \times \mathbb{Z}_q$, and outputs a ciphertext.

The algorithm Sample transforms a high noise ciphertext $(\boldsymbol{\rho}, \tau)$ into a valid Regev's ciphertext under the secret key $\mathbf{s}$.

$\underline{\mathsf{Sample}(\mathbf{s}, (\boldsymbol{\rho}, \tau))}$:

1. Sample $e \leftarrow \chi_{\sqrt{m}\beta}$. Let $\omega_0 = \mathbf{s}^T \cdot \boldsymbol{\rho} + e$ and $\omega_1 = \omega_0 + \lfloor \frac{q}{2} \rfloor$.
2. If $|\tau - \omega_0| < |\tau - \omega_1|$, set $\sigma = 0$. Otherwise, set $\sigma = 1$.
3. Output $(\boldsymbol{\rho}, \omega_\sigma)$, which is a valid ciphertext for the message σ.

The Check algorithm takes as input a public key $\mathsf{pk} = (\mathbf{A}, \mathbf{b})$, randomness $(\boldsymbol{\rho}, \tau) \in \mathbb{Z}_q^n \times \mathbb{Z}_q$, and an alleged ciphertext $(\boldsymbol{\rho}', \omega') \in \mathbb{Z}_q^n \times \mathbb{Z}_q$, and outputs a singlebit denoting acceptance or rejection.

$\underline{\mathsf{Check}(\mathsf{pk}, (\boldsymbol{\rho}, \tau), (\boldsymbol{\rho}', \omega'))}$:

If $\boldsymbol{\rho}' = \boldsymbol{\rho}$ and $|\omega' - \tau| \leq \frac{q}{4}$, accept. Otherwise, reject.

Finally, we describe the EncryptAndExplain algorithm, which takes as input a public key $\mathsf{pk} = (\mathbf{A}, \mathbf{b})$ and a message $\sigma \in \{0, 1\}$ and produces randomness and a ciphertext that are close to the distribution induced by Sample.

$\underline{\mathsf{EncryptAndExplain}((\mathbf{A}, \mathbf{b}), \sigma)}$:

1. Sample $\mathbf{r} \leftarrow \{0, 1\}^m$. Compute $\boldsymbol{\rho}' = \mathbf{A} \cdot \mathbf{r}$ and $\omega' = \mathbf{b}^T \cdot \mathbf{r} + \sigma \cdot \lfloor \frac{q}{2} \rfloor$. Note that $(\boldsymbol{\rho}', \omega')$ is a fresh encryption of σ.
2. Sample $\tau' \leftarrow \mathbb{Z}_q$ subject to $|\tau' - \omega'| < \frac{q}{4}$.
3. Output $((\boldsymbol{\rho}', \tau'), (\boldsymbol{\rho}', \omega'))$.

We now show that these algorithms satisfy each of the conditions of Definition 13.

Complete. Let $(\boldsymbol{\rho}, \tau) \leftarrow \mathbb{Z}_q^n \times \mathbb{Z}_q$ and $(\boldsymbol{\rho}', \omega') \leftarrow \mathsf{Sample}(\mathbf{s}, (\boldsymbol{\rho}, \tau))$. By construction $\boldsymbol{\rho}' = \boldsymbol{\rho}$ and $|\tau - \omega'| \leq \frac{q}{4}$, and so Check always accepts.

Unbiased. We defer the proof that this scheme is unbiased to the full version [RSS18].

Statistically Binding. Let $\mathsf{pk} = (\mathbf{A}, \mathbf{b}) \in \mathcal{VPK}$ with public randomness $\mathbf{A} \leftarrow \mathbb{Z}_q^{n \times m}$. By construction $\lambda_1(\mathbf{A}) > q/4$, so there exists a unique $\mathbf{s}$ such that $\|\mathbf{s}^T \cdot \mathbf{A} - \mathbf{b}^T\| \leq \gamma e_{\max}$. We assume that the above holds for $\mathbf{A}$.

Therefore, it holds that:

$$C_{\mathsf{pk}}^{(\sigma)} = \left\{ (\mathbf{c}, \omega) \in \mathbb{Z}_q^n \times Z_q \ : \ \left\| \mathbf{s}^T \cdot [\mathbf{A}, \mathbf{c}] - \left[\mathbf{b}, \left(\omega - \sigma \cdot \left\lfloor \frac{q}{2} \right\rfloor\right)\right]^T \right\| \leq 2\gamma e_{\max} \right\}.$$

We remark that in this case, $(\mathbf{c}, \omega) \in C^{(0)}_{\mathsf{pk}}$ if and only if $(\mathbf{c}, \omega + \lfloor \frac{q}{2} \rfloor) \in C^{(1)}_{\mathsf{pk}}$. Furthermore,

$$\begin{aligned}
&\Pr_{\rho,\tau}\left[\exists\,(\mathbf{c}_0,\omega_0) \in C^{(0)}_{\mathsf{pk}}, \exists\,(\mathbf{c}_1,\omega_1) \in C^{(1)}_{\mathsf{pk}} \text{ s.t. } \begin{array}{c}\mathsf{Check}(\mathsf{pk},(\boldsymbol{\rho},\tau),(\mathbf{c}_0,\omega_0)) = 1,\\ \mathsf{Check}(\mathsf{pk},(\boldsymbol{\rho},\tau),(\mathbf{c}_1,\omega_1)) = 1\end{array}\right]\\
&= \Pr_{\rho,\tau}\left[\exists\,\omega_0, \exists\,\omega_1 \in \mathbb{Z}_q \text{ s.t. } \begin{array}{c}\left|\mathbf{s}^T\cdot\boldsymbol{\rho} - \omega_0\right| \le \gamma e_{\max},\\ \left|\mathbf{s}^T\cdot\boldsymbol{\rho} - \omega_1 - \lfloor\frac{q}{2}\rfloor\right| \le \gamma e_{\max},\\ |\omega_0 - \tau| \le q/4,\\ |\omega_1 - \tau| \le q/4\end{array}\right]\\
&\le \Pr_{\rho,\tau}\left[\left(\left|\mathbf{s}^T\cdot\boldsymbol{\rho} - \tau\right| \le \gamma e_{\max} + \frac{q}{4}\right) \text{ and } \left(\left|\mathbf{s}^T\cdot\boldsymbol{\rho} - \left(\tau + \left\lfloor\frac{q}{2}\right\rfloor\right)\right| \le \gamma e_{\max} + \frac{q}{4}\right)\right]\\
&\le \Pr_{r}\left[\left(|r| \le \gamma e_{\max} + \frac{q}{4}\right) \text{ and } \left(\left|r + \left\lfloor\frac{q}{2}\right\rfloor\right| \le \gamma e_{\max} + \frac{q}{4}\right)\right]\\
&\le \Pr_{r}\left[r \in \left[\frac{q}{4} - \gamma e_{\max}, \frac{q}{4} + \gamma e_{\max}\right] \cup \left[-\frac{q}{4} - \gamma e_{\max}, -\frac{q}{4} + \gamma e_{\max}\right]\right]\\
&\le 4\gamma\ell\sqrt{m}\beta.
\end{aligned}$$

The first equality follows from the definition of $C^{(0)}_{\mathsf{pk}}$ and $C^{(1)}_{\mathsf{pk}}$ and the description of Check. More specifically, the conditions $\left|\mathbf{s}^T\cdot\boldsymbol{\rho} - \omega_0\right| \le \gamma e_{\max}$ and $\left|\mathbf{s}^T\cdot\boldsymbol{\rho} - \omega_1 - \lfloor\frac{q}{2}\rfloor\right| \le \gamma e_{\max}$ follow from the fact that $(\mathbf{c}_0,\omega_0) \in C^{(0)}_{\mathsf{pk}}$ and $(\mathbf{c}_1,\omega_1) \in C^{(1)}_{\mathsf{pk}}$, respectively. The conditions $|\omega_0 - \tau| \le q/4$ and $|\omega_1 - \tau| \le q/4$ follow from $\mathsf{Check}(\mathsf{pk},(\boldsymbol{\rho},\tau),(\mathbf{c}_0,\omega_0)) = 1$ and $\mathsf{Check}(\mathsf{pk},(\boldsymbol{\rho},\tau),(\mathbf{c}_1,\omega_1)) = 1$ respectively. The next inequality follows from the triangle inequality. Next, we replace $\mathbf{s}^T\cdot\boldsymbol{\rho} - \tau$ by a uniformly random element r of $\mathbb{Z}_q$. Then, we note that r has to belong to a set of size at most $4\gamma e_{\max} \le 4\gamma\ell\sqrt{m}\beta q$, which happens with probability at most $4\gamma\ell\sqrt{m}\beta$. The last inequality then follows.

Simulatable. Let $N = \mathrm{poly}(\kappa)$. Sample $\mathbf{A} \leftarrow \mathbb{Z}_q^{n\times m}$ and $(\mathsf{pk},\mathsf{sk}) = ((\mathbf{A},\mathbf{b}),\mathbf{s}) \leftarrow \mathsf{Gen}(1^\kappa,\mathbf{A})$ and consider the following two experiments:

- For $i \in [N]$, let $(\boldsymbol{\rho}_i,\tau_i) \leftarrow \mathbb{Z}_q^n \times \mathbb{Z}_q$, $(\boldsymbol{\rho}_i,\omega_i) \leftarrow \mathsf{Sample}(\mathbf{s},(\boldsymbol{\rho}_i,\tau_i))$, $\sigma_i = \mathsf{Dec}_{\mathbf{s}}((\boldsymbol{\rho}_i,\omega_i))$. Output $(\mathsf{pk},(\boldsymbol{\rho}_i,\tau_i,\omega_i,\sigma_i)_{i\in[N]})$.
- For $i \in [N]$, let $\sigma'_i \in_R \{0,1\}$. Set $((\boldsymbol{\rho}'_i,\tau'_i),(\boldsymbol{\rho}'_i,\omega'_i)) \leftarrow \mathsf{EncryptAndExplain}(\mathsf{pk},\sigma'_i)$. Output $(\mathsf{pk},(\boldsymbol{\rho}'_i,\tau'_i,\omega'_i,\sigma'_i)_{i\in[N]})$.

In the full version [RSS18] we show that the outputs of these two experiments are computationally indistinguishable.

Computationally Hiding. Given public key $\mathsf{pk} = (\mathbf{A},\mathbf{b})$ and randomness $(\boldsymbol{\rho},\tau)$, the procedure Sample simply computes a fresh encryption $(\boldsymbol{\rho},\omega)$ using the secret-key variant of Regev's scheme. Let $\sigma = \mathsf{Dec}_{\mathbf{s}}((\boldsymbol{\rho},\omega))$. Then similarly to the above proof

$$(\mathsf{pk},\boldsymbol{\rho},\tau,\omega,\sigma) \equiv (\mathsf{pk},\boldsymbol{\rho},\tau',\omega',\sigma)$$

where $\omega' = \mathbf{s}^T \cdot \boldsymbol{\rho} + \sigma \cdot \lfloor \frac{q}{2} \rfloor + e$, with $e \leftarrow \chi_{\sqrt{m}\beta}$ and τ' sampled uniformly such that $|\tau' - \omega'| < q/4$.

Then, since τ' is a randomized function of ω', the computational hiding property of the POCS follows immediately from the semantic security of Regev's encryption scheme.

This concludes the proof of Lemma 8 for $q \equiv 2 \pmod 4$. We describe how to extend the proof to general q in the full version [RSS18]. The main difficulty is to sample the boundary points with the correct probability.

4.4 Putting It All Together (Proof of Theorem 2)

We now complete the proof of Theorem 2. We have shown that all of the conditions of Lemma 4 hold, as follows.

1. By Proposition 5, Construction 5 has a valid set of public keys $\mathcal{VPK}$.
2. By Lemma 8, Construction 5 has a POCS with respect to $\mathcal{VPK}$.
3. By Lemma 6, there is a NIZK for GoodPK.
4. By Lemma 7, there is a NIZK for GoodCT.

Theorem 2 then follows immediately by Lemma 4.

References

[ACPS09] Applebaum, B., Cash, D., Peikert, C., Sahai, A.: Fast cryptographic primitives and circular-secure encryption based on hard learning problems. In: Halevi, S. (ed.) CRYPTO 2009. LNCS, vol. 5677, pp. 595–618. Springer, Heidelberg (2009). https://doi.org/10.1007/978-3-642-03356-8_35

[AFV11] Agrawal, S., Freeman, D.M., Vaikuntanathan, V.: Functional encryption for inner product predicates from learning with errors. In: Lee, D.H., Wang, X. (eds.) ASIACRYPT 2011. LNCS, vol. 7073, pp. 21–40. Springer, Heidelberg (2011). https://doi.org/10.1007/978-3-642-25385-0_2

[APSD17] Alamati, N., Peikert, C., Stephens-Davidowitz, N.: New (and old) proof systems for lattice problems. Cryptology ePrint Archive, Report 2017/1226 (2017)

[BDSMP91] Blum, M., De Santis, A., Micali, S., Persiano, G.: Noninteractive zero-knowledge. SIAM J. Comput. **20**(6), 1084–1118 (1991)

[BFM88] Blum, M., Feldman, P., Micali, S.: Non-interactive zero-knowledge and its applications (extended abstract). In: STOC (1988)

[BKM06] Bender, A., Katz, J., Morselli, R.: Rin signatures: stronger definitions, and constructions without random oracles. In: Halevi, S., Rabin, T. (eds.) TCC 2006. LNCS, vol. 3876, pp. 60–79. Springer, Heidelberg (2006). https://doi.org/10.1007/11681878_4

[BMW03] Bellare, M., Micciancio, D., Warinschi, B.: Foundations of group signatures: formal definitions, simplified requirements, and a construction based on general assumptions. In: Biham, E. (ed.) EUROCRYPT 2003. LNCS, vol. 2656, pp. 614–629. Springer, Heidelberg (2003). https://doi.org/10.1007/3-540-39200-9_38

[BP15] Bitansky, N., Paneth, O.: ZAPs and non-interactive witness indistinguishability from indistinguishability obfuscation. In: Dodis, Y., Nielsen, J.B. (eds.) TCC 2015. LNCS, vol. 9015, pp. 401–427. Springer, Heidelberg (2015). https://doi.org/10.1007/978-3-662-46497-7_16

[BR93] Bellare, M., Rogaway, P.: Random oracles are practical: a paradigm for designing efficient protocols. In: CCS (1993)

[BRV17] Berman, I., Rothblum, R.D., Vaikuntanathan, V.: Zero-knowledge proofs of proximity. IACR Cryptology ePrint Archive 2017:114 (2017)

[BV14] Brakerski, Z., Vaikuntanathan, V.: Efficient fully homomorphic encryption from (standard) LWE. SIAM J. Comput. **43**(2), 831–871 (2014)

[BY96] Bellare, M., Yung, M.: Certifying permutations: noninteractive zero-knowledge based on any trapdoor permutation. J. Cryptol. **9**(3), 149–166 (1996)

[CCRR18] Canetti, R., Chen, Y., Reyzin, L., Rothblum, R.D.: Fiat-shamir and correlation intractability from strong KDM-secure encryption. Cryptology ePrint Archive, Report 2018/131 (2018)

[CGH04] Canetti, R., Goldreich, O., Halevi, S.: The random oracle methodology, revisited. J. ACM **51**(4), 557–594 (2004)

[CL17] Canetti, R., Lichtenberg, A.: Certifying trapdoor permutations, revisited. IACR Cryptology ePrint Archive 2017:631 (2017)

[DDN03] Dolev, D., Dwork, C., Naor, M.: Nonmalleable cryptography. SIAM Rev. **45**(4), 727–784 (2003)

[DN07] Dwork, C., Naor, M.: Zaps and their applications. SIAM J. Comput. **36**(6), 1513–1543 (2007)

[dPL17] del Pino, R., Lyubashevsky, V.: Amortization with fewer equations for proving knowledge of small secrets. In: Katz, J., Shacham, H. (eds.) CRYPTO 2017. LNCS, vol. 10403, pp. 365–394. Springer, Cham (2017). https://doi.org/10.1007/978-3-319-63697-9_13

[FLS99] Feige, U., Lapidot, D., Shamir, A.: Multiple noninteractive zero knowledge proofs under general assumptions. SIAM J. Comput. **29**(1), 1–28 (1999)

[FS86] Fiat, A., Shamir, A.: How to prove yourself: practical solutions to identification and signature problems. In: Odlyzko, A.M. (ed.) CRYPTO 1986. LNCS, vol. 263, pp. 186–194. Springer, Heidelberg (1987). https://doi.org/10.1007/3-540-47721-7_12

[GG00] Goldreich, O., Goldwasser, S.: On the limits of nonapproximability of lattice problems. J. Comput. Syst. Sci. **60**(3), 540–563 (2000)

[GK03] Goldwasser, S., Kalai, Y.T.: On the (in)security of the fiat-shamir paradigm. In: FOCS (2003)

[GK05] Goldwasser, S., Kharchenko, D.: Proof of plaintext knowledge for the ajtai-dwork cryptosystem. In: Kilian, J. (ed.) TCC 2005. LNCS, vol. 3378, pp. 529–555. Springer, Heidelberg (2005). https://doi.org/10.1007/978-3-540-30576-7_29

[GKM+00] Gertner, Y., Kannan, S., Malkin, T., Reingold, O., Viswanathan, M.: The relationship between public key encryption and oblivious transfer. In: FOCS (2000)

[GKP+13] Goldwasser, S., Kalai, Y., Popa, R.A., Vaikuntanathan, V., Zeldovich, N.: Reusable garbled circuits and succinct functional encryption. In: STOC (2013)

[GKW17] Goyal, R., Koppula, V., Waters, B.: Lockable obfuscation. IACR Cryptology ePrint Archive 2017:274 (2017)

[GM84] Goldwasser, S., Micali, S.: Probabilistic encryption. J. Comput. Syst. Sci. **28**(2), 270–299 (1984)

[Gol01] Goldreich, O.: The Foundations of Cryptography - Basic Techniques, vol. 1. Cambridge University Press, Cambridge (2001)

[Gol04] Goldreich, O.: The Foundations of Cryptography - Basic Applications, vol. 2. Cambridge University Press, Cambridge (2004)

[Gol11] Goldreich, O.: Basing non-interactive zero-knowledge on (Enhanced) trapdoor permutations: the state of the art. In: Goldreich, O. (ed.) Studies in Complexity and Cryptography. Miscellanea on the Interplay between Randomness and Computation. LNCS, vol. 6650, pp. 406–421. Springer, Heidelberg (2011). https://doi.org/10.1007/978-3-642-22670-0_28

[GOS12] Groth, J., Ostrovsky, R., Sahai, A.: New techniques for noninteractive zero-knowledge. J. ACM **59**(3), 11:1–11:35 (2012)

[GR13] Goldreich, O., Rothblum, R.D.: Enhancements of trapdoor permutations. J. Cryptol. **26**(3), 484–512 (2013)

[Gro10] Groth, J.: Short pairing-based non-interactive zero-knowledge arguments. In: Abe, M. (ed.) ASIACRYPT 2010. LNCS, vol. 6477, pp. 321–340. Springer, Heidelberg (2010). https://doi.org/10.1007/978-3-642-17373-8_19

[GS08] Groth, J., Sahai, A.: Efficient non-interactive proof systems for bilinear groups. In: Smart, N. (ed.) EUROCRYPT 2008. LNCS, vol. 4965, pp. 415–432. Springer, Heidelberg (2008). https://doi.org/10.1007/978-3-540-78967-3_24

[GVW15] Gorbunov, S., Vaikuntanathan, V., Wee, H.: Predicate encryption for circuits from LWE. In: Gennaro, R., Robshaw, M. (eds.) CRYPTO 2015. LNCS, vol. 9216, pp. 503–523. Springer, Heidelberg (2015). https://doi.org/10.1007/978-3-662-48000-7_25

[KRR17] Kalai, Y.T., Rothblum, G.N., Rothblum, R.D.: From obfuscation to the security of fiat-shamir for proofs. In: Katz, J., Shacham, H. (eds.) CRYPTO 2017. LNCS, vol. 10402, pp. 224–251. Springer, Cham (2017). https://doi.org/10.1007/978-3-319-63715-0_8

[KTX08] Kawachi, A., Tanaka, K., Xagawa, K.: Concurrently secure identification schemes based on the worst-case hardness of lattice problems. In: Pieprzyk, J. (ed.) ASIACRYPT 2008. LNCS, vol. 5350, pp. 372–389. Springer, Heidelberg (2008). https://doi.org/10.1007/978-3-540-89255-7_23

[KW18] Kim, S., Wu, D.J.: Multi-theorem preprocessing NIZKs from lattices. In: Shacham, H., Boldyreva, A. (eds.) CRYPTO 2018. LNCS, vol. 10992, pp. 733–765. Springer, Cham (2018). https://doi.org/10.1007/978-3-319-96881-0_25

[LLM+16] Libert, B., Ling, S., Mouhartem, F., Nguyen, K., Wang, H.: Signature schemes with efficient protocols and dynamic group signatures from lattice assumptions. In: Cheon, J.H., Takagi, T. (eds.) ASIACRYPT 2016. LNCS, vol. 10032, pp. 373–403. Springer, Heidelberg (2016). https://doi.org/10.1007/978-3-662-53890-6_13

[LM09] Lyubashevsky, V., Micciancio, D.: On bounded distance decoding, unique shortest vectors, and the minimum distance problem. In: Halevi, S. (ed.) CRYPTO 2009. LNCS, vol. 5677, pp. 577–594. Springer, Heidelberg (2009). https://doi.org/10.1007/978-3-642-03356-8_34

[LNSW13] Ling, S., Nguyen, K., Stehlé, D., Wang, H.: Improved zero-knowledge proofs of knowledge for the ISIS problem, and applications. In: Kurosawa, K., Hanaoka, G. (eds.) PKC 2013. LNCS, vol. 7778, pp. 107–124. Springer, Heidelberg (2013). https://doi.org/10.1007/978-3-642-36362-7_8

[Lyu08] Lyubashevsky, V.: Lattice-based identification schemes secure under active attacks. In: Cramer, R. (ed.) PKC 2008. LNCS, vol. 4939, pp. 162–179. Springer, Heidelberg (2008). https://doi.org/10.1007/978-3-540-78440-1_10

[MV03] Micciancio, D., Vadhan, S.P.: Statistical zero-knowledge proofs with efficient provers: lattice problems and more. In: Boneh, D. (ed.) CRYPTO 2003. LNCS, vol. 2729, pp. 282–298. Springer, Heidelberg (2003). https://doi.org/10.1007/978-3-540-45146-4_17

[MW16] Mukherjee, P., Wichs, D.: Two round multiparty computation via multi-key FHE. In: Fischlin, M., Coron, J.-S. (eds.) EUROCRYPT 2016. LNCS, vol. 9666, pp. 735–763. Springer, Heidelberg (2016). https://doi.org/10.1007/978-3-662-49896-5_26

[Nao03] Naor, M.: On cryptographic assumptions and challenges. In: Boneh, D. (ed.) CRYPTO 2003. LNCS, vol. 2729, pp. 96–109. Springer, Heidelberg (2003). https://doi.org/10.1007/978-3-540-45146-4_6

[NY90] Naor, M., Yung, M.: Public-key cryptosystems provably secure against chosen ciphertext attacks. In: STOC (1990)

[Pei09] Peikert, C.: Public-key cryptosystems from the worst-case shortest vector problem: extended abstract. In: STOC (2009)

[PV08] Peikert, C., Vaikuntanathan, V.: Noninteractive statistical zero-knowledge proofs for lattice problems. In: Wagner, D. (ed.) CRYPTO 2008. LNCS, vol. 5157, pp. 536–553. Springer, Heidelberg (2008). https://doi.org/10.1007/978-3-540-85174-5_30

[PVW08] Peikert, C., Vaikuntanathan, V., Waters, B.: A framework for efficient and composable oblivious transfer. In: Wagner, D. (ed.) CRYPTO 2008. LNCS, vol. 5157, pp. 554–571. Springer, Heidelberg (2008). https://doi.org/10.1007/978-3-540-85174-5_31

[PW08] Peikert, C., Waters, B.: Lossy trapdoor functions and their applications. In: STOC (2008)

[Rab79] Rabin, M.O.: Digitalized signatures and public-key functions as intractable as factorization. Technical report, Cambridge, MA, USA (1979)

[Reg09] Regev, O.: On lattices, learning with errors, random linear codes, and cryptography. J. ACM **56**(6), 34:1–34:40 (2009)

[RSS18] Rothblum, R.D., Sealfon, A., Sotiraki, K.: Towards non-interactive zero-knowledge for NP from LWE. IACR Cryptology ePrint Archive 2018:240 (2018)

[Sah99] Sahai, A.: Non-malleable non-interactive zero knowledge and adaptive chosen-ciphertext security. In: FOCS (1999)

[Sho99] Shor, P.W.: Polynomial-time algorithms for prime factorization and discrete logarithms on a quantum computer. SIAM Rev. **41**(2), 303–332 (1999)

[Ste96] Stern, J.: A new paradigm for public key identification. IEEE Trans. Inf. Theory **42**(6), 1757–1768 (1996)

[SW14] Sahai, A., Waters, B.: How to use indistinguishability obfuscation: deniable encryption, and more. In: STOC (2014)

[Vad99] Vadhan, S.P.: A study of statistical zero-knowledge proofs. Ph.D. thesis, Massachusetts Institute of Technology, Cambridge, MA, USA (1999)

[VN61] Von Neumann, J.: Various techniques used in connection with random digits, Paper no. 13 in Monte Carlo method. NBS Applied Mathematics Series (12) (1961)

[WZ17] Wichs, D., Zirdelis, G.: Obfuscating compute-and-compare programs under LWE. IACR Cryptology ePrint Archive 2017:276 (2017)

More Efficient Algorithms for the NTRU Key Generation Using the Field Norm

Thomas Pornin[1] and Thomas Prest[2](✉)

[1] NCC Group, Toronto, Canada
thomas.pornin@nccgroup.com
[2] PQShield Ltd., Oxford, UK
thomas.prest@pqshield.com

Abstract. NTRU lattices [13] are a class of polynomial rings which allow for compact and efficient representations of the lattice basis, thereby offering very good performance characteristics for the asymmetric algorithms that use them. Signature algorithms based on NTRU lattices have fast signature generation and verification, and relatively small signatures, public keys and private keys.

A few lattice-based cryptographic schemes entail, generally during the key generation, solving the *NTRU equation*:

$$fG - gF = q \mod x^n + 1$$

Here f and g are fixed, the goal is to compute solutions F and G to the equation, and all the polynomials are in $\mathbb{Z}[x]/(x^n + 1)$. The existing methods for solving this equation are quite cumbersome: their time and space complexities are at least cubic and quadratic in the dimension n, and for typical parameters they therefore require several megabytes of RAM and take more than a second on a typical laptop, precluding onboard key generation in embedded systems such as smart cards.

In this work, we present two new algorithms for solving the NTRU equation. Both algorithms make a repeated use of the field norm in tower of fields; it allows them to be faster and more compact than existing algorithms by factors $\tilde{O}(n)$. For lattice-based schemes considered in practice, this reduces both the computation time and RAM usage by factors at least 100, making key pair generation within range of smart card abilities.

1 Introduction

NTRU lattices are a class of trapdoor lattices that were introduced by [13], as the core object in which the NTRUEncrypt asymmetric encryption algorithm is expressed. Given a monic polynomial $\phi \in \mathbb{Z}[x]$ of degree n, the lattice is

Parts of this work were done when Thomas Prest was an engineer at Thales, and was supported by the projects PROMETHEUS (European Union Horizon 2020 Research and Innovation Program, grant 780701) and RISQ (French Programme d'Investissement d'Avenir, grant P141580).

D. Lin and K. Sako (Eds.): PKC 2019, LNCS 11443, pp. 504–533, 2019.
https://doi.org/10.1007/978-3-030-17259-6_17

generated by two "short" polynomials f and g modulo ϕ. The coefficients of f and g are very small integers (in NTRUEncrypt, they are limited to $\{-1, 0, 1\}$). The polynomial f and g are secret, but their ratio:

$$h = g/f \bmod \phi \bmod q \tag{1}$$

for a given, small integer q, is public. The polynomial f is chosen so as to be invertible modulo ϕ and q. q is not necessarily prime.

NTRU lattices offer good performance characteristics; they have been reused in several other asymmetric schemes. Some of these schemes require the lattice trapdoor to be "complete", which means that beyond knowledge of f and g, the private key owner must know two other short polynomials F and G that fulfill the *NTRU equation*:

$$fG - gF = q \tag{2}$$

A complete NTRU trapdoor is required for example in the signature scheme NTRUSign [12], an identity-based encryption scheme [8], the signature scheme Falcon [18], and the hierarchical identity-based encryption scheme LATTE [4].

Finding the *shortest* solution (for a given norm) is a hard problem; however, computing a solution which is short enough for the purpose of running an algorithm based on complete NTRU lattices, is doable. Solving the NTRU equation is then part of the key generation process.

While the NTRU equation looks simple, solving it in an efficient manner is nontrivial. Existing algorithms for finding a solution [12,21] have time and space complexities that are at least cubic and quadratic in the dimension n, respectively. For typical parameter sizes, this translates in practice into requiring several megabytes of RAM and taking around 2 s on a typical computer.[1] This precludes implementation in many constrained, embedded systems. One could argue that being able to implement the key generation on an embedded device is not too important since one could simply generate it externally and copy-paste the key in the device, but keeping the private key in a tamper-resistant device for its complete lifecycle is often desirable for security (as there is no external exposure at any time) and compliance (e.g. to the FIPS 140-2 norm [16]).

In this article, we show how we can leverage the field norm in polynomial rings to achieve much improved performance for solving the NTRU equation. It allows us to propose two new algorithms based on the field norm, which provide better (time and space) complexities than existing algorithms by quasilinear factors in n (precisely, at least $O(n/\log n)$). As a by-product, we developed an improved algorithm for computing polynomial resultants, when one of the polynomials is a cyclotomic (see Sect. 3). Table 1 compares the asymptotic complexity achieved by our new techniques with existing known methods.

We implemented both the classic resultant-based NTRU solver, and our new algorithms, with similar optimization efforts and tools. This allowed direct measures of the performance improvement of our techniques, which corroborated the

[1] All the timings in this document are provided for a MacBook Pro laptop (Intel Core i7-6567U @ 3.30 GHz), running Linux in 64-bit mode.

Table 1. Comparison of our new methods for solving the NTRU equation with existing ones. B denotes an upper bound on $\log\|f\|, \log\|g\|$. The tag [K] indicates that Karatsuba's algorithm was used for large integer multiplications, and [SS] indicates the Schönhage-Strassen algorithm was used.

Method	Time complexity		Space complexity
Resultant [12]	$\tilde{O}(n(n^2 + B))$		$O(n^2B)$
HNF [21]	$\tilde{O}(n^3B)$		$O(n^2B)$
TowerSolverR (Algorithm 4)	$O((nB)^{\log_2(3)} \log n)$	[K]	$O(n(B + \log n) \log n)$
	$\tilde{O}(nB)$	[SS]	
TowerSolverI (Algorithm 5)	$O((nB)^{\log_2(3)} \log^2 n)$	[K]	$O(n(B + \log n))$
	$\tilde{O}(nB)$	[SS]	

asymptotic analysis: for a typical degree ($n = 1024$), the new methods are faster *and* smaller than the classic algorithms, both by a factor of 100 or more.

1.1 Techniques

Our algorithms rely on repeatedly applying the project-then-lift paradigm, a well-known paradigm in algorithmic number theory and cryptanalysis which consists of projecting a problem onto a subset in which it becomes easier, before lifting the solution to the original set.

In our case, we rely on using the presence of *towers of fields* and *towers of rings.* As an illustration, let us consider the following tower of fields:

$$\mathbb{K}_\ell \ / \ \mathbb{K}_{\ell-1} \ / \ \dots \ / \ \mathbb{K}_1 \ / \ \mathbb{K}_0 = \mathbb{Q}$$

where $\forall i, \mathbb{K}_i = \mathbb{Q}[x]/(x^{2^i} + 1)$, and the associated tower of rings (which are the rings of integers of the corresponding fields) with $n = 2^\ell$:

$$\mathbb{Z}[x]/(x^n + 1) \supsetneq \mathbb{Z}[x]/(x^{n/2} + 1) \supsetneq \cdots \supsetneq \mathbb{Z}[x]/(x^2 + 1) \supsetneq \mathbb{Z}$$

It is well known that the field norm can map any element $f \in \mathbb{Z}[x]/(x^n + 1)$ onto a smaller ring of its tower. This fact is exploited in the "overstretched NTRU" attack [1], where problems are mapped to a smaller ring, then solved, at which point the solution is lifted back to the original ring.

However, what is not exploited in these works is the fact that the field norm plays nicely with towers of fields: for a tower of field extensions $\mathbb{L}/\mathbb{K}/\mathbb{J}$ and $f \in \mathbb{L}$, we have $\mathrm{N}_{\mathbb{K}/\mathbb{J}} \circ \mathrm{N}_{\mathbb{L}/\mathbb{K}}(f) = \mathrm{N}_{\mathbb{L}/\mathbb{J}}(f)$ (where N denotes the field norm). This fact is at the heart of our algorithms.

We first repeatedly use the field norm to project over $\mathbb{Z}$ equations which are originally over $\mathbb{Z}[x]/(x^n + 1)$; this is the *descent* phase. It turns out that these equations can be solved much faster over $\mathbb{Z}$. We then use the properties of the field norm to lift our solutions back in $\mathbb{Z}[x]/(x^n+1)$; this is the *lifting* phase. This simple principle allows us to gain a factor at least $\tilde{O}(n)$ over classical algorithms.

We apply a few additional tricks such as memory-laziness, the use of residue number systems, or the fact that in cyclotomic fields, the Galois conjugates of an element in FFT or NTT representation are straightforward to compute. These techniques make our implementation faster and more memory-efficient.

1.2 Applications

Our new algorithms impact at least four existing lattice-based schemes.

NTRUSign. The first scheme which entails solving this equation in the key generation is NTRUSign [12]. In its current form, this scheme is however insecure, but for reasons independent of the key generation.

Falcon. In the signature scheme Falcon [18], the costliest part of the key generation consists of solving an NTRU equation. Without our techniques, it would require about 2^{33} clock cycles on a recent laptop computer, and 3 MBytes of RAM, for the highest security level, limiting its usability for many embedded devices. As we gain a factor 100 in speed *and* memory, this significantly widens the range of the devices on which Falcon can be entirely implemented.

DLP. The setup phase of the identity-based encryption scheme DLP [8] is identical to the key generation of Falcon. The same remark as above applies.

LATTE. Very recently, Campbell and Groves [4] introduced LATTE, a hierarchical identity-based encryption scheme which essentially combines [8] with the Bonsai trees construction of [5]. At each extraction of a user secret key, LATTE needs to solve a *generalized* NTRU equation. More precisely, given $f_1, \ldots, f_k \in \mathbb{Z}[x]/(\phi)$, it needs to compute $F_1, \ldots, F_k \in \mathbb{Z}[x]/(\phi)$ such that

$$\sum f_i F_i = q$$

and k may in practice be equal to 3 or 4 (see [4, slide 23]). Our techniques can be extended in a straightforward way to solve this kind of equation. The impact for LATTE is even more important than for the aforementioned works, as an authority may need to perform many extractions (typically, one per user and per key renewal period).

1.3 Related Works

The NTRU equation was first introduced and solved in [12].

Another method for solving the NTRU equation was suggested by Stehlé and Steinfeld [21], using the Hermite Normal Form. The most space-efficient algorithm for computing the HNF is due to Micciancio and Warinschi [15]; however, like the method based on resultants, it has quadratic space complexity and quasi-cubic time complexities, and does not solve the RAM usage issue.

The use we make of the field norm is reminiscent of the "overstretched NTRU" attack by [1], except that these works are cryptanalytic and use the field norm once, whereas ours uses it repeatedly and improves cryptographic constructions.

1.4 Roadmap

In Sect. 2, we introduce our notations, and recall the classic resultant-based algorithm; we also describe some known mathematical tools that we will use in our new algorithm. In Sect. 3, we present a novel method for computing specific cases of resultants; our new algorithm builds on this method, and is described in Sect. 4, where we also show how it can be viewed as an optimisation of the classic resultant-based algorithm. Implementation issues are discussed in Sect. 5.

2 Preliminaries

We denote by $\mathbb{Z}, \mathbb{Q}, \mathbb{R}, \mathbb{C}$ the ring of integers and the fields of rational, real and complex numbers. For $a > 0, b > 1$, we denote by $\log_b a$ the logarithm of a in the basis b, with the convention $\log a = \log_2 a$. For an integer $r > 0$, we denote by $\mathbb{Z}_r$ the ring of integers modulo r.

2.1 Polynomial Rings and Fields

Let $\mathbb{Z}[x]$ be the ring of polynomials with integer coefficients (thereafter called *integral polynomials*). Let ϕ be a non-zero monic integral polynomial of degree $n \geq 1$ (i.e. $\phi = x^n + \sum_{i=0}^{n-1} \phi_i x^i$). Euclidean division of any integral polynomial by ϕ is well-defined and yields a unique remainder of degree less than n; we can therefore define $\mathbb{Z}[x]/(\phi)$, the ring of integral polynomials modulo ϕ.

Similarly, we define $\mathbb{Q}[x]/(\phi)$, $\mathbb{C}[x]/(\phi)$ and $\mathbb{Z}_r[x]/(\phi)$. When ϕ is irreducible in $\mathbb{Z}[x]$, it is also irreducible in $\mathbb{Q}[x]$, and $\mathbb{Q}[x]/(\phi)$ is a field. In this article, we will work modulo polynomials ϕ which are irreducible in $\mathbb{Q}[x]$; however, in general, $\mathbb{C}[x]/(\phi)$ and $\mathbb{Z}_r[x]/(\phi)$ are *not* fields.

2.2 Matrices and Vectors

While the point of using polynomial rings to represent lattices is to avoid computations related to matrices and vectors, we will still use such algebraic objects in some proofs.

We will denote matrices in bold uppercase (e.g. $\mathbf{B}$) and vectors in bold lowercase (e.g. $\mathbf{v}$). We use the row convention for vectors.

The p-norm of a vector $\mathbf{v}$ is denoted $\|\mathbf{v}\|_p$, and, by convention, $\|\mathbf{v}\| = \|\mathbf{v}\|_2$. We recall that for $\mathbf{v} \in \mathbb{C}^n$ and $0 < r \leq p \leq \infty$, and with the convention $1/\infty = 0$:

$$\|\mathbf{v}\|_p \leq \|\mathbf{v}\|_r \leq n^{\left(\frac{1}{r}-\frac{1}{p}\right)} \|\mathbf{v}\|_p. \tag{3}$$

For a polynomial $f \in \mathbb{C}[x]/(\phi)$, where ϕ is a monic polynomial of degree n, we denote by $\mathcal{C}_\phi(f)$ the $n \times n$ matrix whose j-th row consists in the coefficients of $x^{j-1} f \bmod \phi$:

$$\mathcal{C}_\phi(f) = \begin{bmatrix} f \bmod \phi \\ xf \bmod \phi \\ \dots \\ x^{n-1} f \bmod \phi \end{bmatrix} \tag{4}$$

When ϕ is clear from context, we will simply note $\mathcal{C}(f)$. One can check that when $\phi = x^n + 1$, the matrix $\mathcal{C}_\phi(f)$ is a skew-circulant matrix.

The operator $f \in \mathbb{C}[x]/(\phi) \mapsto \mathcal{C}(f)$ is a ring isomorphism onto its image. In particular, for all $f, g \in \mathbb{C}[x]/(\phi)$, we have:

$$\begin{aligned} \mathcal{C}(f+g) &= \mathcal{C}(f) + \mathcal{C}(g) \\ \mathcal{C}(fg) &= \mathcal{C}(f)\mathcal{C}(g) \end{aligned} \tag{5}$$

2.3 Fast Integer Multiplication

Our techniques, when applied to solving the NTRU equation, imply the use of large integers. Asymptotic computational costs depend on the time complexity of multiplying two such integers. We denote by $\mathcal{M}(b)$ that complexity, when the size in bits of the two integers is bounded by b:

- if we use Karatsuba's algorithm, then $\mathcal{M}(b) = O(b^{\log_2(3)}) \approx O(b^{1.585})$;
- with the Schönhage-Strassen algorithm [19], $\mathcal{M}(b) = \Theta(b \cdot \log b \cdot \log\log b)$.

Karatsuba's algorithm is more efficient for small values of b, but the Schönhage-Strassen algorithm [19] is asymptotically better. When giving the time complexities of our improved algorithms, we will consider both methods.

It shall be noted that asymptotic complexity is a reasonable estimate of performance only for "large enough" parameters. In our implementations, we found that for typical parameters (degree n up to 1024), the bottleneck was not integer multiplication, but rather Babai's reduction, which entails performing floating-point operations.

2.4 Cyclotomic Polynomials

Most lattice-based cryptographic algorithms that use polynomial rings to represent structured lattices rely on cyclotomic polynomials (some notable exceptions being e.g. [3,20]). Cyclotomic polynomials have some properties that make them ideal for use of the field norm.

Definition 1. *For an integer $m \geq 1$, the m-th cyclotomic polynomial is:*

$$\Phi_m = \prod_{\substack{0<k<m \\ gcd(k,m)=1}} (x - e^{2i\pi(k/m)}) \tag{6}$$

Cyclotomic polynomials have the following well-known properties:

- They are in $\mathbb{Z}[x]$ and are irreducible in $\mathbb{Q}[x]$.
- The degree of Φ_m is $\varphi(m)$, where φ denotes Euler's function: $\varphi(m) = |\mathbb{Z}_m^\times|$.
- If $n = 2^\ell$, then $\Phi_{2n} = x^n + 1$.
- If p is a prime factor of m, then:

$$\Phi_{mp}(x) = \Phi_m(x^p) \tag{7}$$

Since cyclotomic polynomials are irreducible, $\mathbb{Q}[x]/(\Phi_m)$ is a field for all $m \geq 1$; we will call them *cyclotomic fields.*

2.5 The Field Norm

The field norm is the central tool we use in our algorithms, and the key to their efficiency. In this section, we recall its definition, as well as a few properties.

Definition 2 (Field Norm). *Let $\mathbb{K}$ be a number field, and $\mathbb{L}$ be a Galois extension of $\mathbb{K}$. We denote by $\mathrm{Gal}(\mathbb{L}/\mathbb{K})$ the Galois group of the field extension $\mathbb{L}/\mathbb{K}$. The field norm $\mathrm{N}_{\mathbb{L}/\mathbb{K}} : \mathbb{L} \to \mathbb{K}$ is a map defined for any $f \in \mathbb{L}$ by the product of the Galois conjugates of f:*

$$\mathrm{N}_{\mathbb{L}/\mathbb{K}}(f) = \prod_{\mathrm{g} \in \mathrm{Gal}(\mathbb{L}/\mathbb{K})} \mathrm{g}(f) \tag{8}$$

Equivalently, $\mathrm{N}_{\mathbb{L}/\mathbb{K}}(f)$ can be defined as the determinant of the $\mathbb{K}$-linear map $\psi_f : a \in \mathbb{L} \mapsto fa$.

It is clear from the definition that the field norm is a multiplicative morphism. In addition, the field norm is compatible with composition: for a tower of extensions $\mathbb{L}/\mathbb{K}/\mathbb{J}$, it holds that $\mathrm{N}_{\mathbb{L}/\mathbb{K}} \circ \mathrm{N}_{\mathbb{K}/\mathbb{J}}(f) = \mathrm{N}_{\mathbb{L}/\mathbb{J}}(f)$.

For conciseness, $\mathbb{K}$ and $\mathbb{L}$ may be omitted from the subscript when clear from context. For example, when $f \in \mathbb{L}$ and $\mathbb{K}$ is the unique largest proper subfield of $\mathbb{L}$, then we denote $\mathrm{N}(f) = \mathrm{N}_{\mathbb{L}/\mathbb{K}}(f)$. In addition, if $f \in \mathbb{L}$ and $\mathbb{L}$ sits atop a field tower that is clear from context, then we may abusively denote by $\mathrm{N}^i(f)$ the i-times composition of N. For example, if we consider the following field tower:

$$\mathbb{Q}[x]/(x^n+1) \;/\; \mathbb{Q}[x]/(x^{n/2}+1) \;/\; \dots \;/\; \mathbb{Q}[x]/(x^2+1) \;/\; \mathbb{Q} \tag{9}$$

with $n = 2^\ell$, then $\mathrm{N}^i(f)$ sends $f \in \mathbb{Q}[x]/(x^n+1)$ to $\mathbb{Q}[x]/(x^{n/(2^i)}+1)$.

The Case of Cyclotomic Extensions. For cyclotomic extensions, the field norm can be expressed in a form which is convenient for us. Let $m, n > 0$ be integers such that $n|m$, $\mathbb{L} = \mathbb{Q}[x]/(\Phi_m)$ and $\mathbb{K} = \mathbb{Q}[y]/(\Phi_n)$. The morphism $y \mapsto x^{m/n}$ defines a field extension $\mathbb{L}/\mathbb{K}$. The Galois conjugates $\mathrm{g}_a(f)$ of $f \in \mathbb{L}$ are then of the form

$$\mathrm{g}_a(f)(x) = f(x^a) \tag{10}$$

for the set of $a \in \mathbb{Z}_m$ verifying $a = 1 \bmod n$. This provides a simple and efficient way of computing the norm $\mathrm{N}_{\mathbb{L}/\mathbb{K}}(f) = \prod_a \mathrm{g}_a(f)$, especially in FFT or NTT.

In the particular case where $n = 2^\ell$, $\mathbb{L} = \mathbb{Q}[x]/(\Phi_{2n})$ and $\mathbb{K} = \mathbb{Q}[y]/(\Phi_n)$, the field norm is particularly simple to express. Any $f \in \mathbb{L}$ can be "split" into its coefficients of even and odd degrees:

$$f = f_e(x^2) + x f_o(x^2) \tag{11}$$

with $f_o, f_e \in \mathbb{K}$. Noting $\psi_f : a \in \mathbb{L} \mapsto fa$, we have

$$\mathrm{N}_{\mathbb{L}/\mathbb{K}}(f) = \det{}_{\mathbb{K}}(\psi_f) = \det \begin{bmatrix} f_e & f_o \\ y f_o & f_e \end{bmatrix} = f_e^2 - y f_o^2 \tag{12}$$

2.6 Resultants

Resultants are powerful tools in number theory. Among other applications, they allow to keep track of coefficient growth when computing the (pseudo-)GCD of polynomials in $\mathbb{Z}[x]$, and they play a crucial role in a previous algorithm by [12] which solves the NTRU equation. We will see (in Sect. 3) that our first application of the field norm is an efficient algorithm to compute resultants between a cyclotomic polynomial ϕ of degree n, and another polynomial of degree less than n.

Definition 3 (Resultant). *Let f, g be two polynomials in $\mathbb{C}[x]$, of degrees n and m, respectively. We denote their coefficients and roots as follows:*

$$\begin{aligned} f(x) &= \sum_{j=0}^{n} f_j x^j = f_n \prod_{j=0}^{n-1} (x - \alpha_j) \\ g(x) &= \sum_{k=0}^{m} g_k x^k = g_m \prod_{k=0}^{m-1} (x - \beta_k) \end{aligned} \tag{13}$$

The resultant *of f and g is defined by either of these two equivalent definitions:*

1. $\mathrm{Res}(f, g) = f_n^m g_m^n \prod_{j,k} (\alpha_j - \beta_k) = f_n^m \prod_j g(\alpha_j) = (-1)^{mn} g_m^n \prod_k f(\beta_k)$
2. $\mathrm{Res}(f, g) = \det(\mathrm{Syl}(f, g))$, *where* $\mathrm{Syl}(f, g)$ *denotes the Sylvester matrix of f and g:*

$$\mathrm{Syl}(f, g) = \begin{bmatrix} f_n & 0 & \cdots & 0 & g_m & 0 & \cdots & 0 \\ f_{n-1} & f_n & \ddots & \vdots & \vdots & g_m & \ddots & \vdots \\ \vdots & f_{n-1} & \ddots & 0 & \vdots & & \ddots & 0 \\ \vdots & \vdots & \ddots & f_n & g_1 & & & g_m \\ f_0 & & & f_{n-1} & g_0 & \ddots & & \vdots \\ 0 & \ddots & & \vdots & 0 & \ddots & g_1 & \vdots \\ \vdots & \ddots & f_0 & \vdots & \vdots & \ddots & g_0 & g_1 \\ 0 & \cdots & 0 & f_0 & 0 & \cdots & 0 & g_0 \end{bmatrix} \tag{14}$$

The second definition makes it clear that if f and g are integral polynomials, then their resultant will also be an integer.

The resultant of f and g can be computed with the Euclidean Algorithm on polynomials. The Extended Euclidean Algorithm (also called Extended GCD) furthermore keeps track of intermediate quotients in order to yield Bézout coefficients, i.e. polynomials u and v in $\mathbb{C}[x]$ such that $uf + vg = \text{Res}(f, g)$. When f and g are integral polynomials, the Bézout coefficients will also be integral polynomials.

In addition to these definitions, the following proposition will be useful for providing bounds over the resultant.

Proposition 1. *If g is monic with distinct roots over $\mathbb{C}$, then, for all $f \in \mathbb{C}[x]/(g)$, $\text{Res}(g, f) = \det(\mathcal{C}_g(f))$.*

Proof. For a fixed g, all the matrices $\mathcal{C}_g(f)$ are co-diagonalizable:

$$\mathcal{C}_g(f) = \mathbf{V}^{-1} \times \mathbf{D} \times \mathbf{V}$$

Where $\mathbf{V}$ is the Vandermonde matrix associated to the roots of g, and $\mathbf{D}$ is the diagonal matrix which diagonal terms are the evaluations of f over the roots of g. As a consequence, $\det \mathcal{C}_g(f) = \det \mathbf{D} = \prod_{g(\gamma)=0} f(\gamma) = \text{Res}(g, f)$. □

2.7 Fast Fourier Transform and Number Theoretic Transform

The Fast Fourier Transform, and its variant the Number Theoretic Transform, are powerful tools that allow for efficient computations in polynomial rings. The field norm, in particular, can be very simply and quickly evaluated when the operands use the FFT or NTT representation. Most of the speed-ups obtained by our techniques come from the interaction between the field norm and the FFT/NTT.

Let $\phi \in \mathbb{Q}[x]$ be a monic polynomial of degree n, with n distinct roots $(\gamma_j)_{0 \leq j < n}$ over $\mathbb{C}$. For $f \in \mathbb{C}[x]/(\phi)$, its *Fourier Transform* $\hat{f}$ is defined as:

$$\hat{f} = \left(f(\gamma_j)\right)_{0 \leq j < n} \tag{15}$$

The Fourier Transform is an isomorphism between $\mathbb{C}[x]/(\phi)$ and $\mathbb{C}^n$. Therefore, for $f, g \in \mathbb{C}[x]/(\phi)$, the Fourier transform of $f + g$ and fg can be computed by term-wise addition and multiplication, respectively, of $\hat{f}$ and $\hat{g}$.

The *Fast Fourier Transform* (or FFT) is a well-known algorithm for computing the Fourier Transform of f in the special case of $\phi = x^n + 1$ with $n = 2^\ell$ [7,10]. The FFT has time complexity $O(n \log n)$ operations in $\mathbb{C}$; the inverse transform can also be computed with similar efficiency. In particular, the FFT allows for computing the product of two polynomials modulo ϕ with complexity $O(n \log n)$. The FFT can be extended to other moduli, especially cyclotomic polynomials.

The *Number Theoretic Transform* (or NTT) is the analog of the Fourier Transform over the finite field $\mathbb{Z}_r$ for a given prime r. The NTT is well-defined as long as ϕ splits over $\mathbb{Z}_r$; when $\phi = x^n + 1$, it suffices that $r = 1 \bmod 2n$. As in the case of the FFT, the NTT can be computed in $O(n \log n)$ elementary operations in $\mathbb{Z}_r$ for some moduli, in particular cyclotomic polynomials.

2.8 Babai's Reduction

Before we show how to solve the NTRU equation, we present one last tool which plays an important role in this process: Babai's reduction, or rather a generalization of it. This reduction transforms a solution of the NTRU equation into another solution with shorter polynomials. We first define the adjoint.

Definition 4 (Adjoint). *Let $\phi \in \mathbb{Q}[x]$ be monic with distinct roots (γ_j) over $\mathbb{C}$. For $f \in \mathbb{C}[x]/(\phi)$, we define its adjoint $f^\star$ as the unique polynomial in $\mathbb{C}[x]/(\phi)$ such that for each γ_j:*

$$f^\star(\gamma_j) = \overline{f(\gamma_j)} \tag{16}$$

where $\bar{\cdot}$ denotes the complex conjugation.

Existence and uniqueness are easily obtained by noticing that, in FFT representation, computing the adjoint is equivalent to replacing each Fourier coefficient with its conjugate.

If $f \in \mathbb{R}[x]/(\phi)$, then $f^\star \in \mathbb{R}[x]/(\phi)$. Indeed, if γ is a root of ϕ, then $\overline{\gamma}$ is also a root of ϕ, and $\overline{f(\gamma)} = f(\overline{\gamma})$; therefore, $f^\star(\overline{\gamma}) = \overline{f^\star(\gamma)}$ for all roots γ of ϕ. This property is achieved only by real polynomials, i.e. polynomials whose complex coefficients are all real numbers.

The adjoint allows us to define Reduce (Algorithm 1), which is a straightforward generalization of Babai's nearest plane algorithm [2] over $\mathbb{Z}[x]/(\phi)$-modules. For inputs $f, g, F, G \in \mathbb{Z}[x]/(\phi)$, the Reduce algorithm computes F' and G' of close to minimal size such that $fG - gF = fG' - gF'$:

Algorithm 1. $\mathsf{Reduce}_\phi(f, g, F, G)$

Require: $f, g, F, G \in \mathbb{Z}[x]/(\phi)$
Ensure: $F', G' \in \mathbb{Z}[x]/(\phi)$ such that $fG' - gF' = fG - gF \bmod \phi$

1: **do**
2: $\quad k \leftarrow \left\lfloor \frac{Ff^\star + Gg^\star}{ff^\star + gg^\star} \right\rceil$
3: $\quad (F, G) \leftarrow (F - kf, G - kg)$
4: **while** $k \neq 0$
5: **return** F, G

Several iterations may be needed, especially if k is computed in low precision. Indeed, in practice the coefficients of the polynomials F, G can be extremely large before reduction, and it is therefore more efficient to compute k with a low precision (e.g. using `double` values in the C programming language) over approximations of the polynomial coefficients: this allows the use of the FFT representation, where polynomial multiplications and adjoints are easily computed. Each iteration then yields an approximate k value with small coefficients (with scaling). Of course, using floating-point arithmetic means that one could be stuck in an infinite loop, but this is easily thwarted by exiting the algorithm as soon as the norm of (F, G) stops decreasing.

We note that computation of k involves a division of polynomials modulo ϕ. In FFT representation, division is simply applied term by term. Since ϕ is irreducible over $\mathbb{Q}[x]$, no division by 0 occurs here. In practice, though, use of approximate values in low precision may (rarely) yield situations where we end up dividing by 0. As will be explained in Sect. 5.1, occasional failures can easily be tolerated in the context of key pair generation for a cryptographic algorithm.

In this article, we will use Reduce in several places, each time with polynomials f, g, F, G that fulfill the NTRU equation (Eq. 2). If $fG - gF = q$, then, heuristically, the Reduce algorithm computes F' and G' such that the coefficients of F' and G' have about the same maximal size as the coefficients of f and g.

2.9 Solving the NTRU Equation with Resultants

We now present the first known method for solving the NTRU equation (Eq. 2): given f and g in $\mathbb{Z}[x]/(\phi)$, find F and G in $\mathbb{Z}[x]/(\phi)$ such that $fG-gF = q$, where q is a given relatively small integer. Our techniques are best demonstrated by showing how they apply to, and speed up, this classic NTRU solving algorithm.

This method works for any monic ϕ irreducible over $\mathbb{Q}[x]$; it was introduced in [12] and an implementation can be found in [8]. It relies on Bézout equations over $\mathbb{Z}[x]$:

- First, we compute Bézout coefficients $s, s', t, t' \in \mathbb{Z}[x]$, and integers R_f and R_g, such that:
$$\begin{aligned} sf + s'\phi &= R_f \\ tg + t'\phi &= R_g \end{aligned} \tag{17}$$
Since ϕ is irreducible over $\mathbb{Q}[x]$, it is guaranteed that we can enforce the condition $R_f, R_g \in \mathbb{Z}$. The s' and t' polynomials do not actually need to be computed; only s and t are used thereafter.
- We compute the GCD δ of R_f and R_g, along with Bézout coefficients $u, v \in \mathbb{Z}$ such that:
$$uR_f + vR_g = \delta \tag{18}$$
- If δ is a divisor of q, we can then combine Eqs. 17 and 18, yielding a solution to Eq. 2:
$$\left(\frac{uq}{\delta}s\right)f + \left(\frac{vq}{\delta}t\right)g = q \mod \phi \tag{19}$$

Since $\mathbb{Q}$ is a field and ϕ is irreducible over $\mathbb{Q}[x]$, finding solutions $s, t \in \mathbb{Q}[x], R_f = R_g = 1$ to Eq. 17 is doable via the extended GCD. Because $\mathbb{Z}$ is not a field but only an integral domain, we cannot straightforwardly apply the extended GCD on $\mathbb{Z}[x]$. However, by scaling the solutions in $\mathbb{Q}[x]$, one may obtain solutions in $\mathbb{Z}[x]$ which verify $R_f = \text{Res}(\phi, f)$ and $R_g = \text{Res}(\phi, g)$ (see e.g. [9, Corollary 6.21])[2].

---

[2] Several techniques (on-the-fly rescaling, computation modulo small primes, etc.) have been proposed to make the extended GCD more efficient (for an overview, see e.g. [9, Chapter 6]), but they result in the same bounds over R_f, R_g.

In practice, one may get $|R_f|$ and $|R_g|$ to be smaller than $|\operatorname{Res}(f,\phi)|$ and $|\operatorname{Res}(g,\phi)|$, but usually not by much. In the general case, these bounds are tight (e.g. for $f = 1 - kx, \phi = 1 + x$).

Using this method, combined with Babai's reduction to obtain a short solution (F, G), yields the Algorithm 2.

Algorithm 2. $\mathsf{ResultantSolver}_{\phi,q}(f, g)$

Require: $f, g \in \mathbb{Z}[x]/(\phi)$
Ensure: Polynomials F, G such that Equation 2 is verified
1: Compute $R_f \in \mathbb{Z}$ and $s \in \mathbb{Z}[x]$ such that $sf = R_f \bmod \phi$
2: Compute $R_g \in \mathbb{Z}$ and $t \in \mathbb{Z}[x]$ such that $tg = R_g \bmod \phi$
3: Compute $u, v \in \mathbb{Z}$ such that $uR_f + vR_g = \mathrm{GCD}(R_f, R_g)$
4: **if** $\delta = \mathrm{GCD}(R_f, R_g)$ is not a divisor of q **then**
5:     **abort**
6: $(F, G) \leftarrow (-(vq/\delta)s, (uq/\delta)t)$ ▷ At this point, $fG - gF = q$ already
7: $\mathsf{Reduce}(f, g, F, G)$
8: **return** F, G

Correctness. One can show that if ϕ is irreducible over $\mathbb{Q}[x]$, then Algorithm 2 fails if and only the NTRU equation does not have a solution for the inputs (f, g). This will also be true for our new algorithms. Of course, handling such cases is important (and has been studied in [21]), but since our algorithms are "optimal" in this regard (they fail if and only if there is no solution at all), we consider this to be outside the scope of this document.

Lemma 1 (Complexity of ResultantSolver for $\phi = x^n + 1$ and $q = 1$). *Let $\phi = x^n + 1$, $q = 1$, $\deg(f), \deg(g) < n$ and the euclidean norms of f, g be bounded by some value: $\log\|f\|, \log\|g\| \leq B$. Algorithm 2 (ResultantSolver) runs in space $O(n^2 B)$ and time $O(n(n^2 + B)(\log n + \log B)^2)$.*

Proof. We perform a step-by-step analysis of Algorithm 2.

S1. We have $|R_f| \leq |\operatorname{Res}(f,\phi)| = |\det \mathcal{C}_\phi(f)|$ since ϕ is monic with distinct roots. In addition:

$$\begin{aligned} |\det \mathcal{C}_\phi(f)| &\leq \|f\|_2^n && \text{(upper bound)} \\ |\det \mathcal{C}_\phi(f)| &\approx \sqrt{2\pi n}\left[\frac{\|f\|_2}{e}\right]^n && \text{(heuristic)} \end{aligned} \quad (20)$$

For any square matrix $\mathbf{B} = \{\mathbf{b}_1, \ldots, \mathbf{b}_n\}$, we have $|\det(\mathbf{B})| = \prod_i \|\tilde{\mathbf{b}}_i\| \leq \prod_i \|\mathbf{b}_i\|$, where $\tilde{\mathbf{b}}_i$ denotes the orthogonalization of $\mathbf{b}_i$ with respect to the previous rows. In our case:

- The upper bound uses the fact that each row of $\mathcal{C}_\phi(f)$ has a norm $\leq \|f\|_2$.
- For the heuristic approximation, we modelize each row of $\mathcal{C}_\phi(f)$ as a random vector of size $\|f\|_2$, so that the orthogonalization of the i-th row has a norm $\sqrt{\frac{n+1-i}{n}}\|f\|_2$. Of course, in our case the vectors are not independent, however this heuristic gives good approximations in practice.

The proven upper bound yields $\log|R_f| = O(nB)$. We even have $\log|R_f| = \Theta(nB)$ with the heuristic.
To finish the study of this step, we bound $\log\|p\|_\infty$. Since $\mathcal{C}(p) = R_f\mathcal{C}(f)^{-1}$, a straigthforward application of Cramer's rule yields $\|p\|_\infty \leq \|f\|^{n-1}$, so $\log\|p\|_\infty = O(nB)$.

S2. The analysis is identical and yields $\log|R_g|, \log\|s\|_\infty = O(nB)$.

S3. The extended GCD algorithm finds u, v such that $|u| < |R_g|$ and $|v| < |R_f|$. Since $\log|R_f|$ and $\log|R_g|$ both are in $O(nB)$, the same asymptotic bound applies to $\log|u|$ and $\log|v|$.

S6. From the previous items, we have $\log\|F\|_\infty, \log\|G\|_\infty = O(nB)$.

S7. This step can be performed with a space overhead $O(n)$ using Algorithm 1 with precision $O(1)$.

Overall, the logarithms of $|u|$, $|v|$ and of each coefficient of p, s, F, G are in $O(nB)$, so the total space complexity is in $O(n^2B)$.

The time complexity is now easy to analyze. The costliest steps are S1 and S2, and according to [9, Corollary 6.39] they can be performed in time $O(n(n^2 + B)(\log n + \log B)^2)$, which concludes the proof. □

3 Improved Algorithm for Computing Resultants

Our first application of the field norm is an improved algorithm for computing polynomial resultants, which we present in this section. This algorithm, by itself, is not sufficient to significantly reduce the CPU and RAM costs of the classic NTRU equation solving algorithm (ResultantSolver, described in Sect. 2.9); however, it is an important step toward the construction of our improved solver. Moreover, this algorithm may prove useful to other applications that use resultants but not necessarily NTRU lattices.

Let $\phi = \Phi_{pm}$ be the pm-th cyclotomic polynomial for some integers p and m, $n = \varphi(m)$ its degree and $\mathbb{K} = \mathbb{Q}[x]/(\phi)$.

Let $f \in \mathbb{K}$. It is well-known that the field norm $\mathrm{N}_{\mathbb{K}/\mathbb{Q}}(f)$ is equal to the resultant $\mathrm{Res}(\phi, f)$, however we re-explain the intuition here for cyclotomic polynomials. We recall that the resultant of f with ϕ can be computed as:

$$\mathrm{Res}(\phi, f) = \prod_{j=0}^{n-1} f(\gamma_j) \tag{21}$$

where the γ_j values are the roots of ϕ over $\mathbb{C}$.

As noted previously, $\mathbb{K}$ is a field extension of $\mathbb{Q}[x]/(\Phi_m)$ by the morphism $y \mapsto x^p$. We can thus group the n roots of ϕ into n/p sets $\{\gamma_j\zeta^k\}$, each set using a base root γ_j multiplied by ζ_k, for $k = 0$ to $p-1$, and $\zeta = e^{2i\pi/p}$ a primitive p-th root of unity. It is easily shown that these n/p sets are a partition of the n

roots of ϕ. To ease notation, we number here the base roots from 1 to n/p. This yields the following:

$$\mathrm{Res}(\phi, f) = \prod_{j=1}^{n/p} \prod_{k=0}^{p-1} f(\gamma_j \zeta^k) = \prod_{j=1}^{n/p} \mathrm{N}(f)(\gamma_j) \tag{22}$$

Note that the γ_j (the base roots of our sets) are exactly the roots of Φ_m. Thus:

$$\mathrm{Res}(\Phi_{pm}, f) = \mathrm{Res}(\Phi_m, \mathrm{N}(f)) \tag{23}$$

In other words, we can divide the degree of ϕ by p, by replacing f with $\mathrm{N}(f)$.

We may note that, in FFT representation, computing the field norm is no more than multiplying together the Fourier coefficients along the groups into which the roots of ϕ are partitioned.

As we saw in Sect. 2.6, the resultant $\mathrm{Res}(\phi, f)$ can also be defined as the determinant of the Sylvester matrix of ϕ and f. As such, it can be expressed as a polynomial expression of the coefficients of f and ϕ. The result above then expresses an equality of the expressions of $\mathrm{Res}(\Phi_{pm}, f)$ and $\mathrm{Res}(\Phi_m, \mathrm{N}(f))$ that will hold over any other field where Φ_{pm} has n roots. In particular, if f is an integral polynomial and r is a prime such that pm divides $r-1$, then we can perform all computations modulo r; notably, we can use the NTT. In NTT representation, just like in FFT representation, the field norm of f is computed by simply multiplying the NTT coefficients together along the partition groups of the roots of ϕ.

An important special case is $n = 2^\ell$. The cyclotomic polynomial is then $\phi = x^n + 1 = \Phi_{2n}$, and $p = 2$. We can furthermore apply the process repeatedly: we replace $\mathrm{Res}(x^n + 1, f)$ with $\mathrm{Res}(x^{n/2} + 1, \mathrm{N}(f))$, then $\mathrm{Res}(x^{n/4} + 1, \mathrm{N}(\mathrm{N}(f)))$, and so on. We thus obtain a very simple, recursive algorithm for computing resultants of f with $x^n + 1$:

Algorithm 3. $\mathsf{TowerResultant}_n(f)$

Require: $f \in \mathbb{Z}[x]/(x^n + 1)$ with $n = 2^\ell$
Ensure: $R_f = \mathrm{Res}(x^n + 1, f)$
1: **if** $n = 1$ **then**
2:     **return** f_0
3: **return** $\mathsf{TowerResultant}_{n/2}(\mathrm{N}(f))$

If f is an integral polynomial, then algorithm TowerResultant can be computed modulo any prime r such that n divides $r - 1$; this yields the resultant modulo r. Using sufficiently many such small primes allows rebuilding the resultant value with the Chinese Remainder Theorem. Modulo each small prime r, the NTT can be used, with cost $O(n \log n)$ operations in $\mathbb{Z}_r$, followed by $n - 1$ multiplications in $\mathbb{Z}_r$. The total cost will then depend on how many small primes we need, i.e. what is the maximum size of the resultant $\text{Res}(x^n + 1, f)$. The following lemma gives us a bound on that size:

Lemma 2. *Let the* L^1*-norm of* f *be bounded:* $\log \|f\|_1 \leq C$. *Then:* $\log |\text{Res}(x^n + 1, f)| \leq nC$.

Proof. We recall that $\hat{p}$ denote the Fourier transform of p over the roots of ϕ (here, $\phi = x^n + 1$). We have:

$$\|\widehat{\text{N}(f)}\|_\infty = \|(f(\gamma)f(-\gamma))_{\{\gamma\}}\|_\infty \leq \|(f(\gamma))_{\{\gamma\}}\|_\infty \|(f(-\gamma))_{\{\gamma\}}\|_\infty = \|\hat{f}\|_\infty^2 \quad (24)$$

where γ runs over all the roots of $x^n + 1$. Therefore, for any $0 \leq j \leq \log n$, we have $\|\widehat{\text{N}^j(f)}\|_\infty \leq \|\hat{f}\|_\infty^{2^j}$. Using classical properties of p-norms, it follows that:

$$\|\text{N}^j(f)\|_2 = \frac{1}{\sqrt{n/2^j}} \|\widehat{\text{N}^j(f)}\|_2 \leq \|\widehat{\text{N}^j(f)}\|_\infty \leq \|\hat{f}\|_\infty^{2^j} \leq \|f\|_1^{2^j} \quad (25)$$

When $2^j = n$, corresponding to the end of the recursion in algorithm TowerResultant, the result follows. □

Therefore, if the L^1-norm of f is bounded by 2^C, the resultant can be expressed over at most nC bits. The number of required small primes for the computation, using the NTT, is then $O(nC)$, yielding a total time cost of $O(n^2 C \log n)$; space complexity is $O(nC)$ (the size needed to represent the result).

This improved resultant computation can be applied to the classic NTRU equation solver:

- $\text{Res}(\phi, f)$ is computed modulo many small primes r, as explained above.
- The Bézout coefficient s such that $sf = \text{Res}(\phi, f)$ is also computed modulo each r; since $\mathbb{Z}_r$ is a field, f can be inverted modulo ϕ, allowing for computing s efficiently, in particular with the NTT.
- When enough small primes have been used, the complete resultant $\text{Res}(\phi, f)$ can be rebuilt, as well as the Bézout coefficient s, by applying the CRT on all individual monomials.

While this new algorithm reduces the time cost of ResultantSolver, it does not help with the space complexity: indeed, the coefficients of s have all about the same size as the resultant, and there are n of them. We will now show how the field norm yields new recursive formulas for solving the NTRU equation, that allow for a dramatic improvement in space complexity.

4 Improved Algorithms for Solving the NTRU Equation

This section presents new techniques and algorithms for solving the NTRU equation (Eq. 2). These algorithms result from the recursive application of the field norm to the classic NTRU solver itself, building on the improvements made to resultants and described in the previous section.

We will first present the outline and the intuition of our techniques in Sect. 4.1. In Sect. 4.2, we present a recursive algorithm based on our observations, and in Sect. 4.3, we present a slightly slower but more memory-efficient iterative algorithm. Finally, in Sect. 4.4, we will provide analyses for the time and memory requirements of both algorithms.

4.1 Outline

Let $m, p > 0$ be integers, $\mathbb{L} = \mathbb{Q}[x]/(\Phi_{pm}), \mathbb{K} = \mathbb{Q}[y]/(\Phi_m)$ and $\mathrm{N} = \mathrm{N}_{\mathbb{L}/\mathbb{K}}$. Suppose that we have a given integer q and two polynomials $f, g \in \mathbb{Z}[x]/(\Phi_{pm})$, and we want to find $F, G \in \mathbb{Z}[x]/(\Phi_{pm})$ such that:

$$fG - gF = q \tag{26}$$

On the other hand, suppose that for $\mathrm{N}(f), \mathrm{N}(g)$, which are in the smaller ring $\mathbb{Z}[y]/(\Phi_m)$, we already know $F', G' \in \mathbb{Z}[y]/(\Phi_m)$ such that:

$$\mathrm{N}(f)G' - \mathrm{N}(g)F' = q \tag{27}$$

We claim that we can use the solutions F', G' to Eq. 27 to deduce solutions F, G for Eq. 26. Indeed, we recall that $\mathrm{N}(f) = \prod_{\mathrm{g} \in \mathrm{Gal}(\mathbb{L}/\mathbb{K})} \mathrm{g}(f) = ff^{\times}$, where $f^{\times} = \prod_{\mathrm{g} \in \mathrm{Gal}(\mathbb{L}/\mathbb{K})^{\times}} \mathrm{g}(f)$ denotes the product of all the Galois conjugates of f except itself, and we have a similar equality for g. Equation 27 is then equivalent to:

$$ff^{\times}G'(x^p) - gg^{\times}F'(x^p) = q \tag{28}$$

which is an equality in the larger ring $\mathbb{Z}[x]/(\Phi_{pm})$. From this last equation, it follows that $F = g^{\times}F'(x^p)$ and $G = f^{\times}G'(x^p)$ are valid solutions for the NTRU equation.

From these observations, we can now give the outline of our algorithms for solving the NTRU equation: (1) use the field norm to project it to a smaller subring, (2) solve the equation in the smaller ring, (3) use Eq. 28 to lift the solutions back in the original ring. However, and contrary to the "overstretched NTRU" attack [1], we do not perform the projection and lifting steps once, but repeatedly. More precisely:

- we project f, g onto a smaller subring until we reach the ring of integers $\mathbb{Z}$; we call it the *descent* phase;
- once we obtain solutions in $\mathbb{Z}$, we lift them repeatedly until we are back to the original ring; we call this the *lifting* phase.

The multiple projections and liftings are key to the efficiency of our algorithms: performing them once would only yield gains in a $O(1)$ factor, but we will show that their repetition allows to gain factors larger than $\tilde{O}(n)$ in theory, and in practice a factor 100 for a typical value $n = 1024$.

The flow of our two algorithms is summarized in the Fig. 1. The descent phase is represented in the middle column, and the lifting phase is represented in the right column.

$$
\begin{array}{ccccc}
\mathbb{Z}[x]/(x^n+1) & \ni & f,g & \rightarrow & F,G \\
\cup\!\!\mid & & \downarrow & & \uparrow \\
\mathbb{Z}[x]/(x^{n/2}+1) & \ni & \mathrm{N}(f),\mathrm{N}(g) & \rightarrow & F^{[1]},G^{[1]} \\
\cup\!\!\mid & & \downarrow & & \uparrow \\
\mathbb{Z}[x]/(x^{n/4}+1) & \ni & \mathrm{N}^2(f),\mathrm{N}^2(g) & \rightarrow & F^{[2]},G^{[2]} \\
\cup\!\!\mid & & \downarrow & & \uparrow \\
\vdots & \vdots & \vdots & & \vdots \\
\cup\!\!\mid & & \downarrow & & \uparrow \\
\mathbb{Z} & \ni & \mathrm{N}^\ell(f),\mathrm{N}^\ell(g) & \rightarrow & F^{[\ell]},G^{[\ell]}
\end{array}
\tag{29}
$$

Fig. 1. Outline of Algorithms 4 and 5 for solving Eq. 2.

4.2 A Recursive Algorithm

In the special case of $\phi = x^n + 1$ with $n = 2^\ell$, we can apply these formulas with $p = 2$, and then do so again on $\phi' = x^{n/2} + 1$, repeatedly. This yields the TowerSolverR algorithm, expressed as follows:

Algorithm 4. TowerSolverR$_{n,q}(f, g)$

Require: $f, g \in \mathbb{Z}[x]/(x^n + 1)$ with n a power of two
Ensure: Polynomials F, G such that Equation 2 is verified

if $n = 1$ **then**
  Compute $u, v \in \mathbb{Z}$ such that $uf - vg = \mathrm{GCD}(f, g)$
  if $\delta = \mathrm{GCD}(f, g)$ is not a divisor of q **then**
    abort
  $(F, G) \leftarrow (vq/\delta, uq/\delta)$
  return (F, G)
else
  $f' \leftarrow \mathrm{N}(f)$ ▷ $f', g', F', G' \in \mathbb{Z}[x]/(x^{n/2} + 1)$
  $g' \leftarrow \mathrm{N}(g)$
  $(F', G') \leftarrow$ TowerSolverR$_{n/2,q}(f', g')$
  $F \leftarrow g^\times(x)F'(x^2)$ ▷ $F, G \in \mathbb{Z}[x]/(x^n + 1)$
  $G \leftarrow f^\times(x)G'(x^2)$
  Reduce(f, g, F, G)
return (F, G)

The informal explanation of why algorithm TowerSolverR uses much less space than the classic solver (ResultantSolver) is that, at each recursion step, the size of individual coefficients roughly doubles, but the degree is halved, so there are only half as many coefficients to store. The algorithm relies on Babai's reduction (Reduce) to bring back the coefficients of the newly computed (F, G) to about the same size as the coefficients of (f, g) for this recursion level. A formal space complexity analysis is given in Lemma 3.

Correctness. If it outputs a solution (termination is addressed below), the correctness of Algorithm 4 is immediate. Indeed, correctness is clear at the deepest recursion level, and if the algorithm is correct for $(f, g) \in \mathbb{Z}[x]/(x^{n/2}+1)$, then Eqs. 27 and 28 assure us that it will be correct for $(f, g) \in \mathbb{Z}[x]/(x^n+1)$.

Other Cyclotomic Polynomials. Algorithm TowerSolverR can be extended to arbitrary cyclotomic polynomials. Each iteration corresponds to a case where $\mathbb{Q}[x]/(\Phi_m)$ is considered as an extension of $\mathbb{Q}[x]/(\Phi_{m'})$, where m' divides m. The degree is divided by m/m', while average coefficient size grows by a factor approximately m/m'. The exact order in which successive divisions are applied on the degree is a matter of choice.

For instance, if we consider $\phi = \Phi_{2304} = x^{768} - x^{384} + 1$, then the algorithm may first apply a division of the degree by 3, yielding sub-polynomials modulo $x^{256} - x^{128} + 1$, then doing seven degree halving steps to bring the NTRU solving problem down to modulus $x^2 - x + 1$.

On the other hand, an implementation could first perform the seven degree halvings, down to modulus $x^6 - x^3 + 1$, and only then perform the division by 3. Both options have similar algorithmic complexity in time and space, but one may be more efficient than the other, depending on specific implementation context.

Finally, we would like to mention the polynomials of the form $x^p - x - 1$ for a prime p, as used in NTRU Prime [3]. The deliberate lack of nontrivial subfield when working with these polynomials makes it seemingly hard to apply our techniques there in a straightforward way, but a recent work [14] suggest that it might be possible.

4.3 An Iterative Algorithm

Each recursion involves computing $\mathrm{N}(f)$ and $\mathrm{N}(g)$, then saving them while the algorithm is invoked again on these two polynomials. However, all the $\mathrm{N}^i(f), \mathrm{N}^i(g)$ can be recomputed from f, g. Therefore, we may adopt a *memory-lazy* strategy and avoid storing the intermediate $\mathrm{N}^i(f), \mathrm{N}^i(g)$, instead recomputing them when needed. This yields a slower but more space-efficient iterative algorithm, described in algorithm TowerSolverI.

Compared to Algorithm 4, Algorithm 5 therefore performs a balanced trade-off by a factor $\ell = \log n$ between speed and memory.

4.4 Complexity Analysis

We now formally study the complexities of TowerSolverR and TowerSolverI.

Lemma 3 (Space complexity analysis). *Let $q = 1$ and the euclidean norms of f, g be bounded: $\log\|f\|, \log\|g\| \leq B$. We also note $\ell = \log n$. Algorithms 4 (TowerSolverR) and 5 (TowerSolverI) run in space $O(n\ell(B+\ell))$ and $O(n(B+\ell))$, respectively.*

Algorithm 5. $\mathsf{TowerSolverI}_{n,q}(f,g)$

Require: $f, g \in \mathbb{Z}[x]/(x^n + 1)$ with n a power of two
Ensure: Polynomials F, G such that Equation 2 is verified
$(f', g') \leftarrow (f, g)$
for $i \leftarrow 1, \ldots, \log n$ **do**
  $(f', g') \leftarrow (\mathrm{N}(f'), \mathrm{N}(g'))$ ▷ At that point, f' and g' have degree 0
Compute $u, v \in \mathbb{Z}$ such that $uf' - vg' = \mathrm{GCD}(f, g)$
if $\delta = \mathrm{GCD}(f, g)$ is not a divisor of q **then**
  abort
$(F, G) \leftarrow (vq/\delta, uq/\delta)$
for $i \leftarrow \log n, \ldots, 1$ **do**
  $(f', g') \leftarrow (f, g)$
  for $j \leftarrow 1, \ldots, i - 1$ **do**
    $(f', g') \leftarrow (\mathrm{N}(f'), \mathrm{N}(g'))$
  $(F, G) \leftarrow (g'^{\times} F, f'^{\times} G)$
  $\mathsf{Reduce}(f', g', F, G)$
return (F, G)

Proof. We start with Algorithm 4 (TowerSolverR). It is clear that we have the following tower of recursive calls:

$$\mathsf{TowerSolverR}_{n,q}(f, g) \rightarrow \mathsf{TowerSolverR}_{n/2,q}(\mathrm{N}(f), \mathrm{N}(g)) \rightarrow \ldots$$
$$\cdots \rightarrow \mathsf{TowerSolverR}_{1,q}(\mathrm{N}^{\ell}(f), \mathrm{N}^{\ell}(g))$$

We now bound the space needed by internal variables.

1. From Eqs. 3 and 25, each $\mathrm{N}^i(f), \mathrm{N}^i(g)$ takes $O(n(B + \ell))$ bits.
2. We now bound the (euclidean) norm of (F, G). First, we consider its norm *after reduction.* Noting $V = \mathrm{Span}((f, g))$, the vector (F, G) can be uniquely decomposed over $V \oplus V^{\perp}$ as:

$$(F, G) = (\tilde{F}, \tilde{G}) + (\breve{F}, \breve{G})$$

where $(\tilde{F}, \tilde{G}) \in V^{\perp}$, and $(\breve{F}, \breve{G}) \in V$.
We first bound the norm of $(\tilde{F}, \tilde{G})$: a simple computation shows $(\tilde{F}, \tilde{G}) = \left(\frac{f^\star}{ff^\star + gg^\star}, \frac{g^\star}{ff^\star + gg^\star}\right)$. This remains true when we evaluate $\tilde{F}, \tilde{G}$ over 0, so if we note $f = \sum_{0 \leq j < n} a_j x^{-j}$ and $\tilde{F} = \sum_{0 \leq j < n} A_j x^j$, then for any $0 \leq i < n$:

$$A_i^2 = |(x^{-i}\tilde{F})(0)|^2 = \frac{a_i^2}{|(ff^\star + gg^\star)(0)|^2} \leq \frac{a_i^2}{(\|f\|^2 + \|g\|^2)^2} \tag{30}$$

where Eq. 30 uses the following facts:
   - First equality: $A_i = (x^{-i}F)(0)$;
   - Second equality: for any polynomial p, $(x^{-i}p)^\star = x^i p^\star$ and $p^\star(0) = p(0)$;
   - Inequality: for any polynomial p, $pp^\star(0) = \|p\|^2$.

Summing Eq. 30 over all the i's yields $\|\tilde{F}\| \leq \frac{\|f\|}{\|f\|+\|g\|}$. Similarly, we get $\|\tilde{G}\| \leq \frac{\|g\|}{\|f\|+\|g\|}$, which yields $\|(\tilde{F}, \tilde{G})\| \leq 1$. It now remains to bound $\|(\breve{F}, \breve{G})\|$: if (F, G) is reduced using Babai's round-off algorithm, the triangle inequality ensures that $\|(\breve{F}, \breve{G})\| \leq n/2\|(f, g)\|$; it if is reduced using the nearest plane algorithm, the pythagorean inequality ensures that $\|(\breve{F}, \breve{G})\|^2 \leq n/4\|(f, g)\|^2$. In both cases, we have:

$$\|(F, G)\|^2 = \|(\tilde{F}, \tilde{G})\|^2 + \|(\breve{F}, \breve{G})\|^2 \leq 1 + \frac{n^2}{4}\|(f, g)\|^2 \tag{31}$$

and it follows that (F, G) can be stored in space $O(n(B+\ell))$. Of course, we also have to handle (F, G) when it is computed from $F', G', f^\times, g^\times$ and is therefore not yet reduced. We have $\|F\| \leq \sqrt{\frac{n}{2}}\|F'\|\|g\|$ and $\|G\| \leq \sqrt{\frac{n}{2}}\|G'\|\|f\|$. From the inequalities 25 and 31, it follows that (F, G) can be stored in space $O(n(B + \ell))$ even before reduction.

Algorithm 4 needs to store ℓ successive values of $(\mathrm{N}^i(f), \mathrm{N}^i(g))$, each taking space $O(n(B + \ell))$, as well as one set of polynomials F', G', F, G at once, each taking space $O(n(B + \ell))$. The space complexity of Algorithm 4 is therefore $O(n(\ell(B + \ell)))$.

For Algorithm 5, the previous analysis remains valid, except that only a constant number of values $(\mathrm{N}^i(f), \mathrm{N}^i(g))$'s need to be stored simultaneously, as they can all be recomputed from (f, g) in space $O(n(B + \ell))$, according to Lemma 2. The space complexity of algorithm is therefore $O(n(B + \ell))$. □

We now study the time complexities of Algorithms 4 and 5.

Lemma 4 (Time complexity analysis). *With the conditions of Lemma 3, the time complexities of Algorithms 4 (TowerSolverR) and 5 (TowerSolverI) are:*

- $\tilde{O}(nB)$ *for Algorithm 4 with Schönhage-Strassen;*
- $\tilde{O}(nB)$ *for Algorithm 5 with Schönhage-Strassen;*
- $O((nB)^{\log_2(3)}\ell)$ *for Algorithm 4 with Karatsuba;*
- $O((nB)^{\log_2(3)}\ell^2)$ *for Algorithm 5 with Karatsuba;*

We note that while the complexities given with Schönhage-Strassen are much better than with Karatsuba, they are misleading as the $\tilde{O}$ hides constant and logarithmic factors which are not negligible in practice. The complexities given with Karatsuba reflect much more accurately the running times that we observe for typical values of n and B.

Proof. For $i \in [\![0, \ell]\!]$, let $B_i = \log\max(\|\mathrm{N}^i(f)\|, \|\mathrm{N}^i(g)\|)$. Using Eq. 25 and the fact that $\|f\|_1 \leq \|f\|_2^2$, we have $B_j \leq 2^{j+1}B$. The two costliest steps in our algorithms are the descent (computing $\mathrm{N}^i(f), \mathrm{N}^i(g)$ for increasing i) and the lifting (computing $F^{[i]}, G^{[i]}$ for decreasing i).

- *Descent.* Computing $\mathrm{N}^{i+1}(f)$ from $\mathrm{N}^i(f)$ is essentially as costly as an NTT and an inverse NTT, which both take time $O(\frac{n}{2^i}\log(\frac{n}{2^i})\mathcal{M}(B_i))$.

Thus, it can be done in time $D_i = O(\frac{n}{2^i} \cdot \log \frac{n}{2^i} \cdot (2^i B)^{\log_2(3)})$ with Karatsuba, or $\tilde{O}(nB)$ with Schönhage-Strassen (see Sect. 2.3). This step is repeated ℓ times (once for each depth) for Algorithm 4, and $O(\ell^2)$ times ($\ell - i$ times for the depth i) for Algorithm 5.

- *Lifting.* From Eq. 31, we know that $\mathrm{N}^i(f), \mathrm{N}^i(g), F^{[i+1]}, G^{[i+1]}$ have the log of their euclidean norm bounded by $B_i + \log \frac{n}{2^i}$, so computing F, G at the recursion depth i can be done in time $R_i = O(\frac{n}{2^i} \log(\frac{n}{2^i}) \mathcal{M}(B_i + \log \frac{n}{2^i}))$. In both algorithms, this step is repeated once for each depth.

In Algorithm 5, the descent is the costliest part as computing $\mathrm{N}^{i+1}(f)$ from $\mathrm{N}^i(f)$ is done $O(\ell^2)$ times ($\ell - i$ times for the depth i). Its time complexity is therefore $\sum_{0 \le i < \ell} (\ell - i) D_i$, which ends the proof for Algorithm 5.

In Algorithm 4, the lifting is the costliest part as each individual step is slightly more expensive than for the descent. Its time complexity is then $\sum_{0 \le i < \ell} R_i$, which ends the proof for Algorithm 4. □

General Case for q. The analysis above covered the situation where the right-hand side of the NTRU equation is $q = 1$. In the general case, we may target another value of q, usually a small integer. This is done by multiplying values by q at some point in the lifting phase. In the description of algorithms TowerSolverR and TowerSolverI, that multiplication was done right after the GCD, but it could be done later on. In any case, multiplying by q increases the size of polynomial coefficients by $\log q$ bits, and Babai's reduction will in practice absorb these bits. In the worst case, the $\log q$ bits subsist to the last step, implying a space overhead of at most $O(n \log q)$ bits. The same remark applies to ResultantSolver.

Failure probability. We note that Algorithms 4 and 5 can both possibly abort. However, we note that they do so if and only if the NTRU equation has no solution for the inputs (f, g). Indeed, if there exist F, G such that $fG - gF = q \bmod (x^n + 1)$, then $\mathrm{N}^\ell(f)\,\mathrm{N}^\ell(G) - \mathrm{N}^\ell(g)\,\mathrm{N}^\ell(F) = q$ in $\mathbb{Z}$. Thus, if the NTRU equation can be solved, then Algorithms 4 and 5 will not fail and will solve it.

Output quality. An important notion is the *quality* of the solutions (F, G), for example its Euclidean norm or its Gram-Schmidt norm (as defined in e.g. [8,11]). For any of these metrics, our algorithms will output solutions of exactly the same quality as existing algorithms.

Indeed, the set of solutions is of the form $\{(F_0 + rf, G_0 + rg) | r \in \mathbb{Z}[x]/(x^n + 1)\}$, where (F_0, G_0) denotes an arbitrary solution pair. For any element in this set, Algorithm 1 will output the same solution, so the Euclidean norm of the output will be the same for Algorithms 2, 4 and 5. On the other hand, for a fixed input (f, g), all the solutions to the NTRU equation have the same Gram-Schmidt norm (see e.g. [8, Lemma 3]).

5 Implementation Issues and Performances

Our new solving algorithm (TowerSolverI) is implemented as part of the key generation process of Falcon [18], a signature scheme submitted to the NIST call for post-quantum cryptographic schemes [17]. Falcon uses modulus $\phi = x^n + 1$ (with $n = 2^\ell$) or $\phi = x^n - x^{n/2} + 1$ (with $n = 3 \cdot 2^\ell$); these two sub-cases are called "binary" and "ternary", respectively. Our implementation supports the binary case for all degrees from 2 to 1024, and the ternary case for all degrees from 12 to 768; only the higher degrees (512, 768 and 1024) provide sufficient security, but the lower values are convenient to test the correctness of the key generation process.

In the context of Falcon, the target q value for the NTRU equation is fixed to $q = 12289$ (binary case) or $q = 18433$ (ternary case). The coefficients of the secret polynomials f and g are generated with a discrete Gaussian distribution of standard deviation $1.17\sqrt{q/(2n)}$ in the binary case, thus a size of a few bits at most; they are slightly larger in the ternary case, but in practice it can be assumed that they always fit over 8 bits each for normal key sizes.

We implemented TowerSolverI, and measured the costs of the various steps so as to estimate the computational overhead of TowerSolverI when compared to TowerSolverR. We also implemented the classic solver ResultantSolver, as a baseline to estimate the impact of our new techniques based on the field norm. Test system is a MacBook Pro laptop (Intel Core i7-6567U clocked at 3.30 GHz), running Linux in 64-bit mode. Implementations are in C and do not use platform integer types larger than 64 bits. Obtained performance is the following, for modulus $\phi = x^{1024} + 1$:

Algorithm	CPU (ms)	RAM (kB)
Classic algorithm: ResultantSolver	2000	3300
New algorithm (iterative): TowerSolverI	20	30
New algorithm (recursive): TowerSolverR	17	40

The following subsections describe various optimizations and other local techniques that together allow for these substantial performance gains. The source code can also be browsed on the Falcon Web site:

https://falcon-sign.info/impl/falcon-keygen.c.html

5.1 Value Sizes

The analyses presented in Sect. 4 allow computing absolute bounds on the size of intermediate values and resultants. However, these bounds are substantially larger than average cases.

An important point is that, *in the context of key pair generation*, it is acceptable for the solving algorithm to occasionally fail. Indeed, there are unavoidable failure conditions, when (for instance) the randomly generated f polynomial is not invertible in $\mathbb{Z}_q[x]/(\phi)$. If such a case arises, then it suffices to generate new random f and g. Similarly, we may arbitrarily reject (f, g) pairs for which the NTRU equation can be solved, but some internal implementation threshold is exceeded: such rejections imply a reduction of the space of possible keys, but have no significant impact on security as long as rejections are relatively infrequent. Even rejecting half of potential private keys only gives one bit of information to attackers.

Therefore, it is acceptable to *measure* the average maximum size of intermediate values, and use such sizes as the basis for memory allocation, with some margin. For instance, the theoretical maximum bound on the coefficients of f and g at maximum recursion depth (when they are constant polynomials, and equal to their resultants with $x+1$) is about 12000 bits (for $n = 1024$); however, in practice, their average size was measured to be about 6308 bits, with a standard deviation of less than 25 bits. We can thus assume that they will almost always fit in 6500 bits, and may simply reject the very rare cases when that assumption does not hold.

This methodology allows the use of static memory allocation, that offers strong guarantees on memory usage and also helps with making the key generation process memory access pattern uncorrelated with the secret values.

5.2 RNS, CRT and NTT

A *Residue Number System* is a representation of an integer z by storing $z \bmod r_j$ for a number of moduli r_j. Any integer in a range of length no more than the product of the r_j has a unique representation and can be unambiguously recomputed with the Chinese Remainder Theorem. Integers in RNS representation can be added and multiplied by simply computing the result modulo each r_j.

In our implementation, we use moduli r_j which are prime numbers slightly below, but close to, 2^{31}. We furthermore require that ϕ has n distinct roots modulo each r_j; in the binary case, this is achieved by ensuring that $r_j = 1 \bmod 2n$. We precomputed 521 such primes, ranging from 2135955457 to 2147473409.

Computations modulo any r_j can be done with branchless code, which promotes efficiency. In the C language, addition is implemented thus:

```
static inline uint32_t
modp_add(uint32_t a, uint32_t b, uint32_t p)
{
        uint32_t d;

        d = a + b - p;
        d += p & -(d >> 31);
        return d;
}
```

This function computes the sum of `a` and `b` modulo `p`; the operation `a+b-p` is first computed modulo 2^{32}; if the result would have been negative, then the most significant bit will be set; we then *extend* that bit into a full-word mask in order to conditionally add the modulus again if necessary.

For multiplications, we use Montgomery multiplication:

```
static inline uint32_t
modp_montymul(uint32_t a, uint32_t b, uint32_t p, uint32_t p0i)
{
        uint64_t z, w;
        uint32_t d;

        z = (uint64_t)a * (uint64_t)b;
        w = ((z * p0i) & (uint64_t)0x7FFFFFFF) * p;
        d = (uint32_t)((z + w) >> 31) - p;
        d += p & -(d >> 31);
        return d;
}
```

Montgomery multiplication of a by b modulo p computes $ab/R \bmod p$, where R is a power of 2 greater than p (here, $R = 2^{31}$). The parameter `p0i` is a precomputed value equal to $-p^{-1} \bmod 2^{31}$. An integer a modulo p is said to be in "Montgomery representation" if it is kept as the value $aR \bmod p$; converting to and from Montgomery representation is done by computing a Montgomery multiplication with, respectively, $R^2 \bmod p$ or 1. The Montgomery multiplication of two integers which are in Montgomery representation, is equal to the Montgomery representation of the product of the two integers.

The Chinese Remainer Theorem (CRT), given $z_1 = z \bmod t_1$ and $z_2 = z \bmod t_2$, where t_1 and t_2 are prime to each other, allows recomputing z modulo t_1t_2 with the following equation:

$$z = z_1 + t_1((t_1^{-1} \bmod t_2)(z_1 - z_2) \bmod t_2) \tag{32}$$

In our case, we use the CRT to convert an integer back from RNS representation, applying it on the moduli r_j one by one. At each step, we have the value z modulo t_1 and t_2, where:

$$\begin{aligned} t_1 &= \prod_{j<k} r_j \\ t_2 &= r_k \end{aligned} \tag{33}$$

The inverse of t_1 modulo t_2 is precomputed and stored along with the prime r_k itself. The CRT formula above can thus be applied with:

- a reduction of a big integer modulo r_k;
- a subtraction and a multiplication modulo r_k;
- a multiplication of a small integer (modulo r_k) with a large integer (t_1);
- an addition of two large integers.

This process can be done in place, if big integers are represented in basis 2^{31}, i.e. as sequences of 31-bit words; restricting words to 31 bits (instead of 32) also makes computations easier in standard C, where carry flags are not available. The aggregate products of r_j could be precomputed, but they can also be recomputed on the fly, for better space efficiency. If z fits over w words of 31 bits, and is represented in RNS modulo w small primes r_j, then the whole process of converting z back to a big integer in basis 2^{31} has cost $O(w^2)$ step, and is done mostly in place (we need an extra buffer of w words to rebuild the product of r_j, but that value may be shared if we have several integers z to convert).

It shall be noted that applying the CRT with r_j moduli one by one is not the most efficient method with regards to time complexity. For instance, we could assemble the r_j with a balanced binary tree, and use Karatsuba or Schönhage-Strassen for multiplications (each *modular* multiplication can be performed with two *integer* multiplications with Montgomery's method). However, such methods are more complex to implement, and require some extra space. In our implementation, the CRT reconstruction contributes only a small part to the total runtime cost, and can be performed mostly in-place.

In the course of the TowerSolverI algorithm, we often keep polynomials whose coefficients are both in RNS and NTT representations:

- The RNS representation means that a polynomial $f \in \mathbb{Z}[x]/(\phi)$ is replaced with w polynomials $f_j \in \mathbb{Z}_{r_j}[x]/(\phi)$.
- Each such polynomial f_j is furthermore in NTT representation (the moduli r_j where chosen so that ϕ splits over $\mathbb{Z}_{r_j}$, thereby allowing that representation).

As the algorithm goes deeper through the recursion, the degree of polynomials lowers, but the coefficients grow, thus requiring more moduli r_j. A common pattern is the following:

- Some polynomial inputs are provided modulo w small primes r_j and in NTT representation.
- The output is computed modulo these w small primes r_j, again in NTT representation. Moreover, the inverse NTT is applied on the inputs for each r_j.
- When all w small primes have been used, the CRT is applied to rebuild the full input coefficients.
- The rebuilt coefficients are then used to pursue the computation modulo w' more small primes r_j, each time computing the NTT.

5.3 Binary GCD

At the deepest recursion level, the polynomials f and g are plain integers (polynomials modulo $x+1$ are constant), and the NTRU equation becomes a classic GCD computation with Bézout coefficients. Nominally, this algorithm uses repeated divisions, which are expensive and complex to implement. In order to both simplify and speed up that step, we use a binary GCD variant. The algorithm can be expressed as follows:

- Values a, b, u_0, u_1, v_0 and v_1 are initialized and maintained with the following invariants:

$$\begin{aligned} a &= fu_0 - gv_0 \\ b &= fu_1 - gv_1 \end{aligned} \tag{34}$$

Initial values are:

$$\begin{aligned} a &= f \\ u_0 &= 1 \\ v_0 &= 0 \\ b &= g \\ u_1 &= g \\ v_1 &= f - 1 \end{aligned} \tag{35}$$

- At each step, a or b is reduced: if a and/or b is even, then it is divided by 2; otherwise, if both values are odd, then the smaller of the two is subtracted from the larger, and the result, now even, is divided by 2. Corresponding operations are applied on u_0, v_0, u_1 and v_1 to maintain the invariants. Note that computations on u_0 and u_1 are done modulo g, while computations on v_0 and v_1 are done modulo f.
- Algorithm stops when $a = b$, at which point the common value is the GCD of f and g.

This algorithm works only if both f and g are odd; otherwise, we cannot reliably compute divisions by 2 modulo f or g. Applying the principle explained in Sect. 5.1, we simply reject (f, g) pairs that would yield even resultants; this represents a reduction of the key space by a factor of 3, i.e. a loss of about 1.58 bits, which is considered negligible, as far as security is concerned. This rejection is easily done as a preliminary step, in which the resultants $\text{Res}(\phi, f)$ and $\text{Res}(\phi, g)$ are computed modulo 2: analysis of the TowerResultant algorithm in that specific case, when $\phi = x^n + 1$ and $n = 2^\ell$, shows that it suffices to add the coefficients of f modulo 2 (and similarly g).

The algorithm cost is quadratic in the size of the operands. The description above is bit-by-bit; in practice, we see that the decisions in the algorithm depend only on the few highest and lowest bits of each operand at each step. The implementation can thus be made considerably faster (experimentally, by a factor of about 12) by using the high and low bits to compute the action of 31 successive steps, and applying them on the values together with multiplications.

5.4 Babai's Reduction

When reducing candidate (F, G) relatively to (f, g), we must compute a reduction factor k:

$$k = \left\lfloor \frac{Ff^\star + Gg^\star}{ff^\star + gg^\star} \right\rceil \tag{36}$$

The polynomial division can be implemented efficiently in FFT representation with floating-point values. This implies, however, a loss of precision: thus, the resulting k will be only approximate, and the reduction will need to be applied repeatedly until F and G have reached an adequate size or cannot be reduced any further.

In our implementation, we extract the high bits of f, g, F and G and compute k with the FFT and a scaling factor, such that the resulting coefficients for k

are equal to small integers (that fit on 30 bits each) multiplied by 2^s for some integer s. We shall then subtract kf and kg from F and G, respectively.

The computation of kf and kg is the most expensive part of the reduction. We have the choice between two methods:

1. Use a plain quadratic algorithm: if the degree is d, we thus need d^2 multiplications of a big integer (a coefficient of f or g) by a small integer (a coefficient of k).
2. Use the RNS representation and the NTT to compute the multiplication of k by f.

In general terms, throughout the TowerSolverI algorithm, we use polynomials of degree d with coefficients of size w words, such that dw remains roughly equal to n (coefficients double in size when the degree is halved). Babai's reduction will require $O(w)$ iterations (at that point, the size of F and G is about three times the size of f and g). The plain quadratic algorithm involves d^2 multiplications of a big integer (size w words) by a small one, thus $O(d^2w)$ operations per step, and a total of $O((dw)^2) = O(n^2)$. The use of NTT, however, implies the following elements:

- f and g must be converted to RNS and NTT. This is done once for the whole reduction. Conversion to RNS is $O(w^2d)$; the NTT has cost $O(wd \log d)$.
- For each iteration, k must be converted to NTT modulo each of the small primes ($O(wd \log d)$), multiplied with f and g ($O(wd)$), and converted back to big integers for the subtraction ($O(w^2d)$ for the CRT of d values of size w words each).

Thus, the RNS+NTT method has cost $O(w^3d + w^2d \log d) = O(n(w^2 + w \log d))$. At low recursion depth, where w is small and d is large, this method is thus faster than the plain quadratic algorithm; however, at high depth, w becomes large, the CRT cost dominates, and the plain quadratic algorithm becomes faster. Therefore, there is threshold at which implementation strategies should be switched.

In our implementation, we found that the threshold was at depth 4: when the polynomial degree is $n/16$ or more, the NTT method is faster. This threshold heavily depends on implementation details and the involved hardware, and thus should be measured.

5.5 Asymptotic and Real Performance

Asymptotic analysis would call for using big integer arithmetics, and efficient algorithms, e.g. Karatsuba or Schönhage-Strassen for integer multiplications. But such analysis is a valid approximation of real implementation performance only when inputs are "large enough". Our experience, when implementing the algorithms in the case of Falcon, is that practical degrees such as $n = 1024$ are below that threshold. This is why our code uses for instance RNS and a simple quadratic CRT process; our measures indicate that the dominant cost remains Babai's reduction.

With our use of quadratic algorithms for RNS and CRT, the expected asymptotic time complexity (for values of q and coefficients of f and g small enough to be considered "elementary") of TowerSolverI is $O(n^2 \log n)$, while ResultantSolver would use $O(n^3)$. For $n = 1024$, this implies a factor of $n/\log n \approx 100$, which matches measured time.

Similarly, TowerSolverR is theoretically faster than TowerSolverI, since it stores intermediate values instead of recomputing them; but the execution time overhead of TowerSolverI is, in practice, less than 15%. We prioritized space efficiency and used TowerSolverI.

6 Conclusion and Open Problems

We presented the use of the field norm to optimize some computations on polynomial rings, in particular resultants and solving the NTRU equation. A practical consequence of the latter is that the post-quantum signature algorithm Falcon is fully usable on small microcontrollers or even smartcards, since 32 kB of RAM are enough to run our algorithm even for a long-term security NTRU lattice (degree $n = 1024$): all operations related to signatures (signature production, verification, and key pair generation) can fit on such constrained hardware.

We list below some open questions.

Non-cyclotomic polynomials. In our description, we covered the case of cyclotomic polynomials as moduli. The method can be extended to other moduli; in fact, for every modulus $\phi = \phi'(x^d)$ for some $d > 1$, application of the "field norm" can divide the degree by d for purposes of computing resultants and solving the NTRU equation. This holds even if ϕ is not irreducible over $\mathbb{Q}[x]$, i.e. if $\mathbb{Q}[x]/(\phi)$ is not, in fact, a field. The description of the general case remains a problem to explore; however, the use of reducible moduli in NTRU lattices is usually not recommended.

Floating-point arithmetic. Efficient implementation still relies, for Babai's reduction, on FFT and floating-point numbers. Fixed-point representation is probably usable, but the required range and precision must still be investigated. Whether the reduction may be performed efficiently without the FFT is an open problem.

Large integers. While our gains, in terms of memory, are significant, we still need to handle large integers. From an implementation complexity point of view, it would be interesting to get rid of large integers, for example by performing all operations in RNS, without negatively impacting the running time and memory requirements of our algorithms.

Other applications to cryptographic constructions. We think it is worthwhile to investigate whether our techniques can improve the efficiency of other cryptographic algorithms. In addition, just like we provided a constructive application of the field norm (as opposed to [1]), a constructive application of the trace (as opposed to [6]) would be, in our opinion, very interesting. Finally, [14] showed that an algebraic perspective is not necessary in the case of [1]; this raises the question of whether it is in our case.

Applications to cryptanalysis. A final line of research would be to use our techniques to improve the attacks based on the field norm [1], or even on the field trace [6].

References

1. Albrecht, M.R., Bai, S., Ducas, L.: A subfield lattice attack on overstretched NTRU assumptions. In: Robshaw, M., Katz, J. (eds.) CRYPTO 2016, Part I. LNCS, vol. 9814, pp. 153–178. Springer, Heidelberg (2016). https://doi.org/10.1007/978-3-662-53018-4_6
2. Babai, L.: On Lovász' lattice reduction and the nearest lattice point problem. In: Mehlhorn, K. (ed.) STACS 1985. LNCS, vol. 182, pp. 13–20. Springer, Heidelberg (1985). https://doi.org/10.1007/BFb0023990. http://dl.acm.org/citation.cfm?id=18858.18860
3. Bernstein, D.J., Chuengsatiansup, C., Lange, T., van Vredendaal, C.: NTRU prime. Technical report, National Institute of Standards and Technology (2017). https://csrc.nist.gov/projects/post-quantum-cryptography/round-1-submissions
4. Campbell, P., Groves, M.: Practical post-quantum hierarchical identity-based encryption. In: 16th IMA International Conference on Cryptography and Coding (2017). http://www.qub.ac.uk/sites/CSIT/FileStore/Filetoupload,785752,en.pdf
5. Cash, D., Hofheinz, D., Kiltz, E., Peikert, C.: Bonsai trees, or how to delegate a lattice basis. In: Gilbert, H. (ed.) EUROCRYPT 2010. LNCS, vol. 6110, pp. 523–552. Springer, Heidelberg (2010). https://doi.org/10.1007/978-3-642-13190-5_27
6. Cheon, J.H., Jeong, J., Lee, C.: An algorithm for NTRU problems and cryptanalysis of the GGH multilinear map without a low level encoding of zero. Cryptology ePrint Archive, Report 2016/139 (2016). http://eprint.iacr.org/2016/139
7. Cooley, J.W., Tukey, J.W.: An algorithm for the machine calculation of complex Fourier series. Math. Comput. **19**(90), 297–301 (1965)
8. Ducas, L., Lyubashevsky, V., Prest, T.: Efficient identity-based encryption over NTRU lattices. In: Sarkar, P., Iwata, T. (eds.) ASIACRYPT 2014, Part II. LNCS, vol. 8874, pp. 22–41. Springer, Heidelberg (2014). https://doi.org/10.1007/978-3-662-45608-8_2
9. von zur Gathen, J., Gerhard, J.: Modern Computer Algebra, 3rd edn. Cambridge University Press, Cambridge (2013)
10. Gentleman, W.M., Sande, G.: Fast Fourier transforms: for fun and profit. In: Proceedings of the 7–10 November 1966, Fall Joint Computer Conference, pp. 563–578. ACM (1966)
11. Gentry, C., Peikert, C., Vaikuntanathan, V.: Trapdoors for hard lattices and new cryptographic constructions. In: Ladner, R.E., Dwork, C. (eds.) 40th ACM STOC, pp. 197–206. ACM Press, May 2008. https://doi.org/10.1145/1374376.1374407

12. Hoffstein, J., Howgrave-Graham, N., Pipher, J., Silverman, J.H., Whyte, W.: NTRUSign: digital signatures using the NTRU lattice. In: Joye, M. (ed.) CT-RSA 2003. LNCS, vol. 2612, pp. 122–140. Springer, Heidelberg (2003). https://doi.org/10.1007/3-540-36563-X_9
13. Hoffstein, J., Pipher, J., Silverman, J.H.: NTRU: a ring-based public key cryptosystem. In: Buhler, J.P. (ed.) ANTS 1998. LNCS, vol. 1423, pp. 267–288. Springer, Heidelberg (1998). https://doi.org/10.1007/BFb0054868
14. Kirchner, P., Fouque, P.-A.: Revisiting lattice attacks on overstretched NTRU parameters. In: Coron, J.-S., Nielsen, J.B. (eds.) EUROCRYPT 2017, Part I. LNCS, vol. 10210, pp. 3–26. Springer, Cham (2017). https://doi.org/10.1007/978-3-319-56620-7_1
15. Micciancio, D., Warinschi, B.: A linear space algorithm for computing the herite normal form. In: Kaltofen, E., Villard, G. (eds.) Proceedings of the 2001 International Symposium on Symbolic and Algebraic Computation, ISSAC 2001, ORCCA & University of Western Ontario, London, Ontario, Canada, 22–25 July 2001, pp. 231–236. ACM (2001). https://doi.org/10.1145/384101.384133
16. NIST: Security requirements for cryptographic modules (2001). https://nvlpubs.nist.gov/nistpubs/FIPS/NIST.FIPS.140-2.pdf
17. NIST: Submission requirements and evaluation criteria for the post-quantum cryptography standardization process (2016). https://csrc.nist.gov/Projects/Post-Quantum-Cryptography
18. Prest, T., et al.: Falcon. Technical report, National Institute of Standards and Technology (2017). https://csrc.nist.gov/projects/post-quantum-cryptography/round-1-submissions
19. Schönhage, A., Strassen, V.: Schnelle multiplikation großer zahlen. Computing **7**(3–4), 281–292 (1971). https://doi.org/10.1007/BF02242355
20. Smart, N.P., et al.: LIMA. Technical report, National Institute of Standards and Technology (2017). https://csrc.nist.gov/projects/post-quantum-cryptography/round-1-submissions
21. Stehlé, D., Steinfeld, R.: Making NTRUEncrypt and NTRUSign as secure as standard worst-case problems over ideal lattices. Cryptology ePrint Archive, Report 2013/004 (2013). http://eprint.iacr.org/2013/004

Efficiently Masking Binomial Sampling at Arbitrary Orders for Lattice-Based Crypto

Tobias Schneider[1(✉)], Clara Paglialonga[2], Tobias Oder[3], and Tim Güneysu[3,4]

[1] ICTEAM/ELEN/Crypto Group, Université Catholique de Louvain, Louvain-la-Neuve, Belgium
tobias.schneider@uclouvain.be

[2] Technische Universität Darmstadt, Darmstadt, Germany
clara.paglialonga@crisp-da.de

[3] Horst Görtz Institute for IT Security, Ruhr-Universität Bochum, Bochum, Germany
{tobias.oder,tim.gueneysu}@rub.de

[4] DFKI, Bremen, Germany

Abstract. With the rising popularity of lattice-based cryptography, the Learning with Errors (LWE) problem has emerged as a fundamental core of numerous encryption and key exchange schemes. Many LWE-based schemes have in common that they require sampling from a discrete Gaussian distribution which comes with a number of challenges for the practical instantiation of those schemes. One of these is the inclusion of countermeasures against a physical side-channel adversary. While several works discuss the protection of samplers against timing leaks, only few publications explore resistance against other side-channels, e.g., power. The most recent example of a protected binomial sampler (as used in key encapsulation mechanisms to sufficiently approximate Gaussian distributions) from CHES 2018 is restricted to a first-order adversary and cannot be easily extended to higher protection orders.

In this work, we present the first protected binomial sampler which provides provable security against a side-channel adversary at arbitrary orders. Our construction relies on a new conversion between Boolean and arithmetic (B2A) masking schemes for prime moduli which outperforms previous algorithms significantly for the relevant parameters, and is paired with a new masked bitsliced sampler allowing secure and efficient sampling even at larger protection orders. Since our proposed solution supports arbitrary moduli, it can be utilized in a large variety of lattice-based constructions, like NewHope, LIMA, Saber, Kyber, HILA5, or Ding Key Exchange.

1 Introduction

Ever since the first publication by Kocher [24], protection against side-channel analysis (SCA) has become an essential optimization goal for designers of

D. Lin and K. Sako (Eds.): PKC 2019, LNCS 11443, pp. 534–564, 2019.
https://doi.org/10.1007/978-3-030-17259-6_18

security-critical applications. It has been shown numerous times that an adversary, which does not only have access to the inputs and outputs of a system but can also measure some physical characteristics (e.g., timing) of the target, is capable of extracting sensitive information from an unprotected implementation with ease [18]. This affects especially embedded systems, as they (a) allow extensive physical access to the adversary enabling the exploitation of additional side-channels (e.g., power, EM) which requires more sophisticated protection schemes, and (b) often possess only limited resources which makes the integration of dedicated countermeasures a complex task.

One important type of countermeasure in this context is masking [9]. Its core idea is splitting the sensitive information into multiple shares and transforming the target implementation to securely compute on these shares. Based on certain assumptions, it is possible to prove that an adversary needs to combine at least t intermediate values (so called *probes*) of the circuit to extract any sensitive data. In practice, an increase in the number of required probes exponentially increases the attack complexity given a sufficient level of noise in the measurements [32]. The seminal work of Ishai et al. [22] introduces a security model, which identifies the attack situation described above. It introduces the *probing model*, that allows to prove the security of a masked gadget. Still, the imprudent composition of such gadgets can introduce security flaws, due to the extra information that an adversary might be able to extract when using the outputs of a gadget as input to another one. The notion of Strong Non-Interference (SNI), introduced in [5], provides stronger conditions that ensure a secure composition of masked gadgets.

While for common symmetric and asymmetric constructions the application of masking schemes has been extensively examined and achieves a high level of security and efficiency, this is still ongoing research for most post-quantum schemes. First approaches to achieve first-order side-channel security were made [10,11,25,28], but the overhead for higher-order masking of post-quantum cryptography has not been studied, except in [6] for the specific GLP signature scheme [20]. However, GLP has not been submitted to the standardization process for post-quantum cryptography run by the National Institute of Standards and Technology (NIST) [26]. Among those 69 complete and proper submissions to this competition, lattice-based cryptography is clearly the largest group with a total of 29 submissions due to advantages, such as reasonable parameter sizes, simple implementation, as well as advanced constructions like identity-based encryption and homomorphic encryption. The competition explicitly takes into account the ease of integration of physical countermeasures as an evaluation metric [27], which is therefore a primary contribution of this work.

Most of the lattice-based encryption and key exchange schemes rely on the Learning with Errors (LWE) problem or variants like Ring-LWE for which many of them require noise polynomials with small Gaussian distributed coefficients. For small standard deviations, the binomial sampler as presented in [1] and implemented in [2] is the best choice as it has a constant run time by design, is easy to implement and does not require any precomputed tables. However, applying masking schemes to sampling algorithms for protection against side-channel analysis is a non-trivial task. It has been shown in [25] by Oder et al.

that this can easily become even the bottleneck of an implementation, causing a performance overhead of more than 400%.

This reduction in performance stems mostly from the mixture of different masking schemes. Oder et al. initially generate uniformly-random bits by running SHAKE for a given seed. Using a pseudo random number generator (PRNG) is common as a first step in such samplers and, as shown in [25], needs to include side-channel countermeasures as well. From this uniform randomness, the approximated Gaussian randomness is derived, e.g., [1] proposes to subtract the Hamming weight of two uniform bit vectors. For both steps, Boolean masking is an obvious choice, since many PRNGs rely on Boolean operations and the computation of the Hamming weight requires bit-wise manipulations of the shares, which is complex for arithmetic masking (assuming not every bit is separately masked). However, the subsequent operations in the lattice scheme favor arithmetic masking. Therefore, it is necessary to apply a conversion at some point of the protected sampler.

Related work. In [6], Barthe et al. propose the first provably-secure sampler for arbitrary orders. However, the targeted GLP signature schemes requires a uniform sampler, which poses different challenges to the implementer than a binomial one. Thus, their results cannot be straight-forwardly transferred to protect a binomial sampler, as required for many NIST submissions.

One of these submissions is NewHope [1] and its potential for physical protection was evaluated in [25], where, as part of their construction, Oder et al. presented a masked binomial sampler. However, it was heavily-optimized for first-order protection and not easily extendable to higher orders. In addition, their results show that masking such a sampler can severely impact the performance of the whole scheme. Therefore, it is an open problem how to efficiently protect binomial samplers against side-channel adversaries.

While the authors of [25] convert Boolean-masked bits to arithmetic shares, they do not formally specify the conversion algorithm. Such Boolean-to-arithmetic (B2A) conversions have been extensively researched [7,8,12–14,16, 21,23,30,33] as many symmetric primitives mix Boolean and arithmetic operations. However, they focus solely on power-of-two moduli. In contrast, many lattice schemes employ other moduli (not necessarily power-of-two) to allow optimizations. For these cases, it is necessary to apply specific conversions (in the following denoted as $\texttt{B2A}_q$). The first of such conversion algorithms which work with arbitrary moduli was proposed in [6] based on the cubic conversion of [14] and proven to be secure at arbitrary orders. Since these algorithms are a non-negligible part of masking a binomial sampler, any improvements regarding the conversion will also improve the sampling performance.

Our contribution. Our first contribution is a revised version of the quadratic B2A algorithm of [14] which is combined with some of the ideas outlined in [6]. While this is technically straightforward, we still provide the essential proof of security, resulting in $\texttt{A2B}_q$ and $\texttt{B2A}_q$ algorithms with the best asymptotic run time complexity (i.e., $\mathcal{O}(n^2 \log k)$, where k denotes the bit size of the operands and n the number of shares) to date.

As a second contribution, we present a new $\mathtt{B2A}_q$ conversion with a run time complexity of $\mathcal{O}(n^2 \cdot k)$. Our new algorithm is proven to be $t - \mathsf{SNI}$ enabling composition with $n = t + 1$ shares. While its asymptotic complexity is worse than our quadratic adaption of [6], it still significantly reduces the conversion time for relevant values of k. The new algorithm even outperforms the established standard B2A algorithms for power-of-two moduli for certain parameters (e.g., $n \geq 11$ for $k = 32$). Therefore, it is not only relevant for our considered use case, but might also improve the performance of masked symmetric algorithms.

Thirdly, relying on $\mathtt{B2A}_q$ conversions we propose two masked binomial samplers for lattice-based encryption and key exchange schemes. The first sampler is a higher-order extension of the approach from [25], while the second variant uses bitslicing to further increase the throughput. Again, we prove both solutions to be $t - \mathsf{SNI}$ to enable easy composition in larger constructions, e.g., for CCA2-transformations. This results in the first provable SCA-protected binomial samplers at arbitrary orders. Since our proposed solutions support arbitrary moduli, they can be adopted in a large variety of NIST submissions, e.g., NewHope [1], LIMA [31], Saber [15], Kyber [3], HILA5 [29], or Ding Key Exchange [17].

Finally, we present an ARM Cortex-M4F microcontroller implementation of our constructions to evaluate their performance on a popular embedded processor platform. We find that our new $\mathtt{B2A}_q$ conversion improves the performance of the samplers over the adaption of [6] up to a factor of 46, while our new bitsliced sampler improves the performance over a generalized version of the approach of [25] up to a factor of 15. The combination of both approaches results in the currently most-efficient masked binomial sampler. At first-order, it even outperforms the implementation from [25], which is highly-optimized for first-order security, while our contribution provides generic protection for arbitrary orders.

Organization of the paper. In Sect. 2, we start by briefly reviewing the state-of-the-art regarding B2A conversions and masked binomial sampling. In Sect. 3, we provide the adaption of the quadratic $\mathtt{B2A}_q$ from [14] using the prime addition from [6] and its corresponding proof of security. In Sect. 4, our new $\mathtt{B2A}_q$ algorithm is presented and compared to the current state-of-the-art considering both standard and prime moduli. Finally in Sect. 5, we propose our new masked sampling algorithms and conduct a case study using the parameters of the NIST submission NewHope.

2 Background

In this section, we first introduce the notation used throughout this paper and the considered notions of physical security. Then we briefly introduce the B2A algorithms relevant to our work and review the masked binomial sampler of [25].

2.1 Notation

In the rest of the paper we denote with q a prime number, with B2A the standard conversion from Boolean to arithmetic masking and with $\mathtt{B2A}_\mathtt{q}$ the same transformation for prime moduli. We will indicate with k the bit size of the conversion, κ the bit size of the input vectors of the samplers, n the number of shares and t the security order. Moreover, the lower case will be used for Boolean encoding and the upper one for arithmetic encoding. Operations on the whole encoding, i.e., vector of shares, are denoted in bold and performed share-wise, e.g., $\mathbf{z} = \mathbf{x} \oplus \mathbf{y}$. We denote the k bits of a share as $\left(x_i^{(k)} \dots x_i^{(1)}\right) = x_i$, i.e., the least-significant bit (LSB) of x_i is written as $x_i^{(1)}$ (resp. $\mathbf{x}^{(1)}$ denotes the LSB of $\mathbf{x}$).

2.2 Notions of Physical Security

Counteracting side-channel analysis via masking informally means to randomize the information leaked during the computation of sensitive variables in order to make the representation of such variables independent from the actual processed data. The security of a masking scheme has been formalized for the first time by Ishai et al. in [22]. Their seminal work introduces the *t-probing model*, where an adversary is allowed to read up to t wires in a circuit (the so called *probes*). Every sensitive variable s is encoded into n shares s_i, such that the sum of them gives the original masked variable s and only the combination of all the shares gives some information about s. In order to keep this independence throughout the whole circuit, every operation is performed on the shares s_i and, especially in the case of non-linear operations, it makes use of additional randomness, which helps to guarantee that every t-tuple of intermediate variables is independent from at least one of the shares of s. Such transformed gates are commonly called gadgets and, in order to provide sound claims of their composability, they must satisfy the conditions of one of the following definitions.

Definition 1 ($t-\mathsf{NI}$). *A given gadget $\mathcal{G}$ is t-Non-Interfering ($t-\mathsf{NI}$), if every set of t probes can be simulated by using at most t shares of each input.*

Definition 2 ($t-\mathsf{SNI}$). *A given gadget $\mathcal{G}$ is t-Strong-Non-Interfering ($t-\mathsf{SNI}$), if every set of t_1 probes on the internal values and t_2 probes on the output values, with $t_1 + t_2 \leq t$, can be simulated by using at most t_1 shares of each input.*

Both definitions have been introduced in [4] and are refinements of the original definition of probing security, given in [22]. They require the existence of a simulator, which can simulate the adversary's view, without accessing the sensitive variables, using only part of their shares. In particular, the definition of $t-\mathsf{SNI}$ is important when designing a gadget, which is supposed to be part of a bigger algorithm. In this case indeed, using the output of a gadget as input to another one might add sensitive information to the knowledge of the adversary and $t-\mathsf{NI}$ would not be sufficient to ensure global security. On the other hand, the conditions of $t-\mathsf{SNI}$ are stronger, since they require an independence between the number of probes on the output shares and the number of the shares needed to perform the simulation, therefore they allow to compose gadgets securely. In the rest of the paper, we will prove our algorithms to be $t-\mathsf{SNI}$ making them suited to be composed with other gadgets as part of a larger circuit.

2.3 Conversion from Boolean to Arithmetic Masking

The first sound transformation from Boolean to arithmetic masking (B2A) has been proposed by Goubin in [19] and it is based on the fact that the function $\Phi(x, r) : \mathbb{F}_{2^k} \times \mathbb{F}_{2^k} \mapsto \mathbb{F}_{2^k}$ such that

$$\Phi(x, r) = (x \oplus r) - r \mod 2^k \tag{1}$$

is affine in r over $\mathbb{F}_2$. The algorithm is very efficient, since it has a run time complexity of $\mathcal{O}(1)$, i.e., independent of the size of the inputs k. However, the initial algorithm was only proven secure against a first-order adversary ($t = 1$).

The first B2A algorithm secure at higher orders was presented in [14]. Instead of relying on the aforementioned affine relationship $\Phi(x, r)$, the main idea is to first initialize the shares $(A_i)_{1 \le i \le n-1}$ with random samples in $\mathbb{F}_{2^k}$. Then they are used to generate a random encoding $\mathbf{A}'$ of the form $\sum_{i=1}^{n} A'_i = -\sum_{i=1}^{n-1} A_i \mod 2^k$. This encoding is given to a higher-order secure arithmetic-to-Boolean (A2B) conversion algorithm to compute the Boolean shares $\bigoplus_i y_i = \sum_i A'_i \mod 2^k$, which are then added to the input encoding $\mathbf{x}$ via a Boolean-masked addition algorithm. This results in

$$\bigoplus_i z_i = \bigoplus_i x_i + \bigoplus_i y_i = x - \sum_{i=1}^{n-1} A_i \mod 2^k.$$

Using the function $\texttt{FullXOR} : \mathbb{F}_{2^k}^n \mapsto \mathbb{F}_{2^k}$ [14], which securely decodes a given input encoding, the remaining share of $\mathbf{A}$ is set to $A_n = \texttt{FullXOR}(\mathbf{z})$, which completes the transformation given

$$\sum_{i=1}^{n} A_i = \sum_{i=1}^{n-1} A_i + (x - \sum_{i=1}^{n-1} A_i) = x \mod 2^k.$$

In theory, the aforementioned framework can be instantiated with any secure A2B and Boolean-masked addition algorithm. In practice, however, there is only one secure higher-order A2B algorithm to the best of our knowledge, which was also published in the same work [14]. Its underlying concept is rather simple. Each share of the arithmetic input encoding $\mathbf{A}$ is first transformed to a Boolean encoding with n shares. These n Boolean encodings are then added together using a Boolean-masked addition algorithm resulting in a Boolean encoding $\mathbf{x}$ with $\bigoplus_i x_i = \sum_i A_i \mod 2^k$. With a simple addition algorithm this basic version has a cubic complexity of $\mathcal{O}(n^3 \cdot k)$. In [14], the authors also propose an improved version which relies on recursion and has a quadratic complexity of $\mathcal{O}(n^2 \cdot k)$. Instead of summing the input shares A_i sequentially one by one, the main algorithm splits the n shares into two halves of $\lfloor \frac{n}{2} \rfloor$ and $\lceil \frac{n}{2} \rceil$, and recursively calls itself for the two halves. The resulting encodings are then added together as

$$\begin{aligned} x &= \left(A_1 + \cdots + A_{\lfloor n/2 \rfloor}\right) + \left(A_{\lfloor n/2 \rfloor + 1} + \cdots + A_n\right) \\ &= \left(y_1 \oplus \cdots \oplus y_{\lfloor n/2 \rfloor}\right) + \left(z_1 \oplus \cdots \oplus z_{\lceil n/2 \rceil}\right) \\ x &= x_1 \oplus \cdots \oplus x_n. \end{aligned} \tag{2}$$

The complexity of both these B2A and A2B algorithms can be improved by using a more efficient masked addition algorithm, e.g., using the logarithmic addition from [13] reduces the run time complexity of both directions to $\mathcal{O}(n^2 \cdot \log k)$.

An alternative higher-order B2A conversion algorithm relying on the affine relation given in Eq. (1) was recently presented by Bettale et al. in [7] following previous work of [21] and [12]. Since it is not based on the Boolean-masked addition of shares, its run time is independent of the input bit size. This makes it especially efficient for small values of n for which it is possible to achieve a significant speedup over the previous solutions based on [14]. For increasing number of shares, however, the performance of the new algorithm quickly deteriorates given its asymptotic run time complexity of $\mathcal{O}(2^n)$.

Conversion with prime moduli. All the aforementioned approaches assume an arithmetic modulus of the form 2^k, i.e., a power of two, and cannot be directly applied for prime moduli. The foundation for some very basic solutions for $\texttt{A2B}_q$ and $\texttt{B2A}_q$ conversions were given in [25]. However, the algorithms were not strictly formalized, their application is very specific to the presented use case, and their security is limited to a first-order adversary. Therefore, we refrain from giving further details on both algorithms and will only briefly mention their $\texttt{B2A}_q$ approach when discussing the masked binomial sampler in the next subsection.

The first generic solution for arbitrary orders was recently given in [6]. The authors present a new Boolean-masked addition algorithm which works modulo a prime q with $2^k \geq 2q$. Based on this adder, both the A2B and B2A algorithms from [14] can be changed to feature moduli other than a power-of-two. Their $\texttt{B2A}_q$ solution is given in Algorithm 1 which as the approach from [14] relies on an A2B conversion. Due to page limitations, we do not discuss all algorithms necessary for the conversion inside the paper (e.g., FullXOR) and instead refer to their original publications[1]. In their work, the authors only provide the proofs for an adaption of the A2B algorithm from [14] with cubic complexity (cf. Algorithm 2). In Sect. 3, we complement their work by providing the security proofs for an adaption of the conversion algorithm with quadratic complexity (cf. Algorithm 3) which leads to conversions for both directions with currently the lowest complexity of $\mathcal{O}(n^2 \cdot \log k)$.[2]

2.4 Masked Sampler from [25]

The construction of [25] initially uses a Boolean-masked SHAKE core to generate masked pseudo-random bits with a uniform distribution. As defined in

[1] In the full version of this paper, all algorithms are given as supplementary material.

[2] The authors of [6] also hint that the k-independent algorithm of [7] can be adopted to other moduli. However, we did not find a working solution. Nevertheless, an adapted algorithm would share the exponential complexity of the original making it only viable for small number of shares and, therefore, not a generic solution for masking at any order. In addition, the bit sizes considered in our case study are relatively small which would further decrease the benefit of a prime-adjusted algorithm.

Algorithm 1. SecBoolArithModp [6]

Input: $\mathbf{x} = (x_i)_{1 \le i \le n} \in \mathbb{F}_2^k$ such that $\bigoplus_i x_i = x \in \mathbb{F}_2^k$
Output: $\mathbf{A} = (A_i)_{1 \le i \le n} \in \mathbb{F}_q$ such that $\sum_i A_i = x \mod q$

$(A_i)_{1 \le i \le n-1} \xleftarrow{\$} \mathbb{F}_q$
$(A_i)'_{1 \le i \le n-1} \leftarrow q - (A_i)_{1 \le i \le n-1}$
$A'_n \leftarrow 0$
$\mathbf{y} \leftarrow \texttt{SecArithBoolModp}(\mathbf{A}')$
$\mathbf{z} \leftarrow \texttt{SecAddModp}(\mathbf{x}, \mathbf{y})$
$A_n \leftarrow \texttt{FullXOR}(\mathbf{z})$

Algorithm 2. SecArithBoolModp (cubic) [6]

Input: $\mathbf{A} = (A_i)_{1 \le i \le n} \in \mathbb{F}_q$ such that $\sum_i A_i = x \mod q \in \mathbb{F}_q$
Output: $\mathbf{x} = (x_i)_{1 \le i \le n} \in \mathbb{F}_2^k$ with $2^k > 2q$ such that $\bigoplus_i x_i = x$

$(x_i)_{1 \le i \le n} \leftarrow 0$
for $j = 1$ to n **do**
  $(y_i)_{1 \le i \le n} \leftarrow (A_j, 0, \ldots, 0)$
  $\mathbf{y} \leftarrow \texttt{RefreshXOR}(\mathbf{y}, k)$
  $\mathbf{x} \leftarrow \texttt{SecAddModp}(\mathbf{x}, \mathbf{y}, k)$
end for

the specification of NewHope, the sampler takes two 8-bit vectors (x, y) of this pseudo-randomness as input and computes the difference of the Hamming weight between them. Since the subsequent operations of the lattice scheme are performed modulo $q = 12289$, the masked sampler needs to convert from Boolean masking to arithmetic masking modulo the prime q. Again, the $\texttt{B2A}_q$ conversion is not explicitly given and analyzed in [25], but rather directly integrated in the overlying algorithm. In particular, the authors exploit that Boolean-masked bits (x_1, x_2) with $x_1 \oplus x_2 = x$ provide the following arithmetic relation

$$x = x_1 + x_2 - 2 \cdot x_1 \cdot x_2 \tag{3}$$

which is used to transform these Boolean masked bits to an arithmetic encoding modulo q. The resulting masked sampler (cf. Algorithm 4 in [25]) is highly-customized for a first-order adversary and the authors do not provide any discussion on how to extend this approach to higher orders. Our new higher-order $\texttt{B2A}_q$ conversion algorithm, given in Sect. 4, relies on this arithmetic relation as well, but contains further optimizations to significantly improve the efficiency and security at higher orders.

3 Improved Higher-Order $\texttt{B2A}_q$ from [6]

In this section, we discuss the adaption of the $\texttt{B2A}_q$ conversion algorithm with quadratic complexity from [14] to the setting of prime moduli. The basic idea was already proposed in [6] without any concrete instantiation or proof. Nevertheless,

Algorithm 3. `SecArithBoolModp` (quadratic)

Input: $\mathbf{A} = (A_i)_{1 \le i \le n} \in \mathbb{F}_q$ such that $\sum_i A_i = x \mod q \in \mathbb{F}_q$
Output: $\mathbf{x} = (x_i)_{1 \le i \le n} \in \mathbb{F}_2^k$ with $2^k > 2q$ such that $\bigoplus_i x_i = x$

if n=1 **then**
  $x_1 \leftarrow A_1$
end if
$(y_i)_{1 \le i \le \lfloor n/2 \rfloor} \leftarrow \mathtt{SecArithBoolModp}\left((A_i)_{1 \le i \le \lfloor n/2 \rfloor}\right)$
$(y_i)_{1 \le i \le n} \leftarrow \mathtt{RefreshXOR}\left((y_1, \ldots, y_{\lfloor n/2 \rfloor}, 0, \ldots, 0), k\right)$
$(z_i)_{1 \le i \le \lceil n/2 \rceil} \leftarrow \mathtt{SecArithBoolModp}\left((A_i)_{\lfloor n/2 \rfloor + 1 \le i \le n}\right)$
$(z_i)_{1 \le i \le n} \leftarrow \mathtt{RefreshXOR}\left((z_1, \ldots, z_{\lceil n/2 \rceil}, 0, \ldots, 0), k\right)$
$\mathbf{x} \leftarrow \mathtt{SecAddModp}(\mathbf{y}, \mathbf{z})$

we provide the algorithmic description of the adjusted conversion and prove its $t-\mathsf{SNI}$ property to enable comparison with our new approach of Sect. 4.

3.1 Construction

In the original algorithm from [6], `SecBoolArithModp` calls the simple version of `SecArithBoolModp`, i.e., the shares are added sequentially as depicted in Algorithm 2, which leads to a run time complexity of $\mathcal{O}(n^3 \cdot \log k)$. To improve this, we adapt the recursive structure previously discussed in Eq. (2). In particular, the input encoding given to `SecArithBoolModp` is split into two sets of $\lfloor n/2 \rfloor$ and $\lceil n/2 \rceil$ elements. These are then separately given to a new call of `SecArithBoolModp` and the resulting Boolean encodings are summed to derive the correct result. This comes with the advantage that each sub routine processes a smaller number of shares which reduces the complexity of the refresh and addition, decreasing the overall complexity to $\mathcal{O}(n^2 \cdot \log k)$.

The complete $\mathtt{A2B}_q$ algorithm with quadratic complexity is given in Algorithm 3 which would simply replace the call to `SecArithBoolModp` in Algorithm 1 to derive a corresponding quadratic $\mathtt{B2A}_q$ conversion. To map the $\lfloor n/2 \rfloor$ (resp. $\lceil n/2 \rceil$) Boolean shares to the n shares required for the secure masked addition, we choose to rely on the $t-\mathsf{SNI}$-refresh `RefreshXOR` from [6] instead of the `Expand` function from [14]. To this end, the Boolean encodings are first padded with zeros and the resulting n shares are refreshed. An exemplary structure for the case $n = 4$ is depicted in Fig. 2.

3.2 Security

The $t-\mathsf{SNI}$ security of `SecBoolArithModp` in Algorithm 1, when using the quadratic version of `SecArithBoolModp`, relies on the fact that `SecArithBoolModp` itself is $t-\mathsf{SNI}$. Before proceeding with proving that Algorithm 3 is $t-\mathsf{SNI}$, we give the following Lemma.

Lemma 1. *Given a circuit* C *as in Fig. 1, where* `f`, `g` *are* $t-\mathsf{SNI}$ *gadgets and* `h` *is* $t-\mathsf{NI}$*, the circuit* C *is* $t-\mathsf{SNI}$.

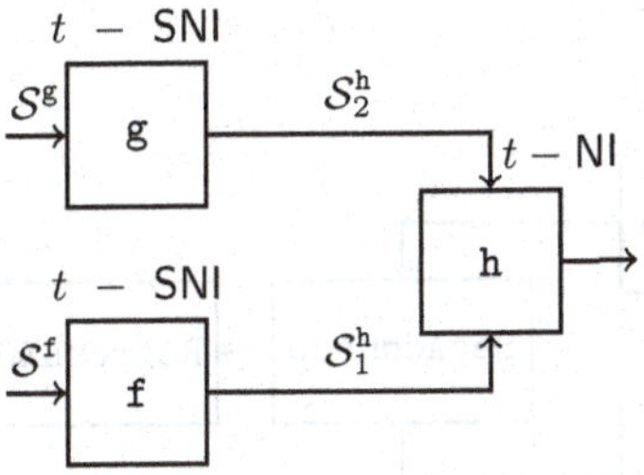

Fig. 1. Recurrent scheme in Algorithm 3

Proof. Let $\Omega = (\mathcal{I}, \mathcal{O})$ be the set of adversarial observations on $\mathcal{C}$, where $\mathcal{I}$ are the probes on the internal values and $\mathcal{O}$ the ones on the output values, with $|\mathcal{I}| + |\mathcal{O}| \leq t$. In particular, let $\mathcal{I}_{\mathtt{f}}$ be the set of probes on f, $\mathcal{I}_{\mathtt{g}}$ the set of probes on g and $\mathcal{I}_{\mathtt{h}}$ be the set of probes on h, with $|\mathcal{I}_{\mathtt{f}} \cup \mathcal{I}_{\mathtt{g}} \cup \mathcal{I}_{\mathtt{h}}| \leq |\mathcal{I}|$.

We prove the existence of a simulator which can simulate the adversary's view by using at most $|\mathcal{I}|$ input shares, analyzing the circuit from right to left.

Gadget h. Since h is $t-$NI and $|I_{\mathtt{h}} \cup \mathcal{O}| \leq t$, then there exist two observation sets $\mathcal{S}_1^{\mathtt{h}}, \mathcal{S}_2^{\mathtt{h}}$ such that $|\mathcal{S}_1^{\mathtt{h}}| \leq |I_{\mathtt{h}} \cup \mathcal{O}|$, $|\mathcal{S}_2^{\mathtt{h}}| \leq |I_{\mathtt{h}} \cup \mathcal{O}|$ and the gadget can be simulated using at most $|\mathcal{S}_1^{\mathtt{h}}| + |\mathcal{S}_2^{\mathtt{h}}|$ shares of the inputs.

Gadget f. Since f is $t-$SNI and $|I_{\mathtt{f}} \cup \mathcal{S}_1^{\mathtt{h}}| \leq t$, then there exists an observation set $\mathcal{S}^{\mathtt{f}}$ such that $|\mathcal{S}^{\mathtt{f}}| \leq |I_{\mathtt{f}}|$ and the gadget can be simulated using at most $|\mathcal{S}^{\mathtt{f}}|$ shares of the inputs.

Gadget g. Since g is $t-$SNI and $|I_{\mathtt{g}} \cup \mathcal{S}_2^{\mathtt{h}}| \leq t$, then there exists an observation set $\mathcal{S}^{\mathtt{g}}$ such that $|\mathcal{S}^{\mathtt{g}}| \leq |I_{\mathtt{g}}|$ and the gadget can be simulated using at most $|\mathcal{S}^{\mathtt{g}}|$ shares of the inputs.

Combining the previous steps of the simulation, we can claim that $\mathcal{C}$ can be simulated by using at most $|\mathcal{S}^{\mathtt{f}} \cup \mathcal{S}^{\mathtt{g}}| \leq |I_{\mathtt{f}}| + |I_{\mathtt{g}}| \leq |I|$ shares of the inputs, completing the proof. □

Proposition 1. `SecArithBoolModp` *in Algorithm 3 is* $t-$SNI, *for* $t = n-1$.

Proof. In order to prove `SecArithBoolModp` to be $t-$ SNI we iteratively split the circuit in sub-circuits $\mathcal{C}_i$, for $i = 2, \ldots, n$ as in Fig. 2, where in particular $\mathcal{C}_n :=$ `SecArithBoolModp` and we prove the thesis by induction on $i \in \mathbb{N}$.

We remark that $\mathcal{C}_2$ is of the form of the circuit in Fig. 1. Indeed `RefreshXOR` is $t-$SNI and `SecAddModp` is $t-$NI, as proven in [6]. Therefore thanks to Lemma 1, the circuit $\mathcal{C}_2$ is $t-$ SNI.

Let us suppose now that $\mathcal{C}_{n-2}$ is $t-$ SNI and we prove the thesis for $\mathcal{C}_n$.

Since the composition of $t-$SNI gadgets is still $t-$SNI, as pointed out in [4], we know that both $\mathcal{C}_{n-2}((A_i)_{1 \leq i \leq \lfloor n/2 \rfloor})$ and $\mathcal{C}_{n-2}((A_i)_{\lfloor n/2 \rfloor + 1 \leq i \leq n})$ composed with the `RefreshXOR` gadget are $t-$ SNI. Therefore, the circuit $\mathcal{C}_n$ can be represented as the circuit in Fig. 1, with f $=$ `RefreshXOR`$(\mathcal{C}_{n-2}((A_i)_{1 \leq i \leq \lfloor n/2 \rfloor}))$, g $=$ `RefreshXOR`$(\mathcal{C}_{n-2}((A_i)_{\lfloor n/2 \rfloor + 1 \leq i \leq n}))$ and h $=$ `SecAddModp`. From Lemma 1 we conclude therefore that $\mathcal{C}_n$ is $t-$ SNI, completing the proof. □

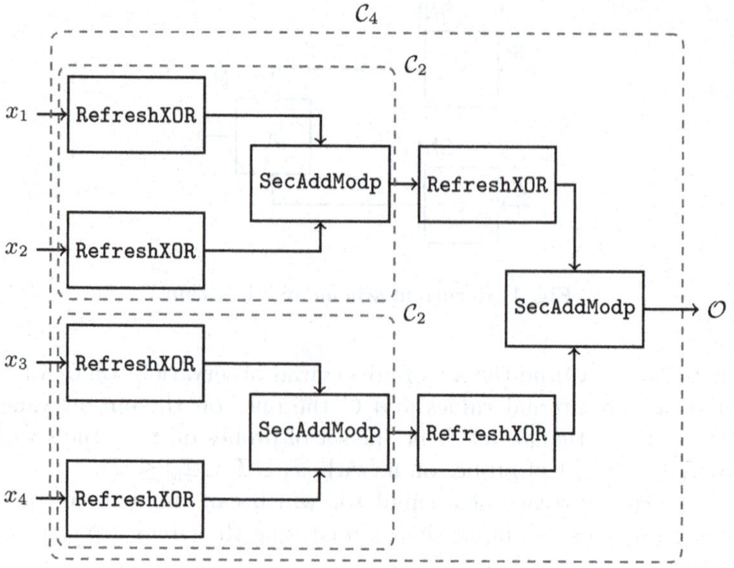

Fig. 2. Structure of SecArithBoolModp in Algorithm 3 for $n = 4$

4 A New $\mathtt{B2A}_q$ Conversion Algorithm

In this section, we present our new $\mathtt{B2A}_q$ conversion algorithm. Initially, we describe how the aforementioned arithmetic relationship of Boolean-masked bits can be used to construct a higher-order-secure conversion algorithm. We use this bit-wise transformation to derive a generic method to convert Boolean encodings to arithmetic encodings for arbitrary bit size k, number of shares n, and modulus q. The security of our solution is extensively proven and the $t-\mathsf{SNI}$ property is shown. In the last subsection, we compare the performance of our proposal not only against the new SecArithBoolModp (quadratic) algorithm for a prime modulus, but also against standard B2A conversions assuming a modulus of 2^k.

4.1 Conversion for $x \in \mathbb{F}_2$

Firstly, we discuss how to securely transform the Boolean shares $(x_1, x_2) \in \mathbb{F}_2$ with $x_1 \oplus x_2 = x$ into arithmetic shares (A_1, A_2) with $A_1 + A_2 = x \mod q$ for some arbitrary modulus q. For conciseness, we will not explicitly indicate every time that the arithmetic operations are done modulo q. To perform the conversion, the Boolean shares are transformed to the arithmetic encodings $B_1 + B_2 = x_1$ and $C_1 + C_2 = x_2$. This results in the following equations

$$\begin{aligned}x &= x_1 \oplus x_2 = (B_1 + B_2) \oplus (C_1 + C_2)\\ &= (B_1 + B_2) + (C_1 + C_2) - 2 \cdot (B_1 + B_2) \cdot (C_1 + C_2).\end{aligned}$$

Algorithm 4. $\mathtt{SecB2A}_{q-Bit}$ (simple)

Input: $\mathbf{x} = (x_i)_{1 \le i \le n} \in \mathbb{F}_2$ such that $\bigoplus_i x_i = x$
Output: $\mathbf{A} = (A_i)_{1 \le i \le n} \in \mathbb{F}_q$ such that $\sum_i A_i = x \mod q$

$(A_i)_{1 \le i \le n} \leftarrow 0$
for $j = 1$ to n **do**
  $(B_i)_{1 \le i \le n} \leftarrow (x_j, 0, \ldots, 0)$
  $\mathbf{B} \leftarrow \mathtt{RefreshADD}(\mathbf{B}, q)$
  $\mathbf{C} \leftarrow \mathtt{SecMul}(\mathbf{A}, \mathbf{B})$
  $\mathbf{A} \leftarrow \mathbf{A} + \mathbf{B} - 2 \cdot \mathbf{C}$
end for

Before deriving the final arithmetic encoding $\mathbf{A}$, we have to sample a fresh random element $R \in \mathbb{F}_q$ to secure the shared multiplication $(B_1+B_2)\cdot(C_1+C_2)$. Now, it is easily possible to compute the shares as

$$A_1 = B_1 + C_1 + R - 2 \cdot B_1 \cdot C_1 - 2 \cdot B_1 \cdot C_2$$
$$A_2 = B_2 + C_2 - R - 2 \cdot B_2 \cdot C_1 - 2 \cdot B_2 \cdot C_2.$$

Extending this simple first-order approach to arbitrary n simply requires a proper refresh and multiplication algorithm, as described in Algorithm 4.

However, similarly as before, the algorithm has a run time complexity of $\mathcal{O}(n^3)$, i.e., cubic in the number of shares, and, therefore, quickly becomes inefficient for increasing security orders. Therefore, we further optimize the simple version of the conversion to increase the performance significantly.

1. Instead of using the $t-\mathsf{SNI}$ refresh RefreshADD for every iteration round, we found that it is sufficient to use a $t-\mathsf{NI}$ refresh for every round and only perform a final $t-\mathsf{SNI}$ refresh at the end. This reduces the complexity of the refresh for every iteration from $\mathcal{O}(n^2)$ to $\mathcal{O}(n)$.
2. Instead of multiplying two complete encodings as $\mathtt{SecMul}(\mathbf{A},\mathbf{B})$[3], we do not refresh x_j and instead compute the component-wise multiplication $\mathbf{A} \cdot x_j$. Obviously, this requires that the encoding $\mathbf{A}$ is independent of x_j, which we achieve with the aforementioned $t-\mathsf{NI}$ refresh. In this way, we save another operation with $\mathcal{O}(n^2)$ and reduce it to $\mathcal{O}(n)$. Furthermore, we can save $n-1$ operations of the addition $\mathbf{A} + x_j$.
3. Similar to the previous conversions, we vary the number of considered shares in each iteration, e.g., for $j = 2$ the operations are done on two shares. Note that we cannot use the same recursive approach as the previous examples, because it would not allow us to employ the second optimization.

The optimized conversion is given in Algorithm 5, which now has a run time complexity of $\mathcal{O}(n^2)$. Its structure is depicted in Fig. 3.

Correctness. We prove the correctness of $\mathtt{B2A}_{q-Bit}$, since the refreshing afterwards does not change the decoded output. The proof is based on the following

[3] SecMul is implemented similar to SecAnd of [14].

Algorithm 5. $\texttt{SecB2A}_{q-Bit}$ (optimized)

Input: $\mathbf{x} = (x_i)_{1 \leq i \leq n} \in \mathbb{F}_2$ such that $\bigoplus_i x_i = x \in \mathbb{F}_2$
Output: $\mathbf{A} = (A_i)_{1 \leq i \leq n} \in \mathbb{F}_q$ such that $\sum_i A_i = x \mod q$
$\mathbf{A} \leftarrow \texttt{B2A}_{q-Bit}(\mathbf{x})$
$\mathbf{A} \leftarrow \texttt{RefreshADD}(\mathbf{A}, q)$

Algorithm 6. $\texttt{B2A}_{q-Bit}$

Input: $\mathbf{x} = (x_i)_{1 \leq i \leq n} \in \mathbb{F}_2$ such that $\bigoplus_i x_i = x \in \mathbb{F}_2$
Output: $\mathbf{A} = (A_i)_{1 \leq i \leq n} \in \mathbb{F}_q$ such that $\sum_i A_i = x \mod q$
1: $\mathbf{A} \leftarrow x_1$
2: **for** $j = 2$ to n **do**
3: $\mathbf{A} \leftarrow \texttt{B2A}^{(j)}_{q-Bit}(\mathbf{A}, x_j)$
4: **end for**

property, already mentioned in Eq. (3). Given $x_1, x_2 \in \mathbb{F}_2$, the XOR between the two bits can be written as $x_1 \oplus x_2 = x_1 + x_2 - 2 \cdot x_1 \cdot x_2$. Generalizing to the case of n values, it is easy to see that

$$\bigoplus_{i=1}^{n} x_i = ((((x_1 \oplus x_2) \oplus x_3) \dots) \oplus x_n) = \bigoplus_{i=1}^{n-1} x_i + x_n - 2 \cdot \bigoplus_{i=1}^{n-1} x_i \cdot x_n \quad (4)$$

Now, adding the output shares of Algorithm 6 we get

$$\sum_{i=1}^{n} A_i = \sum_{i=1}^{n} B_i - 2 \cdot \sum_{i=1}^{n} B_i \cdot x_n + x_n = \sum_{i=1}^{n-1} A_i - 2 \cdot \sum_{i=1}^{n-1} A_i \cdot x_n + x_n$$
$$= \bigoplus_{i=1}^{n-1} x_i - 2 \cdot \bigoplus_{i=1}^{n-1} x_i \cdot x_n + x_n$$

which, for Eq. 4, is exactly $\bigoplus_{i=1}^{n} x_i$.

Security. In the following propositions we show that our conversion scheme $\texttt{SecB2A}_{q-Bit}$ in Algorithm 5 satisfies the $t-\mathsf{SNI}$ property, when $t = n-1$. We underline that $t-\mathsf{SNI}$ ensures that our conversion algorithm can be securely composed in larger circuits.

Proposition 2. *$\texttt{B2A}^{(2)}_{q-Bit}$ in Algorithm 7 is $1-\mathsf{NI}$.*

Proof. Let us suppose that the adversary has exactly 1 probe w in Algorithm 7. This belongs to the following possible groups:

(1) x_1, x_2
(2) B_2

Algorithm 7. $\texttt{B2A}_{q-Bit}^{(n)}$

Input: $\mathbf{A} = (A_i)_{1 \le i \le n-1} \in \mathbb{F}_q$ such that $\sum_i A_i = x$; $x_n \in \mathbb{F}_2$
Output: $\mathbf{C} = (C_i)_{1 \le i \le n} \in \mathbb{F}_q$ such that $\sum_i C_i = (x \oplus x_n) \mod q$

$B_n \xleftarrow{\$} \mathbb{F}_q$
$B_1 \leftarrow A_1 - B_n \mod q$
for $j = 2$ to $n - 1$ **do**
  $R \xleftarrow{\$} \mathbb{F}_q$
  $B_j \leftarrow A_j - R \mod q$
  $B_n \leftarrow B_n + R \mod q$
end for
for $j = 1$ to n **do**
  $C_j \leftarrow B_j - 2 \cdot (B_j \cdot x_n) \mod q$
end for
$C_1 \leftarrow C_1 + x_n \mod q$

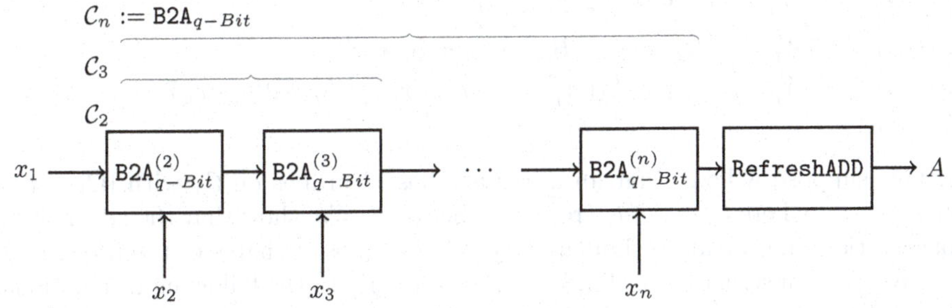

Fig. 3. Structure of $\texttt{SecB2A}_{q-Bit}$ in Algorithm 5.

(3) $B_1 := A_1 - B_2 = x_1 - B_2$
(4) $B_1 \cdot x_2 = (x_1 - B_2) \cdot x_2$, $b := B_1 - 2(B_1 \cdot x_2)$
(5) $B_2 \cdot x_2$, $B_2 - 2(B_2 \cdot x_2)$
(6) $b + x_2 = (B_1 - 2(B_1 \cdot x_2)) + x_2$

We construct a set of indexes I of cardinality 1, by adding the index 1 (resp. 2) if $w = x_1$ (resp. $w = x_2$). The simulation of the probe w, by using at most 1 share of the inputs, is straightforward.

- If the probe w is in group (1), by construction $1 \in I$ or respectively $2 \in I$. Thus the values can be simulated as x_1 (resp. x_2) as in the real algorithm.
- If the probe w is in one of the groups from (2) to (6), thanks to the presence in the computation of w of the random values B_1 or B_2, it is simulated by assigning it to a random and independent value in $\mathbb{F}_q$. □

We remark that the algorithm is not $t-$SNI. Indeed, if an adversary probes the output share $(B_1 - 2(B_1 \cdot x_2)) + x_2 = ((x_1 - B_2) - 2((x_1 - B_2) \cdot x_2)) + x_2$ and the internal value B_2, then the adversary gets the knowledge of two inputs shares, contradicting the definition of $t-$SNI.

In the following proposition we prove that the algorithm $\texttt{B2A}_{q-Bit}$ is $t-$NI.

Proposition 3. $\mathtt{B2A}_{q-Bit}$ *in Algorithm 6 is* $t-\mathsf{NI}$.

Proof. In the following, we denote with $\mathcal{C}_i$ the execution of Algorithm 6 until the ith iteration of the **for**, for $i = 2, \dots, n$, as indicated in Fig. 3. In particular $\mathcal{C}_n := \mathtt{B2A}_{q-Bit}$.

We prove the thesis by induction on the value i. From Proposition 2 the condition is satisfied for the case of $i = 2$.

Let now assume that $\mathcal{C}_i$ is $(i-1)-\mathsf{NI}$ for all $i \leq n-1$ and we show that under this condition $\mathcal{C}_n$ is $t-\mathsf{NI}$ as well. First of all let us denote with $A_j^{(i)}$ the output shares of $\mathcal{C}_i$ for all $i \leq n-1$ and with $j = 1, \dots, n$. We can classify the internal and output values of $\mathcal{C}_n$ in the following groups:

(1) B_j for $j = 2, \dots, n$, r
(2) A_1^{n-1},
(3) $b_1 := A_1^{n-1} - B_2 - \dots - B_j$, with $j = 2, \dots, n$
(4) $A_j^{(n-1)} - r_j =: b_j$, with $j = 2, \dots, n$
(5) $A_1^{(n)} = (A_1^{n-1} - B_2 - \dots - B_n) + x_n = b_1 + x_n$
(6) $A_j^{(n)} = (A_j^{(n-1)} - r_j) - 2((A_j^{(n-1)} - r_j) \cdot x_n) = b_j - 2(b_j \cdot x_n)$
(7) x_n

Let us suppose w.l.o.g. that an adversary has Ω probes on $\mathcal{C}_n$ with $|\Omega| = t = t_1 + \dots + t_n$, where $t_1 + \dots + t_i$ are the probes on $\mathcal{C}_i$. We show that the adversary's observation on $\mathcal{C}_n$ can be simulated by using at most t shares of the input.

We first construct a set of indexes I accordingly to the following instructions: for each probe in group (5), add n to I, and for each probe in group (6), add n to I. The simulation follows the steps below.

- **Step 1.** The probes in group (1) are simulated by assigning them to a random and independent value in $\mathbb{F}_q$.
- **Step 2.** Since by hypothesis $\mathtt{B2A}_{q-Bit}^{(n-1)}$ is $t-\mathsf{NI}$, the probes in group (2) can be simulated by using at most $t_1 + \dots + t_{n-1}$ shares.
- **Step 3.** If a probe is in group (3) and at least one of the $B_2, \dots, B_j$ is not in Ω, then the values can be assigned to a random and independent value. Otherwise, if $B_2, \dots, B_j \in \Omega$, then since $\mathtt{B2A}_{q-Bit}^{(n-1)}$ is $t-\mathsf{NI}$ the probes can be simulated by using at most $t_1 + \dots + t_{n-1}$ shares of the input and the assigned values of $B_2, \dots, B_j$ in Step 1. Otherwise, if a sum $A_1^{n-1} - B_2 - \dots - B_k \in \Omega$, with $k < j$ and $B_{k+1}, \dots, B_j \in \Omega$, then the values can be computed as in the real execution of the algorithm, by using the values $B_{k+1}, \dots, B_j$ assigned in Step 1 and the simulated sum $A_1^{n-1} - B_2 - \dots - B_k$, in one of the phases of this Step.
- **Step 4.** If a probe is in group (4) and $r_j \notin \Omega$, then the values can be assigned to a random and independent value. Otherwise, if $r_j \in \Omega$, then since $\mathtt{B2A}_{q-Bit}^{(n-1)}$ is $t-\mathsf{NI}$ the probes can be simulated by using at most $t_1 + \dots + t_{n-1}$ shares and the value r_j assigned in Step 1.

- **Step 5.** If a probe is in group (5) and $b_1 \in \Omega$, then by construction $n \in I$ and we can compute the value as in the algorithm, by using the b_1 simulated at Step 3 and x_n. Otherwise, if $b_1 \notin \Omega$, we can simulate b_1 as in Step 3, by using at most $t_1 + \cdots + t_{n+1}$ input shares and x_n, since $n \in I$.
- **Step 6.** If a probe is in group (6) and $b_j \in \Omega$, then by construction $n \in I$ and we can compute the value as in the algorithm, by using the b_j simulated at Step 4 and x_n. Otherwise, if $b_j \notin \Omega$, we can simulate b_j as in Step 4, by using at most $t_1 + \cdots + t_{n+1}$ input shares and x_n, since $n \in I$.
- **Step 7.** If a probe is in group (7), by construction $n \in I$ and we can trivially simulate x_n.

In all the steps listed above, we showed that the simulation uses at most t input shares, as required from Definition 1, completing the proof. □

Before proceeding with the next proposition, we remind that the refreshing scheme added at the end of $\texttt{SecB2A}_{q-Bit}$ is an algorithm presented in [6] and proven to be t – SNI. The t – SNI security of $\texttt{SecB2A}_{q-Bit}$ relies exactly on the introduction of this gadget after the computation of $\texttt{SecB2A}_{q-Bit}$. We see below a more detailed security proof.

Proposition 4. *$\texttt{SecB2A}_{q-Bit}$ in Algorithm 5 is t – SNI.*

Proof. The t – SNI security of $\texttt{SecB2A}_{\texttt{q-Bit}}$ easily follows from the fact that $\texttt{B2A}_{q-Bit}$ is t – NI and $\texttt{RefreshADD}$ is t – SNI.

Let $\Omega = (I, \mathcal{O})$ be the set of probes on $\texttt{SecB2A}_{q-Bit}$, where I_1 are the probes on the internal wires of $\texttt{B2A}_{q-Bit}$ and I_2 are the probes on the internal wires of $\texttt{RefreshADD}$, with $|I| = |I_1| + |I_2| \leq t_1$ and $|I| + |\mathcal{O}| \leq t$.

Since $\texttt{RefreshADD}$ is t – SNI and $|I_2 \cup \mathcal{O}| \leq t$, then there exists an observation set $\mathcal{S}^2$ such that $|\mathcal{S}^2| \leq |I_2|$ and the gadget can be simulated from its input shares corresponding to the indexes in $\mathcal{S}^2$.

Since $\texttt{SecB2A}_{q-Bit}$ is t – NI and $|I_1 \cup \mathcal{S}^2| \leq |I_1 \cup I_2| \leq t$, then it exists an observation set $\mathcal{S}^1$ such that $|\mathcal{S}^1| \leq |I_1 \cup \mathcal{S}^2|$ and the gadget can be simulated from its input shares corresponding to the indexes in $\mathcal{S}^1$.

Now, composing the simulators that we have for the two gadgets $\texttt{RefreshADD}$ and $\texttt{SecB2A}_{q-Bit}$, all the probes of the circuit can be simulated from $|\mathcal{S}^1| \leq |I_1| + |I_2| \leq t_1$ shares of the input x and therefore, according to Definition 2, the circuit in Fig. 3 is t – SNI. □

4.2 Conversion for $x \in \mathbb{F}_{2^k}$

While the current solution is very efficient and simple, it only computes the correct results for Boolean encodings of bit values. Otherwise, the arithmetic property does not hold anymore. In order to extend our approach to include arbitrary bit sizes, we apply the previous conversion to each input bit separately and combine with component-wise addition. This trivially results in a complexity of $\mathcal{O}(n^2 \cdot k)$, as we have k calls to $\texttt{SecB2A}_{q-Bit}$. The complete conversion is given in Algorithm 9 and its basic structure for $k = 3$ is depicted in Fig. 4.

Algorithm 8. RefreshADD (based on RefreshXOR [6])

Input: $\mathbf{A} = (A_i)_{1 \leq i \leq n} \in \mathbb{F}_q$ such that $\sum_i A_i = x \mod q$, modulus q
Output: $\mathbf{B} = (B_i)_{1 \leq i \leq n} \in \mathbb{F}_q$ such that $\sum_i B_i = x \mod q$

$\mathbf{B} \leftarrow \mathbf{A}$
for $i = 1$ to $n-1$ **do**
  for $j = 1 + i$ to n **do**
    $R \xleftarrow{\$} \mathbb{F}_q$
    $B_i \leftarrow B_i + r$
    $B_j \leftarrow B_j - r$
  end for
end for

Algorithm 9. $\mathtt{SecB2A}_q$

Input: $\mathbf{x} = (x_i)_{1 \leq i \leq n} \in \mathbb{F}_{2^k}$ such that $\bigoplus_i x_i = x \in \mathbb{F}_{2^k}$
Output: $\mathbf{A} = (A_i)_{1 \leq i \leq n} \in \mathbb{F}_q$ such that $\sum_i A_i = x \mod q$

$\mathbf{A} \leftarrow \mathtt{SecB2A}_{\mathtt{q-Bit}}((\mathbf{x} >> (k-1)) \wedge 1)$
for $j = 2$ to k **do**
  $\mathbf{B} \leftarrow \mathtt{SecB2A}_{\mathtt{q-Bit}}((\mathbf{x} >> (k-j)) \wedge 1)$
  $\mathbf{A} \leftarrow 2 \cdot \mathbf{A} + \mathbf{B} \mod q$
end for

Correctness. Let us assume that $2^k \leq q$. It is easy to see that for each $i = 1, \ldots, n$ the output shares are of the following form

$$A_i = 2^0 \cdot \mathtt{B2A}_{\mathtt{q-Bit}}(x_i^{(1)}) + 2^1 \cdot \mathtt{B2A}_{\mathtt{q-Bit}}(x_i^{(2)}) + \cdots + 2^{k-1} \cdot \mathtt{B2A}_{\mathtt{q-Bit}}(x_i^{(k)})$$

and therefore $\sum_{i=1}^{n} A_i = x \mod q$.

Security. As done for the previous algorithms, we give in the following the proof of security according to the $t-\mathsf{SNI}$ property, for $t \leq n-1$.

Proposition 5. $\mathtt{SecB2A}_\mathtt{q}$ *in Algorithm 9 is* $t - \mathsf{SNI}$, *with* $t \leq n - 1$.

Proof. Proving that Algorithm 9 is $t-\mathsf{SNI}$ follows from the fact that $\mathtt{SecB2A}_{q-Bit}$ is $t-\mathsf{SNI}$ and from the structure of the algorithm itself, depicted in Fig. 4.

First, we define $\mathcal{C}_i$, for $i = 1, \ldots, k$ as in Fig. 4, where $\mathcal{C}_1 := \mathtt{SecB2A}_{\mathtt{q-Bit}}$ and $\mathcal{C}_n := \mathtt{SecB2A}_\mathtt{q}$. We prove the thesis by induction on $i \in \mathbb{N}$.

Thanks to Proposition 4, $\mathcal{C}_1$ is $t-\mathsf{SNI}$.
We suppose now that $\mathcal{C}_i$ is $t-\mathsf{SNI}$ for all $i = 1, \ldots, n-1$ and we prove that $\mathcal{C}_n$ is $t-\mathsf{SNI}$. Let $\Omega = (\mathcal{I}, \mathcal{O})$ be the set of adversarial observations on $\mathcal{C}_n$, where $\mathcal{I}$ are the ones on the internal values and $\mathcal{O}$ the ones on the output values, with $|\mathcal{I}| + |\mathcal{O}| \leq t$. In particular, let $\mathcal{I}_1$ be the set of probes on $+$, $\mathcal{I}_2$ the set of probes on $2\cdot$, $\mathcal{I}_3$ be the set of probes on $\mathcal{C}_{n-1}$ and $\mathcal{I}_4$ be the set of probes on $\mathtt{SecB2A}_{\mathtt{q-Bit}}$, with $\sum_j |\mathcal{I}_j| \leq |\mathcal{I}|$.

We prove the existence of a simulator which can simulate the adversary's view by using at most $|\mathcal{I}|$ input shares. We proceed with the analysis of the circuit from right to left.

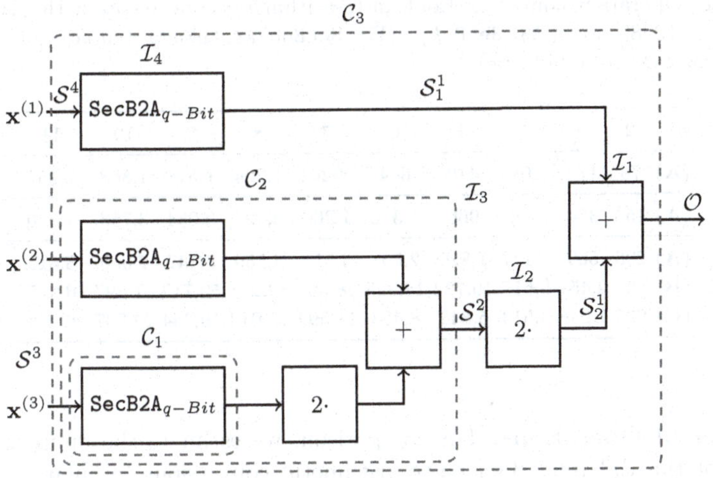

Fig. 4. Structure of $\mathsf{SecB2A}_q$ in Algorithm 9 for $k = 3$.

Since + is a linear operation and $|I_1 \cup \mathcal{O}| \leq t$, then there exist two observation sets $\mathcal{S}_1^1, \mathcal{S}_2^1$ such that $|\mathcal{S}_1^1| \leq |I_1 \cup \mathcal{O}|$, $|\mathcal{S}_2^1| \leq |I_1 \cup \mathcal{O}|$ and the gadget can be simulated using at most $|\mathcal{S}_1^1| + |\mathcal{S}_2^1|$ shares of the inputs.

Since 2· is a linear operation and $|I_2 \cup \mathcal{S}_2^1| \leq t$, then there exists an observation set $\mathcal{S}^2$ such that $|\mathcal{S}^2| \leq |I_2 \cup \mathcal{S}_2^1|$ and the gadget can be simulated using at most $|\mathcal{S}^2| + |\mathcal{S}_2^1|$ shares of the inputs.

Since, for the assumption step, $\mathcal{C}_{n-1}$ is t – SNI and moreover $|\mathcal{I}_3 \cup \mathcal{S}^2| \leq t$, there exists an observation set $\mathcal{S}^3$ such that $|\mathcal{S}^3| \leq |I_3|$ and the gadget can be simulated using at most $|\mathcal{S}^3|$ shares of the inputs.

Since $\mathsf{SecB2A}_{\mathsf{q-Bit}}$ is t – SNI and moreover $|\mathcal{I}_4 \cup \mathcal{S}_1^1| \leq t$, there exists an observation set $\mathcal{S}^4$ such that $|\mathcal{S}^4| \leq |I_4|$ and the gadget can be simulated using at most $|\mathcal{S}^4|$ shares of the inputs.

By combining the steps above, we see that $\mathcal{C}_n$ can be simulated by using in total $|\mathcal{S}^3 \cup \mathcal{S}^4| \leq |\mathcal{I}_3| + |\mathcal{I}_4| \leq |\mathcal{I}|$ input shares, completing the proof. □

4.3 Performance Analysis

We analyze both of our new conversion algorithms regarding the number of required operations and randoms. They are compared to the cubic conversion from [6] for a prime modulus $q = 12289$ as used in NewHope. Furthermore, we compare $\mathsf{SecB2A}_q$ to the conversions from [14] and [7], since they are currently the fastest algorithms for power-of-two moduli secure at arbitrary orders[4].

[4] Note that there are order-optimized algorithms which can provide an even better performance for specific values of t (i.e., Goubin [19] for $t = 1$, and Hutter and Tunstall [21] for $t = 2$). However, for power-of-two moduli our $\mathsf{SecB2A}_q$ is only competitive for larger values of t, and we, thus, exclude these specific examples from the comparison.

Table 1. Operation count for Boolean-to-arithmetic conversions with prime modulo $q = 12289$ for (**A**) $\mathtt{SecB2A}_q$, (**B**) `SecBoolArithModp` (cubic) [6], and (**C**) `SecArithBoolModp` (quadratic).

	n	2	3	4	5	6	7	8	9	10	11	16
$k = 4$	(**A**)	76	174	308	478	684	926	1,204	1,518	1,868	2,254	4,724
$k = 8$	(**A**)	156	354	624	966	1,380	1,866	2,424	3,054	3,756	4,530	9,480
$k = 15$	(**A**)	296	669	1,177	1,820	2,598	3,511	4,559	5,742	7,060	8,513	17,803
	(**B**)	765	2,451	5,617	10,722	18,225	28,585	42,261	59,712	81,397	107,775	326,125
	(**C**)	695	1,948	3,513	5,842	8,483	11,592	15,013	19,354	24,007	29,128	60,973

Number of Operations. For comparison, we estimate the number of operations of the different Boolean-to-arithmetic conversions. Similar to [12], we assume that randomness generation takes unit time, and we do not consider the modulo reductions. For [14] we use the estimation given in [12][5], and for [7] the authors provide a closed equation to compute the number of operations. Our newly-proposed $\mathtt{SecB2A}_q$ has a run time complexity[6] of

$$T_{\mathtt{SecB2Aq}}(n,k) = \frac{9kn^2}{2} + \frac{5kn}{2} - 2n - 3k.$$

We compare the $\mathtt{B2A}_q$ conversions considering the prime modulus from the NIST submission NewHope $q = 12289$. It should be noted that the modular addition `SecAddModp` requires $2^k > 2q$. Therefore, we always call the function `SecBoolArithModp` with $k' = \lceil \log_2 2q \rceil = 15$ in this evaluation. The results are presented in Table 1. It is noticeable that $\mathtt{SecB2A}_q$ outperforms both versions of `SecBoolArithModp` significantly. This is mostly due to the small values of k. It is expected that for larger k the quadratic variant of `SecBoolArithModp` is the most efficient $\mathtt{B2A}_q$ conversion, as it scales with $\mathcal{O}(\log k)$ instead of $\mathcal{O}(k)$. Nevertheless, for our case study we obtain a large performance improvement by using $\mathtt{SecB2A}_q$, since we need to transform either 1- or 5-bit variables.

Additionally, we compare our new algorithms with the state-of-the-art `B2A` conversions assuming a modulus of 2^k for different values of k. The resulting performances are given in Table 2. As expected, the algorithm of [7] outperforms all other solutions for small n. Surprisingly, however, our new conversion $\mathtt{SecB2A}_q$ outperforms the approach of [14] for the considered values of k. We expect that, for larger bit sizes and by incorporating a logarithmic adder, [14] will eventually outperform our approach.[7] Nevertheless, for $k = 32$, which is used in many symmetric algorithms, our $\mathtt{SecB2A}_{q-Bit}$ does provide a performance improvement

[5] Note that there is typo in the final equation: $T'_n = 2n + T_n + B_n + 3n^2 + n$.

[6] In the full version of the paper we derive the complexity of the remaining algorithms.

[7] It was shown in [13] that the logarithmic adder offers a significant improvement over the linear approach for $k > 32$ at first-order.

Table 2. Operation count for Boolean-to-arithmetic conversions mod 2^k for **(A)** $\texttt{SecB2A}_q$, **(D)** Bettale et al. [7], and **(E)** Coron et al. [14]. The bold operation counts indicate that our new algorithm provides the best performance of the considered algorithms for a given value of k.

	n	2	3	4	5	6	7	8	9	10	11	16
$\forall k$	**(D)**	15	49	123	277	591	1,225	2,499	5,053	10,167	20,401	655,251
$k = 1$	**(A)**	**12**	**33**	**63**	**102**	**150**	**207**	**273**	**348**	**432**	**525**	**1,125**
	(E)	56	135	234	374	534	721	928	1,183	1,458	1,760	3,640
$k = 4$	**(A)**	76	174	308	478	684	**926**	**1,204**	**1,518**	**1,868**	**2,254**	**4,724**
	(E)	134	354	636	1,052	1,530	2,098	2,728	3,520	4,374	5,318	11,248
$k = 8$	**(A)**	156	354	624	966	1,380	1,866	**2,424**	**3,054**	**3,756**	**4,530**	**9,480**
	(E)	238	646	1,172	1,956	2,858	3,934	5,128	6,636	8,262	10,062	21,392
$k = 32$	**(A)**	636	1,434	2,520	3,894	5,556	7,506	9,744	12,270	15,084	**18,186**	**38,016**
	(E)	862	2,398	4,388	7,380	10,826	14,950	19,528	25,332	31,590	38,526	82,256

even for standard moduli assuming $n \geq 11$. We further want to note that our algorithm comes with a proof of $t-\mathsf{SNI}$, which allows composability with other modules under certain assumptions [5].

Randomness Complexity. We estimate the number of required random bits for the different Boolean-to-arithmetic conversions. We denote the bit size of the input encoding as k_1 and for samples in $\mathbb{F}_q$, where q is not a power-of-two, we assume $k_2 = \lceil \log_2 q \rceil$ bits. A more detailed discussion of the sampling process of such values is provided in the case study. Again, for [7] the authors provide a closed equation to compute the number of random elements. Our newly-proposed $\texttt{SecB2A}_q$ has a randomness complexity of $R_{\texttt{SecB2Aq}}(n, k_1) = k_2 k_1 (n^2 - n)$.

As before, we initially compare the $\texttt{B2A}_q$ conversions considering the prime modulus from the NIST submission NewHope $q = 12289$. The results are presented in Table 3 and again $\texttt{SecB2A}_q$ outperforms $\texttt{SecBoolArithModp}$. However, it should be noted that all random samples for $\texttt{SecB2A}_q$ are from $\mathbb{F}_q$, while $\texttt{SecBoolArithModp}$ only requires $(n-1)$ random values from $\mathbb{F}_q$ and the remaining are sampled from $\mathbb{F}_{2^{k_1}}$, which can be more efficient depending on the RNG.

In the typical use cases of a power-of-two modulus (like in symmetric crypto), there is no difference between k_1 and k_2 and thus we evaluate the number of RNG calls instead of random bits for this case. The resulting performances are given in Table 4. Again, the algorithm of [7] outperforms all other solutions for small n, while $\texttt{SecB2A}_q$ provides the best performance for certain values of k and n.

Table 3. Required random bits for Boolean-to-arithmetic conversions with $q = 12289$ for (**A**) $\texttt{SecB2A}_q$, (**B**) `SecBoolArithModp` (cubic) [6], and (**C**) `SecArithBoolModp` (quadratic). Note that sampling from $\mathbb{F}_q$ is estimated with $\lceil \log_2 q \rceil$ bits.

	n	2	3	4	5	6	7	8	9	10	11	16
k=4	(A)	112	336	672	1,120	1,680	2,352	3,136	4,032	5,040	6,160	13,440
k=8	(A)	224	672	1,344	2,240	3,360	4,704	6,272	8,064	10,080	12,320	26,880
k=15	(A)	420	1,260	2,520	4,200	6,300	8,820	11,760	15,120	18,900	23,100	50,400
	(B)	1,244	4,933	12,282	24,506	42,820	68,439	102,578	146,452	201,276	268,265	828,210
	(C)	854	2,968	5,922	10,556	16,030	22,764	30,338	40,012	50,526	62,300	137,970

Table 4. Number of RNG calls for Boolean-to-arithmetic conversions mod 2^k for (**A**) $\texttt{SecB2A}_q$, (**D**) Bettale et al. [7], and (**E**) Coron et al. [14]. The bold call counts indicate that our new algorithm provides the best performance of the considered algorithms for a given value of k.

	n	2	3	4	5	6	7	8	9	10	11	16
$\forall k$	(D)	2	7	18	41	88	183	374	757	1,524	3,059	98,286
$k = 1$	(A)	2	**6**	**12**	**20**	**30**	**42**	**56**	**72**	**90**	**110**	**240**
	(E)	9	23	41	66	95	129	167	213	263	318	663
$k = 4$	(A)	8	24	48	80	120	**168**	**224**	**288**	**360**	**440**	**960**
	(E)	15	44	83	141	209	291	383	498	623	762	1,647
$k = 8$	(A)	16	48	96	160	240	336	448	**576**	**720**	**880**	**1,920**
	(E)	23	72	139	241	361	507	671	878	1,103	1,354	2,959
$k = 32$	(A)	64	192	384	640	960	1,344	1,792	2,304	2,880	3,520	**7,680**
	(E)	71	240	475	841	1,273	1,803	2,399	3,158	3,983	4,906	10,831

5 Higher-Order Masked Binomial Sampling

Our sampling algorithms assume that they are given two variables (x, y) that have a length of κ bits and are Boolean-encoded as $(\mathbf{x}, \mathbf{y})$. This is in accordance with many of the aforementioned schemes which rely on a PRNG (Boolean-masked) to produce uniform pseudo-randomness. The sampler needs to compute $\texttt{HW}(x) - \texttt{HW}(y)$ in a secure fashion on these encodings and produce arithmetic shares $\mathbf{A}$ with $\sum_i A_i = \texttt{HW}(x) - \texttt{HW}(y) \mod q$ for a given modulus q to fit the subsequent lattice operations. Since this conversion can be done with any of the aforementioned $\texttt{B2A}_q$ schemes, the algorithms contain a generic function call. Initially, we present a generalization of [25], before proposing a more efficient sampling algorithm based on bitslicing. Both algorithms are proven to be $t-\mathsf{SNI}$ and their performances are compared using NewHope as a case study.

Algorithm 10. $\texttt{SecSampler}_1$

Input: $\mathbf{x} = (x_i)_{1\le i\le n} \in \mathbb{F}_{2^\kappa}$, $\mathbf{y} = (y_i)_{1\le i\le n} \in \mathbb{F}_{2^\kappa}$ such that $\bigoplus_i x_i = x$, $\bigoplus_i y_i = y$

Output: $\mathbf{A} = (A_i)_{1\le i\le n} \in \mathbb{F}_q$ such that $\sum_i A_i = \texttt{HW}(x) - \texttt{HW}(y) \mod q$

1: $(A_i)_{1\le i\le n} \leftarrow 0$
2: **for** $j = 0$ to $\kappa - 1$ **do**
3: $\quad \mathbf{B} \leftarrow \texttt{B2A}_q\left((\mathbf{x} >> j) \wedge 1\right)$
4: $\quad \mathbf{C} \leftarrow \texttt{B2A}_q\left((\mathbf{y} >> j) \wedge 1\right)$
5: $\quad \mathbf{A} \leftarrow \mathbf{A} + \mathbf{B} \mod q$
6: $\quad \mathbf{A} \leftarrow \mathbf{A} - \mathbf{C} \mod q$
7: **end for**

5.1 Generalization of [25]

As briefly discussed in Sect. 2.4, the bits of $(\mathbf{x}, \mathbf{y})$ are transformed separately to arithmetic shares. We extend this approach in Algorithm 10 to be generic for any number of shares n, modulus q, and length of the bit-vectors κ. In particular, we first transform each of the 2κ bits separately to an arithmetic encoding modulo q. These are then summed component-wise to compute the Hamming weight of each variable and the results are subtracted again component-wise.

Correctness. The correctness of $\texttt{SecSampler}_1$ follows directly by the construction of the algorithm. Indeed, since at every iteration of the loop

$$\begin{aligned}\mathbf{A} &= \texttt{B2A}_q\left((\mathbf{x} >> 0) \wedge 1\right) - \texttt{B2A}_q\left((\mathbf{y} >> 0) \wedge 1\right)\\ &\quad + \cdots + \texttt{B2A}_q\left((\mathbf{x} >> \kappa - 1) \wedge 1\right) - \texttt{B2A}_q\left((\mathbf{y} >> \kappa - 1) \wedge 1\right)\end{aligned}$$

we have

$$\begin{aligned}\sum_i A_i &= \sum_i \Big(\texttt{B2A}_q\left((x_i >> 0) \wedge 1\right) - \texttt{B2A}_q\left((y_i >> 0) \wedge 1\right) + \dots\\ &\quad + \texttt{B2A}_q\left((x_i >> \kappa - 1) \wedge 1\right) - \texttt{B2A}_q\left((y_i >> \kappa - 1) \wedge 1\right)\Big)\\ &= \texttt{HW}(x) - \texttt{HW}(y) \mod q\end{aligned}$$

Security. The security of the sampler described in Algorithm 10 can be easily derived from its basic structure and utilization of $t-\mathsf{SNI}$ gadgets.

Proposition 6. $\texttt{Sampler}_1$ *in Algorithm 10 is* $t-\mathsf{SNI}$, *with* $t \le n - 1$

Proof. We point out that the $t-\mathsf{SNI}$ security of both considered $\texttt{B2A}_q$ algorithms, i.e., $\texttt{SecB2A}_{\texttt{q-Bit}}$ proven in Proposition 4 and $\texttt{SecArithBoolModp}$ in Proposition 1, receiving independent inputs, guarantees that every loop of Algorithm 10 represents a $t-\mathsf{SNI}$ gadget and therefore the output $\mathbf{A}$ can be securely injected in the sum of the following loop. □

Algorithm 11. `SecBitAdd`

Input: $\mathbf{x} = (x_i)_{1 \leq i \leq n} \in \mathbb{F}_{2^\kappa}$ such that $\bigoplus_i x_i = x$, $\lambda = \lceil \log_2(\kappa + 1) \rceil + 1$
Output: $\mathbf{z} = (z_i)_{1 \leq i \leq n} \in \mathbb{F}_{2^\lambda}$ such that $\bigoplus_i z_i = \mathtt{HW}(x)$

$(t_i)_{1 \leq i \leq n} \leftarrow 0$
$(z_i)_{1 \leq i \leq n} \leftarrow 0$
for $j = 1$ to κ **do**
  $\mathbf{t}^{(1)} \leftarrow \mathbf{z}^{(1)} \oplus \mathbf{x}^{(j)}$
  $\mathbf{w} \leftarrow \mathbf{x}^{(j)}$
  for $l = 2$ to λ **do**
    $\mathbf{w} \leftarrow \mathtt{SecAnd}(\mathbf{w}, \mathbf{z}^{(l-1)})$
    $\mathbf{t}^{(l)} \leftarrow \mathbf{z}^{(l)} \oplus \mathbf{w}$
  end for
  $\mathbf{z} \leftarrow \mathbf{t}$
end for

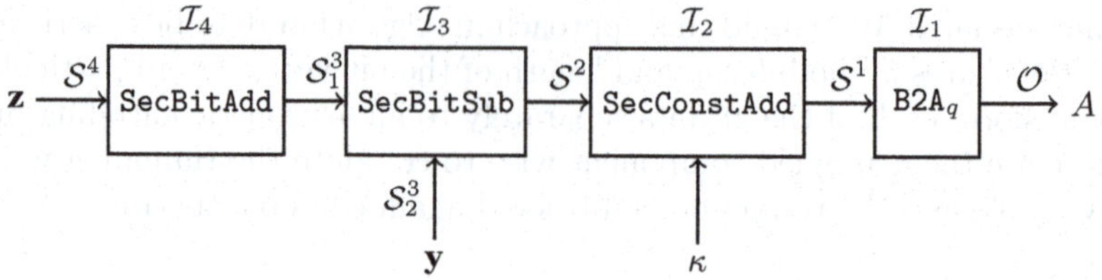

Fig. 5. Structure of $\mathtt{SecSampler}_2$ in Algorithm 15 (lines 1–4).

5.2 New Bitsliced Masked Binomial Sampler

In our improved sampler $\mathtt{SecSampler}_2$, we first compute the Hamming weight of x on the Boolean encodings using bitslicing to significantly increase the throughput. We further improve the performance by directly subtracting the Hamming weight of y from the result, again using bitslicing. In this way, the sampler only requires a single conversion. However, to correctly map the sign of the difference (i.e., negative values would be transformed incorrectly) it is necessary to add κ before converting. A generic algorithm to add such a constant to a Boolean encoding is provided in Algorithm 13. However, for specific values of κ this can be significantly optimized, e.g., for $\kappa = 8$ as in NewHope the addition can be done with only component-wise XOR, as shown in Algorithm 14. Finally, after the $\mathtt{B2A}_q$ conversion, the additional κ needs to be subtracted to recover the correct result, and this can be done component-wise on the arithmetic shares. The complete procedure is given in Algorithm 15. Since the input variables are in a bitsliced format, we directly denote the j-th bit of the l-th share of $\mathbf{x}$ as $x_l^{(j)}$.

Algorithm 12. SecBitSub

Input: $\mathbf{z} = (z_i)_{1 \le i \le n} \in \mathbb{F}_{2^\lambda}, \mathbf{y} = (y_i)_{1 \le i \le n} \in \mathbb{F}_{2^\kappa}$ such that $\bigoplus_i z_i = z$ and $\bigoplus_i y_i = y$, $\lambda = \lceil \log_2(\kappa + 1) \rceil + 1$
Output: $\mathbf{z} = (z_i)_{1 \le i \le n} \in \mathbb{F}_{2^\lambda}$ such that $\bigoplus_i z_i = z - \mathtt{HW}(y)$

$(t_i)_{1 \le i \le n} \leftarrow 0$
for $j = 1$ to κ **do**
  $\mathbf{t}^{(1)} \leftarrow \mathbf{z}^{(1)} \oplus \mathbf{y}^{(j)}$
  $\mathbf{w} \leftarrow \mathbf{y}^{(j)}$
  for $l = 2$ to λ **do**
    $\mathbf{u} \leftarrow \mathbf{z}^{(l-1)}$
    $u_1 \leftarrow \neg u_1$
    $\mathbf{w} \leftarrow \mathtt{SecAnd}(\mathbf{w}, \mathbf{u})$
    $\mathbf{t}^{(l)} \leftarrow \mathbf{z}^{(l)} \oplus \mathbf{w}$
  end for
  $\mathbf{z} \leftarrow \mathbf{t}$
end for

Algorithm 13. SecConstAdd

Input: $\mathbf{x} = (x_i)_{1 \le i \le n} \in \mathbb{F}_{2^\lambda}$, $\lambda = \lceil \log_2(\kappa + 1) \rceil + 1$
Output: $\mathbf{y} = (y_i)_{1 \le i \le n} \in \mathbb{F}_{2^\lambda}$ such that $\bigoplus_i y_i = x + \kappa$

$(t_i)_{1 \le i \le n} \leftarrow (\kappa, 0, \ldots, 0)$
$\mathbf{t} \leftarrow \mathtt{RefreshXOR}(\mathbf{t}, \lambda)$
$\mathbf{y} \leftarrow \mathtt{SecAdd}(\mathbf{x}, \mathbf{t})$

Correctness. The correctness of $\mathtt{SecSampler}_2$ is easy to show.

$$\begin{aligned}\sum_i A_i &= \mathtt{B2A}_q(\mathtt{SecConstAdd}(\mathtt{SecBitSub}(\mathtt{SecBitAdd}(\mathbf{x}), \mathbf{y}), \kappa)) - \kappa \\ &= \mathtt{B2A}_q(\mathtt{SecConstAdd}(\mathtt{SecBitSub}(\mathtt{HW}(x), \mathbf{y}), \kappa)) - \kappa \\ &= \mathtt{B2A}_q(\mathtt{SecConstAdd}(\mathtt{HW}(x) - \mathtt{HW}(y), \kappa)) - \kappa \\ &= \mathtt{B2A}_q(\mathtt{HW}(x) - \mathtt{HW}(y) + \kappa) - \kappa = \mathtt{HW}(x) - \mathtt{HW}(y) \mod q.\end{aligned}$$

Security. Before proving the security of $\mathtt{SecSampler}_2$ in Algorithm 15, we briefly summarize the security properties which its subroutines satisfy.

First we show that SecBitAdd in Algorithm 11 is t – NI and we start the analysis by focusing on its structure. We recall that SecAnd [14] is t – SNI and it receives at every iteration independent inputs (line 7). The output of each SecAnd is added with a XOR to a value independent from its inputs (line 8), therefore the entire inner loop (lines 6–9) represents a t – SNI gadget. This is recursively composed in the outer loop (lines 3–11) providing the outputs $(\mathbf{t}^{(2)}, \ldots, \mathbf{t}^{(\lambda)})$ and preserving the t – SNI property. Additionally, at every iteration of the outer loop, $\mathbf{x}^{(j)}$ is added with a XOR to $\mathbf{z}^{(1)}$ (line 4), resulting in the output $\mathbf{t}^{(1)} = \mathbf{x}^{(1)} + \ldots + \mathbf{x}^{(\kappa)}$. Let us suppose an attacker probes a set of t_1 values $\mathcal{P}_1$ on the shares $(\mathbf{t}^{(2)}, \ldots, \mathbf{t}^{(\lambda)})$ or on the internal values produced during the concatenation of the inner loop, and a set of t_2 values $\mathcal{P}_2$ on the

Algorithm 14. SecConstAdd (optimized for $\kappa = 8$)

Input: $\mathbf{x} = (x_i)_{1 \leq i \leq n} \in \mathbb{F}_{2^\lambda}$
Output: $\mathbf{y} = (y_i)_{1 \leq i \leq n} \in \mathbb{F}_{2^\lambda}$ such that $\bigoplus_i y_i = x + 8$

$\mathbf{y} \leftarrow \mathbf{x}$
$\mathbf{y}^{(5)} \leftarrow \mathbf{y}^{(5)} \oplus \mathbf{y}^{(4)}$
$y_1^{(4)} \leftarrow y_1^{(4)} \oplus 1$

Algorithm 15. $\mathtt{SecSampler}_2$

Input: $\mathbf{x} = (x_i)_{1 \leq i \leq n} \in \mathbb{F}_{2^\kappa}$, $\mathbf{y} = (y_i)_{1 \leq i \leq n} \in \mathbb{F}_{2^\kappa}$, κ, such that $\bigoplus_i x_i = x$, $\bigoplus_i y_i = y$
Output: $\mathbf{A} = (A_i)_{1 \leq i \leq n} \in \mathbb{F}_q$ such that $\sum_i A_i = \mathtt{HW}(x) - \mathtt{HW}(y) \mod q$

1: $\mathbf{z} \leftarrow \mathtt{SecBitAdd}(\mathbf{x})$
2: $\mathbf{z} \leftarrow \mathtt{SecBitSub}(\mathbf{z}, \mathbf{y})$
3: $\mathbf{z} \leftarrow \mathtt{SecConstAdd}(\mathbf{z}, \kappa)$
4: $\mathbf{A} \leftarrow \mathtt{B2A}_q(\mathbf{z})$
5: $A_1 \leftarrow A_1 - \kappa \mod q$

computation of $\mathbf{t}^{(1)}$, with $t_1 + t_2 \leq t$. In particular let t_1^O, t_2^O be the probes on the output values and t_1^I, t_2^I the ones on the internals, with $t_1^O + t_1^I = t_1$ and $t_2^I + t_2^O = t_2$. The $t -$ SNI of the inner loop guarantees that every value in $\mathcal{P}_1$ can be simulated by using at most t_1^I shares of the inputs. On the other hand, because of the linearity of the computation of $\mathbf{t}^{(1)}$, the probes in $\mathcal{P}_2$ can be simulated using at most $t_2^I + t_2^O$ shares of the input. Therefore, by Definition 1, SecBitAdd is $t -$ NI.

Now, since SecBitSub in Algorithm 12 follows the same procedure as Algorithm 11, with the exception of Lines 6 and 7, which simply add a negation to the interested value, then it is $t -$ NI as well.

As for SecConstAdd in Algorithm 13, from [6] we know that RefreshXOR is $t -$ SNI and SecAdd is $t -$ NI. Therefore it is easy to see that the composition of them, as it appears in Algorithm 13, is $t -$ NI. Regarding the optimized version of SecConstAdd in Algorithm 14, here the security comes directly from the fact that the algorithm is linear.

Proposition 7. $\mathtt{SecSampler}_2$ *in Algorithm 15 is* $t -$ SNI, *with* $t \leq n - 1$

Proof. Before proceeding with the proof, we point out that $\mathtt{SecSampler}_2$ is given by the circuit in Fig. 5 with the addition of a share-wise sum between the output share A_1 and the public value $-\kappa$ (line 5 of Algorithm 15). Since the simulation of such value depends only on the simulation of A_1, the security level of $\mathtt{SecSampler}_2$ is not influenced by this additional operation and it corresponds to the one of the algorithm in Fig. 5.

Let $\Omega = (\mathcal{I}, \mathcal{O})$ be the set of adversarial observations on the circuit in Fig. 5, where $\mathcal{I}$ are the ones on the internal values and $\mathcal{O}$ on the output shares, with $|\mathcal{I}| + |\mathcal{O}| \leq t$. In particular, let $\mathcal{I}_1$ be the set of probes on $\mathtt{B2A}_q$, $\mathcal{I}_2$ on SecConstAdd, $\mathcal{I}_3$ on SecBitSub and $\mathcal{I}_4$ on SecBitAdd, with $\sum_j |\mathcal{I}_j| \leq |\mathcal{I}|$.

We prove the existence of a simulator which simulates the adversary's view by using at most $|\mathcal{I}|$ input shares, analyzing of the circuit from right to left.

Since $\mathtt{B2A}_q$ is $t-\mathsf{SNI}$, there exists an observation set $\mathcal{S}^1$ such that $|\mathcal{S}^1| \leq |\mathcal{I}_1|$ and the gadget can be simulated using at most $|\mathcal{S}^1|$ shares of its input.

Since $\mathtt{SecConstAdd}$ is $t-\mathsf{NI}$ and $|\mathcal{I}_2 \cup \mathcal{S}^1| \leq t$, then there exist an observation set $\mathcal{S}^2$ such that $|\mathcal{S}^2| \leq |I_2 \cup \mathcal{S}^1|$ and the gadget can be simulated using at most $|\mathcal{S}^2|$ shares of the inputs.

Since $\mathtt{SecBitSub}$ is $t-\mathsf{NI}$ and $|\mathcal{I}_3 \cup \mathcal{S}^2| \leq t$, then there exist two observation sets $\mathcal{S}_1^3, \mathcal{S}_2^3$ such that $|\mathcal{S}_1^3| \leq |\mathcal{I}_3 \cup \mathcal{S}^2|$, $|\mathcal{S}_2^3| \leq |\mathcal{I}_3 \cup \mathcal{S}^2|$ and the gadget can be simulated using at most $|\mathcal{S}_1^3| + |\mathcal{S}_2^3|$ shares of the inputs.

Since $\mathtt{SecBitAdd}$ is $t-\mathsf{NI}$ and $|\mathcal{I}_4 \cup \mathcal{S}_1^3| \leq t$, then there exist an observation set $\mathcal{S}^4$ such that $|\mathcal{S}^4| \leq |\mathcal{I}_4 \cup \mathcal{S}_1^3|$ and the gadget can be simulated using at most $|\mathcal{S}^4|$ shares of the inputs.

By combining the steps above, we see that $\mathtt{SecSampler}_2$ can be simulated by using in total $|\mathcal{S}^4| \leq |\mathcal{I}_4| + |\mathcal{S}_1^3| \leq |\mathcal{I}_4| + |\mathcal{I}_3| + |\mathcal{S}^2| \leq |\mathcal{I}_4| + |\mathcal{I}_3| + |\mathcal{I}_2| + |\mathcal{S}^1| \leq |\mathcal{I}_4| + |\mathcal{I}_3| + |\mathcal{I}_2| + |\mathcal{I}_1| \leq |\mathcal{I}|$ input shares, proving that it is $t-\mathsf{SNI}$. □

5.3 Performance Analysis

To better compare the two sampling approaches, we derive the run time complexity for both. The calls to $\mathtt{B2A}_q$ and $\mathtt{SecConstAdd}$ are not substituted, since their performance strongly depends on the used parameters, which may allow further optimizations, e.g., Algorithm 14. With $\lambda = \lceil \log_2(\kappa+1) \rceil + 1$, we derive

$$\begin{aligned} T_{\mathtt{SecSampler}_1}(n,\kappa) &= 2\kappa T_{\mathtt{B2A}_q}(n,1) + 6n\kappa, \\ T_{\mathtt{SecSampler}_2}(n,\kappa) &= T_{\mathtt{SecBitAdd}}(n,\kappa) + T_{\mathtt{SecBitSub}}(n,\kappa) + T_{\mathtt{SecConstAdd}}(n,\kappa) \\ &\quad + T_{\mathtt{B2A}_q}(n,\lambda) + n \\ &= T_{\mathtt{B2A}_q}(n,\lambda) + T_{\mathtt{SecConstAdd}}(n,\kappa) \\ &\quad + 7\kappa\lambda n^2 - 7\kappa n^2 + 7\kappa\lambda n + \kappa\lambda - 5\kappa n - \kappa + n. \end{aligned}$$

It is noticeable that $\mathtt{SecSampler}_2$ requires only one conversion of λ bits, while $\mathtt{SecSampler}_1$ consists of 2κ conversion of one bit. This can lead to significant advantages for the former approach assuming small κ as shown in the case study.

Regarding the randomness complexity, we observe a similar trend:

$$\begin{aligned} R_{\mathtt{SecSampler}_1}(n,\kappa) &= 2\kappa R_{\mathtt{B2A}_q}(n,1), \\ R_{\mathtt{SecSampler}_2}(n,\kappa) &= R_{\mathtt{SecBitAdd}}(n,\kappa) \\ &\quad + R_{\mathtt{SecBitSub}}(n,\kappa) + R_{\mathtt{SecConstAdd}}(n,\kappa) + R_{\mathtt{B2A}_q}(n,\lambda) \\ &= R_{\mathtt{B2A}_q}(n,\lambda) + R_{\mathtt{SecConstAdd}}(n,\kappa) + \kappa\lambda n^2 - \kappa n^2 - \kappa\lambda n + \kappa n \end{aligned}$$

5.4 Case Study: NewHope

To concretely evaluate the performance of our proposed sampling algorithms, we conduct a case study using the parameters of the NIST submission NewHope. We set the length of the bit-vectors to $\kappa = 8$ and the prime to $q = 12289$. The same prime can be found in multiple NIST submissions, like Kyber and HILA5.

The parameter κ is usually different though and for Kyber set to 3, 4, or 5 and for HILA5 set to 16. Both sampling approaches are evaluated with the proposed $\mathtt{B2A}_q$ conversions $\mathtt{SecB2A}_q$ and SecArithBoolModp (quadratic). The latter is instantiated with $k' = \lceil \log_2 2q \rceil = 15$ as discussed in the previous section.

We implement all variants on a 32-bit ARM Cortex-M4F microcontroller embedded in an STM32F4 DISCOVERY board with 1 Mbyte of flash memory, 192 kbyte of RAM, a floating-point unit (FPU), and a true random number generator (TRNG). The TRNG needs 40 cycles of a 48 MHz clock to generate a random 32-bit value. The sampling of a true random value runs simultaneously to other computations of the microcontroller. Assuming a sufficient amount of clock cycles between two calls to the TRNG, a sample will be generated without any wait cycles and therefore the average TRNG call will be much faster than 40 cycles at 48 MHz. The maximum clock frequency of the microcontroller is 168 MHz. We use the CYCCNT register of the data watchpoint and trace unit of the microcontroller to measure the performance of our implementation.

To prevent timing leakage, our implementations have a secret-independent running time. In particular, we refrained from using conditional statements or instructions with varying execution time in critical parts of our implementation. We furthermore disabled the data and instruction cache of our target microcontroller. For the implementation of the $\mathtt{B2A}_q$ conversions, we need uniform random numbers mod $q = 12289$. The TRNG of our development board outputs 32 uniform random bits. To sample a uniform random number mod q, we split the 32-bit output of the TRNG into two 14-bit vectors and drop the remaining four bits. We then check whether the first 14-bit vector is smaller than q or not. If yes, we accept and return the value. If not we also check the second value. If this check fails again, we get more true random 32-bit vectors from the TRNG until we find a valid sample. This means that there is a $\frac{q}{2^{14}} = 0.75$ probability of a sample being accepted and a 0.25 probability of a sample being rejected. Such a sampling approach does not have a constant run time, but it still does not introduce a timing leakage, as the time required to generate a valid sample is completely independent from the value of the generated sample.

The results of our implementation can be seen in Table 5, where the comparison for $n = 2$ also includes the masked binomial sampler from Oder et al. [25][8]. It is noticeable that $\mathtt{SecB2A}_q$ outperforms SecArithBoolModp (quadratic) for every order. As discussed before, this huge speed-up is due to the specific parameters of the case study. Indeed the bit sizes of the input $k = 1, 5$ do not fulfill the requirement of $2^k > 2q$, which thwarts its performance since we need to instantiate it with a larger k'. This is especially problematic for $\mathtt{SecSampler}_1$, which requires conversions with $k = 1$. Overall, our $\mathtt{SecSampler}_2$ offers a significant

[8] In contrast to [25], our cycle counts do not include the generation of the input bit vectors. Therefore, our 3,757 cycles for one sample do not match the 6 million cycles for 1024 coefficients reported in [25]. However, as the generation of the input samples is a constant overhead that is independent from the sampling algorithm or the $\mathtt{B2A}_q$ conversion, we decided to exclude it from our measurements.

Table 5. Cycle counts for masked sampling of one binomial distributed coefficient using the B2A conversions (**A**) $\mathtt{SecB2A}_q$ and (**C**) SecBoolArithModp (quadratic). We excluded the generation of the input bit vectors for better comparison as this is a constant overhead for all approaches.

	n	2	3	4	5
	[25]	3,637	-	-	-
$\mathtt{SecSampler}_1$	(**C**)	271,423	638,315	1,076,155	1,758,184
	(**A**)	6,145	13,913	24,397	37,880
$\mathtt{SecSampler}_2$	(**C**)	17,564	40,977	68,914	112,402
	(**A**)	2,649	5,573	9,462	14,587

improvement over $\mathtt{SecSampler}_1$ for both conversion algorithms and it even outperforms the approach from Oder et al. [25], that is highly optimized for $n = 2$. Applying a similar degree of optimization to our proposed sampler for this special case would help to decrease the number of cycles even further.

6 Conclusions

In this work, we initially presented two new conversion techniques to transform Boolean shares to arithmetic shares that work with arbitrary moduli and orders. While the first provides the best asymptotic complexity of $\mathtt{B2A}_q$ algorithm with $\mathcal{O}(n^2 \log k)$, the second proposal offers a significant performance improvement for relevant bit sizes. It can even be applied in symmetric cryptography as for certain number of shares (e.g., $n \geq 11$ for $k = 32$), it outperforms previous work that is optimized for power-of-two moduli. Using these conversions as basis, we further constructed masked binomial sampling algorithms. To evaluate them, we developed implementations for a popular microcontroller platform to obtain realistic performance measurements. Thereby, we show that the combination of $\mathtt{SecB2A}_q$ with our bitsliced sampler outperforms previous work and leads to the currently most-efficient masked binomial sampling algorithm for the considered parameters. Our work helps to better understand the overhead cost for masking of post-quantum cryptography and, thus, is an important contribution for the evaluation of these schemes in the ongoing NIST standardization process.

Acknowledgement. The authors are grateful to the AsiaCrypt2018 reviewers for useful comments and feedback. The research in this work was supported in part by the European Unions Horizon 2020 program under project number 644729 SAFEcrypto and 724725 SWORD, by the VeriSec project 16KIS0634 from the Federal Ministry of Education and Research (BMBF) and by H2020 project PROMETHEUS, grant agreement ID 780701.

References

1. Alkim, E., et al.: NewHope algorithm specifications and supporting documentation. https://newhopecrypto.org/data/NewHope_2017_12_21.pdf. Accessed 09 May 2018
2. Alkim, E., Jakubeit, P., Schwabe, P.: NEWHOPE on ARM Cortex-M. In: Carlet, C., Hasan, M.A., Saraswat, V. (eds.) SPACE 2016. LNCS, vol. 10076, pp. 332–349. Springer, Cham (2016). https://doi.org/10.1007/978-3-319-49445-6_19
3. Avanzi, R., et al.: CRYSTALS-Kyber. Technical report, National Institute of Standards and Technology (2017). https://pq-crystals.org/kyber/data/kyber-specification.pdf
4. Barthe, G., Belaïd, S., Dupressoir, F., Fouque, P., Grégoire, B.: Compositional verification of higher-order masking: application to a verifying masking compiler. IACR Cryptology ePrint Archive, 2015:506 (2015)
5. Barthe, G., et al.: Strong non-interference and type-directed higher-order masking. In: ACM CCS 2016, pp. 116–129. ACM (2016)
6. Barthe, G., et al.: Masking the GLP lattice-based signature scheme at any order. In: Nielsen, J.B., Rijmen, V. (eds.) EUROCRYPT 2018. LNCS, vol. 10821, pp. 354–384. Springer, Cham (2018). https://doi.org/10.1007/978-3-319-78375-8_12
7. Bettale, L., Coron, J., Zeitoun, R.: Improved high-order conversion from Boolean to arithmetic masking. TCHES **2018**, 22–45 (2018)
8. Biryukov, A., Dinu, D., Corre, Y.L., Udovenko, A.: Optimal first-order Boolean masking for embedded IoT devices. In: Eisenbarth, T., Teglia, Y. (eds.) CARDIS 2017. LNCS, vol. 10728, pp. 22–41. Springer, Cham (2018). https://doi.org/10.1007/978-3-319-75208-2_2
9. Chari, S., Jutla, C.S., Rao, J.R., Rohatgi, P.: Towards sound approaches to counteract power-analysis attacks. In: Wiener, M. (ed.) CRYPTO 1999. LNCS, vol. 1666, pp. 398–412. Springer, Heidelberg (1999). https://doi.org/10.1007/3-540-48405-1_26
10. Chen, C., Eisenbarth, T., von Maurich, I., Steinwandt, R.: Differential power analysis of a McEliece cryptosystem. In: Malkin, T., Kolesnikov, V., Lewko, A.B., Polychronakis, M. (eds.) ACNS 2015. LNCS, vol. 9092, pp. 538–556. Springer, Cham (2015). https://doi.org/10.1007/978-3-319-28166-7_26
11. Chen, C., Eisenbarth, T., von Maurich, I., Steinwandt, R.: Masking large keys in hardware: a masked implementation of McEliece. In: Dunkelman, O., Keliher, L. (eds.) SAC 2015. LNCS, vol. 9566, pp. 293–309. Springer, Cham (2016). https://doi.org/10.1007/978-3-319-31301-6_18
12. Coron, J.-S.: High-order conversion from Boolean to arithmetic masking. In: Fischer, W., Homma, N. (eds.) CHES 2017. LNCS, vol. 10529, pp. 93–114. Springer, Cham (2017). https://doi.org/10.1007/978-3-319-66787-4_5
13. Coron, J.-S., Großschädl, J., Tibouchi, M., Vadnala, P.K.: Conversion from arithmetic to Boolean masking with logarithmic complexity. In: Leander, G. (ed.) FSE 2015. LNCS, vol. 9054, pp. 130–149. Springer, Heidelberg (2015). https://doi.org/10.1007/978-3-662-48116-5_7
14. Coron, J.-S., Großschädl, J., Vadnala, P.K.: Secure conversion between Boolean and arithmetic masking of any order. In: Batina, L., Robshaw, M. (eds.) CHES 2014. LNCS, vol. 8731, pp. 188–205. Springer, Heidelberg (2014). https://doi.org/10.1007/978-3-662-44709-3_11

15. D'Anvers, J.-P., Karmakar, A., Roy, S.S., Vercauteren, F.: SABER: Mod-LWR based KEM. Technical report, National Institute of Standards and Technology (2017). https://csrc.nist.gov/Projects/Post-Quantum-Cryptography/Round-1-Submissions
16. Debraize, B.: Efficient and provably secure methods for switching from arithmetic to Boolean masking. In: Prouff, E., Schaumont, P. (eds.) CHES 2012. LNCS, vol. 7428, pp. 107–121. Springer, Heidelberg (2012). https://doi.org/10.1007/978-3-642-33027-8_7
17. Ding, J., Takagi, T., Gao, X., Wang, Y.: Ding Key Exchange. Technical report, National Institute of Standards and Technology (2017). https://csrc.nist.gov/Projects/Post-Quantum-Cryptography/Round-1-Submissions
18. Eisenbarth, T., Kasper, T., Moradi, A., Paar, C., Salmasizadeh, M., Shalmani, M.T.M.: On the power of power analysis in the real world: a complete break of the KeeLoq code hopping scheme. In: Wagner, D. (ed.) CRYPTO 2008. LNCS, vol. 5157, pp. 203–220. Springer, Heidelberg (2008). https://doi.org/10.1007/978-3-540-85174-5_12
19. Goubin, L.: A sound method for switching between Boolean and arithmetic masking. In: Koç, Ç.K., Naccache, D., Paar, C. (eds.) CHES 2001. LNCS, vol. 2162, pp. 3–15. Springer, Heidelberg (2001). https://doi.org/10.1007/3-540-44709-1_2
20. Güneysu, T., Lyubashevsky, V., Pöppelmann, T.: Practical lattice-based cryptography: a signature scheme for embedded systems. In: Prouff, E., Schaumont, P. (eds.) CHES 2012. LNCS, vol. 7428, pp. 530–547. Springer, Heidelberg (2012). https://doi.org/10.1007/978-3-642-33027-8_31
21. Hutter, M., Tunstall, M.: Constant-time higher-order Boolean-to-arithmetic masking. IACR Cryptology ePrint Archive, 2016:1023 (2016)
22. Ishai, Y., Sahai, A., Wagner, D.A.: Private circuits: securing hardware against probing attacks. In: Boneh, D. (ed.) CRYPTO 2003. LNCS, vol. 2729, pp. 463–481. Springer, Heidelberg (2003). https://doi.org/10.1007/978-3-540-45146-4_27
23. Karroumi, M., Richard, B., Joye, M.: Addition with blinded operands. In: Prouff, E. (ed.) COSADE 2014. LNCS, vol. 8622, pp. 41–55. Springer, Cham (2014). https://doi.org/10.1007/978-3-319-10175-0_4
24. Kocher, P.C.: Timing attacks on implementations of Diffie-Hellman, RSA, DSS, and other systems. In: Koblitz, N. (ed.) CRYPTO 1996. LNCS, vol. 1109, pp. 104–113. Springer, Heidelberg (1996). https://doi.org/10.1007/3-540-68697-5_9
25. Oder, T., Schneider, T., Pöppelmann, T., Güneysu, T.: Practical CCA2-secure and masked ring-LWE implementation. TCHES **2018**, 142–174 (2018)
26. National Institute of Standards and Technology. Post-quantum cryptography - round 1 submissions. https://csrc.nist.gov/projects/post-quantum-cryptography/round-1-submissions. Accessed 10 Dec 2018
27. National Institute of Standards and Technology. Submission requirements and evaluation criteria for the post-quantum cryptography standardization process. https://csrc.nist.gov/CSRC/media/Projects/Post-Quantum-Cryptography/documents/call-for-proposals-final-dec-2016.pdf. Accessed 10 May 2018
28. Reparaz, O., Roy, S.S., de Clercq, R., Vercauteren, F., Verbauwhede, I.: Masking ring-LWE. J. Crypt. Eng. **6**(2), 139–153 (2016)
29. Saarinen, M.-J.O.: HILA5. Technical report, National Institute of Standards and Technology (2017). https://csrc.nist.gov/Projects/Post-Quantum-Cryptography/Round-1-Submissions

30. Schneider, T., Moradi, A., Güneysu, T.: Arithmetic addition over Boolean masking towards first- and second-order resistance in hardware. In: Malkin, T., Kolesnikov, V., Lewko, A.B., Polychronakis, M. (eds.) ACNS 2015. LNCS, vol. 9092, pp. 559–578. Springer, Cham (2015). https://doi.org/10.1007/978-3-319-28166-7_27
31. Smart, N.P., et al.: LIMA-1.1: a PQC encryption scheme. Technical report, National Institute of Standards and Technology (2017). https://lima-pq.github.io/files/lima-pq.pdf
32. Standaert, F.-X., et al.: The world is not enough: another look on second-order DPA. In: Abe, M. (ed.) ASIACRYPT 2010. LNCS, vol. 6477, pp. 112–129. Springer, Heidelberg (2010). https://doi.org/10.1007/978-3-642-17373-8_7
33. Won, Y.-S., Han, D.-G.: Efficient conversion method from arithmetic to Boolean masking in constrained devices. In: Guilley, S. (ed.) COSADE 2017. LNCS, vol. 10348, pp. 120–137. Springer, Cham (2017). https://doi.org/10.1007/978-3-319-64647-3_8

Decryption Failure Attacks on IND-CCA Secure Lattice-Based Schemes

Jan-Pieter D'Anvers[1(✉)], Qian Guo[2,3], Thomas Johansson[3], Alexander Nilsson[3], Frederik Vercauteren[1], and Ingrid Verbauwhede[1]

[1] imec-COSIC, KU Leuven, Kasteelpark Arenberg 10, Bus 2452, 3001 Leuven-Heverlee, Belgium
{janpieter.danvers,frederik.vercauteren, ingrid.verbauwhede}@esat.kuleuven.be

[2] Department of Informatics, University of Bergen, Box 7803, 5020 Bergen, Norway
qian.guo@uib.no

[3] Department of Electrical and Information Technology, Lund University, P.O. Box 118, 221 00 Lund, Sweden
{thomas.johansson,alexander.nilsson}@eit.lth.se

Abstract. In this paper we investigate the impact of decryption failures on the chosen-ciphertext security of lattice-based primitives. We discuss a generic framework for secret key recovery based on decryption failures and present an attack on the NIST Post-Quantum Proposal ss-ntru-pke. Our framework is split in three parts: First, we use a technique to increase the failure rate of lattice-based schemes called failure boosting. Based on this technique we investigate the minimal effort for an adversary to obtain a failure in three cases: when he has access to a quantum computer, when he mounts a multi-target attack or when he can only perform a limited number of oracle queries. Secondly, we examine the amount of information that an adversary can derive from failing ciphertexts. Finally, these techniques are combined in an overall analysis of the security of lattice based schemes under a decryption failure attack. We show that an attacker could significantly reduce the security of lattice based schemes that have a relatively high failure rate. However, for most of the NIST Post-Quantum Proposals, the number of required oracle queries is above practical limits. Furthermore, a new generic weak-key (multi-target) model on lattice-based schemes, which can be viewed as a variant of the previous framework, is proposed. This model further takes into consideration the weak-key phenomenon that a small fraction of keys can have much larger decoding error probability for ciphertexts with certain key-related properties. We apply this model and present an attack in detail on the NIST Post-Quantum Proposal – ss-ntru-pke – with complexity below the claimed security level.

Keywords: Lattice-based cryptography · NIST post-quantum standardization · Decryption failure · LWE · NTRU · Reaction attack

This paper is the result of a merge of [14] and [21].

D. Lin and K. Sako (Eds.): PKC 2019, LNCS 11443, pp. 565–598, 2019.
https://doi.org/10.1007/978-3-030-17259-6_19

1 Introduction

The position of integer factorization and the discrete logarithm problem as a cornerstone for asymmetric cryptography is being threatened by quantum computers, as their ability to efficiently solve these mathematical problems compromises the security of current asymmetric primitives. These developments have led to the emergence of post-quantum cryptography and motivated NIST to organize a post-quantum cryptography standardization process, with the goal of standardizing one or more quantum-resistant public-key cryptographic primitives. Submissions originate from various fields within post-quantum cryptography, such as lattice-based, code-based and multivariate cryptography.

Lattice-based cryptography has recently developed into one of the main research areas in post-quantum cryptography. Lattice-based submissions to the NIST Post-Quantum process can be broadly put into one of two categories: NTRU-based schemes (e.g. [39,47]) and schemes based on the learning with errors (LWE) hard problem [36]. A lot of research has been done on their security, such as provable post-quantum secure transformations from IND-CPA to IND-CCA secure schemes [25,29,38,46], security estimates of post-quantum primitives [3,4] and provable reductions for various hard problems underlying the schemes [7,11,32,35,36].

A striking observation is that numerous proposed Key Encapsulation Mechanisms (KEM's) have a small failure probability during decryption, in which the involved parties fail to derive a shared secret key. This is the case for the majority of schemes based on lattices, codes or Mersenne primes. The probability of such failure varies from 2^{-64} in Ramstake [45] to 2^{-216} in New Hope [41], with most of the failure probabilities lying around 2^{-128}. As this failure is dependent on the secret key, it might leak secret information to an adversary. However, reducing this probability has a price, as the parameters should be adjusted accordingly, resulting in a performance loss. An approach used by some schemes is to use error-correcting codes to decrease the failure probability. This leads to a reduction in the communication overhead, but makes the scheme more vulnurable to side-channel attacks.

As suggested by the wide range of failure probabilities in the NIST submissions, the implications of failures are still not well understood. In the absence of a clear evaluation technique for the impact of the failure rate, most NIST submissions have chosen a bound on the decryption failure probability around 2^{-128} based on educated guessing. As far as we know, only NIST-submission Kyber [40] provides an intuitive reasoning for its security against decryption failure attacks, but this approximation is not tight. They introduce a methodology that uses Grover's search algorithm to find ciphertexts that have a relatively high probability of triggering a decryption failure.

1.1 Related Works

The idea of exploiting decryption errors has been around for a long time and applies to all areas of cryptography [9]. For lattice-based encryption systems, the

Ajtai-Dwork scheme and NTRU have been a target for attacks using decryption failures. Hall, Goldberg, and Schneier [23] developed a reaction attack which recovers the Ajtai-Dwork private key by observing decryption failures. Hoffstein and Silverman [24] adapted the attack to NTRU and suggested modifying NTRU to use the Fujisaki-Okamoto transform [18] to protect against such attacks. Further work in this direction is given in [28], [26] and [19]. Fluhrer [17] described an attack against Ring-Learning with Errors (RLWE) schemes. In [15] his work was extended to more protocols and in [8] a chosen-ciphertext attack on the proposal HILA5 [37] was given, using decryption failures.

These attacks are chosen-ciphertext attacks on proposals with only IND-CPA-security and can be thwarted using an appropriate transformation to a chosen-ciphertext secure scheme, such as the Fujisaki-Okamoto transformation [18]. Hofheinz et al. [25] and later Jiang et al. [29] proved a bound on the impact of the failure rate on an IND-CCA secure KEM that is constructed using this transformation, but their bounds are squared in the failure probability in the quantum oracle setting, which seems a very conservative result. Guo, Johansson and Stankovski [22] proposed a key-recovery attack against the IND-CCA-secure version of QC-MDPC, which is a code-based scheme. It uses a distinguishing property that "colliding pairs" in the noise and the secret can change the decryption failure rate.

1.2 Contributions

In this paper we investigate the requirements for KEM's to resist decryption failure cryptanalysis. Having better security estimates can benefit the parameter selection process, resulting in improved security and efficiency. We focus on IND-CCA secure KEM's based on the (Ring/Module-)Learning with Errors and (Ring/Module-)Learning with Rounding paradigms. Nonetheless, the general method can also be applied to investigate the impact of failures on other schemes.

The exploitation of decryption failures of an IND-CCA secure cryptographic scheme proceeds in two main steps: obtaining ciphertexts that result in a decryption failure and estimating the secret based on these ciphertexts. In the first step, an adversary can use failure boosting to find 'weak' input vectors that artificially enlarge the failure rate of the scheme. In Sect. 3, we examine how an adversary can generate these 'weak' ciphertexts that increase the failure probability. We provide a theoretical framework and a Python implementation[1] to calculate an estimate of the minimum effort required for an adversary to obtain one failing ciphertext.

Once ciphertexts that trigger a decryption failure are collected, they can be used to estimate the secret. In Sect. 4, we study how much information is leaked by the collected failures. We develop a statistical model to estimate the secret from the failures and determine the residual entropy of the secret after a

[1] The software is available at https://github.com/danversjp/failureattack.

certain number of failures is collected. The estimate of the secret can be used to construct an easier problem that can be solved faster.

Section 5 combines failure boosting and the secret estimation technique from Sect. 4 to estimate the security of schemes based on (Ring/Module)-Learning with Errors and (Ring/Module)-Learning with Rounding under an attack exploiting decryption failures. We show that an attacker could significantly reduce the security of some schemes if he is able to perform sufficient decryption queries. However, for most NIST submissions, the number of decryption queries required is above practical limits.

In Sect. 6 we propose a new generic weak-key (multi-target) model exploiting the fact that a fraction of keys employed can have much higher error probability if the chosen weak ciphertexts satisfy certain key-related properties. The detailed attack procedure is similar to the attack discussed in the previous sections. It first consists of a precomputation phase where special messages and their corresponding error vectors are generated. Secondly, the messages are submitted for decryption and some decryption errors are observed. Finally, a phase with a statistical analysis of the messages/errors causing the decryption errors reveals the secret key.

In Sect. 7 we apply the model to ss-ntru-pke, a version of NTRUEncrypt targeting the security level of NIST-V. The proposed attack is an adaptive CCA attack with complexity below the claimed security level. We provide a Rust implementation[2] where parts of the attack are simulated.

2 Preliminaries

2.1 Notation

Let $\mathbb{Z}_q$ be the ring of integers modulo q represented in $(-q/2, q/2]$, let R_q denote the ring $\mathbb{Z}_q[X]/(X^n+1)$ and let $R_q^{k_1 \times k_2}$ denote the ring of $k_1 \times k_2$ matrices over R_q. Matrices will be represented with bold uppercase letters, while vectors are represented in bold lowercase. Let $\boldsymbol{A}_{ij}$ denote the element on the ith row and j^{th} column of matrix $\boldsymbol{A}$, and let $\boldsymbol{A}_{ijk}$ denote the kth coefficient of this element. Denote with $\boldsymbol{A}_{:j}$ the jth column of $\boldsymbol{A}$.

The rounding operation $\lfloor x \rceil_{q \to p}$ is defined as $\lfloor p/q \cdot x \rceil \in \mathbb{Z}_p$ for an element $x \in \mathbb{Z}_q$, while $\mathsf{abs}(\cdot)$ takes the absolute value of the input. These operations are extended coefficient-wise for elements of R_q and $R_q^{k_1 \times k_2}$. The two-norm of a polynomial $a \in R_q$ is written as $\|a\|_2$ and defined as $\sqrt{\sum_i a_i^2}$, which is extended to vectors as $\|\boldsymbol{a}\|_2 = \sqrt{\sum_i \|\boldsymbol{a}_i\|_2^2}$. The notation $a \leftarrow \chi(R_q)$ will be used to represent the sampling of $a \in R_q$ according to the distribution χ. This can be extended coefficient-wise for $\boldsymbol{A} \in R_q^{k_1 \times k_2}$ and is denoted as $\boldsymbol{A} \leftarrow \chi(R_q^{k_1 \times k_2})$. Let

[2] The software is available at https://github.com/atneit/ss-ntru-pke-attack-simulation.

$\mathcal{U}$ be the uniform distribution. Denote with $\chi_1 * \chi_2$ the convolution of the two distributions χ_1 and χ_2, and denote with $\chi^{*n} = \underbrace{\chi * \chi * \chi * \cdots * \chi * \chi}_{n}$ the nth convolutional power of χ.

2.2 Cryptographic Definitions

A Public Key Encryption (PKE) is defined as a triple of functions PKE = (`KeyGen`, `Enc`, `Dec`), where the key generation `KeyGen` returns a secret key sk and a public key pk, where the encryption `Enc` produces a ciphertext c from the public key pk and the message $m \in \mathcal{M}$, and where the decryption `Dec` returns the message m' given the secret key sk and the ciphertext c.

A Key Encapsulation Mechanism (KEM) consists of a triple of functions KEM = (`KeyGen`, `Encaps`, `Decaps`), where `KeyGen` generates the secret and public keys sk and pk respectively, where `Encaps` generates a key $k \in \mathcal{K}$ and a ciphertext c from a public key pk, and where `Decaps` requires the secret key sk, the public key pk and the ciphertext c to return a key k or the decryption failure symbol $\perp$. The security of a KEM can be defined under the notion of indistinguishability under chosen ciphertext attacks (IND-CCA),

$$\mathrm{Adv}_{\mathrm{KEM}}^{\text{ind-cca}}(A) = \left| P\left(b' = b : \begin{array}{c} (pk, sk) \leftarrow \texttt{KeyGen}(),\ b \leftarrow \mathcal{U}(\{0,1\}), \\ (c, d, k_0) \leftarrow \texttt{Encaps}(pk), \\ k_1 \leftarrow \mathcal{K},\ b' \leftarrow A^{\texttt{Decaps}}(pk, c, d, k_b), \end{array} \right) - \frac{1}{2} \right| .$$

2.3 LWE/LWR Problems

The decisional Learning with Errors problem (LWE) [36] consists of distinguishing a uniform sample $(\boldsymbol{A}, \boldsymbol{U}) \leftarrow \mathcal{U}(\mathbb{Z}_q^{k_1 \times k_2} \times \mathbb{Z}_q^{k_1 \times m})$ from an LWE-sample $(\boldsymbol{A}, \boldsymbol{B} = \boldsymbol{AS} + \boldsymbol{E})$, were $\boldsymbol{A} \leftarrow \mathcal{U}(\mathbb{Z}_q^{k_1 \times k_2})$ and where the secret vectors $\boldsymbol{S}$ and $\boldsymbol{E}$ are generated from the small distributions $\chi_s(\mathbb{Z}_q^{k_2 \times m})$ and $\chi_e(\mathbb{Z}_q^{k_1 \times m})$ respectively. The search LWE problem states that it is hard to recover the secret $\boldsymbol{S}$ from the LWE sample.

This definition can be extended to Ring- or Module-LWE [30,32] by using vectors of polynomials. In this case, the problem is to distinguish the uniform sample $(\boldsymbol{A}, \boldsymbol{U}) \leftarrow \mathcal{U}(R_q^{k_1 \times k_2} \times R_q^{k_1 \times m})$ from a generalized LWE sample $(\boldsymbol{A}, \boldsymbol{B} = \boldsymbol{AS} + \boldsymbol{E})$ in which $\boldsymbol{A} \leftarrow \mathcal{U}(R_q^{k_1 \times k_2})$ and where the secret vectors $\boldsymbol{S}$ and $\boldsymbol{E}$ are generated from the small distribution $\chi_s(R_q^{k_2 \times m})$ and $\chi_e(R_q^{k_1 \times m})$ respectively. Analogous to the LWE case, the search problem is to recover the secret $\boldsymbol{S}$ from a generalized LWE sample.

The decisional generalized Learning with Rounding (LWR) problem [7] is defined as distinguishing the uniform sample $(\boldsymbol{A}, \lfloor \boldsymbol{U} \rceil_{q \to p})$, with $\boldsymbol{A} \leftarrow \mathcal{U}(R_q^{k_1 \times k_2})$ and $\boldsymbol{U} \leftarrow \mathcal{U}(R_q^{k_1 \times m})$ from the generalized LWR sample $(\boldsymbol{A}, \boldsymbol{B} = \lfloor \boldsymbol{AS} \rceil_{q \to p})$ with $\boldsymbol{A} \leftarrow \mathcal{U}(R_q^{k_1 \times k_2})$ and $\boldsymbol{S} \leftarrow \chi_s(R_q^{k_2 \times m})$. In the analogous search problem, one has to find $\boldsymbol{S}$ from a generalized LWR sample.

2.4 (Ring/Module-)LWE Based Encryption

Let gen be a pseudorandom generator that expands $\text{seed}_{\boldsymbol{A}}$ into a uniformly random distributed matrix $\boldsymbol{A} \in R_q^{k \times k}$. Define enc as an encoding function that transforms a message m into a polynomial representation, and dec as the inverse decoding function. A general (Ring/Module-)LWE based PKE, consisting of a key generation, an encryption and a decryption phase, can then be constructed as described in Algorithms 1, 2 and 3 respectively. The randomness required for the generation of the secrets $\boldsymbol{S}'_B$, $\boldsymbol{E}'_B$ and $\boldsymbol{E}''_B$ during the encryption, is generated pseudorandomly from the uniformly distributed seed r that is given as an input.

Algorithm 1. PKE.KeyGen

Input:
Output: Public key $pk = (\boldsymbol{B}, seed_{\boldsymbol{A}})$, secret key $sk = \boldsymbol{S}_A$).
1) $seed_{\boldsymbol{A}} \leftarrow \mathcal{U}(\{0,1\}^{256})$
2) $\boldsymbol{A} \leftarrow \text{gen}(\text{seed}_{\boldsymbol{A}}) \in R_q^{l \times l}$
4) $\boldsymbol{S}_A \leftarrow \chi_s(R_q^{l \times m}), \boldsymbol{E}_A \leftarrow \chi_e(R_q^{l \times m})$
5) $\boldsymbol{B} = \lfloor \boldsymbol{A}\boldsymbol{S}_A + \boldsymbol{E}_A \rceil_{q \to p}$

Algorithm 2. PKE.Enc

Input: Public key $pk = (\boldsymbol{B}, seed_{\boldsymbol{A}})$, message m, randomness r
Output: Ciphertext $c = (\boldsymbol{V}', \boldsymbol{B}')$
1) $\boldsymbol{A} \leftarrow \text{gen}(\text{seed}_{\boldsymbol{A}}) \in R_q^{l \times l}$
2) $\boldsymbol{S}'_B \leftarrow \chi_s(R_q^{l \times m}), \boldsymbol{E}'_B \leftarrow \chi_e(R_q^{l \times m})$
3) $\boldsymbol{E}''_B \leftarrow \chi_e(R_q^{m \times m})$
4) $\boldsymbol{B}_r = \lceil \boldsymbol{B} \rfloor_{p \to q}$
5) $\boldsymbol{B}' = \lfloor \boldsymbol{A}^T \boldsymbol{S}'_B + \boldsymbol{E}'_B \rceil_{q \to p}$
6) $\boldsymbol{V}' = \lfloor \boldsymbol{B}_r^T \boldsymbol{S}'_B + \boldsymbol{E}''_B + \text{enc}(m) \rceil_{q \to t}$

Algorithm 3. PKE.Dec

Input: Secret key $sk = \boldsymbol{S}_A$, ciphertext $c = (\boldsymbol{V}', \boldsymbol{B}')$
Output: Message m'
1) $\boldsymbol{B}'_r = \lfloor \boldsymbol{B}' \rceil_{p \to q}$
2) $\boldsymbol{V}'_r = \lfloor \boldsymbol{V}' \rceil_{t \to q}$
3) $\boldsymbol{V} = \boldsymbol{B}_r'^T \boldsymbol{S}_A$
4) $m' = \text{dec}(\boldsymbol{V}'_r - \boldsymbol{V})$

Using this general framework, specific schemes can be described with appropriate parameter choices. When the ring R_q is chosen as $\mathbb{Z}_q$, the encryption is LWE-based as can be seen in FrodoKEM [33] and Emblem [42]. A value of $l = 1$ indicates a Ring-LWE based scheme including New Hope [5], LAC [31], LIMA [43] or R.Emblem [42]. If $l \neq 1$ and $R_q \neq \mathbb{Z}_q$, the scheme is based on the Module-LWE hard problem such as Kyber [10]. When referring to Kyber throughout this paper, we will consider the original version that includes rounding. The special case that $\chi_e = 0$ corresponds to (Module/Ring)-LWR-based schemes such as Round2 [6] and Saber [13]. In Lizard [12], a combination of an LWE and LWR problem is proposed. In most (Ring/Module-)LWE based schemes, $q = p$ and no rounding is performed in the calculation of $\boldsymbol{B}$ and $\boldsymbol{B}'$, while t is in most schemes much smaller than q leading to a drastic rounding of $\boldsymbol{V}'$.

We define $\boldsymbol{U}_A$, $\boldsymbol{U}'_B$ en $\boldsymbol{U}''_B$ as the errors introduced by the rounding operations, which is formalized as follows:

$$\boldsymbol{U}_A = \boldsymbol{A}\boldsymbol{S}_A + \boldsymbol{E}_A - \boldsymbol{B}_r\,, \tag{1}$$

$$\boldsymbol{U}'_B = \boldsymbol{A}^T\boldsymbol{S}'_B + \boldsymbol{E}'_B - \boldsymbol{B}'_r\,, \tag{2}$$

$$\boldsymbol{U}''_B = \boldsymbol{B}_r^T\boldsymbol{S}'_B + \boldsymbol{E}''_B + \mathtt{enc}(m) - \boldsymbol{V}'_r\,. \tag{3}$$

Let $\boldsymbol{S}$ be the vector constructed as the concatenation of the vectors $-\boldsymbol{S}_A$ and $\boldsymbol{E}_A + \boldsymbol{U}_A$, let $\boldsymbol{C}$ be the concatenation of $\boldsymbol{E}'_B + \boldsymbol{U}'_B$ and $\boldsymbol{S}'_B$, and let $\boldsymbol{G} = \boldsymbol{E}''_B + \boldsymbol{U}''_B$. An attacker that generates ciphertexts can compute $\boldsymbol{C}$ and $\boldsymbol{G}$ and tries to obtain information about $\boldsymbol{S}$. These variables are summarized below:

$$\boldsymbol{S} = \begin{pmatrix} -\boldsymbol{S}_A \\ \boldsymbol{E}_A + \boldsymbol{U}_A \end{pmatrix}, \quad \boldsymbol{C} = \begin{pmatrix} \boldsymbol{E}'_B + \boldsymbol{U}'_B \\ \boldsymbol{S}'_B \end{pmatrix}, \quad \boldsymbol{G} = \boldsymbol{E}''_B + \boldsymbol{U}''_B\,. \tag{4}$$

After the execution of this protocol, the two parties will arrive at the same key if the decoding $\mathtt{dec}(\boldsymbol{V}'_r - \boldsymbol{V})$ equals m. The term $\boldsymbol{V}'_r - \boldsymbol{V}$ can be rewritten as $(\boldsymbol{E}_A + \boldsymbol{U}_A)^T\boldsymbol{S}'_B - \boldsymbol{S}_A^T(\boldsymbol{E}'_B + \boldsymbol{U}'_B) + (\boldsymbol{E}'' + \boldsymbol{U}''_B) + \mathtt{enc}(m) = \boldsymbol{S}^T\boldsymbol{C} + \boldsymbol{G} + \mathtt{enc}(m)$. The message can be recovered if and only if $\mathtt{abs}(\boldsymbol{S}^T\boldsymbol{C} + \boldsymbol{G}) < q_t$ for a certain threshold q_t that is scheme dependent.

We will say that a (decryption) failure occurred if the parties do not arrive at a common key due to a coefficient of $\mathtt{abs}(\boldsymbol{S}^T\boldsymbol{C} + \boldsymbol{G})$ that is larger than q_t, and will define $F(\boldsymbol{C}, \boldsymbol{G})$ as the probability of a decryption failure given $\boldsymbol{C}$ and $\boldsymbol{G}$ averaged over all $\boldsymbol{S}$, which can be expressed as $\sum_{\boldsymbol{S}} P(\mathtt{abs}(\boldsymbol{S}^T\boldsymbol{C} + \boldsymbol{G}) > q_t \mid \boldsymbol{S})P(\boldsymbol{S})$.

2.5 Fujisaki-Okamoto Transformation

Using the Fujisaki-Okamoto transform [18,25], one can transform a chosen plaintext secure PKE to an IND-CCA secure KEM. On top of the encryption from the PKE, the KEM defines an encapsulation and decapsulation function as described in Algorithms 4 and 5, using hash functions $\mathcal{H}$ and $\mathcal{G}$.

Algorithm 4. KEM.ENCAPS

Input: Public key pk
Output: Ciphertext c, key K
1) $m \leftarrow \mathcal{U}(\{0,1\}^{256})$
2) $r = \mathcal{G}(m)$
3) $c = \texttt{PKE.Enc}(pk, m, r)$
4) $K = \mathcal{H}(r)$

Algorithm 5. KEM.DECAPS

Input: Public key pk, secret key sk, ciphertext c
Output: Key K or $\perp$
1) $m' = \texttt{PKE.Dec}(sk, c)$
2) $r' = \mathcal{G}(m')$
3) $c' = \texttt{PKE.Enc}(pk, m', r')$
4) If $c = c'$:
5) $\quad K = \mathcal{H}(r)$
6) Else:
7) $\quad K = \perp$

3 Weak-Ciphertext Failure Boosting

In this section, we will develop a method to estimate the minimum amount of work to obtain one ciphertext that triggers a decryption failure. In contrast to an honest party that generates ciphertexts randomly, an attacker can search for ciphertexts that have a higher failure probability than average, which will be called 'weak'. As $\boldsymbol{C}$ and $\boldsymbol{G}$ are the only terms with which an attacker can influence decryption failures, the search for weak ciphertexts boils down to the search for weak $(\boldsymbol{C}, \boldsymbol{G})$. However, the pair $(\boldsymbol{C}, \boldsymbol{G})$ is generated through a hash $H()$ with random seed r, and during decryption it is checked whether the generator of the ciphertext knew the preimage r of $(\boldsymbol{C}, \boldsymbol{G})$. Therefore an attacker is forced to resort to a brute force search, which can be sped up at most quadratically using Grover's algorithm [20].

To find a criterion for our search, we sort all possible $(\boldsymbol{C}, \boldsymbol{G})$ according to an increasing failure probability $F(\boldsymbol{C}, \boldsymbol{G})$. This list can then be divided into two sets using a threshold failure probability f_t: weak vectors with a failure probability higher or equal than f_t, and strong vectors with lower failure probability. Let $f()$ be the deterministic function that generates $\boldsymbol{C}$ and $\mathbf{G}$ from the random seed r. For a certain f_t, we can calculate the probability of generating a weak pair: $\alpha = P(F(\boldsymbol{C}, \boldsymbol{G}) > f_t \,|\, r \leftarrow \mathcal{U}, (\boldsymbol{C}, \boldsymbol{G}) = f(H(r)))$, and the probability of a decryption failure when a weak pair is used: $\beta = P(\texttt{abs}(\boldsymbol{S}^T \boldsymbol{C} + \boldsymbol{G}) > q_t \,|\, r \leftarrow \mathcal{U}, (\boldsymbol{C}, \boldsymbol{G}) = f(H(r)), F(\boldsymbol{C}, \boldsymbol{G}) > f_t)$.

The amount of work for an adversary to find a weak pair $(\boldsymbol{C}, \boldsymbol{G})$ is proportional to α^{-1}, but can be sped up quadratically using Grover's algorithm on a quantum computer, resulting in an expected workload of $\sqrt{\alpha^{-1}}$. On the other hand, the probability of a decryption failure given a weak pair cannot be improved using quantum computation assuming that the adversary has no quantum access to the decryption oracle. This assumption is in agreement with the premise in the NIST Post-Quantum Standardization Call for Proposals [2]. The expected work required to find a decryption failure given f_t is therefore the expected number of queries using weak ciphertexts times the expected amount of work to find a weak ciphertext, or $(\alpha \cdot \beta)^{-1}$ with a classical computer and $(\sqrt{\alpha} \cdot \beta)^{-1}$ with a quantum computer. An optimization over f_t gives the minimal effort to find one decryption failure.

3.1 Practical Calculation

For most schemes, the full sorted list $(\boldsymbol{C}, \boldsymbol{G})$ is not practically computable, but using some observations and assumptions, an estimate can be found. The next three steps aim at calculating the distribution of the failure probability $F(\boldsymbol{C}, \boldsymbol{G})$, i.e. what is the probability of finding a $(\boldsymbol{C}, \boldsymbol{G})$ pair with a certain failure probability f. This distribution gives enough information to calculate α and β for a certain f_t.

First, we can remove the hash $H(.)$ in the probability expression by assuming the output of $f(H(.))$ given random input r to behave as the probability distributions (χ_C, χ_G), resulting in: $\alpha = P(F(\boldsymbol{C}, \boldsymbol{G}) > f_t \,|\, (\boldsymbol{C}, \boldsymbol{G}) \leftarrow (\chi_C, \chi_G))$ and $\beta = P(\mathtt{abs}(\boldsymbol{S}^T\boldsymbol{C} + \boldsymbol{G}) > q_t \,|\, (\boldsymbol{C}, \boldsymbol{G}) \leftarrow (\chi_C, \chi_G), F(\boldsymbol{C}, \boldsymbol{G}) > f_t)$.

Secondly, we assume that the coefficients of $\boldsymbol{S}^T\boldsymbol{C}$ are normally distributed, which is reasonable as the coefficients are a sum of $2(l \cdot n)$ distributions that are somewhat close to a Gaussian. The coefficients of the polynomial $(\boldsymbol{S}^T\boldsymbol{C})_{ij}$ will be distributed with mean $\mu = 0$ because of symmetry around 0, while the variance can be calculated as follows, after defining χ_{e+u} as the distribution of the coefficients of $\boldsymbol{E}_A + \boldsymbol{U}_A$:

$$\mathtt{var}((\boldsymbol{S}^T\boldsymbol{C})_{ijk}) = \mathtt{var}(\sum_{i=0}^{l-1}\sum_{k=0}^{n-1} C_{ijk}s_{ijk} + \sum_{i=l}^{2l-1}\sum_{k=0}^{n-1} C_{ijk}e_{ijk}) \tag{5}$$

$$\text{where: } s_{ijk} \leftarrow \chi_s \text{ and } e_{ijk} \leftarrow \chi_{e+u} \tag{6}$$

$$= \sum_{i=0}^{l-1}\sum_{k=0}^{n-1} C_{ijk}^2 \mathtt{var}(\chi_s) + \sum_{i=l}^{2l-1}\sum_{k=0}^{n-1} C_{ijk}^2 \mathtt{var}(\chi_{e+u}) \tag{7}$$

$$= \|(\boldsymbol{E}'_B + \boldsymbol{U}'_B)_{:j}\|_2^2 \mathtt{var}(\chi_s) + \|(\boldsymbol{S}'_B)_{:j}\|_2^2 \mathtt{var}(\chi_{e+u})\,. \tag{8}$$

Therefore, the variance of the coefficients of $\boldsymbol{S}^T\boldsymbol{C}$ for a given $\boldsymbol{C}$ is the same for all coefficients in the same column. This variance will be denoted as σ_j^2 for coefficients in the jth column of $\boldsymbol{S}^T\boldsymbol{C}$. Furthermore, following the Gaussian assumption, the failure probability given σ_j^2 is the same as the failure probability given the jth column of $\boldsymbol{C}$.

In the third step we gradually calculate the distribution of the failure probability. We start from the distribution of the failure probability of the coefficient at the ijk^{th} position given σ_j, denoted with $\chi_{coef\,|\,\sigma}$. This distribution expresses the probability of finding a $\boldsymbol{G}$ so that the failure probability is equal to f_{ijk} given a certain value of $\boldsymbol{C}$ (or equivalently σ_j^2) and can be expressed as follows:

$$P(f_{ijk} \,|\, \boldsymbol{G} \leftarrow \chi_G, \boldsymbol{C}), \tag{9}$$

where:

$$f_{ijk} = P(\mathtt{abs}(\boldsymbol{S}^T \boldsymbol{C} + \boldsymbol{G})_{ijk} > q_t \,|\, \boldsymbol{G}, \boldsymbol{C}) \tag{10}$$

$$\approx P(\mathtt{abs}(x + \boldsymbol{G}_{ijk}) > q_t \,|\, \boldsymbol{G}, x \leftarrow \mathcal{N}(0, \sigma_j^2), \sigma_j^2). \tag{11}$$

The distribution $\chi_{col\,|\,\sigma}$, which models the probability of a failure in the jth column of $\mathtt{abs}(\boldsymbol{S}^T \boldsymbol{C} + \boldsymbol{G})$ given σ_j^2, can be calculated using the convolution of the distributions of the mn individual coefficient failures $\chi_{coef\,|\,\sigma}$ as follows:

$$\chi_{col\,|\,\sigma} = \chi_{coef\,|\,\sigma}^{*nm}. \tag{12}$$

The conditioning on σ_j^2 is necessary to counter the dependency between the coefficients of the columns of $\mathtt{abs}(\boldsymbol{S}^T \boldsymbol{C} + \boldsymbol{G})$, which are dependent as a result of sharing the same variance σ_j^2.

The distribution of failure probabilities in the jth column of $\boldsymbol{S}^T \boldsymbol{C}$, denoted as χ_{col}, can then be calculated using a weighted average over the possible values of σ_j^2 as follows:

$$\chi_{col} = \sum_{l_c} P(f \,|\, f \leftarrow \chi_{col,\sigma}^{*nm}) P(\sigma_j^2 = l_c). \tag{13}$$

Finally we can calculate the full failure distribution χ_{FAIL} as the convolution of the m probability distributions corresponding to the failure distributions of the different columns. This convolution does not have the dependency on σ_j^2 as failures of different columns are independent conditioned on $\boldsymbol{C}$ and $\boldsymbol{G}$, therefore:

$$\chi_{\text{FAIL}} = \chi_{col}^{*m}. \tag{14}$$

From this failure distribution, we can calculate α and β for an arbitrary value of f_t:

$$\alpha = P(f > f_t \,|\, f \leftarrow \chi_{\text{FAIL}}), \tag{15}$$

$$\beta = \frac{\sum_{f > f_t} f \cdot P(f \,|\, f \leftarrow \chi_{\text{FAIL}})}{\alpha}. \tag{16}$$

We want to stress that this calculation is not exact, mainly due to the Gaussian assumption in the second step. More accurate estimates could be obtained with a more accurate approximation in step 2, tailored for a specific scheme. In this case, the assumptions and calculations of step 1 and step 3 remain valid. For the estimations of LAC [31] in subsequent paragraphs, we followed their approach for the calculation of the effect of the error correcting code. Note that this is not an exact formula as the inputs of the error correcting code are correlated through their polynomial structure.

In Fig. 1 we compare the values of α and β calculated using the technique described above, with exhaustively tested values on a variant of LAC128 without error correction. For step 2 of the practical calculation, we use both a Gaussian approximation as well as a binomial approximation that is more tailored for LAC. We can observe that our estimation of the effect of failure boosting is relatively close to reality.

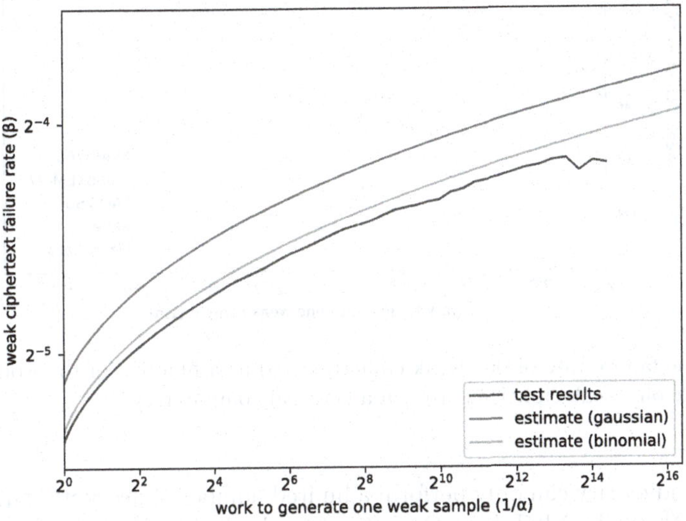

Fig. 1. The failure rate of one weak ciphertext (β) as a function of the work required to generate one weak ciphertext (α) on a classical computer for LAC128 without error correction.

3.2 Applications of Failure Boosting

Failure boosting is a useful technique in at least three scenarios: first, if there is no multi-target protection, second, if the adversary can only perform a limited number of queries to the decryption oracle and third, if the adversary has access to a quantum computer.

In some (Ring/Module-)LWE/LWR schemes, the seed r is the only input to the pseudorandom generator that generates $\boldsymbol{C}$ and $\boldsymbol{G}$. This paves the way to a multi-target attack where precomputed weak values of r can be used against multiple targets: after choosing the parameter f_t, the adversary can generate weak ciphertexts in approximately α^{-1} time ($\sqrt{\alpha^{-1}}$ if he has access to a quantum computer). Each precomputed sample has then a failure probability of β against every target. Figure 2 shows the failure probability of one weak ciphertext versus the amount of work to generate that ciphertext on a classical computer. Multi-target protection, for example by including the public key into the generation of $\boldsymbol{C}$ en $\boldsymbol{G}$ as proposed in Kyber [10] and Saber [13] is a relatively cheap option to resolve this issue.

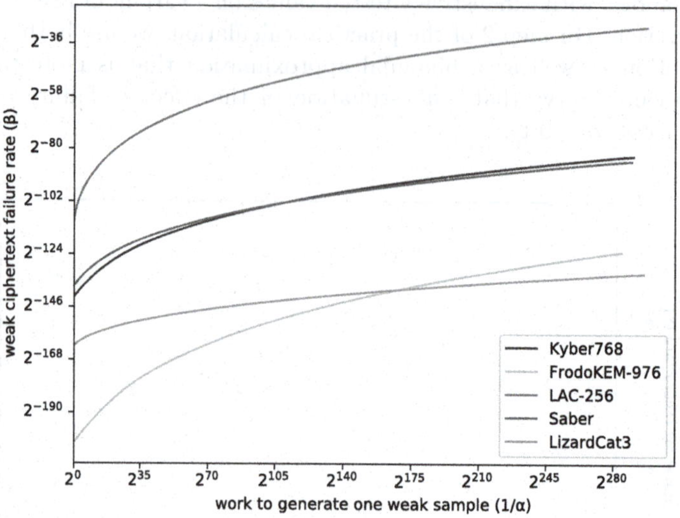

Fig. 2. The failure rate of one weak ciphertext (β) as a function of the work required to generate one weak ciphertext (α) on a classical computer.

If the adversary can only perform a limited number of decryption queries, for example 2^{64} in the NIST Post-Quantum Standardization Call for Proposals [2], the adversary can use failure boosting to reduce the number of required decryption queries. To this end, he chooses the parameter f_t so that the inverse of the failure probability β^{-1} equals the decryption query limit n_d, which results in a probability of finding a decryption failure of approximately $(1 - e^{-1}) \approx 0.63$. To find i failures with similar probability, the failure probability should be brought up so that $\beta^{-1} = n_d/i$. Since the amount of work to generate one input of the decryption query is approximately α^{-1} ($\sqrt{\alpha^{-1}}$ quantumly), the total amount of work expected is $\alpha^{-1}\beta^{-1}$, ($\sqrt{\alpha^{-1}}\beta^{-1}$ quantumly). Figure 3 shows the expected total amount of work to find one decryption failure with a classical computer, versus the failure rate of one weak ciphertext.

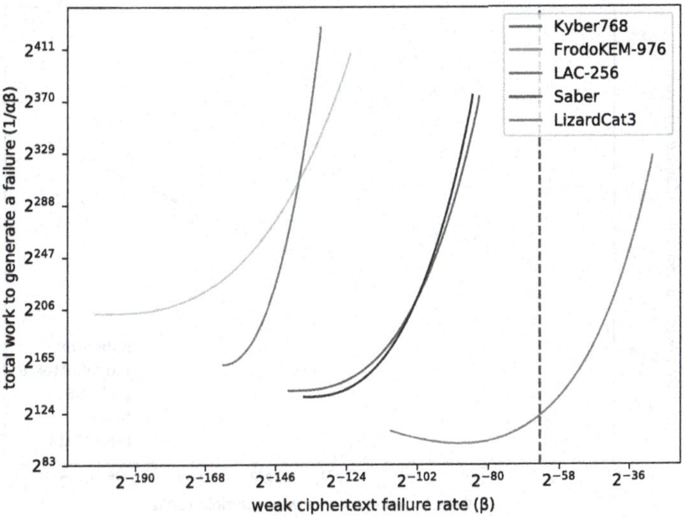

Fig. 3. The expected amount of work ($\alpha^{-1}\beta^{-1}$) on a classical computer, as a function of the failure rate of one weak ciphertext (β). The red dotted line indicates a failure rate of 2^{-64}. (Color figure online)

An adversary with a quantum computer always benefits from failure boosting, as the search for weak ciphertexts can be sped up using Grover's algorithm. However, this speedup is not quadratic if the adversary has no quantum access to the decryption oracle. Figure 4 shows the total amount of expected work to find one decryption failure, versus the amount of work to find one weak ciphertext on a quantum computer $\sqrt{\alpha^{-1}}$.

4 Estimation of the Secret

Finding a decryption failure does not immediately break the security of the KEM, but it does provide extra information to an adversary. In this section we will investigate how much this information leaks about the secret. An adversary that has obtained ciphertexts that produce decryption failures can use them to make an estimation of the secret $\boldsymbol{S}$.

When a failure occurs, we know that at least one coefficient of $\mathsf{abs}(\boldsymbol{S}^T\boldsymbol{C}+\boldsymbol{G})$ is larger than the threshold q_t. This leads to a classification of the coefficients in the set of fail coefficients v_f and no-fail coefficients v_s. To each coefficient at position (i, j, k), a vector of integers $\boldsymbol{s}$ can be associated by taking the coefficients of $\boldsymbol{S}_{:i}$. Similarly, the coefficient can be linked to a vector of integers $\boldsymbol{c}$ calculated as a function of $\boldsymbol{C}_{:j}$ and k, so that the multiplication $\boldsymbol{s}\boldsymbol{c}$ equals that coefficient.

No-fail vectors will contain negligible information about the secret $\boldsymbol{s}$, but failure vectors do carry clues, as the threshold exceeding value of the coefficients of $\boldsymbol{S}^T\boldsymbol{C}+\boldsymbol{G}$ implies a correlation between the corresponding $\boldsymbol{c}$ and $\boldsymbol{s}$. This correlation can be positive, in case of a large positive value of the coefficient, or

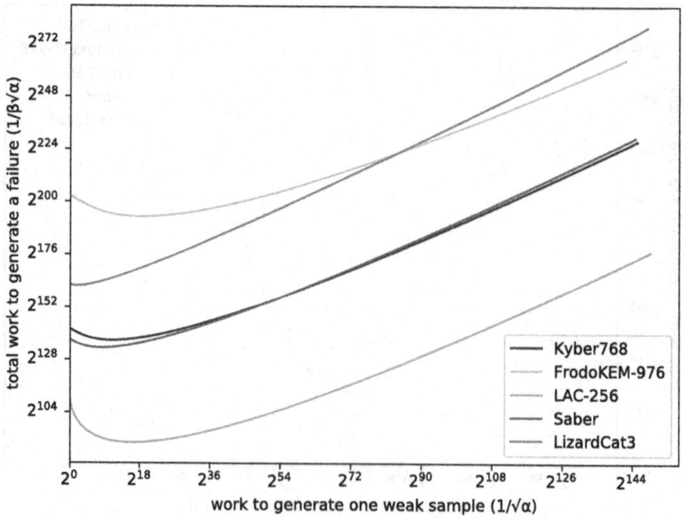

Fig. 4. The expected amount of work ($\sqrt{\alpha^{-1}}\beta^{-1}$) as a function of the work required to generate one weak ciphertext ($\sqrt{\alpha^{-1}}$) on a classical computer.

negative, in case of a large negative value of the coefficient. Consequently, the fail coefficients can be further divided into the sets of positive v_{fp} and negative v_{fn} fail coefficients respectively. Moreover, negative fail vectors can be transformed into positive fail vectors by multiplication with -1. Note that failure coefficients at position (i, j, k) will only contain information about the jth column of $\boldsymbol{S}$, which is why the estimation of the columns of $\boldsymbol{S}$ can be performed independently.

4.1 One Positive Failure Vector

We will first examine the case where we know one positive fail vector $\boldsymbol{c}$ and associated coefficient $\boldsymbol{G}_{i,j,k}$, which we will denote with g. This corresponds to the case where one failing ciphertext and the location and sign of the error is known. The question is how much the knowledge about $\boldsymbol{c}$ and g can improve our estimate of the associated secret $\boldsymbol{s}$. Applying Bayes' theorem and assuming independence between the coefficients of $\boldsymbol{c}$ and $\boldsymbol{s}$ that are on different positions, we can write:

$$P(\boldsymbol{s}_i \mid \boldsymbol{c}, g, \boldsymbol{sc} > q_t - g) \approx P(\boldsymbol{s}_i \mid \boldsymbol{c}_i, g, \boldsymbol{sc} > q_t - g) \tag{17}$$

$$= \frac{P(\boldsymbol{sc} > q_t - g \mid \boldsymbol{s}_i, \boldsymbol{c}_i, g) P(\boldsymbol{s}_i \mid \boldsymbol{c}_i, g)}{P(\boldsymbol{sc} > q_t - g \mid \boldsymbol{c}_i, g)} \tag{18}$$

$$= \frac{P(\sum_j^{j \neq i} \boldsymbol{s}_j \boldsymbol{c}_j > q_t - g - \boldsymbol{s}_i \boldsymbol{c}_i \mid \boldsymbol{s}_i, \boldsymbol{c}_i, g) P(\boldsymbol{s}_i)}{P(\boldsymbol{sc} > q_t - g \mid \boldsymbol{c}_i, g)}. \tag{19}$$

The improved estimates for the coefficients of $\boldsymbol{s}$ can in turn be used to get an estimate $\boldsymbol{s}_{est}$ that minimizes its variance $E[(\boldsymbol{s}_{est} - \boldsymbol{s})^2]$ as follows:

$$0 = \frac{d}{d\boldsymbol{s}_{est,i}} E((\boldsymbol{s}_{est,i} - \boldsymbol{s}_i)^2) \tag{20}$$

$$= 2 \sum_{\boldsymbol{s}_i} (\boldsymbol{s}_{est,i} - \boldsymbol{s}_i) P(\boldsymbol{s}_i), \tag{21}$$

$$\text{or:} \quad \boldsymbol{s}_{est,i} = \sum_{\boldsymbol{s}_i} \boldsymbol{s}_i \cdot P(\boldsymbol{s}_i). \tag{22}$$

The estimate of $\boldsymbol{s}$ gives the estimate of the jth column of $\boldsymbol{S}$, which can be divided trivially in an approximation $\boldsymbol{S}_{A,est}$ of $(\boldsymbol{S}_A)_{:j}$ and $\boldsymbol{E}_{A,est}$ of $(\boldsymbol{E}_A + \boldsymbol{U}_A)_{:j}$. These vectors can be used to transform the original (Ring/Module-)LWE/LWR sample $(\boldsymbol{A}, \boldsymbol{A}(\boldsymbol{S}_A)_{:j} + (\boldsymbol{E}_A + \boldsymbol{U}_A)_{:j})$ into a (Ring/Module-)LWE alike problem with a smaller secret variance by subtracting $\boldsymbol{A}\boldsymbol{S}_{A,est} + \boldsymbol{E}_{A,est}$. This results in the sample $(\boldsymbol{A}, \boldsymbol{A}((\boldsymbol{S}_A)_{:j} - \boldsymbol{S}_{A,est}) + (\boldsymbol{E}_A + \boldsymbol{U}_A)_{:j} - \boldsymbol{E}_{A,est})$, which is a problem with smaller secret $(\boldsymbol{S}_A)_{:j} - \boldsymbol{S}_{A,est}$ and noise $(\boldsymbol{E}_A + \boldsymbol{U}_A)_{:j} - \boldsymbol{E}_{A,est}$. We will call this new problem the simplified problem.

4.2 Multiple Fail Vectors

Having access to m positive fail vectors $\boldsymbol{c}^{(1)} \dots \boldsymbol{c}^{(m)}$ from the same column, with corresponding values of G as $g^{(1)} \dots g^{(m)}$, an adversary can improve his estimate of $P(\boldsymbol{s})$ and therefore obtain a better estimate $\boldsymbol{s}_{est}$, assuming that the failure vectors $\boldsymbol{c}_i$ are independent conditioned on $\boldsymbol{s}$. This corresponds to knowing m failing ciphertexts and the location and sign of their errors.

$$P(\boldsymbol{s}_i \,|\, \boldsymbol{c}^{(1)} \dots \boldsymbol{c}^{(m)}, g^{(1)} \dots g^{(m)}) \approx P(\boldsymbol{s}_i \,|\, \boldsymbol{c}_i^{(1)} \dots \boldsymbol{c}_i^{(m)}, g^{(1)} \dots g^{(m)}) \tag{23}$$

$$= \frac{P(\boldsymbol{c}_i^{(1)} \dots \boldsymbol{c}_i^{(m)} \,|\, \boldsymbol{s}_i, g^{(1)} \dots g^{(m)}) P(\boldsymbol{s}_i \,|\, g^{(1)} \dots g^{(m)})}{P(\boldsymbol{c}_i^{(1)} \dots \boldsymbol{c}_i^{(m)} \,|\, g^{(1)} \dots g^{(m)})} \tag{24}$$

$$= \frac{P(\boldsymbol{s}_i) \prod_{k=1}^{m} P(\boldsymbol{c}_i^{(k)} \,|\, \boldsymbol{s}_i, g^{(k)})}{\prod_{k=1}^{m} P(\boldsymbol{c}_i^{(k)} \,|\, g^{(k)})}. \tag{25}$$

Similar to Eq. 19, $P(\boldsymbol{c}_i \,|\, \boldsymbol{s}_i, g^{(k)})$ can be calculated as:

$$P(\boldsymbol{c}_i \,|\, \boldsymbol{s}_i, g, \boldsymbol{s}\boldsymbol{c} > q_t - g) = \frac{P(\boldsymbol{s}\boldsymbol{c} > q_t - g \,|\, \boldsymbol{s}_i, \boldsymbol{c}_i, g) P(\boldsymbol{c}_i \,|\, \boldsymbol{s}_i, g)}{P(\boldsymbol{s}\boldsymbol{c} > q_t - g \,|\, \boldsymbol{s}_i, g)} \tag{26}$$

$$= \frac{P(\sum_j^{j \neq i} \boldsymbol{s}_j \boldsymbol{c}_j > q_t - g - \boldsymbol{s}_i \boldsymbol{c}_i \,|\, \boldsymbol{s}_i, \boldsymbol{c}_i, g) P(\boldsymbol{c}_i)}{P(\boldsymbol{s}\boldsymbol{c} > q_t - g \,|\, \boldsymbol{s}_i, g)}. \tag{27}$$

In subsequent calculations, each value of the coefficient of g is taken as the maximum possible value.

4.3 Classification of Vectors

The above approach assumes a prior knowledge of the exact position and sign of the errors. This information is needed to link coefficients of $\boldsymbol{C}$ with their corresponding coefficient of $\boldsymbol{S}$. However, this is not always a trivial problem. For most schemes there are three sources of extra information that will allow to perform this classification with a high probability using only a few decryption failures.

Firstly, a large coefficient of $\boldsymbol{G}$ would induce a higher failure probability for the corresponding coefficient of the error term $\boldsymbol{S}^T\boldsymbol{C}+\boldsymbol{G}$. Thus, failures are more likely to happen at positions linked to that coefficient of $\boldsymbol{G}$. Moreover, a positive value of the coefficient suggests a positive error so that $\boldsymbol{c} \in v_{fp}$, while a negative value hints at a negative error, or $\boldsymbol{c} \in v_{fn}$.

Secondly, as vectors $\boldsymbol{c} \in v_f$ are correlated with the secret $\boldsymbol{s}$, they are also correlated with each other. Therefore, vectors $\boldsymbol{c} \in v_f$ are more correlated between each other than a vector $\boldsymbol{c} \in v_f$ with a vector $\boldsymbol{c} \in v_s$. Moreover, a high positive correlation suggests that the vectors share the same class v_{fp} or v_{fn}, while a high negative correlation indicates that the vectors have a different classes. This allows for a clustering of the fail vectors using the higher than average correlation, under the condition that the correlation difference is high enough. This correlation difference is related to the failure rate: a low failure rate implies a higher correlation because only ciphertexts that are highly correlated with the secret lead to a failure rate in this case. For example, Fig. 5 shows an estimate of the correlations between vectors of the classes v_{fp} (pos), v_{fn} (neg) and v_s (nofail) in Kyber768. This approach does not work for schemes with strong error correcting codes (ECC) such as LAC, as the bit error rate before correction is relatively high for these types of algorithms, leading to a relatively low correlation between failure vectors.

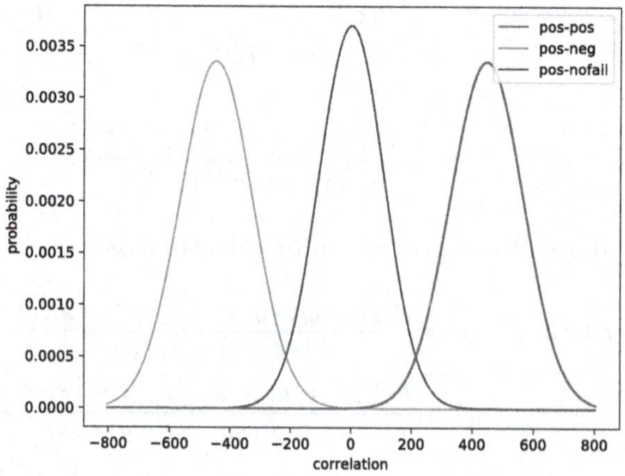

Fig. 5. The probability of a certain value of the correlation between different classes of vectors in Kyber768.

In case of a ring/module structure of the coefficients of $\boldsymbol{S}$, an additional structure arises leading to an artifact in which some pairs of no-fail coefficients within the same polynomial also have high correlation of their corresponding vectors. Imagine a pair of failure coefficients at positions (i, j, k_1) and (i, j, k_2) from different decryption failures a, b, with corresponding matrices $\boldsymbol{C}^{(a)}$ and $\boldsymbol{C}^{(b)}$. The correlation of the vectors $\boldsymbol{c}^{(a)}$ and $\boldsymbol{c}^{(b)}$ can be written as $X^{k_1}\boldsymbol{C}_{:,j}^{(a)T} X^{k_2}\boldsymbol{C}_{:,j}^{(b)} = X^{k_1+k_2}\boldsymbol{C}_{:,j}^{(a)T}\boldsymbol{C}_{:,j}^{(b)}$, from which is clear that the vectors from $\boldsymbol{C}^{(a)}$ and $\boldsymbol{C}^{(b)}$, with respective positions $(i, j, k_1 - t)$ and $(i, j, k_2 + t)$ have the same correlation. The clustering will thus result in n classes, with one class containing the failure vectors. Combining this information with the information of the first method gives an adversary the failure vectors with high probability. Otherwise, an adversary can estimate the secret n times and check the validity of the result using the (Ring/Module-)LWE/LWR problem.

Finally, for schemes that use error correcting codes to reduce their failure probability, side channel leakage during the error correction might reveal information on the presence or position of failure coefficients. Note that if this is the case, it might not even be necessary to obtain a decryption failure since failing coefficients could also be collected on successful decryptions where there is at least one failing coefficient.

4.4 Implications

Figure 6 depicts the relative variance reduction of the secret as a function of the number of positive failure vectors for various schemes. For schemes that have a very low failure probability for individual coefficients of $\boldsymbol{S}^T\boldsymbol{C} + \boldsymbol{G}$, such as Kyber, Saber and FrodoKEM, the variance of the secret drastically reduces upon knowing only a few failing ciphertexts. Assuming that the simplified problem, that takes into account the estimate of the secret, has the same complexity as a regular (Ring/Module-)LWE problem with similar secret variance, we can calculate the remaining hardness of the simplified problem as a function of the number of positive failure vectors as shown in Fig. 7 using the toolbox provided by Albrecht et al. [4] using the Q-core sieve estimate.

The effectiveness of the attack declines as the failure probability of the individual coefficients increases, since the correlation between the secret and the failing ciphertext is lower in this case. This can be seen in the case of LAC, where the individual coefficients have relatively high failure rates due to a strong error correcting code. On the other hand, a failing ciphertext will contain multiple errors, making it easier to collect multiple failure vectors.

Note that once one or more failures are found, they can be used to estimate the secret. This estimate in turn can be used to improve the search for weak ciphertexts by considering $F(\boldsymbol{C}, \boldsymbol{G})$ as $\sum_{\boldsymbol{S}} P(\text{FAIL}(\boldsymbol{C}, \boldsymbol{G}), \boldsymbol{S})$, where $\boldsymbol{S}$ is not sampled from $\chi_{\boldsymbol{S}}$, but from the new probability distribution $\chi_{\boldsymbol{S}_{est}}$. Therefore, the search for weak keys could become easier the more failures have been found. However, we do not take this effect into account in this paper.

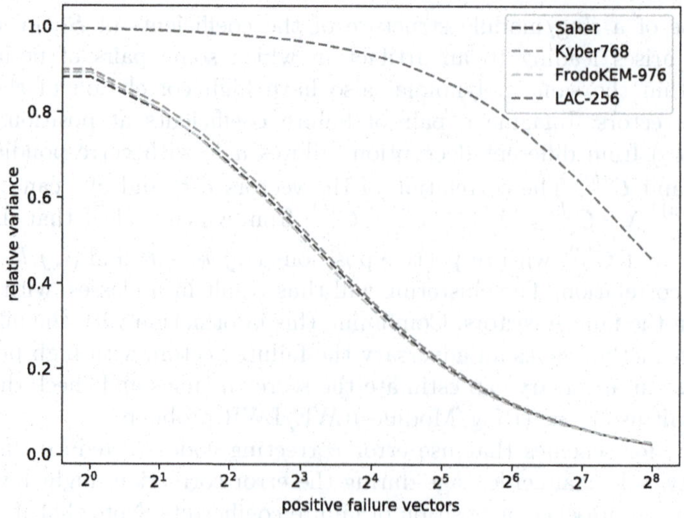

Fig. 6. The relative reduction in entropy as a function of the number of positive failure vectors

5 Weak-Ciphertext Attack

Using the failure boosting technique from Sect. 3 and the secret estimation method from Sect. 4, we can lower the security of a (Ring/Module-)LWE/LWR scheme on the condition that its failure rate is high enough. To this end, we first

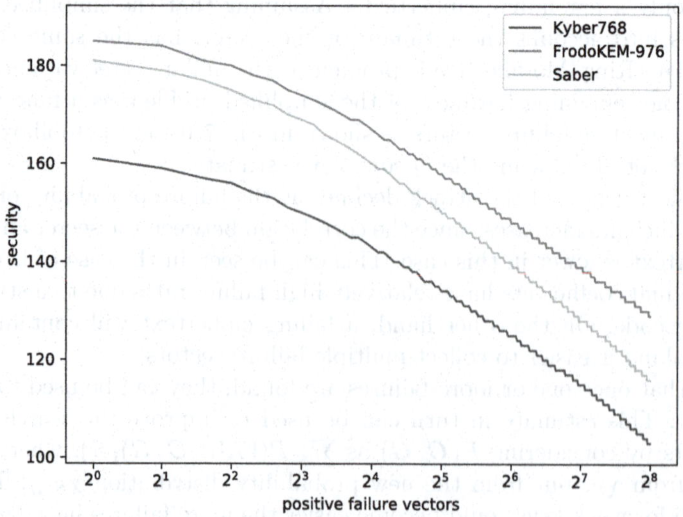

Fig. 7. The hardness of the simplified problem as a function of the number of positive failure vectors

collect i decryption failures using the failure boosting technique, which would cost approximately $i\sqrt{\alpha^{-1}}\beta^{-1}$ work. Then, the exact error position and failure type should be determined for all of the failure vectors using the techniques of Subsect. 4.3. Based on this information, the secret can be estimated, which in turn can be used to simplify the (Ring/Module-)LWE/LWR problem. These last two operations require a negligible amount of work compared to finding decryption failures. Finally, we need to solve the simplified problem, with has a complexity $S_{\text{simplified}}(i)$ as estimated in Sect. 4. The total amount of work is therefore $\mathcal{O}(S_{\text{simplified}}(i) + i\sqrt{\alpha^{-1}}\beta^{-1})$, which is depicted in Fig. 8 as a function of the number of failures i. Note that the practical security of Kyber relies on an error term $\boldsymbol{E}_A$ as well as a rounding term $\boldsymbol{U}_A$. Both are taken into account in the security calculation.

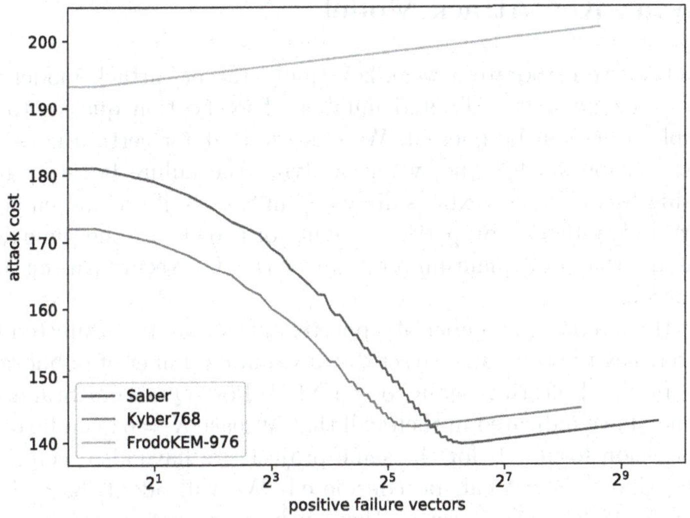

Fig. 8. The full amount of work to break the scheme as a function of the number of collected decryption failures

Table 1 gives an overview of the original hardness of the scheme before decryption failure usage S, and the attack cost $S_{\text{simplified}}(i) + i\sqrt{\alpha^{-1}}\beta^{-1}$ using decryption failures for ideal values of i and f_t, which are calculated through a brute force sweep. The number of collected decryption failures i and the expected number of decryption queries $i\beta^{-1}$ is also included. These values are calculated assuming that the adversary can perform an unlimited number of decryption queries. From this table we can see that the security of Kyber and Saber is considerably reduced. This is due to the fact that finding a failure is easier than breaking the security of the scheme S. For the case of FrodoKEM976, the security is not affected as the work to obtain a failure is considerably larger than breaking the security S.

In other situations such as a multi-target attack or having only a limited number of decryption queries, other values of f_t and i will obtain optimal results. For example in a multi-target attack scenario one would select a higher threshold f_t to be able to efficiently re-use the precomputation work α^{-1} for weak ciphertexts and therefore reduce the overall work. A limit on the number of decryptions n_d could make it necessary to increase the amount of precomputational work α^{-1} in order to reduce the failure rate $\beta^{-1} < n_d/i$. This would make the attack more expensive or might even invalidate it. For example, the NIST Post-Quantum Standardization Process decryption limit is set to 2^{64}, which rules out a decryption failure attack on schemes with a low enough failure rate such as Saber and Kyber, which can be deduced from Fig. 3. As such, the security of this schemes is not affected within the NIST framework.

6 A Weak-Key Attack Model

In this section we elaborate a weak-key (multi-target) attack model when the adversary can only have a limited number of decryption queries to one user but multiple users can be queried. We observe that for certain keys, the error probability can be much higher when applying the failure boosting technique, i.e., choosing 'weak' ciphertexts as discussed in Sect. 3, if the chosen ciphertexts satisfy certain key-related properties. The major targets are the same as before – lattice-based NIST post-quantum proposals with CCA security using some CCA transformations.

We set the maximum number of ciphertexts that can be submitted to a node with a public key to be 2^K and we set the maximum number of public keys in the system to be 2^L. Referring again to the NIST Post-Quantum Standardization Process, they have indicated in their call that at least $K = 64$ can be considered. In the discussion forum [1] for the same project, we have also seen researchers mentioning that $L = 64$ can be considered. We will adopt $K = L = 64$ in the further sections since it seems these values are not questioned, although

Table 1. The security of different schemes with and without decryption failures

	original security	attack cost	reduction factor	decryption failures	decryption queries
Saber	2^{184}	2^{139}	2^{45}	77	2^{131}
FireSaber	2^{257}	2^{170}	2^{87}	233	2^{161}
Kyber768	2^{175}	2^{142}	2^{33}	42	2^{131}
Kyber1024	2^{239}	2^{169}	2^{70}	159	2^{158}
LAC256	2^{293}	$2^{97\dagger}$	2^{196}	$106 \cdot 56$	2^{80}
FrodoKEM976	2^{188}	2^{188}	2^{0}	0	0

† Note that it seems not straightforward for LAC256 to obtain the exact position and type of the errors, which is required to obtain this result

larger values of K and L can give more powerful attacks and could definitely be relevant. For example, comparing with attacks on symmetric schemes, such attacks may require a number of plaintext-ciphertext pairs that are close to the number of possible keys (like 2^{200}), and still they are considered valid attacks.

The proposed attack procedure is split in three steps.

1. Do a precomputation step to establish pairs of messages and corresponding ciphertexts and let informally the set $\mathcal{F}$ denote error vectors corresponding to the different messages, which are equivalent to the $(\boldsymbol{C}, \boldsymbol{G})$ pairs chosen before. These selected error vectors should be with particular properties, e.g, with large norm and/or with several large entries in certain positions, etc.
2. Send the ciphertexts contained in $\mathcal{F}$ and assume that we learn the decrypted messages. Assume further that a subset have been erroneously decrypted (wrong decoding due to too large error) and let $\mathcal{F}'$ be the error vectors causing decryption failure. The cardinality of this set could be larger than average if certain properties (related to $\mathcal{F}$) of the secret vector hold. So we submit the set of ciphertexts to each node holding a public key. The node giving the largest decryption failure rate is selected as the target public key for the attack.
3. Do statistical testing on the set $\mathcal{F}'$ (and possibly the set $\mathcal{F}$) to establish relationships between the secret key and given the noise vectors leading to a decryption failure. Analyzing their correlation, we may be able to recover partial secrets, which can considerably reduce the solving complexity of the underlying hard problem. We are then able to perform a full key-recovery attack via classic approaches such as lattice reduction algorithms.

Note that the above procedure is very close to the weak-ciphertext attack described in the previous sections. One major difference is that here we choose the set $\mathcal{F}$ of 'weak' ciphertexts to be related to the 'weak' keys targeted, while in the prior, the 'weak' ciphertexts are chosen to have a larger decryption failure rate averaged over all keys.

We discuss the three steps briefly. In the precomputation step, we can observe a first difference between different schemes. Most schemes include the public key in the generation of the noisy vectors (as input in the hash function generating the noise). This means that a constructed set $\mathcal{F}$ can only be used for a single public key and a new such set must be constructed for the next public key. For simplicity, we assume $|\mathcal{F}| = 2^K$ and note that the number of nodes with a public key is 2^L. If we set the computational complexity of precomputing a set $\mathcal{F}$ to be 2^λ, the overall complexity of this first step is $2^{\lambda+L}$. On the other hand, there are also schemes where error vectors are generated independent of the public key (e.g. LAC). In such a case the same set $\mathcal{F}$ can be used on all public keys and the complexity is only 2^λ. We could also use Grover's search algorithm to accelerate the pre-computation step, as discussed in Sect. 3. However, since the pre-quantum and post-quantum security goals in the NIST Post-Quantum Standardization Process are different for a certain security level, this quantum acceleration may not help us to break the claimed security level of a submission.

For the second step, the idea is that among many public keys, there will be one where the corresponding secret values have a property that causes more decryption errors than on average. So to increase the decryption error probability to a reasonable and detectable level, we consider that a special property in the secret value is held with probability at least p', where $0 < p' < 1$. We then assume that $p' = 2^{-L}$, so we can expect that this special property in the secret value holds for one public key. As mentioned, with respect to the CCA security, NIST restricts to have at most 2^{64} decryption calls to each user (public key). So in order to distinguish a special property in the secret value corresponding to a public key, one needs to get the failure rate for this case to be larger than 2^{-64}.

Finally, in the statistical testing part, we have a set of error vectors that have caused decryption errors. There seems to be a plethora of methods that can be used to recover secret values. For instance, the strong maximum-likelihood approach has been discussed in Sect. 4 and heuristic approaches can also be applied. A general approach that we can adopt is to consider a smaller part of the secret vector under reconstruction, and select the most probable values for this part, based on the observed error vectors in $\mathcal{F}$. Then one combines such guesses for different parts and builds an approximation of a secret vector. A good approximation will mostly be sufficient as it can be used in lattice-basis reduction algorithms.

We note that in many applications, the challenge is to detect the first decryption failure, since we can usually have adaptive approaches to find more failures afterwards with a lower complexity. This idea is further demonstrated in the next section where an adaptive CCA attack on ss-ntru-pke will be presented, and also in a code-based application [34].

7 A Weak-Key Attack on ss-ntru-pke

We have applied the described weak-key approach and provide the details of attacking ss-ntru-pke, a version in the submission to the NIST Post-Quantum Standardization Process – NTRUEncrypt [47]. Connected is also the provably secure NTRU [44] whose security is based purely on the hardness of Ring-LWE. NTRUEncrypt with different parameter choices has been around for a long time and is one of the most competitive lattice-based schemes when it comes to performance.

Note that our attack in this section is in the pre-quantum (classic) security framework due to the different security goal for NIST-V when Grover's algorithm is considered. We adopt the notations from the NTRUEncrypt submission [47] throughout this section.

7.1 The ss-ntru-pke Scheme

ss-ntru-pke is the version of NTRUEncrypt targeting the highest security level, being 256 bits. This scheme achieves CCA2 security via the NAEP transform [27], a transform similar to the Fujisaki-Okamoto transformation with an additional mask. We give a very brief explanation of the scheme. For most of the description and details, we refer to [47]. In the key generation (see Algorithm 6), two secret polynomials $\mathbf{f}, \mathbf{g} \in \mathcal{R}$ are selected, where the coordinates are chosen from a discrete Gaussian $\mathcal{X}_\sigma$ distribution with standard deviation σ. A public key is formed by computing $\mathbf{h} = \mathbf{g}/(p\mathbf{f} + 1)$.

Algorithm 6. ss-ntru-pke.KEYGEN

Input: Parameter sets PARAM $= \{N, p, q, \sigma\}$ and a *seed*.
Output: Public key $\mathbf{h}$ and secret key $(\mathbf{f}, \mathbf{g})$.
1) Instantiate Sampler with $\mathcal{X}_\sigma^N$ and *seed*;
2) $\mathbf{f} \leftarrow$ Sampler, $\mathbf{g} \leftarrow$ Sampler;
3) $\mathbf{h} = \mathbf{g}/(p\mathbf{f} + 1) \mod q$;

We show in Algorithm 7 the encryption algorithm of ss-ntru-pke and in Algorithm 8 the decryption algorithm, both from the original proposal [47]. In these descriptions, HASH() represents a hash function, and $\mathcal{B}$ represents a set including all binary polynomials with degree at most $N-1$. The Pad() operation is a function to ensure the message has sufficient entropy, and the Extract() operation is the inverse of Pad().

In each encryption of a message $\mathbf{m}$, two polynomials $\mathbf{r}, \mathbf{e} \in \mathcal{R}$ are generated, where the coordinates are again chosen from a discrete Gaussian distribution $\mathcal{X}_\sigma$ with standard deviation σ. This randomness source uses a seed generated as HASH$(\mathbf{m}, \mathbf{h})$. This means that each choice of a message $\mathbf{m}$ will generate also the polynomials $\mathbf{r}, \mathbf{e} \in \mathcal{R}$. Let us denote this by

$$(\mathbf{r}, \mathbf{e}) = \mathbf{G}(\mathbf{m}, \mathbf{h}).$$

Algorithm 7. ss-ntru-pke.ENCRYPT

Input: Public key $\mathbf{h}$, message *msg* of length *mlen*, PARAM and a *seed*.
Output: Ciphertext $\mathbf{c}$.
1) $\mathbf{m}$ = Pad(*msg*, *seed*);
2) *rseed* = HASH$(\mathbf{m}|\mathbf{h})$;
3) Instantiate Sampler with $\mathcal{X}_\sigma^N$ and *rseed*;
4) $\mathbf{r} \leftarrow$ Sampler, $\mathbf{e} \leftarrow$ Sampler;
5) $\mathbf{t} = p \cdot \mathbf{r} * \mathbf{h}$;
6) *tseed* = HASH$(\mathbf{t})$;
7) Instantiate Sampler with $\mathcal{B}$ and *tseed*;
8) $\mathbf{m}_{mask} \leftarrow$ Sampler;
9) $\mathbf{m}' = \mathbf{m} - \mathbf{m}_{mask} \pmod p$;
10) $\mathbf{c} = \mathbf{t} + p \cdot \mathbf{e} + \mathbf{m}'$;

In decryption, with ciphertext $\mathbf{c}$, one computes the message by computing

$$\mathbf{f} * \mathbf{c} = p \cdot \mathbf{r} * \mathbf{g} + p \cdot \mathbf{e} * \mathbf{f} + \mathbf{m}' * \mathbf{f}.$$

A decryption error occurs if $||p \cdot \mathbf{r} * \mathbf{g} + p \cdot \mathbf{e} * \mathbf{f} + \mathbf{m}' * \mathbf{f}||_\infty > q/2$. This basically translates to $||\mathbf{r} * \mathbf{g} + \mathbf{e} * \mathbf{f}||_\infty > q/4$ as $p = 2$ and the last term is much smaller than the first two.

The proposed parameters for ss-ntru-pke for the security level of NIST-V are shown in Table 2. The decoding error probability is estimated to be less than 2^{-80} in [47].

Table 2. Proposed ss-ntru-pke parameters.

N	q	p	$\mathcal{R}$	σ	ϵ	Security
1024	$2^{30} + 2^{13} + 1$	2	$\frac{\mathbb{Z}_q[x]}{x^N+1}$	724	$< 2^{-80}$	V

7.2 The Attack

We now follow the approach of the previous section and describe an attack. The detailed attack is shown in Algorithm 9, where a more efficient CCA2 version is adopted. We define an equivalence relation for two polynomials $u(x), v(x) \in \mathcal{R}$ if $u(x) = x^i \cdot v(x) \pmod{x^N + 1}$, or if $u(x) = -x^i \cdot v(x) \pmod{x^N + 1}$, for $i \in \mathbb{Z}$.

Algorithm 8. ss-ntru-pke.Decrypt

Input: Secret key $\mathbf{f}$, public key $\mathbf{h}$, ciphertext $\mathbf{c}$, and Param.
Output: *result*.
1) $\mathbf{m}' = \mathbf{f} * \mathbf{c} \pmod p$;
2) $\mathbf{t} = \mathbf{c} - \mathbf{m}'$;
3) $tseed = \text{Hash}(\mathbf{t})$;
4) Instantiate Sampler with $\mathcal{B}$ and *tseed*;
5) $\mathbf{m}_{mask} \leftarrow$ Sampler;
6) $\mathbf{m} = \mathbf{m}' + \mathbf{m}_{mask} \pmod p$;
7) $rseed = \text{Hash}(\mathbf{m}|\mathbf{h})$;
8) Instantiate Sampler with $\mathcal{X}_\sigma^N$ and *rseed*;
9) $\mathbf{r} \leftarrow$ Sampler;
10) $\mathbf{e} = p^{-1}(\mathbf{t} - \mathbf{r} * \mathbf{h})$;
11) **if** $||\mathbf{e}||_\infty$ *is big* **then**
 $result = \perp$;
else
 $result = \text{Extract}(\mathbf{m})$;

Algorithm 9. The CCA2 attack against ss-ntru-pke

Input: A number (say 2^{64}) of public keys.
Output: The secret polynomials $(\mathbf{f}, \mathbf{g})$ of one public key.
1) Collect messages/ciphertexts with special form for all public keys;
2) Submit them for decryption and determine a weak public key $\mathbf{h}$;
1') Prepare messages/ciphertexts with special form for this weak key $\mathbf{h}$;
2') Submit them for decryption and collect the decryption results;
3) Use statistical analysis to have a guess $(\hat{\mathbf{f}}, \hat{\mathbf{g}})$ close to the corresponding secret key $(\mathbf{f}, \mathbf{g})$;
4) Use lattice reduction algorithms to recover the secret key $(\mathbf{f}, \mathbf{g})$;

Attack step 1 – pre-computation.
We pick random messages $\mathbf{m}$ and generate corresponding $(\mathbf{r}, \mathbf{e}) = \mathbf{G}(\mathbf{m}, \mathbf{h})$ for a given public key $\mathbf{h}$. We keep only vectors $\mathbf{e}$ equivalent to a polynomial that has the first l (e.g., $l = 2$) positions with the same sign and each with size larger than $c \cdot \sigma$, where c is a constant determining the computational effort of finding such error vectors. These vectors form our chosen set $\mathcal{F}$.

We set $l = 2$ to illustrate the idea in a concrete attack. For one position, the probability that the entry is larger than $c\sigma$ is $1 - \mathrm{erf}(c/\sqrt{2})$. As we can start from any position, the probability to have two consecutive positions with the same sign and entries larger than $c\sigma$ is $p_{\mathbf{e}} = N * (1 - \mathrm{erf}(c/\sqrt{2}))^2/2$. If we set $p_{\mathbf{e}}$ to be 2^{-120}, then c can be as large as 9.193.

Attack step 2 – submit ciphertexts for decryption.
We then send the ciphertexts corresponding to the noise vectors in $\mathcal{F}$ to the decryption algorithm. If the targeted secret key $\mathbf{f}$ is also equivalent to a polynomial that has the first l (e.g., $l = 2$) positions with the same sign and each with size larger than $c_s \cdot \sigma$, where c_s is another constant, then the decoding errors can be detectable. We expect to collect several errors and store their corresponding error vectors $(\mathbf{r}, \mathbf{e})$. The probability to have two consecutive positions with the same sign and entries larger than $c_s\sigma$ is $p_{\mathbf{s}} = N * (1 - \mathrm{erf}(c_{\mathbf{s}}/\sqrt{2}))^2/2$. If we set $p_{\mathbf{s}}$ to be 2^{-64}, then $c_{\mathbf{s}}$ can be as large as 6.802.

If we run 2^{120} precomputation steps for each stored vector with the desired properties, then the overall complexity is 2^{248} since $p_{\mathbf{s}} = 2^{-64}$. Let C_1 denote $2 \cdot c_{\mathbf{s}} c\sigma^2$. We can then have a coefficient in $\mathbf{r}*\mathbf{g}+\mathbf{e}*\mathbf{f}$ whose absolute contribution from these two big entries is at least $C_1 = 2^{25.97}$. We consider the probabilistic behavior of the remaining $(2N - 2)$ positions. As the coefficients of $\mathbf{r}, \mathbf{g}, \mathbf{e}, \mathbf{f}$ are all sampled from a Gaussian distribution with mean 0 and stand deviation $\sigma = 724$, the expected norm of the rest vector in $\mathbf{f}, \mathbf{g}$ with $2N-2$ entries is about $\sqrt{2N-2} \cdot \sigma$. Given a public key, $\mathbf{f}, \mathbf{g}$ is fixed. Thus, this coefficient of $\mathbf{r}*\mathbf{g}+\mathbf{e}*\mathbf{f}$ can be approximated as $C_1 + \Phi_0$, where Φ_0 is Gaussian distribution with mean 0 and standard deviation $\sqrt{2N-2} \cdot \sigma^2$. As the error appears when this coefficient is larger than $q/4$, the error probability[3] can be approximated as

$$P_e = \left(1 - \mathrm{erf}(\frac{q/4 - C_1}{\sqrt{2(2N-2)\sigma^2}})\right) \cdot \frac{1}{2}.$$

We obtain a decoding error probability of $2^{-57.3}$ for this example.

Thus we can obtain about $2^{6.7}$ errors from the 2^{64} decryption trails.

An adaptive CCA attack. If we keep the previous setting, i.e., a CCA1 attack, the cost is larger than 2^{248}. However, we can adopt a much more powerful attack model, namely an adaptive CCA (CCA2) attack, consisting of two phases. In the first phase, the attacker spends half of his computational power to determine a weak key; in the later phase, he would put all his remaining resources into attacking this weak key.

To be more specific, we first prepare 2^{63} messages/ciphertexts for each of the 2^{64} public keys. Then we expect two errors corresponding to one key, which can be claimed as a weak key.

We can also reduce the precomputation work for each key to 2^{89}, if there are 2^{64} public keys. We have $c = 7.956$ and the error probability is $2^{-62.0}$, so we expect to have two errors in the testing stage. We then spend 2^{216} work on another precomputation to have 2^{63} messages with c to be 10.351, done only for this weak key. The error probability in the second phase is estimated as $2^{-53.0}$, so we can have 2^{10} errors. The overall complexity is 2^{217}.

Attack step 3 – statistical analysis.

In this step we will try to recover the secret $\mathbf{f}$. Let us first assume that $\mathbf{f}$ has its two big entries in the first two positions of the vector. Then the position in $\mathbf{e} * \mathbf{f}$ where the error occurs, denoted i_0, is the position where the two significant coefficients in $\mathbf{e}$ and those in $\mathbf{f}$ coincide. We now transform each $\mathbf{e}$ in such a way that its two big entries are also to be found in the first two positions. This is done by replacing $\mathbf{e}$ with the corresponding equivalent vector where the two big entries are in the first two positions. Assuming M decryption errors, this now gives us the following knowledge from the received decryption errors:

$$\sum_{i=2}^{N-1} e_i^{(j)} f_i + N_i^{(j)} > q/4 - 2 \cdot c_{\mathbf{s}} c \sigma^2,$$

for $j = 1 \ldots M$ and where $N^{(j)}$ denotes the remaining contribution to the noise. Finally we note that assuming that $\mathbf{f}$ has its two big entries in the first two positions is not a restriction, as such an $\mathbf{f}$ vector will just be an equivalent

[3] The error can occur in both directions. We omit the term $\left(1 - \mathrm{erf}(\frac{q/4+C_1}{\sqrt{2(2N-2)\sigma^2}})\right) \cdot \frac{1}{2}$ as it is negligible compared with $\left(1 - \mathrm{erf}(\frac{q/4-C_1}{\sqrt{2(2N-2)\sigma^2}})\right) \cdot \frac{1}{2}$ for C_1 a very big positive integer.

vector of the true $\mathbf{f}$. So we need only to recover $\mathbf{f}$ and then check all equivalent vectors.

We next show how to derive more knowledge of $\mathbf{f}, \mathbf{g}$ with statistical tools.

A heuristic approach. As we have assumed that the two big entries in $(\mathbf{f}, \mathbf{g})$ (or $(\mathbf{e}, \mathbf{r})$) are the first two entries, we use $\mathbf{K}$ (or $\mathbf{V}_i$ for $1 \leq i \leq M$) to denote a vector consisting of the remaining $2N - 2$ entries. Thus, the size of $\mathbf{K}$ (or $\mathbf{V_i}$) can be estimated as $\sqrt{(2N-2)}\sigma$.

We adopt the heuristic assumptions from [19] that all the errors are very close to the folding bound $q/4$, meaning that all the messages leading to an error belong to a hyperplane

$$\mathbf{V}_i \cdot \mathbf{K} = \frac{q}{4} - C_1,$$

where C_1 is the contribution from the two significant entries.

Thus, the mean vector $\hat{\mathbf{V}}$ of $\mathbf{V_i}$ should be close to a scaled vector of $\mathbf{K}$, i.e.,

$$\hat{\mathbf{V}} = \frac{\sum_{i=1}^{M} \mathbf{V}_i}{M} \approx \frac{q/4 - C_1}{\|\mathbf{K}\|^2}\mathbf{K}.$$

We can have an estimation $\hat{\mathbf{K}} = \frac{(2N-2)\sigma^2}{q/4-C_1}\hat{\mathbf{V}}$. If we round the entries of $\mathbf{K}$ to the nearest integer in $\mathbb{Z}_q$, we obtain an estimation $(\hat{\mathbf{f}}, \hat{\mathbf{g}})$ of the secret vector $(\mathbf{f}, \mathbf{g})$.

The remaining question is how good this estimation can be? We heuristically answer this question using the central limit theorem.

Each observation $\mathbf{V_i}$ with approximated norm $\sqrt{2N-2}\sigma$ can be viewed as the summation of the signal point

$$\frac{q/4 - C_1}{\|\mathbf{K}\|^2}\mathbf{K},$$

and a noise vector with squared norm

$$(2N-2)\sigma^2 - \frac{(q/4 - C_1)^2}{(2N-2)\sigma^2}.$$

By the central limit theorem, if we have M observations, then the squared norm (variance) of the noise can be reduced by a factor of M. Hence, the error norm should be

$$\sqrt{\frac{1}{M} \cdot \left((2N-2)\sigma^2 - \frac{(q/4 - C_1)^2}{(2N-2)\sigma^2}\right)}.$$

As we consider $\hat{\mathbf{K}}$ instead of $\hat{\mathbf{V}}$, the true error norm should be resized as

$$\frac{(2N-2)\sigma^2}{q/4 - C_1} \cdot \sqrt{\frac{1}{M} \cdot \left((2N-2)\sigma^2 - \frac{(q/4 - C_1)^2}{(2N-2)\sigma^2}\right)}. \quad (28)$$

Using this formula, we can have a candidate with error norm $0.169\sqrt{2N-2}\sigma$, assuming that 1024 errors have been collected.

Table 3. The simulated error rates v.s. the estimated error rates.

q	error rate -estimated-	error rate -simulated-
$q = 2^{29}$	$2^{-9.05}$	$2^{-9.19}$
$q = 2^{29} + 2^{26}$	$2^{-12.64}$	$2^{-12.96}$
$q = 2^{29} + 2^{27}$	$2^{-16.91}$	$2^{-17.09}$
$q = 2^{29} + 2^{27} + 2^{26} + 2^{25}$	$2^{-24.62}$	$2^{-24.57}$

Attack step 4 – lattice reduction.
If $(\Delta\mathbf{f}, \Delta\mathbf{g}) = (\mathbf{f}, \mathbf{g}) - (\hat{\mathbf{f}}, \hat{\mathbf{g}})$ is small, we can recover it using lattice reduction algorithms efficiently. Thus, we obtain the correct value of $(\mathbf{f}, \mathbf{g})$.

If we have the error size to be only $0.169\sqrt{2N-2}\sigma$, as assumed in the previous step, using the LWE estimator from Albrecht et al. [4], it takes about 2^{181} time and 2^{128} memory if one uses sieving to implement the SVP oracle in BKZ. Though the authors of [47] discussed about memory constraint for applying sieving in lattice-based cryptanalysis, we believe it is reasonable to assume for 2^{128} memory when considering a scheme targeting the classic 256-bit security level. Another possibility is to implement the SVP oracle using tuple sieving, further reducing the memory complexity to 2^{117}. The time complexity then increases to 2^{223}, but still far from achieving the claimed 256-security level.

7.3 Experimental Results

We have implemented some of the parts of the attack to check performance against theory. We have chosen exactly the same parameters in ss-ntru-pke as well as in the attack, except for the q value, which in the experiment was set to the values shown in Table 3. The reason being that is we wanted to lower the decryption error rate so that simulation was possible.

We put two consecutive entries in $\mathbf{f}$ each of size $6.2 \cdot \sigma$ and we generated error vectors with two large positive entries each of size $9.2 \cdot \sigma$. For such choice, we first verified the decryption error probabilities, as seen in Table 3. These match the theoretical results well.

Table 4. The simulated error norm v.s. the estimated error norm. ($M = 1024$)

q	error norm $/(\sqrt{2N-2}\sigma)$ -estimated-	error norm $/(\sqrt{2N-2}\sigma)$ -simulated-
$q = 2^{29}$	0.487	0.472
$q = 2^{29} + 2^{26}$	0.391	0.360
$q = 2^{29} + 2^{27}$	0.326	0.302
$q = 2^{29} + 2^{27} + 2^{26} + 2^{25}$	0.261	0.250

Table 5. The simulated error norm v.s. the estimated error norm. ($q = 2^{29} + 2^{27} + 2^{26} + 2^{25}$)

M	error norm $/(\sqrt{2N} - 2\sigma)$ -estimated-	-simulated-
$M = 256$	0.522	0.490
$M = 512$	0.369	0.348
$M = 1024$	0.261	0.250
$M = 1536$	0.213	0.212

For each choice of q we then collected up to $M = 2^{10}+2^9 = 1536$ error vectors and processed them in a statistical analysis step, to get a good approximation of $(\mathbf{f}, \mathbf{g})$. As the heuristic approach described, we first created an approximation of $(\mathbf{f}, \mathbf{g})$, say denoted by $(\hat{\mathbf{f}}, \hat{\mathbf{g}})$, by simply computing $\hat{f}_i = E \cdot \frac{\sum_{j=0}^{M-1} e_i^{(j)}}{M}$ as the value in the ith position. Here E is a constant that makes the norm of the vector to be as the expected norm of $\mathbf{f}$. Clearly, this is a very simple way of exploring the dependence between f_i and e_i, but still it seems to be sufficient.

We have plotted the simulated error norms for various q and M in Figure 9. Furthermore, we show in Tables 4 and 5 the comparison between the simulated error norms and the estimated error norms according to Eq. 28.

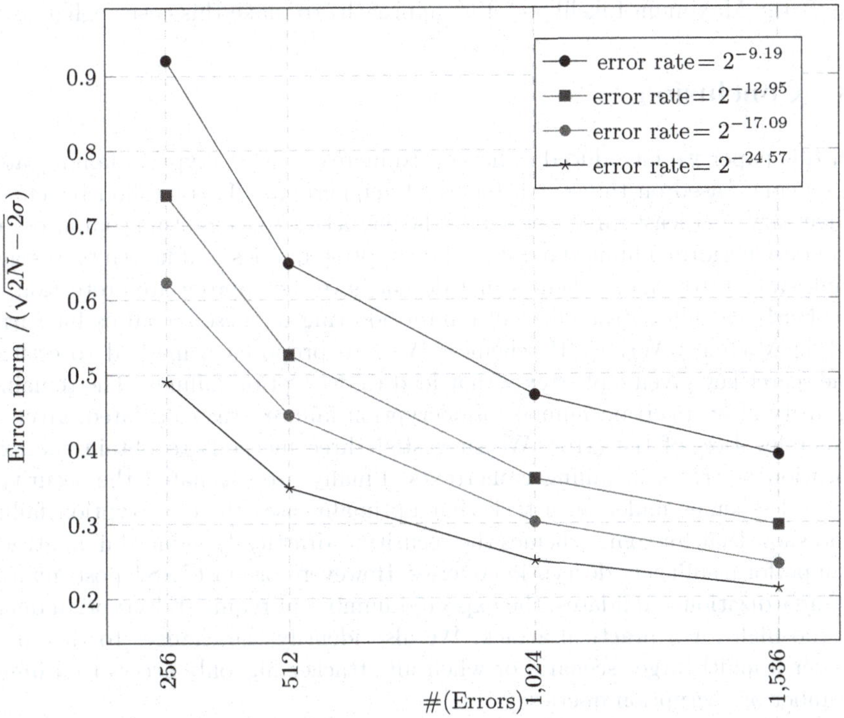

Fig. 9. Error norm as a function of the number of collected error vectors.

In the prior table, M is fixed to 1024 and q varies, while in the latter table, q is fixed to $2^{29}+2^{27}+2^{26}+2^{25}$ and M varies. We see that in all the cases, the simulated data match the estimated data well, though the simulation seems always better than the estimation, i.e., with smaller error norms. Another observation from Table 5 is that the estimation using the central limit theorem becomes more accurate when M becomes larger, which is also very reasonable.

7.4 Summarizing the Attack

The best attack is a CCA2 type attack where we in precomputation use $2^{89+63} = 2^{152}$ operations to derive 2^{63} special ciphertexts that are submitted for decryption. With probability 2^{-64} the secret $\mathbf{f}$ has the desired property of two consecutive big entries. If so, we will most likely see several decoding errors and such a weak key has been detected. When the weak key has been detected, we perform yet another precomputation that uses 2^{216} operations to derive 2^{63} additional special ciphertexts again submitted for decryption. We receive in expectation 1024 decryption errors and the knowledge from the error vectors will allow us to reconstruct $\mathbf{f}$ without too much trouble using lattice reduction algorithms, as experimental results strongly indicated. The overall complexity is thus approximately 2^{217} if the SVP oracle in BKZ is implemented via lattice sieving. Actually, the cost of the lattice reduction algorithms in the final stage is not the bottleneck, since we can employ other powerful statistical tools in Step 3 (e.g., the Maximum Likelihood Test approach) to make this cost negligible.

8 Conclusion

In this paper we introduced a method to increase the decryption failure rate of a scheme, based on the search for 'weak' ciphertexts. This method benefits an adversary in at least three scenarios: if he has access to a quantum computer, if he can only perform a limited number of decryption queries or if he wants to stage a multi-target attack on schemes that do not have the appropriate protection. We explicitly calculated the effect of failure boosting in these scenarios for various (Ring/Module-)LWE/LWR schemes. We also proposed a method to estimate the secret key given ciphertexts that lead to decryption failures. The remaining security after a certain number of decryption failures was calculated, given the exact location of the error. We suggested three methods to obtain the exact location of errors in failing ciphertexts. Finally, we estimated the security of several schemes under an attack that optimally uses these decryption failures and show that for some schemes the security is drastically reduced if an attacker can perform sufficient decryption queries. However, for most NIST post-quantum standardization candidates, the expected number of required decryption queries is too high for a practical attack. We also identify the changes to this attack under a multi-target scenario or when an attacker has only access to a limited number of decryption queries.

We further proposed a generic weak-key attack model against lattice-based schemes, which is slightly different from the previous attack, based on the observation that the error probability can be much higher for certain 'weak' keys. We applied this model to attacking ss-ntru-pke, a version in the NTRUEncrypt submission to the NIST Post-Quantum Standardization Process. Specifically, we have presented an adaptive CCA attack on the claimed 256-bit classic security level (NIST-V) of ss-ntru-pke. This attacking idea can be treated as extension of reaction attacks [16, 22] that already jeopardize the CCA security of MDPC and LDPC based crypto-systems.

Acknowledgements. The authors would like to thank Tancrède Lepoint and the anonymous reviewers for their helpful comments. They would also like to thank Andreas Hülsing for interesting discussions. This work was supported in part by the Research Council KU Leuven: C16/15/058, by the European Commission through the Horizon 2020 research and innovation programme Cathedral ERC Advanced Grant 695305, by the Research Council KU Leuven grants C14/18/067 and STG/17/019, by the Norwegian Research Council (Grant No. 247742/070), by the Swedish Research Council (Grant No. 2015-04528), by the Wallenberg AI, Autonomous Systems and Software Program (WASP) funded by the Knut and Alice Wallenberg Foundation, and by the Swedish Foundation for Strategic Research (SSF) project RIT17-0005.

References

1. NIST Post-Quantum Cryptography Forum. https://groups.google.com/a/list.nist.gov/forum/#!forum/pqc-forum. Accessed 11 Jan 2019
2. Submission requirements and evaluation criteria for the post-quantum cryptography standardization process (2016). https://csrc.nist.gov/CSRC/media/Projects/Post-Quantum-Cryptography/documents/call-for-proposals-final-dec-2016.pdf
3. Albrecht, M., Player, R., Scott, S.: On the concrete hardness of learning with errors. J. Math. Cryptol. **9**, 169–203 (2015)
4. Albrecht, M.R., et al.: Estimate all the LWE, NTRU schemes! Cryptology ePrint Archive, Report 2018/331 (2018). https://eprint.iacr.org/2018/331
5. Alkim, E., Ducas, L., Pöppelmann, T., Schwabe, P.: Post-quantum key exchange – a new hope. In: USENIX Security 2016 (2016)
6. Baan, H., et al.: Round2: KEM and PKE based on GLWR. Cryptology ePrint Archive, Report 2017/1183 (2017). https://eprint.iacr.org/2017/1183
7. Banerjee, A., Peikert, C., Rosen, A.: Pseudorandom functions and lattices. In: Pointcheval, D., Johansson, T. (eds.) EUROCRYPT 2012. LNCS, vol. 7237, pp. 719–737. Springer, Heidelberg (2012). https://doi.org/10.1007/978-3-642-29011-4_42
8. Bernstein, D.J., Bruinderink, L.G., Lange, T., Panny, L.: HILA5 pindakaas: on the CCA security of lattice-based encryption with error correction. In: Joux, A., Nitaj, A., Rachidi, T. (eds.) AFRICACRYPT 2018. LNCS, vol. 10831, pp. 203–216. Springer, Cham (2018). https://doi.org/10.1007/978-3-319-89339-6_12
9. Boldyreva, A., Degabriele, J.P., Paterson, K.G., Stam, M.: On symmetric encryption with distinguishable decryption failures. In: Moriai, S. (ed.) FSE 2013. LNCS, vol. 8424, pp. 367–390. Springer, Heidelberg (2014). https://doi.org/10.1007/978-3-662-43933-3_19

10. Bos, J., et al.: CRYSTALS – Kyber: a CCA-secure module-lattice-based KEM. Cryptology ePrint Archive, Report 2017/634 (2017). http://eprint.iacr.org/2017/634
11. Brakerski, Z., Langlois, A., Peikert, C., Regev, O., Stehlé, D.: Classical hardness of learning with errors. In: Boneh, D., Roughgarden, T., Feigenbaum, J. (eds.) 45th Annual ACM Symposium on Theory of Computing, 1–4 June 2013, pp. 575–584. ACM Press, Palo Alto (2013)
12. Cheon, J.H., Kim, D., Lee, J., Song, Y.: Lizard: cut off the tail! Practical post-quantum public-key encryption from LWE and LWR. Cryptology ePrint Archive, Report 2016/1126 (2016). http://eprint.iacr.org/2016/1126
13. D'Anvers, J.P., Karmakar, A., Roy, S.S., Vercauteren, F.: Saber: module-LWR based key exchange, CPA-secure encryption and CCA-secure KEM. In: Joux, A., Nitaj, A., Rachidi, T. (eds.) AFRICACRYPT 2018. LNCS, vol. 10831, pp. 282–305. Springer, Cham (2018). https://doi.org/10.1007/978-3-319-89339-6_16
14. D'Anvers, J.P., Vercauteren, F., Verbauwhede, I.: On the impact of decryption failures on the security of LWE/LWR based schemes. Cryptology ePrint Archive, Report 2018/1089 (2018). https://eprint.iacr.org/2018/1089
15. Ding, J., Alsayigh, S., Saraswathy, R.V., Fluhrer, S., Lin, X.: Leakage of signal function with reused keys in RLWE key exchange. Cryptology ePrint Archive, Report 2016/1176 (2016). http://eprint.iacr.org/2016/1176
16. Fabsic, T., Hromada, V., Stankovski, P., Zajac, P., Guo, Q., Johansson, T.: A reaction attack on the QC-LDPC McEliece cryptosystem. Cryptology ePrint Archive, Report 2017/494 (2017). http://eprint.iacr.org/2017/494
17. Fluhrer, S.: Cryptanalysis of ring-LWE based key exchange with key share reuse. Cryptology ePrint Archive, Report 2016/085 (2016). https://eprint.iacr.org/2016/085
18. Fujisaki, E., Okamoto, T.: Secure integration of asymmetric and symmetric encryption schemes. In: Wiener, M.J. (ed.) CRYPTO 1999. LNCS, vol. 1666, pp. 537–554. Springer, Heidelberg (1999). https://doi.org/10.1007/3-540-48405-1_34
19. Gama, N., Nguyen, P.Q.: New chosen-ciphertext attacks on NTRU. In: Okamoto, T., Wang, X. (eds.) PKC 2007. LNCS, vol. 4450, pp. 89–106. Springer, Heidelberg (2007). https://doi.org/10.1007/978-3-540-71677-8_7
20. Grover, L.K.: A fast quantum mechanical algorithm for database search. In: Proceedings of the Twenty-Eighth Annual ACM Symposium on Theory of Computing, pp. 212–219. STOC 1996. ACM, New York (1996). https://doi.org/10.1145/237814.237866
21. Guo, Q., Johansson, T., Nilsson, A.: A generic attack on lattice-based schemes using decryption errors with application to ss-ntru-pke. Cryptology ePrint Archive, Report 2019/043 (2019). https://eprint.iacr.org/2019/043
22. Guo, Q., Johansson, T., Stankovski, P.: A key recovery attack on MDPC with CCA security using decoding errors. In: Cheon, J.H., Takagi, T. (eds.) ASIACRYPT 2016. Part I. LNCS, vol. 10031, pp. 789–815. Springer, Heidelberg (2016). https://doi.org/10.1007/978-3-662-53887-6_29
23. Hall, C., Goldberg, I., Schneier, B.: Reaction attacks against several public-key cryptosystem. In: Varadharajan, V., Mu, Y. (eds.) ICICS 1999. LNCS, vol. 1726, pp. 2–12. Springer, Heidelberg (1999). https://doi.org/10.1007/978-3-540-47942-0_2
24. Hoffstein, J., Silverman, J.H.: NTRU Cryptosystems Technical Report Report# 016, Version 1 Title: Protecting NTRU Against Chosen Ciphertext and Reaction Attacks

25. Hofheinz, D., Hövelmanns, K., Kiltz, E.: A modular analysis of the Fujisaki-Okamoto transformation. In: Kalai, Y., Reyzin, L. (eds.) TCC 2017. Part I. LNCS, vol. 10677, pp. 341–371. Springer, Cham (2017). https://doi.org/10.1007/978-3-319-70500-2_12
26. Howgrave-Graham, N., et al.: The impact of decryption failures on the security of NTRU encryption. In: Boneh, D. (ed.) CRYPTO 2003. LNCS, vol. 2729, pp. 226–246. Springer, Heidelberg (2003). https://doi.org/10.1007/978-3-540-45146-4_14
27. Howgrave-Graham, N., Silverman, J.H., Singer, A., Whyte, W.: NAEP: provable security in the presence of decryption failures. Cryptology ePrint Archive, Report 2003/172 (2003). http://eprint.iacr.org/2003/172
28. Jaulmes, É., Joux, A.: A chosen-ciphertext attack against NTRU. In: Bellare, M. (ed.) CRYPTO 2000. LNCS, vol. 1880, pp. 20–35. Springer, Heidelberg (2000). https://doi.org/10.1007/3-540-44598-6_2
29. Jiang, H., Zhang, Z., Chen, L., Wang, H., Ma, Z.: Post-quantum IND-CCA-secure KEM without additional hash. Cryptology ePrint Archive, Report 2017/1096 (2017). https://eprint.iacr.org/2017/1096
30. Langlois, A., Stehlé, D.: Worst-case to average-case reductions for module lattices. Des. Codes Crypt. **75**(3), 565–599 (2015). https://doi.org/10.1007/s10623-014-9938-4
31. Lu, X., Liu, Y., Jia, D., Xue, H., He, J., Zhang, Z.: LAC. Technical report, National Institute of Standards and Technology (2017). https://csrc.nist.gov/projects/post-quantum-cryptography/round-1-submissions
32. Lyubashevsky, V., Peikert, C., Regev, O.: On ideal lattices and learning with errors over rings. In: Gilbert, H. (ed.) EUROCRYPT 2010. LNCS, vol. 6110, pp. 1–23. Springer, Heidelberg (2010). https://doi.org/10.1007/978-3-642-13190-5_1
33. Naehrig, M., et al.: Frodokem. Technical report, National Institute of Standards and Technology (2017). https://frodokem.org/files/FrodoKEM-specification-20171130.pdf
34. Nilsson, A., Johansson, T., Stankovski, P.: Error amplification in code-based cryptography. IACR Trans. Crypt. Hardw. Embed. Syst. **2019**(1), 238–258 (2019). https://doi.org/10.13154/tches.v2019.i1.238-258
35. Peikert, C.: Public-key cryptosystems from the worst-case shortest vector problem: extended abstract. In: Proceedings of the Forty-first Annual ACM Symposium on Theory of Computing, pp. 333–342. STOC 2009. ACM, New York (2009). https://doi.org/10.1145/1536414.1536461
36. Regev, O.: On lattices, learning with errors, random linear codes, and cryptography. In: Gabow, H.N., Fagin, R. (eds.) 37th Annual ACM Symposium on Theory of Computing, 22–24 May 2005, pp. 84–93. ACM Press, Baltimore (2005)
37. Saarinen, M.J.O.: HILA5. Technical report, National Institute of Standards and Technology (2017). https://csrc.nist.gov/projects/post-quantum-cryptography/round-1-submissions
38. Saito, T., Xagawa, K., Yamakawa, T.: Tightly-secure key-encapsulation mechanism in the quantum random oracle model. Cryptology ePrint Archive, Report 2017/1005 (2017). https://eprint.iacr.org/2017/1005
39. Schanck, J.M., Hulsing, A., Rijneveld, J., Schwabe, P.: NTRU-HRSS-KEM. Technical report, National Institute of Standards and Technology (2017). https://csrc.nist.gov/projects/post-quantum-cryptography/round-1-submissions
40. Schwabe, P., et al.: CRYSTALS-Kyber. Technical report, National Institute of Standards and Technology (2017). https://csrc.nist.gov/projects/post-quantum-cryptography/round-1-submissions

41. Schwabe, P., et al.: Newhope. Technical report, National Institute of Standards and Technology (2017). https://csrc.nist.gov/projects/post-quantum-cryptography/round-1-submissions
42. Seo, M., Park, J.H., Lee, D.H., Kim, S., Lee., S.J.: Emblem and R.Emblem. Technical report, National Institute of Standards and Technology (2017). https://csrc.nist.gov/projects/post-quantum-cryptography/round-1-submissions
43. Smart, N.P., et al.: LIMA. Technical report, National Institute of Standards and Technology (2017). https://csrc.nist.gov/projects/post-quantum-cryptography/round-1-submissions
44. Stehlé, D., Steinfeld, R.: Making NTRU as secure as worst-case problems over ideal lattices. In: Paterson, K.G. (ed.) EUROCRYPT 2011. LNCS, vol. 6632, pp. 27–47. Springer, Heidelberg (2011). https://doi.org/10.1007/978-3-642-20465-4_4
45. Szepieniec, A.: Ramstake. Technical report, National Institute of Standards and Technology (2017). https://csrc.nist.gov/projects/post-quantum-cryptography/round-1-submissions
46. Targhi, E.E., Unruh, D.: Post-quantum security of the Fujisaki-Okamoto and OAEP transforms. In: Hirt, M., Smith, A. (eds.) TCC 2016. LNCS, vol. 9986, pp. 192–216. Springer, Heidelberg (2016). https://doi.org/10.1007/978-3-662-53644-5_8
47. Zhang, Z., Chen, C., Hoffstein, J., Whyte, W.: NTRUEncrypt. Technical report, National Institute of Standards and Technology (2017). https://csrc.nist.gov/projects/post-quantum-cryptography/round-1-submissions

Reducing the Key Size of McEliece Cryptosystem from Automorphism-induced Goppa Codes via Permutations

Zhe Li[1(✉)], Chaoping Xing[1], and Sze Ling Yeo[2]

[1] School of Physical and Mathematical Sciences, Nanyang Technological University, Singapore, Singapore
lzonline01@gmail.com, xingcp@ntu.edu.sg
[2] Institute for Infocomm Research (I2R), Singapore, Singapore
slyeo@i2r.a-star.edu.sg

Abstract. In this paper, we propose a new general construction to reduce the public key size of McEliece cryptosystems constructed from automorphism-induced Goppa codes. In particular, we generalize the ideas of automorphism-induced Goppa codes by considering nontrivial subsets of automorphism groups to construct Goppa codes with a nice block structure. By considering additive and multiplicative automorphism subgroups, we provide explicit constructions to demonstrate our technique. We show that our technique can be applied to automorphism-induced Goppa codes based cryptosystems to further reduce their key sizes.

1 Introduction

Since the introduction of public-key cryptography in the 1970's, all the public-key cryptosystems that have been proposed fall into two broad categories, namely, the classical schemes and the quantum-resistant schemes. The former category comprises most of the schemes used today. They are primarily built up from computational number theoretic problems including integer factoring problem and discrete logarithm problem in different groups. While such schemes are generally believed to be secure against classical computers, their security has been shown to be vulnerable to quantum algorithms such as the Shor algorithm [34].

On the other hand, the class of quantum-resistant schemes, as the name implies, includes schemes whose security is not threatened by existing quantum algorithms. Such schemes are further classified by their underlying mathematical problems into various classes including code-based cryptosystems, lattice-based cryptosystems, hash-based cryptosystems, multivariate cryptosystems or schemes based on elliptic curve isogenies [8]. Among these classes, the code-based cryptography is one of the oldest, dating back to the work of McEliece in 1978 [27].

D. Lin and K. Sako (Eds.): PKC 2019, LNCS 11443, pp. 599–617, 2019.
https://doi.org/10.1007/978-3-030-17259-6_20

Essentially, code-based cryptography refers to the class of schemes whose security relies on hard problems in coding theory, such as the general decoding problem. Concretely, the classical code-based encryption scheme works as follows. Let M be a generator matrix of an $[n, k, 2t+1]$-linear code C with a fast decoder. Let S be a $k \times k$ invertible matrix and let P be an $n \times n$ permutation matrix. Let $M' = SMP$. Then, the public key is M' while the secret key comprises the matrices S, M and P. To encrypt a message $\mathbf{x}$, one chooses an error $\mathbf{e}$ with Hamming weight t and computes $\mathbf{c} = \mathbf{x}M' + \mathbf{e}$. To recover $\mathbf{x}$, one first computes $\mathbf{c}' = \mathbf{c}P^{-1}$. Use the decoder with respect to M to decode $\mathbf{c}'$ to obtain $\mathbf{c}'' \in C$. Since $\mathbf{c}'' = \mathbf{x}S$, one can recover $\mathbf{x}$ using S^{-1}.

An alternative but equivalent code-based encryption scheme was proposed by Niederreiter in [31] in which the parity-check matrix instead of the generator matrix was used. In this scheme, a message is converted into a vector of Hamming weight t and encryption is performed by multiplying this vector with the parity check matrix. Once again, decryption is accomplished via a fast decoder while the security is based on the difficulty of the syndrome decoding problem.

The above descriptions only outline the essential ideas of code-based schemes. Variants of these schemes have been proposed to achieve different forms of security such as the CCA2 security [20]. The main advantage of code-based cryptosystems lies in its efficient operations leading to very efficient encryption and decryption. As such, it continues to draw much interest to design new code-based cryptographic primitives. For instance, in the recent NIST submissions, several proposals on code-based key encapsulation mechanisms were proposed [1], including [2,3]. Essentially, any code C used in the schemes must satisfy the main property, namely, it has an efficient decoder using a particular matrix M but multiplying this matrix with a random matrix transforms the corresponding code into a random code. In addition, the code used should not exhibit any structural weakness to recover the private key. The first family of codes suggested by McEliece in [27] is the family of Goppa codes. Subsequently, other families of codes are proposed, including algebraic geometric codes [19], Reed-Muller codes [35], Reed Solomon codes [31], and more recently, MDPC codes [30]. While all these codes have an efficient decoding algorithm, the structures exhibited by some of the codes make them vulnerable to other attacks. Ideally, one hopes to construct public keys with reasonably short lengths such that the underlying structures are properly concealed. Quasi-cyclic MDPC codes are more recent designs that seem promising to achieve these two goals simultaneously. On the other hand, codes such as Reed-Muller codes and Reed Solomon codes, while providing short public keys, have all been broken [23,28]. In terms of security, Goppa codes seem to be the strongest as they have withstood structural attacks since they were first proposed by McEliece. However, they suffer from the disadvantage of having large public key sizes.

As such, it is an interesting problem to consider sub-classes of Goppa codes to better balance the security and public key size requirements. One common approach adopted is to employ quasi-cyclic or quasi-dyadic Goppa codes [7,29] or more generally, codes with a nontrivial automorphism group [6]. Indeed, in [14], the authors showed that existing quasi-cyclic and quasi-dyadic constructions are induced from nontrivial automorphism subgroups of the rational function field. The main advantage to use a code with a nontrivial automorphism group $\mathcal{G}$ is that there exists a subset of basis codewords such that this subset together with their permutations induced by $\mathcal{G}$ form the whole basis of the code. As such, this allows one to use the subset of codewords as the public key instead of the entire basis, thereby reducing the size of the public key. Nonetheless, the size reduction leads to a trade-off with respect to its resistance to structural attacks. In particular, it was shown in [4,14,15] that the public/private key pair of such codes is equivalent to a public/private key pair of another code with smaller parameters. Algebraic cryptanalysis can then be performed on the corresponding codes with smaller parameters and successful attacks following this approach were carried out in [16,17]. As such, one must select the parameters carefully in order to balance the trade-off and to achieve the desired security level [3].

In this paper, we generalize the approach of automorphism-induced code constructions to seek for Goppa codes with compact public key sizes. Instead of finding codes with nontrivial automorphism groups, we will construct Goppa codes that are a union of different subcodes and their permutations. Specifically, we solve the following problem.

Problem 1: Construct Goppa codes C that contain a subset S of linearly independent codewords satisfying the following properties:

- For each $\mathbf{c} \in S$, there exists a set of permutations $\mathcal{P}_{\mathbf{c}}$ such that $\sigma(\mathbf{c}) \in C$ for all $\sigma \in \mathcal{P}_{\mathbf{c}}$;
- $B = \bigcup_{\mathbf{c} \in S} \left(\bigcup_{\sigma \in \mathcal{P}_{\mathbf{c}}} \sigma(\mathbf{c}) \right)$ is a basis of C.

By finding such codes C, one can then use the set S as its public key. Observe that the automorphism-induced codes including the quasi-cyclic and quasi-dyadic codes are examples of the codes we seek. In these cases, all the $\mathcal{P}_{\mathbf{c}}$ are identical and equal to the automorphism group of the code. While this construction allows one to use the set S as the public key, the automorphism group can be exploited to reduce the security of the scheme with respect to algebraic attacks.

This paper seeks to provide other classes of Goppa codes that satisfy the conditions of Problem 1. In our constructions, the sets $\mathcal{P}_{\mathbf{c}}$ are no longer automorphism groups of the codes. Instead, we consider only subsets of permutations of each codeword. In this way, our codes become resistant to the algebraic attacks of [4,14,15] as the folding operation does not lead to an invariant subcode (see Sect. 2.3 for the relevant definitions). Moreover, our construction is generic in the sense that it can be applied to reduce the key size of existing code-based schemes from Goppa codes.

In this paper, we first provide conditions for permutations of codewords to lie in the code. We then construct codes with a partial quasi-cyclic and quasi-dyadic structure. We demonstrate that the codes we construct are not vulnerable to the algebraic attacks of [14,16,17]. Finally, we apply our technique to automorphism-induced Goppa codes to obtain compact and secure Goppa codes. We show with concrete examples that our technique can reduce the public key sizes in BigQuake [3] by at least half.

The subsequent sections are structured as follows. First, we recall Goppa codes and their permutations. We also review automorphism-induced Goppa codes and the associated algebraic attacks. We then present our new construction that exploits subsets of automorphism groups to yield codes with a nice permutation structure. In Sect. 4, we provide a security discussion of our construction. Finally, we present an algorithm that combines our technique with existing quasi-cyclic constructions to obtain Goppa codes with reduced public key sizes.

2 Preliminaries

In this paper, we always assume that $q = 2^m$ for an integer $m \geq 2$. Let $\mathbb{F}_q$ denote the finite field with q elements.

2.1 Goppa Codes

We first review the definition of Goppa codes [27]. In the following, we present a construction that is relevant for this work.

Definition 1 (Goppa code). *Let t and n be positive integers with $t < n \leq q$. Let $g(x) \in \mathbb{F}_q[x]$ be a polynomial of degree t and let $L = \{\gamma_1, \cdots, \gamma_n\}$ be an ordered set containing n distinct elements of $\mathbb{F}_q$ such that $g(\gamma_i) \neq 0$ for $1 \leq i \leq n$. The Goppa code $\Gamma(L, g)$ is defined as*

$$\Gamma(L,g) = \left\{ \mathbf{c} = (c_1, \cdots, c_n) \in \mathbb{F}_2^n : \sum_{i=1}^{n} \frac{c_i}{x - \gamma_i} \equiv 0 \pmod{g(x)} \right\}.$$

The polynomial $g(x)$ is called the Goppa polynomial. When $g(x)$ is irreducible, $\Gamma(L, g)$ is called an irreducible Goppa code. In this paper, we call the ordered set L the Goppa support.

Some of the main properties of Goppa codes are summarized below.

Remark 1. (i) The Goppa code $\Gamma(L, g)$ is a subfield subcode of generalized Reed-Solomon codes. In fact, the class of Goppa codes is a special case of alternant codes.

(ii) The Goppa code $\Gamma(L, g)$ is a binary linear code and has dimension at least $n - mt$, and minimum distance at least $t + 1$.

(iii) If $g(x)$ has no multiple roots, then $\Gamma(L, g)$ has minimum distance at least $2t + 1$. In particular, an irreducible Goppa code $\Gamma(L, g)$ has minimum distance at least $2t + 1$.

Given a Goppa support L and a Goppa polynomial $g(x)$, a parity-check matrix of $\Gamma(L, g)$ is given by $H = VD$, where

$$V = \begin{pmatrix} 1 & 1 & \dots & 1 \\ \gamma_1 & \gamma_2 & \cdots & \gamma_n \\ \gamma_1^2 & \gamma_2^2 & \cdots & \gamma_n^2 \\ \dots & \dots & \dots & \dots \\ \gamma_1^{t-1} & \gamma_2^{t-1} & \dots & \gamma_n^{t-1} \end{pmatrix} \quad (1)$$

and

$$D = \mathrm{diag}(1/g(\gamma_1), 1/g(\gamma_2), \dots, 1/g(\gamma_n)). \quad (2)$$

One of the nice properties of Goppa codes lies in its efficient decodability. In particular, there exists a polynomial-time decoding algorithm for Goppa codes [24] that can decode up to t errors.

Fix $a \in \mathbb{F}_q^*, b \in \mathbb{F}_q, c \in \mathbb{F}_q^*$. For a Goppa support $L \subset \mathbb{F}_q$, let $L' = \{a^{-1}x - b : x \in L\}$. Then, for any $g \in \mathbb{F}_q[x]$, it is easy to check that the Goppa codes $\Gamma(L, g)$ and $\Gamma(L', cg(ax+b))$ are equal. Consequently, for any Goppa code, one can find at least $q(q-1)$ different Goppa supports and monic Goppa polynomials that define the given code.

The following result follows directly from the definition of Goppa codes [24].

Lemma 1. *Fix $L \subset \mathbb{F}_q$. For any two polynomials $g_1(x)$ and $g_2(x)$, one has:*

$$\Gamma(L, g_1(x)) \cap \Gamma(L, g_2(x)) = \Gamma(L, \mathrm{lcm}(g_1(x), g_2(x))).$$

2.2 Permutations of Goppa Codes

In this subsection, we take a look at permutations of Goppa codes.

For a positive integer n, let $\mathcal{S}_n$ denote the symmetric group on n symbols. We let $\mathcal{S}_n$ act on the vector space $\mathbb{F}_2^n$ via

$$\sigma(\mathbf{c}) = \sigma(c_1, \cdots, c_n) = (c_{\sigma(1)}, \cdots, c_{\sigma(n)})$$

for $\sigma \in \mathcal{S}_n$ and $\mathbf{c} = (c_1, \cdots, c_n) \in \mathbb{F}_2^n$. Then, $\sigma(C) = \{\sigma(\mathbf{c}) : \mathbf{c} \in C\}$ is also a code with the same parameters as the code C.

Definition 2. *The automorphism group of a code $C \subseteq \mathbb{F}_2^n$ is defined as*

$$\mathrm{Aut}(C) = \{\sigma \in \mathcal{S}_n : \sigma(\mathbf{c}) \in C \text{ for all } \mathbf{c} \in C\}.$$

In particular, $\sigma \in \mathrm{Aut}(C)$ if and only if $\sigma(C) = C$.

We next show that there exist permutations $\sigma \in \mathcal{S}_n$ such that $\sigma(C)$ is itself a Goppa code.

Let $F = \mathbb{F}_q(x)$ denote the rational function field over $\mathbb{F}_q$. We denote by $\mathrm{Aut}(F/\mathbb{F}_q)$ the automorphism group of F over $\mathbb{F}_q$, i.e.,

$$\mathrm{Aut}(F/\mathbb{F}_q) = \{\sigma : F \to F, \text{ where } \sigma \text{ is an } \mathbb{F}_q\text{-automorphism of } F\}. \quad (3)$$

It is clear that an automorphism $\sigma \in \mathrm{Aut}(F/\mathbb{F}_q)$ is uniquely determined by $\sigma(x)$. It is well known that every automorphism $\sigma \in \mathrm{Aut}(F/\mathbb{F}_q)$ is given by

$$\sigma(x) = \frac{ax+b}{cx+d} \tag{4}$$

for some constants $a, b, c, d \in \mathbb{F}_q$ with $ad - bc \neq 0$ (see [11]). Denote by $\mathrm{GL}_2(q)$ the general linear group of 2×2 invertible matrices over $\mathbb{F}_q$. Thus, every matrix $A = \begin{pmatrix} a & b \\ c & d \end{pmatrix} \in \mathrm{GL}_2(q)$ induces an automorphism of F given by (4). Two matrices of $\mathrm{GL}_2(q)$ induce the same automorphism of F if and only if they belong to the same coset of $Z(\mathrm{GL}_2(q))$, where $Z(\mathrm{GL}_2(q))$ stands for the center $\{aI_2 : a \in \mathbb{F}_q^*\}$ of $\mathrm{GL}_2(q)$. This implies that $\mathrm{Aut}(F/\mathbb{F}_q)$ is isomorphic to the projective linear group $\mathrm{PGL}_2(q) := \mathrm{GL}_2(q)/Z(\mathrm{GL}_2(q))$. Thus, we can identify $\mathrm{Aut}(F/\mathbb{F}_q)$ with $\mathrm{PGL}_2(q)$.

Consider the subgroup of $\mathrm{PGL}_2(q)$,

$$\mathrm{AGL}_2(q) := \left\{ \begin{pmatrix} a & b \\ 0 & 1 \end{pmatrix} : a \in \mathbb{F}_q^*, b \in \mathbb{F}_q \right\}. \tag{5}$$

$\mathrm{AGL}_2(q)$ is called the affine linear group. Every element $A = \begin{pmatrix} a & b \\ 0 & 1 \end{pmatrix} \in \mathrm{AGL}_2(q)$ defines an affine automorphism $\sigma_{a,b}(x) = ax + b$.

The following lemma is straightforward to verify.

Lemma 2. *Let $b \in \mathbb{F}_q$. Then,*

$$\mathrm{ord}(\sigma_{a,b}) = \begin{cases} \mathrm{ord}(a) & \text{if } a \neq 1, \\ 2 & \text{otherwise} \end{cases}$$

We recall the definition of a group action on a set and some of its basic properties.

Definition 3 ([22]). *A group $\mathcal{G}$ action on a set S is a mapping from $\mathcal{G} \times S$ to S to satisfying the following properties:*

(i) $g_1 \cdot (g_2 \cdot s) = (g_1 g_2) \cdot s$ for all $g_1, g_2 \in G, s \in S$,
(ii) $1 \cdot s = s$ for all $s \in S$.

Definition 4. *Let $\mathcal{G}$ be a group acting on a set S. The equivalence class $\{g \cdot s : g \in \mathcal{G}\}$ is called the orbit of $\mathcal{G}$ containing s.*

Remark 2. (i) The orbits of two different elements in S are either equal or disjoint. In particular, S is partitioned into a disjoint union of orbits.
(ii) For $s \in S$, let $\mathcal{G}_s$ denote the stabilizer subgroup of $\mathcal{G}$ that fixes s under the group action, that is $\mathcal{G}_s = \{g : g \in \mathcal{G} | g \cdot s = s\}$. Then, the orbit containing s has $|\mathcal{G}|/|\mathcal{G}_s|$ different elements.

For any element $g \in \mathcal{G}$, the action of g induces a permutation on the set S. In fact, g restricted to any orbit $\mathcal{O}$ is a permutation of $\mathcal{O}$. In particular, let $L = \{\gamma_1, \ldots, \gamma_n\}$ be a disjoint union of $\mathcal{G}$-orbits. Then, for any $\sigma \in \mathcal{G}$ and $1 \le i \le n$, there exists j such that $\sigma \cdot \gamma_i = \gamma_j$. In this case, we will simply denote the corresponding permutation in $\mathcal{S}_n$ as $\sigma(i) = j$.

Definition 5. *Let L be a subset of $\mathbb{F}_q$ containing n distinct elements. For any $\sigma \in \mathcal{S}_n$, we say that L is invariant under σ if $\sigma(L) = L$. If L is invariant under every σ in a subgroup $\mathcal{G}$ of $\mathcal{S}_n$, we say that L is $\mathcal{G}$-invariant. In particular, if L is a disjoint union of $\mathcal{G}$-orbits, L is $\mathcal{G}$-invariant.*

Remark 3. Consider a group action of $\mathrm{AGL}_2(q)$ on $\mathbb{F}_q$ defined by $\sigma_{a,b} \cdot \gamma = a^{-1}(\gamma - b)$. One easily checks that this is a group action. Then, one has $\sigma_{a,b}(x - \gamma) = a(x - \sigma_{a,b} \cdot \gamma)$.

Proposition 1. *Let $\mathcal{G}$ be a subgroup of $\mathrm{AGL}_2(q)$ and let $L \subset \mathbb{F}_q$ be a disjoint union of $\mathcal{G}$-orbits. Let $g \in \mathbb{F}_q[x]$. For any $\sigma \in G$, one has*

$$\sigma(\Gamma(L, g)) = \Gamma(L, g(\sigma^{-1}(x))).$$

Proof. Write $L = \{\gamma_1, \ldots, \gamma_n\}$. Here, it suffices to show that $\sigma(\Gamma(L, g)) \subset \Gamma(L, g(\sigma^{-1}(x)))$. Let $\mathbf{c} = (c_1, c_2, \ldots, c_n) \in \Gamma(L, g)$. By definition, we have:

$$\sum_{i=1}^{n} \frac{c_i}{x - \gamma_i} \equiv 0 \mod g(x).$$

Applying σ^{-1} to both sides of the equivalence relation Remark 3 yields

$$\sum_{i=1}^{n} \frac{c_i}{x - \sigma^{-1} \cdot \gamma_i} \equiv 0 \mod g(\sigma^{-1}(x)).$$

Since L is a union of $\mathcal{G}$-orbits, for each $i = 1, \ldots, n$, there exists some j such that $\gamma_j \in L$ and $\sigma(\gamma_j) = \gamma_i$. Rearranging the equation then gives:

$$\sum_{i=1}^{n} \frac{c_{\sigma(i)}}{x - \gamma_i} \equiv 0 \mod g(\sigma^{-1}(x)),$$

and this proves our desired result.

2.3 Automorphism-induced Goppa Codes

In Proposition 1, suppose further that there exists some $\alpha \in \mathbb{F}_q^*$ such that $g(\sigma^{-1}) = \alpha g$. Then, it follows that $\sigma(\Gamma(L, g)) = \Gamma(L, g)$, that is, σ is in the automorphism group of $\Gamma(L, g)$. In other words, for any $\mathbf{c} \in \Gamma(L, g)$, the permuted codeword $\sigma^i(\mathbf{c})$ lies in the code as well for $i = 1, 2, \ldots$. This property enables one to construct generator matrices of the code exhibiting a nice structure, thereby reducing the public key size of schemes built from these codes.

As such, a common approach to construct McEliece-based schemes with shorter keys is to employ Goppa codes induced by subgroups of $\mathrm{AGL}_2(q)$ (or more generally, subgroups of projective semi-linear groups of $\mathrm{Aut}(F/\mathbb{F}_q)$). For instance, in [6], the author described alternant codes that can be constructed from prescribed automorphism subgroups of which, Goppa codes form a special case. These codes resulted in quasi-cyclic, quasi-dyadic and monoidic alternant codes which were subsequently employed to construct McEliece-based schemes with compact keys [2,3,7,29].

We review the main ideas of this approach below. Here, we are presenting the ideas in a more general manner to facilitate the discussion in the remainder of the paper.

Let $\mathcal{G}$ be a subgroup of $\mathrm{AGL}_2(q)$ of size r. Suppose that there are at least s $\mathcal{G}$-orbits of size r. Let L be a union of s of these orbits and let $n = rs$. Let $t = dr$ for some positive integer d and let $g(x)$ be a polynomial of degree t that is invariant under the $\mathcal{G}$-action, i.e., for every $\sigma \in \mathcal{G}$, there exists $\alpha \in \mathbb{F}_q^*$ such that $g(\sigma(x)) = \alpha g(x)$. From Proposition 1, it follows that for every $\sigma \in \mathcal{G}$, $\sigma(\Gamma(L, g)) = \Gamma(L, g)$. Hence, $\Gamma(L, g)$ is a Goppa code with $\mathcal{G}$ as a subgroup of $\mathrm{Aut}(\Gamma(L, g))$.

One common way to construct the $\mathcal{G}$-invariant polynomial $g(x)$ is as follows. Pick an irreducible polynomial $f(x)$ of degree d. Define

$$g(x) = f(\prod_{\sigma \in \mathcal{G}} \sigma(x)).$$

Then, $g(x)$ is invariant under any $\sigma \in \mathcal{G}$. In [6,14], the authors classified polynomials invariant under some particular subgroups of $\mathrm{AGL}_2(q)$.

Denote the orbits in L by $\mathcal{O}_i$, $i = 1, 2, \ldots, s$. For each orbit $\mathcal{O}_i$, fix a representative β_i. Fix an order in $\mathcal{G}$, that is $\mathcal{G} = \{\sigma_1, \sigma_2, \ldots, \sigma_r\}$. With this order, write $\mathcal{O}_i = \{\sigma_1 \cdot \beta_i, \sigma_2 \cdot \beta_i, \ldots, \sigma_r \cdot \beta_i\}$. It is clear that for any $\sigma \in \mathcal{G}$, σ induces the same permutation for each orbit. We denote this permutation by $\tilde{\sigma}$.

Order the elements in L as $L = \mathcal{O}_1 || \mathcal{O}_2 || \ldots || \mathcal{O}_s = \{(\sigma_1 \cdot \beta_1 \ldots \sigma_r \cdot \beta_1), \ldots, (\sigma_1 \cdot \beta_s \ldots \sigma_r \cdot \beta_s)\}$. Let $\mathbf{c} = (c_1, \ldots, c_n) \in \Gamma(L, g)$. We partition $\mathbf{c}$ as $\mathbf{c} = (\mathbf{c}_{\mathcal{O}_1} || \ldots || \mathbf{c}_{\mathcal{O}_s})$, where each $\mathbf{c}_{\mathcal{O}_i}$ corresponds to the entries indexed by elements in $\mathcal{O}_i$ with $i \in \{1, \ldots, s\}$. Then for each $\sigma \in \mathcal{G}$, $\mathbf{c}_\sigma = (\mathbf{c}_{\tilde{\sigma}(\mathcal{O}_1)} || \ldots || \mathbf{c}_{\tilde{\sigma}(\mathcal{O}_s)}) \in \Gamma(L, g)$.

Next, we seek to construct a generator matrix for $\Gamma(L, g)$ having a nice form. Let k denote the dimension of $\Gamma(L, g)$. Suppose further that $k = n - mt$. Let $k_0 = k/r = (s - md)$.

Consider a generator matrix M of $\Gamma(L, g)$. Without any loss of generality, suppose that M can be put in systematic form (for otherwise, choose other β_i's), that is, $M = (I, B)$, where B is a $k \times (n - k)$ matrix. Label the rows of M by M_i. Define $P(L, g) := \{M_1, M_{r+1}, \ldots, M_{(k_0-1)r+1}\}$. For each $\mathbf{c} \in P(L, g)$, form the matrix

$$\mathbf{c}(\mathcal{G}) = \begin{pmatrix} \sigma_1(\mathbf{c}) \\ \vdots \\ \sigma_r(\mathbf{c}) \end{pmatrix}.$$

Finally, form the generator matrix

$$M(L,g) = \begin{pmatrix} \mathbf{c}_1(\mathcal{G}) \\ \vdots \\ \mathbf{c}_{k_0}(\mathcal{G}) \end{pmatrix},$$

for $\mathbf{c}_i = M_{(i-1)r+1}$. Note that since M is in systematic form, each $\mathbf{c}_i = M_{(i-1)r+1}$ is such that the i-th block is of the form $(1,0,\ldots,0)$ while the other blocks in the first k_0 blocks are $(0,0,\ldots,0)$.

Theorem 1. *The matrix $M(L,g)$ constructed above is a generator matrix of $\Gamma(L,g)$.*

Proof. First, it is clear that for each $\mathbf{c} \in P(L,g)$ and for each $\sigma \in \mathcal{G}$, $\sigma(\mathbf{c}) \in \Gamma(L,g)$. It thus remains to show that $M(L,g)$ has rank k. Observe that for each $\mathbf{c} \in P(L,g)$, $\mathbf{c}(\mathcal{G})$ is an $r \times n$ matrix. Further, $\mathbf{c}(\mathcal{G})$ can be viewed as a concatenation of s $r \times r$ square matrices where each square matrix is in fact $\mathbf{c}_{\mathcal{O}}(\mathcal{G})$ for an orbit $\mathcal{O}$ contained in L. Consider the first k_0 blocks of $\mathbf{c}_i(\mathcal{G})$. By our choice of $\mathbf{c}_i$, we see that the i-th block of $\mathbf{c}_i(\mathcal{G})$ is a permutation matrix while all other blocks are 0. Hence, the first k columns of $M(L,g)$ have the form

$$\begin{pmatrix} A & 0 & \ldots & 0 \\ 0 & A & \ldots & 0 \\ \ldots & \ldots & \ldots & \ldots \\ 0 & 0 & \ldots & A \end{pmatrix},$$

where $A = \mathbf{x}(\mathcal{G})$ and $\mathbf{x} = (1,0,\ldots,0)$. Since the rank of A is r, the desired result follows.

Two particular subgroups of $\mathrm{AGL}_2(q)$ of interest are the multiplicative cyclic subgroup of order $r|(q-1)$ and the additive subgroup of order 2^v for $1 \le v \le m$. Concretely, the former comprises automorphisms of the form $\sigma_a(x) = ax$ for $a \in \mathbb{F}_q^*$ of order r and gives rise to quasi-cyclic Goppa codes [3,7]. In this case, the orbits in the Goppa support L are cosets of the subgroup of $\mathbb{F}_q^*$ of order r and the Goppa polynomial is of the form $g(x) = f(x^r)$ for some irreducible polynomial $f(x) \in \mathbb{F}_q[x]$.

On the other hand, the additive subgroup construction results in quasi-dyadic Goppa codes [2,29]. Let V be any $\mathbb{F}_2$-subspace of $\mathbb{F}_q$ with dimension v. The additive automorphism group consists of automorphisms of the form $\sigma_b(x) = x + b$ for all $b \in V$. Thus, the orbits in L are all cosets of V in $\mathbb{F}_q$, each of size 2^v and the Goppa polynomial is of the form $f(L(x))$, where $f(x)$ is an irreducible polynomial and $L(x) = \prod_{b\in V}(x+b)$.

Observe from Theorem 1 that it suffices to provide the set $P(L,g)$ in order to construct the generator matrix of $\Gamma(L,g)$, that is, these codes are examples of the codes we seek in Problem 1. In other words, when using this code in McEliece-based schemes, the public key size can be reduced. However, matrices with such nice structure also reduce the number of unknowns to mount algebraic attacks, thereby weakening the security with respect to structural attacks. One way to perform algebraic cryptanalysis is to consider the parity-check equations using the parity-check matrix $H = VD$ where V and D are defined in Eqs. 1 and 2, respectively, and treating the γ_i's and $1/g(\gamma_i)$'s as unknowns. One then tries to solve the system of equations using algebraic solving tools such as Gröbner basis algorithms. In the case of automorphism-induced Goppa codes, the unknowns for the Goppa support are reduced to the elements of the subgroup as well as the orbit representatives. At the same time, since $g(a)$ is identical for all a in the same orbit of L, the number of unknowns of the diagonal matrix in Eq. 2 is reduced to the number of orbits. Essentially, it was shown in [4,14] that one can construct Goppa codes with much smaller parameters from these automorphism-induced codes, namely, via folded codes and invariant codes defined as follows.

Definition 6. *Let $C = \Gamma(L, g)$ be a Goppa code induced by an automorphism subgroup $\mathcal{G}$ so that L is a disjoint union of $\mathcal{G}$-orbits. For $\mathbf{c} \in C$, define* $\mathrm{Punc}(\mathbf{c})$ *as the codeword obtained from $\mathbf{c}$ by puncturing on a set of representatives for the orbits in L.*

- *The folded code $\phi(C)$ is the subcode of C defined as:*

$$\phi(C) = \{\mathrm{Punc}(\sum_{\sigma\in\mathcal{G}} \sigma(\mathbf{c})) : \mathbf{c} \in C\}.$$

- *The invariant code $C^{\mathcal{G}}$ is the subcode of C defined by:*

$$C^{\mathcal{G}} = \{\mathrm{Punc}(\mathbf{c}) : \mathbf{c} \in C | \sigma(\mathbf{c}) = \mathbf{c} \textit{ for all } \sigma \in \mathcal{G}\}.$$

Clearly, the folded code is a subcode of the invariant code. In [4,14], it was shown that for the quasi-cyclic case, these two subcodes are identical and equal to $\Gamma(L', f(x))$, where L' is a set of representatives of orbits in L and $g(x) = f(x^r)$ with r being the order of the cyclic subgroup of $\mathbb{F}_q^*$.

3 Partial Quasi-cyclic and Partial Quasi-dyadic Goppa Codes

In this section, we present a more general construction for codes satisfying the properties in Problem 1, namely, we do not restrict to nontrivial automorphism subgroups of the code. In other words, our codes may have trivial automorphism groups but contain subsets of codewords and sets of permutations where these codewords and their corresponding permutations generate the whole code. These constructions will prevent an attacker from finding folded and invariant subcodes of the code.

First, we give a sufficient condition for a permuted codeword of a code to remain in the code.

Lemma 3. *Given a linear code C and a permutation $\sigma \in S_n$, $C' = C \cap \sigma(C)$ is also a linear code. Suppose that C' is nontrivial. For any codeword $\mathbf{c} \in C'$, one has $\sigma^{-1}(\mathbf{c}) \in C$. Further, if $\sigma^{-1}(\mathbf{c}) \in \sigma(C)$, then $\sigma^i(\mathbf{c}) \in C'$ for $i \in \mathbb{Z}$.*

Proof. Since $\mathbf{c} \in C' \subseteq \sigma(C)$, it follows that $\sigma^{-1}(\mathbf{c}) \in C$. In the case where $\sigma^{-1}(\mathbf{c}) \in \sigma(C)$, then $\sigma^{-1}(\mathbf{c}) \in C'$. Based on the fact that $\mathbf{c}, \sigma^{-1}(\mathbf{c}) \in C'$ and σ is a permutation, one can continue to apply σ^{-1} many times and the result is still a codeword of C'.

Remark 4. Suppose that σ has order 2. Then $\sigma(\mathbf{c}) \in \sigma(C) \cap \sigma(\sigma(C)) = \sigma(C) \cap C$.

More generally, let σ_0 be the identity permutation and let $\sigma_1, \ldots, \sigma_l$ be l distinct permutations in $\mathcal{S}_n$. Suppose that for a linear code C, the code $C' = \bigcap_{i=0}^{l} \sigma_i(C)$ is nontrivial. Then for $\mathbf{c} \in C'$ and for all $i = 1, 2, \ldots, l$, $\sigma_i^{-1}(\mathbf{c}) \in C$.

In terms of Goppa codes, one has the following result.

Lemma 4. *Let L be a subset of n distinct elements from $\mathbb{F}_q$. Let $\sigma_1, \ldots, \sigma_l$ be l distinct automorphisms from $\mathrm{AGL}_2(q)$ such that L is invariant under each σ_i, $i = 1, 2, \ldots, l$. Let $g(x) \in \mathbb{F}_q[x]$ be such that $g(x), g(\sigma_1(x)), \ldots, g(\sigma_l(x))$ are pairwise co-prime. Define $G(x) = \prod_{i=0}^{l} g(\sigma_i(x))$. If $\Gamma(L, G(x))$ is nontrivial, then for every codeword $\mathbf{c} \in \Gamma(L, G(x))$, the permuted codeword $\sigma_i(\mathbf{c})$ lies in $\Gamma(L, g(x))$. Moreover, if $\sigma_0 = id, \sigma_1, \ldots, \sigma_l$ form a subgroup of $\mathrm{AGL}_2(q)$, then each $\sigma_i(\mathbf{c})$ lies in $\Gamma(L, G(x))$.*

Proof. From Lemma 1 and Proposition 1, one has

$$\begin{aligned} \Gamma(L, G(x)) &= \bigcap_{i=0}^{l} \Gamma(L, g(\sigma_i(x)) \\ &= \bigcap_{i=0}^{l} \sigma_i^{-1}(\Gamma(L, g)). \end{aligned}$$

Hence, it follows from the above argument that for $i \in \{1 \ldots l\}$ and $\mathbf{c} \in \Gamma(L, G(x))$ lies in the code $\Gamma(L, g)$ as well. For the latter part, if $\mathcal{G} = \{\sigma_0, \sigma_1, \ldots, \sigma_l\}$ is a group, then $\Gamma(L, g(x)g(\sigma_1(x)) \ldots g(\sigma_l(x)))$ is a code with $\mathcal{G}$ as its automorphism subgroup.

There are different ways one can apply Lemma 4 to construct Goppa codes with more permuted codewords. Here, we provide two different constructions.

In the following, we assume that $n = lmt$ for some positive integer l.

Proposition 2 (Partial quasi-dyadic construction). *Let $l = 2^v$, i.e., $n = 2^v mt$ for some positive integer $v \leq m/2$. Let V be a v-dimensional subspace of $\mathbb{F}_q$. Write V as $V = \{b_0, b_1, b_2, \ldots, b_{2^v-1}\}$ with $b_0 = 0$. Let L contain mt different cosets of V under some ordering. Let $g(x)$ be an irreducible polynomial of degree t such that the Goppa code $\Gamma(L, g)$ has dimension $k = n - mt = (2^v - 1)mt$. For $i = 0, 1, \ldots, 2^v - 1$, define σ_i as the automorphism where $\sigma_i(x) = x + b_i$. Define $h(x) = \prod_{i=0}^{2^v-1} g(\sigma_i(x))$. Suppose that the code $\Gamma(L, h)$ is the trivial code. Then, one can construct a subset $P(L, g)$ of $\Gamma(L, g)$ satisfying the conditions of Problem 1.*

Proof. Fix a σ_i with $i \neq 0$ and let $h_i(x) = \frac{h(x)}{g(\sigma_i(x))}$. Let $C = \Gamma(L, h_i(x))$. Clearly, C is a subcode of $\Gamma(L, g(x))$. For each codeword $\mathbf{c} \in C$, one has $\sigma_j(\mathbf{c}) \in \Gamma(L, g(x))$ for $j \neq i$. In particular, $\sigma_j(C)$ is a subcode of $\Gamma(L, g(x))$ for all $j \neq i$ (since the order of σ_j is 2). We claim that for j_1, j_2 such that i, j_1, j_2 are all distinct, one has $\sigma_{j_1}(C) \cap \sigma_{j_2}(C)$ is the trivial code. Indeed, $\sigma_j(\Gamma(L, h_i)) = \Gamma(L, \prod_{e \neq i} g(\sigma_e \sigma_j(x)))$. Thus, by the assumption that the $g(\sigma_i(x))$'s are coprime and Lemma 1, $\sigma_{j_1}(\Gamma(L, h_i(x))) \cap \sigma_{j_2}(\Gamma(L, h_i(x))) = \Gamma(L, h(x))$ which is trivial by our assumption. In addition, since $\dim(\sigma_j(C)) \geq n - (2^v - 1)mt = mt$, it follows that $\dim(\sigma_j(C)) = mt$ for all $j \neq i$. Let $P(L, g)$ be a basis of C. Then, $P(L, g)$ satisfies the conditions of Problem 1 by letting the set of permutations to be $\{\sigma_j : j \neq i\}$.

Proposition 3 (Partial quasi-cyclic construction). *Let r be a positive integer with $r|(q-1)$. Let $n = rmt$. Let H be a subgroup of $\mathbb{F}_q^*$ of order r. Let L be a disjoint union of mt cosets of H in some order. Fix an irreducible polynomial $g(x)$ of degree t such that the Goppa code $\Gamma(L, g)$ has dimension $(r-1)mt$. For each $a \in H$, let σ_a be the automorphism such that $\sigma_a(x) = ax$. Define $h(x) = \prod_{a \in H} g(ax)$. Suppose that the code $\Gamma(L, h)$ is trivial. Then, one can find a set $P(L, g)$ of mt linearly independent vectors that satisfies the conditions of Problem 1.*

Proof. Fix a generator a of H. Define $g_a(x) = \prod_{i=0}^{r-2} g(a^i x)$. Let C be the code $C = \Gamma(L, g_a)$. By Proposition 4, for all $i = 1, \ldots, r-2$, we have $\sigma_{a^i}(\mathbf{c}) \in \Gamma(L, g)$ for all $\mathbf{c} \in C$, that is, $\sigma_{a^i}(C) \subset \Gamma(L, g)$ for $i = 2, 3, \ldots, r$. We claim that $\Gamma(L, g)$ is a disjoint union of $C, \sigma_{a^2}(C), \ldots, \sigma_{a^{r-1}}(C)$. First, we show that for $i \neq j$, $\sigma_{a^i}(C) \cap \sigma_{a^j}(C)$ is trivial. Now, we have $\sigma_{a^i}(C) = \Gamma(L, h_a(\sigma_{a^{-i}}(x))) = \Gamma(L, \prod_{w \neq r-1-i} g(\sigma_{a^w}(x)))$. Similarly, $\sigma_{a^j}(C) = \Gamma(L, \prod_{w \neq r-1-j} g(\sigma_{a^w}(x)))$. From Lemma 1, $\sigma_{a^i}(C) \cap \sigma_{a^j}(C) = \Gamma(L, h)$ which is trivial. Since $\dim(C) \geq n - (r-1)mt = mt$, the claim follows. Consequently, one may choose $P(L, g)$ as a basis of C.

Remark 5.
- In both Propositions 2 and 3, we have $\dim(\Gamma(L, h)) \geq n - \deg(h)m = 0$. In practice, this code is trivial for most cases.
- In fact, one can generalize the results to non-irreducible polynomials g. In this case, one needs to check that the polynomials $g(\sigma(x))$'s are all pairwise coprime for all the automorphisms σ involved.

Remark 6. Just as in Theorem 1, one may transform $P(L, g)$ such that $P(L, g)$ takes the following form. Let

$$P(L, g) = (S_1 || S_2 || \ldots S_{mt-1} || S_{mt}),$$

where each S_i is an $mt \times r$ matrix and for $i = 1, 2, \ldots, mt-1$, S_i is 0 everywhere except at the $(i, 1)$-position. Thus, one may use S_{mt} as the public key.

From Propositions 2 and 3, we see that one can generalize the construction to any subgroup of $\mathrm{AGL}_2(q)$. More precisely, we give the general construction in the next theorem and the proof is similar to the proofs of Propositions 2 and 3.

Theorem 2. *Let t be a positive integer. Let $\mathcal{G}$ be a subgroup of* $\mathrm{AGL}_2(q)$ *and let L be a disjoint union of mt $\mathcal{G}$-orbits under the action of $\mathcal{G}$ on $\mathbb{F}_q$. Let $n = |L| = |\mathcal{G}|mt$. Let $g(x)$ be an irreducible polynomial of degree t such that the code $\Gamma(L, g(x))$ has dimension $n - mt$. Define $h(x) = \prod_{\sigma \in \mathcal{G}} g(\sigma(x))$. Assume that $\Gamma(L, h)$ is trivial. Fix a $\sigma \in \mathcal{G}$ where σ is not the identity automorphism and let $\mathcal{G}' = \mathcal{G} \backslash \{\sigma\}$. Construct $C = \Gamma(L, \prod_{\sigma' \in \mathcal{G}'} g(\sigma'(x)))$. Then, we may take a basis of C as the set $P(L, g)$ in Problem 1 with the set of permutations to be the permutations in $\mathcal{G}'$.*

4 Security Discussion

In general, there are two classes of attacks on McEliece scheme, namely, information set decoding (ISD) attacks and structural attacks. The former attacks were proposed in [32] as a generic decoding attack. Essentially, such attacks seek to perform the decoding directly from the public matrix given. In its most basic form, an adversary tries to guess k positions such that the submatrix restricted to these positions is invertible and the error vector, restricted to these positions, has very small Hamming weight. Such properties will enable the adversary to brute force the error entries at these positions and subsequently, discover the message. Other improvements and variants were later proposed to improve the attack [5,9,10,12,18,21,25,26,36]. So far, the best attack has complexity $2^{0.0967n}$ [26], where n is the code length.

On the other hand, the structural attacks attempt to take advantage of the structure of the specific code used. For random Goppa codes, one can perform a brute force search on the Goppa polynomial and/or the elements in the Goppa support. In [33], an algorithm known as the support splitting algorithm was proposed which can correct permutation of the support elements once the Goppa polynomial and the set of support elements are known.

In addition, one can launch an algebraic attack on a Goppa code C with Goppa polynomial g as follows. Consider the equations:

$$\sum_{i=1}^{n} c_i x_i^j y_i^w = 0 \tag{6}$$

for $\mathbf{c} = (c_1, \ldots, c_n) \in C$, $0 \leq j \leq t-1$ when $w = 1$ and $0 \leq j \leq 2t-1$ when $w = 2$, $x_1, x_2, \ldots, x_n$ are the unknowns for the Goppa support and $y_i = 1/g(x_i)$. Recall that these equations come from the parity-check equations (refer to Eqs. 1 and 2). Hence, solving for the unknowns will give the Goppa support and together with the knowledge of the y_i's will enable one to recover $g(x)$. Thus the challenge remains to solve the above system.

Observe that when $j = 0$ yields k linear equations in the unknowns y_i's. Thus, one way to solve the system is to guess the remaining mt y_i's which results in a system in the x_i's. By considering the k$\lfloor 2\log_2 t \rfloor$ equations which are powers of 2, one can then solve for the unknowns x_i's. The complexity of the approach is asymptotically $O(2^{m^2 t})$. Other approaches exist to solve the system [15,16] but the complexities of these approaches are more difficult to estimate.

As mentioned in Subsect. 2.3, the automorphism-induced Goppa codes are more vulnerable to algebraic attacks as compared to random Goppa codes. This is due to the existence of invariant subcodes which are themselves Goppa codes with smaller supports and lower degree Goppa polynomials. In particular, for an automorphism-induce Goppa code, particularly quasi-cyclic code, such that it has length n, degree t Goppa polynomial and automorphism group of order l, the invariant code has length n/l with degree t/l Goppa polynomial. A thorough security analysis of quasi-cyclic Goppa codes can be found in [3].

For our construction, only subsets of the automorphism subgroup of $\mathrm{AGL}_2(q)$ are used. In particular, we typically remove an element σ from a subgroup $\mathcal{G}$ of $\mathrm{AGL}_2(q)$ (see Theorem 2).

Thus, a similar folding operation will be of the form

$$\sum_{\sigma' \in \mathcal{G}, \sigma' \neq \sigma} \sigma'(\mathbf{c})$$

for any $\mathbf{c}$ in the code. Since the coordinates of $\mathbf{c}$ on each orbit are unlikely to be identical, one cannot use the same trick to puncture the code or to construct an invariant code.

However, one may attempt to mount an algebraic attack on our constructions. In Propositions 2 and 3, suppose that V and H are known, respectively (this assumption is valid as one can exhaustively search for them). Referring to the system of equations in 6 and the structure of the Goppa support as a disjoint union of cosets, the unknowns for the Goppa support are reduced to finding mt representatives in the orbits. However, since our choice of $g(x)$ is such that it is not invariant under any automorphism used in the construction, there is no clear relationship between the y_i's that we can exploit. Consequently, one has to solve a system of equations in mt unknowns in the x_i's and n unknowns in the y_i's. Once again, by exploiting the k linear relationships among the y_i's, one way to solve the system is to perform a brute force search on the remaining free mt y_i's. Alternatively, one can search through all possible mt x_i's and solve the resulting linear equations in the y_i's. In either case, the time complexity is $O(2^{m^2 t})$. Hence, unlike the quasi-cyclic or quasi-dyadic constructions, we see that our constructions do not weaken the security of the codes with respect to algebraic attacks.

5 Practical Implementation Considerations

5.1 Practical Implementation Scheme

Observe that our constructions place some restrictions on the choice of the parameters. For instance, we require n to be an integral multiple of mt. Moreover, the reduction factor is at most $(n - mt)/mt = k/(n - k)$. Thus, to achieve a large reduction size, we need t to be small. However, t needs to be sufficiently large to prevent an exhaustive search on the error vector, or more generally, to guard against the state-of-the-art information set-decoding attacks. In addition, for fixed m and t, n cannot be too large to prevent the distinguishing attack [13]. On the other hand, even though the automorphism-induced codes are more vulnerable to algebraic attacks, the relatively large gap between the complexity of these attacks and the information set-decoding attacks give some room to choose the parameters appropriately for any security level. As such, we propose combining the two constructions to achieve a greater key reduction for a desired security level. The following algorithm gives a possible construction meeting a given security level. Here, we only consider the quasi-cyclic construction as the dyadic construction is similar.

1. Fix a security parameter λ.
2. Fix m such that $q-1=2^m-1$ has small factors.
3. For any two distinct integers l_1 and l_2 with $l_1 l_2 \mid (q-1)$ and $\gcd(l_1, l_2)=1$, do the following:
   - Pick a t_0 satisfying the following two conditions:
     - $\binom{q}{t_0} \geq 2^\lambda$;
     - A $[l_1 l_2 m t_0, (l_1 l_2 - l_1) m t_0, 2 l_1 t_0]$ Goppa code achieves the security level with respect to the information set-decoding attacks.
4. Let $t = l_1 t_0$ and $n = l_1 l_2 m t_0$.
5. Let H be a subgroup of $\mathbb{F}_q^*$ of order $l_1 l_2$ and pick a generator a of H.
6. Let L be a disjoint union of mt_0 different cosets of H and randomly choose an ordering of the cosets.
7. Randomly pick a polynomial $g_0(x)$ of degree t_0. Let $g(x) = g_0(x^{l_1})$.
8. Let $h(x) = \prod_{i=0}^{l_2-2} g(a^{il_1}x)$ and $f(x) = \prod_{i=0}^{l_2-1} g(a^{il_1}x)$
9. Construct the code $\Gamma(L,g), \Gamma(L,h)$ and $\Gamma(L,f)$.
10. If $\dim(\Gamma(L,f)) \neq 0$ or $\dim(\Gamma(L,h)) \neq mt$ or $\dim(\Gamma(L,g)) \neq (l_2-1)mt$, choose another $g_0(x)$.
11. Otherwise, return $\Gamma(L,g)$.

By Proposition 3, for all $\mathbf{c} \in \Gamma(L,h)$ and for $i = 0, 1, \ldots, l_2-2$, we have $\sigma_{a^{l_1 i}}(\mathbf{c}) \in \Gamma(L,g)$. Moreover, $\Gamma(L,h)$ is a quasi-cyclic code induced by a subgroup of H of order l_1. Consequently, one can find a set $P(L,g)$ of cardinality mt_0 such that for all $i = 0, 1, \ldots, l_2-2$, $j = 0, 1, \ldots, l_1-1$, $\sigma_{a^{l_1 i + l_2 j}}(\mathbf{c}) \in \Gamma(L,g)$ whenever $\mathbf{c} \in P(L,g)$. Similar to Theorem 1 and Remark 6, one can construct an $mt_0 \times mt$ matrix that can be extended to a generator matrix of $\Gamma(L,g)$. Consequently, the public key size of such a code is $l_1 m^2 t_0^2$.

In our construction, by our choice of t_0, we ensure that it is secure against a brute force search on all possible $g_0(x)$ and in fact, it is resistant to the existing known structural attacks (see Sect. 4). In addition, we have ensured that the code $\Gamma(L,g)$ is secure against message recovery attacks.

Remark 7. By employing only the quasi-cyclic construction, one gets a public key size of $(l_2-1)l_1 m^2 t_0^2$. Thus, we see that our technique can be further applied to quasi-cyclic constructions to yield more compact public keys.

5.2 Concrete Parameters

We apply our constructions to the parameters in BigQuake [3] to reduce the public key size and to keep the desired security level. We give 3 groups of parameters corresponding to 3 different security levels and each group comprises two code parameters in Table 1. The first is the code parameters from BigQuake [3] and the second is the reduced code parameters we get after applying our scheme to the first code. Now we explain the notations of each column of Table 1 as follows.

- λ: security level of the parameters.
- m: extension degree of the finite field.
- $[n, k, t]$ denotes the resulting Goppa code parameters, n for the code length, k for the code dimension and t for the error correcting ability.
- l_1: the size of the quasi-cyclic group which acts on x.
- l_2: the size of the partial quasi-cyclic group which acts on the Goppa polynomial $g(x)$. This column is not applicable to the BigQuake [3] code parameters.
- ω_{msg}: the logarithm of the work load of ISD, which is computed using the **CaWoF** [37] library.
- *Size*(*bytes*): the resulting public key size.

From Table 1, we can see that our scheme reduces the public key size of BigQuake by at least half. We remark that the parameters given in Table 1 may be vulnerable to other attacks. Here we show the parameters solely to illustrate the power our construction which, to our best knowledge, are secure against current known attacks. In fact, our construction can be applied to most of the existing Goppa codes based constructions to reduce the public key size without compromising the security level.

Table 1. More compact public key parameters by applying our construction to BigQuake

λ	m	$[n, k, t]$	l_1	l_2	ω_{msg}	Size (bytes)
AES128	12	[3510, 2418, 91]	13	NA	132	25389
	16	[12240, 11520, 45]	5	17	143	12960
AES192	18	[7410, 4674, 152]	19	NA	195	84132
	18	[8208, 5472, 152]	19	3	213	49248
AES256	18	[10070, 6650, 190]	19	NA	263	149625
	18	[10260, 6840, 190]	19	3	267	76950

Remark 8. The public key size of the foregoing scheme does not involve the parameter l_2. Therefore one could select a bigger l_2 to keep the public key size and ensure that the increased code parameters n and k will still make the code resistant to, even by a large margin improved and powerful ISD attacks in the future. Alternatively, one is able to exploit this property of our scheme to minimize the public key size by selecting very small l_1 and very big l_2, and increasing

t_0 to some reasonable value. Note that this only applies to big enough m, for otherwise it will suffer from some algebraic attacks. In conclusion, one can vary the parameters l_1, l_2, t_0, m, n appropriately to get a compact public key achieving the desired security level with respect to all known attacks.

Acknowledgements. Chaoping Xing was supported by the National Research Foundation, Prime Minister's Office, Singapore under its Strategic Capability Research Centres Funding Initiative; and the Singapore MoE Tier 1 grants RG25/16 and RG21/18.

References

1. NIST round 1 submissions (2017). https://csrc.nist.gov/projects/post-quantum-cryptography/round-1-submissions
2. Banegas, G., et al.: DAGS: key encapsulation from dyadic GS codes, June 2018. https://www.dags-project.org/pdf/DAGS_spec_v2.pdf
3. Bardet, M., et al.: BIG QUAKE: BInary Goppa QUAsi cyclic Key Encapsulation, April 2018. https://bigquake.inria.fr/files/2018/04/corrected_proposal.pdf
4. Barelli, E.: On the security of some compact keys for McEliece scheme. CoRR abs/1803.05289 (2018). http://arxiv.org/abs/1803.05289
5. Becker, A., Joux, A., May, A., Meurer, A.: Decoding random binary linear codes in $2^{n/20}$: how $1 + 1 = 0$ improves information set decoding. In: Pointcheval, D., Johansson, T. (eds.) EUROCRYPT 2012. LNCS, vol. 7237, pp. 520–536. Springer, Heidelberg (2012). https://doi.org/10.1007/978-3-642-29011-4_31
6. Berger, T.P.: Goppa and related codes invariant under a prescribed permutation. IEEE Trans. Inf. Theory **46**(7), 2628–2633 (2000). https://doi.org/10.1109/18.887871
7. Berger, T.P., Cayrel, P.-L., Gaborit, P., Otmani, A.: Reducing key length of the McEliece cryptosystem. In: Preneel, B. (ed.) AFRICACRYPT 2009. LNCS, vol. 5580, pp. 77–97. Springer, Heidelberg (2009). https://doi.org/10.1007/978-3-642-02384-2_6
8. Bernstein, D.J., Buchmann, J., Dahmen, E.: Post Quantum Cryptography, 1st edn. Springer, Heidelberg (2008). https://doi.org/10.1007/978-3-540-88702-7
9. Bernstein, D.J., Lange, T., Peters, C.: Smaller decoding exponents: ball-collision decoding. In: Rogaway, P. (ed.) CRYPTO 2011. LNCS, vol. 6841, pp. 743–760. Springer, Heidelberg (2011). https://doi.org/10.1007/978-3-642-22792-9_42
10. Canteaut, A., Chabaud, F.: A new algorithm for finding minimum-weight words in a linear code: application to McEliece's cryptosystem and to Narrow-Sense BCH codes of length 511. IEEE Trans. Inf. Theory **44**(1), 367–378 (1998)
11. Chevalley, C.: Introduction to the Theory of Algebraic Functions of One Variable, vol. 6. American Mathematical Society, Providence (1951)
12. Dumer, I.: On minimum distance decoding of linear codes. In: Proceedings of 5th Joint Soviet-Swedish International Workshop Information Theory, pp. 50–52 (1991)
13. Faugère, J., Gauthier-Umaña, V., Otmani, A., Perret, L., Tillich, J.: A distinguisher for high-rate McEliece cryptosystems. IEEE Trans. Inf. Theory **59**(10), 6830–6844 (2013). https://doi.org/10.1109/TIT.2013.2272036
14. Faugère, J., Otmani, A., Perret, L., de Portzamparc, F., Tillich, J.: Folding alternant and Goppa codes with non-trivial automorphism groups. IEEE Trans. Inf. Theory **62**(1), 184–198 (2016). https://doi.org/10.1109/TIT.2015.2493539

15. Faugère, J., Otmani, A., Perret, L., de Portzamparc, F., Tillich, J.: Structural cryptanalysis of McEliece schemes with compact keys. Des. Codes Crypt. **79**(1), 87–112 (2016). https://doi.org/10.1007/s10623-015-0036-z
16. Faugère, J.-C., Otmani, A., Perret, L., Tillich, J.-P.: Algebraic cryptanalysis of McEliece variants with compact keys. In: Gilbert, H. (ed.) EUROCRYPT 2010. LNCS, vol. 6110, pp. 279–298. Springer, Heidelberg (2010). https://doi.org/10.1007/978-3-642-13190-5_14
17. Faugère, J.-C., Perret, L., de Portzamparc, F.: Algebraic attack against variants of McEliece with Goppa polynomial of a special form. In: Sarkar, P., Iwata, T. (eds.) ASIACRYPT 2014. LNCS, vol. 8873, pp. 21–41. Springer, Heidelberg (2014). https://doi.org/10.1007/978-3-662-45611-8_2
18. Finiasz, M., Sendrier, N.: Security bounds for the design of code-based cryptosystems. In: Matsui, M. (ed.) ASIACRYPT 2009. LNCS, vol. 5912, pp. 88–105. Springer, Heidelberg (2009). https://doi.org/10.1007/978-3-642-10366-7_6
19. Janwa, H., Moreno, O.: McEliece public key cryptosystems using algebraic-geometric codes. Des. Codes Crypt. **8**(3), 293–307 (1996)
20. Kobara, K., Imai, H.: Semantically secure McEliece public-key cryptosystems-conversions for McEliece PKC. In: Kim, K. (ed.) PKC 2001. LNCS, vol. 1992, pp. 19–35. Springer, Heidelberg (2001). https://doi.org/10.1007/3-540-44586-2_2
21. Lee, P.J., Brickell, E.F.: An observation on the security of McEliece's public-key cryptosystem. In: Barstow, D., et al. (eds.) EUROCRYPT 1988. LNCS, vol. 330, pp. 275–280. Springer, Heidelberg (1988). https://doi.org/10.1007/3-540-45961-8_25
22. Lidl, R., Niederreiter, H.: Finite fields: encyclopedia of mathematics and its applications. Comput. Math. Appl. **33**(7), 136–136 (1997)
23. Sidelnikov, V.M., Shestakov, S.O.: On insecurity of cryptosystems based on generalized Reed-Solomon codes. Discrete Math. Appl. **2**, 439–444 (1992)
24. MacWilliams, F., Sloane, N.: The Theory of Error Correcting Codes, Volume 2, Part 2. Mathematical Studies. North-Holland Publishing Company, Amsterdam (1978)
25. May, A., Meurer, A., Thomae, E.: Decoding random linear codes in $\tilde{\mathcal{O}}(2^{0.054n})$. In: Lee, D.H., Wang, X. (eds.) ASIACRYPT 2011. LNCS, vol. 7073, pp. 107–124. Springer, Heidelberg (2011). https://doi.org/10.1007/978-3-642-25385-0_6
26. May, A., Ozerov, I.: On computing nearest neighbors with applications to decoding of binary linear codes. In: Oswald, E., Fischlin, M. (eds.) EUROCRYPT 2015. LNCS, vol. 9056, pp. 203–228. Springer, Heidelberg (2015). https://doi.org/10.1007/978-3-662-46800-5_9
27. McEliece, R.J.: A public-key cryptosystem based on algebraic coding theory. Deep Space Network Progress Report 44, pp. 114–116, January 1978
28. Minder, L., Shokrollahi, A.: Cryptanalysis of the Sidelnikov cryptosystem. In: Naor, M. (ed.) EUROCRYPT 2007. LNCS, vol. 4515, pp. 347–360. Springer, Heidelberg (2007). https://doi.org/10.1007/978-3-540-72540-4_20
29. Misoczki, R., Barreto, P.S.L.M.: Compact McEliece keys from Goppa codes. In: Jacobson, M.J., Rijmen, V., Safavi-Naini, R. (eds.) SAC 2009. LNCS, vol. 5867, pp. 376–392. Springer, Heidelberg (2009). https://doi.org/10.1007/978-3-642-05445-7_24
30. Misoczki, R., Tillich, J., Sendrier, N., Barreto, P.S.L.M.: MDPC-McEliece: new McEliece variants from moderate density parity-check codes. In: ISIT, pp. 2069–2073. IEEE (2013)
31. Niederreiter, H.: Knapsack type cryptosystems and algebraic coding theory. Prob. Control Inf. Theory **15**(2), 159–166 (1986)

32. Prange, E.: The use of information sets in decoding cyclic codes. IRE Trans. Inf. Theory **8**(5), 5–9 (1962)
33. Sendrier, N.: Finding the permutation between equivalent linear codes: the support splitting algorithm. IEEE Trans. Inf. Theory **46**(4), 1193–1203 (2000). https://doi.org/10.1109/18.850662
34. Shor, P.W.: Algorithms for quantum computation: discrete logarithms and factoring. In: 35th Annual Symposium on Foundations of Computer Science, Santa Fe, New Mexico, USA, 20–22 November 1994, pp. 124–134 (1994). https://doi.org/10.1109/SFCS.1994.365700
35. Sidelnikov, V.M.: A public-key cryptosystem based on binary Reed-Muller codes. Discrete Math. Appl. **4**(3), 191–208 (1994)
36. Stern, J.: A method for finding codewords of small weight. In: Cohen, G., Wolfmann, J. (eds.) Coding Theory 1988. LNCS, vol. 388, pp. 106–113. Springer, Heidelberg (1989). https://doi.org/10.1007/BFb0019850
37. Torres, R.C.: CaWoF, C library for computing asymptotic exponents of generic decoding work factors, January 2017. https://gforge.inria.fr/projects/cawof/

Key Encapsulation Mechanism with Explicit Rejection in the Quantum Random Oracle Model

Haodong Jiang[1,2,4], Zhenfeng Zhang[2,3](✉), and Zhi Ma[1,4]

[1] State Key Laboratory of Mathematical Engineering and Advanced Computing, Zhengzhou, Henan, China
hdjiang13@gmail.com, ma_zhi@163.com
[2] TCA Laboratory, State Key Laboratory of Computer Science, Institute of Software, Chinese Academy of Sciences, Beijing, China
zfzhang@tca.iscas.ac.cn
[3] University of Chinese Academy of Sciences, Beijing, China
[4] Henan Key Laboratory of Network Cryptography Technology, Zhengzhou, Henan, China

Abstract. The recent post-quantum cryptography standardization project launched by NIST increased the interest in generic key encapsulation mechanism (KEM) constructions in the quantum random oracle (QROM). Based on a OW-CPA-secure public-key encryption (PKE), Hofheinz, Hövelmanns and Kiltz (TCC 2017) first presented two generic constructions of an IND-CCA-secure KEM with quartic security loss in the QROM, one with implicit rejection (a pseudorandom key is return for an invalid ciphertext) and the other with explicit rejection (an abort symbol is returned for an invalid ciphertext). Both are widely used in the NIST Round-1 KEM submissions and the ones with explicit rejection account for 40%. Recently, the security reductions have been improved to quadratic loss under a standard assumption, and be tight under a non-standard assumption by Jiang et al. (Crypto 2018) and Saito, Xagawa and Yamakawa (Eurocrypt 2018). However, these improvements only apply to the KEM submissions with implicit rejection and the techniques do not seem to carry over to KEMs with explicit rejection.

In this paper, we provide three generic constructions of an IND-CCA-secure KEM with explicit rejection, under the same assumptions and with the same tightness in the security reductions as the aforementioned KEM constructions with implicit rejection (Crypto 2018, Eurocrypt 2018). Specifically, we develop a novel approach to verify the validity of a ciphertext in the QROM and use it to extend the proof techniques for KEM constructions with implicit rejection (Crypto 2018, Eurocrypt 2018) to our KEM constructions with explicit rejection. Moreover, using an improved version of one-way to hiding lemma by Ambainis, Hamburg and Unruh (ePrint 2018/904), for two of our constructions, we present tighter reductions to the standard IND-CPA assumption. Our results directly apply to 9 KEM submissions with explicit rejection, and provide tighter reductions than previously known (TCC 2017).

D. Lin and K. Sako (Eds.): PKC 2019, LNCS 11443, pp. 618–645, 2019.
https://doi.org/10.1007/978-3-030-17259-6_21

Keywords: Quantum random oracle model · Key encapsulation mechanism · Explicit rejection · Generic construction

1 Introduction

Indistinguishability against chosen-ciphertext attacks (IND-CCA) [1] is considered to be a standard security notion of a key encapsulation mechanism (KEM). Efficient IND-CCA-secure KEMs are usually constructed in the random oracle model (ROM) [2], where a hash function is idealized to be a publicly accessible random oracle (RO). Generic constructions of an efficient IND-CCA-secure KEM in the ROM are well studied by Dent [3] and Hofheinz, Hövelmanns and Kiltz [4].

The constructions of IND-CCA-secure KEMs in [4] are essentially various KEM variants of the Fujisaki-Okamoto (FO) transformation [5,6] and the REACT/GEM transformation [7,8], which turn a weakly secure public-key encryption (PKE) into an IND-CCA-secure KEM. These constructions can be classified into two categories according to the value for an invalid ciphertext during the decapsulation. One category contains the constructions with explicit rejection which return a rejection symbol $\perp$ when decapsulating an invalid ciphertext, including $\mathrm{FO}^{\perp}$, $\mathrm{FO}^{\perp}_{m}$, $\mathrm{QFO}^{\perp}_{m}$, $\mathrm{U}^{\perp}$, $\mathrm{U}^{\perp}_{m}$, $\mathrm{QU}^{\perp}_{m}$, where FO denotes the class of transformations that turn a PKE with standard security (one-wayness against chosen- plaintext attacks (OW-CPA) or indistinguishability against chosen-plaintext attacks (IND-CPA)) into an IND-CCA KEM, U denotes the class of transformations that turn a PKE with non-standard security (e.g., OW-PCA, one-way against plaintext checking attack [7,8]) or a deterministic PKE (DPKE, where the encryption algorithm is deterministic) into an IND-CCA-secure KEM, m[1] (without m) means $K = H(m)$ ($K = H(m, c)$), $\not\perp$ ($\perp$) means implicit (explicit) rejection and Q means an additional Targhi-Unruh hash [9] (a length-preserving hash function that has the same domain and range size) is added into the ciphertext. The second category contains the KEM constructions with implicit rejection where a pseudorandom key is returned for an invalid ciphertext, including $\mathrm{FO}^{\not\perp}$, $\mathrm{FO}^{\not\perp}_{m}$, $\mathrm{QFO}^{\not\perp}_{m}$, $\mathrm{U}^{\not\perp}$, $\mathrm{U}^{\not\perp}_{m}$, $\mathrm{QU}^{\not\perp}_{m}$.

Recently, the National Institute of Standards and Technology (NIST) launched a Post-Quantum Cryptography Project and published a call for submissions of quantum-resistant public-key cryptographic algorithms including digital-signature, PKE, and KEM (or key exchange) [10]. Among the 69 Round-1 submissions [10], there are 39 KEM proposals. Specially, 25 NIST submissions followed above constructions in [4] to achieve IND-CCA security.

Generic constructions in the ROM have gathered renewed interest in the post-quantum setting, where adversaries are equipped with a quantum computer. In the real world, quantum adversary can execute hash functions (the instantiation of the RO) on an arbitrary superposition of inputs. Therefore, for evaluating the post-quantum security, one needs to perform the analysis in the quantum

[1] The message m here is picked at random from the message space of underlying PKE.

random oracle model (QROM), introduced by [11]. Unfortunately, the QROM is quite difficult to work with, since many proof techniques in the ROM including adaptive programmability or extractability, have no analog in the QROM [11].

Hofheinz et al. [4] first presented two generic KEM constructions in the QROM, $\mathrm{QFO}_m^{\not\perp}$ and $\mathrm{QFO}_m^{\perp}$, where a Targhi-Unruh hash [9] is used to follow the technique in [9,12] to prove the QROM security. However, the security reductions are highly non-tight with quartic loss.

Subsequently, Saito, Xagawa and Yamakawa [13] and Jiang et al. [14] extended the technique in [11] to remove the Targhi-Unruh hash and tighten above security reductions. Jiang et al. [14] presented security reductions for $\mathrm{FO}_m^{\not\perp}$ and $\mathrm{FO}^{\not\perp}$ with quadratic loss from standard OW-CPA security of underlying PKE. Saito et al. [13] proposed a new security notion for DPKE called the disjoint simulatability (DS) security, and showed that the $\mathrm{U}_m^{\not\perp}$ transformation can convert a DS-secure DPKE into an IND-CCA-secure KEM with a tight security reduction. However, above improvements were only achieved for KEM constructions with implicit rejection due to the obstacle that the simulator needs to verify the validity of a ciphertext [13,14].

Among the 25 NIST submissions where the generic constructions in [4] are used, 10 submissions (40%) use generic KEM constructions with explicit rejection [10] including EMBLEM and R.EMBLEM, Lepton, NTRU-HRSS-KEM, BIG QUAKE, DAGS, HQC, LOCKER, QC-MDPC, RQC and ThreeBears. Except ThreeBears [15] which provides a sketch of a QROM security reduction with quadratic loss based on their specific scheme, the other 9 submissions that use the transformation $\mathrm{QFO}_m^{\perp}$ or $\mathrm{QFO}^{\perp}$[2] only have a highly non-tight QROM security reduction with quartic loss.

In this paper, we focus on generic constructions of an IND-CCA-secure KEM with explicit rejection, under the same assumptions and with the same tightness in security reduction as KEMs with implicit rejection [13,14].

1.1 Our Contributions

We present three generic constructions of an IND-CCA-secure KEM with explicit rejection, $\mathrm{HFO}_m^{\perp}$, $\mathrm{HFO}^{\perp}$ and $\mathrm{HU}_m^{\perp}$, from a weakly secure PKE, by revisiting the *plaintext confirmation* method in the QROM (refer to Subsect. 1.2 for details). $\mathrm{HFO}_m^{\perp}$, $\mathrm{HFO}^{\perp}$ and $\mathrm{HU}_m^{\perp}$ are identical with the existing generic constructions with explicit rejection $\mathrm{QFO}_m^{\perp}$, $\mathrm{QFO}^{\perp}$ and $\mathrm{QU}_m^{\perp}$ in [4] except for the hash used in *plaintext confirmation*. In $\mathrm{HFO}_m^{\perp}$, $\mathrm{HFO}^{\perp}$ and $\mathrm{HU}_m^{\perp}$, a conventional hash function works. In contrast, in $\mathrm{QFO}_m^{\perp}$, $\mathrm{QFO}^{\perp}$ and $\mathrm{QU}_m^{\perp}$, the hash function is required to be length-preserving, a Targhi-Unruh hash function. A length-preserving hash function will lead to a significant increase of encapsulation size in the case that the message space elements are strictly larger than a single hash value, e.g., NTRU-HRSS-KEM [16]. Thus, our constructions can directly help to reduce the encapsulation size for these KEM schemes.

[2] Actually, $\mathrm{QFO}^{\perp}$ was not definitely presented by [4]. But, its construction is the same as $\mathrm{QFO}_m^{\perp}$ except that $K = H(m, c)$ and its security can be easily derived from the security proof of $\mathrm{QFO}_m^{\perp}$ in [4].

Table 1. Generic KEM constructions with explicit rejection in the QROM.

Constructions	Underlying security	Security bound
$\mathsf{QFO}_m^{\perp}$ and $\mathsf{QFO}^{\perp}$ [4]	OW-CPA	$q\sqrt{q^2\delta + q\sqrt{\epsilon}}$
Our $\mathsf{HFO}_m^{\perp}$ and $\mathsf{HFO}^{\not\perp}$	IND-CPA	$q\sqrt{\delta} + \sqrt{q\epsilon}$
Our $\mathsf{HFO}_m^{\perp}$ and $\mathsf{HFO}^{\not\perp}$	OW-CPA	$q\sqrt{\delta} + q\sqrt{\epsilon}$
Our $\mathsf{HU}_m^{\perp}$	DS	ϵ

In terms of QROM security reductions, ours are much tighter than the ones of $\mathsf{QFO}_m^{\perp}$ and $\mathsf{QFO}^{\perp}$ in [4], see Table 1. For any correctness error[3] δ ($0 \le \delta < 1$), our obtained security bounds for $\mathsf{HFO}_m^{\perp}$ and $\mathsf{HFO}^{\perp}$ are both $\epsilon' \approx q\sqrt{\delta} + q\sqrt{\epsilon}$ which are much tighter than $\epsilon' \approx q\sqrt{q^2\delta + q\sqrt{\epsilon}}$ in [4], where ϵ' is the success probability of an adversary against the IND-CCA security of the resulting KEM, ϵ is the success probability of another adversary against the OW-CPA security of the underlying PKE, and q is the total number of $\mathcal{B}$'s queries to various oracles. For $\mathsf{HU}_m^{\perp}$, the IND-CCA security of the resulting KEM is tightly reduced to the DS security of the underlying DPKE with perfect correctness[4]. That is, our generic constructions with explicit rejection achieve the same tightness in security reductions under identical assumptions as the corresponding KEM constructions with implicit rejection $\mathsf{FO}_m^{\not\perp}$, $\mathsf{FO}^{\not\perp}$ and $\mathsf{U}_m^{\not\perp}$ in [13,14]. Moreover, we also present tighter QROM security reductions, $\epsilon' \approx q\sqrt{\delta} + \sqrt{q\epsilon}$, for $\mathsf{HFO}_m^{\perp}$ and $\mathsf{HFO}^{\perp}$ based on the IND-CPA security of the underlying PKE.

Accordingly, our tighter QROM security reductions can directly provide more reliable security guarantee for the IND-CCA-secure KEM submissions with explicit rejection where $\mathsf{QFO}_m^{\perp}$ and $\mathsf{QFO}^{\perp}$ are used, e.g., NTRU-HRSS-KEM [16], see Table 2.

Table 2. IND-CCA-secure KEM submissions for which our tighter security reductions of $\mathsf{HFO}_m^{\perp}$ and $\mathsf{HFO}^{\perp}$ can directly provide more reliable security guarantee in the QROM.

Constructions	Submission
$\mathsf{HFO}_m^{\perp}$	NTRU-HRSS-KEM,DAGS,QC-MDPC
$\mathsf{HFO}^{\perp}$	EMBLEM and R.EMBLEM, Lepton, BIG QUAKE, HQC, LOCKER, RQC

1.2 Techniques

The difference between KEM constructions with explicit rejection and implicit rejection is the behavior of the decapsulation algorithm on an invalid ciphertext.

[3] The probability of decryption failure in a legitimate execution of the scheme.

[4] Perfect correctness, i.e., $\delta = 0$ is required by [13]. Here, we just follow this assumption.

In a KEM construction with implicit rejection, a pseudorandom key is returned instead of a rejection symbol $\perp$, which prevents the adversary from judging the validity of a ciphertext by querying the decapsulation oracle. Thus, the simulation of a decapsulation oracle does not need to verify if a given ciphertext is valid or not, and can use an identical hidden random orale H_q to answer the decapsulation queries for both valid ciphertexts and invalid ciphertexts [13,14].

However, in the case of explicit rejection, the simulation of the decapsulation oracle has to first verify the validity of a given ciphertext, which is the key obstacle for the techniques in [13,14] to carry over. Here, before showing how to overcome this obstacle, we first review two general methods [3,4] used in the ROM to achieve an IND-CCA-secure KEM construction with explicit rejection, the γ-*spreadness* assumption and *plaintext confirmation*.

γ-spread. By assuming the underlying PKE to be γ-*spread*, we can obtain a KEM construction with explicit rejection. A γ-*spread* PKE, introduced by Fujisaki and Okamoto [5,6], roughly speaking, requires that ciphertexts (generated by the probabilistic encryption algorithm) have sufficiently large entropy. It plays an important role in the ROM security proofs of the original FO transformation [5,6], and $\mathrm{FO}_m^{\perp}$ and $\mathrm{FO}^{\perp}$ (the KEM variants of FO transformation) in [4]. If the underlying PKE is γ-*spread*, we can easily verify the validity of a ciphertext by checking if the ciphertext is derived by using the randomness produced by the RO [4–6]. In the ROM, adversarial queries to the RO can be recorded by a list, which makes the above checking feasible. Unfortunately, as discussed in [14], in the QROM, it is difficult to learn the actual content of an adversarial RO query.

Plaintext confirmation. Adding an extra hash value of the plaintext to the ciphertext, called *plaintext confirmation*[5], is another method to achieve a construction with explicit rejection. This method was first introduced by [3, Table 4] in the ROM, in the context of a generic construction of an IND-CCA-secure KEM with explicit rejection based on a OW-CPA-secure DPKE, which can be viewed as a simpler version of the REACT construction. Our $\mathrm{HU}_m^{\perp}$ transformation is essentially the same as [3, Table 4].

In particular, a valid ciphertext $c = (c_1, c_2)$ is produced by $c_1 = Enc(pk, m)$, $c_2 = H'(m)$ for some m, where Enc is the encryption algorithm of the underlying DPKE. In the ROM, the validity of a ciphertext ($c = (c_1, c_2)$) can be verified by testing if (c_1, c_2) is contained in a list (m, c_1, c_2), where m is an adversarial query input to H', $(c_1 = Enc(pk, m), c_2 = H'(m))$ is the corresponding ciphertext. However, this verification method will not work in the QROM due to the same reason as in the case of the γ-*spreadness* assumption method that it's hard to learn adversarial query inputs.

In [4], Hofheinz et al. follow Targhi and Unruh's technique [9,12] and simulate H' using a random polynomial of degree $2q_{H'}$ over a finite field $\mathbb{F}_{2^n}$, where $q_{H'}$ is the number of adversarial queries to H' and n is the range size of H'. For a given

[5] This name comes from Bernstein and Persichetti's paper [17].

ciphertext $c = (c_1, c_2)$, the simulator verifies the validity by checking if c_1 lies within the encryptions of the roots of $H'(X) - c_2$. To make H' invertible, H' is required to be length-preserving. Additionally, the technique in [4,9] requires two instances of the one-way to hiding (OW2H) lemma [18, Lemma 6.2], which is a practical tool to prove the indistinguishability between games where the random oracles are reprogrammed. Nevertheless, the OW2H lemma will inherently incur a quadratic security loss. Thus, the security reductions of $\mathrm{QFO}_m^{\perp}$ and $\mathrm{QFO}^{\not\perp}$ in [4] suffer a quartic security loss.

In this paper, we develop a novel verification method for the KEM construction with explicit rejection based on *plaintext confirmation*, and circumvent the learning of adversarial queries. Specifically, the simulator replaces H' by $H'_q \circ Enc(pk, \cdot)$[6], where H'_q is a secret random function that is not given to the adversary. We require $Enc(pk, \cdot)$ to be indistinguishable from an injective function for any efficient quantum adversary. Thus, in the adversary's view, $H'_q \circ Enc(pk, \cdot)$ is a perfect random oracle. Then, we note that if c is a valid ciphertext, $H'_q(c_1) = c_2$, and if c is invalid, then $H'_q(c_1) = c_2$ with negligible probability. Thereby, using H'_q, we can verify the validity of a ciphertext $c = (c_1, c_2)$ just by testing if $H'_q(c_1) = c_2$ or not.

With this novel verification method for the validity of a ciphertext, we can extend the techniques in [13,14] to the constructions with explicit rejection in this paper. Thus, the OW2H lemma is instantiated only once in the security reductions for $\mathrm{HFO}^{\perp}$ and $\mathrm{HFO}_m^{\perp}$, and never used during the security reduction for $\mathrm{HU}_m^{\perp}$, which lead to the same security loss as the corresponding KEM constructions with implicit rejection in [13,14].

Tighter reduction from IND-CPA. Different from the adversary against the OW-CPA security of PKE, the adversary against the IND-CPA security of PKE knows the plaintexts m_0 and m_1 of which one is encrypted to obtain the challenge ciphertext. Thus, the simulator can make an elaborate analysis of the RO-query inputs, e.g., testing whether m_0 (or m_1) has been queried to the RO [4], and determine which one of the query inputs can be used to break the IND-CPA security instead of just uniformly choosing at random. Particularly, in the ROM, [4] presents tight reductions for FO transformations from IND-CPA security of underlying PKE to IND-CCA security of resulting KEM. However, the techniques in [4] require the simulator to maintain a RO-query list which is difficult to implement in the QROM. In our case, we instead use a semi-classical oracle technique (refer to Lemma 3 for details), recently introduced by Ambainis, Hamburg and Unruh [19], to test whether m_0 (or m_1) has been queried. Then, the security bound $q\sqrt{\delta} + q\sqrt{\epsilon}$ is improved to be $q\sqrt{\delta} + \sqrt{q\epsilon}$.

1.3 Discussion

As in prior works [4,13,14], we do not provide a general definition of explicit/implicit rejection on the KEM level. Although on first sight it

[6] Such a non-adaptive RO programming technique is also used in [11,13,14].

seems these notions could be clearly defined, it turns out that capturing implicit/explicit rejection appropriately on the KEM level (rather than on the construction level) is quite challenging. This seems to be mostly due to the fact that the notion of an "invalid ciphertext", on which the definition of explicit/implicit rejection would likely be based, remains elusive as well. Therefore, we only discuss explicit/implicit rejection on the construction level, as was also done in [15,17].

KEMs either have implicit rejection or explicit rejection, or do not satisfy either of these two. The advantages and disadvantages of explicit rejection and implicit rejection for specific KEM constructions have been discussed by [15] and [17]. The goal of this paper is not to take part in this discussion, but rather to expand the proof techniques from KEMs with implicit rejection to KEMs with explicit rejection. In particular, we show security reductions in the QROM for our generic KEM constructions with explicit rejection that preserve the same assumptions and tightness as previously known for KEMs with implicit rejection [13,14].

1.4 Related Work

In a concurrent and independent work, Zhandry [20] presented a proof in the QROM for original FO transformation in [5,6] from OW-CPA security of underlying PKE and one-time security of underlying symmetric key encryption to quantum CCA security of resulting PKE (quantum CCA security of PKE [21] is identical to CCA security except that adversaries can make decryption queries in quantum superpositions). However, the security proofs for KEM variants of FO transformation in this paper were not presented and the tightness was not discussed either. Moreover, their proof techniques are quite different from ours, and require γ-spread assumption of underlying PKE.

1.5 Future Work

We note that the Targhi-Unruh hash is removed in generic KEM constructions with implicit rejection [13,14]. However, a conventional extra hash (although not a Targhi-Unruh hash) is still required in our generic KEM constructions with explicit rejection, just like in the generic construction in the ROM [3, Table 4]. The ThreeBears [15] claims that removing this extra hash will not significantly impact the IND-CCA security of their KEM scheme even though the explicit rejection is used. Indeed, it seems possible that if the underlying PKE has some specific algebraic structure which can be used for the validity verification of the ciphertext, this extra hash can be removed even in a construction with explicit rejection.

In our future work, we will research the specific algebraic structure of the underlying PKE, which can help to achieve an IND-CCA-secure KEM construction with explicit rejection and without this extra hash.

2 Preliminaries

Symbol description. A security parameter is denoted by λ. The abbreviation PPT stands for probabilistic polynomial time. $\mathcal{K}$, $\mathcal{M}$, $\mathcal{C}$ and $\mathcal{R}$ are denoted as key space, message space, ciphertext space and randomness space, respectively. Given a finite set X, we denote the sampling of a uniformly random element x by $x \xleftarrow{\$} X$. Denote the sampling from some distribution D by $x \leftarrow D$. $x = ?y$ is denoted as an integer that is 1 if $x = y$, and otherwise 0. $\Pr[P : G]$ is the probability that the predicate P holds true where free variables in P are assigned according to the program in G. Denote deterministic (probabilistic) computation of an algorithm A on input x by $y := A(x)$ ($y \leftarrow A(x)$). Let $|X|$ be the cardinality of set X. A^H means that the algorithm A gets access to the oracle H. $f \circ g(\cdot)$ means $f(g(\cdot))$.

2.1 Quantum Random Oracle Model

We refer the reader to [22] for basic of quantum computation.

Random oracle model (ROM) [2] is an idealized model, where a hash function is modeled as a publicly accessible random oracle. In quantum setting, an adversary with quantum computer can off-line evaluate the hash function on an arbitrary superposition of inputs. As a result, the quantum adversary should be allowed to query the random orale with quantum state. We call this the quantum random oracle model (QROM), introduced by Boneh et al. [11]. Particularly, [11] argued that to prove post-quantum security one needs to prove security in the QROM.

Tools. Next, we will present several existing lemmas that we will use throughout the paper.

Lemma 1 (Simulating the random oracle [23, Theorem 6.1]**).** *Let H be an oracle drawn from the set of $2q$-wise independent functions uniformly at random. Then the advantage any quantum algorithm making at most q queries to H has in distinguishing H from a truly random function is identically 0.*

Lemma 2 (Generic search problem [14,24,25]**).** *Let $\gamma \in [0, 1]$. Let Z be a finite set. $F : Z \to \{0, 1\}$ is the following random function: For each z, $F(z) = 1$ with probability p_z ($p_z \leq \gamma$), and $F(z) = 0$ else. Let N be the function with $\forall z : N(z) = 0$. If an oracle algorithm A makes at most q quantum queries to F (or N), then*

$$\left|\Pr[b = 1 : b \leftarrow A^F] - \Pr[b = 1 : b \leftarrow A^N]\right| \leq 2q\sqrt{\gamma}.$$

Particularly, the probability of A finding a z such that $F(z) = 1$ is at most $2q\sqrt{\gamma}$, i.e., $\Pr[F(z) = 1 : z \leftarrow A^F] \leq 2q\sqrt{\gamma}$.

One way to hiding (OW2H) lemma [18, Lemma 6.2] is a practical tool to argue the indistinguishability between games where the random oracles are reprogrammed. Following are improved versions of OW2H lemma, recently introduced by [19].

Lemma 3 (Semi-classical OW2H [19, Theorem 1]**).** *Let $S \subseteq X$ be random. Let $\mathcal{O}_1$, $\mathcal{O}_2$ be oracles with domain X and codomain Y such that $\mathcal{O}_1(x) = \mathcal{O}_2(x)$ for any $x \notin S$. Let z be a random bitstring. ($\mathcal{O}_1$, $\mathcal{O}_2$, S and z may have arbitrary joint distribution D.) Let f_S be the indicator function, where $f_S(x) = 1$ if $x \in S$ and 0 otherwise. Let $\mathcal{O}_S^{SC}$ be an oracle that performs the semi-classical measurements corresponding to the projectors M_y when queried with $|x\rangle$, where $M_y := \sum_{x \in X: f_S(x)=y} |x\rangle\langle x|$ $(y \in 0, 1)$. Let $\mathcal{O}_2 \backslash S$ ("$\mathcal{O}_2$ punctured on S") be an oracle that first queries $\mathcal{O}_S^{SC}$ and then $\mathcal{O}_2$.*

Let $A^{\mathcal{O}_1}(z)$ be an oracle algorithm with query number d. Denote Find as the event that in the execution of $A^{\mathcal{O}_2 \backslash S}(z)$, $\mathcal{O}_S^{SC}$ ever outputs 1 during semi-classical measurements.

Let

$$P_{left} = \Pr[b = 1 : (\mathcal{O}_1, \mathcal{O}_2, S, z) \leftarrow D, b \leftarrow A^{\mathcal{O}_1}(z)]$$
$$P_{right} = \Pr[b = 1 \wedge \neg \mathsf{Find} : (\mathcal{O}_1, \mathcal{O}_2, S, z) \leftarrow D, b \leftarrow A^{\mathcal{O}_2 \backslash S}(z)]$$
$$P_{find} := \Pr[\mathsf{Find} : (\mathcal{O}_1, \mathcal{O}_2, S, z) \leftarrow D, A^{\mathcal{O}_2 \backslash S}(z)].$$

Then

$$|P_{left} - P_{right}| \leq \sqrt{(d+1)P_{find}} \text{ and } \left|\sqrt{P_{left}} - \sqrt{P_{right}}\right| \leq \sqrt{(d+1)P_{find}}.$$

Remark: There are several other definitions of P_{right} in [19, Theorem 1]. In this paper, we just need above definition in our security proofs.

Semi-classical oracle. Roughly speaking, semi-classical oracle O_S^{SC} only measures the output $|f_S(x)\rangle$ but not the input $|x\rangle$. Formally, for a query to O_S^{SC} with $\sum_{x,z} a_{x,z}|x\rangle|z\rangle$, $\mathcal{O}_S^{SC}$ does the following

1. initialize a single qubit L with $|0\rangle$,
2. transform $\sum_{x,z} a_{x,z}|x\rangle|z\rangle|0\rangle$ into $\sum_{x,z} a_{x,z}|x\rangle|z\rangle|f_S(x)\rangle$,
3. measure L.

Then, after performing a semi-classical measurement, the query state will become $\sum_{x,z:f_S(x)=y} a_{x,z}|x\rangle|z\rangle$ (non-normalized) if the measurement outputs y $(y \in 0, 1)$.

Lemma 4 (Search in semi-classical oracle [19, Corollary 1]**).** *Suppose that S and z are independent, and that A is a q-query algorithm. Let $P_{max} := \max_{x \in X} \Pr[x \in S]$. Then*

$$\Pr[\mathsf{Find} : A^{O_S^{SC}}(z)] \leq 4q \cdot P_{max}.$$

Lemma 5 (OW2H, Probabilities [19, Theorem 3]**).** *Let $S \subseteq X$ be random. Let $\mathcal{O}_1$, $\mathcal{O}_2$ be oracles with domain X and codomain Y such that $\mathcal{O}_1(x) = \mathcal{O}_2(x)$ for any $x \notin S$. Let z be a random bitstring. ($\mathcal{O}_1$, $\mathcal{O}_2$, S and z may have arbitrary joint distribution D.)*

Let $A^{\mathcal{O}_1}(z)$ be an oracle algorithm with query number d. Let $B^{\mathcal{O}_1}$ be an oracle algorithm that on input z does the following: pick $i \xleftarrow{\$} \{1, \ldots, d\}$, run $A^{\mathcal{O}_1}(z)$ until (just before) the i-th query, measure all query input registers in the computational basis, and output the set T of measurement outcomes. (When A makes less than i queries, B outputs $\perp \notin X$.)

Let

$$P_{left} = \Pr[b = 1 : (\mathcal{O}_1, \mathcal{O}_2, S, z) \leftarrow D, b \leftarrow A^{\mathcal{O}_1}(z)]$$
$$P_{right} = \Pr[b = 1 : (\mathcal{O}_1, \mathcal{O}_2, S, z) \leftarrow D, b \leftarrow A^{\mathcal{O}_2}(z)]$$
$$P_{guess} := \Pr[S \cap T \neq \emptyset : (\mathcal{O}_1, \mathcal{O}_2, S, z) \leftarrow D, T \leftarrow B^{\mathcal{O}_1}(z)].$$

Then
$|P_{left} - P_{right}| \leq 2d\sqrt{P_{guess}}$ *and* $\left|\sqrt{P_{left}} - \sqrt{P_{right}}\right| \leq 2d\sqrt{P_{guess}}$.

2.2 Cryptographic Primitives

Definition 1 (Public-key encryption). *A public-key encryption scheme* PKE $=$ *(Gen, Enc, Dec) consists of a triple of polynomial time (in the security parameter λ) algorithms and a finite message space $\mathcal{M}$.*

- *Gen(1^λ) $\rightarrow$ (pk, sk): the key generation algorithm, is a probabilistic algorithm which on input 1^λ outputs a public/secret key-pair (pk, sk). Usually, for brevity, we will omit the input of Gen.*
- *Enc(pk, m) $\rightarrow$ c: the encryption algorithm Enc, on input pk and a message $m \in \mathcal{M}$, outputs a ciphertext $c \leftarrow$ Enc(pk, m). If necessary, we make the used randomness of encryption explicit by writing $c :=$ Enc(pk, m; r), where $r \xleftarrow{\$} \mathcal{R}$ ($\mathcal{R}$ is the randomness space).*
- *Dec(sk, c) $\rightarrow$ m: the decryption algorithm Dec, is a deterministic algorithm which on input sk and a ciphertext c outputs a message $m :=$ Dec(sk, c) or a rejection symbol $\perp \notin \mathcal{M}$.*

A PKE is determined if *Enc* is deterministic. We denote DPKE to stand for a determined PKE.

Definition 2 (Correctness [4]). *A public-key encryption scheme* PKE *is* δ-correct *if*

$$E[\max_{m \in \mathcal{M}} \Pr[Dec(sk, c) \neq m : c \leftarrow Enc(pk, m)]] \leq \delta,$$

where the expectation is taken over $(pk, sk) \leftarrow Gen$. We say a PKE is perfectly correct if $\delta = 0$.

Next, we define three security notions, one-wayness against chosen-plaintext attacks (OW-CPA) of PKE, indistinguishability against chosen-plaintext attacks (IND-CPA) of PKE, and disjoint simulatability (DS) of DPKE.

Definition 3 (OW-CPA-secure PKE). *Let* PKE $=$ *(Gen, Enc, Dec) be a public-key encryption scheme with message space $\mathcal{M}$. Define* OW $-$ CPA *game* *of PKE as in Fig. 1. Define the* OW − CPA *advantage function of an adversary* $\mathcal{A}$ *against PKE as*

$$\mathsf{Adv}_{\mathrm{PKE}}^{\mathrm{OW\text{-}CPA}}(\mathcal{A}) := \Pr[\mathrm{OW\text{-}CPA}_{\mathrm{PKE}}^{\mathcal{A}} = 1].$$

Game OW-CPA	Game IND-CPA
$(pk, sk) \leftarrow Gen$	$(pk, sk) \leftarrow Gen$
$m^* \xleftarrow{\$} \mathcal{M}$	$b \leftarrow \{0,1\}$
$c^* \leftarrow Enc(pk, m^*)$	$(m_0, m_1) \leftarrow \mathcal{A}(pk)$
$m' \leftarrow \mathcal{A}(pk, c^*)$	$c^* \leftarrow Enc(pk, m_b)$
return $m' =? m^*$	$b' \leftarrow \mathcal{A}(pk, c^*)$
	return $b' =? b$

Fig. 1. Game OW-CPA and game IND-CPA for PKE.

Definition 4 (IND-CPA-secure PKE). *Let* PKE $= (Gen, Enc, Dec)$ *be a public-key encryption scheme with message space* $\mathcal{M}$. *Define* IND − CPA *game of PKE as in Fig. 1, where* m_0 *and* m_1 *have the same length. Define the* IND − CPA *advantage function of an adversary* $\mathcal{A}$ *against PKE as*

$$\mathsf{Adv}_{\mathrm{PKE}}^{\mathrm{IND\text{-}CPA}}(\mathcal{A}) := \left|\Pr[\mathrm{IND\text{-}CPA}_{\mathrm{PKE}}^{\mathcal{A}} = 1] - 1/2\right|.$$

Definition 5 (DS-secure DPKE [13]**).** *Let* $D_{\mathcal{M}}$ *denote an efficiently sampleable distribution on a set* $\mathcal{M}$. *A DPKE scheme (Gen,Enc,Dec) with plaintext and ciphertext spaces* $\mathcal{M}$ *and* $\mathcal{C}$ *is* $D_{\mathcal{M}}$*-disjoint simulatable if there exists a PPT algorithm* S *that satisfies the following.*

- *Statistical disjointness:*

$$\mathrm{DISJ}_{\mathrm{PKE},S} := \max_{(pk,sk)\in Gen(1^\lambda;\mathcal{R}_{gen})} \Pr[c \in Enc(pk, \mathcal{M}) : c \leftarrow S(pk)]$$

  is negligible, where $\mathcal{R}_{gen}$ *denotes a randomness space for Gen.*
- *Ciphertext indistinguishability: For any PPT adversary* $\mathcal{A}$,

$$\mathsf{Adv}_{\mathrm{PKE},D_{\mathcal{M}},S}^{\mathrm{DS\text{-}IND}}(\mathcal{A}) := \left| \begin{array}{l} \Pr\left[\mathcal{A}(pk, c^*) \rightarrow 1 : \begin{array}{r} (pk, sk) \leftarrow Gen; m^* \leftarrow D_{\mathcal{M}}; \\ c^* = Enc(pk, m^*) \end{array}\right] \\ - \Pr[\mathcal{A}(pk, c^*) \rightarrow 1 : (pk, sk) \leftarrow Gen; c^* \leftarrow S(pk)] \end{array} \right|$$

  is negligible.

Definition 6 (Key encapsulation). *A key encapsulation mechanism KEM consists of three algorithms Gen, Encaps and Decaps.*

- $Gen(1^\lambda) \rightarrow (pk, sk)$*: the key generation algorithm Gen outputs a key pair* (pk, sk). *Usually, for brevity, we will omit the input of Gen.*

- *Encaps(pk)* $\rightarrow (K, c)$: *the encapsulation algorithm Encaps, on input pk, outputs a tuple* (K, c), *where* $K \in \mathcal{K}$ *and ciphertext c is said to be an encapsulation of the key K. If necessary, we make the used randomness of encapsulation explicit by writing* $(K, c) := Encaps(pk; r)$, *where* $r \in \mathcal{R}$ *($\mathcal{R}$ is the randomness space).*
- *Decaps(sk, c)* $\rightarrow K$: *the deterministic decapsulation algorithm Decaps, on input sk and an encapsulation c, outputs either a key* $K := Decaps(sk, c) \in \mathcal{K}$ *or a rejection symbol* $\perp \notin \mathcal{K}$.

Next, we now define a security notion for KEM: indistinguishability against chosen-ciphertext attacks (IND-CCA).

Definition 7 (IND-CCA-secure KEM). *We define the* IND − CCA *game as in Fig. 2 and the* IND − CCA *advantage function of an adversary* $\mathcal{A}$ *against* KEM *as*

$$\mathsf{Adv}_{\mathrm{KEM}}^{\text{IND-CCA}}(\mathcal{A}) := \left|\Pr[\text{IND-CCA}_{\mathrm{KEM}}^{\mathcal{A}} = 1] - 1/2\right|.$$

Game IND-CCA	DECAPS(sk, c)
$(pk, sk) \leftarrow Gen$	**if** $c = c^*$
$b \xleftarrow{\$} \{0, 1\}$	**return** $\perp$
$(K_0^*, c^*) \leftarrow Encaps(pk)$	**else return**
$K_1^* \xleftarrow{\$} \mathcal{K}$	$K := Decaps(sk, c)$
$b' \leftarrow \mathcal{A}^{\text{DECAPS}}(pk, c^*, K_b^*)$	
return $b' =?b$	

Fig. 2. IND-CCA game for KEM.

Following the work [4], we also make the convention that the number q_H of the adversarial queries to H counts the total number of times H is executed in the experiment. That is, the number of $\mathcal{A}$'s explicit queries to H plus the number of implicit queries to H made by the experiment.

3 Generic KEM Constructions with Explicit Rejection

Using Targhi-Unruh technique [9], Hofheinz et al. [4] first presented two generic constructions of an IND-CCA-secure KEM with explicit rejection $\mathrm{QFO}_m^{\perp}$ and $\mathrm{QFO}_m^{\not\perp}$ in the QROM, by reducing the OW-CPA security of underlying PKE scheme to the IND-CCA security of resulting KEM with quartic security loss. These two constructions are widely used to achieve IND-CCA security in the NIST Round-1 KEM submissions [10]. Subsequently, Jiang et al. [14] improved above security loss to be quadratic for $\mathrm{FO}_m^{\not\perp}$ and $\mathrm{FO}^{\not\perp}$. For the transformation $\mathrm{U}_m^{\not\perp}$ in [4], Saito et al. [13] gave a tight reduction from the DS security of underlying perfectly correct DPKE to the IND-CCA security of resulting KEM. However, the proof techniques in [13,14] are restricted to the KEM constructions with implicit rejection.

$Encaps(pk)$	$Decaps(sk, c)$
$m \xleftarrow{\$} \mathcal{M}$	Parse $c = (c_1, c_2)$
$c_1 = Enc(pk, m; G(m))$	$m' := Dec(sk, c_1)$
$c_2 = H'(m)$	**if** $Enc(pk, m'; G(m')) = c_1 \wedge H'(m') = c_2$
$c = (c_1, c_2)$	**return** $K := H(m')$
$K := H(m)$	**else return** $\perp$
return (K, c)	

Fig. 3. IND-CCA-secure KEM–I = $\mathrm{HFO}_m^{\perp}[\mathrm{PKE}, G, H, H']$

$Encaps(pk)$	$Decaps(sk, c)$
$m \xleftarrow{\$} \mathcal{M}$	Parse $c = (c_1, c_2)$
$c_1 = Enc(pk, m; G(m))$	$m' := Dec(sk, c_1)$
$c_2 = H'(m)$	**if** $Enc(pk, m'; G(m')) = c_1 \wedge H'(m') = c_2$
$c = (c_1, c_2)$	**return** $K := H(m', c)$
$K := H(m, c)$	**else return** $\perp$
return (K, c)	

Fig. 4. IND-CCA-secure KEM–II = $\mathrm{HFO}^{\perp}[\mathrm{PKE}, G, H, H']$

$Encaps(pk)$	$Decaps(sk, c)$
$m \xleftarrow{\$} \mathcal{M}$	Parse $c = (c_1, c_2)$
$c_1 = Enc(pk, m)$	$m' := Dec(sk, c_1)$
$c_2 = H'(m)$	**if** $Enc(pk, m') = c_1 \wedge H'(m') = c_2$
$c = (c_1, c_2)$	**return** $K := H(m')$
$K := H(m)$	**else return** $\perp$
return (K, c)	

Fig. 5. IND-CCA-secure KEM–III = $\mathrm{HU}_m^{\perp}[\mathrm{DPKE}, H, H']$

In this section, first, we will present three generic constructions of an IND-CCA-secure KEM with explicit rejection, $\mathrm{HFO}_m^{\perp}$, $\mathrm{HFO}^{\perp}$ and $\mathrm{HU}_m^{\perp}$, corresponding the implicit ones, i.e., $\mathrm{FO}_m^{\not\perp}$, $\mathrm{FO}^{\not\perp}$ and $\mathrm{U}_m^{\not\perp}$ in [4,13,14]. Then, assuming OW-CPA security of underlying PKE, we will provide security reductions for $\mathrm{HFO}_m^{\perp}$ and $\mathrm{HFO}^{\perp}$ with quadratic security loss. Particularly, we also present tighter security reductions for $\mathrm{HFO}_m^{\perp}$ and $\mathrm{HFO}^{\perp}$ with the IND-CPA security assumption of underlying PKE. Finally, we will give a tight security reduction for $\mathrm{HU}_m^{\perp}$, from the DS security of underlying perfectly correct DPKE to the IND-CCA security of resulting KEM.

To a public-key encryption scheme PKE = (*Gen*, *Enc*, *Dec*) with message space $\mathcal{M}$ and randomness space $\mathcal{R}$, hash functions $G : \mathcal{M} \rightarrow \mathcal{R}$, $H : \{0,1\}^* \rightarrow \{0,1\}^n$ and $H' : \mathcal{M} \rightarrow \{0,1\}^{n'}$[7], we associate KEM−I $= \mathrm{HFO}_m^{\perp}[\mathrm{PKE}, G, H, H']$, KEM−II $= \mathrm{HFO}^{\perp}[\mathrm{PKE}, G, H, H']$, and KEM−III $= \mathrm{HU}^{\perp}[\mathrm{PKE}, H, H']$, shown[8] in Figs. 3, 4 and 5, respectively. To make the presentation concise, we make the convention that $\mathcal{K} = \{0,1\}^n$.

Remark: Explicit (implicit resp.) rejection[9] means a rejection symbol $\perp$ (pseudorandom key, resp.) is returned for an invalid ciphertext, where we use a construction-dependent definition of invalid ciphertext. For KEM-I and KEM-II (KEM-III, resp.), we say a ciphertext $c = (c_1, c_2)$ is *invalid* if there is no m' such that $(c_1, c_2) \neq (Enc(pk, m'; G(m')), H'(m'))$ ($(c_1, c_2) \neq (Enc(pk, m'), H'(m'))$, resp.).

Theorem 1 (PKE IND-CPA $\overset{QROM}{\Rightarrow}$ (KEM-I IND-CCA). *If* PKE *is* δ-correct, *for any IND-CCA adversary* $\mathcal{B}$ *against KEM-I, issuing at most* q_D *queries to the decapsulation oracle* DECAPS, *at most* q_G (q_H, $q_{H'}$) *queries to the random oracle* G (H, H'), *there exists an IND-CPA adversary* $\mathcal{A}$ *against* PKE *such that* $\mathtt{Adv}_{\text{KEM-I}}^{\text{IND-CCA}}(\mathcal{B}) \leq 2\sqrt{2(q_G + q_H + 1)\mathtt{Adv}_{\text{PKE}}^{\text{IND-CPA}}(\mathcal{A}) + 4\frac{(q_G+q_H+1)^2}{|\mathcal{M}|}} + 4q_G\sqrt{\delta} + \frac{q_D}{2^{n'}}$ *and the running time of* $\mathcal{A}$ *is about that of* $\mathcal{B}$.

Proof. Let $\mathcal{B}$ be an adversary against the IND-CCA security of KEM-I, issuing at most q_D queries to the decapsulation oracle DECAPS, at most q_G (q_H, $q_{H'}$) queries to the random oracle G (H, H'). Denote Ω_G, Ω_H, $\Omega_{H'}$, Ω_{H_q} and $\Omega_{H'_q}$ as the sets of all functions $G : \mathcal{M} \rightarrow \mathcal{R}$, $H : \mathcal{M} \rightarrow \{0,1\}^n$, $H' : \mathcal{M} \rightarrow \{0,1\}^{n'}$, $H_q : \mathcal{C}_1 \rightarrow \{0,1\}^n$ and $H'_q : \mathcal{C}_1 \rightarrow \{0,1\}^{n'}$, respectively, where $\mathcal{C}_1$ is the ciphertext space of underlying PKE scheme. Consider the games in Fig. 6.

GAME G_0. Since game G_0 is exactly the IND-CCA game,

$$\left|\Pr[G_0^{\mathcal{B}} \Rightarrow 1] - 1/2\right| = \mathtt{Adv}_{\text{KEM-I}}^{\text{IND-CCA}}(\mathcal{B}).$$

[7] We assume that G, H, H' are not used in the algorithms of PKE, including *Gen*, *Enc* and *Dec*.

[8] The key generation algorithms *Gen* in KEM-I, KEM-II and KEM-III are the same as the ones in corresponding underlying PKEs.

[9] There may exist some KEMs with neither explicit nor implicit rejection.

Given (pk, sk) and $m \in \mathcal{M}$, define "bad" randomness $\mathcal{R}_{\mathrm{bad}}(pk, sk, m)$ and "good" randomness $\mathcal{R}_{\mathrm{good}}(pk, sk, m) = \mathcal{R} \setminus \mathcal{R}_{\mathrm{bad}}(pk, sk, m)$, where $\mathcal{R}_{\mathrm{bad}}(pk, sk, m) = \{r \in \mathcal{R} : Dec(sk, Enc(pk, m; r)) \neq m\}$. Let

$$\delta(pk, sk, m) = \frac{|\mathcal{R}_{\mathrm{bad}}(pk, sk, m)|}{|\mathcal{R}|}$$

as the fraction of bad randomness and $\delta(pk, sk) = \max_{m \in \mathcal{M}} \delta(pk, sk, m)$. Thus, $\delta = \mathbf{E}[\delta(pk, sk)]$, where the expectation is taken over $(pk, sk) \leftarrow Gen$.

GAMES $G_0 - G_8$	$H(m)$ $//G_2 - G_8$
1: $(pk, sk) \leftarrow Gen; G \xleftarrow{\$} \Omega_G$	1: **return** $H_q \circ g(m)$
2: $G' \xleftarrow{\$} \Omega_{G'}; G := G'$ $//G_1 - G_3$	$H'(m)$ $//G_2 - G_8$
3: $g(\cdot) = Enc(pk, \cdot; G(\cdot))$	1: **return** $H'_q \circ g(m)$
4: $H \xleftarrow{\$} \Omega_H; H' \xleftarrow{\$} \Omega_{H'}$ $//G_0 - G_1$	DECAPS $(c \neq c^*)$ $//G_0 - G_2$
5: $H_q \xleftarrow{\$} \Omega_{H_q}; H'_q \xleftarrow{\$} \Omega_{H'_q}$	1: Parse $c = (c_1, c_2)$
6: $m^* \xleftarrow{\$} \mathcal{M}$	2: $m' := Dec(sk, c_1)$
7: $r^* := G(m^*)$	3: **if** $g(m') = c_1 \wedge H'(m') = c_2$
8: $r^* \xleftarrow{\$} \mathcal{R}$ $//G_6 - G_8$	4: **return** $K := H(m')$
9: $c_1^* := Enc(pk, m^*; r^*)$ $//G_0 - G_7$	5: **else return** $\perp$
10: $m'^* \xleftarrow{\$} \mathcal{M}$ $//G_8$	DECAPS $(c \neq c^*)$ $//G_3 - G_8$
11: $c_1^* := Enc(pk, m'^*; r^*)$ $//G_8$	1: Parse $c = (c_1, c_2)$
12: $c_2^* := H'(m^*)$ $//G_0 - G_1$	2: **if** $H'_q(c_1) = c_2$
13: $c_2^* := H'_q(c_1^*)$ $//G_2 - G_8$	3: **return** $K := H_q(c_1)$
14: $c^* = (c_1^*, c_2^*)$	4: **else return** $\perp$
15: $k_0^* := H(m^*)$	
16: $k_0^* \xleftarrow{\$} \mathcal{K}$ $//G_6 - G_8$	
17: $k_1^* \xleftarrow{\$} \mathcal{K}; b \xleftarrow{\$} \{0,1\}$	
18: $b' \leftarrow \mathcal{B}^{G,H,H',\mathrm{DECAPS}}(pk, c^*, k_b^*)$ $//G_0 - G_4$	
19: $\ddot{G} := G; \ddot{G}(m^*) \xleftarrow{\$} \mathcal{R}$ $//G_5 - G_6$	
20: $\ddot{H} := H; \ddot{H}(m^*) \xleftarrow{\$} \mathcal{K}$ $//G_5 - G_6$	
21: $g(\cdot) = Enc(pk, \cdot; \ddot{G} \backslash m^*(\cdot))$ $//G_5 - G_6$	
22: $b' \leftarrow \mathcal{B}^{\ddot{G}\backslash m^*, \ddot{H}\backslash m^*, H', \mathrm{DECAPS}}(pk, c^*, k_b^*) //G_5 - G_6$	
23: $b' \leftarrow \mathcal{B}^{G\backslash m^*, H\backslash m^*, H', \mathrm{DECAPS}}(pk, c^*, k_b^*) //G_7 - G_8$	
24: **return** $b' = ?b$	

Fig. 6. Games G_0-G_8 for the proof of Theorem 1

Let G' be a random function such that $G'(m)$ is sampled according to the uniform distribution in $\mathcal{R}_{\mathrm{good}}(pk, sk, m)$. Let $\Omega_{G'}$ be the set of all functions G'.

GAME G_1. In game G_1, we replace G by G' that uniformly samples from "good" randomness at random, i.e., $G' \xleftarrow{\$} \Omega_{G'}$. First, let's show that any adversary distinguishing G_0 from G_1 can be converted into an adversary distinguishing G from G' in the following way.

Construct an adversary $B^{\widetilde{G}}(pk, sk)$ against the distinguishing problem between G and G' by taking the accessible oracle $\widetilde{G}$ as G, simulating $\mathcal{B}$'s view and outputting in the same way as G_0 and G_1. We note that for any (pk, sk) generated by Gen, if $\widetilde{G} = G$, $B^{\widetilde{G}}(pk, sk)$ perfectly simulates G_0 and $\Pr[1 \leftarrow B^G : (pk, sk)] = \Pr[G_0^{\mathcal{B}} \Rightarrow 1 : (pk, sk)]$. If $\widetilde{G} = G'$, $B^{\widetilde{G}}(pk, sk)$ perfectly simulates G_1 and $\Pr[1 \leftarrow B^{G'} : (pk, sk)] = \Pr[G_1^{\mathcal{B}} \Rightarrow 1 : (pk, sk)]$.

Thus,

$$\begin{aligned} &\left|\Pr[G_0^{\mathcal{B}} \Rightarrow 1 : (pk, sk)] - \Pr[G_1^{\mathcal{B}} \Rightarrow 1 : (pk, sk)]\right| \\ = &\left|\Pr[1 \leftarrow B^G : (pk, sk)] - \Pr[1 \leftarrow B^{G'} : (pk, sk)]\right|. \end{aligned}$$

Next, we will show that any adversary distinguishing G from G' can be converted into an adversary distinguishing F_1 from F_2, where F_1 is a function such that $F_1(m)$ is sampled according to Bernoulli distribution $B_{\delta(pk,sk,m)}$, i.e., $\Pr[F_1(m) = 1] = \delta(pk, sk, m)$ and $\Pr[F_1(m) = 0] = 1 - \delta(pk, sk, m)$, and F_2 is a constant function that always outputs 0 for any input.

$A^F(pk, sk)$	$\widetilde{G}(m)$
Pick a $2q_G$-wise function f	**if** $F(m) = 0$
$b'' \leftarrow B^{\widetilde{G}}(pk, sk)$	$\quad \widetilde{G}(m) = Sample(\mathcal{R}_{\text{good}}(pk, sk, m); f(m))$
return b''	**else**
	$\quad \widetilde{G}(m) = Sample(\mathcal{R}_{\text{bad}}(pk, sk, m); f(m))$
	return $\widetilde{G}(m)$

Fig. 7. A^F for the proof of Theorem 1

Given any adversary $B^{\widetilde{G}}(pk, sk)$, we construct an adversary $A^F(pk, sk)$ as in Fig. 7. $Sample(\mathcal{Y})$ is a probabilistic algorithm that returns a uniformly distributed $y \xleftarrow{\$} \mathcal{Y}$. $Sample(\mathcal{Y}; f(m))$ denotes the deterministic execution of $Sample(\mathcal{Y})$ using explicitly given randomness $f(m)$. Note that $\widetilde{G} = G$ if $F = F_1$ and $\widetilde{G} = G'$ if $F = F_2$. Thus, for any fixed (pk, sk) generated by Gen, $\Pr[1 \leftarrow A^{F_1} : (pk, sk)] = \Pr[1 \leftarrow B^G : (pk, sk)]$ and $\Pr[1 \leftarrow A^{F_2} : (pk, sk)] = \Pr[1 \leftarrow B^{G'} : (pk, sk)]$. Conditioned on a fixed (pk, sk) we obtain by Lemma 2

$$\begin{aligned} &\left|\Pr[1 \leftarrow B^G : (pk, sk)] - \Pr[1 \leftarrow B^{G'} : (pk, sk)]\right| \\ = &\left|\Pr[1 \leftarrow A^{F_1} : (pk, sk)] - \Pr[1 \leftarrow A^{F_2} : (pk, sk)]\right| \leq 2q_G\sqrt{\delta(pk, sk)}. \end{aligned}$$

As $\left|\Pr[G_0^{\mathcal{B}} \Rightarrow 1 : (pk, sk)] - \Pr[G_1^{\mathcal{B}} \Rightarrow 1 : (pk, sk)]\right|$ can be bounded by the maximum distinguishing probability between G and G' for $B^{\widetilde{G}}(pk, sk)$,

$$\left|\Pr[G_0^{\mathcal{B}} \Rightarrow 1 : (pk, sk)] - \Pr[G_1^{\mathcal{B}} \Rightarrow 1 : (pk, sk)]\right| \leq 2q_G\sqrt{\delta(pk, sk)}.$$

By averaging over $(pk, sk) \leftarrow Gen$ we finally obtain

$$\left|\Pr[G_0^{\mathcal{B}} \Rightarrow 1] - \Pr[G_1^{\mathcal{B}} \Rightarrow 1]\right| \leq 2q_G\mathbf{E}[\sqrt{\delta(pk, sk)}] \leq 2q_G\sqrt{\delta}.$$

GAME G_2. In this game, replace H and H' by $H_q \circ g$ and $H'_q \circ g$ respectively, where

$$g(\cdot) = Enc(pk, \cdot; G(\cdot)).$$

Note that g in this game is an injective function since it only samples from "good" randomness. Thus, the distributions of H in G_1 and G_2 are identical. Therefore,

$$\Pr[G_1^{\mathcal{B}} \Rightarrow 1] = \Pr[G_2^{\mathcal{B}} \Rightarrow 1].$$

GAME G_3. In game G_3, the DECAPS oracle is changed that it makes no use of the secret key sk any more. When $\mathcal{B}$ queries the DECAPS oracle on $c = (c_1, c_2)$ $(c \neq c^*)$, $K := H_q(c_1)$ is returned if $H'_q(c_1) = c_2$, otherwise $\perp$. Let $m' := Dec(sk, c_1)$ and consider the following three cases.

Case 1: $Enc(pk, m'; G(m')) = c_1$ and $H'(m') = c_2$. Since $H = H_q \circ g$ and $H' = H'_q \circ g$, both DECAPS oracles in G_2 and G_3 return the same value $H_q(c_1)$.

Case 2: $Enc(pk, m'; G(m')) = c_1$ and $H'(m') \neq c_2$. In this case, $H'(m') = H'_q(c_1) \neq c_2$. Therefore, both DECAPS oracles in G_2 and G_3 return $\perp$.

Case 3: $Enc(pk, m'; G(m')) \neq c_1$. In G_2, the DECAPS oracle returns $\perp$. In G_3, note that if there exists an m'' such that $Enc(pk, m''; G(m'')) = c_1$, $m'' = m'$ since G in this game only samples from "good" randomness. That is, $Enc(pk, m'; G(m')) = c_1$ which contradicts the condition $Enc(pk, m'; G(m')) \neq c_1$. Therefore, above m'' does not exist. Meantime, we also note that $\mathcal{B}$'s queries to H' can only help him get access to H'_q at $\hat{c}_1$ such that $Enc(pk, \hat{m}; G(\hat{m})) = \hat{c}_1$ for some $\hat{m}$, thus $H'_q(c_1)$ is uniformly random in $\mathcal{B}$'s view. As a result, in this case, $\Pr[H'_q(c_1) = c_2] = \frac{1}{2^{n'}}$ and the DECAPS oracle in G_3 also returns $\perp$ with probability $1 - \frac{1}{2^{n'}}$.

By the union bound, we know that G_2 and G_3 can be distinguished with probability at most $\frac{q_D}{2^n}$. That is,

$$\left|\Pr[G_2^{\mathcal{B}} \Rightarrow 1] - \Pr[G_3^{\mathcal{B}} \Rightarrow 1]\right| \leq \frac{q_D}{2^{n'}}.$$

GAME G_4. In game G_4, we switch the G that only samples from "good" randomness back to an ideal random oracle G. Then, similar to the case of G_0 and

G_1, the distinguishing problem between G_3 and G_4 can also be converted to the distinguishing problem between G and G'. Using the same analysis method in bounding the difference between G_0 and G_1, we can have

$$\left|\Pr[G_3^{\mathcal{B}} \Rightarrow 1] - \Pr[G_4^{\mathcal{B}} \Rightarrow 1]\right| \leq 2q_G\sqrt{\delta}.$$

Let $\ddot{G}$ ($\ddot{H}$) be the function that $\ddot{G}(m^*) = \dot{r}^*$ ($\ddot{H}(m^*) = \dot{k}_0^*$), and $\ddot{G} = G$ ($\ddot{H} = H$) everywhere else, where $\dot{r}^*$ and $\dot{k}_0^*$ are picked uniformly at random from $\mathcal{R}$ and $\mathcal{K}$.

GAME G_5. In game G_5, replace G and H by $\ddot{G}\backslash m^*$ and $\ddot{H}\backslash m^*$ respectively. Note that in this game for $\mathcal{B}$'s query to G (H), $\ddot{G}\backslash m^*$ ($\ddot{H}\backslash m^*$) will first query $\mathcal{O}_{m^*}^{SC}$, i.e., perform a semi-classical measurement, and then query $\ddot{G}$ ($\ddot{H}$). Let Find be the event that $\mathcal{O}_{m^*}^{SC}$ ever outputs 1 during semi-classical measurements of $\mathcal{B}'s$ queries to G and H. Note that the state after semi-classical measurements is exactly the state just before querying $\ddot{G}$ and $\ddot{H}$. Thus, if the event $\neg\mathsf{Find}$ that $\mathcal{O}_{m^*}^{SC}$ always outputs 0 happens, there will be no m^* term for the state just before querying $\ddot{G}$ and $\ddot{H}$ (that is, the amplitude corresponding to $|m^*\rangle$ will be 0) and $\mathcal{B}$ never learns the values of $G(m^*)$ and $H(m^*)$. Therefore, if $\neg\mathsf{Find}$ happens, bit b is independent of $\mathcal{B}$'s view. Hence,

$$\Pr[G_5^{\mathcal{B}} \Rightarrow 1 \wedge \neg\mathsf{Find}] = 1/2 \Pr[\neg\mathsf{Find} : G_5] = 1/2(1 - \Pr[\mathsf{Find} : G_5]).$$

Let $(G\times H)(\cdot) = (G(\cdot), H(\cdot))$, $(\ddot{G}\times\ddot{H})(\cdot) = (\ddot{G}(\cdot), \ddot{H}(\cdot))$, and $(\ddot{G}\times\ddot{H})\backslash m^*(\cdot) = (\ddot{G}\backslash m^*(\cdot), \ddot{H}\backslash m^*(\cdot))$. If one wants to make queries to G (or H) by accessing to $G \times H$, he just needs to prepare a uniform superposition of all states in the output register responding to H (or G). The number of total queries to $G \times H$ is at most $q_G + q_H$. Let $\bar{H}_q$ be the function that $\bar{H}_q(c_1^*) = \perp$ and $\bar{H}_q = H_q$ everywhere else.

$A^{G\times H}(pk, c_1^*, H(m^*), \bar{H}_q)$

$H_q' \xleftarrow{\$} \Omega_{H_q'}$
$g(\cdot) = Enc(pk, \cdot; G(\cdot))$
$c_2^* = H_q'(c_1^*)$
$c^* = (c_1^*, c_2^*)$
$k_0^* = H(m^*)$
$k_1^* \xleftarrow{\$} \mathcal{K}$
$b \xleftarrow{\$} \{0,1\}$
$b' \leftarrow \mathcal{B}^{G,H,H',\textsc{Decaps}}(pk, c^*, k_b^*)$
return $b' =?b$

$H'(m)$

return $H_q' \circ g(m)$

DECAPS ($c \neq c^*$)

Parse $c = (c_1, c_2)$
if $H_q'(c_1) = c_2$
    return $K := \bar{H}_q(c_1)$
else return $\perp$

Fig. 8. $A^{G\times H}$ for the proof of Theorem 1.

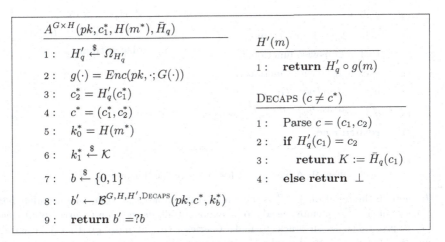

Let $A^{G\times H}$ be an oracle algorithm on input $(pk, c_1^*, H(m^*), \bar{H}_q)$[10] in Fig. 8. Sample pk, m^*, G, H_q, H and c_1^* in the same way as G_4 and G_5, i.e., $(pk, sk) \leftarrow Gen$, $m^* \xleftarrow{\$} \mathcal{M}$, $G \xleftarrow{\$} \Omega_G$, $H_q \xleftarrow{\$} \Omega_{H_q}$, $H := H_q \circ g$ and $c_1^* = Enc(pk, m^*; G(m^*))$. Then, $A^{G\times H}$ on input $(pk, c_1^*, H(m^*), \bar{H}_q)$ perfectly simulates G_4. If we replace $G \times H$ by $(\ddot{G} \times \ddot{H})\backslash m^*$, $A^{(\ddot{G}\times\ddot{H})\backslash m^*}$ on input $(pk, c_1^*, H(m^*), \bar{H}_q)$ perfectly simulates G_5.

Applying Lemma 3 with $X = \mathcal{M}$, $Y = (\mathcal{R}, \mathcal{K})$, $S = \{m^*\}$, $\mathcal{O}_1 = G \times H$, $\mathcal{O}_2 = \ddot{G} \times \ddot{H}$ and $z = (pk, c_1^*, H(m^*), \bar{H}_q)$, we can have

$$\left|\Pr[G_4^{\mathcal{B}} \Rightarrow 1] - \Pr[G_5^{\mathcal{B}} \Rightarrow 1 \wedge \neg\mathsf{Find}]\right| \leq \sqrt{(q_G + q_H + 1)\Pr[\mathsf{Find} : G_5]}.$$

GAME G_6. In game G_6, replace $r^* := G(m^*)$ and $k_0^* := H(m^*)$ by $r^* \xleftarrow{\$} \mathcal{R}$ and $k_0^* \xleftarrow{\$} \mathcal{K}$. We do not care about $\mathcal{B}$'s output, but only whether the event Find happens. Note that in G_5 and G_6, there is no information of $(G(m^*), H(m^*))$ in the oracle $(\ddot{G} \times \ddot{H})\backslash m^*$. Thus, apparently,

$\mathcal{A}(1^\lambda, pk)$

$m_0 \xleftarrow{\$} \mathcal{M}$

$m_1 \xleftarrow{\$} \mathcal{M}$

$b'' \xleftarrow{\$} \{0, 1\}$

$r^* \xleftarrow{\$} \mathcal{R}$

$c_1^* = Enc(pk, m_{b''}; r^*)$

$c_2^* = H_q'(c_1^*)$

$c^* = (c_1^*, c_2^*)$

$k^* \xleftarrow{\$} \mathcal{K}$

Pick a $2q_G$-wise function G

Pick a $2q_H$-wise function H_q

Pick a $2q_{H'}$-wise function H_q'

$g(\cdot) := Enc(pk, \cdot; G(\cdot))$

$b' \leftarrow \mathcal{B}^{G\backslash m_0, H\backslash m_0, H', \text{DECAPS}}(pk, c^*, k^*)$

return Find

$H(m)$

return $H_q \circ g(m)$

$H'(m)$

return $H_q' \circ g(m)$

DECAPS $(c \neq c^*)$

Parse $c = (c_1, c_2)$

if $H_q'(c_1) = c_2$

  return $K := H_q(c_1)$

else return $\perp$

Fig. 9. Adversary $\mathcal{A}$ for the proof of Theorem 1

[10] $\bar{H}_q$ here in the input of $A^{G\times H}$ is the whole truth table of $\bar{H}_q$. One may wonder that the size of $A^{G\times H}$'s memory needs to be exponentially large. Don't worry about this. $\bar{H}_q$ is just taken as an oracle to make queries (with at most q_H times) in actual games. That is, we can also take $\bar{H}_q$ as an accessible oracle instead of a whole truth table.

$$\Pr[\mathsf{Find}\ : G_5] = \Pr[\mathsf{Find}\ : G_6].$$

GAME G_7. In game G_7, replace $\ddot{G}$ and $\ddot{H}$ by G and H. Since $G(m^*)$ and $H(m^*)$ have never been used for simulating $\mathcal{B}$'s view,

$$\Pr[\mathsf{Find}\ : G_6] = \Pr[\mathsf{Find}\ : G_7].$$

GAME G_8. In game G_8, use m'^* instead of m^* for generating the challenge ciphertext, but keep using the original m^* for $G\backslash m^*$ and $H\backslash m^*$, where m'^* is chosen uniformly and independently of m^*. Note that the information of m^* in this game only exists in the oracles $G\backslash m^*$ and $H\backslash m^*$. By Lemma 4,

$$\Pr[\mathsf{Find}\ : G_8] \leq 4\frac{q_G + q_H + 1}{|\mathcal{M}|}.$$

Next, we show that any adversary distinguishing G_7 from G_8 can be converted into an adversary against the IND-CPA security of underlying PKE scheme. Construct an adversary $\mathcal{A}$ on input $(1^\lambda, pk)$ as in Fig. 9. Then, according to Lemma 1, if $b'' = 0$, $\mathcal{A}$ perfectly simulates G_7 and $\Pr[\mathsf{Find}\ : G_7] = \Pr[1 \leftarrow \mathcal{A} : b'' = 0]$. If $b'' = 1$, $\mathcal{A}$ perfectly simulates G_8 and $\Pr[\mathsf{Find}\ : G_8] = \Pr[1 \leftarrow \mathcal{A} : b'' = 1]$. Since $\mathtt{Adv}_{\mathrm{PKE}}^{\mathrm{IND\text{-}CPA}}(\mathcal{A}) = 1/2\,|\Pr[1 \leftarrow \mathcal{A} : b'' = 0] - \Pr[1 \leftarrow \mathcal{A} : b'' = 1]|$,

$$|\Pr[\mathsf{Find}\ : G_7] - \Pr[\mathsf{Find}\ : G_8]| = 2\mathtt{Adv}_{\mathrm{PKE}}^{\mathrm{IND\text{-}CPA}}(\mathcal{A}).$$

Finally, combing this with the bounds derived above, we can conclude that

$$\mathtt{Adv}_{\mathrm{KEM\text{-}I}}^{\mathrm{IND\text{-}CCA}}(\mathcal{B}) \leq 4q_G\sqrt{\delta} + \frac{q_D}{2^{n'}} + 2\sqrt{2(q_G + q_H + 1)\mathtt{Adv}_{\mathrm{PKE}}^{\mathrm{IND\text{-}CPA}}(\mathcal{A}) + 4\frac{(q_G + q_H + 1)^2}{|\mathcal{M}|}}.$$

□

Theorem 2 (PKE OW-CPA $\overset{QROM}{\Rightarrow}$ KEM-I IND-CCA). *If* PKE *is* δ-correct, *for any IND-CCA adversary* $\mathcal{B}$ *against KEM-I, issuing at most* q_D *queries to the decapsulation oracle* DECAPS, *at most* q_G $(q_H,\ q_{H'})$ *queries to the random oracle* G $(H,\ H')$, *there exists a OW-CPA adversary* $\mathcal{A}$ *against* PKE *such that* $\mathtt{Adv}_{\mathrm{KEM\text{-}I}}^{\mathrm{IND\text{-}CCA}}(\mathcal{B}) \leq 4q_G\sqrt{\delta} + \frac{q_D}{2^{n'}} + 2(q_G + q_H) \cdot \sqrt{\mathtt{Adv}_{\mathrm{PKE}}^{\mathrm{OW\text{-}CPA}}(\mathcal{A})}$ *and the running time of* $\mathcal{A}$ *is about that of* $\mathcal{B}$.

Different from $\mathrm{FO}_m^{\not\perp}$, $\mathrm{HFO}_m^{\perp}$ adds the plaintext confirmation and adopts explicit rejection for decapsulation. In [14, Theorem 2], a security proof of $\mathrm{FO}_m^{\not\perp}$ is given. The sole and key obstacle of applying the proof techniques in [14, Theorem 2] to $\mathrm{HFO}_m^{\perp}$ is the validity verification of ciphertext when simulating the decapsulation oracle. Fortunately, this can be overcome with the same verification method used in the proof of Theorem 1. Thus, combing the proofs of Theorem 1 and [14, Theorem 2], we can obtain a proof of Theorem 2, see Appendix A.

Different from the one in KEM-I, the hash function H in KEM-II takes both the plaintext m and the ciphertext c as input. Using the same proof method in [14, Theorem 1], we can divide the H-inputs (m, c) into two categories, matched inputs and unmatched inputs, by judging whether $c = (Enc(pk, m; G(m)), H'(m))$, and replace H by $H_q \circ g$ only for the matched inputs. Then, following the proofs of Theorems 1 and 2, we can derive Theorems 3 and 4.

Theorem 3 (PKE IND-CPA $\overset{QROM}{\Rightarrow}$ KEM-II IND-CCA). *If* PKE *is* δ-correct, *for any IND-CCA adversary* $\mathcal{B}$ *against KEM-II, issuing at most* q_D *queries to the decapsulation oracle* DECAPS, *at most* q_G $(q_H, q_{H'})$ *queries to the random oracle* G (H, H'), *there exists an IND-CPA adversary* $\mathcal{A}$ *against* PKE *such that* $\mathrm{Adv}^{\text{IND-CCA}}_{\text{KEM-II}}(\mathcal{B}) \leq 2\sqrt{2(q_G + q_H + 1)\mathrm{Adv}^{\text{IND-CPA}}_{\text{PKE}}(\mathcal{A}) + 4\frac{(q_G+q_H+1)^2}{|\mathcal{M}|}} + 4q_G\sqrt{\delta} + \frac{q_D}{2^{n'}}$ *and the running time of* $\mathcal{A}$ *is about that of* $\mathcal{B}$.

Theorem 4 (PKE OW-CPA $\overset{QROM}{\Rightarrow}$ KEM-II IND-CCA). *If* PKE *is* δ-correct, *for any IND-CCA adversary* $\mathcal{B}$ *against KEM-II, issuing at most* q_D *queries to the decapsulation oracle* DECAPS, *at most* q_G $(q_H, q_{H'})$ *queries to the random oracle* G (H, H'), *there exists a OW-CPA adversary* $\mathcal{A}$ *against* PKE *such that* $\mathrm{Adv}^{\text{IND-CCA}}_{\text{KEM-II}}(\mathcal{B}) \leq 4q_G\sqrt{\delta} + \frac{q_D}{2^{n'}} + 2(q_G + q_H) \cdot \sqrt{\mathrm{Adv}^{\text{OW-CPA}}_{\text{PKE}}(\mathcal{A})}$ *and the running time of* $\mathcal{A}$ *is about that of* $\mathcal{B}$.

Theorem 5 (PKE DS $\overset{QROM}{\Rightarrow}$ KEM-III IND-CCA). *If* PKE *is deterministic and perfectly correct, for any IND-CCA adversary* $\mathcal{B}$ *against KEM-III, issuing at most* q_D *queries to the decapsulation oracle* DECAPS, *at most* q_H $(q_{H'})$ *queries to the random oracle* H (H'), *there exists an adversary* $\mathcal{A}$ *against the DS security with an algorithm* S *such that* $\mathrm{Adv}^{\text{IND-CCA}}_{\text{KEM-III}}(\mathcal{B}) \leq \frac{q_D}{2^{n'}} + \mathrm{Adv}^{\text{DS-IND}}_{\text{PKE},U_\mathcal{M},S}(\mathcal{A}) + \mathrm{DISJ}_{\text{PKE},S}$, *where* $U_\mathcal{M}$ *is the uniform distribution in* $\mathcal{M}$, *and the running time of* $\mathcal{A}$ *is about that of* $\mathcal{B}$.

Proof. Let $\mathcal{B}$ be an adversary against the IND-CCA security of KEM-III, issuing at most q_D queries to DECAPS, at most q_H $(q_{H'})$ queries to H (H'). We follow the notations Ω_H, $\Omega_{H'}$, Ω_{H_q} and $\Omega_{H'_q}$ in Theorem 1. Consider the games in Fig. 10.

GAME G_0. Since game G_0 is exactly the IND-CCA game,

$$\left|\Pr[G_0^\mathcal{B} \Rightarrow 1] - 1/2\right| = \mathrm{Adv}^{\text{IND-CCA}}_{\text{KEM-III}}(\mathcal{B}).$$

GAME G_1. Replace H and H' by $H_q \circ g$ and $H'_q \circ g$ respectively, where

$$g(\cdot) = Enc(pk, \cdot).$$

As PKE is perfectly correct, g is an injective functions. Thus, $H_q \circ g$ $(H'_q \circ g)$ is also a uniformly random function as H (H') in G_0. Therefore, we can have

$$\Pr[G_0^\mathcal{B} \Rightarrow 1] = \Pr[G_1^\mathcal{B} \Rightarrow 1].$$

GAMES $G_0 - G_3$

$(pk, sk) \leftarrow Gen$
$H \xleftarrow{\$} \Omega_H; H' \xleftarrow{\$} \Omega_{H'}$ $//G_0$
$H_q \xleftarrow{\$} \Omega_{H_q}; H'_q \xleftarrow{\$} \Omega_{H'_q}$
$m^* \xleftarrow{\$} \mathcal{M}$
$c_1^* := Enc(pk, m^*)$ $//G_0 - G_2$
$c_1^* \leftarrow S(pk)$ $//G_3$
$c_2^* := H'(m^*)$ $//G_0$
$c_2^* := H'_q(c_1^*)$ $//G_1 - G_3$
$c^* = (c_1^*, c_2^*)$
$k_0^* := H(m^*)$ $//G_0$
$k_0^* := H_q(c_1^*)$ $//G_1 - G_3$
$k_1^* \xleftarrow{\$} \mathcal{K}$
$b \xleftarrow{\$} \{0, 1\}$
$b' \leftarrow \mathcal{B}^{H,H',\text{DECAPS}}(pk, c^*, k_b^*)$
return $b' =?b$

$H(m)$ $//G_1 - G_3$

return $H_q(Enc(pk, m))$

$H'(m)$ $//G_1 - G_3$

return $H'_q(Enc(pk, m))$

DECAPS $(c \neq c^*)$ $//G_0 - G_1$

Parse $c = (c_1, c_2)$
$m' := Dec(sk, c_1)$
if $Enc(pk, m') = c_1 \wedge H'(m') = c_2$
  return $K := H(m')$
else return $\perp$

DECAPS $(c \neq c^*)$ $//G_2 - G_3$

Parse $c = (c_1, c_2)$
if $H'_q(c_1) = c_2$
  return $K := H_q(c_1)$
else return $\perp$

Fig. 10. Games G_0-G_3 for the proof of Theorem 3

GAME G_2. In game G_2, the DECAPS oracle is changed that it makes no use of the secret key sk any more. When $\mathcal{B}$ queries the DECAPS oracle on $c = (c_1, c_2)$ $(c \neq c^*)$, $K := H_q(c_1)$ is returned if $H'_q(c_1) = c_2$, otherwise $\perp$.

Let $m' := Dec(sk, c_1)$. Consider the following three cases.

Case 1: If $Enc(pk, m') \neq c_1$. In this case, the DECAPS oracle in G_1 returns $\perp$. We note that $\mathcal{B}$'s queries to H' can only help him get access to H'_q at $\hat{c}_1$ such that $Enc(pk, \hat{m}) = \hat{c}_1$ for some $\hat{m}$. Such a $\hat{m}$ that $Enc(pk, \hat{m}) = c_1$ does not exist due to the perfect correctness of underlying DPKE. Thus, $H'_q(c_1)$ is uniformly random in $\mathcal{B}$'s view and $H'_q(c_1) \neq c_2$ with probability $1 - \frac{1}{2^{n'}}$. Therefore, the DECAPS oracle in G_2 returns $\perp$ with probability $1 - \frac{1}{2^{n'}}$.

Case 2: $Enc(pk, m') = c_1 \wedge H'(m') = c_2$. In this case, $H'(m') = H'_q(Enc(pk, m')) = H'_q(c_1) = c_2$. Thus, both DECAPS oracles in G_1 and G_2 return the same value $H(m') = H_q \circ g(m') = H_q(c_1)$.

Case 3: $Enc(pk, m') = c_1 \wedge H'(m') \neq c_2$. In this case, $H'(m') = H'_q(Enc(pk, m')) = H'_q(c_1) \neq c_2$, both DECAPS oracles in G_1 and G_2 return $\perp$.

Therefore, the DECAPS oracles in G_1 and G_2 output different values with probability at most $\frac{1}{2^{n'}}$. By the union bound we obtain

$$\left|\Pr[G_1^{\mathcal{B}} \Rightarrow 1] - \Pr[G_2^{\mathcal{B}} \Rightarrow 1]\right| \leq \frac{q_D}{2^{n'}}.$$

GAME G_3. In game G_3, c_1^* is given by $c_1^* \leftarrow S(pk)$. Then, we can bound $\left|\Pr[G_2^{\mathcal{B}} \Rightarrow 1] - \Pr[G_3^{\mathcal{B}} \Rightarrow 1]\right|$ and $\left|\Pr[G_3^{\mathcal{B}} \Rightarrow 1] - 1/2\right|$ as in the proof of $U_m^{\not\perp}$ [13, Theorem 4.2].

Construct an adversary $\mathcal{A}$ on input $(1^\lambda, pk, c_1^*)$ that does the following:

1. Pick a $2q_H$-wise ($2q_{H'}$-wise) independent function uniformly at random and use it to simulate the random oracle H_q (H_q'). The random oracle H (H') is simulated by $H_q \circ g$ ($H_q' \circ g$), where $g(\cdot) = Enc(pk, \cdot)$.
2. Let $c_2^* = H_q'(c_1^*)$, $c^* = (c_1^*, c_2^*)$, $k_0^* = H_q(c_1^*)$, $k_1^* \xleftarrow{\$} \mathcal{K}$ and $b \xleftarrow{\$} \{0,1\}$.
3. Answer the decapsulation queries by using the DECAPS oracle as in G_2 and G_3.
4. Invoke $b' \leftarrow \mathcal{B}^{H,H',\text{DECAPS}}(pk, c^*, k_b^*)$.
5. Return $b' =?b$.

Obviously, $\mathcal{A}$ perfectly simulates G_2 if $c_1^* = Enc(pk, m^*)$ ($m^* \xleftarrow{\$} \mathcal{M}$) and G_3 if $c_1^* \leftarrow S(pk)$. Therefore,

$$\left|\Pr[G_2^{\mathcal{B}} \Rightarrow 1] - \Pr[G_3^{\mathcal{B}} \Rightarrow 1]\right| \leq \mathsf{Adv}_{\text{PKE},U_{\mathcal{M}},S}^{\text{DS-IND}}(\mathcal{A}),$$

Let Bad be the event that $c_1^* \in Enc(pk, \mathcal{M})$ in G_3. Then, $\Pr[\mathsf{Bad}] \leq \text{DISJ}_{\text{PKE},S}$. We note that if $\neg\mathsf{Bad}$ happens, $H_q(c_1^*)$ is uniformly random in $\mathcal{B}$'s view since queries to H can only reveal $H_q(c)$ for $c \in Enc(pk, \mathcal{M})$. Therefore, $\Pr[G_3^{\mathcal{B}} \Rightarrow 1 : \neg\mathsf{Bad}] = 1/2$. We also note that $\left|\Pr[G_3^{\mathcal{B}} \Rightarrow 1] - 1/2\right| \leq \Pr[\mathsf{Bad}] + \left|\Pr[G_3^{\mathcal{B}} \Rightarrow 1 : \neg\mathsf{Bad}] - 1/2\right|$. Thus,

$$\left|\Pr[G_3^{\mathcal{B}} \Rightarrow 1] - 1/2\right| \leq \text{DISJ}_{\text{PKE},S}.$$

Combing the above bounds, Theorem 5 is proven. □

Acknowledgements. We would like to thank anonymous reviews of PKC 2019 for their insightful comments. In particular, we are also grateful to Chris Brzuska for his kind suggestions which are helpful in improving our paper. This work is supported by the National Key Research and Development Program of China (No. 2017YFB0802000), the National Natural Science Foundation of China (No. U1536205, 61472446, 61701539), and the National Cryptography Development Fund (mmjj20180107, mmjj20180212).

A Proof of Theorem 2

Proof. Let $\mathcal{B}$ be an adversary against the IND-CCA security of KEM-I, issuing at most q_D queries to the decapsulation oracle DECAPS, at most q_G (q_H, $q_{H'}$) queries to the random oracle G (H, H'). Follow the same notations Ω_G, Ω_H,

$\Omega_{H'}$, Ω_{H_q}, $\Omega_{H'_q}$, $\Omega_{G'}$ and $\mathcal{C}_1$ as in the proof of Theorem 1. Consider the games in Figs. 11 and 13.

GAME G_0. Since game G_0 is exactly the IND-CCA game,

$$\left|\Pr[G_0^{\mathcal{B}} \Rightarrow 1] - 1/2\right| = \mathtt{Adv}_{\text{KEM-I}}^{\text{IND-CCA}}(\mathcal{B}).$$

GAME G_1. In game G_1, we replace G by G' that uniformly samples from "good" randomness at random, i.e., $G' \xleftarrow{\$} \Omega_{G'}$.

GAME G_2. In this game, replace H and H' by $H_q \circ g$ and $H'_q \circ g$ respectively, where

$$g(\cdot) = Enc(pk, \cdot; G(\cdot)).$$

GAME G_3. In game G_3, the DECAPS oracle is changed that it makes no use of the secret key sk any more. When $\mathcal{B}$ queries the DECAPS oracle on $c = (c_1, c_2)$ $(c \neq c^*)$, $K := H_q(c_1)$ is returned if $H'_q(c_1) = c_2$, otherwise $\perp$.

GAME G_4. In game G_4, we switch the G that only samples from "good" randomness back to an ideal random oracle G.

Using the same analysis as in the proof of Theorem 1, we can have

$$\left|\Pr[G_0^{\mathcal{B}} \Rightarrow 1] - \Pr[G_4^{\mathcal{B}} \Rightarrow 1]\right| \leq 4q_G\sqrt{\delta} + \frac{q_D}{2^{n'}}.$$

Let $\ddot{G}$ ($\ddot{H}$) be the function that $\ddot{G}(m^*) = \dot{r}^*$ ($\ddot{H}(m^*) = \dot{k}_0^*$), and $\ddot{G} = G$ ($\ddot{H} = H$) everywhere else, where $\dot{r}^*$ and $\dot{k}_0^*$ are picked uniformly at random from $\mathcal{R}$ and $\mathcal{K}$.

GAME G_5. In game G_5, replace G and H by $\ddot{G}$ and $\ddot{H}$ respectively. In this game, bit b is independent of $\mathcal{B}$'s view. Hence,

$$\Pr[G_5^{\mathcal{B}} \Rightarrow 1] = 1/2.$$

Let $(G \times H)(\cdot) = (G(\cdot), H(\cdot))$ and $(\ddot{G} \times \ddot{H})(\cdot) = (\ddot{G}(\cdot), \ddot{H}(\cdot))$. Let $\bar{H}_q$ be the function that $\bar{H}_q(c_1^*) = \perp$ and $\bar{H}_q = H_q$ everywhere else. Define $A^{G \times H}$ as in Fig. 12. Sample pk, m^*, G, H_q, H and c_1^* in the same way as G_4 and G_5, i.e., $(pk, sk) \leftarrow Gen$, $m^* \xleftarrow{\$} \mathcal{M}$, $G \xleftarrow{\$} \Omega_G$, $H_q \xleftarrow{\$} \Omega_{H_q}$, $H := H_q \circ g$ and $c_1^* = Enc(pk, m^*; G(m^*))$, where $g(\cdot) = Enc(pk, \cdot; G(\cdot))$.

Then, $A^{G \times H}$ on input $(pk, c_1^*, H(m^*), \bar{H}_q)$ perfectly simulates G_4. If we replace $G \times H$ by $\ddot{G} \times \ddot{H}$, $A^{\ddot{G} \times \ddot{H}}$ on input $(pk, c_1^*, H(m^*), \bar{H}_q)$ perfectly simulates G_5.

Let $B^{\ddot{G} \times \ddot{H}}$ be an oracle algorithm that on input $(pk, c_1^*, H(m^*), \bar{H}_q)$ does the following: pick $i \xleftarrow{\$} \{1, \ldots, q_G + q_H\}$, run $A^{\ddot{G} \times \ddot{H}}(pk, c_1^*, H(m^*), \bar{H}_q)$ until the i-th query, measure the argument of the query in the computational basis, output the measurement outcome. Define game G_6 as in Fig. 13.

GAMES $G_0 - G_5$

1: $(pk, sk) \leftarrow Gen; G \xleftarrow{\$} \Omega_G$

2: $H_q \xleftarrow{\$} \Omega_{H_q}; H'_q \xleftarrow{\$} \Omega_{H'_q}$

3: $G' \xleftarrow{\$} \Omega_{G'}; G := G'$ $//G_1 - G_3$

4: $g(\cdot) = Enc(pk, \cdot; G(\cdot))$

5: $H \xleftarrow{\$} \Omega_H; H' \xleftarrow{\$} \Omega_{H'}$ $//G_0 - G_1$

6: $m^* \xleftarrow{\$} \mathcal{M}$

7: $c_1^* := Enc(pk, m^*; G(m^*))$

8: $c_2^* := H'(m^*)$ $//G_0 - G_1$

9: $c_2^* := H'_q(c_1^*)$ $//G_2 - G_5$

10: $c^* = (c_1^*, c_2^*)$

11: $k_0^* := H(m^*)$

12: $k_1^* \xleftarrow{\$} \mathcal{K}$

13: $b \xleftarrow{\$} \{0, 1\}$

14: $b' \leftarrow \mathcal{B}^{G, H, H', \text{DECAPS}}(pk, c^*, k_b^*) // G_0 - G_4$

15: $\ddot{G} := G; \ddot{G}(m^*) \xleftarrow{\$} \mathcal{R}$ $//G_5$

16: $\ddot{H} := H; \ddot{H}(m^*) \xleftarrow{\$} \mathcal{K}$ $//G_5$

17: $g(\cdot) = Enc(pk, \cdot; \ddot{G}(\cdot))$ $//G_5$

18: $b' \leftarrow \mathcal{B}^{\ddot{G}, \ddot{H}, H', \text{DECAPS}}(pk, c^*, k_b^*) // G_5$

19: **return** $b' = ?b$

$H(m) // G_2 - G_5$

1: **return** $H_q(g(m))$

$H'(m) // G_2 - G_5$

1: **return** $H'_q(g(m))$

DECAPS $(c \neq c^*) // G_0 - G_2$

1: Parse $c = (c_1, c_2)$

2: $m' := Dec(sk, c_1)$

3: **if** $g(m') = c_1 \wedge H'(m') = c_2$

4: **return** $K := H(m')$

5: **else return** $\perp$

DECAPS $(c \neq c^*)$ $//G_3 - G_5$

1: Parse $c = (c_1, c_2)$

2: **if** $H'_q(c_1) = c_2$

3: **return** $K := H_q(c_1)$

4: **else return** $\perp$

Fig. 11. Games G_0-G_5 for the proof of Theorem 2

$A^{G \times H}(pk, c_1^*, H(m^*), \bar{H}_q)$

1: $H'_q \xleftarrow{\$} \Omega_{H'_q}$

2: $g(\cdot) = Enc(pk, \cdot; G(\cdot))$

3: $c_2^* = H'_q(c_1^*)$

4: $c^* = (c_1^*, c_2^*)$

5: $k_0^* = H(m^*)$

6: $k_1^* \xleftarrow{\$} \mathcal{K}$

7: $b \xleftarrow{\$} \{0, 1\}$

8: $b' \leftarrow \mathcal{B}^{G, H, H', \text{DECAPS}}(pk, c^*, k_b^*)$

9: **return** $b' = ?b$

$H'(m)$

1: **return** $H'_q \circ g(m)$

DECAPS $(c \neq c^*)$

1: Parse $c = (c_1, c_2)$

2: **if** $H'_q(c_1) = c_2$

3: **return** $K := \bar{H}_q(c_1)$

4: **else return** $\perp$

Fig. 12. $A^{G \times H}$ for the proof of Theorem 2.

GAMES G_6

1: $i \xleftarrow{\$} \{1, \ldots, q_G + q_H\}$

2: $(pk, sk) \leftarrow Gen; G \xleftarrow{\$} \Omega_G$

3: $H_q \xleftarrow{\$} \Omega_{H_q}; H'_q \xleftarrow{\$} \Omega_{H'_q}$

4: $H(\cdot) = H_q(Enc(pk, \cdot; G(\cdot)))$

5: $m^* \xleftarrow{\$} \mathcal{M}$

6: $r^* \xleftarrow{\$} \mathcal{R}$

7: $\ddot{G} := G; \ddot{G}(m^*) = r^*$

8: $g(\cdot) := Enc(pk, \cdot; \ddot{G}(\cdot))$

9: $c_1^* = Enc(pk, m^*; G(m^*))$

10: $c_2^* = H'_q(c_1^*)$

11: $c^* = (c_1^*, c_2^*)$

12: $k^* \xleftarrow{\$} \mathcal{K}$

13: $\ddot{H} := H; \ddot{H}(m^*) = k^*$

14: run $\mathcal{B}^{\ddot{G}, \ddot{H}, H', \text{DECAPS}}(pk, c^*, H(m^*))$

15: until the i-th query to $\ddot{G} \times \ddot{H}$

16: measure the argument $\hat{m}$

17: **return** $\hat{m} =? m^*$

DECAPS $(c \neq c^*)$

1: Parse $c = (c_1, c_2)$

2: **if** $H'_q(c_1) = c_2$

3:     **return** $K := H_q(c_1)$

4: **else return** $\perp$

GAMES G_7

1: $i \xleftarrow{\$} \{1, \ldots, q_G + q_H\}$

2: $(pk, sk) \leftarrow Gen; G \xleftarrow{\$} \Omega_G$

3: $H_q \xleftarrow{\$} \Omega_{H_q}; H'_q \xleftarrow{\$} \Omega_{H_q}$

4: $H(\cdot) = H_q(Enc(pk, \cdot; G(\cdot)))$

5: $m^* \xleftarrow{\$} \mathcal{M}$

6: $r^* \xleftarrow{\$} \mathcal{R}$

7: $g(\cdot) := Enc(pk, \cdot; G(\cdot))$

8: $c_1^* = Enc(pk, m^*; r^*)$

9: $c_2^* = H'_q(c_1^*)$

10: $c^* = (c_1^*, c_2^*)$

11: $k^* \xleftarrow{\$} \mathcal{K}$

12: run $\mathcal{B}^{G, H, H', \text{DECAPS}}(pk, c^*, k^*)$

13: until the i-th query to $G \times H$

14: measure the argument $\hat{m}$

15: **return** $\hat{m} =? m^*$

$H'(m)$

1: **return** $H'_q \circ g(m)$

Fig. 13. Game G_6 and game G_7 for the proof of Theorem 2

Applying Lemma 5 with $X = \mathcal{M}$, $Y = (\mathcal{R}, \mathcal{K})$, $S = \{m^*\}$, $\mathcal{O}_1 = \ddot{G} \times \ddot{H}$, $\mathcal{O}_2 = G \times H$ and $z = (pk, c_1^*, H(m^*), \ddot{H}_q)$, we can have

$$\left| \Pr[G_4^{\mathcal{B}} \Rightarrow 1] - \Pr[G_5^{\mathcal{B}} \Rightarrow 1] \right| \leq 2(q_G + q_H)\sqrt{\Pr[G_6^{\mathcal{B}} \Rightarrow 1]}.$$

Rearrange game G_6 into game G_7, see Fig. 13. Clearly, $\Pr[G_6^{\mathcal{B}} \Rightarrow 1] = \Pr[G_7^{\mathcal{B}} \Rightarrow 1]$. Then, we construct an adversary $\mathcal{A}$ against the OW-CPA security of PKE such that $\text{Adv}_{\text{PKE}}^{\text{OW-CPA}}(\mathcal{A}) = \Pr[G_7^{\mathcal{B}} \Rightarrow 1]$. The adversary $\mathcal{A}$ on input $(1^\lambda, pk, c_1^*)$ does the following:

1. Run the adversary $\mathcal{B}$ in game G_7.

2. Pick a $2q_G$ ($2q_H$, $2q_{H'}$)-wise independent function uniformly at random and use it to simulate the random oracle G (H_q, H'_q). The random oracle H (H') is simulated by $H_q \circ g$ ($H'_q \circ g$). Use $G \times H$ to answer $\mathcal{B}$'s queries to both G and H.
3. Let $c_2^* = H'_q(c_1^*)$ and $c^* = (c_1^*, c_2^*)$.
4. Answer the decapsulation queries by using the DECAPS oracle as in Fig. 13.
5. Select $k^* \xleftarrow{\$} \mathcal{K}$ and respond to $\mathcal{B}$'s challenge query with (c^*, k^*).
6. Select $i \xleftarrow{\$} \{1, \ldots, q_G + q_H\}$, measure the argument $\hat{m}$ of the i-th query to $G \times H$ and output $\hat{m}$.

It is obvious that $\mathtt{Adv}_{\mathrm{PKE}}^{\mathrm{OW\text{-}CPA}}(\mathcal{A}) = \Pr[G_7^{\mathcal{B}} \Rightarrow 1]$. Combing this with the bounds derived above, we can conclude that

$$\mathtt{Adv}_{\mathrm{KEM\text{-}I}}^{\mathrm{IND\text{-}CCA}}(\mathcal{B}) \leq 4q_G \cdot \sqrt{\delta} + \frac{q_D}{2^{n'}} + 2(q_H + q_G) \cdot \sqrt{\mathtt{Adv}_{\mathrm{PKE}}^{\mathrm{OW\text{-}CPA}}(\mathcal{A})}.$$

□

References

1. Rackoff, C., Simon, D.R.: Non-interactive zero-knowledge proof of knowledge and chosen ciphertext attack. In: Feigenbaum, J. (ed.) CRYPTO 1991. LNCS, vol. 576, pp. 433–444. Springer, Heidelberg (1992). https://doi.org/10.1007/3-540-46766-1_35
2. Bellare, M., Rogaway, P.: Random oracles are practical: a paradigm for designing efficient protocols. In: Denning, D.E., Pyle, R., Ganesan, R., Sandhu, R.S., Ashby, V. (eds.) Proceedings of the 1st ACM Conference on Computer and Communications Security – CCS 1993, pp. 62–73. ACM (1993)
3. Dent, A.W.: A designer's guide to KEMs. In: Paterson, K.G. (ed.) Cryptography and Coding 2003. LNCS, vol. 2898, pp. 133–151. Springer, Heidelberg (2003). https://doi.org/10.1007/978-3-540-40974-8_12
4. Hofheinz, D., Hövelmanns, K., Kiltz, E.: A modular analysis of the Fujisaki-Okamoto transformation. In: Kalai, Y., Reyzin, L. (eds.) TCC 2017. LNCS, vol. 10677, pp. 341–371. Springer, Cham (2017). https://doi.org/10.1007/978-3-319-70500-2_12
5. Fujisaki, E., Okamoto, T.: Secure integration of asymmetric and symmetric encryption schemes. In: Wiener, M.J. (ed.) CRYPTO 1999. LNCS, vol. 1666, pp. 537–554. Springer, Heidelberg (1999). https://doi.org/10.1007/3-540-48405-1_34
6. Fujisaki, E., Okamoto, T.: Secure integration of asymmetric and symmetric encryption schemes. J. Cryptol. **26**(1), 1–22 (2013)
7. Okamoto, T., Pointcheval, D.: REACT: rapid enhanced-security asymmetric cryptosystem transform. In: Naccache, D. (ed.) CT-RSA 2001. LNCS, vol. 2020, pp. 159–174. Springer, Heidelberg (2000). https://doi.org/10.1007/3-540-45353-9_13
8. Jean-Sébastien, C., Handschuh, H., Joye, M., Paillier, P., Pointcheval, D., Tymen, C.: GEM: A Generic chosen-ciphertext secure Encryption Method. In: Preneel, B. (ed.) CT-RSA 2002. LNCS, vol. 2271, pp. 263–276. Springer, Heidelberg (2002). https://doi.org/10.1007/3-540-45760-7_18
9. Targhi, E.E., Unruh, D.: Post-quantum security of the Fujisaki-Okamoto and OAEP transforms. In: Hirt, M., Smith, A. (eds.) TCC 2016. LNCS, vol. 9986, pp. 192–216. Springer, Heidelberg (2016). https://doi.org/10.1007/978-3-662-53644-5_8

10. NIST: National Institute for Standards and Technology. Post quantum crypto project (2017). https://csrc.nist.gov/projects/post-quantum-cryptography/round-1-submissions
11. Boneh, D., Dagdelen, Ö., Fischlin, M., Lehmann, A., Schaffner, C., Zhandry, M.: Random oracles in a quantum world. In: Lee, D.H., Wang, X. (eds.) ASIACRYPT 2011. LNCS, vol. 7073, pp. 41–69. Springer, Heidelberg (2011). https://doi.org/10.1007/978-3-642-25385-0_3
12. Unruh, D.: Non-interactive zero-knowledge proofs in the quantum random oracle model. In: Oswald, E., Fischlin, M. (eds.) EUROCRYPT 2015. LNCS, vol. 9057, pp. 755–784. Springer, Heidelberg (2015). https://doi.org/10.1007/978-3-662-46803-6_25
13. Saito, T., Xagawa, K., Yamakawa, T.: Tightly-secure key-encapsulation mechanism in the quantum random oracle model. In: Nielsen, J.B., Rijmen, V. (eds.) EUROCRYPT 2018. LNCS, vol. 10822, pp. 520–551. Springer, Cham (2018). https://doi.org/10.1007/978-3-319-78372-7_17
14. Jiang, H., Zhang, Z., Chen, L., Wang, H., Ma, Z.: IND-CCA-secure key encapsulation mechanism in the quantum random oracle model, revisited. In: Shacham, H., Boldyreva, A. (eds.) CRYPTO 2018. LNCS, vol. 10993, pp. 96–125. Springer, Cham (2018). https://doi.org/10.1007/978-3-319-96878-0_4
15. Hamburg, M.: Module-LWE: the three bears. Technical report. https://www.shiftleft.org/papers/threebears/
16. Hülsing, A., Rijneveld, J., Schanck, J., Schwabe, P.: High-speed key encapsulation from NTRU. In: Fischer, W., Homma, N. (eds.) CHES 2017. LNCS, vol. 10529, pp. 232–252. Springer, Cham (2017). https://doi.org/10.1007/978-3-319-66787-4_12
17. Bernstein, D.J., Persichetti, E.: Towards KEM unification. Cryptology ePrint Archive, Report 2018/526 (2018). https://eprint.iacr.org/2018/526
18. Unruh, D.: Revocable quantum timed-release encryption. J. ACM **62**(6), 49:1–49:76 (2015)
19. Ambainis, A., Hamburg, M., Unruh, D.: Quantum security proofs using semi-classical oracles. Cryptology ePrint Archive, Report 2018/904 (2018). https://eprint.iacr.org/2018/904
20. Zhandry, M.: How to record quantum queries, and applications to quantum indifferentiability. Cryptology ePrint Archive, Report 2018/276 (2018). https://eprint.iacr.org/2018/276
21. Boneh, D., Zhandry, M.: Secure signatures and chosen ciphertext security in a quantum computing world. In: Canetti, R., Garay, J.A. (eds.) CRYPTO 2013. LNCS, vol. 8043, pp. 361–379. Springer, Heidelberg (2013). https://doi.org/10.1007/978-3-642-40084-1_21
22. Nielsen, M.A., Chuang, I.L.: Quantum Computation and Quantum Information. Cambridge University Press, Cambridge (2000). Number 2
23. Zhandry, M.: Secure identity-based encryption in the quantum random oracle model. In: Safavi-Naini, R., Canetti, R. (eds.) CRYPTO 2012. LNCS, vol. 7417, pp. 758–775. Springer, Heidelberg (2012). https://doi.org/10.1007/978-3-642-32009-5_44
24. Ambainis, A., Rosmanis, A., Unruh, D.: Quantum attacks on classical proof systems: the hardness of quantum rewinding. In: 55th IEEE Annual Symposium on Foundations of Computer Science - FOCS 2014, pp. 474–483. IEEE (2014)
25. Hülsing, A., Rijneveld, J., Song, F.: Mitigating multi-target attacks in hash-based signatures. In: Cheng, C.-M., Chung, K.-M., Persiano, G., Yang, B.-Y. (eds.) PKC 2016. LNCS, vol. 9614, pp. 387–416. Springer, Heidelberg (2016). https://doi.org/10.1007/978-3-662-49384-7_15

Factoring Products of Braids via Garside Normal Form

Simon-Philipp Merz[1(✉)] and Christophe Petit[2]

[1] Royal Holloway, University of London, Egham, UK
simon-philipp.merz.2018@rhul.ac.uk
[2] University of Birmingham, Birmingham, UK

Abstract. Braid groups are infinite non-abelian groups naturally arising from geometric braids. For two decades they have been proposed for cryptographic use. In braid group cryptography public braids often contain secret braids as factors and it is hoped that rewriting the product of braid words hides individual factors. We provide experimental evidence that this is in general not the case and argue that under certain conditions parts of the Garside normal form of factors can be found in the Garside normal form of their product. This observation can be exploited to decompose products of braids of the form ABC when only B is known.

Our decomposition algorithm yields a universal forgery attack on WalnutDSA^{TM}, which is one of the 20 proposed signature schemes that are being considered by NIST for standardization of quantum-resistant public-key cryptography. Our attack on WalnutDSA^{TM} can universally forge signatures within seconds for both the 128-bit and 256-bit security level, given one random message-signature pair. The attack worked on 99.8% and 100% of signatures for the 128-bit and 256-bit security levels in our experiments.

Furthermore, we show that the decomposition algorithm can be used to solve instances of the conjugacy search problem and decomposition search problem in braid groups. These problems are at the heart of other cryptographic schemes based on braid groups.

1 Introduction

Continuous progress in quantum computing and the prospect of large scale quantum computers necessitate the development of quantum-resistant cryptographic algorithms. Currently, the security of most widespread algorithms relies on the hardness of the discrete logarithm problem, the elliptic-curve discrete logarithm problem or the integer factorization problem. All of these mathematical problems can be solved using Shor's quantum algorithm [41]. Even though quantum computers with sufficient processing power to pose a threat to current cryptographic applications presumably do not yet exist, researchers, intelligence agencies and the industry aspire to develop cryptographic systems that remain safe once

The full version can be found in the IACR eprint archive as article 2018/1142.

D. Lin and K. Sako (Eds.): PKC 2019, LNCS 11443, pp. 646–678, 2019.
https://doi.org/10.1007/978-3-030-17259-6_22

such devices come into being. Current approaches to attain quantum-resistance include cryptography based on codes, isogenies, lattices and multivariate polynomials over finite fields [19,35,37,43]. Another approach are cryptographic systems based on non-abelian groups [22]. Indeed no quantum algorithm to solve the hidden subgroup problem (the core problem solved by Shor's algorithm for finite abelian groups) is known for general non-abelian groups.

The conjugacy search problem is a fundamental decision problem in combinatorial group theory.

Definition 1. Given two braids $X, Y \in B_N$ where $Y = C \cdot X \cdot C^{-1}$ for some $C \in B_N$, the *conjugacy search problem* (CSP) in braid groups is to find $\tilde{C} \in B_N$ such that $Y = \tilde{C} \cdot X \cdot \tilde{C}^{-1}$.

The asserted computational difficulty of the CSP and its variations has inspired many cryptographic primitives on non-abelian groups such as [3,33].

To establish standards for quantum-secure cryptography [39] the National Institute of Standards and Technology (NIST) is currently evaluating public-key algorithms [39]. One of the 20 signature schemes being considered for standardisation is WalnutDSA^{TM} [6] operating on braid groups.

NIST's ongoing standardization project and thus the potential for widespread use of WalnutDSA^{TM} and other braid group algorithms make a thorough security analysis and understanding of the braid group vital. WalnutDSA^{TM} has been analysed before [10,29,34] bringing some weaknesses of the signature scheme to light. However, the attacks could be thwarted by increasing parameters and slightly changing the protocol [40]. A fundamental assumption underlying the security of WalnutDSA^{TM} is that individual factors in a product of three braids are "obfuscated" when they are presented in some normal form.

Our contribution: In this paper, we describe how the Garside normal forms of factors relate to the Garside normal form of their product. Together with an observation based on experiments, we use this to locate single factors in a product of braids and to decompose certain products in braid groups. More precisely, we give an algorithm that can recover the factors of a product $ABC \in B_N$ up to the centre of the group when only B is known.

Signatures of WalnutDSA^{TM} can be written as a braid word $W_1 \cdot E \cdot W_2$, where W_1 and W_2 are secret braids and E is a deterministic encoding of the message. The product is presented rewritten, e.g. in normal form, with the explicit aim of obfuscating individual factors. Our observations imply that W_1 and W_2 can in fact be efficiently recovered up to the centre of the group. Replacing E by the encoding of any other message yields a new universal forgery attack that works within seconds on most random message-signature pairs.

Related work: Braid groups have been suggested for cryptographic purposes for two decades [22] and protocols such as the Anshel-Anshel-Goldfeld key exchange [4] and Ko et al.'s protocol [33] have been studied extensively. A newer protocol sharing some design components with WalnutDSA^{TM} is the Algebraic Eraser [5]. This scheme and the Anshel-Anshel-Goldfeld key exchange have been subject to numerous attacks which were mostly based on representation theory [8,9,31] or on a length-based approach [30,38]. Yet, the same cryptanalytic techniques do not seem to apply to WalnutDSA^{TM}.

Considerable work has been devoted towards a solution of the conjugacy search problem (CSP) in braid groups. Apart from heuristic approaches such as the previously mentioned length-based attacks, the most successful approaches use summit sets [13,24,25].

Responsible Disclosure Process: We provided the designers of WalnutDSA^{TM} with the details of our attack on the 20th of August. They acknowledged that the attack works. To prevent malicious use of our attack on the signature scheme or similar products by SecureRF, we agreed to postpone the publication of our findings until the 21st of November.

Outline: In Sect. 2, we provide preliminary results on braid groups and the Garside normal form. In Sect. 3 we present the current instantiation of WalnutDSA^{TM} and how it was modified to thwart previous attacks. Section 4 gives our algorithm to recover the factors of a braid ABC presented by its normal form when the braid B is known. In Sect. 5 we describe our attack on WalnutDSA^{TM} and discuss potential countermeasures. Section 6 shows how the decomposition algorithm can be used to solve instances of the conjugacy search problem. We conclude our work in Sect. 7.

2 Braid Groups

This section provides preliminary mathematical background on braid groups. In Sect. 2.1 we define braid groups and provide their algebraic presentation. Section 2.2 defines the colored Burau representation of braid groups which is needed to explain WalnutDSA^{TM} but not essential for the understanding of our contribution. In Sect. 2.3 we define the Garside normal form. A reader familiar with braid groups and the Garside normal form may proceed to Sect. 3.

2.1 Artin Presentation

Let N be a positive integer and let B_N denote the braid group on N strands introduced by Emil Artin [7]. Geometrically, the elements of a braid group are the equivalence classes of N strands under ambient isotopy, i.e. we consider two braids the same if we can distort one into the other without breaking any strand. Artin proved that B_N is indeed a group with presentation

$$B_N = \left\langle b_1, \ldots, b_{N-1} \;\middle|\; \begin{array}{l} b_i b_{i+1} b_i = b_{i+1} b_i b_{i+1} \\ b_i b_j = b_j b_i \text{ for } |i-j| \geq 2 \end{array} \right\rangle, \tag{1}$$

where the group operation is given by concatenation of the strings. Thus, we can represent any braid of B_N as a finite, non-unique word in the so called *Artin generators* b_i. Imagining our strands lying in a plane and numbering the strands from left to right, the generator b_i corresponds to the i-th strand crossing over the $(i+1)$-th strand.

Figures 1 and 2 illustrate the relations given in Presentation (1).

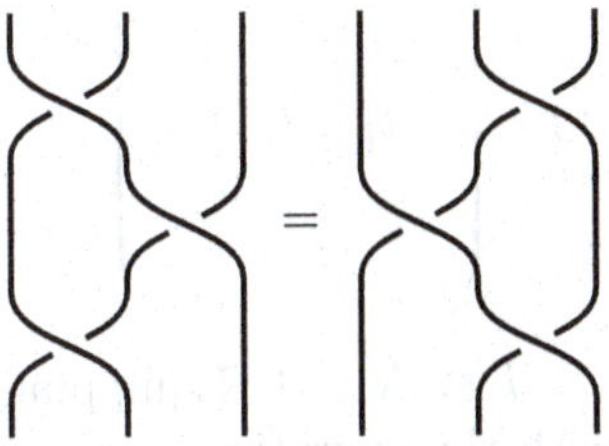

Fig. 1. $b_i b_{i+1} b_i = b_{i+1} b_i b_{i+1}$

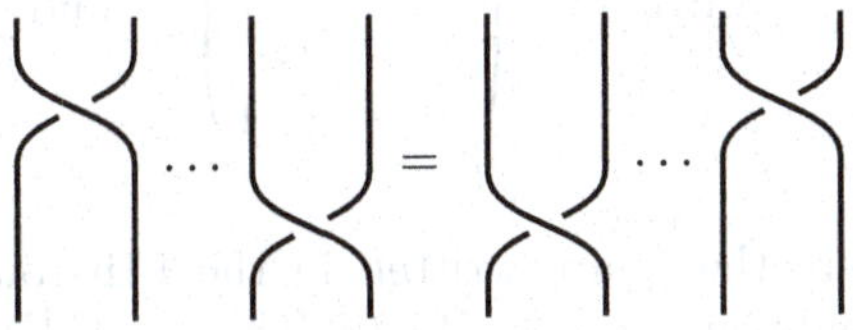

Fig. 2. $b_i b_j = b_j b_i$, if $|i-j| \geq 2$

Note that there is a natural homomorphism sending elements of B_N to the induced permutations in the symmetric group S_N. More precisely, each Artin generator b_i is sent to the transposition $\pi_i := (i, i+1)$. For some braid word $b_{i_1}^{\epsilon_1} \ldots b_{i_k}^{\epsilon_k}$ the induced permutation is $\pi_{i_1}^{\epsilon_1} \ldots \pi_{i_k}^{\epsilon_k}$. Since the corresponding permutations respect the relations in Presentation (1), sending braids to their induced permutations is a well-defined homomorphism. Clearly, this homomorphism from B_N to S_N is surjective. Braids in the kernel, i.e. braids inducing the identity permutation, are called *pure braids*.

It is well known that the group of *pure* braids can be generated by g_{ij}, $1 \leq i < j \leq N$ [12], where

$$g_{ij} := b_{j-1} \cdot b_{j-2} \cdot \cdots \cdot b_{i+1} \cdot b_i^2 \cdot b_{i+1}^{-1} \cdot \cdots \cdot b_{j-2}^{-1} \cdot b_{j-1}^{-1}. \tag{2}$$

The generator g_{ij} may be depicted geometrically as braid where the j-th string passes behind the strings $(j-1), \ldots, (i+1)$, in front of the i-th string and then behind the strings $i, \ldots, j-1$ back to the j-th position.

2.2 Colored Burau Representation

The colored Burau representation of braid groups which we will describe in this section is used to define WalnutDSA^{TM} and its underlying problem. A reader who is mainly interested in the structure being preserved in products of Garside normal forms may want to skip this section.

Let q be the power of a prime and let $\mathbb{F}_q[t_1^{\pm 1}, \ldots, t_N^{\pm 1}]$ be the ring of Laurent polynomials with coefficients in the finite field $\mathbb{F}_q$ with q elements. There exists an action of S_N on $\mathbb{F}_q[t_1^{\pm 1}, \ldots, t_N^{\pm 1}]$, where a permutation acts on the indices of the variables of the Laurent polynomial. That is, for every $\sigma \in \mathsf{S}_N$ and $f \in \mathbb{F}_q[t_1^{\pm 1}, \ldots, t_N^{\pm 1}]$

$$f(t_1, \ldots, t_N) \mapsto {}^{\sigma}f = f(t_{\sigma(1)}, \ldots, t_{\sigma(N)})$$

The action of S_N extends to $\mathsf{GL}_N(\mathbb{F}_q[t_1^{\pm 1}, \ldots, t_N^{\pm 1}])$ by applying it entry-wise. For $\sigma \in \mathsf{S}_N$ and $M \in \mathsf{GL}_N(\mathbb{F}_q[t_1^{\pm 1}, \ldots, t_N^{\pm 1}])$, we denote the action by $M \mapsto {}^{\sigma}M$.

The colored Burau matrices of each Artin generator are defined as follows [6]:

$$\mathsf{CB}(b_1) := \begin{pmatrix} -t_1 & 1 & & \\ & 1 & & \\ & & \ddots & \\ & & & 1 \end{pmatrix} \quad \text{and} \quad \mathsf{CB}(b_i) := \begin{pmatrix} 1 & & & & \\ & \ddots & & & \\ & t_i & -t_i & 1 & \\ & & & \ddots & \\ & & & & 1 \end{pmatrix},$$

where the t_i are written in the i-th row for $2 \le i \le N-1$. Equipping the semidirect product $\mathsf{GL}_N(\mathbb{F}_q[t_1^{\pm 1}, \ldots, t_N^{\pm 1}]) \rtimes \mathsf{S}_N$ with the operation

$$(M_1, \sigma_1) \cdot (M_2, \sigma_2) = (M_1 \cdot {}^{\sigma_1}M_2, \sigma_1\sigma_2),$$

one obtains a group and one can check that the map

$$\begin{aligned} \Phi : B_N &\to \mathsf{GL}_N(\mathbb{F}_q[t_1^{\pm 1}, \ldots, t_N^{\pm 1}]) \rtimes \mathsf{S}_N \\ b_i &\mapsto (\mathsf{CB}(b_i), \pi_i), \end{aligned} \tag{3}$$

where π_i denotes the transposition $(i, i+1) \in \mathsf{S}_N$, extends to a group homomorphism. This group homomorphism is called *colored Burau representation* of B_N [16].

2.3 Garside Normal Form

A *normal form* in a group is a canonical way to represent the elements and thus it provides an opportunity to compare them.

Garside was the first to develop a normal form for braid groups [23] which was improved most notably by Thurston [21] and Elrifai and Morton [20] leading to what is known as the *Garside normal form* today. For further normal forms in braid groups see [11,15,18].

In this section we reproduce some results that led to the development of the Garside normal form to introduce terminology necessary for the explanation of our observation in Sect. 4.

Let B_N^+ denote the monoid of *positive braids* in B_N which are the braids that can be written as a product of positive powers of Artin generators. This is a well-defined monoid as all the defining relations in the presentation of braid groups (1) contain only positive powers of Artin generators.

We denote Garside's "*fundamental braid*" [23] by Δ. Recall that this braid is the unique positive braid in which any two strands cross exactly once and it is of central importance in the Garside normal form. We recall some properties of the fundamental braid due to Garside [23].

Proposition 2. *Let B_N be the braid group on N strands. For $i = 1, \ldots, N-1$, we have*

$$b_i\Delta = \Delta b_{N-i}.$$

In particular Δ^2 commutes with every generator and lies in the centre of B_N. In fact, the centre of B_N is cyclic and generated by Δ^2.

Remark 3. Let τ be the inner automorphism of B_N conjugating elements with Δ, i.e.

$$\tau : B_N \to B_N$$
$$\beta \mapsto \Delta\beta\Delta^{-1}$$

Let $W = b_{i_1}^{\epsilon_1} \dots b_{i_k}^{\epsilon_k} \in B_N$ with $\epsilon_j \in \{0,1\}$. Then the previous Proposition implies

$$\tau(W) = \Delta W \Delta^{-1} = \tau(b_{i_1})^{\epsilon_1} \dots \tau(b_{i_k})^{\epsilon_k} = b_{N-i_1}^{\epsilon_1} \dots b_{N-i_k}^{\epsilon_k}.$$

In particular, τ^2 is the identity automorphism. We will continue to denote this automorphism by τ and call it the *reflection in* B_N throughout this paper.

Proposition 4. [23] *For any generator b_i, $i = 1, \dots, N-1$, we can find positive braids x_i and $y_i \in B_N^+$ such that*

$$b_i x_i = \Delta = y_i b_i.$$

An explicit description of the braids x_i, y_i is given at the same place. Together with Proposition 2 this observation can be used to rewrite any representation of an element of B_N efficiently in the form $\Delta^r P$, where $r \in \mathbb{Z}$ and P is a positive braid that cannot be written as a positive word containing Δ as a subword. Listing all possible words P and choosing the lexicographically minimal one for P yields the initial normal form due to Garside. This algorithm has exponential running time in the number of strands N and the braid length, so it is not completely satisfactory from a computational point of view. However, we have the following natural partial order in the monoid of positive braids.

Definition 5. Let $a, b \in B_N^+$. We write $a \leq b$ if $ac = b$ for some $c \in B_N^+$. We say a is a *prefix* of b. This is a partial order invariant under left multiplication, i.e. $a \leq b$ implies $da \leq db$ for all $d \in B_N^+$.

Let 1 denote the identity in B_N. We see that $1 \leq A$ if and only if $A \in B_N^+$.

Given a partial order as in Definition 5 one may wonder whether there is a greatest common prefix in some sense.

Proposition 6. [23] *For any two elements $a, b \in B_N^+$ there exists a unique element d such that $d \leq a$, $d \leq b$ and that $d' \leq d$ for every common prefix d' of a and b.*

Definition 7. Using the same notation as in the previous proposition, we call d the *greatest common divisor (gcd)* of a and b and we write $d = a \wedge b$.

Elrifai and Morton [20] and Thurston [21] independently developed two different algorithms to compute the normal form of a braid in polynomial time building on top of Garside's results. The centrepiece of their work is to consider the following braids.

Definition 8. The positive prefixes of Δ are called *permutation braids,* i.e. $A \in B_N$ is a permutation braid if and only if $1 \leq A \leq \Delta$.

Permutation braids are exactly those positive braids with any pair of strands crossing at most once and thus uniquely determined by the permutation they induce.

Instead of listing exponentially many representatives and choosing the lexicographically minimal one, the idea of Thurston, Elrifai and Morton was to write a braid word β as a product of permutation braids

$$\beta = \Delta^r A_1 \cdots A_k,$$

where uniqueness is achieved by requiring each letter to appear as far to the left as possible.

Definition 9. A product of permutation braids $A_i A_{i+1}$ is called *left-weighted* if $A_i A_{i+1} \wedge \Delta = A_i$.

That is, if we move any crossing from A_{i+1} to A_i the resulting braid would not be a permutation braid anymore. This allows us to formulate the Garside left normal form.

Theorem 10 (Garside left normal form). *Every braid β can be represented uniquely by a braid word*

$$\Delta^r A_1 \cdots A_k,$$

where $r \in \mathbb{Z}$, $1 < A_i < \Delta$ and $A_i A_{i+1}$ is a left-weighted product for $1 \leq i \leq k$.

Definition 11. Consider the notation of the preceding Theorem 10. We call the integer k the *canonical length* of β and the integer r the *infimum* of β.

For details on the algorithms to compute the Garside left normal form we refer to [20,21]. Using the approach of Elrifai and Morton the normal form of some given positive braid word $b_{i_1} \dots b_{i_k}$ can be computed in time $\mathcal{O}(k^2 N)$, where k is the number of Artin generators of the braid word given. Thurston's alternative but equivalent solution computes the left normal form of a positive braid word given as a product of permutation braids $A_1 \dots A_{k'}$ with time complexity $\mathcal{O}(k'^2 N \log N)$ [21]. Note, this might be faster than the previous algorithm as most permutation braids are a product of multiple Artin generators.

We want to point out that similar observations as the ones we will state in Sect. 4 for the Garside normal form hold for other normal forms such as the Birman-Ko-Lee (BKL) normal form as well. In particular, structure in the BKL normal form can be exploited directly to attack WalnutDSA™ or solve instances of the conjugacy search problem too. However, using the Garside normal form turned out to be slightly more efficient in our experiments which is why we will mean the Garside left normal form when talking about left normal forms for the remainder of this paper.

3 WalnutDSA™

WalnutDSA™ is a digital signature scheme operating on braid groups. It was proposed by Anshel, Atkins, Goldfeld and Gunnels [6]. This Section summarizes the newest version of the signature scheme. In Sect. 3.1 we define E-Multiplication and cloaking elements and state the underlying hardness assumption of WalnutDSA™. The section is not necessary to understand our attack, but these basic building blocks are needed to define the signature scheme itself. Section 3.2 provides details about parameters used and the signature generation and validation. Finally, we will give a brief overview of previous work on WalnutDSA™ showing that our approach is fundamentally disparate in Sect. 3.3.

3.1 E-Multiplication™ and Cloaking Elements

E-Multiplication was first introduced as a one-way function [5] and it is a foundation of WalnutDSA™.

Let $\mathbb{F}_q^\times$ denote the non-zero elements of the finite field $\mathbb{F}_q$. An N-tuple of the form

$$\tau = (\tau_1, \ldots, \tau_N) \in (\mathbb{F}_q^\times)^N$$

will be called "*T-values*" in the following. Given such a tuple, we can evaluate any Laurent polynomial $\mathbb{F}_q[t_1^{\pm 1}, \ldots, t_N^{\pm 1}]$ at τ, denoted $\downarrow_\tau$:

$$\begin{aligned} \downarrow_\tau : \mathbb{F}_q[t_1^{\pm 1}, \ldots, t_N^{\pm 1}] &\to \mathbb{F}_q \\ f &\mapsto f(\tau_1, \ldots, \tau_N) \end{aligned}$$

Similarly, we can evaluate any matrix $M \in \mathsf{GL}_N(\mathbb{F}_q[t_1^{\pm 1}, \ldots, t_N^{\pm 1}])$ to $M \downarrow_\tau$ by doing so entrywise.

E-Multiplication is a right action of the colored Burau group $\mathsf{GL}_N(\mathbb{F}_q[t_1^{\pm 1}, \ldots, t_N^{\pm 1}]) \rtimes \mathsf{S}_N$ on $\mathsf{GL}_N(\mathbb{F}_q) \times \mathsf{S}_N$. We will follow the notation of [6] denoting E-Multiplication with a star: $\star$.

For a single Artin generator b_i, E-Multiplication is defined as

$$(M, \sigma) \star \Phi(b_i) := \Big(M \cdot {}^{\sigma}(\mathsf{CB}(b_i)) \downarrow_\tau, \ \sigma \cdot \pi_i \Big),$$

where $\pi_i = (i, i+1) \in \mathsf{S}_N$ and Φ is the map given in Eq. (3). For a general braid β represented by $b_{i_1}^{\epsilon_1} \ldots b_{i_k}^{\epsilon_k}$ with $\epsilon_j \in \{-1, 1\}$, we define E-Multiplication inductively left-to-right as

$$(M, \sigma) \star \Phi(\beta) := (M, \sigma) \star \big(\mathsf{CB}(b_{i_1})^{\epsilon_1}, \pi_{i_1}^{\epsilon_1}\big) \star \cdots \star \big(\mathsf{CB}(b_{i_k})^{\epsilon_k}, \pi_{i_k}^{\epsilon_k}\big).$$

Remark 12. Following the notation of [6], we write $(M, \sigma) \star \beta$ instead of $(M, \sigma) \star \Phi(\beta)$ for $\beta \in B_N$. Moreover, we denote by $\mathcal{P}$ the map

$$\begin{aligned} \mathcal{P} : B_N &\to \mathsf{GL}_N(\mathbb{F}_q) \times \mathsf{S}_N \\ \beta &\mapsto (\mathrm{Id}, \mathrm{id}) \star \beta. \end{aligned} \tag{4}$$

The security of WalnutDSA™ is based on the computational hardness assumption of the *reversing E-Multiplication* (REM) problem.

Definition 13. Given an ordered pair $(M, \sigma) \in \mathsf{GL}_N(\mathbb{F}_q) \times \mathsf{S}_N$ such that $(M, \sigma) = (Id, id) \star \beta$ for some braid $\beta \in B_N$. The *reversing E-Multiplication* (REM) problem is to find a braid β' such that $(Id, id) \star \beta' = (M, \sigma)$.

In particular inverting the map given in (4) is assumed to be hard. Reversing E-Multiplication is enough to break WalnutDSA^{TM}, indeed we will see that the ability to solve the REM problem allows to forge the signature of one message and that solving two instances of the REM problem allows the recovery of the private key from the public key.

However, our attack on WalnutDSA^{TM} bypasses the problem of reversing E-Multiplication. We will see that our attack works solely on braids and is therefore independent of the colored Burau representation and of the size q of the underlying field $\mathbb{F}_q$.

Another basic building block of WalnutDSA^{TM} are certain braids termed cloaking elements.

Definition 14. A braid is called *cloaking element* of $(M, \sigma) \in \mathsf{GL}_N(\mathbb{F}_q) \times \mathsf{S}_N$, if it stabilizes (M, σ) under the right action of the braid group via E-Multiplication.

In WalnutDSA^{TM} cloaking elements of the following form are generated [40].

Proposition 15. *Let $(M, \sigma) \in \mathsf{GL}_N(\mathbb{F}_q) \times \mathsf{S}_N$. Assume $\tau_a = -\tau_b^{-1}$ for two T-values with indices $1 \leq a < b \leq N$. Let σ_w denote the permutation induced by some braid $w \in B_N$ and let b_i be an Artin generator for $1 \leq i \leq N-1$. If*

$$\sigma_w(i) = \sigma^{-1}(a) \quad \text{and} \quad \sigma_w(i+1) = \sigma^{-1}(b),$$

the braid $w \cdot b_i^{\pm 4} \cdot w^{-1}$ cloaks (M, σ).

Proof. This is an immediate consequence of $\left(\mathsf{CB}_i(\tau_a) \cdot \mathsf{CB}_i(-\tau_a^{-1})\right)^2 = \mathsf{Id}_N$.

Remark 16. Cloaking elements as proposed by the designers of WalnutDSA^{TM} depend only on the permutation σ and not on the matrix M of the element they are stabilizing. Therefore, we will say that some braid cloaks a permutation σ.

For further details on the generation of cloaking elements in WalnutDSA^{TM} we refer interested readers to the original implementation by SecureRF [1] or our implementation in MAGMA [14] (see [36]). However, our attack will be independent of the way cloaking elements are generated.

Concealed cloaking elements are cloaking elements for which the cloaked permutation is not public. Given a braid word W, concealed cloaking elements are added to the word by splitting W into two braid words W_1 and W_2 at a random location and inserting a braid cloaking the permutation induced by W_1 in between.

3.2 The Signature Scheme

Key Generation and Parameter Values. Before any message can be signed, the following system wide public parameters need to be fixed:

- The rank N of the braid group B_N.
- A rewriting algorithm $\mathcal{R} : B_N \to B_N$, i.e. an algorithm transforming a braid word w into an equivalent braid word $\mathcal{R}(w)$. For example, one can use algorithms computing normal forms [11,23], Dehornoy's handle reduction [17] or the stochastic rewriting algorithm introduced in [2].
- A finite field $\mathbb{F}_q$.
- T-values $= \{\tau_1, \tau_2, \ldots, \tau_N\} \in (\mathbb{F}_q^\times)^N$, such that $\tau_a = -\tau_b^{-1}$ for some publicly known integers $1 \le a < b \le N$.
- The number of concealed cloaking elements that will be added.
- A hash function $H : \{0,1\}^* \to \{0,1\}^{2k}$ for some k. Our attack will not depend on any weaknesses of the hash function and therefore we can treat H as a random oracle.

Next, the signer chooses braid words w and w' by choosing uniformly at random l Artin generators or their inverses. The secret key of the signer is the pair (w, w'), while the public key is $(\mathcal{P}(w), \mathcal{P}(w'))$ where $\mathcal{P}$ is the map given in Remark 12. Note, the length of the private braids w and w' is chosen large enough to prevent brute force attacks from being effective.

Later, we will see that the success of our new attack is independent of all parameters but N.

As of the 21st of November 2018, the use of the following parameters is suggested for WalnutDSA^{TM}:

claimed security level	128-bit security level	256-bit security level
N	10	10
q	$2^{31}-1$	$2^{61}-1$
l	132	287
concealed cloaking elts	12	24
H	SHA2-256	SHA2-512

Message Encoding. In order for signatures to provide integrity and authenticity, a signer must encode the message that is to be signed into the signature. The Walnut digital signature algorithm requires the message to be mapped onto a pure braid.

To encode a message in WalnutDSA^{TM} it is hashed using the publicly known hash function H. Then every two bits of the output specify one pure braid generator (see (2)) and the encoding $E(H(m))$ of a message m is the product of all pure braid generators selected. As the exact choice of pure braid generators is irrelevant for our attack we refer to [40] for a full description.

Signature Generation. A signer needs to perform the following steps to generate a signature.

1. Compute the encoded message $E(H(m))$.
2. Generate cloaking elements v, v_1, v_2 as given by Proposition 15 for the identity and the permutations induced by the private braids w, w', respectively.
3. Add the required number of concealed cloaking elements in randomly chosen locations in the braid words $W_1 := v_1 \cdot w^{-1} \cdot v$ or $W_2 := w' \cdot v_2$.
4. Use a rewriting algorithm $\mathcal{R}$ to obtain a rewritten braid word

$$\mathsf{Sig} := \mathcal{R}\big(W_1 \cdot E(H(m)) \cdot W_2\big),$$

which is the signature for m.

Signature Verification. To verify a signature, a receiver computes $E(H(m))$ and checks whether

$$\text{Matrix}\big(\mathcal{P}(w) \star \mathsf{Sig}\big) = \text{Matrix}\big(\mathcal{P}(E(H(m)))\big) \cdot \text{Matrix}\big(\mathcal{P}(w')\big) \quad (5)$$

comparing the matrix parts of $\mathsf{GL}_N(\mathbb{F}_q) \times \mathsf{S}_N$. If both sides of the equation are equal, the receiver accepts the signature as valid. It is easy to check that legitimately produced signatures satisfy (5).

3.3 Previous Work on WalnutDSA™

We want to give a brief overview of previous attacks on the Walnut digital signature algorithm [10,29,34] and the changes they have triggered in the scheme to patch the weaknesses. Moreover, this section shows that our attack uses a completely different approach.

Factorization Attacks. The first attack on a previous version of WalnutDSA™ was published by Hart et al. [29]. In the previous version both secret braids were equal and the public key only consisted of the image of this one secret braid under the map $\mathcal{P} : B_N \to \mathsf{GL}_N(\mathbb{F}_q) \times \mathsf{S}_N$ (see Remark 12).

The attack exploited a malleability property of the signatures, enabling an attacker to forge a signature by solving a factorization problem in a group of matrices. Trying to destroy the malleability property, the designers of Walnut started using two different private braids. However, Beullens [10,40] showed that the following malleability property holds in this case too.

Theorem 17. [10] *Let m, m_1 and m_2 be messages and let h, h_1 and h_2 be the matrix parts of $\mathcal{P}\big(E(H(m))\big)$, $\mathcal{P}\big(E(H(m_1))\big)$ and $\mathcal{P}\big(E(H(m_2))\big)$, respectively. For braids $w_1, w_2, w_3 \in B_N$, we have*

(i) If $h = h_1^{-1}$ and Sig_1 is a valid signature for m_1 under the public key $\big(\mathcal{P}(w_1), \mathcal{P}(w_2)\big)$, then Sig_1^{-1} is a valid signature for m under the public key $\big(\mathcal{P}(w_2), \mathcal{P}(w_1)\big)$.

(ii) If $h = h_1 \cdot h_2$ and $\mathsf{Sig}_1, \mathsf{Sig}_2$ are valid signatures for m_1 and m_2 under the public keys $\big(\mathcal{P}(w_1), \mathcal{P}(w_2)\big)$ and $\big(\mathcal{P}(w_2), \mathcal{P}(w_3)\big)$ respectively, then $\mathsf{Sig}_1 \cdot \mathsf{Sig}_2$ is a valid signature for m under the public key $\big(\mathcal{P}(w_1), \mathcal{P}(w_3)\big)$.

Suppose, an attacker wants to forge a signature for the message m under the public key $(\mathcal{P}(w), \mathcal{P}(w'))$. Clearly, they can compute the matrix $h = \text{Matrix}(\mathcal{P}(E(H(m))))$. Next, the attacker collects pairs of messages and signatures (m_i, Sig_i) that are valid under the same public key. By the malleability properties, it suffices to find a factorization $h = h_{i_1} \cdot h_{i_2}^{-1} \cdot h_{i_3} \ldots h_{i_{m-1}}^{-1} \cdot h_{i_m}$ to get a valid signature for m, where h_i denotes the matrix part of $\mathcal{P}(E(H(m_i)))$.

Such a factorization can be obtained by writing $h \cdot h_1^{-1}$ as a product of elements of the set

$$\{h_i h_j^{-1} \mid i \neq j;\ 1 \leq i, j \leq k\} \subseteq \left\{ \begin{pmatrix} X & Y \\ 0 & 1 \end{pmatrix} \mid X \in \mathsf{GL}_{N-1}(\mathbb{F}_q),\ Y \in \mathbb{F}_q^{N-1} \right\}. \quad (6)$$

An algorithm to solve this factorization problem with time complexity $\mathcal{O}(q^{\frac{N-1}{2}})$ was proposed by Hart et al. [29]. However, the factorizations contained roughly 2^{25} elements of the set given in (6) and consequently the forged signature

$$\mathsf{Sig} = \mathsf{Sig}_{i_1} \cdot \mathsf{Sig}_{i_2}^{-1} \cdots \mathsf{Sig}_{i_{m-1}}^{-1} \cdot \mathsf{Sig}_{i_m} \cdot \mathsf{Sig}_1^{-1}$$

satisfies the verification equation, but can be easily detected due to its enormous length. By imposing an upper limit on the length of valid signatures as was done in the implementation submitted to NIST, the attack was blocked. In contrast, the forgeries produced by our attack will be of the same length as legitimately produced signatures.

Collision Search Attack. Beullens and Blackburn [10,40] realized that the originally proposed 4-bit encoder was not injective and that it mapped to a set of braids where the matrix parts under the function $\mathcal{P}$ were lying in a surprisingly low dimensional, 13 dimensional, affine subspace over $\mathbb{F}_q$. This made the scheme susceptible to a generic collision search attack. More precisely, it was possible to find pairs of distinct messages m_1 and m_2 such that $\mathcal{P}(E(H(m_1))) = \mathcal{P}(E(H(m_2)))$ for sufficiently small q using a generic collision search algorithm. Beullens and Blackburn implemented the collision search due to van Oorschot and Wiener [44] which takes $|\mathcal{P}(E(H(\{0,1\})))|^{\frac{1}{2}} \leq q^{6.5}$ evaluations of $\mathcal{P} \circ E \circ H$.

Recall that a signature is accepted as valid if (5) is satisfied. Given a collision of m_1 and m_2, an attacker can query a signature for m_1 and gets automatically a valid signature for m_2. Consequently, the signature scheme was not existentially unforgeable [28].

To counter the attack the designers of WalnutDSA^{TM} changed the encoder to the 2-bit version described previously, where $\mathcal{P}(E(H(\{0,1\}^*)))$ lies in an affine subspace of dimension $(N-2)^2+1$ [40] over $\mathbb{F}_q$, which is greater than 13 for $N \geq 6$. Together with a significant raise of the parameters N and q, the generic collision search attack became ineffective. Our attack will be independent of q, but we will see that it can be defeated to some extend by further increasing the parameter N.

Reversing E-Multiplication. The last attack presented in [10] solves the underlying problem of WalnutDSA^{TM}, reversing E-Multiplication (REM) [see Definition 13], directly.

Note, it suffices to solve a single instance of the REM problem to forge a signature of a freely chosen message or solve two instances of the REM problem to obtain an equivalent pair of secret braids from the public key. Thus, the hardness of this problem is crucial for the security of WalnutDSA^{TM}.

The attack exploits that E-Multiplication restricted to pure braids is a group homomorphism which maps the chain of subgroups

$$\{e\} = P_1 \subset P_2 \subset \cdots \subset P_N \subset B_N$$

to a nice chain of subgroups in $\mathsf{GL}_N(\mathbb{F}_q)$. Here, $P_i \subset B_N$ denotes the subgroup of pure braids on N strings that can be identified with the pure braids of B_i or, formulated differently, the pure braids that can be written in the generators $b_1, \ldots, b_{i-1}$. Exploiting this subgroup structure, the REM problem can be solved by successively reducing the problem to a smaller subgroup using collision searches. The authors of [10] suggest moreover a slightly finer chain of subgroups for the first reductions which are the most costly ones to improve the performance of the algorithm further.

The resulting attack requires $\mathcal{O}(q^{\frac{N}{2}-1})$ E-Multiplications, and was blocked by a significant increase in the parameters q and N. As mentioned before, our attack will be independent of q and can only be defeated to some extent by increasing N significantly.

Uncloaking Signatures. The most recent attack is due to Kotov, Menshov and Ushakov [34]. They give a heuristic attack which operates purely on braids. The attack removes cloaking elements of a previous version of the Walnut digital signature algorithm without concealed cloaking elements.

The authors observed that cloaking elements in WalnutDSA^{TM} are always generated in such a way that the strands corresponding to the inverse T-values cross each other (see Proposition 15). Since T-values are public, an attacker can trace all strands and find "critical positions" in a signature where there might be a cloaking element. This allows a length-based attack: Note that untwisting the middle part of cloaking elements produces a trivial braid. An attacker guesses the location of cloaking elements and tries to remove them by untwisting the critical position. When multiplying signatures with removed cloaking elements together, more precisely one such signature multiplied with the inverse of another, further elements cancel out. If the remaining word is of significantly shorter length, one has heuristic evidence that the cloaking elements have been removed successfully.

The uncloaking procedure on multiple signatures leads to a system of conjugacy equations in B_N (potentially with errors). Once again this can be heuristically solved using a length-based approach. For earlier work about length-based attacks we refer amongst others to [30,38].

To patch Walnut, concealed cloaking elements, i.e. cloaking elements that are inserted in random locations before and after the encoded message, were introduced. Removing multiple concealed cloaking elements that are not inserted consecutively into the signature appears to be more difficult.

The designers of WalnutDSA^{TM} suggested to insert

$$\kappa \geq \frac{2 \cdot (\text{security level in bits})}{\log_2(N!)} \tag{7}$$

concealed cloaking elements [40]. For $N = 10$ this yields the values given in the table in Sect. 3.2. However, the number κ was estimated under the assumption that one needs to know the permutation of a cloaking element in order to remove it. As this does not hold, the efficacy of this countermeasure has been disputed [40].

We will see that the success of our attack is independent of the number of concealed cloaking elements inserted to the signature the way it was suggested by the designers of WalnutDSA^{TM}. However, we will discuss in Sect. 5.3 that adding a significant number of concealed cloaking elements to the encoded message might thwart our attack at the cost of enlarging signatures and slowing down the signature generation and verification.

4 Decomposition of Products in Braid Groups

The use of normal forms as "obfuscation procedures" in cryptographic schemes such as WalnutDSA^{TM} suggests that properties of single braids are well hidden in the normal form of their product. In this section, we will see that this is in general not the case. More precisely, we will argue that we can expect some (potentially reflected) permutation braids of factors with sufficiently large canonical length to appear in the normal form of their product.

In Sect. 4.1 we prove how the permutation braids of factors relate to the permutation braids of their product. Together with the experimental results of Sect. 4.2 this yields the observation stated in the previous paragraph. In Sect. 4.3 we show how the observation can be exploited under certain conditions to recover the factors of products of the form $ABC \in B_N$ up to the centre $\langle \Delta^2 \rangle$, when B is known. The algorithm to decompose products of braids will be at the heart of our cryptanalysis of WalnutDSA^{TM} in Sect. 5 and our new solutions to the conjugacy and decomposition search problems in Sect. 6.

4.1 Garside Normal Form of Products

Recall that $b_i = \Delta b_{N-i} \Delta^{-1} = \tau(b_{N-i})$ for $i = 1, \ldots, N-1$ by Proposition 2 and Remark 3. Let $\Delta^a \cdot A_1 \ldots A_n$ and $\Delta^b \cdot B_1 \ldots B_m$ be the normal forms of two elements $A, B \in B_N$ respectively. Pushing all Δ's in the product AB to the front yields

$$\begin{aligned} AB = \Delta^a \cdot A_1 \ldots A_n \cdot \Delta^b B_1 \ldots B_m &= \Delta^{a+b} \cdot \tau^b(A_1) \ldots \tau^b(A_n) B_1 \ldots B_m \\ &= \Delta^{a+b} \cdot \tau^{b'}(A_1) \ldots \tau^{b'}(A_n) B_1 \ldots B_m, \end{aligned} \tag{8}$$

for $b' \equiv b \pmod 2$ since τ^2 is the identity map. This is a product of permutation braids by the following Lemma of which we will omit the straightforward proof.

Lemma 18. *Let $1 \le A_1, A_2 \le \Delta$ be elements of B_N. Then $1 \le \tau(A_1), \tau(A_2) \le \Delta$ too. Furthermore, $A_1 A_2$ is a left-weighted product if and only if $\tau(A_1)\tau(A_2)$ is left-weighted.*

Thus, (8) is a product of permutation braids but in general not left-weighted. However, we see that $\tau(A_1) \dots \tau(A_n)$ is a left-weighted product by Lemma 18 and thus the following Lemma is an immediate consequence.

Lemma 19. *Let $\Delta^a \cdot A_1 \dots A_n$ and $\Delta^b \cdot B_1 \dots B_m$ be the left normal forms of the braids $A, B \in B_N$ respectively. Let $b' \equiv b \pmod 2$, then*

$$\Delta^{a+b} \cdot \tau^{b'}(A_1) \cdots \tau^{b'}(A_n) B_1 \cdots B_m$$

is the left normal form of AB if and only if $\tau^{b'}(A_n)B_1$ is a left-weighted product.

Clearly, the condition will not be met for most $A, B \in B_N$. When computing the left normal form of AB in general, new Δ's might be created in the process of computing the left-weighted product of $\tau^b(A_1) \dots \tau^b(A_n) B_1 \dots B_m$. Moving these Δ's to the front results in reflections of *all* leftward permutation braids, which yields the following proposition.

Proposition 20. *Let $A, B \in B_N$ and let $\Delta^a \cdot A_1 \dots A_n$ and $\Delta^b \cdot B_1 \dots B_m$ be their left normal form respectively. The left normal form of AB is*

$$\Delta^{a+b+k} \cdot \tau^{b+k}(A_1) \dots \tau^{b+k}(A_{n-c}) \cdot X_1 \dots X_l,$$

for some integer $0 \le c \le n$ and permutation braids $X_1, \dots, X_l$, where $k \in \mathbb{Z}$ is the number of Δ's that are created when computing the left normal form of $\tau^b(A_1) \dots \tau^b(A_n) B_1 \dots B_m$.

Note that we have $\Delta^k \cdot X_1 \dots X_l = \tau^b(A_{n-C_N+1}) \dots \tau^b(A_n) \cdot B_1 \dots B_m$. The algorithms to compute the Garside left normal form visualize the previous proposition quite well. If $A_1 \cdots A_n$ is a left normal form and we multiply with an Artin generator b_i on the right, this modifies the last permutation braid if $A_n b_i \wedge \Delta \ne A_n \wedge \Delta$. If A_n is not changed all leftward permutation braids are still in left normal form and we are done. If A_n is changed two conditions must be met for A_{n-1} to be changed as well. First, $A_n b_i \wedge \Delta$ must contain another Artin generator b_j in the set of all Artin generators the word can start with compared to $A_n \wedge \Delta$. And second, $A_{n-1} b_j \wedge \Delta \ne A_{n-1} \wedge \Delta$. This process continues inductively to the left until some permutation braid is not changed anymore. If one of the changed permutation braids becomes Δ during this process, it is moved to the front by reflecting all leftward permutation braids.

Remark 21. It is not hard to find particular braids for which the previous proposition does not contain a lot of information as $c = n$. This happens for example, if $B = A^{-1}$ when the product vanishes or if A and B are braids that do not share common strands and thus commute. However, in the next section we will see that for every N and randomly chosen braids $A, B \in B_N$ the expected value for c is bounded independently of n.

Clearly, if c is smaller than n the permutation braids in the left normal forms of A and AB coincide on the left hand side up to reflection. Next, we show that the rightmost permutation braids of the left normal forms of B and AB coincide too. The following Proposition due to Elrifai and Morton provides us with a link between multiplication of a braid on the left and on the right.

Proposition 22. [20] *Let $\Delta^u \cdot x_1 \dots x_m$ be the left normal form of X. Then the left normal form of X^{-1} is $X^{-1} = \Delta^{-u-m} \cdot x'_m \cdots x'_1$, where $x'_i := \tau^{-u-i}(x_i^{-1}\Delta)$ for $i = 1, \dots, m$.*

The braid $x_i^{-1}\Delta$ is called the *right complement* of x_i. Let δ denote the map sending permutation braids to their right complement. It is easy to check that δ induces a bijection on the permutation braids and $\delta^2 = \tau$.

Proposition 23. *Let A, $B \in B_N$ and let $\Delta^a \cdot A_1 \dots A_n$ and $\Delta^b \cdot B_1 \dots B_m$ be their left normal form respectively. The left normal form of AB is*

$$\Delta^{a+b+k} \cdot Y_1 \dots Y_l \cdot B_{c+1} \dots B_m,$$

for some integer $0 \le c \le m$ and permutation braids $Y_1, \dots, Y_l$, where $k \in \mathbb{Z}$ is the number of Δ's that are created when computing the left normal form of $\tau^b(A_1) \dots \tau^b(A_n) B_1 \dots B_m$.

Proof. Clearly, we can show the proposition for A^{-1} and B^{-1} instead of A and B. More precisely, we show that the permutation braids on the right hand side of $A^{-1}B^{-1}$ coincide with the ones of B^{-1}.

By Proposition 20 we know that the left normal form of $B_1 \dots B_m A_1 \dots A_n$ is

$$\Delta^k \tau^k(B_1) \dots \tau^k(B_{m-c}) X_1 \dots X_l, \tag{9}$$

for some $0 \le c \le m$, $k \in \mathbb{Z}$ and permutation braids $X_1, \dots, X_l$. Proposition 22 implies that the left normal form of $(B_1 \dots B_m A_1 \dots A_n)^{-1} = A_n^{-1} \dots A_1^{-1} B_m^{-1} \dots B_1^{-1}$ is

$$\begin{aligned} &\Delta^{-k-(m-c+l)} \cdot X'_l \dots X'_1 \cdot (\tau^k(B_{m-c}))' \dots (\tau^k(B_1))' \\ &= \Delta^{-k-(m-c+l)} \cdot X'_l \dots X'_1 \cdot \tau^{-m+c}(\delta(B_{m-c})) \dots \tau^{-1}(\delta(B_1)), \end{aligned} \tag{10}$$

using

$$(\tau^k(B_i))' = \tau^{k-i}(\delta(\tau^k(B_i))) = \delta^{2(k-i)}(\delta^{2k+1}(B_i)) = \tau^{-i}(\delta(B_i)).$$

Simultaneously, the left normal form of $B_m^{-1} \dots B_1^{-1}$ is $\tau^{-m}(\delta(B_m)) \dots \tau^{-1}(\delta(B_1))$ by Proposition 22. Comparing with (10), we see that the left normal forms of $B_m^{-1} \dots B_1^{-1}$ and $A_n^{-1} \dots A_1^{-1} B_m^{-1} \dots B_1^{-1}$ coincide on the rightmost $m - c$ permutation braids. This finishes the proof.

4.2 Penetration Distance

In this section we provide experimental results to estimate the size of the parameter c in Propositions 20 and 23 for "randomly" chosen braids A and B. We will find that for every N this expectation is uniformly bounded independently of the canonical lengths of the factors A and B.

Since the braid group B_N is infinite for $N \geq 2$, choosing braids at random is a non-trivial task. In practice, there are various ways to choose braids of B_N in a randomized manner. However, different methods result in different probability distributions on B_N.

Recall that every braid word can be rewritten as an element of the monoid of positive braids B_N^+ which we introduced in Sect. 2.3. Let $|x|$ denote the *length* of a positive braid $x \in B_N^+$, i.e. the number of Artin generators occurring in any positive braid word representing x. Since the defining relations of the braid group (and the braid monoid) are homogeneous, this is well-defined.

We start by recalling some results due to Gebhardt and Tawn [27] who studied the Garside normal forms of random braids. They analysed statistical properties of the normal forms of positive braids of length k generated using two methods:

(i) Choose uniformly at random k Artin generators $b_i \in \{b_1, \ldots, b_{N-1}\}$ and concatenate them, i.e. choose uniformly at random a braid word from the set of all positive braid words of B_N^+ of length k. We say that we generate *positive words* of length k uniformly at random.

(ii) Consider the set of all braids that can be represented by a braid word of length k and choose uniformly at random one braid from this set. We say that we generate uniformly at random *positive braids* of length k.

Note, the number of words representing the same element of B_N^+ depends on the element. Therefore, both variants yield different probability distributions on the set of all braids that can be represented by positive braid words of length k.

However, the implementation of the second method is significantly more difficult in practice (see [26] for an algorithm that runs polynomially in N and k) which is why most (cryptographic) applications generate "random braids" similarly to the first method.

Following the terminology of Gebhardt and Tawn, we call conjugation with Δ, i.e. a reflection, of a permutation braid a *trivial change*. We define the *penetration distance* as follows.

Definition 24. [27] For two braids A and B, the *penetration distance* $\mathsf{pd}(A, B)$ for the product AB is the number of permutation braids at the end of the normal form of A which undergo a non-trivial change in the normal form of the product. I.e.

$$\mathsf{pd}(A, B) = cl(A) - max\{i \in \{0, \ldots, cl(A)\} : A\Delta^{-\inf(A)} \wedge \Delta^i = AB\Delta^{-\inf(AB)} \wedge \Delta^i\}$$

where $cl(\cdot)$ denotes the canonical length and $\inf(\cdot)$ the infimum of a braid.

Based on their experiments, Gebhardt and Tawn conjectured the following.

Conjecture 25. [27] *Let $A \in B_N$ be a braid which is randomly chosen from either the uniformly generated random words or from the uniformly generated random braids of length k and let b_i be a randomly chosen Artin generator of B_N. Then the expected penetration distance is bounded independently of the length k of the braid, i.e. there exists some C such that for all k*

$$\mathbb{E}(\mathsf{pd}(A, b_i)) < C.$$

The conjecture raises the question whether there still exists an upper bound for the expected penetration distance of the product AB of two randomly chosen braids or braid words independently of their lengths. That is when B is an arbitrary randomly chosen braid or braid word as well instead of a single randomly chosen Artin generator.

For the purpose of investigating this question, we conducted an experiment in MAGMA [14]. We generated 2.000 instances of pairs of braid words $A, B \in B_N$ for different given lengths using the built-in random function of the braid package in MAGMA. To obtain a "random" braid of given length k, this function chooses uniformly at random a_i from $X \cup X^{-1} \backslash a_{i-1}^{-1}$ for $k = 1, \ldots, k$, where X and X^{-1} is the set of Artin generators and their inverses respectively. In other words, the built-in random function chooses uniformly at random a braid word from the set of all freely reduced braid words of a given length k.

Given such pairs of randomly generated braid words A, B, we computed the product AB and the penetration distance for each particular instance. This was

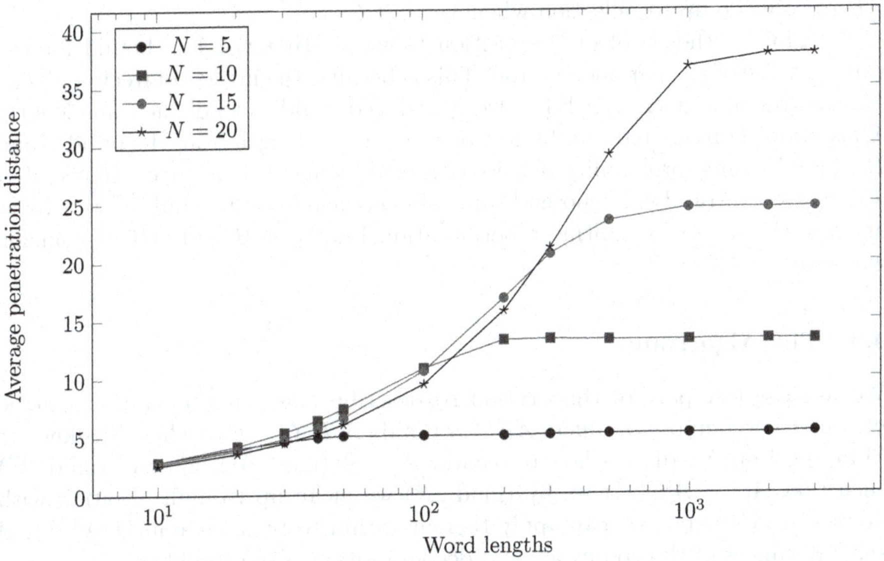

Fig. 3. Average penetration distance after multiplication with braid of given length on the right hand side

done by comparing the permutation braids in the left normal forms of A and AB directly. The diagram in Fig. 3 shows the average penetration distance with respect to the lengths of A and B for different values of N.

We observe that for each N the average penetration distance increases with the word lengths of the random braids and eventually converges to some bound. Furthermore, these bounds increase with the number of strands N of the braid group. Note that for our attack on WalnutDSA^{TM} we will be mainly interested in estimates for $N = 10$ because this is the parameter used.

The convergence suggests that for every N there exists an upper bound for the expected penetration distance of the product of randomly generated freely reduced braid words independently of their lengths.

Conjecture 26. Let $A, B \in B_N$ be braid words that are picked uniformly at random from all freely reduced braid words of length k. Then there exists a $C_N \in \mathbb{N}$ such that for all k, we have

$$\mathbb{E}(\mathsf{pd}(A, B)) < C_N.$$

Plotting the distribution of penetration distances for products of randomly chosen freely reduced braid words for different lengths we noted that most data points are distributed closely around the mean.

Now, Conjeture 26 has significant importance for Proposition 20. Let A and B be two randomly chosen braids of canonical length n and m respectively. Assuming Conjecture 26, i.e. assuming that the expected penetration distance is bounded by some C_N independently of the lengths of A and B, Proposition 20 implies that we expect at least the leftmost $n - C_N$ permutation braids of A and AB to coincide up to reflection whenever $n \geq C_N$.

Looking at the proof of Proposition 23 we see that C_N is a bound for the expected size of the parameter c too. This is because the inverse of freely reduced braid words of a given length is a freely reduced braid word of the same length. Thus, drawing freely reduced braid words of a given length from the braid group B_N has the same probability distribution as drawing their inverses. Hence, if A and B are two randomly chosen braids of canonical length n and m, we expect at least the $m - C_N$ rightmost permutation braids of B and AB to coincide whenever $m \geq C_N$.

4.3 The Algorithm

We use the last part of this section to describe how our observation can be utilised to decompose products ABC of braids $A, B, C \in B_N$, when B is known. More precisely, we discuss how to recover $A' \equiv A \pmod{\Delta^2}$, $C' \equiv C \pmod{\Delta^2}$ such that $AC = A'C'$. Here, by $\pmod{\Delta^2}$ we mean up to multiplication with powers of Δ^2. Later, we can apply this algorithm to break WalnutDSA^{TM} and solve instances of the conjugacy and decomposition search problems.

Let $A = \Delta^a \cdot A_1 \dots A_n$, $B = \Delta^b \cdot B_1 \dots B_m$, and $C = \Delta^c \cdot C_1 \dots C_r$ be the left normal forms of randomly chosen freely reduced braid words $A, B, C \in B_N$.

Assume that m is greater than the C_N given by Conjecture 26. We have discussed in the previous section that we can expect the left normal form of BC to be of the form

$$\Delta^{a+b+k} \cdot \tau^{c+k}(B_1) \dots \tau^{c+k}(B_{m-C_N}) \cdot Y_1 \dots Y_l$$

for some permutation braids $Y_1, \dots, Y_l$ such that $\Delta^k \cdot Y_1 \dots Y_l = \tau^c(B_{j+1}) \dots \tau^c(B_m) \cdot \Delta^{-c}C$ and $k \in \mathbb{Z}$ is the number of fundamental braids Δ that are being created when computing the left-weighted form of $\tau^c(B_{j+1}) \dots \tau^c(B_m) C_1 \dots C_r$.

Now, if the part of the normal form of B that was preserved into BC is of canonical length greater than $C_N + 1$, which we expect to happen for $m \geq 2C_N + 1$, the left normal form of $A(BC)$ is expected to be of the form

$$\Delta^{a+b+c+k+k'} \cdot X_1 \dots X_r \cdot \tau^{c+k}(B_{C_N+1}) \dots \tau^{c+k}(B_{m-C_N}) \cdot Y_1 \dots Y_l \qquad (11)$$

by Proposition 23 and the previous section, where $\Delta^{k'} \cdot X_1 \dots X_r$ is a left-weighted product of permutation braids equal to $\tau^{b+c+k}(A_1) \dots \tau^{b+c+k}(A_n) \cdot \tau^{c+k}(B_1) \dots \tau^{c+k}(B_i)$ if the centre of B equals Δ^2 which we expect for sufficiently long B.

We will keep this notation for the remainder of this section. Let the left normal form of a given ABC be

$$\Delta^u \cdot X_1 \dots X_r \cdot \tau^{c+k}(B_i) \dots \tau^{c+k}(B_j) \cdot Y_1 \dots Y_l,$$

where $u = a+b+c+k+k'$. By the previous discussion, we know that $i-j > 0$ can be expected for randomly chosen freely reduced braid words A, B and $C \in B_N$ with B of canonical length greater than $2C_N + 1$.

It is now a straightforward procedure to recover $A' \equiv A \pmod{\Delta^2}$ and $C' \equiv C \pmod{\Delta^2}$ such that $AC = A'C'$ knowing only B:

1. Compute the left normal forms of B and ABC.
2. Check, whether there is a contiguous subsequence $B_{i_1} \dots B_{i_2}$ of permutation braids of the left normal form of B for some $1 \leq i \leq i_1 < i_2 \leq j \leq m$ in the left normal form of ABC using a string-matching algorithm. If such a subsequence is found, save the location in the left normal form of B and ABC and go to 3. Otherwise, do the same search for contiguous subsequences $\tau(B_{i_1}) \dots \tau(B_{i_2})$ of $\tau(B)$ in the left normal form of ABC.
   If no common subsequence of permutation braids can be found either, we terminate the process and cannot recover the factors. If multiple common subsequences are found, we run the following steps for every of the finitely many possible solution. Notice, the latter is not very likely to happen for randomly chosen braid words and sufficiently long subsequences.
3. Split the braid B or $\tau(B) = \tau(B_1) \dots \tau(B_m)$ at B_{i_1} resp. $\tau(B_{i_1})$ into two parts. Then, do the same for ABC. Denote the parts B_I, B_{II}, ABC_I, and ABC_{II}.
   Note that we find the subsequence $\tau^{c+k}(B_i) \dots \tau^{c+k}(B_j)$ in B or $\tau(B)$ depending on whether $c+k$ leaves residue 0 or 1 modulo 2, since τ^2 is the identity.

Thus, even though we know neither c nor k we can determine the residue of $c+k \pmod 2$ which we denote by $(c+k)'$.
Using the notation of previous paragraphs, we compute

$$\begin{aligned} B_I &:= \Delta^b \cdot \tau^{c+k}(B_1) \dots \tau^{c+k}(B_{i_1}) \\ B_{II} &:= \tau^{c+k}(B_{i_1+1}) \dots \tau^{c+k}(B_m) \\ ABC_I &:= \Delta^{a+b+c+k+k'} \cdot X_1 \dots X_r \cdot \tau^{c+k}(B_i) \dots \tau^{c+k}(B_{i_1}) \\ ABC_{II} &:= \tau^{c+k}(B_{i_1+1}) \dots \tau^{c+k}(B_j) \cdot Y_1 \dots Y_l \end{aligned}$$

4. Compute

$$\begin{aligned} A' : &= ABC_I \cdot B_I^{-1} \cdot \Delta^{-(c+k)'} \\ &= \Delta^{a+b+c+k+k'} \cdot X_1 \dots X_r \cdot \tau^{c+k}(B_{i-1})^{-1} \dots \tau^{c+k}(B_1)^{-1} \cdot \Delta^{-b-(c+k)'} \\ &= \Delta^{a+c+k-(c+k)'} \cdot A_1 \dots A_n \end{aligned}$$

and

$$\begin{aligned} C' : &= \Delta^{(c+k)'} \cdot B_{II}^{-1} \cdot ABC_{II} \\ &= \Delta^{(c+k)'} \cdot \tau^{c+k}(B_m)^{-1} \dots \tau^{c+k}(B_{i_1+1})^{-1} \cdot \tau^{c+k}(B_{i_1+1}) \dots \tau^{c+k}(B_j) \cdot Y_1 \dots Y_l \\ &= \Delta^{(c+k)'} \cdot \tau^{c+k}(B_m)^{-1} \dots \tau^{c+k}(B_{j+1})^{-1} \Delta^{-k} \tau^c(B_{j+1}) \dots \tau^c(B_m) \cdot C_1 \dots C_r \\ &= \Delta^{-k+(c+k)'} C_1 \dots C_r \end{aligned}$$

Since $a+c+k-(c+k)' \equiv a \pmod 2$ and $-k+(c+k)' \equiv c \pmod 2$, we have recovered $A' \equiv A \pmod{\Delta^2}$ and $C' \equiv C \pmod{\Delta^2}$. Using $c \equiv -k+(c+k)' \pmod 2$, we have furthermore

$$A'C' = \Delta^{a+c} \cdot \tau^c(A_1) \dots \tau^c(A_n) \cdot C_1 \dots C_l = AC.$$

The success rate of this decomposition algorithm will be discussed in Sect. 6.

5 New Attack on WalnutDSA™

In this section we want to present our attack on the group-based signature scheme WalnutDSA™ which is an application of the decomposition algorithm we have developed in Sect. 4.

In Sect. 5.1 we present the idea behind our attack on WalnutDSA™, before providing experimental results on the success of our attack in Sect. 5.2. In Sect. 5.3 we discuss how different parameters influence the running time and success rate of our attack and we suggest one potential countermeasure.

5.1 Universal Forgery Attack

Let m be a message with the legitimately produced signature $\mathsf{Sig} \in B_N$. Recall that the braids corresponding to signatures of WalnutDSA^{TM} have a representative braid word of the form

$$\mathsf{Sig} = W_1 \cdot E(H(m)) \cdot W_2,$$

where $E(H(m))$ is the encoded message and $W_1, W_2 \in B_N$ are braids of the form $v_1 \cdot w^{-1} \cdot v$ and $w' \cdot v_2$ with additional concealed cloaking elements inserted. Here, $w, w' \in B_N$ are the private braids of the signer and v, v_1, v_2 are braids cloaking the identity of S_N and the permutations induced by w and w', respectively.

It is easy to see that the braid $\mathsf{Sig}' := W_1 \cdot E(H(m')) \cdot W_2$ is a valid signature for the message m'. Hence, the ability to locate $E(H(m))$ in a legitimate signature and replacing it by $E(H(m'))$ for an arbitrarily chosen message m' gives rise to a universal forgery attack.

To prevent attackers from finding the encoded message by just parsing through the signature, the designers of WalnutDSA^{TM} suggested an *obfuscation procedure*. That is, the application of a rewriting algorithm such as the Garside normal form, BKL normal form [11], stochastic rewriting [2] or Dehornoy's handle reduction [17] to the braid before appending the signature to a message.

Note that rewriting changes only the representative of the same braid. Consequently, normal forms are the strongest way to obfuscate signatures because every attacker can compute them given another representative of the same braid.

Our experimental results in the next section will show that most legitimately produced signatures of WalnutDSA^{TM} are susceptible to the decomposition algorithm described in Sect. 4.3. Since anybody can compute the encoding of a message m, this allows us to recover $W_1' \equiv W_1 \pmod{\Delta^2}$ and $W_2' \equiv W_2 \pmod{\Delta^2}$ such that $W_1' \cdot W_2' = W_1 \cdot W_2$ given only one valid signature $W_1 \cdot E(H(m)) \cdot W_2$ of any m. As $W_1' \cdot E(H(m')) \cdot W_2' = W_1 \cdot E(H(m')) \cdot W_2$, this is enough to obtain forged signatures for any other message m'.

Proposition 27. *Let $W_1 \cdot E(H(m)) \cdot W_2 \in B_N$ be a valid signature for some message m and let $W_1', W_2' \in B_N$ such that $W_1' \equiv W_1 \pmod{\Delta^2}$, $W_2' \equiv W_2 \pmod{\Delta^2}$ and $W_1 \cdot W_2 = W_1' \cdot W_2'$. Then,*

$$W_1' \cdot E(H(m')) \cdot W_2'$$

is a valid signature for any message m'.

Computation of universal forgeries: Given a signature $\mathsf{Sig} = W_1 \cdot E(H(m)) \cdot W_2$ and the corresponding message m, an adversary computes the encoded message $E\big(H(m)\big)$ and uses the procedure described in Sect. 4.3 to recover two braids W_1', W_2' such that $W_1' \equiv W_1 \pmod{\Delta^2}$, $W_2' \equiv W_2 \pmod{\Delta^2}$ and $W_1' \cdot W_2' = W_1 \cdot W_2$. By Proposition 27, this suffices to compute a valid signature for *any* message m':

$$\mathsf{Sig}' = W_1' \cdot E\big(H(m')\big) \cdot W_2'$$

Comparison to legitimately produced signatures: Since W_1 and W_2 are legitimately produced and do not depend on $E(H(m))$, it is impossible to distinguish a forged signature of the form $W_1' \cdot E(H(m')) \cdot W_2'$ from a legitimately produced signature for m'. In particular, the length of our forgeries is the same as the one of legitimately produced signatures.

However, given two signatures one could recognize that at least one was likely forged. Note an attacker can solve this issue by adding an additional concealed cloaking element to W_1 and W_2.

Complexity: In our decomposition algorithm of Sect. 4.3, we need to compute the Garside normal form of Sig and $E(H(m))$ in the first step. Using Thurston's method, this takes time in $\mathcal{O}(|\mathsf{Sig}|^2 N \log N)$ and $\mathcal{O}(|E(H(m))|^2 N \log N)$ respectively. Here $|\cdot|$ means the number of permutation braids of the given positive braid word, not necessarily in left normal form.

The second step of the algorithm requires to find a common contiguous subsequence of permutation braids in the normal forms. Fixing a length Len for the common subsequence that we want to find, the naive algorithm compares $\mathcal{O}(rl)$ products of Len permutation braids, where r and l denote the canonical length of $E(H(m))$ and Sig respectively. We implemented this naive approach in our attack on WalnutDSA™ (see [36]). A more efficient solution is to use the Knuth–Morris–Pratt string-searching algorithm [32]. Running this algorithm on all contiguous subsequence of permutation braids of length Len from the (reflected) encoding and the signature takes $\mathcal{O}(r(l + \mathsf{Len}))$ comparisons of permutation braids.

For WalnutDSA™, we have $|E(H(m))| \leq |\mathsf{Sig}|$. As the number of permutation braids in the Garside normal is minimal compared to other positive braid words we have moreover $r \leq |E(H(m))|$ and $l \leq |\mathsf{Sig}|$ and thus recovering the positions and whether the subsequence of the encoding in the signature is reflected takes $\mathcal{O}(|\mathsf{Sig}|^2)$ comparisons of permutation braids. Since the rest of the decomposition algorithm runs in linear time, the algorithm to forge signatures is dominated by the time it takes to compute the Garside normal form, i.e $\mathcal{O}(|\mathsf{Sig}|^2 N \log N)$.

Note that generating legitimate signatures is quadratic in N too. Moreover, the Garside normal form of a signature might need to be computed as well, depending on the rewriting algorithm used in the generation of WalnutDSA™ signatures.

Improvements: As the encoded message is located in between of two braids W_1 and W_2 of roughly the same size in the signature, we anticipate to find the subsequence of the permutation braids of $\tau^k(E(H(m)))$ roughly in the middle of the signature. Therefore, it is faster on average to start the search for common permutation braids in the middle part of the signature and encoding.

5.2 Experimental Results

We have implemented the relevant parts of WalnutDSA™ and our attack in MAGMA [14]. The source code of our implementations can be found on

GitHub [36]. For our experiments we used the recommended parameters as listed in Sect. 3.2 for the two security levels. In particular, the number of strands N was set to 10.

By Sect. 4 we know that the crucial part for our decomposition algorithm to work is finding a (potentially reflected) contiguous subsequence of permutation braids of the normal form of $E(H(m))$ in the normal form of the signature of m. We generated 1.000 instances of signatures for randomly chosen messages m and both security levels. In our experiment, we were able to locate such a common subsequence of permutation braids in the normal forms of $\tau^k(E(H(m)))$ and $W_1 \cdot E(H(m)) \cdot W_2$ for either $k = 0$ or 1 in all instances. The following table, Fig. 4, shows the canonical lengths of the common subsequences we found for the 128- and 256-bit parameters respectively.

length of common subsequence	128-bit security level	256-bit security level
mean	100	238
minimum	19	153
maximum	142	288

Fig. 4. Lengths of common subsequences of permutation braids of encodings and signatures

To put this into context, we measured the canonical length of encoded messages. For the 128-bit parameters, encoded messages had canonical lengths ranging from 112 to 165 with a mean of 140. The range for 256-bit parameters was 248 to 310 with a mean of 280 permutation braids.

To determine the position of a common subsequence of permutation braids in (reflected) encoded message $\tau^k(E(H(m)))$ and signature Sig, we compared a specified number Len of permutation braids of $\tau^k(E(H(m)))$ and Sig for $k = 0, 1$ at a time. Note that finding common subsequences of a given length is faster than finding all common subsequences of arbitrary lenghts.

The larger the number Len it becomes less likely that a common subsequence appears in the signature just by coincidence. However, we want it to be small enough to actually find a common subsequence in most cases. Fixing $\mathsf{Len} = 15$ turned out to be a good choice in our implementation but taking $\mathsf{Len} = 10$ or 20 leads to almost the same results.

Later, we will see that increasing the number of strands N in the Walnut digital signature algorithm would lead to shorter common subsequences of permutation braids. In this situation we can improve our algorithm to find the common position and whether $k = 0$ or 1 by reducing Len inductively whenever we can not find a common subsequence of permutation braids for $k = 0$ and 1 until we find one or $\mathsf{Len} = 0$.

Testing our entire attack on randomly generated instances, 99.8% of legitimately produced signatures for the 128-bit parameters turned out to allow our universal forgery attack. For the 256-bit security level all 100% of signatures were susceptible.

The algorithm to recover the braids W_1' and W_2' and thus to produce universal forgeries takes time less than a second for the 128-bit and only a couple seconds for the 256-bit parameters.

The higher success rate for the 256-bit parameters can be explained with the output of the hash function being twice as long. This results in the normal form of the encoding containing roughly twice as many permutation braids. Therefore, it is more likely to find a common contiguous subsequence of permutation braids in the left normal forms of the signature and the (reflected) encoded message.

5.3 Countermeasures

Finally, we want to discuss how different parameters of WalnutDSA^{TM} influence the running time and success rate of our attack and we suggest one potential countermeasure. Here, the success rate means the proportion of signatures that allows a universal forgery attack.

Independence from q: Unlike the attacks [10,29], our attack works on the braids only and thus independently of the colored Burau representation. In particular, it is independent of the size q of the underlying finite field $\mathbb{F}_q$.

Increasing the length of the private braids: Increasing the number of concealed cloaking elements or the length of private braids makes both W_1 and W_2 and consequently the signature larger. We see that the running time of our attack is quadratic in the length of the signature and thus it slows down our attack a little bit, while simultaneously enlarging the size of signatures.

We have seen in Sect. 4.3 that the expected number of permutation braids that change non-trivially when multiplying with randomly chosen braid words on the left and right is bounded independently of their length. Therefore, we do not expect enlarging W_1 and W_2 to have a great influence on the success of our attack. Indeed, we generated random instances of Walnut signatures using different lengths for private keys. This did not seem to have any influence on the number of permutation braids found as a common subsequence in the signature and the (reflected) encoding. The success rate of the attack did not change even for very long private braids either.

For private braids randomly chosen from freely reduced words of length 15.000 Artin generators (instead of 287), our attack is still successful within a few minutes while legitimate signatures reach the imposed upper limit for the length of signatures that are being accepted as valid in the current implementation of WalnutDSA^{TM}. Consequently, increasing the length of private braids is not useful to thwart our attack.

Increasing N: Looking at the formula for the running time, increasing N is another way to slow down the attack slightly.

More interesting, however, is that increasing N decreases the success rate. We conducted an experiment generating WalnutDSA^{TM} instances for different values of N. Figure 5 shows the percentage of signatures allowing our universal forgery attack out of 1.500 randomly generated Walnut instances depending on N.

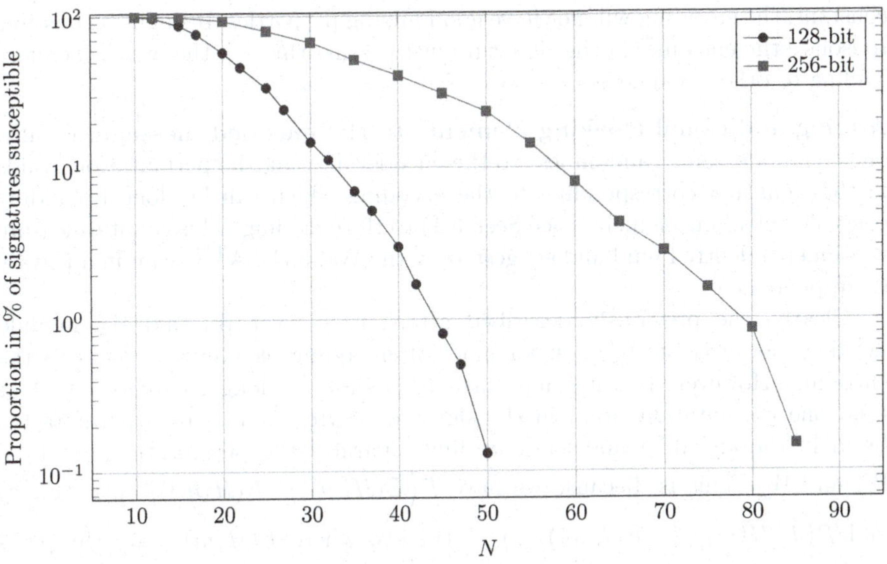

Fig. 5. Success rate of universal forgery attack depending on N

We have seen in Fig. 3 that raising N influences the number of permutation braids that are expected to change when multiplying with braids on the right. For multiplication on the left, we obtained the same result. At the same time the canonical length of the encoding remains constant when scaling up N since it only depends on the length of the output of the hash function used in WalnutDSA™. Combined, this implies that the expected length of the common subsequence of permutation braids of signature and encoding shrinks when raising N. Note that we cannot just reduce the length of the output of the hash function as the signature scheme would become vulnerable to collision search attacks [40].

As our attack does not work anymore once there is no common subsequence of permutation braids left, this explains the decreasing success rate when increasing N. In the 256-bit version the hash function has a longer output and therefore the common subsequence of permutation braids of encoding and signature is larger than in the 128-bit setting. This justifies, why the success probability decreases slower when increasing N for the 256-bit security level. Moreover, we measured the success of our attack by checking whether we recovered the braids W_1 and W_2 modulo their centre successfully. For large N it is more likely that the centre of the encoding $E(H(m))$ does not equal Δ^2 and as we recover braids W_1 and W_2 modulo the centre of $E(H(m))$ this might not be accepted as valid.

Considering our experiment shown in Fig. 5, the success of our attack seems to decrease exponentially when increasing N. However, this would increase the size of the public keys and slow down the signature verification quadratically in N. Moreover, one could fear that with N increasing and the hash output length constant, the encoding will not have good mixing properties. It might be possible to isolate the encoding in the signature just parsing through the braid, therefore leading to other weaknesses.

Adding additional cloaking elements to the encoded message: Finally, one could add some randomness to the encoder altering the permutation braids in the signature corresponding to the encoding which can be done by adding concealed cloaking elements (see Sect. 3.1) to the encoding. This countermeasure was independently found and suggested by the WalnutDSA^{TM} team in a private correspondence.

Clearly, the previously described attack to recover W_1 and W_2 modulo Δ^2 does not necessarily work anymore after adding cloaking elements to the encoding. However, forging signatures is possible as long as we can find at least one permutation braid in the signature corresponding to a permutation braid in the encoding and the encoding separates the permutation braids of W_1 and W_2. This is, because we have $\mathcal{P}\Big(E(H(m))_I^* \cdot E(H(m))_I^{-1}\Big) = (\text{Id}, \text{id})$ and $\mathcal{P}\Big(E(H(m))_{II}^{-1} \cdot E(H(m))_{II}^*\Big) = (\text{Id}, \text{id})$, where $E(H(m))_i^*$ are the parts of the encoding $E(H(m))$ containing additionally concealed cloaking elements. Together with the fact that all encodings are pure braids, we have therefore for $k = 0$ or 1

$$\begin{aligned}\mathcal{P}\Big(&\mathsf{Sig}_I \cdot \tau^k\big(E(H(m))_I^{-1} \cdot E(H(m')) \cdot E(H(m))_{II}^{-1}\big) \cdot \mathsf{Sig}_{II}\Big)\\ &= \mathcal{P}\Big(W_1 \cdot E(H(m))_I^* E(H(m))_I^{-1} \cdot E(H(m')) \cdot E(H(m))_{II}^{-1} E(H(m))_{II}^* \cdot W_2\Big)\\ &= \mathcal{P}\big(W_1 \cdot E(H(m')) \cdot W_2\big).\end{aligned}$$

We know that this still satisfies (5) and thus it is a valid signature for m'. Hence, even though an attacker can not recover W_1 and W_2 up to the centre they can still compute a forged signature for any message m' as long as they find a single permutation braid from the encoding in the signature at the correct position.

Consequently, to counter the attack one needs to make sure that all permutation braids originating from the encoding in the signature are changed. Our experiments show that introducing one cloaking element changes sometimes only 5 permutation braids in their surrounding for $N = 10$. Considering the canonical length of common subsequences measured in Sect. 5, we would therefore expect that at least 30 and 60 additional concealed cloaking elements need to be added for the two security levels. However, it might be necessary to add even more cloaking elements to prevent being susceptible to our attack after applying an uncloaking procedure such as the one due to Kotov, Menshov, and Ushakov [34] to critical positions in the middle of the signature eventually removing concealed cloaking elements.

Altogether, adding additional concealed cloaking elements to the encoding is the best way we found to thwart our attack. Yet, it would slow down the signature generation as all additional concealed cloaking elements need to be generated separately and it would enlarge the signatures of WalnutDSA^{TM}.

6 Application to the Conjugacy and Decomposition Search Problem

Another problem that can be solved using our decomposition algorithm from Sect. 4 is the *decomposition search problem* which can be formulated for the braid group as follows.

Definition 28. Given two elements X, Y of the braid group B_N and two subsets $A, B \in B_N$. The *decomposition search problem* (DSP) is to find elements $a \in A$ and $b \in B$ such that $Y = aXb$.

It is straightforward to construct key exchange protocols based on this problem, assuming that elements of A and B commute with each other [33,42]. Here, our decomposition algorithm of the previous subsection can be used to recover a and b for some instances up to elements of the centre of X, given $Y = aXb$.

Recall that our algorithm to solve DSP by decomposing the braid Y is not only fast but also requires almost no memory. Given B and a product of braids ABC in B_N, the decomposition algorithm of Sect. 4 is dominated by the time it takes to compute the Garside normal form of ABC, i.e. $\mathcal{O}(|ABC|^2 N \log N)$ using Thurston's approach where $|ABC|$ denotes the number of permutation braids a given positive braid word of ABC is written in. Note, that the Garside normal form can be computed even faster in practice [27].

We analysed the success of our decomposition algorithm for randomly chosen braid words A, B and C. To this end we generated uniformly at random freely reduced braid words $A, B, C \in B_N$ of given lengths using MAGMA [14]. Given the product ABC and B, we applied the decomposition algorithm and considered a run successful whenever we were able to recover A and C up to the centre of B_N, i.e. up to multiplication by powers of Δ^2.

Figure 6 shows the percentage of successful recoveries depending on the word lengths of A, B and C for different numbers of strands N. We see that the attack is very successful for sufficiently long randomly chosen braid words reaching 100% success rate. Moreover, we see that this "sufficient" length increases with N. This is no surprise since the bound of Conjecture 26 increases with N as previously noticed. Thus, for words that are shorter it is less likely to find a contiguous subsequence of (reflected) permutation braids of B in ABC.

Moreover, for randomly chosen words B of short length it is more likely that the centre of the braid associated to B does not equal the centre of the braid group generated by Δ^2. Therefore, braids recovered for short B using our decomposition algorithm might not be accepted as valid in our experiments.

Clearly, the conjugacy search problem (Definition 1) is a special case of the decomposition search problem and our decomposition algorithm can be used to solve instances of the conjugacy search problem too. Indeed, a successful run of the decomposition algorithm provides us with a braid $\tilde{C}$ equal to C up to the centre of X, given X and $Y = C \cdot X \cdot C^{-1}$. Consequently $\tilde{C}$ is a solution to the conjugacy search problem, as

$$Y = C \cdot X \cdot C^{-1} = \tilde{C} \cdot X \cdot \tilde{C}^{-1}.$$

Recall that our decomposition algorithm needs a common subsequence of permutation braids of $\tau^k(X)$ and $Y = C \cdot X \cdot C^{-1}$, for $k = 0$ or 1, to work. By Sect. 4.2, we can expect this for braid words X and C that are chosen uniformly at random whenever X has sufficiently large canonical length depending on N. However, in the case of the conjugacy search problem we can apply our decomposition algorithm for some short X as well, exploiting that X and Y are conjugate.

This is because C can be recovered by applying the decomposition algorithm to the braids X^n and $Y^n = (C \cdot X \cdot C^{-1})^n = C \cdot X^n \cdot C^{-1}$ with larger canonical length instead of X and Y, where n is a positive integer. We tested this procedure for randomly generated braid words of a given length X and C. Whenever the decomposition algorithm was not able to find a common subsequence in the permutation braids of $\tau^k(X)$ and $Y = C \cdot X \cdot C^{-1}$ for $k = 0$ or 1, we tried it on X^n and Y^n instead. In our experiments we used $n = 4$ and reran the decomposition algorithm on powers at most 3 times. The result of our experiments can be seen in Fig. 7 and shows clearly that the decomposition algorithm works in the case of CSP for shorter words than for the DSP displayed in Fig. 6.

However, we want to point out that there is not always an n such that X^n and Y^n share a potentially reflected subsequence of permutation braids. Indeed, the minimal counterexample is $N = 4$, $X = b_1$ and $Y = b_2 b_1 b_2^{-1}$, where b_i are Artin generators. We denote permutation braids by their induced permutation. The left normal forms of X^n and Y^n are the products $(1,2)^n$ and $(1,3,2,4)(2,3)^{n-1}(1,3,2)$ respectively, which do not share a single permutation braid.

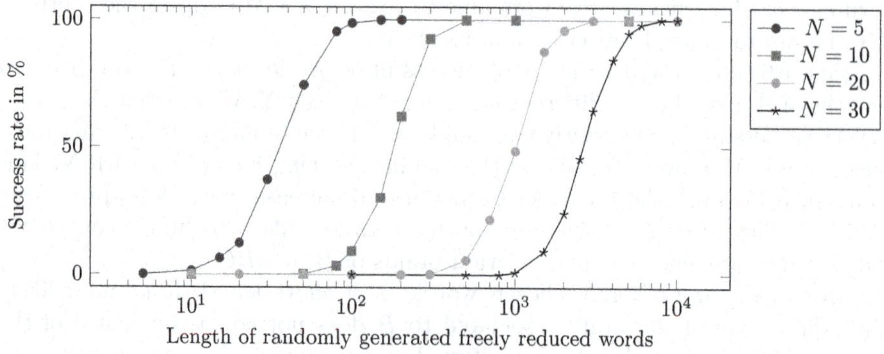

Fig. 6. Success rate of decomposition algorithm for instances of the DSP

Due to the vast use of the CSP, DSP and its variants in the design of cryptographic protocols, studying further applications of our decomposition algorithm and a thorough comparison with other solutions to the conjugacy and decomposition search problem in braid groups will be subject to future work.

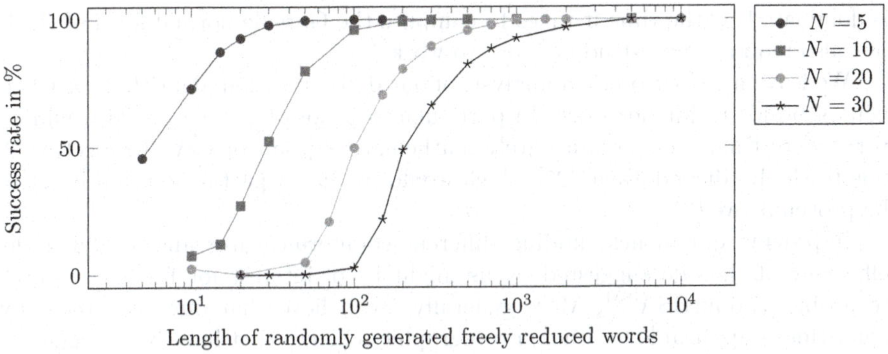

Fig. 7. Success rate of decomposition algorithm for instances of the CSP

7 Conclusion and Further Work

In cryptographic schemes based on braid groups, products of braids are often constructed involving secret braids as factors, and it is hoped that rewriting the product will hide the individual factors. We demonstrated that this is not the case for randomly chosen braid words. We provided an algorithm to compute individual components of products ABC when B is known and ABC is presented in normal form. We expect this decomposition to work for randomly chosen braids A, B and C if B is of canonical length greater than $2C_N + 1$, where C_N is the number given by Conjecture 26. In Sect. 4.2 we estimated C_N experimentally for some values of N.

As an application of our decomposition algorithm we presented a new universal forgery attack on the previously unbroken instantiation of WalnutDSA^{TM}. Given a single random message-signature pair, our attack allows to forge signatures for arbitrary messages within seconds for the 128-bit and 256-bit security levels. Hereby, the forgeries are indistinguishable from legitimately produced signatures. Our experiments showed that 99.8% and 100% of legitimately produced signatures in WalnutDSA^{TM} can be used in our new attack for the claimed 128-bit and 256-bit security levels respectively. In contrast to previous attacks, our attack produces signatures that are identically distributed as legitimate signatures and applies to all versions of WalnutDSA^{TM}. Unlike the previous attacks in [10,29], our attack works on the braids only. Thus, it does not depend on the colored Burau representation of the braid group and is independent of the size q of the underlying finite field $\mathbb{F}_q$. We have further discussed how other parameters influence the success probability and running time of our universal forgery attack. Adding sufficiently many concealed cloaking elements to the encoding may thwart our attack at the cost of increasing the length of signatures and slowing down the signature generation algorithm.

As another application, we provide a new algorithm for solving the conjugacy and decomposition search problems, two problems at the heart of other cryptographic systems based on braid groups [22]. The running time of this algorithm is dominated by the time it takes to compute the Garside normal form of ABC but also requires almost no memory to work.

We leave a full theoretical analysis of our decomposition algorithm for products of braids to further work. In particular, a proof of Conjecture 26 would be very interesting, even from a purely mathematical point of view. Conjecture 25 due to Gebhardt and Tawn [27] which would provide a partial solution is yet to be proven as well.

Improving our attack, finding different countermeasures and studying the efficiency of the one suggested by us might be of interest for further research regarding WalnutDSA^{TM}. More generally, we believe that our decomposition algorithm is applicable to other cryptographic schemes that have been suggested for braid groups. Researching further applications and a thorough comparison of our new solution to the conjugacy and decomposition search problems in braid groups to existing approaches will be subject for future work.

Acknowledgments. The authors would like to thank Ward Beullens and the anonymous reviewers for their helpful feedback. This work was produced as part of a master's thesis of the first author at the University of Oxford. He is now supported by the EPSRC as part of the Centre for Doctoral Training in Cyber Security at Royal Holloway, University of London (EP/P009301/1).

References

1. About SecureRF. https://www.securerf.com/about-us/. Accessed 21 Nov 2018
2. Anshel, I., Atkins, D., Goldfeld, P., Gunnels, D.: Kayawood, a key agreement protocol (2017). Preprint: https://eprint.iacr.org/2017/1162. Version 30 Nov 2017
3. Anshel, I., Anshel, M., Fisher, B., Goldfeld, D.: New key agreement protocols in braid group cryptography. In: Naccache, D. (ed.) CT-RSA 2001. LNCS, vol. 2020, pp. 13–27. Springer, Heidelberg (2001). https://doi.org/10.1007/3-540-45353-9_2
4. Anshel, I., Anshel, M., Goldfeld, D.: An algebraic method for public-key cryptography. Math. Res. Lett. **6**, 287–292 (1999)
5. Anshel, I., Anshel, M., Goldfeld, D., Lemieux, S.: Key agreement, the algebraic eraser, and lightweight cryptography. Contemp. Math. **418**, 1–34 (2007)
6. Anshel, I., Atkins, D., Goldfeld, D., Gunnells, P.E.: WalnutDSA: a quantum resistant group theoretic digital signature algorithm (2017). Preprint available at https://eprint.iacr.org/2017/058, 30 Nov 2017
7. Artin, E.: Theorie der Zöpfe. Abhandlungen aus dem mathematischen Seminar der Universität Hamburg. **4**, 47–72 (1925)
8. Ben-Zvi, A., Blackburn, S.R., Tsaban, B.: A practical cryptanalysis of the Algebraic Eraser. In: Robshaw, M., Katz, J. (eds.) CRYPTO 2016. LNCS, vol. 9814, pp. 179–189. Springer, Heidelberg (2016). https://doi.org/10.1007/978-3-662-53018-4_7
9. Ben-Zvi, A., Kalka, A., Tsaban, B.: Cryptanalysis via algebraic spans. In: Shacham, H., Boldyreva, A. (eds.) CRYPTO 2018. LNCS, vol. 10991, pp. 255–274. Springer, Cham (2018). https://doi.org/10.1007/978-3-319-96884-1_9
10. Beullens, W., Blackburn, S.: Practical attacks against the Walnut digital signature scheme (2018). Accepted to Asiacrypt 2018. Preprint: https://eprint.iacr.org/2018/318/20180404

11. Birman, J., Ko, K.H., Lee, S.J.: A new approach to the word and conjugacy problems in the braid groups. Adv. Math. **139**(2), 322–353 (1998)
12. Birman, J.S.: Braids, Links, and Mapping Class Groups. (AM-82), vol. 82. Princeton University Press, Princeton (1975)
13. Birman, J.S., Gebhardt, V., González-Meneses, J.: Conjugacy in Garside groups I: cyclings, powers and rigidity. Groups Geom. Dyn. **1**(3), 221–279 (2007)
14. Bosma, W., Cannon, J., Playoust, C.: The Magma algebra system I: the user language. J. Symb. Comput. **24**(3–4), 235–265 (1997)
15. Bressaud, X.: A normal form for braids. J. Knot Theory Ramif. **17**(06), 697–732 (2008)
16. Burau, W.: Über Zopfgruppen und gleichsinnig verdrillte Verkettungen. Abhandlungen aus dem Mathematischen Seminar der Universität Hamburg. **11**, 179–186 (1935)
17. Dehornoy, P.: A fast method for comparing braids. Adv. Math. **125**(2), 200–235 (1997)
18. Dehornoy, P.: Alternating normal forms for braids and locally Garside monoids. J. Pure Appl. Algebra **212**(11), 2413–2439 (2008)
19. Ding, J., Yang, B.Y.: Multivariate public key cryptography. In: Bernstein, D.J., Buchmann, J., Dahmen, E. (eds.) Post-Quantum Cryptography, pp. 193–241. Springer, Heidelberg (2009). https://doi.org/10.1007/978-3-540-88702-7_6
20. Elrifai, E.A., Morton, H.R.: Algorithms for positive braids. Q. J. Math. **45**(180), 479–498 (1994)
21. Epstein, D., Cannon, J., Holt, D., Levy, S., Paterson, M., Thurston, W.: Word Processing in Groups (1992)
22. Garber, D.: Braid group cryptography. In: Braids: Introductory Lectures On Braids, Configurations and Their Applications, pp. 329–403. World Scientific (2010)
23. Garside, F.A.: The braid group and other groups. Q. J. Math. **20**(1), 235–254 (1969)
24. Gebhardt, V.: A new approach to the conjugacy problem in Garside groups. J. Algebra **292**(1), 282–302 (2005)
25. Gebhardt, V., González-Meneses, J.: The cyclic sliding operation in Garside groups. Mathematische Zeitschrift **265**(1), 85–114 (2010)
26. Gebhardt, V., González-Meneses, J.: Generating random braids. J. Comb. Theory Ser. A **120**(1), 111–128 (2013)
27. Gebhardt, V., Tawn, S.: Normal forms of random braids. J. Algebra **408**, 115–137 (2014)
28. Goldwasser, S., Bellare, M.: Lecture notes on cryptography. Summer course "Cryptography and computer security" at MIT (1996)
29. Hart, D., Kim, D., Micheli, G., Pascual-Perez, G., Petit, C., Quek, Y.: A practical cryptanalysis of WalnutDSA^{TM}. In: Abdalla, M., Dahab, R. (eds.) PKC 2018. LNCS, vol. 10769, pp. 381–406. Springer, Cham (2018). https://doi.org/10.1007/978-3-319-76578-5_13
30. Hughes, J., Tannenbaum, A.: Length-based attacks for certain group based encryption rewriting systems. arXiv preprint cs/0306032 (2003)
31. Kalka, A., Teicher, M., Tsaban, B.: Short expressions of permutations as products and cryptanalysis of the Algebraic Eraser. Adv. Appl. Math. **49**(1), 57–76 (2012)
32. Knuth, D.E., Morris Jr., J.H., Pratt, V.R.: Fast pattern matching in strings. SIAM J. Comput. **6**(2), 323–350 (1977)

33. Ko, K.H., Lee, S.J., Cheon, J.H., Han, J.W., Kang, J.S., Park, C.: New public-key cryptosystem using braid groups. In: Bellare, M. (ed.) CRYPTO 2000. LNCS, vol. 1880, pp. 166–183. Springer, Heidelberg (2000). https://doi.org/10.1007/3-540-44598-6_10
34. Kotov, M., Menshov, A., Ushakov, A.: An attack on the Walnut digital signature algorithm. Des. Codes Crypt. 1–20 (2018)
35. McEliece, R.: A public-key cryptosystem based on algebraic coding theory. Deep. Space Netw. Prog. Rep. **44**, 114–116 (1978)
36. Merz, S.P.: Non obfuscating power of Garside normal forms (2018). GitHub repository at https://github.com/SimonMerz/Non-obfuscating-power-of-Garside-normal-forms
37. Micciancio, D., Regev, O.: Lattice-based cryptography. In: Bernstein, D.J., Buchmann, J., Dahmen, E. (eds.) Post-Quantum Cryptography, pp. 147–191. Springer, Heidelberg (2009). https://doi.org/10.1007/978-3-540-88702-7_5
38. Myasnikov, A.D., Ushakov, A.: Length based attack and braid groups: cryptanalysis of Anshel-Anshel-Goldfeld key exchange protocol. In: Okamoto, T., Wang, X. (eds.) PKC 2007. LNCS, vol. 4450, pp. 76–88. Springer, Heidelberg (2007). https://doi.org/10.1007/978-3-540-71677-8_6
39. National Institute for Standards and Technology (NIST): Post-quantum crypto standardization (2016). https://csrc.nist.gov/projects/post-quantum-cryptography
40. NIST PQC Forum. https://groups.google.com/a/list.nist.gov/forum/#!forum/pqc-forum. Accessed 21 Nov 2018
41. Shor, P.W.: Algorithms for quantum computation: discrete logarithms and factoring. In: 35th Annual Symposium on Foundations of Computer Science, 1994 Proceedings, pp. 124–134. IEEE (1994)
42. Shpilrain, V., Ushakov, A.: Thompson's group and public key cryptography. In: Ioannidis, J., Keromytis, A., Yung, M. (eds.) ACNS 2005. LNCS, vol. 3531, pp. 151–163. Springer, Heidelberg (2005). https://doi.org/10.1007/11496137_11
43. Stolbunov, A.: Constructing public-key cryptographic schemes based on class group action on a set of isogenous elliptic curves. Adv. Math. Commun. **4**(2), 215–235 (2010)
44. Van Oorschot, P.C., Wiener, M.J.: Parallel collision search with cryptanalytic applications. J. Cryptol. **12**(1), 1–28 (1999)

Author Index